A HANDBOOK OF METHOD
IN
CULTURAL ANTHROPOLOGY

A HANDBOOK OF METHOD
IN
CULTURAL ANTHROPOLOGY

Edited by

Raoul Naroll and Ronald Cohen

Columbia University Press
New York & London

Originally prepared under the auspices of The Council for Intersocietal Studies at Northwestern University.

Library of Congress Cataloging in Publication Data

Naroll, Raoul.
  A handbook of method in cultural anthropology.

  Reprint of the 1970 ed.
  Includes bibliographies.
  1. Ethnology—Methodology.   I. Cohen, Ronald,
joint author.   II. Title.
GN345.N37 1973   301.2   72-12762
ISBN 0-231-03731-7
ISBN 0-231-03749-X (pbk.)

Preface

Although anthropologists often view their own training and discipline with mystical reverence, the discipline as a whole does not have a systematic and cumulative tradition of methodological endeavor. Indeed, there are very few books on method in social and cultural anthropology and almost all of these are devoted to helping the fieldworker collect and describe information on non-Western cultures. These are generally of two varieties. First, there are materials, such as *Notes and Queries* or Murdock's *Outline of Cultural Materials,* that give some idea of the categories of information that anthropologists generally collect data on when conducting ethnographic field trips. For the non-anthropologist, or even the professional, these publications are useful in that they indicate what categories of data collection are regarded as standard in cross-cultural investigations. Second, there are articles, introductions to monographs, and, in a few celebrated cases (Bohannan 1954, Powdermaker 1966, Beattie 1965, and Read 1965), specific books on how an anthropologist managed to get into the fieldwork situation and collect the data that he or she has published on a particular group.

Comparative work in anthropology is as old as or older than the fieldwork tradition, going back to Morgan's work in the nineteenth century through that of Tylor to Hobhouse, Wheeler and Ginsberg, and Murdock and his students in more recent times. Furthermore, small-scale comparisons have always been a central concern of the discipline. Yet, here again, except for a few cases, as in the various works of such as Murdock, Whiting and Child, Moore, and Naroll, no specific work on method has been carried out, and again, as in

fieldwork, there is as yet very little sense of cumulative tradition.

On the other hand, a concern with method and training in anthropology has developed in the past few decades so that summer field schools, fieldwork language training programs and summer institutes on cross-cultural research methods and techniques have now become quite common in the programs of anthropology departments. These training programs indicate a growing awareness that methodological training in anthropology is not something a student should just pick up somehow or other on the way through his graduate training. Rather there must be a definite focus on method, such that the acquisition of professional skills become a clear-cut segment of the student's preparation for a career. Coupled with this awareness, and stimulating it, has been a rapid growth of methodological sophistication in both field research and comparative work in the other social sciences. It is for these reasons, principally, that we have decided to put together a set of materials directed at a full-blown discussion of methodology in social and cultural anthropology.

Having decided to put together a wide range of materials on method, we were immediately faced with the problem of asking what approach we should take to our subject. There are a number of traditional topics that could be covered. In fieldwork there is participant observation, gathering genealogies, gaining rapport, taking village censuses, writing up field notes, writing up the field materials into reports, and so on. In comparative work there are qualitative and quantitative techniques and approaches. In order to present all of these methods and techniques we would in effect have to synthesize the various strands of methodology that have developed in the discipline over the past half-century. This we would then call *the* anthropological method. Probably the best way to do this would be to collect already published materials from a number of disparate sources in journals, books, and unpublished dissertations.

Another approach, the one we have chosen, is more controversial or indeed polemical. In this approach we have worked out a point of view that permits us a more limited perspective on the subject and that helps us to focus on the kinds of techniques and research strategies that we would like to see grow and expand within the discipline.

The first approach, that of synthesizing the present literature, is a worthwhile one and one that still remains to be done. However, it is our view that it would tend to emphasize the uniqueness and separateness of anthropology. We do not deny that this quality exists, and several of the contributions in the volume (see especially the chapters by Honigmann and Mead) investigate this uniqueness. The second approach, a more limited one, stems from our own desire to see anthropology become a progressively more rigorous and scientific branch of the social sciences in general. This means that we have looked to science, and social science in particular, as a guide in determining what our goals and the means to these goals should be. Although lip service has always been paid to these ends, anthropology in particular, but certainly all of the social sciences to some extent, confuse the forest and the trees. It is an undeniable pleasure to know more and more about a particular culture, and, what is more often the case, a small group of people within that culture, but someone, somewhere must eventually ask: Why? Why do we want to know such things; and what goals are we fulfilling in doing so?

One way of answering this question is to take the position that because we did not know such things before, this knowledge increases the store of cross-cultural data available. Certainly comparative research requires as wide a variance and as large a sample of human societies as can be supplied, but the possibilities are endless. How many boards or bricks are in the building you are now living or working in? Would this information add to the store of human knowledge? Obviously

it would, and who can say with absolute assurance that such information would not be useful to social scientists at some future time. Coming closer to our own interests, we can ask: How deep are the nail parings buried among those people who perform this custom? Perhaps we could use this depth as an indicator of the anxiety felt over discarded body parts. Whether or not this is a good indicator, no anthropologist that I know of has in fact recorded and published such information. In other words, observations are limited, always have been, and will become progressively more so as research becomes more theory-directed and less a matter of description. Because this is so, we have decided to orient the subject of methodology primarily toward theory-testing and theory-construction, rather than the analysis and presentation of ethnographic facts.

Even though a major portion of anthropological method has always been directed toward observing, recording, and sometimes explaining why a particular culture was as described, we have decided to stress the use such facts have for proving, disproving, or creating generalizations that transcend any specific culture. In our view, this perspective distinguishes between information and data. The latter is a particular form of information that is justifiably relevant to a scientific problem.

We have chosen this approach, emphasizing problems and theories over detailed descriptions, because we believe there is at present a constant and expanding trend in the social sciences to penetrate disciplinary boundaries and restructure them along lines of common interests or problems. But whether or not disciplinary lines are breaking down or restructuring (as is argued in Chapter 2), a concern with problems and their solution is a growing trend in anthropology, such that explanation has expanded quantitatively during the past fifty years relative to sheer descriptive work. This point has been established in a recent study by Erasmus (1967). He divides explanation into three categories: genetic, idiographic and nomothetic. The first two of these refer to explanations directed toward specific research data taken from a specific site or society. However, the third, that of the nomothetic, refers to general propositions that transcend specific cases. As Erasmus says, such explanations are achieved by focusing on the quality of events that are non-unique, and because they are non-unique, such explanations tend to be comparative (1967:127). Indeed, Erasmus points out that 91 percent of all articles in the nomothetic category were comparative in substantive material and that this too has increased steadily during the last fifty years (1967:130). In other words, a concern with problems that tend to promote explanation applicable across cultures has been on the increase as indicated by actual measurements of anthropological publications over the past fifty years. It is this particular development that informs this book and brings an anthropologist devoted primarily to comparative survey work on large samples of societies (Naroll) to cooperate with one devoted primarily to fieldwork (Cohen). Though each of us uses somewhat different data, our goals are the same, i.e., the creation of generalizations that apply not to *a* culture but across a number of them. To accomplish this end, we must, as Erasmus points out, look for the non-unique categories and create, discover, or posit relationships among them and then ask why such relationships exist. This holds true whether we are asking why X is present among males but not females of one culture or present in some cultures and absent in others, or whether we are asking why there is more of X among males in one culture, or more of it in some cultures. In other words, the comparative perspective is there whether we are doing fieldwork in one or a few societies, or, on the other hand, sampling among a large number of societies.

This does not mean that we feel there are no other worthwhile or serious research goals and methods within anthropology. Obviously there are and they deserve some discussion. Two of these are important and should be noted. First there is the holistic or what we would call the historicist or culture-specific approach, and second there is formal structuralism. The first has been a widespread one in anthropology while the second has a more limited appeal but has received widespread attention.

The holistic approach focuses on *a* culture as the central problem. The object is to study and understand a particular society and its culture historically, socially, economically, politically, psychologically, and even biologically. The assumption is that to understand any one part of the culture we must look at all of the rest of the sociocultural context. Thus the

ethnographer, and even the comparativist who is interested in a limited culture area, has looked at as widely ranging a set of phenomena as possible. They have used any methods and techniques they could find that could be adapted to this problem. This has served to make anthropology open and eclectic. But it has also served to make the accumulation of anthropological knowledge one in which analyses of particular cultures are heaped one upon the other as if the accumulation itself were the goal of the enterprise.

A critical reader might disagree at this point and suggest that often the reason one society is chosen as against another is because of the light it will shed on a particular theoretical problem—and this, too, is part of ethnographic method. We agree with this. But we question whether this traditional approach, even when it is theoretically defined, is the most efficient means of solving problems. In our view the problem must be worked at intellectually, and be clearly defined into its relevant parts so that data can, ideally, provide *yes* or *no* answers to varying solutions or explanations of the phenomena under study. This is again because we see the accumulation and expansion of explanation as our goal rather than ethnographic information in and of itself.

In the case of formal structuralism we have not treated it in detail except as it enters into the discussion of formal taxonomies and the like in ethnoscience. The reason for this is our basic assumption that culture and society as elements of reality are stochastic phenomena operating according to the laws of probability. Explanation must seek therefore to establish relationships among such entities defined as variables and/or constants. Formal structuralism as practiced by Lévi-Strauss or any of his followers assumes that underlying the stochastic quality of the human experience there are formal laws or regularities that explain the statistical tendencies we observe. These laws are derived from moral precepts, or "rules," pertaining to social interaction. Thus social process is the functioning of these "laws." It is interesting to note in this respect that it is most easy to apply such an approach to societies in which the people practicing the rules approximate to 100 percent and the rules themselves apply to 100 percent of the population. Contrarily, we assume that human social and cultural life is dependent upon a great many factors only one of which (albeit an important one) is the moral and ethical precepts applicable to any type of activity. We would not argue with the assumption that there may be regularities underlying statistical tendencies, probabilities, and correlations. But as in the other sciences we see this as resulting from (a) detailed analyses of the statistical properties of observable phenomena, and/or (b) from some symbolic representation of these entities and the theoretical application of a mathematical logic that "lawfully" interrelates them, and from which theorems can be derived. In other words, although the formal structuralist aims at nomothetic theory, we feel it is too narrow in its present applicability, and wrong in its approach because it derives formal laws from moral precepts.

To repeat, because we believe it is an essential distinction, although we appreciate the importance of other approaches and their contributions to anthropology, we have in the main taken the nomothetic position rather than the idiographic or genetic. That is to say, we eschew culture-specific studies with the explanation of the culture as a major goal, and focus instead on the nomothetic goals. Thus our primary goal, which determines the others, is theory-construction—and methodology is our means for searching for and interrelating the non-unique categories that enable us to build theories whose generalizations are applicable across cultures. But within this framework we also tend to avoid nomothetic approaches which we feel do not agree with our basic approach to the nature of social and cultural reality.

Another important epistemological problem is the place of method in the research enterprise. To us, the entire thrust in scientific research involves a series of interrelated phases or intellectual and practical aspects which may apply in any order although the order itself reflects a particular research strategy. These aspects are theory, method, and technique. Theory deals with generalizations, regularities, relationships, that is to say, the nature of phenomena; and it creates, or works toward the creation of, explanations that account for this nature (see Kaplan 1964 and Brown 1963). As Cohen suggests (Chapter 2), it is also the primary goal of science. Method is the means by which knowledge is gained.

In our view, it refers primarily to the logical operations and strategies that provide pathways to theory and to the support or negation of theory once it has been constructed. Technique, or the technology of research, is a more specialized feature of method which the rapid development of data processing, especially in the computer field, has now made into a differentiated aspect of method. A technique is a standardized procedure for producing or manipulating information. Thus, participant observation, TAT, factor analysis, the genealogical method are all techniques. They can be categorized as such because there is a widespread agreement about the way they should be used and wide familiarity with the type of information they can provide for a researcher. In our view they are not, strictly speaking, methods because they do not and cannot, in and of themselves, provide all of the logical strategy necessary for carrying out a research project. For example, why one technique rather than another should be used is also an aspect of method and one not solved by the technique itself. Obviously, one of the most important aspects of method is the choice of technique, but method links all of the aspects of research together—data collection, presentation, research design, analysis and so on—making out of these series or phases a logical set of steps which as a whole is the research method.

Another concept that crosscuts theory, method and technique is that of approach. An approach is an acceptance of one set of assumptions as against another. In this sense it is perhaps the most fundamental quality in the research enterprise since it tends, at least initially, to determine the type of theory, method, or techniques that are to be created and employed. Thus, for example, if we use a psychological approach as opposed to a sociological one, we may be assuming the predominance of psychological determinants. Method and technique are affected by such decisions since they carry out the research task in terms of such assumptions and data collection is in the final analysis determined by the approach. In epistemological terms, an approach, whether stated or not, reflects ultimate beliefs about the nature of sociocultural reality. Thus Homans believes that ultimately sociological and cultural materials can be reduced to psychological materials, while Needham considers such an approach "preposterous" (1962). On the other hand, fundamental differences between approaches should provide growing points for research. Indeed, in the foregoing example Young (1965) has recently designed a study to test the relative explanatory power of "sociogenic" as opposed to "psychogenic" variables with respect to initiation rites.

Our view of method as something in between technology and theory has also informed the choice of materials for the book. We have included some techniques and some discussion of them, but have tried to keep the main focus on how research should be planned and carried out. However, it is important to realize that we do not claim to represent a synthesis of all anthropological method; and that our approach solves some problems but creates others. For example, by opting for methods directed at general theoretical goals, we feel we are emphasizing the non-unique aspects of anthropological research and this joins comparativists and fieldworkers because they both seek categories or units that are cross-culturally applicable. However, it also creates problems in anthropology. The richer, more detailed, lengthier and wider the descriptive range of a case study, the more likely it is to be of use to the comparativist dealing with large arrays of ethnic or societal units. But if fieldworkers become more oriented toward theory-construction and theory-testing, then the range of materials covered, after a cultural context has been researched, must of necessity narrow considerably. To study the Trobrianders is one thing; to study their divorce rate and the theoretically predicted correlates of it is quite another.

Although no clear-cut answers have as yet emerged to such problems, they will in all likelihood stem out of intimate, back-and-forth testing, criticism and cooperation between comparativists and fieldworkers. If both are interested in similar problems, then either in one long-term research project or in several, contributions of both comparativists and fieldworkers can be used to solve problems. Thus at present when comparativists use household organization, they restrict it to traditional categories established by fieldworkers. These can often be scaled or limited by behavioral criteria so that no society would be considered as patrilocal unless 25 percent of the population follows the rule. This would then be considered a low degree of patrilocality while, say 75 percent conformity to the rule would be considered a high degree of conformity. However, when more detailed descriptive data using larger samples of household compositions are collected it may very well transpire that these conventional terms will be dropped and new ones adopted based on statistical clusterings of household personnel and their inter-relationships. Such new conventions would assume that in the future new techniques of data collection and analysis would be standard procedure in such studies, and comparativists would utilize these new, more accurate categories as units in their studies.

In summary, field research in anthropology is developing toward more generally and theoretically oriented field studies which is also the goal of comparative research. For fieldwork this means more rigorously designed studies and a more self-conscious attempt to plan for the methodology involved. Comparative research can both stimulate and be stimulated by such developments. This book represents our attempt to contribute to this process. We also hope that it will provide a basis for discussion among those who agree with us and those who do not. Whatever position the reader takes, we feel he should think about methodological issues; in anthropology, the discussion of them is long overdue.

RONALD COHEN

Evanston, Illinois

BIBLIOGRAPHY

BEATTIE, J.
1965 *Understanding an African kingdom: Bunyoro.* New York, Holt, Rinehart and Winston.
BOHANNAN, L. (Bowen, E. S.)
1954 *Return to laughter.* New York, Harper.

BROWN, R.
1963 *Explanation in social science.* Chicago, Aldine.
ERASMUS, C. J., and W. R. SMITH
1967 Cultural anthropology in the United States since 1900: a quantitative analysis. *South-*

western Journal of Anthropology 23, 2:111–140.

KAPLAN, A.
1964 _The conduct of inquiry_. San Francisco, Chandler.

NEEDHAM, R.
1962 _Structure and sentiment: a test case in social anthropology_. Chicago, University of Chicago Press.

POWDERMAKER, H.
1966 _Stranger and friend: the way of an anthropologist_. New York, Norton.

READ, K. E.
1965 _The high valley_. New York, Scribner's.

YOUNG, F. W.
1965 _Initiation ceremonies: a cross-cultural study of status dramatization_. Indianapolis, Bobbs-Merrill.

Acknowledgments

An edited work such as this requires ultimately the cooperation of many hands. First and foremost we are grateful to the authors of our various chapters who have waited patiently and reacted with forbearance and enthusiasm to our editorial comments. The Council for Intersocietal Studies at Northwestern University provided us with much needed secretarial help during the crucial first stages of the book when correspondence was heaviest. Frada Naroll, Enid Margolis, and Inez Oberteuffer have done much arduous editorial work and to them we owe a special debt of gratitude for helping to put the book into its final shape. Joanne Schipp and Janice Caplan typed and retyped many of the manuscripts after decoding the almost legible handwritten corrections of both the editors and authors.

A more nebulous and diffuse source of "help" has been the intellectual atmosphere or climate of opinion in the social science community at Northwestern University, where the idea of this book was born. In every sense of the word the various social sciences at Northwestern are interwoven into a closely knit community in which a common sense of purpose has emerged and where departmental divisions are literally interwoven by joint appointments and research interests. It was within the ferment and excitement aroused by this atmosphere that both of the editors conceived of creating a handbook on method in cultural anthropology. And it is this general social science orientation which forms the basis of our own approach to the subject matter treated in the volume.

R. N.

R. C.

Acknowledgment is gratefully made to the following publishers for permission to reprint.

AMERICAN SOCIOLOGICAL ASSOCIATION for:
"A Method of Linear Causal Analysis," by Raymond Boudon, *American Sociological Review* 30 (1965), 365–374.

RUSSELL SAGE FOUNDATION for:
"Survey Research and Sociological Anthropology," by John Bennett and Gustav Thaiss, from *Survey Research in the Social Sciences,* by Charles Glock. © 1967.

SOUTHWESTERN JOURNAL OF ANTHROPOLOGY for:

"Outsiders' Judgments; an Ethnographic Approach to Group Difference in Personality," by Robert LeVine, *Southwestern Journal of Anthropology* 22 (1966), 101–116. © Department of Anthropology, University of New Mexico, Vol. 22, No. 2, summer 1966.

and

"An Example of Research Design; Experimental Design in the Study of Culture Change," by George Spindler and Walter Goldschmidt, *Southwestern Journal of Anthropology* 8 (1952), 68–82. © Department of Anthropology, University of New Mexico, Vol. 8, 1952.

WAYNE STATE UNIVERSITY PRESS for:

"Toward a Theory of Political Development," by Raymond Tanter, *Midwest Journal of Political Science* XI, No. 2 (May, 1967), 145–172.

We wish to acknowledge our gratitude to the following publishers and authors who have granted permission to quote selections from their works.

AMERICAN ANTHROPOLOGICAL ASSOCIATION for:

Figure 1 from "Cultural Dimensions: A Factor Analysis of the World Ethnographic Sample," by Jack Sawyer and Robert LeVine, *American Anthropologist* 68 (1966), 726.

AMERICAN ETHNOLOGICAL SOCIETY for:

"Who the Lue Are," by Raoul Naroll, *Proceedings of the American Ethnological Society* (1967), 72–79.

COLUMBIA UNIVERSITY PRESS for:

Trance in Bali, by Jane Belo. pp. 86–88. © 1960.

CONSEIL INTERNATIONAL DES SCIENCES SOCIALES for:

"Comparativists and Non-Comparativists," by André J. F. Köbben, prepared for the symposium on Cross-Cultural Research Tools in Comparative Social Anthropology (Paris, 19–22 September 1966).

HARPER AND ROW for:

"Differences of Perception from Failure of Communication in Cross-Cultural Studies," by Donald Campbell, from *Cross-Cultural Understanding: Epistemology in Anthropology,* by F. S. C. Northrop and H. H. Livingston, eds., pp. 308–336. © 1964.

HARVARD UNIVERSITY PRESS for:

"A Phenomenology of the Other One; Corrigible, Hypothetical and Critical," by Donald Campbell, from *A Logical Point of View,* by Willard van Orman Quine, pp. 42–43. © 1953, 1961, by the President and Fellows of Harvard College.

HUMAN RELATIONS AREA FILES PRESS for:

"Zuni Daily Life," by John M. Roberts. *Behavior Science Reprints,* 1965.

HOLT, RINEHART AND WINSTON for:

"Pattern Matching as an Essential in Distal Knowing," by Donald Campbell, from *The Psychology of Egon Brunswik,* by K. R. Hammond, ed., pp. 83–91, 94–102. © 1966 by Holt, Rinehart and Winston. Abridged and reprinted by permission of Holt, Rinehart and Winston.

INDIANA UNIVERSITY PRESS for:
Foresight and Understanding: An Inquiry into the Aims of Science, by Stephen Toulmin, pp. 110–113, 115. © 1961.

JOURNAL OF CONFLICT RESOLUTION for:
"Cross-Cultural Research on Ethnocentrism," by Donald Campbell and Robert LeVine, *Journal of Conflict Resolution,* 5 (1961), 87–89.

LIVERIGHT PUBLISHING CORPORATION for:
Primitive Religion, by Robert Lowie, pp. 51–53. © 1948 Liveright Publishing Corporation. By permission of Liveright Publishers.

NYDEGGER, WILLIAM F., AND CORRINE NYDEGGER for:
"Observations of Twenty-four Tarong Children," Field Notes (Teofista Castilla, July 29th, 3:06–3:11 P.M., House ⌗14), 1955.

PHILOSOPHY OF SCIENCE for:
"Two Solutions to Galton's Problem," by Raoul Naroll, *Philosophy of Science* 28 (1961), 15–39. © 1961 Philosophy of Science Association.

QUINN, NAOMI for:
"A Day in the Life of a Woman in Capilla Loma," pp. 13–15. Unpublished manuscript.

RIJKSMUSEUM VOOR VOLKENKUNDE for:
Anthropology and the Public: The Role of Museums, by H. H. Frese, p. 69. 1961.

ROYAL ANTHROPOLOGICAL INSTITUTE for:
"New Ways of Presenting an old Idea: The Statistical Method in Social Anthropology," by André J. F. Köbben, *Journal of the Royal Anthropological Institute* 82 (1952), 140.

UNIVERSITETSFORLAGET for:
"Methodological Suggestions from a Comparative Psychology of Knowledge Processes," by Donald Campbell, *Inquiry* 2 (1959), 152–182.

UNIVERSITY OF CALIFORNIA PRESS for:
"Girls' Puberty Rites in Western North America," by Harold Driver. *University of California Anthropological Records* 6 (1941), 21–90.
and
"Culture Elements Distributions. VIII. The Reliability of Culture Element Data," *University of California Anthropological Records* 1 (1938), 205–220.

UNIVERSITY OF ILLINOIS PRESS for:
Life in a Mexican Village, by Oscar Lewis, pp. 63, 64, 65. © 1951.

Contents

PART VII: SPECIAL PROBLEMS OF COMPARATIVE METHOD

Contributors

JOHN W. BENNETT is Professor of Anthropology at Washington University (St. Louis, Mo.). He has done fieldwork in Japan, Israel, Canada and the U.S.

RAYMOND BOUDON, Professor of Sociology at the Sorbonne and Director of the Centre d'Études Sociologiques (Centre Nationale de la Recherche Scientifique), has worked on methodology, logic of social science and the sociology of education.

DONALD T. CAMPBELL, Professor of Psychology at Northwestern University, has done work in social science methodology, psychology of knowledge processes, and measurement of social attitudes, and has collaborated with anthropologists in two investigations.

ROBERT L. CARNEIRO, Associate Curator of South American Ethnology at the American Museum of Natural History, has done fieldwork in Central Brazil and Eastern Peru.

RICHARD P. CHANEY, Assistant Professor of Anthropology at the University of Oregon, has done fieldwork in Mexico.

REMI CLIGNET, Associate Professor of Sociology at Northwestern University, has done fieldwork in Africa and has studied urban sociology and sociology of the family.

RONALD COHEN, Professor of Anthropology and Political Science at Northwestern University, has done fieldwork in Africa and the Canadian Arctic.

GEORGE DALTON, Professor of Economics and Anthropology at Northwestern University, has done fieldwork in Africa on economic development.

HAROLD E. DRIVER, Professor of Anthropology at Indiana University, has done fieldwork in North American Indian ethnology.

ROBERT B. EDGERTON, Associate Professor of Anthropology, Departments of Psychiatry and Anthropology at the University of California at Los Angeles, has done fieldwork in Africa and elsewhere on comparative society, personality development, culture and mental health, and culture and retardation.

MELVIN EMBER, Associate Professor of Anthropology at Hunter College, has done fieldwork in Samoa and cross-cultural studies on marital residence, first cousin marriage and political development.

JOANN FENTON is a graduate student at Northwestern University. She is currently doing fieldwork among the Navaho and in ethnoscience.

WALTER GOLDSCHMIDT, Professor of Anthropology at the University of California at Los Angeles, has done fieldwork in Africa, among American Indians, and in the American rural community.

JOSEF HAEKEL, Professor and Director of the Institut der Völkerkunde at the University of Vienna, has made study trips to the U.S. and Mexico and has done fieldwork in India.

JOHN J. HONIGMANN, Professor of Anthropology at the University of North Carolina, has done fieldwork in Europe, North America and Pakistan.

FRANCIS L. K. HSU, Professor of Anthropology at Northwestern University, has done fieldwork in Chinese, Hindu, Japanese and U.S. cultures.

KENNETH JANDA, Assistant Professor of Political Science at Northwestern University, has done work in information retrieval and data-processing applications to political research, and in international comparative political parties.

ROGER M. KEESING, Assistant Professor of Anthropology at the University of California at Santa Cruz, has done fieldwork in social organization, culture and cognition, and linguistics.

ANDRÉ J. F. KÖBBEN, Professor of Anthropology and Sociology at the University of Amsterdam, has done fieldwork in Surinam and Ivory Coast.

L. L. LANGNESS, Associate Professor of Anthropology in the Department of Business, Government and Society at the University of Washington, has done fieldwork in the New Guinea highlands and among the Clallam in the Northwest coast of North America.

FRANK M. LeBAR is a research associate at the Human Relations Area Files, and a research associate in anthropology at Yale University. He has done fieldwork in Southeast Asia and the Pacific.

ROBERT A. LeVINE, an anthropologist at the Committee for Human Development, University of Chicago, has done fieldwork in Africa, cross-cultural study of socialization, personality development and psychoanalytic anthropology.

CHARLES W. McNETT, JR., Associate Professor of Anthropology at American University, has done archaeological fieldwork in northern Pennsylvania.

MARGARET MEAD, Curator of Ethnology at the American Museum of Natural History, has done fieldwork in Samoa and New Guinea.

JOHN MIDDLETON, Professor of Anthropology at New York University, has done fieldwork in Africa.

DANIEL R. MILLER, Professor of Psychology at the University of Michigan, has done work in child development, psychoanalytic theory, and personality and society.

FRANK W. MOORE, an Executive Director of Human Relations Area Files, has done work in ethnobotany and cross-cultural methodology.

RAOUL NAROLL, Professor of Anthropology at the State University of New York at Buffalo, has done fieldwork in Austria, Germany and Switzerland.

TIMOTHY J. O'LEARY, chief analyst at the Human Relations Area Files, has done archaeological fieldwork in Canada and the United States.

MELVIN PERLMAN, Assistant Professor of Anthropology at the University of California at Berkeley, has done fieldwork in Toro, western Uganda.

RUDOLPH J. RUMMEL, Professor of Political Science at the University of Hawaii, has done work in theoretical international relations and in international conflict.

STUART D. SCOTT, Associate Professor of Anthropology at the State University of New York at Buffalo, has done fieldwork in Polynesia, Guatemala and Mexico.

LEE SECHREST, Associate Professor of Clinical Psychology at Northwestern University, has done work in culture and personality, ecology and behavior, and behavior change.

PATRICIA K. SEGMEN is the Registrar at the Buffalo Museum of Science.

GEORGE SPINDLER, Professor of Anthropology and Education at Stanford University, has done fieldwork in Germany and among American Indians.

RAYMOND TANTER is an Associate Professor of Political Science at the University of Michigan. He has worked on international politics and international aspects of domestic turmoil.

TERRENCE A. TATJE is a Lecturer in anthropology at the State University of New York at Buffalo.

ROBERT B. TEXTOR, Professor of Education and Anthropology at Stanford University, has done fieldwork in Thailand, Indonesia and Malaysia.

GUSTAV THAISS is a doctoral candidate in anthropology at Washington University. He is presently doing fieldwork in Iran.

VICTOR C. UCHENDU, Assistant Professor at the Food Research Institute at Stanford University, has done fieldwork in Nigeria, Ghana, Kenya, Tanzania, Zambia and among the Navaho.

JAN VANSINA, Professor of History at the University of Wisconsin, has done fieldwork in the Congo, Rwanda, and Burundi.

JAMES W. VANSTONE, Associate Curator at the Field Museum of Natural History, has done fieldwork in Alaska and the Northwest Territories.

OSWALD WERNER, Assistant Professor of Anthropology and Linguistics at Northwestern University, has done fieldwork among the Navaho.

DOUGLAS R. WHITE, Assistant Professor of Anthropology at the University of Pittsburgh, has done fieldwork among the Veracruz peasants and fishermen, and the Ojibwa Minneapolitans.

BEATRICE WHITING is a Lecturer on Social Relations at Harvard University.

JOHN WHITING, Professor of Social Anthropology at Harvard University, has done fieldwork in Africa and New Guinea.

PART I

General Introduction

CHAPTER 1

Method in Cultural Anthropology

RONALD COHEN and RAOUL NAROLL

GENERAL INTRODUCTION

This is a book about method in social and cultural anthropology, although its orientation is toward the wider field of social science in general, and ultimately the scientific enterprise as a whole. Methodology within anthropology has always been something of an underdeveloped area. Somehow, by reading, by association, intuition, and being the "right" kind of person to begin with, a student was traditionally supposed to pick up enough understanding of method to carry out field work or comparative analysis. Whereas in other sciences, and increasingly so in the social sciences, a great deal of effort both in research reports and in graduate training programs has dealt with methodological matters, very little of this type of activity has ever interested or bothered most anthropologists.

The result has been twofold: first, students generally recapitulate the methodological learning of the previous generation *at the same rate*. That is to say, the basic technique for teaching methodology has been a "school of hard knocks" approach. The underlying pedagogical philosophy is that it is impossible to either communicate or learn such skills—the incumbent must do it the hard way by going through exactly the same experiences as those who are the acknowledged professionals in the field. This has in turn led to an image of field work as an initiation rite on one side of which is the novitiate, while on the other are the members who, having been through the experience, now have a secret bond that can ultimately be felt, but not totally objectified into a communicable set of ideas and findings.

Second—and stemming out of the first—the traditional anthropological attitude to methodology has led to a non-accumulative or very slowly accumulating tradition which is more akin to that in the humanities than that of the sciences. When method is an important aspect of a research tradition, then specialist writings on this aspect begin to accumulate, and the topic develops a dynamic of its own as well as a research frontier. When this occurs, what may take one researcher years to discover can be taught to his successors briefly and without the difficulties encountered by the original innovator. Anthropologists have felt traditionally that there is some value in having everyone go through the same experience and discover anew the conditions of field work. This is what is meant above by the phrase "at the same rate." It means that if it took five to ten years of experience to produce an anthropologist thirty years ago, it must take exactly the same time to learn the same amount of methodological sophistication at the present time.

The explanation for this conservative approach to methodology within anthropology lies not so much in the basic conservatism of its practitioners as in the conditions of research and the goals of the discipline. Generally, the anthropologist has been the only person capable of collecting and recording information on some remote corner of the earth. This means that the fuller and more widely ranging the record he is able to bring back with him, the better. Besides this, and possibly dependent upon it, is the assumption that cultures are integrated wholes, and to dissect such an entity without knowing all of it produces a high probability of error in the interpretation. Therefore, a technique has been worked out by which the researcher uses his entire experience as a record of the society. This experience can be manipulated to some degree, but basically the person is the chief research instrument.

No wonder then, that the method was difficult to record and develop—it rested ultimately on the person and the personality doing the work. Training could only help to "decenter" the person by making him aware of the great variety of ways and means that have been devised by man in creating his society and culture. At the end of such training, very few if any of the practices known to have been carried out anywhere in the world seem strange to the student. Students were and are prepared not to be shocked, afraid or scandalized by any customs or practices found anywhere in the world. But beyond developing this attitudinal bias, very little else is done to prepare the would-be professional, albeit this decentering process has been an important aspect of training and still is.

However, such training is becoming less important; first of all, because knowledge of different cultures is much more widespread today than when anthropology began. The discipline itself has helped to diminish ethnocentrism among the nonprofessional public. Therefore, there is much less need to train students in the truths of cultural relativism today than there was twenty-five years ago. An example of this is the use of the English word "superstition," whose frequency of use was much greater twenty-five years ago than it is today. The inherently ethnocentric connotation of the word makes it less acceptable to a public that is in fact more cosmopolitan and less ethnocentric than the preceding generation. Secondly, other social scientists are visiting and researching in non-Western areas of the world, making such cross-cultural comparisons common throughout the social sciences. The rapid amount of social change going on in the world today, the lack of isolation of non-Western peoples, and the fact that sectors of their lives are being studied by other social scientists have created something of a crisis in anthropology (Cohen 1967).

The answers are not simple to come by. However, one of the obvious results of world social change on anthropology as a discipline has been the sharpening of problems and a decreased emphasis on the holistic approach, as a fundamental goal of all field work. This in turn has led to more detailed and systematic research on limited sectors of a culture or on a number of cultures, using a comparative approach. Once this development has been admitted, and its impact upon our own field work and comparative research is fully felt, then methodological questions begin to surface rapidly. More limited problems demand more rigorous and systematic research techniques and methodological strategies—and there is very little discussion of such issues available in anthropology itself. This is, in effect, the purpose of this book. We have tried to cover the various kinds of methodological problems that we feel are the most pressing in the field of cross-cultural research at the present time. The book starts out at a very general level, that of epistemology, then narrows to problems of causality, correlation, literature criticism, and the old but still important questions of diachronic versus synchronic analysis. The focus then narrows to field work methodology and moves from there to problems of comparative analysis. In Part I, we have tried to present ideas about knowing. Generally, within such symposia volumes, it is customary to seek the help of one or more of the major philosophers of science in order to obtain a clear picture of epistomology as a special topic of interest. We certainly advise the reader to consult the works of writers like Popper (1959), Kuhn (1962), Brown (1963), and Kaplan (1964). However, it is also our opinion that often as not such writers are not ahead of, but behind, the growth of methodology in a particular discipline. This results from the fact that their task is not so much to invent new ways of knowing, but rather to systematize the methods being developed in the sciences themselves. Thus, the writings of philosophers represent in general, a synthesis of work already developed by the actual scientific yeomen who invent the new ideas, and who often must invent as well new ways of proving such ideas right or wrong. This means that philosophers of science provide us with good texts on conventional epistemological problems in the discipline.

This is not meant to be a criticism of philosophy. When more standardization occurs in anthropological method, then philosophers will be of great help. However, at this stage of its development, anthropology needs to feel its way toward its own logic of inquiry, using critical standards from scientific logic in general and its sister social sciences in particular.

In a chapter devoted to this topic, Naroll supports a stochastic view of reality, such that knowledge is based on an inherent perception of probabilities. The inherent quality of this perception results from the fact that man is part of and adapted to his environment. Thus, his faculty for basing knowledge on probabilities reflects the actual structure of his environment. This point is expanded and made comparative across species by Campbell and his conceptualization of knowing and adaptation as essentially the same process. Thus, human knowing is only a highly specialized facility for achieving what all organisms seek—to succeed at living in their environment, which they do, partially at least, through the aegis of learning.

Focusing in on anthropology, Cohen looks at the ways in which anthropologists claim to learn. Ethnographic descriptions are examined as sets of generalizations, and recommendations are made for their improvement. Various kinds of relationship statements are also examined and finally placed within the purview of a systems approach. However, the system is seen as a heuristic and an analytic device in which boundaries are defined not by empirical data so much as by the requirements of theoretical problems which are in fact today cutting across disciplines and reorienting them. In effect, Cohen asks how generalizations are made in anthropology and how these statements looked at as goals can be improved upon, given the problem that not all possible ethnographic statements can be fully documented. Indeed, it would seem that the most important aspect of ethnography—the way in which traits fit together to form a working sociocultural unit—seems to be left out of formal procedures of note taking and record keeping.

In summary, then, Part I is devoted to the nature of knowledge, and the way in which knowledge is arrived at by man in general, and within anthropology in particular.

GENERAL TECHNIQUE

Part II concerns itself with techniques of importance both to field descriptive work and to comparative studies. Of these, the most important is that of causal analysis. The cause-and-effect concept has come under considerable criticism in the last few decades. Nevertheless, we use it without any hesitation or apology. The distinction between a cause-effect relationship on one hand and a mere association on the other can well be put in terms of probability theory. If two variables are associated, then if you know the value of one, you can make a prediction about the value of the other with better than chance expectation of your prediction being correct. But if Variable A is a cause and Variable B an effect, you can do more than that. First, you must posit as an axiom that you are able at will to change the value of Variable A. Then, you define A as a cause (or causal influence) of B if, and only if, it is true that when you at will produce a change in the value of Variable A, you thereby produce a change in the expectation of the value of Variable B.

Chapter 4 by André J. F. Köbben explores the relationship just set forth between cause and intention. The causal concept is seen as related to the will of the observer. Köbben considers the meaning of the concept of cause in the light of the concept of effect. Effect is examined (1) as the outcome of intention or purpose; (2) as the outcome of intention plus by-products; (3) as the product of actors striving after an unattained object; (4) as the unforeseen accumulation of minor conscious decisions; (5) as the product of coincidence and/or juxtapositions; and (6) as the product of psychophysiological reactions.

Köbben's chapter on the concept of cause closes with a look at the variety of ways in which a group of three or more variables may be causally linked. The mathematical analysis of causal relations between groups of three or more variables is the subject of Boudon's chapter. Boudon's work is extremely important. He offers a general mathematical theory of causal analysis of correlation matrices. In this he reduces to special cases the earlier similar work by Wright, Simon and Blalock. Few anthropologists will be able to follow Boudon's mathematics; for a full understanding, the reader must be familiar not only with matrix algebra but also differential equations. Nevertheless, we urge readers to make their way through it as best they can. They can look carefully at the limits of application which Boudon precisely states. For his theory to be applicable, one must assume that all factors *not* included in the analysis have equal effects upon all those which are included. This assumption is a strong one, as Boudon himself is at pains to make clear. Furthermore, at least one-half of the possible causal explanations must be ruled out by the investigator on nonmathematical grounds. For example, suppose someone is considering the cause-effect relationships underlying the cross-cultural correlations among grassland environments, round houses and patrilineality. Obviously, he may for nonmathematical reasons rule out the possibility that patrilineality is the cause and grassland environments the effect. In other words, he can assume that tribes with patrilineality are not any more likely to seek out grassland environments than those without patrilineality. Given these two requirements, the assumption of *ceteris paribus* and the assumption that half of the mathematically possible relationships among the variables are culturally impossible, Boudon's mathematics permits the investigator to untangle the direction of the remaining relationships among three or more variables.

This then is a partial and restricted but nonetheless powerful solution to the classic problem of untangling causal relationships among correlations. It does not work if we have only two variables; we must have at least three. It is not valid if some variables which are not considered affect unequally the variables which are considered. It is not valid unless the investigator can prime the pump by ruling out at least one possibility among the many. But given these limitations, Boudon's method sorts out causes from effects very nicely indeed.

As an appendix to Boudon's chapter, Naroll presents the special case of influence analysis. This causal analysis method is mathematically narrowly restricted. It applies only to the situation in which several causes independently produce a single common effect.

Its strength lies in its logical component. Where these several causes, though empirically independent factors, are logically related, the special influence analysis model is able to escape the other restrictions of Boudon's general model. Given a stated logical relationship among independent causal factors, it is no longer necessary to make the assumption of *ceteris paribus* nor is it necessary to rule out a priori any of the mathematically possible relationships, in order to test the validity of the influence model. Boudon's chapter is a highly condensed summary of a large subject. Readers who wish to know more should see his other writings (Boudon 1967; Boudon 1968; Boudon, Degenne and Isambert 1967). These other writings deal with nonlinear cases, which are not dealt with here. (The mathematical presentation of Chapter 5 assumes that the correlations are linear rather than curvilinear.)

A final presentation of causal analysis theory is that by Raymond Tanter. Tanter is a political scientist; his data are from a cross-national rather than a cross-cultural survey. (The theoretical problem to which he addresses himself, that of political development, will, however, be of special interest to an anthropological audience.) Tanter's chapter, like Boudon's, is not easy to follow. But students who take the trouble to study it carefully will be fully rewarded. Tanter offers yet another method of causal analysis of correlations. His method depends upon the use of multiple correlations and factor analysis. (Tanter has not explored the possibility of a mathematical relationship between his method and Boudon's. One wonders whether mathematically it too might not be found a special case of Boudon's general model. But that remains to be seen.)

Technical in quite another way from the chapters by Tanter and Boudon is that by Timothy J. O'Leary. O'Leary here copiously fills a long-felt need for a general ethnographic bibliography of bibliographies. He who wishes to learn all he can in a library about the ethnology of any human group should begin his search by consulting this chapter. O'Leary will send him to the regional guides which in turn will list the useful writings in European languages. A survey of O'Leary reveals that the major gaps in ethnographic bibliography today are: (1) the ethnography of Europe itself!; (2) the ethnography of the

Middle East; and (3) the ethnography in the Chinese language of China and its neighbors. The literature on the rest of the world is now fairly well listed in bibliographies.

Once the student, using O'Leary, has gathered together the writings on the human group which interests him, how far can he believe what is written? Chapters by Naroll and Rummel in Part VII, below, consider this problem statistically; their use of data quality control enables statements to be made about patterns of systematic error in groups of statements. But the reader who is concerned with the trustworthiness of any particular statement must use other methods of analysis. Charles Darwin reports that the Yahgans were cannibals. In fact, were they or weren't they? Was Darwin right or wrong? Data quality control methods might well perhaps tell us that errors in statements of this sort tend to be in the direction of mistakenly calling tribes cannibals who are not eaters of human flesh rather than mistakenly denying cannibalism among tribes who are in fact such eaters. But these methods would not tell us whether Darwin was right or Darwin was wrong about the Yahgans. Some American anthropologists, trained primarily as field workers, handle problems of this sort rather simply. If the author is a professional anthropologist, they believe anything he tells them. If not, they pay no attention to him at all. Thus, they would here ignore Darwin on the Yahgan, and in all probability they would here be avoiding an error. But this same rule would lead them to ignore Hyades, Deniker, and worst of all Thomas Bridges. Thomas Bridges, who began as a missionary and ended as a rancher, probably knew more about Yahgan ethnography than any other human being—as I suspect Martin Gusinde himself might well agree. To ignore Bridges' work because Bridges was not a trained anthropologist is essentially to ignore the Yahgans.

Certainly casual travelers have written much nonsense about ethnography. But as Chapter 8 shows, professional anthropologists are by no means immune from error either. There is no escaping the responsibility of evaluating the trustworthiness of every statement by every field worker on its merits. For this heavy task, we have the methods of internal and external source criticism developed in the eighteenth and nineteenth centuries by scholars studying classical antiquity. Sources of information on classical antiquity are notoriously sparse, biased and careless. The art of extracting trustworthy information from such untrustworthy sources was developed to a science by these classical scholars. Their methods were collected in such handbooks as Ernst Bernheim (1908). The most important methodological contribution of the Vienna culture-historical school of ethnologists has been the systematic application of these classical methods to ethnological data. A summary of ethnographic source criticism is here presented for us by the Viennese ethnologist Joseph Haekel.

A classic preoccupation of the culture-historical school of ethnology has been the inferential reconstruction of culture history. In the form of trait distribution studies, this kind of historical study was popular in the United States in the first two decades of this century. In the form of ethnogenic studies, culture-historical studies are highly popular among Soviet ethnologists today. The classic exposition of methods of historical inference about particular cultures by Sapir (1916) has never been superseded. However, Vansina's chapter enlarges and supplements Sapir by focusing on techniques like radiocarbon analysis developed since Sapir's time.

THE FIELD WORK PROCESS

In this section of the book, we have tried to look at field work as a process by which knowledge is achieved. The chapters by Le-Vine, Sechrest and the reprint of Spindler and Goldschmidt's research design point up the difficulties as well as the rewards of more rigorous planning in field work. However, the unfamiliarity of such designs and the general lack of their use in field work deserve some further comments.

Scarcity of rigorous research design in anthropology has very likely been one of its strengths historically. The field worker was simply told to bring back as much material as possible documenting the way of life of the people he had lived among. To plan more rigorously would probably bias observation, it was thought; or even worse, it would prevent the collection of valuable—and often disappearing—data. These data were to form the basis of our record of human variety. Without a full range of such variance across all sectors of social and cultural life, the basis for comparative generalization would be limited. When a case is totally unique, it indicates the possibilities of variation—whereas if there are no data on such a case and no such possibilities can even be conceived of, then comparison is impossible. For example, we have many cases of descent systems changing from matrilineal to other forms, but no record of a patrilineal system ever changing to a matrilineal one. We may then conclude that for some (theoretically important) reason, such change is impossible. However, if one case turns up, then such theorizing must be radically changed in accordance with the new facts.

It is this philosophy of variance that has in the past led to a de-emphasis on research design in field work. The approach inherent in such a philosophy assumes, basically, that the case itself should direct the energies of the researcher, rather than some preordained set of ideas. If any design features were built into field work, they usually were answers to two questions: Has this group ever been studied before? Does it represent a type of society (kinship system, religion, political or economic organization, etc.) that I am "interested" in? The researcher could feel that his work was a contribution to the roster of variance if he could answer *no* to the first (therefore he had a new society), and *yes* to the second (he was adding new data to his "topic of interest").

However, the quest for variance is less exciting than it was twenty-five years ago; surprises in the form of unique cases are hard to come by. Besides, understanding, theory, and explanation did not, unfortunately, grow automatically out of an ever-expanding literature of ethnography. Theory is not an inevitable result of more data even though this view is still held by many anthropologists. For these reasons and more, we are at the stage when more emphasis has to be placed on research design—the stipulation of a particular research strategy by which empirical investigation will lead to theoretical generalizations. This does not mean that we are arguing against an understanding of the cultural context within which more rigorously designed research must take place. To do so would be to reject everything anthropology has contributed to social science. The chapters on research design emphasize instead that

it is possible to build into and add to our older anthropological research "design" (aimed at obtaining more information and expanding the knowledge of human variability). In other words, we do not advocate change so much as growth, and in all likelihood the area of research design is more important than all others in moving anthropology toward more efficient achievement of its long-term theoretical goals.

The chapters on entree into the field (Langness, Middleton, Uchendu and VanStone), on sampling in ethnographic field work (Honigmann), on the art of field work (Mead), and on recording behavior (B. and J. Whiting) all deal more or less with traditional and still almost universally practiced aspects of field work. Whether or not field work moves toward tighter design and more standardized instruments of data collection, these problems of getting into the field situation and living there while in fact using one's ordinary day-to-day life as a research instrument, will still be with us. This is because: all theory-directed data collection still depends on an understanding of the context; and the researcher is in fact living in the society and should use this experience to inform his research focus.

No matter where it is in the world, starting work in a strange community is difficult. Our four contributors to this discussion may not represent the full range of possibilities, but they cover a wide range of field experience on four continents, and at least three of them have different national associations. (VanStone is an American, as is Langness, but the former has lived in Canada and carried out research in the Arctic under the auspices of the Canadian government.) Given this much variation in personal background per researcher and specific research site adds weight to the similarities among the papers. All of the writers stress the importance of going through the proper channels to get to the field, the need to establish a role and the difficulties in doing so, the need to go slow at first and the fact that one's first eager informants are not necessarily or usually the best in the long run. Only one of the four spoke the language of the people living in his research site. Although language in anthropological research has been emphasized for years, it is slowly becoming recognized that only a minority of American-trained field workers become fluent in the language of the people they have lived with. Research is needed to systematically compare across a broad range of topics the quality of field work done by those with and without local language skills. In our opinion, such skills significantly affect the quality of research and most certainly its enjoyment by the researcher.

All of these topics are gone into in much greater detail by Mead in her chapter on the art and technology of field work. Professor Mead takes on the extremely difficult task of trying to assess what makes for a successful field trip, what kind of personality, and personal as well as interpersonal behavior, contributes to such success. For the field work process itself, using the researcher as the center of activity by whom data and theory are produced, this chapter is possibly one of the most important in the entire volume. It is significant and probably not accidental that much of the sensitivity and personally revealing reporting of what an anthropological field trip means as a personal experience has come from women field workers (Bohannan 1964, Powdermaker 1966). It is at least a plausible hypothesis that Western men are more fully absorbed into a culture of success in which they reveal only that which is important to their success goals. Women, being still somewhat alien to the professional world, may find it easier to objectify their roles as alien researchers in the field simply because they occupy a somewhat similar role in their own culture.

Narrowing the problems of participant observation still further, we come to the difficulties of systematic methodology. Traditional anthropological field work has built into its very fiber a conflict between systematic research and the duty to absorb and record the life of a people as it is in fact being practiced. Unfortunately, the people do not have the responsibility of analyzing and categorizing their social and cultural experience and therefore cannot sort their own behavior or responses to questions into neat packages for placement into a filing system or an analytical framework. This is, possibly, the farthest removed that investigation can get from experimental research. In the latter method, the researcher controls a set of independent variables, often one at a time, and observes their effect on a dependent variable. In traditional anthropological field work, of-

ten as not, all variables are varying in response to local conditions. Only by using some of the more rigorous techniques of design discussed by Sechrest, can we obtain some control over this variance.

Given the fact that there is a conflict between systematic research methods and techniques on the one hand, and the blooming, buzzing confusion of social life on the other, then two aspects of the conflict need close attention—sampling and data recording. The traditional anthropological researcher has always had a good deal of faith in the validity and even reliability of the bulk of his observations as these pertain to his community or those small groups of people among whom he has lived. However, it is important to ask if his sampling procedures, based usually on a number of criteria, only some of which have to do with data collection, bias his results. John Honigmann is one of the few anthropologists to have ever addressed himself to this problem. In the chapter devoted to this topic, he outlines the conditions under which traditional techniques of opportunistic sampling are appropriate, and conversely, where other techniques are required by the exigencies of field work. Similarly, the Whitings discuss the means by which detailed observations of everyday behavior can be recorded in a form that is both accurate and amenable to systematic analysis by the researcher. They also make a good case for the recording of actual versus reported behavior by discussing the numerous sources of error that intervene between an act and reports on it by one of the participants being interviewed about the activity.

The rest of Part III is devoted to detailed discussions of more highly targeted research methodology. Once the problem of general contextual research has been faced, then we must link research design to systematic data collection in terms of theoretically stipulated or derived parameters. This does not mean that traditional anthropological work ceases. Participant observation should continue throughout a field work study, aided by note taking, focused interviews, and continuous participation in the social life of the people being studied. However, a major sector of time is also devoted to more problem-oriented data collection using specific techniques directed toward this task. This may involve the use of questionnaires, psychological tests, outsiders' judgments, team research, market surveys, or a host of other standardized techniques.

In Chapter 17 Bennett and Thaiss analyze the place of survey research in anthropological field work and summarize a number of studies that have utilized such techniques. They isolate the conflict between traditional field work methodology and sociocultural survey work in which the former tends to look at all possible variables while the latter demands stringent restrictions on the topics to be investigated. Furthermore, anthropologists are socialized into a disciplinary subculture that stresses close, even intimate relationships with informants while survey research narrows or even eliminates such rapport. The authors attempt to resolve such conflicts and point out that more training in statistical techniques may now be a necessary part of graduate training in anthropology. Other varieties of quantitative data are discussed by Edgerton (on psychological testing) and by LeVine, whose chapter on outsiders' judgments describes a technique for getting at what may be the truths underlying ethnic stereotypes. Again, it should be stressed that we do not support the notion of replacing traditional anthropological field methods with more restricted quantitative techniques. Such naiveté would fly in the face of everything we have learned about cultural differences during the last half-century. However, we do advocate *adding to traditional methods*, i.e., a multi-method approach—and the chapters on survey research methods are central to such considerations.

In this same vein, the chapter by Campbell and LeVine, and that by Perlman point to new methods for creating comparable data from field work materials. Perlman discusses team research in the field and goes into some detail concerning the difficult problem of culture-specific indicators for theoretically relevant variables. Campbell and LeVine report on the work being done in "field manual" anthropology. Here the comparability is built into a field manual which must be filled out by field workers (who may be carrying out research on quite different topics). Such "piggy-back" research may seem like field work at a distance or "abstracted empiricism," but the problem of comparability is a real one—and it is getting worse. Thus, if the bulk of field work is oriented toward theoret-

ically specific problems, thereby focusing and restricting data collection to smaller sets of variables, what will become of the comparability among anthropological publications. Instead of so-called "holistic" ethnography, we are now moving rapidly toward topic-oriented ethnographic data collection, making for comparability within similar topics but not across whole societies simply because an anthropologist happened to have done field work in an area. It is this kind of problem that both Perlman with his team approach and Campbell and LeVine with their field manual methods have attempted to solve.

Often, no matter what the specific technique being used, a problem of translation arises which can be very difficult in the preparation of culture-specific questions or instruments directed for use in a specific culture. Werner and Campbell discuss these problems and their solution at both a theoretical (i.e., what is translation as an interlanguage process of semantic transformation) and a methodological level. The result is a clear-cut set of rules about translation and a set of illustrations concerning the ambiguities that can emerge unless great care is taken with this kind of work.

MODELS OF ANALYSIS

Part IV is in direct contrast to Part III of the book, and for several reasons leans more heavily toward theory than it does toward technique. In Part III, we directed our efforts toward discussions of field work as a set of operations both intellectual and mechanical which had to be carried out in the planning and doing of research. Part IV, on the other hand, is directed toward sets of categories that are relevant when data are to be collected on a special sector of social and cultural life.

These are not meant to be the last word on any of the topics included. Instead they are directed toward a compromise between a holistic descriptive approach, and specific data collection directed at theoretical goals. We assume that in most cases, researchers will be well versed in those categories of data collection that surround or come out of their own particular research problem. Thus, if a research design is directed at political behavior, then the field worker will have already considered a number of theoretical models of the political system that are available in both political science and anthropology. However, specialized knowledge of the religious system or the economic system may be lacking. For purposes of doing research on the general social and cultural context of the society we have therefore decided to present for the field worker a series of chapters that deal in detail with one particular category of social and cultural life. These can then be used as guides to the relevant categories of data that are necessary if the material is to have comparative utility in the discipline as a whole.

Obviously we have presented only a sample of such models and would advise that the field worker equip himself with a number of theoretical texts on the whole range of topics that were traditionally used as chapter headings in ethnographic reports. The wide-ranging eclecticism which expected of an ethnographer that he be a comparative expert in kinship and family life, religion, politics, economics, ecology, technology, art, personality dynamics and history to name only some of the major sectors seems naive in contemporary social science terms. On the other hand, we feel, as did our teachers, that the field worker is quite capable of gathering valuable data across a wide spectrum of social life, but not without help. The kind of aid we wish to offer can be seen then in Part IV. It is not complete, but points up the need for a small library on all aspects of social and cultural life in which the relevant categories of data collection can be spelled out by experts in the field so that the researcher can do justice to this sector when he collects data on it in the society in which he is working.

Three particular models of analysis are included for different reasons. Hsu brings his years of experience to bear on the study of literate civilizations. Here, the sampling difficulties referred to by Honigmann now become so difficult that a qualitatively different order of methodological problem emerges. In large complex civilizations, Hsu assumes there are unifying patterns or common characteristics that thread their way throughout the historical development of the entire culture. These may be more easily and accurately recorded by examining not a small community or a set of them, but through systematic research on society-wide institutions as well as the ideology, literature and art of the culture.

As a technique, ethnoscience has become a widely accepted mode of eliciting in a rigorous way, the means by which a culture structures meaning for the participants in that culture. If ethnoscience is in fact simply a technique, however, then it has the same status as a TAT or a genealogy, and by our editorial standards, it should not be included in a book on methodology. However, we believe that Werner and Fenton have isolated the theoretical goals of ethnoscience so that it is, in their hands, raised to the level of the cross-cultural study of epistemology. At this level, it can be compared with politics, religion, or economics as an important subsector of social and cultural life. However, this derivation of a specific sub-field has not been made heretofore in the literature in such logical and clear-cut terms and therefore requires extra space in our volume so that the authors be allowed to develop their argument and then move toward methodological discussion.

Finally, Roger Keesing's chapter on role behavior is an attempt at a new approach to role analysis. Although the role concept is possibly one of the most fundamental units of analysis in social anthropology and social science in general, it is still somewhat difficult to use as a field tool. This is because the concept basically puts boundaries around a set of activities. Such a set may increase or decrease over time, or be in the process of changing during field observation. This has led to attempts to speak of "subroles" (Bohannan 1963:80) which might delimit such ambiguities. Furthermore, simple interactive approaches based on consensus, or expectations, or complementarity, do not easily get round these difficulties either. As one critic of role theory has pointed out, "Individuals often perceive and act toward role partners as if simultaneous multiple roles were being activated" (Buckley 1967:155). Realizing some of these difficulties, and their magnification for the field worker in a strange culture, Keesing has tried by a combination of behavioral and ethnoscientific techniques to work toward a methodology of role-eliciting that comes closer to sociocultural reality than more traditional field work practices.

LEADING COMPARATIVE APPROACHES

The importance of comparative studies to social science is set forth by André Köbben in his chapter "Comparativists and Non-Comparativists." Social science is a search for valid general theory about human social and cultural behavior. Such theories must commonly begin as the result of the study of a single human society. But, as Köbben shows, two independent studies of the same problem in two unrelated societies often lead to conflicting conclusions. From his study of the Siriono of Bolivia, Holmberg (1950) concluded that hunting and gathering tribes tended to be underfed and obsessed by food. From his celebrated study of Western European nations in the 1880's and 1890's, Durkheim (1951) concluded that, in general, social isolation tends to drive a person to suicide. Hauser's study of the Thai led him to believe that in general the more atomistic a society, the more it would resist modernization. Raulin, studying the people of Gagnia and Daloa, concluded that uprooted peoples would be more interested in modernization than those still at home in the land of their ancestors.

But:

Needham (1954), studying the Punan of Borneo, concluded that hunting and gathering tribes were usually well-fed and unobsessed by food. Asuni (1962), studying the people of western Nigeria, concluded that social isolation had nothing to do with suicide. Adair and Vogt, studying the Zuni, concluded that the less atomistic a society, the more it would resist modernization. De Waal Malefijt, studying the Javanese, concluded that uprooted peoples would be *less* interested in modernization than stay-at-homes.

The most widely respected method of comparative study among anthropologists in the last thirty years has probably been the method of concomitant variations, the so-called "controlled comparisons" method. (Since nowadays other methods also make extensive use of controls, the latter name is misleading.) Here a field study is made of a few neighboring and closely related communities. In the Redfield type of research design, the traits of interest to the investigator vary among the communities while hopefully all other irrelevant traits are constant. In the Eggan type of research design, the traits of interest

to the investigator are constant in all communities studied, while hopefully all other irrelevant factors vary. Widely used and influential as this method has been, hitherto its methodological problems have gone uncriticized. In "A Critical Evaluation of Concomitant Variation Studies," Remi Clignet subjects this method to a searching examination. Clignet looks hard at its problems of typicality, data quality, diffusion, concept definition and causal analysis of correlations.

Regional comparative studies like Boas' pioneering investigation of the myths of the Northwest Coast have quite a different goal from concomitant variation studies. Harold Driver's chapter on culture element distribution studies is a comprehensive review of comparative statistical studies of this sort. The aim of a culture element distribution study is through statistical analysis to uncover the culture history of a region. Trait complexes, centers of diffusion, and culture area classifications are the typical goals. Perhaps the most underappreciated body of anthropological research in this century consists of the magnificent series of culture element distribution studies carried out on the Berkeley campus of the University of California by Kroeber and his students. The findings of these studies turn out to have unexpected dividends for investigators working on theoretical rather than historical problems. As is shown in Chapter 47 below on Galton's problem, these studies establish beyond any doubt whatever the important role of diffusion in establishing cross-cultural correlations.

For world-wide comparative theoretical studies, the cross-cultural survey method, we believe, is the decisive research tool. The history of this method is best set forth in the prize paper by Köbben (1952). Invented, as everyone knows, by Edward Tylor, the method was long cultivated in Amsterdam by S. R. Steinmetz and his students. In England, Tylor was followed by L. T. Hobhouse, whose *Morals in Evolution* (1906) is as undeservedly forgotten as his collaborative work with Wheeler and Ginsberg (1915) is deservedly remembered. To an English writer, Unwin (1939), also belongs the honor of the first formal cross-cultural sample.

But the method as it is practiced today is overwhelmingly the brain child of George Peter Murdock. Murdock's contributions include: (1) The use of formal statistical inference, including coefficients of correlation and tests of significance. (2) The development of systematic continental ethnographic bibliographies. Murdock himself produced the bibliography for North America; his sponsorship and materials played an important part in producing like bibliographies for Africa, South America, Indonesia and Southeast Asia. (3) The formal use of the logical method of postulates, a system of reasoning which carries out Popper's doctrine of deductive reasoning and hypothesis falsification. (4) The *Outline of World Cultures,* the first formal world-wide inventory of the world's ethnic groups. (5) The two most widely used quasi-universes, the World Ethnographic Sample and the Ethnographic Atlas. As Köbben points out, the idea of these universes was anticipated by Herbert Spencer and S. R. Steinmetz; but neither of the earlier attempts was widely productive of further research by others; both Murdock's compilations, in contrast, have been extremely productive. (6) The *Outline of Cultural Materials.* Devised as an indexing tool for the Human Relations Area Files, this topical index to culture has proved much more widely useful than its authors had hoped. (7) Finally, in many peoples' minds, Murdock is associated with the most elaborate and widely used data bank in social science, the Human Relations Area Files. The function and scope of these Files is the subject of Frank Moore's chapter. So widely used are the Files, it is necessary to remind people that cross-cultural surveys *can* be done without them, and often are (e.g., Cohen and Schlegel 1968).

The full force of Murdock's contribution to social science is best seen by studying Textor's *Cross-Cultural Summary.* Here the theoretical implications of thirty-nine cross-cultural surveys are looked at through a massive computer cross-tabulation and cross-correlation. Murdock's Ethnographic Atlas is the sampling and data base for the whole study, and Murdock's World Ethnographic Sample is also used as a source for codings. But to say this is to say the least of Murdock's influence upon this body of work. Most of the studies involved made use of the Human Relations Area Files, which Murdock founded. Most of their authors were students of Murdock's at Yale or Pittsburgh, or students of students of Murdock's. And those who took

no formal classwork from him or Whiting or Ford, learned their trade by studying *Social Structure* or *Child Training and Personality.* The intellectual history of Raoul Naroll is probably typical of this last group. In 1950, Naroll became interested in the cross-cultural survey through reading Hobhouse, Wheeler and Ginsberg. Naroll's teacher, Ralph Beals, advised him to read Murdock. This advice led Naroll to study not only *Social Structure* but also the earlier cross-cultural surveys in the Albert Galloway Keller festschrift, which Murdock edited. (These festschrift papers have lately been most conveniently reprinted in Ford 1967.)

The intellectual impact of George Peter Murdock is then, again, best assessed by a careful study of Textor's *Cross-Cultural Summary* (Naroll 1970). The chapter here by Tatje, Naroll and Textor does not attempt to summarize that impact. It only seeks to look at the implications of the Textor study for comparative method. The Textor study sheds light on the major problems of comparative method. The influence of national character bias upon anthropologists is investigated—a contribution to data quality control. The sampling biases of each of the thirty-nine samples in the study is investigated by comparing each with the other thirty-eight. The influence of cultural diffusion on correlations (Galton's problem) is investigated by correlating sixteen linguistic classifications as subjects with the other variables in the study. But most important of all for comparative method are the implications of the correlations of the so-called "Whiskers" variables. These Whiskers variables were introduced in the earlier cross-national computer survey by Banks and Textor (1963). The name comes from the use of imaginary whisker color to name codings that are random—purely random. For example, half the cultures in Textor's study are coded "cultures that have purple whiskers." The selection of this half was done with a table of random numbers. That purely random designation of whiskers color is the point of the thing. In running thousands of correlations by computer, Textor knew that he could expect through chance alone to get hundreds of "statistically significant" correlations. After all, when we say a correlation is significant at the 5 percent level, we mean that we would expect to get that high a correlation of five trials in every hundred through chance alone, even if in fact the two variables were not correlated at all. If, then, we have the computer run ten thousand correlations, we would expect to come up with five hundred correlations "statistically significant" at the 5 percent level no matter what the data. The Whiskers variables are intended to give the computer a chance to show what it can do with theoretically meaningless data. Theoretically there is no reason to expect tribes that fall among the 50 percent with purple whiskers to have any other common characteristics at all. In fact, the computer did find a number of associations. For example, tribes with purple whiskers are associated at the 5 percent level of significance, with class stratification being based on something other than hereditary aristocracy. The interesting thing about the results of these whiskers variable runs is the fact that they consistently underperformed. They tend to produce fewer of these random correlations than theoretically expected. This point is considered at length in Chapter 34 and is also discussed further on page 941 in the chapter on data quality control.

Yet another cross-cultural compendium far more ambitious and elaborate than that of Textor is being compiled by Douglas White. This compendium is the Societal Research Archives System (SRAS) described in Chapter 35. White began this system while a graduate student at the University of Minnesota; there he was aided and encouraged by his teachers E. A. Hoebel and Pertti Pelto. His SRAS is widely recognized as a tool of great potential use in comparative research.

The validity of categories is a problem which has much concerned both those anthropologists who have done cross-cultural surveys and those who have criticized their work. Most behavioral scientists from other disciplines also give it great weight. Yet it is a problem which persistently traps the unwary and engages the anxious attention of the sophisticated.

Exactly what is meant by the validity of categories? The categories of a cross-cultural survey are its variables. To put it even more sharply, they are the definitions of the variables. Logically, a definition is valid if it is clear and unambiguous, so that we may easily and confidently say that any given object or behavior pattern either is one of the things

defined or is not one of the things defined. The definition may be of a measurement; then we must easily be able to report the value of the variable in terms of the stated measurement scale. However, the logical problem of validity of categories is the least of the problem. Tatje's chapter makes the difficulty clear. He gives the example of the concept "cannibalism." I can define it for a cross-cultural survey thus: If in a given tribe, the people eat human flesh and say it is right and proper to do so, I call them cannibals. If they never eat human flesh, or if they consider eating human flesh wrong and improper, then I say that they are not cannibals. Such a definition is clear. It sets up two criteria, both of which must be fulfilled; if either fails, the tribe is not called cannibal; if both are met, the tribe is called cannibal. Logically, there is nothing wrong with this definition.

Yet its validity in any theoretical cross-cultural survey is most doubtful. Here are some objections to it.

Suppose a missionary reports that the Niam-niam are cannibals but says nothing more. How do we know whether he means they are *eaters* of human flesh or that they also *approve* of eating human flesh? (Some people in the Donner party of immigrants to California in the early 1840's ate the flesh of their companions in order to survive the winter when they were trapped in the snows of the High Sierras. Does that make Americans cannibals?)

What kind of cannibalism is meant? The Donner party used human flesh as an emergency survival ration, as did the sailor in the poem by W. S. Gilbert, who reported himself in at last as, "The bosun tight/ And the midshipmite/ And the crew of the captain's gig." In some tribes human flesh is eaten only for magical purposes, because the people think they will gain a person's qualities if they eat his body or certain parts of it. Eat a brave man's heart and you will be braver yourself. Eat a newborn child, old man, and you will grow younger. In still others, the warriors in battle eat their enemies in order to humiliate them. Nothing was thought a greater disgrace in Fiji 125 years ago than for your enemies to eat you; nothing was a greater triumph than to eat your enemies. (The Fijians might later have pointed out that if General Foch had eaten General

Hindenburg in 1918, there might have been less doubt later on in Germany about which side lost the First World War.) Among still other tribes, human flesh was eaten only as part of a funeral ceremony. People might eat bits of the flesh of a dead father or mother; they said this helped comfort them, helped console them for their loss.

If like Maurice R. Davie (1929) you have a theory that warfare had its origin in cannibalism, clearly you need to think about this second group of questions.

Cannibalism as a category does not describe a behavior pattern which is functionally related to any other behavior pattern or trait. It lumps together a collection of unrelated behavior patterns. Therefore, one cannot learn much, if anything, about the general nature of human society or culture by a cross-cultural survey which has cannibalism for one of its categories. On the other hand, one might well learn something by studying dietary cannibalism, or trophy cannibalism, or funerary cannibalism. By the validity of a category is meant the ability of an investigator to learn something useful about the theoretical problem he is investigating through the use of the category as part of his research design.

The ultimate criterion for validity of categories in cross-cultural surveys then, is set forth in Ember's chapter. That criterion is the usefulness of the category in theory-testing. Cross-cultural surveys, like any other research seeking generalizations, are part of a larger intellectual process of data observation, classification, analysis, and generalization. This process is cyclical: data are observed, classified, analyzed logically (e.g., mathematically), and the results used to test generalizations. Since tests of generalizations rarely if ever are utterly satisfactory, the process immediately begins again. It need not proceed strictly in the order stated. The investigator always finds some work of all four kinds already done and can go on further with any of the four tasks. Classifications are useful which can sort out data in such a way as to make them most amenable to analysis and most parsimoniously generalizable. This last statement is axiomatic, resting on the nature of scientific investigation as an attempt to explain the largest number and variety of observations with the fewest logically and empirically consistent general principles.

For anthropologists today, the most urgent need is a standard set of categories and terms. On many topics, such as kinship, there is a wide agreement about the theoretical importance of a number of categories, but wide disagreement about the names to use for them. Consider the variety of inconsistent technical meanings given to the word "clan." We need to standardize usage to follow the most general and most nearly validated system at hand. In kinship, for example, Murdock's *Social Structure* (1949), with all its faults and shortcomings, is the closest thing we have to a generally validated system. Where theoretical results support the importance of a *new* category, not found in existing literature, then and only then should new terms be introduced. Old terms should not, however, in such cases be given new meanings, for this compounds confusion.

The problem of comparability of categories baffles many anthropologists trained to work in one culture at a time. In describing a single culture, the ethnographer soon learns to use the categories of the culture being studied, rather than those of his own culture, where they differ. In cross-cultural comparisons, where dozens or hundreds of cultures are compared, the narrowly trained ethnographer does not see how he can work with dozens or hundreds of different sets of categories—one for each culture in the sample.

The solution to this problem was worked out satisfactorily in practice by the Yale school a couple of decades ago. Frank LeBar in Chapter 38 presents the working methods used so well at New Haven. But only recently has the Yale principle been given clear statement in Goodenough's rule. Goodenough (1956:37) puts it this way:

What we do as ethnographers is, and must be kept independent of, what we do as comparative ethnologists. An ethnographer is constructing a theory that will make intelligible what goes on in a particular social universe. A comparativist is trying to find principles common to many different universes. His data are not the direct observations of an ethnographer, but the laws governing the particular universe as an ethnographer formulates them. It is by noting how these laws vary from one universe to another, and under what conditions, that the comparativist arrives at a statement of laws governing the separate sets of laws which in turn govern the events in their respective social universe.

For the tyro, anthropologically unsophisticated, the danger to avoid is the danger of supposing that the special categories of one's own culture are suitable for cross-cultural use. They may be, or they may not. The English kin term "mother," for example, denoting as it does a unique relationship always present in every society, is perfectly suitable for cross-cultural comparative use even though in many societies no comparable term is found. Whether or not the Hawaiian language provides a single term distinguishing mother from mother's sister or father's sister, the distinction is theoretically a clear and useful one. On the other hand, as every anthropology freshman knows, the English terms "uncle" and "aunt" are quite ambiguous; the English term "cousin" even more so. In order to decide whether a given concept is cross-culturally useful, one must be clearly aware of the range of functional variation in categorization found in known human societies. Only through systematic comparative study itself can such an awareness be gained. Thus only after carefully examining a wide sample of cultures can one confidently proceed to construct categories. The Human Relations Area Files are a sample particularly convenient for study from this point of view.

The comparativist in cross-cultural surveys, however, need not be further anxious about the problem of cultural context, so widely and properly publicized by Ruth Benedict (1946:42) in her critique of Frazer's *Golden Bough*. Frazer put together a functionally linked system in which each element in the system might come from a different culture. He offered no evidence that the elements occurred together. Field anthropologists familiar with his data often could see immediate and obvious rival hypotheses to explain the functional setting of a given trait. Frazer's method is now, however, no longer in use. Cross-cultural surveys have never used it. By their nature, cross-cultural studies are studies of cultural context, in which one trait from a given culture is compared with another trait of the same culture.

But it is not enough for a category to be theoretically suitable for cross-cultural comparison. It must be operational. That is to say, one must be able to find out enough about a typical society by studying existing library materials so that in practice the classification can be applied. Definitions need to be made extremely precise, so that coders use as little discretion as possible in classifying

particular cultures from field reports. One way out of this difficulty may be to treat the ethnographer as a measuring instrument and to study the characteristics of his report as such. For example, Naroll is currently trying to measure suicide frequency simply by counting the number of words devoted to suicide by ethnographers who mention it at all. Validating such a measure is obviously a difficult matter. Common sense protests immediately that many other factors unrelated to suicide frequency would influence the attention an ethnographer gives to the topic. Yet if suicide wordage is consistently correlated—as it seems to be—with traits not so irrelevantly influenced, such as divorce rules and marriage restrictions, this correlation itself provides validation for such a content analysis approach.

On the other hand, operationalism is not theory construction. As Campbell points out in Chapter 3, it is fundamentally a technique for relating concepts to behavior. Confusing the concept with its operational definition (intelligence is what intelligence measures) maintains theory at its lowest common denominator and enslaves our conceptual development within the confines of contemporary research technology. The warning is clear: because we cannot, at present, operationalize an idea or an insight does not mean that the idea is worthless. It means, instead, that we must strain at the edges of our ingenuity to construct some indicators that have validity in a cross-cultural context.

In fact, cross-cultural surveys are studies of ethnographies rather than of living people. They observe indirectly, "through a glass, darkly." There may well be a methodological advantage to putting our cards face-up on the table, as we do when we study a trait like suicide wordage. For when we do so, it is unmistakably and unforgettably clear that we are directly studying the behavior of field workers, and only indirectly and by inference are we studying the behavior of the people in whom we are interested and whom we seek to understand. Astronomers have long since learned to study photographic plates of the stars, rather than to observe the stars directly. If we think of our work as a study of ethnographies rather than as a study of the native peoples, we will be constantly anxious. We know that ethnographies are immensely less faithful reproducing instruments than astronomical photographs. And our anxiety will be all to the good, for it will lead us to take great care to detect and allow for the large measures of error and distortion which are inevitably involved.

Another problem which we need to keep constantly in mind in constructing categories and developing coding plans is the problem of actual versus theoretical behavior. The peasants of Kaunertal in Tyrol insist that they follow the stem family plan of multi-generational household. In fact, however, a village census reveals no single instance of a stem family household, although several families are eligible (Naroll and Naroll 1962). The comparativist must consider separately for each trait whether he is studying the theoretical system of the people or the system they actually follow. Either choice may be called for by the theoretical problem which interests him. Tatje, LeBar and Ember all give careful attention to the problem involved in the choice.

In any case, however, the comparativist should take care to avoid spurious correlations by confounding the definitions of two traits, so that his definitions themselves produce correlations. For example, in Chapter 40 it was necessary to eliminate occupational subdivision of labor, as found, say in a Samoan canoe-building crew, from a craft-specialty count in order to see if occupational division of labor was correlated with team ramification. Otherwise, the study would have learned nothing, since a correlation between subdivision of labor organized into work crews and team ramification is implied by the very concepts themselves.

Finally, the comparativist must consider carefully whether he cannot somehow scale his variables. For some sorts of problems this may well be utterly impossible. If he is relating residence rules and descent rules, for example—working with the theoretical plans rather than with the actual behavior—he is dealing inescapably with attributes and cannot scale. Often, however, ingenuity and care can yield a practical method of scaling.

Quantification has four main advantages. These will be clear from the other chapters in this book. First, significance tests of increased sensitivity can be used. Since carefully conducted cross-cultural surveys are quite expensive, and since, further, Galton's problem usually limits the size of the usable sample, quantification could make the difference between a study whose significance tests attain conventional levels of significance and one whose tests do not.

Second, an advantage newly discovered by H. M. Blalock (1964:97–126) can be applied. He shows that as data on the relationship between percentage of Negroes and delinquency rate in the United States are successively grouped by counties, states, and regions, increased homogeneity leads to a steady increase in coefficient of correlation. But the slope of the data remains constant. It might then be useful to compute slopes as well as correlation coefficients—especially if the computation is being performed by a computer. However, slopes can be computed only between two quantitative variables.

A third advantage of quantification to the comparativist is the fact that if variables are in quantitative form, he can see whether their relationship is linear or curvilinear. If curvilinear, he can often use some transformation to attain linearity. Linearity is a key assumption of parametric partial correlations. Parametric partial correlations, in turn, form a key element of multiple-variable causal analysis.

A fourth advantage of quantification to the comparativist lies in the freedom from artifacts of arbitrary and varying dichotomy cuts. True, where attributes are all cut near the 50 percent level, these artifacts constitute no problem. But more often than not, they vary widely from 50 percent. Difference in dichotomy cuts of this sort can produce spurious factors in factor analysis.

Several methods of quantification are discussed at length in other chapters in this book. The variable itself may be directly expressible in quantitative form. A Guttman scale may be possible; if not, then usually a Likert scale can be worked out. If several attributes are in quantified form, perhaps they can be combined into an index.

Another method is also possible in cross-cultural surveys. Where the trait concerned can reasonably be supposed to vary in impact upon the ethnographer in direct relationship to its elaboration or importance among the people being studied, the investigator can, as already suggested, attempt to measure this impact by counting the number of words devoted to that topic as well as the number of words in the ethnographer's entire report;

he can thus compute a wordage ratio. Obviously such a ratio would be influenced by the ethnographer's conscious or subconscious interests and attitudes as well as by the culture studied. Where, however, the other factors seem irrelevant to the coding of other variables in the study, the factors would not lead to spurious correlations. For this reason, the wordage ratio method is more useful for *one* only of two variables in a correlation than for both together. In an influence analysis research design, wordage ratio might well be considered for use as the measure of the dependent variable. Obviously, however, where direct quantitative measures of the variable itself are available, they are much to be preferred to the indirect measure of the ethnographer's reactions.

Thus such general problems of categorization as these are the topics of the chapters by Tatje, Ember and LeBar. The remaining chapters focus on specific problems rather than general ones. Naroll's chapter on the ethnic unit of comparative studies focuses on the question: What do we mean by *"a tribe"* or *"a culture"*? For example, is there a general way to answer such questions as "What is the nature of the difference between the Navaho and the Apache?" "Why distinguish between the Pima and the Papago?" The problem was perhaps most neatly put by James Fernandez, in his study of the Fang of Gabon. The Fang lie along a language chain whose dialects grade into Ntumu. Along this language chain are found the people of the Gyem area of the Gabor district. The Ntumu of Bitam say these Gyem people are not Ntumu but Fang. The Fang of Mitzik say they are not Fang but Ntumu. The Gyem people themselves say they do not know whether they are Fang or Ntumu.

Chapter 39 considers ten general criteria which have been proposed for defining whole societies or cultures: (1) distribution of particular traits being studied; (2) territorial contiguity; (3) political organization; (4) language; (5) ecological adjustment; (6) local community structure; (7) widest relevant social unit; (8) native name; (9) common folklore or history; and (10) ethnographer's working unit. The chapter then presents a modified version of Naroll's cultunit concept. The cultunit consists of a group of people (1) who speak mutually intelligible dialects; and (2) who belong to the same state if they

belong to any state at all; or (3) if they do not belong to any state at all, then are in contact with one another through periodic meetings. This concept is demonstrated with two groups of data. First, it is applied to certain difficult special cases in Southeast Asia, discussed by Leach and Moerman. Second, it is applied to the fifty-eight societies in Naroll's War, Stress and Culture sample.

For anthropological theory, perhaps the most important single concept requiring precise definition is that of level of development or civilization. This concept was, for example, the subject of Lewis Henry Morgan's classic —and now universally abandoned—seven-stage taxonomy of (1) Lower, (2) Middle, and (3) Upper Savagery, (4) Lower, (5) Middle, and (6) Upper Barbarism, and (7) Civilization. (See Morgan 1877 and Lowie 1920.) The concept has been the subject of more recent attempts by Childe (1951) and Service (1962). These latter two attempts were supported like Morgan's earlier one by illustrative data often selected because it accorded with the author's thinking. In Service's presentation, the discussion of the band level of development is particularly illuminating (pp. 60–107); for Service, any group without tribal-wide organization which has patrilocal residence is an example of a supposed universal type, while any such group with other rule of residence is an example of disorganization and depopulation inflicted by European contact. Since almost all primitive peoples everywhere suffered severe disorganization and depopulation following European contact, it is easy for Service to select data that support his case. Chapters 40–42 present four other systems of measuring level of civilization. Each of these systems has been tested on a world-wide sample whose selection was uninfluenced by the goodness of fit of the societies concerned with the conceptual system being used.

Naroll's three-trait index of social development is only slightly modified from the original (1956) version. Here the application of this index to a new fifty-eight-society worldwide sample is presented. Again, occupational specialization, organizational ramification and population of the largest settlement are found to have a high log-log correlation with each other.

Chapter 40 also presents Freeman's nine-item Guttman scale of societal complexity.

This scale was modified and improved from an earlier and better known one (Freeman and Winch 1957).

Chapter 41 presents a fifty-item Guttman scale of cultural complexity by Robert L. Carneiro.

Chapter 42 presents a five-level sequence of stages of settlement pattern by Charles McNett.

Each of these measures has some internal evidence supporting its validity. As already said, Naroll's three indicators are highly correlated with one another. The Guttman scales of both Freeman and Carneiro have remarkably few scale errors. (Freeman's scale, like Naroll's index, has the additional support of successful replication on a new sample.) McNett's sequence of stages is shown to be highly correlated with a considerable number of other traits.

But these four measures are all even more strongly supported by their interrelationships. Different though many of them are in concept and technical structure, they correlate well with one another. Clearly, all four are tapping the same underlying factor—the factor of societal complexity, level of civilization. McNett's is the easiest to use. Naroll's is the only ratio scale and has perhaps the clearest linkage with evolutionary theory. Carneiro's is the most elaborate and informative.

These measures of social development were all intended for use in studies of social and cultural evolution. But they have another use as well. Those who study other problems and test other hypotheses often need to control for level of social development. Otherwise they risk testing hypotheses with spurious correlations which in fact only reflect differences in social development. Since social development is so profound and widespread a phenomenon, investigators carrying out cross-cultural surveys of anything else at all would be well advised to use some measure of social development as a control. The use of that measure would be to test the rival hypothesis that the correlations seeming to support their theories in fact merely reflect similarities in development level.

Major data pools like the Human Relations Area Files and the Societal Research Archives System would be much strengthened if all the societies in their samples were coded by all four of these measures. If so,

users could easily apply all four to their studies.

Where no such easy precoded measures are available, comparativists would find McNett's scale quick and easy to apply, and satisfactory for purposes of rival hypothesis control.

SPECIAL PROBLEMS OF COMPARATIVE METHOD

We must place the six chapters of the concluding portion of the *Handbook* in their proper context. To do so, it will be well to list the major problems of comparative method. We distinguish ten such problems. (Of course, many of these ten problems are likewise applicable to other kinds of studies as well.)

1. *The general nature of knowledge.* This problem is discussed in Chapter 2, below. There, the canon of stochastic epistemology is proposed. As part of the general process of inference about the nature of the world outside the mind, a four-part cycle is posited: observation, classification, analysis and theory.

2. *Causal analysis.* As already mentioned, this topic is considered at length by Köbben, Boudon and Tanter in their chapters in Part II.

3. *Chance.* The possibility that chance may be producing seemingly meaningful relationships has been discussed above in connection with the treatment of it by Textor through his use of Whiskers variables. These Whiskers variables seek to offer some control over chance influence upon a large number of correlations. This is one special case of the general problem of evaluating chance as a factor in producing seemingly meaningful relationships. The general topic of the evaluation of chance is, of course, the main concern of an entire branch of mathematics. That branch is mathematical statistics, including the theory of probability. It was especially hoped to include a chapter introducing anthropologists to this topic. However, circumstances prevented our doing so. The consequence is that many of the chapters and much of the reasoning in this handbook will remain unintelligible to anthropologists who know nothing at all of mathematical statistics or probability theory. Nowadays, the basic principles of both these sciences are being widely taught in the high schools, as part of the so-called "new math." The unfortunate truth is that many older anthropologists are simply unequipped to understand the

new anthropology because they do not know the new mathematics on which it is based. Much of this mathematics is new only in the sense that it is new to the high school curriculum. But much of it is absolutely new—unknown to anyone thirty or forty years old.

How serious a handicap this lack of mathematical training can be to our profession is well revealed in a recent paper: "Why Exceptions? The Logic of Cross-Cultural Analysis" (Köbben 1967). This searching review of many leading problems of comparative method devotes (p. 17) about three hundred words to coincidence as a factor in producing correlations and as much more space to the consideration of the influence of uncommon individuals—a "Great Man" theory of ethnology to set beside the "Great Man" theory of history. Had Köbben been trained to think in terms of probability theory, he would probably have perceived that to the large-scale comparativist, "coincidence" and "uncommon individuals" are merely random noise. The use of probability theory and statistical tests of significance measures the net collective impact of *all* random disturbances to correlations. Thus, random sampling error, random observational or coding errors, and random interference through coincidence or random appearance of uncommon individuals—all these tend to lower correlations, and their likelihood of, on the contrary, raising correlations is routinely measured by ordinary tests of statistical significance. The possibility of such distortions must always be present and can never be ignored; but their probability may often be found so small as to be negligible in practice.

Köbben's article proposes that the problem of exceptions to correlations be dealt with by studying only extreme cases. Such an approach would obviously have its uses. But as Blalock (1964:119) points out, extreme case contrasts tend to produce distorted and misleading results. In the scientific division of labor among anthropologists, the study of extreme cases is particularly commended to field workers seeking theoretically significant field situations. For cross-cultural comparativists acquainted with mathematical statistics, the multivariate analysis approach set forth by Boudon and Tanter offers an opportunity to confirm or correct the findings of field workers studying particular extreme cases. Multivariate analysis is precisely intended to

meet the need to which Köbben's paper calls attention. Further, it takes into consideration also the chance factor. Indeed, of the eleven sources of exceptions to correlations listed by Köbben, multivariate analysis in the sophisticated forms presented here by Boudon and Tanter deal with no less than seven: (1) multicausality (Köbben, pp. 12 f.); (2) parallel causality (pp. 13 f.); (3) functional equivalents (pp. 14 f.); (4) intervening variables (p. 15); (5) coincidence (p. 17); (6) personality (p. 17); (7) combination of factors (pp. 18 f.).

4. *Categorization.* Discussed here by Ember, Tatje and LeBar in Chapters 36–38.

5. *Unit of Study.* Discussed by Naroll in Chapter 39—the tribal definition problem.

6. *Data accessibility.* A leading limitation of library studies of theoretical problems lies in the frequent difficulty of finding relevant data. Field work, clinical case studies, or experiments can produce data infinitely more accurate, data much better controlled and data much more copious. But what these other methods of study gain in quantity and quality of data, they lose in data scope. So we turn to cross-cultural library studies, not because the quality of cross-cultural data is good, but rather in spite of the fact that cross-cultural data is often bad.

The problem of teasing usable codes and scales from cross-cultural data is considered by Tatje in his chapter on classification and is touched on as well on pp. 13–17 above in this chapter.

The key point to bear firmly in mind here is that through care and ingenuity often one can tease out a trustworthy and fairly sensitive measure from ethnographic source material even if that material is untrustworthy and insensitive.

7. *Data Quality Control.* The problem of dealing with inaccurate ethnographic sources or errors in coding by comparativists is the problem of Chapter 44. The chapter presents the evidence for the occurrence of error in ethnographic sources; it points up the crucial distinction between systematic and unsystematic error, i.e., bias and random error; and it presents the control factor method of finding and allowing for bias.

While Naroll's chapter focuses on ethnographic data quality control, the chapters by Rummel (45) and Janda (46) focus on that problem in cross-national surveys. Since many comparative anthropologists are interested in comparative studies of developing nations, these two chapters are of considerable interest for their content as well as for the improvements in data quality control method which they present.

8. *Cross-Cultural Sampling*. The frequency of bias in cross-cultural sampling is reviewed by Tatje, Naroll and Textor in Chapter 34. The chapter on cross-cultural sampling by Naroll (43) reviews the problems of sampling bias. A crucial problem in cross-cultural sampling is the bibliographic problem. For a cross-cultural survey, tribes in effect might as well not exist at all if descriptive literature on them is not available in the libraries. Thus any sampling method must provide for choosing tribes about which the needed data is at hand. These days, most cross-cultural samples are drawn from a quasi-universe—a large list of tribes which for many purposes may be taken as a nearly complete list of all tribes about which enough is known for study. The Human Relations Area Files, the World Ethnographic Sample, the Ethnographic Atlas and the Permanent Ethnographic Probability Sample are here considered as sampling universes. Finally, the chapter considers methods of measuring and evaluating sampling bias.

9. *Galton's problem*. This problem is the problem of distinguishing between the influence of cultural diffusion on one hand and functional association on the other. The problem is particularly pressing for cross-cultural surveys and culture element distribution studies. However, as Clignet shows (Chapter 31), it is an urgent problem for concomitant variation studies as well. The urgency of the problem is not fully appreciated until cross-cultural surveys are compared with statistical culture element distribution studies. For example, as Chapter 47 points out, in aboriginal California, partrilinear totemic clans are found invariably and exclusively in tribes (namely the Mohave, the Yuma and the Kamia of the southeast corner of the state) which also play tunes on flageolets, use carrying frames made of sticks and cords, make oval plate pottery, use a large fish scoop, and favor twins. But patrilinear totemic clans are not peculiar to southeast California. They are found scattered around the world in many other places. Would we expect that in Africa, in Eurasia, or in Oceania, wherever we encountered patri-

linear totemic clans, there and there only we would also find people making oval plate pottery, using a large fish scoop, using a squared muller, or favoring twins? Clearly we would not. As Chapter 47 points out, the perfect correlations found between traits comprising selected elements of the southeastern California complex are explained by joint diffusion and only by joint diffusion. How do we know then that correlations between matrilocal residence and matrilineal descent—relations which seem to have a clear functional linkage—might not likewise reflect the influence of joint diffusion, especially since they too are so often found in geographic clusters? That is Galton's problem. It must be solved. It cannot merely be talked away. Chapters 47 and 48 review the history of the problem, examine its logic, and present six solutions to it. Five of these have been presented earlier elsewhere. Both new and important is the sixth solution by Driver and Chaney (Chapter 48).

10. *Multi-universe validity*. Cross-cultural survey results are sometimes questioned on the ground that they represent chiefly the behavior of primitive tribes. Is it not possible that these results might not apply to contemporary people, living in the atomic age of warfare, living in the jet age of travel, and living as well in the electronic age of communication?

From the standpoint of cultural anthropology, all modern nations can be viewed as belonging to a single culture area—Western culture. They share major cultural values like social welfare, democracy, and economic and technological progress. They likewise share a common body of knowledge (chiefly collected in writings in the Latin alphabet). Most important of all they share a common technology, which links them into an economic, political and informational network far tighter than that which in the year 1750 linked the Indians of the Plains into one cultural system, and those of the Northwest coast into another.

This modern Western culture area obviously has many special characteristics which differentiate it from all other human culture areas. The same of course can be said of any other culture area as well, for each is unique. But our own culture area is especially different. Now, these specific differences may well have many implications for social and cultural structure. There seem to be many such differences of which we are aware. There may well be many other differences of which we are not aware.

Thus it is an entirely plausible and pertinent query to ask: Are characteristics of human cultures generally also specifically true of our own civilization? Might not our own civilization present many exceptions to these general rules? These questions are the more forceful since the rules themselves do not pretend to apply invariably to all cultures everywhere and anywhere. No, they only apply as general tendencies to most cultures at most times and in most places.

Thus any generalization from a cross-cultural survey must remain tentative until it is checked against a universe of modern, Western nations—the universe of the cross-national survey. Especially must this be so of any variables which seem to be related to level of social development or processes of culture change. For this reason, our *Handbook* includes chapters by political scientists. These chapters—by Rummel, by Janda, and by Tanter—cope with problems of interest to cultural anthropologists in the context of cross-national rather than cross-cultural surveys. For a general survey of this literature, see Marsh 1967.

Another young discipline which will become increasingly relevant is that of the cross-historical survey. Problems of culture change are diachronic. But both cross-national and cross-cultural surveys are usually synchronic. At best they deal with short spans of change in time. The cross-historical survey, however, commands the full sweep of five thousand years of recorded history among the leading Old World higher civilizations. (Naroll 1967; Naroll 1968; Naroll, Bullough and Naroll 1971; see also Kroeber 1944; Eisenstadt 1963.)

Thus any social science theory which aspires to generality must be checked by a wide variety of methods in a wide variety of cultural contexts. This spirit of "multiple strategy" has characterized the Intersocietal Studies program at Northwestern University, under the successive leaderships of Richard C. Snyder and Richard D. Schwartz. It figures prominently in the writings of Quincy Wright (1942) and of David McClelland (1961).

The ideal test for a major social or cultural hypothesis would be a set of studies: (1) a cross-cultural survey; (2) a cross-historical survey; (3) a cross-national survey; (4) a concomitant variation study; (5) several extreme cases, in which the association concerned is especially high; (6) several exceptions, particular societies in which association concerned is absent. If the hypothesis involves any elements relating the intellectual or emotional behavior of individuals to their cultural and social systems, then (7) case studies of individuals would be needed as well. Finally, (8) the hypothesis should be tested in formal games, like the internation simulation of Guetzkow *et al.* (1963). These games are controlled experiments; herein lies their importance.

If all these approaches yield similar and mutually supporting results, the hypothesis must certainly command the belief of mankind—at least until other studies produce inconsistent or conflicting results. Until hypotheses have been so tested, their results remain tentative and inconclusive.

Cultural anthropology then becomes most meaningful when it is seen as part of a larger body of thought. Cultural anthropology is most meaningful when it forms part of a larger behavioral science.

Because theirs is the most general of the behavioral sciences, anthropologists have a special responsibility to mankind. Most political and economic and social philosophies today rest on obsolete or poorly tested social science. If social science is to provide normative guidance for mankind, cultural anthropology must necessarily form the foundation of the normative structure. This topic is far too large to dwell upon here. We know that today cultural anthropology is widely drawn upon for normative guidance in such matters, for example, as child training. We do not think the state of the art is yet ready for cultural anthropology in particular or behavioral science in general to assume its responsibilities. Our disciplines are still toddlers and this handbook is an attempt to provide one such toddler his primer.

But it is our suspicion that in time to come when cultural anthropologists and other behavioral scientists are able to speak with real authority on the causes of war and peace, of divorce or suicide, of distributing economies and concentrating economies, of social order and social disorder—then they will merely by presenting their case provide mankind with the moral order it now so sorely lacks.

BIBLIOGRAPHY

ASUNI, T.
1962 Suicide in Western Nigeria. *The British Medical Journal*. October 22. Reprinted in *International Journal of Psychiatry* 1, No. 1, January, 1965:52–61.

BANKS, ARTHUR S., and ROBERT B. TEXTOR
1963 *A cross-polity survey*. Cambridge, M.I.T. Press.

BENEDICT, RUTH
1946 *Patterns of culture*. New York, Mentor Books, New American Library.

BERNHEIM, ERNST
1908 *Lehrbuch der historischen Methode und der Geschichtphilosopie*. 6th ed. Munich and Leipzig, Duncker and Humblot.

BLALOCK, HUBERT M., JR.
1964 *Causal inferences in nonexperimental research*. Chapel Hill, University of North Carolina Press.

BOHANNAN, L.
1964 *Return to laughter*. New York, Natural History Press.

BOHANNAN, P. J.
1963 *Social anthropology*. New York, Holt, Rinehart and Winston.

BROWN, R.
1963 *Explanation in social science*. Chicago, Aldine.

BUCKLEY, W.
1967 *Sociology and modern systems theory*. Englewood Cliffs, N.J., Prentice-Hall.

CHILDE, V. GORDON
1951 *Social evolution*. New York, Schuman.

COHEN, R.
1967 Comment on: Anthropological theory, cultural pluralism and the study of complex societies. L. A. Despres. *Current Anthropology* 9:17–18.

COHEN, R., and A. SCHLEGEL
1968 The tribe as a socio-political unit: a cross-cultural comparison. In: M. H. Fried, ed., *Essays on the tribe*. Proceedings of the 1967 meetings of the American Ethnological Society. Seattle, University of Washington Press.

DAVIE, MAURICE R.
1929 *The evolution of war*. New Haven, Yale University Press.

DURKHEIM, EMILE
1951 *Suicide: a study in sociology*. John A. Spaulding and George Simpson, translators. New York, Free Press.

EISENSTADT, S. N.
1963 *The political systems of empires*. New York, Free Press.

FORD, CLELLAN S. (ED.)
1967 *Cross-cultural approaches*. New Haven, HRAF Press.

FREEMAN, LINTON C., and ROBERT F. WINCH
1957 Societal complexity: an empirical test of a typology of societies. *American Journal of Sociology* 62:461–466.

GOODENOUGH, WARD H.
1956 Residence rules. *Southwestern Journal of Anthropology* 12:22–37.

GUETZKOW, HAROLD, CHADWICK F. ALGER, RICHARD A. BRODY, ROBERT C. NOEL, and RICHARD C. SNYDER
1963 *Simulation in international relations: developments for research and teaching*. Englewood Cliffs, N.J., Prentice-Hall.

HOBHOUSE, LEONARD T.
1906 *Morals in evolution*. New York, Holt.

HOBHOUSE, LEONARD T., G. C. WHEELER, and M. GINSBERG
1915 *The material culture and social institutions of the simpler peoples*. London, Chapman and Hall.

HOLMBERG, ALLAN R.
1950 *Nomads of the long bow: the Siriono of Eastern Bolivia*. Smithsonian Institute, Institute of Social Anthropology Publication No. 10., Washington, D.C.

KAPLAN, A.
1964 *The conduct of inquiry*. Chicago, Aldine.

KÖBBEN, ANDRÉ J.
1952 New ways of presenting an old idea: the statistical method in social anthropology. *Journal of the Royal Anthropological Institute* 82:129–46.

1967 Why exceptions? The logic of cross-cultural analysis. *Current Anthropology* 8:3–34.

KROEBER, ALFRED LOUIS
1944 *Configurations of culture growth*. Berkeley, University of California Press.

KUHN, T. S.
1962 *The structure of scientific revolution*. Chicago, University of Chicago Press.

LOWIE, ROBERT H.
1920 *Primitive society*. New York, Liveright.

MCCLELLAND, DAVID G.
1961 *The achieving society*. Princeton, Van Nostrand.

MARSH, ROBERT M.
1967 *Comparative sociology: a codification of cross-societal analysis*. New York, Harcourt, Brace and World.

MORGAN, LEWIS HENRY
1877 *Ancient society*. New York, Holt.

MURDOCK, GEORGE P.

1949 *Social structure*. New York, Macmillan.

NAROLL, RAOUL

1967 *Imperial cycles and world order*. Papers, Peace Research Society (International), 5:83–101.

1968 Deterrence in history. In Dean G. Pruitt and Richard C. Snyder, eds., *Theory and research on the causes of war*. Englewood Cliffs, N.J., Prentice-Hall.

1970 What have we learned from cross-cultural surveys? *American Anthropologist*, Vol. 72, No. 6, in press.

NAROLL, RAOUL, VERN R. BULLOUGH, and FRADA

1971 *Military deterrence in history*. Albany, State University of New York Press.

NAROLL, RAOUL, and FRADA NAROLL

1962 Social development of a Tyrolean village. *Anthropological Quarterly* 35:103–120.

NEEDHAM, R.

1954 Siriono and Penan: a test of some hypotheses. *Southwestern Journal of Anthropology* 10:228–232.

POPPER, K. R.

1959 *The logic of scientific discovery*. New York, Basic Books.

POWDERMAKER, H.

1966 *Stranger and friend: the way of an anthropologist*. New York, Norton.

SAPIR, EDWARD

1916 *Time perspective in aboriginal American culture; a study in method*. Canada, Department of Mines. Geological Survey, Memoir 90. Anthropological Series No. 13, Ottawa, Government Printing Bureau. Reprinted in David Mandelbaum, ed., *Selected writings of Edward Sapir in language, culture and personality*. Berkeley, University of California Press, 1958:389–462.

SERVICE, ELMAN R.

1962 *Primitive social organization*. New York, Random House.

UNWIN, JOSEPH D.

1934 *Sex and culture*. London, Oxford University Press.

WRIGHT, QUINCY

1942 *A study of war*. 2 vols. Chicago, University of Chicago Press.

CHAPTER 2

The Logic of Generalization

RAOUL NAROLL and RONALD COHEN

1. EPISTEMOLOGY
Raoul Naroll

STOCHASTIC EPISTEMOLOGY

To start with, a book on research method may well have a look at the nature of knowledge. The purpose of research is obviously to increase knowledge. But what do we mean by "knowing" and how do we know what we know? Needless to say, these questions constitute that branch of philosophy called epistemology. Their discussion has been a central theme of Western philosophy from Plato and Aristotle through Hume and Kant to Reichenbach and Popper.

The discussion of epistemology by philosophers has usually taken for granted one element in the definition of knowledge. Usually, the question has been in effect framed, "How can we be sure that such-and-such is true?"

No philosopher has provided a generally satisfactory answer to this question, even in its easiest form. The easiest form of the question is: "How can I be sure of what is taking place within my own mind?" To answer this question finally one must dispose of the familiar Chinese paradox. An old sage once was talking to a group of his students. "Last night," he said, "I had a dream. I dreamed I was a butterfly. I flitted from blossom to blossom, reveling in the delicious perfume of the flowers and sipping from their nectar. Then I awoke, and found myself a tired old man." He paused and looked about him at each of his disciples in turn. "Now tell me," he finally asked. "Am I an old man who dreamed he was a butterfly? Or am I a butterfly who *is dreaming* that he is an old man?"

I put it to you that there is no way to answer *with certainty*. There is no way to be *absolutely* sure. There is no final and clear answer to the question: "How do you know that you are not now dreaming?"

The study of optical illusions by Segall, Campbell and Herskovits (1966) further attacks our confidence in our own knowledge. Through a large-scale comparative study of a wide variety of cultures, these three men showed that certain optical illusions are systematically related to cultural background.

You may or may not be persuaded by the foregoing argument. Some people are; others are not. But you must concede, I think, that no answer to the Chinese sage has proved generally convincing. Ever since the basic issues were raised by Plato and Aristotle, thoughtful men in the West have wondered and have disagreed about the basic nature of knowledge.

Thus, after you think about it awhile, you may or may not still feel *absolutely certain* that you are a man or a woman, rather than a butterfly. But you must face the fact that you cannot persuade all your colleagues you know how to demonstrate with certainty the truth of your belief.

There is a tale about another philosopher of ancient times—this one a Greek. The story goes that the old man pondered long on epistemology. "How do I know that I exist? How do I know that bread is good food and wine good drink?" Unable to answer these questions, he refused either to eat or drink anything. And so he died: a martyr to epistemology.

Whether or not there is any truth to this tale, it is nevertheless of the greatest importance. For it points up the epistemological foundation of all scientific research. Some may have no doubt at all that they exist—that they are people and not butterflies. Others may have no doubt at all that bread is good to eat and wine—in moderation—good to drink. But when it comes to the fundamental propositions of science about the general nature of the universe, doubt is the rule rather than the exception. Scientific generalizations are always tentative. There are two accepted models of the logic of scientific inference. The older model is the inductive model of Aristotle. This model holds that scientific generalization consists in reasoning from a number of particulars to a grand general. I have seen hundreds of swans. All swans I ever saw were white swans. Therefore, I conclude that all swans are white. Such was the classic model of inductive reasoning. Philosophers who taught it always emphasized that it did not yield certainty. There was no way to be sure that somewhere else, in the remote undiscovered Antipodes perhaps, there might not be a race of black swans.

The newer model of the logic of scientific inference is that of Karl Popper (1959). Popper argues that true scientific generalization is not inductive at all, but deductive. For example, it strikes him that probably all swans are white. He wishes to test the truth of his idea by systematic study. Therefore he plans a world-wide sample survey of waterfowl, looking for swans. From the general theory it follows by deduction that any particular individual swan must be white. Every new swan observed is a new test of the general theory. If he finds even one black swan, his generalization is refuted. Scientific research consists essentially of attempts to *refute* the scientist's own ideas. The scientist naturally hopes his attempt will fail. But he is not a scientist unless he devises a research plan which is likely to refute his ideas if in fact they are incorrect. If a really thorough and well-designed attempt at refutation fails, then the idea is *tentatively* presumed right. But it is never finally shown to be so. According to Popper and to Aristotle alike, there is no research method which permits generalization with certainty about the world outside the mind from things actually observed to things not so observed.

Thus as scientists we are all in the position of the old Greek who could not be sure that bread is good to eat or wine good to drink. And we must all do as the most skeptical of philosophers in fact do—we must eat the bread and drink the wine anyway, whether it is really good for us or not.

Each of us may conceivably doubt that he is awake and truly observing, not asleep and fantasying. But each of us knows with certainty what he is now feeling—whether his sensations are pleasant or unpleasant. Whether or not the sensations are based on reality or fantasy is beside the point. Each of us, at any moment, knows whether or not he feels comfortable or uncomfortable.

Hunger is uncomfortable, thirst even more so. We all—with the possible exception of one demented ancient Greek philosopher—have a working hypothesis that bread will still the pangs of hunger and wine the pangs of thirst. I *know* I feel hungry. I *think* I am in my kitchen. That *looks like* a piece of bread on the table. As a good Popperian logical positivist philosopher, I proceed to attempt to falsify the hypothesis that in fact I really am in my kitchen, that what I see really is bread on the table, and that such bread is really good to eat. I eat the bread with a bit of raspberry jam, and immediately feel better. My personal hypotheses about hunger, about kitchens and about pieces of bread, already firmly established in early childhood, are once again further supported. My attempt at falsifying my theory of alimentation once again had failed. Happily so. The intervention into what seems to be the real world has not produced any experiences which contradict my alimentation theory: hunger pangs are stilled by food; bread is good food—especially with a little raspberry jam. I do not *know* that this theory is correct, not with certainty. But after so many successful trials, I must conclude with the rest of bread-eating mankind that the probability of its falsehood is very small. Probability estimation is the nub of the matter. The odds now seem to me smaller than ever that my mother was mistaken in this matter. She led me very early in life to believe that bread and jam are good to eat. Nearly fifty years later, after thousands of trials, I have yet to find an instance where bread and jam have disagreed with me.

Technically, the special kind of probability inference involved here is called Bayesian inference. To understand what is meant by Bayesian inference, we must consider for a moment the basic meaning of the probability concept. The classic concept of probability deals with a known universe having known characteristics. Suppose my universe is a glass bowl full of marbles. All marbles are identical in size, shape, weight and all other characteristics, save only color. Exactly half the marbles are black, the other half are white. Then the *probability* concept may be defined in terms of this proportion. Given that the marbles in the jar are well stirred, then what I mean by a probability of 50% is the likelihood or chance that a blindfolded person would have in a single try of obtaining a black marble rather than a white one. This model is an example of *a priori* probability. Before any marbles are taken out of the bowl, it is known what are the proportions of black and white.

Now, the Bayesian kind of probability inference supposes a slightly different model. Again we have a glass jar full of black and white marbles, not differing at all save in color. But this time we do not know what are the proportions of black to white. How can we make judgments about the probability of any given draw yielding a black marble rather than a white one? The probability here may not be determined with certainty. However, inferences may be made about it, which themselves have a certain probability of truth or error. By taking one sample of any desired number from the bowl, statements can be made about the probability that the true proportions of marbles in the bowl are thus-and-so. Such probability reasoning is called *a posteriori* probability reasoning. Its key concept is that of the confidence interval.

For example, suppose that there are clearly a large number of marbles in the jar. I cannot tell how many exactly, but obviously there are tens of thousands. Suppose I stir the marbles thoroughly, and then blindfolded take out only two marbles. Both of them are black. I may conclude from this single trial that the proportion of black marbles to white is at least one to a hundred. Such a conclusion is not certainly correct. But if the experiment is frequently repeated with a wide variety of proportions varying randomly, this conclusion will go wrong on the average only one time in ten thousand.

Thus our basic inference is the probability of a probability. There is less than one chance in ten thousand that the probability of get-

ting a black marble on a blind draw is itself less than one in a hundred. In technical language, the same idea can be put thus: I conclude at the .0001 level of confidence that the probability of getting a third black marble on a third blind draw is at least .01. (This conclusion follows from the binomial theorem of mathematics and may by verified by calculation or by consulting a set of tables of the cumulative binomial probability distribution. See Kenney and Keeping, 1951:14–18, 22 f.)

By a similar calculation, I can conclude that there is a probability of no more than 0.0801 that the true proportion of black marbles to white is greater than 99 to 1. Thus there is in all a probability of 0.9198 (1.0–0.0801–0.0001) that the true probability of getting a black marble on the third blind draw is somewhere in the interval between 0.01 and 0.99 (both inclusive). Such a statement is an example of a confidence interval.

Abstruse this confidence interval concept may be. The work of J. Neyman and E. S. Pearson (1928), it is less than half a century old. Yet I argue that this concept intuitively lies at the root of most "common sense" judgments by people in all cultures.

My argument then runs thus:

Whatever may be the degree of doubt or certainty about the most simple and seemingly obvious facts, there is no doubt in most people's minds about many simple but strong pleasant or unpleasant feelings. Most people know in large measure what they like and what they dislike. They must and in fact they do live their lives on the basis of their judgment—usually intuitive—of the probabilities, of the odds: first, the odds that their perceptions are accurate, or inaccurate; second, the odds that their theories about everyday living —most of which come to them via their culture, of course—are correct or incorrect.

I argue then that all people are intuitive mathematical statisticians and Popperian logicians. All people are constantly constructing theories, testing them against reality, and forming conclusions in their minds about the probabilities concerned—the probabilities of their observations, and the probabilities of their general theories.

Can the mind conduct such subtle and complex inferences intuitively without the thinker being aware of them? Can people who consciously know nothing of probability theory or Popperian epistemology, nevertheless practice both? Make both the very foundation of their daily lives? Can so complex a set of mental operations be possible at an intuitive and subconscious level?

Ask this question of the linguists.

The linguists have taught us all the wonderful regularity and precision of the basic phonetic system of every human language. They have also taught us that this system is regularly learned and differs from language to language. Each language has its own set of phonemes. Each set is a regular pattern produced by various combinations of tongue position, lip position, nasalization and the like. Thus English has nine basic vowel phonemes, produced by a three-by-three matrix of tongue positions. Tongue forward, tongue central or tongue back; tongue high, tongue middle or tongue low. Turkish, on the other hand, has eight basic vowel phonemes, produced by a two-by-two matrix of tongue positions together with a dichotomy of lip positions. Tongue may be high or low; tongue may be forward or back; lips may be rounded or parallel.

Now ask any English speaker to explain the English vowel system as I just have done. Until a few decades ago, none could. Today, only those who have studied linguistic theory can. Almost no English speaker understands the theory of English phonetics. Yet all native speakers practice it precisely.

I argue then that stochastic epistemology is a human universal; that this system of reasoning is found among all people in all cultures. It is this system which English speakers have in mind when they speak of "common sense."

Needless to say, this system is not universally applied to all situations. There are always other epistemologies, in every culture. Each culture has more than one belief system, in other words. But the "common sense" belief system of stochastic epistemology is a system found in all cultures, to deal with much of everyday life. This system of stochastic epistemology is the basis of scientific research. As such, it forms a cultural universal today. And hence one universal value premise. (I use the word "stochastic" here simply to mean "having to do with probability theory.")

All cultures value probability inferences about the world of sensory observation to some extent and for some purposes. Even the most mystical of Hindu ascetics has and uses an empirical stochastic theory of alimentation. He may not eat much, but he generally eats something. He may have little use for the things of this world, but he does need a begging bowl. And that bowl in turn is filled by other Hindus more heavily involved than he in stochastic epistemology—more deeply concerned with observing the world around them and drawing probability inferences about it.

THE NATURE OF KNOWLEDGE

The increase in knowledge may then be thought of as the increase of confidence levels —that is to say, the *de*crease in probability of error—and the narrowing of confidence limits. Such is the measure of how well we know what we know.

The measure of what is worth knowing consists of generality and elegance. The wider the number of phenomena encompassed in a theory, and the simpler the theory, the more general and elegant. Galileo's law of gravity described the movements of falling bodies on earth. Newton's laws of universal gravitation held that Galileo's law was but a special case of a more general set of principles; these same principles likewise implied Kepler's laws of planetary motion. Furthermore, though Newton's basic principles explained much more than Kepler's, they were no more complex.

As scientific anthropologists then, we seek ever more general and more elegant theories of man's culture. We disagree with Evans-Pritchard. He maintains anthropology must become history or it will become nothing. By this he means that anthropology must become exclusively descriptive, idiographic, or it becomes nothing. But we hold on the contrary that history must become anthropology, or it becomes nothing. By that we mean that history must become comparative, theoretical, nomothetic, or it becomes nothing.

For us, the object of both disciplines is identical—the extension of man's knowledge about himself. For us this object is best attained through the empirical testing of the most general and elegant theories of human culture.

As has been said, we hold with Popper and Aristotle that no scientific theory can ever be proved correct. However, as both these philosophers maintain, scientific theories often and easily can be proved incorrect. Scientific research then for us, following Popper, consists of the construction of general and elegant theories together with the systematic attempt to *dis*prove them.

The more general and elegant the theory, usually the easier to disprove it if false.

Hence a general and elegant theory which has withstood a well-designed broad attempt to disprove it is established as a presumption. The canon of parsimony now demands that we take it as though it had been proved, but only until some new evidence comes along to overthrow it. The burden of proof has been shifted to the skeptic. He has, however, only to produce new evidence inconsistent with our theory or a new theory equally consistent with our data, in order to return the burden of proof to the proponent of the theory.

To sum up, scientific research may be said to rest upon the following axioms:

1. The canon of skepticism. Nothing about the world outside the mind of the observer is taken as known or given. Everything must be established by observation.

2. The canon of parsimony. The more general and elegant explanation is preferred to the less general or more complex explanation, other things being equal.

3. The canon of *a posteriori* probability. This is the principle of confidence limits just described.

THE SPIRAL OF THEORY TESTING

The matter of testing theories through observation involves at least four distinct operations.

1. *Theory statement.* Every scientist is a member of a human society with its own culture. Consequently, he comes equipped with a complex set of theories about the real world, furnished by his culture. Some of these may seem to him so manifestly well-tested as to need no further investigation—at least, until a skeptic produces an inconsistent observation or an alternate explanation. For example, we may take the theory current in our own society that bread and jam are good to eat: eating bread and jam not only produces agreeable sensations in the palate, but also stills the pangs of hunger. But very many of these, when looked

at skeptically, appear to rest on very little or very poor evidence, or to conflict with some.

If the scientist is working in a scientific discipline with a history of its own, he soon learns a substantial body of theory under discussion. From this body of theory, he may select particular elements for testing, or he may revise and develop new theories of his own. The latter course is much the rarer, more difficult, and more fruitful, of course.

Scientific research, then, starts with a theory.

2. *Classification.* A theory is a statement of relationships between variables. Such a statement involves concepts which define the variables and the statements of relationships. These concepts explicitly or implicitly form a system of categories, a classification or taxonomy. At the beginning of any science, the scientist has the folk concepts and folk classifications of his mother culture. But it is characteristic of all sciences that they rapidly develop new systems of classification, new concepts—technical language. A scientist may make his major modification to the existing body of theory by developing a new category or set of categories with which to sort out the data.

3. *Observation.* Concepts, classification and taxonomies are mere sorting devices—ways to manipulate data. They have no use in themselves. A new concept is better than an old one if it helps us understand the data better. But by "understand" we simply mean to develop a theory which is more general, more elegant, or more plausible. The making of systematic and accurate observations is thus one of the hallmarks of any science. It is only by applying the *theory* through the *classification* system to our *observations* that a test of theory is possible.

4. *Analysis.* Many theories, particularly of the simpler sort, can be so tested without the aid of any formal logic. For example, the theory of biological evolution rests upon four major bodies of evidence: paleontology, comparative anatomy, embryology and vestigial organs. All four of these bodies of evidence involve a large collection of small theories, elaborate sets of categories, and hundreds of lifetimes of systematic observations. But no special methods of logical analysis are involved. The thought processes, or logical inferences, are all those of ordinary "common sense." On the other hand, Newton's theory

of universal gravitation requires for its demonstration not merely a vast body of astronomical data on the motions of the planets and a number of experiments with falling bodies on earth. It also requires the differential and integral calculus. Unless this particular system of logical analysis—the calculus—is first mastered, Newton's theory cannot be understood.

In the opinion of the present writer, many major theories of human culture will similarly require a thorough grasp of mathematical statistics for *their* understanding.

The spiral. Every new cultural anthropologist, like every other scientist, comes to his work with a considerable body of theory, classification concepts, data observations and methods of analysis. He may properly choose to occupy himself with any one of these four activities alone, if he wishes. Or he may combine two or more of them; most of us do. If his work is fruitful, he will modify the existing state of knowledge to some extent. Perhaps he will contribute new data for use by others. Perhaps he will challenge an existing theory by showing it inconsistent with certain data. Perhaps he will develop new concepts, which permit a more effective test of theory. Perhaps he will apply new methods of analysis to a body of data. Perhaps he will develop new theories.

The key point to grasp firmly in mind is that scientific research consists of all four of these activities, linked together. *The validation of any one activity depends upon the other three.*

New theories are mere idle speculation unless they are tested by collecting data, sorting the data into categories, and analyzing the relationships among the categories. (The analysis need not always be abstruse to be effective; but it must be present.)

New *categories* are mere idle intellectual gymnastics unless they make possible the statement of more elegant, more general or more readily testable theory; and unless, further, this theory is presumptively established by test. Categories are validated by testing the theories they make possible. They have no other service to the scientist. True, it more than once has happened that the categories *led to* the theory. The biological taxonomies of Linnaeus did not rest upon any major theory; but they later were seen to relate directly to biological evolution. The periodic table of chemistry had a like history; later on, new underlying theory made sense of the table.

One way to develop a theory, then, is to develop a system of categories which seem to sort out a vast body of data into a smaller and more manageable grouping.

However, until the categorization has been validated by the theory, it has no further merit than that of an arbitrary indexing system.

New *methods* of analysis are but play toys unless they lead to the validation of more general or more elegant theories, or unless they make more plausible—make a better case for—existing theories.

Finally, new *data* are but a pack rat's trove unless they have relevance to a body of theory. And, in fact, our field workers inevitably collect the data they consider important and ignore the data they consider *un*important. These considerations of importance and unimportance are considerations of relevance to theory.

So scientific research consists of an endless cycle of observation, classification, analysis and theory. But the cycle is a spiral, moving upward. Each turn advances the state of knowledge. Each of us may begin at any point on the spiral he likes. But the value of his work can only be fixed by examining its relevance to the other points.

BIBLIOGRAPHY

KENNEY, JOHN F., and E. S. KEEPING
　　1951 *Mathematics of statistics, Part II*, 2nd ed. Princeton, N.J., Van Nostrand.
NEYMAN, J., and E. S. PEARSON
　　1928 On the use and interpretation of certain test criteria for purposes of statistical inference. *Biometrika* 20A:175, 263.

POPPER, KARL R.
　　1959 *The logic of scientific discovery*. New York, Basic Books.
SEGALL, MARSHALL H., DONALD T. CAMPBELL, and MELVILLE J. HERSKOVITS
　　1966 *The influence of culture on visual perceptions*. Indianapolis, Bobbs-Merrill.

2. GENERALIZATIONS IN ETHNOLOGY
Ronald Cohen

All anthropological research is carried out under the prideful guise of being scientific in theory, substance, and method. Nevertheless, as we rummage about in the literature, it soon becomes clear that the "scientific" quality of anthropology is not uniform, although it may vary systematically in lack of rigor. Difficulties in achieving stringently scientific standards are explained because anthropology is so young compared to the natural sciences or because the material is so complex or because of the difficulties in collecting material in the field. What is an acceptable standard that must be applied to our work, if we wish it to be scientific? And exactly what does science ask of us as an enterprise?

In what is to follow I wish to answer these questions in two ways: first, by setting forth quite briefly a standard for scientific behavior, especially with regard to theory construction. Secondly, and in more detail, I wish to go into the ways in which anthropology had in the past, and may in the future, construct different kinds of theories with varying degrees of explanatory power and varying degrees of potential for further elaboration in order to satisfy the ultimate goal of science which I conceive of as the continuous creation and refinement of ideas and facts that help us to understand the world we live in.

SCIENCE AS A METHOD

As a means for gaining knowledge and understanding, especially in a cumulative sense, science is unexcelled. On the other hand there is probably no such thing as *the* scientific method, and philosophers who have specialized in such matters often refuse us a concise definition because as Kaplan says (1964:27), "There is no one thing to be defined." Some see it as the result of having a certain model of reality (formal, prob-

abilistic, diachronic, synchronic, etc.). Others see it as stemming out of a set of very specific procedures such as operationalism or experimental design. The reason for both its utility as a means for gaining knowledge and the difficulty in defining it stems from its openness and constant changeability. What's "in" today as the most accepted discovery procedure may be "out" tomorrow or be changed into some other kind of scientific device. A model of reality that is useful at one stage of our knowledge may be regarded as less than useless at another. Scientists refuse to stick to just one method, or one procedure, or one concept of reality, and this is the reason it is difficult to pin down exactly what scientific method or *the* scientific method actually is at any one time.

Like religion, science extends or expands the world of sensory experience—but where religion extends and expands our world view to include the supernatural, science extends it to include the data and theories it continually creates. Unlike religion, at least until quite recently, science is by its very nature "open." That is to say, it is in constant tension because of the social organization of scientists and the lack of finality built into its intellectual materials and norms. For their part, scientists may gain rewards by proving each other wrong, by refining (i.e., by limiting or expanding) the applicability of each other's work, by substantiating previously doubtful findings. This in turn produces sanctions against falsification of evidence, and rewards for the careful and truthful recording of observations which provide a base line set of standards for the rise of cumulative knowledge. At the conceptual and general theoretical level, Kaplan (1964:351) claims that there can never be any final answers in science—the process of research is itself an unending one.

The rationale for this stems from a number of properties of concepts and theories: (1) scientific findings and explanations are always partial, and they always leave something out; (2) they are conditioned, i.e., they stipulate what is included in the findings, and

I wish to thank my colleagues in the Department of Anthropology at Northwestern University as well as Professors Harold Guetzkow and Paul Kress who read and made many useful comments on a previous draft of this paper.

then everything else is by definition or implication excluded; (3) there are always approximations, and therefore they always include error; (4) they are independent or uncertain to some extent, i.e., they are always to some degree probable and therefore statistical so that any particular instance has only a likelihood, not a certainty, of occurrence; (5) all scientific findings are to some extent intermediate, i.e., they produce many problems that are unexplained and for which there are at present no data.

These generalizations about the limitations and uncertainties of scientific concepts and theories are, in effect, the fundamental reason underlying progress in any scientific enterprise. The product is a growing body of ideas—more or less integrated, sometimes in conflict—that can be used to describe and understand (within the limits of their defects) the empirical world they were derived from as the enterprise develops. What this means is that empirical reality is too complicated to be understood as it is experienced by ordinary human senses. Science twists, molds, and distorts aspects of reality by fashioning concepts and suggesting interrelationships among them with the hope that this creative reflection will enable us to explain and predict the existential reality of sense experience. As this synthetic product proves progressively more useful, it becomes established as part of the empirical reality it is said to reflect.

This does not mean that any particular research tradition is necessarily a steadily accelerating and cumulating tradition of theory and data. As Kuhn (1962) has shown, scientific traditions move forward in cycles or jumps that range between what he calls "normal" research and "revolutions." Normal research follows fairly clear-cut lines. Problems derive from a known conceptual mass of theory and the results are not terribly surprising. Revolutions take place because traditional modes of theorizing leave out problems that begin to gain in importance, or because there is increasing conflict between interpretations, or because theory becomes heavy and awkward with amendments, or combinations of all of these. Such a crisis produces a stimulus to create new axioms, new modes of posing questions, and new modes of explaining research findings. Given all of these stimuli to change, Kuhn cautions

(1962:150) that even after a "revolution" has occurred it may not triumph because its opponents are unalterably committed to a previous research tradition and thus leave the new approach or theory to younger scientists who are not linked so closely to opposing views. In anthropology, revolutions occurred with the inception of field work and I believe another one is developing because of the rapid changes going on in non-Western societies leading to the disappearance of clear-cut cases of cultural variation.

What I have referred to above as a "synthetic product" is my understanding of the word "theory." Thus it is infinitely easier to use concepts like "Crow kinship terminology" or "segmentary lineage" than to describe the numerous qualities associated with such concepts. As a science begins to find agreement among its practitioners or groups of them, at any time level of its own development, on basic units and concepts, then these become the means for coping with their referents. I would contend that the creation, development, and refinement of such symbols and their interrelationships is the primary goal of science. A group of such symbols, representing aspects of reality and the ideas governing their interrelationships, often conceptualized as well into processual symbols, is a theory. Whether or not the theory is scientific depends ultimately on whether the ideas involved in the theory can be submitted to a test of their validity. The stress here is on the word "ultimately." Obviously there have been many crucial theories in the history of science that could not be tested when they were first proposed. However, science does demand that ultimately theory must stand up before empirical observations, hopefully designed specifically to disconfirm any or all of the propositions contained in the theory.

It is important to note here that I am not suggesting that science replaces reality and nothing else happens. The world of the senses is always there and is constantly referred to through empirical research. Indeed it is this aspect of the enterprise that serves as the executioner of theory. As long as we understand and accept the inexorable mortality of our concepts and theories, we stand in no danger of reification. Scientific theory treated as if it were reality is not hallucination, but heuristic. This pragmatic quality is best appreciated when we have two or more conflicting theories both of which predict and explain the same empirical phenomenon, both of which seem reasonable on a common-sense basis, but both of which stem from different processes, use different concepts, and involve different theoretical relationships.

The goal of science, then, is theory, and theory is treated with greater or lesser confidence by the use of tests devised to disconfirm or substantiate propositions. The development of a science is very crucially bound up with the relations between theory and observations that form the traditions of its research enterprise. These relations are what philosophers refer to when they speak of deductive and inductive science. When we know very little about a topic, investigation proceeds with the goal of discovering its variety in time and space. Once this has been done for a fairly generous number of varieties, we start to classify the phenomena and their subparts, then begin thinking of, and observing ways that they and their subparts are interrelated with each other and other known phenomena. If some of these first ideas about variety and relationships are substantiated, we can, in fact, say that theories are developing. From then on observation is guided more and more frequently by theory. That is to say, in its earliest stages, science is primarily inductive, but its own internal requirements demand more and more deductive work as the enterprise develops. Thus in order to conceptualize X, A, B, and C, and suggest that they are related such that X is a function of (A, B, C), it is important to collect information on just these concepts if we wish to test the validity of a theoretical idea. It may be, of course, that the empirical indicators of each may vary from situation to situation (cf., Perlman's comments on this point in Chapter 19), but other information not related to the theory must be omitted or controlled for if we suspect that it will interfere with the relationships being studied. Another way of saying this is to suggest a generalization: As science develops, there is a constant tendency for more elaborate and refined theoretical development as well as more carefully controlled and theory-directed observation. The goal is theory, the best possible; facts are necessary, but to contribute to science, they must also be "data," i.e.,

information that can be used to confirm or disconfirm a theoretical conclusion.

For present purposes these introductory remarks will suffice to clarify my own particular views on the nature of science as a general cultural institution designed specifically to increase knowledge and understanding in a progressive and cumulative fashion. For further and more detailed discussion on this topic, specialists in the field should be consulted (Hanson 1958, Popper 1959, Gibson 1960, Kuhn 1962, Brown 1963 and Kaplan 1964). The remainder of this paper is devoted to varying models of generalization that are used in social and cultural anthropology.

DESCRIPTIVE MODELS

Nearly two decades ago a writer from psychology, in trying to evaluate anthropology as science, claimed that for the most part, social and cultural anthropology results in descriptive accounts of field trips (Stavrianos 1950). Field reports, she claimed, lack any clear hypothesis or any exact information as to the quantity or quality of the data. In general such reports are also described as lacking in clear conclusions or generalizations. Kluckhohn (1959), in responding to this criticism, suggests that anthropologists view their informants not so much as actors whose behavior must be observed and measured but as documents, or as an art historian treating a new specimen might do when he fits the new item into a recognizable style. He also claims (1959:259) that it is not simply a matter of incidence and distribution, but one of pattern, or in what slightly variant ways the pattern is manifest. In such an analysis, he claims, statistics may even obscure the issue; he then gives the example of American men rising when women enter the room. Data on incidence "simply blur the existence of a minor cultural pattern . . ." (Kluckhohn 1959:260). In effect then, Kluckhohn asserts the independence of anthropology from the type of criticism hurled at it by Stavrianos (1950) because a pattern, and presumably the way the patterns fit together, is qualitatively different from the frequency of occurrence from which the pattern is abstracted, or which expresses the pattern (depending upon its deductive or inductive origins). This is a well-known view in anthropology; in its most elaborate form it is expressed in the work of Lévi-Strauss (1963), who separates social relations as a concept that expresses the statistical findings of empirical reality from social structures, which are abstract patterns derived from a combination of social relations and their ordering by the anthropologist.

If we leave aside the intellectual work performed in this operation and go to the phenomena themselves, then on logical grounds, Kluckhohn treats only one of two possible positions. Pattern emerges from either the statements or behavior of informants. The number of informants who do or do not conform to the pattern is not another kind of datum but simply a refinement of the original one, i.e., a part of it. Since the pattern emerges from a statistically based observation, whether there is one informant or one hundred, it is impossible that a pattern *not* be clarified by increased information about the occurrences from which the observations were originally taken. Let me be perfectly clear about this point because it is the fundamental assumption of the materialist as opposed to the idealist approach in anthropology (cf., LeVine's chapter in this *Handbook*). A social or cultural pattern in the materialist view has a number of elements. First at the most general level it is a regularity or nonrandom occurrence in the sociocultural sphere of human experience. Second, there is to a variable degree an expectation or obligation on the part of actors in society to conform to a range of behavior that is socially recognized to be an acceptable conformity to the expectation. Third, there is an observable set of occurrences which indicate what is the actual degree of conformity to the expected obligation at any one time period. All of these statements involve ranges of variation, as well as expected and observed occurrences—not particularly unstatistical ideas.

If this view is not accepted, or for heuristic purposes another view is taken, such as that of Kluckhohn mentioned above, then quite conflicting "facts" may emerge from the same empirical phenomena. For example, societies differ from being close to zero to close to 100% in the frequency with which they practice cousin marriage. A "structuralist" like Needham (1962) perceives a quite distinct qualitative difference between pre-

ferred and prescribed cousin marriage, i.e., they are different types of obligations and it is the obligation that, for him, determines the pattern. Schneider (1966), on the other hand, claims that both of these are statistically variant results of the same underlying causal forces, and thus the distinction between preferred and prescribed patterns is one of degree and not kind.

Whether a researcher takes one or the other of these views (i.e., how does he treat the statistical variance of the patterns) it is still apparent that a pattern statement is not simply as Stavrianos (1950) claims—a descriptive account. Much more is involved because the pattern that emerges as the descriptive datum is in fact a generalization —akin to those of natural history (Brown 1963). Thus to watch birds is one thing, but to record their behavior and then know within limits when each species migrates southwards is quite another type of knowledge because it grants to its user some level of predictability based on a nonrandom occurrence of the particular phenomenon under observation. Prediction for both bird watching and ethnography is applicable to one case (one species of bird or one society among people). As we shall see, when all generalizations about this one case have been put together, we have what Kaplan (1964:332) has called a pattern model of explanation. In such a model, explanation stems from the degree of fit of each individual pattern to the over-all organization or integration of a set of them. Causal analysis is minimal; we know that such and such regularities occur, i.e., we can predict them, but why they occur is not a necessary part of such a set of generalizations. As I have shown above, what is important here for anthropology is to understand the empirical and theoretical basis of such generalizations. First of all from the materialist point of view they are, as I have said, statistical in nature, i.e., they are statements of probability; and secondly, they rest, ultimately, on the empirical occurrences (also statistical) which form the basis of observation.

Applied strictly to anthropology such generalizations are the basic ingredients of ethnography. Ethnography involves a descriptive summary of the customary practices of a group of people. It is made up of thousands of generalizations having varying degrees of reliability and is based on different amounts of observation and frequency of occurrence. Anthropologists try to document a descriptive or pattern generalization by reference to the behavior from which it was inferred: as Lévi-Strauss (1963:17) says, anthropologists attempt "to enlarge a specific experience to the dimensions of a more general one." The skill with which this is done is perhaps the key standard for judging the scientific status of ethnographic reporting. The point to be remembered here is that there are both data and theory in ethnography, and the variation among ethnographies stems from the validity of the inferences made when the anthropologist moves from data to generalization.

Consider the following example:

According to cultural standards, marriage between individuals of any known degree of blood relationship was considered undesirable, but no punishment was suffered by offenders except social disapproval. (Ray 1963:87)

Presumably the ethnographer has asked the informants about incest and observed a number of cases where the rule has been broken. The only case material actually cited in the report is that given by one informant who said that he could:

. . . remember three men who married their mothers' sisters' daughters. And I know of one who married his mother's sister. Nothing was done about these cases. (Ray 1963:93)

The difficulty with this data and the ethnographic generalization given is quite obvious. Since Ray makes no other statements about incest and gives no other data on the subject, we must assume that he wants us to link the case material with the descriptive generalization. There is no reference to "disapproval" or "laughter" in the data cited although both are stated to be a community reaction to incest. The statement, "No punishment was suffered by offenders," is supported by the informant's statement, "Nothing was done about these cases." On the other hand, the informants' statements give no ground for the incest rule given in the description, viz., "Marriage is forbidden between persons of any known genealogical relation." Indeed the data given suggest the possibility of something quite different, viz., a weakening of the incest barrier (male speaking) in a case of uterine parallel cousins and a possible extension of this to women of the mother's matrilineage. I am not suggesting that this alternative is correct or even that Ray's generalization is wrong—who knows what data he has that are not exhibited in the report? However, for present purposes, this is beside the point. What is important is to note that ethnography does involve generalizations and such theoretical statements require a reasoned argument from data to the resulting inference about patterns.

By contrast to the ambiguity of Ray's generalization, it is instructive to look at a pattern when it is handled with greater precision, as in the following example:

The lateral extension of kinship, that is, the range of relationship within which the expected behavioral norms are regularly observed, tends to follow the line of common identical descent. Half-siblings by the same father are neither expected to show, nor do they show, a similar degree of solidarity of interests to that normally expected and observed between full siblings. As previously mentioned, full siblings differentiate themselves as a group from their half-siblings, and this differentiation is followed by the children. (Smith 1955:46)

The author established the distinction between half- and full siblings on a sample of thirty compounds in a single community (Smith 1955:34). Ten of these with full brothers in them were single authority units, while no divided authority compounds had only full brothers in them. On the other hand, five compounds had half-brothers and divided authority while only three of these had single authority units. The generalization follows logically from the statistical information. Disconfirmation could come from a larger sample in which this relation turned out to be a chance occurrence; or perhaps with better sampling procedures, the direction of relationships might even be reversed. Again this is beside the point. The generalization about half- and full siblings is based on a particular set of observations whose details are given and whose implications are summarized in the generalization. As previously mentioned, ethnography as descriptive theory involves hundreds, even thousands, of such statements. It would be impossible to treat each one as a problem for detailed empirical testing. However, the plausibility of Smith's first generalization about the behavior norms following lines of identical cognatic descent gains in deductive coherence because it not only follows from the author's field work experience, but it is exactly the type of pattern one would logically expect if full brothers maintained their solidarity while half-brothers did not. Thus one way to construct a general theory of one society is to create a pattern model of generalizations validated as well as possible, but especially at key points, and then to derive other related generalizations, obviously with lower confidence limits, but which are fully supported by the documented statements from related generalizations.

For many anthropologists, this method goes no further than the logical derivation of one statement from others as described above. However, such a method has its limitations. Supposing several derivations of equal plausibility are possible, how can we choose between them? For example, supposing the ethnographer has good data on descent group behavior, but his material on voluntary associations is less adequate and he wants to fit both these associational patterns into one over-all set of generalizations. His conclusions about descent may lead him to interpret his non-kin association as (a) an extension or analogue of descent group behavior, or (b) as a cathartic reaction to descent group membership. If he chooses (a) then he stresses the similarities in his data between descent and non-kin group membership; if (b), he may choose to stress the differences.

In order to obviate such difficulties, at least to some extent, anthropologists often try to construct an entire structure or organized whole so that each individual generalization fits into the over-all pattern. As suggested above, this rationale lends credence to less well-substantiated statements. Given the nature of the entire case, as it is theorized to be put together, then it is more likely that each individual pattern should be in the form described, than in any other.

How such an over-all pattern, or integration, is arrived at is not a standardized procedure in anthropology—nor is it mystical. When Ruth Benedict, without the aid of field work, was doing research on Japan which resulted in her book, *The Chrysanthemum and the Sword*,

she saturated herself in Japanese materials of a carefully selected variety: literature, art, projective tests, interviews, etc. After she thought she had denominators that constituted, so to speak, implicit premises cutting across bodies of culture content that were quite different, she then wrote down some hypotheses as to what she should find—and not find—in as yet unexamined data if her initial

formulations were correct. She then sought out fresh materials drawn from the same categories and validated, rejected, or reformulated her initial hypotheses and made at least one more trial run. (Kluckhohn 1959:261)

In my own work on the Kanuri (Cohen 1967) I theorized about halfway through the field work that there were several integrating features that held the individual patterns together. I wrote these down and tried to enumerate all the situations, organizations, and sectors of the society that could provide information to disconfirm these ideas. When these further data tended only to support my "model" I accepted the features as my own integrating or pattern model of the society.

In a more recent and revealing case, that of Barth's attempt to write up Pehrson's field notes, he reports (Pehrson 1966:ix) that he was unable to do so until he actually went to the field site and experienced the culture for himself. He concludes from this that there must be types of information, especially with regard to integrating separate but related ethnographic generalizations, for which anthropologists are trained but for which they do not in fact have any systematic recording techniques. Although Barth may be the first to have stated this problem so openly, it has a familiar ring for anyone who has written an ethnographic report. Thus, as Kaplan admits (1964:333), the pattern model of explanation still leaves a great deal to be desired. It is the perception and subjective feeling that everything is just where it should be that produces a sense of "rightness" for such a theory. It may involve correlations, functional analyses, and perhaps the creation of an entire system; indeed it usually takes in all these. Such generalizations may or may not be as rigorously derived as they are in the discussion of them to follow which involves problems of objective validity and reliability. The crucial question is, as Kaplan says (1964:335), whether the mere think-so (or feel-so) makes a statement so. Even though such subjectivity may be denied (I would only partially admit to it for my own work), there is no simple way out of this weakness in the traditional case study method of ethnography.

The problem of ethnographic generalizations and their synthesis into integrated case studies can now be stated: Is there any way in anthropology to raise the level of validity of all ethnographic statements so the degree of confidence can be raised equally for all such generalizations? I believe there are solutions to these problems. Most of them, however, I will leave until later since they require more fully developed theoretical models, to be discussed below. One method, however, can be discussed briefly here. It requires an idealist basis for theory construction which is outside the purview of this chapter or at least its main thrust. This is ethnoscience, which is dealt with in more detail in Chapter 29. It is idealist in that for the most part workers using this technique have not worked with variability in the occurrences they observe, but have instead set up procedures for establishing formal relations between whatever units they decide to use. In this approach the ethnographer makes a number of assumptions which are crucial to his methodology, and to the position of this approach in the theoretical development of anthropology.[1]

First, it is assumed that the researcher can obtain information about the categories of understanding and meaning in a culture by recording and analyzing concepts reflected in the language. The methodological result of this assumption is that the study is completely restricted to the folk view of the culture. Furthermore, since semantic fields are the phenomena being considered, then no assumptions can be made about their content and all of the interviewing must be conducted in the native language. The study is by definition, then, restricted to the explicit parts of the culture, i.e., to that which can be communicated by language. Second, it is assumed that native concepts (verbal) have some form or structure such that they follow or can be approximated to taxonomic principles or some other formal or logically structured interrelations among semantic components. The methodological consequence of this assumption is to apply taxonomy or some other formal system such as mathematics that can be shown to depict most adequately the ordered relations among the native concepts and their components.

The great advantage of this approach is its objective and systematic means for eliciting the verbal concepts in a culture. It may very

well do this job more efficiently than anything yet produced in anthropology, although there are many precursors to this type of eliciting in traditional ethnographic techniques. By their own admission, however, those using this technique cannot deal with the nonverbal; thus as a valid means of obtaining ethnographic generalizations, ethnoscience has strict limits. It is important to realize that some problems simply have no place in such studies. For example, significantly different behavior by Ego toward two kinsmen for whom he uses the same kin terms could not be discovered using a strictly ethnoscientific analysis of the kinship terminology, since the verbal concepts gloss over these differences (see Keesing's comments in Chapter 23).

There are other problems. While there are well-established means of making traditional anthropological categories of description into useful categories of cross-cultural comparisons, it is not clear how such work could be accomplished with ethnoscientific data, since the recording of this information depends upon (a) the researcher's conceptualization of semantic order in the culture he is studying, and (b) the specifics of the particular culture, i.e., the culture makes the categories. It may be that taxonomies are universal, and/or that other logical structures go along with taxonomy to form a universal set that underlies semantics for the entire human experience—such a goal is both interesting and provocative. But so far even at this level of generality ethnoscience only tells us "what is there," and does not try, as do other models of generalization, to work back to questions, and hopefully to answers, about "why it is there." This does not mean in the end that ethnoscience will not move to this level of explanation either within its own framework, or by combining with more materialist (behavioral) approaches in anthropology. At present it can be welcomed as a delicate instrument for obtaining detailed information about the semantics or folk view of a culture, and is thus a useful addition to the roster of anthropological techniques.

ASSOCIATIONAL MODELS

Ethnographic generalizations are by themselves only best fit statements about the incidence or frequency of occurrences in the society. By themselves, they say little or

[1] I am grateful to Professor Oswald Werner for major help with these assumptions, although the final formulation is my own.

nothing about what goes with what. The simplest levels of relationship between ethnographic generalizations are associational. By this I mean that a correlation is said to exist among two or more phenomena such that a change in one implies a change in the other(s). In strict terms, there is no implication or proof of causal direction, merely an attempt to document the relationship. Thus Gluckman and others have tried to show the relation of descent to divorce rate (Gluckman 1950, Fallers 1957, Cohen 1961), and I (Cohen 1966) have posited a relationship between type of succession and degree of centralization in feudal states.

The problem that emerges almost immediately with correlation is that of measurement. If *a* is correlated with *b,* then to test the relationship, we must be able to show that more or less of one of these implies more or less of the other. In anthropology such correlations are often based on presence and absence statements. Thus "nobles" are said to be present in one type of acephalous lineage societies in Africa but not others (Middleton and Tait 1959). This particular type has clans and admits of heterogeneous origins. We might interpret this to mean that the more heterogeneous the clan origins of an acephalous society, the more likely it is that such a society will have a system of social stratification based on clan affiliation. The hypothesis is a useful one, but the presence and absence of relevant data provide only a gross measure of association such that it is difficult to predict tendencies for more or less association with any confidence. Dichotomous data are not necessarily wrong; indeed sometimes they are the only kind of information available. However, to make such associations more sensitive there is a need to have field data that are scaled, or that can be scaled later on by cross-cultural survey researchers. In the example cited above this means we would want some measure of greater or lesser heterogeneity of clan origins and greater or lesser structuring of social stratification.

Sometimes interesting correlations are uncovered by reinterpreting ethnographic concepts and generalizations. Leach implies this in his work on *Rethinking Anthropology* (1961). However, it is important to be clear just where such analysis takes us and what has to be done to carry it forward—some-

thing Leach does not always do. Thus he tries to show (1961:1–27) that in some patrilineal societies a mother-child relationship is one of affinity, not affiliation—or at least that affinity is a determinant of Ego's relationship to his own mother—an interesting and surprising, i.e., not common-sense, sort of ethnographic correlation. The general condition for such a phenomenon to exist is absorption by the child into the father's lineage. If the son, for example, relates to his divorced mother, he tends to do so as her affine, not her son. Leach does *not* say the relationship resembles that of affinity, or that there are forces tending to create mother-son interaction which symbolize the relation in an affinal form; he says that the relationship "is in sociological terms one of affinity rather than filiation" (1961:14). The best proof, says Leach, of this thesis would be if the son married his own divorced mother, but unfortunately there are no data available to support such a notion. However, there are groups where people have formal requirements at the death of a spouse in which the son fulfills obligations to his mother's lineage when his own father is unable to do so. At such times the son is said to be acting in affinal terms to his mother's group. I would point out in passing that Leach does not show, therefore, that the son acts affinally to the mother, but to her group, which is not quite the same thing and leaves lots of room for the mother-son relations to operate as they do in all societies.

The general problem that Leach raises is an interesting one, but he does not put it into testable correlational terms. He suggests two possible ways for Ego to relate to his mother's descent group in a patrilineal system —through (a) filiation or (b) affinity.[2] Put in the form of a testable hypothesis, we can say that in societies where a mother's tie to her children is weak, because they have strong ties to their father's descent group, then there is a tendency for such children to manifest behavior to her and her descent

[2] This is part of a more general thesis that in any system of kinship and marriage "there is a fundamental ideological opposition between the relations which endow the individual with . . . a 'we' group" (Leach 1961:21) and those that link our group formally to those of others. This dichotomy, he says, is related to symbolic representations in which "our" group is a common substance while relations of alliance to other groups are said to equal some sort of metaphysical influence.

group as if they were not her own children but members of a patrilineage that had a marriage relation to her and her group through one or more of its members. We then operationalize the variables involved, i.e., (a) mother's tie to son, (b) Ego's ties to own patrilineage, (c) affinal relations of husband-father and his patrilineage to wife and her patrilineage, and (d) similarity of son's behavior to mother and her patrilineage, to that of his father and his patrilineage. If we assume as given an inverse relation between (a) and (b), then tests should show that there is a positive correlation between (c) and (d) as predicted. If Leach has touched on something fundamental, then the hypothetical correlation should be checked on limited samples of society using controlled comparisons, on large samples, and even within one society to see if variance in behavior among persons in these roles follows according to the theory.

Several things should be noted in this example. First of all, the relationship that is elicited from "rethinking" ethnographic generalizations and correlations can only be validated by some sort of quantitative procedure. It can be posited by qualitative analysis—indeed this is one of the best ways to discover such relations—but it cannot be made into a fact, that is to say, validated this way. Second, this level of analysis is correlational, i.e., predictive, but not explanatory. Leach gives no plausible reasons beyond some vague notions of dualism stemming out of "we" and "they" groups which might explain why the correlation exists, if it really does. In order to study the reasons why something occurs, we must turn to causes and functional analysis which move beyond correlations to answer questions about "why," not just "how," things occur the way they do.

Before proceeding to such questions, it is important to digress a moment to consider the theoretical and methodological status of quantification. As Kaplan (1965:206) suggests, there is an anti-measurement attitude which consistently argues that measurement is impossible or too inaccurate or premature or only good for dealing with the obvious and so on. When measurements are applied, then a game is begun in which the quantifiers say, "See, we did it!" and the anti-quantification prohibitionists say, "If you can measure it, that ain't it!" And then the latter proceed to show how the phenomena have in fact eluded the measurements. Kaplan (1965:176–206) takes the position now widely held in most of the social sciences and by many philosophers, that all things are measurable, and whether we accomplish the task or not depends not on the thing but our conception of it. The aptness of the measure (i.e., does it measure what it purports to measure?) can be established by one or both of two tasks. First, does the measure itself define the concept? If so, the measure and the concept are the same. Thus for some purposes intelligence is defined as what intelligence tests measure. Second, does the measure predict to other quantities as suggested by a more general theory in which this concept is related to others that have also been measured? It is very unlikely that the network of interrelated quantities could occur as predicted by chance, or by a systematic error in only *one* of the measures. They are either all wrong, or there is a strong possibility that they are all to some extent right.

FUNCTIONAL MODELS OF EXPLANATION

Mechanical relations, or correlations, provide us with a probe that is one step deeper and more satisfactory than a descriptive generalization. However, even though they give us predictive power (i.e., if this, then that), they tell us very little about why, or for what reasons, the relationships exist. Given the massive potentiality of high-speed computers and their ability to handle enormous quantities of information, it is also becoming obvious that a plethora of correlations without any accompanying theory produces very little beyond a slightly more abstract set of descriptions. Thus recent studies such as those by Banks and Textor (1963) do not in themselves explain very much—instead they provide a new form of descriptive information at the correlational level which may be utilized selectively to construct theories for further testing. Anthropology has, for many years, had a semi-evolutionary approach to explanation. Assuming that man-in-society-and-culture adapts to his environment, anthropologists have, in effect, asked what requirements and/or needs are reflected in a functioning way of life. The major goal is posited to be the maintenance or persistence of the phenomena under study, and analysis concerns itself with the discovery of, or inferring of (i.e., more often, imputing) the contributions to maintenance made by each aspect or segment of social life. The functional approach is semi-evolutionary because adaptation was (and is) always implied, but no real technique for studying and analyzing change has ever developed as a clear and logically derived part of the approach. On the other hand, utilizing some notion of "contribution" when analyzing data does go beyond simple correlation to a theoretical statement about the reason(s) why such relations are found.

Before we go any further into the nature of functional analysis, it is necessary to examine the criticism that this particular method of building generalizations is fundamentally an unsound and unscientific procedure even though it has produced sensitive insights beyond the descriptive level (cf., Hempel 1959). Jarvie (1965) claims that functional statements cannot be confirmed or disconfirmed, and therefore as assertions they are unscientific even though they provide plausible explanations. The reason for this is that it is impossible to demonstrate whether the function(s) said to be performed by an institution or custom or other unit of behavior would fail to be performed if the institution or behavior were removed. Without such a test the functional argument is a circular one. Thus:

To be told that the function of church-going is to express and reinforce social solidarity, and the main test of the desire to express and reinforce social solidarity is church-going, is to get into a circle which cannot be broken in favor of a "deeper" explanation. Circular or *ad hoc,* or non-independent testable explanations do not tell us anything new; they are [therefore] methodologically unsatisfactory. (Jarvie 1965:25)

The real difficulty here is that, testable or not, sociocultural reality and actors-in-society *are* purposive in at least some of their actions. Furthermore, actions very often have consequences, and environments do limit the conditions of action if they do not, in some cases, determine them outright. The attack on functionalism, then, is relevant only when a researcher decides that everything must serve a purpose, if not now, then at some previous time. This latter approach leads to a method in which the researcher must elicit, or more correctly impute, purposes to each and every ethnographic generalization in order to explain them.

In order to make this method of inquiry more logical, it is necessary, first, to adopt Kaplan's assumption (1965:365) that teleological analysis is perfectly in order when evidence is presented to tie a particular action with a particular result in a purposive way. Thus, instead of simply imputing or claiming that activity X functions to carry out the purpose(s) Y, we must provide some evidence that such a relationship does in fact exist, i.e., that X does have Y effect(s). This does not mean that we must thoroughly understand the purpose. Purposiveness is part of nature "and can be used to explain other natural phenomena even when we are not in a position to provide, in turn, an explanation for the purposes" (Kaplan 1965:367). Thus Darwin did not explain "survival" although this purposive force was a theoretically useful requirement of nature that helped him to explain biological variation.

In order to clarify what kind of evidence is needed, let us divide teleological explanations up into three subvarieties based on the point of origin of the purposive stimuli.

Motivational. First of all, there are personal actions in which an actor states, or can be evidenced to possess, a goal or set of them. Consequent actions are then related to these purposes, and the actor's functions are fulfilled. Thus if an actor has fully accepted a decision-making role, he wants to carry out such action, and part of the reason such action is performed is because of the actor's motivation to function in this way. Data on motivations, that is to say, intentions or dispositions (cf., Brown 1963) on the one hand, and on their effects on behavior on the other, provide the necessary evidence. In other words we are positing a simple cause and effect relation between the motivations of actors and their subsequent acts, not assuming, of course, that such an antecedent /consequent correlation is a perfect one, or that causation is unidirectional.

Outputs. Second, actions being performed have effects on others and on elements of the situation. I would call such results "output functions." The analysis here is designed to find out what are the consequences of action. The data required are ethnographic generalizations about actions and data (not suppositions) concerning the effects of such action.

This is probably the weakest and most trite area of functional analysis in anthropology because of statements about "maintenance," "contributing to the social order," "maintaining equilibrium," and other vague outputs that are often suggested but not really documented or argued convincingly (cf., Erasmus 1967). What is needed here, ideally, is a research design that includes variation in observed behavior in relation to variation in its posited effects, giving us grounds to relate action to effects in a demonstrable way. If the ideal cannot be reached, then the researcher still has the responsibility to argue hypothetically about what would happen if, for example, his decision-maker did not make such decisions, or did not make enough of them, or make the right ones, and so on, through the gamut of all possibilities, not just the one that creates "stability" or "maintenance of the system."

Examples of such analysis can be seen in two forms: First, where the phenomena are assumed to be static or equilibrated; and second, when this assumption is not made. In its first and most common as well as incomplete version, equilibrium is used as the basic underlying determinant of constituent properties, while in the second, and more rare approach the equilibrium assumption is dropped. As an example of the first approach, we can look at the findings of research on lineage segmentation in Africa. It is now accepted that lineage segments develop natural imbalances in manpower and/or wealth over time. These discrepancies have been shown to be redressed by genealogical manipulation (Bohannan 1952, Fortes 1953), or by contractual arrangements with collateral lineages in which the uterine ties are utilized as a means of uniting weak segments into alliance groups that are equivalent to larger and more powerful ones structured along strict lines of agnation (Lewis 1961). The incompleteness of such work lies in its having taken only one among a number of theoretical possibilities into account. The documentation of this particular theoretical position requires data indicating that the system as observed has, in fact, persisted in its present form for a respectable time-depth. If such data are not available, then whether or not these forces really do "redress" imbalances is based only on the assumption of a stable equilibrium. As I have pointed out else-

where (Cohen 1965b), this may be the most improbable among a number of contending possibilities under conditions of observable change. With this in mind let us suppose that imbalances are not restored or only partially so. What then? Given the equilibrium assumption, such problems are avoided, and the question never comes up. This does not mean that "maintenance" or "persistence" or "equilibrium" are not useful concepts. The studies cited above have made positive contributions, but it does mean that they are incomplete because all the logical, and, perhaps, empirical possibilities have not been explained, and instead forces are assumed into existence which constantly push the interrelated set of variables back to a steady state of balanced opposition between the parts.

In working with the same type of data, but using an evolutionary prospective, Sahlins (1962) argues that segmentary lineages, whether equilibrated internally or not, produce a constant political imbalance between neighboring ethnic groups when one of them has segmentary lineages and the other does not. Instead of looking for "redress," he suggests that a continual advantage in favor of the segmentary lineage group is present and is associated with (produces?) expansionist tendencies such that the segmentary society constantly takes over the territory of its nonsegmentary neighbors. Although there are problems of causal direction and priority in this argument, the hypothesis advanced is testable, and the data upon which it is based can be re-examined to see whether they do provide reasonable grounds for the explanation advanced.

Since the basic approach here is to discover the effects on institutions of behaviors, the most clear-cut demonstration of such phenomena is to be seen in the use of time-lag data, a technique not often used by social anthropologists, with some notable exceptions (Carrasco 1961, and the work of some of the younger social anthropologists using oral history in Africa which will probably provide an antidote to this weakness). Marc Bloch (1961) has used such an approach in his work on feudalism. Thus he gives evidence to show that the introduction of primogeniture in eleventh-century Europe produced tendencies for the decentralization of European monarchies. Habakkuk (1960) claims (again with time-lag data) that the same method of inheritance produced a differential tendency for the later development of migratory and nonmigratory labor, urbanization, and the inception of industrialization in nineteenth-century Europe.

The validity of such studies is embedded in the word "produced." This term implies that a prior occurrence, A, is related to a consequent one, B, by a development or causal sequence. To disconfirm such a contention we must show that A is not prior to B, generally controlled for in time-lag studies, and/or that A has no relation to B which depends on how much other data are available at time A and time B, or whether this condition can be generalized so that the relationship can be tested elsewhere to see whether A precedes B in a number of other similar types of instances.

Requisite Analysis. The third type of functional analysis focuses on the conditions within which actors and institutions must operate. This kind of teleological approach is often called requisite analysis and is purposive in a rather abstract sense since it bears on the purposes being served by requirements of the context in which the phenomena being studied are to be found. Put into terms describing the behavior of the phenomena, we can use the term "adaptation" since the stimuli are coming from the environment or outside the phenomena and they require certain kinds of adjustments or consequent behaviors on the part of the phenomena under study. Again, as in the case of motivational purposes, or outputs, the argument requires a clear-cut delineation of the needs or requirements and their effects—hopefully showing how variations in needs are related to variable effects in the phenomena under investigation.

The most obvious example of requisite analysis is to be seen in the acculturation literature where an ethnic group is presented with a set of new conditions and must respond. Spier's (1958) work on habit channeling among nineteenth-century California Chinese is a case in point. He shows how the Chinese in California changed their tool usage in social situations involving employment by white Americans, but when the Chinese were self-employed or organized into groups amongst themselves for feuding purposes, they used traditional, and in some

cases quite ancient, technology. Another example of the same sort of work are the studies done on millenarian movements (cf., Mair 1959). These materials do have a temporal dimension, and it is possible to see common antecedent—consequent relations which have occurred in a number of cases in many parts of the world.

Perhaps the best-known example is the ecological interpretations of Julian Steward (1955) in which he tries to show how the environment of the American Plateau Region determines the nature of Shoshoni social structure. His argument gains in strength when he adds data on one Shoshoni group at Owens River whose environment was more productive and who also had a more settled and a more complex society than the majority of Shoshoni. However, there is no time-lag built into this study, and so we are left with a correlation analysis even though Steward uses the requisite form of functional analysis to explain his material.

SYSTEMS ANALYSIS

So far in this essay we have dealt with three varieties of generalizations found in anthropology—the ethnographic or probability statements concerning the occurrence of events, the mechanical or predictive correlation, and the functional generalizations that aim at both correlation-prediction as well as explanations which give insight into why correlations should exist. These three are arranged cumulatively, i.e., each succeeding type of generalization includes the methodology of the previous one but adds another qualitatively different set of procedures and strategies to those already given. If we continue this approach, the next step is to move toward some sort of systems analysis in which large numbers of units or components are considered in relation to one another and separated out from their context because as a group these particular components can be made to tell us something that solves an empirical or theoretical problem.

Although the word "system" has been used regularly in anthropology for several decades at least, it has not meant much more than what might be conceived within the scope of functional analysis. However, a number of crucial qualities have been omitted if the word "system" is applied to a set of functional relations. These particular qualities do not stem directly from functional generalizations, but instead can be deduced from two general assumptions about the nature of empirical reality. These are as follows: (a) The attempt to study anything distorts it, and (b) the circular causality criticism leveled at functionalism contains a basic truth that needs recognition in theory construction. What I conceive of as systems analysis takes each of these two problems into account and by doing so leaves us with logical devices for creating less distortion when building our own theories.

Let us begin by defining a system as a set of interrelated parts or units isolated to some degree from their context.[3] For anthropology how each part behaves is derived from ethnographic generalizations, and how these parts interrelate comes from the associational method. The system has, as one of its basic qualities, the idea that as a whole it does "something" or a set of things. If its parts are actors or roles, it satisfies at least some of the internal needs of these parts to a variable degree through time. It also produces effects, and it reacts or adjusts to the needs of its contextual environment. In other words, it functions.[4] However, when we say that the system functions *qua* system, I would argue that we imply two other qualities not previously included in the other types of generalizations and explanations. These are (a) its boundary characteristics, and (b) its feedback mechanisms and their functions.

Boundary maintenance and their characteristics are important in anthropology where empirical observations may not elicit a boundary, and yet such a boundary is needed for many problems of comparison. Thus, as I point out in Chapter 25 on "The Political System," the simplest levels of political complexity interweave political activity into the total role structure of the society so that religion, economics, and political actions are often enmeshed into a single role network. Yet for comparative analysis I need a means of separating out the political system from other activities, i.e., a definition of the boundaries of political activity.

The relation of the parts of a system to phenomena outside it is a measure of the permeability or degree of differentiation of the system from its context or environment, but it must always be remembered that it is the researcher who is isolating the parts from their context in the first instance, not some higher principle of reality or basic quality of existence, even though this may be posited to be the case much later in our investigations. When phenomena defined as parts are more interrelated with each other than with non-system phenomena, then there is a high boundary maintenance. Conversely when parts interrelate closely with contextual or environmental phenomena, and only to a much more limited and lower degree to other system parts, then to that extent boundary maintenance is lowered. When we use such a definition, any set of phenomena can be called a system as long as we can demonstrate their interrelationships to one another.[5]

System boundary, or boundary maintenance, is a concept that separates out phenomena analytically from their context and enables us to study this particular set in terms of a problem focus. The utility of the concept lies in the attention it forces us to pay to the objective fact that *we* have done the separating, and the relation of the system to that from which it was arbitrarily (although logically) abstracted is a matter of some importance. As we shall see below, this is a difficult methodological point, and failure to recognize its implications lead to problems about levels of analysis or to the question of what Gluckman (1964) has called "closed" systems.

What I said above about boundary maintenance being an attempt to cope with the premise that studying anything distorts it now becomes clear. To study something we must

[3] This definition is very similar to that given by Bertalanffy (1956): a system is a set of units with relationships among them. For a recent and detailed discussion of systems theory and its component concepts and hypotheses see Miller (1965a, 1965b, 1965c) and Buckley (1967). In concentrating on boundary, or boundedness, of the system as a crucial aspect that stems from the arbitrary choice of components, I am following some system theorists (Easton 1965) but not others (Tanter n.d.).

[4] In modern machine systems teleology is operationalized through feedback mechanisms. Goal-seeking can be simulated by arranging for a feedback principle which results in the output of a system being modified by the error between output and some present goal (Rappaport and Horvath 1959:89).

[5] Logically one could with this definition posit a system with zero boundary maintenance, but the idea seems of little practical value scientifically for the present. On the other hand, that such systems exist can be seen easily by reducing horoscopes to questions about the empirical relations among their parts.

"pick it up" as it were, in other words take it from its context. But if we have assumed that its very nature and development are closely bound up with its context, then to say we are going to define it from the very beginning as being in relation to that context does less to distort it than if this were not the case. Furthermore there is the even thornier question of whether we "picked up" the right thing or left some of it behind or picked up extras not really included and so on. This is also distortion, and only a clear understanding that it is the investigator who decides on boundaries, i.e., on "thingness," will keep us aware that these parts are related to parts both in and out of the system.

The second quality of systems analysis not present in any of the previous methods of creating generalizations is that of feedback. Where boundary maintenance deals with the relations of parts of the system to one another on the one hand, and to the test of reality on the other, feedback deals with the relations between different kinds of functional interrelationships. Not only do motivations cause actions, actions have effects, and contextual features create limiting or directly causal requirements, but each of these is constantly affecting the other so that causality in the system-in-its-environment is multiple in direction and nature; each cause is an effect, and each effect is also a cause. This is the truism underlying the circular reasoning of functional analysis. If both sides of a causal chain are causes, then logically causality is circular. Unfortunately this makes empirical research much more difficult—but not impossible.

What is needed here are techniques for handling data which we posit as systems so that we can take out functional relations in order to abstract each causal chain separately from the system, or system-in-its-environment, (see Chapters 4 and 5 on causality). The fact that there is already some partially successful work going on in this field means that in the near future it may be possible to include such analyses in our research designs. Thus feedback allows us to visualize and appreciate the complexity of social and cultural materials so that our generalizations can be stated to apply within valid limits. Feedback is, as well, forcing the technologists in our midst to develop a means of handling multiple forces of causality.

Examples of such model building are rare or nonexistent as yet in anthropology, although the idea has been implicit in much of social anthropology ever since the inception of the so-called "organic analogy." Dalton's conception of the economic system (see Chapter 24) or my own adaptation of Easton's political system model are approximations to this ideal of theory construction. The work by Gilbert and Hammel (1966) on simulation of cousin marriages is another good example of an attempt to show all possible combinations and permutations of a multivariable system by creating the conditions under which a set of system variables could interrelate with one another. The computer then allows the researcher to vary one or more of the system variables experimentally to discover what such variance would do to the frequency of different types of cousin marriage. Using this technique, the authors have concluded that about one-half of the frequency of father-brother-daughter marriage can be accounted for by territorial preference, i.e., marrying locally or not, measured at a gross level on societies having these types of input characteristics. Although Gilbert and Hammel have not been able to cope as yet with contextual features, and thus with the problem of boundary maintenance, in any very complicated way, this could be a next step with such a simulation in procedure.

SYSTEMS AND THE LEVELS PROBLEM

Systems analysis, then, is a logical or theoretically based choice of a set of parts whose relation to non-system or environment factors is not natural but delineated for us by the concept of boundary maintenance. If the arbitrariness of systems analysis is accepted, then the matter of levels of analysis—which has exercised social science at least since Durkheim's rules of the sociological method right up to the most recent treatment of the problem by Gluckman (1964)—becomes quickly apparent. This is due to the fact that the choice of a system of interrelated parts presents us immediately with a decision about what to include and exclude from our theoretical and empirical attack on a research problem. Should some variables be excluded because although they may be relevant, they are different "levels" of analysis, or from another area of competence? If the systems approach is to be taken seriously then the decision must be taken to resolve this question in exactly the opposite way to that suggested by the Durkheimian tradition. Let me explain this conclusion. The Durkheimian, or strictly sociological approach is based, in my view, on an epistemology that has almost a paranoid fear of "reductionism" and an honest, but warped, view of the integrity of levels of reality that have been reified because they underpin the professional status of academic disciplines and their development into spheres of "competence." Reductionism is the "sin" of believing that one level of reality can be reduced by findings and explanations of its causal determinants at a simpler level. Since levels of reality (inorganic, organic, psychic, sociocultural) include the previous ones plus new elements not found "below," it is argued that, at some point, the new elements in a level must be explained in terms of causal forces within that level itself. Such arguments have been used, fortunately or unfortunately, to found new disciplines. The new disciplines, like anthropology and to a lesser extent sociology, become expert at certain kinds of data collection on certain kinds of phenomena. Theory and research, especially in social anthropology, have tended to use explanations solely within the social and cultural level of activity. Gluckman calls this methodological caveat "circumscription." He moves beyond the major epistemological problems raised by Durkheim and by reductionism when he states that different

disciplines may study the same events, and even some of the same regularities in these events; but they look for different kinds of interdependencies between the regularities, i.e., for different kinds of relations. (Gluckman 1964:160)

He goes on to say that researchers from various disciplines may talk about psychological, social, cultural, or economic facts but in a strict sense this is not true—what they really mean is that the same events, and sometimes different ones, are being

fitted into various types of systems in terms of one system of reality with different aspects, ... Thus the behavior of workers in a factory has its economic aspect, its political aspect, and its psychological aspect. . . . If one is to succeed in studying society one must split up reality by isolating a particular aspect which presents regularities and is *relatively* [emphasis is that of Gluck-

man] autonomous and independent of other aspects. Having chosen a particular aspect for study, the social or human scientist, who then becomes an economist, sociologist, psychologist, or student of politics, confines himself to that aspect and ignores aspects, and complexities, studied by others. (Gluckman 1964:161)

In this passage Professor Gluckman recognizes many of the pitfalls of Durkheimian reductionism as an argument for remaining within one's own disciplinary bailiwick. He notices, quite rightly, that data for the so-called "different levels," and/or different disciplines, are often collected by observing the same phenomena; whereas, when a biologist reduces his material to physical-chemical components, he records different observations on what are really quite different phenomena. Furthermore Gluckman, by viewing aspects as "relatively autonomous," seems not to be totally unaware (although not completely aware either) of the possibility that such aspects, i.e., the psychological, cultural, social, economic, etc., are not independent natural systems. However, he does not ask the next logical questions, viz., how related or unrelated are they, and what would knowledge of this kind do to solve the theoretical and empirical problems of man's social and cultural existence.

The reason why these questions are not asked has nothing to do with epistemology but is based, instead, on what seems to me to be much thinner ice, namely, professional competence and disciplinary integrity and tradition. Thus in criticizing two of his colleagues for using economic variables he says that he doubts whether they would be able to solve many problems using such variables; indeed even economists "have tried to develop ways of measuring these variables without marked success" (1964:206). However, even if his anthropologist colleagues did solve such problems, "they would be working as economists, . . . not as social anthropologists, and they would have to employ the appropriate techniques and competence, and work within the limits these impose" (1964:206–207). Later on he shows how Kluckhohn's work led to "sterility" and "incompetent trespass into the field of another discipline [viz., psychoanalysis] . . . particularly when its results are compared with the fruitful results of Evans-Pritchard's disciplined refusal to trespass thus" (1964:249). He makes this judgment correctly, because Kluckhohn had none of the psychological data necessary to support his contention, while Evans-Pritchard did gather material to document his generalizations.

To summarize this argument, it seems to me that the problem of levels boils down to two interrelated issues. First of all, social anthropology, it is argued, has its own "level" of analysis; data collection and interpretation have developed a productive tradition of theory by restricting research to this level; second, such a tradition has developed its own disciplinary organizations, its own methodological caveats, its own types of data, and so on. Staying within this boundary, or "closed system," produces results and an ongoing intellectual enterprise as well as a recognizable status in academia. Going beyond these boundaries creates dangers of incompetence and lack of progress toward our final goals of understanding and theory development.

Let me deal with the levels problem first, then the issue of competence which follows deductively from it. If, as I have suggested, systems are, in fact, arbitrary choices of parts, what then determines this choice? The answer is a simple one—the problem to be studied.[6] If the problem is political, then we must ask what such a rubric entails. If the problem is more situationally based, such as it is for Lupton and Cunnison (1964) when they seek to understand the workers' output in a factory, then again the problem defines what should be included. If, instead, the discipline defines the approach, the methods, and the data, we must always be satisfied with either partial answers or multidisciplinary research to fully explore man in society or any particular species of problem.

I submit, however, that reality is not disciplinary. This is a quality of the social structure of academic society which may, or may not, be the ultimate solution to the problems of social science. If kinship and family life are subjects of interest, or politics, or personality, then, as I have argued above, the ultimate goal is development of theoretical systems which tend to explain and eventually replace our present notions and perceptions of these phenomena with more adequate ones in terms of understanding. To do this we must work toward what I have called a "systems approach," or something like it, which isolates elements into an analytically distinct whole; then we must study these as they interrelate amongst themselves and their context. The approach suggested by Gluckman leads logically to political science, and anthropological politics, to economics per se, and to anthropological economics, and so on. But these problems are cross-culturally significant and are foci for empirical research and theory development. This means that eventually problems, not disciplines, must determine theoretical and methodological developments in anthropology and its related fields. It means that anthropologists specializing in certain problems will draw closer to their colleagues in nearby disciplines for theory and method. It also means that ultimately we shall be determined in our methods, not solely by our discipline and its traditions, but by the kinds of data and theory needed to solve these problems. Thus competence is not a matter of tradition, or disciplinary training, but a constantly developing requirement determined by what is studied rather than which professional societies one belongs to.

From the point of view of the other disciplines, it also means that the results of anthropological research on these problems has something to contribute to the developing body of theory growing up across disciplines. Thus the study of new nations in political science requires that a body of information and theory be developed concerning the way in which local politics are incorporating into the new national entity, and the way in which new, politically significant groups have emerged (Cohen 1965a). Anthropological case studies of these traditional politics form an excellent base line for both the political scientist and the anthropologist who wish to study these contemporary developments. On the other hand, those studying such problems today in the field, whether they are from anthropology, sociology, or political science, must do very similar kinds

[6] From another point of view this statement begs the question since we can obviously ask what, then, determines the problem. However, this chapter is meant to be, primarily, a contribution to method, rather than the sociology of science. The reason why scientists choose certain problems is both fascinating in itself and very likely one of the ultimate determinants of developments within science. However, I am restricting myself here to what is, or should be, done when a problem has already been formulated.

of research in which both theory and method begin to merge because the problem itself is a major determinant in the situation.

This discussion hearkens back to the question posed in the section on ethnographic generalization concerning the difficulties of validity in a traditional ethnography. Ethnoscience was mentioned briefly as one method of cutting down on scope while increasing the accuracy of ethnographic work. Perhaps the more common solution to this difficulty comes from the kind of problem orientation discussed above. As theory, method, and data begin to restructure the social organization of social science, only specific aspects of social life will be investigated with any degree of concentration. Anthropology has undoubtedly shown that all problems must be seen in their social and cultural context, but this does not mean that every problem-oriented research project must complete, or carry out, a total holistic ethnography, although some work on context must always be a starting point. This means that anthropological field trips are more and more turning out different varieties of data. First of all, there is the general contextual material for which participant-observation techniques are so well suited. Second, there is the data directed primarily by theory, in which specific and, I would predict, progressively more quantified material is collected. The general background field work will produce the understanding needed to create intelligent measurements, and theory must generate the variables to be operationalized in any particular field work situation.

Such developments are bound to have profound effects on cross-cultural studies. As demonstrated by the work being done on data quality control (Naroll 1962), much emphasis is now placed on assessing the accuracy of ethnographic material and in operationalizing variables from this literature. When, however, there are a number of studies of single cases in which theoretically relevant variables have already been operationalized for each field situation separately, then the comparative job will be simpler and less contentious—simpler because precise data on the variables the comparativist is interested in will be available, and less contentious because the field worker will have performed the operationalization in terms of the culture so that the comparativist will escape the criticism that he has distorted the data to fit his categories. For example, there are theories about divorce rates being related to a system of variables that tend to vary the rate from high to low depending, among other things, on the descent system, fertility of the wife, permissibility of the role structure in the society in general, and so on. Only when a series of studies that quantify the rate is made, and the theoretically related variables in a sample of societies have been chosen to represent ranges of variance for each major variable in the theory, can such a body of ideas be fully tested.

Finally, I should point out that this chapter reflects what I consider to be a major thrust at theory construction in anthropology, indeed, in social science in general. It is not, however, an exhaustive survey of the methods of theory construction. In particular I have avoided idealist approaches such as ethnoscience (dealt with in a later chapter) and the concept of "structure" put forward by Lévi-Strauss (1963). Both of these methods for arriving at generalizations do not make the assumption that between observation and generalization there is a statistical, or probabilistic, quality of reality that must always be accounted for. Before a behavior, or custom, or belief can be put through the procedures of formal analysis of either ethnoscience or structuralism, we must know something about its specific range of occurrence and the variations it displays (cf., Harris 1966:22 and 1968: chapter 20). This intervening quality of variance is a fundamental feature of all phenomena (including, I believe, formal models in the minds of the natives). However, it is not nearly so apparent or crucial to those who utilize either ethnoscience or Lévi-Strauss' structuralism, for they start their assumptions from a different set of premises. At base, then, are totally different conceptions of the ultimate nature of reality and our means of understanding it. Within the materialist approach used throughout this chapter, variance is assumed to be a constant property of all phenomena. Thus formulating a problem for research means asking questions about a variance in terms of other variances that may be causing its behavior. In the formal analysis called for by ethnoscience or by Lévi-Strauss, variance is a "noise-ridden" expression of fundamental regularities or invariant principles that express the ultimate causes of observable reality.

Thus Needham (1962), a follower of Lévi-Strauss, likes to deal with prescribed patterns of behavior, i.e., those that approach 100% correspondence between expectations and actual practice. For him these are purer expressions of the underlying principles, and he does not have to get caught in the cross fire of probabilities in which such correspondences are well below 100%. But how much of the human experience is like this? Should we try to build theories about man's social and cultural life from types of practices that are extremely atypical? Parenthetically, anthropology has not had such notable theoretical success with its most widespread prescription—the incest rule—which obviously does represent something quite fundamental (but what?) in the human condition. However, if this approach is taken seriously then methodology becomes the study and effort to find ways and means of arriving at these formal underlying principles which are said to be expressed in empirical reality. Undoubtedly such approaches have their utility, and it is to the credit of anthropology that it has, less than most of the social sciences, developed no orthodoxy, new or old.[7]

Contention and competition among ultimately different conceptions of reality and the means of developing generalizations means that as a discipline we ourselves appreciate variance in our own midst, and from an evolutionary point of view this is an adaptive, i.e., a "good" way of coping with our problems.

SUMMARY AND CONCLUSION

In this chapter I have briefly gone over the meaning of a scientific approach to understanding. The goal of science is theory, and good theory is a body of ideas that can be submitted, ultimately, to empirical testing. Theory explains and predicts phenomena and is a heuristic device because it can be used as a substitute for the complexities of reality;

[7] I have not chosen to compare these approaches in any detail in this paper because I believe it is more important for the purpose at hand to clarify the phenomenological approach which is the dominant trend in the social sciences today. For a fuller treatment of this subject see Schneider (1965) and Harris (1966 and 1968).

nevertheless it is constantly changing since it has inherent mechanisms in its own social and cultural organization for constant change.

Anthropology is built on the collection of information from field studies. These result in reports which are large collections of ethnographic generalizations. These generalizations are variously accurate and are usually integrated into a coherent set of patterns. The methods of carrying out these two operations of abstraction and synthesis also vary as to accuracy and logical consistency, which leaves the basic data of anthropology in a somewhat unclear position scientifically.

I have started the analysis of anthropological generalization with the methods used to obtain the simplest level of generalization, that of describing a single pattern or regularity among a group of people. Some anthropologists give data upon which such generalizations are based, others illustrate the generalization, others simply state the generalization. In many cases, besides observing a pattern, it is also linked with others to show its agreement and integration into an over-all pattern. This integration or pattern model is in effect a set of correlations whose validity is but poorly known except for the feeling we get as researchers and readers that the entire body of generalizations does fit together in the manner indicated.

From this level of generalization I have moved to the more rigorous methods of creating relationships among ethnographic generalizations or single patterns. The simplest level I have called "associational." Variables are shown to vary with respect to each other. Why this is so is not part of the logic involved in demonstrating that the relationship does in fact hold. The method ultimately involves quantification, because development of the generalization eventually turns on questions of more and less of something. After this level the discussion takes up the functional model of generalization which is designed to cope with questions of correlation but adds statements about cause, i.e., it provides reasons why the relations exist. Functions are divided into (a) those originating with the intentions or dispositions of actors, (b) with the effects of action, and (c) with the requirements of the situation upon the actors. Finally, a systems approach is discussed in which an entire set of variables are theoretically related. The concepts of boundary maintenance and feedback are introduced in order (a) to relate the arbitrarily chosen set of variables to their context, and (b) to take care of the accusation of circular reasoning often directed at functional analysis.

These models have been offered as a replacement for the pattern or synthetic model of traditional ethnography. I believe that they involve much greater limitation in the scale of data collected in the field, but they also involve much greater rigor in the attempt to synthesize ethnographic generalizations into larger sets or systems of interrelationships. If this variety of theorizing continues to expand it means that holistic ethnography does not have a bright future. However, it does mean that the generalizations stemming from field work will be more rigorously developed and more cumulative, stemming as they will from progressively developing theories.

Finally the way in which the limitations are to be applied stems less from the traditions of holistic ethnography than from common interests across the social sciences directed toward a series of problems. These foci, some of which are discussed later in this volume in the section on models of analysis, form the contemporary (they may change in the future) basis for systems analysis. As we have defined it here, this refers to a theoretically derived choice of elements that are posited to be related to one another and relevant to a certain problem. Such a restructuring of the social sciences calls for methodological openness and a lack of concern for disciplinary boundaries.

BIBLIOGRAPHY

BANKS, A. S., and R. B. TEXTOR
1963 Cross-polity survey. Cambridge, M.I.T. Press.

BERTALANFFY, L. V.
1956 General systems theory. Yearbook of the Society for General Systems Research 1:1–10.

BLOCH, M.
1961 Feudal society. London, Routledge and Kegan Paul.

BOHANNAN, L.
1952 A genealogical charter. Africa 22:301–315.

BROWN, R.
1963 Explanation in social science. Chicago, Aldine.

BUCKLEY, W.
1967 Sociology and modern systems theory. Englewood Cliffs, N.J., Prentice-Hall.

CARRASCO, P.
1961 The Civil-religious hierarchy in Meso-American communities: Pre-Spanish background and colonial development. American Anthropologist 63:483–497.

COHEN, R.
1961 Marriage instability among the Kanuri of Northern Nigeria. American Anthropologist 63:1231–1249.

1965a Political anthropology: the future of a pioneer. Anthropological Quarterly 38:117–131.

1965b Review Article. American Anthropologist 67:950–957.

1966 The dynamics of feudalism in Bornu.

Boston University Papers on Africa, Volume II, African History, J. Butler, ed. Boston, Boston University Press.

1967 The Kanuri of Bornu. New York, Holt, Rinehart and Winston.

EASTON, D.
1965 A framework for political analysis. Englewood Cliffs, N.J., Prentice-Hall.

ERASMUS, C. J.
1967 Obviating the functions of functionalism. Social Forces 45:319–328.

FORTES, M.
1953 The structure of unilineal descent groups. American Anthropologist 55:17–41.

GIBSON, Q.
1960 The logic of social enquiry. London, Routledge and Kegan Paul.

GILBERT, J. P., and E. A. HAMMEL
1966 Computer simulation and analysis of problems in kinship and social structure. American Anthropologist 68:71–93.

GLUCKMAN, M.
1950 Kinship and marriage among the Lozi of Northern Rhodesia and the Zulu of Natal. In A. R. Radcliffe-Brown and D. Forde, eds., African systems of kinship and marriage. New York, Oxford University Press.

1964 Closed systems and open minds: the limits of naivety in social anthropology. Chicago, Aldine.

HABAKKUK, H. J.
1960 Family structure and economic change in nineteenth century Europe. In N. W.

Bell and E. F. Vogel, eds., *A modern introduction to the family*. New York, Free Press of Glencoe.

HANSON, N. R.
1958 *Patterns of discovery*. Cambridge, Cambridge University Press.

HARRIS, M.
1968 *The rise of anthropological theory: a history of theories of culture*. New York, Thomas Y. Crowell Co.
n.d. *Emics, etics, and the new ethnography*. Paper presented at the annual meeting of the American Anthropological Association, November 1966.

HEMPEL, C. A.
1959 The logic of functional analysis. In L. Gross, ed., *Symposium on sociological theory*. Evanston, Ill., Row, Peterson.

JARVIE, I. C.
1965 Limits of functionalism and alternatives to it in anthropology. In D. Martindale, ed., *Functionalism in the social sciences*, Monograph 5, American Academy of Political and Social Science.

KAPLAN, A.
1964 *The conduct of inquiry*. San Francisco, Chandler.

KLUCKHOHN, C.
1959 Common humanity and diverse cultures. In D. Lerner, ed., *The human meaning of the social sciences*. New York, Meridian Books.

KUHN, T. S.
1962 *The structure of scientific revolutions*. Chicago, University of Chicago Press.

LEACH, E. R.
1961 *Rethinking anthropology*. London School of Economics Monographs on Social Anthropology No. 22. London, University of London Press.

LÉVI-STRAUSS, C.
1963 *Structural anthropology*. New York, Basic Books.

LEWIS, I. M.
1961 Force and fission in Northern Somali lineage structure. *American Anthropologist* 63:94–112.

LUPTON, T., and CUNNISON
1964 Workshop behavior. In M. Gluckman, ed., *Closed systems and open minds*. Chicago, Aldine.

MAIR, L. P.
1959 Religious movements in three continents. *Comparative Studies in Society and History* 1:113–136.

MIDDLETON, J., and D. TAIT
1958 *Tribes without rulers*. London, Routledge and Kegan Paul.

MILLER, J. G.
1965a Living systems: basic concepts. *Behavioral Science* 10:193–237.

1965b Living systems: structure and process. *Behavioral Science* 10:337–379.
1965c Living systems: cross-level hypotheses. *Behavioral Science* 10:380–411.

NAROLL, R.
1962 *Data quality control*. New York, Free Press of Glencoe.

NEEDHAM, R.
1962 *Structure and sentiment: a test case in social anthropology*. Chicago, University of Chicago Press.

PEHRSON, R. N.
1966 *The social organization of the Marri Buluch*. Compiled and analyzed from his notes by Frederik Barth. Viking Fund Publications in Anthropology No. 43.

POPPER, K. R.
1959 *The logic of scientific discovery*. New York, Basic Books.

RAPPAPORT, A., and W. J. HORVATH
1959 Thoughts on organization theory and a review of two conferences. General systems. *Yearbook of the Society of General Systems Research* 4:87–93.

RAY, V. F.
1963 *Primitive pragmatists: the Modoc Indians of California*. Seattle, University of Washington Press.

SAHLINS, M. D.
1961 The segmentary lineage: an organization of predatory expansion. *American Anthropologist* 63:322–345.

SCHNEIDER, D. M.
1965 Some muddles in the models: or how the system really works. In *The relevance of models for social anthropology*. A.S.A. Monograph No. 1. London, Tavistock. New York, Praeger.

SMITH, M. G.
1955 *The economy of Hausa communities of Zaria*. Colonial Research Studies No. 16. London, Her Majesty's Stationery Office for the Colonial Office.

SPIER, F. G.
1958 Tool acculturation among the 19th century Chinese of California. *Ethnohistory* 5:97–117.

STAVRIANOS, B. K.
1950 Research methods in cultural anthropology in relation to scientific criteria. *Psychological Review* 57:334–344.

STEWARD, J. H.
1955 *The theory of culture change*. Urbana, University of Illinois Press.

TANTER, R.
n.d. *A systems analysis guide for testing theories of international political development*. Paper delivered at the annual meeting of the American Political Science Association, September 1966.

CHAPTER 3

Natural Selection as an Epistemological Model

DONALD T. CAMPBELL

THE NATURAL-SELECTION ORIENTATION

The anthropologist seeking an epistemology or philosophy of science appropriate to his own experiences as observer and theorist, is apt to find orthodox logical positivism inappropriate on many grounds. His reaction may be to adopt a phenomenological or a Verstehen approach, in which most of the burdens of the scientific method are abandoned in favor of a would-be direct intuition of social reality. But if he wants an alternative which retains a hardheaded willingness to confront theories with facts, he will probably find attractive an emerging perspective which frames the process of science in "natural-selection" and "evolutionary" terms. Karl Popper (1934, 1959, 1963) and Stephen Toulmin (1961, 1967) are perhaps the most eminent of the philosophers-of-science espousing such a view.

Some quotations from Popper will illustrate:

According to my proposal, what characterizes the empirical method is its manner of exposing to falsification, in every conceivable way, the system to be tested. Its aim is not to save the lives of untenable systems but, on the contrary, to select the one which is by comparison the fittest, by

This paper has drawn upon several of the author's previous presentations, primarily "Methodological Suggestions From a Comparative Psychology of Knowledge Processes" (1959); "Pattern Matching as an Essential in Distal Knowing (1966); with briefer borrowings from "Variation and Selective Retention in Socio-Cultural Evolution" (1965) "Distinguishing Differences of Perception From Failures of Communication in Cross-Cultural Studies" (1964), and Evolutionary Epistemology" (in preparation), with new material added by the author.

exposing them all to the fiercest struggle for survival. (Popper 1934, 1959:42)

. . . How and why do we accept one theory in preference to others?

The preference is certainly not due to anything like an experiential justification of the statements composing the theory; it is not due to a logical reduction of the theory to experience. We choose the theory which best holds its own in competition with other theories; the one which, by natural selection, proves itself the fittest to survive. This will be the one which not only has hitherto stood up to the severest tests, but the one which is also testable in the most rigorous way. A theory is a tool which we test by applying it, and which we judge as to its fitness by the results of its applications. (Popper 1934, 1959:108)

Toulmin may be an even more appropriate introduction for an anthropologist, because he describes science as cultural evolution.

The ideas of science represent a living and critical tradition. They are passed on from generation to generation, but are modified in the course of transmission. In 1850 Professor Jones teaches physics to his bright young student Smith; and the ideas so transmitted are recognizable ancestors of those which, in 1880, Professor Smith teaches in turn to young Robinson. In each generation, some intellectual variations are perpetuated, and become themselves incorporated into the tradition: this, for the historian, is what constitutes "progress" in science. Likewise for the philosopher of science: some novel theories deserve to survive at the expense of their rivals and predecessors; and the philosopher must analyze the standards by which scientific variants are judged and found worthy or wanting. There is no single, simple test of merit, and it is not for the philosopher to impose one on science; nor can a historian justly criticize earlier scientists for not jumping straight to the views of 1960. For progress can be made in science only if men apply their intellects critically to the problems which arise in their own times, in the light of the evidence and the ideas which are then open to consideration.

The common task which accordingly faces historians and philosophers of science has parallels elsewhere—in Darwinian biology. In the evolution of scientific ideas, as in the evolution of species, change results from the selective perpetuation of variants. Between the physics lectures of Professor Jones in 1850 and those of Professor Smith in 1880 lie thirty years, in which a dozen tentative speculations were considered for every one which survived as a change in the established tradition. For every variant which finds favor and displaces its predecessors, many more are rejected as unsatisfactory. So the question "What gives scientific ideas merit, and how do they score over their rivals?" can be stated briefly in the Darwinian formula: "What gives them survival-value?"

This reformulation suggests new questions and possibilities. To begin with, we know from biology how a variation which confers an advantage on one species in one environment may have no merits at all for another species, or even for the same species in a different environment. So, in science, the same theoretical move can have merit in dealing with one group of problems, and yet prove an obstacle to progress in another field or situation. We met this earlier, when we saw how arguments which had merit in the theory of illumination were out of place in gravitation theory; and theoretical patterns which were largely unfruitful in chemistry subsequently bore fruit in genetics.

Again, biological species survive and evolve, not by meeting any single evolutionary demand, but because they alone, from the available variants of earlier forms, have successfully met the multiple demands of the environment. It is easy to think up possible "advantages" in the abstract: to imagine, for example, how men would benefit from having wings with which they could fly. It is more relevant to calculate the price we should pay for wings: such as the ungainly breast-bone needed to support flight. Only if we do this shall we begin to understand why, in the situation actually existing, surviving species are not even "better-adapted" than they are.

A parallel issue arises in the logic of science. Considering the various merits of a scientific theory singly and in isolation, we may be enticed by abstract but irrelevant ambitions. Why should we not give actual marks—numerical assessments, that is—to rival scientific theories, grading their merits on a scale? Why should we not build up a theory of confirmation, or calculus of corroboration, with which to demonstrate in numerical form the superiority of one theory to another? This dream lies at the heart of much formalized philosophy of science; yet its hopes of fulfilment are strictly limited. Two rival hypotheses may sometimes be so closely related that their relative merits are positively computable: the "significance tests" of mathematical statistics do for us what can be done in this way. But this happens only where the really difficult intellectual problems do not arise. As soon as we broaden our view, and consider situations calling for conceptual innovations, where there are several demands to be satisfied, the idea of an "evidential calculus" for scientific theories becomes unrealizable.

Again, philosophers sometimes assert that a finite set of empirical observations can always be explained in terms of an infinite number of hypotheses. The basis for this remark is the simple observation that through any finite set of points an infinite number of mathematical curves can be constructed. If there were no more to "explanation" than curve-fitting, this doctrine would have some bearing on scientific practice. In fact, the scientist's problem is very different: in an intellectual situation which presents a variety of demands, his task is—typically—to accommodate some new discovery to his inherited ideas, without needlessly jeopardizing the intellectual gains of his predecessors. This kind of problem has an order of complexity quite different from that of simple curve-fitting: far from his having an infinite number of possibilities to choose between, it may be a stroke of genius for him to imagine even a single one. The scientist might, in fact, retort to the logician as the French painter Courbet is said to have replied to the art-critics by commenting that "it is a hard enough matter to paint a picture at all, let alone a good picture." The scientist could here justly reply to formal logicians in similar terms.

The parallel with evolution-theory fits our problem even in unexpected ways. To give one instance only: an inheritable variation sometimes appears in a population first by chance, conferring at that time no particular advantage on its possessors; yet this same variation may subsequently become of extreme value to their descendants as a result of changes in the environment. A feature which, originally, had no merit in this way acquires merit quite unpredictably. The parallel change occurs in science. A classic example of this concerns the notion of "atomic number." When the chemical substances were arranged in order and tabulated, Dalton's successors treated "atomic weight" as the fundamental characteristic of an element. When they had listed the chemical elements in order of atomic weight, it proved convenient to indicate their place in this order, and index numbers were allotted. So, the atomic number of a substance was originally no more than the number in the margin of this list. Had there been twenty or twenty-five elements instead of ninety or more, index letters might have been used instead of index numbers, and the place occupied by a particular substance in Mendelieff's table could have been labelled by its "atomic letter." . . .

Like all great critical activities, science has not one, but a number of related aims; it must try to satisfy these as far as possible in harmony, and it is entitled to take on fresh aims. Any activity so varied in scope has, inevitably, a history with many phases: many legitimate inquiries had to be undertaken before the modern tribunal of experimental verification could have its present-day relevance. There is room in the scientific activity today also for men of many talents. Speculative imagination, scrupulous honesty, mathematical command, logical perspicuity, as well as experimental inventiveness and ingenuity: these are all relevant to the manifold aims of science, in its broadest sense. Here we see the most serious defect in the predictivist account of science: it gives the false impression that the possibilities are closed. Once before, in Hellenistic times, scientists came to see their tasks as restricted to mathematical forecasting: what followed was disastrous. For most of us nowadays the task of understanding nature is a wider one. Prediction is all very well; but we must make sense of what we predict. The mainspring of science is the conviction that by honest, imaginative inquiry, we can build up a system of ideas about nature which has some legitimate claim to "reality." That being so, we can never make less than a threefold demand of science: its explanatory techniques must be not only (in Copernicus' words) "consistent with the numerical records"; they must also be acceptable—for the time being, at any rate—as "absolute" and "pleasing to the mind" (Toulmin 1961:110–115).

The Relationship of the Approach to Philosophy

It is the purpose of this discussion to sketch out a hierarchy of knowledge processes at various biological levels, to examine these for recurrent attributes and differences, and then, considering science as one aspect of a general knowledge process, to make some suggestions of tactics in the attempt to build a social science. Before proceeding, a few comments locating this perspective within the tradition of epistemological issues seems in order.

1) While an aspiration to justify induction in some logical, analytic manner is a continually recurrent one, the bulk of epistemologists and philosophers of science today join Hume in regarding this effort as impossible. Rather, not only are specific inductions matters of synthetic hypothesis of a scientific sort, but this also holds for general principles of efficacious inductive procedure, should any such be found (e.g., Feigl 1956:25–26). All scientific and common sense knowledge is highly presumptive, is never proven, never certain.

2) The general orientation can be called a hypothetical realism. An "external" world is hypothesized in general and specific entities and processes are hypothesized in particular, and the observable implications of these hypotheses (or hypostatizations or reifications) are sought out for verification. No part of the hypotheses has any "justification" or validity prior to, or other than through, the testing of these implications. Both in

specific and in general they are always to some degree tentative. The original source of the hypotheses has nothing to do with their validity: in some sense they were originally blind guesses or a chance mutation. Perhaps the position is not essentially different from a critical realism. No more solid or material physical substance need be assumed than that described by modern physics, but this, for example, is substantial enough to provide some objects which both reflect light and are impervious to the locomotor efforts of fish and man.

3) Whereas a typical philosophical approach initiates the investigation of knowledge process by holding all achieved knowledge in abeyance until the very possibility of any knowledge can first be established, the present approach would assume in general all scientific and commonly accepted knowledge, would assume the achievements of modern physics and biology in particular and would make use of this cumulative achievement in understanding the knowledge process itself. This knowledge is not assumed to be perfect or incorrigible. Rather, the tactic is one of assuming the correctness of the great bulk of knowledge while skeptically examining one fragment. This is the tactic which has enabled physics to continuously build while at the same time correcting its most basic assumptions.

4) While not escaping an interest in primitive fundamentals to knowledge, no primitives are accepted which are not also appropriate to the knowledge processes of the white rat and paramecium. Man's knowledge processes are undoubtedly more complex and efficient than those of his lowly cousins, but they are not expected to be more primitive nor more fundamental. In particular, no immediate, incorrigible, or directly given knowledge is invoked: at all levels knowledge is indirectly, inferentially, and fallibly achieved.

5) Insofar as the enterprise partakes of an epistemology, it is an "epistemology of the other one," to paraphrase Max Meyer's (1921) famous dictum for a scientific psychology. Naess (1936, 1948) has elaborated such a view. In concession to the solipsistic argument, no effort is made to justify "my own" knowledge processes. Rather, the enterprise is one of describing how the organisms under study come to know.

6) At any level, the orientation is one

of describing an organism in an environment. In consistency with behavioristic analyses (e.g., Bergmann and Spence 1944) there is an insistence upon the necessity for separate data series to represent the environment on the one hand (e.g., stimulus-type constructs) and the organism on the other (e.g., response-type constructs) in order that the correlation observed between the two shall not be a tautology. In particular, the rat's learned behavior pattern and the maze are to be distinguished. When this orientation is extended to the scientist in his "maze," the point of view comes dangerously close to what Naess (1935) has criticized as "Labyrintherkenntnistheorie." Perhaps the errors of that position are avoided by treating both the organism's knowledge and the environment-to-be-known as constructs of the scientist of science. The requirement that these constructs be independently definable creates no problem when a rat's knowledge of a maze is under study. But as Naess points out, it does become an important limiting factor when describing the problem-solving behavior of a physicist in a "maze" the description for which one must get from the same physicist. This limit is perhaps avoidable by the study of the problem-solving behavior of scientists at the earlier stages of a now well-developed science. The insistence on the operational independence of "knowledge" and "that-which-is-to-be-known," plus an emphasis upon the indirectness and imperfection of knowing, may characterize my position as a variety of epistemological dualism though I reject their ontological-physical dualism (Lovejoy 1930, Köhler 1938).

7) Although implied in several of the points above, it may help the reader to alert him to the use of the hypothesis that the segments of the total environment known by various organisms by various knowledge processes can overlap, and perhaps usually do. A complete physics would not only map many aspects of the environment neglected in the trial and error problem solving of the paramecium or white rat, but will also map the same aspects of the environment as do these animals, e.g., the impermeability and opaqueness of objects, etc. Von Bertalanffy (1955) has eloquently expounded such a point under the term "perspectivism," in qualifying the relativisms of Whorf (1956) and von Uexküll (1920).

A HIERARCHY OF KNOWLEDGE PROCESSES

There is an emergent position in biology and control theory which sees the natural selection paradigm as the universal nonteleological explanation of teleological achievements, of ends-guided processes, of "fit." Thus crystal formation is seen as the result of a chaotic permutation of molecular adjacencies, some of which are much more difficult to dislodge than others. At temperatures warm enough to provide general change, but not so warm as to disrupt the few stable adjacencies, the number of stable adjacencies will steadily grow even if their occurrence is but a random affair. In crystal formation the material forms its own template. In the genetic control of growth, the DNA provides the initial template selectively accumulating chance fitting RNA molecules, which in turn provide the selective template selectively cumulating from among chaotic permutations of proteins. These molecules of course fit multiple selective criteria: of that finite set of semistable combinations of protein material, they are the subset fitting the template. The template guides by selecting from among the mostly unstable, mostly worthless possibilities offered by thermal noise operating on the materials in solution. Turning the model to still lower levels of organization, elements and subatomic particles are seen as but nodes of stability which at certain temperatures transiently select adjacencies among still more elementary stuff.

Turning to higher levels, the model can be applied to such dramatically teleological achievements as embryological growth and wound healing. Within each cell, genetic templates for all types of body proteins are simultaneously available, competing as it were for the raw material present. Which ones propagate most depends upon the surrounds. Transplantation of embryonic material changes the surroundings and hence the selective system. Wounds and amputations produce analogous changes in the "natural selection" of protein possibilities. Spiegelman (1948) has specifically noted the Darwinian analogy and its advantages over vitalistic teleological pseudo-explanations which even concepts of force fields and excitatory gradients may partake of.

Regeneration provides an illustration of the

nested hierarchical nature of biological selection systems. The lizard's amputated leg regrows to a length optimal for locomotion and survival. The ecological selection system does not operate directly on the leg length however. Instead, the leg length is selected to conform to a vicarious control built into the developmental system, which control was itself selected by the trial-and-error of whole mutant organisms. If the ecology has recently undergone change, the vicarious selective criterion representing the ecological realities will correspondingly be in error. The larger, encompassing selection system is the ecological organism-environment interaction. Nested in a hierarchical way within it is the selective system directly operating on leg length, the "settings" or criteria for which are themselves subject to change by natural selection. What are criteria at one level are but "trials" of the criteria of the next higher, more fundamental, more encompassing, less frequently invoked level.

In its most dogmatic form, the following descriptive epistemology results: there is a nested hierarchy of knowledge processes, the lower (more advanced, less fundamental) of which substitute for the more fundamental, operating as shortcuts. In each process, at each level, there is a variation-and-selective-retention mechanism. The short-cutting substitute mechanisms are themselves the products of a blind-mutation-and-selective-retention process, and as such have no "entailed" status as vicarious knowledge processes. Further, they probe reality still less directly and still more presumptively. At each level there must be a mechanism for (1) variation, (2) selection among variations, (3) preservation and/or propagation of variations. In general, the preservation and variation mechanisms are inherently at odds, some compromise level of each resulting.

The hierarchy of knowledge processes includes the following levels (Campbell 1959, 1960).

Genetic Adaptation

While the processes to be described below are of more obvious epistemic reference, it is important to recognize that genetic evolution itself is also a fundamental knowledge process. Between some virus-type ancestor and the white rat or precultural man, evolutionary processes provided a tremendous gain in practical knowledge of the world, in the temporal and spatial extent of usable forecasts, in what Spencer (1896) designated the "range of correspondences." The process making possible this truly stupendous gain is genetic mutation and selective survival. The invention of bisexuality and heterozygosity represents a distinguishable "invention" (many times independently discovered in various forms of life) in which mutations are cumulated so as to provide a much more rapid adjustment to environmental changes. The process of blind mutation and selective survival must be recognized as a powerful, if slow, inductive procedure. Operating at low efficiency across countless eons, it has produced specific tested and retested assumptions about the nature of reality. These assumptions have been well "probed," but never deductively "proven." In addition, biological evolution has provided other inductive procedures that speed up, abbreviate, and expand the over-all process. These discovered shortcuts include learning, vision, etc., the very workabilities of which in themselves constitute descriptive knowledge of the external world, being mechanisms that would not work in many conceivable worlds.

Non-mnemonic Problem Solving

At the level of Jennings' (1906) protozoan stentor and Ashby's (1952) homeostat, there is a blind variation of locomotor activity until a setting that is nourishing or non-noxious is found. Such problem-solutions are then retained as a cessation of locomotion, as a cessation of variation. There is, however, no memory, no re-use of old solutions. Ashby deliberately took Jennings' paramecium as his model, and describes the natural-selection analogy at this level as follows:

> The work also in a sense develops a theory of the "natural selection" of behaviour-patterns. Just as in the species the truism that the dead cannot breed implies that there is a fundamental tendency for the successful to replace the unsuccessful, so in the nervous system does the truism that the unstable tends to destroy itself imply that there is a fundamental tendency for the stable to replace the unstable. Just as the gene pattern in its encounters with the environment tends toward ever better adaptation of the inherited form and function, so does a system of step- and part-functions tend toward ever better adaptation of learned behaviour. (Ashby 1952:vi)

In a world with only benign or neutral states, an adaptive organism might operate at this level without exteroceptors. Wherever it is, it is trying to ingest the immediate environment. When starvation approaches, blind locomotor activity is initiated, ingestion being attempted at all locations. Even at this level, however, there is needed an interoceptive sense-organ which monitors nutritional level, and substitutes for the whole organism's death. In the actual case of Jennings' *stentor*, chemoreceptors for noxious conditions are present, vicarious representatives of the lethal character of the environment, operating on non-lethal samples or signs of that environment. It is these chemoreceptors and comparable organs which in fact provide the immediate selection of responses. Only indirectly, through selecting the selectors, does life and death relevance select the responses.

At this level of knowing, however, the responses may be regarded as direct rather than vicarious. And as to presuppositions about the nature of the world, the ontology guiding epistemology, perhaps all that is assumed is spatial discontinuity somewhat greater than temporal discontinuity in the distribution of environmental substances: moving around is judged to bring changes more rapidly than staying put. At this level the species has discovered that the environment is discontinuous, consisting of penetrable regions and impenetrable ones, and that impenetrability is to some extent a stable characteristic. The animal has learned that there are some solvable problems. Already the machinery of knowing is focusing in a biased way upon the small segment of the world which is knowable, as natural selection makes inevitable.

Vicarious Locomotor Devices

Substituting for spatial exploration by locomotor trial and error are a variety of distance receptors, of which a ship's radar is an example. An automated ship could explore the environment of landfalls, harbors and other ships by a trial-and-error of full movements and collisions. Using radar, it sends out instead substitute locomotions in the form of a radar beam. These are selectively reflected from nearby objects, the reflective opaqueness to this wave band vicariously representing the locomotor impen-

etrability of the objects. This vicarious representability is a contingent discovery, and is in fact only approximate. The knowledge received is reconfirmed as acted upon by the full ship's locomotion. The process removes the trial-and-error component from the overt locomotion, locating it instead in the blindly emitted radar beam. (The radar beam is not emitted randomly, but it could be so emitted and still work. The radar beam is, however, emitted in a blind exploration, albeit a systematic sweep.) Analogous to radar and to sonar are several echolocation devices in animals. Pumphrey has described the lateral-line organ of fish as a receiver for the reflected pulses of the broadcast pressure waves emitted by the fishes' own swimming movements. The all-directional exploring of the wave front is selectively reflected by nearby objects, pressure-wave substituting for locomotor exploration. The echolocation devices of porpoises, bats, and cave birds have a similar epistemology (Pumphrey 1950, Kellogg 1958, Griffin 1958).

Assimilating vision to the blind-variation-and-selective-retention model is a more difficult task (Campbell 1956). It seems important, however, to make vision palpably problematic, in correction of the common sense realism or the direct realism of many contemporary philosophers, which leads them to an uncritical assumption of directness and certainty for the visual process. The vividness and phenomenal directness of vision needs to be corrected in any complete epistemology, which also has to make comprehensible how such an indirect, coincidence-exploiting mechanism could work at all. Were visual percepts as vague and incoherent as the phosphors on a radar screen, many epistemological problems would be avoided, and from the point of view of an evolutionary epistemology, they are just as vague.

Consider a one-photocell substitute eye such as was once distributed for the use of the blind. To an earphone, the cell transmitted a note of varying pitch depending upon the brightness of the light received. In blind search with this photocell, one could locate some objects and some painted boundaries on flat surfaces, all boundaries being indicated by a shift in tone. One can imagine an extension of this blind search device to a multiple photocell model, each photocell of fixed direction, boundaries being located by a comparison of emitted tones or energies, perhaps in some central sweep-scanning of outputs. To be sure, boundaries would be doubly confirmed if the whole set were oscillated slightly, so that a boundary stood out not only as comparison across adjacent receptors at one time, but also as a comparison across times for the same receptors. (The eye has just such a physiological nystagmus, essential to its function.) Similarly, one could build a radar with multiple fixed-directional emitters and receivers. It would search just as blindly, just as open-mindedly, as the single beam and sweep scanner. In such multiple receptor devices, the opportunities for excitation are blindly made available and are selectively activated.

Blind locomotor search is the primary or direct exploration. A blind man's cane is a vicarious search process, utilizing a less expensive substitute for the blind trials and the wasted movements, removing costly search from the full locomotor effort, making that seem smooth, purposeful, insightful. The single photocell device seems equally blind, although utilizing a more unlikely substitute, one still cheaper in effort and time. The multiple photocell device, or the eye, uses the multiplicity of cells instead of a multiplicity of focusing of one cell, resulting in a search process equally blind and open-minded, equally dependent upon a selection-from-variety epistemology.

The substitutability of cane locomotion for body locomotion, the equivalence of opaque-to-cane and opaque-to-body, is a contingent discovery, although one which seems more nearly "entailed," or to involve a less complex, less presumptive model of the physical world than does the substitutability of light waves or radar waves for body locomotion.

This is, of course, a skeletonized model of vision, emphasizing its kinship to blind fumbling, and its much greater indirectness than blind fumbling, phenomenal directness notwithstanding. Neglected is the presumptive achievement of the visual system in reifying stable discrete objects, stable over a heterogeneity of points of viewing; neglected is the fundamental epistemological achievement of "identifying" new and partially different sets of sense data as "the same" so that habit or instinct or knowledge can be appropriately applied even though there be no

logically entailed identity (Russell 1948, Lorenz 1959, Campbell 1966).

Habit and Instinct

Habit, instinct, and visual diagnosis of objects are so interlocked and interdependent that no simple ordering of the three is possible. Much more detailed work is needed on the evolution of knowledge processes, and such an examination would no doubt describe many more stages than are outlined here. Such a study could also profitably describe the "presumptions" about the nature of the world, or the "knowledge" about the nature of the world, underlying each stage. Certainly the extent of these presumptions is greater at the more advanced levels.

The visual diagnosis of reidentifiable objects is basic to most instinctive response patterns in insects and vertebrates, both for instigation of the adaptive pattern and for eliminating the trial-and-error component from the overt response elements. In a crude way, instinct development can be seen as involving a trial-and-error of whole mutant animals, whereas trial-and-error learning involves the much cheaper wastage of responses within the lifetime of a single animal. The same environment is editing habit and instinct development in most cases, the editing process is analogous, and the epistemological status of the knowledge, innate or learned, no different. Thus one of the great emphases of the empiricists is made irrelevant, but in the form of a more encompassing empiricism. It can be noted that all comprehensive learning theories, including those of Gestalt inspiration, contain a trial-and-error component, albeit a trial-and-error of "hypotheses" or "recenterings" (Campbell 1956).

These general conclusions may be acceptable, but the evolutionary discreteness of the two processes is not as clear as implied nor should instinct be regarded as more primitive than habit. Complex adaptive instincts typically involve multiple movements and must inevitably involve a multiplicity of mutations at least as great as the obvious movement segments. Furthermore, it is typical that the fragmentary movement segments or the effects of single component mutations, would represent no adaptive gain at all apart from the reminder of the total sequence. The joint likelihood of the simultaneous occurrence of the adaptive form of the dozens of mutations involved is so infinitesimal that the blind-mutation-and-selective-retention model seems inadequate. This argument was used effectively by both Lamarckians and those arguing for an intelligently guided evolution or creation. Baldwin, Morgan, Osborn, and Poulton (Baldwin 1902), believing that natural selection was the adequate and only mechanism, proposed that for such instincts, learned adaptive patterns, recurrently discovered in similar form within a species by trial-and-error learning, preceded the instincts. The adaptive pattern being thus piloted by learning, any mutations that accelerated the learning, made it more certain to occur, or predisposed the animal to certain component responses, would be adaptive and selected no matter which component, or in what order, affected. The habit thus provided a selective template around which the instinctive components could be assembled. It is furthermore typical of such instincts that they involve learned components, as of nest and raw material location, etc.

This can be conceived as an evolution of increasingly specific selection-criteria, which at each level select or terminate visual search and trial-and-error learning. For behavior sequences typical of learning, these are as general as drive states and reinforcing stimulations. Even here, the environment's selective relevance is represented in part indirectly, as in the pleasurableness of sweet food (the vicarious and indirect nature of which is shown by animals' willingness to learn for the goal of non-nutritive saccharin, presumably a rare commodity in the ecology of evolution). The habit-to-instinct sequential development would be one of increasingly specific innate subgoals or behavior-selective criteria. Very stable environments over long evolutionary sequences would be a prerequisite for such rigidity of particular selective systems. What we call habit involves more general innate selectors, with the subgoals or subselectors being established by learning. As the more specific subgoals become innately fixed selectors, we describe the behavior as instinctive. Popper in his brilliant unpublished Herbert Spencer Lecture of October 30, 1961, "Evolution and the Tree of Knowledge," makes a creative analysis of the evolution of purposeful behavior which in some ways parallels Baldwin's but is more explicit on the hierarchical selection of selectors. Using a servomechanism model of an automated airplane, he suggests that mutations of "aim-structure" precede and subsequently select mutations in "skill structure."

Visually Supported Thought

The dominant form of insightful problem-solving in animals (e.g., as described by Köhler [1925]) requires the support of a visually present environment. With the environment represented vicariously through visual search, there is a trial-and-error of potential locomotions in thought. The "successful" locomotions at this substitute level, with its substitute selective criteria, are then put into overt locomotion, where they appear "intelligent," "purposeful," "insightful," even if still subject to further editing in the more direct contact with the environment.

Mnemonically Supported Thought

At this level the environment being searched is vicariously represented in memory or "knowledge," rather than visually, the blindly emitted vicarious thought trials being selected by a vicarious criterion substituting for an external state of affairs. The net result is the "intelligent," "creative," and "foresightful" product of thought, our admiration of which makes us extremely reluctant to subsume it under the blind-variation-and-selective-retention model. Yet it is in the description of this model that the trial-and-error theme, the blind permutation theme, has been most persistently invoked. When Mach in 1895 was called back to Vienna to assume the newly created professorship in "The History and Theory of Inductive Sciences," he chose this topic:

The disclosure of new provinces of facts before unknown, can only be brought about by accidental circumstances. . . . (p. 168)
. . . In such [other] cases it is a physical accident to which the person owes his discovery—a discovery which is here made "deductively" by means of mental copies of the world, instead of experimentally. (p. 171)
. . . After the repeated survey of a field has afforded opportunity for the interposition of advantageous accidents, has rendered all the traits that suit with the word or the dominant thought

more vivid, and has gradually relegated to the background all things that are inappropriate, making their future appearance impossible; then from the teeming, swelling host of fancies which a free and high-flown imagination calls forth, suddenly that particular form arises to the light which harmonizes perfectly with the ruling idea, mood, or design. Then it is that that which has resulted slowly as the result of a gradual selection, appears as if it were the outcome of a deliberate act of creation. Thus are to be explained the statements of Newton, Mozart, Richard Wagner, and others, when they say that thoughts, melodies, and harmonies had poured in upon them, and that they had simply retained the right ones. (Mach 1896:174)

Poincaré's famous essay on mathematical creativity espouses such a view at length, arguing that it is mathematical beauty which provides the selective criteria for a blind permuting process usually unconscious:

One evening, contrary to my custom, I drank black coffee and could not sleep. Ideas rose in crowds; I felt them collide until pairs interlocked, so to speak, making a stable combination. (Poincaré 1913:387)
. . . What happens then? Among the great numbers of combinations blindly formed by the subliminal self, almost all are without interest and without utility; but just for that reason they are also without effect upon the esthetic sensibility. Consciousness will never know them; only certain ones are harmonious, and consequently, at once useful and beautiful. (Poincaré 1913:392)
. . . Perhaps we ought to seek the explanation in that preliminary period of conscious work which always precedes all fruitful unconscious labor. Permit me a rough comparison. Figure the future elements of our combinations as something like the hooked atoms of Epicurus. During the complete repose of the mind, these atoms are motionless, they are, so to speak, hooked to the wall; so this complete rest may be indefinitely prolonged without the atoms meeting, and consequently without any combination between them.
On the other hand, during a period of apparent rest and unconscious work, certain of them are detached from the wall and put in motion. They flash in every direction through the space (I was about to say the room) where they are enclosed, as would, for example, a swarm of gnats, or, if you prefer a more learned comparison, like the molecules of gas in the kinematic theory of gases. Then their mutual impacts may produce new combinations. (Poincaré 1913:393)
. . . In the subliminal self, on the contrary, reigns what I should call liberty, if we might give this name to the simple absence of discipline and to the disorder born of chance. Only, this disorder itself permits unexpected combinations. (Poincaré 1913:394)

Alexander Bain was proposing a trial-and-error model of invention and thought as

early as 1855 (Bain 1855). In a very modern and almost totally neglected Theory of Invention, Souriau (1881) effectively criticizes deduction, induction, and "la méthode" as models for advances in thought and knowledge, proposing "le hasard" and voluminous thought trials instead. He offers this phenomenological testimony:

. . . If his memory is strong enough to retain all of the amassed details, he evokes them in turn with such rapidity that they seem to appear simultaneously; he groups them by chance in all the possible ways; his ideas, thus shaken up and agitated in his mind form numerous unstable aggregates which destroy themselves, and finish up by stopping on the most simple and solid combination. (Souriau 1881:114–115)

Note the similarity of the imagery in the final paragraph with that of Ashby as cited under non-mnemonic problem solving above, and that of Poincaré and Mach.

Among the many others who have advocated such a view are Baldwin, Pillsbury, Rignano, Woodworth, Thurstone, Tolman, Hull, Muenzinger, Miller and Dollard, Boring, Humphrey, Mower, Sluckin, and Polya (see Campbell 1960). One presentation which has reached the attention of some philosophers is that of Kenneth J. W. Craik, in his fragmentary work of genius, *The Nature of Explanation* (Craik 1943), a work which in many other ways also espouses an evolutionary epistemology.

The resultant process of thought is a very effective one, and a main pillar of man's high estate. Yet it might be emphasized again that the vicarious representations involved—both environmental realities and potential locomotions being represented in mind-brain processes —are discovered contingent relationships, achieving no logical entailment, and in fine detail incomplete and imperfect. This same vicarious, contingent, discovered, marginally imperfect representativeness holds for the highly selected formal logics and mathematics which we utilize in the process of science.

Socially Vicarious Exploration: Observational Learning and Imitation

The survival value of the eye is obviously related to an economy of cognition—the economy of eliminating all of the wasted locomotions which would otherwise be needed.

An analogous economy of cognition helps account for the great survival advantage of the social form of animal life, which in evolutionary sequences is regularly found subsequent to rather than prior to a solitary form. In this the trial-and-error exploration of one member of a group substitutes for, renders unnecessary, trial-and-error exploration on the part of other members. The use of trial-and-error by scouts on the part of migrating social insects and human bands illustrates this general knowledge process. At the simplest level in social animals are procedures whereby one animal can profit from observing the consequences to another of that other's acts, even or especially when these acts are fatal to the model. The aversion which apes show to dismembered ape bodies, and their avoidance of the associated locations, illustrates such a process. The squeal of a rabbit in the jaws of a dog has no survival value for that rabbit. No big brother rabbits respond with rescue attempts. But it does communicate to the others the unfortunate outcome of this model's exploration and is a functional part of a social knowledge process. The following of scouts who have come back heavy laden illustrates the process for knowledge of attractive goal objects. The presumptions involved in this epistemology include the belief that the model (the scout) is exploring the same world in which the observer is living and locomoting, as well as those assumptions about the lawfulness of that world which underlie all learning.

Also noted in social animals, perhaps particularly in their young, is a tendency to imitate the actions of models even when the outcomes of those actions cannot be observed. This is a much more presumptive, but still "rational" procedure. It involves the assumptions that the model animal is capable of learning and is living in a learnable world. If this is so, then the model has eliminated punished responses and has increased its tendencies to make rewarded responses, resulting in a net output of predominantly rewarded responses (the more so the longer the learning period and the stabler the environment) (Asch 1952, Campbell 1961, 1965).

But even in imitation, there is no "direct" infusion or transference of knowledge or habit, just as there is no "direct" acquisition of knowledge by observation or induction. As Baldwin (1906) analyzes the process, what the child acquires is a criterion image, which he learns to match by a trial-and-error of matchings. He hears a tune, for example, and then learns to make that sound by a trial-and-error of vocalizations, which he checks against the memory of the sound pattern.

Language

Overlapping with both visually and mnemonically supported thought above is language, in which the outcome of explorations can be relayed from scout to follower with neither the illustrative locomotion nor the environment explored being present, not even visually-vicariously present. From the social-functional point of view, it is quite appropriate to speak of the "language" of bees, even though the wagging dance by which the scout bee conveys the direction, distance, and richness of his find is an innate response tendency automatically elicited without conscious intent to communicate. This bee language has the social function of economy of cognition in a way quite analogous to human language. The vicarious representabilities of geographical direction (relative to the sun and plane of polarization of sunlight), of distance, and of richness by features of the dance such as direction on a vertical wall, length of to-and-fro movements, rapidity of movements, etc., are all discovered and contingent equivalences, neither entailed nor perfect, but tremendously reductive of flight lengths on the part of the observing or listening worker bees (Frisch 1950).

For human language too, the representability of things and actions by words is a contingent discovery, a nonentailed relationship, and only approximate. We need a Popperian model of language learning in the child and of language development in the race (Campbell and Walker 1966). Regarding the child, this would emphasize that word meanings cannot be directly transferred into the child. Rather the child must discover these by a presumptive trial-and-error of meanings, which the initial instance only limits but does not determine. Rather than logically complete ostensive definitions being possible, there are instead extended, incomplete sets of ostensive instances, each instance of which equivocally leaves possible multiple interpretations, although the whole series edits out many wrong trial meanings. The "logical" nature of children's errors in word usage amply testifies to such a process, and testifies against an inductionist version of a child's passively observing adult usage contingencies. This trial-and-error of meanings requires more than the communication of mentor and child. It requires a third party of objects referred to. Language cannot be taught by telephone, but requires visually or tactually present ostensive referents stimulating and editing the trial meanings.

Moving to the evolution of language, a social trial-and-error of meaning and namings can be envisaged. Trial words designating referents which the other speakers in the community rarely guess "correctly" either fail to become common coinage or are vulgarized toward commonly guessed designations. All words have to go through the teaching sieve, have to be usefully if incompletely communicable by finite sets of ostensive instances. Stable, sharp, striking object boundaries useful in manipulating the environment have a greater likelihood of utilization in word meanings than do subtler designations, and when used, achieve a greater universality of meaning within the community of speakers. Such natural boundaries for words exist in much greater number than are actually used, and alternate boundaries for highly overlapping concepts abound. Just as certain knowledge is never achieved in science, so certain equivalence of word meanings is never achieved in the iterative trial-and-error of meanings in language learning. This equivocality and heterogeneity of meanings is more than a trivial logical technicality; it is a practical fringe imperfection. And even were meanings uniform, the word-to-object equivalence is a corrigible contingent relationship, a product of a trial-and-error of metaphors of greater and greater appropriateness, but never complete perfection, never a formal nor entailed isomorphism.

Cultural Cumulation

In socio-cultural evolution (Cohen 1962, Mead 1964, Campbell 1965), there is a variety of variation and selective retention processes leading to advances or changes in technology and culture. Most direct is the selective survival of complete social organizations, differentially as a function of cultural and ecological features. More important, however, is selective borrowing, a process which probably leads to increased adaptation as far as easily tested aspects of technology are concerned, but could involve adaptive irrelevance in areas of culture where reality-testing is more difficult. Differential imitation of a heterogeneity of models from within the culture is also a selective system that could lead to cultural advance. The learning process, selective repetition from among a set of temporal variations in cultural practice, also produces cultural advance. Selective elevation of different persons to leadership and educational roles is no doubt also involved. Such selective criteria are highly vicarious, and could readily become disfunctional in a changing environment.

Science

The level of science is but an aspect of socio-cultural evolution. The demarcation of science from other speculations is that the knowledge claims be testable (Popper 1934, 1959) and that there be available mechanisms for testing or selecting which are more than social. In theology and the humanities there is certainly differential propagation among advocated beliefs, and there result sustained developmental trends, if only at the level of fads and fashions. What is characteristic of science is that the selective system which weeds out among the variety of conjectures involves contact with the environment, and is so designed that outcomes quite independent of the preferences of the investigator are possible. It is this feature that gives science its objectivity and its claim to a cumulative increase in the accuracy with which it describes its world.

IMPLICATIONS OF THE NATURAL SELECTION ORIENTATION FOR THE PHILOSOPHY OF SCIENCE

Empiricism, Nativism and the Kantian Categories

Lacking an articulation of the inductive process constituted by biological evolution, the older philosophers with the empiricist insight into the preponderant role of induction in man's achievement of knowledge have emphasized the learning process, and have been wary of any assumptions of innate processes, regarding these as covers for teleological pseudo-explanation, metaphysical vitalism, theism, etc. From the present perspective, this precaution seems unnecessary. The evolutionary ecology leading to instinct development and the ecology providing the selection among responses in trial-and-error learning are in large part the same. The processes do not differ in any epistemological fundamental: both are blindly pragmatic and inductive. Furthermore, what is a learned synthetic induction in one species is an inherited innate synthetic induction in another. The disagreements between Helmholtz and Hering on the innateness of specific visual functions, which were once paralleled by the drawing of philosophical lines, seem now epistemologically irrelevant. As a result, the person of positivist, physicalist, empiricist orientation, looking at the tremendously important evolutionary background of man, can today concede more innate endowment in man's knowledge processes than he has previously been inclined to. Recently several persons from quite different starting points have suggested such an evolutionary reinterpretation of Kant's synthetic *a priori*. (In greater or less explicitness, these include Lorenz 1939, 1943; Baldwin 1902; Waddington 1954; Bertalanffy 1955; Whitrow 1955; Platt 1956; Popper 1957; Pepper 1958: 106–108.) A predisposition toward interpreting events in terms of a three-dimensional space would thus be ontogenetically *a priori*, but not phylogenetically *a priori*. Further, in the sense in which it is now seen, its status as *a priori* gives it no truth status different from that of any other much used inductive inference—but by the same token its selective survival from among countless other mutation-combinations provides an inductively strong credence base. Similarly with regard to causality: to some extent, Hume and Kant can be seen as disagreeing over the psychological fact of whether or not the tendency to perceive cause-effect relationships is learned within the person's own lifetime, or is rather a phylogenetic "learning." Michotte's (1946) research ties up the process with event perception in general, and finds the experience

automatic and indivisible. And from the biological point of view, event perception, as in the perception of motion, is at least as primitive as the perception of discrete objects. Having myself (1963) identified the perception of causality as the phenomenal counterpart of what the behaviorist records as stimulus association through contiguity in conditioning, I would tend to regard it as just as innate as the capacity to learn. But in any event, the argument as to innateness or learnedness is now a problem of psychological fact and of no epistemological relevance.

Except for his relative neglect of the blind variation and selective survival mechanism, Spencer long ago anticipated this development, which must stand as one of the sound contributions of this overproductive man, overaccepted in his own day and overrejected in ours. His point of view can perhaps be most economically presented in the words of a contemporary, Höffding (1900). (The italics are for the most part my own.)

With regard to the question of the origin of knowledge Spencer makes front on the one hand against Leibniz and Kant, on the other against Locke and Mill. He quarrels with empiricism for two reasons: —firstly, because it does not see that the matter of experience is always taken up and elaborated in a definite manner, which is determined by the original nature of the individual; secondly, because it is lacking in a criterion of truth. We must assume an original organization if we are to understand the influence exercised by stimuli on different individuals, and the criterion by means of which alone a proposition can be established is the fact that its opposite would contain a contradiction. In the inborn nature of the individual then, and in the logical principle on which we depend every time we make an inference, we have an *a priori* element; something which cannot be deduced from experience. To this extent Spencer upholds Leibniz and Kant against Locke and Mill; but he does so only as long as he is restricting his considerations to the experience of the individual. *What is a priori for the individual is not so for the race.* For those conditions and forms of knowledge and of feeling which are original in the individual, and hence cannot be derived from his experience, have been transmitted by earlier generations. The forms of thought correspond to the collective and inherited modifications of structure which are latent in every newborn individual, and are gradually developed through his experiences. Their first origin, then, is empirical: the fixed and universal relations of things to one another must, in the course of development, form fixed and universal conjunctions in the organism; by perpetual repetition of absolutely external uniformities there arise in the race necessary forms of knowledge, indissoluble thought associations which express the net results of the experience of perhaps several millions of generations down to the present. The individual cannot sunder a conjunction thus deeply rooted in the organisation of the race; hence, he is born into the world with those physical connections which form the substrata of "necessary truths." Although Spencer is of the opinion that the inductive school went too far when they attempted to arrive at everything by way of induction (for, if we adopt this method, induction itself is left hanging in the air), yet, if he had to choose between Locke and Kant, he would avow himself a disciple of the former; for, *in the long run, Spencer too thinks that all knowledge and all forms of thought spring from experience.* His admission that there is something in our mind which is not the product of our own a posteriori experience led Max Muller to call him a "thoroughgoing Kantian," to which Spencer replied: "The Evolution-view is completely experiential. It differs from the view of the experimentalists by containing a great extension of that view. —But the view of Kant is avowedly and utterly unexperiential." (Höffding 1900:475–476) . . . "It is of no small interest to notice that John Stuart Mill, who at first demurred at Spencer's evolutionary psychology, afterwards declared himself convinced that mental development takes place not only in the individual but also in the race, by means of inherited dispositions. He expressed this modification of his view a year before his death in a letter to Carpenter, the physiologist (quoted in the latter's *Mental Physiology,* p. 486)." (Höffding 1900:457–458)

Independent Invention and the Sociology of Science

The implications of the selective-retention model are, on some points, divergent from those often drawn from evolutionary theory. As we have seen, the blind-variation-and-selective-retention model strongly predicts independent invention for variations and variation-combinations of powerful selective advantage. In the traditional theory of biological evolution, this implication of the natural-selection model is most clearly specified in the fact and concept of *convergent* evolution. Thus the aerodynamic realities and the selective payoff have led winged flight to be independently invented by insects, pterodactyls, birds, and bats; there are apparently ecological niches for both meat eaters and vegetarians (note the convergent evolution of both marsupial wolves and herbivores in Australia); there is apparently an ecological niche for woodpeckers, and so, lacking rivals, Darwin's finches upon Galapagos conver-

gently and independently evolved a pseudo-woodpecker, as well as a number of other non-finchlike forms. The great heterogeneity and the tremendous numbers of variations make almost inevitable the "accidental discovery" of any strongly adaptive form that lies "near" in number of mutation links to any prior form. It further makes it probable that any powerfully adaptive form will be approached from a variety of "directions," providing viable intermediaries exist.

The fact that variation-and-selective-retention theory strongly predicts independent invention, makes it very appropriate to the data on independent discovery and invention in science and technology, as studied by Ogburn and Thomas (1922), Kroeber (1917), Barber (1952) and Merton (1961). Here in a well-studied field of culture history, the application of Darwin's specific contribution to evolutionary theory enables us to legitimately shift our language from cultural *history* to cultural *evolution*. If indeed many persons are, in thought or action, trying many variations on a common body of technology or science, and if a few variation-steps away there is indeed a marvelous device or conceptualization available, then many are likely to encounter it. This becomes no more incredible than that two rats in the same maze discover the same efficient running pattern. A reflexive example: Darwin's theoretical discovery was to him an emotionally exciting insight, so different from ordinary thought yet fitting the problem so well. Spencer and others in his day showed this great admiration for it, and wondered how, coming so close to it themselves, they had missed it. Yet it was so selectively advantageous and available to ordinary thought by such a few steps that it was almost inevitable that others would hit upon it, as indeed they had; not only Wallace, but as Zirkle (1941) has so carefully documented, Empedocles and many more. The discovery was inevitable. The theory would have eventually become generally accepted, even if Darwin had never published. A variation-and-selective-retention theory makes us understand this inevitability. While such data series have been used to emphasize, correctly, a cultural reality independent of individual geniuses, they equally support a Darwinian analogue in socio-cultural evolution. And how much better it is to study the selective system than to impute causal status and free will to the "Zeitgeist" or "cultural bent."

Variation and Opportunism in Science

In general, the rats which emit the widest range of responses learn fastest, and the species with the most rapid mutation rate evolves most rapidly, as long *as the mutation rate is not so great as to jeopardize the already accumulated knowledge.* Note that Point 1, *variation,* and Point 3, *preservation* and *transmission,* are at odds, and that a minimax solution between them must be obtained. For a well-established science, or a very highly evolved organism, the greater weight must be given to transmission, to indoctrination, to training, to passing on what is already known lest that be lost in devoting too great effort to search for innovations. An undeveloped organism or science has less to lose by overexploration (although its less complex achieved base greatly restricts the variety of innovations possible). Were these the only considerations, it is clear that the proportion of graduate student effort devoted to novel experimentation, as opposed to indoctrination, should be greater in the social sciences than in the physical. That the reverse is so should give us reason to question current practice. One excuse for the heavy proportion of indoctrination time in the social sciences is that our store of accumulated wisdom, while not larger in terms of total facts *predicted,* is much harder to transmit, takes longer to memorize and more books to record. Further inspection of the details to which this argument refers will show, however, that this is so in large part just because the social sciences do not yet embody an achieved scientific status and lack the enormously efficient crystallizations of effective predictions which adequate theories represent.

The recognition of the important role of trial-and-error processes in expanding science, and the realistic (albeit "hypothetically realistic") orientation which accompanies such recognition, puts in perspective several narcissistic features of social science making. One of these features is our attitude of disappointment when we learn that someone else has made the same discovery as we. Such disappointment is appropriate for professional "creators" such as poets, novelists, and modern painters, as it is a sign of professional inadequacy. But for persons whose profession is "discovery," not "creation," such independent confirmation shows professional *adequacy,* through demonstrating the validity of one's achievement (insofar as the replication was independent and insofar as both replications were advances, rather than restatements of beliefs already existing in the shared culture). If many persons are engaged in attempting to add to the valid accumulations of a science, then blind trial-and-error, or creative insight, will lead many to the few available solutions at about the same time, and the solution is no less an advance or an achievement for the multiplicity of its discovery. (In mathematics, the discipline of internal consistency plus the accumulation of common achievement, likewise makes independent discovery something to be expected and a sign of validity.)

Another symptom of an inappropriate narcissism which I see in the graduate students in the social sciences, as contrasted with their peers in the biological or the physical sciences, is a greater demand for a narcissistic originality in problem selection and method. But perhaps this is desirable if, in fact, we have as yet no striking achievements worth building on. And as Merton's (1957) study of priority disputes in the history of science shows, narcissism has not been lacking in the successful sciences during their most creative phases, and indeed may play an essential role in maintaining the social institution of science.

Diagnosing Dispositions

In the course of an effort to integrate the concept of *social attitude* with other concepts in psychology dealing with acquired behavioral dispositions (Campbell 1963), it becomes desirable to provide a paradigm for the operational delineation of terms like *attitude* or *habit.* In psychology, too many so-called operational definitions merely specify usual antecedent conditions, and do not point to the distinguishing characteristics of the resultant disposition itself. In particular, a paradigm was needed for attitudes or habits diagnosed by an observer who had *not* watched their acquisition and had *not* seen the environment in which they were learned. The following parable proved to be useful for this purpose, and employs the perspective of a comparative psychology of knowledge processes.

Let us pose to an animal psychologist at one university the problem of diagnosing the habits of an aged and experienced rat shipped to him from another laboratory, with no information as to past environments and reinforcements. The process would be a hit and miss, trial-and-error process. Knowledge that the rat shared some common culture, i.e., that it was a university psychology rat, would make the selections of apparatus somewhat less random. The animal would be placed in a Skinner box while buzzers buzzed and lights flashed, and any combinations that produced increased lever pressing would be taken as symptoms of some habit. The rat might be placed on a Lashley jumping stand while various colors and designs were used as discrimination cards, and if any jumping occurred an effort would be made to find to which card the jumping was most consistent. In similar fashion, T mazes, and runways would be explored. With luck, habits, or significant contingencies between stimuli and response would be encountered. But no matter how clever the research, there would still be the possibility that important, highly specific, and stable habits of the rat would go unnoticed by the diagnostician.

The initial definition of stimulus and classification of response are the experimenter's. They represent classes of objects and classes of behaviors which the experimenter can consistently discriminate (and which he guesses the animal can also). Once he finds some evidence of stimulus-response consistency on the part of the rat, he would typically start varying stimuli and varying his classification of movements in order to approximate more closely the optimal description of the habit. Thus if he found that the rat jumped to a yellow circle he would start varying both the color and the shape to find what maximized the contingency. Likewise, he would try and discover the optimizing classification of response, whether as muscle contraction or locomotor achievement, etc. Although by this trial-and-error he might come closer to the "rat's own" definition of the situation, the final classifications would still be in the scientist's terms and would be limited to classifications which the scientist could make. (He could of course add mechanical aids to his own senses, as in the diagnosis of the responsiveness of various insects and mollusks to the plane of polarization of light.)

Even though the definition of stimulus and response are in the experimenter's language, there is still a verifiability to his diagnosis, through the simple actuarial matter of a significant contingency of stimulus and response. He can, of course, never claim to have reached the optimal classification. But if two diagnosticians disagree, the actuarial approach can say which is the more efficient, which is presumably closer to the original acquisition conditions, or to the "rat's own" definition of stimulus and response.

Note a general limitation on the process: the diagnosis of the rat's habit is only possible insofar as the rat and the scientist overlap to some extent in their classifications of the environment into entities. Were the rat indeed to be responding to constellations of atoms sharing no boundaries with the constellations that the scientist was able to discriminate, the diagnosis of the rat's habits would be impossible. Similarly, learning of the language of another, whether as a child or as an adult, would be impossible if there were not such overlap in the discriminable contours of matter classified in linguistic usage. Thus a color-blind person never completely learns the language of those who discriminate between red and green. The fact that learning a strange language is possible at all sets an empirical limit to the extent of a Whorfian relativism.

While there is not space here for expanding on the implications of this paradigm for attitude and personality diagnosis, it does present another illustration of the ubiquitous necessity of a trial-and-error aspect to knowledge processes. The parable can also serve as a paradigm against which to refer the alternatives of nominalist versus realist interpretations of scientific achievements. It is clear that at every stage, the definitions of stimulus and of response are the inventions or conventions of the scientist. But the contingencies discovered are not therefore arbitrary fictions, and through the iterative process of optimizing the definitions, the final definitions are less "arbitrary" than the original ones might have been, in that they have been selected "by the rat," as it were, from a large array of possible definitions offered by the diagnostician. Bergmann (1957) presents a comparable point of view which can be approximated in these terms: definitions (and operations) are invented, laws relating the operations are discovered. Fruitful definitions are those that produce economically stated laws. The final definitions employed by a science are thus no longer the undisciplined creations of a scientist, but are rather a highly select set, selected from among a very large array of alternates.

Inferred External Entities and Their Verification

At some level in the hierarchy of knowledge processes, the organism tries out the strategy of hypothetically inferring stable entities and processes external to itself. This step may be thought of as occurring first with visual space perception, although there are reasons for putting aspects of it earlier, and also of ruling it out for the simplest forms of eyes. For example, Piaget (1957) finds such hypostatization to some degree absent for the very youngest infants. In any event, the shift in the mode of storage of knowledge and of acquisition of new knowledge is a dramatic one. Below this level, the knowledge embodied in instinct and habit can be regarded as organized in terms of an inventory of specific muscle-contractions to be made to specific receptor-cell activations. Above this level, knowledge becomes distal (Brunswik 1952, 1956), and acquires a reference to objects with specific locations in an extended space beyond the organism's skin. This must of necessity introduce something on the order of central nervous system modeling of the external environment (Craik 1943) which makes possible multiple inter-substitutable diagnostic procedures (the "vicarious functioning" of Brunswik 1952, 1956). That such a highly presumptive and indirect process works is a function of the kind of environment in which the organism locomotes in its search for food and safety. The presumptive reifications involved are, for this ecology, well probed and satisfactory to a high degree of approximation. They make possible efficient locomotion from such a sub-infinity of organism-environment juxtapositions as to certainly have outrun the storage capacity for specific sense-receptor–muscle-contraction rules leading to the same behavior.

It seems likely that the higher cognitive processes developed from vision, and contain residues of its dominance. Visual knowing is strongly given to reification, to the hypostatization of real external entities containing attributes beyond those given to vision. Such realistic bias has been amply justified in the visual diagnosis of middle-sized objects: the inferred attributes when checked by other knowledge processes, such as touch or locomotor effort, are almost always confirmed. However, when a central nervous system machinery based upon this experience is used in other ecological settings, a tendency to reification might be carried over in a way unjustified in this novel ecological setting. Thus symptoms of realism or reification in construct building in the social sciences might be justifiably suspect.

On the other hand, the vividness and phe-nomenal directness (in spite of physical mediateness) of our visual diagnosis of middle-range entities has led many philosophers to grant to the constructs of the visual machinery a special epistemological status not granted to the constructions of other knowledge processes, no matter how well established. In doing this, the clues by which the visual construction of external objects is achieved are left unspecified, so that even were the same criteria of external objectivity to be met, a comparable degree of "reality" would not be granted. In this fashion, the extreme non-reifying nominalist at the level of scientific constructs is apt to be an uncritical direct realist at the level of the visual knowledge of common objects. While the electronic microscope and the radio telescope are providing helpful transitions (few would say that an invisible radio star was less real than a radio-silent visible one), the attitude still occurs among the methodologists of social science.

The cure for both of these unfortunate by-products of visual vividness is to make explicit the kinds of evidence involved in the visual construction of external objects, and then to set up formally equivalent operations for other types of hypothesized entities. The cure is not a total abstinence from theorizing about external processes and entities which are only indirectly known—the cure is rather insistence upon procedures for verifying constructs, for probing or checking the implications of such hypostatization.

My most explicit effort to apply this orientation is to be found in a paper entitled "Common Fate, Similarity, and other Indices of the Status of Aggregates of Persons as Social Entities" (Campbell 1958). There is space here for only the briefest sketch of its argument:

The clues used by the visual perceptual system in diagnosing entityhood have been described by the Gestalt psychologists as proximity, similarity, common fate, and continuity or pregnanz. The latter can be generalized into a criterion of closed boundaries, the first three can be interpreted as criteria for generating boundaries. Labeling component fragments of the stones in a gravel pit and stirring frequently, one could diagnose the separate thinghood of each stone by the high common-fate coefficients among its constituent parts, and by the lower common-fate coefficients between a part of one stone and a part of another, the decline in common-fate coefficients producing a boundary line in a cluster-analysis fashion. Such common-fate coefficients could also be applied to the individuals in an aggregate of persons containing an hypothesized social entity plus hypothesized non-members, and a measure of entityhood achieved of comparable epistemological standing to that of the stone. In parallel fashion, the possible utility of indices based upon similarity and proximity are examined. The many troublesome details of feasible indices must be elided here. The general conclusion is that the status of aggregates of persons as discrete objects or entities can be examined on criteria comparable to those employed in the diagnosis of middle-sized physical objects. In neither case will common-fate indices ever be unity—stones can be broken, etc. In general, some social groups can be stated to be entities upon the same general grounds upon which sticks and stones are so diagnosed. However, the degree of entityhood—the relative height of the intra-entity coefficients to the inter-entity values—would probably be lower for most social groups than for most stones. The coincidence of boundaries based upon several different diagnostic criteria would in addition be less frequent for social entities than for physical ones—and it is upon such multiply confirmed or multiply diagnosable boundaries that the economy of reifying a stone or a group as an entity depends.

If a science of social groups is to be able to usefully employ the attitudes of discovery, problem solving, independent confirmation, and validation of constructs which characterize the successful sciences, such multiple confirmability of boundaries must at least occasionally be achieved. From the evolutionary perspective, it seems clear that the development of vision was predicated upon an environment populated with stable, solid, clear-cut entities—that it could never have developed in a world of fuzzy-edged amoeboid clouds or in a completely fluid homogeneous material space. By analogy, one might guess that the development of any science is predicated upon the discovery of such natural nodes of organization, upon stable discontinuities. If the discreteness and multiple-diagnosibility of entities at the social level turns out upon examination to be lacking, then the possibility of a social science representing a separate level of analysis from the biological or psychological may well be eliminated, but this is not to be decided on the grounds of *a priori* analysis.

Methodological Triangulation and Validity

Like the previous point, this illustration of a methodological principle deriving from a comparative psychology of knowledge proc-

esses makes use of the model of vision. But whereas the previous topic employed monocular diagnostic cues, the present one analogizes from the resolving power of binocular parallax in the perception of distal objects. Like the previous illustrations, the technical details of the methodological requirement are published elsewhere (Campbell and Fiske 1959).

The question of the validity of psychological tests, and in particular the question of their construct validity (Cronbach and Meehl 1955), is clearly a problem for the realist, for the reifying, hypostatizing type that had something in mind which he wanted to measure before he constructed the test, and who, now that the test is constructed, has qualms that it may not be measuring that something perfectly, or even qualms that there may be no such thing as what he was trying to get at. For the thoroughly consistent nominalist, for the extreme single-operationalist, the notions of imperfect measurement, of illusory or nonexistent constructs, are lacking. From the evolutionary perspective one can understand how such reifying, hypostatizing animals as the realist personality testers came to be. But as already emphasized, the cure is not to suppress these animal instincts and drive them into the unconscious only to have them slip past the censor in highly disguised form, but rather to provide an arena in which the inadequacies and unjustified connotations of the hypostatizations are made apparent, as well as whatever justification they may have. To help confront the personality test designer with the degree of validity of his reifying imputations about his test scores, Fiske and I recommend this seemingly arbitrary and dogmatic requirement: To validate a single psychological test, a matrix is required representing all of the intercorrelations among at least two independent methods of measurement each applied not only to the trait in question but also to at least one additional, dissimilar trait.

As are most suggestions for eliminating the unverified or unverifiable baggage of presumptions surrounding scientific and common sense terms, the procedure is a kind of operationism. The requirement calls for a *multiple, probing, delineating* operationism, or what Garner (1954, 1956) has very aptly called a *convergent* operationism. But it stands in disagreement with a rigid single operationism or an extreme *defining* operationism when they are recommended as practical operating procedures for the working scientist. Rather, as in any knowledge process which hypothesizes entities and processes beyond the skin of the organism or beyond the meter readings of the science, all indicators are understood to be both indirect and fallible, and to achieve their estimate of the distal construct only in conjunction with the involvement of other separate processes. Thus while certain complex compensated meters of physics may provide relatively pure measures of single constructs, no single operation is taken as perfectly defining of the distal construct. Instead, the firmness and relative unequivocality of our knowledge of distal constructs comes through a triangulation from two or more operations, no one of which has priority as *the* criterion or *the* definition, and no one of which would be unequivocal without the other.

Were visual perception and memory to operate according to the extreme operationist position, they would avoid any hypostatization of external entities. Each specific pattern of retinal cell excitation would be taken as an ultimate defining term. Instead of showing this restraint, the normal mental processes infer from the visual pattern remote external entities mediately known. But when a single eye views a scene from a single vantage point, the retinal pattern is equivocal for the purpose of inferring such distal objects, for there is a subinfinity of possible external events which would generate the same retinal pattern. Consider the implications of the Ames distorted room (e.g., Beardsley and Wertheimer 1958:433–443). Viewed by a *single* eye from a specific point of vantage, it seems rectangular—but the important thing to note is that from this particular point of viewing there is a large family of *distal* hexahedrons which would produce the same retinal pattern. The distal interpretation of the proximal stimulation is equivocal. A retinal excitation pattern taken as an ultimate defining operation rather than as a mediating cue has no such equivocality. This equivocality is removed, or greatly reduced, when a second point of viewing is introduced, as through the monocular parallax of head movements, through binocular parallax, or, in the Ames room, through exploring the

room's shape with one's hand or a stick. The number of singular constructs about externals which will account for the readings from both sets of operations is, relatively, very limited.

Thus, any single meter or any single psychological test produces readings which are equivocal when employed to infer the status of constructs not exhaustively defined by the measure, or when used as symptoms of something that they do not perfectly represent. The joint employment of maximally *independent* methods focused upon the same construct greatly reduces this equivocality, greatly reduces the number of tenable rival interpretations for *both* sets of measures, and thus indicates the degree of success of the constructual enterprise. Fiske and I have referred to this aspect of validation as *convergent* validation. It constitutes a *methodological triangulation* analogous to what Feigl (1958) has referred to as the "fixing" of abstract concepts in science by a "triangulation in logical space." One might well estimate that *all* of the useful, verified, abstract concepts in the successful sciences are thus established.

The second aspect of the analogy refers to a requirement which Fiske and I call *discriminant* validation, the requirement that specified correlations in the multitrait-multimethod matrix be zero, or at least be lower than the validity values. This requirement has particular importance in psychological testing because of the demonstrated strength of method factors such as halo effects, response sets and apparatus factors. I see in this requirement, and in our means of implementing it, an analogy to the role which contours play in guiding binocular fusion, and in this making binocular parallax usable. To clarify this point, let us consider visual triangulation as it would exist if each eye consisted of a single retinal cell, a single rod or cone, for example. Or let us try to duplicate a triangulation process with two mechanical eyes each consisting of a single photocell, or a fixed radar beam that does no scanning. Or consider a demonstration more feasible in the psychological laboratory in which each eye's view is reduced to a very small area through a reduction screen. Under such conditions, triangulation and binocular parallax would be of no use, false confirmations could not be told from true ones, nor would the retinal evidence provide the guide for the convergence or the aiming of the eyes which it normally does. Analogously, Fiske and I hold that a single validity coefficient, i.e., an isolated correlation between efforts to measure one trait by two different procedures, is uninterpretable. Binocular parallax will not work unless each eye is multiple-celled enough to pick up both thing and non-thing, to provide both figure and ground, to provide contours which can be checked for similarity and thus guide fusion. The analogous background for the interpretation of the validity coefficients is provided by the inclusion of *several traits* in the validation matrix, the most original part of our requirement. Through these, particularly as they generate the heterotrait-heteromethod correlations, the context is provided in which validity coefficients can be interpreted as confirming or disconfirming. (In some of our examples, validity values of .30 indicate some successful triangulation, in others .30 values indicate total failure, depending upon the size of the surrounding heterotrait-heteromethod values.)

While triangulation greatly reduces equivocality, it is not, of course, infallible. The Wheatstone stereoscope in itself demonstrates the condition under which the perceptual system can be led to erroneously infer a single entity when two drawings are actually present. The extreme rarity of such complex coincidences as the stereoscope in the normal ecology of the use of the eye makes this exception trivial in practice. It does however alert one to the absence of any deductive certainty or finality of proof for the distal constructs "confirmed" by triangulation. They only become much more likely through a successful confirmation.

It is perhaps surprising how infrequently discussions of scientific method mention the great importance of confirmation by highly independent procedures, or the fact that remote confirmations are more convincing than ones which involve two very similar apparatuses. The principle does receive occasional mention, however. Margenau comes close with his emphasis upon "bootstrapping" and upon science as an extension of perception, and, in context, by statements such as this: "The greater distance between C_1 and C_2, the greater the departure from triviality in the circuit" (1950:103). Pepper's (1942) concept of structural (as opposed to multiplicative) corroboration seems relevant. Northrop has

the concept of "epistemic correlation" which "joins a thing known in one way to what is in some sense the same thing known in another way" (1949:119). Ayer shows commonsense awareness of the requirement, although no formalization of it, in this aside: "if these sources are numerous and independent, and if they agree with one another, he will be reasonably confident that their account of the matter is correct" (1956:39). Feigl (1958) in his long chapter on the mind-body problem refers in several places to "triangulation in logical space," and it is to be hoped that we can look forward to his providing us with a full development of this most important concept.

Methodological Triangulation in Anthropology

While the purpose of this chapter has been a perspective on science in general, a few illustrations of the last few points from a discussion of cross-cultural comparison (Campbell 1964) seem in order. A naive realistic approach to anthropology would assume that cultural differences were objectively directly available for any and all observers to "see." There would be no awareness of methodological problems, no recognition of the problematic character of knowing about another culture. Such an innocent epistemology could survive neither the experience of extensive fieldwork nor the comparison of interpretations between students of "the same" culture. As in other fields, the rejection of naive realism is made first by a move to complete subjectivity. At this stage, there is recognition of the fact that knowing involves the knower, is shaped by his characteristics. This recognition goes to the extreme of rejecting any other component, i.e., of denying all objectivity to knowledge. The stage of critical or hypothetical realism shares with radical empiricism an emphasis on the subjective relativity of all knowing. It shares with naive realism the aspiration to objective knowledge, invariant over points of observation or instruments. But it recognizes that such constructions will be fallibly known, through a process of hypothetical models only indirectly confirmed. The conditions of confirmation will never provide certainty and will often be totally lacking. From this point of view, scientific knowledge is not immediately available for the asking, but requires very special settings.

The major epistemological and cross-cultural conclusion from the optical illusion study (Campbell 1964, Segall, Campbell and Herskovits 1966) was sort of a "postulate of impotence," that only under the very special condition of great perceptual similarity could one diagnose the particular nature of a perceptual difference; that had the differences been much greater they could not have been distinguished from total failure of communication. It is my thesis that this is not only unavoidably so for the optical illusions task, but is also so for all instances in which it has been learned that one culture differs in a specified manner from another. My methodological recommendation is that this anchoring base of similarities, usually left unconscious, be made explicit at least in methodological examples. This must remain an empty challenge without detailed analysis by anthropologists of instances in which they have successfully diagnosed specific cultural differences.

Professor U. R. Ehrenfels in discussion has pointed out that the Tibetans stick out their tongues to symbolize friendly greeting, whereas for Europeans, the gesture symbolizes contempt. It is argued here that this diagnosis would have been impossible without a similarity in the meaning of the context of behavior, such as the fighting or friendly sharing that followed. Ehrenfels also described the initial conditions in which he observed that the Bulgarians indicate assent by a horizontal wagging of the head, not a vertical one. As a traveler asking if indeed this road led to such a city, his respondents indicated that he was correct both verbally and by head gesture. Had they used only the head gesture he would not have had the context of similarity in which to anchor the striking conclusion that the head gesture was being used in reverse.

Professor León-Portilla has described in conversation the great difficulty in determining the meaning of the Aztec words for body parts because of the different conceptual segmenting involved. He agrees that the successful translation achieved (the successful instances of learning how they classified differently) was only made possible by the fact that many of the body-parts-segments were conceived similarly, including classifying human protoplasm into person-segments and within these the distinctions among arm, leg, head, and body. He reports that a similar situation exists in the study of Aztec religious concepts. The great array of similar religious concepts (León-Portilla 1964) makes possible the comprehension of certain religious concepts quite foreign to our way of thinking.

The achievement of useful hypothetically realistic constructs in a science requires multiple methods focused on the diagnosis of the same construct from independent points of observation through the kind of triangulation discussed above in the section on multitrait multimethod matrix (Campbell and Fiske 1959). This is required because the sense data or meter readings are now understood as the result of a transaction in which both the observer (or meter) and the object of investigation contribute to the form of the data. With a single observation at hand, it is impossible to separate the subjective and the objective component. When, however, observations through separate instruments and separate vantage points can be matched as reflecting "the same" objects, then it is possible to separate out the components in the data due to observer (instrument) and observed. It turns out that this disentangling process requires both multiple observers (methods) and multiple, dissimilar objects of study (Campbell and Fiske 1959).

Applied to the study of the philosophy of a culture, this implies that our typical one-observer one-culture study is inherently ambiguous. For any given feature of the report it is equivocal whether or not it is a trait of the observer or a trait of the object observed. To correct this the ideal paradigm might be shown in Figure 1(a). In the most general model, two anthropologists from different cultures would each study a third and fourth culture. Of the four ethnographies resulting, the common attributes in ethnographies 1 and 3 not shared with 2 and 4 could be attributed to ethnographer A, the common attributes in 2 and 4 not elsewhere present to ethnographer B. Looking at row consistencies in the figure, the common attributes in ethnographies 1 and 2 not present in 3 and 4 could be attributed to culture C as "objectively" known. Attributes common to all four ethnographies are inherently ambiguous, interpretable as either shared biases on the

(a) General paradigm	(b) Reflexive case

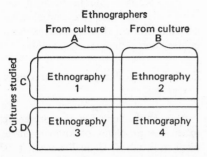

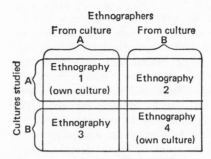

Figure 1. Multiple-Ethnography Schedules to Extricate the Ethnographer-Contributed Content from the Culture-Studied Content.

part of the ethnographers or shared culture on the part of the societies studied. Note the desirability in this regard of comparing ethnologists with as widely differing cultural backgrounds as possible. Insofar as the ethnologists come from the same culture, the replication of results becomes more a matter of reliability than validity, as these terms are used in discussions of psychological tests. Were such a study carried out by using four ethnographers, two from each ethnographer cultures A and B, studying separate villages of cultures C and D to avoid interference and collusion, then the attributes unique to any one of the ethnographies would be attributable to an equivocal pool of village specificities within its culture, to personality specifics of the ethnographer, and interaction of specific ethnographer culture and studied culture. (If only one ethnologist were used from each culture, and if each of the two studied in turn the same village in the target cultures, then the features unique to any one of the four ethnographies would be equivocally due to ethnographer-culture interactions, time-order effects in which the ethnographer reacted differently to his second culture, time-order effects in which the society reacted differently to the second student of it, historical trends, and interactions among these.) The presence of these indeterminacies should neither be suppressed nor be allowed to overshadow the great gains in understanding which such multiple-ethnographer studies would introduce.

While multiplicity of both ethnographer cultures and cultures studied is ideal, it would also be a great gain to achieve only the upper half of Figure 1(a), i.e., two ethnog-

rapher cultures focused on the study of a single target culture. In all such triangulations, we again face the paradox of inability to use differences when these so dominate as to make it impossible to match the corresponding aspects of the reports being compared. The necessity of this common denominator provides one justification for Hockett's advocacy, in discussion, of including material and behavioral and cultural details even in ethnographies focused on the determination of the philosophy of the cultures.

Another version of the multi-ethnographer, multiple-target design is that in which two cultures study each other, as diagramed in Figure 1(b). Usually the focus is on ethnographies 2 and 3, A's report on B and B's report on A. Implicitly, however, A's description of A and B's description of B are contained as bases of reference. There is probably some scientific value to be gained from such reports, even at the level of mutual stereotype sets or of reputational consensus from neighboring peoples (LeVine 1966). Once the evaluative component (each tribe viewing itself as best) is removed, such mutual stereotype sets show remarkable agreement in confirming the direction of group differences.

PATTERN MATCHING IN THE FIT OF THEORY TO DATA

The evolutionary, natural-selection theme may seem to have a bias toward atomistic as opposed to holistic epistemologies. This need not be the case, or if the case, needs to be corrected. The sections just above on triangulation had something of a gestalt emphasis, and this is still more the case in the sections that follow.

Both psychology and philosophy are emerging from an epoch in which the *quest for punctiform certainty* seemed the optimal approach to knowledge. To both Pavlov and Watson, single retinal cell activations and single muscle activations seemed more certainly reidentifiable and specifiable than perceptions of objects or adaptive acts. The effort in epistemology to remove equivocality by founding knowledge on particulate sense data and the spirit of logical atomism point to the same search for certainty in particulars. These are efforts of the past, now increasingly recognized to be untenable, yet the quest for punctiform certainty is still a pervasive part of our intellectual background. A preview of the line argument as it relates to the nostalgia for certainty through incorrigible particulars may be provided by the following analogy. Imagine the task of identifying "the same" dot of ink in two newspaper prints of the same photograph. The task is impossible if the photographs are examined by exposing only one dot at a time. It becomes more possible the larger the area of each print exposed. Insofar as any certainty in the identification of a single particle is achieved, it is because a prior identification of the whole has been achieved. Rather than the identification of the whole being achieved through the firm establishment of particles, the reverse is the case, the complex being more certainly known than the elements, neither, of course, being known incorrigibly.

Evolutionary Perspective on Degrees of Distality

It is convenient for the present exposition to set the problems of knowing in terms of a distinction which Egon Brunswik (1934, 1952, 1956) provided for concepts of stimulus and response in psychology. Figure 2 attempts to present his distinction between proximal stimulus, *s*, and distal stimulus, *S*. For example, this could refer to a distinction between particulate skin-surface, single retinal cell, proximal stimulus events, and objects or events as distal stimuli. A proximal response, *r*, would analogously be a muscle twitch, a distal response, *R*, would be an act, an achievement, a difference effected in the environment.

Brunswik recognized the scientific legitimacy of the search for proximal *s-r* laws, relationships between single retinal cell activation and specific muscle contraction, for example. However, he summarized psychology's expe-

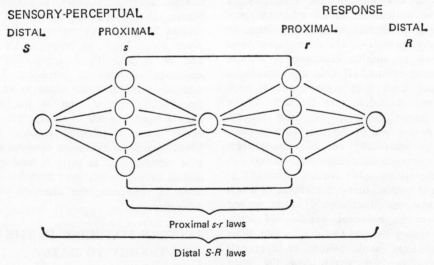

SENSORY-PERCEPTUAL   RESPONSE

DISTAL   PROXIMAL   PROXIMAL   DISTAL

S   *s*   *r*   *R*

Proximal *s-r* laws

Distal *S-R* laws

Figure 2. Brunswik's "Lens Model"*

* The box represents a conceptual organism, with a sensory-perceptual surface (to the left) and a response surface (to the right). The radial lines indicate the multifarious proximal channels alternately (vicariously) mediating the distal achievement. On the stimulus side, these could be illustrated by the multiple inter-substitutable proximal cues for distance or for object color, and so forth. On the response side these could be illustrated by the multiple specific muscle contractions by which the rat might depress a lever, or locomote a runway, and so forth.

rience with the higher vertebrates by the general induction that such laws did not exist; that when computed, these correlations (between presence-absence of stimulus and presence-absence of muscle contraction over a population of occasions) were of zero magnitude. He did not deny the possibility of discovering such laws in any programmatic or logical sense, and in fact emphasized that the behavioral regularities of the lower animals, such as Uexküll's (1934) sea urchins, were of this proximal sort (Brunswik 1956:62). For such coelenterates, the activation of a given tactile receptor cell dependably activates a specific muscle. But for man, the significant *s-r* correlations are to be found at the distal, object-act level, rather than at the proximal level. These significant and impressive (if never perfect) correlations are a major fact that psychological theory must accept. A major self-deception of traditional behaviorisms has been the use of these distal correlations in specious support of theories adequate only to explain proximal ones. A major achievement of Brunswik's perspective is that of maintaining a positivistic, behavioristic orientation without denying the flexible, purposive adaptedness which is characteristic of the perceptual and motor systems of the higher organisms. Smedslund (1953) and Campbell (1954), in defense of a Brunswikian point of view on the problem of "what is learned" and in summary of the research in learning showing the distal character of most learned habits, have emphasized that such distal foci are operationally distinguishable from the proximal.

The achievement of such a point of view meant overcoming special temptations for a person of Brunswik's positivist background. The positivist's militant attack upon vitalism and upon the metaphysical baggage of pseudo-problems made them prone to overlook or deny these less tangible facts of perception and behavior. The particular form that their quest for certainty took was in seeking a certainty of communication, that is, in seeking unequivocally specifiable terms. Proximal stimuli and proximal responses seem much more appealing in this sense than do distal ones. It was Brunswik's achievement to make objective the facts that necessitated the renunciation of this approach to certainty, facts to which many positivists within psychology are still blind. It was his achievement to

have retained both his vigorous positivism, and to have harnessed these "organismic" and "vitalistic" facts as positivistically demonstrated laws. His empirical law of distal achievements through vicarious mediation I accept as established, setting the problem for this essay.

In the primitive coelenterate, the nervous system connects each specific tactile sense organ with a specific muscle. The *s-r* reflexes are adaptive, in that the muscle response changes the relationship between the organism and environment (in some instances leading to tentacle withdrawing, in other instances, contraction and grasping, depending on location, and so forth). While these are distal effects, there is but a single means of mediating them—there are no alternative channels for vicarious mediation. Thus at the proximal level, the correlation holds. Higher forms, even locomotor forms, may possibly preserve this proximal consistency. Loeb (1918) described an ingenious mechanical bug with presumed animal counterparts that flexibly tracked a light. The left eye or photocell activated the right hind leg or wheel, and the right eye, the left hind leg. Thus when both eyes were equally stimulated, locomotion was straight ahead toward the light. If the initial orientation was to one side, the eye receiving the greater amount of light activated the opposite side the more, leading the bug to turn in the direction of the light, up to that point where the eyes were equally stimulated.

But the major stable relationships in the world available for organismic exploitation are consistencies adhering to other objects than the organism itself—consistencies adhering to food objects, shelters, predators, locomotor obstacles, throughways, and so forth. Due to the fluctuating illumination and the variable distance of such objects, proximal stimuli are not optimal indicators of these, nor are proximal responses optimal effectors. Somewhere in the evolutionary hierarchy the available distal relationships come to be exploited, and with this comes a renunciation of rigid one-to-one reflexes at the proximal level. Presumably this has been achieved by the evolutionary level at which image-forming eyes appear. The organism at that point tries out the strategy of hypothesizing stable external objects mediately known, or of behaving in a manner consistent with such hypothesizing.

This is awkwardly conveyed on two counts. On the one hand, the statement is atrociously anthropomorphic. On the other, we so unquestioningly assume the existence of specific external objects—objects with a stability independent of our movements—that we find it hard to accept these as merely the hypotheses of a fallible cognitive apparatus, at best mediately known. We find it hard to comprehend an organism that does not live and locomote in a world of objects. Yet this feature of animal life is clearly dependent upon distance receptors and, in any high degree, upon perceptual constancy mechanisms.

Stimulus-response consistencies, whether instinctive or habitual, are dependent for their establishment and maintenance upon consistencies in the environment, inasmuch as selective survival or selective reinforcement are essential. Initially, only environmental contingencies at the skin of the organism are involved. At higher stages, environmental contingencies at some remoteness from the skin can be diagnosed, and the diagnostic inference becomes to some degree independent of the position of the observing organism. Since it is ecologically true that these less self-centered, more "objective" contingencies are stronger statistically (provide better predictions), there is a selection-pressure in evolution leading to their exploitation, and to the increasingly complex perceptual locomotor apparatus that makes this possible.

Students of science and epistemology have long found it appropriate to tease out the hidden premises underlying the reasoning of scientists and laymen. These premises are often for convenience stated in a language of conscious contents: the scientist presumes order (or partial order) in nature, he presumes that there are fewer causal laws than there are events, and so forth. These premises are unconscious until thus explicated. It is in a similar vein that I use a conscious experience terminology of "hypothesizing" in discussing the implicit presumptions about the nature of the world built into animals at various evolutionary stages (Lorenz 1941, Campbell 1959). These presumptions, these synthetic hypotheses (ontogenetically *a priori* or *a posteriori*), increase with the adaptive radius, the range of correspondences of the organism (Spencer 1896), and represent the increased "knowledge" of the laws of the world, of the

"causal texture of the environment" (Tolman and Brunswik 1935). In these terms, the proximal-level organism in his inherited reflexes modestly assumes some degree of order, some deviation from pure randomness in his environment. At some later level, his ambitious presumptiveness goes so far as to presume the existence of external objects. At this stage, the organism's cognitive apparatus becomes a diagnoser of external entities and processes. At this stage, the puzzling fact of distality and of purposive behavior emerges in full degree. From the standpoint of an amoeba, this is a wondrous, if very presumptive, procedure.

Continuing the evolutionary paradigm, we can note that the higher the level of development the higher the degree of distality achieved, the greater the magnitude of the Brunswik constancy ratio, and the greater the degree to which external events and objects are known in a manner independent of the point of view of the observer. Thus Brunswik (1928, 1956) found the degree of constancy achieved to be higher in older children than younger ones, reaching a maximum around fourteen or fifteen years of age. Thus Piaget (for example, Piaget 1957, Flavell 1963) finds his youngest children failing to reify external objects as having continuing existence and motion when out of sight. With increasing age comes not only increasing hypostatization of external objects, but also of increasing presumption of the conservation of weight and volume, as the child more and more imputes to the world stability under transformations of his point of observation. Thus, within the historical span of human experience, the distality of man's knowledge has been increased by learning and reason over that provided by visual perception. Brunswik both emphasized the marvelous constancy mechanisms of the visual and auditory systems, and at the same time spoke of the "stupidity" of the perceptual apparatus relative to thinking in its rigidity and susceptibility to illusion under ecologically atypical conditions (for example, Brunswik 1934, 1956:88–92). Piaget provides similar evidence. Man's introduction of measuring rods constructed of relatively inelastic quasi solids has freed his knowledge of objects from the ubiquitous compromise with retinal size found in unaided vision (Brunswik 1956:88 and *ad passim*).

The course of science has this over-all trend. The intricacies of measuring instruments and laboratory equipment show a development analogous to that of the vertebrate eye. The addition of specific compensating devices and control features lead meter readings to reflect more and more purely the attributes of the object of study, uncontaminated by the irrelevant specifics, vagaries, and rigidities of the measuring instrument. The concept of a compensated or of an automatically self-calibrating instrument, and the need for continually recalibrating a more primitive one, convey the general spirit of this development. (See Wilson 1952, for specific illustrations.)

Similarly, physical theory has provided in each generation a model of the universe more independent of man's particular position of observation. In the shift from Ptolemy to Kepler this is clear; some see the contributions of relativity and quantum theory and the complementarity principle as reversals in this direction. This is not the position taken here, however. What these developments have done is to convince man that his knowledge of the world is not as completely distal or objective as he had thought, that it is still contaminated by a certain degree of astigmatism (Bachem 1951), and that there are limitations upon the degree of objective knowledge that he can obtain. But note that in many specifics, if not all, the errors of the Newtonian system become correctible when an Einsteinian relativity is adopted, achieving a greater degree of distality, independence of point of observation, and predictive efficacy than that previously held. Oppenheimer (1956) has presented a parallel development in early science. He contrasts Babylonian astronomy with the later Mediterranean versions of Ptolemy and Copernicus. Babylonian astronomy was able to predict the movement of the heavenly bodies with great accuracy, including such subtleties as the eclipses of the moon, without any model of celestial mechanics. This achievement was the product of centuries of bookkeeping, and was based upon vast libraries of detail from which identical sequences and spatial contingencies could be identified as a base for prediction. The great advantage of the model-building astronomies was not one of accuracy (at least initially) but rather one of library space. The same repertoire of predictions could be encompassed with one one-thousandth of the written records. Similarly, while it is conceivable that instinct or learning provide an animal with a fixed response tendency for each possible proximal pattern of stimulation, the central nervous system storage requirements involved for an animal like ourselves with proximal stimulus receptors numbering in the millions, are such as to argue the economy of the more presumptive strategy of creating an approximate model of the environment as a base of prediction. The phenomenal reality of separate external objects for myself, and reputedly for other men, helps convince me that my near relatives probably use this presumptive strategy.

Pattern-matching and Distal Knowing

In the laboratory research on thing constancy, the distal thinghood of the object being judged is never in question—rather only some attribute of it, as its size, shape, or distance. Starting from this setting one misses some of the wonder of the achievement that would be more apparent if one examined an instance in which even the positing of a single thing was equivocal. For note, there is always the alternative of inferring several independent causal sources for the several proximal data, rather than inferring a single common source (Heider 1959).

"Triangulation" is an attractive model which we have already used. From several widely separated proximal points, there is a triangulation upon the distal object, "fixing" it and its distance in a way quite impossible from a single proximal point. Binocular vision can be seen quite literally as such a triangulation.

As Brunswik (1956) emphasized, each proximal stimulation is equivocal when interpreted as evidence of a distal event. For each, there is a subinfinity of possible distal events to which it could be witness. How does the cognitive apparatus decide on the distal focus, decide in what distal bundles to tie the proximal particulars? How do the two proximal sources "know" when they are fixing on one single object rather than two separate ones? Or rather, under what conditions do they "presume" one rather than two? The tentative and partial answer is that this is achieved through a pattern matching. The tentative theme of this paper is that such a pattern matching is involved in all instances of distal knowing, including the achievements of scientific theory. In making this suggestion I join many others. For example, it is an important theme in Craik's (1943) *The Nature of Explanation.* Konrad Lorenz has made a similar point in his paper on "Gestalt Perception as Fundamental to Scientific Knowledge" (1959), a paper which, like the present one, emphasizes the epistemological significance of the evolution of the perceptual constancies. Bertrand Russell has been particularly explicit.

In Russell's (1948) *Human Knowledge: Its Scope and Limits* he starts out as though writing a summary of epistemological problems for laymen. And in the section on language, he seems little changed from his earlier logical atomism. But in the subsequent parts of the book he is again creatively thinking about the problems that have always troubled him. Particularly in his final section on "The Postulates of Scientific Inference" he offers a synthetic theory of inductive knowledge quite in keeping in spirit with that essayed here. While the list of implicit hypotheses about the nature of the world which he offers differs in particulars from one that I might develop, the general effort is similar.

In his "structural postulate" Russell states the principle with which the present discussion deals: "When a number of structurally similar complex events are ranged about a center in regions not widely separated, it is usually the case that all belong to causal lines having their origin in an event of the same structure at the center" (1948:492). His illustrations include multiple copies of photographs, the similar percepts of people viewing a given scene or hearing a given sound, the multiple copies of a given book, the identification of which shadow goes with which man, the assumption of a common culprit in the "brides-in-the-bath" murders, and so forth (Russell 1948:460–475).

As a first example, let us examine again binocular vision via the stereoscope. The stereoscope is ecologically a very unrepresentative sample of possible environments, and is one in which the distal-perceptual apparatus goes awry, in that two separate distal events (the separate pictures each eye views) are misinterpreted as one. In the process, the cues by which oneness is inferred are made more evident.

There are three typical outcomes, if heterogeneous pairs of pictures be allowed: binocular fusion into a single image, double-image superimposition, and a domination of one eye's content to the exclusion of the other. If one starts out with similar simple line drawings that will fuse, this resolution can be destroyed by making one of the drawings more and more different from the other. If there is little detail in the drawings, the failure of fusion may lead to a superimposition of the two contents. For example, if each side has only two vertical lines, under the fused condition only two are seen. If the separation of the two is greatly increased beyond the capacity of binocular resolution, then three or four lines may be seen. If, on the other hand, each eye's view is rich in detail (as when two photographs are used), lack of common contour in the two pictures results in a total suppression of one or the other. It seems clear that the fusion of the two proximal sources into a distal inference is made possible through a process of pattern matching, and does not occur in the absence of a high degree of pattern similarity. Once this high degree of similarity is present to guide fusion, then minor disparities of the correct kind can produce a distal increment through the inference of the third dimension. But without an overwhelming similarity of pattern, such discrepancies cannot be utilized, as the inference of a single common source does not take place.

The above contrasts the matching of congruent patterns with the condition under which patterns are incompatible. We can draw a similar conclusion by comparing the presence of congruent patterns with the absence of any pattern. Consider the use of the stereoscope in connection with a separate reduction screen for each eye, so that a punctiform view of each image is obtained. Under these conditions, no convergence takes place, even though each eye be viewing positions that would be fused if the total patterns were to be seen. Similarly, triangulation upon one of several distal light sources of heterogeneous distance and location would be impossible in a system consisting of two mechanical eyes each made up of a single photocell. Under such conditions, triangulation would be unusable just because of the unresolvable ambiguity as to whether both eyes were looking at the same source. While pattern identity can be misleading, it seems in this setting to be a minimum essential. The multiple-celledness of the retina becomes an essential requirement. No doubt it is true that the greater the degree of pattern similarity the more certain the fusion and the more inappropriate angles of optical convergence that it will overcome. From the point of view of inductive theory, the more elaborate the pattern, the more statistically unlikely a repetition of it through independent chance events becomes, and hence the more implausible the rival hypothesis of twoness becomes, in competition with the hypothesis of oneness.

Monocular processes of distal inference contain upon examination the same dependence upon pattern, and through the utilization of memory, the assumption that repetitions of pattern in time come from a common source. In Wertheimer's phi phenomenon of perceived movement, where two separate events are presented (under certain conditions of spatial and temporal proximity and sequence), the visual system shows bias toward a single-object interpretation so great that the hypothesis of one object in motion becomes more plausible than that of two discrete events. No doubt this effect is the stronger, and occurs over the wider spatial and temporal intervals, the more elaborate the shared pattern of the two stimuli. The recognition of visual events as similar to past ones, and hence the use of memory at all, is dependent upon pattern similarity, and is unavailable to homogeneous fragments. Similarly for patterns extended in time. (Russell calls these "event structures" as distinct from the spatial patterns or "material structures" [1948:464].) Auditory recognition and memory are obviously dependent upon this. In animal brains at least, it seems probable that memory access or memory search is only possible on the basis of some pattern-matching resonance process (Pringle 1951). In mechanical brains, all outcome-controlled processes including memory search are based upon a matching process, in the older machines called "comparing relays." The detail of the pattern involved depends upon the magnitude of the alternative set within which equivocality could take place.

Pattern Matching in Astronomy

Astronomy, our oldest successful science, deals with the most remote and unknowable of objects. It is, therefore, an appropriate place from which to select samples of the utilizations of pattern matching in science.

Consider first the remarkable assurance with which man assumes that he can identify "the same" star upon successive nights, even with the unaided eye. This is the more remarkable (and the more presumptive) because the stars for such instrumentation are so homogeneous a set of objects as to be mutually indistinguishable. It is further remarkable because a given star is continually changing its location, and because the average star is out of range of observation some three-fourths of the time (that is, when below the horizon, when in ascendance during the daytime, and when eclipsed by clouds). It is the rigid pattern of the so-called "fixed" stars that make this possible, or which makes this the preferred interpretation. If indeed the stars were transient events, destroyed each dawn and constituted afresh each evening, then the recurrence across the observed ages of "the same" pattern would be a set of coincidences beyond our credulity. If there were indeed permanent stars, but these moved on a time and space scale corresponding to an enlarged Brownian movement, so that each evening a novel pattern were apparent, then astronomy would not have been the first science to emerge, nor would the confident reidentification of "the same" star on successive nights have taken place. If all the visible "stars" had been planets of our sun (a system that we now understand as simpler and more orderly than that of the fixed stars), the manifest pattern would have been so much less obvious and compelling as to have postponed the hypothesis of reidentifiable sameness for many centuries. It was the grid of the "fixed" stars that facilitated the observation of the patterned meanderings of the "wandering" stars, and enabled their reification as stable particulate substantial entities.

Astronomy's entities at this stage were diagnosed almost entirely (except for the sun and the moon) by external pattern. Each star was unidentifiable in isolation. The frame of the other stars, each in itself unidentifiable, provided the identification through its fixed pattern. In the ecology of our normal vertebrate development, most external entities are diagnosed by recurrence of internal pattern. Today with telescopes, we can so identify nearby planets, and potentially with refined spectroscopes extended into the radio frequencies, we may find internal patterns marked enough to justify the hypothesis of stable thing for some of the fixed stars without the crutch of external pattern. The external pattern of the fixed stars is so strong and redundant that minor discrepancies can provide 3-D gains from successive comparisons, and through such triangulations the distances of stars and the movements of the sun itself have been inferred.

The first achievement of radar reflection from Venus (Price *et al.*, 1959) provides another illustration. It provides a good example because the knowledge process utilized an extremely noisy and fallible channel, and yet was so clear-cut in outcome as to make possible a correction of the prior computations of the distance of the target. Note in ordinary radar (and in television) an interchangeable transition between temporal pattern and spatial pattern, the latter being made possible by the lag in the decay of the phosphorescence on the picture tube. For ordinary uses of radar, the output beam need not be temporally patterned, but can be a constant emission in amplitude and frequency. Its figure-ground patterning comes through the contrasting reflection from object and non-object as the antenna sweeps and resweeps the area. (A single punctiform and unmoving antenna's reception would be uninterpretable, due to the numerous extraneous sources of radio waves.) For the first radar reflection from Venus, this spatial patterning was not used, as not enough contrast to be visible would have resulted, the small angular size of the target and the small energy reflection being parts of the problem. Instead, a temporal pattern was imposed upon the emitting wave. The reception of a radio telescope antenna focused in the direction of Venus was then searched for a matching pattern. The reflected signal was so weak relative to the radio frequency noise of the background that such pattern matching could only be ascertained by a cross-correlation of broadcast and reception which used two-millisecond pulses, present or absent on a fixed quasi random pattern for four and one-half

minutes of transmission. When the cross-correlation was computed with a lag appropriate to the speed of light for the astronomically computed distance, the correlation was not above chance levels. A trial-and-error survey of shorter and longer lags located the optimal lag at a point some 5.0 milliseconds less than expected. At this lag a highly significant cross-correlation repeatedly appeared, indicating a small but significant error in the previous computation of distance. This achievement is a most impressive evidence of the power of pattern matching in identifying recurrences of "the same" thing even when the initial instructions as to "where to look" were in error.

Matching Theory to Data Without Definitional Operationism

Science is the most distal form of knowing. Scientific theories are distal achievements. The processes and entities posited by science (for example, radio stars, neutrinos, atoms, molecules, genes, cells, and so forth) are all very distal objects very mediately known via processes involving highly presumptive pattern matchings at many stages. Such is a summary of the preceding pages. The present section extends this by identifying the over-all relationship between a formal scientific theory and the relevant accumulations of empirical data as one of pattern matching. The resulting interpretation is felt to be compatible with, and to summarize something common among, those several modern philosophies of science that have attempted to retain the "posit" and "put-up-or-shut-up" hardheadedness of pragmatism and logical positivism, without making the error of exhaustive-definitional-operationism (Campbell 1960a). We will but sample from these philosophies, and will not argue here their equivalence upon any grounds other than this one.

It has long been a common property among logical positivisms to describe scientific theory as an internally consistent formal logic (analytically valid) which becomes empirical (gains synthetic truth) when various terms are interpreted in a data language. A variant of this general model is accepted here. The formal theory becomes one "pattern," and against this pattern the various bodies of data are matched, in some over-all or total way.

These empirical observations provide the other pattern, but somewhat asymmetrically. The data are not required to have an analytical coherence among themselves, and indeed cannot really be assembled as a total except upon the skeleton of theory. In addition, the imperfection or error of the process is ascribed to the data pattern, for any theory-data set regarded currently as "true," and except for quantum theory. Theories "known" to be in need of revision, or accepted only as convenient oversimplifications, are conceptually allowed to share the residual matching error. It is as though in the radar reflection from Venus we regarded the known or intended output as the "true" pattern or theory, and the noisy reception as the data. (The asymmetrical conceptual allocation of error between experimental and dependent variables is, however, another problem, receiving explicit treatment in modern statistics.)

This variant of the "interpreted logic" version of logical positivism is in disagreement primarily with those applied variants that have taken an extreme position on "operational definitions." For the "exhaustive-definitional-operationist" if we take his "operational definitions" as defining terms in his formal theory, no error is allowed in the interpretation of theory by data. For him, the admitted imperfection of all scientific theory is located in the strength of the theoretical laws stated, that is, within the kind of relationships which the theory posits. In such a case, it seems doubtful if a formal, analytically consistent theory is possible.

While the categorization may seem to fit, Bergmann (1957) should not be identified as an "exhaustive-definitional-operationist" in any simple manner, for note his criticisms of a similarly extreme operationism (1954) and his condoning of the reification of concepts in physics (1943). Nor should Bridgman (1927), in spite of his temptingly clear expression of this point of view in this quote: "If we have more than one set of operations we have more than one concept, and strictly there should be a separate name to correspond to each different set of operations" (p. 10). The exposition of this discussion will not be hindered by regarding the "exhaustive-definitional-operationist" as a straw man or ideal type useful in clarifying the issues but not to be identified with the position of any actual philosopher of science. While some have in-

directly advocated it when arguing against the errors of other positions, the obvious weaknesses of the position as here presented have probably kept any from direct advocacy.

In contrast to definitional operationism, in the position here advocated the error in matching theory to data is allocated to the imperfect representation of the theoretical concepts by the data series. Where the measurements used by a science have a negligible proportion of error, as in macrophysics and astronomy, the difference in the points of view may be unnoticeable. In any case, focusing the difference upon a decision in the allocation of error makes it obvious that there is no analytically correct choice between the two points of view. As a description of how science has operated, I prefer the present variant, at least as the model of those segments of the physical and biological sciences that have achieved useful formal theory.

Among the logical empiricists, Feigl's critical-realistic version (for example, 1950) is compatible with that here advocated. Hempel (1952:29–50) states the "interpreted logic" position clearly, and has attempted to preserve the values of operationism without accepting a construct-defining version of it. He calls for operational interpretations of scientific terms, allowing these to be partial interpretations. His version of the operationist requirement becomes the requirement that theory be testable, that is, interpretable so that at many points its matching with data be ascertainable. Were he to have explicitly emphasized the inherent mediateness and imperfection of all measurement processes, or to have explicitly recognized the interpretations of theory-terms as fallible, or to have explicitly located the errorfulness on the data side of the matching, his position would be indistinguishable from the one here advocated. Margenau (1950), while not a member of the logical positivist camp, has a point of view regarding the relationship between theory and data that is equivalent on these points. So also are judged to be the positions of Popper (1935, 1959), Quine (1953), Hanson (1958), and Kuhn (1962), some aspects of which will be discussed in more detail below.

Note particularly that there are *two* patterns to be compared—that of theory and that of data, even though in an iterative fashion each has developed in contact with the other. This is in disagreement with those views of science in which theory is viewed simply as a summary of data, that is, as the simple product of inductive generalization. Popper (1959) has effectively discredited such a point of view. Hanson (1958) has emphasized this duality through his stress upon the perceptual aspects of relating theory to data, that is, how differences in theory lead scientists to perceive the world differently, how corrections of outmoded theories must await the availability of an alternative theoretical structure. While there is a subjectivist flavor to much of Hanson's protest, descriptively his portrait of science is a pattern-matching one. His discussion of Kepler's struggles to match theory and data are of particular value, as also are his detailed citations on the shifts in status of specific scientific constructs from empirical law to analytic tautology. The replacement of an old and unsatisfactory theory by a new one has in many instances the characteristic of a trial-and-error process in which total theoretical systems are tried out, being accepted or rejected as a whole. In practice, no theory that has been judged useful in the past of a science is ever rejected simply upon the basis of its inadequacy of fit to data. Instead, it is only rejected when there is an alternative that fits better to replace it. And the fit of the new theory is not perfect, only better. Kuhn (1962) presents similar episodes in the history of science.

Of course, even for theory in physics, the above description has exaggerated the analytic (logical, mathematical) internal consistency of the theory. As Quine (1953) has pointed out, analytic systems contain hidden empirical assumptions. Where the logical or mathematical form of the theory is not complete, considerable revision of specific terms of a theory is possible without necessitating an over-all accept-reject decision. What is important is the recognition of the two-part, two-patterned nature of the process, and the acceptance or rejection of the theory or model upon the basis of some over-all criterion of fit. This is particularly clear in total-theory shifts in science (Kuhn 1962). The model of piecemeal theory revision in its extreme form makes the "theory" no theory at all, but simply a restatement of the data in its full complexity. Theory must instead be a separable pattern from data, with the fit to

data problematic, otherwise testability, predictive power, and parsimony all are lost.

Fringe Imperfection

It is fundamental to the general epistemology here argued that all knowledge is indirect, that all proximal stimulation is equivocal or fallible as a basis for inferring distal objects. This leads to the rejection of those epistemologies based upon any incorrigible sense data or other phenomenal givens, and a parallel rejection of a purely "proximal" science in which scientific constructs be defined in terms of (i.e., exhaustively known through) specific meter readings. Instead, all specific meters are regarded as fallible, corrigible instruments. On theoretical grounds alone, any specific meter can be seen to involve many physical laws other than the construct-relevant one. Keeping these other laws inactive through specific compensations (as in the control of inertial forces in a galvanometer) or through constant conditions, is never achieved to perfection. Wilson (1952) in instance after instance provides specific illustrations of such limitations. Yet this obvious fact is apt to be negated implicitly in a *definitional* operationism. This negation is induced by the need to make explicit the essential relationship of scientific theory to experimental data, overdetermined by a psychic need for certainty. The pattern-matching model for the fit of theory to data provides an explanation of that essential relationship which nonetheless avoids the assumption of certainty for any of the specific data. The imperfection of fit is conceptualized so that any specific meter reading can be regarded as in error, as judged by the pattern matching that minimizes error in general.

Let us consider a case in which we graph together a set of empirical points and a theoretically derived curve and achieve a good correspondence. Some of the points lie above the line, others below, but in general they fit well, and some lie "exactly" on the line. If there is no systematic deviation, we interpret the point-by-point deviations where they occur as error, and would expect such error to occur on some of the "perfectly fitting" points were the experiment to be replicated. While an over-all fit has been required, no single observation point has been taken as an infallible operational *definition* of a theoretical value—all rather are partial and fallible operational representations. Were each taken as "operational definitions," the "theory" would have to be multiple-parametered enough to fit each point exactly—and if selected upon that basis one would need a new "theory" for each new set of data.

In the pattern matching of theory to data we reduce the fringe of error as much as possible, we center theory in the data points so that the fringe occurs without systematic deviation from theory, and we distribute the fringe of error over all of the observational points, potentially. We may end up saying that one observation was "right on," and that another was probably in error. *A priori,* however, any of the points could be wrong. It is through such a process that physicists can throw away "wild observations," an impossibility for a rigid operationist (Kruskal 1960, Campbell 1964). It is through such a process that physics has been able to refine its measuring instruments, a paradoxical event from the standpoint of exhaustive-definitional-operationism. Physics has at any period assumed that the great bulk of its "knowledge" was correct. From this floating platform of overall pattern, it has then challenged and reexamined a particular measurement process. As Neurath said, "We are like sailors who must rebuild their ship on the open sea" (1932). The "anchoring" of theory to data has not at all been achieved through a perfect correspondence at any particular point, but rather through a pattern matching of the two in some over-all way. The matching of the noisy radar reception from Venus with the ideal transmission pattern shows how such a pattern-matching process as cross-correlation can powerfully recognize pattern while still distributing the large fringe of error over every data point. Actual statistics for estimating degree of pattern matching are, of course, not generally available, and the estimate of the human eye from graphed results is still the commonest criterion. The correlation coefficient sets a good example, however, by its equitable allocation of error.

Although Quine doubts the value of the traditional analytic-synthetic distinction which it has been convenient to employ here, he states a perspective upon the relation of theory to data quite compatible with that presented here on a number of points, but in particular, in the handling of fringe imperfection:

Taken collectively, science has its double dependence upon language and experience; but this duality is not significantly traceable into statements of science taken one by one. The idea of defining a symbol in use was an advance over the impossible term-by-term empiricism of Locke and Hume. The statement, rather than the term, came with Frege to be recognized as the unit accountable to an empiricist critique. But what I am now urging is that even in taking the statement as a unit we have drawn our grid too finely. The unit of empirical significance is the whole of science. The totality of our so-called knowledge or beliefs, from the most casual matters of geography and history to the profoundest laws of atomic physics or even of pure mathematics and logic, is a man-made fabric which impinges on experience only along the edges. . . . A conflict with experience at the periphery occasions readjustments in the interior of the field. . . . But the total field is so undetermined by its boundary conditions, experience, that there is much latitude of choice as to what statements to re-evaluate in the light of any single contrary experience. . . . A recalcitrant experience can . . . be accommodated by any of various alternative re-evaluations in various alternative quarters of the total system . . . but . . . our natural tendency [is] to disturb the total system as little as possible. . . . Physical objects are conceptually imported into the situation as convenient intermediaries—not by definition in terms of experience, but simply as irreducible posits. . . . Science is a continuation of common sense, and it continues the common-sense expedient of swelling ontology to simplify theory. (Quine 1953:42–45)

Confirmation and Falsification of Theory

In the positivists' early effort to root out pseudo problems and metaphysics, they produced a testability criterion of meaning, so stated that confirmability of a proposition through the agreement of theory and data become its typical form. But since theories posit general laws whose verification can be only spottily sampled, and also because of the ambiguity introduced through error in data collection processes, this criterion has been challenged, particularly by Popper (1935, 1959). A strict and rigid form of it shares many of the problems of a definitional operationism, and we may regard it as an unsatisfactory statement of how experimental outcomes strengthen our belief in theory.

Popper has advocated instead a falsifiability criterion, in which a theory becomes scientifically meaningful if it is capable of being falsified by empirical data, and in which a theory becomes the better established the more experimental opportunities for falsification that it has survived and the more exacting these probes. Our established scientific theories at any time are thus those that have been repeatedly exposed to falsification, and have so far escaped being falsified. Because of its evolutionary and selective retention analogies, this criterion has appealed greatly to the present writer. As Popper explicitly recognizes (for example, 1959:80–81), falsifiability cannot be held too strictly, as every observation refutes theory if carried out to enough decimal points. Instead, it is a selective retention of theories in competition with other theories, with the magnitude of the tolerable fringe of imperfection dependent upon the sharpness of that competition.

Note that in the pattern-matching model, the theoretical pattern is complete and continuous (with the exception of quantum theory), but the data series may be spotty and incomplete; Kepler actually had data on only a few segments of the path of Mars. If the data confirm the pattern insofar as tested, the theoretical pattern as a whole is made more tenable, including the non-tested segments of the pattern. The fact that theories go beyond the as-yet-observed would not require the rejection of a confirmation criterion in a pattern-matching model, as it would in a more traditionally inductive empiricism. Further, the selective-survival of theories is now perceived to be a selection taking place *in competition with other extant theories.* As Popper (1959), Hanson (1958), and Kuhn (1962) all make clear, it is the absence of plausible rival hypotheses that establishes one theory as "correct." In cases where there are rival theories, it is the relative over-all goodness of fit that leads one to be preferred to another, not the absolute degree of fit of the better.

BIBLIOGRAPHY

ASCH, S. E.
1952 *Social psychology.* New York, Prentice-Hall.

ASHBY, W. R.
1952 *Design for a brain.* New York, Wiley.

AYER, A. J.
1956 *The problem of knowledge.* New York, St. Martin's Press.

BACHEM, A.
1951 Brain astigmatism: a discussion of space and time. *American Scientist* 40:497–498.

BAIN, A.
1855 *The senses and the intellect.* New York, Appleton.

BALDWIN, J. M.
1902 *Development and evolution.* New York, Macmillan.
1906 *Thought and things, or genetic logic.* New York, Macmillan.

BARBER, B.
1952 *Science and the social order.* Glencoe, Ill., Free Press.

BEARDSLEY, D. C., and M. WERTHEIMER (EDS.)
1958 *Readings in perception.* New York, Van Nostrand.

BERGMANN, G.
1943 Outline of an empiricist philosophy of physics. *American Journal of Physics* 11: 248–258, 335–342.
1954 Sense and nonsense in operationism. *Scientific Monthly Monographs* 79:210–214.

1957 *Philosophy of science.* Madison, University of Wisconsin Press.

BERGMANN, G., and K. SPENCE
1944 Psychophysical measurement. *Psychological Review* 51:1–24.

BERTALANFFY, L. VON
1955 An essay on the relativity of categories. *Philosophy of Science* 22:243–263.

BRIDGMAN, P. W.
1927 *The logic of modern physics.* New York, Macmillan.

BRUNER, J. S., J. J. GOODNOW, and G. A. AUSTIN
1956 *A study of thinking.* New York, Wiley.

BRUNSWIK, E.
1928 Zur Entwicklung der albedowahrnehmung. *Z. Psychology* 109:40–115.
1934 *Wahrnehmung und Gegenstandswelt.* Wien, Deuticke.
1952 *The conceptual framework of psychology.* International Encyclopedia of United Sciences. Vol. 1, No. 10, Chicago, University of Chicago Press.
1956 *Perception and the representative design of psychological experiments.* Berkeley, University of California Press.

CAMPBELL, D. T.
1954 Operational delineation of "what is learned" via the transposition experiment. *Psychological Review* 61:167–174.
1956 Adaptive behavior from random response. *Behavioral Science* 1:105–110.

1956 Perception as substitute trial and error. *Psychological Review* 63:331–342.

1957 Factors relevant to the validity of experiments in social settings. *Psychological Bulletin* 54:297–312.

1958 Common fate, similarity, and other indices of the status of aggregates of persons as social entities. *Behavioral Science* 3:14–25.

1959 Methodological suggestions from a comparative psychology of knowledge processes. *Inquiry* 2:152–182.

1960 Blind variation and selective retention in creative thought as in other knowledge processes. *Psychological Review* 67:380–400.

1960 Recommendations for APA test standards regarding construct, trait, or discriminant validity. *American Psychologist* 15:546–553.

1961 Conformity in psychology's theories of acquired behavioral dispositions. In I. A. Berg and B. M. Bass, eds., *Conformity and deviation*. New York, Harper.

1963 Social attitudes and other acquired behavioral dispositions. In *Psychology: a study of a science*. Vol. 6. *Investigations of man as socius: Their place in psychology and the social sciences*, S. Koch, ed., New York, McGraw-Hill.

1964 Distinguishing differences of perception from failures of communication in cross-cultural studies. In F. S. C. Northrop and H. H. Livingston, eds., *Cross-cultural understanding: epistemology in anthropology*. New York, Harper and Row.

1965 Variation and selective retention in sociocultural evolution. In H. R. Barringer, G. I. Blanksten, and R. W. Mack, eds., *Social change in developing areas: A reinterpretation of evolutionary theory*. Cambridge, Mass., Schenkman.

1966 Pattern matching as essential in distal knowing. In K. R. Hammond, ed., *The psychology of Egon Brunswik*. New York, Holt, Rinehart and Winston.

in preparation, Evolutionary epistemology. In P.A. Schilpp, ed., *The philosophy of Karl R. Popper*, in *The library of living philosophers*. LaSalle, Ill., Open Court Publishing Co.

CAMPBELL, D. T., and D. W. FISKE
1959 Convergent and discriminant validation by the multitrait-multimethod matrix. *Psychological Bulletin* 56:81–105.

CAMPBELL, D. T., and E. WALKER
1966 *Ostensive instances and entitativity in language learning*. Multilithed paper for the Seminar on Linguistics, Center for Advanced Study in the Behavioral Sciences, Stanford, Calif.

COHEN, R.
1962 The strategy of social evolution. *Anthropologica* 4:321–348.

CRAIK, K. J. W.
1943 *The nature of explanation*. Cambridge, Cambridge University Press.

CRONBACH, L. J., and P. E. MEEHL
1955 Construct validity in psychological tests. *Psychological Bulletin* 52:281–302.

FEIGL, H.
1950 Existential hypotheses: realistic versus phenomenalistic interpretations. *Philosophy of Science* 17:35–62.

FEIGL, H., and M. SCRIVEN (eds.)
1956 *The foundations of science and the concepts of psychology and psychoanalysis*. Vol. 1 of Minnesota studies in the philosophy of science. Minneapolis, University of Minnesota Press.

FEIGL, H., M. SCRIVEN, and G. MAXWELL (eds.)
1958 *Concepts, theories, and the mind-body problem*. Vol. II of Minnesota studies in the philosophy of science. Minneapolis, University of Minnesota Press.

FLAVELL, J. H.
1963 *The developmental psychology of Jean Piaget*. Princeton, N.J., Van Nostrand.

FRISCH, K. von
1950 *Bees, their vision, chemical sense, and language*. Ithaca, Cornell University Press.

GARNER, W. R.
1954 Context effects and the validity of loudness scales. *Journal of Experimental Psychology* 48:218–224.

GARNER, W. R., H. W. HAKE, and C. W. ERIKSEN
1956 Operationism and the concept of perception. *Psychological Review* 63:149–159.

GRIFFIN, D. R.
1958 *Listening in the dark*. New Haven, Yale University Press.

HANSON, N. R.
1958 *Patterns of discovery*. London, Cambridge University Press.

HEIDER, F.
1959 On perception and event structure and the psychological environment. *Psychological Issues* 3:1–123.

HEMPEL, C. G.
1952 *Fundamentals of concept formation in empirical science*. Chicago, University of Chicago Press.

HÖFFDING, H.
1900 *A history of modern philosophy*, Vol. II. Translated by B. E. Meyer. London, Macmillan.

HOVLAND, C. I.
1952 A "communication analysis" of concept learning. *Psychological Review* 59:461–472.

JENNINGS, H. S.
1906 *The behavior of the lower organisms.* New York, Columbia University Press.

KELLOGG, W. N.
1958 Echo-ranging in the porpoise. *Science* 128:982–988.

KÖHLER, W.
1925 *The mentality of apes.* New York, Harcourt, Brace.
1938 *The place of value in a world of facts.* New York, Liveright.

KROEBER, A. L.
1917 The superorganic. *American Anthropologist* 19:163–214.

KRUSKAL, W. H.
1960 Some remarks on wild observations. *Technometrics* 2:1–3.

KUHN, T.
1962 *The structure of scientific revolutions.* Chicago, University of Chicago Press.

LEÓN-PORTILLA, M.
1964 Philosophy in the cultures of ancient Mexico. In F. S. C. Northrop and Helen H. Livingston, eds., *Cross-Cultural understanding.* Harper and Row, New York.

LEVINE, R. A.
1966 Outsiders' judgments: An ethnographic approach to group differences in personality. *Southwestern Journal of Anthropology* 22: 101–116.

LOEB, J.
1918 *Forced movements, tropisms, and animal conduct.* Philadelphia, Lippincott.

LORENZ, K.
1941 Kants Lehre vom apriorischem im Lichte gegenwärtiger Biologie. *Blätter für Deutsche Philosophie* 15:94–125. Translated in L. von Bertalanffy and A. Rapoport, eds., *General systems,* Vol. III, 1962.
1943 Die angeborenen Formen möglicher Erfahrung. *Z. Tierpsychologie* 5:235–409.
1959 Gestaltwarnehmung als Quelle Wissenschaftliche Erkenntnis. *Zeitschrift für experimentelle und angewandte Psychologie* 6:118–165. Translated as "Gestalt perception as fundamental to scientific knowledge," *General systems,* Vol. VII, 1962.

LOVEJOY, A. O.
1930 *The revolt against dualism.* LaSalle, Ill., Open Court Publishing Co.

MACH, E.
1896 On the part played by accident in invention and discovery. *Monist.*

MARGENAU, H.
1950 *The nature of physical reality.* New York, McGraw-Hill.

MEAD, M.
1964 *Continuities in cultural evolution.* New Haven, Yale University Press.

MERTON, R. K.
1957 Priorities in scientific discovery: a chapter in the sociology of science. *American Sociological Review* 22:635–659.
1961 Singletons and multiples in scientific discovery: a chapter in the sociology of science. *Proceedings of American Philosophical Society* 105:470–486.

MEYER, M. F.
1921 *Psychology of the other one.* Columbia, Missouri Book Co.

MICHOTTE, A. E.
1946 *La perception de la causalité.* Louvain, Inst. sup. de Philosophe, Etudes Psychol. Vol. VI.

NAESS, A.
1936 *Erkenntnis und wissenschaftliches Verhalten.* Oslo, I Kommisjon hos J. Dybwad.
1948 *Notes on the foundation of psychology as a science.* Filosofiske Problemer Nr. 9, Oslo University Press.

NEURATH, O.
1932 Protokollsätze. *Erkenntnis* 3:204–214. Translation in A. J. Ayer, ed., *Logical positivism.* New York, Free Press, 1959.

NORTHROP, F. S. C.
1949 *The logic of the sciences and the humanities.* New York, Macmillan.

OGBURN, W. K., and D. THOMAS
1922 Are inventions inevitable? *Political Science Quarterly* 37:83–93.

OPPENHEIMER, R.
1956 Analogy in science. *American Psychologist* 11:127–135.

PEPPER, S. C.
1942 *World hypotheses.* Berkeley, University of California Press.

PIAGET, J.
1957 The child and modern physics. *Scientists of America* 196:46–51.

PLATT, J.
1956 Amplification aspects of biological response and mental activity. *American Scientist* 44:181–197.

POINCARÉ, H.
1913 *The foundations of science.* New York, Science Press.

POPPER, K.
1935 *Logik der forschung.* Vienna, Springer.
1959 *The logic of scientific discovery.* New York, Basic Books.
1963 *Conjectures and refutations.* London, Routledge and Kegan Paul; New York, Basic Books.

PRICE, R., P. E. GREEN, T. J. GOBLICK, R. H. KINGSTON, L. G. KRAFT, G. H. PETTENGILL, R. SILVER, and W. B. SMITH
1959 Radar echoes from Venus. *Science* 129: 751–753.

PRINGLE, J. W. S.
1951 On the parallel between learning and evolution. *Behaviour* 3:175–215.

PUMPHREY, R. J.
1950 Hearing. In *Symposia of the Society for Experimental Biology,* IV. *Physiological mechanisms in animal behavior.* New York, Academic Press.

QUINE, W. V.
1953 *From a logical point of view.* Cambridge, Harvard University Press.

RUSSELL, B.
1948 *Human knowledge: its scope and limits.* New York, Simon and Schuster.

SEGALL, M. H., D. T. CAMPBELL, and M. J. HERSKOVITS
1966 *The influence of culture on visual perception.* Indianapolis, Bobbs-Merrill.

SMEDSLUND, J.
1953 The problem of "what is learned?" *Psychological Bulletin* 60:157–158.

SOURIAU, P.
1881 *Theorie de l'invention.* Paris, Hachette.

SPENCER, H.
1896 *Principles of psychology.* Vol. I., Part III, General synthesis. New York, Appleton.

SPIEGELMAN, S.
1948 Differentiation as the controlled production of unique enzymatic patterns. *Symposia of the Society for Experimental Biology,* II. *Growth in relation to differentiation and morphogenesis.* New York, Academic Press.

TOLMAN, E. C., and E. BRUNSWIK
1935 The organism and the causal texture of the environment. *Psychological Review* 42:43–77.

TOULMIN, S.
1961 *Foresight and understanding: an inquiry into the aims of science.* Bloomington, Indiana University Press (Harper Torchbook).

1967 The evolutionary development of natural science. *American Scientist* 55:4:456–471.

UEXKÜLL, J. von
1934 *Streifzüge durch die Umwelten von Tieren und Menschen.* Berlin, Springer.

WHITROW, G. J.
1955 Why physical space has three dimensions. *British Journal of Philosophy of Science* 6:13–31.

WHORF, B. L.
1956 *Language, thought, and reality.* Cambridge, Technology Press of Massachusetts Institute of Technology.

WILSON, E. G.
1952 *An introduction to scientific research.* New York, McGraw-Hill.

ZIRKLE, C.
1941 Natural selection before the "Origin of Species." *Proceedings of the American Philosophical Society* 84:71–123.

PART II

General Problems

CHAPTER 4

Cause and Intention

ANDRÉ J. F. KÖBBEN*

The ancient conflicts between free will and pre-destination, between the great man theory and the superorganic are irresolvable. Human beings are neither slaves of culture nor free agents; they are somewhere in between. (Beals and Siegel 1966:5)

THE MEANING OF CAUSE

Statements such as "where A, there B" concerning the correlation between two phenomena A and B, have often been made by anthropologists. Generally we do not stop with merely observing that two phenomena occur together; rather, we proceed to explain. The explanation we give may be—but need not be—of a causal nature. Thus, when we note that agro-towns, such as exist in southern Italy and among the Yoruba in southwestern Nigeria, regularly occur together with insecurity of one sort or another, common sense impels us to say that insecurity is *the cause* of agro-towns having come into existence.[1]

What meaning are we to accord to the term "cause" as used in this sense? Some theorists are of the opinion that it would be wise to treat the notion of causality as primitive or undefined (Blalock 1964:9); others, following Hume and Mill, propound the "invariable sequence" theory, contending that we cannot go further than to state that cause is the antecedent, effect the consequent (Hart and Honoré 1959:12–20). A still more purist standpoint is to view the term "cause" as embodying remnants of primitive animism,

and ban it from the scientific vocabulary altogether. This last viewpoint which Bertrand Russell had already taken in 1913 (MacIver 1942:36) is now quite popular in at least some branches of anthropology. Radcliffe-Brown (1945:37) somewhat deprecatingly says that to conceive of a correlation in terms of cause and effect is in conformity with old-fashioned nineteenth-century ideas. Amusingly, Prince Peter of Greece (1965:102) informs us that "at the London School of Economics" the search for causes is looked upon as pure speculation and banished from the preoccupations of serious scholars. The student should look for correlations only; Prince Peter suggests that it would be quite impossible to obtain a Ph.D. degree if the student looked for causes.

In my opinion this kind of purism impoverishes our analytical tool kit. I even submit that the notion of "cause" is psychologically indispensable to us; we would not even be able to discover regularities of the type "where A, there B" without having an inkling as to the why of the correlation (Nadel 1953:278–279). At least this was so until recently; today we can find such correlations by making the computer correlate everything with everything (Coult and Habenstein 1965; Textor 1967). However, in a way these very computer-produced results are a confirmation of what I said in that they leave us unsatisfied and unconvinced as long as we do not understand why they are linked together.

It may be remarked in passing that the criterion of *invariable sequence* does not bring us very far in anthropology—neither the notion of sequence (the cause being the

* I wish to thank the following persons for valuable suggestions and help: J. F. Boissevain, L. Brunt, J. J. Fahrenfort, L. C. de Nie-Gramer, G. W. Ovink, L. M. Serpenti, K. W. Van der Veen.

[1] More specifically it may be said that insecurity tends to be a necessary condition of agro-towns (Block 1964, Bascom 1955, Hoffman-Burchardi 1964).

precedent, the effect being the consequent), nor that of invariableness. When analyzing, say, a society having agro-towns, we do not observe insecurity first and agro-towns developing out of it as a consequence. We see rather the end product: insecurity and agro-towns occurring *together*, and it may even happen that agro-towns are *still* present, whereas insecurity *no longer* is (Köbben 1967b:17). In other words, generally we cannot draw *post hoc*, only *cum hoc ergo propter hoc*, conclusions in anthropology.

On the other hand, the criterion of invariableness breaks down as soon as we allow the notions of plural and parallel causality. To take the same example: not in all societies where insecurity prevails do agro-towns exist, because more causal factors than this one are needed to make them come into existence. Even if there fails to be a statistically significant correlation between two phenomena A and B, we need not give up the idea that A is one of the factors causing B (Köbben 1967b:12–14).

In assessing the meaning of "cause" as used in anthropology it is best to start with the famous treatise on the subject by Aristotle (Emmet 1958:50–52; Ross 1960:71–75). He distinguishes four species of cause, of which the *causa finalis* is pertinent to our discussion. The final cause is "the plan not yet embodied in a particular thing but aimed at by art or nature." Of final cause *in art* his example is the sculptor who has in his mind the image of the finished sculpture which he is consciously striving to embody while he works the crude stone. Analogously Aristotle postulates a final cause in nature, this being the condition to which inanimate things strive without conscious purpose (such as the tree in winter unconsciously striving to blossom).

Of course we have to reject final causes in nature unconditionally and thus for the natural sciences Bacon's dictum is true that "the inquisition of final causes is barren and like a virgin consecrated to God produces nothing" (Emmet 1958:52). However, since our subject as anthropologists is striving human beings, we have to accept final causes as a fertile explanatory concept (Stegmüller 1962:164–165; Ruhemann 1967:83–84). We cannot say that giraffes have long necks *in order* to reach the leaves of the trees, but we can say that people go to live in agro-

towns *in order* to be safe. It may be pointed out that this difference between the natural and the "social" sciences is much more real than the ones frequently propounded, such as the nomothetic character of the natural versus the allegedly ideographic character of the social sciences (Rickert 1926).

Moritz Schlick (1949:517) denies that there is anything more in the concept of causality than regularity of sequence. He writes:

Metaphysicians regard such regularity as a sign of some peculiar "intimacy" or "tie" between cause and effect, but if the existence of that mysterious "tie" is verified *only* by the observation of regular sequence, then this regularity will be all the meaning the word "tie" actually has and no thinking, believing or speaking can add anything to it.

In his opinion the only difference between an instance in which we do *not* understand why a cause produces a certain effect and one in which we do understand (say, the causal nexus between a certain medicine and the recovery of a patient), is the following. When we do not understand why, we observe only two events, the application of the medicine and, after a lapse of time, the recovery of the patient; whereas when we do understand why, the gap between cause and effect is filled by an unbroken chain of events which are contiguous in space and time. (The medicine comes into contact with the blood particles, these undergo a chemical change, . . . etc.)

Do I agree with Schlick about final causes? Yes, insofar as the purposive actor is simply one chain in the concatenation of events which are contiguous in time and space. On the other hand, for the social sciences final causes may be seen as that peculiar "tie" the metaphysicians are so desperately chasing after. Ontologically there may be nothing special about final causes, but psychologically there is: The curiosity of the observer about how things could have taken shape is best satisfied when the influence of striving actors is demonstrated.

THE MEANING OF PURPOSE

It is one thing to proclaim the necessity of taking final causes into account; it is another to assess their precise meaning. In general, of course, purpose and effect (function) are not identical. Poro Society ceremonies have the function of enhancing tribal cohesion, but it would be naive indeed to think that the tribal elders assembled once in the past and decided to create the Poro society wholesale in order that tribal cohesion be promoted!

As to the relation between purpose and effect, most theorists take a point of view either *too irrationalistic* or *too rationalistic*. An extreme example of the irrationalist viewpoint is the one held by Sumner (1906:3–4) who writes:

Folkways . . . are not creations of human purpose and wit. They are like products of natural forces . . . or they are like the instinctive ways of animals.

Murdock's (1949:197) more moderate position holds that "cultural change is an adaptive process, largely accomplished through the blind trial-and-error behavior of the masses of a society."

One of the objections that may be raised against these and similar formulations is that they do not clarify how such a trial-and-error process really operates. Therefore, Hoebel's (1958:594–595) stand is noteworthy, providing as it does at least the semblance of an explanation. He states that conscious tinkering with the social structure or with gadgetary improvement is uncommon in the world of primitive man and that most inventions result from accidental juxtaposition. He illustrates the principle of juxtaposition primarily by referring to Köhler's experiments with apes. Sultan, the chimpanzee, was presented with two hollow sticks, neither one long enough to reach a banana outside his cage. Both, however, were so fashioned that one could be fitted within the other to make a stick long enough to meet the need. Only when he held the two sticks end to end accidentally did he push the one into the other. "At this critical point his intelligence was equal to the occasion. He could recognize a useful relationship when he saw it. He went to the bars, used his tool and swallowed the banana." Note that this story is meant to characterize invention in human society.[2]

However, it is difficult to account for the variety and complexity of human culture when social institutions are viewed as the product of instinct or blind trial and error.

[2] For other examples of the irrationalistic viewpoint see Opler (1964).

The almost inevitable expedient is to reify culture (or society) by ascribing purposive action to it. In Nadel's (1953:276) felicitous phrase, many anthropologists "make society and culture think for the people." Such reification and the kind of teleology it implies is to be rejected out of hand, as much so as teleological theories in the natural sciences, and for the same reasons. Only if we use such expressions as figures of speech are they at all permissible, and then only provided our formulation leaves no doubt as to the figurative meaning.

The Rationalistic Point of View

In political theory there is an old tradition that conceives of society as if it were the outcome of conscious decision. "It is as if every man should say to every man, I authorise and give up my Right of Governing my selfe, to this Man, or to this Assembly of men, on this condition that thou give up thy right to him, and Authorise all his Actions in like manner. . . ." (Hobbes 1959:89) A similar position is taken by Wittfogel (1957: 17–19); in his book on hydraulic societies he depicts man living in a dry but potentially fertile region as reflecting consciously on the pros and cons of irrigation. "Man compares the merits of the existing situation with the advantages and disadvantages that may accrue from the contemplated change. . . . He proceeds as a discriminating being, actively participating in shaping his future."

Recently Lévi-Strauss (1966:15) in a remarkable shift of viewpoint has put himself resolutely in the ranks of the rationalists:

In my own past work . . . I invoked rather hastily the unconscious processes of the human mind, as if the so-called primitive could not be granted the power to use his intellect otherwise than unknowingly. But [now] . . . I see no reason, just because we know almost nothing of man's protracted past, not to admit that plenty of theoretical thinking of the highest order has been carried on all the time, not among all the representatives of the human species, but among a small minority of learned individuals. Elegant solutions such as the rules of unilateral cross-cousin marriage . . . far from being the recent outcome of unconscious processes, now appear to me as true discoveries.

The great man theory *redivivus!* Still, we may concede Lévi-Strauss several things. First, it is true that in most if not all societies there are individuals who do think intelligently about their own culture; and although most people, when questioned, say that they follow a certain custom because they have always done so, or because their ancestors wish them to do so, or because it is ridiculous not to do so, there are some sophisticated individuals who will give more profound (if not necessarily correct) answers. One may ask whether some cultures are not more suited to generate "primitive philosophers" than others, but that is a question that does not concern us here.

Second, it may be taken for granted that occasionally institutions are consciously created or modified, even in tribal societies. Unfortunately, most of our empirical data come from highly acculturated societies, whose changes may readily be explained as inspired or spurred by modern circumstances, so that they do not prove much about the hoary times Lévi-Strauss talks about. Thus, among Bantu chiefs legislation is fairly common nowadays, having mainly as its aim to fit new social phenomena (such as Christianity, Western education, migrant labor) into traditional society (Gluckman 1963:202). Few cases of chiefs decreeing new rules are known from pre-European days. Schapera (1956:69–70) comments that perhaps other such cases have been forgotten, but that more probably there was seldom need for changes in the existing system in those days.

However—to take an example from another part of Africa—when Ashanti defeated Denkyera in 1701, thereby becoming a more powerful and extensive chiefdom, there was a real need for a more complex political structure. And indeed, the Ashanti legal system and political institutions were reorganized quite consciously. We even know the name of the individual who acted as the Solon to this Athens—the priest Anotchi! (Rattray 1929). True, Anotchi has become a "concentration figure" (Fahrenfort 1927), to whom all kinds of social institutions have been imputed, like the rule of clan exogamy; true also that the mythological accretions need to be removed from the legends about him and about the miracles he wrought. But there is enough in the pertinent oral traditions to convince us that their core is trustworthy.

Finally, I agree with Lévi-Strauss that far too often models about change in tribal societies imply that it occurs gradually, un-

consciously and anonymously through "the unsensed, but nonetheless powerful force of cumulative drives."[3] This cultural drift model seems at least partly to be a function of our ignoring the history of the societies we study. Only infrequently do we catch a society in *flagrante delicto:* seen against the background of its total history our paltry one or two years of fieldwork are just a point in time, insufficient to see much change actually taking place.

Still, *as a general theory* the one advanced by Lévi-Strauss appears to me one-sided and overly rationalistic. Surely not all social institutions have been created by "learned individuals"! It seems more realistic to allow for a scale of possibilities, such as for example the following:

(a) Effect is the outcome of intention (purpose).

(b) Effect is intention plus by-products.

(c) Effect is the product of actors striving after an unattained object, or an object that is by the laws of nature unattainable.

(d) The final effect is the cumulation of minor conscious decisions; it is unforeseen by the actors.

(e) Effect is the product of coincidence and/or juxtaposition.

(f) Effect is the product of psycho-physiological reactions.

These six instances, which may be roughly thought of as lying on a continuum, will be discussed further below. It may be pointed out that they are to be seen mainly as an analytic instrument. Real social situations will oftener grow out of a combination of these instances than out of one of them in its pure form. There will not be many institutions which are entirely the outcome of (conscious) intention, nor on the other hand are there many in which intention is entirely absent. Still, it is important to retain the items (a) and (f) on my scale as the poles of the proposed continuum.

While all the elements of the scale are present in all human societies, they are not equally important everywhere. The more complex a society, i.e. the greater its functional diversification and the more numerous

---

[3] It should be noted however that Herskovits (1955), who propounds the theory of cultural drift with some vigor (506–510, 514), does also allow for the accidental and personal (510–513).

its membership, the greater the role of organizing and thereby of intention (Van Doorn 1956:37–38; Naroll 1956).

THE MEANING OF EFFECT
(a) Effect Is Intention

Modern industrial society is almost unique in that intricate social institutions are created wholesale on the basis of a blueprint. On a smaller scale, however, conscious decisions have given rise and still do give rise to social institutions elsewhere, as in the following example (one may say that *efficient cause,* "that from which comes the immediate origin," and final cause coincide in this case): When a tribesman who has come to live in a West African town feels the need to raise money, he may start a rotating credit association together with, say, twenty other tribesmen. They meet every month and contribute one shilling each to a fund which is immediately handed over to one of their number. The following month another member receives the fund, etc. (Ardener 1964: 201–229). The newly created association has precisely the function it was meant to have, no less, no more. Interestingly, where a similar situation obtains, people have hit upon the same idea, not only in West African towns, but in many other places all over the world.

(b) Effect Is Intention Plus By-Products

More often than not when people act intentionally and attain in fact the purpose they strive toward, there are unforeseen and unintentional side effects, or "latent functions," to use Merton's (1957:63) terminology. These latent functions are generally what matter most to the anthropologist, if only for psychological reasons: such functions are often neither perceived by the members of the society in question nor by the nonprofessional observer.[4]

So it is on this score that anthropology can most easily prove its value. The phenomenon is important because it helps us to understand better the connection between purposive behavior and function. Let us take as an ex-

[4] Merton's (1956:63, 70) discussion of "latent function" is equivocal in that he does not consistently distinguish between unintended and unrecognized consequences.

ample the Djuka of Surinam, who formerly had exogamous matrilineages. Recently people have begun to permit intra-lineage marriages in part of the tribal area, quite consciously and for quite rational motives. Today a man may marry a lineage-sister, unless she is a member of his own lineage-*segment.* Although there is still opposition to overcome, many people express enthusiasm at the new state of affairs and advance good arguments in defense of it. As an informant said: "If you marry someone of another lineage, the children are not for yourself, but if your wife is of your own lineage, the children are, too; besides, both you and your wife can continue to live at home." There is, however, an unforeseen and unperceived side effect, in that the unity of the matrilineal group as a whole is seriously affected. Divorce is common in this society and is regularly accompanied by feelings of resentment between the two families concerned. When a man and a woman from the same lineage divorce, their respective segments take sides and the lineage (the village) is torn by vehement quarreling (Köbben 1967a:20–23).

Again borrowing Merton's (1957:50) terminology, one may say that the unperceived effect in this case is a dysfunction (negative function) for the lineage as a whole. It is important to emphasize that latent functions frequently have this quality. Many anthropologists steeped in the Malinowskian tradition pay more attention to positive than to negative functions and one may say that these anthropologists not only make society think for its members, but also make society look after its members.

(c) Effect Is the Product of Striving After an Unattained/Unattainable Object

Here the Melanesian cargo cults are appropriate examples. The conscious purpose of their prophets is to attain the riches of Western society and the return of the culture hero (or the ancestors) by mystical means. This is clearly a case of "purposes by law of nature unattainable." Still, it is not for nothing that these movements have drawn so much attention from anthropologists as well as administrators and politicians. The actions of the prophets and their followers often have had some or all of these three positive and three negative functions. The three positive ones: (1) revitalization and psychological liberation; (2) the overcoming of tribal and village particularism; (3) preparing the ground for modern political and economical movements. The three negative ones: (1) a hostile attitude toward the powers that be, including noncooperation vis à vis useful governmental services; (2) the bitterness and frustration when the prophecy fails or when the movement is suppressed by force; (3) the unrealistic estimation of the group's power and importance, which may eventually lead to its self-destruction.

(d) The Final Effect Is the Cumulation of Minor Conscious Decision Unforeseen by the Actors

It is this mechanism that Polybius had in mind when he was writing about the Roman constitution and remarked that the Romans had not reached their form of government "by any process of reasoning but by the discipline of many struggles and troubles, *always choosing the best in the light of the experience gained in disaster*" (Haskill 1942: 22–23, my italics). It is possible that Murdock, when talking about the "blind trial-and-error behavior of the masses," had the same process in mind, although his formulation, especially his reference to "the masses," is rather suggestive of instinctive reactions.

In order to demonstrate the process in question I give an extremely simple example, but one that has at least the merit of being based on detailed observation: Agni (Ivory Coast) villagers traditionally had to perform for nobles and village heads *corvée* services such as clearing village paths. More than a generation ago, when cocoa became a cash crop, the Agni began hiring laborers from the Sudan to work their cocoa gardens. In time, when a villager was summoned to *corvée* services, instead of working himself he would send a laborer. The next stage was for an Agni to see if the village headman could provide a laborer and, if so, to offer a day's wages as a compensation. The final step was for the villager to pay taxes in lieu of performing *corvée* services. Interestingly, all three stages I present here, as forming a diachronic series, can still be observed operating side by side in various Agni villages, as a synchronic series. But my main point is the evolution from *corvée* services to taxes

(paid in money), without the Agni having made a conscious decision. My example may seem to suggest that they were innately incapable of "inventing" the new institution. This is certainly not so, but for some reason or another they did not think of it. Similar processes, often in a vastly more intricate form, undoubtedly account for many existing social institutions.

Frequently the complexity of a phenomenon determines whether we have to subsume it under our category *a* ("effect is identical with intention") or under the category *d* here discussed. For example, the Roman constitution in its totality was not devised *in vacuo,* but is the outcome of gradual accumulation (category *d*). However, some of its details certainly were consciously devised in their entirety, so that *considered per se* these are to be put into category *a*.

(e) Effect Is the Product of Coincidence and/or Juxtaposition

Although I do not impute to this factor the preponderant role Hoebel does, there is no denying that coincidence and juxtaposition have been important for improvements in tools and techniques and for the growth of institutions. Since well-documented instances of this process in the primitive world are understandably scarce, the following example from the history of Western invention may serve. In 1835 Daguerre stumbled upon the possibility of making visible the latent image of a photographic plate. He had put away in his chemical cupboard a plate which had been exposed. When he opened the cupboard a few days later he found, to his amazement, the underexposed plate impressed with a distinct picture. By eliminating the various chemicals his cupboard contained he at length established that the vapor from a few drops of mercury spilt from a broken thermometer had worked the miracle. What makes the story interesting is that, as usual, it was not accident alone that made for the invention. For years Daguerre had been obsessed by the idea of fixing the fugitive image, so that when a solution offered itself he was quick to grasp it (Gernsheim 1955:49–50). Without awareness of problem, good luck can be wasted (Kroeber 1948:353–355).

A special case of juxtaposition is what Kroeber has called stimulus invention, which occurs when a culture takes over the idea (the principle) of an invention without its mechanisms, and devises another mechanism to produce the desired result. An example is the Cherokee script: it was evolved by an Indian who had come to realize the value of writing from his contacts with the whites. In Kroeber's (1948:369) words: "without a mark having been set, he would have had nothing to shoot at." In like fashion a script has been developed by a Surinam Bush Negro (Gonggrijp 1960).

Another example of stimulus invention among these same Bush Negroes is rice cultivation. Traditionally they cultivated rice by the slash-and-burn method on high sandy ground; but twelve years ago they began to use the fertile swampy banks of the tidal rivers, which overflow at every flood tide. Consequently these Bush Negroes now produce and sell a surplus of rice. As the inventor admitted himself, he had been inspired to his new technique by the *sawah* system of cultivation such as is applied by the Javanese in Surinam. Still, his method was different in every detail from the Javanese one and took real ingenuity to develop.

(f) Effect Is the Product of Psycho-Physiological Reactions

Instinctive behavior, of which Sumner (1906:3–4) made the most, as we say above, undeniably is accountable for a number of social rules: where situation of anxiety, there magical acts; where extreme segregation of the sexes, there homosexuality is frequent; where society in crisis, there alcoholism is frequent. In these cases one cannot say that the effects (magic, homosexuality, alcoholism) are consciously willed or aimed at; they are rather the direct outcome of a given psycho-physiological state. As Firth (1939:185) observed, when the Tikopians are fishing on the high sea they are in such a state of nervous energy and emotional tension that magical formulas (inviting the fish to bite) are their spontaneous outlet. This is not to say that anxiety is a necessary and sufficient condition for magic. For one thing, once the magic is institutionalized it will be executed even where there are no emotions at all. The same is true for the other regularities mentioned even if for different reasons.

We cannot be sure that in all these in-stances the psychological mechanisms involved were entirely unconscious ones. Conceivably, when in a desperate state, people may consciously think: "Let us drink, so that we may forget the plight we are in." While possible, this is not a very likely origin of alcoholism. Anyhow, whatever its origin (psycho-physiological, or psycho-physiological-cum-intention) the outcome will be similar.

Every human action has, of course, its psycho-physiological basis. In the cases grouped under the categories *a* to *e*, however, there is an intermediate link (or there are intermediate links) between the physiological impulse on the one hand and behavior on the other. Interestingly, Nadel (1953: 276–279) would use the notion of "causality" only where a mechanism in the strict sense of the word gives rise to actions, not where behavior depends on the actor's intentions or awareness for its effectiveness. Presumably he chose this restricted meaning of "causality" in order to conform with the natural sciences. I prefer my wider definition as being more in accordance with established usage.

As anthropologists the nature of the unconscious (or subconscious) background of conscious decisions need not concern us. Nieboer (1910) found that "where slavery, there open resources." By "open resources" he means a situation where there is plentiful land and where few capital goods are required to till the soil. He reasons that in these circumstances the powerful who desire others to work for them have to use physical force to make them do so (Köbben 1967b:12–13). What motives lie at the basis of this desire, whether it is simply the wish to be exempt from hard work themselves, or whether it has to be explained in Freudian or even Adlerian terms is something we should not dabble in, but leave to the psychologist and/or the psychoanalyst. This is not to say that we leave the "real" explanation of human behavior to the psychologist. Ideally, it is up to the latter to state the potentialities of the human species, whereas the social scientist demonstrates which of these potentialities can be realized in a given social framework. In the above example where open resources are present *but there is no stratified social system*, slavery cannot develop. The psychologist's and the social scientist's contribution are of equal importance, though of different

CORRELATION AND CAUSE

It is a commonplace of textbooks to point

(1) A ────────▶ B

(2) A ◀──────── B

(3) A ◀═══════▶ B

Thus, where A and B occur together: (1) A may be the cause of B; or (2) B may be the cause of A; (3) A and B may be functionally interdependent in a self-regulatory system; (4) both A and B may be caused by a third factor; (5) there may be an intervening variable between A and B; (6) A may cause B in combination with a third (fourth, . . . etc.) factor; (7) A and B may be historically rather than functionally related, as in the correlation of maize cultivation and the coiling technique of pottery among the Amerindians (Driver and Massey 1957:339–341; Driver 1967:21); (8) A may be an implication of B, or vice versa. Only the last two of these eight instances do not imply the notion of causality as defined in this paper.

Still, many anthropologists scorn the use of the term "cause" and substitute such words as "function," "interdependency," "concomitant adjustments," as if these had entirely different meanings. Thus Mitchell (1961:261–262), talking about labor migration in Africa, says:

> It may deepen our understanding of labour migrations if we view it and many of its concomitant social manifestations, *not as causes and effects, but rather as concomitant adjustments within a changed social system*. It is virtually impossible to separate out in terms of causes and effects the relationships of labour migration, to marital fidelity, crime, the growth of separatist sects and the hundred and one other changes going on in rural areas in Africa. . . . We should treat with caution overzealous accounts which relate all the social disabilities to the evil effects of labour migration." (Italics added)

out that a correlation between A and B does not mean A *causes* B. I do not propose to identify correlation and cause, although some form of cause lies at the basis of most correlations. The following is an exhaustive list of the possible connections (in which the arrow stands for "causes"):

(4) C⟨ A, B

(5) A──▶C──▶B

(6) A, C──▶B

(7) A hist. B

(8) A ⟩ B

Notwithstanding his wording, Mitchell's message here is really an appeal against monocausal and overly simple explanation, not against the notion of cause-and-effect as such. It is really a plea to consider not only the causal connection sub 1, but also the ones sub 2–6. Thus, the relationship between labor migration (A) and the factors marital infidelity (B), crime (C) and growth of sects (D) should not be represented as:

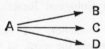

but rather as an intricate knot of causal relations, viz.:

Because the monocausal explanation has for long been a pitfall of the social sciences, Mitchell's warning is well taken. One may however take exception to his suggestion that it is "virtually impossible" to disentangle the knot of causal relations in this and other cases. Although there is some truth in his statement, anthropologists have developed instruments and should develop others: for fieldworkers as well as theorists to assess the precise causal nexus in as many cases as possible is one of the foremost tasks of anthropology, worthy indeed of the attention of serious scholars.

BIBLIOGRAPHY

ARDENER, S.
1964 The comparative study of rotating credit associations. *Journal of the Royal Anthropological Institute* 94:201–229.

BASCOM, W.
1954 Urbanization among the Yoruba. *American Journal of Sociology* 60:446–454.

BEALS, A. R., and B. J. SIEGEL
1966 *Divisiveness and social conflict; an anthropological approach.* Stanford, Calif., Stanford University Press.

BLALOCK, H. M.
1964 *Causal inferences in non-experimental research,* 2nd ed. Chapel Hill, University of North Carolina Press.

BLOK, A.
1964 *Enige aspecten van het geconcentreerde nederzettingspatroon in Zuid-Italië.* MS.

COULT, P. D., and R. W. HABENSTEIN
1965 *Cross tabulations of Murdock's world ethnographic sample.* Columbia, University of Missouri.

DRIVER, H. E.
1967 Comment. *Current Anthropology* 8:21.

DRIVER, H. E., and W. C. MASSEY
1957 Comparative studies of North American Indians. *Transactions of the American Philosophical Society,* 47, Pt 2.

EMMET, D. M.
1958 *Function, purpose and powers.* London, Macmillan.

FAHRENFORT, J. J.
1927 *Het hoogste wezen der primitieven.* Groningen, Wolters.

FIRTH, R.
1939 *Primitive Polynesian economy.* London, Routledge.

GERNSHEIM, H.
1955 *The history of photography.* London, Oxford University Press.

GLUCKMAN, M.
1963 The reasonable man in Barotse law. In *Order and rebellion in tribal Africa.* London, Cohen and West.

GONGGRIJP, J. W.
1960 The evolution of a Djuka-script in Surinam. *Nieuwe West-Indische Gids* 40: 63–72.

HART, H. L. A., and A. M. HONORÉ
1959 *Causation in the law.* Oxford, Clarendon Press.

HASKELL, H. J.
1942 *This was Cicero; modern politics in a Roman toga.* London, Seeker and Warburg.

HERSKOVITS, MELVILLE J.
1955 *Cultural anthropology.* New York, Knopf.

HOBBES, T.
1959 *Leviathan or the Matter, Form, and Power of a Commonwealth, Ecclesiastical and Civil.* London, 1651, reprinted in Everyman's Library (introd. by A. D. Lindsay), London, Dent and Sons.

HOEBEL, E. A.
1958 *Man in the primitive world,* 2nd ed. New York, McGraw-Hill.

HOFFMAN-BURCHARDI
1964 Die Yoruba Städte in Südwest-Nigerien. *Erdkunde* 18:206–253.

KÖBBEN, A. J. F.
1964 *Profetische bewegingen als sociaal protest. In Van primitieven tot medeburgers.* Assen, van Gorcum, chap. 6.
1967a Unity and disunity; Cottica Djuka Society as a Kinship System. *Bijdragen Taal-, Land-, en Volkenkunde* 123:10–52.
1967b Why exceptions; the logic of cross-cultural analysis. *Current Anthropology* 8: 3–19.

KROEBER, A. L.
1948 *Anthropology.* New York, Harcourt, Brace.

LÉVI-STRAUSS, C.
1966 The future of kinship studies. The Huxley Memorial lecture, *Proceedings Royal Anthropological Institute* 13–22.

MACIVER, R. M.
1942 *Social causation.* Boston, Ginn.

MERTON, R. K.
1957 *Social theory and social structure,* 2nd ed. Glencoe, Ill., Free Press.

MITCHELL, J. C.
1961 The causes of labour migration. In *Migrant labour in Africa south of the Sahara.* Abidjan, C.C.T.A.

MURDOCK, G. P.
1949 *Social structure.* New York, Macmillan.

NADEL, S. F.
1953 *The foundations of social anthropology,* 2nd impr. London, Cohen and West.

NAROLL, R.
1956 A preliminary index of social development. *American Anthropologist* 58:687–715.

NIEBOER, H. J.
1910 *Slavery as an industrial system,* 2nd rev. ed. 's-Gravenhage, M. Nijhoff.

OPLER, M. E.
1964 The human being in culture theory. *American Anthropologist* 66:507–528.

PRINCE PETER OF GREECE AND DENMARK
1965 Reply. *Current Anthropology* 6:100–103.

RADCLIFFE-BROWN, A. R.
1945 Religion and society. *Journal of the Royal Anthropological Institute* 75:33–43.

RATTRAY, R. S.
1929 *Ashanti law and constitution.* Oxford, Clarendon Press.

RICKERT, H.
1926 *Kulturwissenschaft und Naturwissenschaft.* Tübingen.

ROSS, W. D.
1960 *Aristotle,* 5th ed. London, Methuen.

RUHEMANN, B.
1967 Purpose and mathematics; a problem in the analysis of classificatory kinship systems. *Bijdragen Taal-, Land-, en Volkenkunde* 123:83–124.

SCHAPERA, I.
1956 *Government and politics in tribal society.* London, Watts.

SCHLICK, M.
1949 Causality in everyday life and in recent science. In H. Feigl and W. Sellars, eds., *Readings in philosophical analysis.* New York, Appleton.

STEGMÜLLER, W.
1962 Einige Beiträge zum Problem der Teleologie und der Analyse von Systemen mit zielgerichteter Organisation. In Yehosha Bar-Hillel, *Logic and Language; studies dedicated to R. Carnap.* Dordrecht, Reidel.

SUMNER, W. G.
1906 *Folkways.* Boston, Ginn.

TEXTOR, R. B.
1967 *A cross-cultural summary.* New Haven, H.R.A.F. Press.

VAN DOORN, J. A. A.
1956 *Een sociologische benadering van het organisatieverschÿnsel.* Leiden, Stenfert Kroese.

WITTFOGEL, K. A.
1957 *Oriental despotism.* New Haven, Yale University Press.

CHAPTER 5

A Method of Linear Causal Analysis—
Dependence Analysis

RAYMOND BOUDON

Among the recent discussion of causal inference in empirical sociological research, the most important are Blalock's works (1961, 1962a, 1963, 1964) and the discussion of asymmetrical causal models between Polk (1962), Blalock (1962b) and Robinson (1962). It appears from these studies that certain problems have not yet been satisfactorily elucidated, and that a somewhat different method can be derived.

For the convenience of readers who may not be familiar with the work of Blalock and others, I shall recall some of the more important points. The core of Blalock's ideas is Simon's (1954:467–479) analysis of the spurious correlation problem in the linear case. Blalock's recent efforts have been especially oriented toward systematic exploration of the consequences of Simon's logic in the more-than-three-variable cases. This is important, of course, since Simon's treatment was confined to the three-variable case and it was not altogether clear whether the linear specification added much to Lazarsfeld's elaboration formula, in this case (Lazarsfeld 1955, Kendall and Lazarsfeld 1950). Blalock was able to show that when one is prepared to admit the linearity of the causal relations, the three-or-more-variables cases may be treated quite easily. Blalock's method, however, takes into account only predictions on the partial correlations that may be derived from a causal scheme.

At this point I began to be puzzled, since from Simon's causal equations, on which Blalock's models are based, it is possible to derive

This article is reproduced with minor changes from the *American Sociological Review*, 30:365–374.

conclusions between variables included in a causal scheme, but also the coefficient of the causal equations. Sociological methodologists tend to overlook these coefficients because their meaning is less obvious than that of partial correlation coefficients.

To see the point more clearly, let us recall Simon's example, in a somewhat different notation. The hypotheses were: x_1 causes x_2 and x_3; x_2 causes x_3. A causal structure of this kind might correspond, for instance, to Durkheim's and Halbwachs' findings on suicide: average age (x_1) appears to affect the propensity to suicide (x_3) both directly and indirectly (with opposite sign) through the variable "extension of family group" (x_2). The corresponding equations would be:

$$
\begin{aligned}
x_1 &= e_1 \\
(1) \quad a_{12}x_1 + x_2 &= e_2 \\
a_{13}x_1 + a_{23}x_2 + x_3 &= e_3
\end{aligned}
$$

where the e_1 terms are "errors" in Simon's terminology. I prefer to speak of implicit factors, i.e., factors not explicitly included in the causal scheme. Although it is embarrassing to treat x_1 as an error term, and consequently x_2 and x_3 as a weighted sum of error terms, it seems much more acceptable to conceptualize the e_1's as factors that act on the explicit variables of the causal scheme without being stated explicitly. Thus, in the previous example, e_3 would measure the effects on propensity to suicide of variables other than age or extension of family group. Now, it seems reasonable to assume that these implicit factors are *specific*, i.e., that each one acts on a single explicit variable, or, in other words, that they are uncorrelated, and if we multiply the equations of (1) by pairs and take the mathematical expectations, we get:

(2.a) $\quad a_{12}E(x^2_1)+E(x_1x_2) \qquad\qquad =0$

(2.b) $\quad a_{13}E(x^2_1)+a_{23}E(x_1x_2)+E(x_1x_3) \quad =0$

(2.c) $\quad a_{12}[a_{13}E(x^2_1)+a_{23}E(x_1x_2)+E(x_1x_3)]$
$\qquad +a_{13}E(x_1x_2)+a_{23}E(x^2_2)+$
$\qquad E(x_2x_3) \qquad\qquad\qquad\qquad\qquad =0$

The term in brackets in equation (2.c), being identical to the left member of equation (2.b), is zero, so that if we solve (2) for the covariances (I shall suppose throughout the paper that variables x_1, x_2, . . . , e_1, e_2, . . . are measured from their means) between age and extension of family group, age and suicide, and extension of family group and suicide, we get, respectively:

(3.a) $\quad E(x_1x_2)=-a_{12}E(x^2_1)$

(3.b) $\quad E(x_1x_3)=(a_{12}a_{23}-a_{13})E(x^2_1)$

(3.c) $\quad E(x_2x_3)=a_{12}a_{13}E(x^2_1)-a_{23}E(x^2_2)$

In his paper, Simon shows that if one assumes that x_1 has no effect on x_3 and, therefore, that the term a_{23} in (3.b) and (3.c) is zero, it is possible to deduce from (3) that $r_{23}=r_{12}r_{13}$, or in other words, that the partial correlation coefficient $r_{23.1}$ is zero.

But this is not the only kind of deduction one may draw. Of course, Simon's purpose was to formalize the idea of spurious correlation. But, from (3), it is apparent that the linear specification, as well as the hypotheses on the implicit factors, permit deductions regarding not only the correlation coefficients, both partial and total, but the coefficients of the equations as well. Indeed, we get from (3), as can easily be seen, three unknown a_{ij} terms and three equations, which can be solved. This suggests that for the purpose of causal analysis it may be worthwhile to estimate and use the "dependence coefficients" (this usage will be justified below) of the causal linear equation. If so, however, why has this method been disregarded by most methodologists, at least in sociology and, as far as I know, economics?

To answer this question, one must first ask what the dependence coefficients measure, and second, what the connection is between the dependence coefficients and the familiar regression coefficients. As the Polk-Blalock-Robinson discussion shows, the connection between dependence and regression coefficients is far from obvious. The difficulty of assigning clear "status" to the dependence coefficients is probably the major reason why they have been overlooked, and why, among the possi-

ble inferences to be drawn from a linear causal structure, those concerning the partial and total correlation coefficients have been considered, while those concerning the dependence coefficients have been ignored.

DEPENDENCE COEFFICIENTS, REGRESSION COEFFICIENTS AND THE IDENTIFICATION PROBLEM

To understand the meaning of dependence coefficients and their connection with regression, one must understand the idea of "identification" (Koopmans 1949, 1950; Wold 1954; Blalock 1964). Let us suppose, for example, that we have a causal structure corresponding to system (1), from which we remove the first equation, leaving:

(4.a) $\quad a_{12}x_1+x_2=e_2$

(4.b) $\quad a_{13}x_1+a_{23}x_2+x_3=e_3$

Now, suppose that in a set of observed data the value of each unity or group on each of the variables x_1, x_2, x_3 is known (for instance, a set of groups where we know, for each group, average age, average extension of family group and suicide rate), and structure (4) holds. This means that, if appropriate values are used for a_{12}, unities plotted in the plane (x_1, x_2) should cluster in the neighborhood of the line $a_{12}x_1+_2=0$. The average closeness of observed points to the line depends on the importance of the implicit factors e_2. In the same way, we should expect observed points plotted in the space (x_1, x_2, x_3) to cluster in the neighborhood of the plane defined by equation $a_{13}x_1+a_{23}x_2+x_3=0$.

This last expectation cannot actually be met however. To simplify, suppose that there are no effects due to implicit factors. In this case, the observed points should lie on the line $a_{12}x_1+x_2=0$, or, in the three-dimensional space (x_1, x_2, x_3), in the plane $a_{13}x_1+a_{23}x_2+x_3=0$. Now, if these equations hold, their sum holds. Thus, we have $(a_{13}+a_{12})x_1+(a_{23}+1)x_2+x_3=0$. More generally the equation $(a_{13}+p_{12}a_{12})x_1+(a_{23}+p_{12})x_2+x_3=0$, where p_{12} may have any value, holds as a consequence of the original equations. This means that the observed points, if the model holds, will lie, not in a specific plane of the space (x_1, x_2, x_3) but in an infinity of planes corresponding to the infinity of possible values of p_{12}.

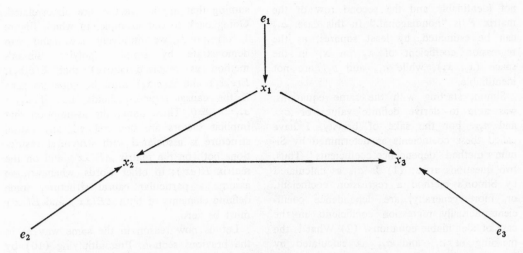

Figure 1. Abstract Structure Corresponding to the Durkheim-Halbwachs Finding on Suicide. Age (x_1) Acts on Extension of Family Group (x_2); x_1 and x_2 Both Act Directly on Suicide (x_3).

The same reasoning applies to system (4): let us substitute for it the system:

(5.a) $$a_{12}x_1 + x_2 = e_2$$
(5.b) $$(a_{13} + p_{12}a_{12})x_1 + (a_{23}p_{12})x_2 + x_3 = e'_3$$

If (4) is true, (5) is true. (Explicitly, the new error term e'_3 in (5.b) is equal to $e_3 + p_{12}e_2$. But to write it explicitly is of no use, since it is impossible to separate e_2 from e_3. For the same reason, we write $Pe = e'$ in equation (7): the explicit components of the new error vector are in this case $e'_2 = e_2$ and $e'_3 = e_3 + p_{12}e_2$.) Thus, if the assumed causal structure holds, the observed points will be close to any plane $(a_{13} + p_{12}a_{12})x_1 + (a_{23} + p_{12})x_2 + x_3 = 0$, where p_{12} may have any value; in other words, the observed points do *not* lie in the neighborhood of any particular plane in the space (x_1, x_2, x_3). As it is impossible to determine a particular set of parameters locating the points in the space (x_1, x_2, x_3), we shall say that the parameters of equation (4.b) are not *identifiable*.

The same argument can be put in matrix form to facilitate further reasoning. Indeed, the system (4) may be translated into the single matrix equation:

(6) $$Ax = e$$
where:

$$A = \begin{pmatrix} a_{12} & 1 & 0 \\ a_{13} & a_{23} & 1 \end{pmatrix}; \quad x = \begin{pmatrix} x_1 \\ x_2 \\ x_3 \end{pmatrix}; \quad e = \begin{pmatrix} e_2 \\ e_3 \end{pmatrix}$$

System (5), on the other hand, may be expressed in the following matrix equation:

(7) $$PAx = Pe = e',$$
where:

$$P = \begin{pmatrix} 1 & 0 \\ p_{12} & 1 \end{pmatrix}$$

From this, we may define identifiability as follows. If, given a causal system $Ax = e$, it is possible to find a nondiagonal matrix P of appropriate dimensionality, so that the product matrix PA has zeros in the same cells as A, i.e., defines the same causal structure, then the coefficients of the linear structure are *not all* identifiable. Reciprocally, if it is impossible to find a nondiagonal matrix P so that PA has the same structure as A, the coefficients of the structure are identifiable: the set of lines, planes and hyperplanes defined by a matrix A is the same as the set of lines, planes and hyperplanes defined by a matrix PA, if P is diagonal.

The phrase *"not all"* can be given a more precise meaning. We have just seen that the coefficients of an equation can be linearly combined with another without changing the causal structure. Hence, if we can find a nondiagonal matrix P, the rows of the latter which depart from "diagonality," i.e., which cannot belong to a diagonal matrix, correspond to the non-identifiable equations. Thus, in the above example, the second equation is not identifiable and the second row of the matrix P is "nondiagonal." In this case, a_{12} can be estimated, by least squares, as the regression coefficient of x_2 on x_1 in the space (x_1, x_2), while a_{13} and a_{23} are not identifiable.

Simon, starting with the same equations, was able to derive definite values of a_{12}, and a_{23}. For the sake of brevity, I have called these coefficients as determined by Simon's method "dependence coefficients." Thus, two questions arise: (1) Is a_{12} as calculated by Simon's method a regression coefficient, or, more generally, are dependence coefficients actually regression coefficients in the case of identifiable equations? (2) What is the meaning of a_{13} and a_{23} as calculated by Simon's method, or, more generally, what do the dependence coefficients mean when no corresponding regression coefficients can be determined?

ARE DEPENDENCE COEFFICIENTS ALWAYS IDENTIFIABLE?

Before answering these questions, we must solve a preliminary problem. In the previous example, dependence coefficients are identifiable, while regression coefficients are not. To what extent can this case be generalized? Are dependence coefficients always indentifiable? One useful device for seeing whether this is so is to multiply equation (6) by x', the row vector that is the transpose of the column vector x. We get the matrix equation:

(8) $Axx' = ex'$

and, taking mathematical expectations,

(9) $E(Axx') = E(ex')$

or

(10) $AE(xx') = E(ex')$

If there are, as in the example of system (4), two equations and three x's, A is a two-rows three-columns matrix and $E(xx')$ is a three-by-three matrix—the matrix of covariances between the explicit and implicit factors, if the latter are measured from their means. $E(ex')$ is the two-rows three-columns matrix of covariances between the explicit and implicit factors again measured from their means.

Now it is clear that, if A contains *a priori* zeros, i.e., if some explicit factors are *a priori* known not to affect certain other explicit factors, $E(ex')$ will contain *a priori* zeros, as-

suming that implicit factors are uncorrelated. Going back to our example, to which Figure 1 corresponds, we intuitively see (and can demonstrate by simply applying Simon's method as reported above) that $E(e_2x_1)$, $E(e_3x_1)$ and $E(e_3x_2)$ must be equal to zero if the causal structure holds, i.e., if $a_{21} = a_{31} = a_{32} = 0$. Thus, under the assumption that implicit factors are uncorrelated, any causal structure is associated with structural restrictions both on the matrix $AE(xx')$ and on the matrix $E(ex')$; in other words, whenever we assume a particular causal structure, some definite elements of both $AE(xx')$ and $E(ex')$ must be zero.

Let us now reason in the same way as in the previous section. Premultiplying (10) by A matrix P of appropriate dimensionality, we get:

(11) $PAE(xx') = PE(ex')$

Of course, if (10) is true, (11) is also true. But the important question is the following: whatever A, can P be a nondiagonal matrix such that $PAE(xx')$ has the same structure as $AE(xx')$ and $PE(ex')$, the same structure as $E(ex')$? If the answer is yes, then both A and every PA obtained by assigning arbitrary values to the nonzero elements of P are acceptable sets of dependence coefficients; hence the dependence coefficients will not always be identifiable. If the answer is no, if premultiplication by any nondiagonal matrix P, whatever A, disturbs the structure either of $AE(xx')$ or of $E(ex')$, then the only acceptable sets of dependence coefficients are the PA's with P diagonal, whence it follows that the dependence coefficients are always identifiable (up to normalization).

Since it can be shown (see appendix for proof) that it is impossible to find a nondiagonal matrix P such that $PAE(xx')$ has the same structure as $AE(ex')$ and $PE(ex')$, the same structure as $E(ex')$, we can state the important result:

When the implicit factors are uncorrelated, the dependence coefficients are always identifiable.

In practice, one may determine these coefficients by using either Simon's method as stated in the first section or equation (10). (Simon's method is to introduce equations of the form $x_1 = e_1$ for the explicit factors that do not depend on any other explicit factor; write the equations for the other explicit factors; multiply equations by pairs;

take mathematical expectations, standardize to substitute correlation coefficients for covariances, and solve for the dependence coefficients in terms of the correlation coefficients and variances. The other method is to state the elements of the $E(ex')$ matrix that are *a priori* known to be zero and pick up corresponding elements of the matrix $AE(xx')$. This method, much less cumbersome than the former, is presented in detail in the last section.)

Before asking what these dependence coefficients measure, I shall add one more remark on Simon's formalization. The matrix notation of equation (6) shows that it is useless to introduce, as Simon does, equations of the type $x_1 = e_1$, i.e., equations expressing the explicit factors not depending on any other explicit factor in the causal scheme. Moreover, this kind of formalization precludes general reasoning on identification, since, if one adds to the matrix A rows corresponding to these factors, it is always possible to find a nondiagonal matrix P^0, such that $P^0 A^0$ has the same structure as A^0. Thus considering the structure in which x_1 causes x_2, and x_1 causes x_3, the corresponding matrix A is:

$$A = \begin{pmatrix} a_{12} & 1 & 0 \\ a_{13} & 0 & 1 \end{pmatrix}$$

Obviously, no matrix derived from this one by one or more linear combinations of the rows will preserve the structure: there is no nondiagonal matrix P such that PA has zeros in the same cells as A. On the other hand, Simon's formalization amounts to building a matrix A^0 such as the following:

$$A = \begin{pmatrix} 1 & 0 & 0 \\ a_{12} & 1 & 0 \\ a_{13} & 0 & 1 \end{pmatrix}$$

which can be premultiplied by a P^0 matrix such as:

$$P^0 = \begin{pmatrix} 1 & 0 & 0 \\ p_{12} & 1 & 0 \\ p_{13} & 0 & 1 \end{pmatrix}$$

without modifying the structure. Here, $P^0 A^0$ has the same structure as A^0.

INTERPRETATION OF DEPENDENCE COEFFICIENTS

We now know that we can always solve for dependence coefficients in terms of observable quantities (correlation coefficients or covariances between explicit factors, and variances of the latter). We also know that when the matrix A is not identifiable, in the sense defined above, these coefficients are clearly not regression coefficients. But we do not yet know whether they are regression coefficients when the A matrix is identifiable. In any case, we shall have to find a general statistical interpretation of these coefficients.

Such an interpretation was put forward by the biologist Sewall Wright (1934, 1954), whose "path analysis," although derived from a different approach, is similar to the method of causal analysis advocated here. (I am grateful to Hanan C. Selvin, who introduced me to Wright's work and stimulated my reflection on causal analysis by his report on "The Logic of Survey Analysis," given in 1964 in Paris—Seminar of the *Centre d'Études Sociologiques* on the epistemology of social sciences. I use the word "dependence" where Wright uses "path," since the expression "path coefficients" or "path analysis" refers to a mere subsidiary computing device, and in my opinion, it obscures the logic of the analysis.) Wright's argument may be paraphrased as follows. Let us first symbolize any causal equation in the form:

(12) $x_1 = a_{1i}x_1 + \ldots + a_{mi}x_m + x_e$

Then, holding constant any variable including the implicit factor x_e except x_i and, say, x_1, we have:

(13) $\sigma^2_{i.23} \ldots {}_{\text{me}} = a^2_{1i}\sigma^2_{1.23} \ldots {}_{(i-1)} {}_{(i+1)}$
$\ldots {}_{\text{me}}$

($N\sigma^2_{1.23} \ldots {}_{(i-1)(i+1)} \ldots {}_{\text{me}}$ is the sum of squares of the distances of the observed points to the regression hyperplane of x_1, or $x^2, x_3, \ldots x_{i-1}, x_{i+1} \ldots x_m, e_e$. As can be seen in Yule and Kendall 1958).

Now let:

$$(14) \quad b^2_{11} = a^2_{11}\frac{\sigma^2_1}{\sigma^2_1}$$

$$= \frac{\sigma^2_{i.23} \ldots {}_{(i-1)(i+1)} \ldots {}_{\text{me}}}{\sigma^2_1}$$

$$- \frac{\sigma^2_1}{\sigma^2_{1.23} \ldots {}_{\text{me}}}$$

If we now suppose that x_1 does not depend on any other factor in the causal scheme, then $\sigma^2_1/\sigma^2_{1.23 \ldots (i-1)(i+1) \ldots me} = 1$: the variance of x_1 is not affected by holding constant factors on which x_1 does not depend. In this case, b_{1i} measures the part of the variance of x_i accounted for by x_1. On the other hand, if x_1 is dependent on some explicit factor(s), it is determined by variables in the system which we wish to hold constant. But holding constant factors on which x_1 is dependent will reduce its variance in the proportion $\sigma_{1.23 \ldots (i-1)(i+1) \ldots me}/\sigma^2_1$. Thus, in general, if we want to state the part of the variance of x_i accounted for by x_1, holding all other factors constant, we have to correct $\sigma^2_{1.23 \ldots me}/\sigma^2_i$ to take into account the reduction of variation in x_1 by holding these factors constant. That is what Wright meant when he wrote that b measures "the fraction of the standard deviation of the dependent variable (with appropriate sign) for which the designated factor is directly responsible, in the sense of the fraction which would be found if this factor varies to the same extent as in the observed data while all others (including residual factors) are constant" (Wright 1934).

Thus, the dependence coefficients, when corrected by the appropriate variances, are really a measure of the *direct* influence of one variable on another in causal scheme. Moreover, we know from the previous section that they can always be determined, if the implicit factors in the scheme are assumed to be uncorrelated.

DEPENDENCE AND REGRESSION COEFFICIENTS IN THE CASE OF IDENTIFIABLE STRUCTURE

The preceding interpretation of dependence coefficients is, of course, valid whether the regression coefficients are identifiable or not. But it is important to see the connection between both kinds of coefficients whenever the latter may be identified. Going back to equation (6), we recall that a structure, or a coefficient matrix A associated with this structure, is identifiable if premultiplication of A by any nondiagonal matrix P is such that PA and A have a different structure. Let us suppose then that the matrix A associated with a causal structure is identifiable. Now, from $E(Axx') = E(ex')$, we can derive a set of equations. If, say, x_i depends on x_j,

we shall have $E(e_i x_j) = 0$, while a_{ji} will be nonzero. Thus, one of the equations allowing for the determination of dependence coefficients will be of the form:

(15) $E(a_{1i}x_1 + \ldots + x_i + \ldots + a_{ji}x_j + a_{mi}x_m) \quad x_j = a_{1i}E(x_1 x_j) + \ldots + E(x_i x_j) + \ldots a_{ji}E(x^2_j) + \ldots + a_{mi}E(x_m x_j) = E(e_i x_j) = 0$

But to estimate the regression coefficients by the method of least squares, one has to minimize the quantity of Q where:

(16) $Q = E(a_{1i}x_1 + \ldots x_i + \ldots + a_{ji}x_j + \ldots + a_{mi}x_m)^2$

Minimizing Q implies that the so-called "normal equation," stating that the partial derivative of Q with regard to a_{ji} is zero, will be satisfied. In symbols:

(17) $\partial Q =$
$\quad \overline{\partial a_{jj}}$
$\quad 2E(a_{1i}x_1 + \ldots + x_i + \ldots + a_{ji}x_j + \ldots + a_{mi}x_m)x_j = 0$

This condition is equivalent to:

(18) $E(a_{1i}x_1 + \ldots + x_i + \ldots + a_{ji}x_j + \ldots + a_{mi}x_m)x_j = 0$

But this is precisely equation (15). Hence, the equations allowing for the determination of the dependence coefficients are the normal equations of regression analysis. Thus, we have the important result:

If a structure is identifiable, the dependence coefficients are regression coefficients; in other words, when the regression coefficients can be identified, the dependence coefficients are regression coefficients.

Wright (1934) has proved a similar theorem. But his approach through "path coefficients" prevented him from seeing the validity of the theorem in the general case. In fact, he proved it only in the case where the postulated causal structure is of the simplest possible form (a set of independent variables acting on a single dependent variable). In this case, a causal structure is always identifiable. But it may be identifiable in much more complex cases as well, and in these cases the dependence coefficients, according to the above theorem, will be regression coefficients.

WHY STANDARDIZE DEPENDENCE COEFFICIENTS?

We have now seen that the dependence coefficients are more clearly interpreted if they are standardized, i.e., if one uses

$a_{ji}(\sigma_j/\sigma_i)$ instead of a_{ji}. This procedure has one disadvantage: the standardized dependence coefficients are no longer equal to the regression coefficients, when the latter can be determined, except when all the standard deviations are equal. But this disadvantage is counterbalanced by the ease of interpretation, and also by the fact that if the unknown terms are the standardized dependence coefficients, the known terms in the equations of dependence analysis will be exclusively correlation coefficients, not variances. To see why this is so, let us go back to equation (15): if we divide the covariances by the appropriate standard deviations to get correlation coefficients, we get:

(19) $a_{1i}\sigma_1\sigma_j r_{1j}+ \; \ldots \; \sigma_i\sigma_j r_{ij}+ \; \ldots \; a_{ji}\sigma^2{}_j+$
$\ldots \; a_{mi}\sigma_m\sigma_j r_{mj}=0$

Setting $a_{1i}(\sigma_1/\sigma_i)=b_{1i}$, $a_{ji}(\sigma_j/\sigma_i)=b_{ji}$, $a_{mi}(\sigma_m/\sigma_i)=b_{mi}$, etc., $a_{1i}\sigma_i\sigma_j r_{1j}$ becomes $b_{1i}\sigma_i\sigma_j r_{1j}$; $a_{ji}\sigma^2{}_j$ becomes: $b_{ji}\sigma_i\sigma_j, \; \ldots \;$; $a_{mi}\sigma_m\sigma_j r_{mj}$ becomes $b_{mi}\sigma_i\sigma_j r_{mj}$; so that

(20) $(b_{1i}r_{1j}+ \; \ldots \; r_{ij}+ \; \ldots \; +b_{ji}+ \; \ldots$
$+b_{mi}r_{mj})\sigma_i\sigma_j=0$

But condition (20) is equivalent to:

(21) $b_{1i}r_{1i}+ \; \ldots \; +r_{ij}+ \; \ldots \; b_{ji}+ \; \ldots$
$+b_{mi}r_{mj}=0$

Thus, the equations of dependence analysis may be constructed in such a way that all the unknown terms are standardized dependence coefficients, and all the known terms, correlation coefficients.

ILLUSTRATION: BLALOCK'S FIVE-VARIABLE CASE

In "Correlation and Causality: the Multivariate Case," Blalock presents three hypothetical causal models in a five-variable situation. For the present purpose of illustration, I shall submit the third model to a dependence analysis. This model is represented in Figure 2. For the substantive meaning of the causal hypotheses embodied in this model, see Blalock 1957 and 1961.

The data . . . were taken from the 1950 Census, the units of analysis being 150 randomly selected southern counties. . . . All relationships were found to be approximately linear. . . . Variable x_1, a crude index of urbanization, is the percentage of the county's population classed as either urban or rural non-farm; x_2 represents the percentage of non-whites in the county. Variables x_3 and x_5 involve measures of white and non-white incomes, respectively (the percentage of families with annual income of 1,500 dollars or more), and x_4 is an index of non-white educational levels (percentage of males 25 and over with more than six years of schooling). (Blalock 1957:677–682)

The corresponding equations, i.e., the matrix equation $Ax=e$ in developed form, are:

(22.a) $a_{12}x_1+x_2 \qquad\qquad\qquad =e_2$
(22.b) $a_{13}x_1+a_{23}x_2+_3 \qquad\qquad =e_3$
(22.c) $a_{24}x_2 \qquad +x_4 \qquad\qquad =e_4$
(22.d) $a_{15}x_1+a_{25}x_2 \quad +a_{45}x_4+x_5 \quad =e_5$

The *a priori* conditions imply that in the $E(ex')$ matrix the elements $E(e_2x_1)$, $E(e_3x_1)$, $E(e_4x_1)$, $E(e_5x_1)$, $E(e_3x_2)$, $E(e_4x_2)$, $E(e_5x_2)$, $E(e_4x_3)$, $E(e_5x_3)$, $E(e_5x_4)$ are zero, yielding ten equations. The equation corresponding to the first zero term would be obtained by multiplying (22.a) by x_1 and taking mathematical expectations:

$$a_{12}E(x^2{}_1)+E(x_1x_2)=E(e_2x_1)=0$$

But, comparing equations (15) and (21) above, we see that we can write directly:

$$b_{12}+r_{12}=0$$

Skipping intermediate steps for other equa-

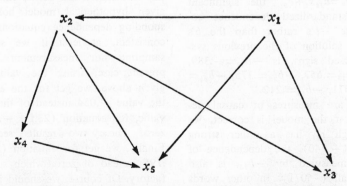

Figure 2. Blalock's Third Hypothetical Structure of Causal Connections Between Variables x_1 (Urbanization), x_2 (Percentage of Non-Whites), x_3 (White Income), x_4 (Non-White Level of Education), x_5 (Non-White Income).

tions we get the following dependence analysis equations:

(23.a) $\quad b_{12}+r_{12} \qquad\qquad\qquad =0$

(23.b) $\quad b_{13}+b_{23}r_{12}+r_{13} \qquad\quad =0$

(23.c) $\quad b_{13}r_{12}+b_{23}+r_{23} \qquad\quad =0$

(23.d) $\quad b_{24}r_{12}+r_{14} \qquad\qquad\quad =0$

(23.e) $\quad b_{24}+r_{24} \qquad\qquad\qquad =0$

(23.f) $\quad b_{24}r_{23}+r_{34} \qquad\qquad\quad =0$

(23.g) $\quad b_{15}+b_{25}r_{12}+b_{45}r_{14}+r_{15} =0$

(23.h) $\quad b_{15}r_{12}+b_{25}+b_{45}r_{24}+r_{25} =0$

(23.i) $\quad b_{15}r_{13}+b_{25}r_{23}+b_{45}r_{34}+r_{35} =0$

(23.j) $\quad b_{15}r_{14}+b_{25}r_{24}+b_{45}+r_{45} =0$

The reader may convince himself that these equations are very easily constructed, and, in spite of their number, fairly easily solved. In fact, the first equation gives b_{12}, the second and the third give b_{13} and b_{23}, etc., so that, in this case, the number of equations to be simultaneously solved never exceeds three.

(Note that the consequences one might draw from the present structure by Simon-Blalock's method are all included in system (23). Thus $r_{14.2}=0$, or $r_{14}=r_{12}r_{24}$ may be derived from (23.a) and (23.d); in the same way $r_{34.2}=0$, or $r_{34}=r_{23}r_{24}$ may be derived from (23.e) and (23.f), etc. But dependence analysis allows also for consequences that are not derivable by Simon-Blalock's method. Thus, the latter may be considered a weak form of dependence analysis, where some equations are ignored and the possibility of measuring causal dependence is lost.)

In our example, the values of the known correlation coefficients, as given by Blalock, are the following: $r_{12}=-.389$, $r_{13}=.670$, $r_{14}=$ .264, $r_{15}=.736$, $r_{23}=.067$, $r_{24}=-.531$, $r_{25}=$ $-.440$, $r_{34}=.042$, $r_{35}=.599$, $r_{45}=.386$.

Now, because the original equations were written in the form, e.g., $a_{12}x_1+x_2=e_2$, rather than $x_2=a_{12}x_1+e_2$, the significant values of the standardized dependence coefficients are the $-b$'s rather than the b's themselves. The solution of the previous system, with reversed signs, is $-b_{12}=-.389$, $-b_{13}=.792$, $-b_{15}=.657$, $-b_{23}=.375$, $-b_{24}=$ .531, $-b_{25}=-.071$, $-b_{45}=.212$.

These values are measures of causal dependence, thus, if the model is correct, we see that although r_{25} has a rather strong negative value ($-.440$), the dependence of x_5 on x_2, as measured by $-b_{25}$, is also negative but small ($-.071$). In other words the proportion of non-whites in the population has, in spite of the correlation, at most a slight depressing effect on non-white incomes. Such a result is, of course, of great importance to sociologists. It shows that dependence analysis is able to deal, not only with spurious correlations in the ordinary sense, but with what we could call partially spurious correlations.

Let us remind ourselves, however, that the validity of a dependence analysis depends on the validity of the hypothetical model. One can sometimes test the model directly by using excess dependence equations; sometimes, too, an interesting result is given, not only by one, but by several plausible models. Thus, the value of $-b_{25}$ is much smaller than the correlation r_{25} in Blalock's three hypothetical models. A dependence analysis similar to that of Blalock's third model above shows that $-b_{25}$ is about $-.101$ in the first model and about zero in the second, compared with the $-.071$ obtained above for the third. Note that in the previous system, the number of equations exceeds by three the number of unknown terms. The solution involved the following equations: (23.a) for b_{12}, (23.b) and (23.c) for b_{13} and b_{23}, (23.e) for b_{24}, (23.g), (23.h), (23.j) for b_{15}, b_{25}, b_{45}. But this leaves unused the three supplementary equations (23.d), (23.f), and (23.i). (In fact, it would have been preferable to use least squares methods to estimate dependence coefficients. But we are not willing here to complicate rationale of the method with estimation problems.) This excess of equations will appear in a dependence analysis whenever the number of causal links in a scheme is smaller than the number $n(n-1)/2$ of pairs which can be built from the n variables. An obvious advantage is that this furnishes a test of the causal model: if a given hypothetical model holds, the corresponding dependence equations should all be consistent, at least if we suppose neither sampling nor measurement error. In the present case, using the values of the b's given above, we get for the equation (23.d) the value $-.054$ instead of the expected zero value, for equation (23.f), $-.003$ instead of zero. These two results seem acceptable. Finally, we get for equation (23.i) the value .195 instead of zero, which seems less satisfactory. Of course, we should judge the goodness of fit by adequate statistical tests, but neither the particular causal model itself nor the estimation problems require attention in this practical illustration of dependence analysis.

CONCLUSION

In the preceding discussion I have solved, hopefully, a number of difficulties regarding linear causal analysis. First, I showed that the coefficients of linear causal equations are regression coefficients when the corresponding equations are identifiable; when they are not, either we can say nothing about the coefficients or we have to introduce the assumption that implicit factors are uncorrelated. We can then determine, not regression, but dependence coefficients. In other words, the concept of dependence coefficient is an extension of the concept of regression coefficient, and while the latter is defined only for identifiable structures the former is defined for both identifiable and unidentifiable structures. In the particular case where causal equations can be identified, regression coefficients may be seen as dependence coefficients. (In the same way, by referring to equation (14) one can easily see that the standardized dependence coefficients, i.e., the b's of (14), may be considered an extension of correlation coefficients.)

The idea of dependence provides us, then, with a method for measuring causal dependence between variables and for testing any particular causal structure, since, unless all pairs of variables are hypothetically connected by a causal link, the method will give more equations than unknowns, allowing thus for a straightforward test of the hypothetical structure. Thus dependence analysis is more powerful than the Simon-Blalock method.

The reader may feel, perhaps, that convincing empirical illustrations are missing; if so, the reason is that moderately complicated causal structures with corresponding data are rather scarce in the sociological literature. I hope that the present report will stimulate further efforts to integrate methodological knowledge on causality as well as a search for more complex causal structures. But I must emphasize that like the Simon-Blalock method, dependence analysis does not provide a way to derive automatically a causal structure from a set of correlation coefficients, but only a way to test a set of *a priori* causal assumptions.

APPENDIX I

Proof of the Theorem: When Implicit Factors Are Uncorrelated, the Dependence Coefficients Are Always Identifiable

Assume that the (i,j) elements of P are all nonzero, and that PA has the same structure as A. The ith equation may be linearly combined with the jth. Moreover, x_{i+1} is causally dependent on x_{j+1}: indeed, since the jth equation defines x_{j+1}, the coefficient of x_{j+1} is not zero in this equation, whence a linear combination of the ith and jth equations will retain the structure of the former only if $a_{j+1,\ i+1}$ is not zero, i.e., if x_{i+1} is causally dependent on x_{j+1}.

Now, in equation (11), premultiplication of $E(ex')$ by P, where P_{ij} is not zero, will substitute a linear combination of the ith and jth rows of $E(ex')$ for the original ith row. But, since x_{i+1} is causally dependent on x_{j+1}, the term of the $(j+1)$th column in the ith row of $E(ex')$ i.e., $E(e_{i+1}x_{j+1})$, is zero, while the term of the same $(j+1)$th column in the jth row is not zero. Hence, premultiplication by P modifies the structure of the ith row, and it is impossible to find a nondiagonal matrix P such that (11) satisfies the structural conditions of (10).

To illustrate this, let us go back to system (4). The corresponding causal structure (see Figure 1) implies $E(e_3x_1)=(e_3x_1)=E(e_3x_2)=0$. That is, using our substantive example, implicit factors acting on the extension of family group are not correlated with age, and implicit factors acting on suicide are correlated neither with age nor with extension of family group. Now, we see from (5) or (7) that we may find a nondiagonal matrix P with $P_{12}\neq 0$, such that PA has the same structure as A, and, of course, $PAE(xx')$, the same structure as $AE(xx')$ (the same coefficients are zero). Now in the equation $PAE(xx')=PE(ex')$, premultiplication by P substitutes for $E(e_3x_2)$ a quantity which we may designate $E(e'_3x_2)$ and which is equal to $E(p_{12}e_2x_2+e_3x_2)=p_{12}E(e_2x_2)+(e_3x_2)$. But, since $E(e_2x_2)$ is not zero, $E(e'_3x_2)$ is zero if and only if $p_{12}=0$. But we have assumed $p_{12} \neq 0$. Thus, premultiplication by P violates the condition derived from the assumption that implicit factors are uncorrelated, according to which x_2 and the implicit factors acting on x_3 are independent.

BIBLIOGRAPHY

BLALOCK, HUBERT M.
1957 Percent non-white and discrimination in the South. *American Sociological Review* 22:677–682.
1961 Correlation and causality: the multivariate case. *Social Forces* 39:246–251.
1962a Four-variable causal models and partial correlations. *American Journal of Sociology* 68:182–184.
1962b Further observations on asymmetric causal models. *American Sociological Review* 27:539–542.
1963 Making causal inferences for unmeasured variables from correlations among indicators. *American Journal of Sociology* 69:53–62.
1964 *Causal inferences in man-experimental research.* Chapel Hill, University of North Carolina.
BOUDON, RAYMOND
1965 A method of linear causal analysis—dependence analysis. *American Sociological Review* 30:365–374.
1967a *L'analyse mathematique des faits sociaux.* Paris, Plon.
1967b A new look at correlation analysis. In Hubert M. and Anne B. Blalock, eds., *Methodology in social research.* New York, McGraw-Hill.
1967c Methods of analysis for panel surveys. *Social Science Information* 6:115–127.
1967d Remarques sur la notion de fonction. *Revue française de Sociologie* 8:198–206.
BOUDON, RAYMOND, ALAIN DEGENNE, and FRANÇOIS ISAMBERT
1967 Mathématique et causalité en sociologie. *Revue française de Sociologie* 8:367–402.
KENDALL, PATRICIA, and PAUL F. LAZARSFELD
1950 Problems of survey analysis. In Robert K. Merton and Paul F. Lazarsfeld, eds., *Continuities in social research.* Glencoe, Ill., Free Press.
KOOPMANS, TJALLING C.
1949 Identification problems in economic model construction. *Econometrica* 17:125–144.
1950 *Statistical inference in dynamic causal models.* In Cowles Commission Monograph No. 10. New York, Wiley.
LAZARSFELD, PAUL F.
1955 The interpretation of statistical relations as a research operation. In Paul F. Lazarsfeld and Morris Rosenberg, eds., *The language of social research.* Glencoe, Ill., Free Press.
POLK, KENNETH
1962 A note on asymmetric causal models. *American Sociological Review* 27:542–545.
ROBINSON, WARREN S.
1962 Asymmetric causal models: comment on Polk and Blalock. *American Sociological Review* 27:545–548.
SIMON, HERBERT A.
1954 Spurious correlation: a causal interpretation. *Journal of the American Statistical Association* 49:467–479.
WOLD, HERMAN O.
1954 Causality and econometrica. *Econometrica* 22.
WRIGHT, SEWALL
1934 The method of path coefficients. *Annals of Mathematical Statistics* 5:161–215.
1954 The interpretation of multivariate systems. In Oscar Kemthorne, Theodore A. Bancroft, John W. Gowen, and Jay L. Lush, eds., *Statistics and mathematics in biology.* Ames, Iowa University Press.
YULE, UDNY, and MAURICE G. KENDALL
1958 *Introduction to the theory of statistics,* chap. 12. London, Charles Griffin.

INFLUENCE ANALYSIS—AN APPENDIX
Raoul Naroll

A special case of Boudon's general system offers an opportunity for adding conceptual to mathematical analysis. This case—called influence analysis—is that in which one variable is a common effect and all the other variables are independent causal factors.

Influence analysis deals only with one kind of influence situation. That situation is the one where a number of functionally unrelated but conceptually similar influences independently produce a given effect. Furthermore, taken together, the effects are additive.

Consider the diseases malaria, yellow fever, typhus, and bubonic plague. They are functionally unrelated: one can fall ill of malaria whether or not yellow fever or typhus or plague is going around the community; the mechanism of any one of these diseases depends in no way on that of the others. Yet one cannot say that the diseases are entirely unrelated; some environments may be especially good both for the Aëdes mosquito which carries yellow fever and the Anopheles mosquito which carries malaria. But while all four of the diseases are functionally unrelated, they are all conceptually similar: they are all produced by microorganisms which travel from person to person by way of insect carriers, and they all frequently cause death. Taken together, they raise the death rate. The mathematical model we have here is that of four independent variables and one dependent variable.

Influence analysis has two components, a statistical component and a logical component. The statistical analysis performs a number of tests to see whether in fact the hypothetical influences have little or no correlation with one another while all are highly correlated with the supposed effect. These tests include (1) a test of the hypothesis that the mean encorrelation (i.e., correlations between influences and effects) is significantly greater than the mean intercorrelation (i.e., correlations among the various influences); (2) a test of the hypothesis that true mean intercorrelation is zero; (3) partial correlations in which each encorrelation is controlled in turn by every supposedly irrelevant influence; and (4) factor analysis. In the factor analysis, as many significant factors are expected as there are hypothetical influences; the hypothetical effect is expected to be moderately loaded on all of these, highly loaded on none. Each of the hypothetical influences is expected to be highly loaded on one and only one factor, so that each hypothetical influence can be matched with a corresponding factor and no factor is identified with more than one hypothetical influence.

If all the foregoing tests turn out in this way (and substantially this result was obtained from my study of thwarting disorientation and suicide, Naroll 1969) and if these relations were predicted in advance of the study (as unfortunately was not true of my suicide study), no rival simple explanation of these statistical ′data is plausible. Any rival hypothesis which would explain this pattern of correlations otherwise than by supposing a cause-effect relationship between the influences and their common effect must posit a number of additional variables at work.

Now, since the number of conceivable additional variables which might be at work is infinite, we can never be sure that our probable cause-effect hypothesis is correct. However, this uncertainty differs only by degree from our uncertainty about the validity of even the best-established scientific laws, such as Einstein's theory of relativity, since Einstein's revision of Newton's laws reminded us that all scientific generalizations are tentative and subject to revision.

The logical analysis which enables us to distinguish between a validated scientific generalization and a mere speculative hypothesis is the canon of parsimony. Other things being equal, we presume that a hypothesis is correct which most parsimoniously deals with all the available evidence—which presents the simplest explanation that accounts for all the data before us. We do not require that a hypothesis account for imaginary but only for actually observed data. Consequently, once a study systematically considers a body of data, if it is consistent with a hypothetical explanation, that explanation stands as validated unless we hear some equally parsimonious rival hypothesis which might explain the data as well.

In other words, a well-conducted scientific study shifts the burden of proof from the investigator to the critic. True, the critic need not *disprove* the hypothesis, he need only produce a rival hypothesis which might with equal parsimony explain the data. Indeed, in practice we do not hold our critics to a very strict standard of parsimony; we lean in the direction of scientific caution by requiring of a critic only that he produce a rival hypothesis which might with nearly equal or almost equal parsimony explain the data. If a critic does even this, we usually feel that he has returned the burden of proof to the investigator.

This matter of the canon of parsimony and the burden of proof is the concern of the logical component of influence analysis. In this research design, if the canon of parsimony is to have its greatest weight, all the hypothetical influences need to be particular taxonomic types of one general category. For example, in my suicide study, I argue that seven traits are correlated with suicide report length while all are uncorrelated with one another. The statistical component consists in showing that this correlation pattern indeed is found by applying the four tests mentioned. The logical component consists in showing that each of these seven unrelated traits is a different example of what I call *thwarting disorientation*—a situation in which social ties are broken, weakened, or threatened in such a way that some individual person is seen by the suicide victim as plausibly to blame for his troubles.

Now, if evidence is produced suggesting that the encorrelations may be artifacts of some sort of bias in the study, this evidence becomes a plausible rival hypothesis. Since there is no intercorrelation between the supposed influences, no *one* methodological bias could explain all these results. Suppose, for example, that inexperienced field workers tend

to overestimate suicide. Take that as an example of a methodological bias. Can we suppose that perhaps such inexperienced field workers also tend to exaggerate divorce freedom, and at the same time exaggerate marriage restrictions, and at the same time exaggerate warfare frequency, and at the same time exaggerate the other three hypothetical influences? Could this single methodological bias explain the results? No. For in such a case, there would be a high intercorrelation among the supposed influences. In the factor analysis, they and the suicide scores would all be highly loaded on a single factor. The factor would be the field worker–experience factor. Thus no one methodological bias could explain *all* these results. Strictly speaking, six other factors are needed. But if a critic establishes the existence of even four or five such methodological sources of artifact, he will shift the burden of proof back to the investigator, since because of our scientific caution we will always be willing to violate the canon of parsimony a little in favor of the critic by speculating that one or two unknown factors (lurking variables) might well explain one or two of the correlations.

BIBLIOGRAPHY

NAROLL, RAOUL
  1969 Cultural determinants and the concept of the sick society. In Robert F. Edgerton and Stanley C. Plog, eds., *Changing* *perspectives in mental illness.* New York, Holt, Rinehart and Winston, pp. 128–155.

CHAPTER 6

Toward a Theory of Political Development

RAYMOND TANTER

The goals of this paper are: 1) to give a brief review of representative comparative studies of developing areas in terms of theories of political development; 2) to determine the relevance of quantitative techniques and the mathematics of causal inference for revision of such theories. One set of means employed in the paper are standard criteria of science, e.g., concept formation, theory construction and explanation. A further set of means are some techniques such as correlational, regression and factor analysis. By applying some of these criteria to the study of developing areas, it is hoped that general knowledge will be enhanced.

Concepts such as mobilization and development are found quite often in the literature without precise empirical referents. The frequency with which these two concepts occur, however, suggests that they are probably theoretically significant even though their referents are sometimes vague. Moreover, the causal sequences linking these concepts with others may not be spelled out explicitly. Hence, it may be difficult to establish the falsity of individual theories because of the lack of precision of the concepts; also, it may be hard to select among competing theories because of the vagueness of the causal orderings. By suggesting precise *tentative* operational definitions and by making explicit alternative causal orderings it is hoped that the theories can be demonstrated as false, and alternative theories can be accepted or rejected. One way of deciding whether to accept a theory is through the use of procedures such as the experimental and/or comparative methods. And when the lan-

This article is reproduced from *Midwest Journal of Political Science* 11:145–172 (1967).

guages of mathematics and statistics are used, it may be possible to make more rigorous deductions and to evaluate predictions more adequately. For example, a recent paper by Hayward R. Alker, Jr. (1966), that provided the inspiration for the present study, illustrates the use of mathematics and statistics in the comparative study of developing areas.

Both non-quantitative and quantitative studies have their origins in comparative inquiry generally. Comparative method refers to the ". . . procedures which, by clarifying the resemblances and differences displayed by phenomena . . . aim at eliciting and classifying a) causal factors in the emergence and development of such °phenomena . . . ; b) patterns of interrelation both within and between such phenomena . . ." (Gould 1964: 116–118).

A goal of the comparative method is the identification of causal factors; thus, it may be thought of as similar in aims to experimentation. Here the primary goal also is to observe invariant relations that obtain between an event to be explained (effect) and one or more initial conditions (causes). The methodology underlying both comparative and experimental methods, then, aims at a type of explanation, where an event to be explained may be deduced or inferred statistically from a set of initial conditions and one or more general laws or tendency statements (Hempel 1962:98–169). The experimental and comparative methods, then, can be used to test the deduction or causal inference. But the goal of explanation and the means of comparative method do not dictate one route by which theories may be discovered. That is, some of the choices are as follows: the *design* may aim at the verification of hypotheses and/or the initial discovery of empirical regularities; the comparisons may be made across units at one point in time (cross-sectional) or within units across time (longitudinal); the *unit* may be at the individual or group levels across a sample or a population; and the *analyses* may be *bivariate* —two variables at a time whether few or many—or *multivariate*—sets of variables are analyzed simultaneously. These distinctions regarding the over-all design, type of comparisons, time units and analyses are not exhaustive nor mutually exclusive. That is, one study may have various combinations according to the purpose of the particular inquiry. For example, a study *could* aim at both the discovery and verification of theories. Mainly discovery in this study is applied to the so-called "fishing expeditions" that aim at discovering empirical regularities among variables by making a minimum number of assumptions, e.g., the assumptions underlying the factor model in some factor analysis studies. Mainly verification is used to indicate studies which directly or indirectly aim at testing one or more hypotheses. For further elaboration of related notions, see Hanson 1958; Friedrich 1966:57–72, and especially 63–68; Snyder 1962:103–172, especially 104–105.

The following discussion, however, is presented only in terms of the principal aim of the designs: mainly theory verification or principally theory discovery.

THEORY VERIFICATION

The fruits of the verification approach to cross-national inquiry have been manifest in productive studies, such as *The Politics of Developing Areas* (Almond and Coleman 1960) and *The Passing of Traditional Society* (Lerner 1958). The key element these studies have in common is that a theory was first set up which then suggested a limited number of concepts and the relationships between them. The researchers then gathered data "to test" explicit hypotheses about these relationships and to make an evaluation of the theoretical significance of these concepts.

For example, in *The Politics of Developing Areas* Almond suggests theories containing concepts such as interest articulation and urbanization. The theoretical significance of interest articulation is examined in political

systems of Southeast Asia, South Asia, Sub-Sahara Africa, the Near East and Latin America. An illustration of the theoretical significance of interest articulation in Latin America is provided by George Blanksten (1960: 431–455; Blanksten 1965; and Mack 1965:225–242, especially 231–232).

Blanksten finds that urbanization has implications for interest articulation: "It is typical of Latin America, that, with the exception of the landowners and the Church, few interests arising in the rural areas are capable of making themselves heard in national politics. In the cities, however, interest groups form more readily and give voice to the demands of urbanized sectors of the population" (Blanksten 1960:477. See also Moore 1963:104–105; Ponsioen 1965:118–119, 126).

An explanation for the proposition that urbanization leads to interest articulation by associational groups may be found in the effect that urbanization has on the social class structure and economic development. For example, Blanksten suggests that urbanization ". . . is a major process in contemporary Latin America and a principal means of Westernization." And, ". . . technological change and economic development have been among the most spectacular forms of Westernization in Latin America." Furthermore, "Economic development weakens the once-rigid lines of separating the social classes; class mobility becomes easier and more rapid; the pastoral Indian moves from the *hacienda* to employment in emerging industries. As economic development multiplies the opportunities open to peoples of Latin America, it broadens their horizons, gives them new roles, alters their patterns of expectation" (Blanksten 1960:470–472; 1965: 131–154; Sorokin 1927 and 1959:85, 532–533; 1928 and 1956:242; Moore 1963:99; Ponsioen 1965:121). An economist provides additional evidence for Blanksten's theory as regards urbanization's direct effects upon the social structure independent of the influence of economic development. For example, Irma Adelman asserts that ". . . changes such as urbanization tend to reduce dependence upon traditional value systems and thereby increase popular receptivity to unfamiliar knowledge, value and skills" (1961:146).

If one were to translate these propositions into causal relationships, they might look like Figure 1, page 116.

Three versions of the propositions are analyzed: Simple Stages, Static Blanksten, and Dynamic Blanksten Theories. In a Simple Stages theory, level of urbanization causes the level of economic development, which in turn leads to social mobilization, and which finally results in political development. Deutsch (1961:493–514) offers a related theory whereby social mobilization causes political development. Deutsch defines mobilization, however, to include phenomena such as urbanization, which in the present study is used as one of the causes of mobilization.

The concept of political development is quite a "slippery" term in the sense that there may be slippage from the concept to the measure. One alternate is to drop the concept of political development and only deal with measures as interest articulation by association groups as well as minority representation and party competition. This writer, however, sees an obligation to find precise empirical referents for such slippery concepts. These measures may be improved or rejected through inquiry itself.

Urbanization is the percentage of population in cities greater than 20,000 for the mid 1950's (Ginsburg 1961:34). Growth rates for the test of the Dynamic Blanksten theory are found in B. Russett, H. Alker, K. Deutsch, H. Lasswell (1964:54–55). Social mobilization is measured by the percentage of the population in the mestizo class, e.g., Indians may become mestizos through intermarriage, migration to the city and adopting the mestizo culture (Blanksten 1960:462–463). The source of the class data is the *Worldmark Encyclopedia of Nations* (1960). A more adequate measure of mobilization may be the *rate* at which Indians are assimilated into the mestizo and white subcultures. In the absence of such rates, however, the proportion of the population mestizo is used as an indicator. The proportion mestizo may be an adequate indicator of mobilization because the Indians probably do not take part in the mobilization process until they become mestizos. Moreover, since "the whites are the landowners, the political leaders and government officials, the clergymen, almost all of the voters and army officers, and about ninety per cent of the people counted as literate," they are not in the process of being mobilized. (Blanksten 1960:470–472. One might say that Latin American "whites" had "arrived"

already.) Mobilization, in this sense, refers to the process whereby people are brought into new situations (as in participation in mass media) such that they become available for recommitment to a different set of values. Thus, the Indians of Latin America may not be available for recommitment while they are living in the rural areas. In addition, the "whites" may not be available for recommitment as such because they generally will accept the values of their subculture rather than share the values of the mestizos or Indians. Thus it is assumed that the higher the proportion of the population mestizo, the more rapid will be the social mobilization process, e.g., the rates at which fomer nonparticipants begin to participate in the modern media so that they become available for recommitment.

Economic development level is measured by gross national product per capita: the total value of goods and services produced in a country during the mid 1950's divided by the population as found in Ginsburg (1961:18). Growth rates for the same data are from B. Russett *et al.* (1964:160–161). Minority representation and party competition is a summed index for the years 1940–1960. The greater the minority representation in legislative bodies and the higher the interparty competition in electing executives, the more "developed" the country is said to be. The index is "a scheme for scoring the nations (in which high scores mean high development) . . . (which) penalize(s) each nation for political instability, which represents 'backsliding,' and reward(s) it for achieving or retaining more complex political forms of organization" (Cutright 1963:253–264, 256). A second measure of political development is interest articulation by associational groups as suggested by Gabriel Almond and coded by Arthur Banks (Almond and Coleman 1960:34; Banks and Textor 1963: 89–90). "Associational interest groups are the specialized structures of interest articulation—trade unions, organizations of businessmen or industrialists, . . . Their particular characteristics are explicit representation of the interests of a particular group, orderly procedures for the formulation of interests and demands, and transmission of these demands to other political structures such as political parties, legislatures, bureaucracies" (Almond and Coleman 1960:34). It is hoped that the measures of interest articulation by associational groups and political representation and party competition, by covering interest groups, parties, legislatures and the executives, might *approximate* part of what is meant by the concept of political development. (No reliability tests were conducted on the two measures of the dependent variable, political development, an important step in developing reliable concepts. Cutright's rules for coding are explicit enough for reliability to be conducted, but Banks does not give as much information on his coding procedure.)

A second version of the propositions, Static Blanksten theory, is a more complex formulation. Here, the *level* of urbanization causes the *level* of economic development and social mobilization; economic development causes social mobilization; and social mobilization causes minority representation and party competition as well as interest articulation by associational groups. A third version, Dynamic Blanksten theory, substitutes growth rates in urbanization and economic development. Tables 1 and 2 contain the correlations and number of nations for each pair of the variables in the three theories. The highest

correlations in Table 1 are with the levels of urbanization and economic development, r=.63; urbanization level and interest articulation by association groups, r=.72; and urbanization level and minority representation/party competition, r=.47. All three correlations are across nineteen nations. No significance tests are applied because the sample is not selected randomly. All distributions are normal, however. Assuming a randomly selected sample, all three correlations *would be* significant at the .05 level of confidence. That is, only five times in one hundred would correlations of that size be expected on the basis of chance.

In contrast to Table 1, Table 2 has only one correlation that would be significant at the .05 level were the assumptions met: r=.61 between urban economic growth across nineteen nations. Also the fewer number of nations for which growth data were available results generally in smaller cases for each of the ten correlations in Table 2. The fact that the correlations generally are low is not as important given the purposes of the present study. That is, an aim is to select among

TABLE 1

CORRELATIONS ACROSS LATIN AMERICAN NATIONS (LEVELS)

Measures[a]	1	2	3	4	5
1. Urbanization Level		.63	—.36	.72	.47
2. Economic Development Level	19		—.30	.42	.29
3. Social Mobilization	16	17		—.26	—.13
4. Interest Articulation	19	20	17		.34
5. Representation/Competition	19	20	17	20	

[a] See text for definitions. The decimal figures (to the right of the principal diagonal) refer to the product moment correlation coefficients. All continuous variables are distributed normally. Variable #4 is a dichotomous measure, where 0=low and 1=high. The point biserial coefficient is obtained when X_4 is paired with the other four variables. To the left of the diagonal are the number of nations upon which the corresponding correlation is based. Although significance tests are not used in the present study, an r of .45 would be significant at the .05 level with an N of 15.

TABLE 2

CORRELATIONS ACROSS LATIN AMERICAN NATIONS (GROWTH)

Measures[a]	1	2	3	4	5
1. Urban Growth		.61	—.03	.17	.31
2. Economic Growth	13		.13	.39	.31
3. Social Mobilization	8	13		—.26	—.13
4. Interest Articulation	9	14	17		.34
5. Representation/Competition	9	14	17	20	

[a] See note in Table 1.

competing versions of a theory linking the same concepts.

Consequently, the theoretical and mathematical assumptions that allow for setting certain of the coefficients equal to zero to achieve a condition where the causal system yields deductions that certain relationships should be zero are of more concern for the moment. Nonetheless, higher correlations would add to the likelihood that the theories are true.

The mathematical equations upon which are based the deductions and predictions in Figure 1 are given in the texts below. (For a more complete discussion of simultaneous equations and causal relationships see Simon 1957; Wold and Jureen 1953; Johnston 1963; Blalock 1960, 1961a, 1962a, 1962b, 1964, 1965. Further technical discussion and applications have been written as well: Polk, Blalock and Robinson 1962:539–547; Simon 1954: 467–479; Beyle 1965:111–116; Cnudde and McCrone 1966:66–72.)

Briefly, the basic mathematical notion is that there is a hierarchical causal relationship. That is, there is a ranking of endogenous variables (within a causal system) defined only by other endogenous variables on which they are dependent singly and in terms of exogenous variables. The highest rank goes to the first causes; these depend only on exogenous variables and residual terms, which are assumed to be uncorrelated. Lower ranked endogenous variables are assumed to depend unilaterally on higher ranked endogenous variables, exogenous variables as well as uncorrelated residual terms. Each variable is defined recursively, i.e., by higher ranked variables, thus the dependent variable cannot cause the independent ones and it is possible to estimate the coefficients of such an equation without taking other equations into account (see Alker 1965:112–129; 1966; Blalock 1964:54–59). There are procedures that can handle reciprocal or feedback causation as well.

Statistically, these mathematical notions can be expressed in terms of the language of partial correlation and regression analysis. The coefficients of any equation in hierarchical systems with uncorrelated random terms can be estimated by least squares without taking other equations into account explicitly. (Least squares is a technique for minimizing the sum of the squared deviations around a line. That is, for any set of points,

there is a line of "best fit," i.e., it minimizes the squared deviation of the points around it. The points in this case would be the intersections of a nation's values on any two variables [Ezekial and Fox 1959:61–63]. The slope, bxy, gives you the predicted change in X for each unit change in Y. The partial slope gives the change in X predicted by Y controlling for or partialing out the effects of other variables [Ezekial and Fox 1959:152–154].) *That is, the partial slopes or net regression coefficients with a hierarchy should be zero if all of the variables of higher causal order are controlled, i.e., partialed out. Moreover, when the net regression coefficient is zero, the corresponding partial correlation is zero as well. Thus the deductions from the theory can be translated into predictions.* That is, $b_{13.2}=0$ is equivalent to $r_{13.2}=0$, thus $r_{13}=r_{12}r_{23}$. In other words, if the partial slope of urbanization on social mobilization holding economic development constant is zero, then the partial correlation is also zero because the numerators are the same for the correlation and regression coefficients. The "dot" means "holding constant." The equation for the first order partial correlation coefficient is:

$$r_{13.2}=\frac{r_{13}-r_{12}r_{23}}{\sqrt{1-r^2_{12}}\ \sqrt{1-r^2_{23}}}$$

The only way for $r_{13.2}$ to be zero is for r_{13} to equal $r_{12}r_{32}$, which is the prediction from the deduction that $r_{13.2}=0$.

The results column of Figure 1 gives the degree of fit for the Simple Stages, Static Blanksten and Dynamic Blanksten theories. While the method does not establish the truth or falsity of either, it does allow for the revision and selection between them.

In the Simple Stages theory, the fit that most approximates the theoretical expectations as indicated by the arrows is that between level of urbanization and social mobilization, holding level of economic development constant. The results compare −.36 with −.19. On the other hand, the fit that least approximates the theoretical expectations is that between urbanization and interest articulation, holding level of economic development *and* social mobilization constant. These results contrast .72 with .05, a difference of .67. To the extent that interest articulation and minority representation/party competition are supposed to measure political development, it appears as if Cutright's minor-

Figure 1
THREE CAUSAL THEORIES OF POLITICAL DEVELOPMENT

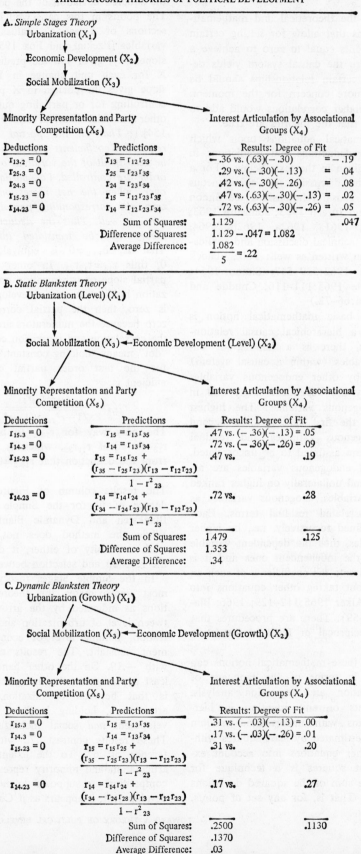

A. *Simple Stages Theory*

Urbanization (X_1)

Economic Development (X_2)

Social Mobilization (X_3)

Minority Representation and Party Competition (X_5)

Interest Articulation by Associational Groups (X_4)

Deductions	Predictions	Results: Degree of Fit	
$r_{13.2} = 0$	$r_{13} = r_{12}r_{23}$	$-.36$ vs. $(.63)(-.30)$	$= -.19$
$r_{25.3} = 0$	$r_{25} = r_{23}r_{35}$	$.29$ vs. $(-.30)(-.13)$	$= .04$
$r_{24.3} = 0$	$r_{24} = r_{23}r_{34}$	$.42$ vs. $(-.30)(-.26)$	$= .08$
$r_{15.23} = 0$	$r_{15} = r_{12}r_{23}r_{35}$	$.47$ vs. $(.63)(-.30)(-.13)$	$= .02$
$r_{14.23} = 0$	$r_{14} = r_{12}r_{23}r_{34}$	$.72$ vs. $(.63)(-.30)(-.26)$	$= .05$

Sum of Squares: 1.129 $\qquad$ $.047$

Difference of Squares: $1.129 - .047 = 1.082$

Average Difference: $\dfrac{1.082}{5} = .22$

B. *Static Blanksten Theory*

Urbanization (Level) (X_1)

Social Mobilization (X_3) ← Economic Development (Level) (X_2)

Minority Representation and Party Competition (X_5)

Interest Articulation by Associational Groups (X_4)

Deductions	Predictions	Results: Degree of Fit	
$r_{15.3} = 0$	$r_{15} = r_{13}r_{35}$	$.47$ vs. $(-.36)(-.13) = .05$	
$r_{14.3} = 0$	$r_{14} = r_{13}r_{34}$	$.72$ vs. $(-.36)(-.26) = .09$	
$r_{15.23} = 0$	$r_{15} = r_{15}r_{25} + \dfrac{(r_{35} - r_{25}r_{23})(r_{13} - r_{12}r_{23})}{1 - r^2{}_{23}}$	$.47$ vs.	$.19$
$r_{14.23} = 0$	$r_{14} = r_{14}r_{24} + \dfrac{(r_{34} - r_{24}r_{23})(r_{13} - r_{12}r_{23})}{1 - r^2{}_{23}}$	$.72$ vs.	$.28$

Sum of Squares: 1.479 $\qquad$ $.125$

Difference of Squares: 1.353

Average Difference: $.34$

C. *Dynamic Blanksten Theory*

Urbanization (Growth) (X_1)

Social Mobilization (X_3) ← Economic Development (Growth) (X_2)

Minority Representation and Party Competition (X_5)

Interest Articulation by Associational Groups (X_4)

Deductions	Predictions	Results: Degree of Fit	
$r_{15.3} = 0$	$r_{15} = r_{13}r_{35}$	$.31$ vs. $(-.03)(-.13) = .00$	
$r_{14.3} = 0$	$r_{14} = r_{13}r_{34}$	$.17$ vs. $(-.03)(-.26) = .01$	
$r_{15.23} = 0$	$r_{15} = r_{15}r_{25} + \dfrac{(r_{35} - r_{25}r_{23})(r_{13} - r_{12}r_{23})}{1 - r^2{}_{23}}$	$.31$ vs.	$.20$
$r_{14.23} = 0$	$r_{14} = r_{14}r_{24} + \dfrac{(r_{34} - r_{24}r_{28})(r_{13} - r_{12}r_{23})}{1 - r^2{}_{23}}$	$.17$ vs.	$.27$

Sum of Squares: $.2500$ $\qquad$ $.1130$

Difference of Squares: $.1370$

Average Difference: $.03$

ity representation/party competition may be a more adequate measure for the Simple Stages theory. Consider the fit of $r_{15.23}=0$ with $r_{14.23}=0$. The prediction using Cutright's measure is off .45, whereas the prediction using the interest measure is off .67. Both measures, however, are explained poorly by the Simple Stages theory. An over-all impression of the degree of fit for this theory can be obtained by summing the squares of the two major columns under results, obtaining the difference and dividing by the total number of rows. For example, after squaring to remove minus signs, one obtains a difference of 1.082. Dividing by five (for the total number of rows), one obtains the average of the difference: .22. This average difference can be compared with the average differences for the other theories. For the Static Blanksten theory, the average difference is .34; Dynamic Blanksten yields an average difference of only .03. This theory asserts that urban growth leads to economic growth and social mobilization, economic growth leads to social mobilization, and social mobilization leads to both interest articulation by associational groups as well as minority representation/party competition. Here, the interest measure yields a more adequate fit than the representation/competition variable.

Figure 2 contains the Revised Simple Stages, Static Blanksten and Dynamic Blanksten theories. The revision of Simple Stages is based upon the assumption that a consequence of interest articulation by associational groups might be to raise the level of minority representation and interparty competition. The average difference does, in fact, go down from .22 to .17 in the revised version. The Static Blanksten theory also improves the fit—the average difference goes down from .34 in Figure 1 to .27 in Figure 2. Here the level of urbanization leads to the level of economic development which leads to social mobilization, interest articulation by associational groups and minority representation/party competition. Social mobilization, thus, affects interest articulation and representation and competition. Almost a perfect fit, moreover, is obtained with the Revised Dynamic Blanksten theory. The average difference is only .02. This theory is the same as the Revised Static Blanksten, with the important exception that the urbanization and economic development variables are rates over time. Thus, the Original or Revised Dynamic Blanksten theories are selected tentatively over the other theories in Figures 1 and 2. (The technique of obtaining the average between theories is admittedly a crude device for obtaining an over-all impression of the adequacy of alternative theories. Significance tests of the size of supposedly zero partial correlations may be applicable if sampling, variance and normality assumptions are met.)

In addition to *The Politics of Developing Areas* (Almond and Coleman 1960) from which the Blanksten theory was selected as representative of the theories contained therein, Lerner (1958; 1957:266–275) presents a theory of political development (participation). He asserts that ". . . the Western model of modernization exhibits certain components and sequences whose relevance is global. Everywhere, for example, increasing urbanization has tended to raise literacy; rising literacy has tended to increase media exposure; increasing media exposure has 'gone with' wider economic participation (per capita income) and political participation (voting)" (Lerner 1958:46). Whether Lerner's theory is called a theory of political development or participation does not matter for the causal analysis to follow. Calling it participation development would round out the definition to include individual participation in elections, interest groups, parties and the executive as well as legislative representation. Furthermore, Lerner adds that "the secular evolution of a participant society appears to involve a regular sequence of three phases. Urbanization comes first, for cities alone have developed the complex of skills and resources which characterize the modern industrial economy. Within this urban matrix develop both of the attributes which distinguish the next two phases—literacy and media growth. There is a close reciprocal relationship between these, for the literate develop the media which in turn spread literacy. . . . Out of this interaction develop those institutions of participation (e.g., voting) which we find in all advanced modern societies" (Lerner 1958:60). For the purposes of this study, Lerner's statements that media has "gone with" economic participaton and the one concernng reciprocity of literacy and media are reinterpreted in light of the one-way causal assumptions.

Figure 2
THREE REVISED CAUSAL THEORIES OF POLITICAL DEVELOPMENT

A. *Revised Simple Stages Theory*

Urbanization (X_1)

↓

Economic Development (X_2)

↓

Social Mobilization (X_3)

↓

Interest Articulation by Associational Groups (X_4)

↓

Minority Representation and Party Competition (X_5)

Deduction	Predictions	Results: Degree of Fit	
$r_{13.2} = 0$	$r_{13} = r_{12}r_{28}$	$-.36$ versus $(.63)(-.30)$	$= .19$
$r_{24.3} = 0$	$r_{24} = r_{23}r_{34}$	$.42$ vs. $(-.30)(-.26)$	$= .08$
$r_{35.4} = 0$	$r_{35} = r_{34}r_{45}$	$-.13$ vs. $(-.26)(.34)$	$= .09$
$r_{14.23} = 0$	$r_{14} = r_{12}r_{23}r_{34}$	$.72$ vs. $(.63)(-.30)(-.26)$	$= .05$
$r_{25.34} = 0$	$r_{25} = r_{23}r_{35}r_{45}$	$.29$ vs. $(-.30)(-.26)(.34)$	$= .03$

Sum of Squares: .925   .054

Difference of Squares: .871

Average Difference: .17

B. *Revised Static Blanksten Theory*

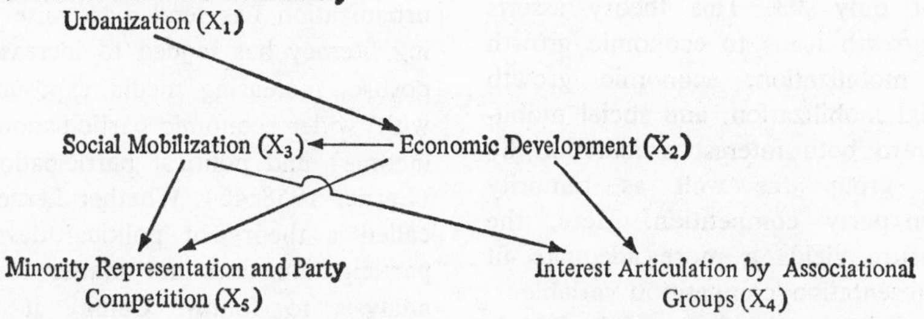

Urbanization (X_1)

Social Mobilization (X_3) ←——— Economic Development (X_2)

Minority Representation and Party Competition (X_5)   Interest Articulation by Associational Groups (X_4)

Deductions	Predictions	Results: Degree of Fit	
$r_{13.2} = 0$	$r_{13} = r_{12}r_{23}$	$-.36$ versus	$-.19$
$r_{14.2} = 0$	$r_{14} = r_{12}r_{42}$	$.72$ vs.	$.26$
$r_{15.2} = 0$	$r_{15} = r_{12}r_{25}$	$.47$ vs.	$.18$
$r_{15.23} = 0$	$r_{15} = r_{12}r_{25}$	$.47$ vs.	$.18$
$r_{14.28} = 0$	$r_{14} = r_{12}r_{24}$	$.72$ vs.	$.26$

Sum of Squares: 1.608   .236

Difference of Squares: 1.372

Average Difference: .27

C. *Revised Dynamic Blanksten Theory*

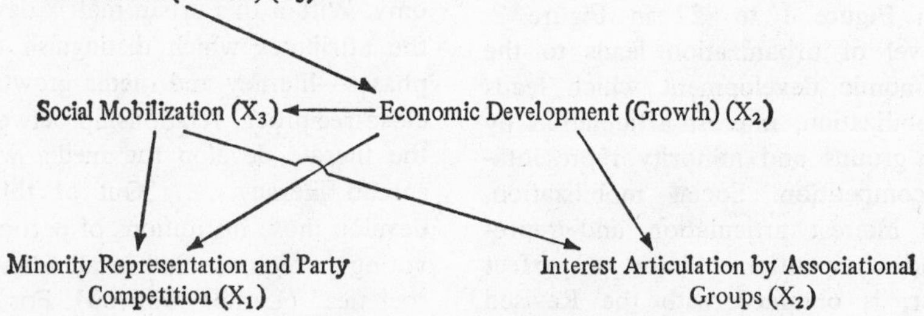

Urbanization (Growth) (X_3)

Social Mobilization (X_3) ←——— Economic Development (Growth) (X_2)

Minority Representation and Party Competition (X_1)   Interest Articulation by Associational Groups (X_2)

Deductions	Predictions	Results: Degree of Fit	
$r_{13.2} = 0$	$r_{13} = r_{12}r_{23}$	$-.03$ vs. $(.61)(.13)$	$= .08$
$r_{14.2} = 0$	$r_{14} = r_{12}r_{42}$	$.17$ vs. $(.61)(.39)$	$= .24$
$r_{15.2} = 0$	$r_{15} = r_{12}r_{25}$	$.31$ vs. $(.61)(.31)$	$= .19$
$r_{14.23} = 0$	$r_{14} = r_{12}r_{24}$	$.17$ vs. $(.61)(.31)$	$= .19$
$r_{15.28} = 0$	$r_{15} = r_{12}r_{25}$	$.31$ vs. $(.61)(.31)$	$= .19$

Sum of Squares: .2509   .1638

Difference of Squares: .0871

Average Difference: .02

Table 3

MULTIPLE CORRELATIONS OF DANIEL LERNER 1949–50 DATA
(N=54)

Dependent Variable[a]	Multiple R	R^2 (X100)[b]
X_1 Urbanization	.61	37
X_2 Literacy	.91	83
X_3 Media Participation	.84	71
X_4 Political Participation	.82	67
		258/4=64.5 per cent

[a] Urbanization—proportion living in cities over 50,000.
Literacy—proportion able to read in one language.
Media Participation—proportion buying newspapers, owning radios, and attending cinemas.
Electoral Participation—proportion actually voting in national elections (averaged over five most recent elections, Lerner, *op. cit.*, pp. 54–68).

[b] By squaring the R's, multiplying by 100 to remove the decimals, summing and dividing by the number of variables (4), one is able to get the percentage of variance that the four variables have in common. The R^2 (X100) column was added to the original table in Lerner to aid the interpretation.

Lerner employs multiple correlational analysis to test the interrelationship of the four variables, but he does not provide a sufficient test of the phasing. Table 3 contains his findings where each of the four measures takes a turn as the dependent variable being predicted by the other three. As can be seen from the multiple correlations and the average per cent of total variance in common, the four measures are interrelated highly. For example, when political participation is predicted by urbanization, literacy and media participation, the multiple correlation is .82 across fifty-four nations. This means approximately 67 per cent of the variation in political participation can be explained by urbanization, literacy and media participation.

Howard Alker does provide tests of the causal sequence for Lerner's theory. Alker builds cumulatively upon Lerner's analysis by applying the Simon/Blalock technique for inferring causality to select between a Simple Stages theory, the Lerner theory and a Revised Lerner theory (Alker 1966). Figure 3 contains the causal arrows for the three theories. Table 4 presents the predictions and the results for the causal analysis using three sets of data.

The first set is Alker's data for eighty-five nations for the late 1950's. His urbanization and literacy are from the *World Handbook* (Russett, Alker, Deutsch and Lasswell 1964: 51–53, 222–223). Media development is a factor index based on per capita radio, newspapers, telephones, as well as other data de-

rived from the *World Handbook* and other sources. Political participation data has two basic ingredients: *World Handbook* data on percentage voting turnout (Russett, Alker, Deutsch and Lasswell, 1964:84–87) and Banks and Textor codes for political enculturation (Banks and Textor 1963:87–88). Banks coded a nation high on political enculturation if it was an integrated and homogeneous polity with little or no extreme opposition, communalism, fractionalism, disenfranchisement or political nonassimilation.

The second set comes from the data of the factor analysis of 236 variables across eighty-two nations in the mid 1950's of the Dimensionality of Nations (DON) project (Rummel, n.d.). The urbanization variable is the same as in the Alker data, both of which come from Ginsburg's *Atlas* (1961). The literacy data for DON uses ten years of age as the base, whereas for the *World Handbook*, fifteen years is used. Media development in DON is measured by newspaper circulation per capita. The political development measure is the Cutright index discussed during the test of Blanksten's theory (Cutright 1963).

The Cutright data for urbanization is the proportion of the population living in cities over 100,000; his communications index is a sum of per capita newspaper readers, newsprint consumption, domestic mail and telephones (data were transformed to allow summing); an education index is a sum of literacy with the number of students per 100,000 enrolled in institutions of higher education.

Figure 3

THREE CAUSAL THEORIES OF NATIONAL POLITICAL PARTICIPATION LEVELS
$(N = 85)^a$

A. *Simple Stages Theory*

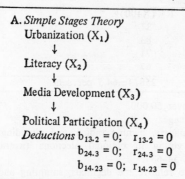

Urbanization (X_1)
↓
Literacy (X_2)
↓
Media Development (X_3)
↓
Political Participation (X_4)

Deductions $b_{13.2} = 0$; $r_{13.2} = 0$
$b_{24.3} = 0$; $r_{24.3} = 0$
$b_{14.23} = 0$; $r_{14.23} = 0$

B. *Lerner Theory*

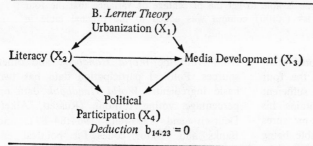

Urbanization (X_1)

Literacy (X_2) ⟶ Media Development (X_3)

Political Participation (X_4)

Deduction $b_{14.23} = 0$

C. *Revised Lerner Theory*

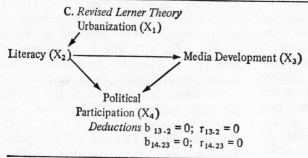

Urbanization (X_1)

Literacy (X_2) ⟶ Media Development (X_3)

Political Participation (X_4)

Deductions $b_{13.2} = 0$; $r_{13.2} = 0$
$b_{14.23} = 0$; $r_{14.23} = 0$

a Reprinted from Alker in 1966.

These data are for the late 1950's across seventy-seven nations. Although there is some overlap in the data from the three studies, and United Nations sources are used primarily by each study, it is interesting to compare the studies in terms of Lerner's theory and the mathematical assumption. The Cutright, DON and Alker data may be ranked in that order if the differences were summed across predictions, but the small range separating the data is exciting evidence of convergence and comparability. The differences may reflect the manner in which the data were combined as in the Alker media development index and Cutright's communications index as contrasted with the DON single measure

of per capita newspaper circulation. Moreover, the dependent variables are the same in the Cutright and DON data—the index of political development; but it is different in the Alker data—political participation levels. Even though this comparison was not perfect, these differences are slight when juxtaposed with the congruity. The analyses of the Blanksten and Lerner theories are examples of the application of causal inference techniques to studies characterized mainly within the theory verification approach. A further set of studies are classified as principally Theory Discovery, and an effort is made to show how the two types of studies may complement one another.

TABLE 4
PREDICTIONS AND RESULTS FOR LERNER'S
THEORY OF NATIONAL POLITICAL PARTICIPATION

Predictions	Results: Degree of Fit		
Theory A	Alker	DON	Cutright
$r_{13} = r_{12} r_{23}$	.41 vs. .41	.76 vs. .67	.74 vs. .68
$r_{24} = r_{23} r_{34}$	.66 vs. .24	.75 vs. .64	.74 vs. .71
$r_{14} = r_{12} r_{23} r_{34}$	.42 vs. .12	.65 vs. .47	.69 vs. .55

Theory B

$$r_{14} = r_{12} r_{24} + \frac{(r_{34} r_{24} r_{23})(r_{13} - r_{12} r_{23})}{1 - r^2_{23}}$$

	.42 vs. .46	.65 vs. .58	.69 vs. .61

Theory C
Same as first prediction in Theory A
Same as prediction in Theory B

THEORY DISCOVERY

In contrast to the verification approach in comparative research, the pioneering cross-national correlation and factor analyses by a psychologist, Raymond Cattell (1949; 1950; Raymond Cattell et al. 1951); a geographer, Brian Berry (1961; 1960); a demographer, Leo Schnore (1961); and political scientists Philip Gregg and Arthur Banks (1965), as well as Bruce Russett (1966), have been geared more to the discovery of theory. It is in this category that the team efforts of the *Atlas of Economic Development* (Ginsburg 1961) the *World Handbook* (Russett et al. 1964), *A Cross Polity Survey* (Banks and Gregg 1965), and the *Dimensions of Nations* (Rummel, n.d.) belong. In these studies no over-all theory is presented. In the selection of variables, however, attention was paid to existing social, economic and political theories. Furthermore, theories were drawn upon to aid in the interpretation of the high interrelationships among the certain variables that clustered together (factors).

What do these studies have to say concerning the interdependency of urbanization, measures of social mobilization, economic and political development expected on the basis of the Blanksten and Lerner theories? In the first Cattell study (1949), the data referred to the period 1837–1937; he analyzed seventy-two variables across sixty-nine nations. Urbanization (frequency of cities over 20,000 per 1,000,000 population, 1927–1937) is associated with a factor on which ratio of service to agricultural occupations also is associated. A factor independent of the one on which urbanization is associated contains a measure of real standard of living, however (Cattell 1949:459–461). Similarly, in a follow-up study where most of the nations with missing data were removed, urbanization and economic development again are on separate factors (Cattell et al. 1951:414–418). But in Berry's analysis, a technological pattern emerged on which are found measures of accessibility, transportation, technology, industrialization, urbanization and the organization of the population (Berry 1960:88; 1961: 113). In addition to Berry, Schnore finds urbanization and development measures highly associated. Schnore selected eleven economic development variables presumably related to urbanization and factored them across seventy-five nations for the early 1950's. The first factor accounted for 90 per cent of the variation in the twelve variables. The variables in order of magnitude of association with the factor are energy consumption, newspaper circulation, motor vehicles, physicians per capita, metropolitanization, literacy, urbanization, non-extractive industry, income per capita, international trade and population growth. The latter was associated only slightly with the others, however. In interpreting his findings, Schnore asserts that this factor might be labeled modernization because of the tight cluster of distinct measures of development and urbanization. Although his analysis is at one point in time, Schnore speculates that ". . . *increasing agglomeration of population in large units would seem to be an intrinsic part of general economic development"* (Schnore 1961:238; italics in original).

Whereas Schnore's study dealt with only twelve variables, Bruce Russett factored fifty-four variables across eighty-two countries for the late 1950's. Russett labeled the first factor economic development. It pulled together the gross national product per capita, measures of media development, literacy, urbanization and a measure of political participation —proportion voting in national elections. The latter, however, is associated only moderately with the economic development factor. In the DON factor analysis of 236 variables across eighty-two nations for the mid 1950's, a general development dimension also emerged. This brought together the same kinds of economic, social and political measures as Russett's (Rummel, n.d.). And in the research using *A Cross Polity Survey,* Gregg and Banks report: "In an earlier factor analysis involving all fifty-seven polychotomous characteristics of the *Survey* and an eleven factor solution, four non-political factors ('Economic Development,' 'Size,' 'Population Density,' and 'Religion') emerged. . . ." The four non-political factors closely correspond to factors identified by Berry (1960, 1961); Rummel (n.d.); Russett (1966); Gregg and Banks (1965:604 fn. 15). A further study is Soares (1964). Soares finds an economic development factor across the states, within Brazil and Venezuela. Urbanization is part of the factor. Soares partials out urbanization, and finds a negative correlation between industrialization and Communist voting (14–16).

The evidence from the Berry; Schnore; Russett; Rummel; as well as Gregg and Banks studies suggests a close interdependency among the measures of urbanization, indicators of social mobilization, and measures of economic and political development. But can the causal *dependency* be explored as precisely by factor analysis as was done with the mathematics of causal inference and the multiple regression and correlation techniques? Although the mathematics underlying the factor model is isomorphic with that of regression analysis, factor analysis is used rarely in causal inference.

The basic equation for factor analysis may be written for the value of variable z_j in standard form for a particular individual $i (i = 1, 2 . . . N)$; i.e.,

$$z_j = a_{j1}F_{1i} = a_{j2}F_{2i} + . . . + {}_{ajm}Fmi + a_jU_{ji}$$

where $F_1, F, . . . Fm$ are m common factors, $U, U_2 . . . U n$ are unique factors, and $a_{j1}, a_{j2}, . . . a_{jm}$ are the loadings or correlations or the variables with the factors. There are n equations of this form, one for each of n variables. Any of these equations may be considered as a classical regression equation, where the dependent variable is the observed variable and the independent variables are the hypothetical factors, i.e.,

$$z_j = B_{j1}F_1 + B_{j2}F_2 + . . . + B_{jm}F_m + B_jU_j \ (j = 1, 2 . . . , n),$$

where z is used to designate the best least squares fit to the obtained variable z and the subscripts are arranged that the position of any regression coefficient is determined uniquely. But the factors are not observed variables as in ordinary regression analysis.

Indeed, Blalock asserts that when used as a causal model, factor analysis is a very restrictive technique. Here, it is ". . . assumed that there are no direct causal links among the indicator variables and that . . . measured variables are caused by the (factor) . . . making the intercorrelations among the indicators completely spurious." Blalock also asks: What if some of the measured variables were also caused by certain of the remaining ones? This would imply that there would be significant intercorrelation remaining after all factors had been extracted (Blalock 1964: 167–168).

Utilizing formulae suggested by Louis Guttman, however, one might be able to obtain evidence regarding the direct causal links among Blalock's indicator variables. That is, one can compute partial regression and correlation coefficients from factor loadings for any pair of variables holding all $n-2$ other variables constant (Guttman 1940:75–99; Guttman and Cohen 1933:169–183).

A statistical version of one of the matrix algebra formulae is as follows:

$$r_{jk.(n-2)} = \sum_{F=1}^{m} \frac{a_j^{F_1} a_k^{F_1}}{\tau F_1}$$

That is, the partial correlation in a factor matrix between any two variables $j, k,$ holding all other variables in the matrix constant $(n - 2)$, is equal to the products of the factor loadings $(a_j^{F_1} a_k^{F_1})$ divided by the eigenvalues (τ) of the respective factors summed across factors, 1 through $m,$ where *m* equals the total number of factors in the unrotated solution. For the mathematical assumptions underlying this formula, see the two articles by Guttman above.

Even though the partials may be computed directly from the loadings, certain *a priori* assumptions still have to be made in order to obtain more equations than unknowns so that deductions and predictions can be made, e.g., some of the coefficients are set equal to zero. To make causal inferences one thus needs "overidentification." The assumptions of temporal sequence and uncorrelated error terms, for example, yield the extra equations that allow for the deductions.

An important consequence for theory construction may emerge from being able to compute the partial coefficients directly from the factors. That is, rather than restricting oneself to only the variables explicitly included in a causal system, and assuming that the excluded variables are uncorrelated among themselves and do not thereby distort the causal inference, one might obtain evidence for or against that assumption by seeing whether the partials vanish when variables not explicitly included in a causal analysis are in fact controlled.

A preliminary examination was conducted for the variables in the Blanksten and Lerner theories above. But the tentativeness of the test precludes drawing strict conclusions at this time. The partial correlations were computed directly from the loadings. In each case the partials vanished, suggesting that the intercorrelations among the measures were either due to underlying factors and/or that the causal analysis of a small number of variables should try to take into account outside variables that may in fact distort the causal inference.

In addition to trying to use factor analysis to obtain partials that may aid causal inferences based upon regression techniques, factor analysis findings themselves may be used to complement those arrived at by regression. In a pilot study, George Blanksten, Raymond Tanter and Lawrence Alschuler conducted a factor analysis across Latin American nations, the results of which may complement the Revised Dynamic Blanksten theory in Figure 2 (Tanter and Alschuler 1965). In principle, one could make predictions concerning the kind of factors one expects, but these predictions generally cannot be made as precisely as is done with the causal inference techniques. That is, it is difficult to set some of the factor loadings equal to zero which would allow certain deductions and predictions as in the case of the causal inference techniques. But factor analysis can suggest which variables one should include in a causal analysis. For example, variables that load highly on different factors are probably not causally related. Moreover, factor analysis prior to regression can aid in the selection of relatively uncorrelated predictors of a dependent variable.

The variables were selected on the basis of concepts used in theories of political development, especially some of those suggested by Almond and Coleman (1960). Data were drawn from the same sources used in analyzing the Static and Dynamic Blanksten theories. Table 5 contains three of the six factors from this pilot study. The six factors accounted for 82.3 per cent of the variance in the thirty-six measures. Each factor may be thought of as a set of highly associated variables that are unrelated generally to other sets. The factor loadings indicated correlations of variables with a factor. These loadings vary between -1.0 and $+1.0$ as does the correlation coefficient if the variables have similar distributions, which is the case.

Mesa 3 computer program was used for the factor analysis. Principal components technique was employed. Unities were inserted in the diagonal of the correlation matrix before factoring. The number of significant factors extracted and rotated is equal to those whose eigenvalues are 1.00. An eigenvalue is a root of a characteristic equation and is equal to the sum of the squares of a factor column (loadings) in the unrotated case. Orthogonal rotation was conducted, i.e., the factors were fitted to clusters of variables with the restriction that the correlation between the factors is zero. The varimax criterion was used to rotate orthogonally to simple structure, i.e., the maximization of high and low loadings. The per cent of total variance under each column is that portion of the variance in all variables which that factor extracts.

From these three factors, the following tentative propositions are offered. As regards

TABLE 5

FACTOR ANALYSIS OF 36 POLITICAL, ECONOMIC, AND SOCIAL VARIABLES ACROSS LATIN AMERICAN NATIONS

FACTOR II	
Factor Loading	Variable[a]
.79	Aggregation by legislature
.72	Per cent population white
.61	Political development (Cutright index)
.58	Gross national product per capita
.58	Per cent population urban (cities≧20,000)
−.56	Per cent growth in rural population
−.58	Per cent population Indian
−.70	Articulation by nonassociational groups
−.74	Per cent population in agriculture
−.82	Articulation by institutional groups
−.94	Articulation by anomic groups
19.00% of total variance	

FACTOR III	
Factor Loading	Variable
1.07[b]	Total urban growth (cities≧20,000)
.95	Medium size urban growth (cities≧10,000≦100,000)
.68	Gross national product per capita (GNP-PC)
.55	Growth in GNP-PC
.50	Aggregation by parties
12% of total variance	

FACTOR IV	
Factor Loading	Variable
1.04	Large size urban growth (cities>100,000)
.88	Per cent decrease in agriculture population
.82	Aggregation by executive
−.50	Political development (Cutright index)
−.47	Per cent of population with 50% of the land
11% of total variance	

[a] See Almond and Coleman 1960; Banks and Textor 1965 for definitions of variables that are not given in the text above. The number of nations ranged between 5 and 20; most correlations however, were based on an N of over 16.

[b] Loadings greater than 1.0 are a result of missing data.

Factor II, nations with high aggregation by legislatures tend to have a high level of minority representation and interparty competition in the election of executives; they tend to be low on articulation by non-associational, institutional and anomic groups. Their populations are largely "white," relatively wealthy, and urban; they tend to have a small per cent of their population in agriculture, small growth in the rural population, and few Indians. Regarding Factor III, nations whose medium-size cities are growing fastest tend to be the wealthiest and to achieve their wealth at a faster rate; they

also tend to aggregate political demands through political parties. And with respect to Factor IV, nations whose large-size cities are growing rapidly tend to lose their agricultural populations fast. These nations also tend to have small numbers of persons owning 50 per cent of the land. Politically, these nations tend to have high aggregation by executive as well as low minority representation and interparty competition in the election of the executive.

One of the most important of these findings is the one relating medium-size city growth to economic development. This adds evidence to that part of the Revised Blanksten theory relating urban growth to economic growth. The portion of the Blanksten theory relating economic growth to social mobilization, representation/competition and interest articulation by associational groups, however, does not receive as much confirmation as the urban growth economic development link. In other words, since the measures of these concepts do not all load on the same factor, this *may* indicate that the five variable theories should take into account a larger universe of variation prior to conducting the causal analysis. In short, the results of the factoring should aid in the selection of variables to include in a causal analysis. And after the causal analysis, one may conduct a further factor analysis to test further the results of the causal inference. For example, a factor analysis might be conducted of the five variables in the original or Revised Blanksten theory to see whether they would yield a single factor. And if the partials do not vanish, this might be further evidence for the causal inference.

SUMMARY

An analysis was conducted of representative comparative studies of developing areas in terms of theories of political development. Studies were classified in terms of the primary aim of their design as mainly theory verification or principally theory discovery.

Such a classification, as previously mentioned, does *not* preclude a researcher from actually pursuing both goals simultaneously, i.e., there may be mixtures of verification and discovery aims in many studies. The distinction is put forth tentatively as a possible aid to the pursuit of knowledge (Snyder 1963:1–23).

The mathematics of causal inference and the statistics of least squares correlation and regression analysis were applied to the theories of George Blanksten and Daniel Lerner and revisions were suggested. Factor analysis studies were examined in terms of their relevance for the discovery of theories of political development. The complementarity of causal inference techniques and factor analysis in theory construction was suggested.

BIBLIOGRAPHY

ADELMAN, I.

1961 *Theories of economic development.* Stanford, Stanford University Press.

ALKER, H., JR.

1965 *Mathematics and politics.* New York, Macmillan.

1966 Causal inference and political analysis. In J. Bernd, ed., *Mathematical application in political science.* Dallas, Southern Methodist Press.

ALMOND, G., and J. COLEMAN

1960 *The politics of developing areas.* Princeton, N.J., Princeton University Press.

BANKS, ARTHUR, and PHILLIP M. GREGG

1965 Grouping political systems: Q factor analysis of *A Cross Polity Survey. American Behavioral Scientist* 9:3–6.

BANKS, ARTHUR, and ROBERT TEXTOR

1963 *A cross polity survey.* Cambridge, Mass., M.I.T. Press.

BERRY, BRIAN

1960 An inductive approach to the regionalization of economic development. In N. Ginsburg, ed., *Essays on geography and economic development.* Chicago, University of Chicago Press.

1961 Basic patterns of economic development. In N. Ginsburg, ed., *Atlas of economic development.* Chicago, University of Chicago Press.

BEYLE, THAD

1965 Contested elections and voter turnout in a local community: a problem in spurious correlation. *American Political Science Review* 59:111–116.

BLALOCK, HUBERT M., JR.

1960 Correlational analysis and causal inferences. *American Anthropologist* 62:624–631.

1961a Correlation and causality: the multivariate case. *Social Forces* 49:246–251.

1961b Evaluating the relative importance of variables. *American Sociological Review* 26:866–874.

1962a Four variable causal models and partial correlations. *American Journal of Sociology* 68:182–194.

1962b Spuriousness vs. intervening variables: the problem of temporal sequences. *Social Forces* 40.

1964 *Causal inferences in nonexperimental research.* Chapel Hill, University of North Carolina.

1965 Theory building and the concept of interaction. *American Sociological Review* 30:374–380.

BLANKSTEN, GEORGE
1960 The politics of Latin America. In G. Almond, J. Coleman, eds., *The politics of developing areas.* Princeton, N.J., Princeton University Press.
1965 Modernization and revolution in Latin America. In H. R. Barringer, G. I. Blanksten, R. W. Mack, eds., *Social change in the developing areas.* Cambridge, Mass., Schenkman.

CATTELL, RAYMOND
1949 The dimensions of culture patterns of factorization of national characters. *Journal of Abnormal and Social Psychology* 44:443–469.
1950 The culture patterns discoverable in the syntal dissensions of existing nations. *Journal of Social Psychology* 32:215–253.

CATTELL, RAYMOND, *et al.*
1951 An attempt at more refined definition of the cultural dimensions of syntality in modern nations. *American Sociological Review* 17:408–421.

CNUDDE, C. F., and D. J. MCCRONE
1966 The linkage between constituency attitudes and congressional voting behavior: a causal model. *American Political Science Review* 60:66–72.

CUTRIGHT, PHILLIPS
1963 National political development: measurement and analysis. *American Sociological Review* 28:253–264.

DEUTSCH, KARL W.
1961 Social mobilization and political development. *American Political Science Review* 55:493–514.

EZEKIEL, M., and K. FOX
1959 *Methods of correlation and regression analysis,* 3rd ed. New York, Wiley.

FRIEDRICH, CARL J.
1966 Some general theoretical reflections on the problems of political data. In R. L. Merritt, S. Rokkan, eds., *Comparing nations: the use of quantitative data in cross national research.* New Haven, Yale University Press.

N. GINSBURG (ed.)
1961 *Atlas of economic development.* Chicago, University of Chicago Press.

GOULD, J.
1964 Comparative method. In J. Gould, W. L. Kolb, eds., *A dictionary of the social sciences.* New York, Free Press.

GREGG, PHILIPP M., and ARTHUR S. BANKS
1965 Dimensions of political systems: factor analysis of *A Cross Polity Survey.*

American Political Science Review 59: 602–614.

GUTTMAN, LOUIS
1940 Multiple rectilinear prediction and the resolution into components. *Psychometrika* 5:75–99.

GUTTMAN, LOUIS, and J. COHEN
1933 Multiple rectilinear production and the resolution into components: II. *Psychometrika* 8:169–183.

HANSON, NORWOOD R.
1958 *Patterns of scientific discovery.* Cambridge, Cambridge University Press.

HEMPEL, CARL
1962 Deductive nomological vs. statistical explanation. In H. Feigl, G. Maxwell, eds., *Minnesota studies in the philosophy of science,* 3:98–169. Minneapolis, University of Minnesota Press.

JOHNSTON, J.
1963 *Econometric methods.* New York, McGraw-Hill.

LERNER, DAVID
1957 Communication systems and social systems: a statistical exploration in history and policy. *Behavioral Science* 2:266–275.
1958 *The passing of traditional society.* Glencoe, Ill., Free Press.

MACK, RAYMOND W.
1965 Race, class and power in the Barbados. In H. Barringer, R. Mack, G. Blanksten, eds., *Social change in the developing areas.* Cambridge, Mass., Schenkman.

MOORE, WILBERT E.
1963 *Social change.* Englewood Cliffs, N.J., Prentice-Hall.

POLK, KENNETH, H. M. BLALOCK, and W. S. ROBINSON
1962 Asymmetric causal models: a three way discussion. *American Sociological Review* 27:539–547.

PONSIOEN, J. A.
1965 *The analysis of social change reconsidered.* The Hague: Mouton.

RUMMEL, R.
n.d. *Dimensions of nations.* Forthcoming.

RUSSETT, B.
1966 Delineating international regions. In J. D. Singer, ed., *Insights and indicators in world politics.* New York, Free Press.

RUSSETT, B., H. R. ALKER, JR., K. DEUTSCH, and H. LASSWELL
1964 *World handbook of political and social indicators.* New Haven, Yale University Press.

SCHNORE, LEO
1961 The statistical measurement of urbanization and economic development. *Land Economics* 37:229–245.

SIMON, HERBERT A.
1957   *Models of man.* New York, Wiley.

SNYDER, RICHARD C.
1962   Recent trends in international relations theory. In A. Ranney, ed., *Essays on the behavioral study of politics.* Urbana, University of Illinois Press.
1963   Some perspectives on the use of experimental techniques in the study of international relations. In H. Guetzkow, C. F. Alger, R. A. Brody, R. Noel and and R. Snyder, *Simulation in international relations: development for research and teaching.* Englewood Cliffs, N.J., Prentice-Hall.

SOARES, GLAUCIO
1964   *Congruency and incongruency among indicators of economic development.* Paper presented at Internation Conference on Comparative Research on Developing Countries.

SOROKIN, PITIRIM A.
1927, *Social and cultural mobility.* New York,
1959   Free Press.
1928, *Contemporary sociological theories.* New
1956   York, Harper.

TANTER, RAYMOND, and LAWRENCE ALSCHULER
1965   *Political, social and economic dimensions of development in Latin America.* Ditto. Evanston, Ill., Northwestern University.

WOLD, HERMAN, and LARS JUREEN
1953   *Demand Analysis.* New York, Wiley.

CHAPTER 7

Ethnographic Bibliographies

TIMOTHY J. O'LEARY

INTRODUCTION

An important part of the anthropologist's equipment is a knowledge of what has already been written in his field, since this knowledge will affect the direction of his research. Bibliographies are of immediate assistance in this respect because they indicate what has, and has not, been written about particular groups or topics and whether any extended reading of the literature will be useful. Perusal of bibliography may also suggest further lines of research without the necessity for going into the literature itself.

What I have tried to do in the following survey is to give a fairly thorough coverage of ethnographic (*not* archaeologic, linguistic or physical anthropological) and related bibliographies on a continental, national and regional level. I have generally eschewed listing bibliographies on the tribal or local level because of the lack of space to do this and because it is expected that these would be covered in the larger bibliographies. However, I have made some exceptions to this rule where the lack of coverage in the larger areas seemed to warrant it, e.g., with the Kurds. The latter decision reflects another policy I have followed—to try to have every part of a major area covered by a bibliography. This results in some areas having a smaller number of bibliographies listed than other areas. Thus, there are fewer listed for the Americas, which are well-covered, than for Europe, which is not.

Since the subject matter of ethnography

I wish to thank Frank M. LeBar, Robert J. Theodoratus and Robert O. Legacé for reading and criticizing an earlier draft of this paper.

covers such a wide range of material in so many related fields, the anthropologist may have to cover more types of written sources of information than is usual with other social scientists. There exist several guides to the general literature of the social sciences which enable the researcher to orient himself within these different fields. Perhaps the most generally useful is that of White *et al.* (1964) which gives a very extended coverage of the major fields (history, economics, and business administration, sociology, anthropology, psychology, education, and political science)—books, reference guides, continuing bibliographies, etc. Lewis (1960) covers some of the same material from the British social science view. Hoselitz (1959) gives probably the best general statement of the development of the social sciences, while Kyle and Donahue (1961) list the major publishing agencies in the field. Guides to the major world areas will be mentioned in the relevant sections below.

Bibliographies of bibliographies are an important aid to the ethnologist. Besterman (1965–1966) is the standard work in this field. It is particularly useful for bibliographies on individual countries or special subjects. The use of this should be supplemented by consulting the *Bibliographic Index*, which appears several times a year and is cumulative.

The general bibliographies available may be classed into two types: cumulative bibliographies and compilations, and annual bibliographies. Major cumulations or compilations which may be consulted profitably include that by the American Universities Field Staff (1960–1961) which is a good annotated bibliography on selected areas; the printed research catalog of the American Geographical Society library (1962) which is excellent for human geography; the printed catalog of the Harvard University Peabody Museum library (1963) which is the best general anthropological bibliography in print; Howe *et al.* (1961) which is a very good selected bibliography of the historical literature; the printed catalog of the School of Oriental and African Studies library (London University, 1963) which covers a major part of the world; and the *Arctic Bibliography*, an extremely fine annotated bibliography which covers the northern regions of the world. Another item which may be classed here is the *Bibliotheca Missionum* (Streit *et al.*, 1916–) which covers the Roman Catholic missionary literature (containing a great deal of ethnographic information) of each continent. These volumes are brought up to date by the annual *Bibliografia Missionaria*.

There are several general continuing bibliographies analyzing the current literature which may be consulted. The *Social Sciences and Humanities Index* (formerly the *International Index*) covers social science and humanities literature in the English language, while the *Reader's Guide to Periodical Literature* (1901–) covers a good deal of the general periodical literature in English. Two German annual bibliographies cover Western-language periodical materials very thoroughly. The *Internationale Bibliographie der Zeitschriftenliteratur* (1897–), issued in two sections treating German and non-German materials, analyzes nearly seven thousand periodicals. The *Bibliographie der Sozialwissenschaften* (1950–) covers economics, politics, sociology, and social psychology, as well as anthropology.

In addition to the above, reference can be made to a number of annual bibliographies and aids which list the current social science literature. The more important of these for ethnographic purposes are the *International Bibliography of Social and Cultural Anthropology* (1956–), the *Internationale Volkskundliche Bibliographie* (1949–), the *Quarterly Check-List of Ethnology and Sociology* (American Bibliographic Service, 1958–), and the *Index to Current Periodicals Received in the Library of the Royal Anthropological Institute* (Royal Anthropological Institute, 1963–). These may be supplemented by the *International Bibliography of Sociology* (1951–), and by the *Novaîa Inostrannaîa Literatura po Istorii, arkheologii i Etnografii* (1960–), for Russian materials.

When working in a specific geographical area, it is a good idea to check the major features of the ethnography of the whole major area. The quickest way, generally, to do this is to read through one of the synthetic regional ethnographies. Doing this will give the researcher an idea of just where the group he is studying fits in with other groups in the area, whether it is aberrant or well within the general range, and will usually give him further bibliographic materials to check. Two of the better world ethnographies are those by Bernatzik (1954) and Biasutti (1959). On another level are the systematic ethnographies being produced by The Akademiîa Nauk SSSR which cover specific regions of the world and which in many cases offer information unavailable elsewhere (Narody Mira, 1956, 1957, 1959, 1960, 1962–1963, 1963, 1964a, 1964b). Similar regional ethnographies will be cited in the appropriate sections without comment.

For treating the regional bibliographies I have rather arbitrarily divided the world into eight sections (Asia, South Asia, East Asia, Soviet Union, Europe, Africa, the Americas, the Pacific), and added a general subject category at the end. Since no single bibliography would be expected to follow this arrangement, readers are advised to check the aids listed for the regions adjoining the region in which they are interested, and also to check the general aids listed above.

BIBLIOGRAPHY

AMERICAN BIBLIOGRAPHIC SERVICE
1958– Quarterly Check-List of Ethnology & Sociology. East Northport, Long Island, and Darien, Connecticut.

AMERICAN UNIVERSITIES FIELD STAFF
1960– A select bibliography: Asia, Africa, East-
1961 ern Europe, Latin America. One volume with supplement. New York.

AMERICAN GEOGRAPHICAL SOCIETY OF NEW YORK
1962   Research catalogue. 16 volumes. Boston, G. K. Hall and Company.

ARCHIV FÜR ANTHROPOLOGIE
1872–   Verzeichniss der anthropologischen Lit-
1904   eratur. Braunschweig, F. Vieweg und Sohn.

ARCTIC INSTITUTE OF NORTH AMERICA
1953–   Arctic bibliography. 13 volumes. Wash-
1966   ington, Government Printing Office.

BECKHAM, REXFORD S., and BECKHAM, MARIE P., COMPILERS
1963   A basic list of books and periodicals for college libraries. American Anthropological Association, Memoir 95, pp. 77–316. Menasha, Wisconson.

BERNATZIK, HUGO A.
1954   Die neue grosse Völkerkunde: Völker und Kulturen der Erde in Wort und Bild. 2nd ed. 3 volumes. Frankfurt am Main, Herkul Verlagsanstalt.

BESTERMAN, THEODORE
1965–   A world bibliography of bibliographies.
1966   4th ed. 5 volumes. Lausanne, Societas Bibliographica.

BIASUTTI, RENATO
1959   Le razze e i popoli della terra. 3rd ed. 4 volumes. Torino, Unione Tipografico-editrice Torinese.

BIBLIOGRAFIA MISSIONARIA
1935–   Roma, Pontifica Biblioteca di Propaganda Fide.

BIBLIOGRAPHIC INDEX. A CUMULATIVE BIBLIOGRAPHY OF BIBLIOGRAPHIES.
1937–   New York, H. W. Wilson Company.

BIBLIOGRAPHIE DER SOZIALWISSENSCHAFTEN
1950–   [Issued with the Jahrbuch für Sozialwissenschaft.] Göttingen, Vandenhoeck und Ruprecht.

ETHNOLOGISCHER ANZEIGER
1928–   Jahresbibliographie und Bericht über die
1944   völkerkundliche Literatur. 4 volumes. Stuttgart, E. Schweizerbart'sche Verlagsbuchhandlung.

HARVARD UNIVERSITY. PEABODY MUSEUM OF ARCHAEOLOGY AND ETHNOLOGY. LIBRARY
1963   Catalogue of the library. 53 volumes. Boston, G. K. Hall and Company.

HOSELITZ, BERT F., ED.
1959   A reader's guide to the social sciences. Glencoe, Illinois, Free Press.

HOWE, GEORGE FREDERICK, et al.
1961   The American Historical Association's guide to historical literature. New York, Macmillan Company.

INTERNATIONAL BIBLIOGRAPHY OF SOCIAL AND CULTURAL ANTHROPOLOGY
1956–   Paris, UNESCO; Chicago, Aldine.

INTERNATIONAL BIBLIOGRAPHY OF SOCIOLOGY
1951–   [1951–1954 published as issues of Current Sociology.] Paris, UNESCO; Chicago, Aldine.

INTERNATIONAL INDEX TO PERIODICALS
1913–   Volume 1–. New York, H. W. Wilson Company.

INTERNATIONAL CONGRESS OF AMERICANISTS, 35TH. EL COMITE ORGANIZADOR
1962   Bibliografía antropológica. Trabajos publicados en México 1955–1962. México.

INTERNATIONALE BIBLIOGRAPHIE DER ZEITSCHRIFTENLITERATUR
1897–   Abteilung A: Bibliographie der deutschen Zeitschriftenliteratur, mit Einschluss von Sammelwerken. Osnabrück, Dietrich.
1911–   Abteilung B: Bibliographie der fremd-
1919,   sprachigen Zeitschriftenliteratur. Osna-
1925–   brück, Dietrich.

INTERNATIONALE VOLKSKUNDLICHE BIBLIOGRAPHIE
1949–   7 volumes. [covers the period 1939/41–
1963   1957/58] Basel, etc.

ISHIDA, EIICHIRO, editor
1961   Minzogaku kankei zasshi rombun sōmokuroku 1925–1959. Tokyo, Nihon Minzokugaku Kyokai.

KYLE, ANDREW, and DONAHUE, GILBERT EUGENE
1961   Guide to source materials and publishing agencies in anthropology. Wayne State University, Monteith College, Working Bibliography Series, No. 2. Detroit.

LEWIS, PETER R.
1960   The literature of the social sciences; an introductory survey and guide. London, Library Association.

LONDON UNIVERSITY. SCHOOL OF ORIENTAL AND AFRICAN STUDIES. LIBRARY.
1963   Library catalog. 28 volumes. Boston, G. K. Hall and Company.

NARODY MIRA: ETNOGRAFICHESKIE OCHERKI
1956   Narody Sibiri. Moskva, Izd-vo Akademiia Nauk SSSR. [English translation published as "Peoples of Siberia," Chicago, 1964.]
1957   Narody Peredneĭ Azii. Moskva, Akademiia Nauk SSSR.
1959   Narody Ameriki. 2 volumes. Moskva, Akademiia Nauk SSSR.
1960   Narody Kavkaza. 2 volumes. Moskva, Akademiia Nauk SSSR.
1962–   Narody Sredneĭ Azii: Kazakhstana.
1963   2 volumes. Moskva, Akademiia Nauk SSSR.
1963   Narody IUzhnoi Azii. Moskva, Akademiia Nauk SSSR.
1964a   Narody Evropeĭskoĭ chasti SSSR. Moskva, Nauka.
1964b   Narody Zarubezhnoĭ Evropy. Moskva, Akademiia Nauk SSSR.

NOVAIA INOSTRANNAIA LITERATURA PO ISTORII, ARKHEOLOGII I ETNOGRAFII
        Moskva, Akademiia Nauk SSSR. Fundamental Naia Biblioteka Obshchestvennykh Nauk.

READER'S GUIDE TO PERIODICAL LITERATURE
1901– Minneapolis, New York, H. W. Wilson Company.

ROYAL ANTHROPOLOGICAL INSTITUTE OF GREAT BRITAIN AND IRELAND. LIBRARY
1963– Index to current periodicals received in the library of the Royal Anthropological Institute. London.

SIEGEL, BERNARD JOSEPH, editor
1959– Biennial review of anthropology. 3 vol-
1965 umes. Stanford, Stanford University Press.

SOCIAL SCIENCE AND HUMANITIES INDEX
1965– Vol. 19– . New York, H. W. Wilson Company.

SOCIOLOGICAL ABSTRACTS
1952– New York, Sociological Abstracts, Inc.

STREIT, ROBERT, et al.
1916– Bibliotheca missionum. Münster in West-phalia and Aachen.

TROPICAL ABSTRACTS
1946– Amsterdam, Royal Tropical Institute.

VOLKSKUNDLICHE BIBLIOGRAPHIE
1918– 14 volumes [covers 1917–1938]. Strass-
1957 burg and Berlin.

WEINREICH, URIEL and BEATRICE
1959 Yiddish Language and folklore; a selective bibliography for researchers. Janua Linguarum, 10. 's-Gravenhage, Mouton.

WHITE, CARL M., et al.
1964 Sources of information in the social sciences, a guide to the literature. Totowa, New Jersey, the Bedminster Press.

ZENTRALBLATT FÜR ANTHROPOLOGIE, ETHNOLOGIE UND URGESCHICHTE
1896– 17 volumes. Braunschweig, F. Vieweg
1912 und Sohn.

ASIA

For Asia as a whole there are few bibliographies, aside from sections in those covering the entire world, as noted above. One perhaps may be cited here, Mezhov's (1891–1894) attempt to classify the materials available at the end of the nineteenth century. The annual bibliography in the *Journal of Asian Studies* keeps abreast of the current literature best in southern and eastern Asia, but does not attempt to cover the northern and western parts of the continent equally. For these areas, reference may be made to the *Novaĭa Inostrannaĭa Literatura po Istorii, Arkheologii i Etnografii*, cited above.

JOURNAL OF ASIAN STUDIES
1957– Bibliography of Asian Studies. [1956 to date] Ann Arbor, Association for Asian Studies.

MEZHOV, VLADIMIR I.
1891– Bibliografiĭa Azii. 2 volumes in 3. St.
1894 Petersburg.

SOUTH ASIA

This area will be treated in three sections, southwest, south and mainland southeast Asia. There is only one general bibliography of southwestern Asia, that by Field (1953–1962), for which a separate subject index exists (Field 1959–1964). Ettinghausen (1954) is a good introduction to the recent literature. Current bibliography may be checked in the *Abstracta Islamica* (1927–) and the *Middle East Journal* (1947–). There are bibliographies on a number of countries and regions, the more useful being Patai (1957) on Jordan, Lebanon and Syria, the Akademiĭa Nauk SSSR (1963) volume on the Kurds, Farman (1951) and Sabā (1951) on Iran, Gay (1875), Hazard et al. (1957) and Loewenthal (1959) on the Arabs and Arabia, Sverchevskaĭa and Cherman (1959–1961) on Turkey, and Pearson (1958) on Islam in general.

For south Asia, reference should be made to Wilson's (1959) survey of bibliographies. Fürer-Haimendorf (1958–1964) is the standard reference work for this area, and may be supplemented for India by Mandelbaum (1949), the Calcutta National Library (1960) volume, Patterson, (1962) and by Kotovskiĭ et al. (1959) for the Russian materials. The UNESCO (1954–) annual bibliographies cover most of south and southeast Asia. Afghanistan is covered by Wilber (1962), while the Tibetan literature is surveyed by Miller (1953).

LeBar (1966) and LeBar et al. (1965) include general surveys of the literature. The basic bibliographies are Embree and Dotson (1950) and Cordier (1912–1932). For Russian materials the Akademiĭa Nauk (1960) volume may be consulted, while Ichikawa (1965) and Irikura (1956) cover Japanese materials. These may be kept up to date in part by consulting the Cornell University Library (1959–) accessions list. Thailand is the best covered of the individual countries with items by Bernath (1964), Chulalongkorn University (1960), Cornell University (1956), Kawabe et al. (1957) and Mason and Parish (1958). For Malaya there is Pelzer (1956) and Cheeseman (1959). Burma is fairly well covered by Trager et al. (1956, 1957). In addition to Cordier (1912–1932), Indochina is partly covered by the U. S. Library of Congress (1950) bibliography and Vietnam by Trần (1966), while Lafont (1964) and Halpern and Halpern (1962) offer a thorough coverage of Laos.

ABSTRACTA ISLAMICA
1927– Appears in Revue des études Islamiques. Paris.

AKADEMIĨĂ NAUK SSSR. INSTITUT NARODOV AZII
1960 Bibliografiĩā ĩUgo-vostochnoĩ Azii. Moskva, Izd-vo Vostochnoĩ Lit-ry.
1963 Bibliografiĩā po Kurdoveniĩū. Moskva, Izd-vo Vostochnoĩ Lit-ry.

BERNATH, FRANCES A.
1964 Catalogue of Thai language holdings in the Cornell University libraries through 1964. Cornell University, Southeast Asia Program, Data Paper 54. Ithaca.

CALCUTTA. NATIONAL LIBRARY
1960 A bibliography of Indology, Volume I, Indian anthropology. Calcutta.

CHEESEMAN, H. R.
1959 Bibliography of Malaya. London, Longmans, Green and Company.

CHULALONGKORN UNIVERSITY. CENTRAL LIBRARY
1960 Bibliography of material about Thailand in Western languages. Bangkok.

CORDIER, HENRI
1912– Bibliotheca indosinica. 4 volumes. Paris,
1932 Leroux.

CORNELL UNIVERSITY. DEPARTMENT OF FAR EASTERN STUDIES. SOUTHEAST ASIA PROGRAM
1956 Bibliography of Thailand. Cornell University, Southeast Asia Program, Data Paper 20. Ithaca.

CORNELL UNIVERSITY. LIBRARY. WASON COLLECTION
1959– Southeast Asia accessions list. Ithaca.

EMBREE, JOHN FEE, and DOTSON, LILLIAN OTA
1950 Bibliography of the peoples and cultures of mainland southeast Asia. New Haven, Yale University, Southeast Asia Studies.

ETTINGHAUSEN, RICHARD, editor
1954 A selected and annotated bibliography of books and periodicals in Western languages dealing with the Near and Middle East. Washington, Middle East Institute.

FARMAN, HAFEZ F.
1951 Iran, a selected and annotated bibliography. Washington, U. S. Library of Congress, General Reference and Bibliography Division.

FIELD, HENRY
1953– Bibliography of southwestern Asia. 7 vol-
1962 umes. Coral Gables, University of Miami Press.
1959– Subject index to bibliographies on south-
1964 western Asia. Coral Gables, University of Miami Press.

FÜRER-HAIMENDORF, ELIZABETH VON
1958– An anthropological bibliography of south
1964 Asia. 2 volumes. Le Monde d'Outre-Mer, Passé et Présent, Quatrième Série, Bibliographies, Volumes 3 and 4. Paris and La Haye, Mouton et Cie.

GANKOVSKIĨ, ĨURII VLADIMIROVICH
1964 Narody Pakistana. Moskva, Nauka.

GAY, JEAN
1875 Bibliographie des ouvrages relatifs à l'Afrique et à l'Arabie. San Remo, J. Gay et Fils.

HALPERN, JOEL M., and HALPERN, BARBARA
1962 Laotian bibliography. Berkeley, Center for Southeast Asia Studies, University of California.

HAZARD, HARRY W., et al.
1956 Bibliography of the Arabian Peninsula. New Haven, Human Relations Area Files.

ICHIKAWA, KENJIRŌ
1965 Southeast Asia viewed from Japan: a bibliography of Japanese works on southeast Asian societies, 1940–1963. Cornell University, Southeast Asia Program, Data Paper 56. Ithaca.

IRIKURA, JAMES K.
1956 Southeast Asia: selected annotated bibliography of Japanese publications. New Haven, Human Relations Area Files.

KAWABE, TOSHIO, et al.
1957 Bibliography of Thai studies. Tokyo, Tokyo University of Foreign Studies.

KOTOVSKIĨ, G. G., et al.
1959 Bibliografiĩā Indii. Moskva, Izd-vo Vostochnoĩ Lit-ry.

LAFONT, PIERRE BERNARD
1964 Bibliographie du Laos. Publications de l'École Française d'Extrême-Orient, 50. Paris.

LEBAR, FRANK M.
1966 The ethnography of mainland southeast Asia: a bibliographic survey. Behavior Science Notes, Vol. 1, pp. 14–40. New Haven.

LEBAR, FRANK M., HICKEY, GERALD C., and MUSGRAVE, JOHN K.
1965 Ethnic groups of mainland southeast Asia. New Haven, HRAF Press.

LOEWENTHAL, RUDOLF
1959 Russian materials on Arabs and Arab countries: a selective bibliography. Der Islam, Vol. 34, pp. 174–187. Berlin.

MANDELBAUM, DAVID.
1949 Materials for a bibliography of the ethnology of India. Berkeley, Department of Anthropology, University of California.

MASON, JOHN BROWN, and PARISH, H. CARROLL
1958 Thailand bibliography. Gainesville, University of Florida Libraries.

MIDDLE EAST JOURNAL
1947– Bibliography of periodical literature.
Washington.

MILLER, BEATRICE D.
1953 A selective survey of literature on Tibet.
American Political Science Review, Vol.
47, pp. 1135–1151. Washington.

PATAI, RAPHAEL
1957 Jordan, Lebanon and Syria: an annotated
bibliography. New Haven, HRAF Press.

PATTERSON, MAUREEN
1962 South Asia: an introductory bibliography.
Chicago, University of Chicago Press.

PEARSON, JAMES D.
1958 Index Islamicus, 1906–1955. Cambridge,
England, Heffer.

PELZER, KARL J.
1956 Selected bibliography on the geography
of southeast Asia. Part III. Malaya. New
Haven, Human Relations Area Files.

ṢABĀ, MOḤSEN
1951 Bibliographie française de l'Iran. 2nd edition. Tehran.

SVERCHEVSKAĪA, A. K., and CHERMAN, T. P.
1959– Bibliografiīa Turīsii. 2 volumes. Moskva,
1961 Izd-vo Vostochnoī Lit-ry.

TRAGER, FRANK N., MUSGRAVE, JOHN K., and
WELSH, JANET
1956 Annotated bibliography of Burma. New
Haven, Human Relations Area Files.

TRAGER, FRANK N., KUBLIN, HYMAN, and KIANG,
LU-YU
1957 Japanese and Chinese language sources
on Burma: an annotated bibliography.
New Haven, HRAF Press.

TRẦN THỊ KIMSA
1966 Bibliography on Vietnam 1954–1964.
Saigon, National Institute of Administration.

UNESCO. RESEARCH CENTRE ON THE SOCIAL IMPLI-
CATIONS OF INDUSTRIALIZATION IN SOUTHERN
ASIA
1954– Southern Asia social science bibliography.
Calcutta.

U. S. LIBRARY OF CONGRESS. REFERENCE DEPART-
MENT
1950 Indochina; a bibliography of the land
and people. Washington.

WILBER, DONALD N.
1962 Annotated bibliography of Afghanistan.
2nd edition. New Haven, HRAF Press.

WILSON, PATRICK
1959 A survey of bibliographies on southern
Asia. Journal of Asian Studies, Vol. 18,
pp. 365–376. Ann Arbor.

EAST ASIA

There are few general bibliographies on
East Asia. Beardsley et al. (1950) is concerned with Japanese material on the area as
a whole, as is Teng et al. (1961). One can
keep up to date by checking through the
annual bibliography in the Journal of Asian
Studies and in the Kyōto University bibliographies (Kyōto Daigaku 1935–). Kimpei's
(1964) bibliography of bibliographies may also
be consulted.

There are a number of works available
on Japan. Cordier (1912) and Wenckstern
(1895–1907) cover the older literature thoroughly. Supplementing these are the Bibliografiīa Īaponii (Vlasov et al., 1960–1965)
for Russian materials, Kokusai Bunka Shinkokai (1959–1964), Tōyōgaku Infomēshon
Sentā (1964), and Webb and Ryan (1965), the
latter being a research guide. In addition, there
is Borton et al. (1954), a selected list in Western languages, and a general bibliography by
the Nihon Gakujutsu Kaigi (1955), one volume
of which is devoted to the social sciences. Sakamaki (1963) has produced a fine volume on
the Ryukyus.

The major reference on China is Cordier
(1904–1908, 1922–1924) which is continued
and supplemented by Yüan (1956, 1958,
1961) and by Lust and Eichhorn (1964).
Russian materials may be located in Skachkov
(1960) while Chinese and Japanese language
references are also covered in Fairbank and
Liu (1950) and Fairbank and Banno (1955).
Additional references can be found in Sun-
zen (1952) and in the shorter bibliographies
by Ku (1946–1948), Liu (1940–1941),
Mickey (1948) and Takemura (1957–1958).
For Korea there are Gerow (1952), Hazard et
al. (1954), and the U. S. Library of Congress (1960). Lee (1961) covers the recent
Korean-language works thoroughly. The U. S.
Library of Congress has also produced a
bibliography on Manchuria (1951).

BEARDSLEY, RICHARD K., et al.
1950 Bibliographic materials in the Japanese
language on Far Eastern Archaeology and
ethnology. University of Michigan, Center for Japanese Studies, Bibliographical
Series, No. 3. Ann Arbor.

BORTON, HUGH, ELISSEEFF, SERGE, and REISCHAUER,
EDWIN O.
1954 A selected list of books and articles on
Japan in English, French and German.
Revised and enlarged edition. Cambridge,
Harvard University Press.

CORDIER, HENRI
1904– Bibliotheca sinica. 4 volumes, with sup-

1908,   plement. Paris, E. Guilmoto.
1922–
1924
1912   Bibliotheca japonica. Paris, Imprimerie National.

FAIRBANK, JOHN KING, and BANNO, MASATAKA
1955   Japanese studies of modern China. Rutland, Vermont, and Tokyo, Charles E. Tuttle Company.

FAIRBANK, JOHN KING, and LIU, KWANG-CHING
1950   Modern China: a bibliographical guide to Chinese works 1898–1937. Harvard-Yenching Institute Studies, Vol. 1. Cambridge.

GEROW, BERT A.
1952   Publications in Japanese on Korean anthropology. Stanford, Stanford University Libraries.

HAZARD, BENJAMIN H., JR., et al.
1954   Korean studies guide. Berkeley and Los Angeles, University of California Press.

KIMPEI GOTO, editor
1964   Bibliography of bibliographies of East Asian studies in Japan. Centre for East Asian Cultural Studies, Bibliography No. 3. Tokyo, Toyo Bunko.

KOKUSAI BUNKA SHINKOKAI
1959– Bibliography of standard reference books
1964   for Japanese studies. 6 volumes. Tokyo.

KU TAO-TSI
1946– A bibliography of Chinese ethnographical
1948   works [in Chinese]. Min-tsu-hsueh Yen-chiu Chi-k'an, Vols. 4 and 6.

KYŌTO DAIGAKU. JIMBUN KAGAKU KENKYŪJO
1935– Tōyō shi kenkyū bunken ruimoku. Kyōto.

LEE, SANG-EUN, et al.
1961   Bibliography of Korean Studies. Seoul, Asiatic Research Center, Korea University.

LIU HSIU-YEH
1940– Selected bibliography of Yunnan and of
1941   tribes of southwest China. Quarterly Bulletin of Chinese Bibliography, New Series, Vol. 1, pp. 83–113, 333–348, 451–464; Vol. 2, pp. 199–225.

LUST, JOHN, and EICHHORN, WERNER
1964   Index sinicus. Cambridge, England, W. Heffer.

MICKEY, MARGARET P.
1948   A bibliography of south and southwest China, with special reference to the non-Chinese peoples and their relation to the peoples of adjacent areas: works in western languages. New York, Viking Fund (microfilm).

NIHON GAKUJUTSU KAIGI, DAI ICHI-BU
1952– Bungaku, Tetsugaku, Shigaku Bunken
1959   Mokuroku—Nihon Minzokugaku Hen. Tokyo.

SAKAMAKI, SHUNZO
1963   Ryukyu: a bibliographic guide to Okina-wan studies. Honolulu, University of Hawaii Press.

SHAFER, ROBERT, editor
1963   Bibliography of Sino-Tibetan languages II. Wiesbaden, Harrassowitz.

SKACHKOV, PETER EMEL'IĀNOVICH
1960   Bibliografiiā Kitaiā. Moskva, Izd-vo Vostochnoĭ Lit-ry.

SUN-ZEN, I-TU
1952   Bibliography on Chinese social history. New Haven, Institute of Far Eastern Languages.

TAKEMURA, T.
1957– Ethnographic bibliography by Chinese
1958   ethnologists on the non-Chinese peoples in south and southwest China [in Japanese]. Shakai Jinruigaku, Vol. 1, pp. 62–74; Vol. 2, pp. 68–75; Vol. 3, pp. 54–61. Tokyo.

TENG, SSU-YÜ, et al.
1961   Japanese studies on Japan and the Far East. Hong Kong, Hong Kong University Press.

TŌYŌGAKU INFOMĒSHON SENTĀ, TOKYO
1964   A selected list of books on Japan in Western languages, 1945–1960. Tokyo, Information Centre of Asian Studies, Toyo Bunko.

U. S. LIBRARY OF CONGRESS. REFERENCE DEPARTMENT
1951   Manchuria, an annotated bibliography. Washington.
1960   Korea, an annotated bibliography. 3 volumes. Washington.

VLASOV, V. A., et al.
1960– Bibliografiiā IAponii. Moskva, Izd-vo
1965   Vostochnoĭ Lit-ry.

WEBB, HERSCHEL, and RYAN, MARGARET
1965   Research in Japanese sources: a guide. New York, Columbia University Press.

WENCKSTERN, FRIEDRICH VON
1895– A bibliography of the Japanese empire.
1907   2 volumes. Leiden, Brill; Tokyo, Maruya.

YÜAN, T'UNG-LI
1956   Economic and social development of modern China: a bibliographical guide. New Haven, Human Relations Area Files.
1958   China in Western literature. New Haven, Far Eastern Publications, Yale University.
1961   Russian works on China in American libraries 1918–1960. New Haven, Yale Far Eastern Publications.

SOVIET UNION

Examination of the literature on the Soviet Union and its component peoples is very complicated, due in part to the many languages involved (e.g., Russian, Georgian, Ukrainian) and to the great time depth in some areas. Reference should first be made to several of the available guides to the literature. The two volumes by Horecky *et al.* (1962, 1965) are good introductions to the literature in Russian and the western European languages. Maichel and Simmons (1962, 1964) is an outstanding annotated guide to Russian reference works and should be consulted for any serious work in the area. Kosven (1947) (in Russian) is a survey and bibliography of Russian ethnographical bibliographies available in the mid-1940's. The only general bibliography in English is the very selective work by Halpern (1961). There are a number of general historical and linguistic bibliographies of use to ethnographers, among which may be mentioned Akademifa Nauk SSSR, Institut IAzykoznanifa (1954–1959, 1958), Akimova (1959), Binkevich (1940), Brodsky *et al.* (1924). Mel'ts (1961), Mezhov (1893) for the older literature, Unbegaun and Simmons (1953), U. S. Library of Congress (1944), and particularly Zelenin (1913). The *Novaia Sovetskaia Literatura po Istorii, Arkheologii i Ethnografii: Literatura, Postupivshaia v Biblioteku* keeps these bibliographies up to date; unfortunately, it is not generally available.

There are continuing national bibliographies for almost every SSR, as well as a number of compendia. Horecky *et al.*, Kosven, and particularly Maichel and Simmons should be checked for these bibliographies. For Ukrainian data to 1916 one may check Andriyevsky (1930); see also Grinchencko (1901), as well as Pelenskyj (1948) for some of the more recent material. For Siberia as a whole, Kerner's (1939) compendium can be checked, as well as Mezhov (1891) for the older Russian material. Jakobson *et al.* (1957) is an outstanding guide to the Paleosiberian peoples, while the *Arctic Bibliography* cited in the general section above covers most of this area.

Some selected bibliographies on individual peoples and nationalities are as follows: Akademifa Nauk Kazakhskoi SSSR (1956), Spelnikov (1951–) and Voznesenskaia and Piotrovskii (1927) for Kazakhstan and neighboring areas; Zdobnov *et al.* (1939–1946) for Buryat Mongolia; Baldaev and Vasil'ev (1962), Akademifa Nauk SSSR, Biblioteka (1963), and Rupen (1964) for Mongolia and the Mongols; Akademifa Nauk SSSR (1959) for Tuvinsk; Amitin-Shapiro (1958) for Kirgi-

zia; Bagrii (1926) for the Caucasus; Anonymous (1935) for the Karakalpaks; Guliev (1962–) for Azerbaidzhan; and Minn *et al.* (1955) for the Samoyed. Luzbetak (1951) contains an excellent annotated bibliography on the Caucasus in English.

AKADEMIĨĀ NAUK KAZAKHSKOĬ SSR, ALMA-ATA. TSENTRAL'NAĨĀ NAUCHNAĨĀ BIBLIOTEKA
1956   Bibliografiĩā izdaniĭ akademii nauk Kazakhskoĭ SSR 1951–1955. Alma-Ata, Izdvo Akademii Nauk Kazakhskoĭ SSR.

AKADEMIĨĀ NAUK SSSR. FUNDAMENTAL'NAĨĀ BIBLIOTEKA OBSHCHESTVENNYKH NAUK
1934– Novaĩā sovetskaĩā literatura po istorii, arkheologii i étnografii: literatura, postupivshaĩā v biblioteku. Moskva.

AKADEMIĨĀ NAUK SSSR. INSTITUT ĨĀZYKOZNANIĨĀ
1954– Bibliograficheskiĭ ukazetel' literatury po
1959   Russkomu ĩāzykoznaniĩū s 1825 po 1880 god. 8 volumes. Moskva, Izd-vo Akademii Nauk SSSR.
1958   Bibliograficheskiĭ ukazatel' literatury po ĩāzykoznaniĩū izdannoĭ v SSSR s 1918 po 1957 god. Moskva, Izd-vo Akademii Nauk SSSR.

AKADEMIĨĀ NAUK SSSR. SOVET PO IZUCHENIĨŪ PROIZVODITEL'NYKH SIL
1959   Bibliografiĩā Tuvinskoĭ avtonomnoĭ oblasti (1774–1958 gg.). Moskva, Izd-vo Akademii Nauk SSSR.

AKADEMIĨĀ NAUK SSSR. BIBLIOTEKA
1963   Bibliografiĩā Mongol'skoĭ narodnoĭ respubliki. Moskva, Izd-vo Vostochnoĭ Lit-ry.

AKADEMIĨĀ NAUK SSSR. SEKTOR SETI SPETSIAL'NYKH BIBLIOTEK
1958– Bibliografiĩā IAkutskoĭ ASSR (1931–
1962   1959). 2 volumes. Moskva, Akademiĩā Nauk.

AKIMOVA, TAT'ĨĀNA MIKHAĬLOVNA
1959   Seminariĭ po narodnomu poeticheskomu tvorchestvu. Saratov, Izd-vo Saratovskogo Gosuniversiteta.

AMITIN-SHAPIRO, Z. L.
1958   Annotirovannyĭ ukazatel' literatury po istorii, arkheologii i étnografii Kirgizii (1750–1917). Frunze, Akademiĩā Nauk Kirgizkoĭ SSR, Institut Istorii.

ANDRIYEVSKY, OLEKSANDER
1930   Bibliografiĩā literaturi e ukrains'kogo fol'klory. Vseukrains'ka Akademiĩā, Nauk, Étnografichno-fol'klorna Komisiĩā, Materialy do Istorii Ukrains'koi Étnografii, 1. Kievi.

ANONYMOUS
1935   Bibliograficheskiĭ ukazatel' literatury po Karakalpaki. Akademiĩā Nauk SSSR, Komissiĩā po Izucheniĩū Estestvennykh, Pro-

izvoditel'nykh Sil., Serifa Karakalpak-skafa, vyp. 8. Leningrad.

BAGRIĬ, ALEKSANDR V.
1926 Narodnafa slovenost' Kavkaza: materialy dlfa bibliograficheskogo ukazatelfa. Baku.

BALDAEV, R. L., and VASIL'EV, N. N.
1962 Ukazatel' bibliografii po mongolovedenifu na russkom fazyke, 1842–1960. Leningrad, Akademifa Nauk SSSR, Biblioteka.

BINKEVICH, E. R.
1940 Ustnoe tvorchestvo narodov SSSR. Bibliograficheskiĭ ukazatel'. Moskva.

BRODSKY, NIKOLAI LEONTEVICH, GUSEV', NIKOLAI ALEKSANDROVICH, and SIDOROV, NIKOLAI PAVLOVICH
1924 Russkafa ustnafa slovesnost' temi—bibliografifa. Leningrad, Izdatel'stvo "Kolos."

DROZDOV, G. N.
1929 Bibliografifa Ural'skogo okruga (ukazatel' pechatnykh rabot zu period 1762–1929 gg.) Ural'skiĭ Okrug i Ego Raĭony, Vol. 2, pp. 49–216. Ural'sk.

GRINCHENKO, B. D.
1901 Literatura ukrainskago fol'klora, 1777–1900. Chernigov.

GULIEV, G. A.
1962– Bibliografifa ètnografii Azerbaĭdzhana (izdannoĭ na russkom fazyke do 1917 goda), chast' 1. Baku, Izd-vo Akademii Nauk Azerbaĭdzhankoĭ SSR.

HALPERN, JOEL
1961 Bibliography of anthropological and sociological publications on Eastern Europe and the U.S.S.R. (English language sources). University of California, Los Angeles, Russian and East European Study Center Series, Vol. 1, No. 2. Los Angeles.

HORECKY, PAUL L., et al.
1962 Basic Russian publications: an annotated bibliography on Russia and the Soviet Union. Chicago, University of Chicago Press.
1965 Russia and the Soviet Union: a bibliographic guide to Western-language publications. Chicago, University of Chicago Press.

JAKOBSON, ROMAN, HÜTTL-WORTH, GERTA, and BEEBE, JOHN FRED
1957 Paleosiberian peoples and languages: a bibliographical guide. New Haven, HRAF Press.

KERNER, ROBERT JOSEPH
1939 Northeastern Asia, a selected bibliography. 2 volumes. Berkeley, University of California Press.

KOSVEN, M. O.
1947 Ukazatel' bibliograficheskikh ukazateleĭ i obzorov literatury po ètnografii narodov

SSSR. Sovetskaifa Etnografifa, 1947, No. 1, pp. 242–248. Moskva.

KRÁL, JIRI
1923– Geografická bibliografie Podkarpatské
1928 Rusi. 2 volumes. Travaux Géographiques Tchèques, 11, 13. Praha.

LUZBETAK, LOUIS
1951 Marriage and the family in the Caucasus: a contribution to the study of North Caucasian ethnology and customary law. Wien, Anthropos-Institut.

MAICHEL, KAROL, and SIMMONS, J. S. G.
1962– Guide to Russian reference books. Vols.
1964 1 and 2. Stanford, Hoover Institution on War, Revolution, and Peace, Stanford University.

MEL'TS, M. Ĭ͞A.
1961 Russkiĭ fol'klor: bibliograficheskiĭ ukazatel', 1945–1959. Leningrad, Izdatel'ski i Otdel Biblioteki Akademii Nauk SSSR.

MEZHOV, VLADIMIR I.
1891 Sibirskafa bibliografifa. Vol. 2. St. Petersburg, I. M. Sibirfakov.
1893 Russkafa istoricheskafa bibliografifa. Vol. 3. St. Petersburg, I. M. Sibirfakov.

MILLER, ROBERT J.
1952 A selective survey of literature on Mongolia. American Political Science Review, Vol. 46, pp. 849–866. Washington.

MINN, EEVA K., et al.
1955 Bibliography of the Samoyed. New Haven, Human Relations Area Files.

PELENSKYJ, EUGENE J.
1948 Ucrainica: selected bibliography on the Ukraine in western-European languages. Memoirs of the Scientific Sevcenko Society, Vol. 158. Munich.

RUPEN, ROBERT A.
1964 Mongols of the twentieth century. Part II: bibliography. Indiana University Publications, Uralic and Altaic Series, Vol. 37, Part 2. Bloomington.

SPELNIKOV, VIKTOR M.
1951– Bibliograficheskiĭ ukazatel' po Kazakhkomu tvorchestvu. Alma-Ata, Akademifa Nauk Kazakhskoĭ SSR.

TOKAREV, S. A.
1958 Etnografifa narodov SSSR. Moskva, Izd-vo Moskovskogo Universiteta.

UNBEGAUN, BORIS O., and SIMMONS, JOHN S. G.
1953 A bibliographic guide to the Russian language. Oxford, Clarendon Press.

U. S. LIBRARY OF CONGRESS. REFERENCE DEPARTMENT.
1944 Russia. A check list preliminary to a basic bibliography of materials in the Russian language. Part V. Folklore, linguistics and literary forms. Washington.

VAKAR, NICHOLAS P.
1956 A bibliographical guide to Belorussia. Cambridge, Harvard University Press.

VOZNESENSKAĬA, ELENA ALEKSANDROVNA, and PIO-
TROVSKIĬ, ALEKSANDR B.
1927 Materialy dlſa bibliografii po antropologii
i ėtnografii Kazakhstana i sredneaziatskikh
respublik. Akademiſa Nauk SSSR, Trudy
Komissii po Izucheniſū Plemennogo Sos-
tava Naseleniſa SSSR i Sopredel'nykh
Stran, 14. Leningrad.

ZDOBNOV, NIKOLAĬ VASIL'EVICH, et al.
1939– Bibliografiſa burſa-mongolii za 1890–
1946 1936 gg. 3 volumes. Moskva, Akademiſa
Nauk SSSR.

ZELENIN, DMITRIĬ KONSTANTINOVICH
1913 Bibliograficheskiĭ ukazatel' russkoĭ etno-
graficheskoĭ literatury o vneshnem byte
narodov Rossii, 1700–1910 gg. Zapiski
Imperatorskago Russkago Geograficheskago Obshchestva po Otdeleniſū Etnografii,
Vol. 40, No. 1. St. Petersburg.

EUROPE

Theodoratus (1969) seems to be the first
general ethnographic bibliography of Europe
to be published since that of Ripley (1899).
In addition to these two items reference
can be made principally to the annual volumes of the *International Volkskundliche
Bibliographie* (cited in the introduction) which,
while ostensibly of world-wide coverage, concentrates on the European material, and to
Peuckert and Lauffer's (1951) review of the
1930–1950 literature. Slavic and East Europe
in general are well covered by a number of
sources, prominent among these being the
annual volumes of the *American Bibliography of Slavic and East European Studies*
(1957–) for the most recent material and
the New York Public Library's printed *Dictionary Catalog of the Slavonic Collection*
(1959) for general coverage. Kerner's (1918)
volume is good for the earlier literature in
the western European languages, with sections
of it being supplemented by Harkins (1953).
Kaloeva (1963) and Voznesenskiĭ (1915)
cover the same area from the Russian point
of view. There are a number of regional
bibliographies which could be cited, the best
of them probably being Balys (1961), Gawełek (1914) and Vassara and Naans
(1961–). The bibliographical coverage of
southeastern Europe is generally poor, aside
from the recent work of Novak (1951) on the
Slovenes, Berze Nagy (1957) on Hungary and
Allodiatoris (1958) on the Carpathian region.
Halpern's selected bibliography of works in
English (cited above) may also be consulted.

The German-speaking areas of Europe are
generally well covered, the primary references here being to the general work of
Bach (1960) and to the various regional
works such as Hauffen and Jungbauer (1931),
Hobinka (1928), Hollander (1924), Mackensen (1936) and Réz (1934, 1935). Switzerland is covered to the early twentieth-century
by Heinemann (1907–1914). Pitré (1894)
covers much the same period for Italy.

Western and northern Europe are spottily
covered. There is almost no ethnographic
coverage of Scandinavia aside from general
items such as Aaltonen (1964) and Neuvonen (1955) on Finland and Grönland
(1961) on Norway. Great Britain is covered
in part by the publications of the Folk-
Lore Society, indexed by Bonser (cited in
subject section below), while Eager (1964)
covers the Irish material. Van Gennep
(1937–1957) offers a very thorough regional
survey of French ethnography with bibliography, while Conover (1940) gives a general
introduction to France. Two good bibliographies (Rousseau 1921; Lempereur, 1949)
cover the Walloons. For the Netherlands
literature, reference may be made to Wabeke
(1951) and Lagerwey (1961).

Some bibliographical information is available on the cultures of the Iberian Peninsula,
with Portugal being the better covered. For
the latter, see Anselmo (1923), Bell (1922)
and Lautensach and Feio (1948) and especially Pereira (1965). For Spain see the
Hispanic Society of America catalog (cited
below under Americas), as well as Foster
(1960), which contains a number of references.

AALTONEN, HILKKA
1964 Books in English on Finland. Turku University Library, Publication 8. Turku.

ALLODIATORIS, IRMA
1958 A Kárpát-medence antropológiai biblio-
gráfiája. Budapest, Akadémiai Kiadó.

AMERICAN BIBLIOGRAPHY OF SLAVIC and EAST
EUROPEAN STUDIES
1957– Vol. 1, 1956 to date. Bloomington, Indiana University.

ANSELMO, ANTONIO JOAQUIM
1923 Bibliografia das bibliografias portuguesas.
Biblioteca do Bibliotecário e do Arqui-
visto, Vol. 3. Lisboa.

BACH, ADOLF
1960 Deutsche Volkskunde. 3rd edition.
Heidelberg, Quelle and Meyer.

BALYS, JONAS P.
1961 Lithuania and Lithuanians: a selected bibliography. Studia Lituanica 2. New York, Frederick A. Praeger.

BARON, KH. A.
1869 Ukazatel' sochineniĭ o korennykh zhitelĭakh pribaltiĭskago kraĭa. Zapiski Russkago geograficheskago obshchestva po otdeleniĭu etnografii, 2, suppl., pp. 1–93.

BELL, AUBREY F. G.
1922 Portuguese bibliography. Oxford, Oxford University Press.

BERZE NAGY, JÁNOS
1957 Magyar népmesetípusok. 2 volumes. Pecs, Baranya Megye Tanácsának Kiadása.

BITTNER-SZEWCZYKOWA, HALINA
1958 Materialy do bibliografii etnografii Polskiej za 1945–1954 r. Lud Vol. 43, supplement. Wrocław.

BORODKIN, MIKHAIL M.
1902 Finliândiâ v Russkoĭ pechati i materialy dlâ bibliografii. St. Petersburg.

CONOVER, HELEN F.
1940 France. Washington, U. S. Library of Congress.

EAGER, ALAN R.
1964 A guide to Irish bibliographical material. London, Library Association.

FOSTER, GEORGE
1960 Culture and conquest: America's Spanish heritage. Viking Fund Publications in Anthropology, 27. New York.

GALLOP, RODNEY
1961 Portugal: A book of folk-ways. Cambridge, at the University Press.

GAWEŁEK, FRANCISZEK
1914 Bibliografia ludoznawstwa Polskiego. Krakow, Akademija Umiejętnosci.

GENNEP, ARNOLD VAN
1937– Manuel de folklore français con-
1957 temporain. 3 volumes. Paris, Picard.

GRÖNLAND, EILING
1961 Norway in English. Norsk Bibliografisk Bibliotek, Vol. 19. Oslo.

HARKINS, WILLIAM EDWARD
1953 Bibliography of Slavic folk literature. New York, King's Crown Press.

HAUFFEN, ADOLF, and JUNGBAUER, GUSTAV
1931 Bibliographie der deutschen Volkskunde in Böhmen. Beiträge zur sudetendeutschen Volkskunde, 20. Reichenberg.

HEINEMANN, FRANZ
1907– Kulturgeschichte und Volkskunde (Folk-
1914 lore der Schweiz. 5 volumes. Bern, Centralkommission für schweizerische Landeskunde.

HOBINKA, EDGAR
1928 Bibliographie der deutschen Volkskunde in Mähren und Schlesien. Beiträge zur

sudetendeutschen Volkskunde, 18, heft 1. Reichenberg.

HOLLANDER, B.
1924 Bibliographie der baltischen Heimatkunde. Riga.

KALOEVA, I. A.
1963 Sovetskoe slaviânovedenie: literatura o zarubezhnykh slaviânskikh stranakh na Russkom iâzyke, 1918–1960. 2 volumes. Moskva, Izd-vo Akademiiâ Nauk SSSR.

KERNER, ROBERT JOSEPH
1918 Slavic Europe: a selected bibliography in the western European languages, comprising history, languages and literatures. Harvard Bibliographies, Library Series, Vol. 1. Cambridge, Harvard University Press.

KRYŻANOWSKI, JULIAN
1947 Polska bajka ludowa w układzie systematycznym. Warszawa, Instytut Literatury Ludowej.

KUNZ, LUDVIK
1954 Ceska ethnografie a folkloristika v letech 1945–1952. Praha, Československá Akademie Věd.

KURI, SALME
1958 Estonia: a selected bibliography. Washington, U. S. Library of Congress, Slavic and East European Division.

LAGERWEY, WALTER
1961 Guide to Dutch studies. s.l.

LAUTENSACH, HERMANN, and FEIO, MARIANO
1948 Bibliográfia geografica de Portugal. Lisboa, Instituto para a Alta Cultura.

LEMPEREUR, EMILE
1949 Essai de catalogue d'une bibliothèque de litterature et de folklore Wallons, 1890–1947. Bruxelles, Editions "Labor."

MACKENSEN, LUTZ
1963 Bibliographie zur deutsch-baltischen Volkskunde. Veröffentlichungen der Volkskundlichen Forschungsstelle am Herderinstitut zu Riga, 4. Riga.

MANNINEN, ILMARI
1932 Die finnisch-ugrischen Völker. Leipzig, Harrassowitz.

NEUVONEN, EERO K.
1955 A short bibliography on Finland. Turun Yliopiston Kirjaston Julkaisuja, no. 7. Turku.

NEW YORK (CITY) PUBLIC LIBRARY. SLAVONIC DIVISION
1939 The Khazars, a bibliography. New York.
1959 Dictionary catalog of the Slavonic collection. 26 volumes. Boston, G. K. Hall and Company.

NICULESCU-VARONE, G. T.
1938 Cei mai de seamă folkloriști Române (bibliografie). Bucureşti, 1938.

NOVAK, VILKO
1951 Slovenska etnografska bibliografija, 1945–1950. Slovenska Etnograf, volumes 3/4, pp. 412–424. Ljubljana.

PEREIRA, BENJAMIM ENES
1965 Bibliografia analítica de etnografia portuguesa. Lisboa, Centro de Estudos de Ethnologia Peninsular.

PEUCKERT, WILL-ERICH, and LAUFFER, OTTO
1951 Volkskunde: Quellen und Forschungen seit 1930. Wissenschaftliche Forschungsberichte: Geisteswissenschaftliche Reihe, Vol. 14. Bern.

PITRÈ, GIUSEPPE
1894 Bibliografia delle tradizioni popolari d'Italia. Torino-Palermo, C. Clausen.

RÉZ, HEINRICH
1934 Bibliographie der deutschen Volkskunde in den Karpathenländern. Beiträge zur sudetendeutschen Volkskunde, 18, heft 2. Reichenberg.
1935 Bibliographie zur Volkskunde der Donauschwaben. Deutschungarische Heimatblätter, Schriftenreihe, 1. Budapest.

RIPLEY, WILLIAM ZEBINA
1899 A selected bibliography of the anthropology and ethnology of Europe. New York, D. Appleton and Company.

ROUSSEAU, FELIX
1921 Le folklore et les folkloristes Wallons. Bruxelles, G. Van Oest and Cie.

SUOMEN HISTORIALLINEN BIBLIOGRAFIA
1940– 3 volumes. Helsingen Seura: Kasikirjoja,
1961 2, 4, 5. Helsinki.

THEODORATUS, ROBERT J.
1969 Selected ethnographic bibliography of Europe. New Haven, HRAF Press.

VASSARA, A., and NAANS, G.
1961– Istoriîa Estonskoĭ SSR. 3 volumes. Tallin, Akademiîa Nauk Estonskoĭ SSR, Institut Istorii.

VOZNESENSKI, SERGEĬ V.
1915 Russkaîa literatura o slavîanstve. Petrograd, N. Karbasnikov.

WABEKE, BERTUS H.
1915 A guide to Dutch bibliographies. Washington, U. S. Library of Congress.

WIRPSZA, ANNA
1961 Zestawienie nabytków Polskiego towarystwa lusoznawczego za okres 1956–1959. Archiwum Etnograficzne, 23. Wrocław.

AFRICA

While there are a number of good individual bibliographies of the area, Africa is not yet well covered as a whole. Only two series of publications attempt to cover the whole of Africa and they are still incomplete. The *Bibliografiîa Afriki* (Milîavskaîa and Sinifśyna, 1964–) covers principally the Russian-language materials, while Jones (1958, 1959, 1960, 1961) covers most of the other languages for the areas she has published. However, since the latter volumes cover only the holdings of the International African Institute with selected other references, recourse must be made to the regional bibliographies for a complete coverage. Murdock (1958) gives a summary bibliography for most of the native groups. The current literature is covered in each issue of *Africa* (1931–), *African Abstracts* (1950–), and the *Bibliographie Africaniste* (Lester *et al.*, 1931–).

Rivlin (1954) offers a survey article for North Africa as a whole, while the France, Ministère de la Guerre (1930–1935), volumes cover certain aspects of French North Africa. Lacoste (1962) is a good bibliography on the Grande Kabylie region. For the rest of North Africa, Bauer y Landauer (1922) covers the older Spanish Morocco material very thoroughly, while Hill (1959) and Coult (1958) cover Libya and the Egyptian Fellah respectively. Blaudin de Thé (1960) offers a fairly small bibliography on the French Sahara, which may be supplemented by Hill (1939) and el Nasri (1962) for the Anglo-Egyptian Sudan and by Brasseur (1964) for Mali.

For Africa south of the Sahara there is a much wider range of material. Reference should be made to the South African Public Library (1961) bibliography of bibliographies for information as to what materials are available. There are a few general bibliographies for this major region. For instance, there is Weischoff (1948), a very useful bibliography in many ways, which was supplemented by Mylius (1952). There is also Forde *et al.* (1956) and Glazer (1964), the latter bring much of the preceding bibliography up to date. A new series of printed cards offered by CARDAN (1966–) will provide an annual bibliography for sub-Saharan Africa. For central Africa there are a number of good bibliographies, especially Tervuren (1932–) on the Congo and neighboring areas, Sanner (1949), Bruel (1914), Santandrea (1948), Heyse (1951), and Lambert (1951). For French West Africa there is the bibliography by Joucla (1937). For south and southeast Africa there is Schapera's (1941) fine bibliography with its supplement by Holden and Jacoby (1950), and Rita Ferreira's (1961) volume on Mozambique.

There are a number of special bibliographies available, among which may be mentioned Jahn's (1965) volume on Neo-African literature, Thieme (1964) and Gaskin (1965) on music, and Edinburgh University (1965) on urbanization.

AFRICA
1931– Bibliography of current publications. London, Oxford University Press for the International African Institute.

AFRICAN ABSTRACTS
1950– London International African Institute.

BAUER Y LANDAUER, IGNACIO
1922 Biblioteca hispano-marroqui. Madrid, Editorial Ibero-africano-americana.

BAUMANN, HERMANN, and WESTERMANN, DIEDRICH
1948 Les peuples et les civilisations de l'Afrique. Paris, Payot.

BLAUDIN DE THÉ, BERNARD M. S.
1960 Essai de bibliographie du Sahara français et des régions avoisinantes. Paris, Arts et Métiers Graphiques.

BRASSEUR, P.
1964 Bibliographie générale du Mali. Institut Français d'Afrique Noire, Catalogues et Documents, 16. Dakar.

BRUEL, GEORGES
1914 Bibliographie de l'Afrique équatoriale française. Paris, E. Larose.

CARDAN (CENTRE D'ANALYSE ET DE RECHERCHE DOCUMENTAIRES POUR L'AFRIQUE NOIRE) and CENTER OF AFRICAN STUDIES, CAMBRIDGE UNIVERSITY
1966– Bibliography cards. Cambridge and Paris.

COULT, L. H., JR.
1958 An annotated research bibliography of studies in Arabic, English and French of the fellah of the Egyptian Nile: 1798–1955. Coral Gables, University of Miami Press.

DESPOIS, JEAN
1958 L'Afrique du nord. 2nd edition. Paris, Presses Universitaires de France.

EDINBURGH UNIVERSITY. DEPARTMENT OF SOCIAL ANTHROPOLOGY
1965 African urbanization: a reading list of selected books, articles and reports. London, International African Institute.

EL NASRI, A. R.
1962 A bibliography of the Sudan 1938–1958. London, Oxford University Press.

FORDE, CYRIL DARYLL, et al.
1956 Selected annotated bibliography of Tropical Africa. New York, 20th Century Fund.

FRANCE. MINISTÈRE DE LA GUERRE. ÉTAT-MAJOR DE L'ARMÉE. SERVICE HISTORIQUE
1930– L'Afrique française du nord. 4 volumes.
1935 Paris, Imprimerie Nationale.

GASKIN, L. J. P.
1965 A select bibliography of music in Africa. London, International African Institute.

GLAZER, KENNETH M.
1964 Africa south of the Sahara: a selected and annotated bibliography, 1958–1963. Hoover Institution Bibliographical Series, 16. Stanford.

HAMBLY, WILFRED DYSON
1937 Source book for African anthropology. Field Museum, Anthropological Series, 26. Chicago.

HEYSE, THÉODORE
1951 Bibliographie du Congo Belge et du Ruanda-Urundi (1939–1950). Bruxelles, G. van Campenhoet.

HILL, R. W.
1959 A bibliography of Libya. Durham, University of Durham.

HILL, RICHARD L.
1939 A bibliography of the Anglo-Egyptian Sudan from the earliest times to 1937. London.

HOLDEN, MARGARET, and JACOBY, ANNETTE
1950 Modern life and customs. [Supplement to Schapera, 1941] Cape Town.

JAHN, JANHEINZ
1965 Die neoafrikanische Literatur: Gesamtbibliographie von den Anfängen bis zur Gegenwart. Düsseldorf, E. Diedrichs.

JONES, RUTH L.
1958 Africa bibliography series. West Africa. London, International African Institute.
1959 Africa bibliography series. North-East Africa. London, International African Institute.
1960 Africa bibliography series. East Africa. London, International African Institute.
1961 Africa bibliography series. South-East Central Africa and Madagascar. London, International African Institute.

JOUCLA, EDMOND A.
1937 Bibliographie de l'Afrique occidentale française. Paris.

LACOSTE, CAMILLE
1962 Bibliographie ethnologique de la Grand Kabylie. Recherches Méditerranéennes, Bibliographies, 1. Paris, Mouton.

LAMBERT, JEANINE
1951 Catalogue de l'Institut d'Études Centrafricaines. Mémoires de l'Institut d'Études Centrafricaines, 4. Montpellier.

LESTER, P., et al.
1931– Bibliographie africaniste. Journal de la Société des Africanistes, Vol. 1–Paris.

LYSTAD, ROBERT A., editor
1965 The African world: a survey of social research. New York, Frederick A. Praeger.

MILÍAVSKAÍA, S. L., and SINÍTSYNA, I. E.
1964– Bibliografiia Afriki. Moskva, Akademiía
Nauk SSSR, Institut Afriki.

MAUNY, RAYMOND
1961 Tableau géographique de l'ouest Africain
au moyen age. Memoires de l'Institut
Français d'Afrique Noire, 61. Dakar.

MURDOCK, GEORGE PETER
1958 African cultural summaries. New Haven,
Human Relations Area Files.
1959 Africa: its peoples and their culture history. New York, McGraw-Hill Book
Company.

MYLIUS, NORBERT
1952 Afrika Bibliographie 1943–1951. Wien,
Verein Freunde der Völkerkunde.

RITA FERREIRA, ANTONIO
1961 Bibliografia etnologica de Moçambique
(das origens a 1959). Lisboa, Junta de
Investigações do Ultramar.

RIVLIN, BENJAMIN
1954 A selective survey of the literature in the
social sciences and related fields on modern North Africa. American Political
Science Review, Vol. 48, pp. 826–848.
Washington.

SANNER, P.
1949 Bibliographie ethnographique de l'Afrique
équatoriale française, 1914–1948. Paris,
Imprimerie Nationale.

SANTANDREA, STEFANO
1948 Bibliografia di studi Africani della mis-
sione dell'Africa centrale. Verona.

SCHAPERA, ISAAC
1941 Select bibliography of South African native life and problems. London, Oxford
University Press.

SOUTH AFRICAN PUBLIC LIBRARY, CAPE TOWN
1961 A bibliography of African bibliographies,
covering territories of Africa south of the
Sahara. 4th revised edition. Grey Bibliographies, 7. Cape Town.

TERVUREN. MUSÉE ROYALE DE L'AFRIQUE CENTRALE
1932– Bibliographie ethnographique de l'Afrique
Sud-Saharienne. [formerly Bibliographie
ethnographique du Congo Belge et des
regions avoisinantes] Tervuren. Belgium.

THIEME, DARIUS L.
1964 African music: a briefly annotated bibliography. Washington, U. S. Library of
Congress.

VANDEWOUDE, EMIEL J. L. M.
1958 Documents pour servir à la connaissance
des populations du Congo Belge. Archives
du Congo Belge, 2. Léopoldville.

WIESCHOFF, HEINRICH ALBERT
1948 Anthropological bibliography of Negro
Africa. American Oriental Series, 23.
New Haven, American Oriental Society.

THE AMERICAS

The bibliographic coverage of the Americas, with the exception of southern Middle
America, is excellent, with several outstanding general and regional bibliographies being
available. An excellent general guide to the
available bibliographies is Gibson (1960). The
most complete bibliographies of books are
the printed catalogs of the libraries of the
Hispanic Society of America (1962), the
History of the Americas collection of the
New York Public Library (1961), and of the
Edward Ayer Collection of Americana and
American Indians in the Newberry Library
(1961). These may be supplemented by Dockstader (1957) for theses and dissertations,
Boggs (1940) for folklore, Bercaw et al.
(1940) for maize cultivation, Edwards and
Rasmussen (1942) for Indian agriculture in
general, Humphreys (1958) for Latin American history, and Work (1928) and the Schomburg Collection (New York Public Library
1962) for the American Negro. Comas Camp
(1953) is a good, selected general bibliography. These bibliographies are kept up to date
by a number of aids, the more important of
which are the *Handbook of Latin American
Studies* (1936–), the *Bibliographie Américaniste* (Rivet et al., 1919–), and Valle's the *Boletín Bibliográfico de Antropología Americana*
(1937–), all of which contain first-class subject bibliographies.

The best available ethnographic bibliographies on North America are those of Murdock (1960) on the Indian tribes and Haywood (1961) on all ethnic groups. Garigue
(1956) is a good introduction to French
Canada while Basler et al. (1960) is a very
helpful aid for the United States of America.
Rouse and Goggin (1947) and Guthe and
Kelly (1963) supplement Murdock for the
eastern seaboard. Miller (1966) is the best
recent bibliography on the North American
Negro.

For Middle America, Bernal (1962) is the
most complete bibliography for the northern
region (i.e., from Guatemala north). This is
supplemented by Boggs (1939) on Mexican
folklore, Ewald (1956) on Guatemala, Lines
(1943) on Costa Rica, Germán Parra and
Jiménez Moreno (1954) on indigenism in the
whole region, Valle (1937–1941) on the
Maya, and Martínez Ríos (1961) on Oaxaca.
The *Handbook of Middle American Indians*

(Wauchope, 1965–) will eventually cover most of this region and will be a major source of information.

South America is covered by two major bibliographies. The first is contained in the first six volumes of the *Handbook of South American Indians* (Steward, 1946–1959) and the second is a more recent compilation by O'Leary (1963). The latter covers continental South America only, but the *Handbook of South American Indians* also contains materials on the aboriginal Caribbean and Central America north to Guatemala. These volumes may be supplemented by several good, regional bibliographies, outstanding among these being Baldus (1954) on Brazil. Others include Fuchs (1964) on Venezuela, Moraes and Berrien (1949) and Pierson (1945) on Brazil, Cortázar (1942) on Argentina, Pereira Salas (1952) on Chile, and Rio de Janeiro (1963) on the Amazon region as a whole.

For the Caribbean area, as indicated above, Steward (1950) may be used for the aboriginal peoples while Comitas (1967) covers the twentieth-century social science literature.

ARGUEDAS, JOSÉ MARIA
1960 Bibliografía del folklore Peruano. Instituto Panamericano de Geografía e Historia, Publicación 230. México.
BALDUS, HERBERT
1954 Bibliografia critica da etnologia Brasileira. São Paulo, Serviço de Comemorações Culturais.
BARCELONA. UNIVERSIDAD
1953– Bibliografía historica de España e Hispanoamerica, Volume 1–. Barcelona, Editorial Teide.
BASLER, ROY P., et al.
1960 A guide to the study of the United States of America. Washington, Library of Congress.
BERCAW, LOUISE O., HANNAY, ANNIE M., and LARSON, NELLIE G.
1940 Corn in the development of the civilization of the Americas. U. S. Bureau of Agricultural Economics, Agricultural Economics Bibliography, 87. Washington.
BERNAL, IGNACIO
1962 Bibliografía de arqueología y etnografía: Mesoamerica y Norte de México, 1514–1960. Instituto Nacional de Antropología e Historia, Memorias, 7. México.
BOGGS, RALPH STEELE
1939 Bibliografía del folklore Mexicano. Boletín Bibliográfico de Antropología Americana, 3, No. 3, appendix. México.
1940 Bibliography of Latin American folklore.

Inter-American Bibliographical and Library Association, Publications, Ser. 1, Vol. 5. New York, H. W. Wilson Company.
BOLETÍN BIBLIOGRÁFICO DE ANTROPOLOGÍA AMERICANA
1937– Volume 1–. México, Instituto Panamericano de Geografía e Historia.
COMAS CAMP, JUAN
1953 Bibliografía selectiva de las culturas indígenas de America. Instituto Panamericano de Geografía e Historia, Publicación 166. México.
COMITAS, LAMBROS
1967 Caribbeana: 1900–1965. Seattle, University of Washington Press.
CORTÁZAR, AUGUSTO R.
1942 Guía bibliográfica del folklore Argentino. Universidad de Buenos Aires, Instituto de Literatura Argentina, Sección de Bibliografía, 1, no. 1. Buenos Aires.
DIÉGUES JÚNIOR, MANUEL
1960 Regiões culturais do Brasil. Rio de Janeiro, Centro Brasileiro de Pesquisas Educacionais.
DOCKSTADER, FREDERICK J.
1957 The American Indian in graduate studies: a bibliography of theses and dissertations. Contributions from the Museum of the American Indian, Heye Foundation, 15. New York.
DRIVER, HAROLD E.
1961 Indians of North America. Chicago, University of Chicago Press.
EDWARDS, EVERETT E., and RASMUSSEN, WAYNE D.
1942 A bibliography on the agriculture of the American Indians. U. S. Department of Agriculture, Miscellaneous Publications, 447. Washington.
EWALD, ROBERT H.
1956 Bibliografía comentada sobre antropología social Guatemalteca 1900–1955. Guatemala, Seminário de Integración Social Guatemalteca.
FUCHS, HELMUTH
1964 Bibliografía basica de etnología de Venezuela. Publicaciónes del Seminário de Antropología Americana, 5. Sevilla, Universidad de Sevilla.
GARIGUE, PHILIP
1956 A bibliographical introduction to the study of French Canada. Montreal, McGill University, Department of Sociology and Anthropology.
GERMÁN PARRA, MANUEL, and JIMÉNEZ MORENO, WIGBERTO
1954 Bibliografía indigenista de México y Centroamerica (1850–1950). Instituto Nacional Indigenista, Memorias, 4. México.
GIBSON, GORDON D.
1960 A bibliography of anthropological bibliog-

raphies: the Americas. Current Anthropology, Vol. 1, pp. 61–75. Chicago.

GUTHE, ALFRED K., and KELLY, PATRICIA B.
1963 An anthropological bibliography of the eastern seaboard, Vol. II. Eastern States Archeological Federation Research Publication, 2. Trenton.

HANDBOOK OF LATIN AMERICAN STUDIES
1936– Vol. 1–. Cambridge, Gainesville.

HAYWOOD, CHARLES
1961 A bibliography of North American folklore and folksong. 2nd edition. 2 volumes. New York, Dover Publications.

HISPANIC SOCIETY OF AMERICA. LIBRARY.
1962 Catalogue of the library. 10 volumes. Boston, G. K. Hall and Company.

HODGE, FREDERICK W.
1907– Handbook of American Indians North of
1910 Mexico. 2 volumes. U. S. Bureau of American Ethnology, Bulletin 30. Washington.

HUMPHREYS, ROBERT ARTHUR
1958 Latin American history. A guide to the literature in English. London, Oxford University Press.

JIMÉNEZ MORENO, WIGBERTO
1937– Materiales para una bibliografía etnográ-
1938 fica de la America Latina. Boletín Bibliográfico de Antropología Americana, Vol. 1, pp. 47–77, 167–197, 289–421. México.

KRICKEBERG, WALTER
1946 Etnología de America. México, Fondo de Cultura Económica.

LINES, JORGE A.
1943 Bibliografía antropológica aborigen de Costa Rica. San José, Universidad de Costa Rica.

MARTÍNEZ RÍOS, JORGE
1961 Bibliografía antropológica y sociológica del estado de Oaxaca. México, Instituto de Investigaciones Sociales de la Universidad Nacional.

MILLER, ELIZABETH W.
1966 The Negro in America: a bibliography. Cambridge, Harvard University Press.

MORAES, RUBENS BORBA DE, and BERRIEN, WILLIAM
1949 Manual bibliográfico de estudos Brasileiros. Rio de Janeiro, Souza.

MURDOCK, GEORGE PETER
1960 Ethnographic bibliography of North America. 3rd edition. New Haven, HRAF Press.

NEWBERRY LIBRARY, CHICAGO. EDWARD E. AYER COLLECTION
1961 Dictionary catalog of the Edward E. Ayer collection of Americana and American Indians in the Newberry Library. 16 volumes. Boston, G. K. Hall and Company.

NEW YORK (CITY) PUBLIC LIBRARY. REFERENCE DEPARTMENT
1961 Dictionary catalog of the history of the Americas collection. 28 volumes. Boston, G. K. Hall and Company.

NEW YORK (CITY) PUBLIC LIBRARY. SCHOMBURG COLLECTION OF NEGRO LITERATURE AND HISTORY
1962 Dictionary Catalog. 9 volumes. Boston, G. K. Hall and Company.

O'LEARY, TIMOTHY J.
1963 Ethnographic bibliography of South America. New Haven, HRAF Press.

PEREIRA SALAS, EUGENIO
1952 Guía bibliográfica para el estudio del folklore Chileno. Archivos del Folklore Chileno, 4. Santiago de Chile.

PIERSON, DONALD
1945 Survey of the literature on Brazil of sociological significance published up to 1940. Joint Committee on Latin American Studies of the National Research Council, American Council of Learned Societies and the Social Science Research Council, Miscellaneous Publication, 4. Cambridge, Harvard University Press.

POBLETE TRONCOSO, MOISÉS
1936 Ensayo de bibliografía social de los paises Hispano-americanos. Santiago de Chile.

RIO DE JANEIRO. CONSELHO NACIONAL DE PESQUISAS
1963 Amazônia—Bibliografía 1614–1962. Rio de Janeiro.

RIVET, PAUL, et al.
1919– Bibliographie Américaniste. Journal de la Société des Américanistes de Paris, Nouvelle Série, Vol. 11–. Paris.

ROUSE, IRVING B., and GOGGIN, JOHN M.
1947 An anthropological bibliography of the eastern seaboard. Eastern States Archeological Federation Research Publication, 1. Trenton.

SPENCER, ROBERT F., et al.
1965 The Native Americans. New York, Harper & Row, Publishers.

STEWARD, JULIAN HAYNES, editor
1946– Handbook of South American Indians.
1959 7 volumes. U. S. Bureau of American Ethnology, Bulletin 143. Washington.

STEWARD, JULIAN HAYNES, and FARON, LOUIS C.
1959 Native peoples of South America. New York, McGraw-Hill Book Company.

TAX, SOL, editor
1952 Heritage of Conquest: the ethnology of Middle America. Glencoe, Ill., The Free Press.

VALLE, RAFAEL H.
1937– Bibliografía Maya. Boletín Bibliográfico
1941 de Antropología Americana, Vols. 1–5, appendix. México.

WAUCHOPE, ROBERT, editor
1965– Handbook of Middle American Indians.

11 volumes. Austin, University of Texas Press.

WISSLER, CLARK
1938 The American Indian. 3rd edition. New York, Oxford University Press.

WORK, MONROE N.
1928 A bibliography of the Negro in Africa and America. New York.

THE PACIFIC

The Pacific is one of the better-covered regions of the world, bibliographically speaking, with a number of good general and regional bibliographies being available. For an idea of some of these, consult Leeson (1954). The most general bibliography is the printed catalog of the library of the Bernice P. Bishop Museum (1964), which covers the whole area, including the countries bordering the Pacific. Taylor (1965) is the single handiest and a uniformly excellent guide to Polynesia, Micronesia and Melanesia, while Lewin (1931) contains a good subject index for these areas. Other bibliographies touching special aspects are Cammack and Saito (1962), Howard *et al.* (1963) and Sachet and Fosberg (1955). Current bibliography may be found in the *Bibliographie de l'Océanie* (O'Reilly, 1946–).

Greenway (1963) is a nearly complete bibliography of aboriginal Australia, and may be supplemented by consulting the *Australian Social Science Abstracts* and Pilling's review work (1962). For Melanesia, Elkin (1953) is an excellent review of research, which may be supplemented by the two Galis bibliographies (1956, 1962), by the Netherlands Ministry (1952) and by McGrath (1965) for New Guinea, and by O'Reilly's (1958) fine bibliography which consists mainly of Japanese works and which should be supplemented by Taylor (1965). Taylor again is the best general bibliography on Polynesia. Luomala *et al.* (1947) is a critical survey of some aspects of the Literature on Polynesia. Good individual bibliographies exist on Hawaii (Hawaii, 1963) and New Caledonia (O'Reilly, 1955).

For Indonesia, the standard bibliography, covering items through 1950, is that of Kennedy (1962), which is partly supplemented by Kleiweg de Zwaan (1923), Bork-Feltkamp (1938) and Suzuki (1958). There is no good ethnographic bibliography on the Philippines. See Houston's (1960) bibliography of bibliog-

raphies, and Eggan *et al.* (1956). Pardo de Tavera (1903) and Welsh (1959) may also be consulted in this respect.

The annual bibliography in the *Journal of Asian Studies* and the Cornell University Library Southeast Asia accessions list (both cited above) cover the Philippines and Indonesia and should be checked.

AUSTRALIAN SOCIAL SCIENCE ABSTRACTS
1946– Melbourne, Australian National Research Council.

BERNICE P. BISHOP MUSEUM, HONOLULU, HAWAII
1964 Dictionary catalog of the library. 9 volumes. Boston, G. K. Hall and Company.

BORK-FELTKAMP, A. J. VAN
1938 Bibliographie de l'Indonésie et de la Mélanésie. Mededeelingen van de Afdeeling Volkenkunde van het Koloniaale Instituut, Extra Serie, 3 (also Internationales Archiv für Ethnographie, 39). Den Haag.

BUCK, PETER H.
1945 An introduction to Polynesian anthropology. Bernice P. Bishop Museum, Bulletin 187. Honolulu.

CAMMACK, FLOYD M., AND SAITO, SHIRO
1962 Pacific island bibliography. New York, The Scarecrow Press.

EGGAN, FRED, *et al.*
1956 Selected bibliography of the Philippines. New Haven, Human Relations Area Files.

ELKIN, ADOLPHUS PETER
1953 Social anthropology in Melanesia: a review of research. London, Oxford University Press.

GALIS, K. W.
1956 Bibliography of West New Guinea. New Haven, Yale University Press.
1962 Bibliographie van Nederlands-Nieuw-Guinea. Den Haag.

GREENWAY, JOHN
1963 Bibliography of the Australian aborigines and the native peoples of Torres Straits to 1959. Sydney, Angus and Robertson.

HAWAII. UNIVERSITY. LIBRARY
1963 Dictionary catalog of the Hawaiian collection. 4 volumes. Boston, G. K. Hall and Company.

HOUSTON, CHARLES O., JR.
1960 Philippine bibliography. Manila, University of Manila.

HOWARD, IRWIN, VINACKE, W. EDGAR, and MARETZKI, THOMAS
1963 Culture and personality in the Pacific Islands: a bibliography. Honolulu, Anthropological Society of Hawaii.

KEESING, FELIX M.
1953 Social anthropology in Polynesia; a review of research. London, Oxford University Press.

KENNEDY, RAYMOND
1962 Bibliography of Indonesian peoples and cultures. 2nd revised edition. New Haven, HRAF Press.

KLEIWEG DE ZWAAN, J. P.
1923 Anthropologische bibliographie van den Indischen Archipel en van Nederlandsch West Indië. Mededeelingen van het Bureau voor de Bestuurzaken der Buitengewesten, bewerkt door het Encyclopaedisch Bureau, 30. Weltevreden.

LEESON, IDA
1954 A bibliography of bibliographies of the South Pacific. London, Oxford University Press.

LEWIN, EVANS
1931 Subject catalogue of the library of the Royal Empire Society. Volume 2. Australia, New Zealand, the South Pacific, General voyages and travels. London, Royal Empire Society.

LUOMALA, KATHARINE, et al.
1947 Specialized studies in Polynesian anthropology. Bernice P. Bishop Museum Bulletin 193. Honolulu.

MCGRATH, WILLIAM A.
1965 New Guineana: or, books of New Guinea, 1942-1965. Port Moresby.

NETHERLANDS MINISTRY FOR OVERSEAS TERRITORIES
1952 Overzicht van de literatuur betreffende Nieuw-Guinea aanwezig in de bibliotheek van het Ministerie voor Uniezaken en Overzeese Rijksdelen. 2 volumes. Den Haag.

O'REILLY, PATRICK
1946- Bibliographie de l'Océanie. Journal de la Société des Océanistes, Vol. 1-. Paris.
1955 Bibliographie méthodique, analytique et critique de la Nouvelle-Calédonie. Société des Océanistes, Publication 4. Paris.
1958 Bibliographie méthodique, analytique et critique des Nouvelles-Hébrides. Société des Océanistes, Publication 8. Paris.

PARDO DE TAVERA, T. H.
1903 Biblioteca Filipina . . . relativos a la historia, la etnografia, la linguistica . . . de las islas Filipinas, de Jolo y Marianas. Washington, U. S. Government Printing Office.

PILLING, ARNOLD R.
1962 Aborigine culture history: a survey of publications 1954-1957. Detroit, Wayne State University Press.

SACHET, MARIE HÉLÈNE, and FOSBERG, F. RAYMOND
1955 Island bibliographies. National Academy of Sciences—National Research Council Publication 335. Washington.

SUZUKI, PETER
1958 Critical survey of studies on the anthropology of Nias, Mentawei and Enggano. 's-Gravenhage, Martinus Nijhoff.

SWEET and MAXWELL
1938 A bibliography of the laws of Australia, New Zealand, Fiji, and the Western Pacific . . . to 1938. London, Sweet and Maxwell, Law Book Company of Australia.

TAYLOR, CLYDE ROMER HUGHES
1965 A Pacific bibliography: printed matter relating to the native peoples of Polynesia, Melanesia and Micronesia. 2nd edition. Oxford, the Clarendon Press.

UTINOMI, HUZIO
1952 Bibliography of Micronesia. Honolulu, University of Hawaii Press.

WELSH, DORIS VARNER
1959 A catalogue of printed materials relating to the Philippine Islands, 1519-1900, in the Newberry Library. Chicago, Newberry Library.

SUBJECT

The best general ethnographic subject bibliography is the printed subject catalog of the Harvard University Peabody Museum library cited above in the general section. There are three other general continuing subject bibliographies which are of interest to ethnologists. These are, in descending order of usefulness, the *Internationale Volkskundliche Bibliographie* cited in the introduction; the U. S. Library of Congress subject catalogs (for books only); and *A London Bibliography of the Social Sciences*. I have listed a few more individual subject bibliographies below. The more important of these seem to me to be Albert *et al.* (1959), Bonser (1961), Conklin (1963), Keesing (1953), Kunst (1959-1960), Nader *et al.* (1966), and the various medical indices (e.g., *Index Medicus*). For an extended listing of such bibliographies, Besterman's bibliography of bibliographies cited in the introduction should be consulted.

ALBERT, ETHEL M., et al.
1959 A selected bibliography on values, ethics and esthetics in the behavioral sciences and philosophy, 1920-1958. Glencoe, Ill., Free Press.

AMERICAN BEHAVIORAL SCIENTIST
1965 The ABS guide to recent publications in the social and behavioral sciences. New York, the American Behavioral Scientist.

BARTLETT, HARLEY HARRIS
1955– Fire in relation to primitive agriculture
1961 and grazing in the tropics: annotated bibliography. 3 volumes. Ann Arbor, Botanical Gardens of the University of Michigan.

BONSER, WILFRED
1961 A bibliography of folklore, as contained in the first eighty years of the publications of the Folklore Society. London.

BRITISH LIBRARY of POLITICAL AND ECONOMIC SCIENCE
1931– A London bibliography of the social
1960 sciences. 11 volumes. London, London School of Economics and Political Science.

CONKLIN, HAROLD C.
1963 The study of shifting cultivation. Pan American Union, Studies and Monographs, 6. Washington.

CURRENT LIST OF MEDICAL LITERATURE
1941– Volumes 1–36. [Superseded by Index
1959 Medicus, New Series] Washington, U. S. Army Medical Library.

DAIKEN, LESLIE H.
1950 Children's games: a bibliography. Folklore, Vol. 61, pp. 218–222. London.

DIEHL, KATHARINE SMITH
1956 Religions, mythologies, folklores: an annotated bibliography. New Brunswick, Scarecrow Press.

DRIVER, EDWIN D.
1965 The sociology and anthropology of mental illness: a reference guide. Amherst, University of Massachusetts Press.

HARVARD MEDICAL SCHOOL AND PSYCHIATRIC SERVICE, MASSACHUSETTS GENERAL HOSPITAL
1962 Community mental health and social psychiatry: a reference guide. Cambridge, Harvard University Press.

INDEX MEDICUS
1879– [Superseded by the Quarterly Cumulative
1927 Index Medicus] New York, Washington.
1960– New Series, Vol. 1–. Washington, U. S. Department of Health, Education, and Welfare.

KEESING, FELIX M.
1953 Culture change; an analysis and bibliography of anthropological sources to 1952. Stanford Anthropological Series, 1. Stanford, Stanford University Press.

KUNST, JAAP
1959– Ethnomusicology. 3rd edition (with sup-
1960 plement). The Hague, Martinus Nijhoff.

MACLEISH, KENNETH, et al.
1940 Anthropology and agriculture: selected references on agriculture in primitive cultures. Agricultural Economics Bibliography, No. 89. Washington, U. S. Department of Agriculture.

NADER, LAURA, KOCH, KLAUS F., and COX, BRUCE
1966 The ethnography of law: a bibliographic survey. Current Anthropology, Vol. 7, pp. 267–294. Chicago.

NETTL, BRUNO
1967 Reference materials in ethnomusicology. 2nd ed., rev. Detroit Studies in Music Bibliography, 1. Detroit, Information Coordinators.

NUTT, ALFRED L.
1906 List of works dealing with the "Early Institutions" side of folklore studies. Folk-lore, Vol. 17, pp. 508–512. London.

QUARTERLY CUMULATIVE INDEX MEDICUS
1927– [Superseded by the Current List of Med-
1952 ical Literature] Chicago, American Medical Association.

SIMMONS, OZZIE G.
1963 Social research in health and medicine: a bibliography. In Freeman, Howard E., Levine, Sol, and Reeder, Leo G., editors, Handbook of Medical Sociology, pp. 493–581. Englewood Cliffs, N.J., Prentice-Hall.

U. S. LIBRARY OF CONGRESS
1955 Library of Congress catalog: a cumulative list of works represented by Library of Congress printed cards. Books: subjects, 1950–1954. 20 volumes. Ann Arbor, J. W. Edwards.
1960 Library of Congress catalog: a cumulative list of works represented by Library of Congress printed cards. Books: subjects, 1955–1959. 22 volumes. Paterson, Pageant Books.
1965 Library of Congress catalog: a cumulative list of works represented by Library of Congress printed cards. Books: subjects, 1960–1964. 25 volumes. Ann Arbor, J. W. Edwards.

CHAPTER 8

Source Criticism in Anthropology

JOSEF HAEKEL

Translated from the German
by Terrence A. Tatje and Emile M. Schepers

A prerequisite for every scientific project is reliable research material. In contrast to the experimental natural sciences, research in the humanities and social sciences depends on sources. These have to undergo critical examination. This particularly applies to history, whose methods, including source criticism, have been developed and built up in the course of time. It was the great service of the German ethnologist Fritz Graebner, who originally came from history, to have first offered a systematic presentation of ethnographic source criticism in his *Methode der Ethnologie* (1911), which followed closely the *Lehrbuch der historischen Methode* of Ernst Bernheim (1908). Graebner tried to place at the disposal of ethnology, which he wanted to regard objectively and formally as a historical discipline, a method of source criticism adequate for its own needs (Graebner 1911:3).

What L. Gottschalk (1945:8 f., 10) said about history would apply *mutatis mutandis* to the objective of ethnology as Graebner (and the ethnological school of thought which he initiated) conceived of it.

The process of critically examining the records and survivals of the past is called historical method. The imaginative reconstruction of the past from the data derived by that process is called historiography. . . . By means of the historical method and historiography the historian endeavors to reconstruct [as] much of the past of mankind as he can. . . . He can never tell the whole story of the actual past (for the records are not complete). . . . With Ernst Bernheim's *Lehrbuch* . . . the modern and more academic discussion of the subject may be said to have begun. Since Bernheim's there has been a number of textbooks on the subject . . . none of them can be said to surpass his masterpiece.

A number of historians have not agreed with this estimate of Bernheim. Gaston van Bulck (1932:14 ff., 194 f.) provided a few supplementary remarks regarding the method of source criticism presented by Graebner; Koppers (1939) concurred essentially with Graebner, but also referred to A. Feder's (1924) *Lehrbuch der geschichtlichen Methode*. Of Koppers' treatment P. Leser (1938:122) observed: "In the whole passage which deals with sources, the divergent concepts of three different scholars are juxtaposed in the classification of sources by Koppers; through this his presentation becomes quite unclear."

An ethnographic source critic should orient himself toward history proper, regardless of whether he regards ethnology as a historical discipline or otherwise. However, he must be aware that there are naturally differences between ethnology and history—as much in technical considerations as in the kind of source materials and tasks of research.

In history we can only comprehend empirically what the sources and relics give evidence of. It would be an illusion to believe that we have before us in historical data the complete progress of a series of events, motives and purposes. What is transmitted is in any case not the whole, nor always the significant. In historical material only excerpts from the full body of factual happenings are presented. These excerpts, as verified by criticims, are all that we know of the historical period in question. (Wagner 1951:219, after J. G. Droysens; see further Collingwood 1955:294.)

Historical source criticism may be broken down into internal and external criticism. Subsumed under external criticism are inquiries into the authenticity of documents and reports, into the kind of source, and into the relations of texts to one another (who copied from whom) (Bernheim 1908:391 ff.; Kirn 1952:53, 59; Gottschalk 1945:28 ff.). To internal criticism belong such questions as the following: What is the credibility of the source and the general reliability of the author (possibly with the aid of biographical statements)? How did the author come by his information? Did he use informants? Did he report from his own experiences? How much was the author *able to* and how much did he *want to* report on the event? How much time lay between the event and the report? (Bernheim 1908:464 ff.; Kirn 1952:53, 59, 63 f.; Gottschalk 1945:36 f.)

Gottschalk gives other important points (1945:36, 38):

Every historical subject has four aspects: the human and personal element, the geographical, the chronological, and the functional. With this in mind the historical investigator combs his document for relevant particulars or notes. . . . To the historian any single detail in any document is good evidence, provided it passes four tests:
1. Was the ultimate source of the detail (the primary witness) able to tell the truth?
2. Was the primary witness willing to tell the truth?
3. Is the primary witness accurately reported with regard to the detail under examination?
4. Is there any external corroboration of the detail under examination?

In general the ability to report the truth depends in part on the spatial and temporal proximity of the witness to the event. But even given these conditions, the competence of the reporter is still the crucial factor (Gottschalk 1945:39). Egocentricity is one source of error; i.e., an author sees the situation from his own standpoint so that a report can be impaired by his bias or prejudice (Gottschalk 1945:41 ff.). A historical report is more credible if it is reinforced by other witnesses; i.e., when two or more independent witnesses report the same fact.

The various ways in which historians classify and define sources will be illustrated by two examples—the classifications of Feder (1924), and of Kirn (1952). Feder classifies sources A) by origin and B) by their cognitive mode:

A. *By Origin*
1. By time:
   a) contemporary sources (contemporary with the historical happenings)
   b) later sources

2. By place:
   a) local sources (those produced at the place of the particular historical event)
   b) distant sources (those produced elsewhere)
3. By the means by which the author gathered the data:
   a) direct or original (primary) sources (if the report is directly connected with the historical fact in question)
   b) indirect or derived (secondary) sources (if the report stems from an intermediary, or otherwise from second or third hand)
B. *By Cognitive Mode*
1. Concrete sources (material objects, culture elements):
   a) relics (culture elements which have a material basis)
   b) survivals (cultural phenomena of a social or spiritual nature)
2. Spoken sources: oral and written communications, traditions and reports

P. Kirn (1952:30 ff.) gives the following classification of historical sources:

1. By origin (whether contemporary or not, whether local or foreign, whether direct or indirect, whether private or open)
2. By content (political or event history, history of law, economic history, art history, religious history, etc.)
3. By purpose (reports, chronicles, annals, documents, biographies, letters, etc.)
4. By cognitive mode (relics or traditions)

By tradition is meant all which arises from the intention to convey knowledge of particular events to the present or future world. All remaining sources fall under the category of relics (e.g., such material sources as artistic monuments, archaeological finds, coins, emblems, etc., and names of distant places and people).

The nature of ethnographic sources and their method of production corresponds only in part to history proper. Graebner has already pointed this out (1911:3). In ethnology (cultural anthropology) we deal to a great extent with concrete sources of real facts, i.e., with cultural traits which the field worker, or another European observer who collects the ethnographic source materials, has directly before him. Since ethnology deals primarily with nonliterate peoples, the reports are based mainly on oral traditions and statements of natives rather than accounts written by them. Thus the greater part of the direct evidence with which ethnology operates are the written reports of field workers and other literate persons. These written accounts are amenable to the same kind of source criticism practiced by historians (cf. also Koppers 1939:90 f.).

While in history the study of events and influential personalities stands in the foreground, in ethnology the point of stress lies in the investigation of the cultural and social life of preliterate peoples. One branch of ethnology, however, namely so-called ethnohistory, seeks to give attention to the history of "events and peoples" of nonliterate peoples by using old—respectively contemporary—documents and reports.

Naturally the historian finds his material mainly in libraries and archives. Even when he can occasionally be an eyewitness to historical events, which of course is seldom, he must continually draw upon the reports of others. Ethnographic source material, gained on the spot from observations and interviews, refers mostly to the present or the immediate past. Through the "direct historical approach" ethnohistory can also bring to light ethnographic materials from earlier times. Considering the growing importance of ethnohistorical studies, the necessity arises for ethnologists to make full use of historical documents in libraries and archives as well as ethnographic field work. Thus Kluckhohn (1945:83) wrote:

With some honorable exceptions anthropologists are notorious among the social scientists for their neglect of library research. Anthropologists have little read, studied, or analyzed any of the [ethnohistorical] documents. . . . Thorough and systematic study might well unearth valuable ethnographic details [from former periods]. . . .

In the same vein W. Fenton (1952:328) says:

. . . cultural anthropology in America has not yet realized its potentialities as a strictly historical science and that the maturity of our discipline depends in part on training ethnologists who will carry the perspective of fieldwork to the library. We must enlist the help of historians to train some ethnologists in historical methods so that our students will be equally at home in the field and in the library and so that they may use the materials and methods of one research activity to enrich the other. . . . The abundant archival resources awaiting the ethnological student have scarcely been touched.

The statements of Graebner, who sought to make use of the principles of historical method for ethnology, still constitute the basis for ethnographic source criticism. Even though the source materials of history and ethnology differ essentially from each other, they share a series of crucial features which make it correct for ethnographic source criticism to follow *mutatis mutandis* the model of historical source criticism. Only the points of emphasis are different. Of course the statements of Graebner (and Koppers) about ethnographic source criticism need various revisions and supplementations, above all with regard to autobiographies of natives, oral traditions, and recorded sources.

THE ETHNOGRAPHIC SOURCES

Following Graebner's (1911:11) terminology, we can distinguish the following types of ethnographic sources:

I. Direct evidence:

These present the complete culture vis-à-vis the field worker, and ethnographic objects in museums and collections.

II. Reports:

1. Written accounts of experiences of ethnographic field work, based on observation and interview. These constitute the core of ethnographic materials.

   a) Complete tribal monographs (holistic approach)
   b) Inquiries into partial aspects of culture and society (particularistic approach)
   c) Reports on research on the same tribe over a time interval (re-studies)
   d) Distributional studies of single culture traits with cartographic inclusions, which were plotted during field studies (see e.g., Schmitz 1960; Tessmann 1930; and Driver, Chapter 32).
   e) Acculturation studies from sociological, functional, psychological and historical viewpoints

2. Dated contemporary (ethnohistorical) reports and documents on ethnic groups or an area (travel reports, missionary reports, records of conquistadors, administrators, merchants, military men, seafarers, etc., colonial records, and geographic and historical works on non-European countries. These begin with the occupation of the country by Europeans and are set forth in chronological order up to the advent of professional field work. This temporal continuum of local historical events makes it possible to bring recent ethnographic data

into relationship with past work. A combination of culture history and event history should be considered. This "direct historical approach" also permits one to make statements about persistence and change, and furthermore about the historical importance of native personages. Where possible a connection with the local prehistory should be sought. Interpretation and conjecture can be carried out together with source criticism.

3. Reports of Chinese, Arabic, and ancient and medieval writers—geographers, historians, travelers, merchants—about peoples who for the most part no longer exist (e.g., Cimmerians, Scyths, Huns, etc.) with the objective of understanding single ethnic groups and their cultural inventories, and reconstructing their histories. At the same time connections with archaeological finds can also be sought. One speaks here of paleoethnography (see Closs 1956; Mänchen-Helfen 1959); but in my opinion the term "archaeoethnology" would be more appropriate.

4. Biographies and autobiographies of natives (complete life histories and reports on only partial sections or episodes of the life of an individual).

5. Oral traditions of natives, which later become fixed in writing.

6. Texts in the native speech with interlineal translation and freer translation, about cultural themes, traditions and biographies.

Among the reports one must also include so-called recorded sources: still photography, moving pictures, drawings, and tape recordings.

SOURCE CRITICISM

Graebner (1911:8 ff.) makes the following remarks about the collecting of ethnographic materials (field work): First, the researcher should have a solid schooling in general ethnological method. It would be wrong to claim that someone is prepared to collect satisfactory ethnographic material merely through "unlimited receptivity" and great knowledge of technical routine. Furthermore, the field worker should practice criticism of his own observations. The research area chosen should be neither too narrow nor too wide. An area with cultural variation is recommended,

but too large an area results in superficiality. And the published results should make critical examination possible. But Koppers (1939:17) remarks that Graebner did not sufficiently assess the difference between the field worker and the armchair anthropologist at home. For the latter the objects and collections brought back by an expedition are the only direct evidence of the culture in question. Cultural phenomena which have no material reflection (social systems, usages, religion, etc.) are direct or firsthand evidence only for the field worker, insofar as he himself can observe and experience them. For others such phenomena become scientifically useful only when they have been described in writing, thus acquiring the character of indirect evidence. As such they conform in principle to the source material of written history and are subject to the usual source criticism of historians.

But neither Graebner nor Koppers has considered the fact that a field worker can also be involved with indirect evidence in his work among a tribe, as when things which he could not directly witness, e.g., the progress of a celebration or a ceremony, are reported to him by informants. A major portion of ethnographic field work reports stem from such communications, i.e., from indirect evidence. On the other hand, the material culture of an ethnic group is also described in ethnographic monographs, even when examples have been brought to a museum as parts of a collection. But indeed, a piece destined for an ethnographic collection first begins to have scientific value as documentation when written statements have been made about its origin, manufacture and use. For this reason it was incorrect for Graebner (1911:24) to write that objects of material culture can be studied directly without the medium of a report, far from their place of origin, in cases when no suitable reports are available. In such cases the objects can only be determined through comparison with already known objects of the same kind.

CRITIQUE OF DIRECT SOURCES

Criticism here refers to two things: The question of authenticity, and the question of setting—the place and time of origin, and function (Graebner 1911:12 ff.; Koppers 1939:99 ff.). The procedures to be followed here are primarily a matter for museum ethnologists, and require extensive specialized knowledge and experience with ethnographic collections.

The Question of Authenticity

Real forgeries of ethnographic objects occur more often than one might suppose (e.g., with African masks). Benign imitations are also common; these fall into three main categories:

1. Imitations of objects which, without being intended to give the appearance of authenticity, only appeal to the public's interest in exotica.
2. Domestic imitations of genuine cultural products of the ethnic group in question.
3. Models of material objects.

According to Graebner falsifications and imitations should be handled in similar ways. The question about models is how close they come to the original in their execution (concerning the value of models as sources see P. Leser 1932). Imitations can have a certain source value if they refer to things which no longer are found in the particular area, or have become very rare. In any case they have museum value, but must be clearly identified as imitations. The construction of models is necessary since many ethnographic objects cannot be brought into a museum because of their large size (e.g., houses) or because they are no longer in use.

In many cases a forgery can be detected from the raw material used, as where a hard-to-work-with material is replaced by another. This can also be the means for detecting a modern, domestic imitation. The authenticity of the production can also be determined by the techniques of manufacture employed. The falsifier or copyist hardly ever succeeds in getting the formal principles and stylistic characteristics of the original completely correct. This would show for example in the uncertain following of line in the imitation of art objects, or in bad taste in the composition of detailed features of the objects. To detect all this, and to judge it, requires a thorough comparison with authentic pieces and excellent specialized competence in technology and artistic ethnology which usually only an experienced museum worker can command.

The Question of Origin, Time and Use

After the question of the authenticity of ethnographic objects is answered, one must still ask whether the item comes from where it is supposed to come; and further, when it was created, and what purposes it served. As a rule objects destined for collections are accompanied by lists and other reports; these belong in the category of indirect evidence, but are nevertheless essential for the evaluation of the material objects. Only through these reports do the objects become scientifically useful. But it is often true that reports appended to a collection of ethnographic material are highly faulty and inexact, or only make quite vague statements about the provenience of the objects. In such cases the characteristic features of the object itself must be examined to determine its approximate identification. But it is also necessary to use source criticism even when place, time and function data are available.

Here again the criteria of material, technique and form are used. The analysis of materials is the task of the natural sciences, functioning as auxiliary disciplines of ethnology. They can answer the question of whether the raw material is really available in the particular area, and can limit it to a definite area in cases where the place of origin of the object is uncertain. One must also ask if a material found in a certain region is actually used in the culture referred to. And one must consider whether the specimen was produced in the area or only acquired as a trade or import good.

More often than the identification of the raw material, the technique by which the object is made makes it possible to unequivocally localize or confirm the ostensible origin. Graebner (1911:27) saw the form and style of the ethnographic object as the most important criterion, since in many cases it is absolutely unequivocal. The expert can often identify objects at first glance, e.g., a Japanese suit of armor, an ax of the Basonge (Central Africa), a shield from the Papuan Gulf (New Guinea), a feather helmet from Hawaii, etc. The identification is facilitated if the object exhibits distinctive decorations. On the other hand it is hard to localize such objects when they appear in approximately similar external form in different areas, especially if the range of variation is slight.

Here one needs a fine feeling for form and a feeling for style, things which are not easily grasped by rational analytic understanding. But once one has acquired the right feeling for the thing, one subsequently also finds the objective features which lie beneath the intuitive impression.

CRITIQUE OF REPORTS

1. External Criticism

Graebner writes (1911:33): "a . . . limited role is played for ethnological reports by the question of time and place of origin as well as of authorship. This is so, whatever problems of this kind may underlie the general principles of analysis of written history—in the broadest sense, including philosophical, paleographic, and other criteria—whose discussion goes beyond the framework of a specific ethnological method." (Cf. Bernheim 1908:391 ff.) Koppers (1939:113) agrees with this position, remarking that

in general, the source of the most decisive material for ethnology, taken from the standpoint of the historian, is the recent past. The methodological operations just mentioned which demand so much attention of the literary historian thus undergo a corresponding simplification in the case of the ethnologist. It is not decisive to know from whose hand it (the report) really originated, even if knowing this does help greatly to clarify the knowledge of the inner worth of the report.

This position cannot remain unchallenged. Graebner and Koppers evidently had only one sort of ethnographic source in mind, namely reports of field work. But even here it is important to know *when* the report was written, even if it confines itself to only the "recent past." In the study of important ethnological questions such as the interaction between continuity and change, and cultural and social dynamics, the date of the ethnographic and ethnohistorical reports is crucial. Likewise it is necessary to know the authorship, i.e., whether an ethnographer proper, a traveler, a missionary or a colonial official was writing. This critical standpoint essentially contradicts what Graebner and Koppers have said about internal criticism of direct evidence.

In the framework of external criticism one must examine how an ethnographic report comes into being, and the dependency relationships between different reports. The verdict on the trustworthiness of a reporter, as well as the verdict on the content of the ethnographic documentation, depends on the answers to these questions. The more a report relies on direct observation the more trustworthy it is, although this depends on how much time elapsed between the observation and the writing. Statements are more credible if they are testified to by several reporters, provided that these reports are independent of one another. This is also true if a phenomenon from a definite region is reported for entirely different times, again provided that the later reports refer to direct knowledge and are not derived from older presentations (see Bernheim 1908:521 ff., 525 ff.). But this is a matter of interpretation which in practice cannot always be separated from source criticism.

Graebner (1911:35) gives an instructive example concerning the dependency relations between two ethnographic sources. It deals with publications of R. Parkinson (1900), and M. J. Erdweg (1902). Parkinson's report appeared two years earlier than that of Erdweg, but both authors show broad verbal correspondences. Parkinson refers generally to the whole area of Berlinhafen in his presentation; Erdweg reports simply the usages of the natives of the island of Tumleo which lies near the north coast of New Guinea (Berlinhafen). The older source, as revealed by the general situation and also from comparison of the two works, is not the article by Parkinson (in spite of the priority of its appearance) but that of Erdweg. Parkinson reports, to be sure, that he got help from missionaries, but is silent about the fact that he had received a finished manuscript from Father Erdweg, who had spent four years on Tumleo as a missionary, and that he had in part transcribed it word for word. Only he erroneously generalized the data valid for Tumleo to the whole Berlinhafen district.

In many cases the chronological relationship of sources to one another provides a starting point for the question of dependence, but as one can see from the example above, this is not infallible. We must judge by other factors, like the degree of verbal or formal correspondence, and biographical data about the authors. Similarity in content of several sources is a sign of borrowing only when this content has a characteristic limitation, e.g., if only certain aspects of the religion of a people are described in them (naturally assuming that the limitation does not lie in the nature of the facts). Similarity in form is another sign of dependence—approximately similar groupings of material, and similar depiction of details, among other things. Even stronger evidence of source dependence is the presence of word for word agreement, and the presence of the same errors. Errors in a source can often be understood only as misinterpretations of the wordage of other sources. From such errors the relationship between particular texts can be discovered. A further criterion for source relatedness is the similar organic integration in which questionable data stand to each other or with the rest of the content. All these techniques follow the model of historical source criticism. (See Graebner 1911:36.)

But the interdependence of pieces of indirect evidence is not only limited to derivation from other well-known reports. Often whole sections of presentations depend not on one's own observations but on information from someone else, perhaps oral, but at any rate unpublished. If in such cases the author does not give his sources, or at least those of the transcribed part of his presentation, then one can only draw conclusions from biographical information, perhaps from the well-known course of a journey, and from formal incongruences in the presentation.

2. Internal Criticism

We deal here not only with the problem of whether the author created from his own observations or from outside sources, but also with the question of *how* he observed and *how* he rendered his own observations and the interpretations of the literature of the field. It is here, as Graebner (1911: 38 f.) pointed out, that the deficiency of autonomous source criticism shows itself. Thus sources of the highest and lowest quality are frequently quoted without distinction in ethnographic works. This can be seen for example in such compilations as Westermarck's *History of Human Marriage* or Frazer's *Golden Bough*. In this kind of voluminous work an intensive, individual criticism of the sources is not possible; one must continually be aware of this and allow for the compilatory character of this kind of work. Even if an author does apply criticism to his

sources, it is serious if this criticism has become unmethodical and subjective. In considering the reliability of a source one must realize above all that when one mistake by the author is in evidence, still further errors are conceivable. But this is no basis for considering the author to be wholly undependable. It is a different matter, however, if several false or inexact assertions are found in a report, which are to be explained by poor observation, bad memory, or carelessness in writing down the observations. We sometimes find ourselves in this position with regard to ethnographic sources which are quite important.

It is important to have regard for errors resulting from the author's bias. The most transparent is the pursuit of definite objectives, e.g., when, as happened in colonial history, the occupier of a country revealed the culture of the natives in the most unfavorable light in order to justify his own actions. This should not be implicitly considered purposeful falsification; it can also be related to auto- or mass-suggestion. Another source of bias lies in the influence that built-in tendencies caused by upbringing and habit exercise on observations in the field. A spirit turned toward the exotic would perhaps incline toward a fantastic interpretation of what he saw and experienced. All statements which display this tendency must therefore be handled with prudence. A rationalistic observer would report ethnographic data in another way.

Of greater significance are the time in which the reporter lived, and his profession. Thus for example reports in the second half of the eighteenth century were colored by the Rousseauan tendency to rediscover the ideal "golden age" of the "primitives." According to L. Vajda (1964:760) false reports and evaluations of foreign peoples by ancient and medieval writers resulted not only from incomplete factual material but also from definite peculiarities of the folk descriptions of the time. These included politico-ideological tendencies, stereotyped, subjective presentations, misunderstood observations, platitudes, speculations and fictions of various kinds. Such shortcomings were uncritically carried over from one report to another. The proportion of truth in such reports is difficult to determine if the usages and way of life of an identified people are reported in a quite plausible way. Thus, in Periplus of Agatharchides an elephant hunt with the aid of "notched tree trunks" is described (i.e., the elephants allegedly leaned against trees to rest and the people were said to fully utilize this peculiarity for hunting purposes). This is probably related to a misunderstood report on a kind of deadfall. This description of an alleged method of hunting was also accepted by other authors, and was unthinkingly ascribed to people who hunted other animals; for example, Julius Caesar's Germans with regard to hunting elks. The passage from Caesar has even gained admittance in a new work as "the oldest evidence of Germanic hunters' yarn," namely in K. Lindner's *Die Jagd der Vorzeit* (1937).

The Chinese annals often give an inadequate picture of the peoples they describe through a sterotyped manner of representation. Once a general report were given about a population in the annals, one would in the future take advantage of this and set it forward again in even later reports. This creates the false impression that the cultures of the people neighboring China remained the same for centuries (Vajda 1964:764 f.).

Graebner notes that the profession and personal inclinations of the ethnographer can have a positive as well as a negative effect on his reporting. In general, that part of a culture receives the best understanding and most adequate description which corresponds to the professional suppositions or interests of the reporter. On the other hand here may lie a source of error, in that the observer may not be able to get out of the conceptual system with which he was brought up and with which he is accustomed, and therefore will not always be right about the real conditions.

A further source of error in ethnographic reporting is bias arising from scientific theories and convictions. This can affect interviews to the extent that things are put down (leading questions) which harmonize with the scholar's theoretical position. This bias can be favored by the use of questionnaires.

An essential demand of source criticism is consideration of the spatial and temporal relationship of the author to the communicated statement. Here the following questions should be asked (Graebner 1911: 43 f.; Van Bulck 1931:17 f., 195 f.): Does the statement result from personal observation or only from hearsay? How much time was available for the collection of material? Was the reported phenomenon observed repeatedly and can it be checked? In evaluating field work reports one must also ascertain what portions of the material originated simply from observation, what was gained in interviews, and what in informal conversation with the people. And one must always bear in mind the selection of informants (Vajda 1964:771): Under what conditions were the interviews obtained? Were there other people present in the discussion with the informant? And of what kind were the informants? Do their statements always agree with directly observed phenomena? What were the possibilities of misunderstanding? How close was the relationship between scholar and informant?

A special problem of source criticism lies in what one should do about contradictory statements by quite good informants about the same subject. In this situation one should consider whether the questions were always asked properly. Perhaps personal conceptions of the questioned people were involved, or local divergences in the opinions of the people. Here one must bear in mind in what region of the tribal area the particular informants are at home; this may possibly clear up seeming contradictions in the formation.

In this context Vajda (1964:772) gives an illustrative example from the Western Sudan. In the 1930's a startlingly rich mystical and symbolic system was brought to light among the Dogon, Bambara and their neighbors by M. Griaule and his students. These tribes were already well known ethnographically from the reports of French ethnologists who had worked with them before 1930. But what Griaule discovered had not been noted by them at that time. It would be unjust however to reproach the earlier scholars for lacking perception. The mythological conception of the world collected by the Griaule expedition was hardly known, or entirely unknown, to the natives who had heretofore been interviewed. Only a small group of knowledgeable old men still possessed comprehensive knowledge of these esoterica. It was just a stroke of luck that Griaule found these informants and got them to talk.

Vajda (1964:770) calls attention to another important aspect of ethnographic source criticism in pointing out the necessary distinction between "functional" and "intentional" data according to Mühlmann's formulation (1938:108 ff.). That is to say, one should try to determine to what extent the phenomena described in a field work report are regarded by the natives as norms or ideals ("intentional" data), and to what degree the practical life of the tribe conforms to them ("functional" data).

Graebner remarks (1911:45) that an objective evaluation of ethnographers' reports and the elimination of the diverse sources of error are not always simple to accomplish, especially when they combine with each other and when it is a matter of weighing them against trustworthy data. The mutual control of the evidence offers a remedy against being overly skeptical of the trustworthiness of reports (cf. Bernheim 1908:524 ff.). On one hand, an unreliable or dubious source can be verified by a satisfactory one. When they are in substantial agreement on common points, there is no cause to mistrust the parts of the presentation not laid down in the better source.

The mutual conformation of several questionable reports is also important. It seems highly unlikely that several reporters should falsely report the same phenomenon or occurrence in exactly the same way; this presupposes naturally that the reports are independent of one another. Thus various reports can be checked against one another. They can also be checked against direct evidence (see Bernheim 1908:531 f.). However, the situation is unfavorable with data transcribed even once. Here, above all, the criterion of general reliability must be employed. With an author whom we know is unquestionably reliable from the parts of his reports which can be checked, we can also generally accept as factual the parts of his communications which cannot be checked. Moreover, no author would easily invent statements which lie outside the scope of his conceptions and realms of thought. The former reliability criterion must be applied with great caution to each single datum which agrees with our previous knowledge (cf. Bernheim 1908:523 ff.). On the other hand, the less the author who made the statements would have expected to find something of the sort, the fewer doubts his report arouses. Reports which cannot be explained

in terms of the characteristic sources of error of a particular scholar, but instead contradict them completely, are especially trustworthy (cf. Bernheim 1908:523).

The great work of Martin Gusinde (1932, 1937) on the Indians of Tierra del Fuego provides an example of the careful application of ethnographic source criticism. First of all, in the introductory chapters on the history of research in Tierra del Fuego, a critical evaluation is undertaken of the reports of the first European travelers and seafarers who visited this region; in which, for example, the power of observation of the famous natural scientist Charles Darwin is judged good—in contrast to other early visitors. Following this is a source-criticism commentary on the ethnographic investigations undertaken in the last fifty years, i.e., since the founding of the missions in Tierra del Fuego. At the same time, the actual situation in which the travelers and scholars made their observations is also described. Of particular importance for the ethnography of Tierra del Fuego was the fact that the Bridges brothers of the Protestant mission became very conversant with the way of life and the language of the natives through long decades of contact with them. Their evidence is therefore judged to be fully believable. For the overwhelming majority of later travelers to Tierra del Fuego the information of the Bridges brothers constituted almost the only source of ethnographic information. Thus J. Cooper called these missionaries the best firsthand authorities on Tierra del Fuego ethnography. Their work also constituted the point of departure for Gusinde's specialized field work carried out in 1918, 1919–20, 1921–22 (together with W. Koppers), and 1922–23, on which he reports in full (with statements about the research conditions) in his two-volume work. Moreover Gusinde gives a thorough account of the activities of the Protestant and Catholic missionaries in Tierra del Fuego, whose knowledge is of great value for an objective judgment of the native religion and standard of living. Gusinde comes to the conclusion that despite the long contact of the Indians with the missions their mentality and their spiritual life had not changed. Only in the last twenty years as a result of increasing European influence have there arisen sharp contrasts between the older and younger generations.

The rich ethnographic material which Gusinde and Koppers were able to uncover on the culture of these Indians facing extinction now appears in this critical framework. Doubtlessly Gusinde's work represents the most detailed description that has ever been made of a South American tribe; the volume on the Selknam (Ona) includes 1176 pages and that on the Yamana (Yahgan) 1500 pages.

In the following section a few remarks will be made about kinds of sources which were not considered or only slightly considered by Graebner and Koppers. We are concerned with so-called restudies, distributional studies of single culture elements, biographies and autobiographies, oral traditions and texts in the native language. The following statements cover not only source criticism proper, which asks only about reliability, but refer also to the interpretation of the sources and to what Graebner designates as "combinational" activity, i.e., "the combining of the data into scientific presentation complexes" (1911:71). These three approaches always overlap.

RESTUDIES

In connection with restudies one must always ask among other things in what temporal relationship to the original research they were carried out, and whether in the same locality within the tribal area or in another settlement area. Have demographic conditions changed during the interval? Was the research situation more or less favorable at the time? Were the same informants used to some extent, or entirely new ones? How long did the restudy take? Were the same research methods used or different ones? Was the restudy undertaken by the same scholar or by another? Can significant differences be seen, in contrast to the results of the first study, and if so, how are they to be explained—on the basis of actual changes in cultural conditions or in the methodology practices?

TRAIT DISTRIBUTION STUDIES

Geographical distribution studies of single cultural elements with trait lists and maps have an important place in the ethnographic literature. At the base of these studies lies a definite conception of culture. For example, M. Herskovits expresses himself as follows on the subject (1954:3 f.):

The approach which holds that culture is to be broken down into traits must be quite different from that of the investigator who conceives of a way of life as an integrated whole, no part of which is to be understood except in its relation to the totality of which it is a part. The significant factor in making the collection of trait lists was the hypothesis that culture is an historical phenomenon which can be understood if the contacts of people are reconstructed. On the other hand, the theoretical position of the functionalists, which maintain that the fabric of a culture is tightly woven, meant that the very concept of the trait was inadmissible, since the aim was to gather materials which revealed the totality the existing patterns of behavior.

There is a certain "atomization" in the drawing up of trait lists in the sense of an unavoidable and more or less forcible breaking up of cultures into their constituent parts —a factor which one should always be aware of when working with distributional studies. Still these studies are useful exercises; they provide overviews of the spatial dispersion of cultural phenomena and thereby reveal a series of ethnographic problems; e.g., the extent to which similar elements are attributable to ethnic contacts or diffusion, the questions of variation of the same cultural phenomenon, and what conclusions can be drawn when a number of elements coincide in their distribution. Such studies are best when elements of material culture are under consideration; the situation is more difficult with phenomena of social life, of the sphere of belief, and of rituals and ceremonies, which are indeed of a good deal more subtle and complex nature and are integrated into functionally related patterns. In any case it is not easy to isolate the appropriate traits for distributional analysis from a complex institution and to manipulate them cartographically or statistically. In this respect distributional studies are often quite disappointing. Often elements which appear in the tables as single words are much too little specified. This shows in the study by Klimek (1935) on culture element distributions in California, among others. For example, the bull-roarer is cited among the listed phenomenon but its varied meanings are not brought out. It would have been necessary here to mention whether the bull-roarer signifies the voice of the supreme being, the thunder, or the spirits; and whether one is dealing with a large or small bull-roarer, since ideological and ritual meanings depend on this.

But from a certain viewpoint an "atomization" of culture in distributional studies can sometimes be counteracted by indicating the context and the interrelationships through explanatory notes in the accompanying text. One should see for example the tables in H. Driver (1941) which refer to the relationship between elements of girls' puberty rites and the ritual situation in Northeast California. It would be desirable, but is not always possible, to take the time factor into account in distributional studies; i.e., to cite the year in which the element was reported. This can be partially accomplished if the year of publication of the sources appears in the bibliography. It is especially necessary to consider the temporal aspect if the material for the distribution list was not taken from recent sources but from publications which are chronologically more widely separated. Considering the high requirements which source criticism stipulates (exact testing of the level of reliability of statements) and the necessity in distributional studies to bring into play wherever possible the total literature of the region (primary and secondary sources) for every single element, it is advisable according to Van Bulck (1931:18, 22, 194) to select a small area for this purpose; moreover he stresses the fact that it is important to take into consideration the cultural context of the element, which naturally cannot be seen from distribution lists.

Such problems are given attention in the work of Driver and Massey (1957:165), which undoubtedly represents an improvement over earlier distribution investigations. They say:

The aim of the present work is to offer a series of broad generalizations about North American Indian cultures together with the data on which they are based. Most of the data are given on a series of schematic maps. . . . A large majority of the maps ignore the time element although, when well known, the broad outlines of temporal change are often given in the text. Where the time element has been worked out in detail by ethnohistorians we have entered dates directly on the maps. It would have been ideal to have drafted a separate map for each subject presented, in order to show where the various tribes were located when the particular traits diffused or were first reported. At the present time there is too

little known about the time element to make this feasible for most of the material. The generalizations offered are of two major kinds, which may be called descriptive and relational. The descriptive generalizations are concerned primarily with the geographical distributions of single traits or small clusters of variants on a single topic. The relational generalizations are concerned with the correlations between the traits of one topic with those of another topic. . . . We believe that a theory of culture which ignores or is unable to account for the geographical distributions presented here falls short of the mark. Needless to say, all the maps contain some errors. Ethnological data are too unrefined to make it possible for anyone to present a broad geographical distribution which will satisfy every critic. We believe, therefore, that there is no such thing as a completely correct distribution.

BIOGRAPHIES AND AUTOBIOGRAPHIES

On biographies and autobiographies of natives Clyde Kluckhohn above all carried out ample source criticism investigations (1945, 1949). To begin with he remarks that all personal documents which originate from preliterate cultures are in some way or another of interest, regardless of whether they were taken down by professional ethnographic field workers or by laymen. The distinction between biographical and autobiographical presentations is often arbitrary however. The editor of such reports must rearrange the raw material with which he is presented in many ways, leaving out and modifying much of it; this is especially true if a life history is received through an interpreter, if one is dealing with something written down by an informant who had only an imperfect knowledge of the European language, if the document originates from a culture in which the feel for chronological progression in reporting is only slightly developed, or if stylistic repetitions and cultural clichés appear. Edited documents of this kind could most honestly be described as "biographies based on materials provided by the subject" (Kluckhohn 1945:81).

By the nineteenth century great interest existed in the life and personalities of leading or outstanding natives, especially those of the North American Indian tribes. Yet,

. . . all these life stories bear internal evidence of editing by white sponsors and are products of highly acculturated individuals. Both biographies and autobiographies, in this early group, are of greater value to the historian than to the ethnographer as to the student of personality-in-culture. Some ethnographic details may be gleaned, but to the psychologically-minded anthropologist all are disappointing. There is much material on the sentiments of the time but painfully little of the personalities. (Kluckhohn 1945:83)

According to Kluckhohn (1945:91) the following questions should be asked in critical examination of biographical materials about natives:

... whether such data as are presented are treated in scientifically respectable fashion; is the reader given the information necessary for judging the trustworthiness of the document? Is the document integrated with other research materials on the people in question? Are interpretations made in accord with a coherent and non-parochial conceptional scheme? Is the document itself sufficiently comprehensive to give more than a schematic picture of an individual's life?

Kluckhohn (1945:94 f.) gives a critical evaluation of the famous autobiography of a Kwakiutl Indian edited by Clellan Ford, *Smoke from Their Fires* (1941), which is of general interest:

Ford did not work through an interpreter, and he provided also a series of unobtrusive, yet highly pointed, notes to the autobiographical document itself. These notes have a consistent theoretical point of departure—essentially that of the rapprochement between psychoanalysis and stimulus-response learning theory. A concluding chapter or two which systematically drew together the inferences permitted by the data, both for the study of culture and for the study of individual psychology, would have enormously enhanced the significance of the book.

Kluckhohn complains about the fact that the means by which the material was obtained are not mentioned in sufficient detail. This raises questions which are also applicable to other field work reports:

To what extent were specific questions asked and what was the nature of these questions? ... How many questions were asked on certain sample working days, and to have a precise list of these questions. What were the working conditions? Were ethnographer and informant alone? Where did they work? Did they work fairly regular hours during an unbroken succession of days? Were the informant's motivations almost entirely economic? With what informal behaviors did he respond to various questions which may have been put to him by the investigator?

But to my knowledge there are hardly any ethnographic monographs in which these stiff

demands are fulfilled on all points. Moreover one must investigate in personal documents of natives how much the life history reflects the cultural pattern and how much it expresses the individual life of the informant with his idiosyncrasies. The most important question is most certainly this: What sort of native does one have before one—the man who is willing to tell his life story to a European? (cf. Kluckhohn 1945:98 f.). According to Kluckhohn (1945:96) one gets the impression in many quite good native autobiographies that the interviews were too guided or too much controlled by the scholar, and that too many questions were put to the informant, to the detriment of an unconstrained rendering of his life memories. So it is recommended that every ethnologist who is interested primarily in the collection of native life histories should carry out this investigation in tribes whose culture has already been recorded ethnographically, since

... the gentle techniques which promote a free flow of spontaneous reminiscences are often incompatible with getting the specific details and the cross-checking of data required in good ethnographic work (Kluckhohn 1945:98 f., 110).

Finally, Kluckhohn refers to still further points in the critical evaluation of autobiographies (1945:112):

Life events have meaning only in their context. This context is, in part, created by the contemporary situation of the subject and by the sequence of experiences which are peculiar to him as an individual. But the context is also determined by the cultural environment.

The use of interpreters creates special problems. Kluckhohn (1945:123) writes:

At worst, an interview carried on through an interpreter resembles an "exchange of telegrams." What the investigator hears will be entirely filtered through a selective screening which is hard to allow for with any precision. The interpreter will suppress or distort both consciously and unconsciously. He will omit what seems to him unimportant or irrelevant. This distortion of translation cannot be prevented unless the whole interview is first recorded in native text and then worked out with a battery of interpreters. Field workers have too often tended to assume that the role of the interpreter was that of a precise or at least a passive instrument. The hazards will be appreciably diminished if anthropologists will give careful and systematic accounts of their interpreters' backgrounds and personalities. However, interpreters can be given a good deal of training and it is astonishing how great improvements can be brought about in an intelligent interpreter.

ORAL TRADITIONS

The source criticism to be carried out here conforms in part to that for direct evidence, but in part special points must be noticed that derive from the intrinsic nature of this traditional material. To begin with we are dealing with the clarification of questions about the credibility of oral traditions with regard to their value as statements and the proportion of truth in them. Every oral tradition goes back to an initial or proto-witnessing of an event or fact in the past on which an eyewitness reported, or else the testimony is based simply on hearsay or a rumor. The report is then handed down orally along a more or less long chain of communication until the scholar gets the tradition from the last informant of the chain as the last or final testimony and fixes it in writing (Vansina 1965:21 f.). For various reasons one must count on distortions and changes of the initial evidence in transmission. The degree to which a tradition is repeated intact depends on its meaning for the society or group in question and how it is transmitted:

In order to assess the value of the testimonies of the informants in the chain of transmission, one must make sure that each has had opportunity of hearing the testimony of the preceding link in the chain, which he is supposed to have repeated. It is usually impossible to know by name all the informants included in a chain, or even to know how many links have been in it. There are, however, cases where this is possible, as when the tradition is the property of one family and is transmitted from one generation to the next of the known genealogy. . . . When transmission is in the hands of a social institution designed for this purpose, one can be confident that the chain is an unbroken one, for the members of the institution are known to each other. (Vansina 1965: 118 f.)

Two types of oral traditions can be distinguished on the basis of the way in which they are reproduced: 1) Traditions in firmly laid down, bound form (fixed texts). These are learned by heart and later transmitted in the same wording; the wording and phraseology are part of the tradition, just as much as is the content itself. 2) Traditions in free, unconstrained form (free texts). Here the importance lies in the content, and the text is not tied to a fixed wording. Hence it can be retold at any time in some other formulation;

what is essential is that the general outline of the text is preserved (Vansina 1965:22 f.).

Oral traditions can also be classified according to their essential features and content; Vansina (1965:142 ff.) has provided the following provisional types, "each with its own limitations, its own bias, and its particular uses for providing a knowledge of the past."

1. *Formulae:* These are stereotyped phrases whose meaning lies as much in the wording as in their appropriate employment. They have fixed texts. Special sacred formulae must be transmitted with great exactness, and sanctions are often applied to ensure faithful reproduction. Such formulae often contain archaic elements and are not intended to give a historical report. But they can throw light on the history of ideas.

1a. Titles. These are formulae which describe the status of a person. They seldom contain historical information.

1b. Slogans. These describe the character of a particular group of people (family, clan, settlement, etc.), and often contain historical statements about the particular group. They belong with fixed texts and can often be understood only in the light of accompanying commentaries.

1c. Didactic formulae. This includes proverbs, riddles, epigrams, etc. They have value as statements in themselves and can also give historical information. Proverbs are sometimes found in sources on legal history; however, for the most part they are restricted to the moral norms of the particular society.

2. *Poetry:* In texts in fixed, artistically poetic form the formal expression of the content plays just as great a role as the actual content itself. Psychological factors and aesthetic qualities in the transmission nevertheless distort the facts of the case which are laid down primarily for expression. In these traditions there are historical statements of a usually somewhat vague and generalized nature.

2a. Historical poetry. Songs and poems of this kind with the intention of reporting historical occurrences are often composed for purposes of propaganda for the elite; this decreases their historical truth value. Frequently they are full of allusions which can often no longer be interpreted.

2b. Panegyric poetry. Poems or songs written for a price are in any case not composed to report historical data. They are put together either in the lifetime of a distinguished person or directly after his death. Characteristic is the liberal use of stereotyped phrases which are supposed to point up the virtue of the person being celebrated. In one respect these traditions constitute a source of information on the social ideals at the time in which they arose. Appended commentaries give more information about historical events.

2c. Religious poetry. Essentially this includes stereotyped forms of prayers, hymns and dogmatic texts, which must be transmitted exactly word for word. Often they are provided with traditional commentaries. Their value lies in the fact that they give a clue to the religion of those who created them. Now and then they contain statements about happenings of the past that are not of a religious nature.

2d. Personal poetry. These poems have no public character. They give free expression of the emotional life of the person from whom they originate. Their transmission usually occurs in irregular ways and distortions of the original form can always occur, no doubt because of the periodically changing artistic tastes of whoever is transmitting the tradition at the time. This kind of traditional material permits an insight into the attitudes toward life of individuals and into the history of emotions and ideas.

3. *Lists:* We are concerned here with place and personal names which are recited in the framework of institutions at ceremonies and other public occasions. For the most part such statements serve to support and strengthen claims to political, social and economic rights. Their historical reliability is therefore not always guaranteed. Lists of place names are the chief source for the study of migrations, but can also give information on the demographic situation in the past. Lists of personal names often refer to genealogies. In view of the political and sociological functions involved here, changes and distortions can easily enter into the oral transmission; moreover one must always consider the fact that mythical elements can be interwoven with them.

4. *Tales:* This category of oral tradition is set down in prose and drafted in free form. It includes very diverse types; but all have in common a certain degree of historical char-

acter. In the first place these traditions serve in the instruction, building up and maintaining of laws, as well as in their justification and verification. With regard to their historical truth value they are nevertheless less reliable. But they often constitute the only source that reports thoroughly on a series of incidents in the past. As official traditions they are brought forth on special occasions and repeated in social groups. Traditions about the history of a locality or group usually do not reach far into the past and are far less subject to open control. Narratives of the histories of families and lineages are useful as explanations of genealogies. When it is possible to combine all available traditions of this kind of a population one can gain a clear picture of the tribal history. One must always take into consideration that historical narratives can always be mixed with mythical and legendary items, especially if questions of origin are involved.

In the source criticism of oral traditions it is important first of all to ask what purpose and what function they fulfill. As completely as possible one should take into consideration the ethnological conditions and value system of the ethnic group from which the traditions stem, and possibly also archaeological evidence. Further one must test to what extent the traditions harmonize with the general conceptions of the population. In so far as they exist detailed written historical reports on the ethnic unit should be brought in and compared with the statements from the tradition.

A further, more important series of questions for source criticism refer to the personality, the social and spiritual milieu, of the final reporters. In this context one must determine from whom and in what manner the informant obtained the tradition, and whether he communicated the tradition intact to the researcher or changed it by personal garnishings or deletions. What social status did the reporter have? If, for example, he is the official speaker of a group one must admit that traditional material would be communicated without change because of the control function of the group. In other cases one must consider the specific situation in which the informant finds himself vis-à-vis the scholar. Can the informant freely transmit the information or must he take notice of the members of his group or tribe? Must the informant expect reactions on the part of his people if he sells traditional material to an outsider? In any case one must reckon with the possibility that for some reason or other the informant transmitted to the scholar only a changed version of the final testimony. To find this out is one of the tasks of source criticism of oral traditions.

The situation is more favorable if a tradition is available in several versions, which can then be compared from a critical point of view. Then the question of the dependency relations of these texts must first be clarified:

The aim is to get a better idea of the relation each testimony bears to the events of which it preserves a record. One therefore only compares testimonies which record the same event or a series of events. Comparison of testimonies will establish their degree of reliability. By means of various dependent testimonies, one can reconstruct the text of the archetype from which they probably all derive. In turn, analysis of variants of the archetype makes it possible to assess the quality of the transmission and the kind of distortions the tradition may have undergone. If the testimonies are independent, comparison of them will lead to a higher degree of certainty as to the reliability of the account of events given by the various traditions. . . . Reliability can be tested either by the textual comparison or by comparison of circumstantial details. . . . (Vansina 1965:120 f.)

Textual comparison of testimonies will have to be carried out in a different manner according to whether the testimony we are dealing with is a fixed or a free text. With fixed texts, the words themselves form part of the tradition, and a word-for-word comparison can be made, following the usages for the comparison of written texts. . . . (Vansina 1965:121 f.) Textual comparison of free texts is more complicated, for here the words do not form part of the tradition. What can be compared are the features which belong to the tradition, namely, plot, theme, episodes, and setting. (Vansina 1955:126, 54–65)

It is a special case when an informant recites various versions of the same tradition. He could have previously received them from his predecessor, but they can also be attributable to himself.

But it is not difficult by comparing the texts of the various versions he has given to discover what the testimony was that was handed down to him and on which his versions were based (Vansina 1965:129 f.)

Regarding a widely distributed tradition one has to ask to what extent one is dealing with diffusion. If this seems plausible, then one must determine under what local influences the particular tradition arose and what ver-

sion is the original (Vansina 1965:133 ff.). When it turns out from comparison that different traditions about the same event are independent of each other, and the individual reports still agree extensively about them, then one can accept as fact that all these pieces of evidence actually transmit a true factual content (Vansina 1965:138).

Another outcome of the comparative process is that different traditions supplement each other, so that a better representation of the described event can be gained. This also results from comparing oral traditions to written sources. About this Vansina (1965:138 f.) writes:

This frequently happens when 19th century written sources are compared with oral traditions. These written sources yet do not sufficiently take into account the incidents attendant upon this event and the effects it produced. The traditions for their part reflect the native point of view, and give a good description of what the intrusion of strangers meant to their society, although they often fail to realize what changes the arrival of the Europeans would bring about.

Finally there is the question of how one infers the specific situation to which the initial evidence refers, and how one can grasp the intentions lying at the bottom of the first report. Vansina (1965:115 ff.) provides the following guidelines for this: Draw conclusions from the content of the final testimonies; examine critically the parallel but independent evidence on the same event or the same fact; try to fathom from the kind of reporting what purposes and aims can be detected at the beginning of the chain of tradition.

Texts in the native language are a category of ethnographic sources of a special sort. Here one must ask how they were recorded —on tape or by being written down according to the words of the informant. What was the linguistic preparation of the translator? To what extent does the free translation correspond with the original text? How was the problem of carrying over terms and phrases which cannot be given literal or adequate correspondence in a European language solved? In general one can say: The ideal requirements that must be made for the scientific utility of a native text is that it be furnished with a specialist's interlinear translation and a free translation, together with explanatory commentary.

RECORDED SOURCES

A critical evaluation of ethnographic texts taken down on tape in the native language is made possible by painstakingly worked out protocols. By the turn of the century the Phonogram Archives of the Austrian Academy of Sciences had already worked out protocol formulae which provided as much for spoken recordings as for musical material. The schema which is here put forward is as follows:

Person Being Recorded: Name, sex, ethnic affinity, place of birth (country), where he grew up, schooling, present place of residence, home of his father, possible bodily peculiarities such as defects (like absence of teeth, results of operations, etc.).

Recording: Type of tape-recording equipment, tape speed, standard or half-gauge number of revolutions, language (dialect), original recorded by whom, technical control by whom. If there are musical insertions in the text, then information about the following must be introduced: vocal music, accompanied or unaccompanied; instrumental music, solo, chorus, one or more voices, kind of voice, instruments.

Subject: Here one should declare what kind of a text is involved, i.e., a short statement of the content (abstract of the translation) and of the cultural context. The question of the content value of the text necessitates an exhaustive characterization of the informant. Moreover, one must take into account how the informant conducted himself before the microphone, to what extent he had inhibitions, and how the procedure of recording was made plausible to him. With tapes in a foreign language it is recommended that the recorder state the theme and the titles of the parts in his own European language before the informant himself begins to speak. In purely linguistic as well as in musical recordings, a middle C on a pitch pipe recorded after the trial gives an exact starting point for the pitch. However, musical passages incorporated in the text must be separately handled according to the principles of ethnomusicology (see Graf 1956, 1958, 1962).

Special exigencies are produced when a man who knows the particular native language listens to a recording for the purpose of making an expert transcription and fol-lowing translation of the text. The extent to which he will be successful depends of course on the tempo and articulation of the words recorded on tape. It is best to undertake the transcription and translation just after the recording, preferably calling on the informant for aid. A problem arises when texts spoken in ecstasy by a shaman are recorded (see Haekel 1966). Unclear points in the translation of texts can be clarified as the opportunity arises with restudies of the tribe.

CRITIQUE OF PHOTOGRAPHY

Above all one must try to determine if the photograph in question is retouched or not. If the negative is at hand this is very easy to determine. If only a copy or enlargement is available then the traces of retouch work must be found through painstaking investigations (with a magnifying glass). The value of a retouched photo as a source is naturally more limited than that of a non-retouched one. With a photograph (copy or enlargement) it is much more difficult to determine if one is dealing with the whole exposure or only with a piece cut out of it. Selective cutting, trimming of pictures, partial enlargements, and "cropping" can fully alter the original meaning and sense of the picture. Copies of parts of another exposure within a picture (picture montage) can usually be detected by the fact that the shadows of the foreign component do not match those of the true exposure (deviating height of the sun, exposure time, light strength, etc.). Retouches, picture cutting and picture montages can be considered falsifications; as such they throw light on the reliability and credibility of the particular source.

In any case the able photographer can more easily falsify his pictures by specific photographic means: suitable choice of films and filters as well as varying distance and object selections. Depending on the color sensitivity of the film (black-and-white as well as color), blond hair can come out pitch black and vice versa. If to the possible choices of film and filter types is added the possibility of artificial lighting there are almost no limits to the possibilities for falsification. But if the critic knows the real colors of objects in the exposure, it is then possible to form conclusions about the method of exposure (and falsification) used.

Exposures with wide-angle lenses create the impression of greater roominess and greater depth in the picture. Exposures with lenses whose focal distances are substantially greater than the diagonal of the negative produce the impression that objects or people, that are in reality far apart, are standing beside each other. A conclusion as to what lens was used can easily be drawn from the comparison of objects of the same size (e.g., both hands of the same person). Naturally all pictures taken at the same spot give the same perspective, no matter what lens is used; it is the association of object with negative format which causes seeming changes in perspective.

BIBLIOGRAPHY

BERNHEIM, ERNST
1908 *Lehrbuch der historischen Methode*, 5th ed. Leipzig.
CLOSS, ALOIS
1956 Abgrenzung und Aufriss einer speziellen historischen Ethnologie. *Zeitschrift für Ethnologie* 81, No. 3. Braunschweig.
COLLINGWOOD, R. G.
1955 *Philosophie der Geschichte*. Stuttgart.
DRIVER, H.
1941 Girl's puberty rites in western North America. University of California, *Anthropological Records* 6:21–90. Berkeley.
DRIVER, H., and W. MASSEY
1957 Comparative studies of North American Indians. *Transactions of the American Philosophical Society* 47, No. 2. Philadelphia.
ERDWEG, M. J.
1902 Die Bewohner der Insel Tumleo, Berlinhafen, Deutsch Neuguinea. *Mitteilungen der Anthropologischen Gesellschaft* XXXII. Wein.
FEDER, A.
1924 *Lehrbuch der geschichtlichen Methode*. Regensburg.
FENTON, WILLIAM
1952 The training of historical ethnologists in America. *American Anthropologist* 54: 328–339.
FISCHER, H.
1961 Das Tonbandgerät in der völkerkundlichen Feldforschung. *Tribus* No. 10. Stuttgart.
GOTTSCHALK, L.
1945 The historian and the historical document. In *The use of personal documents in history, anthropology and sociology*. Social Science Research Council, Bulletin 53. New York.
GRAEBNER, FRITZ
1911 *Methode der Ethnologie*. Heidelberg.
GRAF, WALTER
1956 Musikethnologie und Quellenkritik. In *Die Wiener Schule der Völkerkunde*. Festschrift Wien-Horn.
1958 Zur Quellenkritik beim mündlichen Über-

lieferungsgut. *Wiener Völkerkundliche Mitteilungen* VI. Wein.
1962 Neue Möglichkeiten, neue Aufgaben der vergleichenden Musikwissenschaft. *Studien zur Musikwissenschaft* 25. Wien.
GUSINDE, MARTIN
1931 *Die Feuerland-Indianer I, Selknam*. Anthropos Bibliothek, Expeditionsserie I. Mödling.
1937 *Die Feuerland-Indianer II, Yamana*. Anthropos Bibliothek, Expeditionsserie II. Mödling.
HAEKEL, JOSEF, and C. B. TRIPATHI
Eine Bississenheits—Seance der Rathva Koliin Giyarat (Indien). Österr. Akademie d. Wissenschaften, Philosoph. —Histor. Klasse, Veröffentlichungen der Ethnologischen Kommission, Heft 1. Wein.
KIRN, PAUL
1952 *Einführung in die Geschichtswissenschaft*. Sammlung Göschen, Bd. 270. Berlin.
KLIMEK, STANISLAU
1935 Culture element distribution: I. The structure of California Indian culture. *University of California Publications in American Archaeology and Ethnology* 37:1–70. Berkeley.
KLUCKHOHN, CLYDE
1945 The personal documents in anthropological science. In *The use of personal documents in history, anthropology and sociology*. Social Science Research Council, Bulletin 53. New York.
1949 Needed refinements in the biological approach. In S. S. Sargent and M. W. Smith, eds., *Culture and personality*. New York, Viking Fund.
KOPPERS, WILHELM
1939 The sources of ethnology. In W. Schmidt, ed., *The culture historical method of ethnology*, translated by S. A. Sieber. New York, Fortuny's.
LESER, PAUL
1931 *Entstehung und Verbreitung des Pfluges*. Munster.

1938 Review of W. Schmidt, *Handbuch der Methode der kulturhistorischen Ethnologie. Folklive* II. Stockholm.

LINDNER, K.
1937 *Die Jagd der Vorzeit.*

MÄNCHEN-HELFEN, OTTO
1959 Einige Bemerkungen zur Paläoethnologie. *Central Asiatic Journal* IV, Part 3. Wiesbaden.

MÜHLMANN, WILHELM
1938 *Methodik der Völkerkunde.* Stuttgart.

PARKINSON, R.
1900 Die Berlinhafensektion Neuguinea. *Internationales Archiv für Ethnographie* XIII. Leiden.

SCHMITZ, CARL
1960 Historische Probleme in Nordost-Neuguinea. Huon Halbinsel. *Studien zur Kulturkunde* Bd. 16. Wiesbaden.

TESSMANN, GÜNTHER
1930 *Die Indianer Nordost-Perus.* Hamburg.

VAJDA, LASZLO
1964 Traditionelle Konzeption und Realität in der Ethnologie. In *Festschrift für A. E. Jensen.* München.

VAN BULCK, GASTON
1931 Beiträge zur Methodik der Völkerkunde. *Wiener Beiträge zur Kulturgeschichte und Linguistik* II. Wien.

VANSINA, JAN
1965 *Oral tradition, a study in historical methodology.* Translated by H. M. Wright. Chicago, Aldine.

WAGNER, FRITZ
1951 *Geschichtswissenschaft.* München.

CHAPTER 9

Cultures Through Time

JAN VANSINA

Two types of building blocks can be used in the construction of anthropological theory. The first and obvious one is the ethnographic monograph, usually based on field work by a trained anthropologist. The data gathered are presumed to apply all to one point in time, the "ethnographic present." In fact the fiction goes farther and most studies are timeless. Such a synchronic analysis usually shows the intricate patterns of integration in society just as descriptive grammars trace the forms of language. To achieve this result the anthropologist has had to pick and choose from his notes, all of which to begin with represented only a fraction of reality. This is best expressed in Evans-Pritchard 1940:261, e.g., ". . . but in case it be said that we have only described the facts in relation to a theory of them and as exemplifications of it and have subordinated description to analysis, we reply that this was our intention." The facts are used to illustrate a pattern, a pattern which can either be superimposed from the start—and this is bad ethnography—or stems from the data as interpreted by the ethnographer. Thus the monograph always represents a descriptive model.

The second building block is the historical monograph. It describes the evolution of a culture and abolishes the zero-time fiction. It is then complementary to and indeed follows from synchronic analysis. Such studies are still rare and have been left, by and large, to the care of historians. Our contention is that these diachronic monographs are important to the development of anthropology and research energy should be devoted to this approach. First, as will be seen, it is technically possible to gather the necessary data and put them together for a reconstruction of the past. Secondly, from this material diachronic models can then be elaborated. Such models have subsidiary uses; they provide a check on synchronic models and also provide a means to overcome the prison of the single culture unit. Their major usefulness however is that they lend themselves to comparative study *sui generis*. These comparisons then lead by step-by-step progression to those regularities in society, which all anthropologists worth their salt are trying to discover. Historical monographs as diachronic models are therefore of critical importance for theoretical anthropology.

ASSEMBLING THE DATA

The techniques to gather and evaluate historical data are generally well established. The most common sources are written, iconographic, monumental, archaeological, oral, linguistic, ethnographic or biological in relation to ethnography (McCall 1964 in relation to Africa). Precise rules for applying historical critique to written sources have been formulated by the positivistic historians of the nineteenth century (Bernheim 1908) and updated or adapted by later theorists (Bauer 1928, Bloch 1952, Carr 1964, Feder 1924, Marrou 1961). The major point here is that it is only through a careful appreciation of the document in its full context that its intrinsic value can be appreciated. In this respect some anthropologists have shown a rather remarkable lack of understanding of the nature of historiography. Kroeber (1939) offers probably the most celebrated case of this when he dismisses documents by Spanish missionaries in California in favor of his own observations, made a century and a half later. This certainly shows how ingrained the zero-time notion is among anthropologists!

Oral tradition and eyewitness accounts are sources which usually make the cultural anthropologist feel much more at home. Here again the essence of criticism or historiography is to place the source in its cultural and linguistic milieu, but this milieu happens to be the society the anthropologist is studying at the time he is studying it. In recent years this type of documentation has received much attention (cf., e.g., contributions in *Journal of African History;* Vansina 1961).

Monumental and iconographic sources can be considered along with archaeology, and methods for the use and interpretation of all these data are well established (Atkinson 1953, Leroi Gourhan 1950, Childe 1956). For the important dating methods the journal *Radiocarbon* supplements the more standard accounts. In many parts of the world monuments and iconographic materials have not been fully used yet. An obvious example can be seen in the fact that no one as yet has described material culture and daily life at the court of Benin during the seventeenth century despite the availability of hundreds of bronze plaques which could be used as documents. Also it is often forgotten that cherished objects may be archaeological monuments. In many cases copies will be made when these artifacts are worn out (e.g., in the case of wooden statues, masks and the like), but many of these do not wear out so easily, as seen by the dating of a Dogon (West Africa) mask to 1470±150 A.D. (*Radiocarbon* 1964:4:243; wood). Wooden objects for instance can be used both as a monument and sometimes as a source for iconography concerning dress, decoration patterns, etc.

Historical linguistics and its related techniques have been researched since the early nineteenth century and one can consult the classic by Paul (1909) along with more recent studies such as Bloomfield 1933, Sturtevant 1917, Greenberg 1957, Lehmann 1962, and Sapir 1916. The latter is a classic of its kind and set the pattern for ethnohistorical research in the U.S.A. for the next three or four decades.

Ethnographic data cannot be evaluated so easily since this is the outstanding area where much more work needs to be done regarding methods. The works of the *Kulturhistorische Schule,* Graebner 1911, Van Bulck 1931, Schmidt 1939 and some of the earlier studies in North America, including even Sapir 1916, suffer from two basic defects: the lack of realization that there are no cultural traits similar to molecules in the physical world (Herskovits 1956:170–174) and that every culture is a strongly integrated whole. Under no circumstance can a culture be seen as a Neapolitan cake consisting of layers of cultural sedimentation, because the integrating forces of a culture and the cultural environment which exercises constant (and not interrupted) contact preclude such an evolution. Nevertheless some studies (Spier 1921) show that ethnographic sources can indeed be used. This situation in relation to methodology is best discussed by Herskovits (1956:461–560). We may simply underline here that the very integration of cultures means that no people can mix two cultures in equal proportions at one moment in time. Thus *Mischkulturen* like *Mischsprachen* are nonexistent. Therefore each culture goes back, with regard to its core, to one ancestral culture. The difficulty is that, unlike the linguistic core where phonology and morphology always are at the heart of it, in cultures anything can belong at a given time to the core and the core changes from one culture to another and from one period in time to another. The most that can be said is that usually structures of kinship and territoriality are present as core aspects. On the other hand it is also known that cultures can exhibit some extreme conservatism. In the Middle East archaeologists have found the function of some tools and objects from their diggings by comparison with present-day practice. A hunting camp site of central Africa dated to 2340–2750 B.C. shows a technology which can be paralleled almost perfectly with similar items of Bushman culture in the general area today (Gabel 1965); other examples could be multiplied.

The problem then is to identify what are borrowed features in a culture and if possible put these in a chronological sequence; what are internal innovations and in what order they occurred; and what features were inherited from an ancestral culture whose "reflexes" today would all contribute to this evidence (Vansina 1964b). Obviously if this were to be successfully and completely achieved one would have told the history of cultural change. However, it is only partially possible to achieve this result. The relative chronologies yielded by this type of data are so limited that it becomes difficult even to put them in a common grid for the chronology of even one culture.

The techniques used for construction of chronologies include the tracing of survivals even if metataxis has taken place. Other techniques include distribution patterns of cultural items of which the age area hypothesis is only one variety, and the reconstruction, through comparison, of cultures that are known to have descended from a common ancestral culture, as well as several minor techniques of interpolation and inference. Ethnological data go beyond the status of "conjectural history" and the "40% hypothesis" when they are used in tandem with linguistics and the results confirm one another. In any case the technique of counterproof should be used by which all other explanations could be shown to be much more involved (Ockham's razor) or otherwise much less likely than the selected one. Finally, hypotheses based on cultural evidence should be stated in such a fashion that they can eventually be strengthened by archaeology and/or eventually written data.

The use of biological techniques requires a high degree of competence and detailed discussion is best left to specialists. In general these methods draw conclusions from distribution maps plotting such items as: (a) the wild relatives of domesticated plants and animals; (b) the centers of greatest diversity in domesticated species; and (c) the center of greatest diversity or wild relatives of associated weeds, animal ticks and other parasites. In all cases, including human biology, the genetic situation is at the heart of such reasoning and therefore techniques of population genetics are central to the method. The best the cultural anthropologist can do is to check the data and the general reasoning. Generally his own competence does not go far enough so that he can invent fruitful hypotheses with such data on his own.

The technical question which has been most neglected with regard to historical data is the problem of historical synthesis. How does one draw together data from many different disciplines into a single body of historical reconstruction?

It is not merely a matter of avoiding primary errors of logic such as anachronisms, faulty collection or interpretation of the data, use *pars pro toto*, theological selection of arguments and the like. An example of most of these errors can be found in Heyerdahl 1950, 1952, 1958. Some of these are also discussed in Suggs (1960: 212–224). Heyerdahl's work exemplifies the misuse of evidence which has bred such suspicion of reconstructions based on sets of diverse data. One major error has been too strict an application of Collingwood's imaginative reconstruction. The way in which such a process works is illustrated by the last chapter of *Aku-Aku* in which Heyerdahl shows how romantic daydreaming can lead to an uncontrolled and uncritical selection of data.

The first question to arise in any synthesis is to ask what weight should be given to one piece of evidence in relation to another. Many scholars have felt that whole sets of evidence were *a priori* better than others because the discipline they derived from was somehow more trustworthy. We are a long way from Munro's "The materials with which the archaeologist deals are absolutely free from the bias and the ignorance which so frequently distort the statements of the historian" (Piggott 1965:4). Still Herskovits could say, "The ethnohistorian, in fact, draws on four kinds of resources, those of history, archaeology, oral tradition, and ethnology. The first two may be thought of as giving him his 'hard' materials, which can be taken as much at face value as any of the data of history or archaeology and are subject to the same reservations with regard to their interpretation" Herskovits (1959:230). He argues that "in terms of any index of certainty, the conclusions derived from the ethnographic data must be lodged on a far lower level than those derived from the study of historical documents" (i.e., written materials). What is being weighed are bits of evidence, one pitted against or along another, in a particular situation. But situations vary and it would not be difficult to show cases in which the so often maligned ethnographic materials come out as "hard" evidence, or where any other bit derived from another discipline would make a good show. Thus there is no simple rule of "hard" as opposed to "soft" data for ethnohistory.

In general terms one can only compare

the characteristics of the sets of evidence and actually show their complementarity. In most cultures without writing, written sources give accurate dates for the absolute chronology, but they are written by outsiders and often present an external view of a culture in its most visible aspects only. Iconography, monuments and archaeology yield a somewhat vaguer absolute chronology whilst dealing with evidence relating to environment, economics, and visible artifacts, with some possible data about social structure, political life and religious institutions. Oral tradition is weaker on chronology. It gives us ordinarily a relative chronology whose universe is the people or a subset of that society and it does not go as far back in the past as archaeology does. But its data cover all conscious changes in the culture and this means often some economic, political and even religious changes whereas some slow drifts, in social structure for instance, will not be noticed. Linguistic and ethnographic data are the best tools available to uncover unconscious change in the nonmaterial aspects of a culture and they can be applied to all aspects of culture. However, as chronologies they are always relative and the temporal dimension is often limited such that only two events or situations make up the chronological field. One is earlier than the other is all that can be said, and these situations often cannot be related to other chronologies. This of course is a serious weakness since absolute chronology is the grid of history[1] and relative chronologies will be the more useful the wider their geographical and cultural scale. Still this does not mean that linguistic, ethnographic and biological data are to be set aside, only that the intermeshing of their relative chronologies with wider chronologies must eventually be possible if they are going to contribute to ultimate historical syntheses.

To summarize the real complementarity of ethnohistorical data it may be pointed out that usually only written documents tell us something about the role of an individual in a set of events, oral documents tell us about the motivations leading to events, e.g., wars and present idealized images of individuals involved, whereas impersonal slower changes are better shown in archaeological, cultural and linguistic data. In fact the latter three disciplines usually tell us about succeeding situations whereas the first two deal mainly with events. A practical example is the way in which these data can help to determine the origin of a culture and a people. Oral tradition often gives straightforward detailed data. But they may apply only to leaders, not to the majority of the population. Archaeology adds to this by tracing bulk changes in the culture from its artifacts, and linguistics tells us where the language, and presumably the bulk of the ancestors of the present-day speakers,[2] came from. Written data in cultures without writing are usually simply the repositories of oral tradition at one particular point in time. Ethnological data do not tell us much because they presuppose knowledge from other sources, but once this knowledge exists then ethnological materials can be used to describe the processes by which a particular culture originated from its ancestor(s).

Given then that in every individual case the evidence should be weighed without reference to an *a priori* statement about the value of disciplines, how are such reconstructions made? Usually the synthesis centers heavily around one set of data while others are merely complementary. Thus Suggs' reconstruction of Marquesan history is built around archaeology (Suggs 1962) and the author's *Kuba History* revolve heavily around oral traditions (Vansina 1963). This type of reconstruction is only an intermediate synthesis to be replaced by a genuinely full reconstruction later on when the work is redone.

An ultimate synthesis must take *all* the

[1] Lévi-Strauss (1962:342–348) details the characteristics of the chronological grid and points out the important fact that several grids are involved, and thus several sorts of history result.

[2] As is known, this is no absolute rule. Still, in most cases language, culture and people evolve together. The cultural ancestors are also the physical and linguistic ancestors of the bulk of the people and their modern tongue respectively. Culture and language are more closely tied to each other than any of them to physical population. Yet even in the latter case the link is strong. High prestige, political dominance and a long period of time is necessary for the language of a minority to impose itself on a majority. We believe that this also can happen when population density is low but the minority lives in clusters so that in their immediate environment they are the majority. Given a great length of time they might impose their language and culture on the majority in the whole larger area. Apart from these two situations, though, it is not possible to see how the bulk of a population could lose its language or culture.

available evidence into account. All evidence implies that all of the disciplines mentioned above will be used (and others as well) if they can throw light on the reconstruction such that it becomes eventually a thorough mix of all these data. This can be achieved more easily than it might at first appear. When any evidence of this nature is presented a conscious effort should be made to make out what it represents in terms of other disciplines. For instance, if the cultural data indicate that people in the ancestral society were polygynous and did not share the same house, one would expect archaeologists to find clusters of houses with hearths in each house except the main one in each cluster. That major house was then the dwelling of the husband. If linguistics postulates that several migrations occurred in a small area the correlative evidence from archaeology would be an exact correspondence, say, in successive pottery types. That this actually can be done is well illustrated by the case of the interlacustrine Bantu area, where oral tradition suggests that Nilotic invaders entered the area in the second half of the fifteenth century. This conclusion was not arrived at by relative chronology alone since there was available a selection of absolute dates based on sun eclipses mentioned in the traditions. Archaeological work helped to confirm the date and added some weight to the theory of Nilotic origin because of the type of artifact found, and added strong confirmation to the idea of an invasion (Posnansky 1966).

In this fashion it turns out that the weak chronology of tradition can be bolstered by the use of astronomy and archaeology. Furthermore, this can also be done as well using linguistics and ethnography, whenever items are referred to that can be traced by some artifact or material trace. On the other hand, the interpretation of archaeological data is made within a context of ethnography which often assumes the persistence of features over long periods (Gabel 1965). Such an assumption may be tested by ethnographic studies of the distribution of crucial features involved. Wider distribution generally means longer time depth, although this is not always the case; thus the test is only partial.

If all the data dovetail and confirm one another the result is gratifying because by the principle of independent confirmation, the probability reached by the convergence of independent sources is many times greater than the probability of one line of data only and amounts in practice to certainty. However, care should be exercised to see to it that the data compared are really independent. For instance, if a people say that archaeological deposits such and such are the product of an ancient people named X and Y, oral tradition may depend upon the archaeology. For, if the people knew the sites beforehand they could, and very likely would, have made up an explanation for them and if they had not and human artifacts were discovered, they might conclude logically by themselves that these ought to belong to their predecessors whose name they knew from other oral evidence! The best case of independence is when the oral tradition says that X or Y lived on site A, where nothing is visible today, and then digging on that site uncovers archaeological materials. Similar difficulties can arise for instance between oral tradition and modern ethnographic data. For example, a story has the king of Burundi coming to found the kingdom from the south and passing through places A, B, C, etc., where he founded royal estates of a special kind. It is quite likely that the storyteller, who knows where these sites are today, will have adjusted his story to this knowledge. He thus mentions sites which may not really be mentioned in the original traditions. A detailed comparison of variant stories taken from many informants actually indicates "contamination" of this sort. Thus we can tell when the distribution of archaeological sites and the oral tradition are not truly independent.

It happens also, all too frequently, that data do contradict each other or simply "pass by" each other (McCall 1964:146–148). The first case is rather like the two different results obtained in making a simple sum, and as in that case, one of the results obtained must be wrong. It is not enough that one set of data is wrong; one should show as well, why it is wrong. For instance, an oral tradition may be wrong about the origin of a people because it refers only to the ruling family. It then is not really in flat contradiction with the other data but in fact adds something to them, qualifies them by suggesting that the ruling group is intrusive. This is a very frequent situation which generally indicates that the investigator who complains of the contradiction has not interpreted his data correctly. It is very rare indeed that two types of data will contradict one another when both of them are interpreted rightly. In fact we know of no such case except where the evidence is deliberately falsified, which could happen with both written and oral data.

The "passing-by" of sets of data happens often enough. It means that data which were supposed to cross-check each other are shown not to. For instance, Imbangala traditions in Central Africa include something about a governor or a Portuguese chief Manuel or Miguel. Several interpretations are possible, but in none of these is there any correspondence between events narrated in the traditions and those available in written documents. But as we have already mentioned, written documents do not focus on the same type of events as oral ones. In such cases the result of the confrontation must be limited to show the particular characteristics and inadequacies of each set of data involved, and compared for verification purposes only when truly comparable contents are shown to exist in each.

HISTORICAL RECONSTRUCTION: A DIACHRONIC MODEL

Treatises on historical method are usually laconic about both heuristics (how to find the data) and historical synthesis or reconstruction of the past. This is because the personality and especially the imagination of the investigator loom so large in these operations. He "sees" a problem, gathers the data by imagining where they could be and after evaluation he "puts them together" by imagining how things happened in the past. This process of reconstruction is an abstraction. The vulture in its manifestations acts like discourse in language. The realization of the potentials inherent in cultural "structure" are infinite, and even the most prolix study will never exhaust its content. Which means first that new data can always be adduced to refine a reconstruction and second that any reconstruction of the past, like any description of a culture, has to be a model.

This amounts to saying that all historical monographs are models. This is obviously true for works such as Marc Bloch's study of feudalism or Fustel de Coulanges' *Ancient City*. It is also true of such seemingly true-to-life works as memoirs or biographies. Underlying each of these is a hidden framework which determines that only "relevant" data have been included. The principles of relevance are also those which have presided over the construction of the model. The words of Evans-Pritchard quoted earlier in relation to the anthropological monograph apply just as well here. The most remarkable case is certainly that of Viollet LeDuc who built his models in stone when he restored the French Gothic cathedrals to a point where they represented an ideal which he acknowledged had probably never existed at any given moment of the past (Hubert 1961:1229)!

In practice the scholar feels that a study is "finished" when all the "significant" data have been put into some satisfactory relation with each other. For the culture historian this comes when it is sensed that an answer to the question "What were the major lines of development of this culture?" is provided by his interpretation and synthesis. By "major" is understood what the investigator thinks is major, and this subjective element, present in both anthropology and history, has to be squarely recognized. If only pains are taken to explain what is deemed to be "major," to reveal, in other words, what the postulates are, which presided over the construction of the framework of the model, nothing is really wrong. But the trouble is that it is impossible to provide an overt statement of all the premises and assumptions utilized on an *a priori* basis. We are not consciously aware of all of them. Many are bound to a scholar's *Zeitgeist* and he is no more aware of them than the fish is of the water in which it swims. And yet this unconscious structuring is a major characteristic of all sociological and historical models.

The major difference between a synchronic and a dynamic model stems necessarily from the time element. The diachronic one works with the one "law" in history: that what happened later cannot have influenced what happened earlier (although what *could* happen later often influences earlier action!). A situation A' at a later period in time cannot be a *cause* of an earlier situation A. But A can or cannot be a *cause* of A'.

Historical causality is most correctly described as a chain of related antecedents and consequents. The chain is endless but has to be cut if an analysis is to be made possible. Usually one item or variable in a situation is not the cause of the next situation but a number of interacting variables are. Some of these are known and some, indeed most, are not. Thus to attempt to pinpoint a particular thing and say that this alone was responsible for a particular change is wrong. Instead we say that a bundle of antecedents, a "situation," was responsible for a bundle of consequents in a later "situation." Indeed the assumption of cultural integration opens the door to the possibility that any or all facets of culture, be it a hair style or a world-wide war, involve each other and thus every aspect of culture may be a possible antecedent to a consequent change.

Given this point, what is actually said when historical causes are expressed is that situation A became situation A' because of the known variables $(a, b, c, d \ldots n)$ plus a number of unknown ones in A all of which together produced the identifiable cluster $(a', b', c', d' \ldots n')$ and other unknowns in A'. In a practical case it looks like this: In a congeries of autonomous chiefdoms with similar structure, the central one stood out because it included more people, was bigger and was more central than the others. Later the others were subordinated to the central one. Clearly the change from autonomy to dependence was dependent upon the factors of size, numbers of people, centricity, and maybe some others. This is the story of the Kuba peoples of Central Africa and the central Bushoong chiefdom. But further factors must be added: different and better military institutions for the center and the ideology that one chiefdom should dominate the rest. The obvious next question must then deal with the development of these military institutions, involving antecedents of the antecedents (the introduction of age groups for one) and bringing to light some new antecedents hidden among the unknown factors as well as asking the same questions about the ideology. Clearly a chain of events is involved and the point of departure for the analysis is in practice an arbitrary one. There is also a field or set of unknown factors, and the point at which one decides to limit the investigation is also arbitrary. To travel down the road of intensifying the investigation yields a diminishing return for greater and greater efforts after a certain point, given present data, method, and theory.

At this point, then, other tactics must be utilized. As we shall see, the notion of historical cause is valuable because it complements synchronic causality shown by covariant correlations. The trick is to keep the unknown factors in the historical equations constant. It then becomes quite clear that the known antecedents $(a \ldots n)$ caused $(a' \ldots n')$. This is sound practice and is in fact the cardinal rule of the inductive method used by the natural and physical sciences. It is important to note that the historical method allows us to keep unknown factors more constant than does the synchronic method. This results from the fact that in any given culture the physical environment and the structural framework may not change much over a short time span, whereas in synchronic analysis both are likely to vary. The other advantage of historical causality is that under these circumstances it directly yields a statement in which we can say that a cluster of factors A *caused* the later cluster B whereas the synchronic statement of relationship can only say (without further analysis) that when A changes B also changes. But there is no way of knowing at this stage which of the two sets of factors really controls the other. For these reasons, then, painstaking care should be taken to etch these chains of events clearly in any reconstruction, for they are the "why" of the diachronic model. In other words, whenever a diachronic model is constructed, it is not simply the order of succession of synchronic situations which must be worked out—let us say, describing Mexico in 1492, and the same situation again in 1592. Rather it is to show the chain of events which led from Mexico in 1492 to Mexico in 1592 and justifying the terminal dates in the sequence by showing that they represent periods of comparatively slower change in the chain of events studied.

Perhaps the sources may provide enough information directly when they narrate events, but even so, the picture is usually so complex that at least part of the factors involved have to be inferred. For instance the history of Burundi tells us how Ntare II doubled the national territory between 1800 and 1850 —but not why it happened or how it was possible at that particular time. The chain of causal factors must then be inferred by some form of hypothesis. Maybe the kingdom had changed and become stronger than its neighbors, or maybe the neighbors had weakened? One must then go back to the data and check what indications are available. It is then noted that some neighbors had become weaker and that Burundi had not shown signs of becoming stronger through internal reorganization. This provides a "why" answer, but only in the rough. A full explanation must assume events not recorded in the sources.

Such assumed chains of events are generally recurrent ones. When they are recognized as such they are called "processes" and the more current ones are baptized by labels: "population explosion," "migration," "conquest," "ecological adaptation," to name but a few that grace the current literature. Obviously these labels are simplified expressions describing complex phenomena and should never be tagged to an historical model without the most careful scrutiny. Vagueness in this can lead to quite unwarranted generalizations or even impossible sequences. In fact dynamic models can often be judged by the sophisticated or naive way they tackle such processes. Errors in these matters are most often due to preconceptions or general notions held by the scholar about the nature of culture change. Conversely this means that any historical reconstruction is very much affected by the empirical and theoretical knowledge of culture change held by the scholar at the time of his investigations. Such understanding should of course not be expressed in *a priori* structuring of a process of change which then leads to an *a posteriori* "discovery." The obvious course to follow when a general process applies to a particular situation of change is to investigate if all the conditions of the hypothesis are present and all the antecedents and consequents postulated by the theory of social change are manifest in ways consonant with the theory.

Another major cause of errors in the construction of dynamic models stems from the problem of biased data. The underplaying of the role of the individual or the unique event which occurred where there are no written or oral records is an obvious one. Often, for example, economic factors are overdone simply because more is known about them than about socio-political evolution. Above all there is a tendency to simplify the total picture of a culture as one goes farther into the past and the sources

become scarcer. The latter tendency usually results in the construction of a model showing an increase in over-all cultural complexity, a picture which satisfies us because it coincides with our equation: complexity=progress=trend of history. Such notions as early, developmental, formative, militaristic, expansion, classical, postclassical, in archaeology are illustrations of this level of generalization. However, this notion of progress in history is as much a myth of our culture as the notion of cyclical time, four dynastic reigns deep, is to Burundi or the structural condensation of time in two or three generations to the Australian aborigines. In practice the notion is all the more dangerous in that it is perfectly valid for long time periods and in a world-wide setting. But when the cast is reduced to one culture or one area, and the time to a few centuries, even up to two millennia or so, reality can be quite different. Thus the smaller the time period, the greater the care that should be given to distinguish between the unsupported assumption of a simple-to-complex progression in a diachronic model and clear-cut evidence for such increasing complexity. Only the latter is acceptable.

Dynamic models can be built basically in two ways and in both cases the type of model produced is a structural one. This results from the assumption that the sociostructural framework and the environment condition culture just as morphology and phonemics condition language. They are the framework to be described in a model, that can be either "mechanical" or "statistical," using Lévi-Strauss' terms (1958), but which is always structural.[3] In the first method the scholar may ponder over what happened, recreate the past, fit in the evidence and explain all of it with the simplest and most elegant hypothesis. He then can take his thesis as the outline of his exposé and present all the facts in their appropriate places. But to be thorough he must take the contrary hypotheses into account and then explain

[3] Lévi-Strauss (1958:311–317) distinguished between history, which uses, he says, statistical models, and anthropology, which uses mechanical ones. In fact we believe both use statistical models in a descriptive stage and mechanical ones later. Note I, page 313, gives a bibliography of the dissenters to Lévi-Strauss' view. He expanded these in *La pensée sauvage*, Chap. IX.

why they are less adequate. Only then does this basically narrative form become acceptable, because the assumptions are stated, even though all the reasoning behind the model is not spelled out in detail and the structure of the model often has to be discovered underneath the narrative. Most historians do it this way. The advantage is to underline the subjective aspects of the reconstruction, stress the unique and focus clearly on the chain of causalities. A major disadvantage is that the model itself and the regularities and processes in it may be somewhat obscured, and this is what anthropologists are most interested in.

The second method is to set a starting situation and a final situation, possibly with intermediary stituation floors, and then to adduce the necessary evidence for each of these situations. In effect this becomes a succession of synchronic models. Then the stages are tied one to another by showing how the functional loads were shifted from one synchronic situation to the next one and thereby change occurred, or how structural conflict created changes as conflicts were resolved. Similarly, the investigator may work out how the structure allowed room or opportunity for the entry and acceptance of new elements through diffusion or innovation, or again how readaptation to changed environmental factors took place. Although this is a rather popular approach in anthropology, it has a number of drawbacks. For one thing, it is surrounded by an unnecessary gantry of sophistry and definitions aimed at making certain that all assumptions made are conscious (which is, strictly speaking, impossible) and that purely logical argument be observed at all times. It often underplays the determinative power of the unique, and finally it tends to reduce artificially the chains of antecedent and consequent relations into convenient and often therefore simplified processes. The more theoretical the model the more divorced it becomes from the abstracted reality of the particular case involved and the more assumptions have to be read into the data. But these drawbacks can be avoided as shown by some studies (Smith 1960) and the approach may not be inherently inferior to the previous one. Nor is it superior. My personal inclination, however, lies with the first type of model. Whatever the presentation, the elegance of a dynamic model lies in the way it is able to bring out in all its shadings what the chains of change are, while still preserving the horizontal perspectives of the structure at almost any moment in the period. This is not an easy recipe and in practice the exposition of a dynamic model usually takes a book-length study.

THE USE OF DYNAMIC MODELS

To build up the history of a culture one must start from some sort of synchronic model. But during the operation the emerging historical view helps to correct the synchronic perspective which in turn leads to more refined interpretations of the diachronic system. The relation between the two types of models is that of a dialogue which operates in the form of a dialectic. For instance, an analysis of contemporary government may indicate that effective governing cabinets in modern states usually have ten members or less. One may then propose an hypothesis that only a restricted number of persons can efficiently constitute the final decision-making body in a government. The diachronic analysis shows that indeed whenever the cabinet tended to become larger a new "inner" cabinet arose from it and that whenever institutions lost their crucial functions of government they were then allowed to swell to any size, e.g., the House of Lords in Great Britain. The diachronic analysis thus confirms the synchronic statement and in addition illuminates the process by which the size of the crucial "inner cabinet" evolves (Parkinson 1958:39, Table I; *The Coefficient of inefficiency,* Chap. IV).

In other cases the dynamic view helps to explain some oddities of the synchronic one. When the Bushoong (Congo) political structure is analyzed, it appears that the authority of the king is balanced by his councils. Yet in the actual operation of the political system during 1953, the king obviously held the upper hand. There was a glaring discrepancy between the structure and the practice. A diachronic analysis, however, clearly indicates that this is a recent innovation resulting from the power of the king which developed because he had become a recognized agent of the colonial state. In other words, we are obliged to redraw the synchronic equation of 1953 and take the colonial situation into account (Vansina 1964b).

In some cases two interpretations of a synchronic situation are possible and the diachronic view enables us to see which one is more acceptable. About 80% of Rwanda's population, the Hutu, used to be serfs ruled by an upper caste, the Tutsi. One theory had it that the Hutu accepted their inferior status because a basic premise or configuration, sanction, or theme of society was the inequality of the castes and the mental and hereditary superiority of the upper caste (Maquet 1954:184–196). The other theory was simply that the status of inferiority was accepted because it had been enforced by superior military means. It stresses a structural rather than a mental attitude, and holds that the Hutu do not really accept the premise of inequality (Codere 1962). Rwanda's history shows that the second hypothesis comes closer to reality. Before 1900 much of what is now Rwanda was not under strict Tutsi control and inferiority was not accepted. In the center of the country, on the other hand, the long subservience of the Hutu to the Tutsi, enforced by effective military structures, had led to a common pattern of life in which many Hutu accepted the premise postulated by Maquet. But the chain of causality started from the institutions (military domination) and led to a mental attitude; thus the premise came later rather than the reverse. This implies that as soon as the institutions of dominance decay (as they did under the colonial regime) the mental attitudes might change with some time lag, which they did. The original model then was wrong in the sequence of mental attitude and structure and erred also by considering regional cultural variations to be unimportant. Another instance of the reinterpretation and choice between models through the help of history is the study by Codere (1950) of the Kwakiutl *potlatch*.

Another contribution of diachronic models is that they help to describe the boundaries of a culture unit when it is used in a synchronic model. The problem of defining culture units is a vexing one (Naroll 1964). Generally they have been defined either by postulating an "objective" culture unit from the outside or from the inside. In the first case the anthropologist decides which local communities are more similar in culture and/or language to each other, when this set is compared to others in the area. The congeries are then called a "tribe." Typical examples of these procedures are the Bushmen, Semang, Pygmies, and Lapps. In all these cases members of these "tribes" do not know about the full extent of the ethnic unit and recognize only a smaller unit as their "universe." The subjective view of insiders turns out to be based either on the largest political units (Schapera 1956, e.g., in relation to the South African chief and kingdoms) or on the largest autonomous community felt by insiders to share a similar culture, to be "we" and not "they." By contrast, this definition will make for difficulties in any segmentary society since there is little of a hard and fast line between insiders and outsiders. The arbitrariness of such procedures is shown as well by a case such as Ashanti, where objective similarities lead the investigator to talk about one over-all "Akan tribe" including, among others, the Ashanti. But the kingdom was too big and important so it was made into a separate culture unit. The other Akan are however often labeled Akan because they constitute a number of minor chiefdoms in this area. To confuse things even further, when Akan is used in this latter sense it is often meant to include Ashanti as well!

Whatever culture unit is chosen as the starting point for a diachronic study, it may be assumed that analysis will soon lead to redefinition of the unit almost as a side product of working out its history. If the unit is political the territorial growth or shrinking of the state will show what changes have occurred in the boundaries over time. If it is an "objective" unit, history may show that the unit is not real because the groups which make it up have no common past at all or it may confirm and clarify the unit by showing the exact extent of the common past. If the unit is an insider's point of view it is sometimes possible to show the fluctuations in time of local identification. For instance, the Kongo people of 1600 began to be subdivided, after 1675, by "tribe" into subunits such as the Solongo, Zombo, Soso. This is not a case of better information being available at the later dates. A process of decay occurred in the Kongo kingdom about this time and local loyalties overcame the *esprit de corps* of the one Kongo "nation."

Very often it is not feasible to trace the origins of such "subjective" culture units, when no written documents are available, because the shifts in opinion are largely unconscious and intangible and do not tend to be reported by any corroborative sources. But the concept leaves a trace in local cultural life. If it was really a unit, those who felt themselves insiders should have acted together some time against outsiders and some record of this unity may be available.

Whatever the ethnic unit may be, the major job of a diachronic technique is not to decide pro and con, but to help overcome the tyranny inherent in the very notion of units derived from synchronic analysis. Descriptive anthropology may have stressed the study of cultures in isolation far too much and has certainly missed useful interpretations and limited our understanding of situations: for example, the demonstration by Lévi-Strauss (1949) after Radcliffe-Brown (1930) that a form of transformational theory (Lévi-Strauss 1958:Chap. 3) makes the Australian kinship systems more understandable and certainly shows a logic within them not clearly seen before. On a synchronic level there is no simple way to go beyond a unit which is also the universe of description. The only natural and genuine way to overcome the unit and handle an "area" is an historical one. Even Lévi-Strauss has to admit as much (1964:9) when he says that such comparisons can take place only if historical or geographical (diffusion) ties can be reasonably postulated. Diachronic documentation is the best guide to know how to enlarge one's field of inquiry from one particular "universe" to a larger one, from "village" to "tribe" to "area." It is a guide and it is often used as the justification for doing this. To help overcome the ethnic unit problem is an important contribution that a diachronic approach can make to the comparative study of cultures. In fact, synchronic analysis may already involve the comparative use of diachronic models whose existence is more or less understood as the causal basis for the contemporary unit distributions.

It is hard to exaggerate the contributions that can be made to anthropology by the technique of comparing diachronic models. This is an inductive comparative method, differing from the cross-cultural survey in a *sui generis* way. The steps of the method are: the building of a single larger diachronic model which includes several societies known to descend from a single common ancestral culture (Vansina 1964a). In the model the diversity of the cultures involved in the comparison is totally preserved and no elements are wrenched out of context as they sometimes are in synchronic cross-cultural comparisons. This explains why even for a comparison of two cultures only, it may require a book to set forth a good diachronic model.

The central Kuba and the Lele of Congo are a "simple" case of this sort. Both speak the same language, live in the same environment and superficially at least many features of their cultures are very similar, such as dress, houses, carving, etc. But a sociological analysis shows that the underlying structures are very different one from the other. For example the Kuba are organized in centralized chiefdoms, the Lele in autonomous villages. Even on the level of food production in a similar environment there are differences. The Kuba reap two crops of maize a year, the Lele one; the Kuba fish, the Lele do not; the Lele make finer cloth than the Kuba whose designs are more ornate, etc. (Douglas 1962, 1963; Vansina 1964b). There are good data showing the general evolution of the Kuba since *circa* 1600, especially their political development (Vansina 1963). There is little direct information about the Lele but a number of ethnographic distributions confirm that they have been major innovators in the area. They either invented or (more likely) adopted a system of age-sets and this is correlated with new forms of village government, and polyandry (new). The distribution of the latter institution on the fringes of all peoples bordering on the Lele and throughout Lele land makes it likely that they are the innovators. It is possible to show with present material how the Kuba and Lele cultures have diverged from a common ancestral pattern. This proto-Lele-Kuba society was a type of small and rather weak chiefdom. Each of them (Kuba and Lele) reintegrated constantly new internal or foreign elements into their societies and differentiated eventually from the parent society. It is obvious that cases such as these (and they are, I believe, *legio*) do enrich our knowledge of the dynamics of social change considerably. But such work requires separate treatment. Apart from the two books already devoted to describing synchronic models for Kuba and Lele, a third one is needed to build a satisfying, rich diachronic one showing Kuba and Lele as descendant ethnic groups from a common ancestor.

There is a natural transition from the previous type of comparison to a real one. The Mongo peoples of the Congo basin (numbering at least twenty-five "tribes") are all related one to another and one could presumably try to build up a single diachronic model or a history for all of them. The difference from the Lele-Kuba would be merely one of scope. The same could be done for, e.g., the Western interlacustrine cultures of East Africa. One goes almost unwittingly a step further when an area is considered in which whatever ancestral society there may have been lies much farther back in time. For instance the Lele-Kuba probably separated from the parent culture in the sixteenth century or so. But they belong to a larger congeries of people, which was well differentiated long before that. It would not be wise to reconstruct an ancestral society for the larger group, because it would have to be based on several already reconstructed cultures, which means that the resulting hypothesis would be second or third or nth degrees removed from data. For instance, to describe a common ancestral Bantu society about two thousand years ago by this method would be quite unreal! But an over-all examination of all the cultures in an area would yield specific features about them, realized differently in each culture but still belonging to a common theme. The evidence would show that probably a single ancestral institution might lay at the bottom of these variations on one theme, or it might turn out that diffusion was to be considered. In practice the different realizations of the common theme would be handled as transformations and one would show why each transformation was adopted by each culture, rather than to try to reconstruct the Ur-institution! In such a fashion areas can be enlarged as long as there are good ethnographic and historical reasons for it. One can consider Australia or Bantu Africa or lowland South America or ultimately even the whole of the Americas as one area. In each case the variations of the socio-political structures, religious life, economics, etc., could be recorded and tentative rules about social change, valid for the area, could be set up, rather like those laws in physics which apply only in a given environment.

Another complementary form of a real comparison occurs when the histories of cultures or parts of the cultures in the area are known. We have argued that one of the major steps in handling historical causality is to preserve the unknowns in the equation of the antecedent and subsequent situations, keeping them as constant as possible. If the culture area investigated lies within a single environment such that basic economic production is rather similar, and there are many similarities in the basic social and political patterns, then many of the unknowns in a comparison are held constant (see Chapter 31). A comparison of the separate cultural histories will then show whether the interpretations used to explain one of the cases has more general application to other cases. In practice it is fairly easy to sort out processes which are unique from more general ones even though there may be unknown antecedents working in all cases whose comparability is beyond our reach at this point. For instance, in the Central African kingdoms monarchy was the keystone to the political structure: it was a common antecedent everywhere. So, in most cases, was matrilinearity, except for the Luba among whom patrilinearity made for some unique antecedents. The common factor of kingship, the common ideology of kingship by which the personality of a ruler was so important that fluctuations in the fortunes of the state were closely associated with the succession of personalities on the throne more than to anything else led to remarkably similar profiles in the political history of most of these states. Linked to this was a system of succession whereby frequent civil wars led to a weakening of the state during the *inter regna*, and in many cases states succumbed to foreign intervention during civil wars of this sort. Everywhere too decentralization was so marked that the outer provinces were often semi-autonomous, which explains the lack of a balance of power between the great states and the impossibility of a struggle for the "hegemony." It resulted also in the frequent splitting off of peripheral provinces, whenever the nuclear area was under great stress (Vansina 1966). All of these remarks about Central African states can be said to form a set of regularities or "laws" valid for the area.

A next step might be to compare one area with another where the backgrounds were somewhat different and historical relationship would be nil or remote. For example we might compare the Central African kingdoms with those of Indonesia. If regularities held up after this comparison one could then say about the Central African cases that certain of their common "unknown" factors could be discarded because they did not occur in Indonesia. A good illustration of this sort of comparison is the comparison of Meso-America and the Middle East by Adams (1966). Here regularities are detected quite skillfully and at the same time an explanation is given for differences in the "realization" of the underlying regularities, i.e., in the way they manifest themselves in each area.

Comparisons of some areas with others that are close to them geographically but where no recent historical relationship is involved yields results in between those obtained from intra-areal comparisons and comparisons between areas far away from each other. To compare Central African states with interlacustrine states or West African kingdoms will yield more regularities, and these may be more specific, than in a comparison between Central Africa and Indonesia. The point is that, depending on the problem there is available a marvelously graduated scale of comparisons from very close and similar cultures to the very distant ones. Inductive reasoning can be followed step by step throughout a set of ever-widening "universes" or the researcher can jump steps to test a regularity he suspects to be more fundamental and try it out in a comparison between very different cultures far apart from one another.

By and large there is no doubt that real gains will be made only by a natural progression from the smallest to the biggest levels of universes. For only in this way are regularities tested gradually, refined and re-tested whilst the cultural data are never wrenched out of context. Theoretically the ultimate level would be the world and conclusions might be reached that whenever antecedents $(a \ldots n)$ obtain, x follows. With that would have been established what all anthropologists strive for: a statement with predictive value.

In practice though, it is known that so many variables are at work in human affairs that any particular global constellation of factors will hardly ever occur twice. It is still not certain that what we call the "unique" (*das Einmalige*) is not merely a unique combination of factors which are not unique in themselves. However, this is quite likely, and the consequences of uniqueness must be faced up to. Only in a few fields of history has there been systematic utilization of historical regularities in which decisions are based on such knowledge. The use by the military men of the history of war is a case in point; prediction is achieved by computers who program the several possible initial situations and give a series of probable outcomes.

From the military example and some practice of history, it is obvious that when regularities are proposed as laws this almost never takes the form of: given factors a, b, c, the result will be x, y, z. But rather: given a, b, c, and unknowns, the result will be x, y, z, or t, u, v; and if x, y, z, this will develop into z'; if t, u, v, into t', etc. Such a statement looks like this:

Given the general conditions of the Central African states, the relation between the leadership of the territorial upper level posts and the future evolution of the state will be: first, if these posts are filled with members of the royal lineage they can either become hereditary and lead to another type of territorial control; or the posts are filled every generation by new members of the royal lineage, more closely related to the new rulers, in which case the system can become one of an appointed bureaucracy in which non-royals begin to be appointed, or can persist as before. But, *no case of persistence is known as yet.* Secondly, if the posts are filled by an hereditary principle, the autonomy of the provinces increases and the kingdom can fall apart rather easily. This is also a possible outcome in the first variant of the first case. As long as there is a strong nucleus, however, the system can persist. Thirdly, if an appointed bureaucracy rules, the system is likely to persist as long as tendencies toward inheritance are checked by the court. Since this is difficult to achieve with the powerful royal lineages, a bureaucracy staffed by royals will not last and that is the reason no persistence has been noted.

This set of rules applies to the Central African states. It looks very much like the "rules" one finds in handbooks of chess. And in fact we suspect strongly that all "historical laws" will have to be expressed in the form of a game theory.

One must point out however that even if predictions could be made, the prediction would not be able to come true any longer in the future because in almost all the situations the antecedents would specify a pre-industrial economy, and would not apply to a modern state. Even if control areas were set aside from which no data could be used in the formulation of the rule, such a situation would still hold. If the rule did not apply, a reason for its non-application would have to be stated and incorporated into the rule. No possible predictive test can then be used for those cases. But although it is disappointing, it does not invalidate the procedure.

It has been argued that diachronic models can be built and are worth building not only because they help to improve synchronic models or overcome the difficulties arising from the use of culture units, but mainly because they can be used inductively and comparatively without any loss whatsoever of the fascinating complexity of reality, and without any tearing of features from their natural backgrounds. This method leads to the statement of rules about process, thus fulfilling an essential aim of anthropology. It is however also obvious that much humble collecting of ethnographic data, and much piecing together of "simple" histories and limited diachronic comparisons, will be necessary before any solidly based general rules can be uncovered. And here, as the history of anthropology shows, there is no shortcut.[4]

[4] Most of the illustrations have been drawn from Africa, not that none could be found elsewhere, but because of our greater familiarity with this area. Comparable examples might be adduced from any area in the world.

BIBLIOGRAPHY

ADAMS, R. M.
1966 The evolution of urban society: early Mesopotamia and Prehispanic Mexico. Chicago, Adine.

ATKINSON, R. J. C.
1953 Field archaeology. London, Methuen.

BAUER, W.
1928 Einführung in das studium der geschichte. Tübingen, J. C. B. Mohr.

BERNHEIM, E.
1908 Lehrbuch der historischen methode und der geschichtsphilosophie. Leipzig, Duncker and Humblot.

BLOCH, M.
1952 Apologie de l'histoire ou le métier d'historien. Cahiers des annales 3.

BLOOMFIELD, L.
1933 Language. New York, Holt.

CARR, E. H.
1964 What is history? New York, Knopf.

CHILDE, V. G.
1956 A short introduction to archaeology. London, Muller.

CODERE, H.
1950 Fighting with property. Monographs of the American Ethnological Society, Vol. 18.
1962 Power in Ruanda. In R. Cohen, ed., Power in complex societies in Africa. Anthropologica 4:45–85.

DOUGLAS, M.
1962 Lele economy compared with the Bushong: a study of economic backwardness. In Bohannan and Dalton, eds., Markets in Africa. Evanston, Northwestern University Press.
1963 The Lele of Kasai. London, Oxford University Press.

EVANS-PRITCHARD, E. E.
1940 The Nuer. Oxford, Clarendon Press.

FEDER, A.
1924 Lehrbuch der geschichtlichen methodik. Regensburg, München, Verlag J. Kossel and F. Pustet.

GABEL, C.
1965 Stone age hunters of the Kafue: the Gwisho A site. Boston University African Research Studies No. 6. Boston, Boston University Press.

GRAEBNER, F.
1911 Methode der ethnologie. Heidelberg, C. Winter.

GREENBERG, J. H.
1957 Essays in linguistics. New York, Wenner-Gren Foundation for Anthropological Research.

HERSKOVITS, M. J.
1956 Man and his works. New York, Knopf.
1959 Anthropology and Africa: a wider perspective. Africa, 29 (3):225–238.

HEYERDAHL, T.
1950 Kon-Tiki. London, G. Allen.
1952 American Indians in the South Pacific. London, Allen and Unwin.
1958 Aku-Aku. Chicago, Rand McNally.

HUBERT, J.
1961 Archéologie Médiévale. In C. Samaran, ed., *L'histoire et ses méthodes*, pp. 275–238, 1226–1241. Paris, Gallimard.

JOURNAL OF AFRICAN HISTORY
1960– Cambridge University Press.
1966

KROEBER, A. L.
1939 *Cultural and natural areas of North America.* University of California Publications in American Archaeology and Ethnology, Vol. 48. Berkeley, University of California Press.

LEHMANN, W. P.
1962 *Historical linguistics: an introduction.* New York, Holt, Rinehart and Winston.

LEROI GOURHAN, A.
1950 *Les fouilles préhistoriques: techniques et méthodes.* Paris, Picard.

LÉVI-STRAUSS, C.
1949 *Les structures élémentaires de la parenté.* Paris, Presses Universitaires de France.
1958 *Anthropologie structurale.* Paris, Plon.
1962 *La pensée sauvage.* Paris, Plon.
1964 *Mythologiques: le cru et le cuit.* Paris, Plon.

MAQUET, J. J.
1954 *Le système des relations sociales dans le Ruanda ancien.* Annales du musée royal du Congo belge. Sciences de l'homme. Ethnologie, Vol. I.

MARROU, C. I.
1961 Qu'est-ce que l'histoire? In C. Samaran, ed., *L'histoire et ses méthodes*, pp. 3–36. Paris, Gallimard.
1961 Comment comprendre le métier d'historien. In C. Samaran, ed., *L'histoire et ses méthodes*, pp. 1465–1540. Paris, Gallimard.

MCCALL, D.
1964 *Africa in time perspective.* Boston, Boston University Press.

NAROLL, R.
1964 On ethnic unit classification. *Current Anthropology* 5 (4):283–312.

PARKINSON, C. NORTHCOTE
1958 *Parkinson's law.* London, J. Murray.

PAUL, H.
1909 *Prinzipien der sprachgeschichte.* Halle, M. Niemeyer.

PIGGOTT, S.
1965 *Ancient Europe.* Chicago, Aldine.

POSNANSKY, M.
1966 *Prelude to East African history.* London, Oxford University Press.

RADCLIFFE-BROWN, A. R.
1930– The social organization of Australian
1931 tribes. *Oceania* 1 (2).

SAPIR, E.
1916 *Time perspective in aboriginal American culture: a study in method.* Department of mines, geological survey, anthropological series. Memoir 90, Series No. 13. Reprinted in D. Mandelbaum, ed., *Selected writings of Edward Sapir*, 1949. Berkeley, University of California Press.

SCHAPERA, I.
1956 *Government and politics in tribal societies.* London, Watts.

SCHMIDT, W.
1939 *The cultural historical method of ethnology.* Translated by S. A. Sieber. New York, Fortuny's.

SMITH, M. G.
1960 *Government in Zazzau.* London, Oxford University Press.

SPIER, L.
1921 The sun dance of the Plains Indians: its development and diffusion. *Anthropological Papers, American Museum of Natural History* 16 (7):451–527.

STURTEVANT, E. H.
1917 *Linguistic change.* Chicago. Reprinted 1962, Chicago, University of Chicago Press.

SUGGS, R. C.
1960 *The island civilizations of Polynesia.* New York, New American Library.
1962 *The hidden worlds of Polynesia.* New York, Harcourt, Brace.

VAN BULCK, G.
1931 *Beiträge zur methodik der völkerkunde.* Wiener beiträge zur kulturgeschichte und linguistik, Vol. 2.

VANSINA, J.
1961 *De le tradition orale.* Translated by H. M. Wright, *Oral tradition.* Chicago, Aldine.
1963 *Geschiedenis van de kuba.* Annales du musée royal de l'Afrique Centrale, sciences humaines, No. 44.
1964a The use of process-models in African history. In J. Vansina, R. Mauny, and L. Thomas, eds., *The historian in tropical Africa.* London, Oxford University Press.
1964b *Le royaume kuba.* Annales du musée royal de l'Afrique Centrale, sciences humaines, No. 49.
1965 *Oral tradition.* Chicago, Aldine.
1966 *Kingdoms of the savanna.* Madison, University of Wisconsin Press.

PART III

The Field Work Process

CHAPTER 10

Research Design in Anthropological Field Work

ROBERT A. LEVINE

In experimental studies and quantitative social surveys a research design is an advance plan for organizing the collection of data so that they are maximally relevant to the validity of certain generalizations concerning relations between variables. Field work in social and cultural anthropology only occasionally involves a research design in this sense. More frequently it has been thought of as an exploration into the unknown, in which the investigator must acquire firsthand acquaintance with the background facts of ecology, language, social organization and culture of a people before formulating more specific research goals. In the past, many anthropologists stopped with this exploratory phase, content with contributing another ethnographic description to the archive of cultural variation, or with the intent to return for more specialized investigation at some indefinite future time. This is consonant with a conception of social anthropology as natural history, utilizing naturalistic, exploratory methods of investigation, and producing case studies. There is an increasing tendency, however, to adopt specific goals for field work, formulate intellectual problems that the field work is intended to solve, select groups to work in on the basis of their relevance to these problems, and use methods of study that are susceptible of replication. Exploratory study remains important in anthropology, but more emphasis is now given to the specialized research that uses ethnographic exploration as its launching platform. Even general ethnography is increasingly planned to produce comparable data that can be used in subsequent comparative hypothesis-testing by other investigators. Given these trends, re-

search design in anthropological field work deserves more attention than it has received to date.

This chapter takes up field research design under the four following headings: (a) formulation of a research problem; (b) selection of a region or group in which to study the problem; (c) the exploratory phase of general ethnography; and (d) the problem-solving or hypothesis-testing phase.

FORMULATION OF A RESEARCH PROBLEM

At present social anthropologists are beginning their field work with aims that vary from that of testing a highly specific hypothesis—e.g., litigation rates co-vary with the amount of land held by domestic groups—to that of simply "studying" a people who had never been studied before. Most investigators go to the field with at least a specialized interest in an aspect of culture such as religion, kinship, polity, economy, and knowledge of numerous hypotheses and empirical problems pertaining to that aspect. Their basic procedure is to match their knowledge of hypotheses that *could* be studied *if* there were variation along certain dimensions, with the actual variations they find in the group to be studied; when a correspondence is discovered, a researchable problem has been identified. This matching process may occur before the investigator goes to the field, if sufficient information on the group is available in advance, or during the exploratory phase of field work. All too often it seems to occur very late in field work or even after it, because the anthropologist is too busy collecting data as it comes to stand back from it and say, "What problems might be most fruitfully studied here; what hypotheses could be tested on available variations?" If his omnibus research efforts have been intensive as well as comprehensive, he may have enough data to test hypotheses developed after he has left the field; if not, he may be out of luck without another field trip.

The scientific investigator unacquainted with anthropology may ask, "Why not formulate a single hypothesis or set of hypotheses as precisely as possible before field work?" The usual answer is that the anthropologist planning a field trip is faced with the prospect of making an enormous investment of personal resources in a research setting of which he is likely to be appallingly ignorant beforehand. The more precise his hypothesis, the less the likelihood of his finding variations that would provide an adequate test for it. Many inexperienced field workers (and some experienced ones) have found themselves having to change specialized problems selected prior to field work once they were in the field and then wondering why they went to the trouble of formulating them in advance (except that the granting agency and/or dissertation committee required it). In another discipline, the investigator might change the research setting and retain his original problem, but the anthropological field worker has gone to such efforts to prepare himself for and even travel to his field location, that he is invariably less willing to change the setting than the problem if the two do not match. Even within anthropology, the investigator who uses published ethnographic data to test hypotheses may waste a few weeks of his own and his assistants' time in a blind alley attempting to measure a dimension that does not vary cross-culturally in such a way that it can be measured, but he can and does alter his attack on the problem and try again with relative ease. The field worker, however, having discovered that his hypothesis is untestable in his current field location, must find a way of salvaging some research value from his year or two in the field and the preparation that has gone into it. Hence he is ill advised to put all his eggs in the basket of one hypothesis or research problem unless he knows the field setting very well in advance. These practical considerations comprise the strongest argument against precise *a priori* problem formulation in anthropological field work.

These difficulties in advance planning do not mean that research design has no place in anthropological field work but only that its place must be defined appropriately for the kinds of research situations in which anthropologists operate. In anthropological studies no less than in any other scientific investigations the success of an effort at testing an hypothesis or solving an empirical problem is largely dependent on the adequacy of the research design. Recognizing his unique difficulties in matching his problem interests with the setting in which he will work, the anthropologist must be diligent and ingenious in devising strategies for the construction of workable research designs that are appropriate to his field work.

Several such strategies have been used and are available. First, the anthropologist should develop and be prepared to test an array of hypotheses relevant to his major research interest (e.g., an aspect of culture or behavior) which can serve as alternative foci for field work. Presumably each hypothesis would be of sufficient generality that supporting or refuting it would make a significant contribution to knowledge in the behavioral sciences. At least one of these propositions should be so geared to universal features of human life that it could be tested in a wide variety of if not all societies. Armed with such alternatives, the field worker is not likely to be at a loss if he finds the cultural setting unsuitable for testing his first-choice hypothesis.

Second, the anthropologist should make maximum use of available ethnographic information to select an area of the world and a society where conditions appear most favorable to testing his hypothesis. This procedure is discussed below.

Even if these first two procedures are not followed, every anthropologist has available to him the possibility of dividing his field work (in one or more field trips) into two explicit phases: an exploratory phase in which a specific problem is formulated, a feasible research design is constructed, and field methods are pretested; and an hypothesis-testing phase in which the research design is put into operation. Increasing opportunities for prolonged residence in or repeated trips to field locations make this sequence increasingly possible. It is highly desirable from the viewpoint of effective research design no matter how much pre-field preparation has been done.

The above paragraphs do no more than spell out what is obvious to experienced field workers, yet research design has not yet become institutionalized in anthropological field work, at least partly because the difficulties of advance planning are thought to rule it out. Since these difficulties clearly do not preclude research design, and since the attainment of scientific goals requires it, it is reasonable to conclude that the field worker should strive to formulate a testable hypothesis and devise a research design to test it before he has completed his data collection rather than afterward.

SELECTION OF AN AREA OR SOCIETY FOR FIELD STUDY

Assuming that the investigator has identified a set of related problems and an array of testable hypotheses *prior* to his field work, he is in a position to choose a field location on the basis of the extent to which it provides an adequate testing ground for his hypotheses. What is adequate? A great many theoretically significant hypotheses can be studied in any society, with each replication in another population providing an additional basis for accepting or rejecting the hypothesis. The investigator whose interest lies in such an hypothesis will decide where to work on grounds unrelated to the theoretical problem.

Other problems appear to dictate a choice of society. It has become common for an anthropologist to become interested in a "problem" such as pastoralism and hence select pastoral societies in which to work, or a market economy and select societies having markets, or political leadership and select a group with a centralized state, or culture change and find an area undergoing rapid change, or the relations of a world religion with a tribal cult and select an appropriate area of Asia or Africa. Anthropologists seeking to understand bureaucratic organization, a specialized clergy, polygyny, the couvade, and so forth become field workers in societies where these institutions or customs are conspicuous. This is widely regarded as an advance over the days of general ethnography when field locations were not selected for their problem relevance, and there can be no

doubt that the particular institutions are better understood for detailed studies of them in their most developed forms. To test hypotheses about these institutions, however, we need detailed studies of situations where they are absent or weakly developed for comparison. If every anthropologist were to become interested in a particular institutional pattern and did field work only where that pattern were most elaborated or developed, cross-cultural studies of those patterns would become impossible, for it is from variations in the magnitude of institutional factors that we test hypotheses concerning the functional relations of those factors with other variables. From the viewpoint of cross-cultural studies, old-fashioned general ethnography had the advantage of assuring fairly even coverage on a set list of topics across many societies, whereas intensive ethnography on problem-selected societies prevents comparability.

Quite apart from cross-cultural studies, studying institutions where they are *in*conspicuous has been notably rewarding in modern anthropology. Studies of politics in stateless societies, of descent groups where there are no lineages, of leadership where there are no chiefs, prices where there is no money, of aggression among peaceful peoples, of history and science among the nonliterate and technologically primitive—represent some of the most significant and subtle advances in anthropological understanding during the past few decades. They occurred because field workers did not limit themselves to investigating what was most obvious, elaborated, emphasized, or institutionally developed among the peoples with whom they worked, and at least partly because they had *not* selected a culture to work in on the basis of their strongest research interests. Social anthropology owes much of its intellectual excitement to serendipities such as these, which might be foreclosed by too rigid a matching of problem interest and field setting. Thus we must specify with care what we mean by choosing a field location that provides an adequate testing ground for the investigator's hypothesis.

From the point of view of research design the adequacy of a field setting for studying a given problem bears a direct relation to the amount of variation provided by that setting on dimensions that are relevant to that problem. If the field work is carried out in an area where there is static homogeneity on such dimensions, the investigator will be (without further comparison) in the weakest position to draw valid conclusions about the necessary and sufficient connections existing among the set of variables he has set out to study. Although he will perceive connections that appear inherent in that particular cultural setting, and his informants will convey their sense of relations within their behavior and institutions, he will lack information about what would happen if some of the variables were absent, or present in weaker or stronger form than they are. Without this latter information, he can say nothing about the necessary contingency of one variable on another, and furthermore is likely to be misled by the peculiarities of this one setting into believing that certain variables are correlated when in fact they are not.

An example of this might be the case of a field worker seeking to find the socioeconomic preconditions for a highly centralized state organization. Working intensively in one society organized in this way which had no major internal variations on socioeconomic variables, the anthropologist might see numerous connections between the economy and polity and begin to draw conclusions concerning the social and economic conditions necessary for the development or maintenance of a centralized state. He might subsequently be surprised to find other societies in which these conditions were absent but the state nonetheless existed, disproving his statement that they were necessary. In such a case the field worker might or might not have been right about the observed connections between economy and polity in the case he studied, but be misled by the absence of opportunities for observing political variation into concluding that the connections were necessary and therefore held generally. Another field worker, working in a society high on institutionalized antagonism between the sexes in which women were more frequently believed to be witches than men, might conclude that the latter pattern was caused by the former. Later, it might be brought to his attention that the belief in women's greater propensity for witchcraft is extremely widespread, even among societies lacking institutionalized sex antagonism. This investigator might turn out to be wrong not only in generalizing beyond the single case

of his observation but even within that single case: he could have mistakenly seen the "accidental" co-occurrence of two patterns in a single society as evidence for their being *necessarily* connected.

Even if we assume that these two field workers were sufficiently aware of the relevant ethnographic literature to know that the observed co-occurrences did not prove necessary or invariant relations, the point remains that their field data would not help them decide which of the many co-occurrences they observed were more likely than others to have some necessary connection with each other. In other words, their field settings were badly chosen to reflect on the validity of the types of hypotheses in which they were interested. Unless their goal was to generate hypotheses rather than test them, their research studies were not adequately designed. The plight of such an investigator is similar to that of a medical researcher seeking to establish a causal link between smoking and lung cancer on the basis of a case in which one heavy smoker developed lung cancer. Case studies often raise important questions but do not answer them.

Thus a single society that is homogeneous on the dimensions of concern in the study is clearly an inadequate field setting for an hypothesis-testing investigation. There is no single adequate field setting but only a single guide to the selection of setting—the more variation (in terms of both range and distribution) on the variables to be studied, the better. (One might add: the less variation on dimensions not included in the hypotheses, the better; see Clignet's chapter for a discussion of constants in concomitant variation studies.) In terms of this criterion, there are degrees of adequacy of field settings. A crude example will serve for all of them. Suppose an investigator were interested in the correlates of community size, hypothesizing a number of specific effects that community size has on interpersonal behavior patterns. Five types of field settings, in increasing order of adequacy, can be imagined:

(a) A single community, of whatever size. This would be inadequate because, as argued above, the investigator would not have a firm basis for distinguishing the fortuitous characteristics of that community from those that are necessarily connected with its size.

(b) Several discrete size categories of communities, with *one* representative of each; e.g., a large community compared with a medium and small one. In this type of setting, which involves comparison in a form familiar to anthropologists, some tentative statements can be made about the correlates of size, while recognizing that differences in interpersonal behavior among any three (or five . . .) communities could be due to differences in community characteristics other than size. In other words, unless the other community characteristics are held constant (as in the controlled comparison), they may be confounded with size, leaving the investigator unable to disentangle their respective correlates.

(c) Several discrete size categories of communities (e.g., large, medium, small), with *several* representatives of each. This type of comparison, less frequently made by anthropologists, is more adequate than the previous type because (unless there is a controlled comparison) it gives greater assurance that differences in interpersonal behavior between size categories are due to size rather than to the other community characteristics, which vary both *within* and *between* size categories.

(d) A large and continuous distribution of communities according to size, but within a restricted range of sizes. For example, suppose the field worker could collect data from one hundred communities ranging in size from 300 to 1000 persons, with a fairly even or bell-shaped distribution of communities along the size dimension. It would then be possible to examine the correlations of community size with interpersonal behavior variables using sensitive correlational statistics and without imposing categories devised by the investigator. Conclusions could be drawn on the basis of quantitative evidence as to whether size or other community characteristics were more strongly related to the variables of interpersonal behavior, but the conclusions would be limited to the size range of 300 to 1000 persons.

(e) A large and continuous distribution of communities in an expanded range of sizes. Suppose a field situation similar to the foregoing except that the sample of communities included some between 50 and 300 in size and others up to 20,000. The conclusions concerning the relation of community size

with interpersonal behavior would be similarly expanded.

It should be noted in addition that the more similar are the communities compared in terms of variables other than size, the more certain one can be that correlations of size with interpersonal behavior are not due to other, unstudied variables; but—in the large samples of (d) and (e)—the more dissimilar or heterogeneous (e.g., in ethnic origin) are the communities compared, the more certain one can be that any relation of size with interpersonal behavior is not limited in its generality to any particular set of societies (e.g., those of one area of the world or at one level of socioeconomic development). Thus while the investigator can be unambivalent in seeking maximal variation on the dimensions included in his hypotheses, he faces a more difficult decision concerning dimensions deemed "irrelevant" in advance. For the field worker as opposed to the comparative analyst, practical considerations almost invariably weigh in favor of a "controlled comparison" of neighboring groups resembling each other in many background characteristics. The field worker also faces a practical limitation on the number of units he can compare, and with small numbers it is advisable to hold background factors constant.

In discussing the situation of the anthropological field worker, we usually think in terms of one person operating independently and attempting to master one local language and culture in a period of two years or less. This puts severe limitations on the amount of variation he can cover, but initial selection of the field setting with the maximal-variation principle in mind can increase greatly the field worker's ability to meet the criteria for hypothesis-testing. He can choose an ethnic-linguistic unit that obviously exhibits internal contrasts in which he is interested, with subgroups varying in mode of subsistence (e.g., agricultural vs. pastoral or fishing), descent group organization, political organization (e.g., centralized vs. acephalous), religion (e.g., Islamized vs. pagan), urbanization, or modernization—to mention but a few possibilities. Most of the large ethnic groups of Africa and Asia are fairly heterogeneous internally, so that opportunities for selection of this kind are less limited than ethnographic simplification often suggests. If he visits the area before deciding which group to work with, the field worker can usually discover quickly where he can find the kind of variation he seeks.

Recent ethnographic examples should reassure prospective field workers that they can indeed find theoretically significant intra-ethnic variation. For example, Fallers (1957) and Fallers and Fallers (1960) found among the Soga a subgroup that had had its lineages dispersed by population shifts caused by an epidemic, to compare with a Soga area in which lineage localization was more intact. Their quantitative comparisons of husband-wife separations (1957) and suicide (1960) rates in the two areas provide important evidence for hypotheses relating structurally-generated conflicts and indexes of individual stress. Geertz (1959) found major structural variations among villages in Bali, albeit variations on some common themes, which enable one to gain more insight into the functional relations among aspects of community structure than if the villages had been structurally uniform. Lloyd (1954) notes great variations in political structure among the kingdoms of the Yoruba. The study by Munroe (1964) of couvade among the Black Carib of British Honduras revealed differential participation in the custom, so that it was possible to test some psychological hypotheses by comparing a sample of men who had practiced it with one of those who had not. These examples indicate how internal variations at different structural levels (major ethnic subgroup, village, individual) can be exploited in research designs for testing hypotheses relevant to that level. Psychological anthropologists should take particular note of inter-individual differences in environmental treatment or participation in order to design studies to test their hypotheses, while other social anthropologists should select field settings affording variation at a level appropriate to the nature of the problems they are studying.

Remaining within the limitations of the solitary field worker but going beyond the limits of the single field trip, there is the possibility of finding variation for hypothesis-testing by working with a series of related ethnic groups that differ on certain dimensions of interest. This can be done on successive field trips. It is the "method of controlled comparison" advocated by Eggan

(1954) and illustrated in his work (1941, 1950).

Finally, the field worker can become part of a collective enterprise in which his own research supplies some but not all of the data that enter into a comparative analysis. He can select a group related to, but differing relevantly from, others on which adequate published material is already available. He can agree to collaborate with one or more other anthropologists who work in neighboring groups, using comparable methods of data collection and comparing results. He can collect field data according to the requirements of a field manual (e.g., Whiting *et al.* 1966, LeVine and Campbell 1965) so that his material is pooled with that of others working elsewhere in the world for comparative hypothesis-testing.

With all these, and other, opportunities for finding variation available to the prospective field worker, there appear to be no practical obstacles to the selection of a field setting with the goal of hypothesis-testing clearly in view.

THE EXPLORATORY PHASE OF GENERAL ETHNOGRAPHY

Were general ethnography to be treated like the exploratory phase in any type of study, the major question about it from the viewpoint of research design would be: How can it be organized to facilitate hypothesis formulation, sample selection, the operationalization of concepts in locally meaningful terms, and the development of appropriate research instruments? The apparent consensus among anthropologists that a "basic ethnographic description" of a society is both worthwhile in itself and necessary groundwork for more specialized studies demands prior discussion of what that description is and what contribution it makes to anthropological knowledge.

In collecting the data for a basic ethnographic description, the ethnographer attempts to achieve both *comparability* and *comprehensiveness*. Comparability means that his description of the culture must be in terms that will permit comparison with cultures already described in the ethnographic literature. Each field worker is or should be replicating in his ethnographic groundwork a set of operations carried out by previous field workers in other settings. Such replication enables him to understand what he is finding against the background of his knowledge of world ethnography; it also enables others to use his published descriptions for the purposes of comparative studies. Thus the implicit rules of ethnographic field investigations do not permit the field worker to be completely idiosyncratic in his approach and coverage. He must be guided, at least initially, by past work. This is where comprehensiveness comes in, for general ethnography to date has been governed by the widespread agreement among anthropologists that the field worker should strive for "complete" coverage of the culture or way of life of the people under study, with the recognition that such coverage may be superficial and is always uneven.

Comprehensiveness as a goal of general ethnography makes two demands on the field worker: that he gather data on a variety of topics deemed by anthropological consensus to represent the spectrum of customs, social and cultural institutions, or aspects of culture, and that he investigate distinctive features of the culture. While opinions on aspects of culture to be covered are not unanimous, the strong consensus existing in the field can be seen in the tables of contents of general ethnographic monographs, where chapter headings frequently follow a pattern: habitat and ecology, economy, social organization (including marriage, family, kinship, descent and local groups, status groups, political organization), religion and magic, and the life cycle. Similar patterns are observable for the headings of early chapters presenting contextual material in specialized monographs, although the effects of specialized interests and approaches in disturbing this redundancy are increasingly evident. (For example, chapters on topics like political leadership, law and social control, ethno-ecology, daily routine, child training practices, and psychopathology appear to be more frequent nowadays than in the past.) Formal listings of topics for basic ethnographic description are available in *Notes and Queries on Anthropology* (1951, 6th ed.) and in *The Outline of Cultural Materials* by Murdock *et al.* (1950). These listings tend more toward overrepresenting than underrepresenting the range of topics considered essential background by professional anthropologists; especially in

Murdock *et al.*, little is omitted that anyone has ever thought worthy of inclusion in a general ethnography. The field worker is thus urged to begin by covering a range of established (though crude) categories representing the common denominators of contextual material collected by previous field workers.

The canon of comprehensiveness also enjoins the field worker to go beyond established categories and record whatever local customs or institutions strike him as distinctive compared to other cultures or particularly important in the thinking and behavior of the people he is studying. Such institutions may cut across the conventional categories and appear more important as contexts necessary to understanding local behavior. In order to contribute to the ethnographic record of cultural variation, the field worker must report that which is cross-culturally distinctive, and to provide as meaningful a context as possible for his specialized study he must include that which seems central, focal or integrative in local thought and action. The isolation and description of distinctive features absorbs a great deal of the ingenuity and effort of anthropologists whose aims are primarily descriptive, but from the viewpoint of field research design, it is their contribution to understanding the context in which an hypothesis will be tested that must be stressed.

Within the framework of the demands for comparability and comprehensiveness, the field worker has many options in how he goes about his general ethnographic work and in what he chooses to describe. In other words, he makes many crucial decisions about what is worth recording and what is not. These decisions are often based on a philosophic position in which certain behavioral and cultural phenomena are held to be more real than others; there is an implicitly metaphysical view of the nature of culture according to idealist or materialist premises. The idealist, whether or not he explicitly conceptualizes or acknowledges his ontological assumptions, believes that cultural reality consists in shared mental events such as ideas, beliefs, concepts, and rules that govern, guide, and direct observable behavior, the latter being an imperfect reflection of the former. From this viewpoint, a culture may be thought of as a set of rules governing the speech, thought, and social behavior of a given population. To obtain a basic description of the culture, field work should be designed to discover these rules. A model for this is offered by structural linguistics, in which systematic interviewing of informants of a given speech-community yields the rules of their spoken language. The idealist is inclined to follow this example and work primarily with informants, obtaining generalizations about the concepts and norms that are locally agreed to hold in the spheres of social organization, religion, economy, etc. He will be exposed to observable behavior in these spheres but will concentrate his systematic efforts on discovering the systems of ideas that he believes determine the behavior. The materialist believes that cultural reality consists in the distributions of observable behavioral events in space and time. These distributions, rather than reflecting "higher-order" forces such as ideas, can be reduced to "lower-order" events such as concentrations of energy or of resources convertible into energy; ideologies are built up to justify or rationalize the distributions of resources in a given population adapting to a given environment at a point in time and space. To describe the basic outlines of a culture the materialist believes the field worker should concentrate on the means by which a population is adapting to the physical and social environment in which it is located (and the means used in the past for past adaptations) and the distribution of resources that result from particular adaptation. The ideas and rules current in the population are in many ways derivative from this adaptation and distribution, and are not independent agents determining the course of events. The materialist in his field work is particularly interested in quantitative distributions of actual resources, persons, and other observable objects and events within the population. He may forgo precision about local concepts and norms for precision about the culture "on the ground"—the settlement pattern, demography, economy—which he views as the determining forces in cultural development. The population's system of ideas will be studied later in relation to these material determinants.

If adherence to one or the other of these positions dictated limits to the kind of data

collected, anthropologists of diverse ontological views would produce drastically different material on the same topic or institution. On social organization, for example, the idealist—interviewing informants—would cover indigenous concepts of social structure, groupings, and relationships; the vernacular terms used to denote and classify groups and relationships, the meanings of the terms, and the relations among them; the rules governing marriage, divorce and other recognized social relationships; and the connections between the concepts of social structure and beliefs in other domains such as religion. The materialist would get maps and aerial photographs of the locality to determine the settlement clusters, and carry out census surveys to find out the frequencies of different types of persons (by age and sex), residence patterns, and marital relationships, as well as the composition of households, villages, and—most importantly—the units most centrally involved in the production and distribution of basic resources. On the basis of his field work, the idealist would make statements about the conceptual system underlying the apparent social organization of the group, while the materialist, from his field data, would make statements about the economic purposes and adaptiveness of the operating social structure. Thus the decisions concerning what kind of data on social organization the field worker should collect may be based on his implicit metaphysical position concerning what is real and will certainly affect and restrict what he will be able to report about the social organization of the group studied.

Very few anthropologists do in fact allow their implicit beliefs on the nature of cultural reality to play such an overwhelming role in restricting the data they collect. They tend to be empirical and pragmatic about what is real in cultural domains such as social organization, and they prefer, especially in their background work, to collect data across a broad front of degrees of concreteness and relevance to other domains such as language, economy, and religion. The most frequent solution, particularly in exploratory general ethnography, can be thought of as a common-denominator approach, a diversified sampler of what previous field workers and theorists have considered important types of data to collect. Thus, with respect to the illustrative case of social organization, most anthropologists would agree that general ethnographic coverage should include enough conceptual, normative, and terminological data on the one hand, and demographic or frequency data on the other, to produce an outline of the ideals and actualities of the social structure under study that would be comprehensible to the comparative analyst of social organization.

This common-denominator solution might seem unduly eclectic but has much to recommend it for the exploratory phase of field work. First of all, with a rejection of metaphysical assumptions about what constitutes the real in their subject matter, and with agreement that many contemporary research problems of broad interest to the discipline entail both ideals and actual behaviors, anthropologists have hardly any alternative to straddling the idealist-materialist fence. Secondly, if field workers in their general ethnographic work continue to collect data on both sides of this fence, comparability of field reports is more likely to be maintained for comparative testing of the widest range of hypotheses. Thirdly, the field worker should not foreclose the scope of his exploratory work by his preconceptions, and working back and forth between ideals and actualities and between informant interviewing and observation, keeps him open enough to record contextual data that may prove of great value in designing his final study. A different way of stating this would emphasize that an ideal is not properly understood unless one knows the extent to which it is followed, and an observed behavior pattern is not properly understood if one is ignorant of its normative environment. Finally, some theoretical issues of widely acknowledged significance in anthropology have to do with the amount of discrepancy between ideals and actual behavior, and one obviously must assess both in order to contribute to the ultimate resolution of these issues.

When a field worker has covered in his general ethnographic work the standard range of topics plus strikingly distinctive features, and has approached most topics by informant interviewing and/or observation or survey techniques, he has acquired the essential contextual information and is in a position to design an hypothesis-testing study. General ethnography can be carried on indefinitely, but the field worker who wants to get on with hypothesis-testing work can ask himself: What kinds of variation relevant to an hypothesis of interest have been uncovered so far in my data? Do I need more information about the sociocultural context of these variations to decide whether or not this field setting affords a fair test of the hypothesis? Do I know enough about what factors I want to hold constant and how that can be achieved? Do I need to do some reconnaissance within the ethnic group to find a broader range of variation on some factors or a more suitable context for comparison? These are questions that should be of paramount concern to the field worker toward the close of the exploratory phase. When he feels confident that the gathering of further information will not substantially improve his ability to design an hypotheses-testing study, then he is ready to enter the next phase of field work.

THE PROBLEM-SOLVING OR HYPOTHESIS-TESTING PHASE

For basic instruction in research design in the behavioral sciences the field worker should consult standard works by psychologists and sociologists. The psychological literature (e.g., Underwood 1957) is the most thorough, but it also deals primarily with experimental situations assuming intervention and rigorous control often beyond the possibilities of the anthropological field setting. Sociological and social-psychological writings on design in survey research (e.g., Glock 1967) and on quasi-experimental design (e.g., Campbell and Stanley 1966) are probably the most pertinent to the problems of the anthropological researcher because they deal with naturally occurring variations. If the field worker is in a position to obtain quantitative data relevant to his hypothesis, he may be able to follow the design advice of such treatises quite closely; if not, he can only make a suggestive comparison which approximates the requirements of a hypothesis-testing design and paves the way for future research. Whether or not he can test an hypothesis in the broader behavioral science sense, he will find that the discussions of sample selection, control, measurement effects, and other topics in treatises on research design can contribute to his understanding of how his research problem can best be studied.

This chapter thus leads the field worker to the edge of the pool but does not go into it with him. The following chapters, offering concrete examples of research designs used in anthropological studies, should be more helpful in guiding him through the water. There are, however, five general guidelines that are likely to be useful in the design of a wide range of studies.

Multiplicity of Instances

Since inductive generalization in the behavioral sciences requires more than one case, the field worker should operationalize his crucial variables so that there are as many instances of them as possible within his field setting. In practical terms, this often means reducing a global society-wide concept like centralized political system, market economy, or marital stability, to a dimension on which there is observable variation across territorial or other group divisions, local communities, domestic groups, or individuals. Suppose an ethnographer interested in the workings of a centralized polity finds that he has access to only one case of such a polity in the field, whereas the hypotheses he wants to test concern differences in degree of centralization across societies. He can recast some of these hypotheses into a form in which they make predictions about the behavior and attitudes of groups and individuals varying in the quantity or quality of their participation in the centralized political structures, e.g., communities close to the governmental capital as opposed to those remote from it and less subject to its control; royal, noble and chiefly groups as opposed to commoner strata; political leaders and officeholders as opposed to followers. Testing these hypotheses intra-societally will not solve the comparative problem with which the field worker began, but it will enable him to make some relevant general statements about the subject of interest which hold for the only system to which he has access in the field. By reducing the level of data collection and analysis the field worker has transformed his immediate goals from those of reportage to those of scientific inquiry.

Contemporary sociology (from Durkheim onward) has many examples of large-scale structural and ideological concepts operationalized by variables at a level of analysis at which intra-societal variation can be observed. There is in this procedure no necessary implication of psychological or other kinds of reductionism; the only necessary implication is that the large-scale phenomenon has discernible effects or symptoms at many levels and that indexes may be constructed to measure these effects directly or indirectly. The advantage of the reduction is that by going to a lower structural level one can find a greater number of instances of the effects, and measures taken of these instances can be aggregated for purposes of inductive generalization. Thus there are only two major political parties in the United States, but there are dozens of state party committees, thousands of party officials, millions of party workers, and tens of millions of persons who voted Democratic or Republican, presenting the behavioral scientist with the possibility of aggregating many instances of the category "Republican" or "Democratic" in order to understand American party behavior.

Another possibility for the multiplication of instances is that of pursuing the phenomenon in historical depth. A monarchical political system may have only one king, but if there are detailed royal genealogies going back several centuries, it is possible to obtain data on many instances of kingship, royal succession, and associated variables. For other types of problems, public records may yield a population of instances across time or space.

Multiplicity of Indexes

When scientific consensus on how a variable should be measured has not yet been achieved, it is advisable to measure it in as many ways as possible. If several plausible indicators of the same phenomenon concur in comparisons of empirical cases, then the validity of each is bolstered. Suppose a field worker wanted to compare several communities on a global variable like social disorganization or disintegration; he would be well advised to find several indicators (e.g., crime rates, marital separations, litigation, lack of solidarity, amount of factionalism or interpersonal tension, etc.). If he took only a single index, e.g., crimes of violence, he could be mistakenly assuming that violence in this cultural context is related to social disorganization as measured by other indicators, whereas in fact it might not be. Furthermore, there might be some peculiarity about the recording of violent crimes that produces incorrect comparisons of groups or individuals with one another. The use of several indexes, shown to co-vary in their ordering of groups or individuals, would help dispel these legitimate and serious doubts about the validity of the single index. If the several indexes did not agree, then the field worker would be moved to consider their respective biases on the one hand and reconsider his conceptualization of social disorganization on the other; such thought could not help but augment the validity of his final measurement procedures.

Multiplicity of Tests

Any hypothesis worth testing once in a field situation deserves replication both in that and other settings. Even if measurement error can be ruled out in explaining the positive results obtained in one test of a hypothesis, there is the question of whether the relationship held because of a peculiarity of the setting in which it was studied, i.e., because of other factors confounded with the hypothesized variables. In other words, we want to know how general the hypothesis is, whether it holds across diverse settings. To find this out, we must test it in diverse settings. But the field worker need not throw up his hands and say he has access to only one setting in his field situation. He can create diverse opportunities for testing it by dividing population units along lines of sex, age, acculturation, territorial location, social strata and other locally recognized group boundaries, within each of which the hypothesis can be retested. (Roberts, Sutton-Smith and Kendon 1963 call this procedure subsystem validation; Whiting 1966 gives several examples of it.) The replication is particularly significant when the group within which it is carried out differs in some possibly relevant ways from the group in which the hypothesis was originally confirmed. If confirmation is repeated in the different context, then rival hypotheses (concerning the necessity of those factors that vary across the two settings to the dependent variables) are

disproved, augmenting the likelihood that the original hypothesis is the best available to account for the array of evidence. The more diverse sieves the hypothesis survives, the more confidence it deserves.

Multiplicity of Hypotheses

If the investigator succeeds in replicating positive findings in diverse settings, he is in effect disconfirming alternative hypotheses, as pointed out above. The field worker can make the process of pitting hypotheses against one another more systematic by taking a rival-hypothesis approach from the start; he is advised to do so, since the peculiar conditions of anthropological field work make it difficult to return to the field setting after analysis of one set of data has been completed. Such an approach would involve: (a) explicit formulation of hypotheses in which variation on the dependent variable or variables is predicted by determinants or concomitants other than the one to which he is theoretically committed—such hypotheses can come from rival theories or from logical or common-sense skepticism about his own hypothesis; (b) explicit attempts to measure these rival determinants or concomitants, by finding plausible indexes or symptoms of them in the field situation, so that each instance of the dependent variable can be characterized on these other variables as well as on the ones in his own hypotheses; (c) explicit sampling to generate variation on these rival variables, so as to provide a fair and adequate test of them in the field situation; (d) analyzing results to test the rival hypotheses as well as the investigator's predictions. Setting up a field study that tests not only a single hypothesis but also plausible rivals to it is, more than anything else, what we mean by research design, and it is extremely rewarding in terms of the certainty with which generalizations can be drawn from the study.

Multiplicity of Phase-Specific Conditions

Wherever some groups or individuals are subjected to certain influences that others of the same origin are not, there is the possibility of adapting experimental method for studying this influence. The most obvious naturally occurring experiment of this type is the process of growing up, in which factors internal and external to the organism can be seen to influence its behavior over time. In longitudinal study, individuals are measured before, during, and after these influences, as in a true experiment; in cross-sectional study, successive age grades are taken to represent different phases of influence, and inferences are drawn accordingly. These developmental methods are usable in psychological anthropology without serious modification from their use in intracultural developmental psychology.

The nonpsychological field worker will encounter a variety of social and cultural interventions that are of particular interest to him and of great value in designing research. These include (a) acculturation situations in which some subgroups have become exposed to outside influences while others in the same society have not, (b) immigration situations, in which some individuals or subgroups have moved to a new environment, while others have remained behind in the old one, (c) imposed changes, in which some of the basic conditions of life have been altered by legal decree, by major institutional innovations, or by disasters of one kind or another. If the field worker is present before the exposure, migration, or sudden change, he has the opportunity of doing a longitudinal study, repeating measurements on the same samples before, during, and after the inter-

vention. If he is not present before the onset of the new influence but after it has affected individuals and groups in the society differentially, he can do a cross-sectional study in which unaffected samples are taken to represent the affected ones prior to onset. In such a design he must examine this assumption carefully, taking account of pre-existing differences and self-selection factors if there was not random assignment of the intervention.

CONCLUSION

This chapter was intended as an introduction to field research design for those already schooled in social anthropology. It is often difficult for anthropologists to begin thinking in terms of hypothesis-testing as a major research goal, and even more difficult to realize such a goal in the planning and execution of the field work itself. My intent was to present guiding principles of research design, not to insist that they be followed in every case and under all conditions. Any measure of success in designing field research according to the principles, however, will enable the investigator to reap greater benefits in theoretically relevant information. That such success is not beyond the field worker's grasp is amply illustrated by the following chapters.

BIBLIOGRAPHY

CAMPBELL, DONALD T., and JULIAN C. STANLEY
1966 Experimental and quasi-experimental designs for research. Chicago, Rand McNally.

CLIGNET, REMI
1970 A critical evaluation of concomitant variation studies. This volume.

EGGAN, FRED
1941 Some aspects of culture change in the Northern Philippines. American Anthropologist 43:11–18.
1950 The social organization of the Western Pueblos. Chicago, University of Chicago Press.
1954 Social anthropology and the method of controlled comparison. American Anthropologist 56:743–763.

FALLERS, LLOYD A.
1957 Some determinants of marriage stability in Busoga: a reformation of Gluckman's hypothesis. Africa 27:106–123.

FALLERS, LLOYD A. and MARGARET C. FALLERS
1960 Homicide and suicide in Busoga. In African homicide and suicide, P. J. Bohannan, ed., Princeton, Princeton University Press.

GEERTZ, CLIFFORD
1959 Form and variation in Balinese village structure. American Anthropologist 61:991–1012.

GLOCK, CHARLES Y. (ed.)
1967 Social survey research. New York, Russell Sage.

LEVINE, ROBERT A., and DONALD T. CAMPBELL
1965 Ethnocentrism field manual. Multilith.

LLOYD, P. C.
1954 The traditional political system of the Yoruba. Southwestern Journal of Anthropology 10:366–384.

MUNROE, R. L.
  1964 *Couvade practices of the Black Carib: a psychological study*. Unpublished Ph.D. dissertation, Harvard University.

MURDOCK, GEORGE P., *et al.*
  1950 *Outline of cultural materials*. New Haven, HRAF.

NOTES AND QUERIES ON ANTHROPOLOGY
  1951 6th edition. London, Routledge.

ROBERTS, JOHN M., BRIAN SUTTON-SMITH, and A. KENDON
  1963 Strategy in games and folklore. *Journal of Social Psychology* 61:185–199.

UNDERWOOD, BENTON J.
  1957 Psychological research. New York, Appleton-Century-Crofts.

WHITING, JOHN W. M.
  1966 The cross-cultural method. MS. of revised chapter for G. Lindzey and E. Aronson, eds., *Handbook of social psychology*, 2nd ed. Cambridge, Mass., Addison-Wesley.

WHITING, JOHN W. M., *et al.*
  1966 *Field guide for the study of socialization*. New York, Wiley.

CHAPTER 11

Experiments in the Field

LEE SECHREST

Special problems arise when experiments are conducted in unfamiliar surroundings and on strange populations. The purpose of this chapter is to suggest some approaches to alleviation of such difficulties. At the outset it should be recognized that what is accepted here as an "experiment in the field" covers a very wide range of phenomena. For the purposes at hand an "experiment" is defined as a systematic investigation in which a scientist attempts to determine the effect of some variable (or set of variables) by controlling the circumstances of its occurrence so that a comparison of observations made in the presence and absence of the variable (may) permit an inference concerning its effect. However, the true experiment is often not completely attainable, and there are approximations to it which can be highly informative. Campbell and Stanley (1963) present an excellent discussion of "quasi-experiments" and the rationale which underlies them. The greatest obstacle to the performance of most experiments is in the inability of the experimenter to control the circumstances of occurrence of the variable in which he is interested. In fact, many variables are beyond control in any direct sense, and the experimenter can only control the circumstances of his observations. For example, if one is interested in the effects of acculturation, one will probably be forced to study groups at varying natural levels of acculturation since it is beyond the resources of any experimenter to *produce* acculturation.

It should also be noted that reference

The writer wishes to express appreciation to Dr. Adrienne Barnwell for her helpful comments on this manuscript.

was made above to observations made in the presence and absence of the experimental variable, but that is a stylistic oversimplification. It generally suffices to observe an experimental variable occurring at two levels of strength, and a zero point is not a necessity. Moreover, in many experiments two or more alternative treatments may be compared so that it is again inexact to speak of the presence and absence of the experimental variable. Finally, along these lines we would also note that while the classical experiment called for the manipulation of a single variable, there are no absolute restraints on the size and complexity of an experiment, and if enough subjects are available, any number of variables may be studied simultaneously.

The experiment has proven to be an exceptionally effective strategy for obtaining knowledge in many fields, even if it is not the only one. There is nothing quite so satisfying and persuasive as an experiment with significant outcomes, for from such an experiment it is often possible to conclude that one has knowledge of and can control a factor which is critical to the occurrence of some event. It is not always immediately evident why quasi-experiments are less adequate, but the issue usually boils down to the question whether the evident factors are the critical ones. To use the example suggested above, if two groups are found to differ in level of acculturation, it is difficult to be sure that that is the only difference between them and that acculturation, per se, accounts for any performance differences between them. To point to but one possibility, it may be that acculturation and performance are the result of some other variable such as level or type of motivation.

The important question to be asked (if not answered) is whether an unacculturated group would perform in the same way as the acculturated group if it were exposed to the same acculturating influences, i.e., if the unacculturated group became acculturated. If it is imaginable that even after acculturation the groups might be different, then acculturation is clearly not the variable critical to the performance.

It is important to understand that experimenters in social science very often do not in fact directly manipulate the variables in which they are actually interested. Rather they manipulate some variable which is *assumed* to have a direct relationship to the variable of interest. For example, isolating experimental subjects for a period of time has been used to produce a state of "social deprivation" in a manner analogous to the manipulation of hunger by deprivation of food (Gewirtz and Baer 1958a, 1958b). However, it appears possible that such isolation may produce anxiety and that any subsequent performance effects are attributable to an increased level of anxiety or even "drive" rather than specifically to social deprivation (Walters and Karal 1960, Walters and Ray 1960). One cannot even be certain that the same experimental treatment will produce the same psychological state in all subjects. Thus, in some persons isolation might produce anxiety while in others it might not. Experiments are particularly vulnerable when they involve a great deal of intricacy and produce a high level of awareness in the subject of the experiment as an experiment. Campbell and Stanley (1963) use the term "reactive arrangements" to refer to obvious aspects of experimentation, i.e., to those features of an experiment which themselves produce a reaction in the subject. Ideally, an experimenter should know for certain just what it is he is manipulating, but he should never become complacent about his knowledge.

Purposes of Experimentation

Generally speaking, an experiment becomes desirable when either through observation or deduction some proposition seems likely and when one wishes to eliminate plausible rival hypotheses. For example, Gay and Cole (1967) noted that the Kpelle people of Liberia experienced difficulty with mathematics as taught in school. While they thought it likely that such difficulties stemmed from special features of Kpelle language and culture, it was necessary to eliminate, or at least weaken, the very plausible rival hypothesis that the Kpelle were lacking in native ability. In a series of experiments Gay and Cole were able to show that the latter hypothesis was an inadequate explanation of the mathematical difficulties of Kpelle children.

Strictly speaking, one probably can never absolutely eliminate an hypothesis, and one can certainly never confirm one. Whatever the outcome of an experiment, there are always alternative explanations, e.g., if all else fails, supernatural interventions. It is the task of the experimenter to render implausible those rival hypotheses which initially seem most plausible. The acceptance of one hypothesis comes when all others become implausible, at least from the tenets of the experimenter. Even acceptance of an hypothesis must be tentative because an experimenter may not be aware of all the hypotheses which are plausible rivals to his own, and other experiments may suggest novel interpretations. Indeed, one of the aims of scientific theory is to incorporate previous observations by new hypotheses. Accepted hypotheses are continually confronted by new rivals.

The task of the experimenter is to design an experiment in such a way that plausibility of some hypotheses will be minimized. While it would be highly desirable that *all* but one hypothesis be rendered implausible, that is a goal difficult to achieve. In the true experiment with all subjects assigned randomly to experimental conditions, it may be possible to conclude that only the experimental treatment is a plausible explanation of the results, but such experiments are not as common as one might think, and they are quite impossible for many questions of interest. For example, if one wishes to study the influence of culture on behavior, one can only study those persons resident in cultures of interest. There is no possibility of assigning persons randomly to different cultures (treatments). Thus, a demonstration of differences between cultural groups is vulnerable to explanation in terms other than cultural influence, e.g., difference in heredity, in educational level, in urbanization, in physical health. However, with properly designed investigations it is often possible to call into question the plausibility of *one or more* rival hypotheses. Some of the tactics of such research will be discussed in later sections of this chapter.

The aim of quasi-experiments is to weaken plausible rival hypotheses, if necessary by weakening them singularly through the utilization of experimental groups and procedures which are selectively aimed at one or another of the inadequacies of the basic experimental design. Thus, in their study of mathematical concepts among the Kpelle, Gay and Cole (1967) were able to show that Kpelle children educated in "Western" schools were more like their American counterparts and, hence, demonstrated the importance of educational experience in the phenomena they were investigating. Obviously more data from more experiments will be needed to be persuasive when no one experiment is unequivocally interpretable, but the end result may be a relatively high degree of certainty. A good case in point is the series of investigations which have led most experts to conclude that there is a causal relationship between cigarette smoking and various diseases. Each of the many investigations had important weaknesses, but in aggregate they weaken all the rival hypotheses while leaving the smoking-disease hypothesis uniquely powerful.

It is customary to speak of experimental treatments or conditions as if they were simple, unidimensional variations, but except for the laboratory and sometimes even there, experimental manipulations are global, ill-defined, and understood only in a very general way. Educational techniques, leadership methods, psychiatric treatments, and anti-poverty programs are only some of the more obvious examples of global "experimental treatments." If an experiment shows differences between democratically led and "authoritarian" groups, we still need to know just what the critical variables are. Are democratically led groups different because all members can participate in decision making, because morale is higher, because leaders are warmer and more responsive, or because of any number of other factors or combination of them? Or, to take another example, scarcely anyone who has read the Colliers' (Collier and Collier 1957) report

of the Cornell-Peru Vicos Project would doubt that the intervention had a profound effect on the Indians of Vicos, but the intervention was massive, and it is difficult to know what the really important aspects were. For example, it is at least conceivable that the introduction of new methods of growing potatoes alone could have produced nearly all the change that occurred. The caution that is necessary is that in repeating experiments one may not get the same effects if exactly the same experimental manipulations are not produced. Still, as a general research strategy it is probably best to begin work in a *new* area with the most powerful experimental manipulation possible in order to determine whether any effect at all can be produced. After showing an effect there is time enough to become analytical and discover precisely what produces the effect.

Reasons for Experimentation in the Field

"Experimenting in the field" is here taken to mean any experimentation outside the usual situation and circumstances of the experimenter, but particularly experimentation outside the laboratory with unfamiliar populations. There are six distinct reasons which seem to underlie experimentation in the field and which might entice the researcher out of his familiar environs into novel situations and populations.

First, some experimenters may be led to field experimentation in an attempt to demonstrate the universality of the processes in which they are interested. Lazarus (Lazarus and Opton 1966), for example, has studied stress and mechanisms of defense among American males and has also been able to show that results are very similar for Japanese subjects (Lazarus *et al.* 1967). As yet there has been relatively little field experimentation for the purpose of demonstrating the applicability of Western psychology to other cultures, particularly of a primitive nature, but no doubt such experiments will become more common. E. Bruner and Rotter (1953) have shown the applicability of the Level-of-Aspiration concept to the Navaho. Gay and Cole (1967) have found both similarities and differences in performance of American and Kpelle subjects. J. Bruner and his associates (1966) have shown the relevance of Piaget's theory of conceptual development to populations other than American. Few other examples come to mind.

From the foregoing it follows that one might also do experimentation in the field in order to demonstrate cultural differences. Actually such experimentation has rarely been done, but an important aim of such experiments would be to define cultural boundaries, i.e., to distinguish one culture from another. Although many persons are convinced with justification that too much emphasis has been placed on cultural differences as opposed to similarities, it is still important to elucidate and understand those differences that exist, and experimental procedures applied to important psychological processes may be a route to such understanding.

A third reason for field experimentation is that the experimenter wishes to study certain psychological processes for the light they cast on the population in which he is interested. Thus, Bruner and Rotter (1953) were interested in Level-of-Aspiration among the Navaho largely as a way of getting at identification with and conformity to Navaho society, and Gay and Cole (1967) used a variety of experimental techniques in order to get a better understanding of Kpelle modes of thought. Grinder and McMichael (1963) used some standard experimental procedures in order to study conscience development among Samoan children. One subvariety of such experimentation is for the purpose of testing hypotheses derived from other observations. Gay and Cole developed certain hypotheses from analysis of Kpelle language and were able to test those hypotheses in experimental tasks. The distinguishing feature of these experiments is that they employ well-established experimental procedures in order to increase understanding of another culture.

Still another reason for field experiments is that the experimenter wants access to populations with unique, or at least unusual, characteristics. American and even Western culture and ecology are sufficiently homogeneous that it is often necessary to seek out other populations in order to obtain subjects with radically different experience, outlook, environment, and the like. Such efforts have been most frequent among those persons studying the processes of perception, in part because of the long-standing puzzle-

ment about the role of experience in perception. Perceptual researchers have hoped to locate groups of persons whose experiential histories would cast light on the role of learning in perception. Thus, Allport and Pettigrew (1957) were interested in perceptions of Zulus because of the infrequency of straight lines and right angles in their environment, and they found some evidence for the importance of environment in perception of the trapezoidal illusion. Bagby (1957) studied groups of Mexican and American boys and found that resolution of binocular rivalry was another perceptual phenomenon influenced by experience. Finally, Campbell and his associates (Segall, Campbell and Herskovits 1963; Segall, Campbell and Herskovits 1966) have shown that various perceptual illusions are differently effective in populations differing widely in experience. Campbell (1964) has also contributed an important methodological treatise dealing with problems in identifying perceptual errors. Eventually, as may be seen from the work of Gay and Cole (1967), different cultures may be utilized to test important hypotheses about thinking and problem solving. Work is also being done in areas other than perception. Mischel (1961) was able to collect important data bearing on the effects of an absent father on his son by studying a sample in Trinidad with a markedly high frequency of absent fathers. The advantage to Mischel was that he was able to locate a large number of homes with the father absent with much less effort than would have been required in his own culture. Ultimately many hypotheses from social psychology and the field of personality will probably be resolved in similar field experiments.

A fifth category of field experiments comprises those in which there is an attempt at effecting some social change, and obviously experiments on social change necessitate a field setting. The Cornell-Peru Project (Collier and Collier 1957) gives many examples of attempts which have been made to effect social changes, some of an experimental nature. As will be seen below, in the section on experimental controls, there is a special sense in which many efforts at social change may be regarded as experiments.

Finally, field experiments may be justified because the desired manipulations cannot be made in the familiar surroundings of the experimenter. Thus far there are no especially apparent examples of such experiments, but the possibility has been pointed out by Lyndley Stiles (personal communication, 1967). It may very well be that many experiments in the fields of education, medicine, nutrition, etc., will be possible in environments foreign to the experimenter which would not be possible on his home grounds because of hidebound resistance from conservative interests. Where there are no traditions, innovation is little opposed, and perhaps the best places to try out new systems will be where none at all exist.

EXTERNAL VALIDITY OF EXPERIMENTS

Campbell and Stanley (1963) make an important distinction between the external and internal validity of experiments. Internal validity refers to the specific experimental arrangements which make it possible to be confident that the conclusions drawn from the experiment are justified. External validity refers to the legitimacy of inferences from an experimental result to extra-experimental situations. For example, initial differences in intelligence of experimental groups will imperil the internal validity of an experiment while using subjects enrolled in private schools will imperil external validity insofar as one wishes to generalize to populations other than private school students. There are three general problems relevant to external validity which will be discussed below.

Sampling Problems

Probability theory demands that generalization from a sample to a population be based on observations of a sample drawn randomly from the population. In fact, of course, it is impossible to get a truly random sample from most populations of any interest since those populations exist over time, and there is no way of sampling from portions of a population which do not yet even exist. Other sampling problems, while having solutions possible at least in theory, are nonetheless so severe as to be impossible in practice. Obviously randomness is a desideratum to be approached as closely as possible, but what is obviously important is the rep-

resentativeness of a sample, however it is obtained. Sampling difficulties will be greater in heterogeneous populations, and conversely if one limits generalizations to relatively homogeneous groups, sampling difficulties are lessened.

As was just stated, one partial resolution to the sampling problem is to limit generalizations to populations from which one can draw a reasonably representative sample, but ability to generalize can be established inductively. Thus, if one knows that six propositions have been successfully generalized from a given sample to a population, then it is likely that a seventh may also be generalized. A large proportion of psychological research is done with students in the introductory class as subjects, and while there can be no doubt that the "psychology" that results is somewhat specialized, it is also difficult to point to basic processes which have been shown to be very different in other populations. Apparently samples need not be especially representative demographically in order to be representative in terms of psychological processes.

Still another alleviation of sampling problems is alluded to above. Problems of bias in sampling are likely to be greater for some variables than for others. It is the contention of the writer that sampling should be a source of greater concern for questions involving level of functioning than for questions involving process. For example, suppose one wished to know something about learning ability in a given population. The argument here is that it would be much more likely that a given sample might lead to errors in estimating the overall rate of learning than in estimating the relative importance of variables affecting learning. One can easily imagine obtaining a sample of school children who would yield a completely misleading estimate of learning ability in a population, but it would be rather difficult to find a sample in which higher levels of reward would lead to slower learning. Similarly, one might well come upon samples in which girls were brighter than boys or vice versa, but it would be quite unusual to find a sample in which the expected relative linguistic superiority of girls and mathematical superiority of boys was reversed. One cannot be certain that there will never be sampling biases which affect the inferences which one makes about basic psychological processes, but such biases are probably relatively infrequent. Human populations may not be any less homogeneous psychologically than they are anatomically and physiologically.

The above discussion should not be taken as either an apology for or an invitation to carelessness in research. The only good sampling procedure is the best that is possible under the circumstances, and the better an approximation to a representative sample that can be achieved, the greater confidence the research merits. If one is working in a population of limited size, one can enumerate persons, households, classes, etc., and sample from them. When random sampling is not possible, it is still often possible to obtain subjects who are generally representative of the population of interest. Finally, the method in which a sample was obtained should always be described faithfully, and the ultimate necessity of that description will very nearly ensure that the most egregious sampling biases, e.g., using friends, those who drop by and volunteer, etc., will be avoided.

Generalizations Concerning Treatment Effects

Care must be taken in generalizing about the effectiveness of an experimental treatment unless one can be confident that the treatment will be replicated in all respects. It has already been indicated above that "treatments" involved in experiments are usually and quite necessarily global in nature and that it is often difficult to determine what, if any, are the critical aspects of the treatment. Whatever the obvious variables in an experiment, if it is actually the case that a treatment comprises three factors, then a putative replication of the experiment which includes only one of the variables will not prove successful. For example, several new varieties of rice have been developed which have produced remarkable yields in test plantings, but when they are employed in typical field situations without the correct amounts of water, fertilizer, etc., that obtained in the test setting, they may do worse than established "inferior" varieties. Obviously the prescription for use of a "new, improved" variety of rice may include the implicit expectation that it will be used in conjunction with good irrigation and fertilization practices.

There is still another limitation on generalizations about treatment, namely that what constitutes a "treatment" in one sample may not necessarily do so in another. Many treatments can be defined only in terms of their effects, and the definition of other treatments may be arbitrary. For example, it is possible that one might find a performance which improves with reward in one sample and not in another. But how can one define "reward" without reference to a change in performance? What is rewarding for one group of persons, e.g., a particular form of food, may not be rewarding to another group. It is very likely that some groups of persons are more sensitive to social reinforcements than are others, and differing levels of cooperation dependent upon social feedback can then be expected. Thus, such experimental manipulations as reward and punishment are difficult to define in a way that is independent of the effects they produce. On the other hand, an example of a somewhat arbitrary definition of an experimental variable is defining "practice" in terms of amount of time spent or number of trials on a task. Special care needs to be taken to ensure that practicing subjects are really practicing, and a similar caution needs to be exercised in the utilization of any experimental procedure in groups in which it has not previously been tried and proven.

Reactive Arrangements

The final threat to the external validity of experiments to be discussed here is experimental arrangements which are so special and intrusive that they may yield results which are generalizable only to other similar experimental situations. In fact, there are some who believe that for Americans, at least, merely being in "an experiment" is such a special experience that much of what occurs is determined more by the fact of the experiment than by any more fundamental psychological variables (e.g., Orne 1962). Apparently we are only beginning to understand the psychology of the experiment for American subjects. Just what the meaning of "an experiment" might be for persons from other cultures is very difficult to say.

Certainly we should be cautious in assuming that results obtained under laboratory conditions would generalize to the extra-experimental environment. As a general principle it can be recommended that the "specialness" of experimental situation be minimized and if at all possible subjects should be kept unaware of the fact that they are participating in an experiment. Webb *et al.* (1966) have suggested some of the ways of reducing the reactivity of measurement procedures, and there are many evident ways in which the obviousness of experimental arrangements may be reduced.

For want of a better place to do so, we would also point here to the fact that the experiment is also a very special situation for the experimenter. Not only does experimental routine differ from the experimenter's normal routine so that his interactions are not of the usual variety, but the experimenter is almost certain to have a strong and directional interest in the outcome of his experiment. Whatever his training and conviction about "scientific objectivity," the possibility exists that the experimenter may unwittingly influence the outcome of the experiment. Rosenthal (1966) has demonstrated that the bias of the experimenter can have a subtle, pervasive, and important effect on the outcome of experiments, and he suggests several ways in which experimenter bias may be minimized, one example being to have experimenters with opposite expectations about the outcome of the experiment. The experimenter need not have more than the expectation of getting some particular finding, despite any personal preferences, in order to run the risk of biasing the results he obtains. Experimental results which cannot be generalized beyond a particular experimenter or laboratory are of little value.

Ethics and Experimentation

To suggest the possibility of nonreactive experiments, involving, for example, the possibility that the subject may not even know that he is part of an experiment, raises some difficult ethical problems for many persons. Some of the issues involve very basic questions of values and personal philosophies for which there are obviously no pat answers. One can only suggest that experimentation in the field be guided by a concern for ethics

at least as strong as exists for laboratory experiments. The essential principle is that nothing should be attempted in the way of manipulation that is not absolutely necessary for the experiment and that at the termination of the experiment no subject should be the worse for having participated.

One might also suggest that no greater secrecy or dissimulation be maintained than is absolutely necessary. Moreover, one hopes that the net result of any experiment will be an increment in knowledge that will ultimately make possible improvement of the human condition. If that improvement can be achieved without affront to the dignity and integrity of the individual, then it is worthwhile.

To some the very thought of manipulations such as are common in experimentation is repugnant, implying as they do the superior position of one individual over another. However, all efforts at social change and amelioration imply the same superior-inferior relationship, that one person knows better than another, and that if the disadvantaged person had the knowledge of the superior person, he would behave in the same manner.

Still, it must be admitted that there are risks in experimentation in the field, and that for practical, if no other, reasons dissimulation should be minimized and subjects should be informed of their status. A single "backfire" can ruin a whole research population, ample evidence being extant in the widespread suspiciousness of the possibility of CIA involvement in research.

CONTROL GROUP STRATEGY

The standard experimental strategy for weakening plausible rival hypotheses is to study the responses of some group in which the experimental variable is absent or at some different level and to compare those responses with those of the experimental group. Any difference is, presumably, attributable to the experimental variable. For example, if one is interested in the effect of practice on performance, one can compare the responses of a group permitted practice with a group which is not permitted to practice. Groups introduced into an experiment for the purpose of putting in peril a rival hypothesis are called *control groups,* and the principle involved seems straightforward at first consideration. However, that is far from the case. One of the most common weaknesses of experiments is the utilization of a "control group" without concern for just what is being "controlled" by the group. For example, if we were to study the effect of practice on performance, it would not suffice at all simply to compare groups with and without practice on the critical task. Were we to observe that a group given an initial trial on some task followed by five practice sessions improved in performance as measured by the change between the first and a second test trial, we might think of several different explanations for the findings aside from practice. Perhaps performance would improve over time even without practice; or perhaps performance would improve as a result of "warm-up" of a nonspecific nature; or perhaps performance would improve as a result of increased interest in the task engendered by the first trial. It should be evident that even for such a simple experiment no one control group would be sufficient. Several control groups would be desirable, each putting into jeopardy a separate rival to the practice hypothesis. One group might be given an initial trial followed by a rest period and a second trial; a second control group might be given an initial trial and then "warm-up" exercises on similar tasks; a third group might be given two trials without an interval, etc. The necessity for control groups is limited more than any other way by the ingenuity of the experimenter in thinking of rivals to his own hypothesis and then of creating groups to eliminate those hypotheses.

As was implied earlier and as should be obvious now, an experiment may be worth doing if it offers good possibilities for weakening one or more rival hypotheses even though others will be left. It is characteristic of psychological research that a given experimenter eliminates one rival to his own hypothesis only to find that, like a hydra-headed monster, another rival or two has sprung to take its place, usually instigated by some rival experimentalist. Very few experimenters are capable of developing all the controls that are needed for the first run of an experiment.

There are several kinds of controls which are possible, the most desirable usually being a group selected randomly from the same population as the experimental subjects. However, about as often as not experimental and control groups are constituted from previously existing groups, and it remains to the experimenter to demonstrate the likelihood that the groups were really comparable prior to the experimental manipulation. Thus, it is often the case that experimental and control groups consist of intact classes of school children, in which case experimenters often attempt to demonstrate that the children were equivalent in sex proportions, intelligence, social class, and the like. To the extent that equivalence seems a justifiable assumption the experiment is a legitimate one. It should simply be recognized that nonequivalence of the groups represents a rival hypothesis for any experimental results, and it is plausible to the degree that equivalence has not been demonstrated.

Except in areas of inquiry susceptible to the conservative procedures of the laboratory, it is usually the case that research subjects come in clusters and that clustering often is confounded with experimental variables of interest. Schoolrooms full of children are enticing research populations, but rarely are children assigned randomly to classes, and even if they are initially, their histories will be different from the time of the first class meeting. Statistical tests usually involve the assumption that the probability of any one subject being selected from a population is the same as for any other subject and that the probabilities are independent. When subjects are chosen for research because they are in classes, clubs, villages, or other groups, then sampling is not independent. Then when comparable groups, say classes, from different cultures are compared, the method of clustering is confounded with the variable of interest, i.e., culture, since it is very likely that children are clustered on different bases or for different reasons in different cultures. The sampling-statistical problem in clustering can be met by the expensive but conservative measure of treating clusters as sampling units, e.g., statistical tests might be based on comparisons of performances of classes between two cultures with degrees of freedom being equal to the number of classes. Confounding of method of clustering with an experimental variable can only be examined by the development of internal checks and other comparisons such as are suggested below.

In many experiments a very tempting alternative to the use of separate control groups is the so-called "own-control" design in which each subject is observed under experimental and control conditions so that his responses may be compared. For very good statistical reasons the own-control technique is a good one *if* experimental and control conditions are capable of being presented in both experimental-control and control-experimental orders. That is often the case, e.g., in study of drugs, of perceptual phenomena, etc. However, it is also more often not the case, it being rather more usual that the experimental effect is irreversible, e.g., one cannot assume the decay of practice effects in order to study a person in the unpracticed condition. Hence, several rival hypotheses often remain tenable if one can study persons only in the control-experimental order.

One extremely common variant of the own-control experimental design is some form of time series study in which observations of an experimental population are made for some period of time before and after an experimental intervention, and in which differences are likely to be attributed to the experimental treatment. For example, the delinquency rate in a community may be calculated over a period of years before and after the introduction of some delinquency reduction program, and if the frequency is less after the introduction of the program, the inclination is to regard the program as successful. However, as Campbell and Stanley (1963) show, a mere change is not sufficient. The change must be discrete, of a sharp nature, in order to make implausible the hypothesis of natural and gradual changes over time. Even if the mean delinquency level for the five years subsequent to a reduction program is lower than for the five previous years, the program cannot be judged successful if it appears that the delinquency rate was falling in the pre-experimental years and that the trend simply continues after the introduction of the reduction program. In such a case of a falling delinquency rate, it would be necessary to demonstrate that the rate of decline was more pronounced after the beginning of the experimental program.

Ordinarily a time series experiment requires a relatively long period of observation prior to the experimental intervention, and several observations are necessary. However, there is an exception that is of great importance. In fact, for certain kinds of experiments a "control" group is largely superfluous. When the Cornell-Peru Project researchers arrived in Hacienda Vicos, they found a miserable lot of persons, and after a variety of interventions there can be no doubt that the lot of the Vicos population was greatly improved. Yet, in that experiment there was no control group, and there was, in effect, only a single pre-experimental observation. Who is to say that the changes would not have occurred anyway? Well, probably few persons would suggest seriously that such a view is reasonable. Perhaps an analogy which may be useful in considering such "experiments" is of the chemist who weighs an iron bar, dips it into a liquid, weighs it again, and concludes from a loss in weight that the liquid is an acid that dissolved some of the iron. Where, we may ask, is the "control" group for such an experiment? How do we know that the bar was not in the process of losing weight anyway? The answer, of course, lies in chemical theory as well as in observations of many samples of iron on many occasions, both deduction and induction telling us that iron bars change in weight very, very slowly under normal conditions of storage. Similarly, by induction if not deduction we conclude that change in places such as Vicos occurs very, very slowly unless there is some external intervention. When we are dealing with phenomena with a normally high level of stability, we may infer an experimental effect in the absence of control groups or long-term observations. In such cases plausible rival hypotheses are weakened by appeal to reason. One may only insist that appeals to reason be made with caution and with due regard for the reasonableness of the appeal itself. When at all possible, some evidence to support reason is desirable.

CROSS-CULTURAL COMPARISONS

A special research problem which often arises in connection with experimentation in the field is the desirability of comparing results obtained from two or more samples. Except for the comparison of two samples drawn randomly from the same population, it is always difficult to interpret any differences that are found. Even for such a relatively simple variable as sex, interpretations of differences are difficult. For examples, if male and female college student samples are found to differ on some performance measure, it is naive to suppose that the differences are necessarily attributable to sex per se or even that the nature of the difference is what it seems. If male college students are superior to females on a mathematics test, it is tempting but unsophisticated to conclude that males are superior to females in mathematics ability. However, even assuming that the difference represents a real difference in ability, we cannot be certain that it is attributable to sex. It may very well be that male and female students are drawn from different segments of the population with respect to intelligence, personality, motivation, etc., and hence that any differences in mathematics ability may be the result of those variables rather than of sex per se. In fact, a difference in motivation to perform on mathematics tests may even produce apparent differences in ability where none exist. It should be apparent that if differences between two groups from the same culture are difficult to interpret, then differences between cultures are more than doubly problematical.

There are several important reasons why differences between samples from different cultures are ambiguous with respect to interpretation. First, there is the problem alluded to above: it is difficult to be sure that samples drawn from different populations are drawn from the same segments of the population. Moreover, even when samples are carefully stratified, it is difficult to be at all confident that the basis for stratification is really comparable. Moreover, there are exceptionally intricate issues which arise from population differences in demography. Let us clarify the problems raised above by reference to a fairly typical example of cross-cultural comparison. Grinder and McMichael (1963) reported an investigation of "cultural influence on conscience development" in which they compared responses of Samoan and Caucasian children in Hawaii on a specially devised performance test of "cheating" and on responses to story completion items. Samoan children proved to cheat more often and to relate fewer stories involving remorse, confession, etc. In spite of the fact that all the children were attending a rural school on Cahy, there were admittedly important differences in socioeconomic status between the two groups since the fathers of the Samoan children were unskilled agricultural workers while the fathers of the Caucasian children were in supervisory and administrative positions. Then perhaps the "cultural" differences which were obtained were indicative of the culture of poverty rather than of ethnicity. However, even if Caucasian children whose fathers were unskilled workers had been studied, it is by no means evident that the samples would have been equivalent. It may mean something entirely different to be a Caucasian on the very lowest rung of the SES ladder than to be a Samoan at the lowest rung of the Caucasian ladder. Would it help to compare Samoans at the bottom of their own heap with Caucasians at the bottom of their own? But then isn't it possible that such differences as are associated with economic sufficiency, technological skill, and the like are part of what we mean by cultural differences? Even if we drew truly random samples of Samoans and Caucasians, cultural status would still be confounded with such factors as poverty and attitudes toward it. There are other populations with fairly substantial differences in proportions of young and old persons, of urban and rural dwellers, of Christians and non-Christians, and perhaps even of males and females. Random samples will confound culture with demographic variables, but samples selected so as to mirror each other demographically will not really represent one or both cultures. It is apparent that such problems are plaguing when comparisons are made within cultures as well as when they are made between.

There are some very tentative approaches to the resolution of some of the difficulties mentioned above, but it must be admitted that no final solutions appear to exist.

Studying Process Variables

As was implied earlier, one very useful approach to the comparison of different populations is to study the operations of psychological processes rather than values of parameters. It is difficult to know whether one population is more intelligent than another, but it may not be so difficult to determine the processes underlying different performances. On a complex intelligence measure, for example, one can determine the relative contributions of various aspects of performance to the total variance in scores. One sample may perform relatively well on numerical problems while another performs better on verbal materials. Or one group may be more affected by positive reinforcement while another is more affected by negative. Parisi (1965) found that Italian subjects were equally as responsive as Americans to negative verbal reinforcement, but they were less responsive to positive reinforcement. An overall test of response to reinforcement might or might not show differences, and in any case interpretation of the differences would be difficult since it might be that statements differed in value for the two groups. Gay and Cole (1967) were able to show a number of very interesting differences in mathematical processes between Kpelle and American subjects for whom differences in overall mathematical ability would have been meaningless and of little interest in any case. We expect samples to differ in mathematical ability, but it is not so easily anticipated that one group would have special difficulties with problems whose solution depended on comprehension of the concept "less than." Whenever possible the difficulties inherent in trying to estimate absolute level of performance should be avoided.

Comparison on Supplementary Tasks

It is also very useful to include tasks which are likely to measure variables which provide plausible rivals to the experimenter's hypothesis. Differences or lack of differences on critical tasks may become understandable when performance on other relevant, rival tasks is taken into account. Thus, for example, if it is desirable to estimate and compare intellectual performances in two populations, it must be recognized that differences in cooperation and motivation provide especially plausible rivals to the hypothesis that two groups do or do not differ in intellectual level. The inclusion in an experiment of measures of cooperativeness and motivation unrelated to intelligence will help to clarify whatever results are found. Parenthetically, it should be more widely recognized that a failure to find differences is often no

less in need of explanation than the finding of differences. Poor motivation in a good group and good motivation in a poor group can produce an illusion of *no* difference in the same way that motivational differences can produce illusory differences.

Campbell (1964) has provided some very helpful and ingenious suggestions for ruling out various hypotheses in the cross-cultural study of perception, and many of his suggestions are directly generalizable to other kinds of research. For instance, if it is suspected that the conduct of an experiment will be less careful in one location than another, one can deliberately introduce carelessness as an experimental variable into the conduct of the experiment in the better-controlled location to determine whether it is a significant source of variance. Either through supplementary measures or supplementary experimentation one may be able seriously to impair the credibility of important hypotheses about experimental findings.

Cross-Comparison of Samples

A third approach to at least some sampling problems is to try to sample in such a way that cross-comparisons may be made between samples drawn from different populations. For example, in the Philippines most students do not attend an intermediate school and consequently college students are, on the average, a year or two younger than American counterparts. Many freshmen are only fifteen or sixteen years of age. Therefore, if one wishes to compare Filipino and American college students, age differences exist between samples from the same classes, e.g., sophomores, but amount of college experience differs for samples of the same age. One approach of possible value is to have separate samples of the same age and of the same class, and then to make cross-comparisons. Thus, in an unpublished study of attitudes toward mental disorder the writer found that Filipino-American differences between subjects from the same college were of the same magnitude as differences between subjects of the same age even though freshmen differed from seniors and younger from older students in both populations.

Although, as above implied, one cannot be sure that various demographic statuses have the same meaning in different cultures, there are undoubtedly advantages in arranging data collection in such a way that cross-comparisons can be made on such variables as socioeconomic status, amount of education, age, occupation, etc. Even though no final conclusions might have been possible, Grinder and McMichael (1963) would at least have been at some greater advantage had they been able to compare performance of their Samoan group with other children at a similar socioeconomic level, whether the other children were Caucasian or not. Something of a culturally specific nature is at least implicit in the explicit comparison of *Samoan* and *Caucasian* children that might have been softened by inclusion of other groups such as Hawaiian, Japanese, and Filipino children, all available in Hawaii. Moreover, Caucasian children at a lower socioeconomic level could also have been tested with potentially illuminating results.

Interactions Between Populations and Experimental Arrangements

One final problem in relation to sampling that must be mentioned is that distinct possibilities exist for interactions in a statistical sense between types of subjects employed in experiments and specific experimental arrangements. For example, various kinds of experiments depend in part on the response of the subject to the instruction to "do your best," but it is evident that cultural values may differ in such a way as to bias response to such an instruction. Asch (1937) has described the dislike of Hopi children for open competition and their consequent immunity to instructions to do their best. Thus, if one compared samples of subjects from populations differing in attitude toward doing their best work, any experimental arrangement involving that instruction would result in a sample by instruction interaction. Other hazards lie in the use of reinforcements, either verbal or material, positive or negative, which may differ greatly in value from culture to culture; in employment of tasks in which speed of performance is an important aspect; in the use of apparatus which may be differentially impressive or disturbing; in use of local versus academic dialects; in employment of indigenous versus outside experi-

menters; and perhaps even in doing "an experiment" in the first place.

There is no easy way to prevent such interactions, but careful study of one's populations and of reactions to experimental arrangements may provide important clues to the interpretation of results. One tactic which may be employed in many instances is to include a critical arrangement as part of the experiment itself or to do a separate study of that arrangement. If it is suspected that the ethnic identity or sex of the experimenter is important, then one can have experimenters of different identities or sexes. Although expensive, such measures are far preferable to ending with an experiment which is totally uninterpretable because of unknown biases attributable to experimenter characteristics. Another partial solution to the problem will develop as more and more experimenters work on perfecting and standardizing experimental procedures which are not so susceptible to population biases in attitude.

CONCLUSION

Experimentation as a technique of advancing knowledge has been far overshadowed in field settings by other procedures such as surveys, interviews, ethnographic studies, etc. However, there are many good reasons for encouraging greater frequency of formal experimentation. Experiments, if well done, are often more persuasive than any other data, and they are especially well suited to the rigorous testing of hypotheses developed in other ways. There are many obstacles to the successful completion of experiments, not all of which are unique to the experimental method. For example, sampling problems are just as severe for the survey or questionnaire investigation. Neither elaborate instrumentation nor elaborate use of confederates, deception, etc., is easy to accomplish in the field, and it would appear that in many field settings it will be necessary to keep experiments simple and straightforward. That may be all to the good, especially if it encourages a concentration of effort on the study of basic psychological processes. There is so little we know about populations other than college sophomores that it would be erroneous to attempt to bypass the direct study of such processes as learning, problem solving, interpersonal influence, and response to stress.

The testing of elaborate theoretical deductions can best be done in populations whose basic response characteristics are well known.

It might be wise to reiterate that there is no excuse for research that is careless or even imprecise to a degree greater than that imposed by the conditions of study. Field work may be crude but it need not be sloppy. On the other hand, an experimenter should realize out of modesty that the magnitude of his contribution will be limited but out of pride that the contribution of even a bit of sound data is much to be valued. The serious weakening of one rival to an important hypothesis is well worth accomplishing even if several other rivals are left unimpaired. Field conditions scarcely ever rule out the accomplishment of valuable experimentation when the experimenter has a good grasp of his subject matter and an equally good grasp of the principles by which his science advances.

BIBLIOGRAPHY

ALLPORT, G. W., and PETTIGREW, T. F.
1957 Cultural influence on the perception of movement: the trapezoidal illusion among Zulus. *Journal of Abnormal and Social Psychology* 55:104–113.

ASCH, S. E.
1937 Cited in G. Murphy, Lois B. Murphy, and T. M. Newcomb, eds., *Experimental social psychology*. New York, Harper.

BAGBY, J. W.
1957 A cross-cultural study of perceptual predominance in binocular rivalry. *Journal of Abnormal and Social Psychology* 54:331–334.

BRUNER, E. M., and J. B. ROTTER
1953 A level-of-aspiration study among the Ramah Navaho. *Journal of Personality* 21:375–385.

BRUNER, J. S., ROSE R. OLIVER, PATRICIA M. GREENFIELD, et al.
1966 *Studies in cognitive growth.* New York, Wiley.

CAMPBELL, D. T.
1964 Distinguishing differences of perception from failures of communication in cross-cultural studies. In F. S. C. Northrop and Helen H. Livingston, eds., *Cross-cultural understanding: epistemology in anthropology.* New York, Harper and Row.

CAMPBELL, D. T., and J. C. STANLEY
1963 Quasi-experimental designs in educational research. In N. L. Gage, ed., *Handbook of research on teaching.* Chicago, Rand McNally.

COLLIER, J., and MARY COLLIER
1957 An experiment in applied anthropology. *Scientific American* 196:37–45.

GAY, J., and M. COLE
1967 *The new mathematics and an old culture.* New York, Holt, Rinehart and Winston.

GEWIRTZ, J. L., and D. M. BAER
1958a The effect of brief social deprivation on behaviors for a social reinforcer. *Journal of Abnormal and Social Psychology* 56:49–56.

1958b Deprivation and satiation of social reinforcers as drive conditions. *Journal of Abnormal and Social Psychology* 57:165–172.

GRINDER, R. E., and R. E. MCMICHAEL
1963 Cultural influence on conscience development: resistance to temptation and guilt among Samoans and American Caucasians. *Journal of Abnormal and Social Psychology* 66:503–507.

LAZARUS, R. S., and E. M. OPTON
1966 The study of psychological stress: a summary of theoretical formulations and experimental findings. In C. D. Spielberger ed., *Anxiety and behavior.* New York, Academic Press.

LAZARUS, R. S., M. TOMITA, E. OPTON, and M. KODAMA
1967 Cross-cultural study of stress. *Journal of Personality and Social Psychology* 4:622–633.

MISCHEL, W.
1961 Father-absence and delay of gratification. *Journal of Abnormal and Social Psychology* 63:116–124.

ORNE, M. T.
1962 On the social psychology of the psychological experiment: with particular reference to demand characteristics and their implications. *American Psychologist* 17:776–783.

PARISI, D.
1965 *Social reinforcement and performance in programmed learning in Italy.* Technical Report No. 27, Training Research Laboratory, Urbana, Ill.

ROSENTHAL, R.
1966 *Experimenter effects in behavioral research.* New York, Appleton-Century-Crofts.

SEGALL, M. H., D. T. CAMPBELL, and M. J. HERSKOVITS
1963 Cultural differences in the perception of geometric illusions. *Science* 139:769–771.
1966 *The influence of culture on visual perception.* Indianapolis, Bobbs-Merrill.

STILES, L.
1967 Personal communication.

WALTERS, R. H., and PEARL KARAL
1960 Social deprivation and verbal behavior. *Journal of Personality* 28:89–107.

WALTERS, R. H., and E. RAY
1960 Anxiety, social isolation, and reinforcement effectiveness. *Journal of Personality* 28:358–367.

WEBB, E. J., D. T. CAMPBELL, R. D. SCHWARTZ, and L. SECHREST
1966 *Unobtrusive measures: non-reactive research in the social sciences.* Chicago, Rand McNally.

CHAPTER 12

An Example of Research Design:
Experimental Design in the Study of
Culture Change

GEORGE SPINDLER and WALTER GOLDSCHMIDT

The present paper is a study in methodology.[1] It is an endeavor to present a clear design for interdisciplinary research in the study of that kind of social change commonly called acculturation, as it was used in a study of the Menomini Indians of Wisconsin. It will not include the results of this study, which will be published elsewhere.[2] The presentation of this "experimental design," as we have chosen to call it, is motivated by our firm conviction that the time has come when anthropologists must be more conscious of their methods,[3] must sharpen their tools to fit their increasingly sharpened insights. Specifically they must recognize the need to handle data statistically wherever statistical analyses will serve their purpose, and must recognize the value in the orderly use of such tools as the Rorschach. This is no call—as it has sometimes been—to abandon the time-honored tools of the trade, participant observation and informant, but to integrate with these techniques those of the disciplines of sociology and psychology. Such integration requires the sharp definition of procedures.

It is of no small significance that an increased precision in method brings about a more precise use of words. The general definitions of acculturation are so vague as to hinder its usefulness (Redfield, Linton and Herskovits 1936; Linton 1940).[4] Without endeavoring to impose our definition on others, we find it essential to formulate the term as it is used for the present paper and in the Menomini research. By acculturation we mean the process which takes place within a culture, a population, or a social system, in response to the impact of stimuli from other cultures or populations. We emphasize the term "process" as essential, yet we remember that no process is really ever seen, it is only inferred from an examination of a series of conditions. We emphasize also the fact that we have divorced the acculturative process from the diffusion process (though the phenomena are always associated) by directing our attention to the changes that take place within one culture under the impact of these outside stimuli.

Now, however, there remains the crucial fact that this process has two clearly separate aspects: one deals with the structuring of the relationships between members of the society and is essentially *social* in character; the other deals with the adjustment of the individual to the changing socio-cultural milieu, and is essentially *psychological* in character.

The research design here presented is oriented toward the understanding of the processes of change within a society under the impact of modern American civilization, and is particularly concerned with the adop-

[1] The methodology described in the present paper was worked out by the authors conjointly. The actual field work, the taking and analyzing of the Rorschachs, and other analyses are the work of Spindler, assisted by his wife, Louise Spindler. Acknowledgments are due to the Committee on American Civilization, the Department of Sociology and Anthropology of the University of Wisconsin, and to the Department of Anthropology and Sociology of the University of California, Los Angeles, for their support of the project.

[2] Under preparation by Spindler.

[3] The sociologists have used explicitly experimental designs in research for some time (*vide* Chapin 1947 and Greenwood 1945).

[4] Herskovits 1941 has summarized some of the objections to these earlier formulations.

tion of outward manifestations of cultural and social behavior in their relation to changes in the individual personality characteristics of its personnel, without, for the present, treating either as the independent variable in the situation.

THE RESEARCH LABORATORY

No research ever completely escapes its laboratory setting—certainly not in the social sciences. It will be necessary, therefore, to present the more particular background for which our research design was created.

The 2,731 Menomini Indians live in a heavily timbered reservation of 236,000 acres in east-central Wisconsin. They have felt the direct impact of Western civilization since the mid-seventeenth century, were in exclusive contact with the French from 1667 until 1760, and have been under Anglo-European domination since then. The reserve was created in 1854, and since that time most Menomini have lived on this tract, though a good proportion go to nearby cities for work, and not a few have been more deeply involved in the main stream of the American culture as soldiers and workers in two world wars.

Though such historic factors are admittedly of influence, our research design is not historical, but treats with the implications of change from an analysis of the contemporary scene. Paramount in the present situation is the fact that the economy of the modern Menomini is dominated by the existence of a thoroughly modern sawmill and logging industry, which cuts 25 million cubic feet of lumber each year and affords an annual net income of over a million dollars. Most of the adult males are employed directly in some phase of its operations. Farming, the only other single important source of subsistence for reservation families, adds only about $31,000 a year to the tribe's income. Other miscellaneous sources add an estimated $80,000 to the annual income of the people on the reservation, and these include such occupations as making and selling "curios," running gas stations and "pop" stands, gathering ferns for florists, trapping, and, of course subsistence hunting and fishing.

The lumbering is a modern, high-geared industry, with a variety of employment opportunities. There are foresters, lumberjacks, truck drivers, stackers, saw operators, planers, electricians, mechanics, engineers, warehouse workers, accountants, clerks, stenographers, salesmen, and typists. There are supervisory positions at all levels, from foremen of a six-man logging crew to mill manager. There is a range of salary for full-time, year-around employees from $1,200 to $7,500. Ninety percent of these positions are occupied by Menomini. Of twenty-five higher-level supervisory positions, only five are filled by White men, while a sprinkling of Whites is found throughout the organization.

The presence of this industry, together with other occupational opportunities on the reserve, affords a rather unusual situation —a gamut of economic opportunity from a strictly white-collar, middle-class managerial activity on one hand, through a series of lesser officials, clerks, skilled workers, laborers, adjunct and temporary workers, to persons eking out a living from the land as farmers, hunters and trappers, gatherers of ferns, and the like. The situation offers a gamut from a bridge-playing tea-going group to persons whose life revolves about native-oriented religious cultural forms. Notably, it does not offer a group whose mode of life and cultural form has been uninfluenced by Western culture.

We must note other cultural influences. European religion, thanks to the early French contact, is entirely Catholic; the Protestants have effectively been prevented from exerting a major influence on this aspect of culture. Other religious forces include the Peyote Cult, which came to the Menomini in 1914, the Dream Dance, which was introduced around 1880, and the Medicine Lodge (Mitäwin), which may not be ancient Menomini but contains many old Algonquian elements.

The bulk of Menomini live in Neopit, the site of the reservation headquarters and sawmill, and a minority at Keshena, a residential village. A few dozen families farm in the northeastern section of the reservation. There are scattered dwellings in the forests about Zoar and Crow settlement. The reservation is sprinkled with White residents, mostly men married to Menomini women, with considerable variation in economic standing, but generally in the middle range.

The great range of economic opportunity and achievement makes possible an examination of the effect of these differences. The great contrast with the situation described for the Ojibwa (Hallowell 1942, 1950, 1951 and elsewhere) is that there is a concrete opportunity for goal-realization in terms of middle-class White society. At the same time, the forest's fastnesses protect and preserve the existence of economic activities and cultural forms oriented to (though not identical with) that of the native Northeast.

Of this laboratory situation we were aware in advance, as the Spindlers had spent a summer in the reservation before undertaking the present study. What we wished to do was to regularize the general impression of the various levels of socio-cultural readjustment among the Menomini, and particularly to understand the relationship between these evident differences and the psychological evidences of readjustment.

THE SAMPLE ANALYZED

In a study concerned with cultural variation the problem of sampling becomes crucial unless one is prepared to make consistent observations of all members of the community. In order to eliminate or reduce from our consideration the variables of age, sex and "blood," we took our sample from adult males, all recorded as being at least one-half Menomini. Strictly speaking, our conclusions relate only to a universe of Menomini thus defined. The sixty-eight cases afford a 20 percent sample of the universe thus reduced.

Hence, the persons studied were selected to represent all degrees of observable socio-economic status from the richest to the poorest, and all degrees of cultural participation from Mitäwin to bridge club. The range was established, therefore, in terms of one of the two generic variables that were subject to testing by the research—the sociological. It was not necessary, however, to have each area in this range represented by a constant proportion, and indeed the extreme categories are represented by close to a 100 percent sample. The theoretical advantage of true randomness (which is not gainsaid) had to be subordinated to considerations of rapport, for the intimate social and psychological data demanded required a good relationship between student and subject. The actual process was to obtain introduction from one respondent to another, making

certain to cover the range in terms of manifest social characteristics.

Since the research design was directed toward the establishment of a covariance between two separate aspects of a process, the chief source of bias would be introduced by the unconscious selection of persons of certain personality types. In the absence of a clear predilection as to the nature of the covariance, it seems doubtful if any such bias was introduced. Selection in terms of person to whom the researcher could relate should tend to reduce the variability of the personality types included. The variations actually observed do not give evidence that such bias did, in fact, take place. Selection through refusal to participate could not be considered important since only four persons declined to cooperate.

A "control group" of twelve White men living on the reservation was used. All of these men have made their homes there, work in the mill or run small farms, and are a functioning part of the social structure. All but two are married to Menomini women. They are intermediate in social and economic status.

This control serves as a standard against which all Menomini may be measured, and serves to show the degree to which certain personality patterns appear constant among the Menomini, regardless of the degree of acculturation, as contrasted to persons of distinct ethnic origin. For many purposes a sample of "normal" Rorschach protocols taken by other scholars might have sufficed, and indeed we have not neglected the opportunity to use such data. The development of a control group serves, however, as a check against personal bias in the taking and analysis of the Rorschach. It also holds constant certain obvious environmental and social factors which would not be easy to duplicate in any randomly selected group of protocols from nonclinical studies of Whites.

The control sample has its limitations. Chief among these is the fact that in our society a group of Whites who have selected to live on a reservation and marry Indian women may themselves be considered aberrant. Second is the fact that the sample was perforce quite small. Third, it was comparable in detail only to certain acculturational categories. For these it serves, however, to sharpen certain distinctions, and

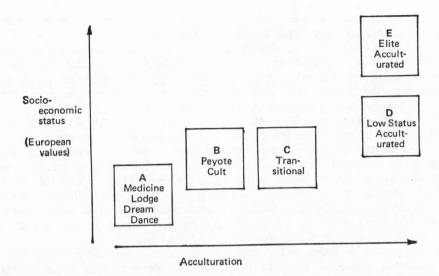

Acculturation

taken in conjunction with the general knowledge of personality expressions in Western society, affords us a measure of difference between Menomini and non-Menomini, regardless of degree of acculturation manifested.

THE SOCIOLOGICAL VARIABLE

What we are here calling the sociological variable has to do with those aspects of the culture which deal with direct behavior in the social interaction system, that is, group orientations and interactions, means of livelihood, possessions and conditions of living. The variation in these aspects of the Menomini culture we have treated as the independent variable, though the research design neither depends upon nor proves the priority of these factors.[5]

The first order of business was to establish a systematic analysis of these social phenomena. To this end we prepared a brief schedule of data covering: amount and source of income; type, condition and facilities in the home; education; knowledge of Menomini language; parental occupation, education, "blood," language, and religion; religious affiliation and participation; knowledge of and belief in native lore and medicines; recreational patterns; group affiliation; and miscellaneous personal data. These items served as criteria for determining the degree of

social acculturation. They reveal the individual's economic status and social participation, as well as his cultural orientation.

The sample population is divisible into five more or less discrete categories in terms of the schedule data; four of them along a continuum of acculturation, and one differentiated on the basis of socio-economic status. The relationship may be expressed in diagrammatic form as follows[6]:

Three of these categories (Medicine Lodge–Dream Dance, Peyote, and Elite) are actually groups, with defined membership and consistent group activities. The other two are not so formulated, but are distinguishable categories on a cultural continuum. The Peyote body itself may be considered as a special group variant of a generically transitional mass.

Of the many social criteria examined, the religious affiliation and orientation was selected as the crucial indicator. A and B of the chart are defined in religious terms; E is made up of persons who participate regularly in services and for the most part are members of the Holy Name Society. The transitional group (C) consists of persons who have had marginal participation in both Catholic and native-oriented religious activities, while the low-status acculturated (D) are persons with exclusive identification with the Catholic Church, but who participate only

[5] Goldschmidt's theoretical predilection is that these social factors are, indeed, the independent variable, though with certain important restrictions in the meaning of that phrase which we cannot discuss here. Spindler's position is more open.

[6] These categories are partially comparable to those defined by Voget (1951) for the Iroquois. The status distinctions are in terms of European values, by which standards the most native-oriented group falls somewhat below the remainder, the elite clearly above.

intermittently in regular services and are not members of the elite Holy Name Society.

That this variation in religious identification acts as an index for a functionally integrated complex of social and cultural factors, is consistent with the theory that religious commitment connotes also a commitment to a cultural system (Malinowski 1945, Hallowell 1950). The validity of the index does not rest upon this theoretical foundation, but is verifiable by statistical procedures. The index chosen was chi-square, which in this case tests whether these categories are significantly differentiated in respect to many other social features such as occupation, home, parental status, recreational patterns, and use of medical facilities, and further, permits statistical expression of association between these specific variables and acculturational categories by coefficients of mean square contingency. Chi-square is most appropriate for such analysis because it depends upon counting rather than adding and averaging attributes—a vital consideration when qualitative or only roughly quantitative data is used.[7] Thus we are able to discover syndromes of objective socio-cultural characteristics for the acculturational and status groups we have defined, and further, to establish the critical points of differentiation and to give a statistical statement of over-all association (in coefficients of contingency) between selected variables and these acculturational categories.

The Medicine Lodge–Dream Dance group, for example, are not only participants in these religious observances, but for the most part its members live scattered in the forest at one end of the reservation in rough shacks, intermittently work for wages, at harvesting or logging, and depend upon subsistence hunting and fishing to supplement their larders. They identify deeply with what remains of the old culture: carry on ancient funeral rites, observe "ghost" feasts for the dead and some menstrual taboos, live under constant threat of witchcraft, repeat the Mana'-

pus tales, and speak Menomini in most social gatherings.

At the other extreme of the continuum are the elite acculturated; men who occupy supervisory or white-collar positions in the mill or agency offices, who have incomes between three and six thousand dollars per year, who have high school educations (or better), who live in excellent, modern frame houses furnished in middle-class style, and who are, almost without exception, members of the Holy Name Society of the Catholic Church. This group provides the effective leadership of the tribe today; nearly all of them have served as members of the advisory council.

These two extreme categories are significantly differentiated by means of chi-square in every one of the twenty-three basic schedule items, with the majority of tests significant at the .001 level or better, or nearly complete mutual exclusion. The categories occupying intermediate position have their own special characters, and exhibit varying degrees of differentiation from each other. This is not the place to present their socio-cultural syndromes and differentiating characteristics, though obviously they are less fully differentiable than the above. These three categories together are broadly similar in socio-economic level. Their members live in frame houses of only fair condition either in the villages or scattered along the highways; their cash incomes range around $1,500 annually and are derived largely from intermittent unskilled labor in the mill or woods.

But within this broad range of socio-economic similarity there are reliable distinctions between the transitional- and low-status acculturated groups in regularity of wage earning and condition of the home. Further, these two categories are very clearly distinct in their relations to the native versus the dominant culture. They are clearly distinguishable in their knowledge of and belief in magic and medicines, their use of medical facilities, and their knowledge and use of the Menomini language, and in each item the transitional element is closer to the old way of life. These distinctions are given time depth by functionally related differences in parental status in respect to language, education, and religion.

Between the Peyote Cult and transitional category there are no reliable socio-economic

[7] Validation involves categorizing responses to each criterion, and comparing each of the five acculturational groups by means of the chi-square with each other (and the White control) for each item available. The sample is small and thus chi-square is subject to error even with Yates' "correction for continuity," but it has greater utility than simple proportions and is far more economical than the calculation of "exact probabilities."

distinctions. It would appear that the membership of the Peyote Cult is actually drawn from personnel in "transition" for whom the stress of this adjustment was especially acute, and if this is the case such similarity would be expected. The distinction here consists of membership definition (the cult is set apart in the reservation community), and in the cultural patterns of Peyotism itself.

Considering the total configuration of differentiations between all five of these categories, it is clear that there is a complex continuum of socio-cultural and economic distinctions running from the Medicine Lodge–Dream Dance to the elite Catholic acculturated group. The divisions of our sample represent distinguishable segments of this continuum with overlap of attributes in the intermediate levels.

Without reference to any specific categories, but for all of the five categories in relation to each other, it is possible to state the indices that differentiate most adequately,[8] and are therefore most positively associated with the defined socio-cultural continuum.[9] They are: knowledge of Menomini lore, witchcraft, and medicine; use of medical facilities; parental status in religion and education; type of games played; type and regularity of occupation; cash income; condition of home; and cooking facilities. Other indices provide distinctions between certain categories but have a less decisive role in over-all differentiation for the five segments together.[10]

Obviously the persons who constitute each category are not stamped from a mold, and will vary among themselves. Yet, statistical handling has made it possible for us to determine whether members of one category differ from those of others, and to establish a complex set of socio-cultural interrelationships within a broad continuum of accultura-

tion that would otherwise not be reducible to objective statement.

The objectivity of definition and the amenability to statistical handling make the use of specific criteria particularly suitable for analysis of this kind. It is important to remember, however, that these items only have meaning in a social and cultural context, and must be used in conjunction with the field methods more traditional to anthropological research. In order that meaningful items could be selected, and in order to understand their meaning in social context the field workers attended Medicine Lodge and Dream Dance ceremonies, participated in Peyote Cult meetings, danced at the "pow-wows" (in reservation terminology), made polite Sunday afternoon social calls, attended "showers" for new brides, each according to the demands of the appropriate social and acculturational level. Through these they arrived at an appreciation of the values, attitudes, social alignments, and interactions of the present Menomini. To give further depth to this understanding, and to reveal in detail some of the personal variables that constitute acculturation at the individual level, seven short autobiographies were collected from subjects carefully selected for their representation of certain important social and psychological processes.[11]

THE PSYCHOLOGICAL VARIABLE

What we are here calling the psychological variable is that aspect of culture which lies within the individual's system of attitudes and persistent organization of bio-emotional and intellectual resources, as these are given meaning in social interaction and orient the individual to his environment. We are not concerned with the qualities of the individual as such, but rather with the uniformities in such "internal" cultural organization and with the consistent diversities as they appear between various groups. To be sure, it can only be observed in the individual, and the uniformities must be recognized as abstractions. Such uniformities in inner personal be-

---

[8] With chi-squares of .001 or better for the total Menomini sample.

[9] Expressed in mean square coefficients of continuity of over .55 (.80 is approximately the highest coefficient obtainable in the size of tables used).

[10] Among the least decisive are: movie attendance and possession of a radio. The prevalence of both items suggests the depth of the impact of Western civilization upon the Menomini. Variations in age and degree of Menomini-White mixture provide the least differentiation of any of the indices. Age is significantly different only for comparisons of A and D; "blood," only for A and E.

[11] An "expressive autobiographic interview technique" was utilized. This technique and its function in the study of acculturation will be discussed in another publication by Louise Spindler, who is largely responsible for its development in this study and has collected five similar autobiographies from women at different levels of acculturation.

havior have elsewhere (Mekeel 1936, Kluck-hohn 1943, Thompson 1948) been treated as "covert culture," as basic personality structure (Kardiner 1939), or in Sapir's terms (1927) as unconscious aspects of social behavior.

Our problem thus becomes one of discovering the degree to which evidences of personality structure vary in relation to the observed variances in the more external and social aspects of the personnel of the group undergoing the acculturative process.[12] We are concerned with problems such as that raised by Hallowell (1949): "Are changes in the modal or basic personality organization a necessary and intrinsic part of the readjustments that acculturation implies, or can acculturation take place without radical changes in personality structure?"

For this purpose we need a tool by which we can infer, with reasonable validity, the dynamic psychological structure of the individuals in our selected cultural setting. An imposing array of clinical studies, an increasing list of experiments, and pioneering attempts in cross-cultural exploration, indicate that the Rorschach Projective Technique is such a tool. Lengthy exposition of the rationale for such application is beyond the scope of this paper. (Hallowell 1945 has covered much of this ground expertly.) We merely note that it has already been used, with varying degrees of success and clarity of purpose in a Guatemalan community, among the Chinese, Hindu, Sikh, Samoans, Chamaro, Alorese, and the Ojibwa (at three different places), Wind River Shoshone, Hopi, Sioux, Papago, Navaho, Kaska, Pilaga, Chamula, and Yakima.

We are not unmindful, either, of the criticisms leveled at those investigations. The Rorschach test does not automatically make a study psychologically penetrating or scientifically useful. It is but a tool, and like all instruments, must be used with care. Many of the studies have been criticized because important variables were overlooked or inadequately defined. Either a few heterogeneous individuals from a population were tested with little or no reference to their status,

roles, or degree of cultural participation or at best the degree of acculturation was impressionistically ordered.[13]

There are those who would say that, as the validity and usefulness of the Rorschach test has not been fully established for our own culture, its use in cross-cultural context is doubly suspect. We agree that caution must be observed in accepting any tool or technique molded in our own cultural setting, but it is well to remember that cross-cultural psychological interpretations are always suspect of hidden assumptions in the form of cultural bias. Use of the Rorschach test forces one to deal with these assumptions explicitly, directly, and on the basis of objectively defined distributions of behavior. At the same time, investigations such as the one reported here have helped to sharpen and set limits to the valid meaning of responses.

Rorschach responses are in themselves data on personal behavior collected under semi-controlled conditions. If two or more groups are differentiated in terms of objective social characteristics and they show internally consistent but statistically differentiable responses to the Rorschach test, then we have a relationship between the social and psychological aspect of human behavior. At the very least it means that the experience patterns of the individual and his perception of these relatively unstructured problems have a direct relationship.

But few of us would be satisfied to stop here. Given differentiating uniformities in two classes of variables under semi-controlled conditions, we are in a position to make interpretations in context, using presently accepted principles derived from the study of society, culture, and the psychological nature of man.

The responses to the Rorschach test are, of course, not "culture-free"; indeed, we do not know what this concept could mean as applied to individual action. It is precisely because the individual's responses are cast in their particular form by his culture that we use such a tool. The ink blots themselves are, or approach being, culture-free (i.e., "unstructured") stimuli. The subject's responses are never culture-free. The protocol is therefore a *personal variant* of a *culturally patterned* response to a *relatively open* situation.

---

[12] It should be quite clear that we are not doing a study of the genetic development of personality in an acculturating population. This might be the next logical problem, but it would require a different research design.

[13] According to Lindesmith and Strauss (1950) this criticism could be justifiably leveled at most "personality and culture" studies.

Interpretation requires, therefore, not only knowledge of the psychological principles from which interpretations are derived, but also knowledge and understanding of the social and cultural field. Problems of "adjustment," for example, must be considered in their functional context.[14] The anthropologist who uses the Rorschach technique cannot merely collect his protocols and leave them with a clinically trained expert for interpretation, but must be trained and equipped to take responsibility for final interpretation.[15]

The Rorschach test, then, was used to discover and delineate the personality characteristics of the same sample of adult Menomini males. One reason for its selection, it was noted, is that standardized indices have been established for the responses, and these can again be handled statistically. And, again, since they are only roughly quantitative, we prefer a counting method to one which adds and averages, and hence used the chi-square technique.[16]

The actual treatment involves setting up categories of patterns or specific scores, such as "Those with three or more human movement responses," and "Those with less than three human movement responses," for each acculturationally defined group, and comparing the distribution of cases. Each score or pattern was tested for significance of difference between each Menomini acculturation category and the White control group, and between each Menomini group and every other one.[17]

This procedure reveals the differentiation among the socio-cultural categories in specific facets of personality structure and function, such as the incidence of breakdown in emotional control, the amount and kind of "inner" life, intratensive-extratensive tendencies, tension levels, intellectual approach, type of control, interpersonal sensitivity, the role of biological drives, affective responsiveness, "anxiety" symptoms, and others of similar nature.

PROBLEMS AND HYPOTHESES

The experimental design of the research in culture change makes possible the testing of a series of hypotheses concerning the relationship between the social and the psychological aspects of this process. At the simplest level, we may examine the direct relationship between the two: Is there differentiation in one aspect and none in another? Does the degree of differentiation in sociological patterns correspond to the degree of differentiation in psychological content?[18] To what extent is homogeneity within an acculturational category with respect to the sociological variable associated with homogeneity in the psychological? At this level of analysis it is not necessary to preserve the sociologically defined categories, for we may relate the evidences of psychological differences to various factors of social participation, religious belief, socio-economic status, and the like. Such questions can be answered without inferential interpretation of the meaning of Rorschach indices beyond the immediate connection between perception and experience.

Other meaningful questions and testable hypotheses may be posited: *Persons in the transitional categories (B and C), alienated as they are from the cultural symbols of their ethnic past and at the same time not having internalized the symbols which constitute the value system of Western society, will exhibit more symptoms of personality disorganization than members of groups closely identified with the symbols of either of these culture types.* Or, again, with the emphasis upon a different aspect of the same general problem: *The least and most acculturated individuals (i.e. groups A and E) will exhibit signs of personality "adjustment," but these adjustments will be of fundamentally different types, presumably because of the divergent cultural expectations.* The rejection or confirmation of these hypotheses, as well as the interpretive-analytic

---

[14] This does not mean that judgments concerning "adjustment" are impossible. We would go beyond elementary relativism, agreeing with Hallowell (1950, 1951) that adjustment as "mental health" is not entirely "culture-bound," and has "universal significance both as a concept and as a value."

[15] Spindler has had two years of formal advanced training in the projective techniques under Dr. Bruno Klopfer.

[16] See Cronbach (1949) and Lewis and Burke (1949) for the reasons why this technique is most usable for Rorschach materials, and what hazards it involves.

[17] In instances where the logic of social and psychological variability is not violated, groups may be lumped together for statistical test, thus avoiding the use of too small *n*.

[18] The use of the same statistical treatment for both sets of variables makes possible a direct comparison of this degree of differentiation.

investigation of the pertinent data, will be a contribution to the understanding of a specific relationship between cultural and personality integration, speaking anthropologically, and societal "massness" and individual "anomie," speaking sociologically.[19]

Extending further a logical series of hypotheses, we suggest: *A basic reformulation of personality takes place in the acculturation process only when the goals and values of the dominant culture are successfully attained.* This formulation builds upon the studies of Hallowell with the Ojibwa, which reveal only personality breakdown and no personality reformulation at any observed level of "overt" acculturation (Hallowell 1949, 1951), and has broad implications for any theory regarding the continuity and malleability of "basic personality structure."

Because of the utilization of a control group made up of Whites living on the reservation we are in a position to consider another significant problem: *Due to a general unity of cultural background among all Menomini not necessarily reflected in the objective indices of socio-cultural adjustment, the Menomini of all levels of acculturation will exhibit significant differences in personality structure from Whites living and working on the reservation, and subject to many of the same social and economic forces.* This will contribute to the understanding of the relative influence of cultural, as compared to social, participation, since the intermediate categories of Menomini and the Whites participate in the same social context, but their cultural origins are distinct.

These represent the most important problems and hypotheses broadly formulated as directives for research before the pertinent data-gathering phases of the study began. They have, of course, been given their present form by reference to the actual field. Other problems have emerged as the analysis of data has proceeded, some of which can be answered as the study now stands, and some of which will need to be investigated further in the field. The research design here described finds its validation in the fact that the problems and hypotheses, both preformulated and emergent, can be investigated and tested

with security. Without the isolation, definition, and relation of variables afforded by such a design, such testing would not be possible.

CONCLUSIONS

The conclusion we wish to stress is the importance of rigorous method to the further study of acculturation. Traditional ethnographic methods would not have yielded useful conclusions to the problem of cultural change that we set ourselves. It is doubtful if we could have arrived at the proper acculturational groups without the use of a schedule and sample data; it is certain that their use could not have been validated without such data, and obvious that the social involvements of these group differentiations could never have been understood. Once established, traditional ethnographic methods were essential to the proper appreciation of the character and meaning of life within the categories, and of course the relation between them.

It is only in the context of such an orderly procedure that the Rorschach technique can give meaningful conclusions. It may be true that homogeneous primitive cultures will yield uniform patterns that do not require such elaborate procedures, but in the dynamics of acculturation it is necessary to regulate its usage. The treatment of the Rorschach test as a kind of Aladdin's lamp by the true believer has resulted in its summary rejection by the disenchanted. There is a middle ground of treating Rorschach data as a measure of an important dimension in the total cultural picture. To do this requires the use of samples, controls, and relationships to other socio-cultural phenomena. Again, we must guard against its use in terms of an ethnocentric standard, remembering our lesson from Benedict that cultural patterns result in different norms. At the same time, we should not forget our Durkheimian lesson, that anomie is a product of mass society, and that an absence (or a duality) of cultural norms may lead to the absence of integration on the personal level.

Finally, we wish to note that the use of a research design has sharpened our conceptual apparatus. By a conscious effort to see acculturation process in an orderly fashion, we were forced to treat as separate entities the

---

[19] These are not simply different ways of speaking of the same thing. Consider, for instance, the relation of such a conclusion to the theory of mass society as currently expressed by Selznick (1951).

socio-cultural and psychological aspects of the situation. In so doing we were led to an examination of the internal variation of each, and to a recognition both of their separations and their interdependence. We recommend particularly to those engaged in integrated research between anthropology and its sister social sciences, and to those anthropologists who are dealing with phenomena related to urban society or Western civilization, that they clarify their procedure and design their research in such a way that their significant questions are answered and that these answers be amenable to checking against other experiments and, insofar as possible, be free from crucial subjective decisions.

BIBLIOGRAPHY

CHAPIN, F. STUART
  1947 *Experimental designs in sociological research.* New York, Harper.
CRONBACH, LEE J.
  1949 Statistical methods as applied to Rorschach scores. *Psychological Bulletin* 46: 393–429.
GREENWOOD, ERNEST
  1945 *Experimental sociology: a study in method.* New York, King's Crown Press.
HALLOWELL, A. IRVING
  1942 Acculturation processes and personality changes as indicated by the Rorschach technique. *Rorschach Research Exchange* 6:42–50. Reprinted in Clyde Kluckhohn and J. A. Murray, eds., *Personality in nature, society, and culture.* New York, Knopf.
  1945 The Rorschach projective technique in the study of personality and culture. *American Anthropologist* 47:95–110.
  1949 *Ojibwa personality and acculturation.* Paper read before the Twenty-ninth International Congress of Americanists. Mimeo.
  1950 Values, acculturation, and mental health. *American Journal of Orthopsychiatry* 20: 732–743.
  1951 The use of projective techniques in the study of socio-psychological aspects of acculturation. *Journal of Projective Techniques* 15:26–44.
HERSKOVITS, MELVILLE J.
  1941 Some comments on the study of culture contact. *American Anthropologist* 43:1–10.
KARDINER, ABRAM
  1939 *The individual and his society.* New York, Columbia University Press.
KLUCKHOHN, CLYDE
  1943 Covert culture and administrative problems. *American Anthropologist* 45:213–227.

LEWIS, DON, and C. J. BURKE
  1949 The use and misuse of the Chi-Square test. *Psychological Bulletin* 46:433–487.
LINDESMITH, ALFRED R., and ANSELM L. STRAUSS
  1950 A critique of culture-personality writings. *American Sociological Review* 15:587–600.
LINTON, RALPH
  1940 *Acculturation in seven American Indian tribes.* New York, Appleton-Century.
MALINOWSKI, BRONISLAW
  1945 *The dynamics of culture change.* New Haven, Yale University Press.
MEKEEL, H. SCUDDER
  1936 *The economy of a modern Teton Dakota community.* Yale University Publications in Anthropology, No. 6.
REDFIELD, ROBERT, RALPH LINTON, and MELVILLE J. HERSKOVITS
  1936 Memorandum for the study of acculturation. *American Anthropologist* 38:149–152.
SAPIR, EDWARD
  1927 The unconscious patterning of behavior in society. In E. S. Dummer, ed., *The unconscious: a symposium.* New York, Knopf. Reprinted in David G. Mandelbaum, ed., *Selected writings of Edward Sapir.* Berkeley, University of California Press, 1949.
SELZNICK, PHILIP
  1951 Institutional vulnerability in mass society. *American Journal of Sociology* 56:320–331.
THOMPSON, LAURA
  1948 Attitudes and acculturation. *American Anthropologist* 50:200–215.
VOGET, FRED
  1951 Acculturation at Caughnawaga: a note on the native-modified group. *American Anthropologist* 53:220–231.

CHAPTER 13

Entree into the Field

RONALD COHEN, L. L. LANGNESS, JOHN MIDDLETON,

VICTOR C. UCHENDU, and JAMES W. VANSTONE

INTRODUCTION
Ronald Cohen

There exists for the initiate no set of hard and fast "rules" for entree into the field. Field situations and field workers constitute two sets of variables. The articles in this section speak for the range of variation to be found in field situations, determined by special circumstances of environmental, cultural and historical setting. Field workers exhibit varying degrees of similarity and dissimilarity in research interests, professional training, cultural provenience and individual temperament, and as Langness suggests, certain types of personality may adjust better to some field situations than to others. In any case, each entree may be said to generate a peculiar set of problems and constraints.

On the other hand, entree implies intrusion and all field workers share the problem of mitigating the effects of their invasion of the field. The authors find the objective of complete acceptance into a community naive if not undesirable, and choose instead to find ways of effecting and maintaining some medium between the insider-outsider statuses of the field worker. Uchendu stresses the importance of ascertaining what the cultural

stereotypes of the field worker are in the community and then of finding ways to neutralize their effects. VanStone suggests embarking upon the field asking culturally relevant questions based upon information already available on the area. Langness points out, on the other hand, some of the pitfalls of an unquestioning acceptance of the literature. In areas where no previous studies have been undertaken and where circumstances permit, Middleton finds it advantageous to assume the role of a child in that culture, wherein he may be "socialized" into the way of life of the people studied.

All the authors concur that the injunction to avoid administration or those in authority in the area can more often inhibit than facilitate the anthropologist's research in the field.

Whereas VanStone and Uchendu discuss field work in light of their experience with cultures which have already been studied by other anthropologists and are more project-oriented, Middleton, having worked in both situations, favors the more traditional, non-project-oriented approach to field work.

1. HIGHLANDS NEW GUINEA

L. L. Langness

. . . Indeed, most of us go into the field so eager to discover the exotic, we seduce our informants so consistently to elaborate the unfamiliar and the strange, that sometimes a kind of *folie à deux*

comes into being between informant and field worker—a tacit and unconscious contract to ignore all practicality and logic. (Devereux 1966: 216)

Prior to 1930 the interior regions of New Guinea were believed to be uninhabited. Even after the discovery of large native populations in these Highlands areas, exploratory patrolling, and limited activity during World War II, there was little contact of importance between most of these people and Europeans until approximately 1950. There had also been little anthropological work done prior to this time, that of Bernatzik (1935), Fortune (1947, 1947a), and the missionaries Vicedom and Tichener (1943–1948) being the exceptions. Partly for this reason, partly because of the flexibility and "openness" of the cultures so often noted, and, perhaps, partly because of the nature of the people themselves, anthropologists, with one or two exceptions, have had little difficulty in gaining entree. Even now Europeans are regarded by most of these peoples with a mixture of respect, curiosity, fear and awe. The anthropologist who lives with them and gains their confidence is a curiosity, a source of pride, a nuisance and a friend all at the same time. The problem, then, is not so much one of entree, but, rather, "How do I cope with all this now that I am here?"

This is not to say, however, that the problems suggested by other contributors to this chapter do not exist; or that there is no suspicion or mistrust at all on the part of the natives. As virtually all of their experience has been either with prospectors, missionaries, administrators, or planters, they initially suspect motives associated with those activities, motives with which they are by no means in sympathy. Little can be done about this beyond mere denial and explanation until sufficient time has elapsed to enable them to learn that the investigator is, indeed, different. Nor is there anything to be gained, as Middleton has indicated, by trying to circumvent the administration or others; or, as VanStone has mentioned, by trying to avoid contact with other Europeans. It is not possible for a European to "go native" and, indeed, were he to do so he would surely be regarded by the natives as ludicrous if not insane. Finally, here, there is no way to avoid being identified with a particular group or faction. After only a brief period of residence, one is so strongly identified with his host group that virtually nothing can be done to change the situation.

Certainly one must approach the situation

through the proper channels—the District Officer, Patrol Officer, and, nowadays, the village councilor. And, of course, proper training and good manners are apropos here just as they are everywhere, as are objectivity, tact, good judgment, and a good deal of respect for your fellow man whoever he may be. Probably a certain type of personality helps to adjust to field work here as there is a great amount of physical contact and many demands on one's dignity, so to speak. There is little privacy. Patience is a must as the languages are difficult, the natives are not given to introspection, they volunteer little, and the eliciting of information is a very frustrating and time-consuming process. Furthermore, as time means little, there is no such thing as making and keeping appointments, and certainly from the point of view of the natives, there is no perceived urgency or necessity to hurry. Finally, the physical demands are great. The terrain is difficult. The people seldom remain in their villages or homes during the day and thus, if you wish to be with, observe, and interview them, it is necessary to accompany them much of the time. This entails considerable crawling in and out of houses, wading rivers, being caught in sudden rains, climbing fences and walking narrow log bridges as well as almost constantly up and down ridges and mountains. One is not only in intimate contact with human beings, but is often equally intimate at times with large numbers of pigs, dogs, chickens, and assorted wildlife including more noxious varieties such as flies, lice, and mosquitoes. Assuming the field worker has the necessary virtues and training there are further problems encountered.

Often the people are eager to help. This can be a problem as they have a tendency to tell you either what they think you want to know or what they can most easily explain. For example, I was repeatedly told that there were three "big lines" at Korofeigu where I was working, "big line" being a pidgin-English word which can for convenience be translated here as a clan. It was soon apparent that there were four such "lines" and that they were, in fact, even clearly separated residentially. When I faced my informants with this observation (and other related facts I had managed to learn) they cheerfully admitted that was correct. They then explained that when the Patrol Officer, years before, had given them village registers,* two of the clans had been living together. Subsequently the two clans separated but no new book had been established. So, as that was the situation in the books, and the situation in the eyes of the only Europeans they had previously dealt with, that was obviously the easiest way to explain it to a new European. This was not an attempt to deceive, they simply were telling it as it was—as Europeans, in a sense, had made it (Langness 1963).

They seldom, if ever, as nearly as I can tell, deliberately deceive; but for a variety of reasons it sometimes appears that they do. This can result, for example, from problems inherent in trying to communicate in pidgin English. During the initial weeks of my field work I repeatedly tried to learn what subgroups were contained within the clan. They repeatedly denied that there were any smaller units than clans. As units smaller than clans are not named, as it turned out, the problem, in part, was the failure to describe adequately in pidgin English what it was I wanted to know. It became apparent to me that there were such units and that they came into operation at certain times and for certain purposes, mainly having to do with marriages, funerals, and the possession of certain ritual items. There is a generic term for them in Bena Bena. But it was not until I managed to overhear this term in a conversation and inquire about it that they admitted to their existence. Again, there was no intent to deceive. The two main factors involved seem to have been an ideology which does not emphasize such units and their failure to understand what I wanted to know.

Their almost total lack of comprehension of what anthropologists are trying to do, coupled with a tendency not to volunteer information in any case, also leads to difficulties. If an informant does not know something he may or may not bother to tell you of his ignorance. Prior to my residence at Korofeigu a geographer had worked there mapping gardens, copies of which were generously made available to me. When later I had occasion to check the maps I determined that although the information about ownership and usufruct was correct, it was

also incomplete. A particular plot of ground said to be owned by one man was in fact a number of smaller plots owned by two or more men. Those smaller plots and the names of the owners did not appear on the maps. As I knew the original informant I asked him to retrace his steps with me and other informants. It turned out he had not known who all of the owners were but, rather than admit his ignorance, had simply given the names he did know. Although he did not intend to deceive, he did admit that he did not think it was important.

This informant was a fairly young man, which raises a further point. Generally speaking, young men know less than older men and thus make less desirable informants. But this is complicated by the fact that most older men do not speak pidgin English and further because older men are not as keen to work as informants or interpreters. This is understandable as older men usually have more responsibilities than younger men, or at least take their responsibilities more seriously. In some areas of the Highlands the investigator is fortunate to find any pidgin speakers at all, and if he does they are invariably young men who do not always possess the information desired. Women are likewise poor informants, as women do not usually speak pidgin and also possess only limited knowledge. Children are often eager to volunteer information but they, too, are unreliable due to ignorance. The ethos of male superiority so characteristic of these cultures can scarcely be exaggerated in its importance and it holds true at all levels—men know more than others.

Women are difficult to work with for other reasons, at least if the investigator is male. There have been, and are, Europeans with native wives and mistresses; and half-caste children, although perhaps not as common as in other parts of the world, do exist. Native men believe that their women are eager to go with European men because of the advantages that accrue to such an action and they are therefore suspicious of attention paid to women. This is not merely sexual jealousy; the men believe that if you have questions it is ridiculous to ask women because women know so little. As men are the source of knowledge, as well as the constant center of attention, this is not difficult to understand. And, while men know that women know

* These are census books kept by the local councilors in which births, deaths, and other facts are recorded each time a Patrol Officer visits.

some things men do not know, such as the facts of menstruation and childbirth, they regard these as either unimportant or as things men should not inquire about. The women tend to agree and thus, even if you do interview them, they tend to be embarrassed and reticent. It is not surprising, then, that so few studies of women have been undertaken in the New Guinea Highlands.

Attitudes and feelings toward Europeans are seldom openly expressed and are difficult to determine. The overwhelming impression one gets from interviewing and on a face-to-face basis is one of acceptance, awe, and respect for European superiority. However, as I have pointed out elsewhere (Langness and Rabkin 1964), when one penetrates the facade a different picture emerges. Special attention must be paid to "unguarded moments" which, although relatively infrequent during the course of field work, probably need to be given great weight in any ultimate assessment of attitudes. The Korofeigans with whom I worked characteristically told me they perceived themselves as inferior to whites and that they wanted to learn from them. My field notes contain dozens of statements to the effect that:

You white men live in good places. Clean places. Our places are dirty. You have good food to eat. Our food is no good. Our places are no good.

Before the whites came we were just children. We did not understand. Now the whites are here and we have councilors. Now we are beginning to understand.

We don't talk good. We just make "kanaka" talk. Our talk is no good. The white men come to teach us and now we will learn.

Even apart from the fact that observations of behavior do not coincide with these statements (although they profess to want to learn, for example, they do not readily send their children to school, etc.), there are reasons for questioning the sincerity of such statements. During moments of extreme excitement or stress, when the facade is momentarily dropped, quite different facts present themselves. Several such occasions arose during the course of my field work. On one occasion a man of about thirty-two was in the final stages of preparing for an important wedding feast he was sponsoring for a classificatory son. Most of the people had congregated. Elaborate plans had been evolved. It was an important event. At the last moment, just as the man started to light the fire for cooking the feast, word was received that everyone was to go immediately to work on the road that passes nearby. How this could occur need not concern us here. Understandably, the man was very angry. He said, "The government work is not our work. This is our work . . . cooking stones." After his initial rage had subsided, but not his anger and disappointment, he confided to me that they had previously discussed moving back in the "bush" where Europeans would not bother them (they thought). The reason they had not done so was simply the fear of being killed by the people already living there. It was quite clear, as it emerged, that this was not just a momentary feeling, that many hours of serious discussion had been spent on this plan. It was equally clear that neither Europeans nor European culture held much enchantment for them. Although several such examples could be given, the point should be already sufficiently clear—the data gathered by normal interviewing and observational procedures, the bulk of what the field worker usually has, should be carefully assessed against observed discrepancies between statement and action and the quantitatively limited but exceedingly important data from "unguarded moments."

VanStone has remarked on the importance of reading about and having prior knowledge of the culture you wish to study. While this may be in general a good idea I would like to point out that it is not without potentially serious consequences. As there has usually been very little available literature, if any, for most New Guinea Highlanders, and as there have been virtually no restudies done of any particular group, most field workers to date have gone to study "their" people having read at best a number of patrol reports and perhaps some geographical survey work or similar non-ethnographic documents. But they have usually read literature available for other groups in the Highlands that have been studied. As the cultures in this area are in many ways homogeneous (and whatever variation does exist has not as yet been very intensively explored), it is very tempting to assume that "your" people must somehow have what others are reported to have. Even if you consciously avoid such an assumption it is nevertheless true that what you have read tends to guide your questioning, at least in the initial phases of field work. This tendency, coupled with relatively inadequate methods of communication, such as pidgin English or limited command of the native tongue, can be frustrating in the extreme. You are never quite certain whether something you would expect to be present truly is not present, or whether you have simply failed to pose the question properly. If you know, for example, that the language group or culture adjacent to the one you are working in has a belief in ghosts, you may tend to insist that "your" people have ghosts; and, if they deny it, what do you make of their denial? There is, of course, the danger that if you are too insistent some informants may agree to have ghosts, if only for your benefit. On the other hand, if you do not repeatedly come back to the question, and try it from different angles and phrase the question in different ways, you may overlook something of importance. Likewise, if you have been told that the people nearby are "aggressive," how much does that influence your perception of the people you are with? As the extremes of behavioral variation even between contiguous groups of people in the Highlands are sometimes difficult to believe, this can be, in fact, a problem of no little importance. It is possible, for example, to find homosexuality in one group whereas in a group only a short distance away it is virtually unknown. Cannibalism, common to one group, is regarded with horror by the people five miles away, and so on.

Finally, an overfamiliarity with, or perhaps one should say an overcommitment to the literature, is related to Middleton's misgivings about problem-oriented research. It is no secret that the profession of anthropology goes through phases in which different kinds of descriptions and explanations tend to be fashionable—evolutionism, historicism, functionalism, etc. The current controversy (just now, perhaps, running its course) over "African models" in the New Guinea Highlands (Barnes 1962, Langness 1964) is an excellent case in point. It was precisely at the time when the literature on segmentary lineage systems had its greatest impact on anthropological thought, the early 1950's, that segmentary lineage societies were reported in the New Guinea Highlands. Furthermore, they were "discovered" by investigators trained primarily in that (essentially British) anthropological tradition. Subsequent researchers, and those trained in other traditions of anthropology, have experienced great difficulty in trying to fit Highlands societies into the so-called African model, and investigators prior to 1950 did not report such societies either. It is true, in this latter case, that work was not carried out in the Highlands, but many would agree with the recent observation of Chowning's that

... the contrasts between the Highlands and the Lowlands or "Seaboard" Melanesia in matters of social organization have been overstated in the past and [that] most of the terms used by Watson to describe social organizations would be equally applicable to both areas. (Brookfield and White 1968:46)

In any case, there is an interesting problem here in the history of ideas, and one which demonstrates clearly the dangers inherent in approaching field work with strong conscious or unconscious but preconceived ideas as to what you expect to find.

Boldness in field work is sometimes necessary, but not at the expense of rapport; good manners are essential, but not at the risk of being wishy-washy; prior training and knowledge are admittedly advantageous, but not if they result in bias.

BIBLIOGRAPHY

BARNES, J.
1962 African models in the New Guinea Highlands. *Man* 62:5–9.

BERNATZIK, H. A.
1935 *South seas.* New York, Holt.

BROOKFIELD, H. C., and J. P. WHITE
1968 Revolution or evolution in the prehistory of the New Guinea Highlands: a seminar report. *Ethnology* 7:43–52.

DEVEREUX, G.
1966 Pathogenic dreams in non-Western societies. In G. E. Von Grunebaum and R. Caillois, eds., *The dream and human societies.* Berkeley, University of California Press.

FORTUNE, R.
1947 Law and force in Papuan societies. *American Anthropologist* 49:244–259.

1947a The rules of relationship behaviour in one variety of primitive warfare. *Man* 47:108–110.

LANGNESS, L. L.
1963 Notes on the Bena council, Eastern Highlands. *Oceania* Vol. 33, No. 3:151–170.
1964 Some problems in the conceptualization of Highlands social structures. *American Anthropologist* Vol. 66, No. 4, Part 2: 162–182.

LANGNESS, L. L., and L. Y. RABKIN
1964 *Culture contact stress: Bena Bena attitudes and feelings as expressed in TAT responses and "unguarded moments."* Paper read to the First International Congress of Social Psychiatry, August 17–22, London.

VICEDOM, G. V., and H. TICHENER
1943– *Die Mbowamb.* 3 vols. Hamburg, Cram
1948 de Gruter.

2: AFRICA
John Middleton

I

To give advice and to make generalizations about ways to carry out anthropological fieldwork in an area as large, diverse, and complex as Africa is in some ways an impossible task. But it is of little use claiming to be perfectionist: anthropologists do have certain generally accepted aims in common, are perhaps fairly similar kinds of people, and do find certain common problems and difficulties. Some of these last are of their own making, others are made by the people whom they study, and still others are made by the members of other disciplines who are jealous of the traditional near-monopoly enjoyed in certain fields by anthropologists.

It is impossible to put down detailed rules for doing anthropological fieldwork. So much depends on the interests, training, and temperament of the fieldworker. If one were to have to mention the most important requirements, the most basic, in my opinion, would be good training and good manners. But let me here assume that the fieldworker has these, and mention some of the factors, both external and internal to the fieldwork situation, that are relevant to research in Africa.

The external factors are principally those of the relationship between the fieldworker and governmental institutions and personnel, both modern and traditional where the last are outside the actual society which is the object of study; between him and religious institutions and personnel, in particular Christian missions and their staff; and between him and educational institutions in the area.

Much has been written of the areas of disagreement between research workers and African governments, when Western anthropologists have been taken as spies or as neo-

colonialist agents. We may assume that all—certainly virtually all—such suspicions are unfounded; but some anthropologists in the past have tried to interfere in local matters, and have left a bad reputation behind them for other anthropologists; other people, usually non-anthropologists, have tried to imply that anthropologists are interested only in the "primitive," a view that is now half a century out of date; and in any case anthropologists can as easily be victims of the Cold War as anyone else. My own field researches were undertaken in two then-colonial countries (Uganda and Zanzibar), and in one independent country (Nigeria). In none of them did I receive any official harassment, although I was certainly the subject of unofficial suspicion as to my motives. But considering the variety of anthropologists and the somewhat strange nature of their calling, it seems to me that there is nothing very remarkable in this. An anthropologist working in any part of the United States (especially if he were an African), would expect similar treatment.

Whereas a government may be suspicious of an anthropologist's interest in contemporary political matters, difficulties may arise also from suspicion by Christian missionaries and by schoolteachers of his interest in traditional "customs," which they are trying to eradicate. I can see no easy way around this suspicion, which is usually based on misunderstanding of what the anthropologist is trying to do. I suspect that many anthropologists are at heart scornful of mission endeavors, and many also give the impression that they alone are experts on traditional culture. But compared to that of many missionaries, the anthropologist's knowledge is often superficial[1]: his skill lies in analysis and interpretation of data rather than in collecting it. After all, while in the field he is in the fortunate position of having nothing else to do with his time.

The internal factors depend largely upon certain features of the society being studied: the degree of remoteness from urban cultures; the nature of the traditional and modern political and other systems; whether or not there are marked differences of wealth and rank; the degrees of literacy, Christian conversion, and the like; the nature of the economy and settlement patterns, whether homesteads are close together or scattered, and whether the people are sedentary or continually on the move; and so on. These factors cannot easily be generalized about, since the range of possible variation is almost unlimited, and there is no need to enlarge on them here.

II

The best way to write this essay is probably to recount some of my own experiences in fieldwork, as examples of what can be done, of what cannot be done, of what could and should have been done. I have worked in three parts of the continent, in areas which present very marked differences of relevance to the problems I am discussing. The first was among a then remote and little-changed people of northern Uganda, the Lugbara; the second was among a fairly sophisticated Muslim people conscious of a long history, the Shirazi of Zanzibar; the third among a sophisticated urban population, that of Lagos, the capital of Nigeria. In none of these cases did I experience any marked color bar, so that my experiences may not be of great interest to those working where such a bar occurs; and I did not work in a state society (Zanzibar was then a state, but an Arab colonial state, and I did little work among the Arabs). In addition, the first two researches were made in countries that were then under colonial rule, which has vanished from most of the continent today.

I chose the Lugbara of Uganda as a first fieldwork people. They were little-known,

and there had been initially no anthropological work done on them[2]; the British Colonial Office and the Uganda Government were willing to finance my fieldwork; so I chose them. I found, by reading the few sources I could find, that they lacked a king or elaborate chiefship; that they had some kind of ancestral cult; that they were grain farmers and sent many labor migrants to southern Uganda to earn cash; that they had had an anti-European cult in the early years of the century; that they spoke a Sudanic language quite unlike the Bantu Swahili which I already knew.

I was given some introductions to people in Uganda by my sponsors in England, and on my arrival in southern Uganda was shown much encouragement by members of the then central government. I never found anyone in the capital who had actually set foot in Lugbaraland, but I was told it was savage, remote, high and cold at night, and was regaled by various secondhand anecdotes about past administrative officers who had gone mad, drunk or permanently sullen while serving there. On my arrival at the district headquarters, the then district commissioner introduced me to the few other government officials and the chief missionaries, then took me on a short tour of the district and introduced me to the principal government-appointed chiefs. One of them suggested that I should stay near his own headquarters, where I could at least learn the main problems with which I should have to cope and where I could start to learn the language. I did this; I bought some simple furniture from the Catholic mission workshops and some canned food from an Indian merchant in Arua (who was later to be one of my most helpful friends), hired a cook, an elderly man with long experience of working for Europeans and a Lugbara of the old school, and moved into my hut, a square hut with mud walls and floor and a thatch roof.

It is important to stress that I was a protégé of the then government. This was deliberate. I have little sympathy with those anthropologists who set themselves up in some kind of personal opposition to government, usually to show that they are anti-colonialist in spirit (who isn't?), free and independent,

[1] This is true especially with regard to knowledge of the vernacular language: one of them in the area of my own fieldwork has published the standard work on Lugbara language (Crazzolara 1960) and several papers on their history and traditions.

[2] The main work was by the late J. H. Driberg (1931), originally an administrator and later an anthropologist.

on the side of the "oppressed" Africans and the like—all this shows far more about the personal insecurity of the anthropologist's psyche than it does about his scholarly or human beliefs and ambitions, or indeed of his sympathy with the people he is studying. Lugbaraland was a closed area, so that no one without government approval could enter it; the Lugbara trusted the then European government a good deal more than they thought they would a future independent government which they feared would be controlled by their hereditary foes from southern Uganda; and without government support I could have done almost nothing. There is no reason to be an uncivil guest, and to be a guest need not involve subjugation of spirit or loss of soul.

The first thing was to learn the language and to be accepted by the Lugbara. I was lucky in one regard: although I knew no Lugbara I could at least speak fluent Swahili. Lugbara-English interpreters hardly existed; but most younger men spoke some form of Swahili, although older people and women rarely did so. It would have been of little use to have worked in Swahili all the time; but it did make the learning of Lugbara, a difficult language, a great deal easier, and it meant that I could immediately converse with a large number of people. If I had been able to have learnt Lugbara before going there, of course, then I should have been a fool not to have done so; but it was not possible in England. To speak the vernacular is the second tool of the fieldworker (the first is to have had reputable anthropological training).

When I went to Lugbara I had no "project." My sponsors in England were wise enough to know that a general ethnographic study is the best way to understand the entire culture of a people of which virtually nothing is known; a "project," which is demanded by so many foundations, is stultifying and a waste of time. So I was free to tackle the culture I saw around me in any way I chose, and I also knew that I had two full years in which to do it. My actual means of doing this were, as I now look back, largely haphazard: I got to know a few people, then their friends and kin, and so widened my acquaintances. I began to realize what were important events and relationships to the Lugbara and what were unimportant ones.

I wandered round the countryside talking people; I learned to drink their beer and e their food, to know the ordinary courtesies of everyday life, to recognize faces when I met them, to know how to behave at burials and death dances, to know how to give and receive gifts and how to behave at markets. If I did any of these things right, I can see now that it was mainly because I let the flow of everyday life take me. I did not try to push certain lines of information which I particularly wanted to know; I let avenues of information open up before me and followed them, since it is only by understanding what are the main emphases of the local culture that one can understand social life at all. I tried, that is to say, to behave as would any polite and well-mannered person behave when a guest in someone else's home; and the Lugbara, who are no fools, saw this and I think appreciated it. A point here is that although I was, as I have said, a protégé of the government, I never used any government-backed authority in everyday matters. I was set traps by the Lugbara to see whether, for example, I would report illicit distilling to the police: I did not do so. But many tests are more subtle than that, and can be very difficult. One is always (or was in colonial days) a European, and to pretend that one can overcome that is a chimera, and a sentimental one at that; I found it best to realize it and to accept it, and to behave with trust toward both sides, both government and missions and to the Lugbara. The fieldworker walks a tightrope of distrust and suspicion, and being a stranger without governmental responsibility, he is always at a disadvantage. It is best to sit it out and to learn to like people. That may sound empty and romantic, but it is still the only way; and it is a way that cannot really be learned: one can do it or one cannot.

In practice what I did was to do as does a Lugbara child, although I cannot claim that it was a self-conscious process. I first acquired kin, since unlike a Lugbara child I was not born into a circle of them. I employed my cook and a general factotum, who wandered around with me as my "Introducer." They were therefore my "sons," so that their fathers were my "brothers," their mothers my "fathers' wives," their sons my "grandsons," and so on. The Lugbara seized on this system immediately, because

...m in which their life is ...p is an idiom, and my situa-...which the idiom could be ...st any other situation in ...nvolved. It may often have ...hem, but it was also some-... .....: and my relationships with people were defined by my kinship relationship to them. This is what a child does, and I followed that example. Like a child too, I learned certain aspects of Lugbara culture in a certain order. First, the household, the crops, the foods, the near kin; next the wider landscape, the stars, the trees and plants and animals, the wider kin; third, the clans and lineages and the ancestors and spirits that also people the world; and with all this, the slow learning of right and wrong, of what is the proper exercise of authority and its relationship to divine power, of the relationship between Lugbara and the outside world, the cosmology in which the small circle of local community life is led. I came to realize that for traditionally minded Lugbara the most important things in their lives, after crops and farming, was the proper observance of moral and religious rules and behavior; I became immersed in divination, oracular consultation, sacrifice. Here I found that I was almost always given my "proper" kinship and lineage status and was expected, of course, to behave according to it: again, I must emphasize that this was not a game. It was real, a part of my and their life that was as real as anything else—my presence there was real enough so why not play it through? By this time I was known over a wide area as the tame European who, because he exercised no overt authority, was yet not a European but "a good man." I had a truck, which became "our truck" and was used by anyone, and I was used also, of course, by chiefs and others as a private mouthpiece to administrative officers and missionaries. Let no anthropologist ever fool himself that he has become a complete member of his local community: he cannot, unless he wishes to cease being an anthropologist altogether. The balance between objectivity and subjective "belonging" is a difficult one; but I find it impossible to give advice—one must play it by ear or go home.

Finally I decided that I had to move to other parts of the country, in order to see Lugbara culture as a whole. I moved, but I could never recapture the first position I had held: everyone knew that I was properly a member of my first community, so how could I become a proper member of another? The range of Lugbara society is so small that it was not easy to trace links between different communities, although it could formally be done and used in certain situations. I lived in three other places, for shorter periods. In the later communities I was much more the "correct" observer, using questionnaires and seeking answers to specific questions in order to fill in gaps in my notes. I was never involved with the community as I had formerly been, never spent hours taping up wounds or merely drinking and chatting; on the other hand, it was far easier to gain rapid information, since I knew what questions to ask.

A few details should be mentioned here. I never had formal "informants" in Lugbara. I never paid people for interviews. I made gifts to people whom I visited, but since they always made return gifts this was not a market transaction. I was known as a historian and a linguist, to collect genealogies and traditions and to learn the various Lugbara dialects. And I took the trouble to maintain proper relations with the government, who throughout gave me all possible help and who never made demands upon me that could have embarrassed me or made my task difficult. For that I must thank the various administrators who were there at the time: without their help I could have done very little.

III

My second fieldwork was very different. It was to make a study of systems of land tenure in the two islands of Zanzibar and Pemba, which composed the then Arab Sultanate of Zanzibar, ruled by an Arab Sultan with the advice of a British Resident. Zanzibar was a country divided in itself between Arab rulers and Shirazi population, and land was a politically difficult and emotional subject. I was given three months for the work (I already spoke Swahili, the vernacular of Zanzibar, so had no language to learn). I was sent out by the British Colonial Office, and immediately accepted as an official fieldworker by the government in Zanzibar: I was given official status and press releases and interviews were arranged for me. After a few days in Zanzibar City, to learn something about the problems as seen from the viewpoint of the government, I vanished to a house set on the sea as far as was easily possible from the city and remained there a month. This was near a large "town," the traditional settlement of the Shirazi, and I spent my days walking through farms learning all I could about the social organization of the town (a subject on which there was then no published information at all) and the practice and principles of farming and land tenure.

Here there was no acquisition of kin or slowly settling into the everyday life of a community. I had little time and a set research task, and had to collect data as fast as I could. As a consequence I learned relatively little about Shirazi culture, only enough to enable me later to prepare a report on land tenure. I found this personally frustrating, since daily I would come across information which would clearly lead on to data which would have been anthropologically exciting, but I had to let the trails grow cold immediately.

After a month, I spent the remainder of the time staying only a few days at a time in some dozen selected "towns" throughout the two islands; then a last week or so in Zanzibar City, staying in a house rented from the Mission; and then back to England to prepare a report on land tenure in the two islands.

I did not, therefore, carry out a full field study. Had I done so, I should have tried to do much the same as in Lugbara. I should have stayed for a long initial period in one settlement, learning the local organization as does a child, and attending everyday social activities, formal and informal, as much as I could. The Shirazi are Muslim, and so, unlike the situation among the Lugbara, I could not attend rites when held in a mosque. I found, however, that as one of the "Peoples of the Book" I was welcomed in theological discussions. I was too ignorant of Islam to achieve much: had I had longer I should have done as much intensive study as I could on Islam, before going to Zanzibar. A non-Muslim who works in a Muslim country would be foolish not to do so. I should also have learned at least the rudiments of Arabic, the court

language of the island: I could then at . have read Swahili in Arabic script.

My third field research was also short, seven months in all, and was a study of Lagos, the federal capital of Nigeria, with emphasis on the position of the Ibo section of the city's population. In Lagos, through the kindness of the then Vice-Chancellor, I was given the post of Honorary Professor at the University of Lagos. This gave me academic sponsorship and respectability; in return I gave a regular course of lectures in anthropology, which introduced me to a circle of faculty and students who gave me much help of every kind. This also gave me a status in the wider community.

To be set down in a strange city of about a million people, when I spoke only English and no local languages, was a shock. The lack of a language did not in this case matter greatly, since English is the lingua franca of Lagos. But the size and ethnic heterogeneity of this hectic capital and seaport were both exciting and confusing. There was no single culture to learn; instead I was faced with a multiplicity of cultures in an urban setting, and so had to learn about a new kind of non-traditional, urban culture, for which my training had not fitted me. I learned what I could about the Ibo of the city, mainly by becoming interested in the activities and history of some of the associations which are so important a part of urban life; I learned relatively little of non-Ibo matters (and Lagos is traditionally a Yoruba city). I did not make elaborate quantitative surveys, for two reasons. One was that the latest available census was at that time fourteen years old, and in a city which had almost trebled its population in that time, the census was little used as a basis for survey work; I did not have time to organize a full-scale census-survey. Perhaps more important, I would not really have known what details to put down on any elaborate survey questionnaire: there is little point in using details which have proved effective elsewhere in a field setting where so little is known as it is about Lagos.[3] But I was able to carry out a brief survey of a few hundred families in selected streets, from different parts of the city and its suburbs, and from different in-

[3] There is one valuable book, by Marris (1961), but it deals mainly with Yoruba of Lagos Island.

rom these I learned a great
qualitative data. In short, I
t study: I now know what
anthropological problems in
city like it, and some of
wers. The most important
..... of study would be the relationship between ethnic groups and "class" structure and
mobility; and the key institution is the "association." To do this work properly, I should
now first visit the rural areas from which
most of the Ibo come, and experience at
first hand something of traditional Ibo culture.
I had to work in a cultural vacuum, and
knew that I was missing much that my informants took for granted and which I could
not actually observe in the urban setting, yet
which affected the everyday behavior of the
Ibo of the city.

IV

As I wrote earlier, I do not think that one
can generalize about ways of starting fieldwork. The main points that I consider relevant I have made in reference to my own
work. Others I have left implicit: that an
anthropologist goes to learn, not to instruct;
that he does not judge or evaluate; that he

tries to minimize the effects of his presence
on the community where he is living. The
main points on the methodology of the actual research seem to me to be two: first,
an anthropologist learns the culture he is
studying as does a child who is learning
about his society, by acquiring kin and neighbors who become parts of a pattern of social
relations of which he is at the center: another way of saying this would be that
an anthropologist can only gain knowledge
of the ways in which people conceive of their
social experience (which is, after all, his
main task) in one way, by being socialized
as is a child. The other is that an anthropologist learns a culture by letting the
people themselves open the doors to it. He
cannot push them open; if he tries, he may
think that he has succeeded, whereas in all
probability the people will merely have let
him think so, out of politeness or fear, while
holding back those parts of it which they
think the more valuable and which are therefore central to it. An anthropologist cannot
learn much in a year or so, however well
trained and however acute an observer; but
if he lets himself be guided by the people, he
can learn at least the essentials of their culture.

BIBLIOGRAPHY

CRAZZOLARA, J. P.
1960 *A study of the Lugbara (Ma'di) language*. London, Oxford University Press.
DRIBERG, J. H.
1931 Yakan. *Journal of the Royal Anthropological Institute* 61:413–421.

MARRIS, P.
1961 *Family and social change in an African
city*. London, Routledge and Kegan Paul.

3: A NAVAJO COMMUNITY
Victor C. Uchendu

We badly need people from [other cultures] to
come and study our American values and *vice
versa*. . . . We have to see a value system from
this point, that point, and the other point. (Kluckhohn, in Tax 1953:340)

Fieldwork among the Navajo Indians of New Mexico and Arizona was done between July 1964 and
June 1965. Grateful acknowledgment is made to the
Rockefeller Foundation whose Fellowship and field
grant made my graduate training in anthropology
possible. The Foundation is not to be understood as
approving by virtue of its grant any of the statements
made or views expressed herein. I thank Professor
B. F. Johnston for his editorial assistance.

Although anthropology is the science of man
—the scientific study of man, his works and
his behavior—it remains, basically, the study
of "other cultures" by students from Western
cultures. This is to say that the non-Western
world has been a traditional laboratory for
Western anthropologists.

This peculiar development in the history of
our discipline has created a characteristic
theme in fieldwork. The problem of field
entrée has revolved around how the Western
anthropologist goes about neutralizing the

effects of the "cultural load" which he bears. As a white man, usually working in a typical colonial setting, he is aware that he is a member of a powerful "out-group" which commands authority and enjoys high status and prestige. He tries to create for himself a different image of a white man who is neither an administrator, nor a missionary nor a trader—the three categories of white men who have influenced the lives of his subjects. It is probably for this reason that some anthropologists advise against any formal identification with political authorities. Malinowski's injunction that the ethnographer must cut himself "off from the company of other white men [because] the native is not the natural companion for a white man" (1961:6–7)—an extreme prescription which is not generally applicable to all field situations —was no doubt influenced by this "fear of white man's power and authority." On the other hand there are a few anthropologists who naively assume that they must "go native" in order to achieve rapport, a point of view that is no longer persuasive.

One critical factor which influences the kind of adjustment which an ethnographer makes in the field is the fact that he is a stranger, an outsider. The "stranger status" is an asset as well as a liability. As Beattie has noted, the importance of "stranger value" in fieldwork lies in the fact that "often people talk more freely to an outsider, so long as he is not too much of an outsider" (1964:87, 1965:18). The initial problem of field entrée, therefore, revolves on how to make oneself "not too much of an outsider." There is no general prescription for achieving this goal. Methods adopted should be consistent with the subjects' definition of a stranger's role—and this is not always clear to an ethnographer, hence the initial blunders—and they should be as unobtrusive as they are informal.

The "stranger status" constitutes a major constraint in gaining field entrée. The kind of constraint resulting from this status is more subtle in covert cultures like the Navajo than in overt cultures like the Igbo. As an Igbo anthropologist, I became quite aware of not only the environmental and cultural contrasts between the Navajo country and the Igbo country but the contrasts in the attitudes of these two societies toward strangers. In Igbo country, strangers are not ignored. They are

questioned as to their whereabouts, their intentions and designs. In the Navajo country, I was completely ignored. Though children were quietly curious about my presence their parents gave the impression that I did not exist. I initiated all the action. I greeted my Navajo contacts only to be made aware that greeting does not command as much value in Navajo society as it does in Igbo society; and that whatever joys are derived from greeting are shared among acquaintances and kinsmen rather than between strangers and Navajo.

My initial contacts with Navajo, under many different settings, made me painfully aware of three facts: First, that it is not good behavior to stare at strangers or to "bother" them. Second, that the exchange of greetings does not guarantee a stranger any hospitality, and that it is not considered "poor upbringing" if a stranger does not exchange greetings with casual acquaintances. Third, that as a stranger I was carrying a heavy "cultural load" which I must lighten if I would have any claim to the confidence of my subjects.

ETHNOGRAPHER'S CULTURAL LOAD

My experience among Navajo Indians convinces me that as fieldworkers, anthropologists are viewed first as bearers of this or that culture and that their role as fieldworkers or professional status as scientists emerges slowly. As culture-bearing animals, ethnographers carry "cultural loads." That is, we share the stereotypes with which our cultures are characterized by our subjects. The challenge posed by the "cultural load" which we bear is that we must find out what our stereotypes are if we are to adopt compensating roles which might neutralize their effects. Viewing the problem in a different perspective, we must try to find out the "content" of our "cultural load," that is the "image" of our culture which our subjects have and the attitudes which they associate with it.

My ethnic background must have been clear to the reader by the few allusions that I have made. I am an Igbo, which is a major ethnic grouping in Nigeria. I have described this culture, and my participation in it, in my book, *The Igbo of Southeast Nigeria* (1965).

Because of the "social visibility" of my skin color, I could not play a covert role in the Navajo country, assuming it was desirable to do so. To most Navajo with whom I came into initial contact, I was just another Negro, a term infrequently used by this literally-oriented culture. The English-speaking Navajo refer to people of my race (Negroes) as "colored guys"; and the Navajo words *Nakaii lizhinii*—a term applied to my race, which means "Black Mexican"—indicate where the Navajo put me in their racial genealogy.

As part of my preparation for the field, I was interested in learning the Navajo image of my race and their general attitude toward outsiders. It was the opinion of my teachers that I could neutralize the "racial factor" by emphasizing my "African-ness" rather than my "Negro-ness," should this become an issue. For me this emphasis was a dilemma because I was not psychologically prepared to separate the two dimensions of my social personality. I turned to the literature on the Navajo and found it unrewarding. Two references only came to hand, and both were equally frightening. Adams' only reference to the Negroes in his Navajo community study was on the role of Negro women as sex objects for Navajo railway workers off-reservation. On this subject he writes:

Especially frequent is the practice of making invidious comparisons between Navajo women and the Negro prostitutes to whom railroad workers have frequent recourse, Negro women being held up as a kind of standard of sexual desirability. Negroes are seldom thought of in any other context at Shonto, and any mention of them is almost invariably an occasion for humor. (1963:76–77)

The Franciscan Fathers, another source of data, are no more complimentary than Adams, though they provide a broader perspective for judging Navajo inter-ethnic and interracial attitudes. They asserted that

for the Zuni and Hopi, the Navajo cherish a sense of natural superiority in addition to a traditional contempt for the latter tribe. The American, though not equal to the Navajo in rank, is respected according to deportment, while the Mexican, with few exceptions, comes in for a considerable share of paternalism. Together with other tribes the Navajo share a genuine contempt for the Negro. (1910:439)

I am calling the reader's attention to my "cultural load," not as a *post facto* rationalization of my field experience but to make him aware of my psychological problems and the concern of my teachers, who, though

quite enthusiastic about the innovation of having an African anthropologist work among an American Indian group, also felt that mistakes which could expose me to physical danger must be avoided. Suffice it to say that my anxiety was unjustified, and that whatever may be the feelings of a few Navajo toward Negroes, the Navajo as a people do not seem to manifest any group hostility against Negroes because they are Negroes. In effect, it was my experience that the "racial factor" was not a major constraint in my gaining acceptance among the Navajo.

ETHNOGRAPHER'S CULTURAL ASSETS

It would be unfair to infer that I had no cultural assets. Although I was a stranger like any other white anthropologist might be, yet I was a "different kind of a stranger." The subject of my research—the pattern of migrant labor activities among the Navajo—called for an "official clearance" and a working relationship with officials and personnel of the Bureau of Indian Affairs. I could not have achieved my goals without this "official clearance" since I needed information from unpublished but useful documents and manuscripts which can only come from these officials. It was with these officials that I found my status as a "visiting foreign scholar" most helpful and fruitful.

My working relationship with the Bureau of Indian Affairs [B.I.A.] personnel was helped by two factors. First, the period of my fieldwork was free from any major "crises" between Navajo and the administration, and the question of being caught up in a web of administrative or political factions did not arise. Second, the head of the Public Health Service, Department of Indian Health, Navajo Agency [PHS-DIH], Window Rock, Arizona, was very anxious to learn what he could about the problems of Navajo migrant workers and he provided me with an unusual "umbrella effect" for any anthropologist.

After satisfying the Bureau of Indian Affairs officials about the legitimacy of my research interests, I used their institutions and channels of communication to gain an orientation into the Navajo country. My major interest, within the first month, was to "know the country," to find my way. I made a few personal contacts, and strengthened the bonds with my guides who filled the multiple roles of interpreters, informants, contact agents and teachers of appropriate "Navajo Ways." The trading posts, the Bureau of Indian Affairs schools, the Indian Hospital, the squaw dances and other ceremonials, and the Navajo Chapter meetings provided me with opportunities to make informal contacts, and especially served the purpose of "exposing" me to my subjects. When the weather permitted, I put on my African robes, to emphasize my "African-ness" as I had been advised. (But the windy weather which sweeps Navajo country in summer proved an enemy to my robes!) Although I seemed to have passed unnoticed in my robes at the initial contacts, it became clear from information reaching me and from the comments of those who became my Navajo friends, that my embroidered robes were commented upon as "items of beauty." The perennial question was: How much did it cost?

During this period of "exposure" the field personnel of the Indian Hospital, and the subagency personnel, Crownpoint, New Mexico, were used to extend my social contacts. The former allowed me to accompany them on their "home visits" and to "field clinics" and many of the patients we visited proved to be migrant families who later became good friends and willing informants. The subagency personnel initiated me into a series of Chapter meetings and allowed me to participate in some of the conferences in which migrant labor problems were discussed with Indian traders.

The important lesson which I learned during the first few months of my fieldwork is that progress in data accumulation is slow. This can be painful to a young anthropologist whose enthusiasm for "getting things moving" might lead to unnecessary frustrations. Every fieldworker has his "phase of frustration." In the Navajo country, this "phase" was for me the "period of exposure." I could not speak the language and therefore could not do much by myself. My guides would not keep regular appointments, and I would drive forty miles or more only to discover that they were gone. When we next met, my delinquent guide would simply grin and no explanation or excuse would be offered. But there are positive factors which help fieldwork among the Navajo. A fieldworker who

takes advantage of these factors, can make much progress in his work.

FACTORS PROMOTING FIELDWORK AMONG NAVAJO

The Navajo have achieved ethnographic prominence through the works of many anthropologists. Fieldwork among them appears to be a continuous activity. The summer attracts many scholars—anthropologists, sociologists and psychiatrists—thanks to the foundation funds, the Department of Health, Education, and Welfare, and the National Science Foundation grants. The effect of these research activities on field entrée is that it has made Navajo aware of the existence of fieldworkers. They may resent their publications insofar as Navajo feel that they and their culture are misrepresented, but they know of the existence of people "who run around asking questions about old ways."

Navajo awareness of the existence of fieldworkers, even though their roles may be misunderstood, and considerable reservations may be expressed about the practical value of what they are doing, has two positive contributions to fieldwork and field entrée. First, the neophyte can be easily directed to the guides and interpreters who have established a partial specialization in helping ethnographers in their work. Second, these guide-interpreters know exactly which informants have the specialized knowledge which is helpful to the ethnographer, which informants are willing or unwilling to discuss which topics, and under what conditions. I chuckled with laughter when one of my guides advised that he would introduce me to my prospective informants as the friend of Professor Barnett. Although I had not met Barnett, yet my guide's ingenious suggestion worked quite successfully. The implication of this is that fruitful contacts which may improve rapport may be established by using scholars who are well known to informants, as referees. In my view, Navajo informants do not regard the ethnographer-informant relationship as a contract which terminates with the exchange of information. They tend to retain a vague feeling of warmth for ethnographers whom they know very well and this relationship can be exploited with great effect by a neophyte.

Although the Navajo society is particularly distrustful, and in fact fearful of strangers, including non-related Navajo, there are certain values in this culture which help field entrée. The non-hierarchical nature of the social structure makes it possible for an ethnographer to start work at any social level—the family, the leaders and men or women. It is not necessary to get a clearance from any traditional authority before one talks to informants. Data collection is essentially an individual bargain with an informant, who may volunteer it or may not. I was impressed with the fact that informants who do not want to volunteer a type of information will say so with little or no expression. There is little deliberate attempt to misinform the ethnographer. I met a few uncooperative medicine men; many were willing and cooperative; and others volunteered what information they had and referred me to medicine men who were more knowledgeable in other fields. I was quite impressed with the honesty of my most knowledgeable medicine man whose life history I recorded. When I requested him to tell me all the facts of his life which he could remember and enjoined on him to hide nothing, he grinned in reply: "We Navajo don't tell everything as long as we are alive. Only the dead tell everything. As long as I live, I must keep some information to protect myself." This sensible statement shows how far a Navajo biographer can go.

The character of Navajo social structure has another implication: it is the limited mediating role of the ethnographer's guide. Anybody who reads Whyte's *Street Corner Society* (1964) will be impressed with "Doc's" power and authority which he wielded to the advantage of his friend, the scientist. Very few anthropologists have been blessed with a "Doc," and ethnographers who work among Navajo Indians will not find a "Doc" because Navajo leaders do not wield much authority.

A frustrating experience I had in Lukachukai, a Navajo community in Arizona, demonstrates this proposition. I was living with a family which is well known to many anthropologists who have worked in this area. My host arranged a two-day *Blessing Way* sing for his son who was visiting from Houston, Texas, where he worked. This was a welcome addition to the *Yiebichie* and *Fire Dance* which attracted me to this part of Navajo country. We concluded an arrange-

ment with the singer about my taping the chants, and it was with this understanding that my host wanted the sing two days earlier than planned so that I could keep my other commitments. At the last minute, the singer changed his mind. He would not let me run the tape after he had intoned the first chant. My host simply told me, as a matter-of-fact: "Hastiin, you people simply visit and leave. I don't have any other place to go. I live here with these people. I can't force him. It is his way. You can watch the ceremony and I will answer your questions later on."

The individualist-orientation of the Navajo is another positive factor that contributes to field entrée. I was aware of the criticisms of some Navajo medicine men by both their practicing colleagues and clients that the "sings" are becoming less effective as curative institutions because anthropologists have taken "souls" out of them. There are critics who blame the increasing "ineffectiveness" of some sings on the drinking habits of the medicine men and their inability to maintain traditional discipline as regards sex code and other religious observances. These criticisms are enough to make rapport with medicine men difficult. However, there are many medicine men who think that they must make their own decision and "help out" enthnographers who seek information. As Reichard notes, the Navajo insists upon self-reliance in certain decisions and "the individual is persuaded; he is not high pressured into a judgment contrary to his own." (1963:xxxix)

And although labels tend to be libels, I would suggest that the "pragmatic empiricism" of Navajo morality and their ethical code which Ladd characterizes as a "Hobbesian system modified by an Epicurean psychology and Spinozistic sociology" (1957: 308) are relevant factors in gaining rapport in a field relationship where payment for information is an established tradition.

A major problem in fieldwork among Navajo is the maintenance of privacy. Kluckhohn noted that "under the right circumstances almost any Navajo will talk about witchcraft" (1944:14). He listed two such conditions: first, the confidence in the person receiving the information and the trust in him that he will not allow idle or malicious gossip to be spread; second, an ideal field setting in which the investigator and a single Navajo informant are involved. All fieldwork problems are not centered on witchcraft. In fact, I wonder whether an ethnographer can learn very much about witchcraft in his first field trip unless he is unusually lucky to be doing his work during a period of crises.

In a country like the Navajo where a one-room hogan is the characteristic dwelling unit, information which is considered "secret" may be difficult to gain in this setting. I found it necessary to do much of my interviewing in my car. With the few medicine men with whom I developed intimate friendly relations, we agreed that I would be bringing them to my house. This was no doubt time-consuming but it proved to be quite rewarding. I remember on one occasion when my medicine-man friend from Mariana Lake, New Mexico, lied to his son's wife that I was taking him to a subagency meeting at Crownpoint—a clear indication that he wanted to protect himself from gossips and from the charge that he was selling his knowledge to outsiders.

OTHER FIELD SITUATIONS

I have so far discussed some of the factors which affect field entrée in the Navajo country, especially the ways these factors affected me as an African anthropologist. We must now examine briefly a few of the many field situations which the nature of my investigation called for and the kinds of demands they made on me in my attempt to gain rapport. I indicated earlier that my focal research interest was on the pattern of agricultural labor migration. This problem called for two different field settings: reservation communities and off-reservation work areas. Although I worked in five different off-reservation work camps, located in two states, I will simplify my presentation by treating these as if they constituted a single field setting. I must warn the reader that what emerges from this is a "composite model," because I made different kinds of adjustments in each work area as the circumstances demanded.

ENTRÉE INTO STANDING ROCK

Standing Rock, New Mexico, is a typical Navajo community, one of the ninety-eight socio-political action units on the reservation. Like many Navajo communities, it is served by three major institutions—the trading post, a B.I.A. School and a Chapter house—each an agent of acculturation and a center for specialized activities.

I gained entrée into this community gradually. The first step in this direction was merely accidental—the fact being that though he lived in Crownpoint most of the year, a guide-interpreter who was most highly recommended to me came from this community. An ex-migrant worker himself, my guide had no difficulty understanding the kind of information I needed. His reputation as one of the few English-speaking Navajo who could "transform" the non-literal English language into a literal Navajo language was an asset in using him to interview the "old ones." Although it was not clear to me first why he took me to certain camps rather than to others, I lost no time in realizing that proximity of kinship guided his choice of informants. Working through the channels of kinship network which he could manipulate, my guide became the bridge between me and the Standing Rock community. I needed just one more guide to map the main kinship groupings in this community.

After a reconnaissance of a few communities in the Crownpoint subagency area, I decided to do more intensive work in Standing Rock, having found it quite representative. By this time, I had known the area for about five months. By an unusual coincidence this community had plans for a new census which it could not finance from its allocation from the Tribal Works Program. The Chapter officials asked my guide whether I could "help them out." This was a tempting offer which promised, not only a maximum of rapport, but a most unusual opportunity for me to visit all the homesteads, get all the information I needed, and provide a needed service for my community.

On December 26, 1964, the local Christmas for this community, I was formally introduced to Standing Rock residents. In a most democratic manner, they affirmed their willingness to cooperate by a standing vote. Although the work took about two months to complete—repeat visits, my guides' flexible working schedule, and the inaccessibility of a few camps during the winter were among the factors—I found this the most rewarding aspect of my Navajo experience. It provided a good example of how a fieldworker can achieve his own research goals through serving his community. It shows too that where the fieldworker's goals and the interest of his community are complementary, *reciprocity* becomes a very effective technique for achieving rapport.

ENTRÉE INTO WORK CAMPS

Fieldwork among Navajo workers in an off-reservation setting has its peculiar problems. The fieldworker must reassure the grower that he is not a spy for the Federal or the State Employment Agencies. He must contend with the Navajo suspicion of the "outsider" and their desire to be left alone. He must adapt his timing of formal interviews to suit the convenience of migrants who work long hours. He must be "sponsored" by a Navajo who understands what the fieldworker wants to do and who can explain this to other Navajo on demand.

The strategy I adopted in many off-reservation work camps was to ensure that the grower agreed to be indifferent to the ethnographer's presence, neither encouraging it nor actively discouraging it—and this is the best that a fieldworker in this situation can expect. As one grower in Phoenix, Arizona, put it, "We are in business, not in research. Our business is very competitive and it comes first before friendship. We cannot allow too many people bothering our 'hands' with questions." This forthright statement may not come from every grower but the sentiments embodied in it are shared by many growers. American agriculture is a big business, not a way of life. Harvest labor is critical and must be available at the right place and at the right time. The presence of an anthropologist may be a disturbing factor.

Showing interest in the migrants' children and working side by side with them on the farm—a direct contribution to the output of each migrant household—were among the many devices used to gain rapport in this setting. Especially among the young men, I discovered that I was not totally a stranger to them. Many had seen my photograph in an issue of the *Navaho Times;* others claimed that they enjoyed my radio talk from Gallup in which I discussed the similarities and the differences between the Igbo and the Navajo acculturation experiences; and for a few, my African robes had advertised me during the Gallup Indian ceremonies.

The younger Navajo workers felt that I shared a common bond of "colonial" culture with them. The frequent questions asked of me were how the white man treated Africans and whether Africans lived on reservations. My answer to the latter question drew not only laughter but serious doubt: The following is an excerpt of the conversation:

"Do you live on reservation?" one Navajo friend asked.

"No. It is the white man who lives on reservation," I answered.

"How did you do this?" another asked unbelievingly.

"The mosquito did it for us," I grinned in reply.

The fact that I bear not only a tribal culture but share a common colonial experience with Navajo provided a common basis for identification with them, minimized Navajo suspicions, aroused their curiosity about Africa and improved rapport. As bearers of tribal cultures we were able to "trade" some exotic information with each other. The Navajo recorded my Igbo folk songs, proverbs and riddles in exchange for their own songs and myths, and what was most important to me, they "helped me out" with the information I needed. It was my young English-speaking Navajo friends who helped to explain to the "old ones" what I was doing and who encouraged them to answer my questions. "We want you to pass your examination. We shall sure help you out with your questions so that you can write your book," were typical remarks.

SUMMARY

As an African anthropologist working among Navajo, I was quite conscious of my "stranger" status and I made no attempt to assume any covert roles. The kind of investigation that interested me and the circumstances under which it was carried out demanded rapport with the B.I.A. personnel and I found this association rewarding. Two important factors which helped entrée among the Navajo were kinship and friendship. My interpreters were drawn from the community in which they have a wide kinship network. They introduced me as a "friend" who needed help and this help was invariably given. Off the reservation, I found that friendship, based on a vague feeling of "colonial" experience, was helpful in gaining rapport with more acculturated Navajo. With their sponsorship, it was easier to gain the confidence of the less acculturated Navajo workers.

Fieldwork among the Navajo fails or succeeds with the kind of contacts an ethnographer is able to establish. The fieldworker or his guide must know the informants well in order to get any kind of information from them. This requires time, it requires patience;

and for the reservation-based Navajo it requires an additional incentive—an informant fee. It is possible to gain the confidence of a few Navajo families during the first field trip to this country. I have good reasons to believe that I achieved this. Whether a fieldworker can achieve more than partial penetration into the life of a Navajo community is a proposition that needs demonstration. This writer did not; but this fact did not place any major constraint in the achievement of my research goal.

BIBLIOGRAPHY

ADAMS, W. Y.
1963 *Shonto: a study of the role of the trader in a modern Navaho community.* Smithsonian Institution, Bureau of American Ethnology, Bulletin 188, Washington, D.C.

BEATTIE, J.
1960 *Bunyoro: an African kingdom.* New York, Holt, Rinehart and Winston.
1964 *Other cultures: aims, methods and achievements in social anthropology.* New York, Free Press of Glencoe.
1965 *Understanding an African kingdom: Bunyoro.* New York, Holt, Rinehart and Winston.

FRANCISCAN FATHERS, THE
1910 *An ethnologic dictionary of the Navaho language.* Arizona, St. Michaels.

KLUCKHOHN, C.
1944 *Navaho witchcraft.* Boston, Beacon Press.

LADD, J.
1957 *The structure of a moral code.* Cambridge, Harvard University Press.

MALINOWSKI, B.
1961 *Argonauts of the Western Pacific.* New York, Dutton.

REICHARD, G. A.
1963 *Navaho religion: A study of symbolism.* New York, Pantheon Books, Bollingen Series XVIII.

TAX, SOL, *et al.* (eds.)
1953 *An appraisal of anthropology today.* Chicago, University of Chicago Press.

UCHENDU, V. C.
1965 *The Igbo of Southeast Nigeria.* New York, Holt, Rinehart and Winston.

WHYTE, W. F.
1964 *Street corner society.* Chicago, University of Chicago Press.

4. ARCTIC AND SUBARCTIC NORTH AMERICA
James W. VanStone

The author's contribution to a chapter on one aspect of fieldwork methodology has been requested on the basis of his field experience in several widely separated areas of the North American arctic and subarctic. The implication is that techniques developed by northern workers to obtain entree into a field situation may in some ways differ from those used by researchers in other areas and that in the north the potential field worker is confronted with special problems. With

The author would like to thank Dr. Wendell H. Oswalt, University of California, Los Angeles, for his helpful suggestions during the preparation of this paper.

this in mind, it is worthwhile to examine the pertinent characteristics of northern peoples which require a special approach on the part of the field worker. Then we can turn to a discussion of various methods of obtaining entree into a field situation to determine which are generally applicable and which have a special application for the areas under discussion.

At first it might seem presumptive to assume that generalizations may be offered about ethnographic fieldwork in an area as large and culturally variable as the American north. Specialists consistently have been aware of the dangers inherent in the tendency to stress the similarities rather than the differences among various arctic and subarctic peoples. And yet it would seem that there are particular problems which affect the entire approach to fieldwork in northern regions and which arise from the environmental, cultural and historical setting. No claim is made that these are unique problems not likely to be faced by field workers entering a field situation elsewhere, but they do serve to set the arctic and subarctic somewhat apart from other areas.

The first of these special circumstances concerns the nature of northern settlements. For combined ecological and historical reasons, the Eskimos and Indians of northern North America are today grouped into small communities where usually from 100 to 300 people live in close proximity to one another and to religious, educational and trade facilities. These villages often are widely separated from one another and, except under certain circumstances and at certain times of the year, are visited infrequently by outsiders. They frequently represent a recent coalescence of population and, as a result, may lack the degree of social cohesiveness that is normally thought to be associated with a community type of settlement pattern. From the standpoint of the ethnographer beginning fieldwork, they represent a very different set of conditions than obtain in the more southerly parts of North America and in other parts of the world. Regardless of initial attitudes toward the ethnographer, the fact of his presence cannot very well be ignored. He is physically present in the small village and will be encountered by nearly all the residents numerous times each day. He will have many opportunities to engage in casual conversation and to join groups of people or individuals as they go about their daily tasks, relax in front of their houses or shop at the village store. Most significant of all, of course, is that he will not need a special reason or appointment whenever he wishes to talk to someone. Unless the people are completely withdrawn and totally unfriendly, it will be difficult for them to avoid him even should they so desire. Friendly relations can often be established casually before the ethnographer moves into the more formal phases of his work.

The importance of this very real advantage was forcibly brought home to me several years ago when I accompanied a colleague on a visit to the Six Nations Iroquois reservation near Brantford, Ontario. Here there was no village or community in the physical sense just described. The houses or small farms inhabited by my colleague's informants were widely separated and spread over a large rural area that closely resembled that inhabited by local whites. It was necessary to drive from one home to another and the opportunity for casual encounters with Indians was virtually nonexistent. Therefore, appointments had to be made and kept and spontaneity in interpersonal relations was not achieved until after the ethnographer had worked in the area for a long time.

In the north it would be quite possible to carry on fieldwork in as formal a manner as one might desire. Nevertheless, the whole process of meeting and getting to know one's informants and making oneself known is much easier where the settlement pattern is characterized by the small community. Thus entree into the field is easier and need not depend entirely on prior contacts, recommendations or similar introductions. Even the smallest communities can grow, however, and it is characteristic of the north today that large, cosmopolitan centers have emerged. These large settlements are also beginning to attract the attention of ethnographers who frequently miss the informality of small communities and have to adjust their field techniques accordingly. The Honigmanns, for example, mention the impersonality of Frobisher Bay as compared to smaller Eskimo and Indian communities where they have worked (Honigmann and Honigmann 1965:5).

Another circumstance which is certain to be different for every ethnographic area is the particular outlook which a people have toward the dominant culture of which they are not yet a part, and the nature and history of contacts with that culture. It almost goes without saying that students who work with northern peoples do not encounter the type of political awareness that is so characteristic of Africa and parts of southeast Asia, an awareness which has its roots in an oppressive colonial past and looks toward a future made bright by the fact that a formerly dependent people are taking their destiny into their own hands. The very idea of an anthropologist and his interest in "primitive" societies may be repugnant to a people who see themselves on a footing of intellectual and political equality with those who would "study" them. The Eskimos and northern Indians, on the other hand, have to a large degree been overpowered by the highly complex Euro-American culture which surrounds them. In some areas, and for a variety of reasons, this has resulted in the creation of a depressed and apathetic minority, while in others historic circumstances have allowed the retention of a viable culture which looks hopefully toward the future but has its roots firmly in the past. It has been my experience that in neither case is the ethnographer likely to encounter implacable hostility once his role is understood. It is probably as true in northern North America as elsewhere that the root of nearly all the difficulties experienced by indigenous peoples in adjusting to modern life can be found in the history of their relations with the white man. And yet for the most part they maintain friendly relations with individual members of the dominant culture and desire to interact with them on the basis of a free and equal exchange of opinions and ideas. The ethnographer, if he is careful and moves slowly, will usually have little difficulty in establishing mutually satisfying relations with the northern peoples among whom he is going to work.

Because of the relative lack of sophistication of northern peoples, however, the ethnographer may have some difficulty in establishing his role in a community and adequately explaining his presence. Until recently, most Eskimos and northern Indians had contact with only certain categories of outsiders, usually missionaries, schoolteachers, traders, bush pilots, doctors, nurses, and in some areas, soldiers and law enforcement agents. Therefore, when an outsider enters a village there is quite naturally a tendency to try to place him into one of these familiar categories, particularly if he has not adequately explained the reasons for his visit. For example, Wendell Oswalt, at the beginning of a lengthy residence in Napaskiak, an Eskimo village on the Kuskokwim River in southwestern Alaska, discovered that initial hostility on the part of the villagers was due to the fact that many people thought he was an undercover agent for the United States Fish and Wildlife Service or perhaps a "secret missionary" (Oswalt 1963:168). He had not explained the reason for his residency in terms that would be understandable to his informants and they were fitting him into familiar categories of outsiders. Because he appeared to be reticent and secretive about his presence, they naturally believed that he belonged to some category of outsider of which they would disapprove. Of course, as a community's world view widens, the people become familiar with a larger number of occupations and professions and can more easily classify outsiders. Nevertheless, they may have only certain types of behavior patterns for dealing with such people and this can make initial contacts difficult for the ethnographer. Oswalt also relates how the people of Napaskiak treat any resident white as they would a schoolteacher and it is difficult to alter this firmly established type of relationship (Oswalt 1963:169).

A final point that might be considered here with special reference to fieldwork in the north is what has been called the nonanthropological aspect of anthropological research. Charles Hughes has written with reference to his fieldwork in the village of Savoonga on St. Lawrence Island in the Bering Sea that

the anthropologist gathering his data does not work in separation from others of his kind. . . . Rather, he daily works with people, often in a small village, where he is close to what in one sense is his "problem," what in another sense are his neighbors. Whatever else he may be, he is a *person* in the village, one with domestic tasks and requirements and (presumably) the normal human complement of needs and reactions; these attributes are often as important in the success or failure of his research as is the quality of ideas and material obtained. (1960:26)

Every field ethnographer knows the truth of the above statement and to dwell on it in detail would be unnecessary and also beyond the scope of this essay. It would probably also be unprofitable to argue whether these nonanthropological aspects of fieldwork are more difficult to deal with under severe environmental conditions, such as those in the arctic, than they are in other areas. Hughes refuses to state categorically that they are and it would be presumptuous of anyone to do so. Nevertheless, the ethnographer planning fieldwork in northern regions must realize that not only initially, but continually a great deal of his time is going to be spent in making himself comfortable in his environment. But then much of the villagers' time is spent this way also, and as soon as the ethnographer's life even begins to approximate that of those around him he begins to have a common ground for achieving mutual understanding.

In spite of my attempts to discuss particular problems facing field workers in northern areas, it will be apparent that parallels for much of what has been said can be found in other areas and, indeed, have been dealt with by Benjamin D. Paul in his excellent article on field relationships (1953:430–451). This only indicates that there are many sound and time-tested methods for gaining entree into a field situation that are generally applicable regardless of the area. Paul speaks in general terms about such basic factors as introductions and establishing a role; his principles applied to the field situation in the first arctic community in which I worked, and have been equally applicable in all other communities with which I have become familiar since that time. It would be a very dull ethnographer, however, who did not learn a few new things as he gained experience in establishing working relationships with new informants. The fact that, in this particular case, these new ideas are little more than elaborations on Paul's is a tribute to the value of this author's work.

One of the most significant points that Paul makes with regard to the problem of introductions is that it is almost always unwise for the ethnographer to attempt to avoid those regional administrators or others in authority in the area of his fieldwork on the grounds that to associate with them would jeopardize his standing with the people with whom he intends to work. This is certainly true as far as northern areas are concerned even though here, as elsewhere, there are many government officials, traders and missionaries, among others, for whom the people do not have much respect and who themselves have very little understanding of those with whom they work or for whom they exercise administrative functions. Nevertheless, such persons may be of considerable assistance in the field and, as Paul suggests, can cause a good deal of trouble if, for some reason, they begin to suspect the motives of the ethnographer. It has been my experience that Eskimos and northern Indians are likely to think it strange if one white resident of a village does not associate with the others. In one village where I worked the people had a very strong dislike of the trader but nevertheless not only did not object to my associating with him, but very obviously expected me to do so. Also, I have known several administrators who were extremely sensitive about their work and looked upon the ethnographer as a threat to their official position and prestige in the villages. This is particularly apt to be true if both the administrator and the ethnographer are government employees. Not to make a special effort to meet and talk with all of these individuals could result in serious obstacles being placed in the way of the ethnographer, or in loss of valuable information and perhaps a useful perspective. Therefore it is a safe generalization in the north, as elsewhere, that the ethnographer should always work through the existing channels of authority when he is beginning his fieldwork. This, of course, not only includes administrators and resident whites, but also "chiefs," village councils and other official individuals and groups within the community. To do otherwise is almost invariably interpreted as high-handed behavior and results in the making of enemies just when friends are most needed.

There are two problems which always confront an ethnographer before he begins his fieldwork and which are particularly acute with reference to the north. These concern the time of year he should begin his work and where he is to live after he arrives in the field. With regard to the first, it may be that the researcher has little choice. If he is a student or professional academic he may have to work during the summer months whether it is the ideal time or not. If he is planning more extended fieldwork, however, he must realize that most arctic and subarctic peoples still follow a modified seasonal round of subsistence activities to which wage labor may have been added in recent years. This means that at certain times of the year the villagers are very busy and will have little time to talk to the ethnographer. At other times the people may be absent from their settlements for extended periods and at still others there may be little work to do and much leisure time. In most areas of Alaska today, for example, summer is a period of intense activity. In the north where there is much military construction, the men will leave their villages to seek work either at the military sites or in the urban centers, while in southwestern Alaska some villages are virtually deserted while the people take part in the commercial salmon fishery at certain coastal points. Among the northern Athabascan Indians of the western Canadian subarctic, on the other hand, people are less actively involved in wage labor and summer may be a period of relative inactivity. The same is true of many Canadian Eskimo communities.

Whatever may be the particular seasonal pattern of a given region, however, the ethnographer, if he has a choice, should begin his fieldwork at a time when potential informants will have the leisure to work with him and when he will not be unduly interrupting their essential subsistence activities. Admittedly this is not always possible, but by planning his time carefully, the ethnographer can often make the best of short periods of leisure that people do have and at least avoid such a fatal mistake as to arrive in a village when there is no one there at all.

When we turn to a consideration of where the ethnographer should live when he comes to work in a northern community, it is obviously not possible to give an answer that can be applied in all circumstances. For work that involves only summer residence, the problem is relatively simple. The ethnographer can bring his own tent and pitch it in the village. In many northern areas he will find many villagers living in tents during the summer too. For a more extended stay, the problem is more complicated. Obviously the ethnographer should avoid living at the school or with one of the permanent white residents because usually the villagers will not feel free to visit him in these places and the natural interaction with people for which he is striving will be seriously impaired. Field workers have long paid lip service to the desirability of living with a family and there can be no doubt that such an arrangement does have some advantages, particularly where learning the language and observing family life are concerned. However, in northern communities, as in many other places, houses are small and very crowded. The ethnographer living with a family may find that his opportunities to meet and interact with those outside his own household are restricted; and the crowded living conditions,

in addition to the demands that they might make on his ability to adjust personally, also may make it difficult for him to write up his notes and successfully carry out other aspects of his work in an orderly fashion. To me it seems much more reasonable for the ethnographer to rent a small cabin of his own, centrally located if possible, where he can receive visitors, have private interviews with informants if he so desires, and also have a little privacy for himself. This latter point can assume considerable importance if the period of fieldwork is a long one. In all Eskimo and northern Indian communities where I have worked, it has been invariably true that informants have talked much more freely to me when we were alone than in the presence of others. In most northern communities too, it is relatively easy for the ethnographer to rent a cabin since there are always some families who have moved to the urban centers and are glad of the opportunity to rent their village houses. Once he has his own place in the settlement, he is immediately caught up in the daily tasks of all villagers and begins to make the contacts based on mutual interests that will be the basis for his work.

It has been my experience that in many communities throughout the arctic and subarctic it is becoming increasingly easy for the ethnographer to establish his role in a community without resorting to the various subterfuges and circumlocutions suggested by Paul. As noted above, the world view of northern peoples is expanding rapidly and so are the number of roles with which people are familiar. The increased education that is now available to young people is particularly helpful in this regard since the presence of even a few educated individuals in a community invariably helps to pave the way for the ethnographer. On more than one occasion in widely separated arctic and subarctic communities I have had high school or trade school students, home for their summer vacations, explain to their elders the purpose behind my questions and my interest in village life. The role of anthropologist may not be well understood, but that of "scientist" is rapidly coming to have the same magic halo around it for Eskimos and Indians as it does elsewhere. If the "scientist" also happens to already know something about the area in which he is about to work, his prestige may rise very rapidly indeed.

And this brings me to what I have found to be one of the most successful ways of gaining entree into a field situation—namely, by becoming as well informed as possible about one's area before entering the field. Most of us make an effort to learn something about the community or area in which we intend to work before we go into the field, and if we have been specializing in a particular area, the chances are that we may know a good deal in a general way. But we seldom have the inclination or the time to undertake the really thorough type of preparation that can pay real dividends when we are attempting to gain the interest and cooperation of informants in the field. This was brought home very graphically to me by my own recent experiences in carrying out archaeological and ethnographic investigations in the Nushagak River region of southwestern Alaska. My field interests shifted to the Nushagak after I had worked among the Eskimos of northwest Alaska and western Hudson's Bay and among the Chipewyan Indians in the Great Slave Lake region of the Northwest Territories. I also had two seasons of archaeological work in southwestern Alaska but actually knew very little about the specific historical background and present-day culture of the Nushagak River Eskimos. My general knowledge of Eskimo culture helped me to establish reasonable working relations with informants in the past, but I had always felt that, given the opportunity, I would like to be truly familiar with all the literature on a given area before entering the field rather than attempting to gather this data after the fieldwork. This opportunity presented itself for the simple reason that I was not able to obtain financing for my Nushagak work until a year later than I expected. With the extra time at my disposal, I set about collecting all the information on the Nushagak River and its inhabitants that I could find. This included a great deal of historical material, scattered ethnographic accounts of the nineteenth century, data on the geography and resources of the area, reports of missionaries and traders, some archaeological information, etc. I was literally steeped in the Nushagak before I had ever set foot on the banks of the river. As a result, I had a very accurate idea of

what I would find and how I would go about solving my research problems. But more important than that, I possessed a fund of information that immediately impressed all the Eskimos with whom I came in contact and encouraged them to take me and my interests seriously. Old people were intrigued and flattered by my knowledge of the past and their memories were successfully jogged to my very real advantage. Family heads and younger men were much easier to approach when they found that I could discuss with some intelligence the subjects which interested them most. It was thus fairly easy for me to establish my role as an interested and informed student of Eskimo culture who desired to add to his knowledge on selected topics about which he already knew enough to ask intelligent questions and pursue promising lines of inquiry. Subjects of interest to the ethnographer could be discussed on a level that did not bore the informant, and those who could not help me were interested enough to pass me along to those who could. The success of the field investigations was assured.

There is no doubt that in the north, as elsewhere, the ethnographer's knowledge of his area and the culture of the people in it also helps to set him apart from the casual tourist, government employee, construction worker, etc. Since the Second World War, the northern regions of both Canada and the United States have been the focus of a tremendous population expansion associated for the most part with increased resource utilization and military construction. In winter many of these people return to the south or to the large population centers in the north. But in summer a virtual continuous flow of nurses, government officials, technical specialists and just plain tourists pass through the villages; most of them ask the same vacuous questions of the Eskimos or Indians and receive a set of vacuous replies. It is more difficult than one might think to jar informants away from these conditioned responses. The ethnographer's knowledge of his area gives him the right to be taken seriously when he enters the field situation and makes his initial contacts with informants.

In discussing pre-fieldwork preparation, I have been referring primarily to the beginning ethnographer who is anxious to equip himself not only to impress and stimulate his informants, but also to make the information he will obtain more meaningful to him. The ethnographer with previous experience in a given area possesses a number of distinct advantages but also possibly some disadvantages. The advantages are similar to those discussed above, but the disadvantages may derive from the fact that he often knows more about a culture than the people themselves. At first glance this might seem to be a slightly ridiculous or even an impossible situation. And yet as rapid acculturation takes place and the old generations are replaced by young people with little interest in the past or knowledge even of those aspects of culture that still may play some part in everyday life, the experienced ethnographer may come to possess more knowledge and information than most of the native peoples with whom he will come in contact. I have found this to be true in northern areas where the deculturation process is progressing nearly as rapidly as it is anywhere else in North America. While doing fieldwork in a village on the northwest coast of Alaska, for example, it soon became apparent that I knew more about local Eskimo material culture than most of the Eskimos with whom I talked. Fortunately my primary research interests did not include material culture except very marginally. Nevertheless when talking with informants and the subject of artifacts came up, I had to be extremely careful, particularly with older people, not to offend them by contradicting their statements about old objects recovered from a nearby archaeological site, or to pretend that the knowledge of a white man was greater than their own on this subject. Similarly any informant can quickly become offended if he thinks that he is not being taken seriously. The ethnographer must learn and practice tact which generally means that he will have to listen to a certain amount of what might, rather impolitely, be called "baloney" before he can guide the informant to a subject on which the latter can speak with authority. Being intelligently informed is fine, but there is nothing to be gained by playing the "expert." However, perhaps the amount of care and tact required for such a situation is no greater than that which the sensible person uses in his everyday dealings with people anywhere.

Also related to the problem of obtaining entree into a field situation in northern communities are the advantages to be derived from combining archaeology, or at least archaeological survey, with ethnographic fieldwork. This is, of course, simply one way of establishing a role and a number of arctic specialists have found it useful and unobjectionable to the people. The field worker moves around a good deal in the course of a survey and usually has a chance to visit many villages and talk with a wide variety of people. His interests often turn the conversation to discussions of aboriginal subsistence or settlement patterns and this can easily lead to more contemporary subjects.

It will be noted that nothing has been said so far about the desirability of knowing the native language when working in northern communities. As a matter of fact, I can think of few ethnographers who have been even partially equipped to carry on interviews with informants in Eskimo or in any of the Athapaskan languages. This is in marked contrast to other parts of the world, particularly Africa and southeast Asia, where a knowledge of the native language is essential for successful anthropological fieldwork. The fact is that in all northern communities, except for a few in the central Canadian arctic, English is spoken by virtually everyone and field workers have seldom felt that a knowledge of the language was worth the time and trouble necessary to acquire it. And yet without doubt there are many circumstances where such knowledge would be extremely useful, particularly for those field workers concerned with ethnography, settlement pattern studies, archaeological survey and other areas of culture where much of the data must be obtained from elderly informants. Although many old people may speak some English, there can be no doubt that much more detailed information could be obtained and a freer exchange of ideas achieved if the informants could be approached in their own language. Interpreters are seldom sufficiently skilled, interested or sympathetic to bridge successfully the gap in understanding between the anthropologist and an elderly Eskimo or Athapaskan-speaking informant.

Although face-to-face contacts between whites and Eskimos or whites and Indians have greatly increased in recent years and Euro-American visitors are no longer a rarity in most northern communities, the ethnographer will often discover that if other anthropologists have preceded him, they will be remembered by the villagers. This is of course partly because some anthropologists came into the arctic and subarctic areas at a time when few other whites paid extended visits to the communities. One thinks, for example of Knud Rasmussen and Aleš Hrdlička in Alaska, Cornelius Osgood and Richard Slobodin among northern Athabascans, Kaj Birket-Smith and Rasmussen in the Canadian arctic. But generally it has been my experience that all previous anthropologists are remembered even when the villages where they worked were relatively large and cosmopolitan. Probably it is because they meet more people and stay longer than most other whites who are not permanent residents. At any rate, the important point here is that the ethnographer newly arrived in a northern community very frequently has a ready-made means of entree; namely to associate himself with his predecessor. When beginning fieldwork in northwest Alaska, I obtained an immediate friendly response from the Eskimos by simply mentioning the names of Rasmussen and Froelich Rainey; the same situation occurred on Nunivak Island in the Bering Sea when I told the Eskimos that the work I wanted to do would be somewhat similar to that done by Margaret Lantis fifteen years earlier. Along the Nushagak River the name of Aleš Hrdlička stood me in good stead even though he had spent only two weeks on the river more than thirty years before the time of my visit. Of course, if one hopes to benefit from the presence of an anthropological predecessor in one's community, it is necessary that the earlier field worker have left a good reputation behind him. Fortunately, this is almost invariably the case in the north. Whether it will continue to be so is, of course, up to those of us who are presently doing fieldwork in the area. The researcher should continually keep in mind that the impression he creates in the communities in which he works will greatly influence the efforts of those who come after him. If he has benefited by association with those who have come before, then he should be more aware than ever of his responsibility

to those who follow. An anthropologist who behaves crudely without regard for the feelings of those among whom he is working can spoil a community for anthropological work for many years to come. This is just as true in the north as it is in any place else in the world.

It should be clear from what has been written here that the author has experienced no real difficulties in gaining entree into field situations in northern communities. This is in spite of the fact that a number of ethnographers have vividly described the difficulties they encountered in doing ethnography with northern peoples (Osgood 1953, Honigmann 1946). Such references have usually been to Indians, though difficulty in working with Indians has not inevitably been encountered (see Honigmann 1949). Eskimos have, for the most part, a record of friendly tolerance toward outsiders and this continues even today when their villages are often deluged with visitors during the summer months. Northern Indians, although distinctly more reserved, have, in terms of my experience, been willing to accept the ethnographer and even to become friendly with him once it is obvious that there is nothing to fear from him or to be lost or gained by association with him. Since the Indians' relationships with whites have most frequently been on a superior-subordinate basis involving all the anxieties that are inherent in this type of relationship, the ethnographer may find that he must work to remove these anxieties before good rapport can be established. Perhaps the key to successful entree into a field situation anywhere is not to expect too much. If the ethnographer can establish his role by one means or another within a reasonable amount of time, and also create enough interest in his work so that he can find informants who will help him, he should not worry if he does not seem to be gaining "complete" acceptance by the villagers. Froelich Rainey's statement (1947:231) about his fieldwork at the Eskimo village of Point Hope in northwest Alaska seems to sum up the situation very well indeed. "We certainly failed to become an integral part of village life. We were, however, received as an exotic addition to the community, and, after some time as such, we managed our inquiries in an atmosphere of friendly acceptance. . . ."

BIBLIOGRAPHY

HONIGMANN, J. J.
1946 *Ethnography and acculturation of the Fort Nelson Slave.* New Haven, Yale University Publications in Anthropology.
1949 *Culture and ethos of Kaska Society.* New Haven, Yale University Publications in Anthropology.

HONIGMANN, J. J., and I. HONIGMANN
1965 *Eskimo townsmen.* Ottawa, Canadian Research Centre for Anthropology.

HUGHES, C. C.
1960 *An Eskimo village in the modern world.* Ithaca, Cornell University Press.

OSGOOD, C.
1955 *Winter.* London, Hale.

OSWALT, W. H.
1963 *Napaskiak, an Alaskan Eskimo community.* Tucson, University of Arizona Press.

PAUL, B. D.
1953 Interview techniques and field relationships. A. L. Kroeber, ed., *Anthropology today.* Chicago, University of Chicago Press.

RAINEY, F. G.
1947 The whale hunters of Tigara. *Anthropological Papers of the American Museum of Natural History,* Vol. 41, Part 2. New York.

CHAPTER 14

The Art and Technology of Field Work

MARGARET MEAD

Anthropology as a science is entirely dependent upon field work records made by individuals within living societies. This is true whether we think of anthropology as a science as beginning with so-called armchair theoreticians, like Tyler and Spencer, or prefer to date anthropology from the time that scientifically trained anthropologists began to make their own observations in the field. It is true when an anthropologist works entirely with statistical analyses of materials in the Human Relations Area Files; the materials with which he worked would not be in the files unless someone had made the field observations. It is true when the ethnohistorian or the archeologist attempts to deal with the inferential material of epitaphs or grave sites; in these cases field work on other, in some sense comparable living cultures, is invoked as explanatory. Furthermore the model of the field worker, as a single trained observer living for a specified period within and observing an ongoing community whose members share a single culture, different from his own, and organizing and integrating his observations and records of the behavior of living identified individuals, is basic to anthropological methods. Actual field conditions often vary from this model; there is a pair of field workers rather than a single worker, residence is at a distance from the community being studied, the individuals being studied are not part of a community, verbal accounts are substituted for actual observation of events, the culture is not different from his own, observations are informal and unorganized and there is no time limit on the duration of the observational period, and the individuals from whom he gets his information are not fully identified in relation to each other. Such field work is to that extent not typical field work, and the self-judgment of the field worker and the judgment of those who use his work will be appropriately qualified. "His account is based on reports received from three informants while the ship was in port," "The informants were living on the reservation of another tribe, which I was only able to visit twice," "The town was one with which I had been familiar since childhood but in doing this research I attempted to take the role of an anthropologist," are typical reservations.

The classical model of the field worker's task thus imposes its own imperatives, and these in turn act as criteria for the selection of techniques and as limiting conditions on the personality and performance of the field worker himself.

TRAINING

The basic training for an anthropological field worker should have provided an understanding of what a whole culture is, the categories of analysis and the methods of observation that have hitherto been found useful, and an open-ended expectation that the culture that he studies will be subject to observation and analysis, will be found to be systematic and to show identifiable regularities, and will be different in some unpredictable respects from any culture that has yet been described. He should have learned that the regularities which he will be able to find will depend upon the nature of his field observations, and that failure to be inclusive, failure to follow up implications in the field, failure to obtain enough of the same kind of material, or enough different kinds of material, may prevent his results being usable for the purposes for which he wanted to use them and for purposes to which others, now and in the foreseeable future, may want to put them. He will also have learned that under classical conditions a field worker visits a field once; he has had no predecessors who have worked under the same conditions and with the same assumptions and tools, and he will have no successors who can replicate his work. Even if he himself returns twenty years later to the same spot, neither he himself nor his tools will be the same and the conditions in the community of observation will be vastly changed. Therefore to the uniqueness of the particular culture studied must be added the uniqueness of the observer, the period and the circumstances and the technology of observation. As his task is to observe the whole, however much he may then specify a particular problem within the whole, each observation assumes unique importance within the spatial-temporal constellation which he is attempting to observe. There are no dry runs, no expendable bits of information. Even information which is later found to have been inaccurate is valuable as data on the state of the field worker's knowledge and understanding at the time it was recorded. Furthermore the value of each observation is a function of all other observations that have been made; additionally valuable if they have both been recorded—by any technical means—and consciously attended to by the field worker, so that the relationship of this particular item to other items is known. Thus the field worker is engaged in building a systematic understanding of the culture he is studying, weighing each new item of information, reacting to each discrepancy, constructing hypotheses about what he may encounter next. This systematic understanding—his total apperceptive mass of knowledge—provides him with a living, changing, analytical system which simultaneously correctly or incorrectly files information received—a hitherto unnoted kinship usage, a new design on a pot, a different cadence in a public speech—and so defines the search for new information. As he is attempting to build an understanding of the whole, before specializing in any aspect, it follows that the greater the degree of simul-taneity of observations on many aspects of the culture, the higher the chance of using the cross-referencing provided by parallels, e.g., in slang and ritual usage; or by contrast, e.g., in the behavior of unmarried men compared with the behavior of married men, or of chiefs in contrast to commoners.

The field worker, before he goes into the field, should be familiar with the way in which different anthropologists have used quite different methods, not only the technical film and tape, but in their selections of observation points, in their relative use of listening or looking, in their dependence upon observed or described events, in the extensive exploration of the repertoire of a few informants or in the use of most of the people in a village, in the continuous examination and analysis of information gained so far, or in the accumulation of enormous masses of data with no conscious and articulate analysis of the relationship of the parts. Such recognition of the differences in the methods and results of different field workers is essential if the new field worker is to find a style of his own, one that is appropriate to his own temperament and skills, the conditions under which he will have to work, the problem with which he is involved, and the technical aids to which he has access. All the possible paraphernalia of modern field work, both the physical paraphernalia of cameras, tape recorders, and instruments, and the sometimes equally encumbering set of possible analytical methods which he takes with him, will be useless unless he first sees himself, and his trained capacity to observe and record in some systematic way in relation to the living texture of the life he has come to study, as central to the research. In experimental work in a laboratory, a disciplined accuracy may be substituted within a well-designed experiment, for this type of continuous awareness and understanding. It cannot be done in the field.

His preliminary training must therefore include a systematic experience of enhanced awareness of his own culture, and his place, or places in case of generational or national mobility, within his own culture. Historically, anthropologists tended to rely upon students developing such awareness in the course of their exposure to other anthropologists and to anthropological materials. This was somewhat like those forms of psychiatric training that prepare a physician to diagnose and treat psychotics merely by exposure to hospital and treatment situations. Anthropology is, however, hindered by its very nature—the distance, uniqueness and isolation of the field experience—from such a full use of inexplicit apprenticeship training, and something more formal is required today. The student who analyzes his own socio-cultural position, so that he is able to think about it with disciplined detachment, will be a better-prepared recording instrument when he is asked to use his own responses as ways of recognizing, diagnosing, and analyzing the behavior of the members of a strange culture. Such analysis will also help him to understand what is required from the field worker in the way of a balance between empathic involvement and disciplined detachment. Detachment which permits discrimination and preference among the people of the community but bars out any formation of primary relationships with them, is particularly difficult to prepare a field worker for. An attempt to look at his own cultural experience and his own close relationships to members of his family, is one way of highlighting the new and different sort of relationship into which he will enter. Also coming to a realization of the extent to which he has seen aspects of the world through the eyes of one parent, or a teacher, friend, lover or husband or wife, may help him to decide on ways in which he can structure his position in a village so as to see with the eyes of others, what is going on around him.

ARRIVAL

When the field worker arrives in his field, work begins immediately; there are first impressions that will not be repeated and so must be recorded, human ties come into being and are hard to break later. An alternative to such immediate readiness and response is some brief residence in a part of the society where he does not plan to work. This is sometimes recommended, but it separates the sharpness of initial insights from the actual locus of intensive research and is by so much a loss. An imaginative grasp of what each event can and must mean is more satisfactory. So the field worker has to realize that he will witness or take part in a limited and unpredictable number of events, feasts,

marriages, initiations, sorcery cases, drownings, accidental deaths. He will have no way of knowing which of these will ever recur, and so he must get as much from each as possible, and on as many levels. A first birth for instance must be examined, if possible, for the medical midwifery involved, behavior of individuals under stress, kinship behavior, ritual, for birth as such, and in relation to all other *rites de passage,* economics. At the same time all the special and idiosyncratic factors—that the father was away, that the only good midwife had just died, that the newborn was the first grandchild of a chief, that the birth occurred on an unlucky day, etc.—must be taken into account. The more extensive the field worker's appreciation of the multitude of facets of a single event that can be analyzed, the more extensive his possible demands on technology can be, and also the more considered his refusals of concentration on one technical recording device in such a way as to interfere with taking other essential aspects of the event into account.

All of his work will also be related to time. His arrival separates sharply the period of observation from all that has come before. On his ability to observe some accompaniments of the passing of time—a change in the way a child is spoken to before and after the loss of its first milk tooth, a difference in the way an old man is handed his evening cup of kava one week before and three months after he gives up his title—will depend his later possibility of rounding out from those events which he has seen, an understanding of those which he has not seen. Every event no matter how small must be placed exactly in time, so that all events may be related to each other. The more technical the aids and varieties of recording and testing that are used, the more essential this becomes, as tapes, stills, cine-film, casual pencil and paper observations, sequences within some ongoing ceremony, can only be satisfactorily cross-indexed by reference to clock time. So a basic field work methodology, stemming from the original need to place each event, in terms of the ongoing actuality and the state of sophistication of the field worker, of placing each item of record, by date, hour and minute is simply intensified to hours, minutes and seconds as each new technology is added. If the time records are complete, an aberrancy in a projective test protocol discovered years later may be checked against a clinic visit record and a photograph which shows unusual depression the day after or the day before the protocol was taken.

A field trip is defined by its expected duration; the field worker will be measuring his pace from the start against a relatively fixed number of months, or occasionally years, with the additional proviso that the field trip may be interrupted by illness, some natural catastrophe—an earthquake—an epidemic, or increasingly, by political events. Each day is not only a given number of days from the beginning of the trip, and an estimated number of days from its probable end, but has also to be seen as a possible last day for data gathering. If the field worker learns to keep these three temporal considerations in mind, he is less likely to postpone writing up, cross-checking, cataloguing, and listing of codes and abbreviations, and less likely to begin enterprises which are technically impossible to complete because of the time they would consume, or the number of unforeseen eventualities which they do not take into account.

RECORDING

Events in the outer world, relayed by post or radio, significant natural events, like the beginning of a new season, a flood, the field worker's own health and mood, the development of a new hypothesis, a fresh insight, a change in technique, a broken exposure meter, stimulation from a book or article, all form part of the field record. Sensitive attention to recording them is one way of enhancing the field worker's awareness that he himself, his own stability and well-being, are inextricably part of the observations which he is making. The ability to register progress of some sort is often essential to the field worker's morale, and progress may be noted in counting up the thousands of words of vocabulary mastered, a tantalizing problem resolved, a bad cut healed instead of turning into an ulcer, a tiresome order got off so that a replacement of film will arrive in time. Types of record-keeping which emphasize the interconnectedness of the events under observation, the progress of the field worker in observing them, his health and mood, and the effectiveness and efficiency with which the complexity of self-maintenance is being dealt with, therefore serve a double purpose.

Before the field worker goes to the field he should have a solid documented knowledge of the way his individual talents and skills relate to the field work task. Such skills include: memory for faces, ability to reproduce nonsense material from memory, ability to reproduce sensible material from memory, relative memory for things seen and things heard, ability to write and observe simultaneously, width of vision, ability to predict what will happen behind one by the expressions of the faces of those in front, tolerance for continuous observation of the same type—e.g., kneeling with smoke in one's eyes for four hours recording trance behavior, sitting immobile and alert for half-hour intervals when a Rorschach card is exposed and no response is forthcoming, listening for one of two orchestras to stop—attention span inside which attention is of the same quality, ability to attend to an unpleasant situation, susceptibility to disqualifying disgust reactions, ability to resist the impulse to interrupt an unpleasant or disturbing sequence of behavior, tendency to identify in a partisan fashion with preferred individuals, etc. Each particular identified skill, or skill deficit, can then become the basis for choice of technique, in addition, of course, to choice of problem. Gross defect such as a poor ear or a very poor memory for nonsense syllables may well rule out work in music or certain kinds of linguistics, but beyond the question of gross defect, a field worker may decide that he wishes to use technical devices to increase his best skill, or to supplement his least skill. For example, someone who already has a fine visual memory may want to use photography so as to be able to communicate to others that which is indelibly registered in his own memory, where someone who depends primarily on his auditory capacities may feel that he will have little use for still or cinematograph records of events for the observation of which he did not depend on his eyes. But the sophisticated use of these extensions means that the field worker has to know such possible relationships and make such choices consciously. The true visualizer either has to give up if he is to use a camera and learn to let the camera record for him, because looking and photographing are incompatible, or learn to look with a view to taking a single condensed significant photograph. (Compare the photographs taken in Bali by Colin McPhee [Plates VIII, IX, X] that represent a condensed vision, with Gregory Bateson's lone sequences from a fixed stance, taken to supplement a less visual memory and provide data for later analysis [Plates I, II, III, IV, VII, XI, XIII, XIV], with Ken Heyman's photography [Plates XIV, XV, XVI] in which his photography and his observation are inextricably combined.)

Choice of methods of recording interviews involve another sense of choices if one elects to interview and write up afterwards; the material will always lack the precision which makes it possible for someone else to analyze it further. A handwritten verbatim transcript slows the informant down and results in a tremendous loss of stylistic features, such as repetition and dramatic pauses, but the material is immediately visible for analysis for the field worker who prefers to see the words about which he wants to think. A tape, in addition to being always subject to the risk of a defect in the machine recording, means listening—at the same speed as the original interview—before any analysis can be done, and transcription before useful cross-comparisons of widely separated images or phrases can be attempted. Here the question of auditory memory span is very important, whether cadences, for example, can be carried easily in the field worker's memory through an interview of an hour's length.

In the choice of recording methods that extend and amplify and make precise the capabilities of the different senses, and sensory specific memories, it is important to keep in mind the extent to which simultaneity is almost always sacrificed if attempts are made to obtain greater precision. If, for example, a field worker is trying to keep up with a complex series of events, and part of the record—say discussions with informants about what is happening—is on tape, part is on film which will have to be sent away to be developed, and part on still photography which he has no time or is unwilling to take the time to develop, then it is sometimes weeks or months later before he can cross-check for relevant details. He doesn't know whether he has a record of a given event at all, if it is on cine-film. So, paradoxically, the better memory a field worker has for multi-sensory detail, the safer it is to use tape and photography to record unique ongoing events. (These considerations do not of course apply to those cases in which events can be scheduled, lessons, bathing babies, making a carving, giving a Gesell test, and the expected method of recording planned for and allowed for. Here loss is also lamentable but doesn't affect the field worker's capacity to follow nonrecurring events. Plans which separate methods to be used for such nonrecurrent events and for events which may be reliably expected to recur, or to be periodically reproducible, thus become an essential part of field work design.)

All such considerations can be referred to the field worker's primary task of grasping as much of the whole as possible—whole language, whole community, a whole initiation, a whole illness, magical measures, death, mourning, etc. Simultaneity and speed have to be striven for, and accommodations between temperamental preferences and capacities worked out. The faster the language is learned, which means the more hours a day are initially devoted to it, the better it will be learned and the more ongoing events can become meaningful, but also the sooner the community is mapped and censused, the better each individual can be placed, and the more kinds of behavior are observed or inquired about, the more intelligible each becomes. Field workers whose preferences are for long sustained work on one subject, or with one informant, will have to learn to stand interruption, and those who take interruptions very easily will have to guard against the easy rewards of what may in the end result in lack of depth. Differences of this sort are important not only in strictly intellectual terms but in matters of change of pace, or depth of emotional involvement. It is very tempting to turn from contemplating a woman who has had her arm cut off by an angry husband, to note a new use of kinship term or buy a handful of beans.

Thus at any point the technology of field work is related to the art of field work, and this in turn with the mental and physical well-being of the individual field worker. Historically, anthropology has depended upon a sink-or-swim kind of training, first exposure to the literature and two or three professional anthropologists to interpret it, then a field trip, all alone, isolated and out of communication, on which the field worker either did or did not do good work, and from which in either event he might return either competent for future work or forever spoiled for it. Such methods served reasonably well when the technical skills required were minimal, when field workers themselves had lived closer to the actualities of life than is true of modern urban-bred students, when the areas where primitive peoples were found were less politically sensitive, and when the number of methods, tests, instruments, and models available to the student was much fewer. Today, when nine-tenths or more of a budget is spent before the field worker sets out, when his choice of technology and his skill in using it is crucial, when health is a matter of using the right drugs and not merely using a mosquito net, or boiling water, when unanticipated political complications, or failure to make approaches at the right level may ruin a whole field plan—preparation assumes a very different position in the career line of a young anthropologist (American Anthropological Association, 1966). Because of the enormous number of choices open to him, in equipment, in instruments, in approaches, field work is very much more difficult and it is a first necessity that everything that can be learned before going into the field should be. This means that students should be encouraged to explore systematically their own capacities and tolerances for isolation, for lack of privacy, for exposure to strangeness of all sorts. If they have never seen a badly hurt person, or a birth or a death, this deficiency of experience which constitutes an unpredictable hazard if encountered in the field, can be made up for by a few days' observations in the emergency ward and other parts of a hospital. Memory style, ability to record and watch, memory span, all can be explored. Then modern equipment, tape recorders, and various kinds of film and sound film can be tried out, and if they are to be used, mastered as a technique and in terms of the particular individual instrument. No field worker should ever take a kind of instrument that he hasn't mastered or a particular instrument he hasn't used into the field. A large amount of the waste, inefficiency, and often despair of modern field work results from a too-hurried departure, and untested and unfamiliar equipment sent into the field.

And it is important to set up the entire technology in advance; the kind of dry box to be used, the method by which films are to be mailed home, who is to project and report on the quality of the film after it is developed, methods of checking the state of cameras by developing small bits of film in the field, and communications which will make accurate, quick replacement possible. Every additional piece of equipment, or complexity of analytical methods, requires more foresight and also more backstopping for spare parts, a new kind of punch card, a new projective object which cannot always be anticipated. Only by combining the kind of planning which gave Raymond Firth eleven months on an island to which no ship came, with only one essential forgotten object, a pair of scissors, with the most careful backstopping from the technicians of museums, universities or technical firms, can the modern field trip, with its diverse equipment and multiple methodological possibilities, be handled efficiently. Universities are just beginning to realize that professional backstopping is essential if field workers are not to be left fuming and impatient for months, with broken equipment, or appropriate new plans which cannot be carried out. Each technical addition both extends the field worker's capabilities and increases the chances of frustration, waste motion, lack of systematic integration of his essential comprehension of the totality of the culture within which he is working.

FIELD SCHOOLS

If pre-field preparation is essential, questions arise about field training schools, summer field trips, quasi-supervised field work such as has been carried out in recent years by various U.S. institutions. Except for supervised practice with equipment, which can be done more economically out of the field, such field training fails to simulate the most essential aspect of field work; absolute responsibility for one's own choices and own mistakes, and complete respect for the permanent value of the work that one is doing and the people among whom one is doing it because they are contributing to a unique record. Field schools cannot reproduce these special conditions. Instead, in many instances they tend to blunt the student's sense of the urgency of his work, the very sense of responsibility which has carried young and inexperienced field workers through tremendous hardships, difficulties and frustrations. Under present-day conditions, the best way to give a student a sense of what he will encounter in the total field situation, is to give guidance and provide experimentation in live situations involving no pseudo-responsibility, with the techniques that he must choose among, insist on adequate learning of technical skills, such as photography, administration of projective tests, etc., and rely upon a concentrated absorption of the best and most diverse monographs, systematically discussed in terms of the methods used when they were written and available today.

Membership on a team, where there is real responsibility for part of a major field expedition is, of course, an entirely different matter. Here work in a real field situation can be combined with supervision and apprenticeship learning, and provide experience that will be useful for multi-disciplinary team research in more conventional settings. The classical field experience of total responsibility for a whole culture, hitherto unrecorded and destined for rapid change, remains, however, the best preparation for anthropological contributions to multi-disciplinary research. This is so in spite of the occupational handicaps in multi-disciplinary work of anthropologists so trained, such as a tendency to dichotomize the group being studied, who are treated with respect, and outsiders, government, mission, traders, all others, on whom the hostility that must be suppressed in disciplined field work, is given free vent. These occupational handicaps may be compensated for in other ways. Anne Roe's sample of anthropologists taken in the early 1940's (Roe 1953), while perhaps somewhat skewed, revealed a rather high paranoid component, easily understandable in a profession which demands a capacity to synthesize apparently unrelated items, and an ability to maintain a relatively even emotional state toward a circumscribed group of subjects. The presence of large amounts of objective materials that can be independently analyzed—films, tapes, long still sequences—can act as a check upon too facile systematizing, and the sense of omnipotence which sometimes accompanies being the only authority on some small unrecorded people. The tendency of anthropologists to identify with their tribe, or village, and to get involved in destructive relationships with the rest of the wider community, in incipient political movements and cargo cults, and in irresponsible feuds with other field workers in between field trips can be reduced by much greater insistence by those students learning to include every level, and every individual whom they will encounter on the way to and in the field—missionary, agricultural officer, airline pilot, schooner captain, trapper, tax collector—as intrinsic parts of the field situation, to be dealt with responsibly because of the need of maintaining long-time open-ended relationships.

PERSONAL RELATIONSHIPS

Another recurrent field problem which is becoming more acute as marriage and parenthood occur earlier within the academic professions, and grants become more generous, is the relationship of field work to personal relationships, and to the question of working alone, or taking a working wife, or a nonworking wife, with or without children, into the field. Ideally this is a problem which should be thought out before marriage. Then the type of marriage attempted can be consciously related to field plans; a man or woman hoping to do field work to complete their professional initiation into anthropology, could then postpone a marriage with a spouse who did not wish to do field work, or accelerate it so that a field trip could precede parenthood. However, partly because so many anthropologists enter the profession late, and from other fields, partly because a field trip represents tremendous demands on a nonprofessionally trained woman, many other kinds of situations continually face future field workers and grant-giving institutions.

The position of the lone field worker who spends many months or over a year alone in an isolated village, completely immersed in its ongoing life has certain advantages over that of a pair of workers. It is easier for the village to take him in, easier to fit him into a canoe or on a hunting trip. The requirements of an individual for food and sleep are very much simpler than even the most rudimentary household in which a husband and wife need some privacy, some level of personal communication and some pleasurable living arrangements. Furthermore, the lone worker is forced to rely on the villagers for company; he will spend much more time in the men's house, or out hunting, simply because he is lonely. He is likely to learn the language more quickly and to speak it better, and for certain types of individuals this kind of companionship with people centuries removed in experience has great poignancy and charm (Read, 1965). On the other hand, such work leaves little room for self-criticism; taking stock of progress is much harder. One is, of course, entirely dependent upon one pair of ears and eyes; if two events are taking place at the same time only one can be attended, and often it is impossible to cover two crucial aspects of the same ceremony. The culture will be experienced and systematized through one temperament, one sex, one age, and one set of personality preferences. The lone field worker, if he is wise, will set up substitutes for dialogue, in frequent correspondence either with a friend, who is or has been in the field, or with a senior colleague interested in the same problems or the same area. Sometimes it is possible to maintain a dialogue by reading extensively in other ethnologists' work. Intensive reading of single pieces of work, or other work on the same area, seems less likely to promote flexibility, and more likely to harden into dogmatic argumentativeness. Writing short articles for publication, or revising or reading proof on previously written work, also stimulates self-awareness and self-criticism.

But the necessary requirement of maintaining a certain distance from every member of the village, a requirement that is crucial to the quality of the work, and sometimes also to the actual safety of the field worker, weighs much more heavily on the isolated field worker. Any interruption from a passing member of his own society is welcomed; distant ports or European centers may beckon continuously, judgment about individuals or issues in the village be obscured. In an ideal situation, several field workers would be located perhaps a half day's journey apart, and be able to meet and talk exhaustively every two weeks or so. When such possibilities do exist, the very possibility removes the sense of isolation and strain and the field worker may actually decide against such a scheduled trip because something important is going on in the village. However congenial the isolation may be, working far removed from any chance for affection or intellectual interchange, often in ill health,

often with the burden of trying to save a dying child or a badly hurt person, frequently frustrated by nonfunctioning equipment, nonarrival of shipments, no news from home, failure to hear about a job or a research appointment, is a difficult, trying task, and should be prepared for as such.*

If a field worker is not to work alone, and include in the sacrifices he makes, absence from a family which he has already acquired, or a gnawing anxiety about whether his girl will wait for him, then the next most practical field pattern is to work with a spouse who is equally well trained but complementary in skills and special interests. When such partnerships are successful, the adequacy of the material is multiplied not by a factor of two but something more like a factor of five; work and methods can be complementary, the insights of each and the information acquired by each, inform the other. Such partnerships are, however, emotionally expensive, make enormous demands upon each partner, and often use up relationships that might have lasted far longer under less exacting conditions. The more completely each becomes involved in the culture, the greater the danger that a positive identification or an aversion, magnified on a cultural scale, may also complicate the marriage. However, marriages seem to stand such pressures better than partnerships with colleagues of the same sex, where there is less complementarity, more rivalry, and more strain on a small village or a limited

* I have worked in the field entirely alone, with no companion of any kind, only twice; on my first field trip to Samoa in 1925, and on my most recent field trip in 1965. The request to write this article reached me in the field and I had an opportunity to think over the difficulty of working alone, even under optimum conditions such as I had in 1965. I was in a village where a house had been built to match my needs, where I knew and trusted the entire village, had learned the language thirty-seven years before, was not dependent on any complex equipment because the films and tapes had already been collected. The people were orderly and law-abiding, there was an outboard motor to rush a sick child into the hospital. The only urgency lay in the ordinary hazards of life in a community of over four hundred, where someone was always being born, or dying, marrying or quarreling, and the principal work hazard was the possibility that the great feast which I had waited three months to see would not come off because a storm might scatter the canoes. All very minor matters compared with what a young field worker, uncertain of every skill, surrounded by incomprehensible strangers, responsible for himself, his work, the future, faces. Yet I still counted it difficult.

number of informants. Children of any age add tremendous hazards to field work. The better medical care becomes, the less willing parents are to forego it, and most field trips with children are tremendously reduced in efficiency because of worry, hurried trips to obtain medical care, early termination, etc. The more we know about the effect of early experience in forming children's minds and character, the less desirable it seems to expose a child to the massive, and very slightly correctable impact of a culture alien enough to repay anthropologically his parents' sacrifice in living there.

Teamwork involving a group of anthropologists and possibly other behavioral scientists with different specialties appears on first inspection to be the ideal way of doing a simultaneous study from many points of view of a single living culture, or of a number of contiguous and related cultures where a specialist can move with some ease from one to another. Where lingua francas and bridging languages are highly developed, as in New Guinea, India, parts of Africa, Indonesia, Malaysia, many of the specialties such as formal linguistic work, ethnomusicology, ethnobotany, physical anthropology studies, full-length expository films, and even some kinds of psychological testing, can be done on a team basis. There may be either short trips of the specialists to field sites where an ethnologist is already well entrenched, or planned expeditions in which several ethnologists work parallel to each other, establish the necessary basic knowledge of the culture, and the specialists move from one such base to another. Because the problem of language is the principal barrier to overcome, such specialists should work, if possible, within limited areas, with the same bridging languages and over-all type of linguistic problem, where their field stays can be prepared for by identifying and training native interpreters and factotums. Where the basic work has been well organized and adequate, maps, censuses, personnel lists, genealogists are all available, the identification of suitable informants, subjects, patients, within the thoroughly known local population can be provided for in advance, the inclusion of the specialists' visits in the field plan makes it possible for the ethnologist doing the basic work to devote the necessary time to organizing and illuminating the work of the visiting specialist. The availability of such specialists

enormously reduces the load on the single worker with a problem that requires some particular mass of material that has to be collected by expert techniques. The graduate student today faced with preparation for his first field trip and a bewildering variety of fascinating problems and tried and untried techniques, often feels so overwhelmed that he, in a sense, gives up before he goes to the field. The partial publications of later years, the monograph on the whole culture which is promised and never completed, reflect the extent to which the modern field worker is bogged down by the contemporary version of the demand for inclusiveness that has always both burdened and stimulated the single field worker. Where in the past, he was expected to bring back adequate descriptive material on every aspect of the culture, from Panpipes to omen dreams, the increasing use of anthropological material by other disciplines and the increasing use of instruments and techniques from related disciplines has resulted in a wholly unrealistic demand that the field worker becomes a specialist in specialties ranging from projective tests, botany, agriculture, child development and growth, nutrition and serology with all the associated methodology and high-level technology. The slow development of the teamwork that would relieve this situation can be explained not only by the relatively small funds that have been available for anthropological expeditions, but also by the discrepancy between the classical model of the field worker who studies the whole culture, all alone, in continuous and uninterrupted relationships with a small community, and the extent to which specialization requires a surrender both on the part of the field worker responsible for the basic culture and on the part of the specialist, of some of this inclusiveness and responsibility. It is of course inevitably surrendered, as far as materials go, when an anthropologist works in a modern complex culture, in cities into which previously primitive people are moving, or in areas—like the Southwest of the United States—where many kinds of field workers have worked for a long time.

An ideal team situation could be set up in areas like Bali, where it would be possible to develop a team of literate and expert Balinese assistants. Visiting specialists with very narrow interests, such as, for example, endocrinologists, serologists, etc., could still be installed in a village base camp of their own, and have an opportunity to see a live culture in operation. But such field situations require the maintenance of a field base over time, with very highly developed briefing materials and briefing specialists, a large population, good transportation and living conditions attractive enough to make a stay of several years attractive to the anthropologists and shorter periods taken from a high-level academic career worthwhile for the specialist.

In areas like New Guinea where a roughly similar culture is shared by a good many localized groups, or in areas like Mexico or parts of the Caribbean, where it is possible to find relatively autonomous villages sharing a common culture but varying in specific respects, parallel field work with different specializations—ecology, law, child development, cinematography—can be carried on, with individuals or pairs working in not too widely separated villages, and each providing organized material as background for the other's work. How well this sounds in theory and how poorly it works in practice serves to highlight the essential nature of classical anthropological field work in which the fit between the field worker and the people he studies, or between a pair of field workers and the people they study, is so special, so idiosyncratic, so dependent upon the way event and incident in the life of field worker and people are related one to the other, that the inclusion of others, which requires fixed time scales, abrupt interruptions of unforeseen cycles of ceremony or developing insight, is almost too difficult to bear. To the good field worker, thoroughly established within the ongoing life of his village, every minute is precious, every outside demand on his attention an unbearable interruption. This extreme and almost inevitable individualism needs very strong motivations to overcome it: a desire for companionship as strong as the demand for uninterrupted concentration, a genuine intellectual need for what the specialist will discover that is related to his problem as he sees it and a kind of generosity which is not necessarily an accompaniment of the personality type of those who make the best field workers.

Teaching projects with arbitrarily chosen teams working on imposed problems with a tight time schedule give graduate students some forewarning of what the requirements of any type of cooperation in the field will be. Furthermore working with a variety of technical aids on such a team provides a way of thinking about just how many and what kinds of aids an individual or a couple will actually want to use in the field. Some appreciation of the practicality of using a variety of technical aids is as essential a preparation for field work as is an understanding of one's individual skills which technical aids can extend and supplement.

AUDIO-VISUAL AIDS

As we have seen, major and continuing problems for the field worker are learning to estimate how much time to put into any type of observation or interviewing, as compared to how much time to put into some other type, and gaining a working knowledge of the ratio between the time and technology of the recording and the time taken to process it, in the field, and later, out of the field. All audio-visual technologies are capable of collecting enormous amounts of material, of far greater permanent value, than can the field worker's unsupplemented pencil and paper recording. It is scientifically unforgivable to record by a poorer method, e.g., an adaptation of European musical notation to non-European music rather than recording also by a tape recorder so that the music can be analyzed for decades and possibly centuries to come, as the questions change and methods of analysis are more refined. Similarly to refuse to make films of dancing, or spatial relationships among people, and rely only upon verbal descriptions or complicated notations—like Laban (1956)—in the field is equally inadmissible. The imperfect processing, while permitting immediate comparative work, interposes a screen between the material and any future more refined analyses. The same considerations apply to professional projective tests; if the tests are used, the original protocols in the language in which the test was administered are the basically valuable data, coding and scoring are devices for immediate comparisons, but alone, without the protocols on which they are based, are equally short-lived in their usefulness. If the basic overriding condition, that all cultural materials are uniquely valuable—even if they are dietary records of school children of German mothers and Irish fathers as compared with the children of

Irish mothers and German fathers in an upstate Pennsylvania town in 1940—and worth saving in the most complete form possible, then the relative value of complete mechanized recording and any human mediated recording or scoring falls into place. But once this initial choice is clear, there is still the question of how and when to use mechanized recording and what kind of on-the-spot supplementation is needed if it is to be of continuing use for analysis by the original field worker and by others.

In general it may be said that for the single field worker to use any form of mechanization which effectively prevents his paying adequate attention to an ongoing event and recording the total context and the personnel is unjustified. Either he must be able to set his tape going, put his cine-camera on a tripod, connect the clicks of his still camera with a tape recorder so the exact time is registered, or dictate simultaneously into a lapel microphone, or he will be better off—in terms of the whole event, to confine his recording to what he can get down with a pencil. A magnificent film of an argument at a village meeting but without notes on who the speakers were, and with a tape untranscribed in the field and untranscribable—in any meaningful sense—is wasteful of field work and of film. A small amount of film with all the personnel and conditions carefully specified, and the accompanying tape transcribed and annotated in the field is worth masses of film not so annotated. A safe rule for the lone field worker is to use no more mechanized recording than he can fully annotate in the field, which means that systematic note taking has to accompany every kind of recording or filming. Major advances in single worker technology come with sound film systems, and carefully worked out devices for built-in annotations (whisper mikes on a separate tape, visible clocks which can be photographed periodically, extra cameras ready for photographing in color a completed Lowenfeld mosaic test, etc.). But the more complex and perfect the technology, the more time the technology takes and the less other field work gets done. Recurrent scenes such as bathing a baby where the baby is bathed every day, or a trance which occurs three times at every feast, where all the basic material on cultural form and personnel has been gathered, are particularly suitable for intensive work that at the same time will not sacrifice valuable material on ongoing events. Singlehanded recording, even of events all the details of which are known beforehand, presupposes an extraordinarily high level of technical knowledge and skill on the part of the field worker.

A team of two makes parallel note taking and mechanical recording immediately more feasible; a team of three, one dealing with sound and one with film, or one with sound film and one with selected and supportive stills or background film shots, while the third does the essential note taking, produces ideal results. But a team of three or four individuals with primarily technical skills is more suitable for the inclusion in a longer field trip for an intensive short period of work, and comes under the heading of the kind of specialists whom it is more economical to import briefly. For making sound films, or even silent films of high quality, which will preserve the record of the life of a people either for exposition or for future analysis, a real sound-film team of specialists in anthropological film making are required—such as the composite effort of two ethnologists, film maker, still photographer, and sound man, used in making *Dead Birds* (Gardner, 1964).

In all specialized work the requirement of including an ethnologist already familiar with that particular milieu (or locale) should be followed. Attempts to say a culture is so well known that it is reasonable to back some specialized forms of recording, such as the anecdotal collections and questionnaires which the Whitings attempted to standardize while giving the field workers permission to follow their own research bents, are highly unsatisfactory. The real ethnologist immediately goes to work on the culture which means shifting from an *etic* to an *emic* level. But an ethnologist already familiar with the local milieu can shift fairly easily to facilitating the collection of standard materials by some other specialist or other technical method. And the visiting specialist is far less tempted than is the ethnologist who knows the culture intimately to readapt his instruments and by so doing sacrifice their principal *raison d'être,* comparability with other cultures. In turn, it follows that a student who wants to do a cross-cultural problem that is highly specialized and requires the mastery and application of some laborious technique would do better to work in association with a field worker who was working on a whole culture than to attempt to combine mastering a whole culture and doing a highly specialized piece of work. Alternatively the work on the whole culture can be done first and the period of intensive testing, filming, collecting ethnobotanical samples, etc., treated, in effect, as a second field trip building on the knowledge and rapport of the first.

The classical field trip in which the anthropologist working within a small known community is able to follow the complete round of season and ceremonial and to witness all the major *rites de passage,* and comes to feel, by the simultaneity and cross-referencing of his observations, a growing sense of mastery of the whole culture, remains the referent of *all* types of anthropological work. As a result all work which does not meet this requirement contains, in a sense, a built-in frustration, as a student goes out to study market women in a growing African city, or the ethnobotany of a Malayan village, or works on a team studying cultural deprivation in a ghetto slum situation in an American city. To the extent that he has learned what studying a whole culture is and is able to keep the parts of the whole culture that he is not studying in mind, he may also be supported rather than only frustrated, but the frustration is undoubtedly there, and unavoidable, unless we wish to sacrifice one of the principal strengths of anthropology, working with whole cultures.

So far I have considered the technology of field work almost exclusively from the standpoint of the field worker, the choices and possibilities confronting him. It is, however, useful to reverse the process, and ask what does modern technology make possible that the field worker, with a commitment to the preservation of records of cultural uniqueness, should therefore try to do. Here we may distinguish between what the new techniques permit the single field worker to do himself, and the extent to which they enlarge further usefulness of the materials he collects. As to his own records, subject to the considerations mentioned above, mechanized methods of data collection give him far more data, far more precise data, and inexhaustible supplies of material on which he can work for the rest of his life. The future usefulness of field data for different kinds of exploitation, many of them unanticipated

at the time the field work was done, is a direct function of the extent to which material can be collected in large, sequential and simultaneous natural lumps on which no analytical devices of selection have operated. So 1,200 *consecutive* feet of film is better than a 500, a 200, a 100 foot roll; 100 feet on a battery-operated camera is better than 100 feet taken with six rewinds and re-selections. Long verbatim texts are more valuable than many short verbatim texts; tapes which contain many other kinds of information are more valuable than several hand-recorded verbatim texts. Only materials which preserve the original spatial-temporal relationships are virtually inexhaustible as sources for new hypotheses and ways of testing old hypotheses. The more material is codified by the method of selection, as when sample scenes, standard-length anecdotes, standard interviews, standard tests, are used, the more immediately useful it may be in relation to some hypothesis, and the less its permanent value.

As our new methods of recording are coinciding with the disappearance of the most distinctively different and isolated cultures, the collection of such permanent records becomes even more essential. It becomes a reasonable demand on the field worker to bring back as much of such material as he can properly annotate and organize so that it can be used in the future. The requirement of adequate annotation interlocks with the requirement that for the field worker's efficiency he should not collect material which he cannot integrate and organize. This then leaves each field worker with his own problem of selecting the technology he will use, when and how much he will use it and how he will integrate problem or theme with the technological collection of objective materials. In making this selection, in relation to his particular culture, his own capabilities and deficits, the theme or problem on which he is working, etc., the question is one of balance between his "subjective" contribution, that is, using his own brain to cross-reference millions of items of observation, to his "objective contributions," that is, the collection of materials that can be handled by other single brains without the further intervention of his own, and ultimately by various sorts of computerized techniques. There seems no reason to believe that the "objective" materials which are suitable for other computers—including the brains of other individual anthropologists or other behavioral scientists—are intrinsically more accurate than his subjective digest, but they are subject to replicative analysis. Replicative analysis takes the place in the study of unique behavioral records, of replication of experiments in the experimental sciences. A single properly annotated and filmed sequence of a mother and child can be subjected to finer and finer analyses, as kinesics, proxemics, and other forms of movement analysis are developed. The same sequence, unchanging, forever there to be observed, will permit hundreds of "experimental analyses" many years apart and long after the original field worker is dead. Part of the skill in this kind of field work lies in the selection for such permanent records—either made by the field worker or by specialists called in for the purpose—of crucial behavior sequences within the culture he is studying. Their lasting value will largely depend upon how specific they are to the culture itself, and how standard and cross culturally applicable the techniques of researching which are used. Types of filming only possible under very special light conditions, tests which fit a particular culture but are not generally applicable, will lower the permanent value of the results.

As our sound-film techniques are perfected and sound cameras become available which are within existing field work budgets, it will be possible to aim at one further possibility, the creation of selected corpora of material —visual, auditory, verbal, projective, ethnemic—so that students of the future may be given the kind of experience of whole cultures which today is provided by live field work, and contact with those who have done live field work. Isolated cultures, unique in every detail, are bound to disappear and the conservation of ways of learning from them is therefore all the more essential.

So the problems and possibilities of field work change. As technical difficulties are overcome, new difficulties of choice enter in. The larger the number of anthropologists working at any given period, the more the standardizing and dulling effect of competition enters in. The more anthropology becomes one of the recognized and lucrative professions, the more field work is likely to become assimilated to an initiation imposed upon a reluctant novice, rather than the golden opportunity for a unique intellectual adventure, which it seemed to earlier generations. And the more change there is in motivation, the less available the older work becomes as model and stimulant. Yet in spite of all the handicaps of competition, and professionalization, the ability to do good field work still depends, as it always has, on a deep involvement with a task so exacting that no efforts, no amount of brilliance or imagination, no battery of technical aids, no depth of commitment and sense of responsibility will ever be enough to permit any individual to do what is there to be done. Those who are attracted by the inexhaustibility of the task, will continue to be so. Training and preparation can only armor them against the paralysis of too many choices, the familiar problems of isolation and temperament fit or non-fit with a particular culture, the hazards of political partisanship or emotional involvement with the groups they study. The intellectual fascination of the task itself does the rest; under this fascination the most unlikely people tolerate tremendous hardships and bring back brilliant work. Those who do not experience this delight would be wise to shift to another kind of research. Clinicians working with missionaries have found that degree of commitment is a better predictor of adjustment in difficult foreign fields, than freedom from neurotic, or even from psychotic components. Similarly, in anthropology, sheer delight in the task is probably the safest predictor we have of field work success.

SOME KINDS OF FIELD PHOTOGRAPHY— BALI, 1936–1958

In illustrating my discussion of these uses of still photography I have decided to use photographs from one culture, by a number of field workers with different interests, extending over a period of twenty years. The choice of Bali was made for a number of

LIST OF PLATES

1

2

4

3

6

5

PLATE I
Bali: Elevation and Respect
Bateson, 1936–1938

(This appeared as Plate 10, *Elevation and Respect I,* from *Balinese Character: A Photographic Analysis,* by Gregory Bateson and Margaret Mead.)

This illustrates the Balinese systems of hierarchy and respect. In addition to the system already noted, according to which the inland-east *(kadja-kangin)* is the most honored direction, a great deal of attention is paid to elevation, and the head is ceremonially the most sacred part of the body. Respect is expressed by lowering the self or elevating the respected person.

Every Balinese, in all his personal relations, continually orients himself in terms of the cardinal points and the relative elevation of the various persons.

1. A man looking at an airplane. In looking up at this strange and surprising object, he has, from habit, put his hands in a posture of ceremonial respect (cf. Fig. 5).
I Wajan Keloepcos, of Bedoeloe.
Bajoeng Gede. July 3, 1936.   1 T 14.

2. The Goenoeng Agoeng, the central mountain of Bali. This mountain is regarded as an abode of gods, and links together the system of cardinal points and the system of elevation. The cardinal points differ from ours in that, though east *(kangin)* and west *(kaoeh)* are determined by the rising and setting of the sun, the other two directions *(kadja* and *kelod)* are determined by reference to the central mountain. In Bajoeng Gede and South Bali generally, *kadja* coincides with the European "north" and has been so translated in this book. In North Bali, however, *kadja* coincides with the European south, and *kadja kangin,* the most honored direction, is southeast. The translation "inland-east" is applicable in both cases.
Photograph from near Bajoeng Gede.
June 17, 1937.   11 R 27.

3. Trance dancer *(sangiang)* on a man's shoulders. The two little girls who dance in trance are to some extent sacred in ordinary daily life and they must avoid going under aqueducts or suspended chicken roosts. In trance, when they are "possessed" by angels *(dedari),* they become much more sacred; their commands are obeyed and they dance, not only on the ground but also elevated on men's shoulders. Most men normally avoid carrying a grown woman, and women's clothes must not be put on top of men's clothes. *Sangiang* dancers cannot dance after puberty, and the reason given for this rule is that men would not "dare" to carry them on their shoulders.
I Misi on shoulders of I Lasia.
Bajoeng Gede. May 26, 1937.   9 O 32.

4. Painting of a *sangiang* dancer being carried. Here the respect is expressed not only by elevation but also by the use of umbrellas.
Painting by I. B. Kt. Diding, Batoean; bought Feb.24, 1938. Picture 119.

5. Comic servant *(kertala,* cf. Pl. 13) in Balinese drama, in position of respect *(soembah),* waiting for the entry of his prince.
Dendjalan. May 26, 1936.   1 I 13.

6. The dream of a Brahman artist. The dictated text of the dream is as follows:
"Another time I dreamt of burning a body. The dead man had never once helped (others). Lazy so to speak, and he died. And no citizens went to visit *(medelokin)* there. I carried (him) to the cemetery and came to the cemetery; and, when I got there, there were all the citizens, all together; and I was stared at by the citizens. They would not lift the firewood for the burning. And so I alone, I burnt him. And while it was burning, I mumbled to myself. The citizens were still there, far off. That's how—when alive, too lazy to help the neighbors, and now stared at by the citizens."
Note that the artist has represented himself as lower than the assembled citizens, and that in the dream he is both the "lazy" man and the man who does the burning. This painter was unusually preoccupied with caste, because he had broken a serious caste rule in stealing the wife of another Brahman.
Painting by I. B. M. Togog of Batoean; bought Aug. 26, 1938.

1

PLATE II
Balinese Child Development
Bateson, 1937–1939

(This appeared as Plate II, *I Karba,* from *Growth and Culture:
A Photographic Study of Balinese Childhood,* by Margaret Mead
and Frances Cooke Macgregor. Photographs by Gregory
Bateson.)

This plate carries I Karba from a period of active happy exploration, carrying off the mallet, exploring the drum of a visiting orchestra (Figs. 1 and 2), exploring the legs of the photographic tripod (Fig. 4), through the period when his parents' teasing, his mother's borrowing a baby to make him jealous (Fig. 6), begin the period of withdrawal, which is shown in the photograph taken a year later (Fig. 7), when Karba no longer responds to teasing efforts to provoke him, but sits, sulkily, among the other children. But even in this period of withdrawal through which Balinese children characteristically go, his gaze is level and appraising; he is withdrawn into himself, but still presents a picture of a well-integrated child. In this picture (Fig. 7) he is still unweaned, and if his mother does not become pregnant, may wean himself gradually, as he becomes old enough to follow his father out to the fields and spend long hours away from his mother.

1 and 2. I Karba, 16 months, with his father (Nang Oera) and a musician, left, from an orchestra accompanying a *djoget* (girl dancer with whom villagers dance). The road in front of our house. Karba plays with the drum (Fig. 2).
6/9/37.   11 M 20, 11 N 2.

3. I Karba, 17½ months, with his mother's sister (Men Singin) and I Karsa, left (Karba's double cousin, son of Men Singin). Taken in our yard under the banana tree.
7/15/37.   12 Q 29.

4. I Karba, 20 months, playing with legs of our tripod and a cup. Nang Sama's yard.
10/9/37.   16 X 21.

5. I Karba, 20 months, standing alone. Our yard.
10/11/37.   17 H 15.

6. I Karba, 24½ months, being suckled by his mother (Men Oera), who is teasingly dandling I Marta, 14 weeks, daughter of Karba's father's brother. Marta's father (Nang Marti) in background.
3/1/38.   21 R 15.

7. I Karba, 36 months, with I Ridjek, I Riboet, age unknown, and I Gati (his back to camera), in Nang Karma's yard. Ridjek is Gati's next oldest sister who lives with her maternal grandparents and cares for Riboet, Karba's half sister and half double cousin.
2/12/39.   36 E 31.

2

3

4

5

6

7

1

3

PLATE III
Balinese Squatting Style
Bateson, 1937–1939

(This appeared as Plate XXV, *Squatting,* from *Growth and Culture: A Photographic Study of Balinese Childhood,* by Margaret Mead and Frances Cooke Macgregor. Photographs by Gregory Bateson.)

In their squatting behavior there is found one of the most marked differences between Balinese and American children. The Balinese squat is much lower, the buttocks often resting on the ground (Figs. 1, 4, 7), and the squatting position occupies a different position in the maturational sequence. American children tend to go from frogging to creeping to all fours or to standing, with the squat following later; the Balinese children, with hardly any creeping, go from sitting to squatting to standing, rising from the squat rather than sinking down into it. Here again a number of factors can be mentioned as explanatory: the presence of squatting as a usual form among Balinese adults, the wide spread of the hips that is associated with being carried on the hip for such a long period, the narrow circle within which a Balinese child is usually permitted movement so that movement up may be substituted for movement away from a given position, the extreme fluidity of Balinese movement, and the emphasis that has been placed on balance during the time the child was learning to stand alone.

5

6

7

8

1. I Karba, 18½ months, and I Marti, 16 months, with a *kapeng* (a copper coin) in our yard. Notice the very low squat, buttocks touching the ground.
8/20/37.   14 L 15.

2. I Karba, 20 months, and I Ngendon, 11 months, playing with ball and spoon. Our yard.
10/11/37.   17 I 27.

3. I Kenjoen, 17 months, and I Marti, 16 months, in our yard. Same scene as in Fig. 1. Playing marbles.
8/20/37.   14 M 24.

4. I Marti, 11 months, in wide low squat, playing with I Karba, 13½ months. Our yard.
3/21/37.   6 C 9.

5. I Tongos, 10½ months, pausing in a near squat, after going on all fours, one leg dragging. I Karba, 20 months, standing with ball.

In Nang Goenoeng's yard, afternoon of play.
10/9/37.   16 Y 38.

6. I Sepek, 10½ months, squatting and maintaining his balance without his hands touching. In own yard, at his delayed *otonin* ceremony. His father (Nang Degeng) watches, holding the next older child (I Leket) sprawled in front of him.
4/30/37.   7 S 39.

7. I Marta, 14½ months, squatting and looking over her shoulder. Own yard.
2/11/39.   35 T 29.

8. I Raoeh, 25½ months, squatting, arms in balancing position, in front of his older brother (I Goenoeng) while his child nurse (I Poendoeh) does the hair of his mother (Men Goenoeng). Own yard.
3/3/38.   22 E 29.

PLATE IV
Bali: Child Nurse
Bateson, 1937

(This appeared as Plate 79, *Child Nurse,* from *Balinese Character: A Photographic Analysis,* by Gregory Bateson and Margaret Mead.)

The major role which small girls play in social life is as nurses. Chiefly they carry around their own younger siblings, but if there is no other baby in the house where a girl lives, she will borrow other babies to carry. There is a great deal of interchange of babies so that, though a baby may leave home in the hands of one girl, it will pass through the hands of many others before one of them brings it back to the mother.

The relationship between child nurse and baby is not of such a kind as would result in introjection of a personalized super-ego. The baby learns limpness—that when the nurse is playing "crack-the-whip" (called *"goak-goakan"* or "flock of crows"), it is best not to stiffen any muscles—and it learns to sleep if the child nurse has a temper tantrum.

The baby is treated mostly not as a person capable of learning by reward and punishment, but simply as a more or less awkward bundle.

Even when the child nurse plays with the baby, her attitude toward it is the characteristically Balinese delight in stimulating some responsive object. She treats the child as an autocosmic symbol. This may be described as treating the child as "different from the self" (except insofar as one's own body or its parts are autocosmic symbols), but the relationship between Balinese child nurse and baby is still very far from being comparable to the relationships in which, in Western cultures, the image of some adult is introjected to form a personalized super-ego. For the Western type of character structure, it is surely necessary that there be great contrast between the two persons. This occurs where the baby is looked after by adults, but where the baby is looked after by children only a little older than itself, the contrast is necessarily less.

1 to 9. A child nurse with her younger sister. Both children came to our house to get treatment for some minor infection of the eyes (such infections are very common in the mountains during the extreme dry season), and both were a little fretful on this particular day. In addition, the child nurse was still learning her task, and was not yet fully skilled in the art of fixing the two ends of the sling under the baby.

In Figs. 1 to 3. the baby is yelling, and the nurse, trying to quiet her, disturbs the set of the sling.

In Figs. 4, 5, and 6, the nurse is adjusting the sling. She has the two ends hanging down from her shoulder, and she raises the baby high. Then she wraps the ends across the baby's nates, and pulls them up between the baby's legs, so that when the baby is again lowered, its weight will hold the ends in place.

In Figs. 7 and 8, the baby is limp and asleep.

In Fig. 9, the baby has awakened and is crying, but the child nurse now pays no attention—by fixedly looking in the opposite direction.

The whole series covers about two minutes of behavior.

I Gati with her younger sister, I Kenjoen, aged 520 days.

Bajoeng Gede. Aug. 19, 1937. 14 B 1, 2, 3, 4, 5, 6, 7, 8, 9.

1

2

3

4

5

6

7

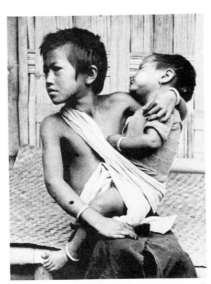

8

9

PLATE V   6

Bali: Studies of a Trance Medium
Belo and Mershon, 1930's

(These appeared as figures 1, 2 and 6, *Intaran District,* from *Trance in Bali,* by Jane Belo.)

Distinguished for its *sadegs,* trance mediums and trance doctors, whose services constitute an essential part of the religious ceremonies of the district. The mediums, some of them experienced older women, noted for their dancing, were held in high respect in their community.

1. Djero Plasa, *Koelit Kajangan.*
2. Djero Plasa dancing. (*Photo by Jack Mershon.*)
6. Djero Plasa dancing in the temple during a trance séance. (*Photo by Jane Belo.*)

Djero Plasa is a woman of perhaps seventy years of age (Figs. 1 and 2). At times, in the temple, she seems a much younger woman. But in observing her on other occasions, watching her movements in ordinary life, one realizes that she is indeed very old. Her personality is so strong that she dominates not only the entire group of *sadegs,* but in fact the whole assemblage in the temple. When she enters the gate, everyone seems at once to be aware of her presence. Like the perfect old actress that she is, she does not fail to play up to her audience. She takes, and holds, the center of the stage.

Djero Plasa is an excellent dancer, and one of the characteristics of her behavior in trance is her tendency to break into the postures of the dance. She may even get up from the formal séance during the period of trance and do a turn in the center of the court. She may, after coming out of trance, join with the other women in the ritualistic dances. Occasionally she goes into trance on her way to the temple and, on her arrival, dances her way into the temple court.

She has a great sense of humor. In her ordinary contacts she makes many jokes and thrusts at her colleagues, and the quality of wit and pointed allusion she introduces also into her ceremonial performances. It seems to add to her quickness in handling any situation in which others are concerned and in keeping for herself the position in the limelight.

Her speech is eloquent; she is well versed in the phrases of the "high language." She has a deep, mannish voice and a laugh that leaves no doubt that she is really amused. In the practice of ritual she is devout, and undeviating in her role of one "possessed by a god." She is very clear in her mind about what is the proper custom and order in the ceremonial. Frequently she interrupts the officiating priest in the performance of his rites, tells him that he is doing it wrong, and proceeds to tell him what is right. Rarely have I seen her fail to carry her point.

77

78

79

80

81

PLATE VI
The Kris Dance
Belo, 1937

These appeared as Figures 77 through 81. *Village of Pagoetan,* from *Trance in Bali,* by Jane Belo.

77. The Kris dancers fall down before Rangda the witch
78. The witch advances
79. The dancers rise and draw their krisses
80. They rush to attack Rangda
81. Neka about to "eat" a live chicken

In this plate, Jane Belo followed through a sequence of events of a single ceremony in Pagoetan, December 16, 1937. It is the Pagoetan trance ceremonies of December 16, 1937, and February 8, 1939, on which the film, *Trance and Dance in Bali,* by Gregory Bateson and Margaret Mead, filmed by Gregory Bateson and Jane Belo, is based.

In the following plate, *Trance: Attack on the Self,* Gregory Bateson analyzes, through the use of photographs from a variety of scenes, the attack on the self, which forms part of this sequence.

PLATE VII
Trance: Attack on the Self
Bateson, 1936–1938

(This appeared as Plate 57, *Trance: Attack on the Self*, from *Balinese Character: A Photographic Analysis*, by Gregory Bateson and Margaret Mead. It is the third in a series of four plates on Trance.)

The men return, still in a somnambulistic state, and after a few simple ballet maneuvers, they strut about singly. Suddenly, first one and then another gives a loud yell and turns upon his own chest the kris with which he attacked the Witch. This in-turned aggression is accompanied by a roaring noise and posturing in which the body is suddenly and repeatedly bent backward with a rising movement of the arms (Fig. 3). In this action, the accent is on the upward motion of the arms and on the forward thrust of the pubis. After a few seconds of this activity, the man will start strutting again, tense and silent, only to revert, with another loud yell, to his spasmodic posturing. Some men actually fall backward onto the ground with an extreme backward bending of the trunk, and lie on the ground writhing in some sort of orgasmic climax.

Meanwhile the women have also turned their krisses on themselves. But their behavior differs from that of the men in that they accent the *downward* bending movement, while the upward and backward movement, which is accented by the men, is, in the women, only a recovery or preparation for another downward movement of the hands, a forward bending of the trunk and a withdrawal of the pubis. This difference and the writhing behavior of the men indicate a close relation between this trance behavior and sexual climax. We have noted that the tendency of children to look for climaxes of affection and anger is frustrated and probably in some sense repressed. It is probable, therefore, that this conventionalized trance behavior is a return to patterns of behavior which have been extinguished or inhibited.

1. Native painting showing the stages of going into trance. The man standing to the left of the Witch is attacking her with a kris in his hand; the man on the ground has presumably just fallen from the attempt to stab her; and the man on the right holds two krisses and has turned them on himself. The Witch herself is apparently preening her hair with her right hand while she waves her cloth with the left.

Painting by I Goesti Njoman Lempad of Oeboed.

Dated by the artist "March, 1938."

2. Portrait of a man *before* the attack on the Witch. He is taking part in the preliminary ballet and holds a kris raised high in his right hand. Note that the pursing of the lips at this stage has an extrovert or aggressive appearance sharply contrasting with the apparent introversion on the faces of men actually in trance.

Dendjalan. May 26, 1936.   1 J 22.

3, 4, 5, and 6. A series of postures of a man in trance.

Fig. 3 shows the high point of his krissing movement. His back is bent far back; the point of his kris is against his chest; and he holds the handle of the kris with both hands high above his head. In dancing in this way with the kris, there is, so far as we could observe, very little flexor tension in the biceps. Instead there is a strong pronator tension in both arms, which holds the point of the kris against the man's chest. If the man's body were not there, the point of the kris would move downward in an arc with the center in the man's hands. In the background of Fig. 3 is a second man jumping in the air and yelling at the moment of transition from strutting to krissing himself.

In Figs. 4 and 5, the man struts with his kris held against his upper arm by the cramped supination of the forearm.

In Fig. 6, he is jumping. This man performed a series of consecutive jumps in this posture.

Dendjalan. Nov. 23, 1936. 3 I 14, 18, 25, 28.

7. A man krissing himself. In contrast with the high degree of tension shown in Fig. 3, a number of men kris themselves in this very "offhand" manner, using only one hand. Some of the obscene carvings show postures very closely related to this. In the background, the priest, who was looking after the men in trance and giving them holy water, has himself gone into trance and is being supported by two club members who are not in trance.

Dendjalan. May 26, 1936.   1 K 2.

8. A small boy in a tantrum. This photograph illustrates the relationship between krissing behavior and tantrum behavior. In both we find the extreme backward bending of the body and the climax.

Men Goenoeng holding I Raoch.

Bajoeng Gede. Oct. 12, 1937.   17 N 37.

9. Men krissing themselves on the ground. This photograph was taken at a religious ceremony (the so-called *"perang dewa"* or "fight of the gods"), but the trance behavior is nominally the same as in the Witch drama. It appears that in this village, the conventional climax position on the ground is lying on the belly, instead of on the back as in Pagoetan.

B2keabali. Oct. 17, 1936.   2 X 13.

1

2

3

4

7

8

5

6

9

107

50

PLATE VIII
Musicians in Bali
McPhee, 1930's

These appeared as Figures 107 and 50 from *Music in Bali,* by Colin McPhee.

Figure 107 shows *Kulkulan* playing the great wooden gong used to summon villagers to ceremonial meetings.

Figure 50 shows paired drums, Kendangs lanang and wadon in the *gamelan pelègongan.*

54

55

56

PLATE IX
Drumming Hand Postures
McPhee, 1930's

These appeared as Figures 54, 55 and 56, taken from a series of five photos on drumming hand postures, from *Music in Bali*, by Colin McPhee.

54. Krèmpèng Stroke
55. Krumpung stroke
56. Pek stroke

42

43

PLATE X
Continuity in Form of Musical Instruments
McPhee, 1930's

These appeared as Figures 42 and 43, which show the continuity through time of the form of musical instruments, from *Music in Bali,* by Colin McPhee.

42. Kajar in the *gamelan pelègongan* (see Plate IX)

43. Kajar and *suling gambuh* (flute), as shown in stone figures at Sukawati village

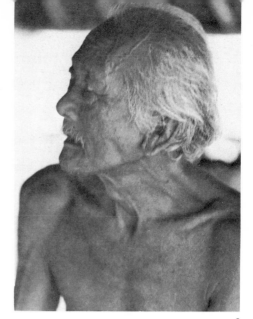

1

2

3

4

PLATE XI
Balinese Artists
Holt, 1950's

1. Ida Bagus Njana of Mas, 1956 CH 688
2. Gusti Njoman Lempad of Ubud, 1956
CH 627
3. Scene from the Brayut Story. Ink drawing
by Gusti Njoman Lempad, Ubud, Bali, 1950.
Collection of A. M. Bruyns. 13 x 9½.
4. Carving by Ida Bagus Njana of Mas, 1955
CH 157

1

PLATE XII
Visual and Kinaesthetic Learning
Bateson, 1936

(This appeared as Plate 16, *Visual and Kinaesthetic Learning II,*
from *Balinese Character: A Photographic Analysis,* by Gregory
Bateson and Margaret Mead.)

Teaching by muscular rote in which the pupil is made to perform the correct movements is most strikingly developed in the dancing lesson.

Mario of Tabanan, the teacher in this sequence, is the dancer chiefly responsible for the evolution of the *kebiar* dance which has become very popular in Bali in the last twenty years. The dance is performed sitting in a square space surrounded by the instruments of the orchestra, but though the principal emphasis is upon the head and hands, the dance involves the whole body, and Mario has introduced a great deal of virtuosity into the difficult feat of rapid locomotion without rising from the sitting position. The chief faults in the pupil's dancing are that he dances only with his head and arms, and does not show the disharmonic tensions characteristic of the dance.

This sequence of photographs illustrates two essential points in Balinese character formation. From his dancing lesson, the pupil learns passivity, and he acquires a separate awareness in the different parts of the body.

1. The pupil dances alone while Mario watches in the background. Note the imperfect development of the pupil's finger posture.

2. Mario comes forward to show the pupil how it should be danced.

3. Mario urges the pupil to straighten up the small of his back. Note that this instruction is given by gesture rather than by words.

4. Mario's hand position and facial expression while demonstrating.

5. Mario takes the pupil by the wrists and swings him across the dancing space.

6. Mario makes his pupil dance correctly by holding his hands and forcing him to move as

he should. Note that Mario is actually dancing in this photograph, and that he postures with his fingers even while holding the pupil's hands. The position of Mario's left elbow in these photographs is characteristic of the tensions developed in this dance.

7. Mario even assumes the conventional sweet impersonal smile of the dancer while he moves the pupil's arms and holds the pupil tightly between his knees to correct his tendency to bend the small of his back.

8. Mario again tries to correct the pupil's tendency to bend his back.

I Mario of Tabanan teaching I Dewa P. Djaja of Kedere.

Tabanan. Dec. 1, 1936. 3 O 11, 13, 14, 17, 21, 22, 23, 25.

3

4

5

6

7

8

PLATE XIII
Balinese Industrialization
Bateson, 1937

(This appeared as Plate 6, *Industrialization,* from *Balinese Character: A Photographic Analysis,* by Gregory Bateson and Margaret Mead.)

Closely connected with the Balinese love of crowded scenes is the tendency to reduce all tasks to separate stages with a definite sequence of bodily movements necessary at each stage. The movements are then performed smoothly and fast, laughing and singing, with a minimum of conscious attention to the task. There is also a tendency to arrange matters so that a maximum number of items can be accomplished simultaneously. Thus the Balinese habit of muscular rote behavior combines with their love of busy and active crowds to give something which we might call "mass production" methods. Their "mass production" differs, however, from our own in lacking any emphasis on efficiency. There are always many more people present, e.g., at the cooking for a feast, than are necessary; and people enter and leave the working group constantly and casually.

1. A Brahman priest (*pedanda brahmana boda*) making holy water (*toja pengentas*) for cremation ceremonies. He sits with several dozen pots of water in front of him, going through his prayers. He prepares one pot of special holy water, which then is diluted into all the pots.

Batoean. Aug. 24, 1937.   14 V 16.

2. Preparing offerings for a ceremony (*metjaroe*) to purify the house yard. First a large number of little leaf trays are folded and stitched; then the trays are laid out; then each tray is filled (as in photograph) from mass stores of each appropriate object. One woman puts a special kind of cake in each tray; another distributes little puddings; another betel; and another flowers, etc.

Men Minab and Men Lemek in foreground; I Maring looking up; I Rendoet behind I Maring.

Bajoeng Gede. July 14, 1937.   12 P 13.

3. Men preparing bamboo pegs for marking out the land in the annual sharing of the temple land.

Left to right: Nang Singin; Nang Soni; Nang Ringin; Djero Keneh in background.

Bajoeng Gede. April 27, 1937.   7 K 3.

4. Three carvings of a man with a duck in one hand and a flag for herding ducks in the other. This subject was for a time very popular with Balinese carvers working for the tourist market. These three specimens were all made by the same artist. It is usual to make such carvings in parallel stages. First, the carver collects a number of suitable pieces of wood; then he roughly carves all of them; next, he finishes the carving on all; and finally polishes them.

Carved in Pajangan.

Bajoeng Gede. June 9, 1937.   11 O 28.

5 and 6. Scenes at a post-mortuary ceremony (*metoeoen*) in which the dead speak through the mouth of the village priestess (*Djero Balian*) in trance. Women prepare piles of banana leaf plates, each with a little cooked rice and a stick of *sate* (cf. Fig. 8). One woman holds the plates; another adds the rice; another, the *sate;* and when each pile of plates is complete it is passed up to the priestess who holds it a moment and speaks as a particular ghost. After the priestess has spoken, the pile is broken up; all the rice is put together in a basket, the *sate* in another basket, and the leaf plates are passed back to the beginning of the work line to be stacked again with more rice and *sate*. Each pile must have the correct number of layers according to the number of deaths in that household since the ceremony was last held (3 plates for one death; 5 for two; 7 or 9 for three; 11 for four deaths, etc). The work involves rapid mechanical movements in cooperation and is accompanied all the time by counting. A European participating is rapidly reduced to a slightly dissociated state.

Bajoeng Gede. July 10, 1937.   12 G 26, 13.

7. Girls shredding tree fern leaves for cooking at a wedding. The leaflets must be stripped from the stalks.

I Gedir; I Njantel; and I Renoe.

Bajoeng Gede. Aug. 18, 1937.   13 P 30.

8. Mass production of *sate* for a tooth-filing ceremony. *Sate* are small sticks on which meat is spiked or pulped food is smeared. Here several hundred such sticks of food are being cooked simultaneously over a long narrow charcoal fire. They are held in place by sticking them into a banana stem. They must be turned from time to time. Note the folded posture of the boy pausing in this task.

On the extreme right, I Tompelos; others not identified.

Batoean. Sept. 30, 1937.   16 G 3.

1

2

3

4

5

6

7

8

1

2

PLATE XIV
Field Work Postures
Bateson, 1937, and Heyman, 1958

1. Margaret Mead with a group of women waiting for a ceremony in Bajoeng Gede, March, 1937, showing kinaesthetic adjustment to the group. Photo by Gregory Bateson, 4-z-3.
2. Margaret Mead in Bajoeng Gede, December 1957. Photo by Ken Heyman, R-11187-13BB6 #8.

1

2

3

PLATE XV
Twenty Years Later
Heyman, 1957–1958

(These are photographs taken by Ken Heyman, when he and
Margaret Mead made a return visit to Bali in December, 1957,
and January, 1958.)

1. The Kris Dance in which the trancers no longer go into trance, but simply imitate trance. Staged by the Balinese themselves for tourists to photograph. R-11187-BR3 #3

2. N. Oera, the father of I Karba (Plate II, Fig. 1), holding the child of I Karba, while I Gati (the child nurse in Plate II) suckles her own child. R-11187-BF22 #36

3. Teaching a group of dancers in the schoolyard in Den Pasar. Group teaching is replacing the expensive individual teaching shown in Plate XII. R-11187-BG7 #15

1

2

3

PLATE XVI

Dressing for the Dance

Heyman, 1957–1958

1. R-11187-BP11 #33
2. R-11187-BP10 #11
3. R-11187-BP11 #14
Photos by Ken Heyman.

reasons. It was in Bali in 1936 that we made the shift from a short series of photographs designed for illustration to a large corpus of photographs taken in rapid sequence and designed as primary research data (Bateson and Mead 1942; Mead 1939c; Tax and others, eds., 1953).

I have kept as close as possible to the form in which these pictures were originally published in all cases where they have been published before. The numbering within a plate corresponds to the original, as does the spelling. Modern Balinese spelling differs in several respects from the spelling used before the establishment of the Republic, but for the old sources I have kept the exact usage of the period. (*Traditional Balinese Culture*, edited by Jane Belo, 1969, contains a complete transformation into the modern spelling and can be used by anyone interested in conforming to earlier and later publications.) The plate or figure numbers from the original are preserved in the descriptive captions which precede the section. Acknowledgment is made to Gregory Bateson, Claire Holt, Frances Macgregor, Ken Heyman, The New York Academy of Sciences and the executors of the estates of Jane Belo Tannenbaum and Colin McPhee for permission to use photographs from *Trance in Bali* and *Music in Bali*.

It was from the Balinese corpus of some 28,000 stills that it was possible to investigate some of Gesell's hypotheses without going into the field to do new work (Mead and Macgregor 1951). Field workers with highly varied interests and different kinds of photographic skills have worked in Bali. Jane Belo (Belo 1960) has assembled the photographs of a whole group of people, including talented visitors to Bali; Colin McPhee systematically made photographs related to music (McPhee 1966), and Claire Holt to art (Holt 1967). In the collection of papers written by the group who worked together during the late 1940's I have illustrations which illuminate the period (Belo, ed., 1969). Several of the field workers used cine-film also, and films exist which make comparisons possible (Bateson and Mead 1952 a-f). The corpus of Balinese stills will be available for research for years to come. Finally, Ken Heyman went with me to Bali for a return visit in 1957-1958, and returned again in 1968, thus providing the special dimension

of growth of identified individuals. These can be compared, for example, with films and stills of real trance in the late 1930's and films and stills of theatrical representations of trance in the 1950's.

There are however certain cautions that are necessary in using Bali, even as one model for field photography. The Balinese are unusually photogenic and tend to compose in groups so that half the work of photography is done for the photographer. They were unself-conscious about photography, accepting it as part of a life which was in many ways always lived on a stage. They are beautiful in European terms and their light brown skin is easy to photograph and presents none of the sharp contrasts provided by exceedingly dark or exceedingly light skins, especially in very deep shade, on beaches, at high noon, or under glaring sunlight.

Indonesia provided technical services of a high order. Although the whole Bateson corpus was developed in the field, from 35 millimeter to bulk film cut and wound in the field, there were facilities available for printing and for the development of cine-film in the 1930's.

In other parts of the primitive world many of these conditions do not obtain: photography may be deeply resented, conditions for the preservation of films may be very difficult, cameras may deteriorate, situations may be much less manageable, as ceremonials which take place at night in very confined spaces, or a field worker who lacks photographic rapport and may not be able to work close up. We cannot ask every field anthropologist to be either a great photographer or a specialist in photographic rapport, which is very special in character. In such cases, it may be useful to ask a well-trained and experienced field photographer to visit the field while the anthropologist is there to direct his attention to appropriate subjects. I have very little doubt that when other forms of field work can be combined with a particular skill such as a cine skill, these produce the most economical and satisfactory results. But there are enough accidents of personality involved in field work in any event not to multiply such demands. Photography gives an opportunity for the nonverbal field worker to bring back magnificent research data. But each field worker should test and know his limits in the use of the camera.

BIBLIOGRAPHY

The following bibliography includes items cited and
deemed relevant to this chapter.

ABEL, THEODORA M., and RHODA MÉTRAUX
1956 Pruebas projectivas en una communidad
rural: Montserrat. *Criminalia* (Mexico)
22:100–108.
1959 Sex differences in a Negro peasant community: Montserrat, B.W.I. *Journal of
Projective Techniques,* 23:127–133.

ADAMS, RICHARD N., and JACK J. PREISS
1960 *Human organization research: field relations and techniques.* Homewood, Ill.,
Dorsey Press.

AMERICAN ANTHROPOLOGICAL ASSOCIATION
Symposium on field training, Thursday,
November 17, 1966, Sixty-fifth annual
meetings of the American Anthropological Association, Pittsburgh, Pennsylvania, November 17–20, 1966.

BALIKCI, ASEN
1969 *The Netsilik Eskimos.* Garden City,
N.Y., Natural History Press.

BARTLETT, FREDERIC C., and others (eds.)
1939 *The study of society: methods and problems.* London, Kegan Paul, Trench,
Trubner.

BASCOM, WILLIAM R.
1941 Anthropology and the camera. In Willard
D. Morgan, ed., *The complete photographer.* Chicago, National Educational
Alliance.

BATESON, GREGORY
1936 *Naven.* Cambridge, England, Cambridge
University Press; 2nd edition, 1958, Stanford, Stanford University Press, reprinted
1966, Stanford, Stanford University Press.
1937 An old temple and a new myth. *Djawa*
17:291–307.
1941 Experiments in thinking about observed
ethnological material. *Philosophy of Science* 8:53–68.
1947 Sex and culture. *Annals of the New
York Academy of Sciences,* 57, Art.
5:647–660.

BATESON, GREGORY, and MARGARET MEAD
1942 *Balinese character: a photographic analysis.* New York, New York Academy of
Sciences; reissued 1962.
1952a *A Balinese family.* Character Formation
in Different Cultures Series, New York
University Film Library, 16mm, 17 min.,
sound.
1952b *Bathing babies in three cultures.* Character Formation in Different Cultures

Series, New York University Film Library, 16mm, 9 min., sound.
1952c *Childhood rivalry in Bali and New
Guinea.* Character Formation in Different
Cultures Series, New York University
Film Library, 16 mm, 20 min., sound.
1952d *First days in the life of a New Guinea
baby.* Character Formation in Different
Cultures Series, New York University
Film Library, 16 mm, 19 min., sound.
1952e *Karba's first years.* Character Formation
in Different Cultures Series, New York
University Film Library, 16 mm, 20
min., sound.
1952f *Trance and dance in Bali.* Character
Formation in Different Cultures Series,
New York University Film Library, 16
mm, 20 min., sound.

BEALS, RALPH L., and Executive Board
1967 Background information on problems of
anthropological research and ethics. *Fellow Newsletter* (American Anthropological Association) 8:1–13.

BELO, JANE
1935 A study of customs pertaining to twins
in Bali. *Tidschrift voor Ind. Taal-,
Land-, en Volkenkunde* 75:483–549.
1949 *Bali: Rangda and Barong.* Monographs of
the American Ethnological Society, 16.
New York, Augustin.
1953 *Bali: Temple festival.* New York, Augustin.
1960 *Trance in Bali.* New York, Columbia
University Press.
1969 *Traditional Balinese culture.* New York,
Columbia University Press.

BENNETT, JOHN W.
1948 The study of cultures: a survey of technique and methodology in field work.
American Anthropologist 13:672–689.
1960 Individual perspective in field work; an
experimental training course. In Richard
N. Adams and Jack J. Preiss, eds.,
Human organization research. Homewood, Ill., Dorsey Press.

BIRDWHISTELL, RAY L.
1952 *Introduction to kinesics: an annotation
system for analysis of body motion and
gesture.* Louisville, University of Louisville.
1958 Family structure and social mobility.

Transactions of the New York Academy of Sciences, Ser. 2, XXI, No. 2.

1959 Contribution of linguistic-kinesic studies to the understanding of schizophrenia. In Alfred Auerback, ed., *Schizophrenia: an integrated approach*. New York, Ronald.

1962 An approach to communication. *Family Process* 1:194–201.

1963 The kinesic level in the investigation of the emotions. In Peter H. Knapp, ed., *Expression of the emotions in man*. New York International Universities Press.

BOHANNAN, LAURA

1958 Political aspects of Tiv social organization. In John Middleton and David Tait, eds., *Tribes without rulers*. London, Routledge and Paul.

BOHANNAN, LAURA, and PAUL BOHANNAN

1953 *The Tiv of Central Nigeria*. London, International African Institute.

BOWEN, ELENORE S. (LAURA BOHANNAN)

1954 *Return to laughter*. New York, Harper; reprinted 1964, Natural History Library, Garden City, N.Y., Doubleday.

BYERS, PAUL

1964 Still photography in the analysis of behavioral data. *Human Organization* 23: 78–84.

1966 Cameras don't take pictures. *Columbia University Forum* 9:27–31.

CASAGRANDE, JOSEPH B. (ed.)

1960 *In the company of man. Twenty portraits by anthropologists*. New York, Harper; reprinted 1964, New York, Harper and Row.

CHAPPLE, ELIOT D.

1953 The standard experimental (stress) interview as used in interaction chronograph investigations. *Human Organization* 12:23–32.

COLBY, BENJAMIN N.

1966 Cultural patterns in narrative. *Science*, 151, 3712:793–798.

COLLIER, JOHN, JR.

1957 Photography in anthropology: a report on two experiments. *American Anthropologist* 59:843–859.

CONDOMINAS, GEORGES

1965 *L'exotique est quotidien*. Paris, Plon.

CUSSLER, MARGARET

1948 The documentary film and the scientist producer. *American Anthropologist* 50: 364–365.

DENNIS, WAYNE

1940 *The Hopi child*. New York, Appleton-Century; reprinted 1965, Science Editions, New York, Wiley.

DOLLARD, JOHN

1935 *Criteria for the life history*. New York, Peter Smith.

DUBOIS, CORA

1944 *The people of Alor*. Minneapolis, University of Minnesota Press; reprinted 1961, New York, Harper and Row.

DYHRENFURTH, NORMAN

1952 Film making for scientific field workers. *American Anthropologist* 54:147–152.

FIRTH, RAYMOND

1936 *We, the Tikopia*. London, Allen and Unwin; reprinted 1963, Boston, Beacon Press.

1957 (ed.) *Man and culture; an evaluation of the work of Bronislaw Malinowski*. New York, Humanities Press; reprinted 1964, New York, Harper and Row.

1959 *Social change in Tikopia*. New York, Macmillan.

FORCE, ROLAND B.

1960 Methodology. [In] Leadership and cultural change in Palau. *Fieldiana: Anthropology* (Chicago Natural History Museum) 50:171–181.

FORTUNE, REO

1935 *Manus religion*. Memoirs of the American Philosophical Society, Vol. 3; reprinted 1965, Lincoln, University of Nebraska.

GARDNER, ROBERT

1964 *Dead birds*. Cambridge, Peabody Museum, Harvard University. Distributed by Contemporary Films, New York, 16 mm, 83 min., sound, color.

GARDNER, ROBERT, and KARL G. HEIDER

1969 *Gardens of war*. New York, Random House.

GEERTZ, CLIFFORD J.

1960 *The religion of Java*. Glencoe, Ill., Free Press; reprinted 1964, Glencoe, Free Press.

GLADWIN, THOMAS, and SEYMOUR B. SARASON

1953 *Truk: man in paradise*. Viking Fund Publications in Anthropology, No. 20, Wenner-Gren Foundation for Anthropological Research.

GLUCKMAN, MAX

1964 *Closed systems and open minds*. Edinburgh, Oliver and Boyd.

1965 *Politics, law and ritual in tribal society*. Chicago, Aldine.

GOLDSCHMIDT, WALTER, PHILIP W. PORTER, SYMMES C. OLIVER, FRANCIS P. CONANT, EDGAR V. WINANS, and ROBERT B. EDGERTON

1965 Variation and adaptability of culture. *American Anthropologist* 67:400–447.

GORER, GEOFFREY

1938 *Himalayan village*. London, Joseph; reprinted 1967, New York, Basic Books.

1955 *Exploring English character*. New York, Criterion Books; London, Cresset Press.

1965 *Death, grief and mourning*. Garden City, N.Y., Doubleday; London, Cresset.

GORER, GEOFFREY, and JOHN RICKMAN
1949   *The people of great Russia.* London, Cresset Press; reprinted 1950, New York, Chanticleer Press; 1962, New York, Norton.

HALL, EDWARD T.
1959   *The silent language.* Garden City, N.Y., Doubleday; reprinted 1961, New York, Fawcett Publications.
1963   A system for the notation of proxemic behavior. *American Anthropologist* 65: 1003–1026.
1966   *The hidden dimension.* Garden City, N.Y., Doubleday.

HENRY, JULES
1940   A method for learning to talk primitive languages. *American Anthropologist* 43: 635–641.
1949   Cultural objectification of the case history. *American Journal of Orthopsychiatry* 19:655–673.

HILGER, M. INEZ
1954   An ethnographic field method. In Robert F. Spencer, ed., *Method and perspective in anthropology.* Minneapolis, University of Minnesota Press.
1966   *Huenun Ñamku: an Araucanian Indian of the Andes remembers the past.* Norman, University of Oklahoma Press.

HITCHCOCK, JOHN T., and PATRICIA J. HITCHCOCK
1960   Some considerations for the prospective ethnographic cinematographer. *American Anthropologist* 62:656–674.

HOGBIN, H. IAN
1935a Adoption in Wogeo, New Guinea. *Journal of the Polynesian Society* 44:208–215.
1935b Native culture of Wogeo: report of field work in New Guinea. *Oceania* 5:308–337.
1936   Adoption in Wogeo, New Guinea. *Journal of the Polynesian Society* 45:17–38.
1943   A New Guinea infancy from conception to weaning in Wogeo. *Oceania* 13:285–309.
1945   Marriage in Wogeo, New Guinea. *Oceania* 15:324–352.
1952   Sorcery and succession in Wogeo. *Oceania* 23:133–136.

HOLT, CLAIRE
1967   *Art in Indonesia.* Ithaca, Cornell University Press.

JABLONKO, ALLISON
1968   *Dance and daily activities among the Maring people of New Guinea: a cinematographic analysis of body movement style.* Ph.D. thesis. New York, Columbia University.

KARDINER, ABRAM
1939   *The individual and his society.* New York, Columbia University Press.

KENNEDY, PETER, ALAN LOMAX and GEORGE PICKOW
1952   *OSS, OSS, WEE OSS.* Made in Padstow, Cornwall, May 1, 1952, for the English Folk Dance and Song Society. Distributed by the New York Country Dance Society of America, 16 mm, 25 min., sound, color.

LABAN, RUDOLF VON
1956   *Principles of dance and movement notation.* New York, Sweetman; London, Macdonald and Evans.

LAMBERT, WILLIAM W., and LEIGH MINTURN
1964   *Mothers of six cultures: antecedence of child rearing.* New York and London, Wiley.

LEACH, E. R.
1954   *Political systems of highland Burma.* Cambridge, Harvard University Press; reprinted 1965, Boston, Beacon Press.

LÉVI-STRAUSS, CLAUDE
1948   The Nambicuara. In Julian H. Steward, ed., *Handbook of South American Indians,* Vol. 3. Washington, Smithsonian Institution, Bureau of American Ethnology, Bulletin 143, pp. 361–370.
1961   *A world on the wane.* London, Hutchinson; republished 1964 as *Tristes tropiques: an anthropological study of primitive societies in Brazil.* New York, Atheneum.

LEWIS, OSCAR
1951   *Life in a Mexican village: Tepoztlán restudied.* Urbana, University of Illinois Press; reprinted 1963, Urbana, University of Illinois Press.
1953   Controls and experiments in field work. In A. L. Kroeber, ed., *Anthropology today.* Chicago, University of Chicago Press.
1959   *Five families: Mexican case studies in the culture of poverty.* New York, Basic Books; reprinted 1965, New York, New American Library.
1960   *Tepoztlán, village in Mexico.* New York, Holt, Rinehart and Winston.
1961   *The children of Sánchez.* New York, Random House; reprinted 1961, New York, Random House.
1966a *La vida.* New York, Random House.
1966b The culture of poverty. *Scientific American* 215, 4:19–25.

LOMAX, ALAN (ed.)
1968   *Folksong style and culture.* Symposium Vol. No. 88. Washington, American Association for the Advancement of Science.

LOWENFELD, MARGARET
1954   *The Lowenfeld mosaic test.* London, Newman Neame.

LOWIE, ROBERT H.

1922 *Crow Indian art.* Anthropological Papers of the American Museum of Natural History, Vol. 21, Part 4.

1935 *The Crow Indians.* New York, Farrar and Rinehart; reissued 1956, New York, Rinehart.

1945 *The German people.* New York, Farrar and Rinehart.

1959 *Robert H. Lowie, ethnologist: a personal record.* Berkeley, University of California Press.

1966 Scholars as people: dreams, idle dreams. *Current Anthropology* 7:378–382.

MALINOWSKI, BRONISLAW

1922 *Argonauts of the western Pacific.* London, Routledge; reprinted 1961, New York, Dutton.

MCPHEE, COLIN

1935 The "absolute" music of Bali. *Modern Music* 12:163–169.

1936 The Balinese *wajang koelit* and its music. *Djawa* 16:1–50.

1937 *Angkloeng* music in Bali. *Djawa* 17:322–366.

1938 Children and music in Bali. *Djawa* 18:1–15; reprinted 1955 in Margaret Mead and Margaret Wolfenstein, eds., *Childhood in contemporary cultures.* Chicago, Chicago University Press.

1939 *Gamelan*-muziek van Bali, Ondergang-schemering van een Kunst. *Djawa* 19:183–185.

1940 Figuration in Balinese music. *Peabody Bulletin,* Ser. 36:23–26.

1944 In this far island, Pt. 1. *Asia and the Americas* 44:533–537.

1945 In this far island, Pts. 2–8. *Asia and the Americas* 45:38–45, 109–114, 157–162, 206–210, 257–261, 305–309, 350–354.

1946 *A House in Bali.* New York, John Day.

1948 *A club of small men.* New York, John Day.

1949a Dance in Bali. *Dance Index* 7, Nos. 7–8:156–207.

1949b Five-tone *Gamelan* music of Bali. *Musical Quarterly* 35:250–281.

1966 *Music in Bali.* New Haven and London. Yale University Press.

MEAD, MARGARET

1931 The primitive child. In Carl Murchison, ed., *A handbook of child psychology.* Worcester, Mass., Clark University Press.

1933a More comprehensive field methods. *American Anthropologist* 35:1–15.

1933b Where magic rules and men are gods. *The New York Times Magazine,* June 25, 1933, 8–9, 18.

1935 Review of *The riddle of the sphinx,* by Géza Róheim. *Character and personality* 4:85–90.

1937 (ed.) *Cooperation and competition among primitive peoples.* New York and London, McGraw-Hill; reprinted enlarged edition 1961, Boston, Beacon Press.

1938 *The Mountain Arapesh. I. An importing culture.* Anthropological Papers of the American Museum of Natural History, Vol. 36, Part 3; to be reprinted with Vol. II. Garden City, N.Y., Natural History Press.

1939a Men and gods of a Bali village. *The New York Times Magazine,* July 16, 1939, 12–13, 23.

1939b Native languages as field-work tools. *American Anthropologist* 41:189–205.

1939c Researches in Bali, 1936–1939. *Transactions of the New York Academy of Sciences,* Ser. 2, 2, No. 1:24–31.

1939d Review of *Himalayan village,* by Geoffrey Gorer. *Oceania* 9:344–353.

1939e The strolling players in the mountains of Bali. *Natural History* 43:17–26, 64.

1940 *The Mountain Arapesh. II. Supernaturalism.* Anthropological Papers of the American Museum of Natural History, Vol. 37, Part 3; to be reprinted with Vol. I as Vol. II. Garden City, N.Y., Natural History Press.

1941a Review of *The Hopi child,* by Wayne Dennis. *American Anthropologist* 43:95–97.

1941b Review of *The individual and his society,* by Abram Kardiner. *American Journal of Orthopsychiatry* 11:603–605.

1942 Educative effects of social environment as disclosed by studies of primitive societies. In E. W. Burgess, ed., *Environment and education.* Chicago: University of Chicago Press.

1946 Review of *A house in Bali,* by Colin McPhee. *The New York Times Book Review,* September 29, 1946, p. 7.

1947 *The Mountain Arapesh. III. Socio-economic life, and IV. Diary of events in Alitoa.* Anthropological Papers of the American Museum of Natural History, Vol. 40, Part 3; to be reprinted as Vol. III. Garden City, N.Y., Natural History Press.

1949a *Male and female.* New York, Morrow; reprinted 1955, New York, New American Library.

1949b *The Mountain Arapesh. V. The record of Unabelin with Rorschach analyses.* Anthropological Papers of the American Museum of Natural History, Vol. 41, Part 3; reprinted 1968 as Vol. I. Garden City, N.Y., Natural History Press.

1952 The training of the cultural anthropologist. *American Anthropologist* 54:343–346.

1954a Research on primitive children. In Leonard Carmichael, ed., *Manual of child psychology*, 2nd ed. New York, Wiley.

1954b The swaddling hypothesis: its reception. *American Anthropologist* 56:395–409.

1955 Applied anthropology, 1955. In Joseph B. Casagrande and Thomas Gladwin, eds., *Some uses of anthropology: theoretical and applied*. Washington, Anthropological Society of Washington.

1956a *New lives for old: cultural transformation—Manus, 1928–1953.* New York, Morrow; reprinted 1966, New York, Morrow.

1956b Some uses of still photography in culture and personality studies. In Douglas G. Haring, ed., *Personal character and cultural milieu*, 3rd ed. Syracuse, Syracuse University Press.

1959a *An anthropologist at work: writings of Ruth Benedict.* Boston, Houghton Mifflin.

1959b Apprenticeship under Boas. In Walter Goldschmidt, ed., The anthropology of Franz Boas. American Anthropological Association, Memoir No. 89, pp. 29–45.

1959c Bali in the market place of the world. *Proceedings of the American Academy of Arts and Letters and the National Institute of Arts and Letters* Ser. 2, No. 9, pp. 286–293.

1959d *People and places.* Cleveland and New York, World Publishing Company; reprinted 1963, New York, Bantam Books.

1961– *New lives for old.* Horizons of Science
1962 Series, I, No. 6, Princeton, N. J., Educational Testing Service, 16mm, 20 min., sound, color.

1963 Anthropology and the camera. In Willard D. Morgan, ed., *The encyclopedia of photography*. New York, Greystone Press.

1964 *Continuities in cultural evolution.* New Haven, Yale University Press; reprinted 1966, New Haven, Yale University Press.

1966 Anthropologist in the field. Review of *stranger and friend*, by H. Powdermaker. New York, Viking Press. *Holiday* 39:113–115.

MEAD, MARGARET, and PAUL BYERS
1968 *The small conference: an innovation in communication.* The Hague, Mouton.

MEAD, MARGARET, and FRANCES C. MACGREGOR
1951 *Growth and culture: a photographic study of Balinese childhood.* New York, Putnam.

MEAD, MARGARET, and RHODA MÉTRAUX
1953 *The study of culture at a distance.* Chicago, University of Chicago Press.

MEAD, MARGARET, and MARTHA WOLFENSTEIN (eds.)
1955 *Childhood in contemporary cultures.* Chicago, University of Chicago Press;

reprinted 1963, Chicago, University of Chicago Press.

MÉTRAUX, RHODA
1957 Montserrat, B.W.I.: some implications of suspended culture change. *Transactions of the New York Academy of Sciences*, Ser. 2, XX, No. 2.

1968 Malinowski, Bronislaw. In David L. Sills, ed., *International encyclopedia of the social sciences*, Vol. 9. New York, Macmillan and Free Press.

MÉTRAUX, RHODA, and THEODORA M. ABEL
1957 Normal and deviant behavior in a peasant community: Montserrat, B.W.I. *American Journal of Orthopsychiatry* 27:167–184.

MÉTRAUX, RHODA, and MARGARET MEAD
1957 *Themes in French culture: a preface to a study of French community.* Stanford, Stanford University Press.

PIKE, KENNETH L.
1947 *Phonemics: a technique for reducing languages to writing.* University of Michigan Publications in Linguistics, Vol. 3.

POLUNIN, IVAN V.
1965 Stereophonic magnetic tape recorders and the collection of ethnographic field data. *Current Anthropology* 6:227–230.

POWDERMAKER, HORTENSE
1939 *After freedom.* New York, Viking Press.
1966 *Stranger and friend.* New York, Norton.

READ, KENNETH E.
1965 *The high valley.* New York, Scribner's.

REDFIELD, ROBERT
1950 *A village that chose progress: Chan Kom revisited.* Chicago, University of Chicago Press; reprinted 1962, Chicago, University of Chicago Press.

REDFIELD, ROBERT, and ALFONSO VILLA ROJAS
1934 *Chan Kom: a Maya village.* Carnegie Institution of Washington, Publication No. 448; reprinted abridged edition 1962, Chicago, University of Chicago Press.

ROE, ANNE
1953 *A psychological study of eminent psychologists and anthropologists, and a comparison with biological and physical scientists.* Washington, American Psychological Association.

RÓHEIM, GÉZA
1934 *The riddle of the sphinx.* London, Hogarth.

1941 The psycho-analytic interpretation of culture. *International Journal of Psycho-Analysis* 22, Part 2:147–169.

ROWE, JOHN H.
1953 Technical aids in anthropology: a historical survey. In A. L. Kroeber, ed., *Anthropology today*. Chicago, University of Chicago Press.

SCHWARTZ, THEODORE
1962 *The Paliau movement in the Admiralty Islands, 1946–1954.* Anthropological Papers of the American Museum of Natural History, Vol. 49, Part 2.
1963 Systems of areal integration: some considerations based on the Admiralty Islands of Northern Melanesia. *Anthropological Forum,* 1:56–97.

SCHWARTZ, THEODORE, and MARGARET MEAD
1961 Micro- and macro-cultural models for cultural evolution. *Anthropological Linguistics* 3:1–7.

SEBEOK, THOMAS A., ALFRED S. HAYES, and MARY CATHERINE BATESON (eds.)
1964 *Approaches to semiotics.* The Hague, Mouton.

SLATER, MARIAM K
n. d. *Effects of field work on the anthropologist as a humanist.* Symposium AAAS, Section H, Washington, December, 1966.

SMALLEY, WILLIAM A.
1960 Making and keeping anthropological field notes. *Practical Anthropology* 7:145–152.

SORENSON, E. RICHARD, and D. CARLETON GAJDUSEK
1966 The study of child behavior and development in primitive cultures. *Supplement to Pediatrics* 37:145–243.

STURTEVANT, WILLIAM C.
1959 A technique for ethnographic note-taking. *American Anthropologist* 61:677–678.
1964 Studies in ethnoscience. In A. Kimball Romney and Roy G. D'Andrade, eds., Transcultural studies in cognition. *American Anthropologist,* Special Publication 66:99–131.

TAX, SOL, and others (eds.)
1953 Technological aids in anthropology. In *An appraisal of anthropology today.* Chicago, University of Chicago Press.

TURNBULL, COLIN M.
1961 *The forest people.* New York, Simon and Schuster; reprinted 1962, Natural History Library, Garden City, N.Y., Doubleday.
1965a *The Mbuti Pygmies.* Anthropological Papers of the American Museum of Natural History, Vol. 50, Part 3.
1965b *Wayward servants.* Garden City, N.Y., Natural History Press.

TURNER, V. W.
1957 *Schism and continuity in an African society. A study of Ndembu village life.* Manchester, Manchester University Press.

WARNER, W. LLOYD
1937 *A black civilization.* New York, Harper; reprinted 1964, New York, Harper and Row.

WATSON, JAMES B.
1963 A micro-evolution study in New Guinea, *Journal of the Polynesian Society* 72:188–192.

WAX, ROSALIE H.
1960a Reciprocity in field work. In Richard N. Adams and Jack J. Preiss, eds., *Human organization research.* Homewood, Ill., Dorsey Press.
1960b Twelve years later: an analysis of field experience. In Richard N. Adams and Jack J. Preiss, eds., *Human organization research,* Homewood, Ill., Dorsey Press.

WERNER, OSWALD
1961 *Ethnographic photography.* M.A. thesis. Syracuse, Syracuse University.

WHITING, BEATRICE B. (ed.)
1963 *Six cultures: studies of child rearing.* New York and London, Wiley.

WILLIAMS, THOMAS R.
1965 *The Dusun: A North Borneo society.* New York, Holt, Rinehart and Winston.
1967 *Field methods in the study of culture.* New York, Holt, Rinehart and Winston.

WYLIE, LAURENCE
1957 *Village in the Vaucluse.* Cambridge, Harvard University Press; reprinted 1964, New York, Harper and Row.
1966 (ed.) *Chanzeaux: A village in Anjou.* Cambridge, Harvard University Press.

CHAPTER 15

Sampling in Ethnographic Field Work

JOHN J. HONIGMANN

TWO KINDS OF SAMPLING

An ethnographer cannot avoid selecting some people, objects, or events for study, thereby renouncing, for a time at least, the possibility of studying others. From a vast range of possibilities, he takes up work in a particular tribe, village, or town; questions certain respondents; employs a few informants; observes some artifacts, situations, or behavioral events, and makes observations at restricted times. If the word "sampling" is used so broadly, then field workers are constantly sampling the universe of people, situations, objects, and behavioral events with which they are occupied. Seldom, however, do they keep track of how they drew a sample or report its composition. Even statements as general as my pseudonymous list of principal Kaska Indian informants and subjects (Honigmann, 1949:27) and Margaret Mead's (1928:250–252) "neighbourhood maps" identifying the adolescent and preadolescent girls she observed, are rare. An anthropologist characteristically extends his remarks beyond his sample and talks about "the" Kaska Indians and Samoan girls or about child rearing, quarrels, and pottery techniques in general—as though he had studied the community, category, or topic exhaustively. The usual spoken implication is that for his problem, the sample adequately represented a larger universe of actors, topics, culture patterns, techniques, or other units under study and therefore could provide reliable information about that universe as it existed at a particular time. A statistically conscious observer might object and point out that for a sample to be considered in a strict sense representative of the universe whence it came, it must have been selected in a suitable manner. Anthropologists are likely to respond by protesting that it is not they who decide what persons or events to use as source of data; such decisions are practically made for them when certain individuals volunteer their help, some groups extend welcome, and some techniques happen to be accessible to observation (Festinger and Katz 1953:173). That units force themselves on a researcher's attention is merely a figure of speech. It overlooks the field worker's readiness to respond positively or negatively to certain cues in the field situation and ignores his active involvement in deciding how to respond to environmental opportunities or when to surrender to unbreachable limitations.

However strongly some stimuli "compel" the ethnographer's attention, it will repay him to be aware of the character of his sample, beginning with the basic distinction between nonprobability and probability methods of drawing it. The first term refers to sampling in the general sense in which I have so far used the word. Probability sampling designates a method that specifically intends every unit in the universe under study to have the same known probability of being studied. If the universe totals 100 people, houses, hours, or garden plots, and we want to study 10, then the probability of any unit being included in the sample is 1 in 10. Actual selection of a probability sample follows definite rules, the most important one requiring the units of the sample to be drawn at random; hence the familiar name for such sampling, random sampling. The unparalleled advantages of probability sampling, which recommend it for certain kinds of social science research, will be pointed out in due course. My object in this chapter is to review both types of sampling as they have been or can be applied in ethnography. I shall develop, first, how anthropologists use and defend use of nonprobability sampling methods in studies of culture and then review random sampling. Since certain procedures connected with defining the universe to be sampled before actual sampling begins are common to both probability and nonprobability sampling, they will be mentioned in both places.

NONPROBABILITY SAMPLING

Selecting a Place to Work

If cultural anthropology is ultimately concerned with achieving generalizations applicable to man in general, then sampling begins when an ethnographer chooses to explore the lifeways of one social aggregate rather than another and, having made that choice, narrows down his objective to look for a locality to settle in. John Beattie (1965:3–13) chose Bunyoro on the advice of an Africanist after discovering that another anthropologist had already begun to work with the group of his first choice. Out of the many local communities constituting Bunyoro, he sought one that, as far as he could judge at the time, was "reasonably representative . . . as typical as possible of rural Bunyoro." Judgment sampling of this sort, which seeks to meet specific criteria, is most likely to be successful when it is informed by expert knowledge. Beattie, being a novice, gained such knowledge from others, a relatively rich literature undoubtedly assisting him in making his choice. He also wanted a community off the main roads and away from bureaucratic centers, yet reasonably accessible. Criteria for selecting a site may follow logically from the research problem and accompanying theory. Southall and Gutkind (1956:ix–x) in their survey of Kampala sought two areas for their sample survey, one to represent the densest type of uncontrolled and primarily African urban settlement in the Kampala area and the other an intermediate situation representing a transition toward maximal density from a previously

rural comunity. In 1952 I went to Pakistan to study the impact of U.S. informational films on rural audiences, the country itself having been designated for me by an agency in the State Department (Honigmann 1953:2). Available time would permit me to pay reasonably close attention to only three villages and I determined to concentrate them in West Pakistan. Here I sought to sample as much of heterogeneous territory as possible by studying one village in three of the most populous provinces out of the ten or so political units then constituting the country's west wing. This allowed me to include three major languages in my sample; for, I asked myself, if the country possessed several languages how did films containing only Urdu narration communicate their content? When it came to selecting villages, logistics and a sufficient degree of isolation from urban influence became critical guides in judging suitability. In Karachi, Lahore, Peshawar and an upcountry town, I sought to make contacts with knowledgeable people who could recommend a village that would be accessible to a mobile unit carrying projection equipment. Guarantees of welcome and a place to live also influenced my decision where to settle. Specifications for an eligible unit to study may be even more explicit, like those Whiting and his associates (1966: chap. 6) demand for a primary social unit or P.S.U. (cf. Firth 1951:49). Defined as a stable social group located within a larger social group, consisting of about thirty mutually interacting families set off from the larger society by some social factor in such a way that they conceive of themselves as a kind of social unit, a P.S.U. must provide the investigators with variables both antecedent and consequent to child rearing. It represents a culture "cut down to manageable size." Factors of temporal stability and spatial homogeneity listed in decreasing order of importance are: territorial unity; membership in a common kinship group, like a clan; membership in a common school district; common religion; membership in a common economic association; membership in the same social class; and membership in the same recreational group.

Once he settles down in a locality and begins to work, an ethnographer has no way of knowing how the behavior patterns and artifacts he observes represent the social system's larger culture, except as reading or informants extend his knowledge. Yet he may title his monograph to refer to the culture or social system as a whole, only in the prefatory pages incidentally designating the precise universe he investigated.

Selecting People to Study: Judgment and Opportunistic Sampling

Further sampling occurs when the field worker chooses steady informants, perhaps following criteria like those Tremblay (1957) specifies for key informants or else working with whoever turns up and shows a readiness and ability to provide information. Note that I am not so much drawing a distinction between the degrees of intensiveness with which an anthropologist works with people—the informants who are steadily employed and may become practically surrogates of the field worker compared to those only casually observed or engaged in conversation. I am stressing the deliberateness with which any subjects are chosen. Informants selected by virtue of their status (age, sex, occupation) or previous experience, qualities which endow them with special knowledge that the ethnographer values, are chosen by a type of nonprobability sampling best called judgment sampling. The ethnographer uses his prior knowledge of the universe to draw representatives from it who possess distinctive qualifications. He may, for example, select informants or subjects according to class strata, occupational status, sex, age, or length of residence in the community. Spindler (1955:10–11) to a large extent employed judgment sampling in obtaining sixty-eight adult Menomini males, all recorded as being at least one-half Menomini Indian. He selected subjects "to represent all degrees of observable socioeconomic status from the richest to the poorest; and all degrees of cultural participation," or acculturational status. While he would have preferred to draw his sample by some random method, he knew it to be even more important to have subjects of different economic and cultural status with whom he could establish rapport sufficient to obtain the intimate social and psychological data his research problem demanded. He later allowed his subjects a hand in choosing additional respondents:

At each sociocultural level, a few known individuals, friendly to me, were treated with first, then a minimum of three names of other persons was obtained from them and at least one of these persons was obtained as a case, using his acquaintance with the first subject as a means of introduction. These cases in turn designated other possibilities. A number of other cases were "picked up" as contacts were made in many casual conversations.

Spindler recognized the possibility of bias serious enough to affect the outcome of his research arising from the possible selection of persons corresponding to certain personality types. Unconscious selection of persons to whom he could relate, he acknowledges, would have tended to reduce the variability of personality types in his sample. However, inspection of his data gave no evidence that such selection actually operated, except for the fact that only four people he chose declined to cooperate with him. Another example of judgment sampling comes from my own experience. In Frobisher Bay, Baffin Island, I had available abundant payroll records of the town's largest employer of Eskimo labor, the government. My wife and I sampled them for only four months, July and December (1962) and March and May (1963). We sought to cover the year without over-representing the summer season when employment is very high and winter when jobs are scarce (Honigmann and Honigmann 1965:70). Definite limits restrict the extent to which judgment sampling can be applied before the field worker knows something about the composition of the universe being investigated. The population may have to be carefully stratified to allow sufficient representation for important constituent categories, as well as explicitly defined, for example to determine who is a Menomini Indian or what summer and winter are at the latitude of Frobisher Bay. Anthony F. C. Wallace (1952:40–41) is exceptionally clear concerning the way he went about choosing a sample that represented the age and sex distribution of Tuscarora Indians, to whom he proposed to administer Rorschach tests. His census revealed a total of 353 persons sixteen years and older who were sociologically Tuscarora. (He specifies the conscious rule by which he decided who in that sense was a Tuscarora.) Then he calculated the number of records necessary to preserve in the sample the same proportions that existed in the population at large, calculating these figures on the expectation that he could deal with a total of about 100 persons (or Rorschach records). He first allowed an informant to select individuals of requisite age and sex. Later, as Wallace got to know more people, he himself suggested subjects for testing. He justifies logically his belief that these methods of selection introduced very little bias, though once his guide shocked him by commenting on twenty persons who had already been tested, saying they represented the "better element" of Tuscarora society. Apparently the assistant used the word "better" to describe people whom he personally knew and liked and therefore had chosen. This revelation distressed Wallace less than the thought that "better element" might have referred to socioeconomic levels, to which he had given no consideration in preparing his sampling design.

Nonprobability judgment sampling demands a clear-cut definition of the universe about which the sample is intended to provide information. Such a decision is often difficult to make. What is the community and where are its boundaries? (See Leighton *et al.* 1963:40.) How are people in a P.S.U. connected? How shall a Tuscarora Indian be defined? What situations are likely to be most rewarding with certain kinds of information? I will have more to say about the critical judgment required in designing sampling frames in the section devoted to random sampling.

If the concept of sampling is strictly limited to some such *deliberate* selection of typical or representative units, then an anthropologist's partly self-selected informants or subjects for observation are not obtained by sampling at all. However, I have already indicated that I propose to ignore such strict usage. The term "opportunistic sampling" is available for the familiar process by which field workers find many of the people who provide them with ethnographic information. Such sampling follows no strict, logical plan (Parten 1950:242–245). The perimeters of the sampled universe are poorly drawn and the procedure itself is so situationally variable, as well as being idiosyncratically influenced by the personal qualities of the particular ethnographer, that it becomes well-nigh impossible for another person to replicate. I recall one use of opportunistic sampling dur-

ing my first ethnographic trip to West Pakistan. The abundant visitors who voluntarily came to my home served as respondents for innumerable questions; I sought to plumb their motivations and other personality characteristics, and in some cases begged them to take the Rorschach test. Occasionally I solicited my guests with my interview schedule (that had been prepared for a random sample) to learn if they had attended the motion-picture showings and if so what they had seen and heard. Responses from such opportunistically selected subjects were kept separate from those of randomly selected subjects. Subsequently I compared both samples, as I will report later in this chapter. My wife and children also utilized invitations to the homes of relatively well-to-do or high-ranking families as opportunities to observe certain aspects of domestic life and to obtain other information, though success in such matters depended on the extent to which hosts were bilingual or could be conveniently interviewed through a bilingual relative. Such opportunistic sampling can also be called chunk sampling, meaning that the researcher resourcefully seizes any handy chunk of the universe that promises to reward him with relevant information: he observes whatever children or mothers are available, visits receptive households, tests willing adults, records remarks he overhears or has volunteered to him, and attends almost any public meetings, church services, and entertainments that he happens to hear about. But since this method calls for acting opportunistically in all such situations, we might as well call it opportunistic sampling.

Judgment and opportunistic, nonprobability sampling represent degrees of deliberateness exercised in choosing informants, subjects, situations, or behavioral events. One type does not exclude the other. Opportune social contacts may be exploited for the special knowledge they possess, as my wife and I did with the lawyers, farmers, teachers, Islamic scholars, women, and political leaders we met in Pakistan. The information provided by such casually selected respondents is interpreted or evaluated according to the status he or she represents and it possesses limited value until significant dimensions of the person's status have been identified. I shall have more to say about identifying opportunistically selected people or situations and about interpreting the information they provide. Such procedures, which in effect convert opportunistic into judgment samples, have been called distinctive of ethnographic field work.

Selecting Behavior and Situations to Observe

I have spoken about sampling places and people in nonprobability fashion but only incidentally have I mentioned sampling behavioral episodes themselves (which, to be sure, always include people). An ethnographer from time to time deliberately assigns himself to observe particular situations and events. Undoubtedly he initially learns much about an as yet unfamiliar culture by seizing convenient opportunities to study behavior and artifacts that catch his eye and ear. Casual observations of cattle returning to the village, men plowing, carpenters repairing a cart wheel, and mothers interacting with children eventually serve him to construct ethnographic statements about agriculture, industries, and child rearing. Informants may themselves be asked to sample by reporting cases of certain kinds of behavior they have observed, thereby extending the ethnographer's observational range. The photographs and drawings of objects in published monographs report "typical" samples chosen by nonprobability methods. "Typical" in this sense means that an object has been selected for illustration because the author judges it characteristic of the class of objects to which it belongs. In the same way, a typical wedding, game, or other behavioral event may be written up at length. (On the other hand, an episode occurring only once during the researcher's presence in the community is better reported as a single case without any assumption about its typicalness unless informants provide comparative information.)

Sampling for behavior can be quite systematically organized when the ethnographer goes into the field equipped with a carefully planned research design. Whiting and his associates (1966: chap. 5) in a field guide they prepared for studies of socialization in five cultures list a number of observations to be made of children, the object of which is to learn about prescribed situations that arise in various settings in which children spend their day and about how they respond in such situations. "Settings" means general cultural activities limited by time and place (e.g., sleeping, breakfast, playing in the schoolyard after school, etc.), and "situations" designates specific social conditions that instigate responses. Twelve situations likely to promote responses are specified, including assaults, insults, hurts, encounters with difficulties, requests for help, and reprimands. The manual contains procedural rules for identifying such situations and responses in culturally specific terms as well as instructions for classifying the data. An observer is told to construct a schedule of a child's typical day in the P.S.U. where he is working and where he is able to identify specific children. The schedule will indicate settings to be sampled for the situations they contain. He is instructed to make twelve five-minute observations on each child spaced as widely as possible over time and setting to yield a one-hour sample of each child's behavior. The field worker has a problem of distributing his time among the various settings in a way that will maximize observation in settings yielding the richest data and still cover a representative sample of the child's activities. In general, he is told to divide his time in proportion to the time children spend in each setting, to under-sample settings (like sleeping) where the twelve situations occur rarely or where response varies little, and to over-sample settings where situations occur abundantly and response varies greatly. He is also advised to photograph and even to take movies of the most frequent settings a child encounters in a community. The twelve five-minute observations are expected to indicate frequency with which the twelve prescribed situations arise and the probability with which each type occurs. The data will later permit cross-cultural analysis of differences in the probabilities of occurrence as well as differences between subgroups and individuals belonging to the P.S.U. The fact that instructions had to be altered after the ethnographers had reached the field and begun to report on problems facing them in their various locations indicates the difficulty anthropologists face in preplanning their sampling and general research designs before learning something about the culture.

Evaluating Nonprobability Sampling in Anthropology

Nonprobability sampling in ethnography along with associated practices like reliance on nonquantitative procedures and on unimodal patterns of behavior undoubtedly constitute the most debated technique in the field worker's armamentarium. Not only do persons in adjacent disciplines voice skepticism but also, particularly when certain kinds of research like national character studies are involved, anthropologists themselves (Mandelbaum 1953:182). Critics point out that judgment and opportunistic sampling allow no way of knowing precisely the degree to which a sample corresponds to the universe it represents and therefore casts doubt on the reliability, perhaps even the general validity, of the information it provides. To argue that a sample of six hundred Vassar College girls mostly of middle-class background adequately reflects the predominantly middle-class culture of the United States doesn't compensate for the lack of any empirical information about, say, lower-class girls (Codere 1955:65–67). Wallace (1952:42) sampled to ensure a representative age and sex distribution in his adult Tuscarora protocols but did he not invite serious bias to enter his sample by allowing his assistant to select 43 percent of the tested subjects? Bias so introduced may indeed be minor, but the degree to which those subjects represented the Tuscarora adult universe in other than age or sex characteristics must remain clouded by some doubt. Many anthropologists have been troubled by such criticism. Yet most of us continue to use judgment and opportunistic samples and I would not dream of suggesting we cease. We use such samples not primarily because our field problem is usually so enormous and our time so limited that we can't afford to use the several probability samples that our multifaceted research would require in order to be clearly representative. Our adherence to traditional anthropological field-work methods of sampling rests on the assumption that the questions put in research can frequently be satisfactorily answered through samples selected by nonprobability methods.

Why should we expect that nonprobability sampling will work in the study of technology, social structure, and idea systems as anthropologists commonly pursue such topics? What logical reason do we have for believing that judgmental and more casually chosen samples will provide an ethnographer with satisfactory factual information about particular cultural systems? As a minimum definition of satisfactoriness, I would demand that the empirical propositions in an ethnography be objectively replicated in a high proportion of cases. While some notable differences of fact have indeed arisen between anthropologists who have reported on the "same" culture, when the few restudies we have are considered, the extent of agreement between professional investigators who have reported on the "same" culture (given a loose, unstandardized criteria of agreement) seem to outweigh disagreements.[1] This indicates that anthropological sampling works and is to a tolerable degree reliable, given the current standards of ethnographic reliability and my qualitative method of appraising reliability. The question I ask is: Why does it work as well as it does? A general answer holds that a common culture is reflected in practically every person, event, and artifact belonging to a common system. In a community, nearly every source of data an ethnographer consults—each informant, subject, event, and artifact—in some degree or in some way reveals consistencies with many other sources (corresponding to the same or a different type) that he consults. Accounts of child rearing by several informants partially fit together with one another and agree with observed instances of child rearing. The fit may not be as perfect as the interlocking of pieces in a jigsaw puzzle, but such an analogy is nevertheless useful. A Sindhi landlord's actions, though vastly different from his tenant farmer's, meshes with certain aspects of the latter's, and the landlord's luxurious rural dwelling is in some respects comparable to the tenant's hovel or referable to the tenant's labor, passivity, powerlessness, etc. It is with such consistencies and comparable aspects abstracted from the sample that we build up an integrated picture of a culture. No two reporters use the same facts in the same way, but some of the same facts recognizably appear in different anthropologists' treatments of the same culture or social system. Use of judgment and opportunistic samples in field work is predicated on the researcher's primary interest in

[1] I believe Kroeber originally made this point.

the *system* of behavior rather than in the way behavioral traits or individuals with specific characteristics are distributed in a known universe whose systematic nature is either taken for granted or ignored (cf. Kroeber 1957:193). If the system is composed of subgroups, then such subgroups are sampled for whatever information they can contribute concerning the whole system.

The person who has most tried to explain how traditional anthropological sampling works is Margaret Mead.[2] Confining her discussion mainly to the selection of people by nonprobability methods, she points out the vital importance of identifying informants by salient characteristics they possess which are capable of affecting the validity of information they produce. (The same rule, as I will bring out later, applies to certain kinds of cultural products.) Hence accomplished ethnography calls for "skill of evaluating an individual informant's place in a social and cultural whole and then recognizing the formal patterns, explicit and implicit, of his culture expressed in his spontaneous verbal statements and his behavior" (Mead 1953: 646). When the sample is a human being, his identification is made in terms of more than his representative status or social characteristics.

... the validity of the sample depends not so much upon the number of cases as upon the proper specification of the informant, so that he or she can be accurately placed, in terms of a very large number of variables—age, sex, order of birth, family background, life-experience, temperamental tendencies (such as optimism, habit of exaggeration, etc.), political and religious position, exact situational relationship to the investigator, configurational relationship to every other informant, and so forth. Within this extensive degree of specification, each informant is studied as a perfect example, an organic representation of his complete cultural experience. This specification of the informant grew up historically as a way of dealing with the few survivors of broken and vanished cultures and is comparable to the elaboration with which the trained historian specifies the place of a crucial document among the few and valuable documents available for a particular period. ... (Mead 1953:645–655)

Again like a historian working with documents, an anthropologist drawing information from expressive cultural products like novels or films notes salient characteristics of their authors "so as, in the end, to be able to discount . . . individual differences" (Mead 1961:19). A single life history is representative of a community's culture to the degree that the individual it portrays has been involved in experiences common to other (not necessarily all) individuals. To that degree, the subject's life history becomes a model of his culture which the anthropologist can use in building *his* model (Mead 1953:653). Even a relative stranger, like the Hudson's Bay Company manager serving an Indian community in northern Canada, or the visiting missionary, becomes representative in the sense that he is capable of providing information about the Indians' culture, but his special cultural and social position must be known and carefully considered in appraising what he says or does (Mead 1951b: 77).

Such diverse sources of data open ethnography to the charge that it relies on unstandardized modes of procedure and is haphazard or impressionistic in its approach, charges that Mead (1955) takes pains to rebut when she emphasizes that an anthropologist in his work follows rules different from those employed in other social sciences but doesn't operate totally without discipline. The ethnologist who combines information from novels, from living informants, and even utilizes his own personal experience in another culture to construct his final model of the culture or social personality may have sampled informants and behavioral settings opportunistically, but he did not do so haphazardly if he kept in mind what his sources represented. Safeguards in anthropological sampling include cross-checking information one receives from different sources, using every datum to test the soundness of the model as it is built and comparing each to data employed before, examining it for inconsistencies, contradictions, and incongruities. "Anthropological sampling is not a poor and inadequate version of sociological or socio-psychological sampling, a version where *n* equals too few cases," Mead (1953:654) claims, *"it is simply a different kind of sampling."*

With so much importance put on identifying salient characteristics of human samples in field work, it becomes imperative for the ethnographer to keep records of

[2] Her views mainly appear in Mead 1951b, 1953, 1954, 1955, 1961; and Mead and Métraux 1953:1–53. See also Zelditch 1962.

the people he studies—not merely their names but generous amounts of biographical and other data relevant for understanding information they provide. Indexing of field notes not merely by categories like those given in the *Outline of Cultural Materials* but by names is essential so that the full set of notes referring to any individual can be used to augment formal biographical data available about him and thus round out knowledge of him that will help to place any particular behavior or statement referring to him in the fullest possible, meaningful context. What X tells me on one occasion is apt to assume special significance once I know certain of his previous behavior and have retrieved it from my records. In this way, long-term research in single communities will someday benefit through comprehensive data banks established for persons and for entire families.[3] When the ideal of full, individual identification becomes unrealizable, as in studying a large community like a nation or city involving many subjects who therefore must remain for the most part anonymous, other methods can be employed to achieve a similar result. Mead (1953:652) suggests random sampling, or "positional studies in which small complex parts of the total structure are carefully localized and intensively studied," like organizations or several shops in a factory. Or else "the intensive analysis of segments of the culture which are unsystematically related to each other and overlap in a variety of ways" are consulted (in Russian national cultural studies such segments have included novels, proceedings of the Communist party congress, and controls on Soviet industry). Rhoda Métraux (1943:88) also speaks of positional sampling used to interview specific groups for information about food habits, including grocers and persons waiting in line to register for ration cards. In a heterogeneous social system, therefore, work in any sampled subgroup is done knowing, or while learning, salient characteristics of that subgroup with respect to the whole, just as in sampling persons or cultural products. Special attention might have to be given to a subgroup if its members are playing a particularly decisive political role in a nation.

[3] For an example see the use Goldfrank (1948) makes of such information in analyzing versions of myths.

Anthropological methods of sampling, Mead (1952:402–403, 1953:655) maintains, are logical as long as the fieldworker expects mainly to use his data not to answer questions like "how much" and "how often" but to solve *qualitative* problems such as discovering what occurs, the implications of what occurs, and the relationships linking occurrences. Anthropological sampling serves the ethnologist who is primarily engaged in searching for patterns that occur and recur in diverse sets of social relations, "between employer and employee, writer and reader, and so on," including between parents and children (Mead 1953:655). Such patterns can be constructed from information provided by identified living informants augmented by bits of data obtained from cultural productions, like paintings, plays, or movies. The latter data are "cross-integrated" with observed behavior and statements provided by informants (Mead 1951a:109, 116). She illustrates from linguistics: "If one wants to know the grammatical structure of a language, it is sufficient to use very few informants about whom the necessary specified information has been collected; if one wants to know how many people use a certain locution or a particular work in preference to another, then sampling of the wider type is necessary. . . ."

Mead's account of judgment sampling stops short of demonstrating how the information so obtained is utilized in ethnographies in ways that avoid undue overgeneralization. It hardly suffices to be told that "any cultural statement must be made in such a way that the addition of another class of informants previously unrepresented will not change the nature of the statement in a way which has not been allowed for in the original statement" (Mead 1953:648), or to be warned that the representativeness of the informants must be included in statements, as for example, " 'These statements are made about the culture prevailing in the rural south among people living in communities of less than twenty-five hundred people.' " Can all new information by hitherto unrepresented samples be anticipated? How precisely can samples be identified in ethnographic statements? I doubt if such rules can regularly be followed when large amounts of information must be reported. Such criticism, however, may be unfair, for one of the crucial problems in traditional anthropological method, and one we understand very poorly due no doubt to the extent to which a personal element is involved, is precisely the matter of what happens to data after they have been collected in the field and prior to the point where they turn up in the stylized prose of a monograph.

It is well to guard against using the term "anthropological sampling" without bearing in mind that no probability methods of sampling apply in anthropology only to the extent that ethnographers in fact pursue research interests like those stated, or interests consistent with ends such sampling can serve. I think it noteworthy that Mead does not defend nonprobability sampling by referring to the predominant homogeneity of small-scale communities which renders random sampling unnecessary (see, however, Mead 1932:10–12). Neither homogeneity or heterogeneity by itself constitutes a sufficient basis for choosing between probability or nonprobability sampling methods. We may safely assume that in any community, regardless of whether it is large or small in scale, individuals embody or enact culture differently, and so do families. To that extent, a degree of heterogeneity is universal. A research problem that seeks to capitalize on internal ("intracultural") variations of behavior between a fairly large number of individuals or families in communities of any scale would undoubtedly find probability sampling advantageous.

PROBABLITY SAMPLING

Selecting a Sample[4]

A probability sample is called for whenever it is useful to know within precise margins of error how often units (people, artifacts, activities, attitudes, or opinions) with particular features occur in a universe of such phenomena that is too large or for some other reason difficult to investigate *in toto*. The word "features" covers any question that can be incorporated in an interview schedule and any variable to which an observer can give attention. The carefully planned process of selection used to obtain a probability sample comes close to creating a miniature,

[4] In describing how probability samples are selected I follow mainly Parten 1950:116–122 and Riley 1963: 284–287.

unbiased replica or cross-section of the sampled phenomena. Due to the underlying mathematical theory of probability sampling,[5] such samples can be employed with considerable, known confidence for the light they throw on the universe from which the sample was drawn. Laws of chance or probability, rather than expert knowledge or self-selection, govern the way representatives of that universe are chosen. The very role that chance plays in drawing the sample can be known. Put another way, the probability sampling tells us what percent of the time we can expect our sample to be representative of the universe from which it is drawn. Such practical and mathematical advantages are important reasons for the widespread use of sampling in science. In what follows I will be mainly concerned with random sampling, the best known method of probability sampling. In this method, each unit in the sampled universe enjoys an equal chance of being drawn.

In preparing to choose a probability sample by random selection, the first step is to construct a sampling frame. A sampling frame is the sampled universe drawn together in some convenient fashion for sampling. It often differs from the target universe, that is, from the total population which the anthropologist may be studying. In a moment I will bring up some of the problems connected with generalizing from the sampled universe to the target universe. Here it suffices to say that all the safety we enjoy in making statistical inferences from the random sample to the sampled universe disappears once we extend knowledge gained from the sample beyond the sampling frame to the target universe. The sampling frame may consist of a stack of newspapers, a herd of cows (if the object is, say, to discover milk yield), a street map of a city, or a list of people. A satisfactory census or other enumeration of people may already be available in the community or at some capital to serve as a sampling frame. If not, or if the census is suspected to be incomplete, the field worker will have to make his own enumeration. He can often save time in doing so by utilizing available

[5] For the theory of sampling see any of the following: Deming 1960; Hansen, Hurwitz, and Madow 1953; Kerlinger 1965: chap. 4; Kish 1953; Wallis and Roberts 1956: chaps. 4, 10, and 15; also Naroll's chapter on statistical inference in this volume.

knowledge, as Fortes and his coworkers (1947:177) did when the Ashanti survey began its enumeration using lists of household heads taken from the tax rolls. Often it proves too difficult or impossible to construct a sampling frame that coincides with the target universe which the ethnographer is studying. Baeck (1961:162) was interested in the consumption patterns of well-to-do Congolese in Leopoldville but restricted himself to drawing a sample of government clerks earning incomes above a certain figure who were also household heads. He used a payroll list as his frame. His sample, of course, included no other occupations that may have been represented among well-to-do Congolese. Peter Marris (1961:xii–xiv) would have preferred to sample households in Lagos, but because he found no adequate list of such units he had to settle for individuals drawn from a census. In Pakistan I wanted to know about both men's and women's presence at, and reaction to, the motion pictures shown in the three villages I had selected, but purdah did not permit me to construct sampling frames including women's names. In Frobisher Bay we wanted to know about Eskimo drinking but could best find out about Eskimo men who had received permits to deal with the Territorial liquor store. We used a 100 percent sample of such people (Honigmann and Honigmann 1965:204 ff.).

There is danger of error whenever the researcher generalizes beyond the sampling frame. To avoid or reduce such error, the ethnographer may specify the relationship between the sampling frame and the target universe, for example, the degree to which well-to-do Congolese are represented by government clerks earning above a certain figure. He may decide to restrict his conclusions to the sampled universe, at that point shedding all interest in the target universe. We did this to a large extent when under the heading of "Eskimo drinking" I confined most of our discussion to purchases made by permit holders in Frobisher Bay, merely indicating that there were some teetotalers and that a small, unknown amount of illegal home-brewing occurred. The ethnographer may also, if time permits, increase the number of sampling frames in order to cover as large a portion of the target universe as possible. In Leopoldville, for example, he

might have added to the payroll list a tax list of household heads and drawn from it a random sample of householders who pay amounts above a certain figure. If one employs the sampling frame to make wider generalizations, it can be done by basing what is said on well-founded knowledge of the target universe and of the subject matter being studied. Thus because many Pashto-speaking male respondents in Pakistan failed to understand the film track's Urdu narration, it was even less likely that Pashto-speaking mature women would; their seclusion, I reason, has allowed them little opportunity to learn Urdu. Often the sampling frame represents a more or less satisfactory compromise between studying the target universe directly and utilizing available sources of information or working within time limits available to the ethnographer. Compromise cannot go to all lengths. Frames must possess some relevance to the problem being investigated if they are to be useful. For a researcher interested in the inheritors of land, a list of *all* taxpayers or households won't do; he needs a sampling frame of persons who have inherited land or a list of estates whose owners he can track down to solicit the required information (cf. Leach 1958). One is justified in wondering what Geoffrey Gorer (1955) accomplished by way of getting to know about "English character" with a sampling frame consisting of 10,524 questionnaires returned by persons who in response to an appeal published in a popular newspaper, consented to complete such an instrument.

Sampling frames are sometimes hard to construct because the universe itself (e.g., well-to-do Congolese in Leopoldville) is conceptually ambiguous. Much thought has to be given to formulating rules concerning what is to constitute the frame and why. Are men working away from the village to be included in the household? Should I include members of satellite villages in the universe to be sampled? What time limits are sufficient or required for my problem? Solutions to such questions depend on the research objectives and on knowledge of relevant factors in the community's culture and history. For example, in Frobisher Bay it was very desirable to have data on liquor purchases that went back before the date when new regulations entered into force; such data would enable me to tell what difference, if any, the regulation made. Obviously previous knowledge of an area and its history will provide valuable guidance both for constructing sampling frames and for generalizing beyond them (cf. Smith 1963). If the essence of art lies in applying skill to overcome limits imposed by one's tools, materials, and personal resources, then designing a sampling frame calls for considerable art.

The sampling frame contains all the units or observations that will be sampled; the sample contains the number of units actually studied (including those that can't be found or refuse to collaborate). Step two in collecting a sample consists in determining how many such units are needed (assuming that circumstances do not permit a 100 percent sample) and then randomly drawing that number from the frame. Sample size depends on the amount of variability in the sample and the degree of confidence that the research wishes to establish for his results. In general, the larger the sample, the smaller the probable error and the greater the confidence attached to the results. However, beyond a certain size, gains to be expected rapidly decline, making large samples relatively inefficient to use. Listing units in the frame and assigning each a serial number or numbering houses and blocks permits convenient sampling by use of a table of random numbers (Wallis and Roberts 1956: 631 ff.), for to draw a large number of cases by lot would be a clumsy, time-consuming procedure. A list or series of items, like pages or newspapers, can be random-sampled by numbering them or numbering areas of the page and lines of type. This is an appropriate place to point out that sampling pages, newspapers, or printed lines by selecting units at regular intervals is not true random sampling because the selection of each unit fails to be independent of the others. Regular-interval sampling is random only if the arrangement of the series is free from bias, for example, if the pile of newspapers has been mixed so that choosing every seventh does not result in only Sunday papers being drawn. Similar precautions must be taken in stopping to question people or vehicles at regular intervals, when the interviewer must also be cautious that he does not depart from the sample design and unconsciously show partiality in making his selection. In sampling a list of names at regular intervals, danger lies in oversampling the initial letter and omitting the least common letters. Returning to random sampling procedures, a numbered grid placed over a large-scale map allows random selection of places to be visited for investigation. In two-stage or multi-stage sampling, once such places are randomly chosen their constituent units are again random-sampled. Peter Marris (1961:xiv) contemplated drawing a grid over a plan of Lagos and sampling the squares. However, the density of population made this unthinkable; each square would have included too many people to sample further and an adequate sampling frame would have been hard to construct.[6]

No matter how carefully drawing occurs, bias resulting in a misleading sample, one that under- or over-represents certain kinds of units, cannot be completely eliminated. Failure of people to respond or to be located, inaccessibility which deters an interviewer from going to certain places, and the readiness of some respondents to cooperate all contribute to bias. I respect the fortitude of my Pathan assistant in a large North-West Frontier village as he patiently accompanied me on long treks across hot fields in search of respondents whose wells and fields we had located through inquiring in the market place. Even then we couldn't locate an unallowably large proportion (26 percent) of the sample which had been chosen from a voter's list, the validity of which I came to doubt (Honigmann 1953:57).

Stratified Random Sampling

The simplicity characteristic of simple random sampling disappears when the basic method which I have described is applied in more complex circumstances, for example, in national samples of public opinion. It would be merely academic for me here to go into such variations of random sampling as area or cluster sampling.[7] However, I will briefly describe one well-known variation, stratified random sampling, because it is likely to be helpful in ethnographic research. This

[6] For more on the mechanics of drawing samples see Parten 1950:265–272, 277–280.
[7] For information on these and other methods see Hansen, Hurwitz, and Madow 1953 or Parten 1950.

type of probability sampling occurs when the universe under study is heterogeneous; that is, the units vary in characteristics which are apt to be significant for the problem being studied. For example, a population contains persons of different ages or members of different ethnic groups. These features, the investigator suspects, might influence other features that he is studying. He takes care to draw a sample that will proportionately represent the likely significant features in the universe. He divides the sampling frame into strata or categories (cells), each homogeneous with respect to a certain characteristic. Then he draws a random sample of proportionate size from each cell. In a small Sindhi village of about five hundred persons my initial census of males eighteen years old or more revealed a population stratified in six tiers: noncultivating landlords; cultivating landholders; tenant cultivators; craftsmen and tradesmen, including domestic servants; Marwari, a Hindu enclave; and Brahui-speaking transients living on the settlement's outskirts. My sample of forty subjects represented each of these categories in proportion to its weight in the total population. Circumstances, however, made it impossible to complete interviews with each designated respondent, the suspicious Brahui putting themselves beyond reach (Honigmann 1953: 10–11). Constructing a frame for stratified random sampling obviously requires prior knowledge about the composition of the universe so that its probably significant characteristics can be defined. To a very large extent I relied on my Sindhi-speaking assistant for such knowledge.

Advantages and Disadvantages of Probability Sampling

Major justification for using probability samples in any discipline lies in the precision with which they allow inferences drawn from the sample to the sampled universe to be statistically grounded. Speaking less exactly: when sampling is used to control for bias, one is relatively safer in generalizing from the few to the many. As I pointed out, such safety vanishes upon leaving the sampled universe (or sampling frame) in order to extend results to a larger aggregate of which the frame itself is but a part, unless one knows precisely how the frame fits the target universe. Probability sampling can conveniently and confidently answer questions concerning the frequency with which features are distributed in a large population: the number of people who possess certain amenities in their homes, are gainfully employed, possess certain cognitive and emotional traits as measured by the Rorschach test, or immigrated to the community in various years. The technique need not involve people directly. It can, for example, be effectively used to discover the number of times a certain value or sentiment is expressed in newspaper editorials and reports of political speeches during an election campaign (Garrett and Honigmann 1965). Beyond such descriptive use, probability methods are even more important for the way they lend themselves to discovering predictive relationships in a given universe. Do mental health ratings vary with income or with other indicators of socioeconomic status? (Srole *et al.* 1962:32 ff., 210 ff.) Hypotheses following from such questions can often be confidently tested with the aid of samples drawn by some method of random selection.

Probability sampling may be to some extent inappropriate when the aim of research is to understand a social or cultural *system* to whose operation or dynamics individual actors or artifacts offer only clues. When interest then lies in discovering the logical relationship that exists between norms, statuses, organizations, or patterns of overt behavior, both deviant and non-deviant, the incidence of those phenomena is not a crucial question. Such a problem is little concerned with generalizing data from a few to the many units comprising a universe. Research problems, however, rarely correspond solely to quantitative or qualitative matters. It is rare that results obtained through one procedure can't be enlightened by results obtained in another way. Consequently, it will more often than not be advantageous to apply probability methods along with other fieldwork techniques. At least, one will be wise always to weigh carefully the possibilities in using or not using probability sampling and in estimating its relative advantages and disadvantages.

A latent function of probability sampling deserves attention. The careful planning it requires forces an investigator to give much thought to what he wants to learn about, and why. Therefore it is especially appropriate to problem-oriented research where it helps in defining the crucial variables which, in turn, are often few enough to allow an adequate sampling frame to be efficiently constructed.

Turning now to disadvantages, the care and time required to construct sampling frames which in the end probably don't fully cover the target universe must certainly be taken into account (Hill 1963:8, Parten 1950:111–112, 225–226). Perhaps it would be more efficient to sample opportunistically, carefully identifying the pertinent characteristics of the informants, particularly if precise estimates of frequency are unimportant. Furthermore, in culturally unfamiliar social systems, an adequate sampling frame can't be constructed until much preliminary study has been done. By that time the knowledge to be gained by probability sampling may be very small pickings indeed, especially if research is not problem-oriented. The relatively few variables involved in problem-oriented research constitute an advantage that allows an adequate sampling frame to be efficiently constructed. In comparison, it is very difficult if not impossible to sample by probability techniques for all the information that is pertinent when studying a total culture. In our study of town-dwelling Eskimo in Frobisher Bay we would have needed a staff of several people and much more time than we had to cover by probability sampling all the sources we actually explored; that is, to sample the local radio station's output, school-attendance records, aims and goals of the town's various organizations, activities and learning opportunities in the various shops, earnings and expenditures, amount of fresh food that full- and part-time hunters brought in, attitudes of Euro-canadians toward Eskimo, child rearing, and so on.[8]

Although several large-scale random sample surveys have been successfully conducted under conditions of extreme suspicion and fear (cf. Southall and Gutkind 1956:235), in some parts of the world people randomly selected for interviewing would very likely so often refuse to answer questions that the

proportion of uncompleted interviews would destroy the sample's representativeness. There will always be some people in a random sample who refuse to provide information for which they are solicited or who will be unavailable for interviews. They, in fact, did not have a chance equal to that of the more willing of the sample to be interviewed. Confidence in the results of a random sample is seriously impaired if the proportion of noncollaborators becomes too high, say 10 percent of the total sample or more (Cochran, Mosteller, and Tukey 1954). The implication then is that those who responded constitute a select and unrepresentative selection. In a study of sexual behavior they are, perhaps, the high performers, exhibitionists, or extroverts who distort what actually occurs in the universe (cf. Himelhoch and Fava 1955: chaps. 7–11). Resistance to being interviewed, I suspect, is likely to be frequently encountered in relatively small-scale communities. When it occurs, it springs not only from hostility or suspicion but also from inexperience with, and little taste for, the kind of introspection, reporting, and forethought that people in a different type of society so effectively manage when they are asked to respond to a host of apparently unrelated questions (Lerner 1958:147). We failed largely to overcome such unwillingness in Frobisher Bay Eskimo and as a result could barely complete even a simple household census.

Probability and Nonprobability Samples Compared

It is interesting to look at two experiments in field work which employed both probability and nonprobability samples under controlled conditions. A hypothesis I tested with data obtained in three Pakistan villages predicted that random and opportunistic samples would be significantly different in composition (Honigmann and Honigmann 1955). Results show that male subjects appearing in the combined opportunistic samples for the three villages differed in socioeconomic status from those in the combined random sample. The combined random sample shows 9, 60, and 31 percent of the respondents coming from the upper, middle, and lower socioeconomic respectively. In comparison, the opportunistic samples drew

---

[8] I forbear going into arguments concerning the validity of responses obtained by use of questionnaires. For discussions of this question see Vidich and Bensman 1954 and Zelditch 1962.

17, 46, and 37 percent of the respondents from those strata. Apparently, by querying men who came to our attention, spoke English, and proved to be willing informants we had especially shown a bias for the uppermost stratum. Why lower-status men were also over-sampled is not clear. I can only suggest that my intention to avoid unduly representing high-status people made me zealous in contacting men from the opposite end of the continuum. I also compared the Sindhi and Punjabi to see if the random and opportunistic samples would be different not only in composition but in two types of response: attendance at the film performances and number of people showing correct awareness of the government presenting the films. (For this purpose I did not use data from the North-West Frontier Province village where sampling had proven to be very difficult.) Differences at the .05 level of probability or lower occurred with respect to both types of response. This suggests, by the logic of probability sampling, that I would have been mistaken had I relied solely on the opportunistic sample to inform me about the behavior of village population from which those helpful and informative men came.

Among Cree Indians in Attawapiskat in 1955 I used Card II of the Behn Rorschach Test to discover whether information obtained from a random adult sample (N=20) in response to a controlled stimulus would differ significantly from adults opportunistically selected (N=23) (Honigmann and Carrera 1957).[9] I predicted that the samples would differ in respect to eight scored response categories (e.g., animal content, human content, total responses, incidence of color, incidence of rejection). Differences between the means of the random and opportunistic

[9] The Wenner-Gren Foundation for Anthropological Research supported the field work in Attawapiskat.

samples turned out to be statistically nonsignificant. However, a second test hints that the stimulus itself was nondiscriminatory; for when the two Cree Indian samples were compared to ninety-six undergraduate college students, no significant differences showed up between means of those two groups.

From these experiments it is possible to conclude that the more homogeneous the universe, the more likely it is that probability and nonprobability samples will manifest similar characteristics and results. The reason is clear: the small variability in the universe means that all respondents are likely to respond in similar ways to the same situation.[10] The more stratified the universe, the more likely that probability and nonprobability samples drawn from the same strata will respond similarly. Again the reason is clear: the relative homogeneity within each stratum means that all respondents coming from it are likely to respond in similar ways to the same situation. Presumably anthropologists in small-scale homogeneous communities take advantage of the community's slight variability when they sample opportunistically and generalize from the sample to the population at large. When Margaret Mead, speaking of large-scale heterogeneous social systems, advises carefully identifying pertinent characteristics of opportunistically chosen informants, she is in effect saying that the anthropologist who confronts considerable variability must create and sample more categories in which variability is reduced. Sampling opportunistically from homogeneous strata reduces the possibility that different results would be obtained between probability and nonprobability samples.

[10] I am indebted to Donald R. Ploch for the following conclusions and for a very critical and helpful reading of the section dealing with probability sampling.

BIBLIOGRAPHY

BAECK, L.
  1961 An expenditure study of the Congolese Évolués of Leopoldville, Belgian Congo. In Aidan Southall, ed., *Social change in modern Africa*. London, Oxford University Press.

BEATTIE, JOHN
  1965 *Understanding an African kingdom: Bunyoro*. New York, Holt, Rinehart and Winston.

COCHRAN, WILLIAM G., FREDERICK MOSTELLER, and JOHN W. TUKEY
  1954 Statistical problems of the Kinsey report. *Journal of the American Statistical Association* 48:673–716.

CODERE, HELEN
1955 A genealogical study of kinship in the United States. *Psychiatry* 18:65–79.

DEMING, W. EDWARDS
1960 *Sample design in business research.* New York, Wiley.

FESTINGER, LEON, and DANIEL KATZ (eds.)
1953 *Research methods in the behavioral sciences.* New York, Dryden Press.

FIRTH, RAYMOND
1951 *Elements of social organization.* London, Watts.

FORTES, M., R. W. STEEL, and P. ADY
1947 Ashanti survey, 1945–46: an experiment in social research. *Geographical Journal* 110:149–179.

GARRETT, SUE GENA, and JOHN J. HONIGMANN
1965 *Pakistani values revealed in the 1964 national election.* Manuscript.

GOLDFRANK, ESTHER S.
1948 The impact of situation and personality on four Hopi emergence myths. *Southwestern Journal of Anthropology* 4:241–262.

GORER, GEOFFREY
1955 *Exploring English character.* London, Cresset Press.

HANSEN, MORRIS H., WILLIAM N. HURWITZ, and WILLIAM C. MADOW
1953 *Sample survey methods and theory,* Vol. 1, *Methods and Applications.* New York, Wiley.

HILL, POLLY
1963 *The migrant cocoa-farmers of Southern Ghana.* Cambridge, England, University Press.

HIMELHOCH, JEROME and SYLVIA FLEIS FAVA
1955 *Sexual behavior in American society.* New York, Norton.

HONIGMANN, JOHN J.
1949 *Culture and ethos of Kaska society.* Yale University Publications in Anthropology, No. 40.

1953 *Information for Pakistan, report of research on intercultural communication through films.* Chapel Hill, Institute for Research in Social Science, University of North Carolina. Mimeographed.

1964 Survival of a cultural focus. In Ward H. Goodenough, ed., *Explorations in cultural anthropology.* New York, McGraw-Hill.

HONIGMANN, JOHN J. and RICHARD CARRERA
1957 Another experiment in sample reliability. *Southwestern Journal of Anthropology* 13:99–102.

HONIGMANN, JOHN J., and IRMA HONIGMANN
1955 Sampling reliability in ethnological field work. *Southwestern Journal of Anthropology* 11:282–287.

1965 *Eskimo townsmen.* Ottawa, Canadian Research Centre for Anthropology, University of Ottawa.

KERLINGER, FRED N.
1965 *Foundations of behavioral research.* New York, Holt, Rinehart and Winston.

KISH, LESLIE
1953 Selection of the sample. In Leon Festinger and Daniel Katz, eds., Research methods in the behavioral sciences. New York, Dryden Press.

KROEBER, A. L.
1957 *Ethnographic interpretations 1–6.* University of California Publications in American Archaeology and Ethnology 47, No. 2.

LEACH, EDMUND R.
1958 An anthropologist's reflections on a social survey. *Ceylon Journal of Historical and Social Studies* 1:9–20.

LEIGHTON, DOROTHEA C., JOHN S. HARDING, DAVID B. MACKLIN, ALLISTER M. MACMILLAN, and ALEXANDER H. LEIGHTON
1963 *The character of danger.* New York, Basic Books.

LERNER, DANIEL
1958 *The passing of traditional society.* New York, Free Press of Glencoe.

MANDELBAUM, DAVID G.
1953 On the study of national character. *American Anthropologist* 55:174–187.

MARRIS, PETER
1961 *Family and social change in an African city.* London, Routledge and Kegan Paul.

MCCALL, D.
1961 Trade and the role of wife in a modern West African town. In Aidan Southall, ed., *Social change in modern Africa.* London, Oxford University Press.

MEAD, MARGARET
1928 *Coming of age in Samoa.* New York, William Morrow.

1932 *The changing culture of an Indian tribe.* Contributions to Anthropology, No. 15. New York, Columbia University Press.

1951a Research in contemporary culture. In Harold Guetzkow, ed., *Groups, leadership and men.* Pittsburgh, Carnegie Press.

1951b The study of national character. In Daniel Lerner and Harold D. Lasswell, eds., *The policy sciences.* Stanford, Stanford University Press.

1952 Some relationships between social anthropology and psychiatry. In Franz Alexander and Helen Ross, eds., *Dynamic psychiatry.* Chicago, University of Chicago Press.

1953 National character. In A. L. Kroeber, ed., *Anthropology today.* Chicago, Chicago University Press.

1954 The swaddling hypothesis: its reception. *American Anthropologist* 56:395–409.

1955 Effects of anthropological field work models on intercultural communication. *Journal of Social Issues* 11 (No. 2): 3–11.

1961 National character and the science of anthropology. In Seymour M. Lipset and Leo Lowenthal, eds., *Culture and social character*. New York, Free Press of Glencoe.

1964 The idea of national character. In Roger L. Shinn, ed., *The search for identity: essays on the American character*. New York, Harper.

MEAD, MARGARET, and RHODA MÉTRAUX
1953 *The study of culture at a distance*. Chicago, University of Chicago Press.

MÉTRAUX, RHODA
1943 Qualitative attitude analysis. In Margaret Mead, ed., *The problem of changing food habits*. National Research Council, Bulletin 108.

PARTEN, MILDRED
1950 *Surveys, polls, and samples*. New York, Harper and Row.

RILEY, MATILDA WHITE
1963 *Sociological research, Vol. I, a case approach*. New York, Harcourt, Brace.

SMITH, RAYMOND T.
1963 Review of family structure in Jamaica: the social context of reproduction, by Judith Blake. *American Anthropologist* 65:158–161.

SOUTHALL, AIDAN
1961 *Social change in modern Africa*. London, Oxford University Press.

SOUTHALL, AIDAN W., and PETER C. W. GUTKIND
1956 *Townsmen in the making*. East African Studies, No. 9.

SPINDLER, GEORGE D.
1955 *Sociocultural and psychological processes in Menomini acculturation*. University of California Publications in Culture and Society, Vol. 5.

SROLE, LEO, THOMAS S. LANGNER, STANLEY T. MICHAEL, MARVIN OPLER, and THOMAS A. C. RENNIE
1962 *Mental health in the metropolis*. New York, McGraw-Hill.

TREMBLAY, MARC-ADÉLARD
1957 The key informant technique: A non-ethnographic application. *American Anthropologist* 59:688–701.

VIDICH, A., and J. BENSMAN
1954 The validity of field data. *Human Organization* 13 (No. 1):20–27.

WALLACE, ANTHONY F. C.
1952 *The modal personality structure of the Tuscarora Indians*. Bureau of American Ethnology, Bulletin 150.

WALLIS, W. ALLEN, and HARRY W. ROBERTS
1956 *Statistics: a new approach*. New York, Free Press of Glencoe.

WHITING, JOHN W. M., et al.
1966 *Field guide for a study of socialization in five societies*. New York, Wiley.

ZELDITCH, MORRIS, JR.
1962 Some methodological problems of field studies. *American Journal of Sociology* 67:566–576.

CHAPTER 16

Methods for Observing and Recording Behavior

BEATRICE and JOHN WHITING

PROBLEMS IN OBSERVATION

How many times does a field worker have to observe the behavior of individuals before he can feel confident in writing a general descriptive statement? Should he observe the same people in the same place doing the same things, or can he combine incidents which have the same class of individuals and are in comparable settings? What kind of observations should the field worker make if he wishes to make statements about the frequency of some type of behavior or the probability of its occurrence? Rules of evidence for generalizing are an endemic problem of anthropological field work and there are general rules concerning the stability of measures which apply to all ethnographic materials. This chapter, however, is concerned specifically with the rules of evidence for generalizing about behavior and will consider techniques for standardizing observation, when to use these techniques, how often, when and where to observe, how to record and how to analyze records.

One might begin by asking if anthropologists are really concerned with behavior. Since the turn of the century they have been settling in communities and learning about social patterns by participating in the daily life. Participant observation is a technique associated with the profession. The purpose of observation, however, has been to describe culture or social structure rather than behavior itself, and hence, anthropologists have been satisfied with non-systematic observation.

Their interest in behavior, in general, is limited to insights it might give about the cognitive maps shared by individuals in a society or to understanding the nature of the social groups which regulate the lives of individuals. Bronislaw Malinowski, who was one of the first anthropologists to live for an extended period in complete isolation in a functioning preliterate society, speaks for many of his colleagues when he describes the relation of behavior to the domains of interest to anthropologists. He writes, "In ethnography, the distance is often enormous between the brute material information—as it is presented to the student in his own observation, in native statement, in the kaleidoscope of tribal life and the final authoritative presentation of the results" (Malinowski 1922:3-4).

The ethnographer has in the field, according to what has just been said, the duty before him of drawing up all the rules and regularities of tribal life; all that is permanent and fixed; of giving an anatomy of their culture, of depicting the constitution of their society. But these things, though crystallized and set, are nowhere formulated. There is no written or explicitly expressed code of laws, and their whole tribal tradition, the whole structure of their society, are embodied in the most elusive materials—the human beings. (Malinowski 1922: 11)

The observation of behavior and the questioning of informants as to the behavior observed are data from which one deduces the conscious or unconscious models which govern the religious, economic, social and political life of members of a society. An ethnographer, then, does not present descriptions of individual behavior. He collects samples of various types of behavior in his search for understanding the cognitive and social structural regularities. His field notes abound with the record of events, incidents which caught his eye or were relevant to his interest at the moment, but he seldom includes the concrete examples in his monograph.

Ethnographies are based primarily on a combination of these observations and extensive interviewing. The anthropologists observe behavior and then attempt to assess its meaning, generality and frequency. Consider an example of the type of incident recorded in field notes:

Met A and his wife on the path. She was carrying a bundle of wood in tump line—X, her male child, about 2½, was on her hip. A carried a spear. They were walking along single file, A in the lead.

A typical anthropologist records in his mind that the wife is the burden carrier and walks behind her husband. He will keep his eyes open to see if this is always the case or if A is more demanding or less considerate of his wife than other men. He will inquire from informants as to whether this is the usual practice, find out whether it is prescribed or preferred behavior, etc. If the incident is "typical" it will appear along with other observations in the form of a statement which may read: "Women are considered inferior to men. They are the burden carriers and are expected to walk behind their husbands. A man who allows his wife to walk ahead of him would be considered henpecked or 'silly.' "

Note that the anthropologist does not feel compelled to tell you how many times he observed such behavior or how many people he interviewed so that he could write the phrase "wives are expected to walk behind their husbands." If he felt obliged to present such evidence for every statement in his monograph his task would be insurmountable and ethnographies would never be written. The reader must trust the ethnographer's judgment as to when such generalizations are possible.

There is an implicit assumption that a field worker living in his community constantly checks his observations of behavior against his deductions as to the regularities of life and where there are discrepancies, discusses them with informants. If, for example, he is interested in the status relation of husband and wife, he may ask a series of questions about etiquette, order in walking along paths

or through doors, order of serving meals, greeting patterns, burden-carrying patterns, etc. If the rules are clearly prescribed, he has few problems; but if they are not verbalized or clearly prescribed, he has to spend time observing in relevant settings. If the ethnographer's goal is the discovery of the cognitive map shared by categories of individuals in a society, he uses his observations of behavior primarily as he probes in interviewing. If, on the other hand, he sees culture as an unconscious model which governs the interaction of individuals and which no member of the society can describe, he has to depend more heavily on observation. In this later case, if he does not sample systematically and count instances of behavior, he has to depend on coherence as an index of validity. If he does choose to observe systematically, his task is time-consuming. Recently, more field workers seem willing to make this necessary investment of time.

This present growing interest among anthropologists in the systematic recording and analysis of behavior seems to have been initiated by two groups of anthropologists— those interested in culture and personality and those interested in the relation between what has been referred to as the *ideal* and the *manifest*, i.e., cultural models and normative behavior. The latter interest has led both American and British anthropologists to collect systematic statistics concerning residence, choice of marriage mates, social or work group affiliations, divorce and suicide rates, etc. Since records of these types of behavior do not exist in preliterate societies, anthropologists have become the local census takers and record keepers and are collecting and recording the type of behavior ordinarily analyzed by sociologists in complex societies (see Rivers 1906, Kroeber 1917, Bohannan 1954, and Leach 1961). Such material, however, is usually collected by interviewing, asking individuals to report their own behavior or the behavior of others. This interest in normative behavior, however, may well lead these anthropologists to undertake sysematic observation when they become interested in behavior which informants are unable to report. It is interest in this type of behavior which has led students of culture and personality to devote more time to the observation and recording of behavior. They have turned to estimates of frequency and predilection for certain modes of behavior as indices of personality. For example, Mead (1930), in discussing the personality of the Arapesh, has discussed patterns of oral behavior; in discussing Balinese character, Bateson and Mead (1942) have leaned heavily on various nonverbal behaviors; Whiting *et al.* have depended primarily on measuring the frequency and preference for certain types of behavior as measures of personality dimensions (Whiting *et al.* 1956, 1966).

Within the decade, the above researchers have been joined by the physical and biological anthropologists who have been studying primates (see Altman 1962, 1967, and DeVore, ed., 1965). A third group who have contributed to the recent attempts to observe and record behavior are students of nonverbal communication or metalanguage such as Birdwhistell (1952, 1954), Pike (1954) and Harris (1964). It should be noted that both the students of animal behavior and the metalinguists cannot possibly collect the data they need by interviewing and hence share basic methodological problems with the students of culture and personality.

These new research interests call for a new methodology. For example, some of the major criticisms leveled at students of culture and personality have been that they see what they want to see, that they are biased by their theories of personality development and that they observe and report selectively. It is true that these researchers have been discriminatively criticized—perhaps because their theories have been more salient—since all anthropologists have been guilty of lacking systematic sampling techniques and checks on reliability and depending almost completely on coherence validity. It is obvious that anyone interested in scientific anthropology will need to face up to these problems and develop new research instruments.

Techniques for systematic observation and the recording of behavior have been developed by social and child psychologists who have been interested in predicting behavior, but in order to make standardization possible they have confined their observations primarily to controlled settings such as the laboratory and school (see Wright's review article, 1960). Recently, however, influenced by Barker and Wright, they are venturing into natural settings. This latter work (1951, 1954,

etc.) underlines some of the problems endemic to observing in such settings. Their specimen records take hours to make, hours to transcribe and many more hours to analyze. For the investment of man-hours of skilled labor one must ask whether the returns are compensatory. In the Six Culture Study, we collected approximately three thousand five-minute specimens of behavior. It has taken us years to complete the analysis. Several anthropologists who have collected extensive and valuable observation material have published the raw data without analysis undoubtedly primarily because they found the task too time-consuming (see Roberts, *Zuni Daily Life,* 1956). (It is no wonder that anthropologists invented the ethnographic interview—a device whereby informants report on their own behavior and the behavior of others, assess its frequency, comment on its relation to the perception of norms and consider the consequences of deviation from this norm.)

Since systematic observation is such a time-consuming task the ethnographer must carefully weigh the advantages and disadvantages of investing part of his preciously short stay in the field in such work. What considerations, then, should lead him to decide that systematic observation is necessary? It seems as if there is one clear criterion and that is the inability of an informant to give relevant or valid data in a domain of interest to the ethnographer.

The informant may be unable to describe the pattern of behavior for one of six reasons: (1) he and the ethnographer have no language which is adequate—e.g., vocabulary to describe kinesthetic behavior or elaborate ritual behavior; (2) there is no clear generalized pattern of behavior—e.g., patterns exist but vary by age, sibling order, residence patterns, etc., and hence an informant cannot see or the ethnographer is unable to evoke the regularities; (3) the informant is unaware of—e.g., cannot verbalize—his behavior and the behavior of others in a particular domain—e.g., socialization; (4) the informant is unable to report things he does *not* do which may be of special importance—ignoring lower caste persons, ignoring a child's requests for help, etc.; (5) he is unable to report behavior validly because there is a conflict between ideals, rules and norms and he defends in order to resolve the conflict, thus reporting ideas rather than the actual frequency of incidents; (6) he attempts to generalize from his past experience and is not able to remember accurately.

Let us consider these problems individually. The first is best exemplified by cookbooks, do-it-yourself manuals and books on how to ski, skate, etc. Anyone who has tried to cook a soufflé with the aid of a cookbook and has never watched a friend or Julia Child knows that the common vocabulary for describing culinary techniques is inadequate. Similarly, film or direct observation make verbal descriptions of how to putty a window or ski easier to comprehend.

The second problem is difficult, not because the informant cannot report his own beliefs, values and practices but because they vary with age groups, or household types, sibling order, etc., and no one informant has experience in all the patterns. The ethnographer can only discover the pattern by sampling various categories of people. Although he may depend on ethnographic interviews for his data, systematic observation in standard settings may enable him to determine which category of individuals to interview.

The third and fourth type of problem, namely being unaware or unable to verbalize or unable to report behavior one does not perform, can be well illustrated in the domain of socialization. It has been found that even the most verbal and educated of U. S. Orchard Town mothers (Fischer and Fischer 1963, 1966) are unable in formulating general statements about socialization to perceive some of the clear regularities in their behavior. One might hypothesize that tremendous individual variation made it impossible to generalize in these areas but our findings in the Six Culture Study indicate that although the individual variations are great, the societal differences are also clear (see Minturn and Lambert, *Mothers in Six Cultures*, 1964, and forthcoming volume on *Children's Behavior in Six Cultures* by Whiting *et al.*, in preparation). It seems, rather, that these mothers are unaware of some of their implicit values, of many of their teaching techniques, and of many of their patterns of interaction with the members of their family, all of which they frequently share with other mothers in the community.

Parents teach values and beliefs and trans-

mit habits without being aware of what they are doing. The unconscious components of human communication have been documented by clinicians, anthropologists and linguists such as Sullivan (1953), Bateson (1956), Birdwhistell (1952, 1954), Pike (1954) and recently and most cogently by Robert Rosenthal in his book on experimental bias (1966). Those anthropologists who are interested in the transmission of culture or covert social practices need to observe these unconscious patterns of communication.

Furthermore, as Bateson *et al.* have pointed out (1956), the overt and covert messages communicated by socializers may be contradictory. Clinical psychologists and family psychotherapists can give numerous illustrations of interaction among parents and children where the conscious parental training procedure and the actual training are at odds. A mother will state her belief that aggressive behavior on the part of her son is unacceptable but will subtly reinforce this behavior. Orchard Town, U.S.A., mothers, for example, are prone to such conflicting messages in their training of *self-arrogation*, consciously disliking such behavior but actually teaching their children to show off and brag (e.g., mother to four-year-old: "Show Mrs. X the pretty pictures you made in school today") (Whiting *et al.*, in preparation).

A further problem stems from the fact that parents cannot report adequately on acts which they do not perform. For example, they may not report the fact that they fail to respond to requests for help from their children. That ignoral is an important technique in socialization is underlined by the recent study of Imamura (1965) who found in a study of a matched sample of sighted and blind children a significant correlation between the frequency of ignoral behavior on the part of the mothers and succorant behavior (appeals for help) on the part of the child. Similarly, mothers may not tell you that they ignore crying between what they consider normal intervals of feeding.

Examples of problem five, defensive distortion, can be found in any society in many domains. Rationalization, justification, denial and other defense mechanisms influence informant's statements. A good example is the Nyansongo mother who claimed her baby was upset for only one day by abrupt weaning, when in fact, as observed by R. LeVine

(1963:150–151), the baby cried and fussed for several weeks. Similarly, the Nyansongo mothers distorted when they reported that they punished disobedience severely when in fact they were observed to ignore disobedience more than half the time (see Whiting *et al.*, in preparation).

Many such cases may reflect semantic misinterpretation rather than unconscious distortion. Thus the Rajput mother who claims that her children do not work may not consider tending young siblings or running errands "work"; however, it may equally well be that she believes upper caste people should not work and hence under-reports the chores her children do. To decide between these explanations requires both exploration of linguistic domains and systematic observations of behavior (see Minturn and Lambert 1964).

Distorted memory of past events, problem six, may also effect the ethnographic interview. Even time-conscious American mothers cannot remember when they weaned their babies or taught them table manners (see Haggard *et al.* 1960, Robbins 1963, and Radke-Yarrow 1963). The consistency of distortion may be valuable evidence of beliefs and values if one knows its discrepancy from behavior. Thus, the Orchard Town mothers who value independence and self-reliance consistently reported that their children could dress and toilet themselves earlier than we have reason to believe is accurate, while the Rajput mother, who does not share these values and does not encourage self-reliance, distorted in the opposite direction, consistently overestimating the age at which the children learned these skills. On a more mundane level a sample of Harvard graduate students' wives in Cambridge consistently underestimated the time they spent watching TV and overestimated the time they spent reading (B. Whiting 1967).

Considering these six problems and accepting the fact that observation is time-consuming, one should devise a technique for determining whether or not direct observation is necessary. In domains of interest to the anthropologist, he should test the informant's ability to report his own behavior and the behavior of others. I am sure that anthropologists have been doing this informally but it seems wise to systematize the procedure. For example, in the domain of socialization, an ethnographer should observe in a home

and then interview the mother on the following day about her techniques for handling socialization problems which actually occurred the previous day during the observation period. Where there are discrepancies the ethnographer can discuss them. The mother may explain that her report reflects the usual pattern and that the observer's presence distorted behavior or she may disagree with or not understand his perception. Continued observation and interviewing will indicate those areas where mothers are competent reporters.

That there may well be some simple rules of thumb concerning problem areas is suggested by a recent study of the time budgets of a group of graduate students' wives in Cambridge (B. Whiting 1967). It appeared that mothers could report events and describe behavior which occurred once a week or even once a day more accurately than they could describe behavior which occurred more frequently especially if it occurred simultaneously with other types of behavior. The mothers remembered when they went out for the evening and what they did or when they went marketing and who they met, but could not remember when they read to their children, played with them or performed other routine activities. It may be that informants in general are better able to report their behavior in less routinized areas of life.

When the ethnographer decides that an informant cannot report his behavior or the behavior of others validly in a domain of theoretical concern, he is faced with decisions about where, when and whom to observe, on what to focus and how to record.

WHAT TO OBSERVE—TYPES OF SYSTEMATIC OBSERVATIONS

Techniques of observation may be classified with four major categories: those that focus on *acts,* those that focus on *persons,* those that focus on *places,* and those that focus on the *object* of group attention. The first two major types can be further subdivided according to whether a single or several acts or persons are to be observed. Thus, the observer may be interested in a molar-type activity such as housebuilding or a ceremonial dance, or he may be interested in more molecular units, discrete acts such as greeting, insulting, etc. Similarly, if the focus is on persons the observer may concentrate on an individual as a representative of a status or category, or on a dyad, or on a group. The six types, then, would include those that focused on: (1) an activity; (2) a category of acts; (3) the object or person which is the center of attention of a group; (4) an individual as a representative of a status category; (5) a dyad; (6) a setting. (Observing a group usually involves scanning individuals and hence is not included as a separate category.)

Let us consider each of the six types. An *activity* (type 1) is defined here to include events such as ritual performance or a game with formal rules that have a discernible beginning and end, a stated goal, and agreed-upon statuses and roles. It includes technological processes such as housebuilding, gardening, and cooking, and formal transactions such as buying and selling produce or arranging a marriage. Suppose, for example, one is interested in describing a game. First of all, games usually fit the category of behavior which the informant cannot report to the ethnographer's satisfaction. Anyone who has attempted to learn a game without visual cues knows how difficult it is. Examples of unsatisfactory descriptions of games based on verbal reports alone are to be found in the field notes of young ethnographers of the thirties, who recorded, for example, descriptions of the stick games as dictated by elderly American Indian informants. Bob Newhart's fantastic conversation between Abner Doubleday, the inventor of baseball, and Olympic Games, Inc., parodies the problem. Doubleday's description is reported somewhat as follows:

A pitcher and a catcher throw a ball back and forth and a player from the other side stands between them with a bat and may or may not swing at it depending on whether or not it looks like a "ball"—i.e., below the knees and above the shoulders. Three strikes and the player is out—or four balls (no explanation could be given as to why 4 instead of 3 balls). If the player hits the ball, he runs as far as he can before someone catches it, as long as it is "fair" (Bob Newhart 1960). (Then follows an abortive attempt to explain "fair" which includes white line, etc.)

In general, the test for the adequacy of a description of a game is the ability to enable someone to play it. With this goal in mind, the ethnographer observes and interviews until he feels able to play the game himself (granted he has the necessary skills).

His description will include personnel and rules for their selection, material apparatus, rules, goals and skills.

If the interest is oriented to classifying the game along the cross-cultural dimensions suggested by Roberts *et al.* (1963) (see Bibliography for list of articles), the test of adequacy is whether one can judge the degree to which the game involves physical skill, strategy, chance or competition. The test of adequacy is ability to use the cross-cultural scales.

If the anthropologist wishes to compare societies throughout the world along dimensions of preoccupation with strategy, chance or physical skill, he needs additional information from which to estimate how often people play the game and who chooses to play it. Here it is probably possible for people to report their behavior validly and hence it will be a timesaver to ask various categories of adult informants to estimate how frequently they played the various types of games. If one is interested in children's games, on the other hand, and if one finds from observation that their verbal reports as to how often they play the game are far from accurate, the anthropologist will have to do more extensive observing.

Type 2 focuses on more molecular categories of acts. Let us assume that our ethnographer wants to contrast a series of games on the degree of overt competitiveness of the players. Having observed the games, he isolates a series of discrete acts which he labels as "competitive behavior" and which might include instrumental pushing and hitting, exhortative or critical comments to team-mates, insulting behavior to opponents, argumentativeness with the umpire, elation or dejection about outcomes, etc. Using these categories of acts he samples the performances of players of the games he wishes to contrast. More frequently, observation of discrete molecular acts is made in settings where the interaction of individuals is casual rather than being part of a game or ritual. For example, one observes the competitiveness of Rajput men as they sit around the men's sleeping platforms smoking or the competitiveness of a group of mothers as they sit around chatting.

Type 3 observation focuses on the target of the attention of a group. In a game, for example, the observer would follow the person in possession of the ball. Good examples of this type of observation and ones which are more typical of the ethnographic domain are to be found in the work of Bales and other students of small groups (Homans 1950, Thibaut and Kelly 1959, etc.). In analyzing the structure of groups, decision making and general resource mediation, Bales (1950) concentrates on the individual who is holding the floor at the moment. So, in a court session, an ethnographer's observations would center in sequence on the prosecutor, the judge, the defendant, the witness or whoever holds the stage, recording their interaction with other individuals or groups of individuals.

Turning to the two types which focus exclusively on people, type 4 includes those observations of individuals which are made in order to generalize about the behavior of categories of people. Suppose the ethnographer wishes to contrast the behavior of men and women during a ritual. His attention will turn to discrete individuals, scanning the women who are present and the men and noting their activities. If he wishes to further distinguish between categories of men and women—for example, married versus unmarried—he scans individuals whose marital status he knows or can determine at some later date.

The observation of dyads (type 5) concentrates on the interaction or lack of interaction between two individuals as members of categories. Thus the ethnographer observes maternal uncles and nephews whenever they meet and notes who initiates interaction, the nature of the interaction and its effect on the behavior of the other member of the dyad. Avoidance behavior is a typical concern of ethnographers which is usually dyadic in nature.

Type 6 observation is focused on a setting. The ethnographer deploys himself at a water hole, a market place, a chief's court or the living room of a house and describes who comes and goes and what they do. Roberts' running accounts of daily life as observed in Zuni households (1956) is an example of this type. One can generalize about life in the central room of Zuni matrilineal extended families from an analysis of these records.

The observer should decide before beginning to record which type of observation

he is going to make. He may change his focus systematically, but if he does not plan in advance, his behavior record will often be uninterpretable. We have found it advisable to use different notebooks for different types of observations so that the change of techniques is clearly indicated.

WHERE TO OBSERVE: THE CHOICE OF SETTING

The interest of the ethnographer determines not only which of these six types of observations are best, but also where he should station himself to make the observations most efficiently. He needs a schedule for the community so that he can determine where to go at what time of day on what day of the week. For observational studies the *daily routine chart* is as essential as a genealogical chart is for the study of kinship. Various time and space maps are necessary for choosing where to observe: a ceremonial and social events calendar, a seasonal chart of economic activities, and daily routine charts for different categories of individuals. The degree of detail in any one of these charts will depend again on theoretical interests. In socialization studies we have found that by a combination of interviewing and observing in various households one can map the settings where various members of the family are to be found during the day, the people who are apt to be with them and the activities that are probably taking place (Whiting *et al.,* in preparation; see also Lewis 1951:62–72, for example of daily routine chart of a household). If the observer is interested in the father-adolescent son dyad, for example, he can judge from the schedule the best time to observe in the household and when else he might go. If he is interested in a particular type of interaction he may further predict from preliminary observation where this category of behavior is most apt to occur. If, for example, the ethnographer wishes to observe a mother's teaching techniques he should select that period of the day when mother and child interact frequently. We have found that the routine in most households is such that one can predict these periods with a fair degree of success.

It should be noted that setting affects behavior. We have found that some types of behavior are more frequent in one setting than another (Whiting *et al.*, in preparation). For example, helping and other nurturant categories of behavior occur more frequently in the house and immediate yard. Peer aggression is more apt to occur when adults are absent and the children are outdoors. Schoolrooms are very restrictive and certain categories of behavior occur rarely in this setting. In sum, preliminary observations in various settings will help the ethnographer choose the best place to station himself.

If the ethnographer rarely observes the type of behavior he wishes to record he should consider eliciting it experimentally. Strodtbeck's (1951) decision-making experiments among the Navajo are an example of this technique. It would have been impractical to wait around until an occasion arose when the researcher had the good fortune to hear a husband and wife discuss a family problem, but it was possible to introduce a controversial topic and observe the ensuing attempts to resolve the conflict. In the Six Culture Study we attempt to measure a child's tendency to be self-reliant. Our measure called for observing how a child responded to "encountering difficulty" (see Whiting *et al.* 1966). If he attempted to resolve the situation himself rather than asking others to help him or becoming angry or giving up, he was rated as self-reliant. Unfortunately, the frequency with which children encountered difficulty during the course of our sampling of their behavior in various settings was so infrequent that we either did not observe the child at all in the situation or observed him on such few occasions that we could not judge the typicality of his response. Furthermore, the degree of difficulty encountered varied greatly. Ideally, devising a simple experiment seems the best strategy for such a variable—preferably one in which the experimenter can pretest to ascertain how difficult the task is for an individual so that some standard can be set for comparing individuals in the society and across societies.

HOW MANY OBSERVATIONS ARE NECESSARY: SAMPLING PROBLEMS

The number of observations of a given type one makes depends on the generalizations one wishes to make. A good technique is to write a hypothetical statement and analyze its logical implications. We have noted that being able to describe a game or a technological process so that the reader can perform the activity is a possible criterion for sampling in type 6 observations. If the ethnographer is doing type 6 observations and concentrating, for example, on who attends a market, he observes until he feels satisfied that when he sets out to visit the market place he can predict fairly accurately the people he will meet. If he wants to generalize about *markets* he must visit other market places. If the same category of people appear in the same proportions in this sample, he can probably make a generalization, but he should draw the reader's attention to the number of markets he has observed.

If he wishes to compare the behavior of categories of people who frequent *a* market place, contrasting old women of the grandparent generation with child-bearing women with adolescent girls with preadolescent girls, the sampling problem is more difficult. How many adolescent girls, for example, should he observe in order to generalize about some aspect of their behavior? It could be that he has no choice since only four or five adolescents visit this specific market place. If there are more, he should sample six and if he finds that this aspect of their behavior is similar he can assume that the other adolescent girls will also behave similarly and he can write a summary statement about this type of behavior with some degree of confidence. (Again he should note the size of the sample.) If, on the other hand, each of the six girls behaves differently in the domain he is observing, he is unable to make a general statement and should increase the sample, observing more adolescent girls. He may now discover regularities or he may not and may decide that there are no observable *categorical* patterns of behavior in the domain —i.e., that being an adolescent girl is not an important variable in predicting the particular type of behavior in the market place. In sum, the number of observations will depend on the similarity of the behavior across members of the category selected for study.

Similarly if one is interested in acts, the number of observations of each individual will depend on the stability of the behavior unit in an individual across time. Will the same individual exhibit the same amount of aggression, as operationally defined by the ethnographer, from one day to the next so that the ethnographer can generalize about the individual's behavior? If the variation is great for one observation period to another, more observation periods will be necessary. It may be that the ethnographer will discover that he cannot generalize across all settings and that his statements will have to be qualified. For example, in the Six Culture Study, we had a sample of twenty-four children in each of six societies. These children were observed on an average of fifteen times on different days for five-minute periods (Whiting *et al.*, in preparation). We scored as one category of behavior attempts on the part of a child to help or dominate another child when the sample child's motivation seemed to be nurturant or responsible. When we contrasted a child's score in the first half of the observational periods with his score in the second half, the agreement was around .5. If, on the other hand, we controlled for setting and contrasted only the first and second halves of observations made at the child's home or in his own yard, the agreement was .7. We are able, therefore, to make general statements contrasting this type of children's behavior in the six cultures in these settings with more confidence that we have a stable measure (see Whiting *et al.*, in preparation).

Paired comparison is another useful technique for determining how many individuals to observe. In the Six Culture Study, we wanted to contrast the nurturant-responsible acts of boys and girls of the same age. A good strategy would have been to do a series of comparisons of pairs. If in a boy-girl comparison, girls consistently exhibited this behavior more frequently than boys, the ethnographer could feel reasonably confident in making a generalization. If, however, the differences were not so consistent, he would have to sample a larger group and in so doing might discover, as our analysis in the Six Culture Study indicates, that the sibling order of the child is also an important variable and that a boy with many younger siblings may be as nurturant-responsible as a girl (Whiting *et al.*, in preparation).

Lee and Ruth Munroe and Sara Nerlove (Nerlove 1969) have recently used paired comparison to good advantage in a study of sex difference in the setting occupancy of

Marigoli children. They matched girls and boys by actual age and recorded where each matched pair was at the same hour on fifteen different days. In all age groups the boys were further away from home than the girls.

PROBLEMS OF RELIABILITY— TRAINED ASSISTANTS

The problem of the reliability of measures is a ticklish one for an anthropologist who frequently works alone. If he is trying to observe systematically, he may have grave problems, for example, trying to keep the focus of his observation consistent. The problems vary with the domain of interest, type of observation and the number of observations he makes. In general the more complex the domain on which the observer is focusing and the more observations he needs to make, the more the specific definition of the area of focus is apt to change. In *activity*-type observations, for example, the problem of reliability is not so important as in more molecular *act*-type observations. By the tenth observation of an individual the original operational definition of aggression, for example, may have subtly changed. Furthermore, the observer may be developing new and interesting theories as he observes which will bias his observations or he may have become particularly fond of or hostile to sample individuals. Ethnographers are advised to read Robert Rosenthal's (1966) recently published volume on experimental bias in order to get some idea of the pitfalls.

Simultaneous observation and recording by two or more individuals is the recommended procedure for attempting to control both for slippage in definition of focus and observer bias. In the field, in naturalistic settings, however, there are many conditions which make simultaneous observation difficult. Assuming one has a colleague or has found assistants to train, natural settings are often disrupted by *one* observer, let alone two or three. If one attempts to set up experimental settings similar to those devised by experimental psychologists in our own society, one encounters the problems of the stilted and unnatural behavior that often occurs in our own laboratories, but may be exacerbated in other parts of the world because people are less accustomed to such settings.

If possible, native assistants should be found and trained to observe. They are helpful not only in assessing slippage and bias, but also in collecting a large sample of observations. Arthur Wolf in his study of Taiwan found it possible to train college students to make observations similar to those made in the Six Culture Study (Whiting *et al.* 1966). Okorodudu (1966) in a study of achievement motivation among the Kpelle of Liberia trained local high school girls to observe and record the frequency of the occurrence of sixteen types of mother-child interaction. In training the girls she interviewed them about the Kpelle linguistic categories for the acts which a mother does for and with a child of various ages. All of the girls had cared for younger siblings and had acted out most of the behavior themselves. In training the girls she asked them to describe in detail the type of behaviors which were included in these different categories of child care. She then explained to the girls the types of behavior she wished to observe and record. She visited the homes of sample children with the girls and again discussed the desired categories using examples from the observations they had made together. They continued to observe together until there was 80 percent agreement on coding categories.

THE ROLE OF THE OBSERVER

To what degree should the observer attempt to be unobtrusive while making systematic observations? In naturalistic settings it is impossible to be invisible since screens and one-way mirrors are impractical. The choice is primarily between interacting or attempting to remain aloof. The two extremes are exemplified by *One Boy's Day* (Barker and Wright 1951) in which the observer interacts with the child, and the Six Culture Study (Whiting *et al.* 1966) in which the field workers attempted to remain aloof from all interaction. Since the former was sampling one day rather than returning to observe the same child on several occasions, the strategy of interacting was probably wise. If the observer plans to return on numerous occasions he is probably advised to discourage all interaction. The field teams in the Six Culture Study had various degrees of success in remaining non-involved (Whiting *et al.* 1966). In Khalapur, India, it was difficult for Leigh Minturn since the

women, being confined to the courtyard by purdah, received visitors with eagerness. In New England the privacy of the isolated nuclear family made it especially difficult for the Fischers to be unobtrusive. It was less difficult in Tarong, Philippines, since visiting was very frequent. The first few times, however, it was difficult to dissuade the families from sending the children out of the house since this was and is considered etiquette. Observing was easiest in Taira, Okinawa, since the house and yards were visible from the streets and the Maretzkis could often stand there and record without being noticed. In all cases it appeared as if the children became accustomed to having the observers around and although we have no concrete evidence, they seemed to behave more naturally after two or three observation sessions.

HOW TO RECORD

Assuming that the ethnographer has decided to study some aspect of the culture which requires systematic observation (and has decided on the most fruitful settings for making his observations), how should he record the observations? Should he try to write down everything he sees? Should he write paragraphs in simple English? Should he depend on cameras, tape recorders, or video tape, or should he use some recording device like the Chapple Chronograph (1940) or Bales' recorder (1948)? Should he use a timing device such as that designed by Gewirtz (1965) or a stop watch? Advice on these questions depends on many contingencies, but there are several basic principles.

(1) Do not try to record everything you see. In training anthropology students to observe we have found that it is initially difficult to convince them that they cannot see and record everything that happens. Once they have witnessed an accident or other unusual event, however, and listen with care to the varied reports of eyewitnesses, they begin to grasp the problems. When they have actually done simultaneous observations and recording with another student, they are convinced that they need to decide on policies for omission or inclusion. It is often easiest to proceed by deciding what *not* to record.

(2) Do not try to observe on molar and molecular levels at the same time. For example, on the one hand, detailed observa-

tional records of the interaction of dyads will not include satisfactory descriptions of games; on the other hand, long specimen records like *One Boy's Day* (Barker and Wright 1951) may not be detailed enough for interactional analysis.

(3) There is no one best way to record and it is possible to vary one's techniques systematically. It is recommended that the observer have several types of observations and recording techniques which he alternates systematically while observing. He should be careful to mark his records carefully when he changes from one technique to another.

If you are coding while observing, it is wise to bring back simple running descriptions of typical observational periods as illustrations of your scoring system. We strongly recommend having such a descriptive record of all your types of observations accompanied, if possible, by video tape and recordings. Such protocols will give the context to both your precoded material and to your verbal descriptions, will illustrate your method, and may be used as checks on observer bias.

(4) Analyze your data as you collect it. It may be impossible to do this for all your observations but at least attempt a large enough sample to insure that you are recording what you need for analysis and that your system is not so complex that it will require an unrealistic number of hours for analysis. Records of observations in themselves are of little value if you do not have time to analyze them. The social science archives are filled with unanalyzed tapes, films and protocols. Roberts (1956) published his raw data hoping it would be of use to anthropologists, but I know of only one study which used his data to generalize about behavior (Whiting 1966). So often these stored records, as in longitudinal studies, do not include the crucial details which the analyst wishes since the studies were not designed with the same variable in mind.

In sum, decide how you want to analyze the data before you begin lengthy systematic observation. If you have not decided and wish to sample the universe, running English paragraphs such as anthropologists have recorded for years in their notebooks are as good as any record. They will probably consist primarily of acts which are salient at the moment and which are relevant to some developing generalization you wish to make about some aspect of life. See Mead for suggestions as to methodology (1940:330–332). If, on the other hand, you have decided on a specific interest or interests, make sample observations and then attempt to code them. This will tell you whether you are observing and recording the relevant details.

HOW LONG TO OBSERVE

Do not try to observe and record for too long a period as we have found that fatigue reduces reliability. The optimal observational period will vary with the type of observation. In activity-type observations, for example, the ethnographer may find it best to stick with the observation from start to finish of the game, ritual, or technological process. If it is an activity which occurs frequently, the ethnographer can return to observe another full cycle or he can select to observe those segments of the activity which he finds on analysis he does not understand.

For some molecular-type observations it is possible to sample long periods of time if the technique of recording is simple. For example, one can spend several hours in a household recording who initiates interaction with whom if one does not record the content of the behavior initiated. On the other hand, if one is recording details of interaction and attempting to observe what instigates an individual's behavior, recording for more than fifteen minutes at a time is not advisable.

HOW TO BUILD A CODE

In order to analyze molecular types of observational material, it is necessary to score the records in a standard way. The usual procedure is to decide on units and compute the frequency and rate of occurrence of these units. More complicated analyses may include an analysis of the sequence of occurrence of units (see Lambert 1960). In analyzing the material, unless the number of observations is small, we recommend developing a code which can be converted if desired for use in computer programs. Our experience with codes in the Six Culture Study illustrates some of the typical problems.

The aim of the Six Culture Study was to explore and to test hypotheses about the relation of the various techniques of child rearing used in the six societies to the personality characteristics of children between the ages of three and ten. In order to measure personality we decided rather than using the standard tests such as Rorschach, TATs, Draw-A-Man, etc., we would observe behavior systematically and rate personality characteristics on the basis of preference for and frequencies of the occurrence of certain types of behavior as observed in naturalistic settings (see Whiting *et al.* 1966). We selected nine types of behavior on the basis of previous cross-cultural work by John W. M. Whiting and Irvin L. Child. The types are modeled most closely on Henry A. Murray's needs and presses as described in *Explorations in Personality* (1938). They include nurturance, succorance, responsibility, dominance, submission (obedience), self-reliance, sociability, achievement, and aggression (for definition, seen Whiting *et al.* 1966:9–11).

The detailed history of the development of the code for one of these behavior systems, namely *nurturance*, will serve as an example. Selected as one of the important dimensions of personality, it was defined transculturally as follows: "In the presence of knowledge that someone else is in a state of need or drive, nurturance consists of tendencies to try to alleviate this state in the other person" (Whiting *et al.* 1966:10). Observations in the field were recorded in simple English paragraphs and the ethnographers were asked to use few inferential adjectives and adverbs. An interpreter usually accompanied the field worker to help him translate verbal behavior. The following observation is an example of a five-minute observation.

Mitsuko is an eight-year-old Okinawan girl who lives in Taira (for ethnography, see Maretzki 1963) with her mother and father and paternal grandmother, and three younger sisters: a six-year-old, Hatsue, a four-year-old, Mariko, and a three-month-old infant. The observation was made about three o'clock in the afternoon at the Yamagawa well. There are five other children at the well: an eight-year-old girl cousin, Ikuko; a nine-year-old girl, Tsuyako; a five-year-old girl, Masami; a seven-year-old boy, Terumitsu; and a six-year-old boy, Atsushi. The observation is focused on Mitsuko.

Mitsuko stands at the well's edge looking down at the water; she has left Mariko (sister, 4) standing at the edge of the concrete foundation (which is quite slippery). Mariko calls to her, "Sister, sister" in a whining voice. Mitsuko comes back to where Mariko is standing, puts her arms around her and asks her what she wants. Mariko says, "Ummm," and points over to the well. Mitsuko asks, "Want to go over there?" Mariko answers, "Hmm" (yes). Mitsuko takes her around the shoulders and leads her slowly and carefully over the slippery concrete to the water. Terumitsu (B7) says affectionately, "Little Mariko." Atsushi (B6), standing nearby, says, "I'm taller than her," and goes up to measure himself against her. Mariko stands smiling. Terumitsu drops the wooden dipper he has in his hands and runs over to Atsushi saying, "But I'm taller than you!" and he stands himself against Atsushi who stands smiling. Mitsuko smiles and leads Mariko protectively back over the slippery concrete to the ground. As they reach the edge both slip and nearly fall. Mitsuko's grip tightens and they both reach safe ground without falling. Terumitsu sloshes water over the well's concrete overhang. All laugh and watch. Mitsuko stands watching. Terumitsu comes over and asks her if she wants to continue his waterplay. Tsuyako (G9) stands to the back of her singing one song after another to the baby on her back who is crying. Mitsuko scratches her head and watches Tsuyako. Mariko turns to Mitsuko and asks Mitsuko to take her again to the water's edge. Mitsuko does not look at her. Mariko grabs hold of Mitsuko's hair to get attention. Mitsuko crouches and continues listening and watching Tsuyako. Ikuko (G9) comes up to her and asks her to wear her shoes for a while. She starts to put one shoe on then turns to Mariko and says, "Here, Mariko, hold on to this one." Mariko takes it and holds on while Mitsuko puts one shoe on. Terumitsu comes over and pours water over Mariko's feet as she smiles. Mitsuko says, "me next, me next!" and takes off the shoes. Terumitsu pours another dipperful of water, half over Mitsuko and half over Mariko's feet. Mitsuko with clean feet, now puts on the shoes. (Maretzki 1955)

It was agreed that Mitsuko nurtured her four-year-old sister in this protocol. The specific nurturant acts consisted of responding to her sister Mariko's calls for help, approaching Mariko and putting her arms around her and asking her what she wanted, and helping her across the slippery concrete.

On the basis of these and other specific examples of behavior we devised a code for nurturance which included: gives help (including giving food or object if obviously nurturant), gives emotional support or affection, gives information instrumental to nurturance, gives approval and gives permission. Each five-minute record was scored for the presence of these acts as well as a child's reactions to requests for help from others. The total frequency of these acts in all the observation periods focused on a given child was totaled and a rate per minute score was computed. The frequency of many of the discrete acts, however, was very low so they were combined into two macro-scores —one, giving help; the other, giving emotional support—on the basis of several criteria: (1) if they were considered related theoretically; (2) if they were highly correlated with one another; (3) if in the factor analysis they appeared with high loadings in the same factor; (4) if two coders used the categories interchangeably; and (5) if the new macro-categories could be reliably scored by independent coders.

In the above list, for example, giving permission was omitted from the summary nurturance score because it was not highly correlated with giving help or giving emotional support. For later comparisons across the six societies, giving help and giving support were combined into a single category of macro nurturance since neither one occurred with sufficient frequency for comparison among the boys and girls in all six societies. Furthermore, these two types of nurturant behavior were highly correlated. In other words, the coding procedure started with a broad transculturally defined variable which was divided into specific observable acts which were reported in the protocols collected in all six societies. These specific acts were used in the original code for each five-minute observation. In the final analysis the discrete acts were recombined into two macro nurturance categories (for discussion see Longabaugh 1966, and Whiting *et al.*, in preparation), so that each of the 134 children in the six societies received a rate score for nurturant behavior.

In 1961 at the Laboratory of Human Development, Longabaugh devised a code for interaction which he used in analyzing the behavior of mother-child dyads from different types of households. This code consisted of six modes of behavior: gives, seeks, withholds, accepts, ignores, rejects; and three resources: information, support and direction (Longabaugh 1962). It could be coded reliably while observing and there were significant differences between different household-type dyads on these dimensions as measured in one five-minute period of observation in a controlled setting. We have since devised a modification of this code which can be used

in naturalistic settings (see Antonovsky *et al.* 1966, mimeo.).

A very simple, but interesting code was devised by Ridington during a summer's field work in the Barbados (1964). She observed in different types of households and recorded the number of times adults and children initiated verbal interaction with one another. She did not attempt to record the content of this verbal interchange but found significant differences in amount of interchange between adults and children in the two types of households.

In sum, there is a constant interaction between types of codes, types of recording and types of observation. A cumbersome time-consuming method of recording and coding may lead one to devise a new technique of observation. Thus, as a possible measure of maternal nurturance to infants we would recommend a simple measure of the latency of a mother's response to her infant's crying which could be easily recorded with a stop watch. For older children, if we want to compare maternal nurturance, we would recommend selecting one or two settings when the mother is busy and recording her responses to requests for help from the children. It is always wise where possible to have a variety of methods of measuring the same type of behavior. The more numerous the independent measures one uses the more certain one is of generalizations in that domain of behavior.

ILLUSTRATIONS OF TYPES OF RECORDS OF BEHAVIOR

Included below are examples of records of behavior which have been published by anthropologists. A comparison of these protocols will illustrate some of the points made in this chapter. The first example is a household activity chart published by Lewis in *Life in a Mexican Village* (1951:63–71). The focus of these observations was the economic activities of a Tepoztlán household. Lewis was interested in making a general statement about the division of labor in the household when it operated as an economic unit. The record is taken in half-hour periods from the time the first person rises until the last person goes to bed. The activities of the four members of the household during each time period is noted in simple English

Table 1

A SYNCHRONIC RECORD OF THE ACTIVITIES OF EACH MEMBER OF A TEPOZTECAN FAMILY

Time March 28	Father	Mother	Eldest Daughter	Second Daughter	Youngest Daughter
A.M.					
6:00-6:30	In bed	Rises, makes fire and coffee	In bed	In bed	In bed
6:30-7:00	Rises, feeds cattle, takes them to pasture.	Goes to buy bread, sweeps patio	Rises, sweeps kitchen, prepares utensils	Rises, goes for milk	In bed
7:00-7:30	Drinks coffee	Serves husband and self coffee	Grinds corn, makes tortillas	Drinks coffee, cuts and stores dried fish	Rises, washes, combs hair
7:30-8:00.	Hauls water, shells corn for mules	Resumes sweeping patio	Grinds corn, makes tortillas	Smooths and folds laundered clothes	Breakfasts
8:00-8:30	Breakfasts	Combs hair, breakfasts, serves others	Grinds corn, makes tortillas	Breakfasts	Goes to school
8:30-9:00	Talks with investigator	Cuts squash for animals. cooks squash, shells corn	Grinds corn, makes tortillas	Makes beds	At school
9:00-9:30	Goes to bed	Arranges squash in market basket	Breakfasts	Sweeps porch	At school
9:30-10:00	In bed	Arranges squash in market basket	Washes dishes	Washes arms and feet, combs hair	At school
10:00-10:30	In bed	Goes to market to sell corn and squash	Prepares corn for grinding	Accompanies mother to market to make purchases	At school
10:30-11:00	In bed	At market	Prepares and cooks stew	At market	At school
11:00-11:30	In bed	At market	Prepares and cooks stew	At market	At school
11:30-12:00	In bed	At market	Prepares and cooks stew	Returns home, polishes nails	At school
P.M.					
12:00-12:30	Feeds mules	At market	Grinds corn	Talks with recorder	Returns home
12:30-1:00	Rests	At market	Makes tortillas	Feeds chickens	Does nothing
1:00-1:30	Rests	Returns home, prepares lunch	Makes tortillas	Helps with tortillas	Does nothing

Table 1 (continued)

Time P.M.	Father	Mother	Eldest Daughter	Second Daughter	Youngest Daughter
1:30-2:00	Eats and talks with recorder	Serves and eats	Makes tortillas	Eats	Eats
2:00-2:30	Eats and talks with recorder	Serves and eats	Eats	Eats	Goes to school
2:30-3:00	Reads prayers	Serves and eats	Eats	Sews	At school
3:00-3:30	Goes to bed	Hauls water for animals	Washes dishes	Sews	At school
3:30-4:00	In bed	In bed	Washes dishes	Sews	At school
4:00-4:30	In bed	Cleans dried gourds	Shells corn, prepares dough	Sews	At school
4:30-5:00	Reads prayers	Cleans dried gourds	Shells corn, prepares dough	Sews	At school
5:00-5:30	In bed	Cleans dried gourds	Mends her clothes	Sews	Returns home
5:30-6:00	In bed	Feeds turkeys	Mends her clothes	Sews	Reads
6:00-6:30	In bed	Cuts squash for animals	Knits	Sews	Talks to friends
6:30-7:00	In bed	Mends blouse	Knits	Sews	Talks to friends
7:00-7:30	In bed	Goes to visit mother	Grinds corn	Goes for bread	Knits
7:30-8:00	In bed	Sits in kitchen, talks with girls	Makes tortillas	Prepares coffee	Knits
8:00-8:30·	Gets up to drink coffee	Serves coffee to family and self	Eats	Eats	Eats
8:30-9:00	Goes to bed, takes medicine and foot bath	Prepares medicinal drink and foot bath for husband	Washes dishes	Knits	Knits
9:00-9:30	In bed	Goes to bed	Goes to bed	Knits	Knits
9:30-10:00	In bed	In bed	In bed	Goes to bed	Goes to bed

Table 1 (continued)

Time March 29 A.M.	Father	Mother	Eldest Daughter	Second Daughter	Youngest Daughter
6:00-6:30	Rises, feeds cattle	Rises, puts up coffee	Rises, makes fire, sweeps kitchen	In bed	In bed
6:30-7:00	Drinks coffee	Hauls water, goes for bread	Grinds corn	Rises, goes for milk	In bed
7:00-7:30	Hauls water	Has coffee and bread	Grinds corn	Waters plants, has coffee and bread	Rises and washes
7:30-8:00	Takes cattle to pasture	Goes to wash clothes at lavaderos	Makes tortillas	Sweeps, makes beds	Eats
8:00-8:30	Breakfasts and talks with family	Washes clothes	Makes tortillas	Goes to pick flowers	Goes to school
8:30-9:00	Feeds animals	Washes clothes	Breakfasts	Goes to pick flowers	At school
9:00-9:30	Looks for carpenter's tools	Washes clothes	Prepares beans	Goes to pick flowers	At school

phrases. Lewis does not describe how he made the record but part of it must have been based on interviewing and part on observation.

The activities are summarized by number of hours spent by each of the three women on six types of activities: farm work, trading or selling, marketing, sewing and knitting, and church attendance (Lewis 1951:72).

The second illustration is a daily routine record made by Naomi Quinn in an Indian household in the province of Chimborazo in the Ecuadorian Sierra (1966, MS). The observation was made as part of a pilot study on the relation of woman's economic tasks to the teaching of responsibility and the assignment of tasks to children. As in the Lewis records the focus is on activities but in this case it is primarily on activities of one woman rather than all the members of the household. The central actor is the woman of the house as she performs her tasks and assigns them to various members of the household. The activities of her husband and children are noted secondarily and in less detail. Parts of the day were sampled on a series of days since it was found exhausting to make such detailed records for more than about six hours at a stretch. The units of time used in recording were not standard but were based on convenience which corresponded in general with changes of the focus of attention of Josefa, the woman being observed. The activities are described in more *molecular* dimensions than in the Lewis record and since the focus is primarily on one person it is not possible to construct synchronic record of the other members of the house in similar detail. This demonstrates the need for *a priori* choice of focus of attention. Increasing the details in the description of activities of a single individual cuts down on the possibility of recording the activities of several individuals at the same time.

The following excerpts from Quinn (1966, MS:13–15) present the cast of characters, the setting and the first few hours observed on Thursday, April 5, 1962. The observation on this day continued until 11:00 A.M. The notes in parentheses in the left-hand column were added after the observations were made.

The third illustration is taken from *Zuni Daily Life* (Roberts 1956). This document includes a day's observation in each of three

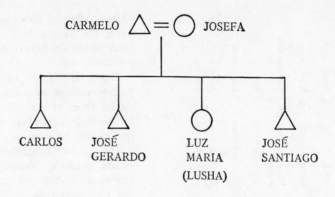

CARMELO △ = ○ JOSEFA

CARLOS   JOSÉ   LUZ   JOSÉ
          GERARDO   MARIA   SANTIAGO
                      (LUSHA)

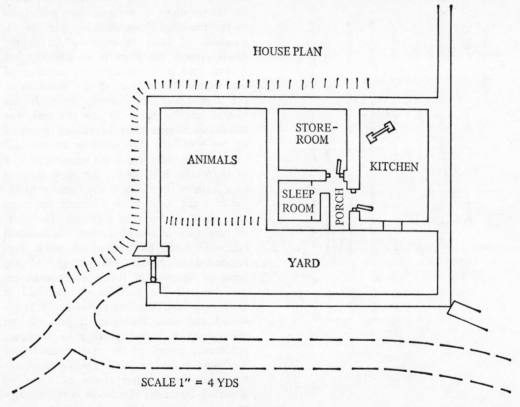

HOUSE PLAN

ANIMALS

STORE-
ROOM

KITCHEN

SLEEP
ROOM

PORCH

YARD

SCALE 1″ = 4 YDS

Figure 1.

Zuni households and two separate days of observation at a sheep camp run by the members of one of the households. The observations were made with several purposes in mind: to contribute to the knowledge of daily life, including child care, technology, animal husbandry, division of labor, etc., and to advance the study of small group cultures, in this case, the household (Roberts 1956:2). The observers, Roberts and his Zuni interpreter, stationed themselves in one of the rooms in the household and took turns dictating their observations onto a tape recorder in simple English phrases. The observers focused on "the principal centers of group interaction and activity" (Roberts 1956:5). They did not attempt to record all verbal behavior.

The observations start when the first member of the household rises and ends when the last goes to bed. As in the Quinn record the time is noted at irregular intervals based on what seems to be convenience. The observers scanned the cast of characters. It

Table 2

Day I, Thursday, April 5, 1962

Duration	Location	Activity
5:30-5:45	storeroom	Josefa and Carmelo are dressing; José Santiago is sitting in the storeroom, but the other children are still in bed.
(Gerardo is sleeping over at Marika's, which he does occasionally when he feels like it. Marika, a crippled sister of Josefa's, lives alone in the next house.)		
5:50-6:19	kitchen	Josefa carries José Santiago into the kitchen. She peels potatoes with José Santiago on her lap; Carmelo has gone outside to sweep the front yard.
(This is done every morning by Carmelo with the help of Carlos, whose job it is supposed to be.)		
6:00-6:05		Carlos and Luz Maria come into the kitchen, Luz carrying her clothes; Josefa interrupts potato peeling to dress Luz Maria. Carmelo calls to Carlos very sternly four or five times to go to doctrine class, and Josefa insists, "Run, run!" but Carlos just sits huddled in the kitchen, looking miserable.
6:19-6:25	storeroom	Josefa washes the potatoes; Carlos goes outside to help his father.
(Josefa said Carlos has complained it was too cold to go.)		
6:25-6:27	kitchen porch kitchen sleeping room kitchen	Josefa tells Luz Maria to bring in fuel but gets no response; she puts José Santiago on her back and goes herself, bringing in a load of firewood, which is stored on the porch, and a load of straw for kindling, from the sleeping room.
6:27-6:50		Josefa tends the fire; Luz Maria is playing with José Santiago on his mother's back and Josefa tells her to stop several times without looking up.
6:35		Josefa knocks José Santiago's head gently against Luz Maria's and laughs.
6:43	sleeping room kitchen	Josefa tells Luz Maria to bring in more straw, again getting no response; Josefa goes herself; Carmelo has gone for water at the faucet and to buy bread and sugar for me at the store.
(The water faucet from which the family's water supply is carried, and at which Josefa washes her clothes, is some 60 yards away, at the edge of the road; it is reached by a path which follows one of the ravines downhill. The store is just across the road from the faucet.)		
6:50-7:00		Carlos enters; Josefa puts a pot with two eggs and a pot of potatoes on the fire (the eggs are for me), searches for utensils, adds salt, while Carlos tends the fire.
7:00-7:13		Carlos goes out to help his father; Josefa cuts an onion into the potatoes, and tends the fire.
7:10		Josefa calls Carmelo but gets no answer.

Table 2 (continued)

Duration	Location	Activity
7:13-7:24	storeroom	Josefa hunts for a *mano* (stone pestle), finds it and grinds salt; Luz Maria and José Santiago stay in the kitchen.
7:24	porch	Josefa dumps a box of potatoes over into a sack, to use the box for my table.
7:24	kitchen	Josefa tests the food; she gives a potato to José Santiago.
7:25		Josefa takes plates down from a shelf; she sends Luz Maria for Carmelo; Luz Maria goes out and comes right back.
7:27		Josefa gives another potato to José Santiago.
7:28		Josefa serves Luz Maria a bowlful of potatoes; she serves the eggs to me.
7:29		Josefa calls Carlos angrily; he enters, and she serves him.
7:30		Josefa gives a third potato to José Santiago.
7:32		Josefa takes José Santiago off of her back and sets him on a blanket in the center of the kitchen; she gives Carlos seconds.
7:33		Josefa serves me potatoes.
7:35		Carmelo enters and serves me bread and coffee-milk with sugar and *manzanilla* (an herb). Josefa serves Carmelo, gives Carlos thirds and serves herself.
7:37		Josefa serves Carlos a fourth bowlful, telling him to hurry, for school; she serves Carmelo seconds, and offers Luz Maria a second bowlful, which Luz refuses; Josefa eats it herself.
7:37-7:50		Carlos leaves for school; Josefa offers Luz Maria seconds, which she now accepts.
7:50-7:52		Josefa puts away the plates.

(Carmelo is working for Sr. Portalancia, planting potatoes, and the patron wants all the men to eat in the fields, because he is in a hurry to finish the planting. So Josefa now begins to prepare a lunch to bring to the fields.)

Duration	Location	Activity
7:52	porch kitchen	Josefa carries in more potatoes.
7:52-8:10		Josefa peels potatoes.
8:10-8:20	yard	Josefa looks to see if the men are going to work; Carmelo follows her out; Josefa gathers together Carmelo's things; in the kitchen, the baby is whining.
8:20-8:25	path outside gate	Josefa talks to Carmelo and watches him go.

Table 2 (continued)

Duration	Location	Activity
8:27	kitchen	Josefa adjusts Luz Maria's skirt.
8:30-8:35	yard kitchen	Josefa splits a board with a pick; the baby is crying; Josefa carries the wood inside.
8:35-8:40	porch	Josefa cleans José Santiago, who has urinated, with a cloth and carries him out onto the porch, where she cleans him off more thoroughly; she puts him on her back; he stops crying.
8:40	sleeping room kitchen	Josefa gets a load of straw.
8:40-8:55	kitchen storeroom kitchen porch kitchen	Josefa makes a fire, puts rice in a pot, adds water and puts the pot on the fire; she yells at Luz Maria to go out for an onion, with no result; she goes for herself, bringing back an onion and cutting it; she goes for a strainerful of potatoes, Luz Maria following her; she gives some beans to Luz Maria.
9:00-9:25		Josefa nurses the baby, on her lap, while peeling potatoes; José Santiago falls asleep on her lap.

appears that rather than compulsively rotating their attention on individuals they allowed it to be drawn to salient events, returning to scanning when no particular episode demanded attention. It will be noted that this record is as *molecular* in its description as the Quinn protocols but less selective in the type of activities and details which are recorded. It can also be noted that there are fewer interactional sequences. It is almost as if one had a series of juxtaposed stills instead of a record of continuous action—the result of scanning rather than restricted focus.

The following is an excerpt from the record of Household A which begins at six-fifteen in the morning.

TABLE 3
THE DAY—MAY 3, 1951

COMMENT.

The dictating machine was initially placed in ER, and an extension cord was run through the east window to the next-door neighbor's house where it was plugged into a power source. There was enough cord to move the machine to CR but not to WR.

The first observation was made at 0615 on a fair, clear morning, and the last at 2129, so the report covers slightly more than fifteen hours of continuous observation. Notes were made by the author and his Zuni interpreter (AdElSo27). When the interpreter's remarks are presented, the time designation will be followed by his code designation. Unless otherwise indicated, the comments are by the author. The asterisk after a time notation indicates that the time has been estimated.

THE RECORD.

0615

Mo51 and FA68, who slept in the east bed in ER, are up now.

FaYoBr53 and Da10 are sleeping in the same bed in the southwest corner of CR.

So14 and FaElBr73 are asleep in their respective beds in CR.

Fa68 is making a fire in the ER heating stove.

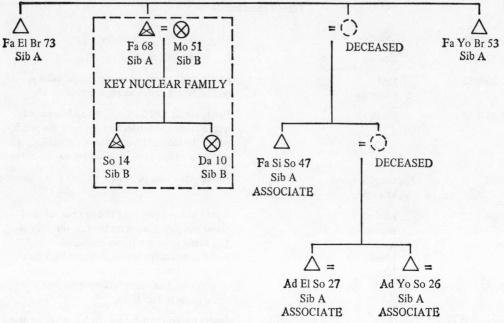

Figure 2. Members of Household A

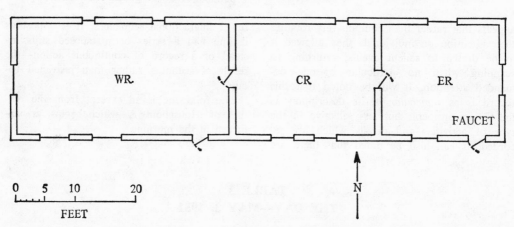

Figure 3. Floor Plan of House A

Mo51 is moving into CR to make a fire in the CR cooking stove. She removes the ashes from the stove.

0617—(AdElSo27A)*

Mo51 almost tripped on the extension cord crossing ER.

0617*

Fa68 put wood in the ER heating stove and then put kerosene on the wood. He lighted the fire with a match.

Da10 is just waking.

0620

There is no activity in the village, and the streets are quiet.

Mo51 is putting her black manta on over her dress.

Fa68 is dressed in his shirt and trousers, but he is not wearing shoes.

Da10 is putting on her skirt before she gets out of bed. Now she climbs out of bed. She is wearing a blue blouse and a green-plaid wool skirt, but not socks or shoes. Although she has a bed of her own, she didn't sleep in it last night. Instead she slept with FaYoBr53. She asks her mother where her socks are.

Mo51 is now fully dressed in her black oxfords, brown stockings, manta, green dress, red belt, red-checkered apron in front, and earrings.

Fa68 puts on his socks, and he is just putting on his shoes. He was wearing long, winter underwear when he arose.

0625

Da10 has on her socks and shoes and is standing by the ER heating stove.

Fa68 put his shirt inside his trousers, went to the ER water tap, filled a bucket with water, and then placed the bucket on the ER heating stove to heat water for washing. Now he is taking out the ashes from this stove.

Mo51 came into ER and removed the bucket from the ER stove. She carried the water to the CR cooking stove and poured the water into the large, white, enameled coffeepot sitting on the top of the stove and placed the coffeepot directly over the fire.

FaYoBr53 is now peering up from his blanket.

Mo51 took the bucket back to the ER tap and filled it. She then brought it back to the ER heating stove where Fa68 had originally placed it.

Fa68 moved into CR. He is now putting more wood in the CR cooking stove fire.

The fire is now roaring in the ER heating stove.

Fa68 returns to ER and at the washstand runs some cold water from the tap into the white, enameled washbasin. He moves the washbasin to the smaller washstand, rolls up his sleeves, unbuttons his shirt, picks up a bar of hand soap, and washes his hands.

Mo51 is still working with her hair.

FaElBr73 just sat up in bed.

0628

Fa68 is also washing his face.

0628—(AdElSo27A)

Fa68 continues washing his face and hands. Now he is brushing his teeth. He emptied the water into the slop bucket and pours clean water into the basin again. He continues to wash his face and to brush his teeth. Having finished washing, he dries his hands with a towel hanging on the south side of ER. He asked Mo51 if she were going to wash her face too.

0630

FaElBr73 is sitting on the edge of his bed dressed in his long, winter underwear.

So14 is still sleeping.

FaYoBr53 is awake, but he isn't up.

Da10 walks to the ER washstand and fills the white, enameled washbasin with cold water.

Mo51 has just finished braiding her pigtail.

Fa68 comes back with a towel from ER.

Da10 is washing her hands with bar soap.

Mo51 stepped outside. She is now walking south to the woodpile.

Fa68 walked into WR, closing the door, and then returned to CR.

Mo51 returns to the house. She had looked to see if any wood was already chopped, but since there was none, she came back.

Fa68 picked up his butcher knife in CR, walked over to the worktable, opened the drawer, and took out a file with a handle. He is now sharpening the knife.

Mo51 is just beginning to clean off the CR table.

Da10, who has finished washing her hands and face, is drying her face with a towel.

0636—(AdElSo27A)*

Fa68 is cutting up the mutton, which was hanging in WR, for breakfast.

Mo51 uncovered half of the CR dining table by folding back the oilcloth.

Fa68 returned from WR and placed the mutton on the exposed half of the table (CR) to cut the mutton into pieces for frying.

Mo51 and Fa68 are discussing the preparation of the mutton. They are now stating that the intestines of the sheep just butchered tasted like hot chili, hot pepper. They claim it's due to eating the sagebrush all the time because there's no grass that the sheep could eat to have the meat be more tender instead of tasting like a hot pepper.

Da10 got the chewing gum from the drawer of the dresser and is now chewing it.

So14 just now woke up, but he still isn't up from his bed.

FaElBr73 got up and went into WR although his shoes still weren't tied and his shirt wasn't tucked in.

Da10 picked up her jacket or coat and wanted to go to school. Mo51 told her that she was still too early.

0640

FaElBr73 is already wearing his headband. Fa68 is still cutting mutton on the CR dining table.

Mo51 went into ER, picked up the white, enameled washbasin, returned to CR, put some warm water in it from the container on the CR stove, and went back to the ER washstand.

Da10 is wearing her coat and is moving about. She had considered going to school without breakfast. AdElSo27 said that sometimes she doesn't eat breakfast. Da10 walked to the box containing bananas, picked up one banana, and walked outside.

0641

Although we were mistaken, it was thought that Da10 was going to school. School doesn't start until nine o'clock. Mo51 says that Da10 is doing some work for her teachers and probably that is why she left early.

Mo51 washed her face.

FaElBr73 is making his bed. He is dressed in a cotton shirt, headband, denim trousers, and work shoes.

Fa68 is dressed in a work shirt, wool trousers, and work shoes, but he is not wearing a headband.

Mo51 goes to the CR dresser and takes out some lard. Now she has moved the coffeepot back on the CR stove and is putting some lard into the large frying pan.

0645

Everyone is up except So14, who is beginning to stir, and FaYoBr53, who is still in bed. The mutton is now cooking in the frying pan.

FaElBr73 has made his bed, but this is the only bed which has been made this morning. Da10's bed is made because she didn't sleep in it last night.

Fa68 is still cutting up mutton.

Mo51 is frying the mutton in the large frying pan.

FaElBr73 is just putting on his belt.

FaElBr73 went to the ER washstand and picked up a cup. He pours some water into the washbasin and is now walking to the ER heating stove to get some warm water from the bucket placed there by Mo51.

Fa68 went into WR and brought back two good-sized onions to be cut up and fried with the mutton.

Mo51 suggested that one onion would be enough. Mo51 places a lid over the frying pan for quicker cooking of the food.

Fa68 tried to cut up the onions, but he didn't make much progress.

Mo51 has taken his place and is now cutting up the onions.

FaYoBr53 is sitting on his bed. He hasn't begun to dress.

FaElBr73 finished washing his face and hands. He is now drying them with the towel.

Fa68 is adding more wood to the CR cooking stove fire. He carries the shoulder of mutton from which he has been cutting pieces for breakfast back into WR.

After FaElBr73 finished drying his hands, he emptied the water from the washbasin into the slop bucket.

Fa68 asked where a different bucket was. They told him that it might be outside.

FaElBr73 is now brushing his teeth.

0651*

FaYoBr53 is sitting up in his long, winter underwear and is putting on his trousers.

FaElBr73 is still brushing his teeth. He took a drink of water earlier this morning too.

0652

Fa68 picked up a bucket. He is going to the water tap to fill the bucket with water.

So14 is yawning.

Fa68 takes his bucket of water outside. He intends watering the sheep in the pen south of the house.

Mo51 has now wiped off the entire CR table.

Fa68 has finished cutting up the meat and onions. There are two butcher knives, a rag, and a plate of onions on the CR table.

FaYoBr53 is putting on his shoes.

So14 pulled on his trousers as he sat on his bed.

FaElBr73 is standing by the stove.

Fa68 returns and refills his bucket.

Da10 just entered the house. She still has her banana. She didn't go to the school.

AdElSo27 is washing his hands and face.

0655

Fa68 enters (probably CR) with a broom and dustpan.

Mo51 removes the onions from the table so that no dust will get on them.

FaYoBr53 stands up and walks toward the ER washstand.

FaElBr73 comes into CR and gets a little sack (it may contain medicine).

AdElSo27 is drying his hands.

FaYoBr53 obtained some cold water in a basin from the ER tap for washing, then went to the ER heating stove and added hot water from the bucket.

Mo51 has gone to the outdoor privy northeast of the house.

FaElBr73 went outside.

Fa68 is sweeping the CR floor.

So14 has awakened, but he is still in bed.

FaYoBr53 is washing his hands with hand soap. He is not wearing his shirt, but he has rolled up his long, underwear sleeves.

Fa68 is sweeping. He sweeps the dust into a dustpan and then empties the pan into the CR cooking stove.

Da10 is eating her banana.

Outside FaElBr73 is walking north to HC, a household with which he is affiliated.

Fa68 is standing at the CR stove stirring the mutton and onions.

FaYoBr53 is washing his face.

So14 has put on his trousers and shirt.

Fa68 is adding wood to the CR cooking stove fire.

FaYoBr53 is wiping his face with the hand towel which hangs by the mirror to the west of the ER door.

So14 is now up, wearing shirt, socks, and trousers.

0700

So14 is winding (and possibly setting) the alarm clock.

Fa68 went into WR and then out through the WR door to empty the waste water.

There is smoke coming from many chimneys in the village now, but there still is little activity on the road to the south.

Da10 threw the banana peel into the slop bucket.

So14 walked to the ER washstand. He now has some water in the white, enameled washbasin and is washing his face and hands with hand soap.

FaYoBr53 stepped outside dressed in his undershirt, trousers, and socks. He is going to the outdoor privy.

Fa68 is still watering the sheep. He took another white, enameled pail, the same pail which contained the slop water.

So14 has finished washing and is drying his face while he sits on his bed.

Fa68 returned to WR with the pan.

FaYoBr53, Mo51, and FaElBr73 are out of the house.

0705

Fa68 picks up his hat in WR and puts it on. He walks into CR and over to the stove where he removes the lid of the pan and stirs the mutton and onions which are cooking.

Da10 watches him.

So14 is looking at a comic book called "Topix."

Fa68 rinsed out the small coffeepot. Then he obtained some "McCormick Tea" from the CR cupboard. He puts some tea in the coffeepot. Then he pours some hot water from the large coffeepot on the CR stove into the little coffeepot. He puts the lid on the coffeepot. He looks at the large coffeepot, takes it to the ER washstand from CR, empties the remaining water, and washes out the coffeepot with water, putting the waste water into the slop pail.

AdElSo27 says that Fa68 frequently aids in getting breakfast. Now Fa68 is putting spoonfuls of coffee into another white, enameled coffeepot. He walks over to the CR stove and adds hot water to the pot. He puts this coffeepot on the stove next to the coffeepot serving as a teapot. He gets the lid and puts it on the coffeepot.

Mo51 returned and walked into CR.

0710

Mo51 goes to the CR cupboard and gets out the dishes for setting the table—among them the little cream pitchers, the Zuni Salt Lake salt.

Fa68 walks outside.

Mo51 puts a platter on the table.

So14 is just sitting.

FaElBr73 returns to the house.

Fa68 is outside chopping wood.

There is little activity outside, but a few persons have walked down the road.

Mo51 set out seven bowls.

FaElBr73 comes back into CR, picks up a chair, and sits down on it.

FaYoBr53 comes back into the house.

Mo51 is still setting the table.

FaYoBr53 walks over to his bed, takes off the pillows, and starts to straighten it.

So14 is outside the house.

FaYoBr53 is making his bed.

Fa68 comes in with some wood which he puts into the ER heating stove.

FaElBr73 is just sitting quietly.

Da10 is sitting in a chair which she has pulled up to the CR table.

Mo51 is cutting a loaf of Zuni bread.

Fa68 fills the water bucket on the ER heating stove. He now walks into CR.

So14 just entered ER from outside.

Mo51 is putting fried mutton and onions into a bowl.

FaYoBr53 is still making his bed.

Fa68 just put back the frying pan lid.

0715—(AdElSo27A)

The table is now set for breakfast.

Da10 put some fried meat on her plate.

Mo51 used the dipper to get some warm water from the ER heating stove.

Fa68 put some tea in a cup for himself.

FaYoBr53 got a banana from the box.

So14 has one too.

The seating arrangement at HA's dining table is: FaElBr73, east end; Da10 and Fa68, north side; So14, west end; FaYoBr53 and the author, south side.

Fa68 rose and looked in the cupboard for some more cream, but there was none.

A comparison of the details of these first three types of records will emphasize some of the differences in central focus and detail of recording. Let us compare the first half hour in the three records.

The entry in the Lewis record is 13 words long, in the Quinn record, two paragraphs— a total of about 46 words. (The information in parentheses was added later.) For the comparable length of time, Roberts has approximately 1200 words or close to ninety-five simple English sentences while Quinn's has about six subject predicate units. The differential length of the Roberts and Quinn protocols is due to the fact that Roberts tries to include all the minutiae of daily life. He notes, for example, the color of clothing, and reports where his characters are standing and sitting, the temperature of the water they use to wash their faces, etc. Quinn is interested in naming and timing the tasks which the mother performs and naming activities of the husband and the children but skips ethnographic details unless she thinks they are particularly relevant to her interest.

LEWIS: *Life in a Mexican Village*

Time	Father	Mother	Eldest Daughter	Second Daughter	Youngest Daughter
March 28 6:00–6:20	In bed	Rises, makes fire and coffee	In bed	In bed	In bed

QUINN: *A Day in the Life of a Woman in Capilla Loma*

Day 1, Thursday, April 5, 1962

Duration	Location	Activity
5:30–5:45	storeroom	Josefa and Carmelo are dressing; Jose Santiago is sitting in the storeroom, but the other children are still in bed.
(Gerardo is sleeping over at Marika's, which he does occasionally when he feels like it. Marika, a crippled sister of Josefa's, lives alone in the next house.)		
5:50–6:19	Kitchen	Josefa carries Jose Santiago into the kitchen. She peels potatoes with Jose Santiago on her lap; Carmelo has gone outside to sweep the front yard.
(This is done every morning by Carmelo with the help of Carlos, whose job it is supposed to be.)		

ROBERTS: *Zuni Daily Life*

See accords for 0615–1645, reproduced above.

In appraising the observations, let us ask what we learned from these observations which we could not have discovered more efficiently by interviewing. What can we say about behavior on the basis of these protocols?

It is interesting that the Zuni father actually helped with the cooking and firemaking in contrast to the men in Tepoztlán and Ecuadorian households. If this is accepted behavior in Zuni, however, we could have easily discovered it by ethnographic interviews. If, however, helping with cooking is not prescribed but proscribed then both the husband and wife might have been loath to admit the extent of the husband's help. Having made the observation in one household, it would be necessary to sample others in order to discover whether the husband's behavior was idiosyncratic or a typical deviation from a stated ideal and norm. (In Household B the men helped with the fire but not cooking and in Household D the father helped with the fires and a twenty-two-year-old son-in-law helped set the table for breakfast. In the sheep camp there were no women and the men did the cooking. However, I would only conclude from the three cases that if I were interested in this domain I should observe more households and probably control for the number and ages of the women in the household and the number of small children.)

If one is interested in time budgets, the estimates informants give re daily activities is often far off. If one is interested, for example, in how long it takes to prepare breakfast, observation may be necessary. In Tepoztlán the family had coffee one half-hour after rising and the tortillas one and one-half hours later. In Capilla Loma, Josefa served potatoes, coffee and bread two hours after rising. In the Zuni household, it took one hour to cook mutton, onions and coffee.

If one is interested in the number of responsibilities a woman has, observation is also probably essential. The Quinn record illustrates the number of things Josefa does at once: care for a year-old baby, dress a four-year-old, remind an eight-year-old, peel potatoes, etc. In Zuni Household B where there is a child near Josefa's baby's age, there are a grandmother and three aunts available to care for him while breakfast is being prepared.

If one is interested in the details of handling an infant or child, both the Roberts records in Household B (Roberts 1956:45–78) and Quinn records are inadequate because the focus is not exclusively on the child. The following entries in Zuni Household B concern the one-and-one-half-year-old infant boy.

0623: YoSo8 walks in to South East Room carrying ElDa So1½ wrapped in a pink baby blanket. After washing her hands, ElDa21, the baby's mo, picks up the baby and carries him to the northwest bedroom.
0628: Mo51, the baby's grandmother, told her 14 year old daughter, YoDa10, to pick up ElDaSo 1½, her nephew, and she went in and did so;
0705: ElDaSo1½, the baby, was fussing. His aunt aged 10, YoDa10, picked him up and took him into the South central room.
0715: The baby's grandmother, Mo51, finished breakfast and picked up ElDaSo1½, her grandson, who was being held by YoDa10.

Contrast these static descriptions with the following protocols recorded by Corinne Nydegger and her interpreter TS (Nydegger and Nydegger 1955). It focuses on Teofista, the three-year-old daughter of Petra (House 14). The grandmother Maria (House 15) who lives next door is present.

Protocol—⚡Intimate
Teofista Castillo
July 29—3:06–3:11 P.M.
House ⚡14

TS and I are seated on the porch of house ⚡14, chatting with Petra, Teofista's mother (14-0) and her grandmother, Maria. Teofista is in the bedroom of the house, presumably napping.

Petra	TS
CN	Maria
sala	bedroom

Wails can be heard from the bedroom, increasing in volume.

Maria goes into the house and Petra explains to TS that Teofista occasionally wakes up and finds herself alone, always cries and has to be picked up when this happens.

Maria comes back to the porch, carrying Teofista, who looks almost asleep but is still wailing loudly.

Maria puts Teofista in Petra's lap, resumes her seat.

Teofista continues to weep and wail, Petra trying to hush her with quiet: "Don't, don't."

Teofista roars: "I don't like! I don't like!"

With her eyes closed and appearing to be asleep, she continues to wail.

Petra smiles, rocks Teofista a little, says softly: "Don't cry now. Are you not ashamed?"

Teofista repeats, almost indistinguishably wailing: "I don't like! I don't like!"

CLUSTER OF HOUSES (PART OF HAMLET WHICH INCLUDES 12 OTHER HOUSES).

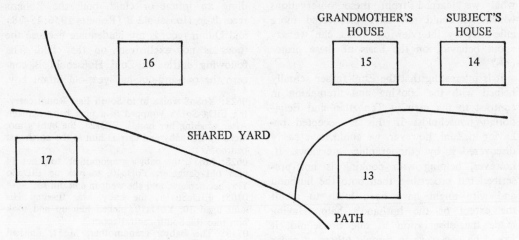

THE MALE HEADS OF HOUSEHOLDS 13, 14, 16 AND 17 ARE SONS OF HOUSEHOLD 15.

HOUSE PLAN (ADAPTED FROM HOUSE PLAN, FIGURE 1, NYDEGGER AND NYDEGGER 1966)

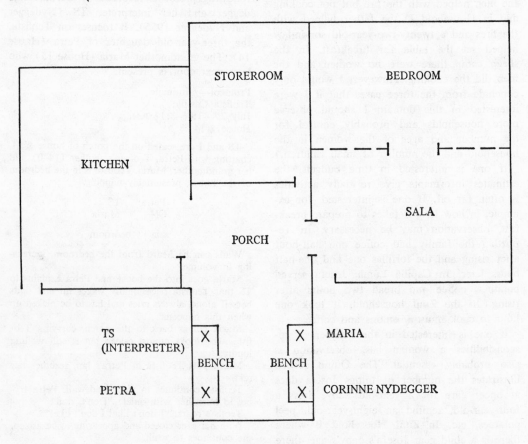

FIGURE 4

Maria laughs, goes to Petra and tries to take Teofista.

Teofista hits and wiggles, refuses to be picked up.

Petra shrugs, smiles and Maria laughs, sits again.

Teofista continues the wailing in an even rhythm, occasionally broken by a sob or two.

Petra jiggles her a bit, says: "See, mother of Elizabeth (me) is smiling at you."

Teofista closes her eyes tightly, wags her head and increases the wails.

Maria says: "Let's go and see Foling." (Felisa Castillo, cousin, 17, who lives next door.)

Teofista howls: "I don't like!"

Maria laughs, Petra smiles, rocks Teofista.

The wails subside to a low moaning.

She scratches her leg, whimpering a bit and looking very miserable.

Justo, Teofista's brother aged 5, below the porch, pounds one of the porch posts with a stick.

Petra says sharply to him: "Pssst!"

Teofista stops wailing, appearing to have gone to sleep.

After a moment, the wails start again.

Petra, getting annoyed by now, says: "La! Stop now, my child! Are you not ashamed!"

Teofista roars: "Not ashamed!" angrily.

She opens her eyes, looks at me, blinks a bit, closes her eyes again.

She whimpers as before, but considerably subdued.

She again scratches her leg, then rubs her eyes, scrubbing at them with both hands.

Turning, she angrily pounds Petra's chest with her fists, whimpering.

Petra pulls back a bit, smiling, settles Teofista again.

Teofista settles down a bit, watches Loreto (17-3) and Asuzena (16-3) (girl cousins aged 3 who live next door) run past the house laughing.

Suddenly she turns, no longer crying, and pounds Petra again as hard as she can.

Petra says: "Ay!" and forcibly resettles her.

Breathing heavily, Teofista leans back against Petra, shading her eyes with her hands.

She sits this way, sulky and half-asleep, as Petra rocks her slightly.

The observer in this case keeps her eyes on the child and does not attempt to report the behavior of others unless it is addressed to the child or seems to be the focus of the child's interests. In order to know how typical Teofista's behavior on this occasion was we would have to sample other instances. If we wanted to generalize about the behavior on first awaking from a nap we would have to visit other days at the same time hoping to find the same people around. If we were interested in dyads, for example, the grandmother–three-year-old female grandchild dyad, we would have to sample their interaction on a series of occasions in different settings.

The next illustration is of a different type of observation, one which has a longer history in anthropology. It is focused on ceremonial or ritual behavior, behavior which from the earliest time field workers have attempted to describe in their own words, as they were never satisfied with just the verbal accounts of informants. Mead and Bateson and their research assistants developed the most carefully thought out methodology for such observations. It is described by Mead (1940:238) as follows:

The investigator may make a running record of the behavior of a group of individuals against a time scale. Where cooperative field work is being done, a parallel photographic or Cine record, or a combination of the two may be added to this. The observations may be parceled out among a number of observers, one taking ceremonial behavior, another informal behavior not immediately oriented to the ceremony, another recording only verbatim conversations, or another following a single individual through the same period. (This is the method which is now being used in our Balinese researches by Mr. Bateson, Miss Jane Belo, Mrs. Katharane Mershon, and myself, with the addition of three trained literate native observers, I Made Kaler, Goesti Made Soemoeng, and I Katoet Pemangkoe, working in shifting cooperative combinations. In this method at least two people always work on a given ceremonial occasion, and they work selectively, against a time scale. The result is either: scenaria, conversational record, with or without photographic, Leica only, or Cine and Leica combined.)

The most recent publication on Bali ritual behavior based on records collected using this method is a volume on *Trance in Bali* published by Jane Belo in 1960. It includes many examples of the recorded observations. Included below is a sample of one of the records of the ritual behavior of the preadolescent trance dancers (Misi and Renoe) in Bajoeng Gede, a mountain village in central Bali which was studied by Mead and Bateson from 1936 to 1939. The performance from which the illustration is given was recorded in July, 1936, by Mead (MM), Bateson (GB) and a Balinese secretary (MK). It was filmed by Bateson and photographs were also taken on a Leica. The dance begins at 3:52 P.M. and continues until 5:55. The following is an excerpt. Jane Belo has added comments on the film so that the reader can imagine what the record would be like if the film was also available.

Sanghyang Performance of July 13, 1936 (From Notes of MM, MK, Cine Film #20, #21 of GB, LEICA 2 A, GB)

This was the performance which was ordered by MM and GB in order that they might see the West Club dance, since Tjibloek, the elder of the two girls, appeared to be on the verge of puberty. They had asked that the performance begin in the early afternoon because they wanted to photograph it. The day before it was to take place Tjibloek began to menstruate. The show was held up, too, for other reasons: the orchestra had been lent out, and it was necessary to borrow another one; the offerings were not right; the crowd necessary for the singing was slow to assemble. Once MM and GB went off in a huff, left the temple, and went home, for it seemed that the performance would never take place.

MM About half an hour later I Lasia came to say that both Renoe and Tjibloek were there. . . . We went back, to find Renoe inside looking very sulky and cross, and Tjibloek looking over the temple wall, and were told that she could not enter the temple because she was menstruating, but that Renoe would dance. So we started in.

3:52 P.M. They started to dress Renoe. She was trembling violently.

4:00 Nang Karma starts praying. Singing begins. Each stickholder puts his hands on the stick, Nang Saboeh to the east, I Moedri to the west.

4:05 Cine shots of Renoe dressing and trembling.

4:10 Renoe brought up to the délings (puppets).

4:11 She puts her hands on the stick.

4:13 Renoe begins to sway. Nang Karma sprinkles her.

4:15 She starts swaying with her head free and begins stamping with the stick.
Shift to a more stamping rhythm, back to swaying, then stamping again, swaying.

JB The film of this part shows Renoe, her body rounded and her head bent toward the pedestal, her arms only agitated at first by the vibration of the stick. Soon the vibration extends to her head, which seems to shake. Then, as she goes further into trance, and the swaying from side to side increases in violence, she loosens up so that her head rolls on her neck, and the shaking motion is discontinued. This is the moment which MM noted as "swaying with head free."

The film shows her swaying several times to the left, then, with a compensatory swing, far over to the right, and again to the right, before she achieves the full abandoned fling of her body all the way from one side to the other. As she begins the thumping motion on the pedestal, she leans forward, toward it, and her head goes forward loosely as she pounds. Again she goes into the side-to-side motion, so strongly carried away that the girl behind her, who is supporting her under the armpits, is carried from side to side too in the swaying motion. As Renoe leans toward the pedestal, thumping, her head rolls forward with the forward motion, down, almost on her arm, back, down, and down again. The pedestal rocks.

MM noted:
4:16 Stamping again. Another song. So violent she missed the pedestal.
4:18 Renoe falls back, OUT.

JB The film shows her fallen back against the attendant, quite limp. The attendant shifts her position, lifting her a little on her lap, to which Renoe responds, or fails to respond, with rag-doll flexibility. Her head rolls forward. Then it lolls back against the attendant's shoulder.

MM noted:
4:20 Renoe's head is swaying. Her headdress is put on. She leans back.
4:22 Singing. She starts to sway. She is stood up, picked up, carried on shoulder to our sanggah (household shrine).

JB The leica series shows the putting on of the headdress. Renoe is leaning back as they bind the cloth around her head, and, as they adjust the headdress, her head is still lolling. One arm, over the shoulder of an assistant, dangles limply. Further shots with the cine camera show her as she is lifted, seated on the shoulder of the man who is to carry her, still limp. He holds her legs as he rises from the crouching position and walks away, but her arms dangle loosely, she does not hold on to him, and even her feet hang down without any tension in them.

MM noted:
4:25 She begins to dance in our sanggah.
4:30 Change of step. She is dancing better than I have ever seen her, but MK thinks it is just because of the presence of the gamelan (orchestra).

JB The film shows her flinging her arms downward and back to alternate sides in a motion like the one the Balinese call tajoengan, "as when someone is walking and swinging his arms," yet she is standing in place. She twists her head, turns her body from side to side, as if dissatisfied. Then she raises her arms in the side-to-side motions, lifting them high over her head (an unusual gesture in Bali) and flinging out the ends of the scarf which hang from her hips with grace and abandon. As she goes into the side step, njerégség, her little feet, now extremely active, seem to race across the dance space. Someone has given her her fan, which she was without in the early moments of the dance and which, perhaps, she was gesturing for as she flung her arms about.

MK noted at this time:
When we reached Tuan's sanggah, the sanghyang was sung to, and the song was the one which con-

tains *"kotés-kotés"* (side bend and down flung arms). The *sanghyang* did *kotés-kotés*. I Sadia came up bringing the fans. One fan was given to Renoe. I Pajoe adjusted her headdress. She was sung to, then, the song *"sampar wanten"* [meaning unknown], and she was not pleased by it. Then there was the song *"déwa ajoe,"* still she was not pleased. Now she was played to by the *gamelan*. She wanted it. After the *gamelan* played, again *"déwa ajoe"* was sung. Again it was not wanted. Then the singers sang the song *"menjerégség"* (side step). The *sanghyang* did *njerégség* (side step). After that she did not want to perform. Nang Karma called out, *"Mesolah, Ratoe, apang tiang nenten doekaina ring I Toean"* (Perform, Your Highness, that I may not be blamed by Tuan).

MM
4:45 Renoe demurs again and is asked if she would like to go back to the temple. She would. We approve. Back to the temple.
4:47 Crowd shout warning as she is carried through the gate. It is said that she wants Tjibloek. Crowd is enjoying this impersonal bullying.
4:50 Renoe whispers. Everyone laughs. Whispers again.
MK I heard it said that the *sanghyang* wanted to touch (to bring in trance). The women and girls ran away. It was the *sagnhyang's* desire that Misi should dance with her.
MM Renoe stamps in temper. Whispers again. I Misi was lifted (?) over the wall and came down the east side of the crowd. Renoe fell upon her and shook her furiously, nearly pulling her head off. Misi went into trance almost immediately, went limp, and was carried over and dressed hastily, Renoe standing with eyes closed, in a position of petulance, occasionally stamping and waving her fan. Misi's eyes are twitching.
5:01 Crowd is growing. Djero Balian [old priestess, who is also a trance spokesman of the gods] comes in.
5:07 Both little girls begin to dance. Misi dances backward, trips over a child and falls limp. Ngemboet goes over and re-dresses her. GB remarks "Misi *believes* in it." Renoe stands with eyes closed while Misi is dressed. *After headdress is put back* on her head, holy water is brought, and it is sprinkled.
5:10 Misi's head lollops back while the headdress is sprinkled.
5:12 Dancing again. Crowd of girls keeps shrinking back from the dancers. Renoe whispers to Misi.
5:14 Music changes to *gamelan* and flute.
5:15 Dancers stop. Begin again. Renoe is dancing with eyes a little open, Misi as if her eyes were closed and she conscious.
5:17 Change to singing. A baby, I Ngenoe (approximately nineteen months) on the south side with his mother is waving his hands and imitating the dancers. [The baby is the small brother of Misi.]

5:19 Change of song. Renoe tells Misi to demur. Whispers. Fascinated, the baby Ngenoe dances out into the center, going up to Renoe, who doesn't see him and knocks him down. He is picked up wailing by Wadi [older trance dancer] and returned to his mother. Crowd shouted warnings when he fell. Renoe takes no notice. Dancing again.
5:21 Renoe in tantrum. I Lasia offers his shoulder, bends his knees several times, but is not accepted. Renoe goes over to a group of girls and sits on a girl's shoulder. She points and demands to be taken up. The girls laugh hard. I Lasia kneels again. She still refuses him. Misi falls backward on the girls. She doesn't want to be carried. Men Polih goes to her, persuades her to dance, to stand up. She wants her to dance on shoulders. Misi refuses. Men Polih demands. Misi simply flops over backward. Men Polih is angry at the refusal. Ngemboet offers himself. He is refused.
5:25 Misi still refusing to dance on shoulders. She stands up near the girls and dances in place, as if she would have a safe place to fall if necessary. Renoe is dancing more and more violently and boisterously, seated on the girl's shoulder. Renoe demands that Misi get up on a girl's shoulder. Nang Karma asks why Renoe is so wild and is told she wants to be carried by I Lameg and I Lameg refuses. Ngemboet offers to carry her. He is refused. I Lasia lifts her finally, dragging at her ankles.
5:27 Renoe drops her fan. Misi goes limp, in the face of attempts to make her dance on shoulders. Men Polih in exasperation lifts her up in her arms and dances with her. Renoe gets down.
5:31 Renoe goes and flops backward on the arms of a group of girls. Wadi is ordered to lift her up and does. Wadi dances with her in her arms. Renoe is really too heavy for her, and she has to shift her constantly. I Lasia offers to take her from Wadi. Renoe refuses. Renoe flops about wildly in Wadi's arms. Misi is dancing, stiff and formal, in Men Polih's arms. Men Polih puts Misi down. Renoe gets down. Renoe goes and climbs on I Lasia's shoulders, and points with fan at Misi. Nang Ngetis offers to Misi and is accepted. Both are up. Misi is now dancing very well on shoulders. The baby, I Ngenoe, follows them out again, the same tranced look on his face. Men Soeni grabs him back crossly.
5:32 Change in music, and both change their style of dancing.

During the three years that Mead and Bateson studied the village of Bajoeng Gede, they were able to record many similar performances of the little girl trance dancers. They were able to contrast performances of the same girls on different occasions as well as comparing the individual girls. On the basis of these comparisons they are able to generalize about the stability of the ritual over time and the amount of idiosyncratic behavior. Jane Belo, on the basis of similar observations made of a series of performances in Kajoe Kapas, is able to make statements about the similarities and differences between the two villages in the following specific details of the ritual behavior:

Smoking and vibration of (the) puppets on the string as a prelude, then going into trance (of the two children), the putting on of the headdresses, the dancing and refusing to dance to the proffered musical accompaniment, the keeping the eyes closed, the communication with each other by whispering, the taking off of the headdresses, and the being brought out of trance, the return to the normal state (1960:181).

Jane Belo does not discuss any attempts to code the observations in a standard manner but it is obvious that Mead, Bateson and the author did extensive informal coding. They obviously noted the presence, absence and sequences of activities such as smoking, vibration of the puppets, etc., cited above. The comments both here and in other publications by Bateson, Mead and Belo (see Bibliography) also suggest hours spent in analyzing gestures and choreography. It would be useful if they had published some of the informal codes they used in their analyses. Formal codes for these types of behavior with intercoder reliability might help the researcher evaluate his records and suggest not only types of behavior sequences for particularly close scrutiny but other methods of recording. It may be, for example, that new techniques for recording choreography would be useful.

SUMMARY

In conclusion, although anthropologists have always depended on observation to collect data from which to construct a description of the culture of a society, few have attempted systematic observation using standard sampling techniques, recording devices, and methods of analysis. At present anthropologists interested either in: (1) the relation of culture to behavior, (2) measuring the personality characteristics of individuals, (3) analyzing socialization techniques, (4) describing nonverbal behavior, or (5) any other area in which informants find it difficult or impossible to describe their own behavior or the behavior of others validly, are becoming aware of the value of such standardized observations.

This article advises ethnographers not to embark on systematic observation which is laborious and time-consuming unless they are convinced that informants cannot report their own behavior or the behavior of others reliably. It was noted that there were six reasons why the informant might not be able to do this: (1) he had no adequate vocabulary to describe the behavior; (2) he could not perceive the regularities in behavior and hence could not generalize about categories of people; (3) he was unaware of his behavior in certain domains; (4) he could not report acts he did not perform; (5) he distorted because of conflict between ideals and reality; and (6) he could not remember relevant past events. It was recommended that the ethnographer check to see if informants could report accurately in a domain before making a decision to observe systematically.

The article outlines six types of observations: those focused on (1) an activity, (2) an act or several acts, (3) the target of a group's attention, (4) a person as a representative of a category of persons, (5) a dyad, and (6) a setting. It recommends that all field workers make detailed *daily routine charts* to aid them in selecting a time and a place to observe. It discusses problems of sampling and recommends training native assistants. It discusses techniques of recording and advises field workers to bring home descriptive records as examples but recommends that observers use a variety of types of observations and techniques of recording and analyze at least a sample of their protocols to determine whether they were adequate and can be analyzed efficiently.

Above all, if one intends to make systematic behavioral observations in the field, one cannot successfully approach the task in a casual manner. It is a complex and technically demanding method that requires both planning and practice.

BIBLIOGRAPHY

ALTMAN, S. A.
1962 A field study of the sociobiology of Rhesus monkey, Macaca Mulatta. *Annals of the New York Academy of Sciences* 102, 2:338–435.
1967 *Communication among primitives.* Chicago, University of Chicago Press.

ANTONOVSKY, H. F., JOHN WHITING, BEATRICE WHITING, and BARBARA AYRES
1966 *Coding interaction.* Mimeo.

BALES, R. F.
1950 *Interaction process analysis: a method for the study of small groups.* Cambridge, Mass., Addison-Wesley.

BALES, R. F., and H. GERBRANDS
1948 The interaction recorder. *Human Relations* 1:456–463.

BARKER, R. G.
1954 *Midwest: its children.* New York, Row, Peterson and Co.
1963 (ed.) *The stream of behavior.* New York, Appleton-Century-Crofts

BARKER, R. G., and H. WRIGHT
1951 *One boy's day.* New York, Harper and Row.

BATESON, GREGORY
1941 Experiments in thinking about observed ethnological material. *Philosophy of Science* 8, 1:53–68.
1956 Some systematic approaches to the study of culture and personality. In D. G. Haring, ed., *Personal character and cultural milieu.* Syracuse, Syracuse University Press.

BATESON, GREGORY, DON D. JACKSON, JAY HALEY, and JOHN WEAKLAND
1956 Toward a theory of schizophrenia. *Behavioral Science* 1, 4:251–264.

BATESON, GREGORY, and MARGARET MEAD
1942 *Balinese character—a photographic analysis.* New York, Special Publications of the New York Academy of Sciences, II.

BELO, JANE
1960 *Trance in Bali.* New York, Columbia University Press.

BIRDWHISTELL, RAY L.
1952 *Introduction to kinesics.* Louisville, University of Louisville Press.
1954 *Kinesics and communication.* Explorations, No. 3, Toronto.

BOHANNAN, PAUL
1954 *Tiv farm and settlement.* London, Her Majesty's Stationery Office.

CHAPPLE, ELIOT D.
1940 Measuring human relations: an introduction to the study of interaction of individuals. *Genetic Psychological Monographs* 22:3–147.

DEVORE, IRVEN (ed.)
1965 *Primate behavior—field studies of monkeys and apes.* New York, Holt, Rinehart and Winston.

FISCHER, JOHN, and ANN FISCHER
1963 The New Englanders of Orchard Town, U.S.A. In Beatrice Whiting, ed., *Six cultures.* New York, Wiley. See also paperback edition, Vol. V, Six Cultures Series, 1966.

GEWIRTZ, J. L., and B. HAVA
1965 Stimulus conditions, infant behaviors, and social learning in four Israeli child-rearing environments. In B. M. Foss, ed., *Determinants of infant behavior III.* London, Methuen.

GUMP, PAUL V., PHIL SCHOGGEN, and FRITZ REDL
1963 The behavior of the same child in different milieus. In R. G. Barker, ed., *The stream of behavior.* New York, Appleton-Century-Crofts.

HAGGARD, ERNEST, *et al.*
1960 On the reliability of the anamnestic interview. *Journal of Abnormal and Social Psychology* 61, 3:311–318.

HARRIS, MARVIN
1964 *The nature of cultural things.* New York, Random House.

HOMANS, GEORGE C.
1950 *The human group.* New York, Harcourt, Brace.

IMAMURA, SUDAKO
1965 *Mother and blind child—the influences of child-rearing practices on the behavior of preschool blind children.* New York, American Foundation for the Blind.

KROEBER, A. L
1917 *Zuni kin and clan.* New York, The Trustees of The American Museum of Natural History.

LAMBERT, WILLIAM W.
1960 Interpersonal behavior. In Paul H. Mussen, ed., *Handbook of research methods in child development.* New York, Wiley.

LEACH, EDMUND RONALD
1961 *Pul eliya.* Cambridge, Cambridge University Press.

LEVINE, ROBERT, and BARBARA LEVINE
1963 Nyansongo: a Gusii community in Kenya. In Beatrice Whiting, ed., *Six cultures.* New York, Wiley. See also paperback edition, Vol. II, Six Cultures Series, 1966.

LEWIS, OSCAR
1951 *Life in a Mexican village.* Urbana, University of Illinois Press.
LONGABAUGH, RICHARD H. W.
1962 *The description of mother-child interaction.* Ph.D. thesis presented to the Graduate School of Education of Harvard University.
1963 A category system for coding interpersonal behavior as social exchange. *Sociometry* 26, 3:319–344.
1966 The interaction world of the chronic schizophrenic patient. *Psychiatry* 29, 1: 78–99.
1966 The structure of interpersonal behavior. *Sociometry* 29, 4:441–460.
MALINOWSKI, BRONISLAW
1922 *Argonauts of the western Pacific.* London, G. Routledge and Sons, Ltd.; New York, E. P. Dutton.
MARETZKI, THOMAS, and HATSUMI MARETZKI
1955 *Observations of 24 Tairan children.* Field notes.
1963 Taira: an Okinawan village. In Beatrice Whiting, ed., *Six cultures.* New York, Wiley. See also paperback edition, Vol. VII, Six Cultures Series, 1966.
MEAD, MARGARET
1930 *Growing up in New Guinea.* New York, Morrow.
1935 *Sex and temperament in three primitive societies.* New York, Morrow.
1940 *The mountain Arapesh: I. an importing culture; II. supernaturalism; III. diary of events in Altoa.* Anthropological Papers of The American Museum of Natural History 36, 37 and 40.
1946 Research on primitive children. In L. Carmichael, ed., *Manual of child psychology.* New York, Wiley.
MINTURN, LEIGH, and JOHN T. HITCHCOCK
1963 The Rajputs of Khalapur, India. In Beatrice Whiting, ed., *Six cultures.* New York, Wiley. See also paperback edition, Vol III, Six Culture Series, 1966.
MINTURN, LEIGH, and WILLIAM W. LAMBERT
1964 *Mothers of six cultures.* New York, Wiley.
MURRAY, H. A., *et al.*
1938 *Explorations in personality.* New York, Oxford University Press.
NERLOVE, SARA BETH
1969 *Trait dispositions and situational determinants of behavior among Gusii children of southwestern Kenya.* Ph.D. thesis, Department of Anthropology. Stanford, California, Stanford University.
NEWHART, BOB
1960 Nobody will ever play baseball. *The Button-down mind of Bob Newhart,* Warner Bros. Records.

NYDEGGER, WILLIAM, and CORINNE NYDEGGER
1955 *Observations of 24 Tarong children.* Field notes.
1963 Tarong: an Ilocos barrio in the Philippines. In Beatrice Whiting, ed., *Six cultures.* New York, Wiley. See also paperback edition, Vol. VI, Six Culture Series, 1966.
OKORDUDU, CORAHANN
1966 *Achievement training and achievement motivation among the Kpelle in Siberia: a study of household structure antecedents.* Ph.D. thesis presented to Graduate School of Education, Harvard University.
PIKE, K. L.
1954 *Language in relation to a unified theory of the structure of human behavior,* preliminary edition. Glendale, Calif., Summer Institute of Linguistics, 2 vols.
QUINN, NAOMI
1966 *A day in the life of a woman in Capilla Loma.* MS.
RADKE-YARROW, MARIAN
1963 *The elusive evidence.* Presidential address to the Division of Developmental Psychology, American Psychological Association, Philadelphia.
RADKE-YARROW, MARIAN, and H. L. RAUSH (eds.)
1962 *Observational methods in research on socialization processes—a report of a conference.* Sponsored by the Committee on Socialization and Social Structure of the Social Science Research Council.
RAUSH, H. L.
1958 *On the locus behavior—observations in multiple settings with residential treatment.* Paper presented at the Annual Meeting of the American Orthopsychiatric Association.
RAUSH, H. L., A. T. DITTMAN, and T. J. TAYLOR
1959 Person, setting and change in social interaction. *Human Relations* 12, 4:361–379.
RIDINGTON, ANTONIA KERA
1964 *The relation of household structure to child-rearing practices in St. Christopher, Barbados.* Honors thesis, Department of Anthropology, Harvard University.
RIVERS, H. R.
1906 *The Todas.* London and New York, Macmillan.
ROBBINS, L. C.
1963 The accuracy of parental recall on aspects of child development and of child-rearing practices. *Journal of Abnormal and Social Psychology* 66, 3:261–270.
ROBERTS, JOHN M.
1956 *Zuni daily life.* Behavior Science Reprints. New Haven, Conn., HRAF Press.
ROBERTS, JOHN M., M. J. ARTH, and R. R. BUSH
1959 Games in culture. *American Anthropologist* 61:597–605.

ROBERTS, JOHN M., and BRIAN SUTTON-SMITH
1962 Child training and game involvement. *Ethnology* 1:166–185.

ROBERTS, JOHN M., B. SUTTON-SMITH, and A. KENDON
1963 Strategy in games and folk tales. *Journal of Social Psychology* 61:185–199.

ROMNEY, KIMBALL, and ROMAINE ROMNEY
1963 The Mixtecans of Juxtlahuaca, Mexico. In Beatrice Whiting, ed., *Six cultures.* New York, Wiley. See also paperback edition, Vol. IV, Six Culture Series, 1966.

ROSENTHAL, ROBERT
1966 *Experimental effects in behavioral research.* New York, Appleton-Century-Crofts.

STRODTBECK, FRED L.
1951 Husband-wife interaction over revealed differences. *American Sociological Review* 16, 4:468–473.

SULLIVAN, HARRY STACK
1953 *The interpersonal theory of psychiatry.* New York, Norton.

THIBAUT, JOHN W., and HAROLD H. KELLEY
1959 *The social psychology of groups.* New York, Wiley.

WHITING, BEATRICE
1963 (ed.) *Six cultures.* New York, Wiley.
1967 *Time budgets of Harvard graduate students' wives—an exploration in methodology.* Mimeo.

WHITING, JOHN
1961 Socialization process and personality. In Francis L. K. Hsu, ed., *Psychological anthropology.* Homewood, Ill., Dorsey Press.
1966 The learning of values. In Evon Vogt and Ethel Albert, eds., *Peoples of Rimrock.* Cambridge, Mass., Harvard University Press.

WHITING, JOHN, et al.
1954 *Field guide for a study of socialization in 5 societies.* Cambridge, Mass., Lab of Human Development, Mimeo. See also in paperback edition, Vol. I, Six Culture Series, New York, Wiley, 1966.
n.d. Behavior of children in six cultures. In preparation.

WOLF, ARTHUR
Ph.D. thesis. Ithaca, N.Y., Cornell University.

WHYTE, W. F.
1960 Observational field work methods. In Paul H. Mussen, ed., *Handbook of research methods in child development.* New York, Wiley.

WRIGHT, HERBERT F.
1960 Observational child study. In Paul H. Mussen, ed., *Handbook of research methods in child development.* New York, Wiley.
1967 *Recording and analyzing child behavior.* New York, Harper and Row.

CHAPTER 17

Survey Research in Anthropological Field Work

JOHN W. BENNETT and GUSTAV THAISS

INTRODUCTION[1]

This contribution is an essay on the applicability of survey research methods to various anthropological research modalities[2] and includes a review of current anthropological studies in which survey techniques have been used. We exclude from discussion the fields of archeology and physical anthropology, although it must be noted that the basic technique of survey research—the collection of comparable "bits" of information from a sample of a defined universe—has been utilized in these fields for a long time. However, the human populations investigated by archeologists and physical anthropologists are typically defined not in terms of their observable behavior but in terms of material objects and techniques, and biological phenomena, respectively. New studies of micro-evolutionary processes require the simultaneous investigation of social behavior and biological traits, and here survey methods are of great value. We shall not consider these studies here, but many of our observations pertain to them insofar as we discuss the application of survey methods to the social segment.

[1] The writers wish to acknowledge the assistance of their colleague, Don Bushell, Jr., who participated in the development of basic ideas for this paper.
[2] We identify these materials as "anthropology" by the professional allegiances of their authors, by the adherence to field-work methodology, and by a respect for the largest possible context for the specific data collected. At the same time, we acknowledge strong tendencies toward merging of methodological and theoretical views in the social sciences (Schwab 1954, Sofer and Sofer 1955, Vidich and Shapiro 1955, Bennett and Wolff 1956, Lang and Kunstadter 1957). However, the separate professions are as distinct as ever, if not more so.

This paper will consist of: (1) a discussion of the "holistic-depictive" approach in anthropology and the special difficulties attending the use of survey methods therein; (2) a review of recent anthropological and near-anthropological studies in which survey techniques have been combined with other methods; and (3) a brief consideration of comparative cultural studies in which elements of survey methodology are present.

Therefore, we are considering survey research in two main contexts: *first*, as a methodological entity in its own right which may be contrasted with another methodological entity—field-holistic or depictive research—in anthropology; and *second*, as a body of specialized techniques which can be adapted to various anthropological objectives. That is, we shall hold that while in certain anthropological research modalities survey methods as an entity, with their distinctive logic and epistemology, are wholly or partly inappropriate, in other contexts one or more of the techniques can be used with profit.

SURVEY RESEARCH AND HOLISTIC DEPICTION IN ANTHROPOLOGY

The methodological approach of modern anthropology includes a particular method—field work—and a major objective: a respect for cultural context. This approach consists today of a number of other separable but interrelated objectives and methods, some of which, considered to be in conflict, have contributed to theoretical controversy in the discipline. Thus, anthropological studies include: (a) depictive reconstruction of whole cultures, with an emphasis on intensive observation and informal interviewing methods. The "social systems" constructed by some anthropologists imply somewhat different objectives but in this generalized context can be taken as part of the approach; (b) studies of parts of cultures or social systems, made in pursuit of specialized theoretical objectives, and employing sharply defined techniques as well as the more exploratory techniques; (c) a view of the human subjects of the research as individual persons, with interest in their unique historical qualities (an approach especially associated with (a)); and (d) a view of the human subjects as groups or populations about which to generalize (associated with both (a) and (b), but perhaps especially (b)). Sometimes the sub-approaches (a) and (b) are placed in opposition, as in the controversy between the holistic "cultural character" school and the analytical social anthropologists. Others see no particular conflict between them, and regard the methods and approaches as complementary.

Conceived as an entity, survey research is a method which in essence requires the presentation of a standardized stimulus to a human population selected on the basis of defined criteria. The information sought is generally defined in terms of the stimulus or topic, rather than in terms of the unique qualities of the population. That is, there is typically more interest shown in the topic of the survey than in the population itself, and this concern for the topic requires attention to the methodology and theory of the research in advance of the actual study. Topics to be researched need to be defined with great precision, since complete control over relationships between factors bearing on the topic is desired. Broad theoretical assumptions concerning certain common factors in the populations to be surveyed generally lie behind the research. We shall usually refer to these various techniques with the term "extensive."

The (a) plus (c) modality of field-holistic research can be viewed as a methodological entity, and we shall call it *holistic depiction*. Associated with holistic depiction are a number of data-gathering techniques which have in common a certain exploratory approach, i.e., the movements of the investigator are adjusted to the rhythms of everyday life, and not to the demands of a structured instrument. Among these "intensive" techniques are observation, participant and other-

wise; general, "open-ended" interviewing or simple talk; visitations of people and events, including photography and sound recording; the keeping of diaries, and kindred devices. These techniques are all adjusted to a residential form of investigation, rather than laboratory or door-to-door. They should not be viewed as "traditional," or "imprecise," as some social scientists have done, but rather as simply another approach to the gaining of knowledge of social behavior (Bennett 1948). We shall subsequently refer to this entire body of techniques with the term "intensive."

All of the primary data of sociocultural anthropology come from studies made in living societies in their natural setting; and, although not all the studies aim at presenting the literal "whole" of a culture or society, there remains the objective of describing as inclusive a context as possible. Holistic depiction is done in a way which focuses the attention of the anthropologist, and his reader, on the human subjects of the research and their unique milieu or in their milieu conceived as unique for purposes of study. The logic of such studies requires the investigator to consider the individual subjects as persons, and therefore they are not, in any fundamental or ultimate sense, simply a "population." The relationship of topics to the subject-person is typically complex: classically, in holistic depiction the topics of inquiry flow from the interaction of the investigator with his subjects, and it is felt that neither topics nor particular theoretical concepts should bias the study. An extreme example of this approach is found in Bateson's *Naven*, where the field-work phase of social experience with the subjects was prolonged into a post-field work intellectual experience, in search of the problems of the research and their solution (Bateson 1936). While this case is hypertypical, its general aspects are visible in all the major ethnological treatises. Often actual or pseudonymic names of particular persons studied are used (in contrast to the merged anonymity of the subjects in survey research), and the emergence of problems and methods for their solution in the course of the field work is documented. An example is the graphic presentation, via actual case studies, of the conflicts between matrilineal kinship and father-son relationships in Malinowski's (1929) *Sexual Life of Savages in Northwestern Melanesia*.

It has been argued that, notwithstanding fundamental differences in holistic and survey research, extensive survey research techniques can and should make a desirable adjunct to intensive ethnological field work. Major hypotheses, especially those concerning the typicality or representativeness of certain attitudes and behavior patterns, at least could be checked with the use of an instrument providing a standard stimulus applied to carefully selected groups of informants. An example of the application of such methods to what is, on the whole, an ethnological study of a human social group, is Dore's (1958) *City Life in Japan*. We do not know whether Dore would answer to the title of "anthropologist" or "sociologist," but in any case he used a carefully constructed interview schedule to obtain responses to important questions in the study. This material is introduced at strategic points in order to illustrate and to buttress conclusions derived from observational and other intensively gathered field data. In a few cases the survey data are themselves the initiators of key interpretations or hypotheses.

The skillful accommodation between extensive and intensive methods in Dore's study was made possible in part by the fact that he was working within an urban population—a population possibly culturally more integrated than those of most Western cities, but similar in most respects. The methods of survey research are often made easy of application by the existence of populations which can be stratified by various well-known criteria such as education and socio-economic factors. The variables in modern urban or urbanized populations the world over are thus the common ground out of which survey research methodology arises; the fact that some of these population-stratifying characteristics do not exist or cannot be easily determined, being objects of study in themselves in some of the societies studied by anthropologists, can be a practical difficulty in the use of such methods.

A related issue is the difficulty of getting people to respond to questionnaires in the absence of a well-defined cultural tradition of "opinion" or "attitude." In the early post-World War II years, ambitious survey researchers made several international studies of attitudes, using the same schedule in several languages. Some of these studies were failures; others were sharply criticized as unreliable due to the fact that respondents in some countries simply had no understanding of the question-and-answer situation. Societies with strong collectivist patterns, where the person is more a committed member of a group than an autonomous, thinking individual, are exceedingly difficult to survey at the cultural or psychological levels, although surveys of other types of data present no particular difficulty. However, these cultural limitations on interviewing tend to disappear as countries and peoples lacking national institutions begin to acquire them.[3]

The survey researcher, either in his own country or in the form of a native team of interviewers, is generally working within a known cultural context, and assumes that the respondent accepts him as a fellow member of the larger society and responds in an appropriate manner. The anthropologist usually cannot make this assumption, since, at least at the beginning, he is a "foreigner," an outsider, even in cases where he is studying a society or subculture of his own tradition: he must assume that the people he talks to will color their remarks to a varying degree on the basis of their perception of his foreignness. Hence, by constant checking of statements and observations, the anthropologist finds it necessary to seek out the "truth"; whereas the survey researcher, on the whole, assumes that he is obtaining it through his tested instrument.

A special difficulty in the use of extensive survey research methods by the holistic-depictive anthropologist lies in the large number of variables with which he habitually concerns himself. The survey instrument is generally confined to a few variables, conceived

[3] An especially dramatic example of this type of change occurred in Japan immediately after World War II. The Occupation had no difficulty introducing and using public attitude survey techniques, because the Japanese took to them with enthusiasm. The Japanese citizen, newly emancipated, welcomed the opportunity to sound off; and newspapermen, political scientists, psychologists, and others went about the task of finding out about the attitudes of the population with vigor and determination. The long-suppressed tendencies in these directions, developing through the years of industrialization under authoritarian and traditionalist governments, demanded an outlet; and survey research became, for a time, a major public and political symbol of the right to have ideas and the right to find out about them. (See Passin 1951.)

as related to a limited number of objective dimensions. Answers provided for hypotheses are thus limited in scope: hence the frequent criticism of survey research made by anthropologists as being narrow in content and methodologically constricted. Bateson's *Naven* provides an extreme case once again; the full interpretation of the ceremonial reported in this monograph includes dozens of variables, found related to one another by intensive qualitative analysis. The relevant dimensions of the behavior examined are, moreover, not the typical "objective" and oral "public" data utilized in survey research, but "private" emotive patterns, gestures, states of being, perspectival orientations, and the like. It is difficult to see how survey research could possibly contribute to a complex study, as *Naven* is, of ceremonial transvestitism. This difficulty would inhere even in the case of anthropological studies of economics (supposedly an "objective" topic), where complicated forms of gift-giving, prestige competition, subtle interpersonal exchanges, and so on form the essence of the study (Burling 1962).

Still another difficulty centers around the nature of the data regarded by the anthropologist as significant for interpretation. In survey research, the critical interaction takes place between the interviewer and the respondent; in anthropology too this is important, but even more important are interactions between the subjects themselves. That is, the anthropologist *observes* social behavior in the actual social setting (the archetypical case is Bateson-Mead, *Balinese Character*), and interprets the sociocultural whole as much from this type of data as from oral responses to questions. Techniques of observation of subject-subject interactions are not available in a survey approach, and the anthropologist is forced to be skeptical of informants' accounts of such interaction.[4]

Thus, the anthropologist's view of oral statements of informants is sometimes in conflict with the conception held by the survey researcher. By and large, the latter must place considerable trust in the oral report; or he may hold that his sample is constructed in such a way that falsifications are distributed so that they cancel each other. On the other hand, when the anthropologist is concerned with the literal truth of oral statements, he may utilize survey techniques with considerable profit, since these will require him to sample a number of informants, systematically chosen. Actually all good field workers follow a "survey research" approach, in this sense of using more than one informant, whether they construct statistical samples or not.

However, the anthropologist is just as frequently concerned with an entirely different aspect of oral statements—their indirect or oblique representations. Truth is no object here; the concern is for subtle symbolism and negative evidence, or even in the fact of lying as revelatory of cultural stresses (Passin 1942). The intensive nature of the methodology in this context leads toward conversation, not survey of opinion, and intensive participation with particular individuals chosen on the basis of their unique or strategic personal qualities and roles. Survey methodology in the strict sense is not appropriate in these situations.

Another argument leveled against survey methods by some anthropologists is based on the small size of the populations studied in many field researches. The small size of the community permits a saturation sample; every individual and family can be talked with at some length. Hence, it is sometimes argued, there is no need for an interview schedule which is seen, in this type of criticism, simply as a device to obtain data from a large number of individuals in a brief period of time. This is one function of a schedule, but by no means the only one. The criticism misses an important point; the schedule is fundamentally a means of obtaining responses to standardized stimuli, so that comparisons between responses can be controlled. Hence, there is no important *theoretical* objection to the use of schedules in small populations when it is desirable to obtain comparative response data on particular topics—whether or not an actual sample is used.

The resistance displayed by many anthropologists to the idea of a sample is also somewhat questionable due to the fact that, even in cases where not everyone in the community is interviewed, the large number that is may come to constitute an adequate sam-

[4] A possible blending of extensive techniques and intensive observation appears to be emerging in the recent methodological approach called by various terms: cognitive analysis, systematic ethnography, componential analysis, ethnoscience. We discuss this approach later.

ple: there is no reason why this implicit sample should not be treated as such, and the responses analyzed comparatively with the usual survey methods. Kluckhohn used these implicit samples, as well as formal samples, during his many years of work on the Navaho. In some of his publications he used percentages of responses from the implicit or accumulated samples of informants in order to demonstrate salience of attitudes and other phenomena (Kluckhohn 1938, Henry 1951, Streib 1952).

Another problem concerns the social atmosphere of field work. The anthropologist is typically concerned with establishing personal relationships with his subjects, not the formal contacts found in survey research. It has been argued that standardized questionnaires, used at the beginning of a field study, provide a suitable means for meeting individuals, and quite often this can be and is done. However, there are other ways of getting acquainted; once a routine is established and channels of information developed, the use of a schedule can disrupt relationships. The field worker may feel that it is too artificial and formal a technique; it violates the personal mood already established.[5] A related objection concerns the rather extensive commitment of time required to plan, pretest, and administer a schedule.

Thus, the informal, probing techniques associated with holistic-depictive research are typically flexible and eclectic, whereas the techniques in survey research are highly disciplined. Field work as a method is typically unpredictable because the movement of the researcher in the natural society is to some extent unpredictable. Hence he may find it difficult to accept the particular discipline of a particular methodological procedure. Rather

[5] One reader of this paper objected that this argument is fallacious insofar as clinical psychologists and psychiatrists use instruments, and do not thereby disrupt relationships with their patients. This point, often voiced by people who have never done intensive field work, misses the important differences between the role situations in medical practice and participant field work. In the former, the relationship is one of doctor and patient, and of course the patient will take a test if the doctor asks him to—it is in his interest to do so. In the field, the informant is the *host*, not the patient, and the field worker the *guest*, not the doctor. The latter sits at the feet of the informant, as it were, and has no control over him. A discussion of the consequences of this relationship is found in Evans-Pritchard (1940:9–15).

than resisting discipline, however, he is in a position to try out many different disciplined approaches, discarding or keeping them on the basis of a simple pragmatic test—whether they contribute to general enlightenment, or secure a needed slice of data.

There is, of course, a final issue here—the extent to which intensive methodology is psychologically more congenial for certain types of workers. There seems little doubt, though there is no definite proof, that intensive ethnographic research is a style of operation which requires certain subjective skills for maximum accomplishment; and, conversely, that extensive methodology is best used by individuals who remain at a calculated distance from their human subjects (Mead and Métraux 1953).

METHODS IN COMBINATION: A REVIEW OF THE LITERATURE

We have already pointed out that survey methods taken as single techniques can be of use in anthropological research, even when holistic-depictive interests are dominant. However, when anthropological research moves toward the (b) plus (d) modality described on p. 317—that is, toward problem-oriented studies of parts of culture and toward methods which to some degree accept the subjects as groups or populations—the possibilities of fusion of survey and intensive approaches become greater. Perhaps a majority of anthropological work today is carried out in the atmosphere of problem-orientation; and, insofar as this is the case, the use of prepared interview schedules, scales, and analytical procedures becomes more common. A check of the contents of the *American Anthropologist* over the past six years showed that about one-third of the research articles in the field of sociocultural anthropology were based upon data acquired by the use of such instruments. Nearly all of these articles were segments of larger studies, segments in which specific hypotheses were tested with the use of instruments on a survey basis. In many cases, it was not possible to tell whether the hypotheses were formulated in advance of field work or during it, but in any event they *were* formulated and appropriate methods developed. Some of the anthropologists who do this type of work would probably hold to the position that the overall depictive study cannot, in any comprehensive sense, utilize structured survey instruments, but that the segmental studies of particular phases of the research can do so with profit.

Such fusion of methods has characterized social research for many years. Malinowski, for example, in his *Argonauts of the Western Pacific* (1922) and *Coral Gardens and Their Magic* (1935), discussed the use of what he called the "method of statistic documentation of concrete evidence." This somewhat cumbersome concept involved, among other things, the use of village censuses to obtain data on the quantifiable aspects of village life, such as the number and type of dwellings, household composition, information on gardening practices, and other similar types of data. Because of Malinowski's great influence in anthropology and especially with regard to field-work methods, most anthropologists have since used one or another technique of this kind. Lists and censuses have become standard in anthropology, useful not only for the data to be collected but also because they enable the anthropologist to get to know the community and establish rapport relatively quickly.[6]

Anthropologists have also turned to survey methods in their recent move to study "complex societies"—that is, in doing field work in the population aggregates of contemporary nation-societies. This venture has been accompanied by considerable methodological difficulty, insofar as the methods used by anthropologists in the field-holistic tradition have been inappropriate to large populations —or at least, there has been a serious problem of representativeness created by the intensive work with single small population units. Hence survey techniques become necessary and desirable. At the same time, however, the anthropologist chafes under the restrictions created by survey methods, since he desires to pursue his typically complex questions and hypotheses, which contain far more variables than can possibly be handled in surveys, or at least in surveys done on any reasonable basis of time and money.

In any case, the prototype of all survey research combined with intensive field work on modern populations is the *Mass Observation* technique, as it existed in Harrison's original format (Madge and Harrison 1939). Workers were often drawn from the actual social segments to be studied, and then sent back to the field to conduct the interviews and participant observation. The published reports of this work were a matrix of survey tables and participant reports. The "panel study," a somewhat related approach developed in public attitude surveying, combined formal interviewing with personal acquaintance and informal conversation with a constant group of respondents.

An example of problem-oriented segmental research on a modern society, where the community becomes the "sample" rather than the "object" in itself, is recounted in a paper by Vidich and Shapiro (1955) on a study of stratification in an American small town by an anthropologist who used participant observation techniques and a sociologist using survey techniques (see also Arensberg 1961). Both investigators accepted the problem and the general objective of the testing of a "theory" of social stratification as measured by prestige ratings. The anthropologist (Vidich) obtained his prestige ratings by assigning each person in a random sample a rating on the basis of his and his assistant's general knowledge of the community and its residents. The sociologist (Shapiro) obtained his ratings by administering a sociometric-type questionnaire to the same sample. The two systems of ratings agreed on the whole, and each, according to the authors, provided complementary data. The anthropological data gave considerable meaning and depth to the survey data; and the latter secured a more representative spectrum of prestige positions (it was found that the anthropologist apparently had not made adequate contact with lower-class groups). The authors conclude that the two approaches are complementary and should be used in juxtaposition and not in competition.

However, attention should be called again to the fact that *both* investigators accepted the general problem and theoretical objective

[6] For conflicting statements on "when to use" survey devices in field studies see Landy (1959) and Streib (1952). Some examples of more recent monographs—such as Mitchell (1956), Fraser (1960), Anderson and Anderson (1964)—show quite clearly how social survey methods, especially the community census technique, supplement intensive methods in order to establish a clearer picture of the culture under consideration. For discussions of the use of the village census survey and quantitative methods in anthropology, see Richards (1935), Schapera (1935, 1957), Firth (1954), Keller (1960) and Schade (1960).

of the study in a frame described by our (b) plus (d) modality. Consequently, this comparison of field-holistic and survey methods is not complete. A more adequate test would have required the anthropologist to make his own study independently, work out his own system of classifying social groups in his own way and with his own "sample," with the sociologist doing likewise, and their final results compared. It is probably safe to say that the anthropologist *would* have made some sort of stratification analysis, since stratification seems to be an inherent feature of American communities, although one could always argue that one must never make such assumptions, however familiar the context. The holistic-depictive anthropologist would typically question the relevance of all such pre-research constructs as "stratification" since they tend to bias the results by providing categories for data collection which are derived from the observer and not from the observed. It is conceivable, therefore, that the convergence of the results obtained in intensive and extensive methodologies in this case was due to the adherence by the anthropologist to the sociological frame of reference and sampling concept. If this were true, then his prestige ratings were basically the "same" as those obtained by the sociometric survey: they were simply an inspectional survey.

A related example exists in the status data from the two studies of Plainville, made at a fifteen-year interval by Withers (West [Withers] 1945) and Gallaher (1961). Both studies were done with intensive methods, that is, neither investigator utilized survey instruments in the strict sense to obtain a picture of the stratification situation. Withers, however, identified a definite system of "social classes," whereas Gallaher denied that such a system of definite groups existed, preferring the concept of "status rank," in which every individual is assigned a fluctuating position along an infinitely graded continuum between two extremes. When Withers did his study, the recognition of social class in U.S. society was *de rigeur*. However, we cannot know for sure whether Gallaher is more correct than Withers, since the time interval could have blurred the boundaries of an actual stratification system. In any case, the research points up the need for extreme care in the use of theoretical concepts of classifica-

tion in holistic research, and the anthropologist has a point when he warns against the pre-commitment to such concepts inherent in the use of many types of survey instruments. Commitment to highly specific theories and hypotheses provides a classification of data in advance of the study and, if the objectives emphasize the "discovery" of the community or culture, flowing out of its existential state into the experiences of the observer, and thus to the write-up, then pre-existing theories may become a filter which prevents much of importance coming through.

On the other hand, the Withers-Gallaher studies suggest a criticism of field methods in which a needed survey-type discipline is lacking. The ambiguity in the differences between the two approaches to stratification and status is due in part to the fact that structured instruments apparently were not used in either study, alone or in combination with the observational field methods. If Withers had used a schedule of some kind, and if this could have been replicated by Gallaher, considerable light would have been shed on the problem discussed above. The case illustrates the potential usefulness of a combination of the extensive survey approach with intensive field investigation. Even more, the case points up the frequent confusion between holistic and problem-oriented research. It is one thing to aim at a holistic depiction of culture with the personalized, exploratory style which is typical of this type of research as a distinct methodological entity. However, whenever theoretical concepts borrowed from external frames of reference are to be used—e.g., "stratification"—then the researcher has an obligation to utilize the instruments and the logic appropriate to these frames, for better or for worse. This type of confusion also existed in the earlier culture-and-personality research, where many of the problems which required disciplined techniques were studied in holistic-depictive style.

At this point we shall present our topical review of current anthropological literature in which survey methods have been used to advantage. The review is not exhaustive, but the majority of important items have been analyzed and presented as typical of the available resources. The purely quantitative surveys usually contain fairly complete information on technique—the choice and reliability of the sample, and the formulation and administration of questionnaires (for example, see Smith 1962). In reports which combine extensive and intensive techniques (see Wilson 1941–1942), the survey methods are usually (but not always) described, but the intensive methods, hardly ever (i.e., the precise techniques used in participant observation, informal and focused interviewing, etc.).[7]

In anticipation of our conclusions, we may say that the use of survey methods as revealed by the literature suggests that anthropologists use them as they approach certain kinds of problems—those concerned with change, and especially in societies which are part of larger national frameworks. Insofar as anthropologists have done such work, their efforts blend with those of non-anthropologists studying similar phenomena. Thus, we have included a number of scholars from other fields in our review, for example: sociologists Dore (1958), Bose (1962) and Lerner (1958) and political scientist Frey (1963). Delving further back into the literature, the study which classically represents this disciplinary fusion is *Middletown* (Lynd and Lynd 1929). The Lynds, as sociologists, lived and worked in the community for eighteen months, sharing in its life, collecting abundant survey and statistical materials, and making use of the intensive techniques familiar to the anthropologist.

Community Studies

After World War II a noticeable shift in research interests took place as more anthropologists became interested in the study of complex societies. Among the major reasons for this trend were the emergence of new nations and the rapid rate of change in developing areas.

The most common form of anthropological research in complex societies has been the community study. This approach, however, has come under serious attack not only from anthropologists but from other social scientists as well. The French sociologist Dumont, writing about recent field work in India, attacks "the uncritical choice of a number of anthropologists of the village as the frame of inquiry," arguing that this approach

[7] For consideration of the problem of partial reportage of method in anthropological research, see Stavrianos (1950).

is a simple heritage of the discipline's classic, tribe-inspired, overemphasis on local groups in contrast to more extensive research (Dumont and Pocock 1957). From another perspective, the development economist Higgins, frustrated by the difficulty of determining to what extent the results of community-based studies of economic change in one region of rural Java may be generalized to refer to Indonesia as a whole, complains:

If anthropologists are to be genuinely helpful to economists seeking to understand the relationship between culture and economic behavior, their scope and method must be substantially changed. . . . They must find short cuts to generalization. The traditional methods of the anthropologists confine them to intensive and prolonged study of small geographic regions. If their scientific standards are to be met, that cannot be helped. But some training in statistical methods, and particularly in sampling techniques, might enable them to distinguish the strategic variables which correlate highly with everything else in the culture and thus characterize it. Thus armed, anthropologists would need less time to find out whether neighboring (communities) are different or the same. If they are the same, the anthropologist can move on; if they are different, more prolonged study may be necessary. (Higgins 1959)

While anthropological methods are undergoing re-examination, there remain many anthropologists who will state, with Casagrande, that

I am not suggesting that we sell our birthright for statistics and surveys. Both can be instructive, but our distinctive research contribution and our particular strength lies in the intensive study of small groups and I assume that our work will continue to be anchored to the natural community. (Casagrande 1959)

Comments of this kind notwithstanding, the investigation of small communities in complex societies often involves a more rigorous and a more self-conscious methodology than has been characteristic of tribal studies. Ryan has used a questionnaire approach in attempting to examine the attitudes of Sinhalese peasants toward modernization, surveying about 100 households in a village near Colombo with respect to their opinions concerning both traditional practices and innovative behavior (Ryan *et al.*, 1958). A similar but much more ambitious study was undertaken by Frey, a political scientist, who surveyed more than 450 Turkish villages in an attempt to determine the attitudes of Turkish peasants toward modernization. The author, in discussing the reasons for the project, states that

the nation is currently in the anxious "second stage" of its contemporary revolution; having largely accomplished the modernization of elite elements, it is attempting to bring its peasantry into active social and political participation on supra-village levels. Information about peasant attitudes and conditions of life—more profound than that obtained by the national census and more general than that garnered from the few good anthropological studies—is urgently required. (Frey 1963)

Frey included eight basic areas of inquiry in the final interviewing schedule: communications, personal background, attitudes toward development, other relevant psychological traits, socialization, position in and conception of environing social structure, politicization, and religiosity.

In his discussion of the way in which patterns of caste ranking are affected by the structure of the local community in which they appear, Marriott (1960) used both the results of a survey he had conducted of the opinions of some 300 persons in two Uttar Pradesh villages as to the ranking of thirty-six locally represented castes, and a correlation based on data from secondary sources of population size and number of castes in 151 villages from five regions in India and Pakistan. In a study of conflict and solidarity in a Guianese plantation, Jayawardena (1963) used a combination of formal and informal interviewing methods as well as a survey conducted to elicit information on the demographic and social characteristics of his respondents and to ascertain their degree of involvement with the courts. The author was interested in the study of the factors that cause social conflict, the forms it takes, and the social consequences of such behavior.

The Youngs (1960a, 1960b) administered a "structured" questionnaire to a sample of community officials in twenty-four Mexican villages in connection with their study of rural reactions to the growth of industrialization in one of the states of central Mexico. They then used the results as well as various types of census data to construct a Guttman scale of economic contact between various villages and the factory center, to set up indices of absolute and relative social change in the villages, and to obtain an objective measure of village "morale."

Lerner (1958), combining survey techniques with depth interviews, has produced a typology of "traditional," "transitional," and "modern" societies, derived from studies of communities in the Middle East. It might well serve as a heuristic model of social and cultural change to be tested in other developing areas. Lerner considers the interrelationship of historic, cultural, economic, and technological factors in the individual drive to modernity. He points to sociocultural regularities in the passing of traditional society and in the psychological processes of transition to modernity, emphasizing the individual desire for change among "transitionals" and elites in the Middle East. He also notes the survey findings that rural people are "unhappier" than urban people, as opposed to conventional dichotomies of urban anomie versus rural stability. Lerner concludes that in the Middle East traditional society is passing because relatively few want to maintain the traditional rules.

A final example of the community study, this one done in India by the sociologist Bose (1962), attempts to test by the use of survey methods certain postulates of Redfield's folk-urban continuum. In Redfield's model the peasant society is considered to be intermediate between the folk society and the urban society. In such a society there are some persons who have the value systems expected in a folk society and there are others who have the value systems of an urban society. In Bose's study, it was postulated that people with folk value systems would resist change in agricultural techniques and those with urban value systems would accept it. To test this hypothesis, a random sample of eighty farmers was selected from a list of owners cultivating three acres of land or more. A questionnaire of thirty items was used for eliciting responses. The results of the study support the hypotheses that the value orientation of a people has a relation to technological change and that people with tradition-oriented, folk-type values are more resistant to change than people with urban-oriented values.

This is an interesting piece of research, but it invites certain basic criticism. It is a matter of doubt as to whether Redfield's categories of "folk" and "urban" can be taken as empirical types or putative types for the purposes of constructing survey instruments. It is not always clear what Redfield himself had in mind, but there seems little doubt that in large part he was concerned with an image of man and human diversity, and not with the empirical typing of actual communities. In a sense Redfield was pointing to features of all societies; all men have both "folk" and "urban" characteristics, just as all men have anxiety in some degree. In part, Bose's study represents an instance where the choice of extensive methods was partly inappropriate to the particular problem. Intensive, exploratory, and introspective research might have been better adapted to the task. Or if his objective was to type communities quantitatively, types other than "folk" and "urban" would have been more suitable.

Urbanization Studies

One aspect of the study of complex societies and the anthropology of development—and an area of research which anthropologists have largely ignored until recently—is that of urban society and the process of urbanization. The most extensive research on this topic has been done in Africa by British and British-trained anthropologists. Much of this research is undertaken for practical, administrative objectives, such as collecting information to be of use to the national government or municipality. Other pieces of research are more theoretical in nature and are concerned with the formulation of hypotheses and the provision of material capable of comparative analysis, although they may incidentally provide data useful for administrative objectives. Most of the following studies present combinations of extensive and intensive methods.

Fortes (1948) states that the purpose of the Ashanti survey was "to get a broad general picture of the social and political structure of Ashanti today, and to investigate in greater detail those aspects in which ecological and economic factors play the biggest part." In addition to the customary methods of collecting information from selected informants, observation and participation in group activities and so forth, much use was made of questionnaires and other prepared inquiry forms. Fortes notes that the collection of numerical data was necessary not only because of the large scale of the Ashanti survey, but also because of the variability of social relationships in a rapidly changing society. In studying land tenure, for example, the broad principles could be ascertained from discussions with informants, but the actual operation of these principles varied from case to case, owing to the presence of conditions and circumstances not allowed for by the general rules. Hence, it was necessary to attempt to measure the strength of the different forces of change.

Busia, a Ghanaian sociologist, conducted a social survey of Sekondi-Takoradi (Ghana) in 1947–1948. The objectives of the research were primarily practical, to elucidate problems with which the government was concerned, such as urban living conditions, the cost of living, and the effect of crowded urban conditions upon juvenile delinquency. Busia further states that he tried to combine the methods of the social survey with those of the social anthropologist:

> In collecting our information, we have used all the five techniques most generally used in the collection of social data: direct observation of behavior, examination of documents, "free" interview, questionnaires and interview by schedule. (Busia 1950)

Because the study was designed to elucidate practical problems, the facts were presented as briefly as possible and only those have been included in the monograph which throw light on such problems.

An investigation sponsored by the Institut d'Etudes Centre-Africaines and directed by Balandier (1952), a social anthropologist, had two main objectives: first, the gathering of precise information on the African population of Brazzaville, Congo, and an analysis of the problems which characterize the two main areas of the city; second, the inquiry was conceived as part of a larger research program into the social evolution of the Bacongo peoples. Quantitative methods, based on questionnaires and schedules, were used in collecting all basic data. Other methods included the collection of life histories, and the administering of Rorschach, intelligence, and sociometric tests. No mention is made of direct and participant observations.

Mitchell, an anthropologist on the staff of the Rhodes-Livingstone Institute, conducted a survey of four Copperbelt mining towns in 1953 and 1954. The surveys were designed to give statistical information on such topics as occupation, religion, tribe, marital status, education, wages, and length of residence in the mining towns. A supplementary schedule obtained information on literacy and reading preferences. A 10 per cent random sample of houses in the four towns was used to represent the population. After the surveys were completed, intensive anthropological studies of a selected sub-sample of households were made (Mitchell 1953, 1954).

A study done in East London (South Africa), this one some years later by Pauw (1963), sought information on the family among urbanized Bantu. The first part of the study consisted of the application of a questionnaire to a sample of 202 individuals representing 109 different households. Information was sought on demographic characteristics of the population as well as sociocultural variables dealing with marriage, the household, and the family. Further data were gathered about preceding generations who had moved from the rural areas to the town. After these data were tabulated, 14 households representative of different cultural and structural types were selected for more intensive study.

We shall now turn to two additional African studies whose methods are unusually well described: *Jinja Transformed* by the Sofers (1955) and *An Experiment in Methodology in a West African Urban Community* by Schwab (1954).

According to the authors of the Jinja study:

> The study of Jinja had three main objectives: (a) to collect data likely to be of use to government in framing policy; (b) to contribute to the general body of scientific knowledge concerning social process and social relations in urban societies with multi-racial populations; (c) to experiment in methods of social research. (Sofer and Sofer 1955)

The practical aspect of the study concerned the attempt to gather data on such questions as the effects of the employment of women on African social structure, why African workers prefer monthly to weekly wages, whether tenants in the African housing estate would like to have communal plots to cultivate, whether Africans receive adequate attention at the local hospital, and what fuel Africans use and where they secure it. Statistical information was requested by the government regarding African incomes and rentals, and the number of children in need of educational facilities.

The theoretical aspects of the study attempted to test hypotheses concerning a multi-racial and multi-cultural society undergoing rapid growth and change. The authors hoped that their findings might be of some use to researchers using comparable methods to build up theories or universal principles applicable to all such societies.

With regard to experimentation in methods of social research, the authors felt that the investigation should be conducted by a combination of the methods of the quantitative social survey and of more intensive field work:

> The employment of sample survey methods becomes necessary when it is desired to collect systematic numerical facts relating to the characteristics of a population as a whole and when that population is large in relation to research resources and heterogeneous in respect of the characteristics in which the investigator is interested. If the population is small, it is possible to investigate all the units involved. . . . (In intensive field work) there is greater concentration on qualitative data not susceptible to expression or analysis in quantitative form. . . . (Sofer and Sofer 1955)

The Sofers go on to discuss how the data obtained through survey methods for the understanding of the dynamic aspects of town administrative problems is limited in scope:

> If depth of insight is to be obtained into the problem situations and processes of urban life, survey methods need to be supplemented by the intensive fieldwork of the trained observer, involving lengthy and/or repeated contact with individuals and groups. This necessity can be illustrated with reference to problems associated with immigration. It is possible through survey methods to ascertain such facts as the tribes, religions, age and sex composition, geographical origins, standard of living and occupations of the immigrant population, but less easy to discover significant material relating to the immigrant's transition to urban life, or to the effects of the new environment on his relations with his wife and his control over his children. Again survey methods can establish the labour resources of the population in terms of manpower and training, but can help only to a limited extent to account for the productivity of the labourer, a question not only bound up with nutrition but also with such factors as the social atmosphere of the job and familial incentives to higher production. (Schwab 1954)

The Sofers conclude their discussion of methods by stating that it is "valuable to use both groups of methods in urban social research."

Schwab (1954) attempted, in his "intensive

anthropological survey of the social and economic organization of Oshogbo," to integrate the social survey with intensive anthropological methods. The study was undertaken because it was felt that there was a need to study large, urban areas in Africa which have undergone extensive and systematic contact with Western culture, and which consequently are important foci for cultural change. "Because of the complexity and size of the Oshogbo community and the tremendous variation in and fluidity of norms of present-day Oshogbo social life," the use of quantitative measurement, "however approximate or crude," was necessary. Intensive observational methods were judged inadequate in and of themselves, and had to be augmented by additional techniques which could better sample the complexity and variability of the community. Further, as a consequence of changes taking place in social relationships and value patterns, it became necessary to speak of a continuum of norms existing in the community, since there no longer existed any uniformity of patterns. It was therefore hoped that, by developing sampling and other quantifying devices, Schwab and his associates could get at some measure of isolation of the various dependent and interdependent variables that entered into the changing social relationships and make some effort to assess their strength.

Initially Schwab devoted much effort to getting the consent of the community for the study and establishing effective rapport with the people of Oshogbo. This latter involved several weeks of meeting and talking with as many individuals as possible, until Schwab no longer seemed to be regarded as a stranger. After this period of attempting to allay suspicion, the author began to question and interview people in a more systematic manner:

The main purpose of these inquiries was not to secure detailed or even, in some instances, very precise information, but to obtain general knowledge necessary for the initiation of a census. Since there were no records available, a sample census was considered essential to secure basic demographic and other social data. The objectives of the sample census were not to enumerate heads, but rather to obtain the characteristics of the community, and to collect reliable and representative data concerning family organization, occupational structure, and the religious, educational and age composition of the community. From the census, a sub-sample of families was to be chosen, with selection being made on the basis of economic differentiation of the male heads of the households. These selected families were to be subjected to intensive investigation for the remainder of the survey. (Schwab 1954)

While the research was in progress, Schwab overcame many of the difficulties encountered in doing survey research in underdeveloped areas.[8] Eventually there were 6,241 individuals in the census out of a total population of about 70,000. The data were obtained largely through the use of schedules in the form of guides to the problems under investigation, and also through the use of questionnaires:

Questionnaires, however, had only a limited scope, for they were employed primarily for the collection of factual data that lent themselves easily to quantification. Thus questionnaires were utilized to obtain such information as the number and percentage of children's deaths, the incidence of divorce, and certain economic data. However, after some experience with questionnaires in the field, it became apparent that they could not be employed in a situation where the material was in any way qualitative or complex, as in the study of the kinship system or other complex institutions. In these circumstances the schedules were used which suggested the lines the investigation should follow and set the minimum limits for the information required. (Schwab 1954)

Schwab goes on to state that he feels that where questionnaires were used the interviews tended to be directive, but where the guides were used they were non-directive. This may have been disadvantageous since it

[8] We may briefly describe a few of these problems. The inevitable problem of "Why me?" arose among respondents because the people of Oshogbo were unable to comprehend why they were chosen in preference to residents of some other compound. As a result they refused, at first, to cooperate. A further problem was that it was necessary to secure the permission of the entire corporate group of which the respondent was a member before interviewing could proceed. In addition, people refused to enumerate wives and children and when they did so, children under five were often omitted since they were not considered permanent members of the family because of the high death rate among young children. Respondents were also frequently chastised by other members of their group or compound for being "informers" and hence others in the area were reluctant to give information. Most of these difficulties were overcome by repeated visits to the compounds and by enlisting further aid from influential leaders of the community. In addition, Schwab was able to convince his population that he had no official government capacity and was in no position to levy taxes or impose laws. See Stycos (1960) for further discussion of such problems.

may have produced uneven results; but, on the other hand, Schwab says that excellent rapport was established which probably led, ultimately, to more complete knowledge.

For another study of urban areas we move to the islands of the West Indies. To determine whether the family systems of three West Indian societies conform to a single model of family and domestic relations, M. G. Smith (1962), an anthropologist, undertook an extensive social survey of three large samples: 224 households of Carriacou, 215 households of Grenada and 1,440 Jamaican households. A tremendous amount of work went into the collection of the data in order to insure representativeness, comparability, and full documentation of all interpretations and analytic statements. The book offers a somewhat different approach to the study of West Indian family life than is usually presented and is also, in part, a criticism and refutation of the methods and results of others who have tackled the same analytic problems. Because of the great variation of family types (at least hypothetically) and because of the sociological and cultural diversity of the populations and their sizes, it was deemed necessary to undertake a social survey. As far as we have been able to discern, depth or intensive observational studies were not made.

Applied Anthropology

Anthropologists have also concerned themselves with the role of anthropology in administration and economic development. This role has primarily been advisory and to a large extent, because of the socio-political situation, concerned chiefly with the administration of colonial areas and dependent peoples. The work of the British anthropologists falls into this category and was discussed in the section on urban studies. Here we shall concern ourselves with the few studies which have been done by anthropologists and other social scientists concerned with administration, community development, and health programs in developing areas.

Lewis, known primarily for his work in rural and urban Mexico, did a study of village life in northern India to gather data which would be useful and enlightening to Indian government administrators (Lewis 1958). A social survey was conducted in order

to determine the demographic and sociocultural variables of the village. Such data as sex, age, clan, caste, and age at betrothal were collected. For those villagers involved in agriculture such variables as amount of land owned, size of cultivated units, amount of land rented in and amount of land rented out, and number of oxen and bullock carts were collected. At the conclusion of the census, a socio-economic scale was developed with the aid of the census data. With this scale Lewis and his colleagues were able to select a sample of thirty households which was representative of all the major socio-economic variables in the village, and undertake an intensive qualitative study.

A similar piece of research was done by Dube (1955) in the state of Hyderabad in south-central India. A social survey was carried out in the village of Shamirpet, the data of which were used to select a sample of 120 families representing different castes and levels of income, education, and urban contacts. These families then became the subjects for intensive anthropolitical investigation. Dube also used survey data collected by other specialist members of his research team, including information from a diet and nutritional survey, a survey of village agriculture and its problems, and a survey of animal care and health. These additional data provided important leads for intensive investigation within the sub-sample.

Mangin (1960) and his associates, one of whom was an anthropologist, undertook a study of the effects on mental health of migration to urban areas:

In collaboration with Humberto Rotondo, a psychiatrist from the Ministry of Health, and Jose Matos Mar, an anthropologist from the University of San Marcos (Lima, Peru) a study of one *barriada* (a squatter settlement) was carried out during 1958 and 1959. In addition to traditional anthropological methods such as observation, conversation and participation, we administered five questionnaires, including the Cornell Medical Index, to a selected sample of 65 of the 600 families.

The author states that the material has not yet been systematically analyzed but he does present tentative findings. For example, in noting that there seemed to be much ambivalence toward marriage and the family, Mangin states:

A common contradiction that may not be as contradictory as it first appears is that in which one encounters verbalization about happiness and enjoyment only with wife and children from the very same men who habitually beat their wives and children. Violence toward wife and children is the most frequently encountered form of violence in Peru and, in many cases, there was no hint of it in the questionnaires. This was one of the many occasions where the questionnaires became valuable only in conjunction with the observational data of the anthropologist. (Mangin 1960)

Seppilli, of the University of Perugia, Italy, reports on a study of fertility in a rural Mexican community:

The study of fertility is part of a larger research program designed to examine the dynamics of male and female roles and of family organization in a changing rural society. (Seppilli 1960)

Analysis of the phenomena under investigation was achieved through a "dynamic methodology based on an interdisciplinary approach, combining cultural anthropology and other social sciences contributions." A random sample of the population (3,361 inhabitants) was taken with a ratio of 1:6 between the sample and the universe. The final sample—after refusal and absentees—consisted of 143 family units representing 566 individuals. Questionnaires were then administered to the sample. Special questionnaires were also administered to a sample of school children. Additional intensive techniques were carried out in order to integrate and deepen the general data.

And finally, Scotch and Geiger (1964) discuss the results of an interdisciplinary cross-cultural study which attempted to establish the relationship between cultural processes or factors and the processes in the pathophysiology of disease. The instrument used for the study was the Cornell Medical Index, which was applied to probability samples of two general population groups—urban and rural Zulu. The C.M.I. questionnaire (made up of 195 questions on physical and emotional symptoms) was modified for use in the non-Western setting. Scotch (1960), in another survey study among the Zulu, reports on the relation of sociocultural factors to hypertension. These reports are the result of an extensive epidemiological study conducted in the Union of South Africa.

National Character

National character studies developed out of applied research in World War II, and were initially founded on culture-and-personality theory. In this section we shall discuss a few studies that have made methodological contributions.

In a study of English national character, Gorer (1955) used a questionnaire consisting of opinion and attitude questions. His procedure in obtaining respondents was somewhat unique since he introduced the questionnaire in a widely read weekly newspaper asking for cooperation. About 11,000 completed forms were returned, of which some 5,000 were analyzed. Gorer did not submit his questionnaire to other national populations and, in any case, he seems to take it for granted that their answers would be different from those of the English. In 1948 Gorer did a study of *The American People* which was based mainly on rather impressionistic methods. However, he used data from the *Fortune* magazine surveys as a check on certain of his hypotheses.

Lanham (1956) sent detailed questionnaires on child training devices to parents in a Japanese community, using the schools as an intermediary. The results convincingly disproved the La Barre and Gorer suppositions on the social pervasiveness of the strictness of Japanese child rearing, especially toilet training.

Stoetzel (1953, 1955) obtained data on the outlook of Japanese youth after the war, and its attitude toward etiquette (*giri*). Stoetzel's results concerning *giri* deserve special mention since he utilized the survey technique to test certain holistic-depictive findings of Benedict (1946):

We thus see that contrary to the findings of Benedict's anthropological investigation, the technical interpretation of "giri" is recognized by only a little over one-third of the Japanese people (35%). Moreover, when we consider the distribution according to age and place of residence we find (a) that country-people far more often refrain from defining "giri" than townspeople; (b) that they give technical replies much less often, but give "popular" replies almost equally often; (c) that young people are less familiar with "giri" than their elders, either in the technical sense or in the more usual acceptation. This leads to the conclusion that, if "giri" is really the culture trait so precisely defined in "The Chrysanthemum and the Sword"—a definition endorsed by 35% of present day Japanese—it is a feature which is dying out; at the same time, as it survives to a greater extent in urban than in country communities, it would appear to be an aristocratic rather than a popular feature, spread among the people in the more or less recent past by literary and intellectual means. (Stoetzel 1955)

In this example, as in the pieces by Bose and Lanham, we may observe the value of survey techniques in attempting to test generalizations and hypotheses obtained by intensive and observational methods. In such studies, the possibility is raised of using surveys as explanatory rather than purely descriptive devices. While anthropologists might benefit from the application of explanatory-type survey methods, considering the ambiguity of some aspects of their own intensive methodology, there are great difficulties in refining hypotheses and problems in order to make them amenable to the disciplined technology of survey research. As we noted in the first section of the paper, many of the anthropologist's conclusions are statements of tendency, or global conclusions of great textural complexity, which resist dissection. However this may be, whenever the anthropologist proposes a conclusion of relatively simple and explicit dimensions, he has an obligation to utilize survey research to give it a final test.

Multi-ethnic Field Research

Another important arena for the use of survey research instruments is the comparative multi-ethnic regional field study. Such studies are made in relatively large regions inhabited by a number of different subcultures, ethnic groups, tribes, or neighborhood groups. The objectives are to compare responses of the different groups to the natural environment, the effect of differing cultural traditions on a similar economy, and related problems. Examples are the Harvard Five Cultures studies, the research program directed by Steward on Puerto Rico (Steward 1956, Kluckhohn and Strodtbeck 1961),[9] and the current study of a region in southwestern Saskatchewan by the senior author of this chapter.

In the last case, a single basic survey instrument—a detailed open-ended interview schedule—was administered to a large sample of persons and families from each of the several ethnic, religious, and occupational groups in the region. This schedule included

[9] Vogt and Albert (1966) contains a complete bibliography of the Five Cultures project, and a review and critique of its methods.

questions relating to each of the important problem-areas of the research program. A basic regional foundation was thus laid for the interpretation of the very different slices of data obtained by many other methods from the separate cultural groups. The distinctive adaptations and problems of these groups required variant approaches—the Indians were studied as a deprived minority, the ranchers as a problem in the nostalgic persistence of frontier ideology, the farmers as a case of political sophistication in a rural setting, the Hutterites as a problem in the influence of communal organization on economic efficiency, and so on.

Socialization

Landy (1959) presents an "exploratory-descriptive ethnographic study of socialization, or cultural transmission and learning, in a rural Puerto Rican village within the context of its culture and social structure." As to the method of investigation, Landy states, ". . . contrary to ethnographic tradition, we found it helpful at the outset to take a census of the community or universe. . . ." The census covered many categories of demographic, sociological, and psychological data and it also proved useful as a means of establishing contacts with every family in the community. From the census data, eighteen lower-class families were selected according to certain specific criteria in order to provide representation of this segment of the population, and then subjected to intensive observational and interviewing studies.

General Remarks

There appears to be general consensus among the authors examined in this section that the choice of field methods is *not* an either/or proposition. The authors recognize that an adequate field study is not conducted on the basis of a single technique, gathering a single kind of information, but rather that different types of data require different approaches. This is borne out by the methodological sequence displayed by most of the reviewed studies. The investigator's initial approach to the community was designed to obtain general impressions of the culture through personal contacts and observation. When the investigator felt the time was appropriate, a census was conducted, its categories based on the qualitative data at hand —that is, the perceived cultural and social-structural patterns largely determined the choice of a method of sampling and the structure of the samples, as well as the recruitment of interviewers of various origins and the precautions to be taken in approaching the persons questioned. The pre-tests of the instruments assisted in evaluating the initial qualitative judgments. After the completion of the census, a sub-sample was selected for intensive depth studies. In some of the researches, questionnaires and schedules were used as instruments for eliciting responses; in others, intensive observational techniques were used; while in still others, a combination of the two methods was employed.

We noted also that social surveys illustrate the use of quantitative techniques in testing anthropological hypotheses—the studies of Bose which attempted to test postulates of Redfield's folk-urban continuum, and of Stoetzel concerning the generality of Benedict's conclusions on Japanese culture. Other research opportunities provided by survey data will accrue in the use of the growing number of social survey data archives in the United States and Europe. The data libraries at the University of Michigan, the University of California at Berkeley, Yale University, and the University of Cologne select certain topics or areas for special emphasis. Thus Berkeley specializes in survey data from underdeveloped areas in Asia and Latin America; Ann Arbor emphasizes data based on consumer behavior and political behavior; the Yale collection combines survey data with extensive holdings of demographic and official statistics from many countries (see Scheuch 1963). Admittedly there are many problems involved in the use of survey data cross-culturally, but there is considerable scope for experimentation with regard to such matters as the applicability of survey methods developed in Western cultures to non-Western areas, the optimum combination of survey with intensive field-work techniques, and the sequence in which both types should be undertaken. Schwab's study provides an excellent example of such experimentation.

Survey methods enable the investigator to define the nature and extent of the various cultural traits and permit an analysis of social differentiation, while intensive methods permit the deepening of knowledge of the "social facts" or approach to, in Malinowski's phrase, "the imponderabilia of actual life."

If anthropology has a message for survey research, it is this: delay the construction of schedules of all kinds until something is known about the cultural context of the phenomenon under study; do not assume that all slices of social actuality are always identically responsive to theoretical constructs; remember that all such constructs are, in the last analysis, human conceptions of the social situation at one place and time, and their relevance to a new situation must always be a problem for investigation (Bennett 1961).

If survey research has a message for anthropology, it is this: first, often context can be known in general terms, known sufficiently well to permit the use of instruments which will materially aid in the checking of particular hypotheses, or hasten the collection of certain types of data. It is not always necessary to know the culture in detail; the intelligent and well-educated observer can operate on the basis of our growing comparative knowledge of cultures and social systems. Second, whenever specific hypotheses are to be tested in field work, the anthropologist has an obligation to construct and utilize instruments which will adequately represent the population under study.

SOME MARGINAL APPLICATIONS

Analytic Comparison

Research which aims at a comparison of two or more cultural or institutional systems is often problem-oriented research, which, as we have already seen, is susceptible to the application of survey research methods. Comparison requires the investigator to exert controls over the data in ways which are not needed in depictive studies of single systems. Some comparative studies are *post hoc;* they are performed on data already collected, and this fact also requires the exertion of disciplined control and the logical conception of cultural data as composed of analytical bits, more or less representative of particular "populations."

In anthropology, the comparative approach has a history going back to Tylor (1889), who "surveyed" marriage customs and found "adhesions" which indicated, in his view, historical connections. Another classical instance was Morgan's (1871) monumental attempt to study kinship on a comparative basis by sending a questionnaire around the world to missionaries and administrators in contact with non-Western peoples. The "culture element surveys" of the California anthropologists Kroeber and Driver (1938), and their precursors, the "trait analysts" like Spier (1921; also, Bennett 1944); the grand-scale comparators like Hobhouse, Wheeler, and Ginsberg (1930), and their modern descendents, Murdock (1949), Driver and Massey (1957), Whiting and Child (1953), are all important representatives of this trend.

It is important to note that the comparative analytic survey made on secondary cultural data has always occupied a controversial position in anthropology. During the 1930's, the trait analysis work of the preceding decades was subjected to a detailed criticism which still hangs over it like a cloud (Leach 1960). The essence of this criticism was that culture cannot be segregated into simple, single items, since culture is by nature a complex configurational or functional whole—or at least an entity in which the bonds between the parts are so unique that to break them arbitrarily in favor of a rationalistic classification is to falsify the nature of the entity. In spite of criticism, the secondary comparative survey has persisted in anthropology, and has undergone considerable refinement. The extent of this refinement can be grasped from a comparison of the "culture element survey" work done by Kroeber and Driver (1938) in the 1930's and 1940's and the recent volumes on the American Indian by Driver and Massey (1957). A contemporary study of broader scope, with considerable methodological sophistication, has been done by Swanson (1960).

The criticisms were correct insofar as the analysts attempted to define single cultures as mere assemblages of traits. However, the criticisms missed the point when the comparative dimension of analysis was in view, for it is difficult to compare cultures *as wholes*. Some kind of classification—implicit or explicit—of their elements is necessary. The nature of this classification is the vital issue, and it is true enough that the early classificatory schemes like Wissler's (1923) "universal pattern" were jejune and biased. However, classifications based on the recog-

nition of enduring or typical functional relationships among institutions, among institutions and habitat, or among interaction patterns associated with recurring status relationships in many societies, are another story altogether. Classifications of this kind should, as a general rule, precede rather than follow analytic comparison: the partnership between the "anthropologist" and the "survey researcher" is thus once more demonstrated.[10]

Systematic Ethnography

A related and possibly significant new approach has developed in recent years, especially among linguistic anthropologists, that provides a new approach to the problem of classification. This approach has been labeled "the new ethnography" or "ethnoscience" by its devotees. Essentially, what this new approach involves is the systematic collection of data on how the natives of a given culture themselves classify and structure their material and social universe. Thus, the anthropologists are trying to get at a refinement of the empirical basis of comparative study, by providing more surely valid descriptions of the individual systems on which comparative study must depend. It is the classificatory principles discovered in ethnography which should be compared, not the occurrence of categories defined by arbitrary criteria whose relevance in the cultures described is unknown (Goodenough 1956).

An example here might help to clarify this problem. Murdock (1949), in discussing one of his findings, states that if a tribe, for example, under the influence of a more powerful culture accepts a new method of production, its rule of residence will soon change, for this is the first response to altered conditions. Now, Murdock's categories of residence are based on the conventional ethnological concepts of patrilocal, matrilocal, bilocal, etc.; but the "ethnoscientists" state that the principles by which people choose where to reside may involve considerations not only of genealogical tie (which underlie traditional categories) but also features of ecology, social role, and other expectations and obligations (Hymes 1964). It is therefore essential to resist the temptation to assign an aspect of a native culture too easily to a

[10] See Eggan (1954) and Forde (1959) for the classic anthropological view of these matters.

familiar category. Such methodological errors often result from not investigating the full range of phenomena. In order to correct for these methodological errors, many anthropologists are using standardized stimuli with selected samples in order to control for as many of the variables as possible. In addition, other systematic ethnographers are endeavoring to amend intensive methods of investigation with quantitative techniques. Here the stress is placed upon techniques which can measure the degree of consistency of utterances and behavior at various levels of explicitness. This requires a survey type of approach, wth greater care given to problems of representativeness than may be the case for more informal studies (see Cancian 1963, Metzger and Williams 1963, Ackerman 1964, Burling 1964, Frake 1964, Romney and D'Andrade 1964, and Sturtevant 1964).

CONCLUSION

In this chapter we first described aspects of anthropological research which do not readily conform to the extensive methodology of survey research, and indicated that often this situation becomes the focus of polemic attacks—the "anthropologists" condemning "sociologists" and "behavioral scientists" for meaningless abstractions and excessive counting; the "sociologist" accusing the "anthropologist" of sloppy method and unwarranted generalization. It is clear from the review of problem-oriented research that anthropologists in respectable numbers have abandoned the holistic-depictive approach, and consequently accept whatever methods are useful in pursuing the problem of interest. Change and other aspects of dynamics constitute the primary focus of these problems; such interests require more analytic procedures than do the depictive studies.

At the same time, certain continuities in anthropological research regardless of modality are evident and suggest that anthropology for the time being retains a distinctive viewpoint while also showing acceptance of a more self-conscious methodology. The bulk of research has been done on foreign soil and, in nearly all cases, respect for cultural context accompanied the survey operations. These two features—the foreign environment for research and respect for cultural context—are anthropological specialties in the sense that the academic anthropology departments are equipped to foster and train students in the appropriate procedures. Other social sciences, while evincing increased interest in non-Western research, are not so well equipped to handle this type of work and often call upon the anthropologist as a team member in interdisciplinary projects.

Underlying these features are deeper issues, also suggested by some of our early discussion. The nature of the anthropologist's engagement with culture in the context of intensive method carries with it certain sources of insight and understanding which are simply not available in extensive methods. It is hoped that this difference of approach can be preserved in the social sciences. Often the advocates of one grand social science imply, perhaps unconsciously, the abandonment of any type of *verstehen* and the substitution of the computer or the social survey. It matters little whether the torch is kept alight by people who bear the label "anthropologist," or some other; but the need for a *variety* of approaches and methods in the social sciences is critical. Those periods of social science which displayed a marked unity of outlook have been the theoretically sterile periods: the last half of the nineteenth century, with its "evolutionary" presumptions for all the social sciences, is the most familiar; another was the "historical" period of anthropology, particularly the first two decades of the twentieth century. The human reality must be apprehended by a variety of viewpoints, not by one alone, because this very reality is always in part a construct, always in part an image, and only by encouraging difference in perspective and approach can one obtain the needed richness of imagery, and consequently, theory.

BIBLIOGRAPHY

ACKERMAN, CHARLES
1964 Structure and statistics: the Purum case *American Anthropologist* 66:53–65.

ADAMS, R. N., and J. PREISS (eds.)
1960 *Human organization research: field relations and techniques.* Homewood, Ill., Dorsey Press.

ANDERSON, R. T., and B. G. ANDERSON
1964 *The vanishing village, a Danish maritime community.* Seattle, University of Washington Press.

ARENSBERG, C. M.
1961 The community as object and as sample. *American Anthropologist* 63:241–264.

BALANDIER, G.
1952 Approche sociologique des 'Brazzavilles noires': étude preliminaire. *Africa* 22, 1: 23–34.

BATESON, GREGORY
1936 *Naven: a survey of the problems suggested by a composite picture of the culture of a New Guinean tribe, drawn from three points of view.* London, Cambridge University Press.

BATESON, GREGORY, and MARGARET MEAD
1942 *Balinese character: a photographic analysis.* New York, New York Academy of Sciences.

BENEDICT, RUTH
1946 *The chrysanthemum and the sword: patterns of Japanese culture.* Boston, Houghton Mifflin.

BENNETT, J. W.
1944 The development of ethnological theory as illustrated by studies of the Plains sun dance. *American Anthropologist* 46:162–181.
1948 The study of cultures: a survey of technique and methodology in field work. *American Sociological Review* 13:672–689.
1961 Individual perspective in fieldwork. In R. N. Adams and J. J. Preiss, eds., *Human organization research: field relations and techniques.* Homewood, Ill., Dorsey Press.

BENNETT, J. W., and K. H. WOLFF
1956 Toward communication between sociology and anthropology. In W. L. Thomas, Jr., ed., *Current anthropology.* Chicago, University of Chicago Press.

BLALOCK, H. M., JR.
1960 *Social statistics.* New York, McGraw-Hill.

BOSE, S. P.
1962 Peasant values and innovation in India. *American Journal of Sociology* 67:552–560.

BURLING, ROBBINS
1962 Maximization theories and the study of economic anthropology. *American Anthropologist* 64:802–821.
1964 Cognition and componential analysis: God's truth or hocus-pocus? *American Anthropologist* 66:20–28.

BUSIA, K. A.
1950 *Report on a social survey of Sekondi-Takoradi.* London, Crown Agents.

CANCIAN, FRANK
1963 Informant error and native prestige ranking in Zinacantan. *American Anthropologist* 65:1068–1075.

CASAGRANDE, J. B.
1959 Some observations on the study of intermediate societies. In V. F. Ray, ed., *Intermediate societies.* Seattle, American Ethnological Society Publications, University of Washington Press.

DORE, R. P.
1958 *City life in Japan: the study of a Tokyo ward.* Berkeley, University of California Press.

DRIVER, H. E., and W. C. MASSEY
1957 Comparative studies of North American Indians. *Transactions of the American Philosophical Society,* New Series 47, 2: 165–456.

DUBE, S. C.
1955 *Indian village.* London, Routledge and Kegan Paul.

DUMONT, L., and D. POCOCK (eds.)
1957 *Contributions to Indian sociology,* Vol. 1. Paris-Oxford, Institute of Social Anthropology.

EGGAN, FRED
1954 Social anthropology and the method of controlled comparison. *American Anthropologist* 56:743–763.

EISENSTADT, S. N.
1961 Anthropological studies of complex societies. *Current Anthropology* 2, 3:201–222.

EVANS-PRITCHARD, E. E.
1940 *The Nuer.* Oxford, Clarendon Press.

FIRTH, R.
1954 Census and sociology in a primitive community. In *Problems and methods in demographic studies of preliterate peoples.* Proceedings of World Population Conference, United States, Paper 6:105–227.

FORDE, DARYLL
1959 The anthropological approach in social science. In M. H. Fried, ed., *Readings in anthropology,* Vol. 2. New York, Crowell.

FORTES, M.
1948 Ashanti social survey: a preliminary report. In M. Gluckman and J. M. Winterbottom, eds., *Human problems in British Central Africa,* Vol. 6. Northern Rhodesia. Rhodes-Livingstone.

FRAKE, C. O.
1964 Notes on queries in ethnography. *American Anthropologist* 66, 2:132–145.

FRASER, T. M., JR.
1960 *Rusembilian: a Malay fishing village in southern Thailand.* Ithaca, Cornell University Press.

FREY, F. W.
1963 Surveying peasant attitudes in Turkey. *Public Opinion Quarterly* 27:335–355.

GALLAHER, ART, JR.
1961 *Plainville fifteen years later.* New York, Columbia University Press.

GEERTZ, CLIFFORD
1961 Studies in peasant life: community and society. In B. J. Siegel, ed., *Biennial Review of Anthropology.* Stanford, Stanford University Press.

GOODENOUGH, W. H.
1956 Residence rules. *Southwestern Journal of Anthropology* 12:22–37.

GOODMAN, L. A., and W. H. KRUSKAL
1954 Measures of association for cross-classification. *Journal of the American Statistical Association* 49:732–764.

GORER, GEOFFREY
1948 *The American people: a study in national character.* New York, Norton.
1955 *Exploring English character.* New York, Criterion Books.

GOULDNER, A. W., and R. A. PETERSON
1962 *Notes on technology and the moral order.* New York, Bobbs-Merrill.

HENRY, JULES
1951 Economics of Pilaga food distribution. *American Anthropologist* 53:187–219.

HIGGINS, B. H.
1959 *Economic development: principles, problems and policies.* New York, Norton.

HOBHOUSE, L. T., G. C. WHEELER, and MORRIS GINSBERG
1930 *The material culture and social institutions of the simpler peoples.* London, Chapman and Hall.

HOTCHKISS, J. C.
1964 Studies of language and culture in Highland Chiapas, Mexico. In V. E. Garfield, ed., *Proceedings of the 1963 Annual Spring Meeting of the American Ethnological Society.* Seattle, University of Washington.

HUNTER, MONICA
1936 *Reaction to conquest: effects of contact with Europeans on the Pondo of South Africa.* Part 2, An urban community. New York, Oxford University Press.

HYMES, D. H.
1964 A perspective for linguistic anthropology. In Sol Tax, ed., *Horizons of anthropology.* Chicago, Aldine.

JAY, PAUL
1963 Tahitian fosterage and the form of ethnographic models. *American Anthropologist* 65:1027–1046.

JAYAWARDENA, CHANDRA
1963 *Conflict and solidarity in a Guianese plantation.* London, Athlone Press.

KELLER, S.
1960 Der zenus als quelle sozial-anthropologischer untersuchungen. *Homo* 11, 1.

KLUCKHOHN, CLYDE
1938 Participation in ceremonials in a Navaho community. *American Anthropologist* 40: 359–369.

KLUCKHOHN, F. R., and FRED STRODTBECK
1961 *Variations in value orientations.* Evanston, Ill., Row, Peterson.

KROEBER, A. L., and H. E. DRIVER
1938 The reliability of culture element data. *University of California Anthropological Records* 1:205–220.

LANCASTER, LORRAINE
1961 Some conceptual problems in the study of family and kin ties in the British Isles. *British Journal of Sociology* 12: 317–331.

LANDY, DAVID
1959 *Tropical childhood: cultural transmission and learning in a rural Puerto Rican village.* Chapel Hill, University of North Carolina.

LANG, G. O., and PETER KUNSTADTER
1957 Survey research on the Uintah and Ouray Ute reservation. *American Anthropologist* 59:527–532.

LANHAM, B. B.
1956 Aspects of child care in Japan: a preliminary report. In D. G. Haring, ed., *Personal character and cultural milieu.* 3rd rev. ed. Syracuse, Syracuse University Press.

LEACH, E. R.
1960 Review of S. H. Udy, Jr., *Organization of work: a comparative analysis of production among non-industrial peoples.* *American Sociological Review* 25:136–138.

LERNER, DANIEL
1958 *The passing of traditional society: modernizing the Middle East.* Glencoe, Ill., Free Press.

LEWIS, OSCAR
1958 *Village life in Northern India: studies in a Delhi village.* Urbana, University of Illinois Press.

LYND, R. S., and HELEN LYND
1929 *Middletown: a study in contemporary American culture.* New York, Harcourt, Brace.

MADGE, CHARLES, and T. H. HARRISON
1939 *Britain by mass observation.* London, Penguin Books.

MALINOWSKI, BRONISLAW
1922 *Argonauts of the Western Pacific: an account of native enterprise and adventure in the archipelagoes of Melanesian*

New Guinea. London, Routledge and Kegan Paul.

1929 *The sexual life of savages in north-western Melanesia: an ethnographic account of courtship, marriage and family life among the natives of the Trobriand Islands.* New York, Liveright.

1935 *Coral gardens and their magic: study of method of tilling in the Trobriand Islands.* London, Routledge and Kegan Paul.

MANGIN, W.
1960 Mental health and migration to cities: a Peruvian case. *Annals of the New York Academy of Sciences* 84, 17:911–917.

MARRIOTT, MCKIM
1960 *Caste ranking and community structure in five regions of India and Pakistan.* Monograph No. 23. Poona, India, Deccan College Post-Graduate and Research Institute.

MEAD, MARGARET, and R. B. MÉTRAUX
1953 *The study of culture at a distance.* Chicago, University of Chicago Press.

METZGER, DUANE, and G. E. WILLIAMS
1963 A formal ethnographic analysis of Tenejapa Ladino weddings. *American Anthropologist* 65:1076–1101.

MITCHELL, J. C.
1953 An estimate of fertility among Africans on the Copper-belt of Northern Rhodesia. *Human Problems in British Central Africa* 13:1–29.

1954 The distribution of African labour by area of origin on the copper mines of Northern Rhodesia. *Human Problems in British Central Africa* 14:30–36.

1956 *The Yao village: a study in the social structure of a Nyasaland tribe.* Manchester, Manchester University Press.

MORGAN, L. H.
1871 *Systems of consanguinity and affinity in the human family.* Smithsonian Contributions to Knowledge, Vol. 17. Washington, D.C., U. S. Government Printing Office.

MURDOCK, G. P.
1949 *Social Structure.* New York, Macmillan.

1957 World ethnographic sample. *American Anthropologist* 59:664–687.

1959 Introduction. In S. H. Udy, Jr., ed., *Organization of work.* New Haven, Human Relations Area Files Press.

NAROLL, R.
1962 *Data quality control: a new research technique.* Glencoe, Ill., Free Press.

PASSIN, H.
1942 Tarahumara prevarication: a problem in field method. *American Anthropologist* 44:235–247.

1951 The development of public opinion research in Japan. *International Journal of Opinion and Attitude Research* 5:20–30.

PAUW, B. A.
1963 *The second generation: a study of the family among urbanized Bantu in East London.* Fairlawn, N.J., Oxford University Press.

PETTITT, G. A.
1946 Primitive education in North America. *University of California Publications in American Archaeology and Ethnology,* Vol. 43.

RICHARDS, A.
1935 The village census in the study of culture contact. *Africa* 8:20–33.

ROMNEY, A. K., and R. G. D'ANDRADE
1964 Cognitive aspects of English kin terms. *American Anthropologist* 66, 2:146–170.

RYAN, B., *et al.*
1958 *Sinhalese village.* Coral Gables, University of Miami Press.

SCHADE, H.
1960 Sozial-anthropologie—ergebnisse einer zenus-untersuchung. *Homo* 11.

SCHAPERA, I.
1935 Field methods in the study of modern culture contacts. *Africa* 8:315–326.

1957 Marriage of near kin among the Tswana. *Africa* 27:139–159.

SCHEUCH, E.
1963 Data archives: problems and promise. Chairman of the Proceedings of the Eighteenth Conference on Public Opinion Research. *Public Opinion Quarterly* 27:641–643.

SCHWAB, W. B.
1954 An experiment in methodology in a West African urban community. *Human Organization* 13:13–19.

SCOTCH, N. A.
1960 A preliminary report on the relations of socio-cultural factors to hypertension among the Zulu. *Annals of the New York Academy of Sciences* 84, 17:1000–1009.

SCOTCH, N. A., and H. J. GEIGER
1964 An index of symptom and disease in Zulu culture. *Human Organization* 22:304–311.

SEPPILLI, T.
1960 Social conditions of fertility in a rural community in transition in central Mexico. *Annals of the New York Academy of Sciences* 84:959–962.

SMITH, M. G.
1962 *West Indian family structure.* Seattle, University of Washington Press.

SOFER, CYRIL, and RHONA SOFER
1955 *Jinja transformed: A social survey of a multiracial township.* East African Studies 4. London, Kegan Paul, Trench and Truber.

SPIER, L.
1921 The sun dance of the Plains Indians: its development and diffusion. *Anthropological Papers of the American Museum of Natural History,* Vol. 16, Part 7.

STAVRIANOS, B. K.
1950 Research methods in cultural anthropology in relation to scientific criteria. *Psychological Review* 57:334–344.

STEWARD, J. H., *et al.*
1956 *The people of Puerto Rico: a study in social anthropology.* Urbana, University of Illinois Press.

STOETZEL, JEAN
1953 The contributions of public opinion research techniques to social anthropology. *International Social Science Bulletin* 5, 3:494–503.

1955 *Without the chrysanthemum and the sword: a study of the attitudes of youth in post-war Japan.* New York, Columbia University Press.

STREIB, G. F.
1952 The use of survey methods among the Navaho. *American Anthropologist* 54:30–40.

STURTEVANT, W. C.
1964 Studies in ethnoscience. *American Anthropologist* 66, 2:99–131.

STYCOS, J. M.
1960 Sample surveys for social science in underdeveloped areas. In R. N. Adams and J. J. Priess, eds., *Human organization research: field relations and techniques.* Homewood, Ill., Dorsey Press.

SWANSON, G. E.
1960 *The birth of the gods: the origin of primitive beliefs.* Ann Arbor, University of Michigan Press.

TYLOR, E. B.
1889 On a method of investigating the development of institutions applied to the laws of marriage and descent. *Journal of the Royal Anthropological Institute* 18:245–269.

VIDICH, A. J., and GILBERT SHAPIRO
1955 A comparison of participant observation and survey data. *American Sociological Review* 20:28–33.

VOGT, E. Z., and ETHEL ALBERT
1966 *People of Rimrock: a study of values in five cultures.* Cambridge, Harvard University Press.

WEST, JAMES (Carl Withers)
1945 *Plainville, U.S.A.* New York, Columbia University Press.

WHITING, J. W., and I. L. CHILD
1953 *Child training and personality: a cross-cultural study.* New Haven, Yale University Press.

WILSON, GODFREY
1941– *An essay in the economics of detribalisation in Northern Rhodesia.* Rhodes-Livingstone Papers. Nos. 5 and 6. Northern Rhodesia, Rhodes-Livingstone.

WISSLER, CLARK
1923 *Man and culture.* New York, Crowell.

YOUNG, F., and R. YOUNG
1960a Two determinants of community reaction to industrialization in rural Mexico. *Economic Development and Cultural Change* 8:257–264.

1960b Social integration and change in twenty-four Mexican villages. *Economic Development and Cultural Change* 8:366–377.

CHAPTER 18

Method in Psychological Anthropology[1]

ROBERT B. EDGERTON

Psychological anthropology is a large and rapidly expanding field that is continually adding a great variety of interests to the long-standing concern of "culture and personality" with typical or modal personality. To review and evaluate method in this field today is a task that could please no one—except possibly those who condemned Sisyphus—for no sooner is such a labor completed than a new review and a new appraisal become necessary. Nonetheless, the task is at hand and it is not without purpose, for in psychological anthropology, perhaps even more so than in other areas of anthropology, questions of method are absolutely fundamental; they are fundamental because, in addition to all the reasons why method is always important, this field has been characterized by its involvement with specific, psychological methods of data collection.

Indeed, if anthropology in general has been guilty of saying too little about its methods, psychological anthropology, or its ancestor, culture and personality, has said (and has claimed) too much about its methods. For many years, questions of method, such as those involving the correct utilization of sundry projective techniques, have been discussed and have led to more general considerations of methodology and research design. Unfortunately, the inheritance of this long methodological concern is a mare's-nest in which views conflict, methods proliferate, publications accumulate, and dismay grows apace. Psychological anthropology is still, like much of the larger anthropology of which it is a part, a field in which findings are subject to a bewildering variety of interpretations, and the logic of inference is often neither clear nor consistent. And much that is done in the name of method continues to be shrouded in mystery by the practice of partial and imprecise reporting of the procedures of data collection and analysis. As a result, even the most enthusiastic practitioner in the field today would have to admit that psychological anthropology for the most part remains a demi-science in which assertion often rules the day, and full verification of propositions or findings remains an illusion far beyond the horizon of forseeable progress.

Yet, there is another dimension to the picture. The same criticisms that I have directed to psychological anthropology can be applied to most, if not all, of the fields in anthropology. And, research in psychological anthropology is increasingly marked by the serious efforts of many investigators to achieve a precision of method and sophistication of methodology to match the best of the behavioral sciences. Thus, progress is being made, slowly, but, we have reason to think, surely.

THE SCOPE OF THIS REVIEW

In a field that is so large, so ambiguously defined, so heterogeneous, and so rapidly

[1] Psychological anthropology is a term that displeases some anthropologists (including the present author) who feel that so-called "psychological" studies in anthropology should be renamed to better indicate that anthropological studies of the individual should be integrated with and directed toward an understanding of sociocultural systems. Nonetheless, the term is widely used and understood as a designation for a sub-field in anthropology. It is used here to refer to studies done in that sub-field, not as an endorsement of the term, nor of many of the studies done under its aegis.

changing, no review can be comprehensive. Therefore, what follows is a selective account, but one that attempts to touch upon the range of methods in current practice. Consequently, unlike many earlier reviews, this chapter is not confined to "projective techniques" (cf. Henry and Spiro 1953, Henry 1961, Kaplan 1961, Lindzey 1961). To deal here solely with the so-called projectives would accord them a unity they do not possess and a significance they no longer merit in the expanding field of psychological anthropology.

Some areas of research that are generally considered to fall within the domain of psychological anthropology are omitted here because they (e.g., linguistic models, ethnoscience and its ethnopsychological variants, and correlational analyses of the kind exemplified by the work of Whiting and his associates) are treated in appropriate detail elsewhere in this volume.

The main portion of this chapter will be devoted to an evaluation of methods of eliciting or recording data. Although it is axiomatic that any plan of data collection should be integrated with a plan of data analysis, the scope of this chapter does not permit systematic description or evaluation of the many considerations that relate to the analysis of data. The final section of the chapter will discuss the field as a whole and will suggest a reorientation of research methods.

PROJECTIVE TECHNIQUES

Since the appearance of *Anthropology Today* which contained Jules Henry's and Melford Spiro's (1953) survey of the use of "projective tests" in field research, any number of similarly focused surveys have been written. In 1961, two of the most thoughtful and thorough of these reviews appeared (Kaplan 1961, Lindzey 1961). Anyone interested in the use of projective techniques in cross-cultural research would be well-rewarded by reading these two reviews, as both Kaplan and Lindzey make observations of the greatest relevance. In so murky an area as this, however, it may be appropriate that these two eminently sound psychologists disagree somewhat in their conclusions regarding the value of projective techniques in anthropological research. For example, although Lindzey covers his flanks adroitly with some sincerely pessi-

mistic comments, his tone concerning the cross-cultural use of projectives is not entirely negative (1961:327–328):

Is there a general verdict concerning the use of projective techniques in anthropological research? It is a gray world in which we live! There are both good and bad aspects to the history of association between these instruments and this area of research. Although one may hope that research yet to be conducted will resolve many of the present ambiguities, one must, for the moment, leave the verdict to the individual observer. Those with high standards and a cathexis for rigor and empirical control will surely consider projective techniques guilty as charged and view them as possessing little or no demonstrated merit in this setting. Those who resonate to sensitive speculation and believe there is still a place for unadorned descriptive inquiry in the social sciences may well conclude that projective techniques have made defensible contributions to anthropological research and that their continued use is fully warranted.

My own impression is that studies involving the most sophisticated use of these instruments in this setting (for example, Gladwin & Sarason, 1953; Spindler 1955; Wallace 1952) provide a clear justification for the anthropologist displaying renewed interest in projective techniques. Unfortunately, I must add that such studies at present are vastly outnumbered by those in which these devices do not appear to have made a legitimate investigative contribution.

Although Lindzey is at best a left-handed admirer of projectives in anthropological usage, Bert Kaplan, a skilled and experienced field researcher among the non-Western peoples, takes a severely negative position (1961:252):

My judgments about the cross-cultural use of projective tests have been very harsh. I have looked for the positive values in these tests and found them very scant. I have looked at the difficulties in their use and found them to be enormous, and have concluded that as these tests are being used and interpreted at present, only a modicum of validity and value can be obtained from them.

Harsh words, indeed, but not unreasonably so. There are worthy cross-cultural uses of projectives, many more than the three that Lindzey mentioned, but most studies employing projectives have not only failed to meet rigorous standards of scientific method, they have failed to measure up even to minimal common-sense criteria of adequacy in the collection or interpretation of data.

In the years since Kaplan's and Lindzey's reviews were published, there have been some changes in the use of projective methods in cross-cultural research. Although these developments are hardly so momentous that either Lindzey or Kaplan could be expected to change his evaluation of projectives, they are nonetheless worthy of comment.

THE RORSCHACH

Although recent studies offer us little that could be regarded as a methodological advance beyond the work of Wallace (1952), Gladwin and Sarason (1953), or Spindler (1955), Rorschach research has come to reflect an increased concern with sampling, with the comparability of the "test situation," with the reliability of scoring systems, and with the demonstrable validity of the interpretations. For an introduction to the variety in recent work, one might examine the collaboration of Miner and DeVos (1960) in their Algerian research, that of Helm et al. (1963) among the Slave Indians, the psychoanalytically tinged work of Boyer and his colleagues (1964) with Apache shamans, and the retrospective concern of Williams and Williams (1965) with the Rorschach test situation.

The competing interpretive schemes of Klopfer and Beck continue to be employed, but we also find some use of a Piotrowskian mode of interpretation (Bricklin and Zeleznik 1963) and innovative quantitative schemes (e.g., DeVos 1955). Perhaps the most significant of these innovations is found in the work of Holtzman et al. (1961). Holtzman's "ink-blot test" attempts to overcome many of the methodological difficulties that have bedeviled the traditional Rorschach. For example, the traditional Rorschach offers the respondent ten standard ink-blots and permits him to give as many or as few responses to each blot as he wishes. The characteristic result is a highly skewed distribution that fails to achieve even ordinal properties of measurement. In an effort to correct this difficulty, the Holtzman technique employs forty-five blots, for each of which only one response is recorded. These blots also provide greater variety in color and configuration than the Rorschach—e.g., the Holtzman blots avoid the bilateral symmetry that characterizes the Rorschach and they also employ a great many pastel colors. Edgerton (1965) has modified the traditional Rorschach in order to utilize some of Holtzman's suggestions for improved

reliability and statistical treatment of the responses, and others, for example Leininger (1966) in her research with the Gadsup of Highland New Guinea, have successfully employed the Holtzman blots in non-Western societies, but for the most part, the promise of the Holtzman technique has not been widely examined in cross-cultural research.

In general, anthropologists seem to be less enamored of the possibilities of the Rorschach than they were ten or even five years ago. Perhaps they have become aware that concern over the validity of the Rorschach is not limited to its cross-cultural use; validity studies of the Rorschach as a clinical tool are likewise often negative (Meehl 1959, Zubin 1954). On the other hand, the use of the Rorschach by foreign researchers has increased. Cheng's (1958) ambitious study of the Ami on Formosa is but one of many such examples.

An anthropologist who is about to depart for the field today, may still pack the Rorschach away in his field kit, but that kit is now much more crowded by other techniques, and in the competition for space, it appears that the Rorschach plates are more and more often left at home.

VERSIONS OF THE TAT

If the popularity of the Rorschach is waning, the use of versions of the TAT is, if anything, on the increase. Almost without exception, those anthropologists and psychologists who have evaluated the various projective techniques in cross-cultural research have been more favorably disposed toward TAT-like techniques than they have toward the Rorschach, or for that matter, most of the other projectives. This more positive evaluation seems to derive from the belief that less is claimed in terms of the "depth" of psychodynamic meaning of TAT responses, and the fact that the interpretation of TAT protocols tends to be seen as possessing both greater reliability and validity. The continued use of TAT-like techniques seems to reflect a widespread faith in the usefulness of such data-eliciting devices.

Redrawings of the standard Murray TAT set are now routine preparation for many research problems, and there has been a rapid accumulation of knowledge concerning effective design and administration of picture stimuli techniques in cross-cultural research (Henry 1956, Sherwood 1957, Goldschmidt and Edgerton 1961, Spindler and Spindler 1965). Methodological innovations in the use of the TAT as a means of eliciting "personality" data also continue to appear: for example, the work of Caudill (1962) in Japan, Stycos (1964) in Haiti, and DeVos and Wagatsuma (1959, 1961) in their Japanese research.

However, the most marked trend in the use of TAT-like picture stimuli techniques is the use of such devices to elicit responses that are relevant to social-psychological and cultural questions, rather than responses relevant primarily to personality; TAT-like picture stimuli have been found useful in the investigation of attitudes, values, beliefs, and role-behavior of many sorts—all viewed as social and cultural phenomena rather than expressions of individual or "group" psychodynamics. When picture-stimuli are directed to this more social level of inquiry, they are designed to maximize the dramatic impact of realism, as would ideally be provided by a photograph, and they avoid the "projective" ambiguity that is characteristic of traditional TAT pictures. Investigators who have employed these techniques have shown unusual regard for research design and "objectivity." Significant in this development is the work of Fried (1954), Goldschmidt and Edgerton (1961), Parker (1964) and Spindler and Spindler (1965). This latter article by the Spindlers contains an excellent review of developments in these techniques, including the various rationales for their use.

Other standard projective techniques, despite periods of popularity in the past, are now only occasionally employed. An exception is sentence completion, not because it is used so often (a recent use of sentence completion techniques is Leichty's [1963] comparison of U.S. and Vietnamese children), but rather because a version of it was accorded such a central role by Phillips in his study of personality in a Thai village (1965). Phillips' detailed and stimulating study used sentence completion as a fundamental data collection technique. Although the generality of Phillips' conclusions has been questioned (Keyes 1966), his work is nonetheless an intriguing blend of theory and method—especially so, because Phillips refers to his version of sentence completion as (1965:126–127) "an ideal

technique for studying the range and variation of human personality. Here is an instrument the units of which seem to have true cross-cultural stimulus value and the responses to which seem genuinely comparable from one human group to another." Skeptics—among whom the reviewer must be counted—will find Phillips' claim an overly enthusiastic one, but the search for a universally applicable projective technique is venerable, and even though the haystack is large and the needle is small, it will undoubtedly continue. Unfortunately, if the fate of this sentence completion technique is similar to that of other projectives for which universal applicability was claimed, the critical multi-cultural examination of the technique will be some time in coming, for in this field the prevailing mood is to innovation, not replication.

Human figure drawing is still employed, as in the work of Dennis (1960) with the Bedouin, Badri and Dennis (1964) and Badri (1965) in the Sudan, and Preston (1964) with the Northwest Coast Eskimo. However, all these researchers are psychologists, not anthropologists. Except for an occasional enthusiastic recommendation, such as that by Barnouw (1963) for the House-Tree-Person test, human figure drawing seems to have fallen into disuse among anthropologists.

Examples of the use of other projectives can still be located—Garcia-Vicente (1960) used the Lowenfeld Mosaic in Angola, Gregor and McPherson (1963) administered both the Porteus Maze and Gestalt Continuation tests to nonliterate aborigines in Central Australia, and Ervin and Landar (1963) used word association techniques among the Navaho. And variants continue to appear, as in Rosenberg's (1962) modification of psychodrama, called "ethnodrama."

But some of the standard projectives—for example, doll play—have virtually disappeared from view. The problems in the use of doll play are effectively set forth by the contrasting arguments of Landy (1956), who takes a negative view, and Ritchie (1957), who argues for the use of the technique. The arguments revolve around the economy of the technique (its cost in time, energy and money) and the problems of interpretation. Here, even more so than with most projectives, validation studies are lacking.

Even though projective techniques continue to be used in cross-cultural research, they no longer exercise the dominance over psychological anthropology that they once did. There are many reasons for their loss of popularity. Their dubious validity is but one, their expense to administer is another, and their association with theories of "depth" psychology is yet another. Still another, perhaps equally important reason, is that most of the projectives have been associated with the study of typical personality, and psychological anthropology is no longer centrally concerned with typical personality. Other interests, and thus other methods, have grown up alongside the projectives, and have begun to take over center stage.

TRENDS AND DEVELOPMENTS IN METHOD

Current interests and methods in psychological anthropology are formidably diverse. For example, the traditional concern with early socialization has broadened to include a cross-cultural inquiry into child development. Such developmental research seems to be more typically European than American, as, for example, in the work of Cawley and Murray (1962) on Piaget and Inhelder norms, or Geber's (1962) African research that has employed Gesell and Terman-Merrill techniques. However, American students are showing increasing interest in the social and cultural, rather than principally pediatric, implications of these research procedures, and Mead's contributions in this area are well known.

Other developing methods have had broad cultural and psychological significance. Hall's study of "proxemics," for example, suggests a method for measuring some of the most fundamental, unconscious, and hence elusive, features of man's conduct (Hall 1963). Although empirical research in proxemics—how man unconsciously structures microspace—has scarcely begun (e.g., Watson and Graves 1966), the potential of such research, as with Birdwhistell's earlier and related studies of kinesics (1952), is undeniably great.

A similarly important development has taken place in psycholinguistics where research has increasingly taken on general psychological and cultural relevance. One psycholinguistic approach will be mentioned here because of its significance and frequent utilization as a cross-cultural technique for the investigation of questions of general psychological significance. Osgood's Semantic Differential Technique for the study of the "dimensions of semantic space" frequently has been employed cross-culturally (Osgood 1964) and its popularity appears to be growing (Helper and Garfield 1965, Strodtbeck 1966). The technique's appeal lies, in part, in its relative ease of cross-cultural applicability and replicability, and, in part, in the great challenge of the posited universal basis for its three factors—Evaluation, Potency and Activity. Osgood and his coworkers applied factor analysis to their accumulated data and arrived at three independent factors which they believe can describe the connotative meaning of any concept. Thus they offer a three-dimensional map of semantic space within which, they argue, any word can be located. The technique's appeal also lies in its potential usefulness as a technique for the study of meaning, in both its cognitive and affective aspects.

Important developments have also occurred in the analysis of fantasy productions. The analysis of art as a projective system has received relatively little attention in recent years (for an exception, see Kavolis 1964). However, the analysis of other fantasy productions, particularly folk tales and mythology, has been marked by some methodologically noteworthy changes. The general work of Jacobs (1959) and Fischer (1963) has received considerable attention already, and work by others continues. For example, Parker (1962) has applied TAT scoring techniques to the analysis of Eskimo and Ojibwa mythology, and following the earlier work of McClelland and Friedman (1952), Price-Williams (1965) has completed an analysis of aggression in the child-rearing practices and folklore of the Tiv. Building upon Spiro's (1960) suggestion, Price-Williams' research in Nigeria is an interesting effort to discover links between socialization, folklore and witchcraft in terms of a theory of psychological displacement. Price-Williams finds that traces of the aggression which is sharply discouraged in Tiv childhood, appear in Tiv folklore; he suggests that in adult life overt conflict between kin is displaced through witchcraft accusation. The formulation is scarcely original, but the methodology which combines field research with multi-judge ratings of folk tales, is a useful step toward an improved understanding of the relationship of fantasy productions to displaced aggression. For a recent sampling of research in mythology see Jacobs and Greenway (1966).

In another study based upon Nigerian data, LeVine (1966) has extended the McClelland-Atkinson n Achievement scoring procedures to dreams, specifically to dreams collected from 342 male secondary students, representing the Hausa, Ibo and Yoruba. In considering the hypothesis that differences in the incidence of n Achievement between ethnic groups correspond to differences in their traditional status mobility systems, LeVine has offered a commendable example of the potential of methodologically rigorous dream research for the investigation of basic problems in the study of motivation. LeVine and his colleagues provide us with a promising means of scoring verbal fantasy productions and, to their credit, they examine alternative hypotheses with refreshing candor. The result is a noteworthy inquiry into possible tribal differences in personality, one that should stimulate further research with n Achievement scoring techniques.

A most significant development—not only for the study of folklore but for anthropological research in general—is exemplified by Colby's work in the application of computer techniques to the analysis of folk texts. Improvements in computers and computer language have now made unbelievably massive data handling not only feasible but routine. Colby has utilized the General Inquirer System of Stone and colleagues (Stone et al., 1966) in a search for basic patterns in folk tales. This computer system employs a dictionary of entry words grouped into conceptual units that can be tallied, compared to and retrieved from the sentences in which they occurred in the original text, and graphically presented for visual comparison. The capacity, speed and flexibility of the latest generation of computers are enormous, and while content analyses of folk tales are hardly new, Colby's use of computer systems for content analysis is a promising advance. Colby has already analyzed folk tales from several cultures (1966a, 1966b) and is now attempting to develop improved computer techniques for the analysis of cultural materials such as TAT protocols, dreams, autobiographies and photograph-elicited texts. As Colby (and many others) have shown, the use of computers will not only vastly facilitate data analysis, it will also redirect data collection procedures in the field, quite possibly to a degree that we cannot yet comprehend.

Still another kind of development is represented by the multidimensional model for the study of games that has been put together by Roberts, Sutton-Smith and colleagues. This model for game analysis (which should not be confused with game theory), like many earlier emphases within "culture and personality," stresses the articulation of one mode of conduct—in this case, games—with others, such as folk tales (Roberts et al., 1963) or child training (Roberts 1962). But this model is far more complex than most of those that preceded it: it is both observational and experimental; it employs mathematics and symbolic logic; it is based upon intuitive inference, yet it is both subject to and is a means of empirical verification (Sutton-Smith and Roberts 1964, Roberts et al., 1965). Some of the basic assumptions of the approach are these (Sutton-Smith and Roberts 1964:14):

... some of the major concepts that children have about competition are drawn from their experiences with games; that games are model forms of real competition; and that the model function of games occurs because games, as well as the styles of competition of which they serve as models, are expressions of cognitive attitudes towards competition that arise out of the characteristic interaction of child-training processes and cultural prescription. . . .

Even though this approach is subject to a number of the same criticisms that have plagued its psycho-functional precursors, it is methodologically more sophisticated than earlier studies.

The foregoing brief account of developments has necessarily omitted a great deal that is of methodological significance, but it has attempted to provide appropriately diverse examples of trends that have general methodological relevance for psychological anthropology. Two of the most pronounced of these trends have been reserved for final treatment; they are (1) the rapid emergence of cross-cultural studies of perception, and (2) the increased utilization of interview methods.

After a long interruption following the work of Rivers at the turn of the century, the ten years following the work of Lenneberg and Roberts (1956) have witnessed a substantial outpouring of cross-cultural research in perception. For example, the work of Allport and Pettigrew (1957) on the trapezoidal illusion among the Zulu, was followed by Hudson's (1960) more general African research. Turnbull's (1961) intriguing anecdote about the inability of an Mbuti Pygmy to correlate size-constancy and distance was followed by Bonte's (1962) research on the relative susceptibility of 50 Bashi Africans and 100 Mbuti Pygmies to the Müller-Lyer illusion. In the same year, Schwitzgebel (1962) investigated the perceptual abilities of Dutch and Zulu adults on a variety of tasks including length estimation, size matching, time estimation, and the location of the Gottschalk embedded figures. Unfortunately, Schwitzgebel's methodology is imprecisely reported. Price-Williams (1962) had Tiv children perform various sorting tasks that indicated the abstractness or concreteness of their modes of classification. Doob has continued his earlier interests in African perception and communication by examining eidetic imagery among the Ibo (1964) and Kamba (1965). However, the most comprehensive and widely comparative work in the cross-cultural study of psychophysics, particularly in the perception of geometric illusions, is that of Segall, Campbell and Herskovits (1963, 1966). These and other studies of visual perception have been primarily the work of psychologists, but the possible social and cultural implications of perceptual differences both between and within cultures should attract more attention from anthropologists, for if perceptual abilities are as sensitive to cultural influences as these studies suggest, then it is imperative that we understand the sources of these perceptual differentia as well as the possible effects of such differences upon intra- and inter-cultural communication.

The method that has shown the greatest growth as a technique in psychological anthropology is the interview. While projective techniques have declined in use, interviewing has grown proportionately. Indeed, there are so many versions of interview techniques in current usage that it is impossible to do more than touch upon the variety of approaches now being taken. These approaches range between the semi-structured, intensely intimate format of Oscar Lewis (1959, 1966), to the highly structured impersonality of survey research. The work of Lewis, from Tepoztlán to Puerto Rico, is too well known to need further review; others, however, are less well known. For example, a somewhat similar technique developed by Roberts and Arth (1966) is known as "dyadic elicitation." This technique consists in having one member of the "native culture" ask a question of another member in privacy, but while a tape recorder

is in operation. The resulting tapes are later translated from the native language into English. The approach has some obvious advantages over standard interviewing practices, but it also has some disadvantages, principally its high cost in terms of time and money. As Roberts and Arth (1966:40) point out:

This technique is probably best used in selected instances where it is difficult to get appropriate responses from informants by ordinary means, where texture is desired, and where there is concern with the actual transmissions of culture from teacher to pupil within the interactive network of the society.

Other interview techniques have taken quite different forms. For example, "hypothetical situation" techniques, although often criticized for posing unreal or out-of-context situations, have continued to be employed and have been improved. Two recent and inventive instances are available in the work of Berndt and Fernandez. Berndt (1966) asked the Gunwinggu and "Murngin" of Australia to imagine that they were in a storm at sea in which they and various relatives were in a boat about to sink. Respondents were then asked whom they would save, if only one person could be saved. Fernandez (1966) made similar use of what he called the "ultimate circumstances situation" with a contrastive sample of Dartmouth students and Zulu. In Fernandez's employment, a disastrous situation (drowning, public nudity, etc.) is presented and the respondent is asked to choose which one of several close relatives he would help if he could aid only one.

Another recent, but quite different, technique is Freed's "role profile test" (1965). This procedure, as used with Washo and Mohave respondents, requires that cards bearing the kin terms for various relatives be ranked on each of sixteen questions (e.g., "Which relative is most likely to help you if you need it?"). The technique is flexible in that it can be adapted to any number of interests and the orderings that result from the ranking procedure are easily treated statistically.

Survey research interview methods have also come into prominence, although the versions employed have varied widely. The work of Rogers and Frantz (1962) is an example of standard survey procedure. Rogers and Frantz selected a probability sample of 500 from the whole of the adult white population of Southern Rhodesia. Even though their research was not basically psychological, their concern with attitudes toward race relations has considerable psychological relevance. Many other researchers have employed similarly standard survey methods, particularly with relatively urban populations.

Edgerton (1965) has extended survey procedures, including probability sampling, to the study of a pastoral and a farming community within each of four tribal societies in East Africa. A structured interview was administered to 505 respondents (both men and women) in privacy, and under standardized conditions. The interview, consisting of eighty-six questions, included both open-ended and forced-choice questions that were intended to elicit personality-relevant responses. Even extremely unacculturized, pastoral tribesmen were able to respond to these questions with little apparent difficulty.

LeVine and Campbell's extensive cross-cultural study of ethnocentrism provides another variant of interviewing technique. These investigators have utilized several sources for interview data in what they term "reputational ethnography"—e.g., judgments by ethnic groups concerning other ethnic groups, visitors' judgments about the groups they visit, self-report judgments by each group on itself. LeVine (1966) has reported upon one such interview procedure with thirty tribes in Uganda, Kenya and Tanzania, ten in each of the three countries. LeVine's interviews were administered by a Nairobi survey research organization (subcontracting of this sort is itself an innovation) to fifty respondents in each one of the thirty societies. Respondents were asked about those ten tribes in their own country as well as four "well-known or bordering groups from the other countries." Although LeVine's findings are preliminary, his interviewing methods are intriguing, especially in view of the high agreement between a number of tribes in the "reputational" attribution given. LeVine also reports that his findings concerning preoccupation with witchcraft, relative independence of action and the expression of aggression for certain tribes are "remarkably similar" to the findings reported by Edgerton (1965).

Survey interviewing methods have also been extensively used in recent psychiatrically oriented cross-cultural research. For example, MacLean (1966) has reported the results of a sample survey of attitudes toward hospitals and healers among 400 men and 106 women in an unacculturated area of Ibadan. Parker and Kleiner (1966) have collaborated in the use of survey interviewing methods with a large sample of Negroes in Philadelphia. Parker and Kleiner's data collection procedure and over-all research design provide an unusually solid foundation for their analyses of the sociological and psychological dimensions of psychiatric disorder. Chance's utilization of a revision of the Cornell Medical Index (CMI) as a means to an understanding of personality adaptations among the Eskimo (1965) and the Chinese of Taiwan (Chance, Rin and Chu 1966) is also noteworthy. In both studies, Chance and his colleagues employed the CMI within a research design that included probability sampling, a substantial N (sample size on Taiwan was 488), and careful interviewing technique.

In a series of major studies, Leighton and his colleagues have approached the study of psychiatric disorder from Nova Scotia to West Africa by means of a highly structured interviewing procedure set within a design featuring both survey procedures and "depth" interviewing (Leighton et al. 1963). These extensive studies implicate such a variety of data collection procedures that they should be read not only by those with an interest in cross-cultural psychiatry but by all who are concerned with methodology. An overview of the approach is now available in Murphy and Leighton (1965).

Whether the researcher in psychological anthropology turns to the interview as his basic data collection technique or merely as one of many information-gathering devices, methods of interviewing remain fundamental to his craft. And whether interviewing is regarded as an art or a science, detailed reviews of interviewing procedures, such as that recently offered by Richardson et al. (1965), become essential reading.

SOME AREAS OF NEGLECT

Some techniques continue to be accorded little interest in psychological anthropology. For example, there has been little utilization of complex mechanical devices for recording observations, such as Chapple's interaction recorders (1962), although such devices could be useful in more urban non-Western settings, as, for example, in research with school children. Even such simple, precise, yet flexible techniques as the Q-sort seldom make an appearance in non-Western field research, where they could easily be adopted to a number of interests (e.g., MacAndrew and Edgerton 1964, Silberman 1966). More important, two major areas of methodological concern remain relatively undeveloped; these are: case studies and observational studies.

Although case study method stands in higher regard in anthropology than it does in sociology or most branches of psychology, nonetheless, relative to other methods in psychological anthropology, it is neglected (Honigmann 1961, Langness 1966). Despite the accumulation of autobiographical materials, the volume of published case study material has not kept pace with the rate of publication in other areas of method. More critical is the failure to make systematic, concerted use of the case materials that have been published. Case studies continue to be thought of as ancillary procedures, useful in a secondary role and possessed of their own validity, but not as techniques around which psychological research ought to be organized, and not as "methods" warranting full equality in the armamentarium of "behavioral science."

Of course, there are impressive difficulties in all of the techniques of biography reconstruction that are so crucial to retrospective case study methods, but these difficulties are, in principle, no more insuperable than those that our other, more "objective," methods present. Case studies need not remain outcasts in our family of methods. Whether they take a longitudinal, cross-sectional, or historical form, they can be quite as rigorously objective as our other, more fashionable, methods. In this regard, perhaps Langness' (1966) recent call for more complete exploitation of life history material will be taken seriously.

The relative underdevelopment of objective techniques of observation is understandable to a degree, for the development of such methods is truly formidable outside of a small-group, "laboratory" research situation. Still, it is remarkable that so few of the methods employed in psychological anthropology are observational. The work of John and Beatrice Whiting, and their colleagues, in the study of socialization is a step in the direction of comparability of units in field observation, but even the Whitings' studies have yet to achieve the status of a fully operationalized, cross-culturally comparable, observational

method (cf. Mead 1964). This should not be taken as a criticism of the Whitings, who have contributed a great deal to the observational study of socialization (e.g., Whiting and Whiting 1960, and Whiting 1963); nevertheless, their interviewing tactics remain more explicit and detailed than their observational procedures. Others, notably Hall (1963) in his proxemic analysis and Harris (1964) in his search for "cultural things," have made advances in the specification of relevant and comparable units of observational analysis, as well as providing operationalized (or operationalizable) notational systems for recording what is observed.

Yet our efforts to develop objective observational methods have lagged, and we have even failed to take full advantage of existing techniques. For example, psychological anthropologists still make little use of behavior rating scales (such as those employed by Richardson 1966, or Brookover and Back 1966), for the precise recording of behavior within limited spheres of action. Furthermore, despite the ardent pleas of Mead (1956) and many others, as well as some useful research applications (Bateson and Mead 1951, Mead and Heyman 1965), the camera is strikingly underutilized in psychological anthropology. Finally, we have not yet made much use of the model for minute observational description of the sort that Barker and Wright (1951) called "psychological ecology." This approach calls for a microscopic report—massively detailed—of all those actions displayed by one person (and those with whom he interacts) within a very limited period of time. The technique is expensive and time-consuming, yet it is capable of producing the kind of detail that may be required if we are to discover otherwise hidden relationships.

Psychological anthropologists, like all anthropologists, observe behavior, but when they think in terms of "objective" methods, they turn elsewhere, to other and simpler sources of data. I believe that the single greatest weakness of psychological studies in anthropology is the failure to develop and employ replicable techniques of observation.

AN APPRAISAL

It used to be lamented that the cross-cultural study of personality and other psychological interests was handicapped by a lack of methods. Thus, while it was sometimes said that it is a poor carpenter who blames his tools, it was argued in rebuttal that one could not expect the Taj Mahal to be built with one's bare hands. This argument is heard less often today for we now have tools galore. Indeed, there are signs that psychological anthropology may go the way of much of sociology, where it often appears that method is permitted to dictate the choice of problem. However, we also see indications that psychological anthropologists are becoming more concerned with methodology, especially with well-conceived research design as a strategy of problem solving, rather than concentrating upon methods to be used, much as a virtuoso would practice finger exercises. Recent research, published and in process, confirms this shifting orientation. At the same time, there is growing concern with problems such as validity (e.g., McEwen 1963), reliability (e.g., Young and Young 1961), bias (e.g., Schwab 1965), inference (e.g., Strodtbeck 1964) and a general search for universally applicable procedures, or "meta-methods."

In all of this developing concern with methodology, there is an explicit or tacit acceptance of the social or behavioral science version of what is basically a nonsocial paradigm of proper scientific procedure (Kuhn 1962). We are learning to work within this paradigm better and better, and we are acquiring useful knowledge as we do so. There is much to be pleased about in these developments, yet as we look ahead, there is also reason to be uneasy.

Psychologists, particularly social psychologists, are going to non-Western societies in ever increasing numbers. In the preceding pages I have only rarely identified names as belonging to anthropologists or psychologists. The field of psychological anthropology is so multidisciplinary that to have to would have been both tedious and invidious. Perhaps this degree of disciplinary mix is fitting. Perhaps even greater fusion would be helpful. For many reasons, however, I doubt it. For one thing, we, as anthropologists, stand in danger of finding ourselves reduced to the status of second-rate psychologists, as, to stretch a point, the "primitive" section on social psychology in the American Psychological Association. Joking aside, surely, we cannot reasonably expect that we can very often utilize psychological methods better than the psychologists themselves. Therefore, if psychologists continue to go into non-Western societies, how can we do better than they? The answer, I suspect, is that we cannot, as long as we use *their* methods and *their* paradigm of scientific procedure.

Recommendations that we as anthropologists must attend more carefully to the methodological strictures of psychologists, and other behavioral scientists, should be heard. We must be more concerned with our purposes as anthropologists, and methodology is central to whatever we do. We must, that is, become more self-conscious about our procedures, but I do not think that we shall find all of the answers to our problems in a more faithful adoption of the methods or methodologies of psychology, or, for that matter, any other science.

That we in psychological anthropology have thus far depended upon these disciplines for our methods is undeniable. It is also curious, because while we have never subscribed to Vernon's shibboleth that "words are actions in miniature," these techniques are almost without exception means of eliciting words— that is, answers to our projective stimuli or our semi-projective questions. Words may not be small deeds, but neither are they insignificant, and it is well that our techniques improve constantly as valid, reliable means of measuring what men say, and that we improve in our use of them.

But why should we as anthropologists focus upon words instead of actions? In urban settings where these word-focused methods were first applied, it is manifestly easier to collect word data than action data, and it is also easier to analyze these data within the existing standards of scientific procedure. It is also easier to do so in the field, as long as we are bound by these same essentially hypothetico-deductive procedures.

It is here that I demur, along with Yehudi Cohen (1966) who questions our devotion to a paradigm of science that derives from the nonsocial sciences, and with Margaret Mead (1962) who has consistently advised us to avoid a premature reduction of the complexity of our social and cultural subject matter by the use of the oversimplified methods common to psychological anthropology. In this regard I could do no better than to quote from Irwin Deutscher, in his recent presidential address to the Society for the Study of Social Problems. Speaking of the development of method in the social sciences, Deutscher says (1966:244):

There was a time earlier in this century when we had a choice to make, a choice on the one hand of undertaking neat, orderly studies of measurable phenomena. This alternative carried with it all of the gratifications of conforming to the prestigious methods of pursuing knowledge then in vogue, of having access to considerable sums of monies through the granting procedures of large foundations and governmental agencies, of a comfortable sense of satisfaction derived from dealing rigorously and precisely with small isolated problems which were cleanly defined, of moving for 30 years down one track in an increasingly rigorous, refined, and reliable manner, while simultaneously disposing of the problems of validity by the semantic trickery of operational definitions. On the other hand, we could have tackled the messy world as we knew it to exist, a world where the same people will make different utterances under different conditions and will behave differently in different situations and will say one thing while doing another. We could have tackled a world where control of relevant variables was impossible not only because we didn't know what they were but because we didn't know how they interacted with each other. We could have accepted the conclusion of almost every variant of contemporary philosophy of science, that the notion of cause and effect (and therefore of stimulus and response or of independent and dependent variables) is untenable. We eschewed this formidable challenge. This was the hard way. We chose the easy way.

Because the easy way is not necessarily the right way, I object to a fusion of "psychological" anthropology (indeed, I object to the term) with psychology or any other discipline. The strength of anthropology, and its purpose, has always been the contextual study of the complexity of man's-relations-in-soci-

ety, now and over time. I believe, with Spiro (1961), that this is the same purpose that should dominate psychological anthropology. By a continued employment of our currently accepted methods of data collection in psychological anthropology, we atomize our context and simplify man's relationships. This is too great a price to pay.

At the risk of seeming to be parochial, I suggest that we must find our own paradigm of methodology, one that permits us to retain our sense of the context, complexity, and interaction of social, cultural and psychological phenomena. We must not become the victims of method, especially not of methods of disciplines that are not devoted to the solution of our problems. Our concern ought to be with the solution of *our* problems, by whatever methods satisfy *our* purposes.

I suggest further that we will play ourselves false as anthropologists as long as our methods and our concern for "objectivity" lead us to the exclusive study of words, rather than actions. We must continue to study words, especially as they reflect the perceptual-conceptual world of non-Western peoples, but we must also devise means of observing what people do, and how their actual behavior relates to what they say. To do so is admittedly taking the hard way.

If psychological anthropology is to remain a part of anthropology, of the study of man-in-society-and-culture, rather than becoming merely a cross-cultural version of psychology, it must establish its own paradigm of methodology, and that paradigm, even though it may differ from currently accepted canons of procedure in behavioral science, must permit us to get on with the study of words *and* deeds, with all of their contradictory complexity.

BIBLIOGRAPHY

ALLPORT, G. W., and P. F. PETTIGREW
1957 Cultural influences on the perception of movement: the trapezoidal illusion among Zulus. *Journal of Abnormal Social Psychology* 55:105–111.

BADRI, M.
1965 Influence of modernization on Goodenough Quotients of Sudanese children. *Perceptual and Motor Skills* 20:931–932.

BADRI, M., and W. DENNIS
1964 Human-figure drawings in relation to modernization in Sudan. *Journal of Psychology* 58:421–425.

BARKER, R., and H. WRIGHT
1951 *One boy's day. A specific record of behavior.* New York, Harper & Bros.

BARNOUW, V.
1963 *Culture and personality.* Homewood, Ill., Dorsey Press.

BATESON, G., and M. MEAD
1951 *Films on character formation in different cultures.* New York, New York University Film Library.

BERNDT, R.
1966 *Dominant social relationships among the Gunwinggu and "Murngin" of aboriginal Australia.* Paper prepared for Wenner-Gren Symposium No. 35, Kinship and culture.

BIRDWHISTELL, R.
1952 *An introduction to kinesics.* Louisville, University of Kentucky Press.

BONTE, M.
1962 The reaction of two African societies to the Müller-Lyer illusion. *Journal of Social Psychology* 58:265–268.

BOYER, L., B. KLOPFER, E. BRAWER, and H. KAWAI
1964 Comparisons of the shamans and pseudo shamans of the Apaches of the Mescalero Indian reservation: a Rorschach study. *Journal of Projective Techniques and Personality Assessment* 28:173–180.

BRADLEY, D.
1964 Problems of recognition in Bantu testing. *Perceptual and Motor Skills* 19:718.

BRICKLIN, B., and C. ZELEZNIK
1963 A psychological investigation of selected Ethiopian adolescents by means of the Rorschach and other projective tests. *Human Organization* 22:291–303.

BROOKOVER, L., and K. BACK
1966 Time sampling as a field technique. *Human Organization* 25:64–70.

CAUDILL, W.
1962 Patterns of emotion in modern Japan. In R. J. Smith and R. K. Beardsley, eds., *Japanese culture: its development and characteristics.* New York: WGFAR Viking Fund Publications in Anthropology, 34.

CHANCE, N.
1965 Acculturation, self-identification, and personality adjustment. *American Anthropologist* 67:372–393.

CHANCE, N., HSIEN RIN, and HUNG-MING CHU
1967 Modernization, value identification, and mental health: a cross-cultural study. *Human Organization* (in press).

CHAPPLE, ELIOT D.
1962 Quantitative analysis of complex organizational systems. *Human Organization* 21:67–87.

CHENG, FA-YA, CHU-CHANG CHEN, and HSIEN RIN
1958 A personality analysis of the Ami and its three subgroups by Rorschach test. *Acta Psychologica Taiwanica* 1:131–143.

COHEN, Y.
1966 Macroethnology—large-scale comparative studies. In J. Clifton, ed., *Introduction to cultural anthropology: essays in the scope and methods of the science of man.* Boston, Houghton Mifflin.

COLBY, B.
1966a Cultural patterns in narrative. *Science* 151:793–798.
1966b The analysis of culture content and the patterning of narrative concern in texts. *American Anthropologist* 68:374–388.

DENNIS, W.
1960 The human figure drawings of Bedouins. *Journal of Social Psychology* 52:209–919.

DEUTSCHER, I.
1966 Words and deeds: social science and social policy. *Social Problems* 13:235–254.

DEVOS, G.
1955 A quantitative Rorschach assessment of maladjustment and rigidity in acculturating Japanese Americans. *Genetic Psychology Monographs* 52:51–87.

DEVOS, G., and H. WAGATSUMA
1959 Psycho-cultural significance of concern over death and illness among rural Japanese. *International Journal of Social Psychiatry* 5:5–19.
1961 Value attitudes toward role behavior of women in two Japanese villages. *American Anthropologist* 63:1204–1230.

DOOB, L.
1964 Eidetic images among the Ibo. *Ethnology* 3:357–363.
1965 Exploring eidetic imagery among the Kamba of Central Kenya. *Journal of Social Psychology* 67:3–22.

EDGERTON, R.
1965 "Cultural" vs. "ecological" factors in the expression of values, attitudes and personality characteristics. *American Anthropologist* 67:442–447.

ERVIN, S., and H. LANDAR
1963 Navaho word-associations. *American Journal of Psychology* 76:49–57.

FERNANDEZ, J.
1966 *Bantu brotherhood.* Paper prepared for Wenner-Gren Symposium No. 35, Kinship and culture.

FISCHER, J. L.
1963 The sociopsychological analysis of folk tales. *Current Anthropology* 4:235–296.
1965 Psychology and anthropology. In Bernard Siegel, ed., *Biennial review of anthropology.* Stanford, Stanford University Press.

FREED, S.
1965 A comparison of the reactions of Washo and Mohave respondents to an objective technique (Role Profile Test) for measuring role behavior. *Transactions of the*

New York Academy of Sciences, Ser. II, 27:959–969.

FRIED, JACOB
1954 Picture testing: an aid to ethnological field work. *American Anthropologist* 56:95–97.

GARCIA-VICENTE, J.
1960 Le mosaic Lowenfeld test parmi les noirs de l'Angola. *Revue de Psychologie Appliquée* 10:77–91.

GEBER, MARCELLE
1962 Test de Gesell et Terman-Merrill appliques en Uganda. In A. Mermiot, ed., *The growth of the normal child during the first three years of life: modern problems in pediatrics,* Vol. 7. Basel, S. Kareer.

GLADWIN, T., and S. SARASON
1953 *Truk: man in paradise.* Viking Fund Publications in Anthropology, No. 20.

GOLDSCHMIDT, W., and R. EDGERTON
1961 A picture technique for the study of values. *American Anthropologist* 63:26–45.

GREGOR, A., and D. MCPHERSON
1963 The correlation of the Porteus Maze and the Gestalt Continuation as personnel selection tests of peripheral peoples. *Journal of Psychology* 56:137–142.

HALL, E. T.
1963 A system of the notation of proxemic behavior. *American Anthropologist* 65:1003–1026.

HARRIS, M.
1964 *The nature of cultural things.* New York, Random House.

HELM, J., G. A. DEVOS, and T. CARTERETTE
1963 *Variations in personality and ego identification within a Slave Indian kin-community.* National Museum of Canada, Bulletin 190, Contributions to Anthropology, Part II, pp. 94–138.

HELPER, M., and S. GARFIELD
1965 Use of the semantic differential to study acculturation in American Indian adolescents. *Journal of Personality and Social Psychology* 2:817–822.

HENRY, J., and M. E. SPIRO
1953 Psychological techniques: projective tests in field work. In A. L. Kroeber, ed., *Anthropology today.* Chicago, University of Chicago Press.

HENRY, W.
1956 The Thematic Apperception Technique in the study of group and cultural problems. In H. Anderson and G. Anderson, eds., *An introduction to projective techniques.* Englewood Cliffs, N.J., Prentice-Hall.
1961 Projective tests in cross-cultural research. In Bert Kaplan, ed., *Studying*

personality cross-culturally. New York, Row, Peterson.

HOLTZMAN, W., J. THORPE, and E. HERRON
1961 *Inkblot perception and personality.* Austin, University of Texas Press.

HONIGMANN, J.
1961 North America. In F. L. K. Hsu, ed., *Psychological anthropology.* Homewood, Ill., Dorsey Press.

HUDSON, W.
1960 Pictorial depth perception in subcultural groups in Africa. *Journal of Social Psychology* 52:183–208.

JACOBS, M.
1959 *The content and style of an oral literature. Clackamas Chinook myths and tales.* Viking Fund Publications in Anthropology, No. 26.

JACOBS, M., and J. GREENWAY (eds.)
1966 *The anthropologist looks at myth.* Austin, University of Texas Press.

KAPLAN, B.
1961 Cross-cultural use of projective techniques. In F. L. K. Hsu, ed., *Psychological anthropology.* Homewood, Ill., Dorsey Press.

KAVOLIS, V.
1964 Art styles as projection of community structure. *Sociology and Sociological Research* 48:166–175.

KEYES, C.
1966 Review of *Thailand peasant personality,* by H. Phillips. *American Anthropologist* 68:793–794.

KUHN, T.
1962 *The structure of scientific revolutions.* Chicago, University of Chicago Press.

LANDY, D.
1956 Methodological problems of free doll play as an ethnographic field technique. In A. F. C. Wallace, ed., *Selected papers of the Fifth International Congress of Anthropological and Ethnological Sciences.* Philadelphia, University of Pennsylvania Press.

LANGNESS, L.
1966 The life history in anthropological science. In G. and L. Spindler, eds., *Studies in anthropological method.* New York, Holt, Rinehart and Winston.

LEICHTY, M.
1963 Family attitudes and self-concept in Vietnamese and U.S. children. *American Journal of Orthopsychiatry* 33:38–50.

LEIGHTON A., et al.
1963 *Psychiatric disorder among the Yoruba.* Ithaca, Cornell University Press.

LEININGER, M.
1966 *Convergence and divergence of human behavior; an ethnopsychological study of two Gadsup villages in New Guinea.*

University of Washington, unpublished doctoral dissertation.

LENNEBERG, E., and J. ROBERTS
1956 *The language of experience: a study in methodology.* Supplement to International Journal of American Linguistics, Memoir No. 13.

LEVINE, R.
1963 Culture and personality. In B. Siegel, ed., *Biennial review of anthropology.* Stanford, Stanford University Press.
1966 Outsiders' judgments: an ethnographic approach to group differences in personality. *Southwestern Journal of Anthropology* 22:101–116. Reprinted in this volume.

LEWIS, O.
1959 *Five families: Mexican case studies in the culture of poverty.* New York, Basic Books.
1966 *La vida. A Puerto Rican family in the culture of poverty.* New York, Random House.

LINDZEY, G.
1961 *Projective techniques and cross-cultural research.* New York, Appleton-Century-Crofts.

MACLEAN, C. M. U.
1966 Hospital or healers? an attitude survey in Ibadan. *Human Organization* 25:131–139.

MCCLELLAND, D., and G. FRIEDMAN
1952 A cross-cultural study of the relationship between child-training practices and achievement motivation appearing in folk tales. In G. Swanson, T. Newcomb, and E. Hartley, eds., *Readings in social psychology.* New York, Holt.

MCEWEN, W.
1963 Forms and problems of validation in social anthropology. *Current Anthropology* 4:155–183.

MEAD, M.
1956 Some uses of still photography in culture and personality studies. In D. Haring, ed., *Personal character and cultural milieu.* Syracuse, Syracuse University Press.
1962 Retrospects and prospects. In T. Gladwin and W. Sturtevant, eds., *Anthropology and human behavior.* Washington, D.C., Anthropological Society of Washington.
1964 Review of six cultures: studies of child-rearing. In B. B. Whiting, ed., *American Anthropologist* 66:658–660.
1965 *Family.* New York, Macmillan.

MEAD, M., and F. MACGREGOR
1951 *Growth and culture: a photographic study of Balinese childhood.* New York, Putnam.

MEAD, M., J. W. M. WHITING and B. B. WHITING
1960 Contributions of anthropology to the methods of studying child-rearing. In P. Mussen, ed., *Handbook on research methods in child development.* New York, Wiley.

MEEHL, P.
1959 Structured and projective tests: some common problems in validation. *Journal of Projective Techniques* 23:263–267.

MINER, H., and G. DEVOS
1960 *Oasis and casbah: Algerian culture and personality in change.* Anthropological Papers, Museum of Anthropology, University of Michigan, No. 15.

MURPHY, J. M., and A. H. LEIGHTON (eds.)
1965 *Approaches to cross-cultural psychiatry.* Ithaca, Cornell University Press.

OSGOOD, C.
1964 Semantic differential technique in the comparative study of culture. In A. K. Romney and R. G. D'Andrade, eds., Transcultural studies in cognition. *American Anthropologist* 66:171–200.

PARKER, S.
1962 Motives in Eskimo and Ojibwa mythology. *Ethnology* 1:516–523.
1964 Ethnic identity and acculturation in two Eskimo villages. *American Anthropologist* 66:325–340.

PARKER, S., and R. KLEINER
1966 *Mental health in an urban Negro community.* Glencoe, Ill., Free Press.

PHILLIPS, H.
1965 *Thai peasant personality.* Berkeley, University of California Press.

PRESTON, C. E.
1964 Psychological testing with Northwest Coast Alaskan Eskimos. *Genetic Psychology Monographs* 69:323–419.

PRICE-WILLIAMS, D. R.
1962 Abstract and concrete modes of classification in a primitive society. *British Journal of Educational Psychology* 32:50–61.
1965 Displacement and orality in Tiv witchcraft. *Journal of Social Psychology* 65:1–15.

RICHARDSON, F. L. W., JR.
1966 Recollecting vs. "live" recording: organizational relationships of a surgeon. *Human Organization* 25:163–179.

RICHARDSON, S. A., B. S. SNELL, and D. KLEIN
1965 *Interviewing. Its forms and functions.* New York, Basic Books.

ROBERTS, J.
1962 Child training and game involvement. *Ethnology* 1:166–185.

ROBERTS, J., and M. ARTH
1966 Dyadic elicitation in Zuni. *El Palacio* 73:27–41.

ROBERTS, J., M. ARTH, and R. BUSH
1959   Games in culture. *American Anthropologist* 61:597–605.

ROBERTS, J., H. HOFFMANN, and B. SUTTON-SMITH
1965   Pattern and competence: a consideration of tick tack toe. *El Palacio* 72:17–30.

ROBERTS, J., B. SUTTON-SMITH, and A. KENDON
1963   Strategy in games and folk tales. *Journal of Social Psychology* 61:185–199.

ROGERS, C., and C. FRANTZ
1962   *Racial themes in Southern Rhodesia: the attitudes and behavior of the white population.* New Haven, Yale University Press.

ROSENBERG, J.
1962   Ethnodrama as a research method in anthropology. *Group Psychotherapy* 15: 236–243.

SCHWAB, W. B.
1965   Looking backward: an appraisal of two field trips. *Human Organization* 24: 372–380.

SCHWITZGEBEL, R.
1962   The performance of Dutch and Zulu adults on selected perceptual tasks. *Journal of Social Psychology* 57:73–77.

SEGALL, M., D. CAMPBELL, and M. J. HERSKOVITS
1963   Cultural differences in the perception of geometric illusions. *Science,* Ser. II, 139: 769–771.

1966   *The influence of culture on visual perception.* Indianapolis, Bobbs-Merrill.

SHERWOOD, E.
1957   On the designing of TAT pictures, with special reference to a set for an African people assimilating Western culture. *Journal of Social Psychology* 45:161–190.

SHONTZ, F.
1965   *Research methods in personality.* New York, Appleton-Century-Crofts.

SPINDLER, G.
1955   *Sociocultural and psychological processes in Menomini acculturation.* Culture and Society Series, Vol. 5, Berkeley, University of California Press.

SPINDLER, G., and L. SPINDLER
1963   Psychology and anthropology: applications to culture change. In S. Koch, ed., *Psychology: a study of a science.* Vol. 6, *Investigations of man as socius: their place in psychology and the social sciences.* New York, McGraw-Hill.

1965   The instrumental activities inventory: a technique for the study of the psychology of acculturation. *Southwestern Journal of Anthropology* 21:1–23.

SPIRO, M.
1961   An overview and a suggested reorientation. In F. L. K. Hsu, ed., *Psychological*

Anthropology. Homewood, Ill., Dorsey Press.

STONE, P., et al.
1966   *The general inquirer.* Cambridge, M.I.T. Press.

STRODTBECK, FRED L.
1964   Considerations of meta-method in cross-cultural studies. In A. K. Romney and R. G. D'Andrade, eds., Transcultural studies in cognition. *American Anthropologist* 66:223–229.

STRODTBECK, F., and D. GOLDHAMER
1966   *Approaches to the objective study of cultural values.* Prepared for Midwest Universities Institute for Cross-Cultural Research and Training in Sociology held at Bloomington, Indiana, July 8, 1966.

SUTTON-SMITH, B., and J. ROBERTS
1964   Rubrics of competitive behavior. *Journal of Genetic Psychology* 105:13–37.

TURNBULL, C.
1961   Some observations regarding the experiences and behavior of the BaMbuti Pygmies. *American Journal of Psychology* 74:304–308.

WALLACE, A. F. C.
1952   *The modal personality structure of the Tuscarora Indians as recorded by the Rorschach test.* Bulletin No. 150, Bureau of American Ethnology.

1962   The new culture-and-personality. In T. Gladwin and W. Sturtevant, eds., *Anthropology and human behavior.* Washington, D.C., Anthropological Society of Washington.

WALLACE, A. F. C., and R. FOGELSON
1965   The identity struggle. In I. Boszormenyi-Nagy and J. Framo, eds., *Intensive family therapy.* New York, Hoeber Medical Division, Harper and Row.

WATSON, O. M., and T. GRAVES
1966   Quantitative research in proxemic behavior. *American Anthropologist* 68: 971–985.

WHITING, B. B., ed.
1963   *Six cultures: studies of child rearing.* New York, Wiley.

WILLIAMS, H. H., and J. R. WILLIAMS
1965   The definition of the Rorschach test situation: a cross-cultural illustration. In M. E. Spiro, ed., *Context and meaning in cultural anthropology.* New York, Free Press.

YOUNG, F. W., and R. C. YOUNG
1961   Key informant reliability in rural Mexican villages. *Human Organization* 20: 141–148.

ZUBIN, J.
1954   Failures of the Rorschach technique. *Journal of Projective Techniques* 18: 303–315.

CHAPTER 19

The Comparative Method:
The Single Investigator
and the Team Approach

MELVIN L. PERLMAN

INTRODUCTION

Comparative cross-cultural field studies can be carried out by a single investigator, by a team of researchers, or by a combination of both. Each approach has its advantages and limitations and these complement one another. In this chapter I suggest that the amount of systematic knowledge we already have of the important variables for a given problem will indicate which approach is likely to produce the most fruitful results in comparative studies. I maintain that when we have sufficient knowledge of which variables are likely to be the most important a combination of the two approaches is best, and I suggest how such a combination could work in practice. If, however, we are investigating complex problems of world-wide scope likely to involve many variables and we have little or no knowledge of the importance of some of them, then our research will be largely of an exploratory kind. In such exploratory research the experiences of a whole team are most valuable, assuming they have

An earlier version of this paper was read at the American Anthropological Association Meeting in Denver, November 1965. This paper is based on fieldwork carried out in Uganda in 1959–1962 when I was a Research Fellow of the East African Institute of Social Research, Makerere University College. The latter stages of the research were supported by a Research Training Fellowship from the Social Science Research Council and a Graduate Fellowship from the National Science Foundation, and the support of these organizations is gratefully acknowledged. I want to thank Paula Foster for her valuable assistance in supplementing and interpreting my Acholi data, and am very grateful to Laura Nader, Nelson Graburn, John Beattie, Aidan Southall, Richard Stern, and David M. Schneider for many helpful suggestions in the preparation of this manuscript.

first done intensive field research—each member having knowledge of a different part of the world. Such exploratory research on problems of broad scope could and should be followed up, of course—once most of the important variables are discovered—by research of a more specific and focused character.

Team Research

There are several types of team research and I refer to only one in this paper.[1] Team research can mean that all or most of the members of the team do research in all societies investigated, as for example in Leighton's Stirling County study (Leighton and Macmillan 1952, Leighton 1955, Hughes 1960), or in the comparative *Study of Values in Five Cultures* (Vogt and Albert 1966). Or, it can mean that a large number of people each do research in one of a large number of societies over an extended period of time, as for example in the cross-cultural study of ethnocentrism (LeVine and Campbell 1965). When I use the term team research in this chapter I do not mean either of these two types, but rather a third type in which each member of a small team goes out to study a different society at about the same time as other members, as for example in the study of child rearing in six cultures (B. Whiting 1963, Minturn and Lambert 1964, and J. W. M. Whiting *et al.*, 1966), or in the culture and ecology in East Africa project (Goldschmidt 1965).

[1] Even though I do not deal specifically with other types of team research in this paper, I believe that many (though not all) of the points made here are nevertheless relevant for any type of team research.

The definition of this third type of team research need not imply that all the field-work is done at exactly the same time; it may be done over a period of a few years. It does imply, however, that the members of the team (at least most of them) have been chosen in advance and that their number is not so large as to preclude their getting together for effective face-to-face communication; the number of researchers might fall between five and fifteen. Such a team is therefore somewhat different from that in the second type of team approach as exemplified in the cross-cultural study of ethnocentrism; in this latter study it is hoped that eventually fifty researchers will participate, and they have not been chosen in advance.

Furthermore, team research is a matter of degree. In one sense every individual researcher is part of a "team" in that he is an organic part of a community oriented toward the scientific study of societies. Insofar as this orientation obliges the single researcher to make as explicit as possible the evidence on which he bases his conclusions and hypotheses, his contribution to the store of comparative propositions is enhanced. At the opposite end of the continuum the ideal might be a small highly organized group of researchers who have similar interests and training, and whose personalities are such as to facilitate a high degree of cooperation. We know, however, that such an ideal cannot easily be achieved in practice. Comments about team research in this chapter should be understood to refer to the latter part of this continuum, though not its extreme end; that is, I do not mean to include something here which should be impossible to achieve in practice. I do believe, however, that it is worth-while stating what would be desirable even if it appears difficult to achieve in practice. Such a statement may help us to move in that direction.

Nevertheless, the difference between what may be desirable in principle and what can actually be achieved in practice points to one of the fundamental differences between the single investigator and the team approach. So much the better, for example, if we can achieve a high degree of cooperation within a team project; we should strive to achieve such a goal. But this may be very difficult in practice, and this is where we can see the advantage of the single investigator. That is,

he has an important *practical* advantage, even though *in principle* a team might achieve this; the importance of practical considerations in doing fieldwork, and of differences of personality, interests and training are likely to mean that the single investigator will maintain this advantage. At the same time the team should move in the direction of trying to achieve as much coordination and cooperation as is practically possible.

I have not made an exhaustive study of the procedures of even the third type of team research, but I shall raise some questions arising out of the relevant literature, of which there is not a great deal.[2] As there is not much published about specific procedures used in cross-cultural team research, I have tried to speak informally with a few anthropologists who have been members of different team projects in order to gain additional information.

Criteria for a Useful Comparative Method

I shall assess the differing merits of the team approach as opposed to that of a single investigator essentially in terms of two criteria: (1) how well does the method facilitate the formulation of concepts sufficiently general to permit comparison and generalization, but which nevertheless do not distort the picture of social interaction in particular societies, and (2) the degree to which the method provides for as much control as possible over the analytical framework while insuring that increased control does not result in the elimination of any significant variable.

I do not claim that these criteria are the only ones by which we could assess the usefulness of comparative methods, though I believe they are among the most important. Nor would I claim that either criterion is really new, for surely any comparative method is more useful to the extent that it facilitates the formulation of valid generaliza-

[2] There are publications on interdisciplinary team research which deal with the team aspects of the problem, but they do not usually do so within the context of the complicating problems of cross-cultural comparisons. One recent volume that does, however, is the *Field Guide for a Study of Socialization* (1966) by John W. M. Whiting *et al.* On interdisciplinary team research see especially Luszki 1958 (includes annotated bibliography) and Luszki 1960.

tions about the phenomena being compared. Also, the importance of greater control over the analytical framework has been suggested before, notably by Eggan in his article on the method of controlled comparison (1954).[3]

I believe that not enough attention has been given to the other aspect of my first criterion, namely the risks of distortion. There is some awareness of this problem, however; for example, it is explicitly mentioned in the book *Mothers of Six Cultures* (Minturn and Lambert 1964:1–4). The danger of distortion still deserves to be strongly emphasized; it is important both because in choosing general concepts we do not want to present a distorted picture of social interaction in any particular society and because, if the concepts chosen do not correspond sufficiently closely to the data, any generalizations formulated are less likely to hold true when put to the test of prediction.

With these considerations in mind, then, I emphasize two familiar points which correspond to the two criteria: (1) the importance of the researcher's maintaining a high degree of flexibility in the formulation and reformulation of concepts and indices while he is still in the field collecting data, and (2) the importance of setting up controls in the analytical framework only after an initial period of exploratory research in the field.

Let me briefly contrast in broad terms what I consider to be the major advantages and limitations of each approach. First, one of the advantages of the team approach is that generalizations can be tested in more societies, and each time a hypothesis holds true it will be established with greater certainty. Secondly, because each member of the team can spend a relatively longer period in the field, a team of researchers as a whole can gain a more intimate knowledge of the languages and cultures of many societies. To the extent that the lack of such intimate knowledge prevents the single researcher from gaining reliable data, the team has an incontestable advantage; if the reliability of the data as originally collected can be questioned,

no valid generalizations can be made either for a single society or for many.

The team approach also has certain limitations, at least as presently practiced. First, it is difficult to achieve effective face-to-face communication between the members while the data are still being collected. This decreases the flexibility with which changes can be made in the research design. A second limitation is that differences in the personalities, interests, and training of the members may militate against achieving three important objectives: (1) a unity of conception of the problem or problems, (2) agreement on societies to be included in the study for reasons of a strategic comparison, and (3) the obtaining of data that will be to a high degree validly and usefully comparable.[4]

Conversely as to advantages, a single investigator can remain very flexible about making changes in the research design as he goes along, and furthermore, no differences of personality, interests, or training are involved. But a single investigator is limited— at least from a practical point of view—to investigating a small number of societies. This means both that generalizations can be less broadly established and that, because of limitations in time and knowledge of languages, the risk of obtaining unreliable data is increased.

In this paper, then, I emphasize, elaborate, and illustrate points already made by others concerning important criteria for a useful comparative study. Then I suggest a practical way to achieve more fruitful comparative research by taking cognizance of these important criteria for different types of problems. For focused problems of known dimensions, the efforts of a single investigator should be combined with those of a team to maximize their differing advantages and minimize their differing limitatons; for explora-

---

[8] Indeed much of what I have to say is not new to anthropologists even though they may not have seen it explicitly stated in print, for until relatively recently anthropologists have not often been primarily or explicitly concerned with methodology in their published writings (see Adams and Preiss 1960:vii, x, and Gulliver 1965:78).

[4] See B. Whiting 1963:3, 12, as well as Goldschmidt's comment (1965:408) that it is with considerable pride that he finds that the members of his team remain on good speaking terms. There is the risk that different members of a team will measure different aspects or qualities of any variable under investigation. Compare with Evans-Pritchard (1963: 10), who states that "a further difficulty which all who try to compare things [customs] rather than qualities or aspects of things is that they can . . . be alike with regard to some features and unlike with regard to others, so that the classification which necessarily precedes comparison depends on which criteria are selected."

tory research on problems of unknown dimensions, the team approach should be emphasized because here the advantages of the single investigator are not relevant. Finally, I discuss some further implications of the distinction—not an absolute but a relative distinction—between focused and exploratory research, especially the way each contributes differentially to the systematic advance of our knowledge.

FLEXIBILITY IN THE RESEARCH DESIGN

I turn now to the matter of *flexibility to make changes in the research design while data are being collected*. If a team of researchers has agreed ahead of time—in a published field manual for example—upon concepts and indices for measuring certain variables, it may be difficult for them to make changes while in the field because of the difficulties of effective face-to-face communication. Without this contact their loyalty to the team and to the idea of bringing back what they consider comparable data may prevent them from making changes, both in concepts and in indices of measurement. Or, if they do make changes on an individual basis, their data may be of low comparability.

For example, we know that in the study of child rearing in six cultures field notes were mailed in periodically to a central clearing house at Harvard, specifically to help insure comparability of data; also, field problems were discussed by correspondence. Yet, in spite of the central clearing house and of all the prior planning and work on the research design, "the data are not always comparable" (B. Whiting 1963:3, 12). This is not to minimize the degree of comparability that has been achieved in this very important and pioneering study in team research, but one wonders if even greater comparability might have been achieved had the fieldworkers and the senior investigators all come together at regular intervals for face-to-face communication during the progress of the fieldwork (cf. John W. M. Whiting *et al.*, 1966:118).

It is clear from the conclusion to *Mothers of Six Cultures* (Minturn and Lambert 1964: 290–293) that new and unanticipated variables were uncovered, and these were deemed to be extremely important in the end. My point is that some of these variables might have been discovered earlier while the data collection process was still going on, if revision of the research design had been fostered by regular face-to-face communication. No doubt the importance of some of these variables came to light only through the analysis and writing up of the material, and this is to be expected. Some unanswered questions will always remain. But by revising the research design through face-to-face communication as we go along we will significantly increase our chances of providing validly comparable data to answer a larger number of questions.

A single researcher can be more flexible as the research progresses, more free to work out his concepts and indices as he goes along. With some personal knowledge of all the societies in the study, he can adequately work out concepts that will permit valid comparison among them, while insuring that the concepts chosen do not distort the reported attitudes and behavior of any particular people in the study. For example, in my comparative research in Uganda,[5] as I moved around the country—which I did several times, going back and forth from one society to another—I constantly revised the questionnaire that I used, found out what kinds of data were coming out of the court records in one society, and then returned to other societies to get comparable answers and court data.

It may be that a variable can be measured most reliably by a particular index in one

[5] My comparative study of marriage and family life in Uganda followed a more intensive one in a single district, Toro, where I spent about two years in 1959–1961. Major comparative data were collected in four other districts (Buganda, Kigezi, Lango, and Teso) in each of which I spent from one to two months. Finally, I visited all remaining districts of the country, doing a quick survey for a few days in each. My major purpose in this survey was to assure that I had not completely missed any major variable. I should emphasize that in spite of the very short period spent in each of the remaining societies, I consider that I was able to obtain useful information. In each society, I interviewed about fifteen people representing a cross-section of the society for two hours each and also collected whatever documents were available. Perhaps the most important point is that the survey was undertaken at the very end of my third year in Uganda, and by that time I knew enough about the problems involved to be able to probe much more deeply in a short time than would otherwise have been possible.

society, but by some other index in another society. For example, in my study of marriage in Uganda, I discovered among the Toro that many girls of marriageable age were going to live in the homes of young men, even though no bridewealth had been paid and even without the tacit consent of their fathers. I was interested in the changing status of women and one very important aspect of this was their degree of independence from parental (especially paternal) authority. As marriages had been arranged for children by their parents in the past, and as even now girls are expected to pay deference to the wishes of their parents, I decided that the percentage of conjugal unions in which a girl chose her own partner would constitute at least one useful index of the degree of her independence from parental authority. Other indices were also used, but for the purposes of this discussion I shall confine myself to this one.

When I came to study the Acholi of Northern Uganda, I assumed at first that I would be able to use the same index. Further inquiry revealed, however, that, although it was not the most usual or preferred type of marriage, an elopement (without the consent of the girl's parents) existed traditionally among the Acholi. The existence of an indigenous Acholi term, *keny poro*, for this type of marriage, was further evidence that it was not very new, as it was in Toro. This cast some doubt on the feasibility of using an increase in the frequency of this type of union as a reliable index of the degree to which a girl was becoming increasingly independent of her parents' authority. Further inquiry showed that although there was some correlation between the two, this correlation did not hold in any ultimate sense. That is, it became quite clear that Acholi girls deliberately elope in order to choose their own spouses, often against the wishes of their parents. Furthermore, elopement gives the young man the upper hand and this means that the bridewealth may eventually be slightly lower than it would have been otherwise. This may be taken as evidence, then, that these girls are expressing some independence of their own and a corresponding defiance of parents' authority. However, this is not the whole story because if the young man continues to refuse to pay the bridewealth, the girl will not wait longer than

about a year before returning to her father's home. My informants did not know of a single case in which a girl ultimately refused to return to her father's home if the bridewealth had not been paid. The main reasons for her return were strong public opinion and, especially, family pressure. The family might threaten to cut off all the rituals and eventually invoke a curse that she would have no children, that the young man would have no luck in hunting, and that she would bring misfortune upon the whole family. The belief in this curse is still very strong in Acholi, even among those of some education, and it serves as a strong buttress for the authority of parents.

The comparative data from Toro indicate that usually the bridewealth is never paid, and even when it is, it is quite clear that a girl would influence her young man to pay the bridewealth mainly out of concern for her respectability and his, and not because she had been moved by her parents' authority. And if it came to a choice, she would certainly not give up living with the man of her choice either for motives of respectability or because of concern for her parents' authority. In the past, Toro parents also had a curse at their disposal, but the belief in this curse is no longer sufficiently strong among the Toro to prevent a girl from asserting complete independence from parental authority in marital affairs. In Toro, then, the percentage of conjugal unions in which the girl (rather than her parents) chooses her own partner remains a crucial index, whereas whether or not the bridewealth is ever paid is not a reliable index of her independence from parental authority. Among the Acholi, the opposite is true: although an increasing number of Acholi girls are choosing their own conjugal partners, and this is an indication of a willingness *to attempt* to defy parental authority, in the end the most reliable index is whether or not the bridewealth is eventually paid.

In this situation different indices are likely to provide the most reliable measure of a single variable in different societies. Or, in the Acholi case, probably a combination of the two indices would most accurately reveal the subtle changes that are taking place. Subtleties in the data such as I have described cannot usually be predicted in advance.

To take another example, it might be supposed that the concept of illegitimacy would be useful in discussing any society and would also permit comparisons between societies. In Toro, however, it clearly presents a distorted picture of the views of these people. The Toro use the term *abana baheru*, "children of the outside," referring to any child born outside a conjugal union. Contrary to the generally accepted view,[6] these Toro children lose no birthrights; the attitude toward them is not at all adverse, and in adult life they suffer from no disabilities arising from their birth out of wedlock. For some purposes, then, the Toro cannot be compared with many other societies by reference to the concept of illegitimate children because that concept fuses two separate notions: (1) born out of wedlock and (2) loss of birthrights, which remain entirely distinct in Toro. In my own writings about the Toro I have referred to them simply as children born out of wedlock.

I am not arguing that researchers, whether as individuals or as members of a team, should not attempt to formulate concepts and indices in advance of fieldwork. Such a procedure can be very useful in guiding them to ask appropriate questions, to make some generalizations, and to test hypotheses. Inevitably we all take some ideas to the field with us; what counts is the degree to which these ideas are formally incorporated in advance of fieldwork into a relatively rigid research design. I am arguing that although researchers must take working definitions of concepts and suggested indices with them to the field, they must also be in a position to remain sufficiently flexible to change those concepts and indices where necessary while still in the field. In the team approach such changes should be made in close consultation with all other members of the team. I maintain that in cross-cultural research it will usually be necessary to make such changes because it is only after the subtleties in the

data have been laid bare that researchers are really in a position to make judgments about which concepts and indices are the most suitable.

Admittedly, it could be argued that a single researcher cannot be sufficiently familiar with the complexities of several societies to make adequate and reliable judgments of the kind I have indicated would be necessary. My own experience leads me to believe that this would not always be so, although certainly there are practical limits to the number of societies and languages that a single investigator can study adequately.

CONTROL OVER THE ANALYTICAL FRAMEWORK

I turn next to the second criterion for a useful comparative method, namely, that it provide *as much control as possible over the analytical framework without the elimination of any significant variable*. This question of control can be seen from different points of view. In a recent publication, also on the comparative method, Eggan has stated that "research design can play a more conscious role in our scholarly programs than it has so far. . . . we need to evaluate the variant hypotheses now in circulation in terms of the data already available, and to look for field situations which will enable us to select the more promising for further testing and refinement" (1965:369). Looking at the question of control from this point of view, a highly controlled comparative study could be achieved through the prior selection of societies having similarities and differences known to be relevant to the hypotheses to be tested.[7]

Such prior selection can be valuable, however, only for those problems about which we have sufficient knowledge of crucial variables. If we make selections without such knowledge, then we risk eliminating societies that have unanticipated variables which might prove very significant. Where crucial variables are unknown, a representative sample cov-

---

[6] See Robert Bierstedt (1964:386), who states that legitimacy denotes "the condition of being a child presumably lawfully begotten or born in wedlock, having or involving full filial rights and obligations. . . . Virtually all societies distinguish between legitimacy and illegitimacy of birth and apply sanctions to the parents and in many instances to the children. There is a large literature on the legal aspects of illegitimacy in various countries and in various periods of history, but *no problem of definition*" (my italics).

[7] Compare Zelditch's recent statement that "the intensive comparative study samples 'purposively,' as distinct from randomly. Cases are chosen to satisfy certain specific criteria of the investigator, and accordingly can be chosen so that they are the most strategic, and also so that cases compared are matched on characteristics known at the time to be relevant" (1964:465).

ering as many differences as possible would be best, although if a few variables are known or at least suspected to be very important, societies exemplifying these should certainly be included.

I would maintain—again because of subtle differences in cultures that cannot be predicted in advance—that the crucial choice of societies to be included in a comparative study cannot usually be made adequately on the basis of the literature alone. Ideally this choice would require, in addition, some research in the field, such as a survey or pilot study. And this is precisely where a single investigator can perhaps make a valuable contribution, assuming that the problem is sufficiently well defined and focused.

For example, I have made a survey of all the societies in Uganda with specific reference to marriage and family life. I would not claim that all the related problems are well defined and focused. Nevertheless, were I asked to make recommendations for an intensive comparative study along these lines, I would definitely include the Acholi because they are very different from other Uganda societies in at least one crucially important variable, in regard to the stability of marriage. Acholi judges seem to be the only ones in Uganda who have the authority and power to refuse to grant divorce in court and to make the judgment hold. Further, I would recommend that only one of the Nyoro, Toro, or Ganda be included because of their basic similarity in most aspects of marriage and family institutions, as well as similarities in independent variables causing change in these institutions.

The study of child rearing in six cultures was based on several earlier studies, and the research design was fairly well defined and explicit; one wonders whether some survey research in the field by one or perhaps more of the senior investigators could have led to a more strategic choice of societies. We know that the final choice was a compromise between the advantages of previous coverage, personal interests, and the attempt to provide for a great range of differences (B. Whiting 1963:3). Perhaps with more explicit knowledge gained in the field, senior investigators would have been able to demonstrate to members of the team specific reasons for a choice in the interest of making valid comparisons that would have prevailed over rea-sons of personal interest (cf., J. W. M. Whiting et al., 1966:123).

Several or all members of a team could also do such survey or what might be called exploratory research. This would appear to be most useful for problems of broad scope and unknown dimensions, problems for which we are unsure of the important variables. I understand from my informal inquiries that in the Culture and Ecology in East Africa Project some exploratory research was done by two members of the team specifically in order to make the final selection of four societies from a list of ten possibilities, which itself was based upon exhaustive research in the literature.[8] It cannot be expected that such exploratory research can uncover all the important variables in so complex a problem but, although final judgment must await full publication of the results, this research seems so far to have been very useful in helping the investigators choose societies for a strategic comparison. For very complex problems the whole period of intensive fieldwork may be considered as a kind of "exploratory" research in the sense that, although some hypotheses can be tested, many others are only formulated as questions without sufficient data to test them. For example, it is noteworthy that *Mothers of Six Cultures* begins with the statement that "this book reports an adventure in research exploration . . ." (Minturn and Lambert 1964:1). Many hypotheses will have to be tested in future or continuing studies, by either the same or different investigators, as has already been specifically suggested in the study of child rearing in six cultures (B. Whiting 1963:12–13, Minturn and Lambert 1964:292–293). This is, of course, the way in which science progresses; we must build upon earlier studies.

Looking now at the question of control from another point of view, a team would be able to provide control over more variables than a single investigator, simply because the number of societies that the latter could investigate is limited. That is, when there are too few cases, the possibilities of controlling many variables are severely limited and the danger of spurious correlation is much in-

[8] This and other information on the Culture and Ecology in East Africa Project has been kindly provided by Edgar Winans, and I here record my appreciation to him.

creased. For example, the field manual for the cross-cultural study of ethnocentrism points out that there is "a wide range of variables which appear in various theories as causes or correlates of ethnocentric hostility and imagery," and that it is expected a large sample of societies will be included in this study (LeVine and Campbell 1965:40, 42). One of the reasons a large sample of societies is needed is to gain greater control over the many variables involved. For such problems, if we have only a few societies in the comparative study there is little chance of manipulating the variables as many times as would be necessary to gain sufficient knowledge of the precise effects of each variable.

We should be in a position to manipulate operative variables and turn some of them into parameters for increased control over the data. But whether this is a justifiable procedure will depend upon our having enough knowledge of each variable to support the judgment that it is sufficiently similar in all societies so that we may validly assume that there will be no differing effects upon the dependent variable. The services of a single investigator could be particularly valuable here, especially for problems of limited scope involving only a few variables. With his knowledge of several societies, he could suggest which operative variables could most usefully be turned into parameters, and for any particular variable he could judge whether it would be sufficiently similar in all societies being compared.

Such judgments could also be made, of course, by a team of researchers working together as a group. And it could even be argued that their judgments would be likely to be more sound because of their greater familiarity with particular societies, especially for more complex problems involving many variables. The main disadvantage of this approach would be that typically they would not get together again until after the field research was finished. At that stage it would be impractical if not impossible to implement any changes that would require additional data collection.

SINGLE INVESTIGATOR AND TEAM APPROACHES COMBINED

I have suggested that the advantages and limitations of the two approaches discussed in this paper complement one another, and that the best comparative studies may well use a combination of both, if we have sufficient knowledge of the important variables. I turn now to a suggestion of how I think such a combination could work in practice. The single investigator is particularly valuable once the important variables for specific and focused problems have been ascertained. With ideas of a number of possible research problems in mind, stemming from a detailed study of the literature, he can do extensive research in an area in which he has previously done intensive fieldwork in one or two societies. In this way a single mind and conception of the problems are brought to bear on diverse data that are nevertheless somewhat familiar from previous experience in the area. He can gather sufficient information upon which to base a judgment both about the problems on which to concentrate and about the societies in which it would be most useful to do more intensive research. If we are to make systematic advance in *comparative* studies, we cannot choose societies for fieldwork only because no one has yet done fieldwork among them, or on the basis of personal interest; we must choose them systematically and strategically so that we can more effectively define parameters to test hypotheses. Having studied certain problems in depth, both in the literature and in the field in at least one or two societies, the single investigator should be in a position to choose societies for intensive research, the data from which should constitute a highly controlled comparative study because of the prior selection of similarities and differences known to be relevant.

It is also possible for a number of colleagues to come together as a team, discuss the problems they want to investigate, and then each one go out as a single investigator to the area or continent of his competence to do exploratory research. They could keep in close contact with one another even while in the field and each could return with a recommendation for the society or societies from his area that should be included in the study.

When investigating problems about which we have relatively little knowledge, making it difficult to choose variables strategically, we would want to choose societies representing many differences, each suspected of containing important variables. For this purpose it would be advantageous in the exploratory research to use a whole team of researchers, members of which have some experience in and knowledge of somewhat different parts of the world. Such a team could profitably initiate and concentrate on research involving problems of broad scope and unknown dimensions in order to provide knowledge of the important variables; this could then lead to more specific and focused projects in future studies.

Returning to problems for which we have sufficient knowledge, and following the first suggestion above, the single investigator, then, could become a member of a team, doing intensive research in one society himself; or he could become the principal investigator, finding others to do fieldwork in the societies he had selected for the comparative study. Or following the second suggestion, each member of the team could undertake to do intensive research in the society he selected, if there was only one society from his area, or he could find additional researchers to do the same if he had recommended more than one society. In either case, it would of course be important for members of the team to get together in advance and work out comparable questions to be asked and in general to insure, so far as possible, that a unity of conception of the problem or problems be maintained. Then, to gain the flexibility to make changes in the research design which is so crucial to the success of any comparative study, the members of the team—even if located in different parts of the world—could come together a few times to communicate and exchange ideas and information while the data collection process is still going on. That is, they should remain in as close contact and consultation as possible at every stage of the research. And this need not add much, if any, to the cost; for example, the number of members of the team could be reduced by one, and the funds used instead to provide air fares if necessary for the other members of the team to remain in close contact. Even if all the members of the team are not in the field at the same time, the whole team can still get together for face-to-face communication.

An example is provided in the procedures used in the American Kinship Project under Schneider at Chicago.[9] The data were collected over a two-year period, from the fall

[9] I am indebted to Nelson Graburn for this information on the American Kinship Project, and it is quoted here with the permission of David M. Schneider.

of 1961 to the fall of 1963. From six to eight investigators met informally three or four days a week with the principal investigator or among themselves to discuss their data as they were being collected. Hypotheses, types of data to collect, and ways to collect any particular type of data were constantly being talked about and modified during this period. It is my impression that the data for this project are highly comparable. It appears to me that this constant revision of hypotheses and data collection procedures is one of the main reasons for the high comparability of the data. Admittedly, all the data were collected not only in one society but also in one city, Chicago; but the group of middle-class families interviewed included families which varied according to several important criteria, including ethnicity. My point is that this principle of revising the research design while the data are being collected can be very effectively employed also in cross-cultural research. Indeed it can be argued that such revision is even more necessary for cross-cultural research than for research in a single society.

With regard to the Culture and Ecology in East Africa Project, I understand that the team did meet together twice during the course of the fieldwork and that this was considered helpful in working out schedules and rethinking the hypotheses involved. I would add that such meetings can also help to build and maintain an *esprit de corps,* which is so essential to the obtaining of comparative data. This point is related to the importance of attempting to overcome differences in personalities, interests, and training.

Sociologists and social anthropologists have often been divided into two camps: the theory builders and the fact finders. Those who emphasize theory may complain that, although we have endless facts, they often contradict one another and they do not give us cumulative knowledge and increase our powers to predict. Those who emphasize fact-finding may complain that the therorists base their conclusions upon *a priori* assumptions and hypothetical models that are so divorced from the real world as to have little value. In suggesting that we revise our concepts while in the field, I am in effect making a recommendation for a practical way to bring these two camps together so that they can merge theory and data into a unified whole, for it is this, of course, that is the hallmark of the most significant and the most useful social science.

EXPLORATORY AND FOCUSED RESEARCH

Finally, I should like to emphasize again the difference between research on a clearly defined and focused problem for which it is possible to have a highly controlled comparison, on the one hand, and exploratory research, on the other. As already stated, this is a relative and not an absolute distinction, which is nevertheless useful. Exploratory research can most usefully be carried out by a whole team, and must precede the more highly controlled type of focused research.

There may be a tendency to relegate exploratory research to second place in the hierarchy perhaps precisely because it is not sufficiently focused, because—not being able to predict just where such research may lead—one cannot have sufficient confidence that it is likely to lead to "productive" results, measured especially in terms of hypotheses tested. It is granted that one must be wary of the use of the term "exploratory" as a cover for ill-conceived research designs on problems about which we already have considerable knowledge of the important variables. But there is a difference between this and a valid attempt to discover variables on a problem of broad scope about which we have relatively little knowledge.

Certainly a more highly controlled and focused comparison is to be preferred if it is likely to lead to a greater advance of our knowledge. But the criteria for this must not be thought of exclusively in terms of the number of hypotheses tested, but also of the number of important though unanticipated variables discovered; and it could be argued that the latter must precede the former.

When the degree of control and focus in the comparison is given too much weight as a criterion, the research design may be so rigid as to lead to a rejection of a hypothesis without providing much information about other possibly important variables; but if the design is conceived from the beginning in more flexible terms it will encourage researchers to pose diverse questions in many related areas, and these are likely to provide more information on unanticipated variables. The degree of rigidity or flexibility in the research design should be directly correlated with the amount of systematic knowledge we already possess about the problem under investigation. The more we know, the more rigidly we can profitably control and focus the comparison; the less we know, the more flexible we should make the research design to encourage the discovery of new and unanticipated variables.

Anthropologists are particularly well suited to flexible exploratory research, in part because of their experience in many societies in diverse parts of the world, which leads to an awareness of how little systematic knowledge we have of many important problems on a cross-cultural basis, and in part because of the anthropologist's tradition of studying particular social interactions within the context of a whole social system, which lends itself easily to the search for unanticipated variables.

I have examined the differing advantages and limitations of the team approach and that of the single investigator according to two criteria. Concerning the first criterion —sufficient flexibility—one of the main advantages of a single investigator (and this is possible only for a focused problem) is his single and unified conception of the whole problem. With some personal knowledge and experience of all the societies involved and with great flexibility to make changes, he is probably best able to choose concepts that, on the one hand, are sufficiently general and, on the other hand, allow for the particularities of societies. The choice and sharpening of particular concepts (and the consequent elimination of alternative ones) are especially crucial for focused research in which a main goal is to test hypotheses.

In exploratory research, however, we may still be mainly interested in searching for unanticipated variables and corresponding concepts to locate the dimensions of the problem more adequately; also, for any particular variable, we seek many alternative concepts at the beginning so that when the time comes to focus the research an adequate choice of particular concepts can be made for comparative purposes.

In *exploratory* research, then, the services of a single investigator are likely to be less valuable than those of a whole team precisely because the members of a team hold somewhat differing original conceptions of the problems, often related to their differing experiences in various parts of the world. In exploring a problem we need to take account of all these differing conceptions in order to document the breadth of its dimension and to more adequately choose particular concepts that will accommodate them. Obviously, this sometimes involves dividing the problem into several parts or aspects for more adequate analysis. In any case, one of the goals of exploratory research is to insure that the concepts ultimately chosen will not leave out of consideration —and thus distort—social interaction in specific and sometimes widely differing societies.

The second criterion—maximum control over the analytical framework without the elimination of any significant variable— strongly highlights the difference between focused and exploratory research. In focused research one assumes that the important independent variables are known and thus a controlled comparison can be set up to test their effects on the dependent variable. In such research the single investigator has an advantage, at least at the beginning, in his experience in several societies, which enables him to choose a few societies strategically for a highly controlled comparative study, matching differences and similarities known in advance to be relevant for hypotheses to be tested. At a later stage, however, because of the limitations in the number of societies and languages that a single investigator can study adequately, a team would be best because each member would do the intensive fieldwork in his chosen society. When a whole team does the research the data are likely to be more reliable for each society studied; also, as there will be more societies included, it will be possible to control more variables, and propositions can be established with greater certainty. Thus for focused research a combination of the team approach and that of the single investigator is recommended.

As to exploratory research on problems of broad scope and unknown dimensions in which we are primarily attempting to discover as many unanticipated variables as possible (although we should also test hypotheses wherever feasible), the team has an incontestable advantage over the single investigator because its members have knowledge and experience of many parts of the world. With regard to the second criterion, increased control over the analytical framework is not really possible until we have done some exploratory research to make sure that we will not be eliminating any significant variable; therefore, exploratory research is especially related again to only one aspect— the latter—of the second criterion.

In this chapter I have enumerated the complementary advantages and limitations of the team approach and that of a single investigator in comparative studies. I have assessed the differing merits of these two approaches according to two familiar criteria, which I have emphasized and illustrated. On the one hand, I have concluded that for focused problems of known dimensions a combination of these approaches would be most fruitful; this is the type of research that is likely to be productive of tested hypotheses. On the other hand, for problems of broad scope and unknown dimensions, exploratory research, which is likely to be productive of important although unanticipated variables, is necessary, and an emphasis on the team approach is likely to be most fruitful.

The distinction between focused and exploratory research is not an absolute one, but it does indicate the differing ways in which each contributes to our systematic knowledge. Both these contributions are important, though exploratory research should precede focused research. There may be a tendency to favor focused research because it is the end product and because there is a hope that the exploratory research can be based on existing literature—a hope that is unjustified for most cross-cultural comparisons. Exploratory research in the field is definitely necessary, it should be done by a whole team of researchers, and anthropologists are among the most qualified to carry it out.

It may be objected that anthropologists have been doing exploratory research for a long time, and that it is rarely followed up by focused research. This is true, but they have been doing it mainly as individuals, and I suggest that it is precisely because such research has not been done as part of a team effort that we have not made much progress toward focused research.

I stated earlier that team research is a matter of degree; it is on a continuum from individuals working as part of the scientific community to the small organized group involved in a high degree of cooperation; the latter is an ideal often very difficult to achieve in practice. I now add that the ends of this continuum appear to be correlated with the relative distinction between exploratory and focused research. Insofar as we are able to overcome the difficulties and to achieve highly cooperative research in cross-cultural comparisons, to that degree also we shall be able to achieve highly focused research cross-culturally, with results in terms of tested hypotheses.

It has been suggested that whether one does individual or team research is largely a matter of intellectual and psychological predisposition (Adams and Preiss 1960:5, 22–25), and not all anthropologists will (nor should they) do team research. Nevertheless —assuming practical difficulties can be handled adequately—highly focused cross-cultural research is likely to be most successful when carried out by a team (or a combination of individual and team approaches) specifically organized for this purpose, rather than by the (sometimes tenuously) combined efforts of researchers working basically as individuals, even if, as individuals, we all belong to the "team" of the scientific community.

BIBLIOGRAPHY

ADAMS, RICHARD N., and JACK J. PREISS
  1960 *Human organization research: field relations and techniques.* Society for Applied Anthropology. Homewood, Ill., Dorsey Press.
BIERSTEDT, ROBERT
  1964 Definition of "legitimacy." In J. Gould and W. L. Kolb, eds., *A dictionary of the social sciences.* New York, Free Press.
BOHANNAN, PAUL
  1957 *Justice and judgment among the Tiv.* New York, Oxford University Press.
EGGAN, FRED
  1954 Social anthropology and the method of controlled comparison. *American Anthropologist* 56:743–763.
  1965 Some reflections on comparative method in anthropology. In M. Spiro, ed., *Context and meaning in cultural anthropology.* New York, Free Press.
EVANS-PRITCHARD, E. E.
  1963 *The comparative method in social anthropology.* The Hobhouse Lecture for 1963. London, Athlone Press.
GOLDSCHMIDT, WALTER
  1965 Theory and strategy in the study of cultural adaptability. *American Anthropologist* 67:402–408.
GULLIVER, P. H.
  1965 Anthropology. In Robert A. Lystad, ed., *The African world: a survey of social research.* African Studies Association. New York, Praeger.
HUGHES, CHARLES C.
  1960 *People of cove and woodlot; communities from the viewpoint of social psychiatry.* New York, Basic Books.

LEIGHTON, ALEXANDER H.
  1955 Psychiatric disorder and social environment: an outline for a frame of reference. In *Psychiatry, Journal for the Study of Interpersonal Processes,* Vol. 18. Baltimore.
LEIGHTON, ALEXANDER H., and ALLISTER MACMILLAN
  1952 People of the hinterland: community interrelations in a maritime province of Canada. In Edward H. Spicer, ed., *Human problems in technological change.* New York, Russell Sage Foundation.
LEVINE, ROBERT A., and DONALD T. CAMPBELL
  1965 *Ethnocentrism field manual* (April 1965).
LUSZKI, MARGARET BARRON
  1958 *Interdisciplinary team research; methods and problems.* National Training Laboratories. New York, New York University Press.
  1960 Team research in social science: major consequences of a growing trend. In Richard N. Adams and Jack J. Preiss, eds., *Human organization research: field relations and techniques.* The Society for Applied Anthropology. Homewood, Ill., Dorsey Press.
MINTURN, L., and W. LAMBERT
  1964 *Mothers of six cultures.* New York, Wiley.
SCHAPERA, I.
  1953 Some comments on comparative method in social anthropology. *American Anthropologist* 55:353–362.
VOGT, EVON Z., and ETHEL M. ALBERT (eds.)
  1966 *The people of Rimrock: a study of values in five cultures.* Cambridge, Harvard University Press.

WHITING, BEATRICE (ed.)

1963 *Six cultures, studies of child rearing.* New York, Wiley.

WHITING, JOHN W. M., IRWIN L. CHILD, WILLIAM W. LAMBERT, *et al.*

1966 *Field guide for a study of socialization.* New York, Wiley.

ZELDITCH, MORRIS

1964 Cross-cultural analysis of family structure. In Harold T. Christensen, ed., *Handbook of marriage and family.* Chicago, Rand McNally.

CHAPTER 20

Field-Manual Anthropology

DONALD T. CAMPBELL and ROBERT A. LEVINE

INTRODUCTION

The title refers to an emerging solution to the growing problem of data comparability in anthropology.

The use of comparative method in social anthropology, whether in enumerative cross-cultural surveys like those of Murdock (1949) and Whiting and Child (1953) or in more qualitative controlled comparisons (Eggan 1954, Clignet, Chapter 31 in this volume), has depended heavily on published ethnographic reports that attempted to describe "the whole culture." The current trend among anthropologists, however, is toward specialized field work that produces publications on a narrower range of cultural materials. No longer can it be assumed that if so-and-so has studied the Wazungu, his monograph will cover topics ranging from basketry to folklore and from cross-cousin marriage to child rearing; it is more likely to be on Wazungu market organization, ritual structure, or ethno-botany, with only an introduction summarizing other aspects of culture. One reason for this change is that standards of ethnographic reportage have risen. Even with the average period of field work moving toward two years, only a few aspects of a culture can be thoroughly detailed by modern standards. Another and more questionable reason for the shift to specialization is the newer goal of attempting to test a behavioral science hypothesis framed in terms of specific variables rather than remain at the level of descriptive ethnog-

raphy. Ironically, the attempt to be scientific in this manner sometimes reduces the scientific value of the end product, for single case studies or even two-culture comparisons are hopelessly equivocal for hypothesis-testing (see Campbell 1961, Campbell and Stanley 1966) and can only be viewed as generating hypotheses for future research unless a large sample of subgroups or individuals is studied (see LeVine, Research Design in Anthropological Field Work, Chapter 10 in this volume); whereas the narrowed scope of ethnographic coverage diminishes the potential utility of the data for future comparative analyses on unanticipated topics.

Each student doing field work for his dissertation goes into a unique area, studies it with a unique set of methods, to which his own unique personality contributes heavily, and now must focus upon a unique hypothesis and a unique content. The resulting idiosyncrasy in an ethnographic report has as a result little chance of being interpretable as due to differences in culture. Were there consensus as to the scientific hypotheses most needing testing, so that several replications were available for each hypothesis, the situation would be more encouraging. But the narcissistic demands for originality, characteristic of all of the underdeveloped sciences, insures that almost every study be of a different hypothesis. The result is that current ethnography is doing less to improve the Human Relations Files than the advances in methodological sophistication and ethnographic detail would suggest, and is not providing the needed new statistical degrees of freedom for cross-validating the discoveries made in our continual resorting of the old

The preparation of this chapter has been supported in part by a grant from the Carnegie Corporation of New York to Northwestern University.

cases. From the point of view of comparative social science, the situation is chaotic. We must seek out and further those mechanisms which provide ways for getting comparison back into ethnographic research.

One alternative is coordinated full-time research as exemplified by Whiting's Six Cultures study (Whiting *et al.*, 1966; B. B. Whiting *et al.*, 1963; Minturn and Lambert 1964) and Watson's (1963) four-culture micro-evolution studies in the New Guinea Highlands. In these, ethnographers dedicate a full year or so to coordinated, comparable field work. While this may remain an ideal, it provides no general solution to the problem. On the one hand, the number of cultures is too small for the quantitative testing of hypotheses with an N of cultures. (Note that in Minturn and Lambert's work, degrees of freedom based upon individual differences within cultures are the major basis of hypothesis testing— just as they are in quantitative studies in psychology within our own culture.) For another, if comparability is rigidly adhered to, the work itself becomes unpleasant both through its rigid control and through the very large commitment to a number of inevitably inappropriate research decisions made prior to acquaintance with the local scene. When the researcher did not himself participate in making these wrong decisions, the impositional burden is even greater. Furthermore, this approach tends to inhibit the exploratory quality of field work and the following up of unanticipated leads suggested by the culture itself, which constitute for many the most personally rewarding aspect of anthropological research.

The most generally available solution of this problem would seem to be part-time collaborative research, in which the field worker devotes a small part of his time to doing research designed to replicate or parallel that of another. There are several possible arrangements for these. A single research project can solicit cooperation from numerous anthropologists. Thus Herskovits (Segall, Campbell and Herskovits 1966) secured the cooperation of some twenty anthropologists who contributed one week's time in the field to collecting optical illusion data. In the Cooperative Cross-Cultural Study of Ethnocentrism, directed by the present authors, some twenty to thirty cooperating anthropologists are subsidized for an extra two months' stay in the field devoted to collecting comparable data.

Many more modes of securing part-time commitment to collecting explicitly comparable data are needed. At the low cost end, one could consider five-man dissertation teams, each member of which agreed to spend four months toward the end of his stay collecting data at the rate of one month each for his four teammates. Each student would end up with profound acquaintance with his own area, plus explicit comparison data on his own topic for his own culture and four other areas. But there is no reason why anthropology should be less expensive than physics, perhaps the contrary. So scandalous is the lack of explicitly comparable material in current research that we should have deliberate funding policies designed to foster it. Most anthropologists' major field experience is also their first. A funding policy could send students overseas for a master's degree research year designated as an apprenticeship experience not requiring theoretical or topical originality, and in which they would replicate the methodology of an existing study as nearly as possible in their own novel area. Where possible, the author of the original research would be financed to spend a starter month and a terminal month with the replicator, to achieve as much comparability and interpretability of differences as possible. While in many instances mentor and replicator would come from the same institution, a discipline-wide coordinating council might well set funding priorities on the studies and locations most important for replication. The inevitable extension of the period of graduate training this would produce need not be a liability if a professional salary is paid during field work. If the dissertation is done in the same arena after a year back at school, the dissertation field work period could perhaps be shortened back to a one year stay. In the first two or three years after the doctorate field experience, the ethnographer frequently has need of a short-term or full-year return to his familiar field. Replication funding of such return trips on a fifty-fifty time-split would be very well received, half of the time being devoted to replication tasks, half to the ethnographer's personal scholarship.

So extreme is our need for comparable

data that such developments are bound to increase in frequency and extensiveness. With them should come a technology of guiding research at a distance so as to maximize comparability. This technology we are tentatively designating under the term "field-manual anthropology." In the second edition of this Handbook (1980?), there will be definitive articles on the subject. For the present we can only illustrate possible approaches and raise some anticipatory problems, in advance of those substantive outcomes that may eventually enable us to choose among alternative methods.

Field manuals, at least in the sense of questionnaires to Europeans residing among exotic peoples, go back into the last century. Morgan (1871) sent a questionnaire on kinship to missionaries and administrators around the world. Allen (1879:204 ff.), studying color vocabulary, asked correspondents in Asia, Africa, America, and the Pacific Islands, "Can they distinguish between [e.g.] blue and green?" and "Have they separate names for blue and green?" Magnus (1883) sent both a questionnaire and color samples to traders and missionaries. Leach (1961) provides the following report on Frazer:

Early in his career, Frazer engaged in "original research" in that in 1887 he issued a printed questionnaire entitled, *Questions on the Manners, Customs, Religions, Superstitions etc. of Uncivilized or Semi-civilized Peoples*. Later versions of the same document were sent out in 1888, 1889, and 1907. The recipients appear to have been for the most part missionaries and colonial administrators. The title page of the original pamphlet bears the following: "Answers to all or any of the following questions will be gratefully received by J. G. Frazer, M.A., F.R.G.S., Trinity College, Cambridge, England. N.B.—As the Questions have been drawn up to elicit information about a large range of peoples, it is probable that many of them will not apply to the particular people with which you are acquainted. Mr. Frazer proposes to publish the results of his enquiries. Full acknowledgement will be made to those who have favoured him with answers and printed copies will be forwarded to them." In fact, Frazer does not appear to have made any systematic use of the answers he obtained to these circulars, though presumably some of this information is incorporated in his earlier writings. In the expanded volumes which make up his later work, the source material is provided almost exclusively by the published work of previous writers. (Leach, 1961:384)

Notes and Queries (Royal Anthropological Institute, 1874; 6th edition, 1951) might

possibly be regarded as a field manual, for certainly it has had as its goal increasing the interpretable comparability of field work, even though it partakes of the foregone goal of "complete" ethnographies. The field manual most widely available and most useful as a model is that used in the six culture study on child rearing (prepared in 1954, published as Whiting *et al.*, 1966). While of limited topical focus, it is designed to cover over one year of field work. A very narrowly focused field manual covering five types of optical illusion has also been published (Herskovits, Campbell and Segall 1969). Widely distributed in multilith duplication is the 248-page *A Field Manual for cross-cultural study of the acquisition of communicative competence* (Slobin *et al.*, 1967). These are no doubt but a sample of a much larger range of "field manuals" that have been employed in various studies.

Our strategy in the present chapter will be to first present a sample section, constituting about one-third of our own field manual (LeVine and Campbell, 1965). This in itself will present some methodological issues and our reasons for resolving them as we did. Following this, we will discuss more general problems and strategies.

The goal of the Cross-Cultural Study of Ethnocentrism is to collect data descriptive of pre-colonial indigenous intergroup relations, including such specific topics as history of intergroup conflict, intergroup cooperation and economic exchange, social distance, stereotypes, and intergroup hostility, and as potential predictors, data on social structure, child-training methods, etc. (See Campbell and LeVine 1961, 1965; LeVine 1965; Campbell 1965, 1967.) As a matter of anticipatory apology, it can be stated that appearances to the contrary notwithstanding, the field manual has gone through four versions, with data collection experience contributing to each of the three revisions. An initial version with sample data collection preceded the version published in 1961 (Campbell and LeVine 1961). That article was conceived of as a complete field manual, with a review of relevant literature on ethnocentrism, an inquiry schedule with some two hundred questions, and methodological argument. When this proved too exacting for field workers to squeeze in on their own research time, funds to subsidize field work were solicited. Securing these led to a re-examination of the literature (Campbell and LeVine 1965) and an expansion of the topics covered to reflect the details of the competing theories. This expanded version was used by Nelson Graburn among the Eskimo and Naskapi, by James Watson in the New Guinea Highlands, by Satish Saberwal among the Embu of Kenya, and by ourselves among the Gusii of Kenya. These ethnographers participated in a revision conference which modified and reduced the field manual to its current form. Among the evidence used were back translation efforts from four of the five groups. If we still do not want to claim

exemplary perfection for it, it is because revisions do not always improve—in correcting one weakness others are inadvertently created—and because some problems set by theoretical interests are not readily solved. As to the stilted and banal language, this is a result of an effort to achieve unambiguous and interpretable English (see Werner and Campbell, Chapter 22, in this volume). But good or bad, a concrete example will help. In the next few pages we provide extensive excerpts from our *Ethnocentrism Field Manual* (LeVine and Campbell 1965). The first portions provide general instructions to collaborators; the latter ones, instructions for informant interviews.

ETHNOCENTRISM FIELD MANUAL

FIELD WORK PROCEDURE

Selection of the groups of reference

This field manual is designed for use by an ethnographer who has already done extensive field work in a given group of non-industrial people inhabiting a region where the political-military units were free of superordinate control until 1880 or later. The tasks described herein do not involve his working outside of that group, although in some cases he will have collaborators doing the same work among neighboring groups. In some areas there will be ambiguity concerning the type of boundary or level of grouping to be employed for defining the "ingroup," i.e., the group on which the ethnographer and his informants are reporting, and the "outgroups," i.e., the groups of which the informants report traditional ingroup images and relations. For example, in some stateless societies, the ingroup could (from the viewpoint of political autonomy, social distance, and military conflict) be a village, and the outgroups could be surrounding villages, even though those villages are very similar in language and culture, and even though beyond them there are pronounced linguistic and cultural boundaries. Such an ingroup-outgroup definition would mean that the results of the Ethnocentrism Inquiry Schedule (Section IV) would not be descriptions of "inter-tribal," "inter-societal," "inter-cultural," or "inter-ethnic" relations and images in the usual senses of those terms, but rather inter-group relations at an *intra-cultural* level. On the other hand, another ethnographer in the same situation could take the local boundaries designated by ethnographic and linguistic convention—the "tribes" or "cultures" of the region—as distinguishing ingroup from outgroup and have his informants report on the entire cultural or ethnolinguistic entity and its relations with and images of the other such distinct entities in the region, disregarding the inter-group relations at lower levels (except insofar as they come up in

Section IV as internal inter-community aggression). In this case, the images of culturally similar enemy groups would not be included in the data. Both alternatives are arbitrary and have disadvantages from the viewpoint of comparative study.

In Section III.A. an interview strategy is presented for finding the levels of grouping most salient to informants from the local group with which work is started. It is not anticipated, however, that this will solve the problem for the ethnographer, for informants may well produce long lists of outgroups defined by various criteria, some being more inclusive than others. In III.A.8. there is a procedure for reducing the list of outgroups—and defining the ingroup for purposes of the study. In applying this procedure to his specific case the ethnographer should be guided by the principle that it is as undesirable to focus entirely on the relations of small, culturally similar groups when dissimilar groups were known to the people traditionally as it is to focus entirely on inter-cultural relations and images when culturally homogeneous segments were independent military groups with sharp social boundaries. Where the situation is this ambiguous, the principle dictates that both culturally similar *and* dissimilar groups be included in the list of outgroups and that the ingroup be defined at a level lower than that of the cultural-linguistic boundary. If there is a multitude of culturally similar groups in the immediate vicinity (e.g. politically autonomous villages or "sub-tribes") but a relatively small number of culturally or linguistically distinct groupings in the whole region, it would be preferable to include only a few of the similar groups and all of the more dissimilar recognized entities.

Selection of communities within the ingroup

Since the final working definitions of the ingroup under study and the outgroups referred to may come out of the preliminary interviewing itself, the selection of a community or area in which to begin interviewing is crucial. If the first informants are from a marginal area located unusually near a linguistic boundary, they might give quite a different list of local groupings than centrally located informants. A similar problem arises if the first subgroup worked with has a peculiar history of migration or of political dominance or subordination which sets it apart in terms of intergroup experience from other subgroups of the ethnographically designated unit. Considerations of personal convenience will undoubtedly play a part in the ethnographer's decision as to where to start work, but he may have options and the following principles can serve as a guide:

1. Unless the ingroup is so small that all of its segments are very near ethnolinguistic boundaries, central communities are preferable to peripherally located ones.

2. A community or segment with a history of intergroup experience (e.g. migration) which appears in advance to be typical of that for the ingroup as a whole is preferable to one deemed atypical in this regard.

3. All information the ethnographer has or acquires concerning peculiar factors which might have influenced the segment relations with or perceptions of the intergroup environment should be explicated in detail in the materials he provides the project.

4. If the segment chosen for initial work is atypical, a special effort (apart from subsequent work described in the following section) should be made to do at least one ethnocentrism interview (Section III) with an informant in a different subgroup that is more typical in its intergroup experience to the ethnic group as a whole.

5. If the ethnic group is highly centralized, e.g. a monarchy with a royal court, then the first informants should be chosen from the politically dominant sector without regard to typicality.

Selection and description of informants

On the basis of the responses of initial informants to the survey of outgroups (III.A), a series of final working definitions of the ingroup and outgroups should be arrived at. Where the ingroup unit decided on (according to the procedure outlined in III.A) is a segment of the ethnographically defined unit rather than the whole, then informants should be chosen *exclusively from that segment,* apart from any special effort to compensate for atypicality (mentioned above). If the ingroup unit decided on coincides with the ethnographically defined unit, then informants may be chosen from any of its segments, and the greater the diversity of segments they come from, the better. Thus we are saying: although the ethnographer may use differing levels of ingroup-outgroup boundaries in *questioning* his informants, he must *select* informants on the basis of a single ingroup boundary consistently adhered to.

The cross-checking of informants' accounts represents a major methodological interest of the CCSE as well as an important control on the reliability of the data; it is therefore essential that the informants be interviewed independently, with no informant having prior knowledge of another's responses to the questions he is about to be asked. This does *not* rule out group interviews, with notes on degree of consensus among multiple informants, but it does mean that anyone present at such a session can not be used as a full independent source of information on the same topics (subsequent reports of disagreement with the group's consensus should of course be welcome). In selecting *informants,* the ethnographer should use the following desiderata as a guide:

1. *Expertness on the traditional culture.* The informants are *not* to be selected per se as a representative cross-section of the population, but rather as experts on the traditional culture. Thus if there are official or semi-official trained custodians of the oral history, these may be ideal.

2. *Articulateness, willingness, and perspective.* Not all persons who fully participated in a culture can report on it fluently. Articulateness and willingness obviously are required. Interest in the content in history, in the contrast of cultures and in culture change, may all be requisite to a willingness to talk in detail, to search old memories, etc. We cannot summarily rule out the use of marginal persons as informants, although the source of bias and limitation which may accompany this should be noted. (In interview section III.H. we suggest a deliberate supplementary use of inter-ethnic migrants.)

3. *Age.* Insofar as articulateness and willingness are not jeopardized, the older the informant, the better for our purposes. Every informant should have reached adulthood before the group came under colonial or national administration.

4. *Role and status in the community.* First priority should be given to old persons who once occupied central political positions in the community. Persons who currently are politically active may be suspect of distorting past beliefs and actions so as to better justify current political stands and alliances. While past political responsibles have top priority, if useful informants are sufficiently available, the four replications should be spread over social roles and statuses. Thus traditional followers and soldiers, as well as leaders, should be used. If religious leaders, military leaders, peacetime leaders, judicial leaders, etc. were differentiated, some use of all types would seem desirable. Note that while we aim at four or more complete replications of the interview content, these may be spread over 10 or 20 informants, as it is not expected that one informant will go through all interview content.

5. *Sex.* Males should be used exclusively for all sections except M, for which there should be two female and two male informants.

The ethnographer is likely to find that it is easier to use numerous informants, breaking the interview up into parts, rather than getting all of the material from only four or five. The main advantages are reduction of informant fatigue and elimination of the insult of asking for information the informant feels he has already given.

The evaluation of the informant interviews will be greatly facilitated if the ethnographer makes notes concerning relevant aspects of each informant's background, interview performance, and local reputation. The following points should be covered.

1. Age and travel experience. This can be obtained from—or in the case of age, laboriously worked out with—the informant himself, and has proved in some field situations to be a good way of beginning with an old informant. Dating his age by a local event calendar is essential for assessing his reliability in reporting memories of particular occurrences and customs. The details of his travel experience are indispensable for understanding the extent to which his accounts are based on idiosyncratic experience, including direct contact with foreign peoples, or on second-hand information and conventionalized folk beliefs. Obtain a crude life history of the informant in terms of where he has lived from childhood onward, who he saw there, etc. Allow him to elaborate at any length he chooses on his contact experiences, without directing him to use group names that he does not spontaneously mention.

2. Interview performance. An anthropologist develops a way of judging the honesty, frankness, and capability of his informants in a particular culture and such intuitive judgments, even if closer to impressions than demonstrable evaluations, are extremely important to record. In recording them, the ethnographer should keep in mind the following informant qualities: (a) comprehension of questions; (b) fluency of answers; (c) memory for detail; (d) ability to distinguish what he knows from what he does not know or conversely, tendency to fabricate in the absence of knowledge; (e) internal consistency of answers; (f) tendencies to distort, exaggerate or conceal any or all types of information; (g) general willingness or unwillingness to talk or to continue after a short period of time (e.g. does he become bored and then give short answers?).

3. Local reputation. This involves judgments by others who know the informant that bear on the reliability of his answers. For example, is he known as honest or dishonest, a man who knows much or little about the past? Do his family, kin group, or other connections and loyalties make him more likely to bias answers in particular ways? The ethnographer will probably obtain this kind of information in the course of selecting his informants, and it is essential to record it.

In addition to these general evaluations of informant characteristics, insertions should be made in parenthesis in the interview text concerning particular replies which are dubious, biased, or based on misunderstanding.

Selection of interpreters

The considerations of competence and absence of bias mentioned for the choice of informants are also relevant to the choice of interpreters. He should be a native speaker of the local language, this being more important (because less obvious to the ethnographer) than his English competence. If he is a local outgrouper, his own ethnicity may affect the informant's answers and his own translations, especially for a content such as ours. Even so, each interpreter is a biased vehicle, and for this reason, in the replication of interviews, a replication through different interpreters each time is desirable. This may not be feasible in all cases, but should be striven for. (The double-translation procedure, described below, will provide some feeling for how important this requirement is.)

Data collection procedure

Although most of the data will be collected through informant interviews, with only the background material in Section V derived from observation by the ethnographer and from documentary records, several different procedures will be followed for informant interviewing. On some topics (indicated below) there are set interview schedules which are to be translated into the vernacular (and then translated back into English by a different bilingual as a check on the original translation) as accurately as possible. On other topics the ethnographer will be free to devise his own interviewing strategy and schedule, so long as he obtains data to answer the questions which are asked of him in this manual. In either event he is to record the responses (or their English translation) in detailed field notes.

ETHNOCENTRISM INQUIRY SCHEDULE

Methodological Introduction

In this section and Section IV which follows, the ethnographer is asked to obtain the information indicated. It is intended that he ask such questions and use such approaches as are required to achieve this goal. Public opinion poll procedures are neither feasible nor sufficient. The job is not done when a specified question has been asked and an answer given, if the required information has not been obtained. Similarly, if this informant has already provided the information required, there is no need to ask the question. (But note that at least four independent reports on each topic are wanted.)

Because of this, in a previous version of this section, the questions were addressed to the ethnographer rather than to the informant or respondent. The present version differs in providing suggested wordings in English for starter-questions to be asked of the informant. This is done for two purposes. On the one hand, for most topics the ethnographer has at some point to frame a question for his interpreter to relay, and in the haste of the face-to-face situation may employ a colloquial, elliptical, or ambiguous English. It may therefore be convenient to have a ready-worded statement in English.

Second, a specific English wording is needed for the *double-translation task*, to provide the original version with which to compare the English back-translation. Even where one is using a tried-and-true interpreter, this procedure is highly desirable, if only because of the often forgotten ambiguity of colloquial English, and because of the often subtle distinctions required in the inquiry.

For such a concentrated and focused inquiry there are lacking the opportunities to cross-check and to learn by listening and observation which normal ethnography provides. Thus it is particularly important to be sure that when new topics are introduced, the starting question is as close to that intended as is possible.

In what follows, those portions in quotes are for use in the double-translation task. They are to be translated by one interpreter into the local language, and then independently translated back into English by a second interpreter. If the interpreters are literate, both of these steps can be done in writing. If they are not, the first translation into the local language (but not the original English) can be spoken into a tape recorder, and this record subsequently played to a second interpreter who then interprets into English. The oral process is much more disappointing in outcome than is the written process and is not to be preferred. However, fifteen-minute samples of the oral process provide an enlightening screening test for potential interpreters, and one which has face-validity to the candidates involved.

As a supplementary project, the process of double-translation is being studied in its own right. For this purpose, where feasible, the records of the process are desired. Most important is a copy of the first English back-translation, no matter how poor it may be. As this back-translation is used in discussion with the interpreters in revising the local language version, it will help if the English back-translation is red-penciled to indicate the nature of its errors. If the error seems to have occurred in the initial step from English to local language, mark it I.E. (in-error); if the error is in the translation from the local language back into English, mark it O.E. (out-error).

With two interpreters doing written translations, the double-translating and the subsequent corrective editing will probably take from five to seven days. The original English questions can be divided between the two for in-translation, and they can back-translate each others' in-translations. It may be found helpful in achieving adequate translations to substitute the actual name of the ingroup, and the name of some specific outgroup where (ingroup) and (outgroup) are indicated in the version here presented, before turning the original English questions over to the interpreter. For field use, however, the local-language version should make easy and clear the substitution of different outgroups from phase to phase of the inquiry. A final edited local-language version can be usefully used in the actual interviewing of informants, if the interpreter is literate. The interpreter can keep a copy in front of him to refer to for the agreed-upon starter wording, for use as indicated by the ethnographer who may be able to start an inquiry by merely designating the question number. Of course, once any given topic has been started, the follow-up questioning must be extemporized by ethnographer and interpreter until proper comprehension and response is achieved.

For many of the topics that follow, more alter-native wordings and probes are offered than will actually be needed in many interviews. On other topics, there is but a sampling of possible probes that might prove useful.

The English wordings provided are often stilted, awkward, and childish. In part at least, this is due to efforts to provide a completely explicit English, as through repeating nouns instead of using pronouns which are so often ambiguous in their reference. Even so, in double-translation task it will occasionally be necessary to provide altered English wordings before the interpreter can make his first in-translation. Where this is so, a note of these changes is needed for the double-translation study.

Before the comparison of the two English-language versions and subsequent editing of the local-language versions of Sections III and IV, the ethnographer should conduct the II.A. and II.B. interviews on concepts of social organization and aggression, in order to sharpen the ethnographer's awareness of available terminology in the local language for these conceptual domains. For example, among the Gusii, the II.B. interview uncovered the common usage of the same verb for "injure" and "kill" and led to insertion in the Gusii-language questions of explicit reference to death where "killing" rather than "injury" was the intended meaning.

In conclusion, let it be emphasized again that while specific queries to the informant are provided throughout, it is important to regard these as topic indicators addressed to the ethnographer, who is to use those tactics and wordings that seem to him optimal in achieving the information required.

A. Survey of Outgroups

The effort in this section is to get from the informant in an as unprejudiced manner as possible a traditional vocabulary of groups. No uniformly successful approach has been found, and it may be expected that some of the entries into the problem will draw a blank. The first few questions approach the problem in an open-ended manner, from several diverse starting points. Later questions are more specific and directive. If earlier questions have elicited partial or complete answers to subsequent ones, the questioning should be modified accordingly. Terms for outgroups and ingroups should be recorded in the vernacular.

A.1. (Original people)
A.1.1. "According to the beliefs of your ancestors before the Europeans arrived, who were the first human beings in the world?"
A.1.2. "Where did the first human beings live?"
A.1.3. "What language did the first human beings speak?"
A.1.4. "What other parts of the world were there?"
A.1.5. "Where did the other peoples (groups) come from?"
A.1.6. "Where did these other peoples live?"
A.2. (Languages)

A.2.1. "According to the beliefs of your ancestors in the time before the Europeans, what peoples spoke different languages from each other?" (If this draws a blank, then ask:)

A.2.2. "Did all the peoples speak the same? Which ones spoke differently from one another?"

A.2.3. "Which peoples could not understand one another?"

A.2.4. "Which peoples spoke differently but were able to understand one another?"

A.2.5. (If not previously given:) "Which peoples could your ancestors understand?"

A.2.6. "Which ones could they not understand?"

A.2.7. "Among the peoples your ancestors *could* understand, which ones spoke differently (said words differently, had a different way of talking) from your ancestors?"

A.3. (Groupings by warfare)

A.3.1. "In the days of your fathers and grandfathers, which peoples (group) fought wars with which other groups?"

A.3.2. "Against which peoples (groups) did your ancestors go to war?"

A.4. (Groups that have disappeared)

A.4.1. "Were there any tribes or peoples known to your ancestors long ago that have since disappeared?" (For each such:)

A.4.2. "Where did they live?"

A.4.3. "What language did they speak?"

A.4.4. "What caused them to disappear?"

A.4.5. "Where did they go?"

A.5. (Migration of ingroup)

A.5.1. "When did the (ingroup people) come to this land?"

A.5.2. "Where did they come from?"

A.5.3. "What people lived on this land before the (ingroup people) came?"

A.5.4. "Why did those people leave?"

(In this question and following ones, the ethnographer must choose a vernacular term for the ingroup. The decision will often be an arbitrary one, but one which is important for the study. If there was a traditionally centralized political organization, the term should be for the most inclusive continuous political organization. If not, it should be for the most inclusive designation carrying feelings of belonging, group membership, loyalty, pride, etc. Language group designations are acceptable in the absence of political structures, if the feeling of membership is present.)

A.6. (Neighboring peoples)

A.6.1. "Before the coming of the Europeans, what groups lived next to the (ingroup) people?" (Probe for neighbors in all directions.) For each of the immediately adjacent groups:

A.6.2. "What group lived beyond the (specific outgroup)?" (By asking what group lived beyond each mentioned group, a map of the area should be filled out with names of groups for three levels of adjacency, if possible. More remote groups should be learned of if known. It is important, however, for the informant to distinguish between his present knowledge and the knowl-

edge had by his people at the time of first European contact.)

A.7. When the informant's ready inventory of outgroup names has been exhausted, ask about knowledge of and names for other outgroups which you as an ethnographer know to have existed in the area.

A.7.1. "Did the (ingroup) know about the——— in those days?"

A.7.2. "By what names did they know them?"

A.8. (Reducing the list of outgroups)

In some inquiries, the same groups will be mentioned again and again in the preceding questions, and the ethnographer will therefore have little problem in selecting some ten or more outgroups, about which to conduct the basic inquiry. In other areas, the names dredged up will differ greatly from question to question, and a much larger list of potential outgroup names will result. In this instance, a process of selecting and combining names will be necessary. In some cases, several subgroup names will have been obtained, and an inclusive name may be found that can be used instead. In other cases of strong similarities among groups but inclusive name lacking, one typical group might be taken as a representative, the similars being omitted on the presumption that the stereotypes and attitudes evoked would be essentially the same. If there are centralized state organizations among potential outgroups, these should certainly be employed. Lacking these, warfare groupings should be given high priority. Linguistic units territorially compact are also acceptable.

There may be instances in which ambiguity exists as to whether a given segment should be regarded as an outgroup neighbor or as a part of the ingroup. In such instances, it is well to remember that one of the goals of the inquiry is the testing of hypotheses dealing with the effect of cultural similarity on ethnocentric hostility. For this reason, it is desirable to have among the outgroups as much diversity as possible, including some highly similar to the ingroup. From this point of view, it would be desirable to have as one of the outgroups a neighboring people sharing the same language culture.

With these criteria in mind, the ethnographer should select some ten to fifteen outgroups for the subsequent inquiry. These should include all of the adjacent outgroups and those one degree removed. If cutting is needed, representative samples from more remote outgroups can be used.

A.9. Masterlist of outgroups

In accordance with the guiding principles set forth above, prepare a masterlist of outgroups to be asked about in subsequent questioning. Sections B and C, which follow, are to be repeated asking about each outgroup in turn. There may be ten or fifteen or more such outgroups in some areas. Even if spread over several sittings, fatigue and boredom may very well lead to more perfunctory responses to outgroups asked about last. If the order of inquiry were systematic, this fatigue would be confounded with such factors as proximity, size, importance, etc., leading to spurious relationships. For this reason the order in which outgroups are treated should be changed for each informant, and should ideally be random with regard to nearness, size, etc. It is recognized, however, that the requirements of salience in maintaining informant rapport at crucial stages may require deviations. However, we are providing a randomization plan which should help. With the A.9. masterlist of outgroups are sets of random numbers to be used in ascertaining interview order where feasible. The outgroups can be listed in any order, e.g. as mentioned by the informant, etc. Not all rows will be filled, of course. For the rows filled, interview first about that outgroup which has the lowest number in the column corresponding to the informant being interviewed. Outgroup order should be recorded in the field notes. If there are more than 20 outgroups, randomly select 15 for inquiry. These should include all of the immediately adjacent outgroups, and a random selection at each of the further removes. Where the remoteness of the outgroup, and the informant's general denials of knowledge make it foolish to ask some of the very specific questions, these can be eliminated at the ethnographer's discretion. The general evaluative and introductory question should not be skipped, however.

Options for distributing sections B and C among informants

It may seem too tedious to give both sections to the same informants about each outgroup. In this case, each of these sections (preceded by Section A) should be given to separate informants, running through all of the outgroups on one section with this same informant. (An alternate division of content in which one informant would answer B and C for part of the outgroups, would be undesirable because it would reduce the comparability among outgroups, confounding it with informant differences.) Use of both Sections B and C for all outgroups with a single informant is acceptable if informant's patience is sufficient.

Where B and C are used separately, not only should *each* informant be asked A, but each should also be asked D. The informants asked about B should also be asked about F. This is for reasons of comparability between ingroup and outgroup trait descriptions.

B. Imagery of the Outgroup

(B and C to be asked about each outgroup in turn. Use the traditionally commonest specific designation. If there are two terms of equal currency, use the more proper, less abusive term.)

B.   "For a while now, our questions will all be about the (specific outgroup) people."

B.1.   "What were all the names and nicknames used by the (ingroup) to refer to the (specific outgroup)?"
        (For each name:)

B.1.1. "What other meanings does that name have?"

B.1.2. "Why were they called that name?"

B.1.3. "Were there other peoples called by the same name?"

B.2   "Did the (ingroup) like or dislike the (specific outgroup)?"

B.3.   "What did the (ingroup) people think were the virtues and good characteristics of the (outgroup) people?"

B.4.   "What did the (ingroup) people think were the sins, the weaknesses, and the bad characteristics of the (outgroup) people?"

B.5.   "In what ways were the (specific outgroup) people different from the (ingroup) people?"
        (Record the spontaneous ordering of topics, then probe especially as indicated in B.5.1. through B.5.18. For the first few we explore alternative wordings of the basic comparisons, and then essay a standard question form. (When the respondent gives an answer which characterizes but one of the groups under comparison, ask him how the other group was on this trait.)

B.5.1. "In what ways did the (outgroup men) dress differently from the (ingroup) men?"

B.5.2. "In what ways did the (outgroup women) dress differently from the (ingroup women)?"

B.5.3. "In what ways were the (outgroup people) different from the (ingroup people) in their physical appearance?" (Probe for skin color, physiognomy, body build, bodily mutilations, etc.)

B.5.4. "In what ways was the (outgroup) language different from the (ingroup) language?"
        "In what ways were the (outgroup) people different from the (ingroup) people in——?"

B.5.5. "ways of getting food to eat?" (farming, livestock, hunting, fishing, collecting.)

B.5.6. "customs of eating?"

B.5.7. "rules about marriage?"

B.5.8. "circumcision of boys?"

B.5.9. "circumcision of girls?"

B.5.10. "rules and prohibitions about love-making between boys and girls?"

B.5.11. "rules about sexual relations?"

B.5.12. "customs of urination and defecation?"

B.5.13. "ways of teaching children?"

B.5.14. "customs of fighting in wars?"

B.5.15. "political organization?"

B.5.16. "drinking alcoholic beverages?"

B.5.17. "crafts, manufactures, artisans?"

B.5.18. "their houses and how they were built?"

B.5.19. "how they treated foreigners?"

B.5.20. "pride in themselves?"

B.6   "Were the (outgroup) people ever used as good examples in teaching (ingroup) children? Did (ingroup) people ever say to their children, 'Be like the (outgroup) people'? For what things, ways of acting, was this done?"

B.7.   "Were the (outgroup) people ever used as a bad example in the teaching of (ingroup) children? Did the (ingroup) people ever say to their children, 'Don't be like the (outgroup) people'? For what things, ways of acting, was this done?"

B.8. "When (ingroup) parents were trying to frighten their children into being good, did they ever mention the (outgroup) to their children? Did the (ingroup) people ever say to their children, 'The (outgroup) will get you if you don't stop being bad' or 'I will give you away to the (outgroup) if you are bad'?"

B.9. "Did the (ingroup) people fear the (outgroup)?"

B.10. "Were there any of the (ingroup's) troubles or problems which the (ingroup) blamed the (outgroup) for?"

B.11. (This shifts to the knowledge of reciprocal stereotypes, to the ingroup's knowledge of the outgroup's view of the ingroup.)

B.11.1. "What did the (outgroup) people say about the (ingroup)?"

B.11.2. "Did the (outgroup) people like the (ingroup)?"

B.11.3. "Were the (outgroup) people afraid of the (ingroup)?"

B.11.4. "Did the (outgroup) people blame the (ingroup) for troubles of the (outgroup)?"

B.11.5. "What names did the (outgroup) have for the (ingroup) people? What did these names mean?"

C. Traditional Relationships with the Specific Outgroup

(Asked about each outgroup, just as B. This should be modified insofar as a given informant has already provided the information.)

C.1. Peaceful relationships with the specific outgroup:

C.1.1. (If needed)
"What types of contacts and relationships did the (outgroup) people have with the (ingroup) people?"

C.1.2. (To be asked for adjacent outgroups only)
"In those long ago days before the Europeans came, where was the boundary between (outgroup) land and the (ingroup) territory? How could one recognize this boundary? How had this boundary been decided upon?"

C.1.3.1. "Did the (ingroup) have any common organizations with the (outgroup) people, such as clans, religious societies, age groups, blood-brotherhoods?"

C.1.3.2. "Did the (ingroup) ever have military alliances with the (outgroup)?"

C.1.4. "What things did the (outgroup) trade with the (ingroup)?"

C.1.5. "Did any of the (ingroup) wizards, prophets, diviners, healers, priests, or sorcerers practice among the (outgroup) people, in the days before the Europeans

came? Did any (outgroup) persons come to learn sorcery, witchcraft, divination, or other kinds of magic from (ingroup) experts?"

C.1.6. "Did any (outgroup) wizards, prophets, diviners, healers, priests, or sorcerers practice among the (ingroup) people?" "Did any (ingroup) persons visit among the (outgroup) to get help from (outgroup) wizards, prophets, diviners, healers, priests, or sorcerers?" "Did any (ingroup) persons go to learn sorcery, witchcraft, divination, or other kinds of magic from (outgroup) experts?"

C.1.7. "Did the (outgroup) people have any of the same religious beliefs as the (ingroup) people? Did they worship any of the same spirits and gods?"

C.1.8. (If conceivable)
"Did people from the (ingroup) ever work together with people from the (outgroup)? On what sorts of activities?"

C.1.9. "Did (ingroup) people ever join (outgroup) people for feasts or celebrations?"

C.1.10. "Were there games, contests, or competitions between (ingroup) people and the (outgroup) people? What were these?"

C.1.11. "Did the (outgroup) people provide gifts, tribute, slaves, children, brides, or services to the (ingroup) people? Were these obligatory or voluntary?"

C.1.12. "Did the (ingroup) provide gifts, tribute, slaves, children, brides, or services to the (outgroup)? Were these obligatory or voluntary?"

C.1.13. "How many of the (ingroup) could understand the (outgroup) language?"

C.1.14. "How many of the (outgroup) could understand the (ingroup) language?"

C.1.15. "Did the (ingroup) regard any of the (ingroup's) laws, customs, gods, tools, crops, domesticated animals, handicrafts, songs, words, methods of divination and sorcery, etc. to have originated among the (outgroup)? Were these regarded as good or bad?"

C.2. Migration and intermarriage with the specific outgroup:

C.2.1. "Were there any men or women who lived with the (ingroup) in those long ago days who were born as one of the (specific outgroup)? What were they called? What was their position? Were they slaves, servants, or just like other (ingroup) members? Were they given land? Were these migrants treated the same as (ingroup) members under (ingroup) laws? Were their children treated as (ingroup) members? Why did they move? How many such migrants were there?"

C.2.2. "Were there men or women born (ingroup) members who lived with the (outgroup) people? What was their position? Were they slaves or servants or like other (outgroup) persons? Why did they live there? How many such migrants were there?"

C.2.3.1. "Could (ingroup) men marry (outgroup) women? Where would such a couple live, among the (ingroup) or among the (outgroup)?"

C.2.3.2. "Could an (outgroup) man marry an (ingroup) woman? Where would they live?"

C.2.4. "Could a man be a member of both the (ingroup) and the (outgroup) at the same time?"

C.2.5. "Did the (ingroup) allow (outgroup) people to come as visitors into (ingroup) territory?"

"Did the (outgroup) allow (outgroup) people to come as visitors into (ingroup) territory?"

"Were there certain places in (ingroup) territory where (outgroup) visitors were not allowed to go?"

"Were such (outgroup) visitors allowed into (ingroup) houses?"

"Were such (outgroup) visitors allowed to eat or drink with (ingroup) people?"

C.2.6. "Did the (ingroup) allow (ingroup) persons to go as visitors to (outgroup) territory?"

"Did the (outgroup) allow (ingroup) persons to go as visitors into (outgroup) territory?"

"Were there certain places in (outgroup) territory where (ingroup) visitors were not allowed to go?"

"Were such (ingroup) visitors allowed into (outgroup) houses?"

"Were such (ingroup) visitors allowed to eat or drink with (outgroup) persons?"

C.3. Hostile and predatory individual acts toward the outgroup:

C.3.1. "Did the (ingroup) in those days encourage or prohibit (ingroup) men to steal, raid, or take cattle, food, and tools from the (outgroup) persons?"

C.3.2. "Did the (outgroup) in those days encourage or prohibit (outgroup) men to steal, raid, take cattle, food, and tools from the (ingroup)?"

C.3.3. "Did the (ingroup) people encourage or prohibit (ingroup) men to rape, seduce, or steal women from the (outgroup)?"

C.3.4. "Did the (outgroup) people encourage or prohibit (outgroup) men to rape, seduce, or steal from the (ingroup)?"

C.3.5. "Did the (ingroup) people encourage or prohibit (ingroup) men to kill (outgroup) persons?"

C.3.6. "Did the (outgroup) people encourage or prohibit (outgroup) men to kill (ingroup) persons?"

C.3.7. "Did (ingroup) persons use witchcraft or sorcery against (outgroup) persons?"

C.3.8. "Did (outgroup) persons use witchcraft or sorcery against (ingroup) persons?"

C.4. Warfare relationships with the specific outgroup:

In addition to the general questions outlined below, the ethnographer should use this opportunity to encourage the informant in describing specific encounters (particularly major ones or typical ones) as fully as possible and in outlining a chronology of intergroup conflicts which will help in the military history of the region, as described in IV.E. below.

C.4.1. (If necessary by this time) "Was there ever fighting between the (outgroup) people and the (ingroup) people?" (Ask even if no tradition of formal warfare exists.)

C.4.2 "What were the causes of these fights, these wars?"

C.4.3.1. "What were the goals for which the (ingroup) people fought? Did they fight for defense? for revenge? for wrongs? for trophies? to prove manhood? for booty and plunder? for captives? for slaves? for political control of that region?"

C.4.3.2. "What happened when an (ingroup) man killed an (outgroup) man in war? Were there rituals he had to perform? Were there special honors awarded him? Were body parts of the dead enemy taken as trophies?"

C.4.4. "What were the goals for which the (outgroup) fought?"

C.4.5. "What weapons were used? How were they used? Were spears thrown from a distance? or was the fighting close in, hand-to-hand? Were attacks announced to the enemy? or was stealth and ambush used?"

C.4.6. "What did the (ingroup) do with (outgroup) war captives?"

C.4.7. "What did the (outgroup) do with (ingroup) war captives?"

C.4.7.1. "In these fights, was there anything a man could do to keep from being killed when enemy warriors had him surrounded?"

C.4.8.1. "In such fights, did any of the (ingroup) men or women help the (outgroup)?"

C.4.8.2. "In such fights, did any of the (outgroup) men or women help the (ingroup)?"

C.4.9. "How many men were killed in such a war? What damage did wars cause? Were houses destroyed, crops ruined, etc.?"

C.4.10. "How did such wars end? How was peace made?"

D. Rankings of Outgroups

In this section, for up to ten of the most important groups (if more than this have been covered in A, B, and C), we aspire to a complete ranking of groups on a few particularly important features. For all topics, D.1. through D.8. a complete ranking is wanted, although tied ranks will be accepted. The sample wording provided is illustrative rather than complete. For D.1. through D.5. be sure that the ingroup is included in the ranking.

D.1. "We have talked of many tribes or groups, the——, the——, the——, (etc. specific outgroups) and the (ingroup). Of all of these groups, which one had the most land, the largest territory?"
"Which group had the next most land?"
"Which group ranked third in land?"
"Which group had the least land?"
"Did (outgroup A) have more land or less land than (outgroup B)?"
"Of these groups, which ones had less land than the (ingroup)?"

D.2. "Of all of these groups, which one had the most people?"

D.3. "Of all of these groups, in which one was there the largest city or village? What was the name of that city? How many people lived in that city?" (Get the name, if known, and population of the largest city in each group, as of the days before Europeans, as well as the rankings of these cities.) If specific known cities are not available, ask, "Which group had the largest villages? How many people lived in one of the largest villages?" and secure ranks in terms of largest village size.

D.4. "Of all of these groups, which one was strongest in political power and war strength?"

D.4.1. "Of all of these tribes, which one was wealthiest?"

D.5. "Of all of these tribes, which one was the most virtuous, moral, and good?"
For the following, D.6., D.7., D.8., the ingroup is not to be included in the ranking, but is instead an external referent.

D.6. "Of all of these tribes, which one was the most similar to the (ingroup) in customs and ways of life?"

D.7. "Of the languages of all of these groups, which language was the most similar to the (ingroup) language? Which was most different?" Crude bases of ranking are provided earlier in the several coverings of B.3.3.

D.8. "Of all of these groups, which group did the (ingroup) people like the best in the days before the Europeans came? Which did they dislike the most?" (Etc.)

E. Bipolar Trait Inquiry for Groups Collectively

In this section, the inquiry centers about traits which may or may not have been spontaneously mentioned by the respondent in Section B, thus serving as a cross-check, and more particularly to attempt to move the respondent into a language of character traits. The ethnographer should have in front of him (and the interpreter in front of him in the decided local-language usage) a list of the groups for which B and C have been done. The goal will be to get the informant to consider the status of *all* of the tribes or outgroups on the trait in question. The basic language will be bipolar: Thus we will first ask a question such

as, "Of all of the tribes which we have been talking about including the (ingroup), which ones did the (ingroup) regard as Dirty, and which ones did they regard as Clean?" If some tribes are mentioned in each class, then ask about the unmentioned ones, "Were the (specific outgroup) regarded as Dirty or Clean?" An intermediate category of "neither" or "in between" or "average" is acceptable if the tribe has been specifically mentioned. Full record should be made of the informant's responses, and restatements of the trait in his own words are to be recorded. If the informant states that all are Dirty, this should be recorded as such, and indeed certain theories predict that all outgroups will be perceived in the same way on certain traits. However, in such instances follow-up questions should ask, "Which tribe was thought to be the most hard-working?" etc. Even if the initial questions have provided two or three groups, it is desirable where informant interest and discrimination permit to follow up by asking for the extremes. "Which tribe was the dirtiest?" "Which tribe was the cleanest?"

Order effects, fatigue effects, attention and recency of reminder effects, all create bias in such an inquiry, particularly in a section such as this where abstractions are involved. This bias as it affects differential attention to groups can be reduced if the ethnographer's inquiry and reminder list is in the different order specified in A.9. for each separate informant and if in reminding on different traits, the groups are offered in changing orders. To prevent order and fatigue effects from uniformly piling up on certain traits, we request the ethnographer to *reverse the order of items E.1. through E.17. every other* time he administers them, *keeping the numbers the same* regardless of order. To assure accuracy in analysis, the interview record should spell out the trait name.

For items E.1 to E.17. use this general stem:
"Of all the groups we have mentioned, including the (ingroup), which groups did the (ingroup) in those old days believe to be ——?"
The only exceptions for the use of this general stem are items E.5., E.6., E.11., and E.12., which have "men" or "women" beside them. For these, use one of the following stems with the appropriate sex:
"Of all the groups we have talked about, which groups did the (ingroup) believe to have —— men/women?"
Or if that does not translate smoothly, "Of all the groups we have been talking about, which groups did the (ingroup) think to have men/women who were ——, and which men/women who were ——?"

E.1. "Peaceful among themselves
or
Quarrelsome among themselves"

E.2. "Peaceful with neighboring tribes
or
Quarrelsome with other tribes"

E.3. "Honest and trustworthy
among their own people
or
Dishonest and treacherous among
their own people"

E.4. "Honest and trustworthy in
dealings with foreigners and
strangers
or
Dishonest and treacherous in
dealings with foreigners and
strangers"

E.5. "Hardworking men
or
Lazy men"

E.6. "Hardworking women
or
Lazy women"

E.7. "Brave
or
Cowardly"

E.8. "Dirty, filthy
or
Clean, sanitary"

E.9. "Stupid
or
Intelligent, clever"

E.10. "Weak physically
(muscle strength)
or
Strong muscled"

E.11. "Handsome, beautiful men
or
Unattractive, ugly men"

E.12. "Handsome, beautiful women
or
Unattractive, ugly women"

E.13. "Had strong magical powers
or
Had weak magical powers"

E.14. "Friendly, warm, hospitable
or
Unfriendly, cold, inhospitable"

E.15. "Sexually restrictive,
controlled
or
Sexually immoral"

E.16. "Cruel
or
Not cruel"

E.17. "Distrusting of others,
suspicious
or
Trusting, gullible"

F. Questions About the Ingroup Parallel to B

F.1. "What names did the (ingroup) people use
in naming themselves? What did they name
their own tribe?" For each name: "What
was the meaning of that name? What other
meanings did that name have? In what ways
would the (ingroup) use that name?"

F.2. "What did the (ingroup) people think were
the good characteristics of the (ingroup)
people?"

F.3. "What did the (ingroup) people think were
the sins, weaknesses, and bad characteristics
of the (ingroup) people?"

G. Evaluation of Trait Pairs Used in E

(Ask for each of the pairs in E.) "Did the
(ingroup) people in those long ago times think
it better (more virtuous) to be ——— or ———?"
Explain if necessary that groups differ in what
things they regard as good. Get explanations on
unlikely or puzzling responses. In records use
numbers G.1. through G.17. in parallel to E.1.
through E.17. (Campbell and LeVine 1965:1–9
4–39.)[1]

[1] For perspective on the field manual excerpts here
given, the section headings of omitted sections are as
follows:

II. Interviews with Bilingual Informants on Relevant
Vernacular Terminology
   A. Concepts of social organization
   B. Concepts of aggression
III. H. Special interview for outgroup member
IV. Interviews on Internal Features of the Group
   I. Aggression
   J. Sexual behavior
   K. Other behavior patterns
   L. Beliefs and rituals
   M. Child rearing practices
   N. Authority patterns
V. Geographic and Ethnographic Background Ma-
terials
   A. Sketch map of region
   B. Report on geographical and ecological setting
and features of region
   C. Report on "objective" group differences
within the region
   D. Report on linguistic differences within the
region
   E. Report on military history
   F. Background data on the group studied

METHODOLOGICAL CONSIDERATIONS

1. *Indigenous instances and the retrospective focus.*[2] Casual observations of daily
events offer convincing evidence that there

[2] We are indebted to *The Journal of Conflict Resolution* for permission to reprint, with modification,
pages 86–90 of Vol. 5, 1961 (Campbell and LeVine
1961), as points 1, 2, and 3 in what follows.

is no foreseeable shortage of material for
the student of intergroup hostility. Why then
this strenuous effort to get data under the
expensive conditions of anthropological field
work, and with a focus upon traditional
rather than current group relations? The
answer is comparable to that motivating all

cross-cultural work. For testing hypotheses about social process and group structure, the maximum heterogeneity of cultural forms is needed. Furthermore, the greater the independence among the instances, the more powerfully do the data probe the theory. The westernization of the world brings with it new and powerful ethnocentrisms. Both through processes of diffusion and through reactions to a common outgroup, we may soon have available only widespread replications of two or three basic cultural forms of intergroup imagery. Thus through reaction to a similar pattern of domination, a common pattern of anti-colonialism is absorbing more and more of the ethnocentric energies of peoples in the underdeveloped areas. For historical reasons, this pattern is fused with anti-Western-Europeanism, anti-Caucasianism, anti-capitalism, and (from our point of view) anti-democratic-bloc-ism, since the white Western-European capitalistic democracies have been the colonial powers. Europe's traditional class warfare ideology (containing many ethnocentric features) has been diffused to become one base for new-nation nationalistic ethnocentrism, since indigenous peoples with colonial domination have for years found their most accessible allies in the labor movements of the colonial nations ruling them. This couples readily with the diffusion of the East-West, communist-capitalist bloc conflict pattern. Moreover, a dominant diffusion item has long been the European model for the national state. With these powerful and highly relevant foci for ingroup-outgroup identification, the currently irrelevant and obstructing traditional local jealousies will be under strong acculturation pressure, and their elimination will become a major goal of all educational systems. While the dynamics of ethnocentrism will no doubt remain, the researcher may be soon faced with but one or two universally diffused instances, a trivial numerical base upon which to build empirical generalizations. It is thus the intent of the present study to place its major focus upon the pattern of intergroup relations such as might have existed prior to European contact. While there is also an interest in the most salient current ingroup-outgroup orientations, the interview is oriented toward a retrospective recall of traditional patterns.

There is correspondingly an emphasis upon

obtaining large numbers of ethnic groups. It would be desirable, for example, to have as many as one hundred groups as a basis for the study of relationships. The numbers employed in many cross-cultural studies are very small numbers, coupled with the very large number of hypotheses tested (cross-tabulations made), allow for very striking relationships to appear which are purely the product of capitalization upon chance. The problem is the same whether qualitative interpretations or quantitative scores are used. For tests of hypotheses dealing with individual differences or life history variables in rats or men, the supply of instances is so great that the science will never exhaust its ability to test hypotheses. For the sciences of culture and social organization, this is not the case, however, and every unique culture is needed in the record before it disappears.

2. *Number of respondents: anthropological vs. survey-research standards.* In the very first draft of the inquiry schedule distributed to a large number of interested social scientists (Campbell and LeVine 1961:82) for comments, we suggested that it be used "as an informant interview to be administered to as few as two to five individuals." This phrase drew no comment from the anthropologists responding, presumably because it was within the normal bounds of field work practice (although crowding the upper limits of redundancy). It did draw criticism from experienced survey-researchers and psychologists with cross-cultural field work experience who insisted upon larger numbers of interviews within each group, with perhaps twenty to fifty as a minimum. We do, of course, endorse the desirability of as many interviews as possible if other equally important values are not sacrificed. The other values almost certain to be sacrificed are: first, the number of ethnic groups studied, and second, the number of topics about which ethnographic data are collected. With the expense of anthropological field work and with interviews proceeding at a rate of two or three per month, we have asked for four replications of each part of the schedule, conducted through several interpreters if possible. Less than half of our collaborators have actually met this standard. Some have stopped after one very good informant, requiring urgent

persuasion to get up to our practical minimum, two.

The choice point of more reliable data on fewer instances or less data on more instances is one which correlational field studies of all types face, and is one for which in some instances a mathematical solution of optimal strategy is possible. Transposed to the correlational study of individual differences it becomes the relative advantage of increasing the number of questions dealing with the same attitude asked of each respondent (and thus increasing the reliability of the attitude score) versus using the same energy to increase the number of persons interviewed. The increase in reliability will increase the magnitude of correlations obtained, thus increasing one's confidence in (or the statistical significance of) the relationship. Increasing the number of cases upon which the relationship is based, even though it does not affect the magnitude of the correlation, has a similar effect upon confidence (or statistical significance). Neither relationship is linear. Estimating the reliability of the measure and the magnitude of the "true" correlation, the optimal strategy can be determined for the specific instance.

In our situation, the "reliability" of relevance becomes the correlation across the population of cultures of data supplied by two interviewers (technically, the intraclass correlation). The higher this reliability, the less the gain from duplicating interviews within a culture. With regard to this, we tentatively make the assumption that this reliability is greater when the respondent takes the role of "informant," reporting upon the group consensus, than when the focus is upon his "own opinions" and upon individual differences in attitude within the culture. This assumption is potentially open to empirical check. (For a quantitative comparison of informants in an across-groups correlational study within our own culture, see Campbell 1955.)

To put the argument another way, the greatest increment in knowledge occurs when we shift from zero informants to one informant. From there on, there is diminishing utility or informational increment for each new informant. While some similar diminishing utility function holds for the social scientist in adding new cultures, this latter resource is so much scarcer as to be much more precious. Looking at the present achievements of cross-cultural correlational study, we note that striking relationships have been established upon the basis of data much less systematic and reliable than that called for in our suggested four-informant interviews. Furthermore, the need for more data which one feels in studying such research is pre-eminently for cross-validation upon a new set of cultures, as opposed to better data within each of the cultures already studied, although admittedly both needs are felt.

3. *Uniformity of interview administration and confounded error.* Another place where survey procedures and anthropological field work traditions may be at cross-purposes has to do with the rigidity or the uniformity with which the inquiry schedule is administered. With each ethnic group introducing both a different language and a different cultural model into which the informant interview is interpreted or rationalized, it is of course recognized that interviews will be inevitably less uniform than in survey research work within the United States. At the same time, our schedule asks for more uniformity between ethnographers than is now the case in anthropological field work. In guiding the inevitable compromise it seems well to make explicit some of the issues, the values, and the hazards involved.

On the side of flexibility for the ethnographer to re-ask, restate, explain, and cross-examine informants, and to eliminate questions which the informant has already answered incidentally, we have these arguments: The communication problems involved are tremendous. There is no point in collecting data which the ethnographer does not trust, answers to questions which he believes are evasive or deceitful. Insistence upon a very rigid adherence to a schedule, requiring an exact usage of the printed words whenever an English-speaking interpreter is used, etc., might easily defeat its purpose in providing data which the ethnographer himself believes to be worthless. Uniformity may in some instances reduce rather than enhance the interpretability. For instance, suppose we learn that the A's regard the B's as "greedy" in the course of a garrulous monologue elicited by some tangential question—a monologue which an opinion pollster might shut off by saying, "We'll come to those topics later." We would be more certain of this item in such a case than if it had been only later elicited by the taciturn naming of B's in a routinized response to "greedy" in the long list of traits. Similarly, consider that two respondents have alleged B's to be greedy— we will have greater confidence in this result in the case in which two different interpreters were used, or in which two different translation terms for "greedy" have been used, than for the case in which exactly the same procedures have been employed. This preference is an extension of that by which we would feel greater confirmation from agreement between two separate informants than from agreement between repetitions of the interview with a single informant. The principle involved may be designated that of "heterogeneity of irrelevancies," or the "diversification of biases" (LeVine, Chapter 21, Outsiders' Judgments: An Ethnographic Approach to Group Differences in Personality, this volume). The more irrelevant factors have been randomized, the less likely we shall mistake the effect of one of them for the effect of the factors we seek to investigate.

Such encouragements of diversity must not be confused with the perhaps greater danger that systematic deviations from the interview schedule (e.g., deviations running through all of the interviews done in a given culture, or all done by a given ethnographer in several cultures) could generate spurious relationships. Thus if the ethnographer always gives the same concrete illustration to a too-abstract question, the effects of this illustration may systematically bias the results, giving the interviews a higher consistency and reliability, but one that is spurious. Heterogeneity *within* the interviews of a single ethnographer are thus no necessary threat to validity and may even lead to gain, while *heterogeneity between ethnographers* when systematic within any one ethnographer, will be a source of decreased validity. The systematic idiosyncracies of the interpreter are probably an even more likely source of bias than are those of the ethnographer, and the use of several interpreters is essential.

4. *The ethnographer's awareness of the purpose of the study.* There is increasing awareness of the possible bias in field work of strong commitment to pre-observational hypotheses, or of knowing the study designer's purposes (e.g., Rosenthal 1966). These considerations might have lead us to keeping the ethnographer uninformed of our hypotheses. They did not, and in fact we went to the other extreme of providing each collaborator with a two-hundred-page review of competing theories on ethnocentrism and intergroup conflict. We justified this as follows:

The following chapters attempt an assembly of propositions from a number of social science theories, applicable to the general content area of ethnocentrism, particularly as testable with anthropological data. These chapters in their present form are far from being polished or definitive analyses and employ a variety of expository styles. They should, nonetheless, be of use to collaborators in the Cross-Cultural Study of Ethnocentrism in illustrating some of the potential range of issues and modes of analysis to which the data being collected are relevant.

One function should be to increase the ethnographer's sensitivity to relevant observations not specifically covered in the field manual. Another utility is that through knowing the interpretative use to which the data are to be put, the ethnographer should be in a better position to note misleading aspects of the data collected and to provide warnings as to their interpretation. In addition, it is also hoped that this over-view of a number of theories might result in a type of enlightened objectivity. The problem of bias is always present whenever an observer goes into an ambiguous situation as a strong partisan of a single theory. One control for this sometimes employed is to keep the field worker in the dark as to the purposes and hopes of the study designers. This approach is not judged to be feasible in the present study and would, we believe, result in a poorer quality of data, a mechanical collection of answers to questions often misleading or uninterpretable in that form. Instead, it is hoped that the recognition of multiple competing theories will create a theoretically motivated concern for collecting those data that will help decide among them, an objectivity resulting not from ignorance of theoretical issues, but rather from an awareness of a multiplicity of competing theories, with no one of which is the investigator so emotionally identified that disconfirmation becomes personally ego-deflating. We believe that the effort of preparing this analysis has helped move us from being defensive partisans of a single theory to more of an objective concern for the comparison of competing theories in the adequacy with which they fit the data. (Campbell and LeVine 1965:1–2)

All field-manual studies we know of, including the one on optical illusion (Segall *et al.* 1966), have taken a similar position concerning informing field workers about hypotheses, but the Whiting *et al. Field Guide* does not include competing hypotheses. In that study the field teams and senior investigators constituted a research group with a single theoretical orientation that could have biased the research, but part of their shared viewpoint was a strong skepticism about the empirical validity of their own hypotheses that was considered an adequate antidote to the apparent theoretical bias.

5. *Degree of specification of procedures.* The excerpts above represent a current extreme in the direction of specification of field work procedures. Most of the field manuals specify the information wanted rather than how to go about getting it. The Whiting *et al. Field Guide* is divided into sections on cultural data, where the information desired is specified, and sections on individual measures where methods are made more explicit. Our field manual also eliminates specific instructions on data collection techniques when it comes to those classes of information which are professionally central to social anthropology, as on sociopolitical structure, territorial units, household organization, leadership, and societal complexity. Even in the sections sampled above, we definitely do not aspire to the degree of specification typical of the public opinion surveys of sociologists. This is seen in our apology for suggesting specific questions, in our statement that these specific second-person wordings are intended to inform the ethnographer as to the content we want, and in our emphasis that it is the information we want, no matter how obtained.

Nonetheless, the degree of specification is extreme, and it is probably on this issue that the major future methodological controversies will center. Epistemological issues are involved. On the one hand is the logical positivist's demand for completely explicit operations, and with this the search for certainty in explicit particulars. This extreme we certainly reject (Campbell, Chapter 3, this volume), and recognize that the matching of particulars across cultures must certainly depend upon a prior, context-dependent matching of whole patterns. Ludicrously useless would be a cross-cultural comparison of yes-no answers to an isolated single question administered by a stranger who had just arrived. We acknowledge our context-dependence by requiring that our inquiry be done by an anthropologist thoroughly familiar with the area, and that he not accept answers he believes are wrong or based upon a misunderstood question.

Favoring methodological explicitness is a general perspectival relativism which most anthropologists would accept. A given object will be seen differently from different perspectives, and we gain increased comparability when we are able to maximize perspectival comparability. Ideally we would use several independent methodological perspectives in every setting (the use of the anthropologist's wife as a field worker is a recurrent example), but where we cannot, to specify the perspective used, and to attempt parallel perspectives, perhaps removes one needless irrelevant source of differences in cross-cultural comparison.

Even with our degree of explicitness, the data we get are disappointingly far from the comparability of public opinion interviews done within the United States. We may not, in fact, be achieving more comparability than do the other field manuals which pay attention only to what to learn, not how to learn it. A chance to compare may become available. In James Watson's micro-evolution study in the New Guinea Highlands several of his collaborators have also done the ethnocentrism inquiry. While Watson's group did not technically use a "field manual," they did prepare some hundred pages of memoranda (Watson *et al.* 1961–1962) designed to increase comparability among the four ethnographies. We should be able to compare the comparisons on content covered by ours. No doubt both provide greater comparability than that achieved through content coding of ethnographies done for other or more general purposes.

Our collaborators uniformly report that working with our field manual is *much* more fatiguing, both for them and for the informant, than is ordinary field work. Most of them advise us, however, not to relax our standards or efforts for comparability. Why should the fatigue be so much greater? The answers are very revealing for the whole approach. An important feature is *whose* agenda of interests sets the course of conversation. In ordinary field work, as in friendly discussion in general, the local informant's interests predominate, the anthropologist willingly learning of those topics seeming most interesting to his newfound friend. In field-manual ethnography, the ethnographer (or more properly, the field-manual designer) sets the agenda. While in our field manual, we have tried to relax this rigidity, the contrast with ordinary field work becomes great. A second reason for field-manual fatigue comes from a distinction between listening and asking. Many topics and content areas are best and most validly learned of by listening, not asking—by passively waiting for the topic to come up incidentally and indirectly. The field-manual approach is just not suited for such topics, and cannot claim to be an all-purpose tool. A third and most important reason has to do with the method of establishing the *absence* of a given trait. In the quantitative cross-cultural studies based on the Human Relations Area Files or other ethnographic reports, absence is determined sometimes by the ethnographer's report on the trait's absence, but more often on his failure to mention it. Even where the ethnographer explicitly states an absence, his evidence may essentially be a failure to see or hear mention of the trait. Granted the incompleteness of all ethnographies, there is great ambiguity about absences. The field-manual approach, at least as used by us, asks directly about presence or absence. This is fine where the trait is present, and often brings up interesting features that might never have spontaneously emerged. But where the trait is absent, the interview becomes very frustrating, with the informant and ethnographer unable to be sure they are understanding each other.

The fatigue of field-manual ethnography sets very real limits on the amount of it that can be scheduled. Our two-month commitment is probably at the upper limit or beyond.

6. *Variations in data quality and the observational base.* Even with the most realistically designed field manual and the most dedicated professional field workers, there is likely to be considerable variation among field workers in their levels of acquaintance with and experience in the cultures and communities studied, and this is bound to affect the quality of the data they produce. In terms of Naroll's (1962) criteria of ethnographic data quality, field workers will vary in the total length of time they spend in the field, their mastery of the local language, and their exposure to the cultural behavior of comparative interest. The more experienced and knowledgeable field worker who has undergone a more thorough socialization into the culture of the group can bring a more complete contextual understanding to the tasks the field manual demands of him and, theoretically, obtain a more valid set of data for comparative analysis. For a project like the Cross-Cultural Study of Ethnocentrism, in which the focus is on past history to be reconstructed from informant interviews, data quality can be largely controlled in the ways discussed above. For projects with a contemporaneous focus like the Six Culture Study, however, in which observational data and informant accounts are combined, special problems arise: What relative weights does the field worker assign to what he has actually witnessed as opposed to what he has been told about by informants? Does not the field worker with a longer and more intensive field experience have a greater observational base from which to assess the accuracy of his informants' accounts and on which to build more searching and meaningful interviews? A reading of the field workers' comments in the *Field Guide* by Whiting *et al.* (1966) leaves no doubt that these issues arise and must be faced by the comparative analyst. We raise these problems in passing not to solve them, for our ethnocentrism study has given us no special competence to discuss them and they should be treated at length elsewhere, but because they must be taken seriously into account by any designer of a field manual dealing with contemporary patterns of cultural or individual behavior. Insofar as the field manual is simply a set of instructions for administering a psychological test, like the optical illusion study of Segall *et al.,* (1966), this type of problem is of little urgency, but when the manual is an attempt to make conventional ethnography more comparable, like the cultural part of the Six Cultures Field Guide, then it demands detailed attention in the manual's instructions. Current trends in ethnographic data collection would seem to recommend treating ethnographic observation in a given behavioral domain, and the recording of informants' views of behavior patterns in that domain, as separate tasks and independent data source to be checked against one another.

7. *Publication rights and "ownership" of data.* Collaborative projects present special problems in regard to publication, around which there have been serious conflicts and

frustrations. Occasionally there are bitter misunderstandings about "ownership" of the data, or about the relative importance in the collaborative product of the study designer or the data collector. More frequent are frustrating delays due to the bottleneck of unified or joint publication.

Our recommendation in this situation is an explicit recognition of ownership of dual rights, with the field worker free to publish what he has collected. Such a policy has been applied without noticeable harm in the optical illusion study (Segall *et al.*, 1966), in which several of the cooperators published on their own data prior to the major report, one scooping the project by as much as seven years. In that study the collaborators donated their own time, but even where they are salaried research associates, this seems to be an optimal solution.

In most collaborative comparative studies, as in our own, there is a natural division of labor furthering this decision. There is the intensive specialization on a specific culture, which we can conceptualize as a vertical dimension of concern and the primary focus of the ethnographer. Orthogonal to this is the horizontal interest of the field-manual designer, a comparison across cultures on a narrow band of data.

In an effort to make explicit many issues which we believed to have caused misunderstandings in other studies, we prepared, and have generally used, the following "contract":

STATEMENT OF AGREEMENT WITH COLLABORATORS

Because of the novel relationship involved in this study, it seems well to reach agreement in advance on issues which in some previous studies have provided bases for misunderstanding when not made explicit at the beginning.

1. *Mutual rights to use of data.* Although the ethnographer is employed as a research associate of the Study, and is thus obligated to provide the Study with a copy of all field notes (including interview records, etc.) collected during the period of employ, he is also free to retain a copy of all such field notes, and is free to publish articles and books based upon these field notes, as long as such publication contains an acknowledgment of the support provided by this project and involves no restrictions of copyright or otherwise which would restrain the Study from utilizing the data for its purposes.

2. *Obligations of the ethnographer.* The ethnographer is obligated to turn over promptly to the Study all the field notes, interviews, back-group information, etc., which are specified in the Study's field manual, and to cooperate in providing such supporting information as may be required to make the data comprehensible for the central comparative analysis. (He is not obligated by this agreement to provide subsequently an ethnographic write-up of his field material. It is hoped, however, that he will take responsibility for a regional ethnography covering the material he has collected.)

3. *Obligations of the Study to the ethnographer.* The Study is obliged to provide the ethnographer with a copy of all field notes and interview records where the sole copy or recording has been turned over to the Study for transcription. The Study is obliged to provide the ethnographer with a copy of all summaries made of his materials. The Study is obliged to acknowledge the participation of the ethnographer in all publications utilizing material which he has collected. Were a publication to be focused solely on material collected by him (as in an instance where the Study takes responsibility for the write-up of the regional ethnography) the ethnographer is to be offered the status of co-author even though he may have made no contribution to the writing (although even in this case his editorial comments will be solicited).

4. *Privileged material.* The Study recognizes that the moral obligations of the ethnographer to his informants may result in the restriction from publication of privileged material. However, the Study reserves the right to utilize such material in those uses which prevent identification through pooling the data from peoples all over the world.

8. *Recording and transmitting of field notes.* The most common mode of recording the field notes has been by paper and pencil during the interview with the ethnographer filling out and transcribing as soon as possible afterwards. This initial note-taking is in English if the ethnographer is working with an interpreter. If he is working directly in the local language, his field notes may be in English by on-the-spot translation, or are more likely in the local language and require translation later.

The use of a tape recorder during the interview produces ampler notes, not necessarily more coherent, and adds listening and transcribing time to an already tedious process. A technique used in one instance for obtaining rather full records in work through interpreters is as follows: In the interview itself, the interpreter made on-the-spot oral translations, which the ethnographer then used to guide further inquiry. The whole interchange in both languages was taped. Later, the interpreter played the tape back step-by-step, writing out a more detailed translation of the informant's responses. This written translation process takes four or five hours for every hour transcribed, and is best undertaken with a staff of two or three interpreters. It is reasonable field work investment where such resources are available, and would probably now be our recommended procedure where the ethnographer is to work through interpreters, and perhaps even where not. Rough though these translations may be, they are usable. Postponed translating, to be done by the ethnographer himself, is certainly the most expensive of all.

There are ethnographers with a capacity for working sixteen hours a day, who get their field notes into presentable form by editing and typing them each night while their informants sleep. Such ethnographers are ready to turn over their field notes to us as soon as the field work is done. We have encountered one or two of these, but most have found it necessary to postpone the editing and translating, often for years. We should have scheduled a one- or two-month salaried period, augmented with secretarial funds, for editing the two months of field work, and for supplying the information requested in the non-interview parts of the field manual.

The form in which the data are turned over to the project need not, of course, be as field notes. It could also be in the form of integrated ethnographic essays addressed to the questions raised, and based upon all of the information at the ethnographer's disposal. The specification of field notes was made primarily in an effort to avoid the long delays which ethnographic writing entails. By and large, our coders would find essays easier to code than field notes, because an essay is consistent, integrated, and interpreted. The essay may very well be argued to be a more accurate portrayal than the more voluminous field notes upon which it is based, and with some of which it disagrees. To regard the field notes as a firmer scientific base is perhaps like looking for greater clarity by examining the details of the television picture with a magnifying glass.

Not only are field notes weaker in their particularity and consistency, they are also less interpretable to coders for other reasons —they are framed in perspectives and reference levels unknown to the coder, in a language which is only superficially shared. The language and perspectives of the ethnographer's essay is much more certainly shared by the coders. The translation process has been carried one step further.

We are not seriously suggesting that ethnographic essays be substituted for field notes as the mode of data exchange. The increased delays in delivery would make that utterly unfeasible. But if it were to turn out that the field-manual approach were to be less effective in establishing cross-cultural correlations than are the published ethnographies of the Human Relations Area Files (we are not anticipating that this will be so), this issue would be focal.

The superior clarity of the ethnographic essay is of course in part specious. The integration and gestalt achieved reads more persuasively whether accurate or not. Consider the analogy of the television-transmitted pictures from Lunar Orbiter: the transmission is full of random static, and of systematic features that are due to the mechanics of the process, not the moon. The computer programs that "clean up" these pictures pick up statistical regularities that they attribute to the moon, and discard small discrepancies from these as error. The pictures end up more interpretable, and in this case no doubt more valid. But a certain degree of forced overclarification, of falsification, is no doubt involved. These computer programs would produce some degree of pattern and order even were the input pure static, just as do factor analysis programs when fed random numbers instead of data. Analogously, many of the perceived patterns of culture are imposed by the mind of the observer.

Field-manual anthropology must continue to explore alternatives in the means of communicating between the anthropologist's field experience and the coding categories relevant to theory. Tangentially it may be remarked that our big expansion of the field manual between the published 1961 version that was used in the field in 1963 and 1964, was due to the inclusion of content specifically related to our propositional analysis of competing theories. Much of this proposition-specific content produced extremely awkward interview questions which were then eliminated in our fall 1964 revision conference, moving the schedule back to a more general content-area focus.

One alternative is to let the ethnographer do the coding. Questionnaires to anthropologists asking them to be informants after they have returned from the field have met with only mixed success, and are not what we are suggesting. Suppose one sent to the ethnographer in the field, as a kind of field manual, coding instructions such as one would provide an analyst working with HRAF material. This would include for each dimension clear-cut illustrations of each coding category or of extreme and intermediate points on a rating scale. These illustrations would be extensive excerpts from published ethnographies, providing context as well as specifics. The ethnographer's assignment might then be to do enough inquiry of his own devising to do a decision on each dimension—or he might do this as a supplement to a focused inquiry schedule such as presented here.

BIBLIOGRAPHY

ALLEN, G.
1879   *The colour-sense: its origin and development*. London, Trubner.

CAMPBELL, D. T.
1961   The mutual methodological relevance of anthropology and psychology. In F. L. K. Hsu, ed., *Psychological anthropology: approaches to culture and personality*. Homewood, Ill., Dorsey Press.
1965   Ethnocentric and other altruistic motives. In D. Levine, ed., *The Nebraska symposium on motivation 1965*. Lincoln, University of Nebraska Press.
1967   Stereotypes and the perception of group differences. *American Psychologist* 22: 812–829.

CAMPBELL, D. T., and R. A. LEVINE
1961   A proposal for cooperative cross-cultural research on ethnocentrism. *Journal of Conflict Resolution* 5 (1):82–108.
1965   *Propositions about ethnocentrism from social science theories*. Northwestern University, mimeo.

CAMPBELL, D. T., and J. C. STANLEY
1966   *Experimental and quasi-experimental design for research*. Chicago, Rand McNally. Reprinted from N. L. Gage, ed., *Handbook of research on teaching*. Chicago, Rand McNally, 1963.

CLIGNET, R.
1970   A critical evaluation of concomitant variation studies. In this volume.

EGGAN, F.
1954   Social anthropology and the method of controlled comparison. *American Anthropologist* 56, 5, Part 1.

HERSKOVITS, M. J., D. T. CAMPBELL, and M. H. SEGALL
1969   *Materials for a cross-cultural study of perception*, 2nd ed. Indianapolis, Bobbs-Merrill.

LEACH, E. R.
1961   Golden bough or gilded twig? *Daedalus* 90:371–387.

LEVINE, R. A.
1965   Socialization, social structure, and intersocietal images. In Herbert Kelman, ed., *International behavior: a social psychological analysis*. New York, Holt, Rinehart, and Winston.
1966   Outsiders' judgments: an ethnographic approach to group differences in personality. *Southwestern Journal of Anthropology* 22 (2):101–116. Reprinted in this volume.
1970   Research design in anthropological field work. In this volume.

LEVINE, R. A., and D. T. CAMPBELL
1965   *Ethnocentrism field manual*. The Cross-Cultural Study of Ethnocentrism, supported by a grant from the Carnegie Corporation of New York to Northwestern University.

MAGNUS, H.
1883   *Über ethnologische untersuchungen des farbensinnes*. Breslau.

MINTURN, L., and W. W. LAMBERT
1964   *Mothers of six cultures: antecedents of child rearing*. New York, Wiley.

MORGAN, L. H.
1871   *Systems of consanguinity and affinity in the human family*. Smithsonian Contribution to Knowledge, Vol. 17. Washington, U. S. Government Printing Office.

MURDOCK, G. P.
1949   *Social structure*. New York: Macmillan.

NAROLL, R.
1962   *Data quality control: a new research technique*. Glencoe, Ill., Free Press.

ROSENTHAL, R.
1966   *Experimenter effects in behavioral research*. New York, Appleton-Century-Crofts.

ROYAL ANTHROPOLOGICAL INSTITUTE OF GREAT BRITAIN AND IRELAND, A COMMITTEE OF
1874   *Notes and Queries on Anthropology*. London, Routledge and Kegan Paul. 1st ed., 1874; 6th ed., 1951.

SEGALL, M. H., D. T. CAMPBELL, and M. J. HERSKOVITS
1966 *The influence of culture on visual perception.* Indianapolis, Bobbs-Merrill.
SLOBIN, D. I., S. M. ERVIN-TRIPP, J. J. GUMPERZ, J. BRUKMAN, K. KERNAN, C. MITCHELL, and B. STROSS
1967 *A field manual for cross-cultural study of the acquisition of communicative competence.* University of California, Berkeley. Multilith, second draft.
WATSON, J. B.
1963 A micro-evolution study in New Guinea. *Journal of the Polynesian Society* 72:188–192.
WATSON, J. B., *et al.*
1961– *New Guinea micro-evolution studies.*
1962 Memoranda, 3, 4, 5, 9, and 10, work papers parts I, II, and III, September 18, 1961, to August 25, 1962. Duplicated,

Department of Anthropology, University of Washington.
WERNER, O., and D. T. CAMPBELL
1970 Translating, working through interpreters, and the problem of decentering. In this volume.
WHITING, B. B., I. L. CHILD, W. W. LAMBERT, and J. W. M. WHITING
1963 *Six cultures: studies of child rearing.* New York, Wiley.
WHITING, J. W. M., and I. L. CHILD
1953 *Child training and personality: a cross-cultural study.* New Haven, Yale University Press.
WHITING, J. W. M., I. L. CHILD, W. W. LAMBERT, A. M. FISCHER, C. NYDEGGER, W. NYDEGGER, H. MARETZKI, T. MARETZKI, L. MINTURN, K. ROMNEY, and R. ROMNEY
1966 *Field guide for the study of socialization.* New York, Wiley. Multilith edition 1954.

CHAPTER 21

Outsiders' Judgments: An Ethnographic Approach to Group Differences in Personality

ROBERT A. LEVINE

Despite recent advances in psychological anthropology, behavioral dispositions such as personality traits, attitudes, motives, and values often prove elusive to cross-cultural measurement. The knotty methodological problems involved in scientifically conscientious culture and personality work have caused many potentially interested anthropologists to flee to subject matters, such as social structure and language, in which there is more agreement concerning units of analysis and measurement procedures. Those who have not fled frequently seek aid from psychological testing procedures, but without entirely allaying doubts concerning the reliability and validity of instruments such as projective techniques for cross-cultural research. The difficulty of achieving intersubjective agreement on measuring instruments makes it imperative that psychological anthropologists search widely for methodological solutions which seem truly appropriate to cross-cultural study rather than adhere rigidly to routines imported from the psychology of individual differences. The method proposed in this article may be viewed as a radical solution, the exposition of which will serve to emphasize the importance of the search itself.

On the surface, there would seem to be nothing further from what we are seeking

This article is a working paper of the Cross-Cultural Study of Ethnocentrism, supported by a grant from the Carnegie Corporation of New York to Northwestern University. The ideas presented herein derive from the general analysis of knowledge processes set forth by Donald T. Campbell (1965). Campbell originally suggested the relevance of his analysis to intercultural perception of group differences in personality and encouraged the present author in attempting a systematic application.

in the measurement of cross-cultural differences in personality than the images, beliefs, and stereotypes which ethnic groups hold concerning each other. We are likely to judge the "objective" or "scientific" character of a piece of culture and personality work by its attempts to depart from and its independence of the popular stereotypes of outgroups which are widespread among non-anthropologists of all cultures. Yet there are conditions under which most anthropologists are prepared to accept, albeit tentatively, an intuitive attribution of a distinctive behavioral disposition to the members of a group, viz., when the attribution is made by a professionally qualified ethnographer on the basis of an adequate field experience. The terms "professionally qualified ethnographer" and "adequate field experience" can be defined in terms of attempts to reduce certain kinds of bias which are believed to operate in intercultural perception. A "professionally qualified ethnographer" is a person who (a) has learned to suspend moral judgment and ingroup loyalty while obtaining knowledge about cultures other than his own, (b) has had experience in generalizing from an array of specific ethnographic facts reported by others to a pattern characteristic of a group, (c) has had experience in comparing characteristic patterns of one group to those of another with respect to a common dimension of culture or social structure. The first qualification is supposed to reduce his tendency to make *loyalistic misperceptions* of foreign cultures. In these, the observer makes incorrect generalizations about the other group because he wants to prove his own group's superiority (through exaggerating differences or overemphasizing the outgroup's deviation from his own group's standards) or to justify the opposition or oppression by his own group to the outgroup. The professionally qualified ethnographer is presumed to be free of this bias motivated by ingroup loyalty and is in this respect deemed *a priori* a more accurate observer of outgroup behavior than an average person from the same culture. The second and third qualifications are supposed to reduce the tendencies to conclude mistakenly that some particular act or practice indicates a general pattern and to overlook relevant acts or practices—"errors of hasty judgment" characteristic of untrained observers. Thus we trust the ethnographer's attribution of a behavioral disposition to a group more than that of a non-ethnographer, in part because we assume that the ethnographer's training has reduced his susceptibility to the biases referred to as "loyalistic misperception" and "errors of hasty judgment."

"Adequate field experience" is extended exposure to diverse aspects of the functioning and thought of a group through observation, conversation, and "participation." This kind of experience is alleged to reduce further (though not eliminate) the possibility of the ethnographer's concluding that certain acts or practices form a general pattern when in fact they do not or of omitting in the formulation of a general pattern certain acts or practices which are actually related to the ones included—the "errors of hasty judgment" mentioned above. Just as the "professionally qualified ethnographer" is contrasted with the untrained observer, so "adequate field experience" is contrasted with a casual visit in terms of the probability of forming accurate generalizations. Furthermore, anthropologists are aware that field experience does not allow for perfect accuracy and that such experiences vary widely in adequacy. The established professional consensus is that the longer the ethnographer's residence in the field situation and the greater his command of the local language, the more adequate is the field experience. The effects of these variables on ethnographic judgments of group behavior have been shown in cross-cultural study (Naroll 1962). The general point is that the greater the exposure of the ethnographer to the particularities of a group's acts and beliefs, the less likely is he to make incorrect general statements con-

cerning the patterning of those acts and beliefs. But the likelihood is not reduced to nil.

Now, the ethnographer in the field situation depends in part on another type of observer: the informant. What is an "informant"? He is usually a group member who, due either to generally superior inductive and verbal skills or to a life history which has exposed him to the types of behavioral contrasts in which we are interested (e.g., "cultural marginality"), is capable of drawing generalizations from the particularities of his social environment and communicating them to an ethnographer. The good informant is less likely than the ethnographer to misjudge ingroup behavior because of inadequate duration of residence or inadequate knowledge of the local language—he lacks these biases to which ethnographers as outsiders are susceptible. However, he is so close to the events on which he is reporting that other biases enter: his position in society and individual life history may cause him to misperceive the larger group and its functioning, both as error resulting from a parochial point of view (with concomitant lack of awareness that other points of view exist) and as the motivated result of subgroup loyalties. The ethnographer reduces the net bias in his informants' accounts by diversification of informants, i.e., selecting informants who vary in social position, aspects of life history, and subgroup loyalty. Those points in which such diverse informants agree are accepted as probably valid unless the ethnographer has good reason to believe that a common bias is operating. One such common bias is the loyalistic misperception of ingroup behavior by informants, their tendency to glorify or justify the entire ingroup. The ethnographer has two defenses against this— a request for details and particulars, the response to which may reveal inconsistencies in generalization, and independent observations of the events concerned.

This somewhat tortuous reconstruction of ethnographic epistemology suggests that it is widely, if implicitly, recognized by anthropologists that biased human observers (such as ethnographers and informants) can produce acceptable generalizations concerning group behavior so long as their biases are known and there is a strategy available for eliminating, reducing, or controlling these biases. The biases of ethnographers are controlled through strategies of training (i.e., rehearsal of the processes of ethnographic generalization and comparison) and of criteria for exposure to the culture under study (length of residence in the field, knowledge of the local language). Working with his informants, the ethnographer employs a strategy which can be called the *diversification of biases,* in which misperceptions not widely shared cancel each other out, leaving a net information yield of generalizations supported by agreement among informants. If such generalizations are not regarded by the informants as particularly favorable to the group, the ethnographer may be inclined to accept them and to offer them to his professional colleagues as validated statements concerning group behavior. If the generalizations appear to involve ingroup glorification, the ethnographer will suspect his informants of shared loyalistic misperception and may have recourse to strategies for eliminating this bias, viz., the elicitation of fine-grain detail which can be examined for consistency with the reported general pattern, and ultimately with independent firsthand observations by the ethnographer *or others who are known not to share the loyalistic biases of the ingroup informants.* In addition, informants are likely to share another bias in perception which does not lead them to report falsehoods but only causes them not to report existing behavior patterns that appear to them universal and obvious because they are unacquainted with cultural contexts in which these behavior patterns are absent. This bias can only be eliminated by the use of an outside observer, be he the ethnographer or some other exotic person, preferably from a cultural context dissimilar to the one under study.

Ethnography, then, does not presume to be an infallible knowledge-gathering process but is most accurately seen as a series of operational strategies for reducing the biases known to affect human judgments of group behavior. If this view of ethnography be accepted, then the beliefs which outsiders hold concerning another group's behavior should not be dismissed as possible sources of data concerning that group; rather, we should ask, to what biases are outsiders susceptible, and what strategies can be devised for eliminating them? In considering these questions below, two types of outside judg-ments are distinguished: those of visitors or immigrants from another culture and those of informants from neighboring ethnic groups who may not have firsthand acquaintance with the group on whose behavior they are reporting. The use of the latter types of judgment for obtaining descriptions of group behavior is termed "reputational ethnography."

THE JUDGMENTS OF VISITORS AND IMMIGRANTS

It is widely accepted in anthropology that there are certain advantages to an ethnographer being a foreigner to the culture he is studying. The advantages are thought to be a broader comparative perspective, a freshness of approach to the cultural behavior under study, a greater tendency to question and investigate what an insider might take for granted. Before applying this line of reasoning specifically to non-ethnographic visitors, it is necessary to examine the psychological processes involved in the general case.

If a foreign visitor to an ethnic group engages in interaction with members of the group during his period of residence in their territory, he will inevitably be confronted with certain differences between his own group and theirs. This is because, in the course of his being socialized into his own culture, he has acquired a large number of interactive habits and expectations. In a foreign culture, some of these habits will prove inappropriate and some of the expectations will not be fulfilled. Each failure of a habit to lead to its usual goal, each instance of unfulfilled expectation, will teach him something about the foreign culture and its system of expectations. In order to make a minimal adaptation to the foreign environment, he will need to acquire a new set of habits and expectations, however fragmentary, and this acquisition will occur though trial-and-error matching of his own behavior patterns with those of the host group and through the direct tuition of guides who will spontaneously, or at the visitor's request, instruct him in behavior appropriate to their culture. It is important to note that, if his old habits and expectations worked in the new environment, he would not be required to notice behavioral differences between his culture and theirs; but if his usual responses do not work, *even the least curious visitor must notice such behavioral differences.* Insofar as the behavior required is dissimilar from that of his own group, he will perceive his own newly acquired habits and expectations as sharply discontinuous from those he uses at home. This sharp discontinuity in interactive patterns will enable him to comment on behavioral differences between his own group and the foreign group, but he is likely to formulate such a comment in terms of a distinctive attribute of the foreign group, taking his own group's patterns as the understood background against which the foreign group is contrasted. (This is as true of ethnographers, who traditionally treat in more elaborate detail customs which deviate from their own—but without making the comparison explicit—as it is of untrained visitors who innocently treat foreign customs as bizarre deviations from the universally appropriate norms of their own group.) Thus the position of the visitor as an adaptive organism in a new environment leads him inevitably to notice contrasts between old and new environmental demands, but he tends to conceptualize the contrast as an attribute of the foreign group.

It follows from this reconstruction of the visitor's experience that the visitor will be able to report more attributes (valid or not) of the group he visited (a) the more behavioral domains and role relationships in the group's sociocultural system he has sampled through participation, (b) the more intense his participation (or the less he is relieved of having to conform to group norms), and (c) the greater the dissimilarity between his own group's habits and expectations and those of the foreign group. Furthermore, the types of attributes on which he can report will correspond to the behavioral domains in which his interaction with the foreigners took place. Thus a trader may be able to comment on the honesty, efficiency, and intelligence of a foreign group with which he has dealt but have less to say about their domestic morality.

Of course the professional ethnographer's capacity to comment on the behavior of a group with which he has done field work goes far beyond the limits of his actual participation in role relationships and various cultural domains, because he samples many of these vicariously through questioning and nonparticipant observation. He may acquire through participation the habits and expectations appropriate to the roles of adult male or female, guest, host, employer, friend, community member, and fictionalized kinsman, but he is likely to learn the response patterns involved in marital roles, religious behavior, and many aspects of economic and political life only through active verbal inquiry and observation of the role performances of others. Since it is his explicit task to sample the habits and expectations of the group in each behavioral domain in any way he can (while conforming to some implicit ethical standards for ethnographic work), his task has a much less confining effect on his perceptions than that of the average single-purpose visitor such as the trader. On the other hand, however, the high status he is frequently accorded and his professional ethics may keep from the ethnographer's view areas of behavior which are perceived by other visitors who feel freer to follow their impulses and manipulate people. Furthermore, in areas of widespread multilingualism, a local trader may begin his visit to a people with considerable knowledge of their language, whereas the ethnographer usually knows little of it when he arrives.

From the above discussion it appears evident that there is sufficient overlap between the experiences of the ethnographer and that of the non-ethnographic visitor to consider seriously whether there are conditions under which we would be prepared to accept reports on group behavior by such visitors.

Any particular non-ethnographic visitor is likely to misperceive or inaccurately report group behavior for the following reasons: (a) insufficient duration of residence and hence insufficient opportunity to observe group behavior, (b) insufficient total interaction with members of the foreign group because of an enclave living pattern in the foreign territory, (c) loyalistic bias due to unfriendly or oppressive relations between the visitor's group and the foreign group, (d) functionally limited opportunities for observation because of specialized task orientation such as trading, (e) too great similarity between his own culture and that of the outgroup, so that he is prevented from perceiving their behavior as having distinctive attributes, (f) too great dissimilarity between his own culture and that of the outgroup, so that he perceives global contrasts and misses nuances of outgroup behavior, (g) personal motives and anxieties, (h) influence by beliefs of his own group concerning the outgroup.

If these biases can be eliminated or controlled, then visitors' reports should provide acceptable data on group behavior. This may be achieved through the following operations: first of all, set minimum criteria for length of residence and amount of interaction so that those visitors whose visits were very short or who never ventured from enclaves of foreigners are automatically rejected as informants. Second, select a set of visitor-informants varying on the following dimensions: (a) degree of amity-enmity between visitor's group and outgroup in question, (b) types of functional relations or role relationships between the visitor and outgroup members, (c) amount of cultural similarity (and spatial distance) between visitor's group and host group. This will result in a set of visitors: some of whom come from friendly, some from unfriendly groups; some of whom come to the group as traders, some as spouses of members, some as teachers, some as employers, etc.; some of whom come from culturally very similar groups, some from moderately similar groups, some from dissimilar groups; some from adjacent groups, some from a moderate distance, some from far away. Third, interview each of this diverse set of visitor-informants on the behavioral characteristics of the group in question. The biases peculiar to each group represented or to individual informants should appear as disagreements among the informants; the attributions on which all agree, having failed to be canceled out by diversification, cannot be regarded as resulting from any of the biases mentioned and can thus be accepted as characteristic of the group unless explained by some shared bias. Furthermore, wherever the only disagreements are those of visitors from particular groups deviating from the majority view in a direction predicted by the bias which they were selected to represent, then the view of the majority may be considered to have been upheld.

The assumption behind this type of analysis is the same as that made by the ethnographer cross-checking informants' accounts, viz., that the likelihood that a heterogeneous set of observers, systematically chosen so as to represent the maximal diversity of biases in perception, made identical misperceptions is slight enough to recommend our accepting their common judgments until we have positive evidence which contradicts them. In the case of personality characteristics, which are so difficult to assess reliably across cultures, this method would appear to yield as strong evidence as any research instruments currently in use, at least on the external aspects of social character, without the problems of instrument effects and observer intervention that bedevil cross-cultural methodology.

REPUTATIONAL ETHNOGRAPHY

When ethnic groups in a region interact, they inevitably develop images of each other, and these images become institutionalized as part of the belief systems of their respective cultures. In this section the problem to be considered is whether the reputations which groups acquire among neighboring peoples can be used by the anthropologist as a measure of behavioral differences within a region. Now, as compared with judgments made by a visitor, an ethnic group's image of a neighboring people is extremely indirect knowledge, since it is a set of beliefs concerning remote phenomena with which firsthand acquaintance may be slight or nonexistent. On the one hand, it can be argued that if a set of, say, ten ethnically distinct tribes have inhabited an area long enough and have had some opportunities for interaction, their images of each other will naturally tend to be comments on the most striking contrasts and incompatibilities among them, including contrasts in customs, behavioral expectations, moral standards. According to this argument, the fundamental information on which the image will be based is that of the visitors (or hosts) who have firsthand experience with outgroup members and who, having matched their own habits and expectations against those of the outgroup, formed a concept of that group in terms of the divergences noticed. This intercultural experience is then relayed to other group members in terms that they will understand, i.e., as deviations from behavior patterns which are most familiar to them. Over time, this relayed information is sharpened and leveled to its common elements, i.e., to those attributes on which various visitors are in greatest agreement and which, therefore, are relayed to the stay-at-homes most frequently. In this view, then, the institutionalized images of outgroups are likely to contain numerous grains of truth, if interpreted as statements of behavioral *differences* between groups rather than as absolute attributes of the group under discussion.

A contrary view is that the institutionalized images which groups develop of each other are autistic fantasies representing the motives, impulses, anxieties of the ingroup projected onto outside objects which are so ill-known and therefore ambiguous that they provide a perfect medium for the expression of internal dispositions. In this view the images, as they develop, act to block the reception of new information, except that which supports the highly valued (cathected) image already formed. Over time the images become unrealistic, rigid stereotypes, which give psychic gratification to ingroup members but cannot fruitfully be mined for fact.

Rather than accept either of these views of outgroup perception in a region, I should like to follow the procedure used earlier in this article by examining the possible sources of bias in such perception and searching for strategies to eliminate the bias. However, regardless of whether it proves possible to reduce the bias, the images themselves are of intrinsic interest to the ethnographer as part of the belief system of the people whose culture he is investigating.

It must first of all be admitted that territorially separate groups are unquestionably more susceptible to perceptual biases of insufficient contact and experience than are visitors. Fortunately, however, the groups in a region are not all *equally* susceptible to these or the other biases mentioned below, so that it is possible to examine the differential effects of varying degrees of such biases. In this discussion I assume that the images of outgroups are obtained through standard ethnographic interviews with informants in each group and that each informant's account will be partly dependent on his own personal amount and kind of experience with the outgroup on which he is reporting—a type of bias which can be controlled in the manner presented above for visitor-informants. This discussion, however, is focused on biases of entire groups rather than individual informants.

The biases affecting intergroup perception

within a region include the following: (a) those due to remoteness or insufficient contact; (b) loyalistic bias resulting from the history of amity and enmity, including military relations, between groups; (c) specialized opportunities for observation due to functional specialization of intergroup contact, as in trade, military alliance, or intermarriage; (d) degree of cultural similarity (if too little, resulting in failure to notice nuances; if too much, failure to perceive distinctive attributes).

If one is investigating a region which contains at least ten ethnic groups, then it should be possible to maximize diversity in at least some of these biases. If informants from all of the ethnic groups in the region are interviewed concerning each of the others, then for each group one should have judgments from adjacent groups and groups of several degrees of proximity; from friendly and hostile groups; from groups which were trading partners, others which were military allies, etc., with the group in question; from culturally similar and dissimilar groups. Agreements across all groups could be regarded as strongly confirming the attribute in question but might be rare, due to the powerful effects of the biases. The ethnographer would want to compare the responses intensively to detect the effects of each type of bias. If he discovered, for example, that the attribution of some characteristic varied directly and continuously with the proximity of the reporting groups to a particular group, then he might decide to accept the reputation on that trait established among the closer neighbors. If he found that only the most hostile groups deviated from the agreement of the others, he might decide to accept such agreement in the face of their deviation. Similarly plausible grounds could be used for assessing the relative weights of bias and valid perception with respect to the known distribution of particular biases among the reporting groups. Many internal checks on bias are available in the analysis of this kind of reputational data. Thus if groups attribute a trait which they clearly regard as good to a group they dislike, this favors acceptance of the attribution more than its assertion by friendly allies.

Having sifted the judgments through the sieve of diverse biases twice—once to yield net agreements and once to examine the effects of specific biases on specific types of judgments—the ethnographer has yet another stratagem for eliminating bias in the intergroup perceptions, viz., checking the self-reports of the group against its reputation among outgroups. In previous articles (Campbell and LeVine 1961, 1965) it was suggested that two groups could have mutually confirming images of each other while reversing the evaluative connotations of the attributes involved. Thus, in the example presented there, the English may see Americans as intrusive and themselves as respecting the privacy of others, while Americans in turn see the English as unfriendly and themselves as friendly and open-hearted. Or, in the example of Bruner (1956), the Hidatsa Indians view the Anglo ranchers as stingy, while the latter view the Hidatsa as improvident. In these cases there is "latent agreement" on the differences between the groups, which is revealed by allowing the expectable loyalistic value biases to cancel each other out. The ethnographer can examine the self-report data of a group and its images of other groups who have judged it to discover in what respects it may be agreeing with its outgroup judges on the behavioral differences between them while reversing the values assigned to the attributes. Where he finds reciprocal images or latent agreement on the direction of the difference, he may feel that an outgroup judgment has been confirmed.

Thus the basic procedure of reputational ethnography is to compare each judgment by each group with (a) the judgments of all the other groups taken together, (b) the judgments of groups deemed to have more and less of biases which should have an effect on the particular variable, (c) the judgment by the judged group of itself on that variable, and (d) the judgment by the judged group of the judging group on that variable.

Reputational ethnography may well prove a more powerful tool for bias reduction in culturally heterogeneous regions with a high degree of functional specialization than in regions where fewer biases are naturally diversified. Nonetheless, in every region groups vary in degree of proximity to each other and usually in degree of amity and enmity as well, so that there is some scope for

assessing and therefore reducing the effects of bias.

POSSIBLE USE OF OUTSIDERS' JUDGMENTS IN PSYCHOLOGICAL ANTHROPOLOGY

Outsiders' judgments are not presented here as a substitute for traditional ethnography in those areas of cultural behavior where it is strongest, but rather as a supplement in those areas where traditional ethnography and orthodox psychometrics are weakest, viz., in the assessment of personality differences between culturally distinct populations. This novel procedure has the advantage over ordinary ethnography of introducing an explicit comparative approach from the very start of the data collection and the advantage over psychological testing of using standard ethnographic techniques of data collection and inference, in which all professional social anthropologists are trained.

It is inimical to the spirit of this article to suggest that the proposed procedure be used in isolation from other methods of measurement. I would propose a multi-method approach to the measurement of personality differences in a region. Four methods of measuring each personality variable could be employed: (1) reputational judgments by each ethnic group of each other, (2) visitors' judgments on each group; (3) self-report judgments by each group on itself; (4) other methods of psycho-diagnosis (projective and semi-projective instruments, dream analysis, life histories, behavior observations) applied to all the ethnic groups. These methods could be seen as varying along a subjective-objective dimension from the frankly personal judgments of individual visitors, through the "emic" or locally agreed-upon group judgments, to the "etic" instruments of psychological assessment. In this approach, each method would be regarded as yielding genuine data of tentatively acceptable validity. Ultimately, the results of the four methods would be compared in an attempt to achieve convergent validation.[1] However, the reputational judgments and self-reports might be collected as part of a preliminary survey of a region, in order to

[1] Validation of psychological measurement through convergent findings of different methods is systematically demonstrated in Campbell and Fiske (1959).

uncover quickly and tentatively personality differences among the component peoples which can be intensively studied—if sufficiently interesting—in later investigation.

ILLUSTRATIONS OF THE APPROACH FROM AN EAST AFRICAN STUDY

Concrete illustrations of reputational judgments and self-reports can be given from a preliminary analysis of data collected in an attitude survey of thirty East African ethnic groups by Marco Surveys, Ltd., Nairobi, for the Cross-Cultural Study of Ethnocentrism. While the survey method differs greatly from ethnography, the present examples are of inference procedures equally applicable to both. Ultimately, the survey data will be most useful in the study of visitors' judgments, but those results are not yet available.

The thirty groups constitute a connected chain from Uganda through Kenya to northern Tanzania. Fifty respondents from each of ten groups in each country were interviewed in the vernacular concerning the ten groups in their own country and four well-known or bordering groups from the other countries. One part of the interview involved naming which of the fourteen groups under discussion was highest on each of forty-eight traits; it is from preliminary tabulations of these responses that the following examples are drawn. Since only one group could be named for each trait, the scatter of choices is considerable, even within ethnic samples. For purposes of this analysis, it is regarded that group A attributed a particular trait to group B if more than one-third of the respondents in the group A sample made the attribution and if group B received a higher number of choices than any other group.

A Kikuyu-Luo difference in thriftiness provides an example of what might be called "maximal validation." For the trait description, "thrifty, like to save money," eight of the ten Kenya groups named the Kikuyu as highest; for the description, "lacking in thrift, like to spend money," five Kenya groups named the Luo. Since no other group received more than one attribution from within Kenya on either of these traits, this represents substantial agreement across peoples varying in distance and friendliness to the

groups named. It is also notable that the Teso of Uganda, who live near the Kenya border, made the same judgments. Most importantly, however, the Kikuyu and Luo themselves were among the groups making both attributions. In other words, the Kikuyu and Luo both agree that the Kikuyu are highest on thriftiness and the Luo lowest. Thus the consensus of outgroup judgments is confirmed by the self-reports of both ingroups and their judgments of each other. This multiple agreement cannot be due to any of the types of bias outlined above and must be accepted as representing a real behavioral difference between the two groups until convincing evidence to the contrary is produced. The unanimity of judgment by groups that are presumably characterized by diverse biases leads to calling this maximal validation.

A less certain but still convincing form of cross-validation occurs when the attribution of a "negative" trait by neighboring groups is confirmed by the ingroup. For example, the Kamba agree with their adjacent Kenya neighbors, the Kikuyu and Embu, that they (the Kamba) are the group most "interested in using witchcraft and poison." In Tanzania, the Sukuma also agree with their immediate neighbors, the Nyamwezi and Tanzania Luo, in assigning this trait to themselves. The Tanzania Masai are regarded by their neighbors, the Arusha, Meru, and Pare, as the most "sexually loose, immoral" group, and the Masai themselves agree. The Kenya Luo join with six other Kenya groups in naming themselves as highest on the trait description, "proud, despise other people." In Uganda, all ten groups, including the Ganda, attribute this trait to the Ganda. Whether or not we assume that such a trait is negatively valued by the ingroup, the concordance of self-attribution with neighbors' judgments rules out the possibility that the latter are due solely to loyalistic misperception and strengthens the inference that a real difference between the ingroup and others is involved. If there were data to demonstrate conclusively that the ingroup respondents believed themselves to be admitting a failing of their group, but one that was so pronounced it was useless to conceal it, this would further strengthen the inference.

More serious problems of validation are raised where ingroup confirmation is absent.

For example, seven of the ten Uganda groups name the Ganda as highest on the trait description, "They appear to be friendly but backbite and are two-faced, hypocritical." The Ganda do not agree, but the item is so negatively stated that we would not expect any people to attribute it to themselves. (In fact, among the thirty groups only one, the Soga, contains a sizable number of respondents who attribute it to their ingroup.) We can easily account for the Ganda disagreement in terms of loyalistic bias. Despite the varying distances and experiences of the seven groups to the Ganda, however, it is hard to rule out the suspicion that their consensus represents shared bias resulting from past or present political alignments rather than a real behavioral difference. This suspicion is buttressed by the fact that the two least politically active groups, the Karamajong and Teso, are the only two that do not agree with this attribution. Thus we cannot accept this consensus without further information.

Other illustrations are free of apparent shared biases. For example, five Uganda groups judge the Ganda as most "sexually loose, immoral"; the Ganda themselves do not agree. The five groups include all adjacent neighbors and more remote groups (Teso, Karamajong). Furthermore, the Gusii of Kenya and the Pare of Tanzania also attribute this trait to the Ganda, indicating that the reputation is not confirmed to participants in the same political system. Although it may be that the Ganda are a target for the projected sexual fantasies of those groups (like the Gusii) in which sexual behavior is relatively restricted, their selection as such a target by such diversely located groups requires explanation. In the absence of such explanation, the outgroups' judgment can be accepted as indicating a real difference in sexual behavior patterns between themselves and the Ganda. A similar case concerns the Kenya Luo as "interested in using witchcraft and poison." Two of their adjacent neighbors, the Gusii and Kipsigis, judge them highest on this, as do four Uganda groups, the Teso, Soga, Acholi, and Karamajong. Although the Luo themselves do not agree, this consensus among diverse groups strongly suggests some genuine cultural differences.

Although the attitude survey itself did not include "objective" measures of group personality against which to check the reputational judgments and self-reports, some of its findings appear to be concordant with those of the personality testing done by Edgerton (1965a, 1965b) for the Culture and Ecology in East Africa Project. His extensive battery of interview questions and projective tests was administered to each of 505 persons drawn from both agricultural and pastoral communities in each of the following groups: Sebei of Uganda, Pokot and Kamba of Kenya, and Hehe of Tanzania. The Kamba are the only group included in both his study and the present one.

Edgerton (1965b) found a strong preoccupation with witchcraft among the Kamba, confirming the attribution of their own judgments and those of their neighbors mentioned above. He also found in general that the Bantu (i.e., Kamba and Hehe) are "more concerned with sorcery-witchcraft" than the Kalenjin (Sebei and Pokot, Edgerton 1965a: 443). This conforms generally to our finding that Bantu groups (Kamba, Sukuma, Sambaa, and others) are, apart from the Nilotic Luo, the only ones with reputations of this type, whereas Kalenjin (Nandi and Kipsigis) and other groups of the "Nilo-Hamitic" (Great Lakes Sudanic) language family (Masai, Karamajong, Teso, Arusha) are hardly ever named in this connection.

In comparing persons from pastoral and agricultural communities, Edgerton found "the more pastoral the economy, the more that society will maximize and value independence of action for its male members" (1965a:446). Most of the groups included in the present survey are predominantly agricultural, with the Masai and Karamajong as the most conspicuous exceptions. In all three countries, there is a high degree of cross-group consensus in naming one of these groups (Masai in Kenya and Tanzania, Karamajong in Uganda) as most "brave" and "independent, disobedient, and unruly." Furthermore, Edgerton's finding that pastoralists express aggression more directly and freely than agriculturalists (1965b) is concordant with our findings that the Masai and Karamajong were most frequently named as most "cruel" (in all three countries) and that the Masai (in both Kenya and Tanzania) were most frequently named most "hot-tempered."

Thus, with respect to aggressive and independent behavior, the judgments of East

African groups concerning each other are remarkably similar to the conclusions arrived at by Edgerton through direct personality assessment. This suggests that there is a correspondence between the reputations of groups and their personality as measured by tests and projective interviews.

The foregoing illustrations are crude examples of an approach that needs to be made more systematic and applied with great care and thoroughness if it is to be optimally effective. Imperfect as they are, they indicate that outsiders' judgments are a promising source of new data for psychological anthropology.

BIBLIOGRAPHY

BRUNER, E. M.
1956   Primary group experience and the process of acculturation. *American Anthropologist* 58:605–623.

CAMPBELL, DONALD T.
1965   Pattern matching as essential to distal knowing. In K. Hammond, ed., *Probabilistic functionalism: the psychology of Egon Brunswik.* New York, Holt, Rinehart and Winston.

CAMPBELL, DONALD T., and D. W. FISKE
1959   Convergent and discriminant validation by the multitrait-multimethod matrix. *Psychological Bulletin* 56:81–105.

CAMPBELL, DONALD T., and ROBERT A. LEVINE
1961   A proposal for cooperative cross-cultural research on ethnocentrism. *Journal of Conflict Resolution* 5:82–108.

1965   Perception of outgroup attributes. In *Propositions about ethnocentrism from social science theories.* Mimeo.

EDGERTON, ROBERT B.
1965a   Cultural vs. ecological factors in the expression of values, attitudes and personality characteristics. *American Anthropologist* 67:442–447.

1965b   *An ecological view of witchcraft in four East African societies.* Paper presented at the African Studies Association annual meeting, October 28.

NAROLL, RAOUL
1962   *Data quality control.* New York, Free Press.

CHAPTER 22

Translating, Working Through Interpreters, and the Problem of Decentering

OSWALD WERNER and DONALD T. CAMPBELL

INTRODUCTION[1]

A standard fare of anthropological linguistics of the last thirty years has been the so-called Sapir-Whorf hypothesis. Briefly, it asserts that human beings speaking different languages do not live in the same "real" world with different labels attached: they live in different worlds—language itself acts as a filter on reality, molding our perceptions of the universe around us. German linguistic philosophers have called this molding more picturesquely *die Sprachliche Zwischenwelt*, the language's "world in-between" man and reality (e.g., Gipper 1963).

It is not our purpose to go into a theoretical discussion of linguistic relativity. We will touch on the hypothesis only indirectly. If the Whorfian hypothesis is interpreted literally, translation from one language into another is

This research was in part supported by grant MH-10949-3 from the National Institutes of Health, and by the Council for Intersocietal Studies, operating at Northwestern University under a grant from the Ford Foundation.
[1] The most extensive treatment of translation that we know of is Nida (1964). We understand that a new edition of his book, which is out of print, is in preparation. This work contains an extensive bibliography on translation, including machine translation. An extensive bibliography is also to be found in Hymes (1964:98). Problems of decentering which are the major foci of this paper and to a much lesser extent ethnographic translation are barely touched on by Nida. Both types of translation need more research. Whereas ideas about decentering translation are relatively new and unexplored, currently in anthropology "ethnoscience" addresses itself largely to lexical problems and ethnographic translation (see Werner and Fenton's article on "Ethnoscience" in this volume).

impossible. For the purposes of epistemology, Quine (1960) details this position. However, no one in practice subscribes to such an extreme view, just as no one is stopped by the epistemologist's parallel conclusion that certain knowledge is impossible.

Translation of a source language into a target language is a crucial undertaking for anyone interested in cross-cultural research. Our main purposes therefore will be (1) to identify some types of translation relevant to the problems of social science, (2) to discuss translation problems in the light of some recent developments in the theory of human language, more specifically in transformational generative theory, (3) to include some experience with translation gained by social scientists in cross-cultural research, and (4) to make specific recommendations of how some of these difficulties might be overcome, at least in part. The ideas and techniques which we propose are far from being thoroughly tested. While they are offered here as advice, they are also presented in the spirit of hypotheses, and as a call for systematic research into the translation problems faced by social scientists.

While consideration of the specific uses of translation is postponed until after the presentation of the theory, there is one specific distinction of goals which needs mention at this point. On the one hand, there is the *symmetrical* or *decentered* translation aiming at both loyalty of meaning and equal familiarity and colloquialness in each language. On the other hand, there is *asymmetrical* or *unicentered* translation, in which loyalty to one language, usually the source language, dominates. While neither ideal is ever achieved, wide differences in practice do occur.

As an undesirable example of asymmetrical translation, consider the typical practice in translating English language "personality tests" into foreign languages. If equivalence to the original "standardized" form is demanded, there results an awkward, exotic target-language version—the only solution, we shall argue more in detail below, is to regard the English version as itself continually open for revision in the process of preparing "equivalent" tests, i.e., of decentering the translation effort. But the ethnographic translation of songs, ceremonies and oral literature, is appropriately and in principle asymmetrical, as Bohannan (1954:819) pointed out. A product which was colloquial and familiar in its original language is appropriately translated into something exotic and unnatural in the investigator's language. This exotic quality may appropriately include retention of native terms, thereby teaching the reader a new vocabulary when the concepts are unavailable in his language. To do otherwise, to achieve the sometime literary ideal of equivalent typicality in the new language, would be to fail to communicate the fundamental information of cultural difference. Of course, as Voegelin and Voegelin (1960:68) have pointed out, some of the exotic material is no doubt due to the interpreter's poor comprehension of social science terms in the investigator's language, a needless and misleading source of error.

The goal of symmetrical translation is an ideal held out for much literary translations. As such, it almost inevitably involves a supra-linguistic translation of culture symbols. Nida (1964:166) calls this kind of translation "dynamic equivalence." That is, a culture symbol in the source language is translated into a culture symbol in the target language which evokes the same functional response. Bohannan (1954:815) cites the example of the murder mystery where the British detective could identify a lady in the dark by her pronunciation, whereas in the American version, a street light had to be invented in order for the detective to see, because in America it is impossible to tell a lady in the dark. Similarly, in Navaho a coyote may be identified with witchcraft, while in European languages and cultures a black cat might perform the same function; or, in the translation of proverbs and poetry: English "once in a blue moon" becomes in Spanish "every time a bishop dies." This type of translation is often necessary in literature and in Bible translation, where the result should read like a native original even though remote in space and/or time. In other words, translation also means providing an understanding of cultural empathy, where content, context and style may have to be adjusted to the receptor culture.

While for ethnographic translation, asymmetrical translation is required, for most other purposes of anthropological field work, decentering and symmetrical translation is the goal. Decentering implies a de-emphasis of the investigator's language in such a way that the system of symbols supersedes a single culture. At best, decentering eliminates the distinction between source and target language and stresses equivalences. Intra-lingual paraphrase as a basis for translation, multiple-stage translation and back-translation are some of the methods for decentering. These will be discussed below.

The goals of decentered translation are akin to those of ethnoscience. While anthropological linguists no longer go into the field looking for the local language synonyms of "aunt," "cousin," and "brother-in-law," forcing the information acquired into a European category system, similar asymmetries do still occur. The methods of ethnoscience (see Chapter 29, Method and Theory in Ethnoscience or Ethnoepistemology) seek to avoid such ethnocentrism, and to pinpoint "meaning" without translation, by making the lexical system or "field" explicit. The "meanings" of words follow from lexical and semantic relations of a given field. They can be comprehended nonverbally. On the other hand, the explicitness of fields and "meanings" across languages allows for more accurate decentering of translation, because the overview of an entire lexical field allows for better choices of equivalent or near-equivalent expressions, especially if the lexical fields are explicitly known in *both* languages.

THE TRANSFORMATIONAL GENERATIVE THEORY OF LANGUAGE[2]

Transformational theory addresses itself to the "projection problem." That is, a synchronic description of a language should take into account and should explain the native speaker's ability to interpret a potentially infinite number of sentences he has not heard before. An important corollary of this aim is that linguists no longer investigate the structure of some arbitrary corpus of linguistic data, but turn to the investigation of the speaker's ability or implicit knowledge about his language. The theory attempts to specify explicitly what a native speaker actually knows about his language. This is to be sharply distinguished from what he can casually report of his knowledge. A grammar, which in this view is a part of a theory of language, is a formal device which is constructed by the linguist in somewhat analogous fashion to a child, who, from a finite number of utterances, constructs a theory that, with finite means, is capable of interpreting (predicting) a potentially infinite set of sentences never encountered before.

Such grammars are defined as a system of a finite set of grammatical rules which are recursive; they therefore enumerate recursively the sentences of a language, and automatically (by means of an algorithm) assign a structural description to every sentence. This is analogous to the rules (algorithm) of multiplication which are applicable to an infinite set of any two arbitrary numbers.

Recent investigations (e.g., Lakoff 1966) demand that the rules should assign some index of grammaticality to the generated sentences, because a large number of sentences of small deviance from grammaticality are perfectly understandable. Such slightly ungrammatical sentences occur often in native speech, and/or the speech of foreigners. It is part of a speaker's linguistic competence to be able to interpret (for example, by editing, or by grammatically rearranging) such sentences.

Empirical investigation of languages indicates that the class of possible grammars for the description of human languages is severely limited. At present, grammars of at least the formal complexity of transformational grammars are necessary to enumerate the sentences of a language economically, and more importantly, to assign the correct parsing or structural descriptions to these sentences. These structural descriptions are crucial for the correct interpretation of sentences, because they specify such notions as subject, predicate, object, and other grammatical relations (better known as parts of speech).

Transformations establish relationships— syntactic relationships—between sentences. For the establishment of these relationships, the native speaker utilizes his knowledge of grammatical relations such as subject, predicate and object, etc. In fact, the definition of grammatical relations by the base component of the grammar is the primary justification for the introduction of transformations contained in the transformational component.

The base generates a set of sentence-like structures of the common deep structure which contains the basic underlying meanings. The transformations take these sentence-like structures and change them into (surface) structures of actual sentences. These actual sets of sentences, related transformationally, are different non-lexical (without the change of particular words—see below for examples) paraphrases of the same basic "meaning."

The severe limitations on the class of possible grammars lead to the discovery that in addition to substantive universals, such as, all languages of the world possess consonants and vowels, there are formal universals; e.g., that transformations are rules of a special, very restricted type found in all human languages. This insight implies what is known in social science as "Grand Theory." More precisely, it leads from theories of specific languages to linguistic meta-theory, or to a *universal grammar of human language.*

Language universals are crucial for translation. At some future date, there may exist a general theory of human language. It will contain all features that are universal to all languages. Grammars of individual languages

---

[2] The basic source is, of course, Noam Chomsky, but for the nonspecialist his major works (e.g., Chomsky 1965) may not be the best introductions. A good nontechnical introduction to transformational generative grammar is to be found in J. J. Katz (1966). Other articles which are relatively easy to follow are: Chomsky (1967), Chomsky (1968), Postal (1964), Schachter (1964) and possibly Lees (1957), Bach (1964), and Koutzoudas (1966).

will then contain only information idiosyncratic to specific languages.

Perhaps the most revolutionary insight of transformational theory is the great formal similarity of human languages, particularly in their deep structure or base component. The latter most closely reflects the semantic structure of sentences. We will deal with deep structure in detail below. The apparent baroque exoticism, the painfully learned and easily forgotten long lists of irregular forms, etc., are relatively superficial features of languages. They are results of various accidents in the courses of the historical process of language change. A highly schematic representation of currently accepted universal theory of language is shown in Figure 1 as follows:

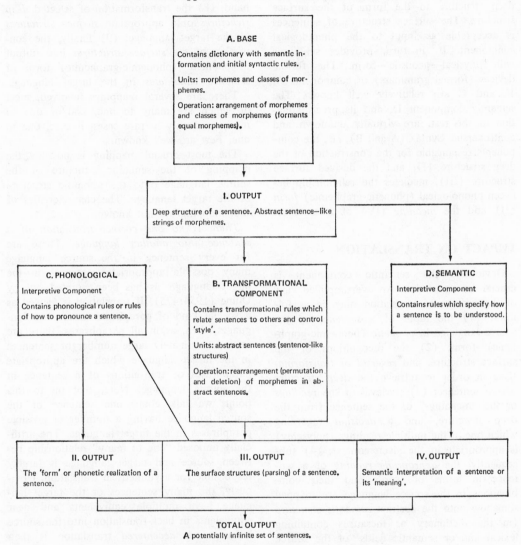

A. BASE

Contains dictionary with semantic information and initial syntactic rules.

Units: morphemes and classes of morphemes.

Operation: arrangement of morphemes and classes of morphemes (formants equal morphemes).

I. OUTPUT

Deep structure of a sentence. Abstract sentence—like strings of morphemes.

C. PHONOLOGICAL

Interpretive Component

Contains phonological rules or rules of how to pronounce a sentence.

B. TRANSFORMATIONAL COMPONENT

Contains transformational rules which relate sentences to others and control 'style'.

Units: abstract sentences (sentence-like structures)

Operation: rearrangement (permutation and deletion) of morphemes in abstract sentences.

D. SEMANTIC

Interpretive Component

Contains rules which specify how a sentence is to be understood.

II. OUTPUT

The 'form' or phonetic realization of a sentence.

III. OUTPUT

The surface structures (parsing) of a sentence.

IV. OUTPUT

Semantic interpretation of a sentence or its 'meaning'.

TOTAL OUTPUT

A potentially infinite set of sentences.

Figure 1. Schema of a Unified Theory of Language

The base component of the theory provides the deep structure of sentences (see Figure 1). This is a postulated structure which specifies all necessary semantic relations, and is introduced because it simplifies description. The semantic interpretive component operates on the deep structure of sentences, i.e., it takes the abstract sentence-like deep structures and provides them with "meanings." This is accomplished by projection rules which describe how the individual meanings of words from the dictionary component of the base are to be combined, and thus provide sentences with "meaning." The "meanings" of sentences are invariant across transformations; that is, invariant to the only two operations which are performed by transformations on the deep structure: (1) deletions and (2) permutations of some of the morphemes (formants) or classes of morphemes of the deep structure. The transformations introduce various redundancies (e.g., grammatical government) and put the deep structure in the form of the surface structure. The surface structure of sentences is acceptable as input to the phonological component. It, in turn, provides sentences with physical—acoustic—form. The formal devices (formal grammars) of components A, B, and C are relatively well known. The semantic component D, and its precise relation to the rest, are virtually unknown and controversial. Syntax (A and B), i.e., the components responsible for the construction of the deep structure (I), and the derived surface structure (III), mediates the relationship between phonological (phonetic-graphemic) *form* (II) and the *meaning* (IV) of a sentence.

IMPACT ON TRANSLATION

Obviously, the semantic component is crucial for translation. An oversimplified view of the process of translation may be as follows: (1) the input of a *sentence* of the source language in *phonetic* (phonemic-graphemic) form; (2) the recognitions of the surface structure, and *reversal of transformations* in order to retrieve the *deep structure* of the sentence; (3) retrieval of the *readings* or the "meanings" of the sentence from the deep structure, and a *decision* regarding which one of the multiple readings (polysemy) is appropriate in the given context; (4) subsequently, the *appropriate reading* of a sentence in terms of words and their combinations in the source language are mapped somehow onto the abstract *semantic structure* (in the dictionary or thesaurus containing lexical and/or semantic fields[3] of the source language; (5) the *semantic structure of the source language in turn is mapped onto the semantic structure of the target language.*

[3] Currently only some lexical fields are known. These are especially taxonomic lexical fields of words connected by a relation "X is (a kind of) Y" which form connected tree graphs. It is assumed here that as yet unknown semantic relations may underlie lexical fields. (See Chapter 29 of this volume.)

This mapping is the "trick" of translation. Now an equivalent sentence of the target language needs to be produced; (6) retrieval of possible appropriate mappings in the target language from the semantic structure; (7) generation of possible *deep structures appropriate* to carry the content of a reading or several readings and a decision regarding the deep structures available for the task on hand; (8) the transformation of selected *deep structures* onto appropriate *surface structures* in the target language; (9) finally, the conversion of the *surface structures* into output in *phonetic* (phonemic-graphemic) form of *sentence candidates* in the target language.

There are several mappings involved, most of which are many to one, and/or one to many, and only in rare cases, if ever, one to one. Few are well known.

The most crucial mapping is possibly the mapping of the semantic structure of the source language onto the semantic structure of the target language. The characteristics of that mapping are not known.

There is no one correct translation of a sentence into another language. There are for every sentence in the source language many possible appropriate sentences in the target language, as has been pointed out by Quine (1954:475). If translation is viewed as a special kind of paraphrase across two languages, then, as in all paraphrases, there are an indeterminately large number of sentences in the target language which are appropriate paraphrases or translations of a sentence in the source language. Note, that up to this point, we talk about one sentence of the source language having a number of possible paraphrases in the target language. The artificially imposed "one to many" relationship between source and target language is largely responsible for asymmetrical translation. Obviously, the many sentences of the target language have multiple equivalents and near equivalents in back-translation into the source language. A *decentered* translation is then viewed as a *set* of equivalent or near-equivalent sentences of the source language corresponding to a similar set of sentences in the target language. In decentered translation therefore we need to look for a "many to many" relation between equivalent or near equivalent sentences in both source and target language. In fact, the "many to many" mapping of decentered translation is intended to eliminate the distinction of source and target language. It makes the two versions in different languages (more) coordinate.

The set of most appropriate sentences expressing the content of an original sentence, or the correspondences of two coordinate sets of sentences, will change as the culture of the target language changes (assuming invariance of the source language). This is responsible for frequent assertions that every age needs its own translations: as the target culture changes, with it change literary (or rhetorical) style and intellectual milieu, and both affect standards of excellence in translation, that is, the subset of most appropriately corresponding sets of sentences. Of course, by the same criterion, within the source language, every age needs its own paraphrase.

Translation is therefore not simply code switching, where one code is unambiguously retrievable if the other is given. The world of different speakers is not just the same world with different labels attached. Exact translation is therefore impossible in principle. The crucial problems are methods, techniques, etc., by which the quality or approximation of translation may be improved, particularly in strictly synchronic translation. The rest of this section will deal with some insights into the nature of language which may yield better, and perhaps more accurate, translations.

Deep Structure

The similarities which languages display in their deep structure are striking. The differences observed, particularly when learning a new language, that is, the unexpected complexities and irregularities, are surface phenomena, due mostly to historical accident. The deep structure specifies the unique shared structure closest to the semantics of a set of sentences which are *syntactic paraphrases* of each other. This kind of paraphrase, of entire or of parts of sentences, must be a regrouping without new words, that is, without the use of synonyms.

Translation may be simplified if all complex sentences are decomposed into their constituent simple sentences.[4] This process should

[4] Nida (1964:68) makes a similar suggestion for the simplification of translation, although his reasons are not theoretically justified.

be carried out as far as possible, as illustrated below. Simple sentences are presumably closer to the deep structure, hence, semantic structure, of languages and tend to be considerably more similar than are complex sentences. The distance of a simple sentence from the abstract deep structure presumably varies from language to language. (Such distance may be measured, perhaps, by the number of obligatory transformations that need to be applied in order to get simple sentences most directly from their deep structure.)

Ambiguity

Transformational theory deals with ambiguity explicitly, and recognizes two basic types.

Syntactic Ambiguity, that is, sentences generated by different sequences of applications of the rules of the grammar, may have, in the end, identical phonetic (phonemic-graphemic) shape. In other words, sentences with different deep structures may have identical surface structures. For example:

(i) The shooting of the hunters was terrible.[5]

This sentence is ambiguous in at least two ways. That is, in the underlying deep structures, *either* "hunters" is the *subject* of sentence (ii), and is one of the constituent sentences which makes up sentence (i):

(ii) The hunters were shooting.

or in the other derivation, "hunters" is the *object* of sentence (iii) and is also one of the constituent sentences which make up sentence (i):

(iii) The hunters were shot (by an unspecified agent).

Or, put in the active voice:

(iv) An unspecified agent shot the hunters.

However, the above sentence (i) is, in fact, at least four ways syntactically ambiguous.

(v) (The fact that (the hunters were shooting) was terrible.)

(vi) (The fact that (an unspecified agent shot the hunters) was terrible.)

(vii) (The way (the hunters were shooting) the subject of (i))

(viii) (The way (an unspecified agent shot the hunters) was terrible.)

[5] This example was taken from Fodor and Katz (1964).

Constituent sentences are between parentheses.

Because recognition of syntactic ambiguity is crucial to translation, but is difficult to detect (although context helps), decomposition of any complex sentence, as illustrated by sentences (v) to (viii), also aids translation.

If we translate sentence (i), into German, part of the ambiguity is resolved:

(i) The shooting of the hunters was terrible.

(ix) Das Schiessen der Jaeger war schrecklich.

(x) Das Erschiessen der Jaeger war schrecklich.

There is a certain finality about being shot in German which English does not possess.

The process of translation in itself may help resolve ambiguity. That sentences in different languages are differently ambiguous is an argument for decentering by comparing sets of lexical paraphrases from both languages (see below).

Lexical Ambiguity is due to the fact that the same lexical item may have several "meanings," while the structure of the sentence in which the word occurs remains the same:

(ix) John has guts to go there.

This sentence, although ambiguous in at least two ways syntactically, is also lexically ambiguous. The lexical ambiguity is due to the interpretation of guts as John's intestines, someone's intestines now possessed by John, or John's intestinal fortitude. The syntactic ambiguity is due to different interpretations of "to go there."

Lexical ambiguity may be easier to detect, but is so common, that *ambiguous sentences are the rule rather than the exception. This goes for all languages. Sentences in different languages are differently ambiguous*. Simple sentences aid also in the detection of lexical ambiguity.

Paraphrase

Analogous to ambiguities, there are two types of paraphrase relations: syntactic and lexical.

Syntactic Paraphrase, paraphrase retaining the same lexical items rather than substituting synonyms, is essential in the decomposition of complex sentences into their constituent simple sentences. It is based on the speaker's knowledge that such paraphrases are "mean-

ing" equivalents. Transformations formalize this equivalence. Sets of sentences related transformationally (by syntactic paraphrase) are the clues linguists use to reconstruct the deep structure of a language. Thus, the sentence "The hunters were shooting" is a constituent sentence of "The shooting of the hunters was terrible." Possible syntactic paraphrases of the "The hunters were shooting" include:

(xi) The shooting of the hunter . . . (or the subject of (i))

(xii) The hunter's shooting . . .

(xiii) That the hunters were shooting . . .

(xiv) Were the hunters shooting?

(xv) Who was shooting?

(xvi) Who was doing what?

and possibly others. All of these sentences, or parts of sentences, are derived from the underlying deep structure identical or similar to the deep structure of sentence (ii) "The hunters were shooting." This is another way of saying what has been known for a long time, namely, that complex propositions or sentences are composed of embedded and/or conjoined simple propositions or sentences (Chomsky 1966:35, 1966: footnote 70).

Syntactic paraphrase illuminates the compositional nature of complex sentences. It is helpful in the decomposition of complex sentences in accordance with our rule that translation of complex sentences requires simplification into smaller constituent sentences. Although translation may be viewed largely as a form of lexical (synonymous) paraphrase (below), syntactic paraphrase may also be important for translation. It may be closely related to sociolinguistic styles of usage.

Lexical Paraphrase, also called synonymous paraphrase, because of its employment of synonyms, is essential in the decomposition of the senses of complex concepts into component senses. This method is an aspect of componential semantic analysis (e.g., Goodenough 1956, Lounsbury 1956, Sturtevant 1964, Colby 1965). It is based on the native speaker's knowledge that certain words "mean the same" as certain other words or phrases, sentences, or paragraphs. For example, synonymous paraphrase and the relation "is a" between two words reveals the two "meanings" of the English word "queen":

(xvii) A queen (1) *is a* king's wife.

(xviii) A queen (2) *is a* female king.

On more familiar grounds of componential analysis, or the analysis of kinship terms:

(xix) My **father** *is an* ancestor of mine (lineal), and he *is a* senior of mine (*ascending generation*), and he *is* immediately above me (*one link*), and he *is a* man (*male*).

The terms within parentheses are the commonly listed components of the definition of the term "father" in the Yankee kinship system.

Lexical paraphrase is important in the discovery of what a term signifies. This insight may be particularly useful if good dictionaries of the target language are not available. At least key terms may be defined this way. It is the case that the longer the paraphrase, the more restricted its occurrence, because the less likely there is to be ambiguous interpretation. For example:

(xx) "dry"

is ambiguous and has a wider range of occurrence than one of its paraphrases:

(xxi) "devoid of moisture"

The longer paraphrase of a term (e.g., "devoid of moisture" for "dry") is more readily translatable, because it is more specific, than the total range connotation and what-have-you of the original term "dry" (e.g., "dry" wine is not "devoid of moisture").

A subtype of lexical paraphrase is *partial synonymous* or *partial lexical* paraphrase. If total synonymous paraphrase describes the so-called definition of a good monolingual dictionary, then partial synonymous paraphrase describes similarities of definition or "lexical or semantic field" relations of a "thesaurus." Present-day thesauri are not notable for their systematic approach to the "field" problem; what constitutes similarity of definition is not rigorously specified.

Partial paraphrases of

(xxii) My father went to town.

in the Yankee kinship system are:

(xxiii) The man went to town.

or

(xxiv) The woman went to town.

The sentence "The man went to town" is a closer (partially synonymous) paraphrase of "My father went to town" than "The woman went to town," because the first two share more attributes (components), i.e., in the first case, *animate, human,* and *male;* in the second case, only *animate* and *human.* Note that "The man went to town" and "The

woman went to town" are closer paraphrases of each other—the difference is the component of sex—than "My father went to town" and "The man went to town," which differ by many more specific components, such as *ancestor, one generation removed,* etc.

Note however that on another level "The man went to town" includes "My father went to town" as special case, but does not include "The woman went to town." It may thus be possible, as long as we are dealing with hierarchic taxonomies or classificatory systems within the vocabularies of languages, to rigorously define paraphrase distance. This may require more than one parameter.

Partial lexical paraphrase may be particularly important for translation. Often in the target language a more generic term of the source language is lacking and a more specific term of the target language has to be substituted. Conversely, often a more general term has to be used in lieu of a specific term in the source language.

Going up and down the scale of specificity is *not* unusual in monolingual speech:

(xxv) "The *gorilla* escaped again. We are unable to build cages strong enough to restrain the *animal.* But even if we did, the *beast* is too clever. I don't think *apes* should be kept in cages anyway. Why not ship the *brutes* back to the jungle."

Although it is considered good style in English writing not to repeat terms too often, this is not true of spoken English, at least not to the same degree, and is certainly not true of most non-European languages.

The Navaho concept ba'álíil is an example for the need of restricting the word's "meaning" by reducing the generality of partial translations: the concept overlaps with the English concept of "power," and is often translated by "supernatural power"; but it is not all power—only supernatural and not all supernatural power, but only that power contained in the performance of ceremonials, in witchcraft, or in the acts of ghosts. It cannot be possessed by a human being—it can only be transmitted by a chanter, a witch, or it may be possessed by a ghost.

In this view, part of the translation problem is a more general case of lexical or partial lexical paraphrase. At times, when the cultural gap of source and target language is great, encyclopedic cultural information needs to be included in the paraphrases. This is often done by translator's notes.

Semantics

We dealt with semantic questions in the sections on lexical paraphrase and partial paraphrase. This section deals further with finding lexical (word) equivalences.

Many bilingual dictionaries do not contain definitions in the target language if it is the investigator's language. The information in the investigator's language are only *translation labels*. Conklin (1964:29–30) warns of confusing the two concepts. Translation labels serve only as identification tags which may mark two lexical items as same or different. They are the very first step in lexicography. A definition, on the other hand, must list information that gives all possible "meanings" (polysemy), homonyms, synonyms and antonyms. That it should also give taxonomic information and possibly further information is discussed in Werner and Fenton (Chapter 29 in this volume).

Traditionally definitions are of the form of giving a concept's genus and species. The binary definitions of the Linnean system are based on this principle. In our view (see also Werner and Fenton in this volume) this is extremely limiting. A definition must contain a *whole series* of genus and species, or taxonomic information. If we envision a taxonomy as a complex tree structure then one part of the definition of a term is the path from the highest possible node of a taxonomy to the term to be defined. This path is a *chain* of genus-species relationships. In addition—a second part of every definition—is the subtree which is dominated by, or of which the term to be defined is, the most general one—that is, all possible paths from the term to be defined to the most specific terms available. Other possible candidates for relationships used to define terms are described in Casagrande and Hale (1967), Werner (1967) and in Werner and Fenton (in this volume).

A taxonomic definition—including the path from the highest dominating node to the term to be defined plus the subtree dominated by the term—pinpoints some of the semantic problems of translation. By "dominating" we mean that x can *dominate* y semantically such that "y is a kind of x."

In order to be translation equivalents, two terms should have identical referents and be embedded in identical taxonomic systems. This requirement is almost never fulfilled.

Current work in ethnoscience seems to imply, however, that the situation is not as hopeless as this extreme view of linguistic relativity would indicate (Perchonock and Werner 1969). There seems to be a great amount of agreement between languages in the naming of very specific terms and many general terms. For examples, we get the following Navaho-English agreements:

    hináanii — animals or animate beings
                (literally "things that live")
    tł'ízí — goats

correspond closely and symmetrically without forcing unusual or awkward expressions onto English or Navaho.

The intermediate categories of Navaho have no such ready equivalents and the awkwardness is forced on the English circumlocutions:

    hináanii — animals, animate beings
dominates
    naagháaii — walkers, beings that walk
dominates
    naaldlooshii — walkers, beings that trot on
    all fours, domesticated animals
dominates
    tł'ízí — goats

The classifications *between* the most general and the most specific present the greatest problem to translation. Between sets of languages taxonomic decentering by going either up or down the scale of generality in the process of adjusting *both* language (source and target) versions may decenter the translation. Since the overlaps and contrasts are probably specific with reference to any two languages it remains to be seen if this kind of decentering can be extended to more than two languages at one time.

In order to accomplish taxonomic decentering one requires at least some rudimentary knowledge of the systems of classification in *both* languages. Methods for accomplishing this are discussed in Werner and Fenton (in this volume). However, these methods, or extensions of them, to abstract terminological systems and verbs are only marginally relevant or fail completely.

Activities

Translation of activities (verbs) is often complicated. "The detective dialed the number" is difficult to translate into a culture that doesn't have detectives. A longish paraphrase of "detective" may, however, be simpler than the description of the dialing of a number in a culture without telephones. Ethnographies often neglect this point: "Solang (a Micronesian) built a canoe" is a different statement than "Peter Sloan built a canoe (using the plans in the last issue of *Popular Science*)." The two men were doing quite different things, which is obscured by the parallelism of the two statements.

We understand the implication of many sentences because we know the culture. But "John plants corn" with the backup of Iowa farm technology is only marginally equivalent to "Ashkii plants corn" if Ashkii is a traditional Navaho, who starts in the center of the field and plants by hand and digging stick, in ever increasing spirals, singing sacred songs to assure a plentiful harvest. Many apparent translation equivalences are equivalent only in the most abstract sense. The specifics may be radically different. However, the specifics may be most crucial in translation, especially in translation for social science research— for example, for the study of technological change. (For a detailed discussion see Werner 1966.) Nevertheless, the fact that translation *is* possible may be due to a considerable overlap in the abstract senses of vocabularies of the languages of the world. That at least degrees of approximation in translation are possible may be evidence that as yet undiscovered but postulated semantic universals do exist.

Context

Longacre (1958) has observed in relation to Bible translation that long passages are easier to translate than short ones.[6] Long passages allow for better expression of semantic equivalences than overly short ones. That is, the longer the text the less it is open to ambiguous interpretation.

In our experience *all methods of decentering translation are interpretable as methods for providing more context in both languages.*

A Bible translation is relatively fixed and asymmetrical in that the original is beyond editing. However, in most social science ap-

[6] See also Quine (1953, 1963:59): ". . . a retreat to longer segments tends to overcome the difficulty of ambiguity or homonymy," and Campbell (1964: 330).

plications of translation, we would like to emphasize, decentering and hence editing of the original schedule is unavoidable and desirable. This principle extends to a potential revision of all previously constructed language versions of all social science translations of schedules after every last language translated into.

The concept of translation as a mapping from many acceptable sentence paraphrases of the source language to many acceptable sentences of the target language is a method for providing more context. Every new sentence in the appropriate set allows for pinpointing more precisely the intended "meaning" and facilitates translation. Informally, this method is often used with questionnaire schedules when the subject cannot comprehend the question (e.g., LeVine and Campbell 1965:14). The interviewer paraphrases (interprets) with or without the benefit of a language barrier. Translation between sets of equivalent sentences formalizes this procedure.

Back-translation is a special case of the mapping of equivalent sets of sentences in one language onto a set in another. Failures of back-translation (e.g., Phillips 1959) indicates that (1) the translation is not decentered (as in the case of the parlor game "telephone" where a message is translated back and forth with "dismal" i.e., funny results), or (2) that due to "reverse translations" (Voegelin and Voegelin 1954), the interpreters have translated one of the many unacceptable paraphrases of the original message in the investigator's or in the source language during the first translation (from investigator's to native language), during the second (back-translation from native to investigator's language), or more likely during both translations.

Taxonomic decentering is also a provision of more context. It places every term into a lexical and/or semantic field. That is, each term which is to be translated is presented in the context of sets of dominating (more general) and subordinate (more specific) concepts. Adjustment of lexical items in both source and target versions with regard to their degree of generality, or conversely, specificity, is accomplished by reference to the taxonomic context. The seeking of equivalences in two languages requires adjustments in both.

Multiple-stage translation (Voegelin and

Voegelin 1954), if applied to texts of an editable source-language version, together with taxonomic decentering as an additional stage, becomes a third method for decentering: multiple-stage translation proceeds in general in four steps:[7]

(1) *A morpheme to morpheme translation* of the source language text.

(2) *Reordering* of the source language translation to maximally approximate the target language.

(3) *Deletion* of items which are redundant or untranslatable in the target language.

(4) *Addition* of grammatical items which are necessary to make the target language version smooth.

A decentered multiple-stage translation would allow adjustments in the source language by shifting to other acceptable paraphrases at each of the steps (2), (3) and (4) in such a way that the number of necessary deletions and additions is minimized and/or reduced to trivial cases of redundancy such as agreement between noun and adjective in number or gender in some languages.

Multiple-stage translation requires considerable linguistic sophistication and a thorough knowledge of the morphemes of the two languages in question. Intuitive knowledge of interpreters with respect to morpheme identification and morpheme boundaries is not reliable in most languages with complex (word) grammatical structures. However, the need for morpheme to morpheme translation may be reduced by analyzing complex sentences into underlying constituent simple ones. At the present state of our knowledge it appears that linguistically untrained or minimally trained interpreters may be more reliable in this operation. Multiple-stage translation is therefore a powerful decentering method only if a linguist is available to the project.

USING AN INTERVIEW SCHEDULE WITH AN INTERPRETER

This section discusses the utilization of an interview schedule with a competent bilingual interpreter. It presumes as a starting point a preliminary interview guide in the investigator's language. For the purposes of

the illustrations, this will be English, and the target language Navaho. The first task is the reformulation of the English version. Suggested steps:

(1) *Get a good dictionary and a good thesaurus of English* (or the investigator's language).

(2) *Break down all complex sentences into constituent simple sentences.* Utilize syntactic paraphrase in doing so. *This will make translation more difficult* because the translator is forced to stick close to a non-adjustable original. (Translations of Pushkin's verse or of Ernest Hemingway's prose are considered difficult by professional translators because both authors use a so-called diaphanous style, i.e., short sentences [David Stampe, personal communication].)

If decentering of the schedule is sought, the lexical and syntactic paraphrase of the simple sentences may commence at this point. For this, it is important to have at least one consultant-interpreter who identifies with the project and is familiar with every phase of it.

An interpreter is not an adjunct to a cross-cultural–cross-language project, he is central to its success. It takes time and patience to learn to *work with* an interpreter. In a strange culture, he is like a seeing guide to a blind man.[8] Ideally he should be a bilingual, linguistic-cultural expert and colleague, in every sense of the word a confidant of the project. Such a person is more important than any of the "rules" we are here proposing (Herskovits 1955:335, Mead 1942, and others).

An interpreter-translator should be chosen on the basis of his competence in the target language rather than in English. There are some horror tales in circulation (e.g., Kennedy and Leighton 1957) of interpreters who spoke passable English, but did not do well in their supposedly native language. It is the investigator's job to train and to teach the interpreter the crucial English vocabulary of the research plan, as well as the philosophy and rationale of the research.

Even in simple cultures, people and interpreters are specialized. One interpreter may

---

[7] Voegelin (1954) suggests eight steps; however, Voegelin and Voegelin in one of their more recent papers (1967:2185) reduce the steps to four.

[8] In the Mead (1939) and Lowie (1940) controversy we side squarely with Robert Lowie's suspicions concerning one's own linguistic competence for sensitive eliciting. The danger of "reverse translation," and therefore of error, is great.

know one cultural domain better than another. It is very difficult to find an interpreter's weak spots. If he is a part of the project, he should be given time off to bone up on a topic (cultural domain). Interviewing of (dialogue with) native specialists, with tape recordings is a practical procedure. An expansion of such training can be accomplished by translation of portions of the tapes into English (or the contact language) combined with a discussion with other staff members about the objectives of the project.

(3) *Eliminate all metaphoric and idiomatic expressions.* The literal translation and analysis of metaphors is an important aspect of asymmetrical translation of the ethnographic material. However, metaphors and idioms complicate the task of decentering unnecessarily because they increase the range of semantic domains.

(4) *Look up every word of the simple sentences—or at least every key word—in the dictionary AND the thesaurus* and include two sets of possible paraphrases for each sentence: (a) *paraphrases which are acceptable* and (b) *paraphrases which are not.* The researcher must then present the interpreter with *both* sets and with instructions that the translation should be close to one or more of the acceptable paraphrases and should include no unacceptable ones. The sentences should then be back-translated several days later or by another interpreter. Check if the back-translation falls within the range of acceptable paraphrases.

Here are some examples from a health survey among the Navahos:

(xxvi) Did you ever have the measles?

"Did" is an auxiliary and is part of the English interrogative construction. "You" is the second person singular. No further comment is needed except parenthetically that in some languages, different degrees of honorifics may have to be substituted depending on who is being addressed.

In place of "ever" the paraphrase "at any time" is permissible; "at all times," "always," "in any case," and "at all" are not. The two thesauri we consulted are not very helpful— no useful entries.

Acceptable paraphrases of "have": "experience," "acquire," "obtain(?)"; our own additions, "afflicted with," "suffered from," "possess." No selections from the thesauri were appropriate with perhaps "enjoy" (?), and "succumb to" coming close.

Unacceptable paraphrases: "hold in possession," "control," "own," "be under certain obligation," "bear," "beget," "be in certain relation to," "entertain in the mind," "perform," "participate," "give expression to," "exercise," "maintain," "assert," "learn," "approve," "tolerate," "allow," "cause to go," "cause to be," "cause to effect," "hold in a position of disadvantage," "hold advantage over." From the thesauri: "include," "accommodate," "teem with," "occupy," "hold," "own," "submit," "yield," "bend," "resign," "defer to," "accede," "know," "ken," "scan," "wot."

"Measles" will be discussed below. Let us assume for the moment that it is unambiguous. Following is a list of some acceptable paraphrases based on the lists above.

We obtained the closest translation into Navaho from Werner's research assistant, Mr. Kenneth Begishe:

(xxvii) łichíí’ ’ąąh ha’ajeehísh łah nidoolna’?
        a   b   c   d   e

(a) *red* (b) *on something unspecified* (c)

(xxvii)

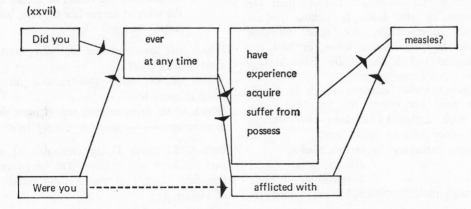

comes up and out in *plural form* and interrogative marker -ísh (d) *at one (some) time* (e) *it caught you.*

Freely: *Did measles at any time catch you? Did you ever catch or did you ever contract the measles?* Note that "catch" and "contract" were not among the acceptable paraphrases, although both are acceptable and coordinate with "acquire." This kind of deficiency of dictionaries is amplified in bilingual dictionaries, especially those of "exotic" languages. All present-day dictionaries and thesuari leave a lot to be desired.

Dictionaries of languages other than the best known, and even these, should be treated with the utmost suspicion. For example, the translations (a), (b), and (c) in sentence (xxvi) above, together are translated in most Navaho dictionaries as "measles." It took several weeks of intensive field work to have Mr. Leslie Cody finally translate it as "some kind of measles," i.e., any kind of contagious red rash!!! In this example of interviewing by questionnaire, a listing of the observable symptoms may have been more appropriate.

The situation is even worse in the case of "meningitis." The Navahos at least know measles and (a), (b), and (c), in (xxvii) are most frequently applied to cases of "actual" measles. A translation of "meningitis" is to be found in at least three Navaho dictionaries, but is meaningless to most Navahos. The translation was done from an English monolingual medical dictionary apparently by the following steps: First look up "meningitis"; it is described as "inflammation of the meninges." Inflammation in Navaho literally is *"it is getting red."* Second look up "meninges"; it is "the membrane covering of the brain"; the best Navaho equivalent for "membrane" is *"its covering."* The resultant *the covering of the brain is getting red* is literally interpretable, but most Navahos wonder how one would know, or how the membrane (which they know from sheep's brains) could ever get red.

Another lexical example which is funny, if it were not tragic: the following entry has been copied by at least two Navaho dictionaries from an earlier one:

(xxix) hachaan yitl'iz *excreta harden,*
                  pile up, piles,
                  hemorrhoids   (sic)

Although most "untutored" Navaho interpret

(xxix) as *constipation,* a few "trained" medical interpreters invariably render it as *hemorrhoids.*

A final example will deal with syntactic paraphrases, the decomposition of complex sentences and an approximation of decentering between English and Navaho. The example is from the Kluckhohn-Strodtbeck Value Orientation Schedule: The item is a text rather than an isolated question. The larger context of a text facilitates translation.

The entire original schedule (Kluckhohn and Strodtbeck 1961:81–82), Version (1):

LIVESTOCK DYING   *man-nature:* Item MN1

One time a man had a lot of livestock. Most of them died off in different ways. People talked about this and said different things.

A
(Subj) Some people said you just can't blame a man when things like this happen. There are so many things that can and do happen, and a man can do almost nothing to prevent such losses when they come. We all have to learn to take the bad with the good.

B
(Over) Some people said that it was probably the man's own fault that he lost so many. He probably didn't use his head to prevent the losses. They said that it is usually the case that men who keep up on new ways of doing things, and really set themselves to it, almost always find a way to keep out of such trouble.

C
(Obj) Some people said that it was probably because the man had not lived his life right—had not done things in the right way to keep harmony between himself and the forces of nature (i.e., the ways of nature like the rain, winds, snow, etc.).

Which of these reasons do you think is most usually true?
Which of the other two reasons do you think is more true?
Which of all three reasons would most other persons in —— think is usually true?

Item 4. Livestock Dying (man-nature) subpart B.: Man over Nature: The back-translation into English of the Navaho translation of version (1).

(1 & 2) One time a man's (a stranger) livestock was existing (when) almost all died from different causes, it is said.

(3) When people talked about it, they spoke differently, it is said.

(4a) Some spoken thus, it is said:

(4b) That man, the one who owned the livestock, because he himself was that way caused (was the reason for) that so many of his livestock are gone, they said, it is said.

(5 & 6) Thus, the point is, that if any man is just (to himself) following the new ways, and if he does thus, his livestock will not die away (from him) in the aforementioned way, it is said.

Although no attempt was made in this case to eliminate metaphorical and idiomatic expressions in advance, note how quickly they are eliminated as essentially "untranslatable."

The back-translations point up these flaws of the English original. "He didn't use his head" is difficult to translate because it is not entirely clear what paraphrases would be acceptable to the authors of the schedule. Furthermore, Navahos think with their noses. "Really set themselves to it" complicates the issue more than is necessary. The referent of the "it" is far from clear: It may refer to a general statement in the sense of "apply themselves" or specifically to "apply the new ways."

The simplified version, version (2), derived directly from the English original, version (1):

(1) One time there was a man.

(2) He (the man) had a lot of livestock.

(3) Most of the man's livestock died.

(4) (The man's) livestock died in different ways.

(5) People talked about this.

(6) People said different things.

(7) Some people said:

(8) (The man) Lost many (of his livestock).

(9) It was the man's own fault.

(10) (The man) probably didn't use his head.

(11) (The man) didn't prevent his losses.

(12) (Some) men keep up on new ways.

(13) (Some) men really set themselves to it. (The new ways?)

(14) (Such) men almost always find a way.

(15) (Such) men keep (thus) out of trouble.

Note that the short sentences reduce the chances of ambiguous interpretation and that this in itself centers the translation.

The free English back-translation of the Navaho translation of version (2) after replacement of "he didn't use his head" by "he didn't think . . ." and "set themselves to it" by "persist with the new ways . . .":

(1) There was once a man (stranger) living, it is said.*

(2) He had a lot of livestock.

(3) Almost all of his livestock died.

(4) His livestock died in different ways.

(5) The people talked about this.

(6) The people spoke in many different ways.

(7) Some of the people spoke thus:

(8) A lot of his livestock died.

(9) It happened because of the way the man was himself.

(10) Perhaps he never thought (made plans) about it (the livestock).

(11) He lost the livestock without doing anything about it.

(12) Those men who do things according to the new ways,

(13) and those men who really stick to it (persist),

(14) a way out happens for them.

(15) Thus, disaster (event) just passes over them.

In the Southwest, "disaster" in the situation which is described, seems much more appropriate than the colorless "trouble." Mr. Kenneth Begishe claims version (2) was considerably more difficult to translate into Navaho than version (1). Even superficial investigation shows that the translation of version (2) comes closer to the English original than version (1). The Navaho as the English of version (2) is choppy and slightly offensive aesthetically. The English is reminiscent of first-grade readers. However, this flaw may be well worth the greater accuracy of the translation. Furthermore, the simplified version may be more appropriate for a wider range of respondent's intelligence.

* "It is said" should follow all sentences, but is omitted in the above sentences.

The first round (several translation rounds back and forth are conceivable) of an English-Navaho decentering may look something like this in the English version, version (3):

(1) There once lived a man.
(2) He had a lot of livestock (cattle).
(3) Almost all of his livestock (cattle) died (perished).
(4) His livestock (cattle) died in many different ways.
(5) The people talked about this.
(6) The people spoke in many different ways (about him). (The people said many different things about him.)
(7) Some of the people spoke thus:
  (8) A lot (many) of his livestock died (perished).
  (9) It happened because of the way that man is.
(10) Perhaps he never thought about (planned for) his livestock (cattle).
(11) He lost his livestock (cattle) without doing something about their dying (perishing).
(12) Those men who do things according to the new ways,
(13) and those men who really persist with the new ways,
(14) they usually find a way out.
(15) In this way they avoid disaster (disaster passes them by).

Note that the availability of paraphrases in English makes the above schedule also a better monolingual English instrument. By "circumlocution," paraphrase increases redundancy, but also increases context. By this method, the number of possible ambiguities of interpretation are reduced. Longacre's (1958) principle of ease of translation with more context implies that context narrows the meaning of a "text" by greatly circumscribing ambiguity, that is, the possible appropriate interpretations.

OTHER USES OF BACK-TRANSLATION IN FIELD WORK WITH INTERVIEWERS

The social scientist who finds himself needing to interview through interpreters while knowing little or nothing of the target language is in a relatively helpless situation, utterly dependent upon his interpreters, unable to judge their skill, and unable to instruct them in the quality of translation he requires. In this setting, the technique of back-translation offers him some degree of discipline. After the investigator has prepared an interview schedule in his most translatable English, following the above instructions, he now sets two interpreters to work, one translating the first half into the local target language, the other the second half. This completed, each then works with the translated local-language versions of the other, translating these back into English. (These can be written translations, if interpreters are literate in both languages, or spoken into tape recorders, copying so as to produce a monolingual tape in the local language for the back-translator to work on.) The investigator thus ends up with two versions in his language, and through them a triangulation on to the local-language version, which almost certainly must be adequate if the two English versions are.

The investigator immediately gains some insight into the quality of his translators. Both are validated where the back-translation is adequate. Where not, a three-way conference about each item, discussing the into-translations and back-translations, will achieve a consensus as to the specific problems. These will cumulate into evidence of general ability which the interpreters themselves will accept as valid. There is probably no better way of selecting among a surfeit of candidates for the job of interpreting.

The results of such first-round back-translations are usually distressingly poor, as Phillips (1959) reports in one of the very few published discussions of the method, and as our experience confirms. Unlike Phillips, however, we accept this usually poor quality as something the investigator needs to be confronted with and as a testimony to the value of back-translation rather than a reason for avoiding it. Certainly the more informal ways of having one translator check the translations of another give the investigator more confidence in the translator's competence, but this is probably misleading. The investigator has no control over shared misconceptions, professional reluctance to criticize another professional, local loyalty in exploiting a rich outsider, etc. Back-translation gives him a very considerable (although, to be sure, not complete) control over quality even when he knows nothing of the local language.

Back-translation will instructively inform

the investigator of what part of his content can be successfully asked and what part of his social science interest is uncommunicable, at least with the translation talent available. It will force a realistic abandonment of many subtle distinctions that cannot be communicated. It will further an active revision of the English language "original."

Back-translation is the most powerful tool available to the investigator in training his interpreters. Teaching requires the ability to note errors, and only through back-translation can the investigator do this unless he is exceedingly expert in the local language. A week or so spent in back-translating in the whole range of the investigator's area of interest produces a great advance in interviewer sophistication and willingness to discuss the equivocalities of specific translation problems. Without this, the interpreter uses the face-saving posture of dogmatic professional certainty.

Even for that majority of anthropologists who use no preset inquiry schedule but who use interpreters in extempore interviewing which follows the respondents' leads—and for the bulk of field work this is undoubtedly the best method—the discipline of back-translation seems desirable for the reasons given above. Dependence upon interpreters without such checks undoubtedly leads to a great deal of self-deception as to the translation quality. (Ethnoscience techniques, in limiting all inquiry to the local language, avoids these problems at the expense of such great tedium that it rarely is used as the only method.) Even if the back-translation effort produces no standard questions for use in interviewing, it produces an appropriate set of local-language translations of the investigators' key concepts.

Another specific use of back-translation is as a short-cut approach to ethnotaxonomy in a given domain (LeVine and Campbell 1965). The investigator prepares a list of terms and near-synonyms in a given domain (e.g., interpersonal aggression). One bilingual generates as many as possible local-language translations for *each* term. Another bilingual generates as many as possible English-language translations of each local-language term. The investigator then has his original English-language taxonomy plus the heterogeneous sets of English back-translations, which he

seeks to make sense of by hypotheses about the local-language taxonomy.

Back-translation, for all its power, is not foolproof. Even after an inquiry schedule item has successfully been back-translated, later use in the field will turn up ludicrously mistranslated items. It is instructive to consider how these are noted. One depends upon context and assumptions of already achieved knowledge and consistency to judge a given response bizarre, off the subject, irrelevant. When tracked down, these errors often turn out to be due to established translation-dictionary equivalents which have been used both in the into-translation and the back-translation.

These translation-dictionary rules come from standardized schoolroom and Bible-reading "solutions" to difficult but recurrent translation problems. Such errors are avoided by the less-schooled interpreter who has never seen a translation-dictionary, who has learned each language by participation rather than instruction, and who thus translates English-to-local-language. (Other sources of error may be due to local-language polysemy, which may be particularly great for its written form.) Note that the greater the context and redundancy provided, the more chance to note interpreter errors. Coherent descriptive narratives are best for this, short-answer questions poorer. Yes-no answers provide so little opportunity to verify respondent comprehension as to be worthless in work through interpreters.

More research is needed on the whole technique of back-translation, and more detailed collecting and reporting of existing experience. The present authors will volunteer their services as a clearing house for such experience. Ideally such records would include as a minimum the English original and the first English back-translation, with errors marked as "into" errors or "back" errors. From a large sampling, recurrent "into" errors would add to our principles of writing maximally translatable English. Our experience to date justifies the recommendations given above as to simple sentences, repetition of nouns rather than use of pronouns, avoiding metaphor and colloquialisms, avoiding the English passive tense, avoiding the hypothetical phrasings of the subjunctive tense, avoiding questions in which an abstract category concept is used to elicit specific instances in the response (such questions assume ethnotaxonomic universals, which misleading assumption may explain the widespread belief that local languages lack abstract terms typical of European ones). A list of frequently mistranslated English words would also result, for which words like "like" (affection or similarity), "kind" (considerate or variety), "people" (persons or ethnic group), would be included.

A history of the method is also needed. It has undoubtedly been several times independently invented. Anthropologists guiding opinion polls in Japan for the U.S. military government were using it by 1946 (John W. Bennett, Personal Communication). Stern and D'Epinay (1948) provide the earliest published description we have encountered. It has been frequently used, although without much methodological discussion (Jacobson 1954, Schachter 1954, Duijker 1955, Ervin and Bower 1952, Cantril 1965, Mitchell 1965, Almond and Verba 1963). Phillips (1959) has provided the only anthropological discussion of the method of which we are aware.

TRANSLATION OF PERSONALITY, ATTITUDE AND ABILITY TESTS

Cross-cultural research using psychological instruments has been greatly hampered by the concept of "standardized tests," i.e., the belief that there are well-developed all-purpose comparison instruments for which valuable "population norms" have been collected. This notion of "standardized tests," the almost magical assumption that psychological tests could measure directly and perfectly what they claimed to measure, has led to a most unfortunate ethnocentric asymmetry in the translation of such instruments. The version in the investigator's language (e.g., English) has been regarded as inviolable. A mischievous brand of logical positivism has even regarded it as the operational definition of the scientific construct intended (Campbell 1966, Campbell and Fiske 1959, Webb *et al.* 1966). As a result, all of the translation effort has been directed toward representing it loyally in the target language. Figurative, metaphoric translation, in which target-language idioms have been substituted for analogous idioms in the original, has been avoided due to fear of losing an item-by-item identity. Illustrative referents

have been retained even though they represented familiar objects in the original language but exotic objects in the target language. Thus a fundamental asymmetry has resulted in which familiar, colloquial, accessible test items in English become exotic, awkward, and difficult items in the target language.

For intelligence tests, it becomes obvious that equivalently able persons will do more poorly on the target-language version. For other types of tests, the direction of distortion cannot be specified without considering their specific content, but is no doubt equally important. The cure requires treating the original-language version as itself up for revision. Such revision and item-selection processes will no doubt produce an original version which is more banal, less subtle, more explicit, less colloquial, less idiomatic, less metaphorical, and with less extreme items. This may produce a test which is less reliable and less valid for original-language use. It will require collecting new original-language comparison groups on the new instrument. But certainly it is better to have comparable data on two banal tests, than to have noncomparable data because only one is banal.

The prevalence of the unconscious assumption of the unmodifiability of the original-language version is shown in a discussion by Berrien (1969) in a generally excellent article. "Iwahara was faced with another complicating problem when translating the Edwards (*Personality Preference Schedule*) statements into Japanese. The items pertaining to heterosexual interest were too crude and blatant for the Japanese sensibilities. He, therefore, wrote new statements which pertained to heterosexual interests that were more acceptable in that culture. Under those circumstances, is it still more legitimate to compare the Japanese results with those of Americans?" (Berrien 1967:39) In his extended answer to this question, involving suggested solution of bicultural construct validation, he fails to consider the solution of collecting new United Statesian data on well-translated versions of the milder Japanese items.

Back-translation provides a most useful technique for suggesting revisions of the original, as well as revisions of the first translation effort. It also provides an epistemological model for the difficult process of decentering. Consider an original test, its first translation, and the first back-translation.

We now have two original-language versions. Which should we use in our original-language data collation? The researcher, comparing the original and the first back-translation, will certainly prefer the original. But which is more comparable to the target-language version? Undoubtedly the back-translation—because of its comparably *poor* quality, for one thing. *If* translation is possible, then the researcher should be willing to collect data using the back-translation. Any qualms he has about this he should have about the translated version too.

The back-translation concept considered as multistage iterative process provides an ideal conceptualization of decentered translating. In addition to a large supply of competent bilingual translators, ideally some with each first language, there would be monolingual translation-judges in each of the languages. These judges would have the power to say when any double-translation was adequate by comparing the two versions in his language. Translation revision efforts would be made until he was satisfied. Figure 1 illustrates such a process. Essential to the decentering process is the monolingual judge in the target language. Without him, with only the judge in the original language (usually the investigator himself), the process would still produce a unicentered product, although less so than if the first original-language version were kept unmodified.

The strategy of cultural comparison has to be one of competitive interpretation of obtained differences, in which differences in culture attitude or personality is only *one* of the possible explanations. Imperfections of translations will ubiquitously appear among the plausible rival hypotheses. As with such rival hypotheses in general (Segall, Campbell and Herskovits 1966, Frijda and Jahoda 1966), studying the effects of deliberate variation may help rule this out. Thus, if for a multiple-item attitude test, the same cultural difference occurs on each item, translation imperfection ceases to be a plausible hypothesis. Note here two recommendations: first, in favor of multiple items over single items, and second, analysis of results by item rather than solely by total score. So strong is the likelihood of translation-imperfection, that even in the public-opinion survey format, where typically a single item represents a concept, one should use at least two items per concept, each pair sharing no key words but by intention as identical as possible in meaning.

A suggested tactic for confirming the equivalence of translation is to have bilinguals respond to the items in both languages (e.g., Schachter 1954). Used as a formal statistical approach, the goal should not be identity at the item-by-item level, but rather equivalence of means and variances, plus appropriate correlations between scores on

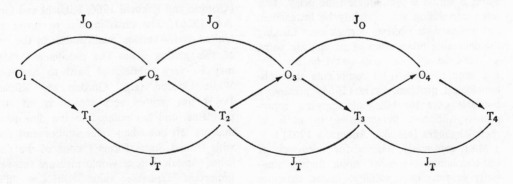

J_O J_O J_O

O_1 O_2 O_3 O_4

T_1 T_2 T_3 T_4

J_T J_T J_T

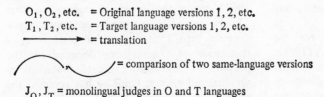

O_1, O_2, etc. = Original language versions 1, 2, etc.
T_1, T_2, etc. = Target language versions 1, 2, etc.
⟶ = translation

⌣ = comparison of two same-language versions

J_O, J_T = monolingual judges in O and T languages

Figure 2. An iterative sequence of back-translations

the two forms. Bentz (1955) and Lonner (1968) report translations of standard personality and interest scales which approximate these requirements. In Bentz's study, using sixty bilingual Latin American executives, the cross-language correlations after a five-month delay averaged .57 for the six scales of the Allport and Vernon Study Values, in contrast with the test-retest values for the original scale after three months' delay (on an unspecified population) of .74. Parallel values for the Kuder Interest Scales were .75 vs. .90 (over two months). In Lonner's study the average cross-language correlation of sixty-two scales on the Strong Vocational Interest Blank, administered in German one month later in English to eighteen European psychologists, was .80, in comparison with English test-retest correlations over one month on a much less homogeneous group which averaged .91. Both Lonner and Bentz write as though optimal translation would bring the cross-language correlations up to the same level as test-retest values. But surely this is unreasonable, for as we have emphasized, a translation at best can be no more similar than a paraphrase in the same language. If one has constructed an original-language paraphrase for each item, and if these are then separated into a Form A and Form B, the cross-language correlation of Form A should be at best as high as the within-language correlation of Form A with Form B across a comparable time delay. This latter correlation will certainly be lower than an ordinary test-retest correlation. Lacking the deliberate preparation of paraphrase pairs, an odd-even split of items could be used for the same purpose. (To complicate the epistemological problem, Ervin (1964) presents a plausible case for bilinguals showing appropriately different personalities in each of their languages [see also Anderson 1967].)

Most commonly, claims for adequacy of test-translation are based upon finding similarity in reliability, validity, factor structure and other statistics for the forms in both languages. This is fine when successful, and can be quite unequivocal evidence for both the universality of the trait and for the adequacy of translation. Gough (1966a, 1966b) has provided quite impressive parallel validations. But even in these, the disadvantages of a unicentered anchoring on the United States version of the test creates am-

biguities. Thus while the "Femininity" scale was designed for use as a personality trait within sexes, sex differences are relevant to its validity. For the U.S. form, the sex difference is indicated by a point biserial correlation coefficient of .71. For other countries, the values were significant, but lower: France, .52; Italy, .47; Norway, .62; Turkey, .47; Venezuela, .58. If the instrument had been *de*centered (with the U.S. version as subject to editing as the others, with items being suggested equally from the commonly observed sex differences in interests in each country, with statistical item selection being done jointly for all countries, etc., and with multicentered back-translation editing), then we might interpret this finding as demonstrating that sex differences in interests were much the greatest in the United States, and were the least in Italy and Turkey. What we know anthropologically leads us to believe the reverse to be true, and that the .71 value reflects merely the cultural bias of the test, it having been constructed just so as to maximize sex differences within the United States, naturally did this less well in dissimilar cultures.

Where procedures such as factor analysis or item selection are involved, in a decentered test development procedure, these should be carried out in both languages, and only those items showing up on the same factors in both cultures used in computing factor scores (Gordon and Kikuchi 1966, Kikuchi and Gordon 1966). The unwillingness to revise the United States version again stands in the way of this getting done. The unicentered biases may be very subtle and hard to root out. While Gordon (e.g., Gordon and Kikuchi 1966) has written very sensitively on such problems, and has pointed to the dimensions that get left out when value studies start only with United States forms ("none of the published American tests would measure the very important Japanese value 'Giri' or 'filial piety'"), he has in a later study (Gordon 1967) made the error of concluding that Chinese personalities were in fact more homogeneous than United Statesian ones, using a translation of Q-sort items designed for the purpose of maximizing United Statesian individual differences. Until he has reversed the process, developing Q-sort items in China to maximize Chinese differences and then translated these for the United States administration, no such conclusion is warranted.

Special problems emerge with special features of tests, which are perhaps only metaphorically translation problems, but are illustrative of fundamental problems in cross-cultural equivalence. The Edwards Personality Preference Schedule, like many of the better personality tests, is designed to avoid meaningless self-flattery through forcing the respondent to choose among pairs or triads of statements equated for social desirability. Berrien (1966), in building a Japanese version, had the translated items scaled for social desirability in Japan, and then used these quite-different values to assemble the items into different pairs. This was undoubtedly the correct thing to do if one wanted a test for use in making differentiations among Japanese. But for developing a test to compare the United States and Japan, it was wrong, for had the procedure been perfectly executed there would have been no value or need differences between the cultures (and within each culture, the mean of each value or need would have been the same [Kikuchi and Gordon 1966]). His intermediate-stage data on Japanese and United States differences in social desirability ratings of the items were the relevant facts for describing cultural differences in personality. Similarly, Cantril's (1965) self-anchoring scales, supposedly an improvement in cross-cultural comparability, are no doubt useful for within-country comparisons, but by making all comparisons relative to the local adaptation level and frame of reference, they obscure the differences that would otherwise be found.

There has recently been emphasis on the importance of nonverbal indicators of attitude (e.g., Webb *et al.* 1965) and advocacies of increased use of nonverbal tasks in cross-cultural research as a method of avoiding the translation problems which verbal materials present (Frijda and Jahoda 1966). Along with the latter is an emphasis on the desirability of using tasks which can be communicated by gesture. Construed as advocacy of avoiding an overdependence on verbal methods by supplementing and cross-validating them by alternate means, this is to be strongly supported. Nonverbal and observational methods have imperfections that are different from those of verbal procedures, and this makes possible a methodological

triangulation which filters out the systematic irrelevancies associated with any one method (Campbell and Fiske 1959, Webb *et al.* 1965). But any advocacy of nonverbal tasks and observation as a substitute for (rather than a supplement to) verbal methods must be rejected, for these nonverbal procedures have their own irrelevant and misleading components, just as serious as those of verbal procedures (Webb *et al.* 1965).

Particularly should the notion be rejected that no translation is required for nonverbal tasks and gestural instructions. The actual status is the reverse—such instruments require fully as much translation as do verbal materials, but the art of translating them is nowhere near as fully developed. Nonverbal intelligence test items are in general not more independent of culture than are verbal ones—usually they are more culturally specific, more unicentered. In the TAT personality test in which pictures are used to which stories are told, the pictorial content is very culture-bound. Efforts to cure this by making new pictures appropriate to specific cultures have not helped the problem of comparison, for the possibility remains that the differences in response are due to the differences in the pictures (Lindzey 1961, Doob 1965). In the end, a projective personality test with the verbal instruction "Tell me a story about a little boy and his mother" is more translatable than the TAT technique stimulating such stories by means of a picture stimulus. (This is claimed in full recognition of the difficulties which even this simple example would encounter.) Gesture surely often works for simple communication between persons sharing no languages—yet, gesture too is a culturally specific, with some New Guinea groups pointing with eyes and not understanding pointing with fingers, with Bulgarians indicating assent with the side-to-side head motion we use to indicate negation, with Tibetans indicating approval by sticking out their tongues, etc.

SUMMARY

The theory of generative grammars, an emphasis on deep structure and paraphrase, has lead to numerous criticisms and recommendations in the practice of ethnographic translation, in working with bilingual informants, in working through interpreters, and in translating of research instruments. In these recommendations have recurred the themes of multiple paraphrases in the source and target languages, of back-translation, and of "decentering."

BIBLIOGRAPHY

ALMOND, G., and S. VERBA
1963 *The civic culture: political attitudes and democracy in five nations.* Princeton, N.J., Princeton University Press.

ANDERSON, R. B. W.
1967 On the comparability of meaningful stimuli in cross-cultural research. *Sociometry* 30, 2:124–136.

BACH, E.
1964 *An introduction to transformational generative grammar.* New York, Holt, Rinehart and Winston.

BARIOUX, M.
1949 Experience in the Time International Survey: techniques used in France. *Public Opinion Quarterly* 12:715–718.

BENTZ, V. I.
1955 *A comparison of the Spanish and English versions of the Sears Executive Battery.* Chicago, National Personnel Department, Sears, Roebuck and Company. Mimeo.

BERRIEN, F. K.
1966 Japanese and American values. *International Journal of Psychology* 1, 2:129–141.
1967 Methodological and related problems in cross-cultural research. *International Journal of Psychology* 2, 1:33–43.

BOHANNAN, P. J.
1954 Translation: a problem in anthropology. *The Listener,* May 13, 815–816.

CAMPBELL, D. T.
1964 Distinguishing differences of perception from failures of communication in cross-cultural studies. In F. S. C. Northrop and H. H. Livingston, eds., *Cross-cultural understanding: epistemology in anthropology.* New York, Harper and Row.
1966 Pattern matching as an essential in distal knowing. In K. R. Hammond, ed., *Egon Brunswik's psychology.* New York, Holt, Rinehart and Winston.

CAMPBELL, D. T., and D. W. FISKE
1964 Convergent and discriminant validation by the multitrait-multimethod matrix. *Psychological Bulletin* 56, 2:81–105.

CANTRIL, H.
1965 *The pattern of human concerns.* New Brunswick, N.J., Rutgers University Press.

CASAGRANDE, J. B., and K. L. HALE
1967 Semantic relationships in Papago folk-definitions. In D. Hymes and W. E. Bittle, eds., *Studies in southwestern ethnolinguistics.* Cambridge, Mass., Mouton.

CHOMSKY, N.
1957 *Syntactic structures.* Cambridge, Mass., Mouton.
1965 *Aspects of the theory of syntax.* Cambridge, Mass., MIT Press.
1966 *Cartesian linguistics.* New York, Harper and Row.
1967 The formal nature of language. In E. H. Lenneberg, ed., *Biological foundations of language.* New York, Wiley.
1968 *Language and Mind.* New York, Harcourt, Brace & World, Inc.

COLBY, B. N.
1965 Ethnographic semantics. *Current Anthropology* 7:3–32.

CONKLIN, H.
1964 Ethnogenealogical method. In W. H. Goodenough, ed., *Explorations in cultural anthropology.* New York, McGraw-Hill.

DOOB, L. W.
1965 Psychology. In R. Lystad, ed., *The African world: a survey of social research.* New York, Praeger.

DUIJKER, H. C. J.
1955 Comparative research in social science with special reference to attitude research. *International Social Science Bulletin* 7:555–556.

ERVIN, SUSAN M.
1964 Language and TAT content in bilinguals. *Journal of Abnormal Social Psychology* 68:500–507.

ERVIN, S., and R. T. BOWER
1953 Translation problems in international surveys. *Public Opinion Quarterly* 16:595–604.

FODOR, J. A., and J. J. KATZ
1964 *The structure of language.* Englewood Cliffs, N.J., Prentice-Hall.

FRIJDA, N., and G. JAHODA
1964 *International Journal of Psychology.*
1966 On the scope and methods of cross-cultural research. *International Journal of Psychology* 1, 2:109–127.

GARVIN, P.
1962 *Natural language and the computer.* New York, McGraw-Hill.

GIPPER, H.
1963 *Bausteine zur Sprachinhaltsforschung.* Düsseldorf, Pädagogischer Verlag, Schwann.

GOODENOUGH, W. H.
1956 Componential analysis and the study of meaning. *Language* 32:195–216.

1964 (ed.) *Explorations in cultural anthropology.* New York, McGraw-Hill.

GORDON, L. V.
1967 Q-typing of Oriental and American youth: initial and clarifying studies. *Journal of Social Psychology* 71:185–195.

GORDON, L. V., and A. KIKUCHI
1966 American personality tests in cross-cultural research—a caution. *Journal of Social Psychology* 69:179–183.

GOUGH, H. G.
1966a A cross-cultural analysis of the CPI Femininity Scale. *Journal of Consulting Psychology* 30, 2:136–141.

1966b An appraisal of social maturity by means of the CPI. *Journal of Abnormal Psychology* 71, 3:189–195.

HERSKOVITS, M. J.
1949 *Man and his works.* New York, Knopf.

HYMAN, H.
1947 World surveys—the Japanese angle. *International Journal of Opinion and Attitude Research* 1, 2:18–30.

HYMES, D. (ed.)
1964 *Language in culture and society.* New York, Harper and Row.

HYMES, D., and W. E. BITTLE (eds.)
1967 *Studies in southwestern ethnolinguistics.* Cambridge, Mass., Mouton.

JACOBSON, E. H.
1954 Methods used for producing comparable data in the OCSR: Seven-Nation Attitude Study. *Journal of Social Issues* 10: 40–51.

1960 Cross-cultural contributions to attitude research. *Public Opinion Quarterly* 24: 205–223.

KATZ, J. J.
1966 *The philosophy of language.* New York, Harper and Row.

KENNEDY, D. A., and A. M. LEIGHTON
1957 Pilot study of cultural items. In *Medical diagnosis, a field report.* USPMS Division of Indian Health, Health Education Branch.

KIKUCHI, A., and L. V. GORDON
1966 Evaluation and cross-cultural application of a Japanese form of the Survey of Interpersonal Values. *Journal of Social Psychology* 69:185–195.

KLUCKHOHN, F. H., and F. STRODTBECK
1961 *Variations in value orientations.* Evanston, Ill., Row, Peterson.

KOUTZOUDAS, A.
1966 *A Beginner's Manual for Writing Transformational Grammars.* New York, McGraw-Hill.

LAKOFF, G.
1965 *On the nature of syntactic regularity.* Harvard Computation Laboratory Report, NFS-16:II-4.

LAMBERT, W. E.
1955 Measurement of the linguistic dominance of bilinguals. *Journal of Abnormal Social Psychology* 50:197–200.

LAMBERT, W. E., J. HAVELKA, and C. CROSBY
1958 The influence acquisition contexts on bilingualism. *Journal of Abnormal Social Psychology* 56:239–244.

LEES, R. B.
1957 Review of Chomsky 1957. *Language* 33:375–408.

LEVINE, R. A., and D. T. CAMPBELL
1965 *Ethnocentrism field manual.* The cross-cultural study of ethnocentrism, supported by a grant from the Carnegie Corporation of New York to Northwestern University.

LINDZEY, G.
1961 *Projective techniques and cross-cultural research.* New York, Appleton-Century-Crofts.

LONGACRE, R. E.
1958 Items in context—their bearing on translation theory. *Language* 34:482–491.

LONNER, W. J.
1968 The SVIB visits German, Austrian and Swiss psychologists. *American Psychologist* 23:164–179.

LOUNSBURY, F.
1956 A semantic analysis of Pawnee Kinship usage. *Language* 32:158–194.

LOWIE, R.
1940 Native languages as ethnographic tools. *American Anthropologist* 42:81–89.

MEAD, M.
1939 Native languages as field work tools. *American Anthropologist* 41:189–205.

MEAD, M., and G. BATESON
1942 *Balinese character: a photographic analysis.* New York Academy of Sciences Special Publication.

MITCHELL, R. E.
1965 Survey materials collected in the developing countries: sampling measurement, and interviewing obstacles to intra- and international comparisons. *International Social Science Journal* 17:677.

NIDA, E.
1945 Linguistics and ethnology in translation. *Word* 1:194–208. Reprinted in Hymes 1965.
1964 *Toward a scientific theory of translating.* New York, J. J. Brill.

OSGOOD, E. E.
1962 Studies on the generality of affective meaning systems. *American Psychologist* 17:10–28.

OSGOOD, E. E., and T. A. SEBEOK (eds.)
1954 *Psycholinguistics: a survey of theory and research problems.* A Morton Prince Memorial Supplement to the Journal of Abnormal Social Psychology 49.

PERCHONOCK, N., and O. WERNER
1969 *Navaho systems of classification: some implications for ethnoscience. Ethnology* 8:229–242.

PHILLIPS, H. P.
1959 Problems of translating and meaning in field work. *Human Organization* 18:184–192.

POSTAL, P.
1964 *Harvard Education Review*

QUINE, W. V.
1953 *From a logical point of view.* New York, Harper Torchbooks.
1960 *Word and object.* New York, Wiley.
1964 Meaning and translation. In J. A. Fodor and J. J. Katz, eds., *The structure of language.* Englewood Cliffs, N.J., Prentice-Hall.

SCHACHTER, P.
1962 In P. Garvin, ed., *Natural language and the computer.* New York, McGraw-Hill.

SCHACHTER, S.
1954 Interpretative and methodological problems of replicated research. *Journal of Social Issues* 10:52–60.

SEGALL, M. H., D. T. CAMPBELL, and M. J. HERSKOVITS
1966 *The influence of culture on visual perception.* Indianapolis, Bobbs-Merrill.

STERN, E., and R. L. D'EPINAY
1948 Some polling experiences in Switzerland. *Public Opinion Quarterly* 11:553–557.

STURTEVANT, W. C.
1964 Studies in ethnoscience. *American Anthropologist* 66, 2:99–131.

VOEGELIN, C. F.
1954 Multiple stage translation. *International Journal of American Linguistics* 20:271–280.

VOEGELIN, C. F., and FLORENCE M. VOEGELIN
1960 Selection in Hopi ethics, linguistics, and translation. *Anthropological Linguistics* 2:48–77.
1967 *Anthropological linguistics and translation.* To honor Roman Jakobson:2159–2190. Paris, Mouton.

WEBB, E. J., D. T. CAMPBELL, R. D. SCHWARTZ, and L. B. SECHREST
1966 *Unobtrusive measures: nonreactive research in the social sciences.* Chicago, Rand McNally.

WERNER, O.
1966 Pragmatics and ethnoscience. *Anthropological Linguistics* 8, 8:42–65.
1967 Systematized lexicography: the use of computer-made concordances. *American Behavioral Scientist* 10:5–8.

PART IV

Models of Ethnographic Analysis

CHAPTER 23

Toward a Model of Role Analysis

ROGER M. KEESING

INTRODUCTION

The Problem

Since the publication in 1951 of Ward Goodenough's *Property, Kin and Community on Truk,* anthropologists have been confronted by the challenge of describing social interaction in terms of an underlying cultural code. Though we have made some progress, the internal structure of cultures as cognitive systems remains largely a mystery, and we are still far from attaining Goodenough's goal of "a grammar of social interaction."

Cultures, so conceived, consist largely of "norms"—"rules" epistemologically and logically parallel to the rules of a grammar. How these principles for treating patterns in the phenomenal world as meaning-laden messages and decoding them, and for constructing appropriate behavior sequences, are cul-

Earlier versions of this paper were presented to the Philadelphia Anthropological Society (November 19, 1967) and a Social Science Colloquium at Northwestern University (February 22, 1968). Parts of it derive from Keesing 1966c and Keesing 1967c. Field work on Malaita and analysis of Kwaio data have been supported by the U. S. Public Health Service, Ford Foundation, Social Science Research Council, and National Science Foundation. I am indebted to my Kwaio collaborator Jonathan Fifi?i; to members of my Stevenson College Seminar "Changing Hats Inside Your Head"; and to many colleagues who have contributed to my thinking about roles or made suggestions on earlier versions of the paper—among whom Gregory Bateson, Ronald Cohen, Daniel Crowl, William Davenport, Meyer Fortes, Charles Frake, William Geoghegan, Ward Goodenough, George Grace, John Haviland, Paul Kay, and Duane Metzger had had a particularly prominent influence on the final version.

turally organized is a problem we are only beginning to explore.

This paper asks whether cultural principles for behavior are ordered in terms of "roles": and if so, how we can decipher this ordering in an unfamiliar culture. It derives directly from Goodenough's initial (1951) and recent (1965) examinations of "status" and "role" as elements in cultural systems, and the conceptual revisions he proposes; and from my recent attempts among the Kwaio of Malaita, British Solomon Islands, to carry further his pioneer work.

Since both my conceptual scheme and the theory of culture that gives it meaning are based largely on the work of Goodenough, a review of his approach will serve to introduce my own analysis.

Goodenough's Approach to "Status" and "Role"

The foundation of Goodenough's approach to "roles" is his narrow and rigorous conception of culture as a system of norms— existing only in the cognitive world of our subjects, the "ideational order," as contrasted with the realm of observable events (including behavior), the "phenomenal order."

Culture consists of standards for deciding what is, . . . for deciding what can be, . . . for deciding how one feels about it, . . . for deciding what to do about it, and . . . for deciding how to go about doing it. (1961a:522)

Otherwise phrased, culture consists of

the forms of things that people have in mind, their models for perceiving, relating and otherwise interpreting them (1957:167) . . .

of ideal forms . . . propositions about their inter-relationships, preference ratings regarding them, and recipes for their mutual ordering as a means to desired ends. (1964:12)

Invoking this distinction rigorously, Goodenough perceives at the outset that most usages of "status" and "role" incorporate elements from both the ideational and phenomenal orders. That is, "roles" and "statuses" have characteristically been treated as elements of *social*, not cultural, systems. Goodenough, in contrast, proceeds directly to structural analysis of the normative systems on which "role behavior" is based (1965).

He notes, first, that the concept of "status" has confounded two elements that need to be analytically separated: on the one hand, a social position or category; and on the other, the rights and duties associated with that position. Goodenough shows that viewed as cultural orderings, sets of positions and sets of rights and duties are distinct and formally separate. For a culturally distinguished social position, Goodenough introduces the term *social identity*. "Status" pertains not to positions, but to rights and duties and the rules for their cultural distribution.

Goodenough goes on to note the pervasive and unfortunate tendency to deal with social positions singly (e.g., "the role [or status] of the doctor"). As some previous theorists have noted, the cultural principles governing action in a social position vary according to the position of *alter*.

. . . A physician's rights and duties differ considerably depending on whether he is dealing with another physician, a nurse, a patient, or the community and its official representatives. If a status is a collection of rights and duties, then the social identity we label "physician" occupies a different status in each of these identity relationships. (1965:4)

Goodenough discusses the way in which each social identity has certain culturally defined matching identities an alter can assume. Each matching pair of social identities comprise an *identity relationship*.

Goodenough focuses on *status relationships*, which are the reciprocal relations of right and duty distributed in an identity relationship. He shows how the duty-statuses (and the implied reciprocal right-statuses) of each identity relationship are amenable to formal analysis, and how they can be perceived to fall into wider patterns of status-ordering. He shows formally the necessity of treating social

identity relationships and status relationships as separate—though interlocking—systems (1965:8).

Goodenough illustrates how in actual behavioral settings ego is likely to occupy a number of coalescing social identities in the same interaction. A man never interacts solely as "physician" (e.g., to "nurse"). He is at the same time "adult" and "male" as well. This additive or combinational property of culturally defined positions and associated statuses has not been adequately studied—in part because of our failure to distinguish systematically the cognitive code for behavior from its expression in concrete situations. Goodenough calls the composite identities assumed in a given interaction the actor's *social persona* (1965:7).

Goodenough goes on to show how the formal organization of status relationships can be analyzed by an ethnographer, and how the models so derived can render intelligible subtle and complex patterns of interaction in an alien culture.

FINDING SOCIAL IDENTITIES IN AN UNFAMILIAR CULTURE

The Ethnographic Task

I went to the field armed with a number of methodological and conceptual schemes that seemed promising. Among them was a preliminary version (1961b) of Goodenough's paper. In attempting to implement his suggestions, I quickly discovered that his method depends on our being able to discover what are the social identities and identity relationships in an unfamiliar culture; and that this task is neither simple nor amenable to some conventional method. The problem, then, was: How does an ethnographer find what social identities and identity relationships there are in an alien culture, and what their behavioral entailments are?

Note that we are not dealing with "roles" as properties of *social systems*, positions in a social network that individuals are "stepping into." If we were, we could be relatively arbitrary about our analytical task. Rather, we are dealing with social identities and statuses as elements in a formally ordered system of *norms*—ideas "in people's heads." If we are to anticipate what actors who share an unfamiliar culture will do, we need to approximate *their* model of their social universe: what kinds of situations there are, what capacities they conceive themselves and others to be acting in, and what acts are possible and appropriate. Though we cannot assume all of our actors have identical cognitive mappings of this universe of social relationships, a model that replicates the common general outlines and formal properties of their variant versions will best allow us to anticipate the events in that universe.

That being the case, I could not simply invent a formal method for deciding what "roles" there were in Kwaio culture. I knew my intuitions would not suffice as a method —for in dealing with another culture our intuitions are often misleading. I hoped to be able to devise a method which was public and potentially replicable, which reflected the unique structure and categories of the culture under study, and which met high standards of ethnographic adequacy.

Most sociologists who have used the "role" concept seem to have regarded the identification of "roles" as unproblematical, probably in part because they usually share the cognitive code of their subjects. Attempts to define "roles" operationally seem either arbitrary or culture-bound or both. Nor can we even assume that our theatrical metaphor of "role" and the cognitive processes it implies are universal. We must begin by facing squarely the possibility that the whole notion of "role" is a product of our own culture biases, an artifact of our "folk sociology," and that projecting it on other peoples may severely distort their cultural and social orders.

It was with these traps in mind that I set about to find what "social identities," if any, there were in Kwaio culture. Goodenough's own definition of "social identity" as "an aspect of self that makes a difference in how one's rights and duties distribute with respect to specific others" (1965:3) seemed promising only if one could first discover patterns of rights and duties. I quickly ran into difficulties of the following sorts.

Difficulties in Isolating Social Identities

(1) It is usually difficult and often impossible to elicit and analyze rights and duties unless you already have a working (if not final) model of social categories or positions, on the one hand, and categories of situations, on the other. You can study the distribution of rights and duties between *individuals* X and Y; but unless you can sort out the several identity relationships in which they may interact, and the categories of situations in which various rules and principles come into play, you cannot effectively order the rights and duties so elicited.

(2) Linguistic labels do not turn out to be reliable indicators of social identities. In Kwaio, what most of us would want to call social identities are often not monolexemically labeled. There is a label for "priest," but not for "diviner" or "curer," and so on. Such difficulties preclude simple use of ethnographic semantics or a corpus composed solely of utterances in inferring a society's roster of social identities (cf., Metzger and Williams 1963a).[1] On this point, Goodenough's original Trukese analysis and discussion of methodology is instructive (1951: 114–119); but serious problems remain.

(3) Cultural codes for behavior do not consist solely of paired positions, on the one hand, and the rights and duties that distribute in these relationships, on the other. There must be sets of norms that tell the occupant of a position *what to do*: what can or should be done, in what sequences, in particular situations. I have referred elsewhere to such norms as "operating norms" (1965a). Note that we are not considering sets of operating norms to be *elements of* social identities. That would be to compound the confusions perceived by Goodenough.

Goodenough's use of "status" requires some clarification. When he speaks of "rights and duties" he does so in the broadest sense. His model is a linguistic one, in which some distinctions are obligatory—without them meaning is changed or obliterated. Other distinctions are optional, and ranges of free variation and style are possible. Rights and duties here are the boundaries of behavior not in a strict jural sense but in this communicational sense.

However, in his actual analyses of Trukese status systems, he deals with scales of sexual and social distance that are more like jural boundaries than rules for "grammatical" behavior. There seems a gulf between what

[1] Goodenough himself would not rely on monolexemic labels to distinguish descriptive categories for ethnographic discourse—a point on which he has differed from many others who have followed his pioneer work in ethnographic semantics.

Goodenough describes as status relationships and "what you have to know in order to operate as a member of the society" (Goodenough 1957:168) in each of its social identities.

Many operating norms pertaining to "role behavior" seem to escape Goodenough's analytical net. In fact they would have to, since much of our "role behavior" is not oriented directly toward alters (and hence cannot be conceptualized in terms of reciprocal right and duty). To conceive what a Kwaio feast-giver must know to stage a feast, or what a Kwaio gardener must know to build a garden in terms of "obligatory" rules or right and duty, seems awkward at best.

If we dilute the notions of "right" and "duty" so that they work that widely, they are no longer powerful enough where we most need them. In the sense of jural boundaries, they serve us better. We find the same rights of precedence, authority, distance, and the like manifest in many identity relationships of a culture. They cross-cut the specifics of role behavior between student and school principal, soldier and commanding officer, defendant and magistrate, or between buyer and salesman and tenant and landlord. Moreover these boundaries of right and duty and their manifestation in different contexts are amenable to formal analyses, such as Goodenough's, that sort out constants and essentials from particularities. We can then say that in some or all of these "jural" respects the occupants of two different social identities have the same *status* vis-à-vis a pair of matching social identities.

This renders "status" a powerful analytical tool. But it is precisely this power to sort constant formal features from particularities that requires us to devise another means for describing the operating norms that specify these particularities. In Kwaio culture, at least, I found contrasts in operating norms as important in defining social identities as contrasts in the boundaries of right-and-duty.

(4) Social identities differ in the qualifications or principles for assuming them. This provides still another set of differentiae which could be used—instead of, or in addition to, rights and duties—in distinguishing social identities. As we will see, invoking this criterion we could be led to distinguish as separate social identities "positions" with identical jural entailments, or to join, as elements of a single identity, "positions" with different jural entailments.

(5) We cannot hope to arrive—by analysis of rights and duties or any other means—at a simple roster of a culture's social identities and identity relationships. Here Goodenough's ethnographic optimism is probably misleading. A main reason is that social identities are ordered in hierarchies of class inclusion. Rights and duties and operating norms are differentiated not only situationally, but according to the taxonomic level on which the identity is defined. We can illustrate this with the "role of the doctor" in American culture. While this is perhaps a unitary social identity on one level, we clearly must make cognitive discriminations between types of doctors (specialists of various sorts, doctors vs. dentists, medical doctors vs. chiropractors, etc.). Within the setting of a hospital we might encounter distinctions between (staff) physician vs. intern. We would find particular kinds of doctors in particular positions. The taxonomic level at which distinctions are relevant behaviorally will vary according to situation and identity relationship. The rights and duties of a hospital patient in dealing with a physician may be roughly the same with any doctor (e.g., the patient need only discriminate doctors from nurses, orderlies, secretaries, visitors, other patients, etc.). The rights and duties and appropriate behavior for the doctor who enters the doctor-patient relationship may vary sharply according to his position on the staff and his relationship to the case (consultant, etc.). In identity relationships with other doctors, a physician may have to make even finer discriminations of social identity. Yet, returning to the highest level of the hierarchy, he will have *some* rights and duties with respect to any doctor with whom he interacts professionally.

The same hierarchical structuring begins to emerge when we examine situations or contexts. We have not so far deciphered the code whereby any culture defines situations; and this restricts our knowing just what structures are involved. However, some taxonomic ordering seems likely, intermeshed with the hierarchical structure of social identities. Elements of this structuring will emerge in the course of our analysis.

(6) The analytical value of distinguishing positions and their behavioral entailments is

that occupying the position can then be assumed to imply enacting the role. Thus most students of role theory have assumed an isomorphism and linkage between sets of positions and sets of behaviors.

But this heightens and renders more critical our problem of discovering what positions are culturally salient. For if we use lexical labels to infer positions, we must optimistically hope that applicability of the position-label means applicability of a set of operating norms. I will illustrate ethnographically that this is not necessarily the case; but this is something we already know from the study of kinship terminologies (Keesing 1968 b). If we define positions by contrasts in rights and duties, we will create a partial isomorphism by definition; but as we have seen, other operating norms may still contrast.

If we wish to establish the invariant relationship between position categories and behaviors most students have assumed, we must begin with behaviors and isolate behavioral equivalence-classes—"categories" that have predictable behavioral entailments, whether the categories are explicit or implicit. We can then search for evidence that such schemata reflect the cognitive ordering of native actors. If not, we can seek other modes of order, which may include "positions" defined by other means. But if we do, we must abandon the assumption that occupying the position entails applicability of a behavioral pattern.

A Proposal for Conceptual Clarification

At this point, I would suggest—though not insist on—the potential utility of reintroducing the term "role" to denote the operating norms associated with a social identity relationship. If we did so, we could speak with considerable conceptual rigor of:

(1) Paired social *positions* (social identity relationships).

(2) The distribution of rights and duties in such relationships (status relationships) that provide jural boundaries for behavior.

(3) The operating norms appropriate to the occupants of paired positions (role relationships).

Such a conceptual clarification would enable us to perceive that roles are a subclass of operating norms (which would also include, for instance, norms about the *assumption*

of social identities). Furthermore, though *status* could not be usefully considered except in pair relationships, analytic contexts could arise where we would want to treat *roles* singly (so we could say, e.g., that a man goes to barber's college to learn the role of a barber—which includes not only cutting hair, but buying equipment from barbers' supply houses). We could use the term "composite role" for the combined behavioral patterns appropriate to a social persona. This differs somewhat from Goodenough's usage (1965:16). But I feel it is more flexible and useful, and corresponds reasonably well to one set of traditional sociological usages, to the intuitions of our folk sociology, and to the theatrical metaphor that provides the label (cf., role vs. part or character).

TOWARD A METHODOLOGICAL SOLUTION

I should make clear at this stage that I have not arrived at a perfect discovery procedure, and solved all of these problems. I have, I think, explored them to a point where I can raise some new questions and suggest some further paths for exploration.

Nor is it at all clear that we should strive and hope for an explicit "automatic" discovery procedure that produces these or other elements of a cultural description. This is a point to which we will return (p. 441). But at least inductive methods can be useful ways of asking early questions and mapping out alternative possibilities.

Let us take as a paradigmatic model of the problem a case where we observe a pair of individuals interacting; and by observation and verbal eliciting we are able to arrive at some idea of the patterns of reciprocal behavior in which they engage. Let us say that A is B's mother's brother. We note that A provides for B during frequent long visits with his household, instructs him in certain techniques and imparts esoteric knowledge to him, makes gifts to him, sacrifices pigs raised by B to propitiate their common ancestors, loans B money, and so on. Our problem is: are A and B engaged in one role relationship or several? How can we sort out the identity relationships in which they are interacting (if more than one), and discover the entailments of each?

We are armed, at this stage, with fore-knowledge that:

(1) We cannot expect to find a simple one-level roster of social identities; there may not, in any useful sense, be a finite roster at all.

(2) There are sets of cultural categories about "kinds of people" that may not correspond to social identities (if we conceive these as labeled or unlabeled position categories with invariant behavioral entailments): "little old lady," "social climber," "uncle" and the like are social categories, but they may not be social identities.

To use our paradigmatic example, A may fall into the labeled social categories 'uncle' (to B), 'rich man,' 'priest,' 'old man'; and also 'adult,' 'relative,' 'man,' 'living person,' 'right-handed person,' etc., etc. The list may for practical purposes be infinitely extensible; some of these categories may have no behavioral entailments of any social consequence; and some of the position-categories that are crucial in terms of rights and duties or other behavioral rules (e.g., A and B's relationship as "lender" and "borrower") might in their culture be unlabeled.

How, then, do we sort out what identity relationships actors using a cultural code quite different from ours are acting in? We need to know whether the acts performed by A and B are a combination of several elements that need not go together. Hence, we will have to look at other pairs of individuals to find what operating norms go together in invariant packages. Some elements of A and B's relationship may apply to any priest who sacrifices to a client (whatever their kinship relationship); some may apply to any person who borrows money from another; some to any old man vis-à-vis a young one; some to any pair of relatives; some to any mother's brother and his sister's son; and so on.

This calls for a means of distributional analysis across ranges of data, and for a focus on atypical circumstances rather than typical ones: on mother's brothers who are young men, on priests who are not close relatives, on co-residents who are not kinsmen, etc. We need a way of teasing apart strands that are often twisted together and interwoven, a way to sort behaviors that *always* go together from behaviors that *sometimes* or *usually* go together. Only then will

we arrive at position-categories with invariant behavioral implications. This requires that we distinguish social identities ultimately on the basis of recruitment criteria. If meeting criteria (a), (b) and (c) determines the applicability of a set of behavioral norms (say, in one situation), and meeting the same criteria determines the applicability of a different set of norms in another situation—then a person who enacts the first set will predictably enact the second as well. This is the invariance we are seeking. This "position," whether labeled or not, is what we want provisionally to call a social identity (cf., section (6) above). We can then ask whether the knowledge of our actors is organized in this manner.

But empirically, we cannot begin with recruitment criteria. We must begin with *acts* and *situations*. Let me illustrate the sort of distributional analysis that proved useful in the field, with a situation that is relatively neat and discrete, and a set of behaviors that are explicit and identifiable—a Kwaio 'mortuary feast.'[2] We will consider shortly the added difficulties in studying more messy domains of social behavior.

How do we determine what social identities and identity relationships are represented in a Kwaio 'mortuary feast'? First, let us be clear once again that if we are talking about social identities as patterns in the cognitive worlds of our actors—not in the realm of observable phenomena—then we are concerned not directly with the behavior enacted at feasts, but rather with the conceptual code of which the behavior is an expression. If the feast itself represents a cognitive isolate, then a first question we will want to ask is what acts and events are included within it. In observing the enactment of such a feast, we will see many patterns of interaction that turn out not to be "part" of the feast at all. We will want some way of determining that the man borrowing betel-chewing supplies from a friend is engaging in an act temporally and spatially—but not cognitively—included within the feast. Here the kinds of eliciting described in the literature of "ethnoscience" proved quite effective. That is, one can elicit verbal descriptions of how feasts are, or should be, given;

[2] For information on Kwaio society, the reader should consult my papers listed in the bibliography. Single quotes indicate glosses for Kwaio categories.

one can record simulated interaction concerning feasts (Metzger and Williams 1963b); one can elicit statements about a feast before it occurs, while it is occurring, and after it has occurred; one can create hypothetical situations exploring the permutations of an observed event; and so on. Observation of repetitions of the same event also aids in distinguishing the "contexts within contexts" (Keesing 1965b) that are conceptually separate, but may be physically included. This sorting out presented me with no grave difficulties.

A second step is to determine at what taxonomic level the performance of acts differentiates actors. If we observe a man carving portions of pork and passing them to a helper with instructions about who is to get each piece, are we dealing with one social position or two or three? Here we have two labels: *xwalia boo*, 'carve the pig,' and *tolinia boo*, 'divide the pig.' Does this mean we have two social identities here? Reflection will show that this procedure will not work. The occupant of a single social position in our society—say a desk clerk—may fill out forms and put the carbon copies in the file. How, then, are we to make this distinction? Kwaio have no monolexemic label for "carver" or "divider," or both, so this will not work. Different operating norms govern carving and dividing; but different norms govern filling out forms and filing them, so this will not work.

As we have suggested, the best criterion turned out to be whether the same person invariably performed both acts. That is, if you observe a dozen repetitions of carving and dividing, and the same person always does both, you can say with some confidence that these are elements of the same role. It turns out that in Kwaio culture, one person may carve and another person divide. The latter then rewards the former for his services, unless he is an immediate kinsman (see pp. 436–440). This can be determined from either intensive verbal eliciting, observation of repeated occurrences, or—as I found most effective—from a strategic mixture of the two. Moving back and forth between verbalized norms and empirical events that may deviate from them proved a most effective means of eliciting the many qualifying clauses and conditions that modify normative rules of thumb.

Here once more we should emphasize that we are concerned with cognitive appropriateness, not manifest behavior. It may be that on occasion some physical disability, lack of knowledge, etc., precludes an actor doing those things his fellows feel he normally would or should do. We must be prepared to distinguish this form of partial substitution from cases where an appropriate separation into component elements is culturally specified. We will return to this problem shortly.

Let us assume that we can achieve relative success, as I did, in such sortings—so that we can identify those clusters of acts invariably (or appropriately) performed by the same actor. Are we on our way toward success? Perhaps, but we are in danger of falling into one of the traps perceived by Goodenough—talking about positions without attention to the polar positions of the other parties to the interaction. There are not always alters involved: operating norms tell a man how to fell a tree or carve a pig whether or not others are present (which could perhaps lead us to talk about identities that are "cultural" but not "social").

But most of those acts we record are *communications*, and in our analysis we soon find networks of reciprocal pairs. We discover, by keeping track of the parties to interaction, that those persons who receive portions of pork from the man supervising distribution are the ones who presented him three or four hours earlier with shell valuables; and that the order of pork distribution and the portions presented correspond to the value of the shell money each contributed. Through careful analysis, at least for a large-scale event like a Kwaio 'mortuary feast,' complex but distinguishable clusters and networks emerge. For each position or pair of positions one can elicit statements about procedure, rights, and duties. To do so, one must usually use the terms for acts with which analysis began. In Kwaio culture, at least, I usually found no ready-made linguistic labels at this level for the *positions* (though there are some notable exceptions).

What assurance have we, in the absence of such labels, that our actors conceive of what is (or should be) going on in terms of social identities? Perhaps, cognitively, there are in most cases simply acts that are to be performed and recipes for deciding who should perform them. What we infer to be "social positions" could simply reflect isomorphism or major overlap in the "recruitment principles" for performing certain acts. Perhaps we have forced our theatrical metaphor of "role" onto a cognitive process that is rather different, and simpler. Perhaps our actors conceptualize in terms of social positions, if at all, only where they have monolexemic labels for such positions.

We will return to this problem. For the moment, let us see what we can do with the pairs and networks we have uncovered. One of the problems we face is whether these provisional social identities and identity relationships occur in any other settings. Does the same sequence of acts occur in other contexts? Is it possible that though some or all of the acts in another context are different, they are enactments of the same role? The man who administers a sacrament to men of the host descent group at our feast is the same man who in other settings addresses the spirits or sacrifices pigs on their behalf. Is he a "priest" in both?

Here we are dealing with the distribution of elements in different environments, a problem formally similar in several respects to that of traditional phonemic analysis in linguistics. A phone is an element of sound distinctive in a specified environment. Phones that differ, but never contrast in the same environment, are considered to be in complementary distribution. Given certain conditions, principally some phonetic relatedness, they can then be considered allophones or a single phoneme.

If we consider a culturally defined event or situation to be an environment, and isolate what are the distinctive social categories, we can then proceed to ask whether some of these may be environmentally conditioned "allo-identities" of a single social identity that occurs in other environments as well.

Though the analogy is useful in posing the problem as one of distributional analysis, it has important limitations. The criterion of contrast in a single environment cannot be directly applied. Some social identities contrast with others in the sense that they are mutually exclusive: the Kwaio man who administers the sacramental rite to descent group men at a mortuary feast is never the same man who administers a similar rite to the women. However, there are many sets of acts that *can be* performed by the same person even though they frequently are performed by different people. We have, in fact, suggested that social identities might be defined by a reverse criterion of contrast: only if two sets of acts *never* appropriately contrast, in the sense that different people perform each set, would they be considered to reflect a single social identity.

How, then, to tell whether two positions distinguished in this way—in different environments—are "allo-identities" of a single social identity? If each position is labeled—and the label is the same—then we can presume they are conditioned variants of a single social identity. This is the case with the Kwaio social identity *wane naa ba'e* ('priest'), who administers the sacramental rite to men, sacrifices pigs, communicates with spirits, etc.

One advantage we have in such distributional analysis is that we are observing actual named individuals occupying these positions. To simplify slightly the explication of cumbersome analytical steps, we have talked about positions singly. We should here recall that we are treating paired positions; and that we observe pairs of actual individuals occupying them. One strong clue that we are dealing with "allo-identities" is that the same individuals occupy the positions vis-à-vis one another in the different settings.

A further analytical lead is that the acts in the two environments are often themselves interrelated. In Kwaio society, we observe individual A applying a leaf poultice to B, and can elicit the fact that A *gulaa* ('is curing') B. Some weeks or months later, in a different setting, we find B presenting A with a small feast, and can elicit the fact that B *daula'i* A. Our informants can tell us that this transaction is *kwaena*, 'payment for services rendered,' in return for the act of 'curing.' Though there is no Kwaio lexeme denoting the position of either A or B, we might well want to label them "curer" and "patient."

Finally, the linking of "allo-identities" can be aided by the frequent partial overlap of the acts in different environments. If acts 12, 13, 14, and 15 are associated with a social position in one environment, we may find 12 in a different environment (with the same participants) and 14 in a third environment. Other sorts of linkage also emerge—as when all the environments (situations or contexts) in which paired positions occur share some defining characteristic (e.g., are "sacred").

What we have done is to sketch some criteria, admittedly not precise, akin to the criteria which lead to grouping allophones into a single phoneme. Though we could render these more precise, there probably would still often be, as in phonemic analysis, several alternative solutions.

We have sketched procedures which, if refined, would enable us to distinguish social positions that potentially contrast in particular environments; and then, looking at the range of environments, to regroup as positional variants of a single social identity related social positions that are in complementary distribution.

Such procedures operate on a single analytical level, separating and regrouping on the basis of distributional criteria. But in addition to contrasting at a single analytical level, both social positions and environments are taxonomically ordered in hierarchies of class inclusion. A pediatrician is also a kind of physician; and a coming-out-party is a kind of party.

Are these higher-order categories like "physician" also social identities? And if so, how are we to isolate them using the methods we have sketched? These higher-level categories principally involve not specific behavioral patterns, but broad rights and duties. Starting at the lower levels, we work upward analyzing rights and duties in search of levels where social positions have the same jural entailments. Such a procedure involves asking (implicitly or of our informants) "kind of" questions: the man who sells fish at a Kwaio 'market' is a kind of what? He is a kind of "seller," and we find that he shares some rights and duties with people who sell other scarce goods in Kwaio society. The criterion of hierarchic class inclusion implies that all the entailments of "seller of fish" apply to "seller of land." The ordering of situations in taxonomic hierarchies provides further clues in such analytic procedures. Sometimes what the procedure we outlined earlier leads us to distinguish as separate social identities are units in the same taxonomic hierarchy, so that

they merge at higher levels. This would be true, say, of the physician in charge of a hospital case and a consulting specialist. Both, at a higher level, are physicians. At other times the distinguished social identities fall into separate taxonomic hierarchies.

A PRELIMINARY ASSESSMENT

Rather than attempting to refine and formalize such methods, let us reflect at this stage on what it is we have achieved by them, what problems they entail, and what difficulties emerge if we try to generalize such chains of analysis to the whole cultural range of situations and events.

Before we proceed further, however, let us be clear that our objective is *primarily* to learn something about the way cultural knowledge about social interaction is organized and stored. It may or may not prove possible (or even desirable) to convert a set of strategies and concepts for exploring this cultural ordering into an explicit, formal discovery procedure. Our subjects learn their culture without one. Exploration of a method that works well in the neatest segments of a culture may be strategically useful if we use it as a source of guidelines and conceptual clarification, while it might mislead and unduly restrict us if we sought to apply it rigidly to all segments. With these reservations let us see what we have accomplished and what problems remain.

First, because of the way we distinguished social positions, we can assume that occupying the position entails applicability of the role. This invariant linkage between position and role has been assumed by most students of "status" and "role," as we have noted, though it is a precarious assumption seldom made explicit. But we have devised a method for *creating by definition* an invariance that otherwise would be uncertain. If the method is feasible, it identifies "positions" because they are behavioral equivalence classes. The question would then be not whether the positions have behavioral implications, but whether native actors employ such position-categories in storing and processing cultural knowledge of appropriate behavior.

But first, let us see what problems we would encounter in trying to analyze the full range of ethnographic phenomena using the methodological and conceptual guidelines we have sketched.

We used for illustration a culturally discrete and labeled kind of event—what Frake calls a "scene" (1964:112). The kind of distributional analysis we illustrated would—to be strictly applied—require a finite list of such "scenes." The Kwaio 'mortuary feast' constitutes a "scene," composed of component smaller "scenes" (e.g., the pork distribution, the performance of music). So, it would seem, is a domestic meal or a 'sacrifice.' However, we encounter over and over again in Kwaio culture "scenes" that have no common monolexemic labels—though labels can be coined in many cases by productive morphemic processes (e.g., *me?e*, 'chew betel' *me?e+—na*, 'betel chewing'). Moreover, we find continua of scale and discreteness, whereby at one extreme a model of separate "scenes" seems to fit well; while at the other extreme it seems forced on the data. To talk about the interaction of friends as a discrete "scene," for instance, seems inappropriate to the Kwaio material.

What we need, apparently, is a theory of the cultural definition of situations; and so far we have made little progress in this direction. Concepts like "scene" seem most appropriate to events that are culturally *created* and *staged*—e.g., the 'mortuary feast'—and least appropriate to the ever varying, kaleidoscopic patterns of circumstances that human beings *encounter* in everyday life. For the latter, instead of a finite set of ideal-type situations against which empirical percepts are matched, we probably will need a more complex model. Perhaps it will be formally akin to the generative devices of a grammar, whereby an infinite series of unique definitions of situations can be produced by the operation on a finite set of elements of a finite set of rules of combination.[3] Perhaps it will entail multiple levels, where invariant formal models of situations coded at very deep levels are modified by flexible surface structure rules to adjust to the particularities of empirical situations (Bateson 1968). I will explore these problems in greater detail elsewhere. For the moment, it suffices to observe that we could not, without distorting the data, produce a finite yet complete set of "scenes" for Kwaio culture

[3] This possibility was suggested to me by George Grace.

to which we could apply the methods for inferring social identities we have sketched.

A parallel difficulty derives from our inference of social identities from specific sequences of acts. Just as not all situations are neat and discrete "scenes," so not all interaction entails specified behavior sequences. At the extreme is the relatively unstructured interaction of friends, who clearly are not enacting a set of recipe-like instructions. But if there is a continuum of behavioral specification, even in the middle of it roles entail something more diffuse than simply sets of specified behaviors. Goodenough's approach to this problem (in practice if not in principle) is to specify the boundaries of such relationships, and not their behavioral content. While this is often useful, it runs afoul of the tendency for the boundaries to become thinner and more vaguely defined as one proceeds down this continuum.

A third general problem with this strategy of identifying behavioral equivalence classes is that it leads us, as we observe sequences more and more carefully, to make finer and finer distinctions—to "shred out" more and more social identities into component parts as we find instances where two or more actors perform separately sequences we had previously seen enacted by a single actor.

I recorded many cases in which a behavioral sequence that everyone insisted should be performed by a single actor was performed by two—because the appropriate actor was physically incapable or because he lacked the requisite skill or knowledge. We need some nonarbitrary and clear line between cases like these, which we would want to call appropriate exceptions to the unitary performance of a single role; and cases where we want to distinguish separate social identities even though, due to overlap in recruitment principles, they often or usually coalesce. Since this has to do with standards of appropriateness in the eyes of native actors, it is analogous to the much-debated questions of degrees of grammaticality and their empirical assessment in transformational linguistics. Empirically ours is a messy problem, but at least on principle there seems a way out. Where the division of behaviors usually performed by a single actor among two or more actors follows lines of cleavage *established by and standardized in the culture*, then we are dealing with separate social identities; where the division is random or unsystematic (according to whether the principal actor is blind, feeble, incompetent, immature, crippled, etc.), we are dealing with *ad hoc* modifications of a single social identity.

This leads, in turn, to a more general problem. We have suggested a cutoff point for the fractionation and multiplication of social identities. But do the "social identities" we have isolated at this level have any cognitive salience, or have we carved out segments that are too fragmentary and low-level? The frequent absence of linguistic labels at this lower level, even though higher-level "positions" are characteristically labeled, clearly gives ground for concern.

The problem can be illustrated with an American example. Books and chapters in guides to etiquette have dealt at great length with "the father of the bride" and his role in the marriage. Yet if we examine actual weddings we find that frequently the specified acts are performed by persons other than the father. If this is the adoptive father, foster father, uncle, or some other surrogate for the father, we have no analytical problems. But sometimes these acts are divided among two or more persons. Such divisions often take place in cases of divorce or when the father is dead. If a girl whose parents are divorced is married before she is legally of age, her stepfather might finance the marriage and give the bride away while her father legally consents to the marriage. We have a legal category "guardian" for someone empowered to make such commitments. But by the method we have outlined, we would have to identify an unlabeled category of "bride-giver" as a separate social identity (since the person(s) who give the bride away would not *necessarily* perform any other acts in the marriage sequence); and this intuitively seems awkward (but cf., the labeled position "best man," whose part in the marriage is conspicuous but almost equally limited).

Before we discard this method too hastily, however, let us recall that when these component parts in the wedding sequence must be sorted out in such atypical cases, there are standard principles (codified for some segments or strata of society by Emily Post, Amy Vanderbilt, etc.) for deciding who should do what. In a nonliterate society, bereft of etiquette books, *people must know these things*. They must know the component elements into which these typically composite "roles" are to be carved up, and they must have principles for deciding who appropriately performs each element. These sorting-out procedures, in short, are part of the culture, and an adequate cultural description must incorporate them.

At this stage we have isolated fragmented social positions and their role entailments which our actors apparently *can* distinguish, and higher-level positions, combining these fragments, which our actors more often label and customarily *do* distinguish. The problem is how we are to use such "positions" in describing a culture—bearing in mind our quest for cognitive salience but also the challenge of making sense of the atypical and improbable as well as the typical, as native actors are able to do. Four observations will be useful at this stage:

(a) Children learning their culture—like ethnographers learning someone else's—learn the typical and standardized patterns first, and gradually learn the exceptions to "rules of thumb" and "ideal roles."

(b) Our consciousness of "role playing" is largely confined, first, to the typical labeled composite "positions" of our culture; and second, to positions of higher levels of taxonomic hierarchies (like "physician"). Intuitively we apparently perceive the lower-level implicit "positions" as *patterns of acts* (like giving the bride away) rather than *capacities in which we act*.

(c) The composite "positions" in which we ourselves and those close to us habitually interact become particularly standardized in our conceptual world. But each of us also continually encounters alters who represent unfamiliar or unlikely composites, and we must behave appropriately toward them.

(d) Since only the low-level "position" elements in these composites have invariant behavioral entailments—that is the way we identified them—we either must pay serious attention to them descriptively or abandon the assumption that occupying a position entails a predictable role.

If (a) and (b) suggest the wisdom of focusing on the standardized, typical "roles" of a culture and the corresponding positions, (c) and (d) suggest that we would be wise to examine carefully the alternative of focusing on the lowest-level component elements and the principles for constructing atypical combinations.

In what follows, I will explore, illustrate, and evaluate this second alternative—what I call for brevity a "building blocks" model. I will argue that it has significant advantages over the alternatives I have attempted and perceive at present. There are too many unknowns in a theory of culture structure for us to be more than exploratory and speculative. But at least I believe the "building blocks" model leads us to ask the right questions and place the proper demands on our descriptions.

The "building blocks" model would take as social identities the lowest-level positions with invariant behavioral entailments. It would view them as the constituent units in the construction of composite "social persona," and would give "grammatical" rules for their combination.

The tendency for social identities to coalesce empirically is due in large measure to an overlap in principles for assuming each. The first priorities or principles in typical circumstances may be the same—so that they diverge only in unusual circumstances

In terms of this model, I would argue, as Goodenough himself did, that actual interaction is not typically in single social identity relationships, but in *combinations of* social identities (his "social personae"):

Finally, we must consider that the parties to a social relationship do not ordinarily deal with one another in terms of only one identity-relationship at a time. The elderly male physician does not deal with a young female nurse in the same way that a young male physician does, and neither deals with her as a female physician does. In other words, identities such as old, adult, young adult, man, and woman are as relevant as are the identities physician and nurse. Some identities are relevant to all social interactions. In my culture, for example, I must always present myself to others as an adult and as a male. This meaning that I am ineligible for any identity that is incompatible with being adult and male. (1965:7)

It is culturally probable combinations of social identities, the standardized social personae of a culture, that characteristically are conscious and monolexemically labeled: the prepackaged units of a culture. Our familiar "roles" often represent the coalescence of whole series of social identities, general and specific, and a merging of their entailments. Let us take "father." Not only may "father" (vis-à-vis his children) combine two or more social identities like "guardian," but also more

general social identities entailing certain rights and duties: man (vs. woman), and adult (vs. child). While father is always male and adult, other ideal social persona are grouped probabilistically. Thus the category "doctor" tends cognitively to imply maleness, and a female physician (like a female gas station attendant) continually generates some cognitive dissonance as she encounters alters using a probabilistic code.[4]

But what is most revealing is our ability to create new combinations. Some are improbable, some rare, and a few probably unique. The point is that instead of taking a small set of ready-made social identities as the basic units of cultural inventory, we would view our actors as continually *creating* "social personae" (or whatever we choose to call them) out of the elements provided by the culture. We would focus not simply on the elements of the social identity system but also on the "grammatical" rules for their combination.

Goodenough foresees this challenge:

Among the various identities that I . . . possess and that are compatible with these two, not all are compatible with one another nor are they always mutually exclusive as to the occasions for which they are appropriate. The result is that for any occasion I must select several identities at once, and they must be ones that can be brought together to make a grammatically possible composite identity. (1965:7)

This dynamic of the combination of social identities is crucial partly because the entailments—jural and behavioral—of identities may change as they combine with others. That is, "social personae" may have emergent properties. A Kwaio example will be useful here. Using the inductive procedures we outlined we can identify the identity relationship LITIGANT : LITIGANT[5] (there are higher and lower taxonomic levels here as well). When two litigants are also close kin, this sets up the combination LITIGANT–CLOSE KINSMAN : LITIGANT–CLOSE KINSMAN. Yet many of the obligations and expectations of close kin conflict with— but in principle override—the expected roles

[4] Discussion of this phenomenon at the Philadelphia Anthropological Society turned up a male student who had recently encountered a female gas station attendant and filled his car's gas tank himself; and that led to an interesting examination of the Freudian implications of filling 'er up.
[5] I have adopted as a convention this way of indicating Kwaio social identity relationships.

of litigants, so that litigation is (or should be) constrained. If CURER and PATIENT are also close kinsmen, it is inappropriate for the CURER to impose the fee to which he is normally entitled. This highlights the fact that using such a model we may talk about social identities combining into composites; but what are really crucial are the rules for creating *composite roles*, i.e., for combining the sometimes conflicting behavioral entailments of the positions.

The Kwaio example illustrates, incidentally, a general tendency in societies of this scale for obligations and duties of kinship to override other identity relationships. This tendency is the empirical basis for many generalizations about the importance of kinship in primitive societies. I feel it also partly accounts for Goodenough's success in inferring social identities by asking about the rights and duties of particular named individuals vis-à-vis specific alters. With context not otherwise specified, his subjects apparently chose identities based on kinship as the appropriate responses—though each of the inhabitants of Romonum probably occupies a number of social identities vis-à-vis every other in various situations.

We can also see why controversies have persisted regarding the relationship of kinship terms to behavior. Behavioral rules apply to social identities. Kinship terms may be, but often are not, labels for social identities. At close genealogical distance, or in ideal circumstances, correspondence between the two systems is high; while beyond this the genealogical net and a social identity system (usually involving residence, genealogical distances, chronological age, etc., as well as genealogical relationships) may increasingly diverge. There may be an ideal conception of a "mother's brother" just as there is an ideal conception of a "father"; but alter's assignment to this kinship category does not necessarily imply applicability of these idealized avuncular behavior patterns. The role of the "mother's brother in South Africa" may represent a complex composite that incorporates the social identities ADULT, MAN, MEMBER OF MOTHER'S PATRILINEAGE, RESIDENT OF NEIGHBORING SETTLEMENT, CLOSE COGNATIC KINSMAN, and so on, as well as a member of a particular kin type that falls in a particular kinship category. Other members of that category who lack some or all of these additional characteristics may appropriately act quite differently toward ego.

This dynamic process whereby we create combinations of social identities to meet the ever varying demands of situations also would render comprehensible the relevance of social identities at different taxonomic levels. A social identity at a lower level *implies* the rights and duties of all higher levels. In the formulation of "social personae" we combine not only horizontally, in the merging of coordinate social identities, but vertically, in the merging of taxonomic levels.

It is worth illustrating with Kwaio data the sorts of phenomena that emerge as we move up taxonomic hierarchies from the lowest-levels of distinguishable social identities.

A frequently sold item is the areca nut, used for betel chewing. A recurrent, if microscopic, "scene" is the sale of these nuts, in exchange for shell beads. Some rights and duties of the man who buys and the man who sells are specific to the sale of this item in this context (e.g., the duty of the seller to provide betel pepper leaves to the purchaser upon request). We could, at this microcosmic level, define ARECA SELLER : ARECA BUYER as an identity relationship. However, some rights and duties apply to BUYER and SELLER regardless of the commodities changing hands. Note the formal similarity here to Goodenough's analysis of property-transaction types in Truk as in complementary distribution (1951:61–64).

Another example illustrates greater complexity. Using the method we outlined studying 'mortuary feasts,' we could identify a social identity PRINCIPAL FEAST-GIVER. This is the man who sponsors the feast and in whose settlement it is held. First, we may note that there are several different kinds of 'mortuary feasts' he could decide to give; and each has not only different behavioral entailments but implies some contrasts in rights and duties vis-à-vis other participating identities. This, then, could take us down one step to a sort of basement taxonomic level. Second, another cluster of rights and duties vis-à-vis GUESTS applies not only to the man who gives a 'mortuary feast' but also the man who gives a 'marriage feast' or a 'housebuilding feast.' These include, on the part of feast-giver, providing shelter, firewood, and water; and on the part of the guest, observing certain minimal standards of ritual conduct and purity that differ from those of an everyday visitor. We could call those the rights and duties of FEAST-GIVER and GUEST. Yet this leads to still a higher level. The sponsor of *any* gathering (not only a feast) assumes certain jural responsibilities for those who come to it. If one of these guests is killed or injured on the way to or from the gathering (e.g., by a snake bite), the sponsor is jurally responsible and must pay compensation. This enables us to speak of SPONSOR and GUEST as social identities on this highest level (above which there are only the minimal rights and duties between *any* two Kwaio).

We see in this sketch the sort of complexity we encounter if we seek to use a schema of social identities in any detailed cultural description. To those who would counter that all this is far too complicated I would reply in two ways: First, we need not, in all descriptive contexts, treat all levels of social identity hierarchies—the problem for us as for native actors is to find the relevant levels. Second, the competence of native actors implies such complexity, whether we like it or not. They may have some radically different way of organizing such distinctions cognitively, but they clearly are able to make them.

We can make another observation about lexical labeling. On these taxonomic hierarchies of social identities, as in the clustering of composite identities, labels are applied probabilistically at those levels where they are most likely to make most difference—particularly in the middle range. Where we move higher or lower in these hierarchies, descriptive phrases are likely to be produced in lieu of monolexemic labels.

Further, in a complex social system, social identities are likely to be labeled at a higher level by those outside a particular subsystem than by those within. In this connection we might recall the earlier example of an American hospital.

We have not, of course, demonstrated that an approach based on minimal behavioral equivalence-classes—the "building blocks" model—replicates the cognitive organization of native actors. We have not demonstrated that such a model is ethnographically feasible, in terms of discovery procedures or constructing a written description. Nor have we demonstrated that native actors operate in terms of "roles" at all.

Before we return to a final evaluation of the methods and models we have sketched, and particularly the question of cognitive salience, an extended ethnographic illustration will show how the "building blocks" model can be used in cultural analysis. Appropriately, since we have touched at several points on "the role of the father," we will examine this problem in Kwaio society.

THE ROLE OF THE KWAIO FATHER

Our question put simply, is this: Is "father" a Kwaio social identity (in a cognitively salient and ethnographically useful sense); or is a Kwaio father in fact occupying two or more different social identities vis-à-vis his children?

We begin with the methodological observation that in analyzing the social identity system of a culture, we do not begin in a state of complete ignorance regarding human biology, other human societies, or the culture we are studying.

The method of analysis I sketched requires general familiarity with a culture—the cast of characters and the "scenes," in addition to the language. Thus though we phrased the method as one step-by-step induction, in practice it is much more one of rigorously testing hypotheses we have already derived from learning the general outlines of the culture.

So by the time I began to analyze the social identity system, I knew that most Kwaio children had living fathers, that usually they lived in the same household, and that at various phases in the domestic cycle fathers characteristically performed a number of acts vis-à-vis their children. They also paid a midwife for birth of the child, provided food and domestic services, administered discipline in various forms, paid for curing and sacrifices, paid compensation for misdeeds by children, received compensation for offenses against children, taught skills and valuable knowledge, gave taro planting stock, pigs, and other scarce goods, received the major share of daughters' bridewealth, paid a major share of sons' bridewealth, and so on. I observed, of course, variations in style, affect, and detail within individual families; but running through them there were consistent threads of right and duty, behavior and reciprocation, expectation and obligation, between fathers and children.

But was it possible that Kwaio fathers were

in fact occupying two or several identities vis-à-vis their children, and that "father" was a composite identity or social persona consisting of components that overlapped empirically with high probability?

Analysis of the range of "scenes" or situations involving fathers and children provided many clues. Most revealing were those households that diverged from the typical nuclear family structure. It was on these that I focused my attention, using my observations on nuclear family households as a background and control.

One set of clues came from those cases where the father of children was no longer living. I examined who performed those acts "normally" performed by father, across the range of relevant contexts.

In four households, children lived with a stepfather. I observed that this man performed some, but not all, of the acts I had seen fathers perform. Particularly in contexts involving jural action, a different man performed acts I had seen fathers perform: in three cases, a kinsman of the deceased father; and in one case, a kinsman of the mother.

In nineteen households a foster father was providing for children. In some of these households, I observed the foster father acting much as fathers act, across the whole range of contexts, though I recorded some differences especially in the transmission of property (before and at death). In some foster households, however, I observed a separation out of jural acts, as in households with stepfathers.

Some further clues were gleaned from the few cases of divorce and subsequent custody by maternal kin for which I was able to obtain evidence, and from informant's statements about what *would* happen if a divorced woman who maintained custody of her children remarried. More extensive evidence came from several other households where the father was living but not raising his child. Three of these were cases where a man had given one or several of his children to a kinswoman to raise.

Finally, I studied three interesting cases where, though the father and his child were living in the same household, the father was subordinate within the household to a senior man. In one case, a young man's wife died and he took their young child back to his father's household. In a second case, a similar pattern resulted from divorce. In the third,

the wife's death was again the cause, but the senior man of the household was the widower's older brother. Here some acts normally performed by Kwaio fathers were seen to be performed by the father; while others were performed by the older man in whose household he was living.

By using these atypical Kwaio household alignments as "natural experiments" in the possible permutations of the social order, and studying patterned variations in behavior across the range of cultural contexts, I arrived at three major distinctive components of "the role of the Kwaio father," which I will treat as separable social identities.

(1) Head of household.

(2) Guardian.

(3) "Father" (of which more shortly).

Here I will summarize briefly the jural rights and duties, and non-jural rights and obligations, of these social identities. (These categories "jural" and "non-jural" are given precise ethnographic definition in Keesing 1965a.) Detailed specification of operating norms would require an analysis in terms of contexts, which is beyond the scope of this paper (*vide* Keesing 1965a).

HEAD OF HOUSEHOLD (: HOUSEHOLD MEMBER)

(1) Represents household interests, and controls household property, in the "public domain." Thus exercises controlling interests in the corporation of which ego is a member.

(2) Contributes labor, services, and property for subsistence of household members. However, unless he is obligated *in some other capacity* to provide subsistence to them, he acquires the right to claim ultimate repayment for these services.

(3) Is entitled to contributions of labor, for subsistence production, from household members as they are physically able.

(4) Imposes discipline over children, in household and daily affairs, *not* to include inflicting physical injury.

GUARDIAN (: WARD)

(1) Exercises primary control over ego in jural matters and acts as spokesman for ego's kin. Ths involves demanding compensation for offenses against ego, taking the lead in paying for offenses by ego, and making decisions about ego's jural status.

(2) For a female ego, exercises control over her sexuality until her marriage. Is entitled to transfer, or refuse to transfer, sexual and other rights through her marriage. Supervises

distribution of bride-price. Acts as spokesman, from among her kin, over the residual rights they retain over her sexuality, life, and well-being.

Further details on the GUARDIAN are provided in Keesing (1965a) and Keesing (1967b).

FATHER (: CHILD)

JURAL

(1) Transmits to the child natal rights of agnatic and cognatic descent (see Keesing 1966b, 1967c) relationships to kin and ancestors, and rights in property-owning corporations of which he is a member.

(2) Child has a right to inherit property created or held in full title by ego. (The oldest son acts as "steward" of such property on behalf of his siblings.)

NON-JURAL

(3) Should give children, without expectation of reciprocation, scarce goods such as pigs to raise, taro shoots to plant, etc.

(4) Should provide subsistence, normal costs of curing, etc., for children without expectation of reciprocation.

This latter social identity is relatively complex, and well illustrates some of the hierarchical and other structures we encounter in such analysis. We will analyze these phenomena fragmentarily for purposes of illustration, since a full description would take us far afield.

What we labeled "FATHER" could more accurately be labeled IMMEDIATE KINSMAN, MALE, SENIOR GENERATION. Immediate kinship is defined in a schema of four degrees of cognatic kinship: *immediate, close, distant,* and *peripheral.* Some rights, duties, and obligations attach to each of these degrees. Thus on one level each degree of kinship defines a social identity. For instance, the duties of ego to a man to whom he is PERIPHERAL KINSMAN are that should this kinsman be killed by someone, ego must abstain from interacting with the killer until the ancestors that joined him to the decedent have been compensated. This is a minimal duty, and those to closer kinsmen are more demanding.

Like some status relationships studied by Goodenough on Truk, these relationships prove to be scalable (1965). Each successively closer kinship distance to ego entails all the rights and duties of those more distant, plus new ones. Thus, the duties of close kin subsume the duties of distant and peripheral kin and expand upon them.

At a lower taxonomic level, more specific social identities are created by cross-cutting factors. Sex is one, so that some rights and duties are defined at the level MALE IMMEDIATE KINSMAN : FEMALE IMMEDIATE KINSMAN. Others are defined in terms of generationality: SENIOR IMMEDIATE KINSMAN : JUNIOR IMMEDIATE KINSMAN; and still others are defined in terms of the paradigmatic intersection of sex and generationality (MALE SENIOR IMMEDIATE KINSMAN, etc.). Kwaio, like Americans, lack lexical labels for some of these positions. It is interesting that Kwaio lack a "parent" category.

Two important points about such hierarchical structurings arise at this stage. First social identities frequently must be defined within *contrast sets,* not in isolation. Second, the level of contrast that will be relevant to a particular descriptive task will vary considerably. At one point we may be interested in "father," at other times with "parent."

The separation of entailments for "father" into jural and non-jural components has interesting implications. Let us begin by distinguishing the shorthand label "father" from the cultural concept 'father,' which denotes the legitimately recognized begetter of a child (*maʔa neʔe lafia*). Kwaio recognize that this conceivably could be someone other than the biological parent, and in the rare cases when a child is 'illegitimate' (*futabono-bono*) it has no 'father' in this sense. A man who fathered an illegitimate child during my stay, and paid heavy compensation to the mother's kin, now has no recognized relationship to the child.

'Father' invariably occupies the social identity MALE SENIOR IMMEDIATE KINSMAN as long as he is alive (though as his children become 'adult' and he becomes 'old,' the behavioral implications change progressively until the directionality of dependency is reversed). The only rare exception to this occurs when a child is 'adopted.' His 'father,' if alive, remains in that category but he ceases to occupy the social identity MALE SENIOR IMMEDIATE KINSMAN. All entailments of that social identity, jural and non-jural, are transferred (Keesing 1967b).

When 'father' dies while his children are still dependents, he discharges at his death the jural duties of passing on rights over property and relationships to ancestors. In a sense, 'father' actually—in passing from the living to the dead—continues to act as a jural link to ancestors, shrines, and territories; while his own property will have been transmitted before or at death.

At this stage, then, the jural elements of paternal duty have been enacted with finality; and only the non-jural elements remain to be assumed by a surrogate. This is the obligation assumed when a surviving relative volunteers to 'foster' dependent children (Keesing 1967b). Assignment of a child is made by the GUARD-IAN from among prospective fostering kin, according to principles I have analyzed in detail elsewhere (1967b).

A stepfather also assumes these non-jural components voluntarily, under usual circumstances—if indeed the widowed mother has been permitted to keep custody of her children (Keesing 1967b). Moreover, since the non-jural components of parental obligation are generally similar for "mother" and "father," an unmarried woman who 'fosters' a child is assuming these obligations as well.

The key transaction-type involved in these non-jural entailments of "parenthood" is a kind of nonreciprocal giving: nonreciprocal in that it creates no specific obligations of return. In Kwaio culture, pigs, shell money, taro planting stock, tools, and similar items are supplied by parents (or others acting like parents) to children. The Kwaio category for such transactions is fa?awelaa, lit., "cause to be [in the position of] a child"—and is used whether or not the giver is actually parent of the recipient.

In a more detailed analysis, it is possible to factor out a fourth component of the "role of the father," though for present purposes this need only be sketched. This is the social identity MOTHER'S HUSBAND. Unless ego's stepfather is also HOUSEHOLD HEAD, this social identity is of little relevance. A minimal and fragile step kin relationship is created that makes appropriate use of the kin term ma?a, also used for 'father.' But relationship to mother's husband is terminated at mother's death, and it is not transitive, in the sense that it does not serve as a link to the stepfather's kin (other than his children by a former marriage), his ancestors, or his property. All of the entailments of being MOTHER'S HUSBAND are subsumed within the entailments of being MALE SENIOR IMMEDIATE KINSMAN.

We can sort them out by looking at cases where mother is divorced and has remarried (so father and stepfather can be compared); at cases where a remarried widow lives with her children and cases where she does not; and so on. Given this feature of inclusion, we could treat these as two components of the role of "FATHER," separable in some circumstances (as we did with the jural and non-jural components).

Goodenough (1965) shows how his formal analysis of status relationships in Trukese culture enabled him to interpret successfully a complex and (to native onlookers) surprising sequence of interaction. My analysis enabled me to make sense of a case that, without such analysis, would have caused me great puzzlement.

A man named ?Oimae was allowed to 'foster' the young daughter of a deceased relative. Another man, more closely related, was acting as GUARDIAN. When the girl was a teen-ager, ?Oimae made an indecent sexual suggestion to her and she left angrily to live with another relative. Several years later, the girl was married. When an initial bridewealth payment was made, and distributed by the GUARDIAN to the girl's relatives, ?Oimae was not given a share. He angrily demanded that he be included in the distribution. The GUARD-IAN retorted that the girl had sworn ritually that ?Oimae was not to be given a share. The two men, in protracted litigation, advanced their claims. The GUARDIAN demanded purificatory compensation for xwaisulafinaa, 'sexual insult,' committed earlier against the girl. ?Oimae countered with a demand for compensation for the subsistence he had provided for the girl while he was 'fostering' her. Eventually each paid compensation to the other, in roughly equal amount.

What was happening here, in terms of our analysis? ?Oimae's expectation that he would receive a large portion of the girl's bridewealth derived from his assumption of the non-jural components of the social identity "FATHER." In this identity, ?Oimae was obligated to provide subsistence; but in return, he could expect to be treated as an IMMEDI-ATE KINSMAN in the distribution of bridewealth. When the girl, through the GUARDIAN, refused to recognize him as such, she was redefining his position as that of HOUSEHOLD HEAD. But in this identity, she would have become jurally obligated for the subsistence he provided her;

hence his claim, which she and the GUARDIAN could not then reject, for compensation for her subsistence.

This litigation would not, I think, have been similarly comprehensible had I treated "father" as a single undifferentiated social identity. Only by distinguishing these components analytically could we make sense of what happened; and only by making similar distinctions—however this was managed cognitively—could our subjects have maneuvered the way they did.

What we have treated as separate social identities of course merge empirically with high frequency. Furthermore, it is clear that in a sense being a father is more than simply "the sum of its parts." The standard or normal identity combinations of a culture often have emergent properties—and if these properties are not easy to define analytically, they inspire innumerable poems and bonds of sentiment. The "building blocks" model is as able to comprehend such properties as a more conventional treatment of "the role of the father." But it also enables us to make sense of the whole range of ethnographic variation. By focusing on the typical, we sacrifice the power to understand the atypical. The "building blocks" approach reveals how and why the typical occurs, while rendering intelligible the full range of possibility.

SOCIAL IDENTITIES AND CULTURAL THEORY

Our analysis so far has proceeded through these major steps:

(1) We described a series of difficulties we had encountered in trying to describe the social identities and roles of a culture.

(2) We sketched the outline of a method that—at least in the distinguishable "scenes" of a culture—isolated minimal social positions with predictable jural and behavioral entailments.

(3) We examined, and illustrated ethnographically, a model that would take these minimal positions as social identities and would focus on the rules and dynamics whereby they combine as constituents in composite social personae.

We are now in a position to evaluate the procedures and models we have examined, in the light of wider problems of cultural description. This will lead us to consider, necessarily sketchily, some of the major ques-

tions that lie along the frontiers of cultural theory. These include:

(1) What will be the shape and design of a cultural description?

(2) What is the relation of such a cultural description to the overall goals of ethnography?

(3) How are we to attain such a cultural description, and how is its adequacy to be evaluated? Specifically, what is the place in this enterprise of (a) an explicit inductive methodology; and (b) direct evidence of "psychological validity"?

(4) What is the place of "roles" and "social identities" in such a cultural description, and what evidence is there that the procedures and concepts we have sketched will be productive?

It is worth making explicit at the outset the four major sources of the premises that underlie this discussion: the cultural theory of Ward Goodenough; the developing theories of generative grammar, especially the work of Noam Chomsky; recent research on communication by Gregory Bateson; and the descriptive models of "ethnoscience."

The Goals of Cultural Description

An analysis of roles and social identities, following the direction we have sketched or some other, would comprise a portion of a cultural description. To be able to evaluate the place of segments within a wider whole, we must have some conception of the scope and design of the whole.

Following Goodenough, I conceive "culture" to consist of organized knowledge: of patterns *for* behavior, not patterns *of* behavior. A cultural description is thus a "cultural grammar," a statement of

. . . what one must know in order to generate culturally acceptable acts and utterances appropriate to a given socio-ecological context. (Frake 1962a:85)

But this hides many ambiguities. What is "knowledge"? How is "what one must know" to be set out? How does the "cultural grammar" deal with individual variations in cultural codes, and with the fact that no individual knows all of "his" culture? What is the relation of "the cultural grammar" to patterns of actual behavior, and to the overall goals of ethnographic description?

These questions have been most squarely

dealt with in the domain of language, especially in the work of Chomsky. In Chomskyan terms, a cultural description is a theory of cultural *competence* (1965:3 ff.). To paraphrase him, a cultural grammar is a model of the cultural knowledge of an idealized actor-observer, in a community completely homogeneous in culture, who knows its culture perfectly. If we follow the Chomskyan model, a "cultural grammar" would describe, with a set of explicit elements and rules, the organized knowledge that enables this idealized actor-observer to produce appropriate ("grammatical") acts and correctly interpret observed events and acts. Apparently in other cultural domains, as well as in language, this competence permits the construction and decoding of an infinite set of behaviors (though for many domains the extent of such creativity remains problematical). Such cultural competence underlies *performance*, observable behavior. (The same general contrast had been drawn by Saussure with *langue* and *parole*.) But since actual actors have variant versions of the code and diverse patterns of motivation, and since many factors affecting performance (sociological, demographic, economic, ecological, etc.) are external to the code, a grammar of cultural competence does not "predict behavior" or account for all patterns of performance (Chomsky 1965, Kay 1965).

Though the ultimate concern of a "cultural grammar" in a sense is "ideas in people's heads," the model of idealized actor-observer demands a description of culture as a system of "extrinsic thought" (Bateson 1967:765), not phrased in terms of the psychological operations of the individual actor. "Culture," then, is an abstract model *derived from* the ideational order, not that order itself. This point has, I think, been insufficiently clear in the writings of Goodenough.

Whether the cultural code is to be described from the standpoint of the actor is important in evaluating "role" and "social identity." Will an ethnography be phrased as a set of rules for making decisions, for "generating" behavior, for "navigating in the world" (Keesing 1967a, 1967b)? Chomsky emphasizes that his grammatical model does not "generate" in this sense, that it is not a "speaker model" (1965:9). Whether at this stage we can or should follow Chomsky here is problematical, a point to which we will re-

turn. We can at least be aware of the ambiguity in the goal of a description that will tell

. . . what you have to know in order to operate as a member of the society (Goodenough 1957: 168) . . .

. . . what one must know in order to respond in a culturally appropriate manner in a given socio-ecological context. (Frake 1962b:54)

With regard to the scope of the cultural grammar and its relationship to the overall tasks of the ethnographer, it is worth examining carefully Chomsky's competence-performance distinction. First, Chomsky is concerned with delimiting what is linguistic competence from what is not. He excludes from this domain many areas of competence that are cultural but not linguistic; and almost inevitably, these become confounded with the (for Chomsky negatively-defined) class of performance. If the competence-performance distinction, and Goodenough's "ideational-phenomenal" distinction, are to be parallel and useful, it must be on grounds of epistemology, not content. The distinction between linguistic and non-linguistic competence becomes relatively arbitrary. This problem is examined in detail in Hymes (n.d.).

It is further worth observing, and emphasizing more strongly than Chomsky, that it is an ultimate concern with the wider framework of performance that gives meaning to a competence theory. Hymes has made this point very well in his call for "an ethnography of speaking" (1962, 1964). Because so many aspects of non-linguistic behavior are not direct reflections of the cultural code, such a concern with performance is particularly crucial in cultural anthropology. To use a classic anthropological example, a competence theory of *kula*-ing in the culture of the Trobriands or Amphletts or Dobu would give rules for "grammatical" *kula* exchanges in that segment of the system; but it would tell us nothing about the entire *kula* ring, the economic principles that affect patterns of choice, or the actual flow of valuables. Nor would a competence model of Trobriand culture tell us what villages, or districts, or lineages, or gardens there are—only the "grammatical" rules for residing, descending, gardening, etc. I emphasize this point because in many ethnoscience writings the need to place a competence description in the framework of performance has not been made sufficiently clear. The "cultural grammar"—far as we are from achieving it—then is only one segment of the total concern of the ethnographer. It is a crucial element in our understanding of events, processes, and behavior; but it does not by itself constitute that understanding.

Whatever the overall design of the "cultural grammar," and we have only the sketchiest notion of what it may turn out to be, we can be sure it will be highly complex. Based on what we know of language, we can expect that most elements of the cultural code are unconscious, in the sense that native actors are not aware of and cannot verbalize them (cf., Chomsky 1965:8–9). The methodological implications of this fact will concern us shortly. Furthermore it seems quite possible that, as Bateson (1968) has cogently argued, the coding of cultural knowledge at the lowest levels of unconscious thought is qualitatively different from coding at higher levels —characterized by a logic of relations, not of things; and iconic, rather than digital, coding. Basic premises are the least accessible and the least amenable to linguistic or other digital representation; and what is most familiar or most constant is sunk to the deep levels of "habit" (Bateson 1968). This adds new dimensions of complexity to the "cultural grammar." This usefully leads into questions of methodology.

Methodology and Evaluation in Cultural Analysis

Discovery Procedures

We began, in our quest for "social identities," with the hope of (1) devising a rigorous and explicit inductive methodology for (2) discovering descriptive units and "rules" that replicate the cognition of native actors. In asking about the means for attaining the "cultural grammar," we can introduce these problems of discovery and validity.

Two sharply contrastive positions on methodology—and specifically the possibility of rigorous and explicit discovery procedures—are held by proponents of "ethnoscience" and by Chomsky. Ethnoscientists, particularly Metzger and Williams, have argued that to make cultural descriptions more than impressionistic journalism, we need explicit and agreed-upon methods for analyzing a corpus

of data. If the data are public and the method explicit, then the ethnography is potentially replicable by another analyst.

But Chomsky has argued in various ways against the possibility of such unbroken inductive chains from data to theory in linguistics; and it is highly doubtful that they play an important part in any developed science (cf., Bar-Hillel 1964:205–211). He argued cogently (Chomsky 1957:50–56) against the "grammar producing machine" sought by the linguistics of the 1950's. He showed that the most we could hope for is an evaluation procedure that enables us to choose between two alternative descriptively-adequate theories. More recently, he has placed great emphasis on moving from "descriptive adequacy" (a theory satisfying the criteria for the class of possible correct solutions) to "explanatory adequacy" (a theory chosen from this class on the basis of such criteria as simplicity, generality [in terms of a theory applying to all languages], and correspondence with intuitions of native speakers) (Chomsky 1965: 24–27, 1966:12–24).

With regard to discovery procedures, Chomsky has noted that "no adequate formalizable techniques are known for obtaining reliable information . . . concerning the linguistic intuition of the native speaker" (which must be the principal test of adequacy) (1965:19). At best, he is prepared to admit the possibility of some operational procedure yielding results corresponding to the intuitions of native speakers in clear cases, and hence useful in analyzing "unclear and difficult cases" (1965:19). Chomsky concludes that "there is no reason to expect that reliable operational criteria for the deeper and more important theoretical notions . . . will ever be forthcoming" (1965:19).

Chomsky further emphasizes the contrast between the intuitions of native speakers and their ability to verbalize grammatical rules:

Although . . . the speaker-hearer's linguistic intuition is the ultimate standard that determines the accuracy of any proposed grammar, linguistic theory, or operational test, it must be emphasized . . . that this tacit knowledge may very well not be immediately available to the user of the language. (1965:21)

Chomsky's methodological precepts can be summarized as:

(a) Rejection of the possibility of formal

and explicit discovery procedures to arrive at competence theories;

(b) Emphasis on whether a proposed theory *works* (not how it was derived);

(c) Focus on intuitions of native speakers in judging descriptive adequacy and in formulating evaluation criteria for choosing between alternative theories.

What conclusions we draw about the possibility or desirability of formal and explicit discovery procedures depends on our epistemic premises and our conception of the scientific enterprise. My present position, considerably different from the one that guided my initial field work, is this. Formal discovery procedures will be very useful where they are possible and when they work. But the criteria for "possible" and "work" must lie outside of any proposed methodology (cf., Chomsky 1965:37 ff.). Rather than devising a method that uncovers structure in some cultural segment or domain, and setting out to apply it to the whole (cf., componential analysis or Metzger and Williams' eliciting frames), we should keep constantly in mind the widest ranges of cultural competence and the scope of cultural systems. A self-imposed methodology that works for kinship or folk taxonomies but does not uncover the structuring of other domains or more basic premises will not suffice for cultural description, though it may provide conceptual clues and guidelines. We must seek to discover the architecture of the whole, not solve the easiest puzzles to show the virtues of methodology. The many ways that have turned up to describe segments of a language which do not fit into an adequate overall grammar should haunt the ethnographic methodologist.

Most of all, we need to use all evidence available to a child learning his culture. Like Chomsky with regard to language, I find it surprising that human beings can learn their cultures (cf., Chomsky on "acquisition models," 1965:30–34, 53–59, Hymes n.d.). That they are able to do so may well require some "pre-programming" of a "universal cultural grammar" from which they learn the applicable rules. We do not know, and we probably cannot find out until we learn a great deal more about cultural competence and cultural structure (cf., Chomsky's use of the black box theory, 1965:30 ff.). If we as ethnographers can decipher another culture, it is because we:

(a) Share this pre-programming with our subjects, to the degree it exists and persists (cf., Bateson 1967:765); and (as anthropologists) supplement it with comparative knowledge of cultural variation and structure;

(b) Have intuitions about our own culture (one of the class of possible cultures); and

(c) Have access to all the forms of data the native culture-learner can use.

Ethnographic methodology can and should help us control for the biases of our own culture and render more quick and efficient the business of testing and evaluating which the native culture-learner carries on over a period of many years. But we will be in grave difficulty if our method is so restrictive that it precludes our using intuitions, hunches, trial-and-error, non-linguistic cues, and all other means of culture-learning used by native actors.

Psychological Validity

Let us turn now to the question of "psychological validity" in evaluating cultural descriptions. That may tell us something about how to tell if a methodology "works" in this wider sense, and something about our quest for social identities and roles.

Can we distinguish formally adequate descriptions of cultural structure from those that replicate the cognition of native actors? Is "psychological validity" a feasible goal, and can evaluation criteria be devised that will attain such validity?

The extreme "hocus-pocus" and "God's Truth" positions derive from fundamentally different basic assumptions about epistemology and the nature of science. My own position is that "psychological reality" could realistically imply not a single correct solution shared by all native actors (because they have no magical means of finding out what is in each other's heads); but a range of cognitively possible solutions that produce roughly equivalent results.

Many formally possible solutions fall outside this range. Careful eliciting, controlled use of our own and our subjects' intuitions, use of artificial eliciting stimuli (like the ethnologist's manipulated and contrived models of birds of prey), and advances in cognitive psychology can help us to sort out what is cognitively possible, and cognitively salient, from what is not. Furthermore, we know from descriptive linguistics that there are many possible "solutions" to segments of cultural data that fail ultimately because they do not fit into a total theory of competence. Thus in finding possible solutions to pieces of the puzzle we must keep constantly in mind the whole design into which they must fit. The range of alternative solutions to the whole puzzle must be much narrower than the range of solutions of sub-segments. Since the former range constrains native actors, we must seek to discover and work within these constraints.

Following Chomsky, I agree that we want to go as far as we can to attain "psychological validity." However, it seems clear to me that *at some point* we will have to be prepared to opt for heuristic value rather than replication of the cognition of our subjects. This is because:

(a) Cultural descriptions are inevitably directed to *some* heuristic purpose other than exhaustiveness and cognitive validity. This implies a selectivity and focus that generates a gap between ethnographic account and cognitive ordering of native actors.

(b) Furthermore, a cultural description is ordered in a single linear sequence (successive pages). This raises problems of internal arrangement that probably render a written ethnography markedly different in basic structure than the cognitive organization of cultural knowledge (cf., Chomsky 1967:102 ff.).

(c) Moreover, an ethnographic description is inevitably written in a metalanguage foreign to the cognitive world of the native actor, though it may employ many elements of his language. This metalanguage may be based on another natural language; but large portions of it could be phrased, e.g., in a mathematical or logical metalanguage.

(d) Finally, if Bateson is right about unconscious thought, there may well be aspects of cultural coding that lie quite outside the kinds of ordering we can describe with the mathematics and logics Western man has formalized. I myself suspect that Chomsky's efforts to describe language in logico-mathematical terms may in the long run fall far short of accounting for linguistic competence or the intuitions of native speakers because segments of language are coded in ways we have not yet learned to decipher. The very *task* of description may of necessity transcribe the coding at the lowest levels of unconsciousness in terms of higher-level metalanguages (Bateson 1968).

The point, then, is that "cognitive validity" cannot be a realistic hope in ethnographic description if it is taken to mean that the description is to replicate on paper what goes on neurophysiologically, or perceptually, in the heads of our subjects.

We are facing a particular kind of "black box" problem: one where we do not seek a total descriptive theory of what is (or might be) in the box; but rather seek to account for only a limited segment of the outputs, in—as it were—a non-electronic language. We cannot, by the nature of the problem, find out what is in the black box. Our tests of "psychological validity" are epistemologically similar to the test inputs a communications engineer devises to narrow the range of what might be in the box. What we are seeking is an analog or model of some elements of what might be in the black box, described as if they were "extrinsic" to it (Bateson 1967:765). The task is rather like communicating with a computer through an input-output device, and trying to build a theory of how it is programmed and what information is stored in it; and phrasing that theory in a metalanguage (like Fortran) that is quite different from the electronic coding in the computer.

If a culture comprises a black box problem to an ethnographer, it constitutes one to each child learning to operate as a member of his society. As in any interesting black box problem, there is no single possible solution—for ethnographers or native actors. Criteria for choosing among possible solutions cannot simply invoke "psychological validity"—for that is to beg the question. They must be part of a general theory for describing that set of related black boxes, apparently similar in overall design, that are human cultures.

Since so much writing in ethnoscience has stressed the importance of using lexically-labeled categories in cultural description—and has implied that such labeling is the best index of "psychological validity" and "emic" analysis—a final comment on this point is called for.

From what linguists have told us about unconscious grammatical rules and categories, there is no reason to assume that cognitively crucial units of cultural structure are labeled, conscious, or verbalizable. If Bateson is right about the layering of consciousness and unconsciousness, it is particularly clear why many of them should *not* be. What we should demand of a cultural theory, in my view, is not that all of its analytical units be folk categories. Rather, the theory must incorporate models of unconsciousness and should *account for labeling on the levels where it occurs.* Folk categories should, in this view, be among the outputs of the black box for which the theory accounts; but folk sociology, like folk grammar, is probably a limited surface layer of the cultural whole. Even the intuitions of native actors in test situations can be invoked only on certain levels of the description, as in linguistics.

Roles and Social Identities in Cultural Description

"Role Behavior" and Cultural Competence

Having surveyed—though not solved—the mysteries of the nature and design of the "cultural grammar" and how it might be attained, we can now evaluate how social identities and roles would fit into this design and how the models and methods we have sketched measure up to this task.

Let me extend and modify the analogy of cultural analysis as a black box problem in order to explore some aspects of cultural competence crucial to the question of roles. Imagine a society as consisting of a large number of similar communications devices (e.g., computers) linked in a network so that they exchange messages with each other and their environment. Each "black box," as a sending and receiving device, has a set of rules for constructing and deciphering messages.

A general property of the competence of these black boxes with which the observer must contend in devising a theory of these rules is that devices are able to decode messages from one another and the environment, and construct messages, they have never encountered before. The linguistic aspects of such creativity have been explored by Chomsky (1957, 1965).

More specifically, the elements of competence for which we seek to account in talking about roles and social identities include:

(a) The ability of devices to decipher a pattern of messages from one another and the environment as defining a *context;* consensus on the context is crucial to further message exchange (Bateson 1955, 1956, 1958, 1963).

(b) The ability of devices to transmit in different *modes* such that:

[1] any device has a repertoire of modes in which it can transmit (a subset of the total set of modes defined in the code);

[2] each mode entails a special subset of rules for message exchange;

[3] messages transmitted in a mode can be correctly decoded only if the receiver is communicating in a matching mode (the code defines matching modes in pairs and networks);

[4] the coding of modes and contexts is interlocked, so that modes or their entailments are context-specific.

The term "mode" is intentionally vague at this stage, since our problem is to discover what the nature of these modes is and how information about sending and receiving in them is organized.

Let us add to this analogy two pieces of evidence. First, we [Anglo-Americans] are intuitively aware of moving in and out of these modes; and of something (the "self" or "real self" or "person") which is distinct from the mode we are using and which endures despite shifts in mode. This duality can produce consciousness of a gulf between mode and person (Natanson 1966a, 1966c). These intuitions have produced, on the level of folk sociology, the metaphor of "man as an actor" (Natanson 1966a).

Second, we are conscious of and have labels for some of the modes or capacities in which we "act." "Butcher, baker, and candlestick maker"—and "teacher," "seller," and "leader" —are intuitively salient categories that relate to this mode selection (the major features of which might or might not be conscious).

Beyond this, what these modes are like in terms of cognitive storage and processing and what segments of our cultural knowledge are coded in terms of such modes remains largely a mystery. Herein lies our problem.

The "Building Blocks" Model Re-Examined

A full analysis of Kwaio social identities, using methods I have illustrated and employing a "building blocks" descriptive model, is not yet possible. There are, as we will see, too many unsolved problems and unknown factors. It is possible, however, to push considerably beyond the illustrative segments given here, in the direction of "grammatical" and contextual rules and the specification of operating norms (cf., Keesing 1965a for a preliminary attempt to do so).

My analyses so far convince me that the "building blocks" model moves us a long way toward accounting for these elements of cultural competence noted above. I am not prepared to argue that this is the only, or even the best, path in that direction; at this early stage, we should explore many strategies.

One alternative would be to analyze behavior in terms of *positions* only for the labeled, standardized, conscious position-categories. We could then include in our description principles for dismantling the standardized roles into component patterns of *acts* performed by different persons in atypical cases; but without the implication that these component clusters of acts define implicit *positions*.

As we have shown, such a model requires us to abandon the assumption that occupying a position-category entails enactment of a specified role. The role entailments become ideal or probabilistic, not invariant.

The focus on typical, standard, labeled positions has guided most social scientists who have used the "role" concept. In its usual form such an approach does not seem likely to lead us toward an adequate theory of competence. It leads us, I think, to adopt a relatively static view of role enactment. That is, we have a limited array of ideal position-types and their probable (but not invariant) behavioral entailments. Role behavior involves sort of extrapolation and interpolation around these ideal-types. When situation and ideal-type differ sufficiently, the ideal can be sorted into components; but the basic process consists in matching a set of ideal-types against ever-changing and varying empirical situations. Moreover, since this model focuses on labeled categories, it deals primarily with the realm of consciousness—at least with higher levels of cognitive storage and processing. Bateson's warnings about the distortions and selectivity of consciousness come to mind here (1968).

We will suggest shortly a descriptive model that would treat as social identities only the standardized position-categories of a culture, but would account more effectively than these usual treatments for the ranges of possible variation and the dynamics and creativity of actual interaction.

But it is worth emphasizing again the promise of the "building blocks" model. If we consider the minimal and invariant lower-level components to be social identities, we are led to a dynamic view. Social identities become, in a sense, analogous to phonemes: they are minimal units of invariant contrast that are the constituent units of larger constructions. We are led to focus not on the units themselves—because they are fragmentary and often unlabeled, and moreover distributed across different levels of taxonomic hierarchies—but rather on their combination into larger units. They are, like most interesting elements of language, unconscious. Yet unusual situations or "messages" can bring out our intuitive ability to make distinctions at lower levels where necessary (cf., Chomsky on the triple ambiguity of "I had a book stolen," 1965:21–22).

We become better able to describe not only the hierarchical structuring of social identities and their roles, but also the way such hierarchies are articulated with the differentiation of subcultures. Let me illustrate. A nurse in a particular hospital may perform several differentiated roles the details of which are specific to a particular segment of this hospital. Yet she is also a nurse on a higher level, and the knowledge she would carry with her if she moved to a hospital in a different city is also part of the social identity system. To talk about "the role of the nurse" is to sacrifice the power to make sense of the low-level and specific as well as the high-level and general, and to show how they combine dynamically in "constructing" appropriate behavior.

The flexibility of the "building blocks" model also suggests ways to transcend the limitations of a strictly dyadic approach to identity relationships. First of all, in addition to treating identity relationships involving parties like corporations, governments, and supernaturals (as discussed by Goodenough), we can manage relationships where an alter is quite diffuse (Nadel 1957). Second, we can treat social identities as elements in *complex networks* that may have structural properties beyond those of the component dyads. The first step toward such complexity is introduced when a pair in an identity relationship enter into an identity relationship with a third party (e.g., two opponents and a referee). The possibility of a "grammatical" treatment of such networks in terms of immediate constituents and "syntactic" rules is opened up here.

The "building blocks" model, at this point, may seem to require formidable descriptive complexity. Taxonomic hierarchies, contexts-within-contexts, grammatical rules for combining social identities into social personae and for combining identity relationships into wider networks—all these correctly imply analytical labyrinths we have scarcely explored in our illustrative segments. To this I can only say that the complexities that have emerged in the study of grammars—subsegments of cultural codes—should lead us to expect, not shrink from, such intricacies.

Within the selected and simplified domains I have used to illustrate the method of distributional analysis and the "building blocks" model, promising results have been attained. The problems, of course, lie in the simplifying assumptions we have made for the sake of argument, and in the challenge of fitting these segments into a wider design. It is to these problems that we now turn.

Our Simplifying Assumptions

We have simplified by assuming: (a) a complete set of cultural "scenes"; (b) a perfected discovery procedure to find social positions with invariant behavioral implications; and thus, (c) that every position *has* a set of behavioral implications. Furthermore, (d) we have been using "behavioral implications" and "entails" simplistically as though occupying the position produces *enactment* of the role instead of mere *applicability* of the role. These are sweeping assumptions that do not correspond to the Kwaio (or American) data. In asking about the place of the "building blocks" model we have sketched in the wider design of a cultural description, we will be asking about the necessity of these (empirically invalid) assumptions, and about ways to transcend them, as well as about the place of this segment in the whole.

The Need for a Theory of Contexts

As we have noted, the most glaring deficiency in our understanding of cultural competence is the lack of any adequate theory concerning *contexts*. "Scenes" are a subset of a broader class of contexts, and a theory of how scenes are culturally defined must be part of a theory of context definition. Essential to that theory, I believe, will be a creativity or productivity that enables human actors to define situations they have never

encountered. If we view contexts as defined by patterns of messages, the analogy with linguistic creativity becomes clear. This makes simple enumeration of situation-types impossible, and defeats any rigid discovery procedure that relies on a finite list of discrete "scenes." But if this bodes ill for formalizing a discovery procedure, it may bode well for the "building block" model as a whole—since a parallel is quickly apparent. Furthermore, both Bateson's and Chomsky's recent writings give reason to hope that the coding of situations at lower levels may be more neat, simple, and invariant than the particularities of situations suggest. The elements may be clearly structured and discrete; and their matching of empirical complexity may be based on "syntactic" rules of combination and on modifying surface-structure rules. Advances toward a theory of cultural competence in defining contexts are clearly needed before a conceptualization of roles and a methodology for studying them can be carried beyond a provisional stage. But we can begin this enterprise with high hopes that since these principles are cognitively stored, they will prove amenable to formal description; and that since human beings growing up in a society are able to learn them, so will the scientific observer. This is a major task for social scientists in many disciplines in the next decade, and anthropologists would do well to watch closely the progress on this frontier by researchers like Garfinckel, Goffman, and Barker and Wright. I accord this challenge to social science the highest priorities.

Roles and Role Enactment

A second deficiency in the "building blocks" model as presently stated is that it assumes that each position (if we could identify them all) has a describable set of behavioral entailments. Yet Kwaio and American evidence indicates that positions vary greatly in the detail of behavioral specifications embodied in the role. For some positions, the role resembles a set of instructions on things to do (and ways to do them). But that is perhaps one end of a continuum; and at the other end, the relationship between friends can be characterized in part by the *lack* of specific behavioral entailments. We noted earlier Goodenough's suggestion that rights and duties can be used to specify the boundaries of such roles, even where content is diffuse. But empirically, we find often (perhaps characteristically) that where roles are most diffusely defined, so too are their boundaries.

Further, our assumption that occupying the position entails *enacting the role* implies an invariance that does not exist empirically. There is that whole dialectic, on a conscious level, between perceived "self" and role-playing "agent" (Natanson 1966b). The gulf between self and role player may be wider or narrower, depending on the individual, the circumstances, and the role.

Identity Relationships as Contexts

One avenue toward a solution of these problems, which emerged long after my return from the field, derives from the work of Bateson. Sequences of message-exchange between organisms involve not only the exchange of information, but also communication about the context of message-exchange. On this level of "metacommunication" (Bateson 1955), premises about the relationship of the communicating organisms and about the first-order messages are established. The metamessage "this is play," for example, places a "frame" around (i.e., defines a context for) the messages it accompanies that labels them as fictional; hence acts that are overtly hostile become "just play" (Bateson 1955, 1956, cf., Natanson's "zones" 1966a:335).

A social identity relationship can perhaps best be viewed not only as entailing a set of behavioral rules (message-exchanging instructions) but also as defining a *communications context* (a set of premises *about* message exchange). The minimal property of a social identity relationship may not be a specific set of behaviors to be performed by each actor; but rather a defined context for (set of premises about) message exchange. Let me illustrate.

The relationship between friends is governed not by a set of acts that are to be performed, but rather a shared set of understandings about the relationship. Friends can, in fact, do almost anything consistent with these premises: the rule of behavior is to "be yourself," even in a society where "being yourself" and "role playing" are considered antithetical in folk sociology. If we define the premises of "friendship," we define the identity relationship.

Another interesting example is the classic anthropological "joking relationship." The social identities involved may well be labeled by kinship categories (e.g., brother- and sister-in-law). But their *roles* entail not specific things to do, but a set of premises *about* whatever they do. The warning "you're going too far" may in Goodenough's sense indicate that the boundaries of the relationship are being transgressed; but it may also indicate that the premises of the relationship are in danger of being violated and must be reaffirmed or even renegotiated (cf., the fascinating discussion of "smile when you say that!" in Bateson 1956). Bateson has explored extensively what can happen when such metacommunication generates paradoxes of abstraction (1955, 1958, 1963, Bateson *et al.*, 1956).

If we view identity relationships as defining communications contexts as well as behaviors and rights and duties, we provide a hope for escape from a number of problems we have encountered.

First, a theory of social identities becomes part of a theory of contexts. As progress is made toward understanding how contexts are culturally defined and how information about them is stored and exchanged, we can hope to achieve increasing sophistication in handling roles and social identities and their relationship to the cultural definition of situations.

Second, we are able to transcend the assumption that assuming a social identity automatically entails enacting its role: because the contextual premises of the identity relationship *define* the relation of the actor to the role. This is one of three sources of "distantness" between "person" and "role player." Another is the variable commitment of individuals to the rules and premises of the cultural code, and its component segments. A final source is the combination of social identities into social personae where this entails some incompatibility of component roles, context-premises, or both. Where circumstances lead to assumption of a social persona whose role entailments are internally contradictory or whose component contextual premises are not the same, interesting phenomena (include Goffman's "role distance") occur. If a husband is drying dishes when his hard-drinking buddy arrives to take him to a poker game, a *macho* relationship conflicts with his domestic role—and he counters with a meta-assertion (characteristically joking) that dissociates him from the domestic role.

Interestingly, this process characteristically entails formulation of a *higher-order set of premises about the combination of roles* (and the relationship of actor to them) that may contradict, yet override, the premises of the component relationships.

Third, formal similarities, contrasts, and contradictions in the communications contexts established by the identity relationships of a culture may be crucial in the "grammatical" rules for building social personae. To use Goodenough's example, two men may be boss and employee during the day; yet the employee may, on one evening a week, be his boss' commanding officer at a National Guard meeting. Given incompatible premises for the two relationships, they will rigidly compartmentalize them. The warning that one should not transact business with a friend is a reminder that the premises—not the behavior—conflict. Yet it is quite "grammatical" for business associates to *develop* close social ties, to transact business during a round of golf.

"Primary Roles" as Cultural Templates

One major objection to the "building blocks" model of roles could be that it takes persons like father and mother, whose relation to ego is so basic and crucial, and subdivides their "roles" into fragments on the basis of unusual cases.

Any theory of roles must recognize the importance of these primary and basic relationships: but that does not mean our proposed model is wrong. As we have noted, it is quite possible to deal with emergent properties of composite roles. Some useful clues again come from Bateson's recent writing on unconscious thought (1968). He argues that the deepest levels of cultural knowledge are coded in pure-relational terms, with these relations manipulated and symbolized in terms of metaphors that give them content. If he is right, then father-child, mother-child, sibling-sibling (or friend-friend) relationships may well serve as metaphoric models for basic relational patterns of dominance, dependence, symmetry, asymmetry, and the like. The recurrent triadic relational patternings explored by Freilich (1964) come to mind as well. Exploration of this path would take us far afield. We can speculate at least that:

(a) The metacommunicative context established by an identity pair specifies (among other things) abstract formal relationships between the parties like dominance-submission, friend-friend, symmetrical rivalry, dependence-succorance, high-low, etc.

(b) These formal relationships apply over a large range of identity pairs, singly or in combination (e.g., Freilich's "high status friend").

(c) Such relationships may be coded formally at the deepest levels of unconscious thought, but without specification of the *content*.

(d) Role relationships learned in early experience become models and metaphoric expressions of these basic relational patterns, providing templates for further role learning and enactment (Schneider and Homans 1955).

None of this, I believe, is inconsistent with a model that views the roles of mothers and fathers as composites. Father is male, authoritarian, adult, etc., as well as genitor; and ego learns basic elements of his relationships to other males, other authoritarians, and other adults from his father even though only he may represent a composite of all these elements.[6]

"Building Blocks" and Conscious Role Playing

A remaining major question we have touched on several times is whether it is appropriate to speak of the lower-level implicit "building blocks" in terms of "social identities" and "roles." For with this approach, the positions dwindle in importance and become more akin to mental pigeonholes in which rules for behavior are stored than "social selves" we step into. "Social identity" and "role" seem to imply that the actor is conscious that he is performing in a socially conventional mode, and that he has a "self" distinct from that mode.

I am more concerned with discovering the structure of the cognitive systems our cultural competence implies than with the labels one bestows on the elements of that structure. I believe that:

(a) Our cultural competence requires that we have a much more complex structure for "role behavior" than our conscious models suggest.

(b) A theory that accords primacy to our conscious models will severely distort our understanding of cognitive operations. Thus, if "role" and the like are to refer only to

[6] Nor is it incompatible, I think, with psychoanalytic theories.

modes and mode-switching at a conscious level, our preoccupation with roles is probably misdirected. For it seems likely that such conscious role-playing is an epiphenomenon of underlying processes and ordering.

(c) We need instead a wider theory which accounts for cultural competence by inferring an underlying unconscious structure; and which in the process accounts for those selected, partial, and often distorted segments that rise to consciousness. This is not to deny the importance of controlled use of the intuitions of native actors; but that is very different from taking at face value the constructs of folk sociology.

In any case, I know of no convincing evidence from non-Western societies where "role playing" and a distinction between "real self" and "social self" are basic notions of folk sociology. It seems quite possible that these are Western embroideries overlying and disguising universal but unconscious cognitive elements and processes. My own feeling is that we should concentrate on the structures men's cultural competence and observed behavior imply, and not worry overmuch whether our folk metaphors are appropriate labels for our metalanguage.

This question, however, raises an important alternative possibility we have mentioned but have not yet explored. Perhaps we have been going astray in trying to infer *positions* at these lower levels. Perhaps there are, at lower levels of cognitive coding, sequences and complexes of acts to be performed, and rules for how to do them, and who should do them—but no ordering in terms of positions or capacities. Perhaps this whole idea of "position" is an epiphenomenon at higher levels, the result of clusterings of acts, rights, and duties that typically but not invariably go together.

But our "positions" have receded in importance as they have become fragmentary and proliferated, and this alternative may not be significantly different. "Positions" have become, in our analysis, indexing-labels or pigeonholes in which reciprocal premises, rules and expectations are stored—not the masks and costumes of "man as an actor." They are then the constituent units of higher-level constructions.

The main alternative this new approach suggests, in terms of the overall ordering of cultural knowledge, is a greater emphasis on

"*scenes*" and the sequences of acts that must be performed in staging them, rather than on *social identities* an actor moves in and out of as he passes through scenes.

These alternative ways of looking at cultural structure—one focusing on scenes, with actors moving through them, the other on actors moving through scenes—parallel in an interesting way Chomsky's distinction between a model of an idealized speaker-hearer and a speaker-model. The "building blocks" model would not necessarily be actor-oriented, and at least predisposes us to look at dyads. But the whole notion of moving in and out of roles pushes us toward an actor-orientation.

The possibility of a description that corresponds more directly to the speaker-hearer model of generative grammar has been suggested in an exploratory paper by John Haviland (n.d.). He suggests that the cultural grammar ultimately might be phrased in terms of "tableaux" (which somewhat resemble Frake's "scenes"). These include sets of "staging instructions" that specify the complexes of acts performed in each. Who does what is determined, in such a model, not by a set of precoded "roles" but by contingent circumstances—by who is available and eligible to do what and knows how. Haviland suggests the possible use of critical path programming in formally describing such patterns of contingency. To return to our Kwaio mortuary feast, we would be led not to view "carver" and "divider" as social identities; but rather to see these as things which must be done by someone within a "feast plan." The cultural grammar sets out the feast plan and assumes that its idealized actor-observer knows how to perform all the acts of his culture. (Rules for performing these acts would of course have to be set out in any attempt at exhaustive cultural description.)

This alternative is challenging and promising. However, before we can explore it further, we will have to make a good deal of headway toward a theory of contexts and situations.

Is a Formal Discovery Procedure Feasible?

We have illustrated a discovery procedure that works relatively well in some domains and situations, yet in its present form clearly cannot be generalized so that it works everywhere.

Is it possible or desirable to formulate a

discovery procedure that will work everywhere? No answer would satisfy every specialist. My own position is that we are likely to refine our methodologies when we get a better theory of cultural competence and cultural structure, not arrive at that theory by some preconceived inductive methodology. Advances in a theory of how cultures define situations, for instance, will greatly expand our methodological horizons. To paraphrase Chomsky, inductive methodologies will only explore the order of surface-structures; and what we need are theories of deep-structure that narrow the range of possible surface-structure rules (cf., Chomsky 1965; Werner and Fenton, Chapter 29, this volume).

The kind of method I have sketched provides in my view not a rigid discovery procedure that could be used everywhere, but rather a conceptual clarification of what we are seeking to find. Exploration of the implicit premises and behavioral entailments of identity relationships will require insight and imagination, not simply rigorous induction. We will have to take as basic a kind of circularity and inference by approximation where we make provisional inferences about social identities to analyze rights and duties, provisional inferences about "scenes" to distinguish social identities, and so on.

Two final provisos about method are needed. First, if we are to admit the legitimacy of methodologies that are not formal and rigorously inductive, it must be because we place much higher demands than are usual in anthropology on testing our theories to see if they work. We must demand invariant relationships, attempt to account for complex phenomena and unusual outcomes, and use intuitions and judgments of appropriateness by native actors. What becomes important is

whether a theory works, not how we arrived at it. How we are to choose among alternative theories that work becomes a crucial part of our theory.

Second, we must recognize and accept that we are in the early phases of studying cultural structure. Like the analyses of early linguists, our work will probably be superseded many times in the years to come. The better answers, when they come, will probably derive from better understandings of the overall structure of cultural systems and the formal models required to describe them, and of cultural competence and its neurophysiological correlates, not from refined methodologies for studying segments of the whole.

What we can do now is set out the problems in exploratory fashion and map out alternative approaches and designs for solving them. We need now not a standardization of methodology or theory—it is too early for orthodoxy—but rather concerted assaults on the problem from as many sides, with as many strategies, as possible. We need—when confronted with analytical alternatives—to present descriptive segments that demonstrate the implications of the possible choices, and invite further structural restatement (cf., Bock 1967, for a related but somewhat different model of role analysis).

Most of all, we must avoid the temptation to retreat into artificially neat and narrow domains and segments. We have had too many programmatic statements and snatches of illustrative ethnography (like those I have presented). In their place, we should strive to produce systematic descriptions of large segments of cultures that bring to light the complexities of cultural structure and competence and begin to reveal what kinds of models we will ultimately need.

BIBLIOGRAPHY

BAR-HILLEL, J.
1964 *Language and information.* Reading, Mass., Addison-Wesley.
BATESON, G.
1955 A Theory of play and fantasy. Symposium. American Psychiatric Association, *Psychiatric Research Reports* 2:39–51.
1956 The message "This is play." In *Second*

conference of group processes. The Josiah Macy Jr. Foundation.
1958 The new conceptual frames for behavioral research. In *Proceedings of the Sixth Annual Psychiatric Institute.* New Jersey Psychiatric Institute, Princeton.
1963 Exchange of information about patterns of human behavior. In Fields and Abbott, eds., *Symposium on information storage*

and neural control. Springfield, Ill., Charles C. Thomas.

1967 Review of C. Geertz, Person, time and conduct in Bali: an essay in cultural analysis. *American Anthropologist* 69: 765–766.

1968 *Style, grace and information in primitive art.* Paper presented at Wenner-Gren "Conference on Primitive Art."

BATESON, G., *et al.*
1956 Towards a theory of schizophrenia. *Behavioral Science* 1:251–264.

BOCK, P. K.
1967 Three descriptive models of social structure. *Philosophy of Science* 34:168–173.

CHOMSKY, N.
1957 *Syntactic structures.* The Hague, Mouton.
1965 *Aspects of the theory of syntax.* Cambridge, M.I.T. Press.
1966 *Topics in the theory of generative grammar.* The Hague, Mouton.
1967 Some general properties of phonological rules. *Language* 43:102–128.

FRAKE, C. O.
1962a Cultural ecology and ethnography. *American Anthropologist* 64:53–59.
1962b The ethnographic study of cognitive systems. In T. Gladwin and W. C. Sturtevant, eds., *Anthropology and human behavior.* Washington, D.C., Anthropological Society of Washington.
1964 A structural description of Subunum religious behavior. In W. Goodenough, ed., *Explorations in cultural anthropology.* New York, McGraw-Hill.

FREILICH, M.
1964 The natural triad in kinship and complex systems. *American Sociological Review* 29:529–540.

GOFFMAN, E.
1961 *Encounters: two studies in the sociology of interaction.* Indianapolis, Bobbs-Merrill.

GOODENOUGH, W.
1951 *Property, kin, and community on Truk.* New Haven, Yale University Publications in Anthropology No. 46.
1957 Cultural anthropology and linguistics. In *Report of the seventh annual round table meeting on linguistics and language study.* Georgetown University, Monograph Series on Languages and Linguistics No. 9.
1961a Comments on cultural evolution. *Daedalus* 90:521–528.
1961b *Formal properties of status relationships.* Paper presented at the annual meeting of the American Anthropological Association, November 16, 1961, Philadelphia.
1964 Introduction. In W. Goodenough, ed.,

Explorations in cultural anthropology. New York, McGraw-Hill.

1965 Rethinking status and role. In M. Banton, ed., *The relevance of models for social anthropology.* London, Tavistock.

HAVILAND, J.
n.d. *Explorations in generative ethnography.* Unpublished MS.

HYMES, D.
1962 The ethnography of speaking. In Thomas Gladwin and William Sturtevant, eds., *Anthropology and human behavior.* Washington, D.C., Anthropological Society of Washington.
1964 Introduction: Toward ethnographies of communication. In John Gumperz and Dell Hymes, eds., *The ethnography of communication.* Washington, D.C., Anthropological Society of Washington.
n.d. *On communicative competence.* Unpublished MS.

KAY, P.
1965 Ethnography and the theory of culture. *Bucknell Review* 19:106–113.

KEESING, R. M.
1965a *Kwaio marriage and society.* Unpublished Ph.D. dissertation. Harvard University.
1965b Comment on Colby. *Current Anthropology* 7:23.
1966a Kwaio kindreds. *Southwestern Journal of Anthropology* 22:346–352.
1966b *Kwaio descent groups.* Unpublished MS.
1966c *The role of the Kwaio father.* Paper presented at annual meeting of the Southwestern Anthropological Association, April, 1966, Davis, Calif.
1967a Kwaio fosterage. Forthcoming in V. Carroll, ed., *Adoption in Eastern Oceania.*
1967b Statistical and decision models of social structure: a Kwaio case. *Ethnology* 6:1–15.
1967c *Shrines, ancestors, and non-unilineal descent on Malaita.* Paper presented at annual meeting of the American Anthropological Association, December 1, 1967, Washington, D.C.
1967d Christians and pagans in Kwaio, Malaita. *Journal of the Polynesian Society* 76:82–100.
1968a Step kin, in-laws, and ethnoscience. *Ethnology* 59:59–70.
1968b Word tabooing in its cultural context. Forthcoming in D. Marshall, ed., *Anthropology and Austronesia.*
1968c Descent groups as primary segments. Forthcoming in C. Jayarwardena *et al.*, eds., *Essays in honour of H. I. Hogbin.*
1968d *On quibblings over squabblings of siblings.* Paper presented at annual meeting

of the American Anthropological Association, November, 1968, Seattle.

METZGER, D., and G. WILLIAMS
1963a Tenejapa medicine I: the curer. *Southwestern Journal of Anthropology* 19:216–234.
1963b A formal analysis of Tenejapa Ladino weddings. *American Anthropologist* 65:1076–1100.

NADEL, S. F.
1957 *The theory of social structure*. New York, Free Press.

NATANSON, M.
1966a Man as an actor. *Philosophy and Phenomenological Research* 26:327–341.
1966b Anonymity and recognition: toward an ontology of social roles. In W. von Baeyer and R. M. Griffith, eds., *Conditio humana*. Springer-Verlag, Berlin.
1966c Alienation and social role. *Social Research* 33:375–388.

REUSCH, J., and G. BATESON
1951 *Communication: the social matrix of psychiatry*. New York, Norton.

SCHNEIDER, D., and G. HOMANS
1955 Kinship terminology and the American kinship system. *American Anthropologist* 57:1194–1208.

CHAPTER 24

The Economic System

GEORGE DALTON

This essay is addressed to the problems confronting the anthropologist doing fieldwork in the mid-1960s who has a special interest in studying the economy of the people among whom he works, what information to collect and how to analyze it. It will suggest a theoretical framework with which to make comparisons between small subsistence and peasant economies, and refer to works which may be regarded as models of ethnographic description and theoretical analysis. We begin by discussing the scope and content of economic anthropology and go on to describe the salient characteristics of industrial capitalism as a base with which to compare primitive and peasant economies.

SCOPE AND CONTENT OF ECONOMIC ANTHROPOLOGY

Economics, Anthropology, and Economic Anthropology

Methodological and theoretical questions— what is the scope of economic anthropology? should anthropologists incorporate the conceptual language of conventional economics in their analyses?—have been contentious issues for thirty years, going back to Firth's survey of economic anthropology in 1939 (*Primitive Polynesian Economy*, Chap. 1), Goodfellow's book in the same year (*Principles of Economic Sociology*), and Herskovits' *Economic Life of Primitive Communities*

In writing this paper, I have had to repeat much of what I said in two other papers, "Economics, Anthropology, and Economic Anthropology," and "Theoretical Issues in Economic Anthropology."

(1940, Chap. 2). The issues raised in these works were never resolved. They remained dormant until 1957 when Polanyi's symposium volume appeared (*Trade and Market in the Early Empires*), and touched off the second round of disputes which continue to the present.

It is necessary to point out the underlying reasons why these theoretical difficulties persist before going on to discuss a set of conceptual categories in expository fashion.

It is not sufficiently realized how complex economic anthropology is, how wide and diverse is the scope of its subject matter. Economic anthropology is concerned with the structure and the performance of hundreds of primitive and peasant economies—studied at different points in time, in all parts of the world—under static and dynamic conditions.

By structure I mean the organization of the economy: the transactional modes used to allocate land and labor, to arrange work, and to dispose of produce—in short, processes of production; also, market processes, external trade activities, and money uses. Structure also refers to the connections between economic and social organization, what Polanyi calls "the place of economy in society."

By performance I mean the quantifiable results of economic processes: how much and what kinds of subsistence, commercial, and prestige goods get produced; how equal or unequal is the distribution of income. Performance also relates to the productivity of labor, land, and other resources.[1]

[1] There seems to be no equivalent in the conventional subjects of anthropological inquiry such as kinship, religion, and polity, to what is here meant by the quantifiable performance of the economy. The closest

By primitive economies, I mean the Tro-briand and Tiv types, whose principal modes of transacting labor, land, tools, and produce are socially obligatory gift-giving (Mauss' *prestation,* and Thurnwald's reciprocity), and redistribution through political or religious leaders. These are economies in which the bulk of resources and produce are transacted in nonmarket spheres.

By peasant economies I mean those in Latin America described by Tax (1963) and Wolf (1966), and in Asia by Firth (1946), where commercial (market) transactions for resources and produce are quantitatively important, and so cash transactions, the pricing of land and tools, and wage-labor are common.

But this is not all. There are two basically different sets of conditions under which anthropologists analyze primitive and peasant economic structure and performance. The first is relatively static conditions, by which I mean before modernizing activities take place—what anthropologists sometimes refer to as traditional economy. (Malinowski describes the traditional internal and external economy of the Trobriands, although some commercial activities organized by Europeans —pearl fishing and plantation agriculture— were present.)

The second focus of analytical interest is the modern sort of economic change, and development: the enlargement of production for sale, the adoption of Western technology and applied science, and other modernizing activities (Geertz 1962, Epstein 1962).

For the most part, we are only at the beginnings of systematic analysis of these several aspects of primitive and peasant communities: organization, performance, primitive economy, peasant economy, traditional forms, change and development.

Despite the complexity and diversity of the subject matter, some writers search for a universally applicable theory of economic anthropology as though it were a Holy Grail, which once found, would shed the grace of understanding of all economies, those hundreds studied by anthropologists, as well as the dozens of developed, industrialized capitalist and communist economies studied by economists.

TABLE 1
SUBJECTS ANALYZED IN ECONOMIC ANTHROPOLOGY

1. Socioeconomic Structure: Primitive-Static Economies
   Peasant-Static Economies

2. Economic Performance: Primitive-Static Economies
   Peasant-Static Economies

3. Socioeconomic Organization and Economic Performance in Primitive and Peasant Economics Compared to Industrial Capitalism

4. Processes and Problems of Change, Growth, and Development in Primitive and Peasant Economies

What is required . . . is a search for the general theory of economic process and structure of which contemporary economic theory is but a special case. (LeClair 1962:1186)

Such a position indicates an insufficient appreciation of the complexity of the subject matter of economic anthropology and misunderstanding of conventional economics (which until recently was concerned exclusively with our own type of economy, industrial capitalism). Economics contains no such notion of a general or universal theory which in any sense is addressed to widely different processes and problems. Price theory is concerned with the determinants of price under different market conditions. Aggregate income theory considers an utterly different process: What determines national income for one

one comes is simple enumeration, e.g., frequency of murder, theft, or divorce. The distinction between organization and quantifiable performance applies to all economies, those studied by anthropologists, economists, and historians.

year? The concepts employed are different even though they relate to the same economy. So too for growth theory. And when economies different from our own are analyzed— Soviet economy, the underdeveloped economies of India or Nigeria—additional theoretical concepts are invented to deal with what is special to their structures or performance.

Economists employ several sets of theoretical concepts because of the different structures, processes, and problems studied: the structures and performance of industrial capitalist, industrial communist, and underdeveloped national economies, under static and dynamic conditions. Economic anthropology also requires several sets of theoretical concepts because it too is addressed to different structures, processes, and problems.

Of all the fields labeled social sciences, economics and anthropology are the least alike in their traditions, methods, and emphases. The mainstream of economics relates almost exclusively to our own kind of economy since it achieved its present industrialized form. Price theory, income theory, growth theory, money and banking, public finance, etc., consider the processes of large-scale, nationally-integrated, industrialized, capitalist economies. With the exception of writers such as Veblen and Galbraith, economists exclude institutional matters relating to social organization and culture from their analytical interests. These are relegated to industrial sociology and business administration. Even the few economists who concern themselves with economic history and comparative economic systems usually focus on the post-industrial period in Europe and America. There is no tradition in economics of detailed fieldwork, area studies, or concern with small-scale communities. Neither is there concern with what anthropologists mean by folk-views and psychologists mean by human behavior. Economists almost never have occasion to incorporate the work of sociology and psychology, except for the recent work on the institutional aspects of economic development (Hagen 1962).

There are two main positive traditions in economics. The first is the creation of formal theory of an abstract sort, which increasingly is stated in mathematical models. The second is a pragmatic concern for policy-making, a sensitivity to current problems of importance, such as depression and inflation. Keynes' work (1936), of course, is a clear example of formal analysis designed to make policy. A more recent example is the creation of economic development theory in response to the problems of developing the national economies of Africa, Asia, and Latin America. In almost all these ways anthropology has a radically different tradition. Theory in anthropology is neither highly abstract nor usually stated in mathematical terms. The empirical knowledge of anthropologists focuses on societies and cultures other than our own, and fieldwork is an important part of training and research. Most frequently the unit of analysis is a small community, not the nation-state. Anthropologists are concerned with human behavior and folk-views and have broad interests in culture and society—kinship, religion, polity—which makes anthropology much closer to sociology and psychology than is economics. Finally, there is no pragmatic tradition in anthropology. Policy-making has not been a principal interest in theory-building.

When anthropologists argue that conventional economics is *applicable* in economic anthropology, they have three things in mind (LeClair 1962, Burling 1962). The first is peasant economies (Firth 1946, Tax 1963), where market dependence for livelihood is important, cash transactions frequent, and commercial activities familiar. Where there is wage-labor and purchase and sale of land and produce, the conceptual categories of conventional price theory are obviously applicable, and the generalizations of economics about price and income formation, relevant. But the same is not true for primitive economies (the Tiv and the Trobriand Islanders) whose main sectors of economy are not organized by the market mode of transaction.

Conceptual categories of conventional economics are also adaptable to measuring economic performance. Here too, in peasant economies one can measure the money value of income generated (output produced) in the commercial sectors of production and distribution (Firth 1946), and arrive at the local community equivalents of national income and gross national product sums and their components, as conventionally measured for the United States. For primitive economies, measurement of community output is possible in terms of quantities of each sort of good produced, but not in national income accounting terms (because of the absence of cash transactions). So too with attempts to measure productivity of resources, such as output per man-year or per acre (Salisbury 1962). A third way anthropologists "apply" conventional economics is simply to use the terminology of economics, such as "maximize," "economize," "scarcity," and "rational choice" to describe *whatever* economic processes and activities they find in primitive and peasant societies:

> The elements of scarcity and choice, which are the outstanding factors in human experience that give economic science its reason for being, rest psychologically on firm ground. . . . Our primary concern in these pages is to understand the cross-cultural implications of the process of economizing. (Herskovits 1952:3, 4)

To assume that what economists mean by "scarcity," "choice," and "economizing" in our own economy are universally present in all economies is simply to misunderstand these terms. To apply these concepts to primitive economies lacking market organization of land, labor, and production is to equate *all purposeful activity* with "economizing," and then to conclude that the apparatus of economic theory is applicable because economizing activities have been identified:

> From this point of view, we are "economizing" in everything we do. We are always trying to maximize our satisfactions somehow, and so we are led back to the notion that economics deals not with a type but rather with an aspect of behavior. This economic view of society becomes . . . the model for looking at society. It is a model which sees the individuals of a society busily engaged in maximizing their own satisfactions—desire for power, sex, food, independence. . . . (Burling 1962:817–818)

This is to distort the meaning of economic activities in primitive societies. Priests become stockbrokers maximizing piety instead of profit. Bridewealth becomes the price one pays for sexual and domestic services. Indeed, when market language is used to describe all activities, the distinction between marriage and prostitution is blurred because the superficial point that both entail acquiring services for material payment receives undue emphasis (Dalton 1966).

Theory in economic anthropology is in its infancy despite the fact that the ethnographic literature of case studies is enormous, rich, and diverse. Indeed, even the obviously important connections between economies studied by anthropologists and those studied by historians of preindustrial Europe and Asia have hardly been touched (Goody 1963, Beattie 1964, Cohen 1966). Only in the last few years have we begun to construct a theoretical framework which, in systematically comparing traditional economies with our own, yields insights of the sort got in analyzing traditional kinship, polity, and religion. Moreover, the second large branch of the subject, processes of socioeconomic change, growth, and development as small communities "modernize" and become integral parts of nation-states, is even less developed.

Like economics, economic anthropology borders at one end on historical description of economies that have long since been transformed, and at the other on quantitative measurement and dynamic processes of present-day economies undergoing change and development. There is ample room for complementary theoretical approaches because of the many structures, processes, and problems that comprise economic anthropology.

Developed, Industrial, Capitalism

Whether the anthropologist is interested in the structure and performance of traditional primitive or peasant economies, or in their change, development, and modernization, it is necessary for him to understand the salient characteristics of the industrial capitalist countries of North America and Western Europe. These serve as an indispensable base of comparison. Here we can only sketch in a few basic points.

Scale. The United States has a national economy whose component units, millions of households and thousands of business firms, are thoroughly integrated through purchase, sale, lending, borrowing, and investment transactions. The socioeconomic unit most frequently analyzed in economic anthropology, the small-scale village community or tribal segment, is almost never the unit analyzed in economics. In economics microanalysis is of single prices, commodities, or firms, not small-scale geographical segments of the larger national society. The village, county, or town in America or Britain is not an interesting unit for economic analysis because it lacks a self-contained economy. Moreover, the nationally integrated developed economies take part in an international economy through sustained import and export transactions of resources, products, finance, and capital.

The large scale of national and international economy is the spatial expression of extreme division of labor: individual persons specialize in one occupation; individual firms produce one or few goods, geographical regions and nations specialize in producing fewer goods than they consume. The result (within and between national economies) is higher productivity and an extreme degree of interdependence.

Organization: Market Integration. The organizational fact of central importance in industrial capitalism is the existence of a network of local, regional, national, and international markets through which prices of resources and products are determined which guide production decisions. All the ingredients of production are organized for purchase at money price (resource and labor markets); all the produce of factories and farms is sold at money price (product markets). Natural resources, skilled and unskilled labor, machines and buildings, transport, communications, power, insurance, manufactured goods, and the specialist services of doctors, entertainers, repairmen, etc., are organized for purchase and sale. In developed economies, subsistence production—production for self-use—is a tiny proportion of total output, confined to do-it-yourself repairs and craft hobbies, and the shrinking farm sector.

Money. The type of money used and the functions it performs in developed capitalist economies are consequences of the crucial structural fact of market integration. One cannot begin to understand the role of money in our own economy without first understanding the role of markets.[2]

The primary function of dollars or francs is to serve as means of (commercial) exchange, which simply reflects the high frequency and wide range of purchase and sale of resources, goods, and services. The other commercial functions of money—store of (commercial) value, standard of (commercial) value, means of (commercial) payment, etc.—similarly reflect the accounting and pricing procedures characteristic of economies integrated by market exchange. So too with the

secondary features of dollars and francs. That our money is finely divisible and easily portable reflect the wide range of prices that exist and the extreme frequency of household and business firm purchases. That our money has noncommercial functions—that payment of taxes and fines to government, for example, are made with the same money used for ordinary commercial purchases—reflects another structural feature of national capitalist economies: that all levels of government purchase goods and services on the private market, as do households and business firms.

Technology. Technology means tools and knowledge. Both take special forms in advanced capitalist economies. The machines of applied science, from irrigation equipment to computers, contribute to the relatively high productivity of advanced capitalist economies. That machines are also relatively *expensive and long-lasting* has economic and sociological implications of importance.

Where expensive, long-lasting modern machinery is in use, so too is the factory system and institutional arrangements to assure a continual supply of labor and material resources necessary to work the machines; either a market system exists to supply inputs and purchase the outputs of the machines (as in capitalism), or its functional equivalent as in the central planning arrangements in Soviet economy. One important difference between machine-using American economy and machine-using Soviet economy is in these organizational arrangements (economic institutions) necessary to service machine technology and its accompanying factory system.

The second aspect of technology, knowledge, is reflected in the economy in the range and sophistication of the skills accquired by the blue-collar and white-collar labor forces, in the institutionalized research directed toward the creation of new products and techniques of production, and in the continual innovation of production lines.

Performance. The material performance of developed capitalism is finely measurable because of the ubiquity of pricing in money terms. Just as the single business firm draws up detailed statements of profit and loss (based upon cost accounting), and balance sheets showing the value of its asset holdings and debts, measurements of the quantifiable performance of the national economy are drawn up. National income accounts, input-

[2] Money objects are used in economies very differently organized, e.g., the U.S., the U.S.S.R., the Tiv. Where money objects are employed differently, organized differently, and carry out different functions, underlying economic organization is different. See Einzig (1948), Quiggen (1949), and Dalton (1965).

output tables, and balance of payments accounts are three such measurements. They quantify important information about the structure and performance of the national economy.

The familiar fact of the high productivity of the developed capitalist economies deserves emphasis as a salient characteristic; but another descriptive fact should be stressed as well: the enormous *range* and variety of goods and services produced. Hundreds of thousands of consumer, producer, and government goods and services are regularly produced. Finally, developed capitalist economies experience continual growth per capita in annual production, at a typical rate of between 1 and 3 per cent (principally because of net capital investment, improved technology, and improved skill and knowledge). This means that the people can expect continual increases in their real material income, indeed, something like a doubling of real income every thirty-five years.

Traditional, Subsistence Economies

A recent article (Cook 1966) criticizes those of us who are still analyzing in detail the structure of traditional subsistence economies such as the Trobriand Islands in Malinowski's time. In the mid-1960s very few such economies exist intact, almost all of them undergoing various kinds and degrees of economic, social cultural, and technological change.[3]

First, I point out that this issue seems not to arise in other branches of anthropology: anthropologists do not criticize each other for studying traditional political organization or traditional religion because—like traditional economy—they are now undergoing change. Indeed, why study history, then, since it is

[3] Although there are very few pure subsistence economies in the mid-1960s, economies in which commercial transactions are entirely absent, there are a good many primitive economies (especially in Africa) in which half or more of total income comes from subsistence production, and peasant economies in which smaller, but significant amounts of subsistence production are the rule. In the early 1950s, a U.N. agency reported that ". . . between 65 per cent and 75 per cent of the total cultivated land area of tropical Africa is devoted to subsistence production" (United Nations 1954:13). In the 1960s, the problem of transforming subsistence agriculture in Africa is still very much a matter of concern. See Yudelman (1964); also, Clower, Dalton, Harwitz, and Walters (1966).

concerned with forms of social organization no longer in being?

Questioning the usefulness of analyzing traditional economies is an example of an odd double standard in anthropology. Anthropologists who would condemn out of hand a theoretical approach which regarded primitive religion or political organization as simply being variants of European religions and polities to be analyzed in the conceptual language of Christianity and democracy, nevertheless approach primitive economy as though it were a variant of capitalism to be analyzed in the conceptual language of supply, demand, elasticity, capital, maximizing (bride) price, etc. (LeClair 1962, Pospisil 1963).

Anthropologists have old and new reasons to study the organization of traditional, subsistence economies, even in the 1960s when these are changing. One old reason is precisely the same that justifies their studying any aspect of traditional social organization and culture —religion, polity, kinship, language: to find out how these are (or were) organized in as many societies as we can and then make analytical generalizations about these, and compare them with our own Western systems. But there are at least two special reasons why it is important—even at this late date—to study traditional primitive economies.

I assert that the theoretical portion of economic anthropology has been poorly done. Compared to the theoretical writings on kinship, economic anthropology is underdeveloped. I do not mean to suggest that theoretical light began to dawn only with the publication of *Trade and Market in the Early Empires.* Malinowski (1921, 1922, 1935), Mauss (1954), and Firth (1929, 1939, 1946)—to name only the outstanding—have made contributions of great importance. But much was not done, and much of what was done was done poorly. And it is Polanyi's work on modes of transaction, money, markets, external trade, and operational devices that has begun important new lines of analysis, and, indeed, has allowed us to clear up some old muddles such as "primitive money" (Polanyi 1957, 1968; Dalton 1965) and economic "surplus" (Pearson 1957; Dalton 1960, 1963).

Another reason why it is necessary for us still to be concerned with traditional subsistence economies stems from the unfortunate fact that several of the early writers who sought a theoretical framework with which to analyze primitive and peasant economies (Goodfellow 1939, Herskovits 1952), turned to writings on post-industrial economic theory for conceptual guidance instead of writings on preindustrial European economic and social history. Pirenne (1936), Weber (1950), Bloch (1961, 1966), and Polanyi (who was an economic historian) have more to teach anthropologists about preindustrial economies than do Marshall (1920), Robbins (1935), or Knight (1941).

The peoples and communities of Africa, Asia, Latin America, and Oceania traditionally studied by anthropologists are experiencing the several kinds of change entailed in economic development, industrialization, urbanization, and the formation of nation-states. Anthropologists are increasingly concerned with the processes and problems of present-day socioeconomic change. There is a rapidly growing literature of theory and case studies (Smelser 1963, Douglas 1965, Brokensha 1966). Indeed, anthropologists have returned to places they did fieldwork in twenty or more years earlier, to study socioeconomic change (Firth 1959, 1966).

I suggest that analytical insights and generalizations about change and development have to be based on firm understanding of traditional socioeconomic organization (Dalton 1964, 1965b). Change is always change of what is; and what is, depends on what has been: "Any planned growth is embedded in a set of institutions and attitudes which come from the past" (Keyfitz 1959:34).

One can illustrate the point from European and American experience. How is it possible to understand the causes and consequences of those New Deal, Fair Deal, or "Great Society" changes in the U.S. economy and their counterparts in the English and Scandinavian welfare states, except by knowing the structure and performance of nineteenth- and early twentieth-century capitalism in Europe and the U.S.? How is it possible to understand the impact of Western money on subsistence economies in Africa unless one first understands the nature of indigenous money and its uses, which, in turn, requires knowing how indigenous economy functioned before the monetary incursion (Douglas 1958, Bohannan 1959). So too, in order to understand why litigation over land rights sometimes occurs when land is first made subject to contractual purchase and sale, one has to know the nature

of land tenure before land was made marketable (Biebuyck 1963).

Processes of modernization—industrialization, the expansion of commercial production—ramify into all segments of society and culture. Many of the anthropological studies being undertaken are addressed to two broad questions, both of which require knowledge of traditional, "pre-modernization" structures: (1) What are those features of traditional social organization, culture, polity, and economy which make for receptivity or resistance to technological, economic, and cultural innovations (Douglas 1965)? (2) What are the "impacts"—processes of sequential change—on traditional social organization and culture when a group undertakes enlarged production for sale, the use of Western money and technology, and incorporates other such innovations (Epstein 1962, Firth and Yamey 1964, Gulliver 1965)?

A THEORETICAL FRAMEWORK FOR ECONOMIC ANTHROPOLOGY

A theoretical framework for economic anthropology which is judged widely to be useful must be clear about the similarities and differences between our economy and primitive and peasant economies, about the relevance of conventional economics to economic anthropology, and it must contain an explicit statement of the matters to be analyzed in economic anthropology.

Economic Anthropology as Part of Comparative Economy

The economies of direct interest to anthropologists are the large set of subsistence and peasant communities in Africa, Asia, Latin America, Oceania, and the Middle East. The focus of analytical interest is either their traditional structure and performance before serious Western incursion (Malinowski 1922, 1935), or matters relating to socioeconomic change and development (Hunter 1961, Firth 1966). In either case there is an important literature outside of anthropology. The fields within economics which provide complementary information are preindustrial economic history (Takizawa 1927, Postan 1966), comparative economic systems (Carr 1951, Myrdal 1960, Grossman 1967), and the institutional literature of economic development (Lewis 1955, Myrdal 1957, Hagen 1962). Economic anthropology is best done within a framework of comparative economic systems which draws on all economies of record. The analysis of preindustrial and developing

TABLE 2
ECONOMIES OF RECORD AND SOCIAL SCIENCE SUB-FIELDS

ECONOMIES OF RECORD

Scale	Economy of Record	Sub-field in Social Science
Small-Scale	Primitive and Peasant, Before Modernization	Economic Anthropology; Pre-industrial Economic and Social History (e.g., Europe and Asia)
Small-Scale	Primitive and Peasant, Change and Development	Economic Anthropology; Applied Anthropology; Economic Development; Economic History
Small-Scale	Utopian [4]	European and American History
National	19th Century Capitalism	Economic History; History of Economic Thought; Classical and Neoclassical Economic Theory; Industrial Sociology
National	Welfare State and Fascism	Comparative Economic Systems; Economic History; Modern Economic Theory; Industrial Sociology
National	Communist	Soviet Economy [5]; Comparative Economic Systems; Industrial Sociology

SUB-FIELD IN SOCIAL SCIENCE

[4] The important connections between the structure of traditional, primitive economies and utopian communities (Noyes 1870, Bestor 1950, Bishop 1951, Nordhoff 1961) have never been systematically analyzed. Both are small-scale economies whose internal organization is of nonmarket sorts; where production processes—especially land tenure, work organization, and produce allocation—express social relationships. It is this feature which makes writers like Nyerere (1964) and Senghor (1964) assert that traditional African communities had a "socialist" ethos.

[5] Soviet economy has developed as a separate field of specialization within economics. See Nove (1962).

economies is now scattered in various branches of economics, history, sociology, and anthropology, all of which contribute information of use to the broad range of topics considered in economic anthropology (see Table 2).

What Is an Economic "System"?

I shall discuss some of the conceptual categories I think most useful in economic anthropology, indicate the questions they help answer, and the leading ideas they are associated with (see Table 3).

One of many semantic difficulties in economic anthropology is that the word "economy" (like the words "society" and "culture") has no size dimension attached to it. We can speak of the economy of a hunting band comprising a few dozen persons or the economy of Communist China comprising several hundred million.

Whatever the size of the economy it will have several features in common, three of which are of special interest.

(1) Whether the human group is called band, tribe, village, or nation, and whether its economy is called primitive, peasant, capitalist, or communist, it consists of people with recognized social and cultural affinities —kinship, religion, language, neighborhood— expressed in some sort of shared community or social life. This means that two kinds of goods and specialist services[6] must be provided for use within the community (however defined): food and other material requisites of *physical* existence, and goods and services for religion, defense, settlement of disputes,

[6] The concept of "services" causes difficulty in economic anthropology, (as do the concepts of "capital" and "market") because the term is used to cover a wide range of items or activities in our own economy, only a few of which are found in primitive economies. In our own economy, the term "services" is used to describe ordinary labor, mechanized utilities (telephone and electricity services), the services performed by craftsmen and professional specialists, e.g., dentistry, TV repairs, musicians; and also the functions performed by political and religious office-holders. In our own economy, all but the latter services are organized for purchase and sale. In relation to primitive and peasant economies, I prefer to use the term "specialist services" to refer to those provided by craftsmen, such as blacksmiths, wood carvers, and dancers, and those provided by persons performing political, religious, and ritual roles.

rites of passage, and other aspects of *social* and community life. The acquisition or production of material items and specialist services necessary for physical and social existence are never left to chance because neither individuals nor communities can survive without them. It is for this reason that it is useful to regard all communities or societies as having economic systems. The word "system" refers to structured arrangements and rules which assure that material goods and specialist services are provided in repetitive fashion. One task of economic anthropology is to spell out these rules and systematic arrangements for that set of societies of interest to anthropologists.

(2) A second similarity among economies is that they all make use of some form(s) of natural resources (land, waterways, minerals), human cooperation (division of labor), and technology (tools, and knowledge of production or acquisition processes). Each of these features is structured: the use of tools, natural resources, and division of labor require social rules—specified rights and obligations. The rules for the acquisition, use, and transfer of rights to land, we call "land tenure"; the rules specifying human cooperation in production processes, we call "work organization"; the existence of tools and technical knowledge in any economy means that there will be rules for their acquisition, use, and transfer.

Two general points emerge: The rules specifying rights of acquisition or usage of any of these components of an economy *may* be expressions of kinship or political relationships, in which case the economic component is inextricably related to the social (both observable activities and folk-views will indicate if such is the case), and we have a *socioeconomic* practice, institution, or process. Aboriginal arrangements for land tenure in parts of Africa are obvious examples, where land is acquired through kinship right or tribal affiliation (Schapera and Goodwin 1937:157, Bohannan 1954). Secondly, what we call economic organization is the set of rules in force through which natural resources, human cooperation, and technology are brought together to provide material items and specialist services in sustained and repetitive fashion.

(3) A third similarity is the incorporation of superficially similar devices and practices in economies differently organized. Economies as different as the U.S., the U.S.S.R., and the Tiv make use of market places, foreign trade, monetary objects, and devices for measuring and record-keeping.

In summary, all societies of record—those studied by anthropologists, historians, and economists—have structured arrangements to provide the material means of individual and community life. It is these structured rules that we call an economic system. Economic anthropology delineates these social rules of economy by first describing activities and folk-views, and then analyzing processes and relationships in the small-scale, preindustrial communities of the underdeveloped world, and makes comparisons between primitive, peasant, and the industrialized developed economies of the West. So too with comparing the components of economy: the allocation of land and labor, the organization of work, the disposition of produce, and the organization and usage of forms of money, markets, and external trade.

There are very important differences among economies, however, differences in structure and in performance, and much valuable analysis lies in contrasting economies with regard to the following: technology, size, and physical environment; transactional modes used to allocate resources, organize work, and dispose of produce. In comparing performance, questions such as these are relevant: what is the range of goods and services produced; what are the relative quantities produced; how equally or unequally is real income distributed, and why?

Traditional, Primitive Economies: Structure and Performance

The questions about primitive economies of most interest to anthropologists relate to their organization (structure), and to comparisons of their organization with other types of economy (peasant, and industrial capitalist). With regard to their performance, one can say less of interest. One can indicate the relatively narrow range of goods and specialist services produced or acquired; the level of output and fluctuations in output can be measured in real terms of quantities produced (Deane 1953, Reynders 1963); input

measures can be devised (Salisbury 1962), indicating amounts of equipment used in production processes, and work-days employed, and so arrive at some indicators of productivity. Dietary standards may be scrutinized (Richards 1939). Some impressions of the equality or inequality in real income distribution can be conveyed. But given the absence of Western money and pricing and the relatively few resources used and goods produced, these measures of performance can only be rough indicators stated in terms of the resources and product units themselves.

The Scale of Primitive Economies

It is this smallness of scale, so hard for a modern European to grasp imaginatively, which is the fundamental characteristic of primitive life. . . . (Wilson 1941).

There are some useful distinctions to be made among traditional economies. Much of the literature of primitive economies[7] describes those without centralized polities— "tribes without rulers"—Malinowski's Trobriands being the most minutely described case in the literature. In saying that most primitive economies without centralized polity are small, one means several things: that the economy of the Tiv, the Nuer, or the Trobriand Islanders is small relative to modern, nationally-integrated economies of Europe and America; that most (but not all) resource, goods, and service transactions take place within a small geographical area and within a community of persons numbered in the hundreds or thousands. It is true that external trade with strangers—sometimes, as with the Kula, carried out over long distances—is common. But, typically, it is intermittent, petty, and confined to very few goods. It is rare (except in peasant economies) for foreign trade transactions to be frequent, quantitatively important, or essential to livelihood.

[7] The literature of primitive (subsistence) economies —traditional economies most different from our own —is richest for Africa and Oceania, for small-scale communities rather than kingdoms and empires, and for agriculturalists rather than hunters, gatherers, etc. Malinowski's work (1921, 1922, 1926, 1935; also Uberoi 1962) is the single best source. On the economies of kingdoms and other politically centralized societies, see Nadel (1942), Maquet (1961), Arnold (1957a and b), and Polanyi (1966).

There are two other ways in which primitive economies are small-scale. Frequently there are one or two staple items (yams in the Trobriands, cattle among the Nuer) which comprise an unusually large proportion of total produce. It is common for these important staples to be produced within the small framework of village, tribe, or lineage. Lastly, primitive economies are small in the sense that a relatively small number of goods and services is produced or acquired—dozens of items and specialist services rather than hundreds of thousands as in developed, industrial economies.

There are mutually reinforcing connections between the size, structure, and performance of an economy. Two widely shared characteristics of the small economies anthropologists study are a simple level of technology (compared to the industrial economies of the West), and the fact that they are frequently geographically or culturally isolated (again, compared to those of Europe and North America). The absence of sophisticated machines and applied science, and of extreme labor specialization characteristic of national economies numbering their participants in the millions, means a relatively low level of productivity. Two direct consequences for primitive (and some peasant) economies of their level of technology and small size are that their peoples are sharply constrained in production activities by physical resource endowment (ecology), and that their peoples depend greatly on human cooperation for ordinary production[8] processes as well as in emergencies such as famine and personal misfortune.

A second consequence of low-level technology combined with small size and relative isolation from other economies is the extent of mutual dependence among people sharing many relationships: economic arrangement in primitive economies are intimately related to kinship and polity. The primitive economy is

[8] The extraordinary dependence on immediate physical environment for livelihood made it seem reasonable for an older generation of anthropologists to use classifications such as gathering, hunting, fishing, pastoral, and agricultural "economies." These categories do not classify according to *economic organization,* but rather according to principal source of subsistence, physical environment, and technology. Note that if we used these categories for developed economies, the U.S. and the U.S.S.R. would appear in the same category, both being manufacturing and agricultural "economies."

"embedded" in community relationships and is not composed of associations separate from these (Dalton 1962, 1964).

Association is a group specifically organized for the purpose of an interest or group of interests which its members have in common. . . . Community is a circle of people who live together, who belong together, so that they share not this or that particular interest, but a whole set of interests wide enough and comprehensive enough to include their lives (MacIver 1933:9, 10, 12, quoted in Nadel 1942:xi).

Some points may here be underscored: (1) That set of economies which I have consistently called "primitive" or "subsistence" economies require for the analysis of their *organization* conceptual categories which are socioeconomic because material and service transactions are frequently expressions of kinship, religious, or political relationships. (2) Two general features of primitive or subsistence economies are the pervasive social control of production and distribution, and the assurance of subsistence livelihood to persons through the social determination of labor and land allocation and the social right to receive emergency material aid in time of need. These points have frequently been made in other terms: to Tönnies, primitive economies are *Gemeinschaft* rather than *Gesellschaft;* to Maine, they are characterized by status rather than contract; to Weber and MacIver, they are communities rather than associations; to Karl Polanyi (1944: Chap. 4, 1957), the economy is "embedded" in the society; to Raymond Firth (1951:142), the formula is: "From each according to his status obligations in the social system, to each according to his rights in that system."

Primitive economies are so organized that the allocation of labor and land, the organization of work within production processes (farming, herding, construction of buildings and equipment), and the disposition of produced goods and specialist services are expressions of underlying kinship obligation, tribal affiliation, and religious and moral duty. Unlike the economist who can analyze important features of industrial capitalism (such as price and income determination) without considering kinship and religion, the economic anthropologist concerned with the *organization* of primitive economies finds there is no separate economic system that can be analyzed independently of social organization.

The ways in which tools and implements are acquired, used, and disposed of is another point of contrast between primitive, peasant, and industrial capitalist economies. Typically in primitive economies tools are either made by the user himself, acquired for a fee from a specialist craftsman, or, as is sometimes the case with dwellings, storehouses, and canoes, acquired from a construction group specifically organized for the task. The construction group providing ordinary labor as well as the services of craftsmen specialists is remunerated either by the host providing food (Thurnwald's *Bittarbeit* and barn-raising in the American West), or food and luxury tidbits (tobacco, betel), or these as well as payments in valuables or special-purpose money to the craftsmen-specialists (Dalton 1965). I mention here that Western cash is not paid, that the making of tools, canoes, and dwellings is an occasional event rather than a continuous activity, that the construction workers do not derive the bulk of their livelihood from providing such services; that the tools, canoes, and buildings when put to use do not yield their owners a cash income, and that, typically, the implements are used until they are physically worn out, when they are either repaired or discarded. Unlike peasant economies (Firth 1946) there is nothing like a secondhand market for tools and buildings in primitive economies.

Polanyi's analytical distinctions between reciprocity, redistribution, and (market) exchange and their application to specific cases have been written up in detail (Polanyi 1944: Chap. 4, 1947, 1957, 1966; Dalton 1961, 1962, 1965b). Unfortunately, they have been misconstrued as applying to transactions of produce, only (Smelser 1959, Burling 1962, Nash 1966). These socioeconomic categories apply to inanimate resource and labor allocation, and to work organization as well as to produce disposition—to production as well as to distribution of goods and craft services (LeClair 1962). It is misleading to regard "systems of exchange" as something apart from production processes because exchange transactions enter into *each* of the three component processes of production (Dalton 1962, 1964).

Consider any production process: automobile manufacturing in the U.S., yam-growing in the Trobriands, collective farming in the U.S.S.R., Malay peasant fishing, or cattle raising among the Nuer. All these production lines require the allocation of land, labor, and other resource ingredients to the production processes; the organization of work tasks within the production process; and the disposition of the items produced. Among the Tiv, land allocation for farming in accordance with lineage affiliation is as much a "reciprocal" transaction as yam-giving as part of *urigubu* obligation is in the Trobriands.

Primitive States: Internal Redistribution and External Administered Trade

As in other branches of anthropology, the typical unit of analytical interest in economic anthropology is a relatively small group, the tribe, the lineage segment, the village community. There is a small, internal economy to be analyzed whether our focus of interest is a primitive economy without centralized polity (such as the Tiv), a primitive economy within a centralized polity, such as the local farming communities in Nupe (Nadel 1942), or a peasant economy, such as the Malay fisherman (Firth 1946). To be sure, persons or groups within each of these small economies may carry out transactions with outsiders—external trade, tax and tribute payments to outside political authorities—but it is meaningful to distinguish between internal (local community or lineage) transactions and those external to the local group, however defined.

In primitive economies within centralized political authority—what Polanyi called archaic societies and Fortes and Evans-Pritchard (1940) called primitive states—there are socioeconomic transactions in addition to those found within the local community and between local communities. These are of two principal sorts, transactions between the political center and its local constituencies, and external trade transactions between the political center and foreigners (Arnold 1957a, 1957b; Polanyi 1963, 1966). The local constituents pay tribute to the political center—ordinary subsistence goods, luxuries reserved for elite usage, labor for construction projects and military service—and usually receive from the center military protection,

TABLE 3
A SUMMARY OF CONCEPTUAL CATEGORIES AND RELEVANT QUESTIONS IN ECONOMIC ANTHROPOLOGY

I. A. *Traditional Economies*
    1. Primitive, without centralized polity (Tiv)
    2. Primitive, with centralized polity: chiefdoms, kingdoms, empires (Nupe, Bantu, Inca)
    3. Peasant (Malay fishermen, Latin American peasantries)

  B. *Analytical Distinctions for Primitive and Peasant Economies*
    1. *Organization*
      i. Size of economy; technology; natural resource endowment.
      ii. Transactional modes (reciprocity, redistribution, market-exchange; dominant-integrative modes distinguished from petty modes).
      iii. Production processes: (a) allocation of resources (land acquisition, use, and transfer; labor acquisition and use; the acquisition, use, and transfer of tools and equipment). (b) work organization. (c) disposition of produce. (d) specialist services and their remuneration.
      iv. Organization and role(s) of external trade (reciprocal gift trade; politically administered trade; market trade).
      v. Organization and role(s) of internal markets and market places (marketless economies; petty market places; small-scale market-integrated economies. Resource markets and produce markets).
      vi. Organization of money and money uses (distinctions between general-purpose and special-purpose monies; between commercial and non-commercial uses of money; relation of money uses to transactional modes).
      vii. Operational devices: record-keeping, accounting, and measurement devices (quipu strings, pebble counts); devices of culture contact (silent trade, border markets, ports of trade).
      viii. Prestige economy contrasted with subsistence economy (transactional spheres and conversions; bridewealth; ceremonial transfers; valuables and treasure items as special-purpose monies).
      ix. The relation of economic to social organization (the place of economy in society): social control of resource allocation, work organization, and product disposition; social guarantee of livelihood through resource allocation and the provision of emergency subsistence.

    2. *Performance*
      i. Number of goods and specialist services produced or acquired.
      ii. Level of output; fluctuations in output; frequency or dearth of famine (emergency devices in dearth of famine: use of trade partners for emergency gifts; use of less-preferred foods; emergency conversions, e.g., sale of treasures and people for food).
      iii. Distribution of real income: how equal or unequal?
      iv. Distribution of subsistence goods contrasted with distribution of prestige goods (spheres of exchange; conversion between spheres).
      v. Growth in total product.

  C. *Special Points Relating to Traditional, Peasant Economies*
    1. The nature of market organization and dependence contrasted with national, developed market economies; why "penny capitalism" is an appropriate description of peasant economy.
    2. Peasant economy and culture before and after the Industrial Revolution.
    3. The mixture of traditional and market economy; of traditional and modern technology; of traditional social organization and culture and elements of modern culture.
    4. Primitive economy and society in contrast to peasant economy and society, and in contrast to industrial capitalist economy and society.

II. *Socioeconomic Change, Growth, and Development: Sequential Process Analysis*
1. Two fields of economic development: economics (national development—from above), and anthropology (community development—from below).
2. The reasons for the complexity of the subject of change, growth, and development.
3. The distinctions between degenerative change, economic growth, and socioeconomic development.
4. The nature of the initial incursions: change, growth, and development are initiated from outside the small community.
5. The frequent case of primitive economies becoming peasant: growth without development.
6. What constitutes "successful" community development?

judical services, and emergency subsistence in time of local famine or disaster.

Where there is a centralized political authority there is a redistributive sector to be analyzed which has no counterpart in primitive economies without a centralized polity (i.e., that are not chiefdoms, kingdoms, or empires). Indeed, where there is an intermediary elite between the king (his royal household economy and his domain), and the rank-and-file villages or tribal segment constituencies which express their political subordination through tax and tribute payments and other upward transactions, there are socioeconomic sectors that some writers call feudal (Nadel 1942, Maquet 1961, Cohen 1966), although others question the usefulness of so labeling them (Goody 1963, Beattie 1964).

Peasant Culture and Economy

Writers on peasantry (Redfield 1956, Wolf 1966) emphasize the special nature of peasant personality and culture as that which distinguishes peasant from primitive: the semi-isolation from urban culture with which it shares religion and (in Europe) language; that peasants and peasant communities are the subordinate rank and file, so to speak, of larger political groupings, so that in Latin America, Europe, and India there are political authorities externally located who exercise some formal political jurisdiction over the peasantry.

It is important to note that if we confine ourselves to cultural aspects such as religion, language, and political subordination, we can point up what is common to an enormous

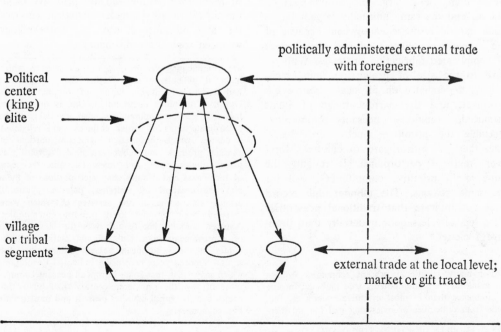

Political center (king) elite

village or tribal segments

politically administered external trade with foreigners

external trade at the local level; market or gift trade

number of peasantries, and at the same time justify the use of the special category, peasant culture, by showing it is different in these ways from primitive culture. Trobriand Island culture has none of the religious, linguistic, and political characteristics so far enumerated for peasants. To go further, however, requires some special distinctions because of the long periods of historical time over which groups called peasant by social analysts have existed intact, and because there are other criteria used to differentiate peasant from primitive and modern.

One line of demarcation is the Industrial Revolution. All peasantries before the Industrial Revolution occurred in their regions used primitive technology, differing in no important way from the technologies used by those groups (Tiv, Lele, Nuer) anthropologists identify as being primitive. Let us call peasant communities as they existed before the Industrial Revolution in their regions, "traditional" peasantries. Then we can point out immediately that traditional peasantries, although differing from primitive societies in those cultural ways specified earlier, were like primitive communities in their use of simple (machineless) technology, their units of production (principally but not exclusively agricultural) being small, and the number of items produced within a peasant community being relatively few. In traditional peasantries as in primitive communities, there is the same reliance upon one or two staple foodstuffs which comprise a large proportion of total output, and the same unusually large reliance upon natural resource endowment because of the simple technology used and the absence of complicated fabrication processes. With regard to the size of production units, technology, dependence on physical resource endowment, and the narrow range of items produced, traditional peasant communities resemble the primitive much more closely than they do with regard to culture. Moreover, material performance is roughly the same as in primitive communities, and for the same reasons. The ethnographic record does not indicate that traditional peasantries were typically less poor materially than primitive societies.[9]

[9] For many traditional peasant economies (village communities), it is undoubtedly true that real income is no higher than in most primitive economies. But, aside from difficulties of measuring real output, there

If we consider peasantries since industrial technology was introduced to their parts of the world, two points become evident. The range of differences among communities still called peasant widens considerably, so that many peasant communities become less homogeneous with regard to technology, economy and culture. Specifically, one finds in some recently studied peasant communities mixtures of modern and primitive practices within the same community: some households use modern technology, some do not; some households as production units increase specialist production of cash crops for market, while some still produce a significant quantity for their own consumption; some persons acquire literacy and new skills, others do not. Some peasant communities are changed significantly due to growth and development in their regions and nations (Myrdal 1957, Chaps. 2, 3).

What anthropologists mean by peasant culture is clear; what they mean by peasant economy is not clear.

By a peasant economy one means a system of small-scale producers, with a simple technology and equipment often relying primarily for their subsistence on what they themselves produce. The primary means of livelihood of the peasant is cultivation of the soil. (Firth 1951:87)

But this is a perfect description of the Lele (Douglas 1965), the Tiv (Bohannan and Bohannan 1968), and the Trobriand Islanders in Malinowski's time—all are primitive economies. If we are to make analytical sense of the large literature of economic anthropology we need some finer distinctions.

are complicating features of peasant society which make it difficult to say whether many peasantries had consistently higher levels of output than is typical in primitive communities. One is due to the fact that peasant communities seem invariably to be subordinate units of larger political (and religious) groupings, which means that significant portions of peasant produce and labor are paid "upward" as taxes, tributes, rents, and tithes. The elite recipients of such taxes and tributes channeled portions of them into the creation of churches, palaces, pyramids, armies, etc., some of the services of which were received back by the local peasant communities. Another complicating feature was the slow growth of improvements in agricultural and marketing techniques in some European peasant communities for several hundred years before the Industrial Revolution, which may mean that some European peasant communities of say, the eighteenth century, had higher incomes than is typical of other peasant and most primitive economies.

It is as useful to distinguish between peasant and primitive economy as it is to distinguish between peasant and primitive culture. The *economic* organization of a peasant community has two sets of distinguishing characteristics:

(1) Most people depend for the bulk of their livelihood on production for market sale or selling in markets; purchase and sale transactions with cash are frequent and quantitatively important; and, frequently, resource markets are present: significant quantities of labor, land, tools, and equipment are available for purchase, rent, or hire at money price. It is the relative importance of markets for resources and products and of cash transactions that is the principal feature of difference between peasant and primitive *economies*. It is this feature which gives peasant economies their crude resemblance to the least productive of our own farming sectors and which justifies Tax's appropriate phrase, "penny capitalism." But in all other ways relating to productive activities, peasant economies—especially traditional peasantries—more closely resemble the primitive than they do the modern: small-scale, simple technology, a narrow range of output, a few staples comprising the bulk of output, unusual reliance on physical resource endowment because of the absence of applied science and the technology of extensive fabrication; low levels of output—poverty and material insecurity.

(2) What strikes the economist is that although the rudiments of capitalist (i.e., market) economy are present and important in peasant communities, they are *incomplete* and *underdeveloped* compared to market organization in a modern national economy. By incomplete is meant that within a given peasant community, some markets may be absent or petty—land may be frequently purchased or rented but labor is not (Chayanov 1966), or vice versa; and that subsistence production may still be quantitatively important in some households. By underdeveloped is meant the absence of facilitative institutions and social capital of advanced capitalist countries: on the one hand, banks, insurance companies, and stock markets; on the other electricity, paved roads, and educational facilities beyond the elementary school. In peasant communities the extent of economic, cultural, and technological inte-

gration with the province and nation is markedly less than is the case with hinterland communities in developed nations.

In summary, peasant society, like primitive society (and also feudalism, *jajmani* in village India, and slavery) is a socioeconomic category (Firth 1964:17). If we include peasantries of all times and places within our analysis, then it is fair to say that peasant culture is more homogeneous and distinctive than is peasant economy (Fallers 1961). The spectrum of peasantries is wide, and contains varying mixtures of primitive and modern institutions. At one end are those in medieval Europe—the Russian mir, the feudal village (Bennett 1962) and some of present-day Latin America, which are peasant cultures (in religion, language, political subordination) with primitive economies (because of the absence of market dependence and cash transactions). There are also cases of peasant economy with a primitive culture, as in the early transition period of African groups enlarging their cash-earning production while retaining their tribal organization and culture (Fallers 1961, Dalton 1964, Gulliver 1965).

Community Change and Development

The most promising area for fruitful interchange and collaboration between economics and anthropology is the field of economic development. Most development economists, however, are interested in processes and problems of *national* economic growth and development that have little in common with anthropologists' interest in local community social and economic change. But a growing number of economists are working on matters requiring anthropological insight: creating an industrial labor force, transforming subsistence agriculture (Yudelman 1964), devising policies for investment in educational facilities. Others are devising techniques of measurement and analysis to show the connections between sociopolitical organization and economic development (Adelman and Morris 1965, 1967). And yet other economists are making use of anthropology, sociology, and psychology to analyze—what is for economists—an unusual range of processes and problems entailed in economic growth and development (Myrdal 1957, Hagen 1962).

Matters relating to what I shall call socioeconomic change, growth, and development at the local community level conventionally appear in anthropology under the headings of evolution, diffusion of innovations, social change, culture change, culture contact, acculturation, and applied anthropology. There are two points about this literature of socioeconomic change that I should like to emphasize.

The subject is extraordinarily diverse and complicated. One need only look at some recent symposium volumes (Southall 1961, UNESCO 1963) to see that a wide range of complex processes is considered: urbanization, industrialization, commercialization, national integration. Moreover, these processes take place over much longer periods of time than anthropologists customarily remain in the field, and their analysis requires consideration of the nation-state and the policies of central government which impinge on the small group —the village or tribe—that traditionally has been the principal focus of interest in anthropology.

The case studies of socioeconomic change reach back to the early days of European colonization of Africa (Schapera 1934, Hunter 1961), Latin America (Chevalier 1963), and Asia (Boeke 1942), when neither political independence was a fact nor economic development of indigenous peoples an explicit intention. Indeed, in these respects, we need only refer to the American Indians. At this end of the spectrum are case studies of socioeconomic change taking place in villages which are now parts of independent nation-states whose central governments are bent on economic development and modernization. Moreover, there are many cases of piecemeal change, where a new cash crop or a new school or a new religion is introduced in an otherwise traditional community (Dalton 1964), and cases of comprehensive community development, such as the famous case of Vicos (Holmberg 1965).

Given the complexity and length of the processes, the very large number of case studies on record, the dynamic nature of the subject, and the changed political and economic *national* conditions under which local community development now proceeds, it is not surprising that relatively few theoretical insights and conceptual categories with which to analyze socioeconomic change have been contrived. Three notable contributions are

Myrdal (1957), Hagen (1962), and Smelser (1963).

The subject of socioeconomic change is unusual in another way, as well. Those of us in the social sciences who work on problems of economic development and modernization hope not only to come to understand these processes, but also to use such knowledge to reduce the social costs of economic improvement. Therefore, this extension of the traditional concerns of economic anthropology into processes of socioeconomic change and development has policy implications to an extent that is unusual in anthropology (Erasmus 1961, Goodenough 1963, Arensberg and Niehoff 1964).

What is also true is that each of us—the anthropologist, the economist, the sociologist —comes to a novel problem situation such as change and development in an African village community with two kinds of professional knowledge, the theory of one's subject, and an intimate knowledge of some portion(s) of the real world. The economist (typically) comes with price, income, growth, and development theory, plus his knowledge of the structure and performance of his own and perhaps several other economies. If he is a specialist in economic history or Soviet economy (Gershenkron 1962), he brings with him knowledge of the sequential processes through which England, Japan, Russia, or the U.S. developed. When he comes to examine local development in an African community, he is struck by similarities to and differences from what he is already familiar with.

First, there is no counterpart in conventional economic analysis to the study of local community change and development. European and American villages and townships —the local community counterparts of the Tiv lineage segment or an Indian village— are never the focus of analytical concern. Economics is about national economies and the component activities of business firms and households thoroughly integrated with their national economies through purchase and sale transactions. Immediately we can feed back into our new concerns knowledge that we know is important from our old ones. Empirically, *how do small groups—the tribe, the village—become part of a regional or national economy?*

Similarly, local community change or development seems never to be a "natural" process of imminent expansion of the village or tribe, but rather the local community's response to incursion from outside itself. Whether it is the conquistadores' invasion of Peru four hundred years ago, or Cornell University's somewhat more benevolent invasion of Vicos fifteen years ago, or European colonial incursion into Africa, or the slave-raider, missionary, or merchant who comes, the process of community change starts with impingement from without. Therefore, a second question we can feed back to the empirical case studies is, *what is the nature of the initial incursion which starts the processes of socioeconomic change, and to what extent does the character of the initial incursion shape the sequential changes that follow?*[10]

Most of the ethnographic case studies fall into one of three broad categories that I shall designate (i) degenerative change; (ii) growth without development; and (iii) socioeconomic development. The three categories —which are really ideal types—are not stages of progression. Moreover, they are clearly overlapping. Some of the empirical literature fits neatly into these categories, some does not. My point is to make sharp analytical distinctions, and to do so I must oversimplify.

Degenerative Change

One way to understand what constitutes successful community development is to consider cases of obvious failure.

Leach remarks somewhere that peoples, tribes, and communities change, but very rarely do they become extinct. Rome fell to the barbarians but Italian villages survived. There are cases in which epidemic disease or brutal conquest decimated communities to the point of extinction, but they are few and will not concern us.

One reason why "culture contact" and applied anthropology are tainted subjects to some anthropologists is because so much of the early literature consists of European and American incursions which produced decimation, misery, and community degeneration

among indigenous groups (Rivers 1922, Jaspan 1953).

Native [Fiji] society [in the 1880s] was severely disrupted by war, by catastrophic epidemics of European diseases, by the introduction of alcohol, by the devastations of generations of warfare, and by the depredations of labor recruiters. (Worsley 1957:19)

By degenerative change I mean severe disruption of the traditional life of a community over several generations with accompanying indicators of novel sorts and frequencies of personal and social malaise. I do not postulate frictionless bliss in the traditional society; but whatever conflicts and malaise were generated by traditional society—warfare, vendetta, sorcery—were coped with by traditional institutions (Malinowski 1926), without prolonged disruption of ordinary life. Where degenerative change occurs, it is, obviously, because the situation is such that traditional institutions designed to deal with traditional sorts of stress and conflict are unable to deal with the novel change because it embodies forces which are at the same time irreversible and overwhelming to traditional organization.

The extreme cases are marked by military conquest and displacement of traditional political authority by conquerors who neither understand nor respect the culture of the traditional society they now control. The indigenous people are unable to resist imposed changes, are prohibited from pursuing rituals or activities which are meaningful and integrative within traditional society, and are forced to pursue new actvities (e.g., working in mines and plantations) which are not integrative—do not fulfill social obligation and so reinforce social relationships—in traditional society (Steiner 1957).

For the sting of change lies not in change itself but in change which is devoid of social meaning. (Frankel 1955:27)

Degenerative situations and the psychological processes of individual and group reaction to them have caught the attention of many writers, perhaps because the consequences are so dramatic. Having lost the primary ties of meaningful culture, social relationships, and activities (Fromm 1941), and forced into meaningless activities and degrading helplessness, the cultural reaction to the intolerable and bewildering changes are

[10] A third general point of significance I believe to be the time rate of change which is experienced (Polanyi 1944: Chap. 3). This is not, however, independent of the other features of the transformation process.

fantasy, aggression, withdrawal, and escape (Smelser 1963). And so we have the ethnography of cultural disintegration, from the Pawnee Ghost Dance to Melanesian cargo cults[11] and Navaho alcoholism.

If one examines these cases of degenerative change from the viewpoint of community development, several features stand out:

(a) *The nature of the initial incursion.* In cases of severe degenerative change, the initial incursion causes cultural decimation: military conquest, political subjugation, and severe disruption of usual activities. A by-product of the incursion may be material worsening, or, indeed, slight material betterment. But in these cases the economic consequences are really beside the point because the force of change is perceived and felt to be cultural deprivation of valued activities, and the community's subjugation to militarily superior foreigners with hostile intentions and contempt for indigenous ways. The foreigners may come with the intent to deprive the people of gold or land. But typically it is not the deprivation of gold or land which causes the deep disruption.

Not economic exploitation, as often assumed, but the disintegration of the cultural environment of the victim is then the cause of degradation. The economic process may, naturally, supply the vehicle of the destruction, and almost invariably economic inferiority will make the weaker yield, but the immediate cause of his undoing is not for that reason economic; *it lies in the lethal injury to the institutions in which his social existence is embodied.* The result is loss of self-respect and standards, whether the unit is a people or a class, whether the process springs from so-called "culture conflict" or from a change in the position of a class within the confines of a society. (Polanyi 1944:157. Italics added)

The nature of the initial incursion seems invariably important, not only to the generation experiencing the initial impact but also in shaping the sequences of socioeconomic change in which successive generations live (Hagen 1962). The group's cultural memory of what they regard as early injustice is long (Schapera 1928), and sometimes is nurtured several generations later (Colson 1949).

(b) *The absence of new economic, technological, and cultural achievement.* Several

writers have described the essential features of degenerative change in general terms: the incursive shock prevents the traditional society from functioning in customary ways without providing substitute ways which are meaningful to the people in terms of traditional culture (Frankel 1955, Steiner 1957). The incursion is disintegrative to traditional organization without providing new forms of organization which reintegrate the society along new lines (Smelser 1963). These are useful ways to state the problem. But much detailed analysis of socioeconomic change needs to be done: What are the sequential processes of disintegration and subsequent reintegration? Which specific features of traditional society are most vulnerable? How long do these processes take? Under what conditions has reintegration taken place? We are here concerned with historical processes to be analyzed in sociological terms. The problems require explicit concern with long stretches of calendar time and with sequential process analysis of old and new economy, technology, polity, social organization, and culture.

Degenerative change does not mean that some people believe themselves to be worse off materially or culturally under the new conditions. Some people are made worse off during any kind of social change. Rather, it means that the old society ceases to function in important ways, the folk-views of most people perceive the changes as worsenings, and in no important area of social or private life has there been significant absorption of new culture (e.g., literacy), new technology and economy (e.g., new farming methods and enlarged production for sale), which create social reintegration. Neither is degenerative change necessarily a permanent state of affairs. Worsley (1957a) argues that Melanesian cargo cults, despite their traumatic symptoms of malaise, misunderstanding of European economy, and distorted religiosity, contain the beginnings of wider political organization of an anti-colonial sort which may possibly evolve into more orthodox and productive political activity (see also Hagen 1962).

Growth Without Development

Most of the case studies of community change reported in the literature differ from

[11] Cargo cults are complicated movements expressing several aspects of fission and fusion. Here, I simply want to emphasize that among other things, they are symptoms of malaise that indicate deep misunderstanding of the processes of modernization through which Western goods are acquired.

the one described above in two principal ways. First, the incursion was not severely disruptive of traditional society. The Trobriands (during Malinowski's residence), the Tiv (at the time of Bohannan's fieldwork), and many other groups carried on their traditional activities largely intact for generations after the foreign presence was felt. A second difference from cases of degenerative change was that the peoples became engaged in new cash-earning activities (principally growing cash crops and selling wage-labor), and that this was the *only* innovation of importance adopted. Subsistence economies became peasant economies as cash earnings and dependence for livelihood on market sale of crops or wage-labor grew, while traditional culture and society remained largely intact (except for those changes induced by the enlarged commercial production or cash-earning).

Here we have the two salient features experienced by a large number of primitive societies: untraumatic incursion which allows ordinary activities, ceremony, and social relationships to continue on much as before; and enlarged cash-earning activities without the concomitant adoption of improved technology, literacy, or any of the other important accoutrements of "modernization" (Gulliver 1965). I call this situation "growth without development." The community's income grows somewhat because of its enlarged sales of crops or labor, but those structural changes in economy, technology, and culture necessary for sustained income growth and the progressive integration of the local community with the nation, are not forthcoming. During the period when cash income grows while old culture, values, and folk-views remain initially unchanged (because literacy, new vocational skills, new lines of production, new technology, are not adopted), there are some characteristic responses generated. We can illustrate them by drawing on a very large literature—cash income growth without economic and technological development is a very frequently experienced set of events following contact with European culture.

1. The use of new cash income for old status prerogatives (bridewealth, potlatch).

2. New conflict situations (land tenure litigation).

3. The undermining of traditional arrangements providing material security through

social relationships (cash-earning and individualism).

Typically, cash income is earned by individual or household activities rather than lineage or large cooperative group activities (such as canoe building and reciprocal land clearing). Writers on peasant economy (Yang 1945: Chap. 7, Chayanov 1966) stress the economic importance of the *family household* as a production unit, for good reasons. The growth of dependence on market sale of labor or crops for livelihood means the lessened dependence on extended kin, age-mates, friends, and neighbors—in a word, lessened dependence on wider social relationships—to acquire labor or land to use in production processes.

Secondly, the form of income, Western cash, is utterly different from anything known in traditional marketless economies. It is indefinitely storable, and so provides material security for its individual owner. It can be used to purchase a variety of goods and discharge a variety of obligations which no money-stuff or treasure item does in primitive economy. Not only a potentially enormous range of European imports—gin, tobacco, canned foods, steel tools, crucifixes, transistor radios—school fees, and colonial taxes, but also traditional subsistence goods (foodstuffs), traditional prestige-sphere services, obligations, and positions (e.g., bridewealth), and natural resources (land), and labor, all become purchasable or payable with cash. This is what is meant by Western cash being a "general purpose" money (Dalton 1965). The process of acquisition as well as the transactional use or disposition of Western cash in formerly primitive economies breaks down the traditional separation between spheres of subsistence and prestige goods and services (Firth 1958: Chap. 3, Bohannan 1959).

The use of new cash income for old status prerogatives, new conflict situations, and the undermining of traditional arrangements providing material security are related consequences of earning cash income within an otherwise traditional setting. For example, that bridewealth has come to be paid in cash rather than, as formerly, in high-prestige items such as cows, indicates the great importance placed on cash (and what it will buy and pay for). The *social* consequences of such displacement are several. Consider the contrasting situations before and after cash displaces traditional valuables as bridewealth. Indigenously, bridewealth in cows could be got by a young man wanting to marry, only by soliciting the required cows from kin, friends, elders, chiefs, i.e., by drawing on social relationships and thus creating obligations to repay them (reciprocate) in some form (e.g., labor service, clientship, etc.). After cash becomes acceptable as bridewealth, young men can raise their own cash and pay their own bridewealth, thus weakening their dependence on traditional superiors.

Indigenously, where bridewealth required the payment of prestige goods, the items (such as cows) could be disposed of by the bridewealth recipients in very few ways. Cows (like kula bracelets) could only be exchanged or paid within the prestige sphere which was narrowly circumscribed. But cash received as bridewealth has no such limitations. It can be used for traditional prestige goods or traditional subsistence goods, or any of the array of new goods. Bohannan (1959) has pointed out the moral ambivalence which results in the changed situation where bridewealth receipts in cash can be spent on low-echelon goods.

Socioeconomic Development

Economists can answer the question "What constitutes successful development"? with little difficulty. Their unit of analysis is the nation-state, and their base of reference is the already developed nations of North America and Europe. The indicators of successful development from the viewpoint of economics are impersonal, having little to do with folk-views, attitudes, social relationships, or culture. Successful development is characterized in terms of the country's yearly percentage rate of growth in gross national product, the size of per capita income and its distribution, and the use of advanced technology in major production lines.

If the anthropologist is asked "What constitutes successful development"? the answer is more difficult. The anthropologist's unit of analysis is the tribal or village community, not the nation-state[12]; the anthropologist is not only concerned with economy and technology, but also with folk-views, attitudes, social relationships, or culture. And he does

[12] Clifford Geertz's work is a notable exception.

not use as a base of reference for successful development the already developed nations of Europe and North America. Moreover, the anthropologist is analytically concerned with the social process of economic development and sensitive to its social and cultural costs.

Community Integration with the Region, Nation, and the Rest of the World

There is no such thing as a small-scale community's development independently of the large units of economy and society external to the tribe or village. The several kinds of change that constitute modernization all entail integration with external groupings, i.e., enlarged dependence upon external groups with whom new economic and cultural transactions take place.

Sustained income growth for the local community requires enlarged production for sale to regional, national, or international markets, and a return flow of consumption goods, producer's goods, and social services (health and education) purchased with the ever increasing cash income. The community becomes economically integrated with (and dependent upon) the regional, national, and international economy through a continual enlargement and diversification of purchase and sale transactions. These can be enlarged and made to grow only with the use of improved technology (tools and technical knowledge) acquired or purchased initially from outside the local community. Moreover, the experience of a significant growth in income seems frequently to be a necessary pump-priming condition if traditional groups are to become willing to take the risk of producing new kinds of crops and goods, or old ones with new and relatively expensive and unfamiliar techniques of production. Primitive and peasant unwillingness to change production is frequently a sensible expression of their poverty and material insecurity. They cannot afford unsuccessful experiments. The old techniques are not very productive, but they keep the people alive. One of the important lessons of the unusual (and unusually quick) development progress in Vicos (Holmberg 1965) was that the *Cornell group* assumed the financial risk of planting improved varieties of potatoes. The demonstration effect of the sharp increase in the value product of the new potatoes convinced the people of Vicos to follow suit. A legitimate role for any central government wanting to accelerate local community development is for it to bear some portion of the financial risk of economic and technological innovation.

The local community's integration politically is yet another aspect of successful community development. But when central government acts only as a tax gatherer, the local community is likely to perceive any governmentally initiated project to expand community output as a device to increase taxes, and therefore to be resisted. Here too there must be demonstration effects: that government can provide the local community with important economic and social services and confine itself to taxing only a portion of enlarged income forthcoming.

Lastly, there is a cultural integration with the larger society: learning new language, new vocational skills, education, private and public health practices, and acquiring a participant awareness of alternatives, events, and institutions of the larger world.[13]

What must transpire for development to be successful is fairly clear. What perhaps deserves emphasis is that successful development from the economist's viewpoint is compatible with successful development from the anthropologist's vewpoint. Anthropologists are concerned with minimizing the social costs of community transformation, and with the desirability of the community's retaining its ethnic identity in the new society of income growth, machines, and literacy. But we know from examining the sub-cultures in already developed nations, such as Japan, England, the U.S.S.R., and especially the U.S. (with its unusual ethnic diversity), that the retention of identity in both new and old institutional forms is compatible with modern activities The point surely is to work with those levers of new achievement which the people themselves perceive as desirable, higher income through new economic and technological performance, and wider alternatives through education. If such developmental achievements are in fact incorporated, those features of traditional culture and social organization incompatible with the new are sloughed off without the personal and community malaise that characterize degenerative change and growth without development.

Social policy has . . . to assure that the individual in losing both the benefits and the burdens of the old society acquire no weightier burdens and at least as many benefits as he had in his previous station. (Okigbo 1956)

SUMMARY AND CONCLUSION

There are several points I should like to emphasize by way of summary and conclusion.

Theoretical analysis in economic anthropology is in its beginnings. Descriptive ethnographies exist in abundance, but it is only in the last ten years that concepts, generalizations, and attempts at systematic comparison have been forthcoming in something like a sustained analytical literature. Indeed, we are now getting university courses and textbooks devoted to the subject. But interest in the subject has grown faster than a satisfactory theoretical framework, a situation which generates disputes over basic methodological and conceptual issues (Dalton 1967).

The scope of economic anthropology is extremely wide. The set of economies of interest comprises thousands of villages and tribal segments all over the underdeveloped world. Part of the task of theory is to group these into a few clusters by creating an analytical typology, just as economists group national economies when they consider comparative economic systems. The distinctions between primitive and peasant economies, between organization and performance, and between traditional (relatively static) economies and those undergoing socioeconomic change, growth, and development were described in some detail. Moreover, to make analytical sense out of primitive and peasant economies the anthropologist must have a firm understanding of conventional economics and of the structure and performance of industrial capitalism.

There are special methodological and conceptual problems in the study of socioeconomic change, growth, and development. Anthropologists and others are contriving new ways to study socioeconomic change at the local community level because of the com-

---

[13] Gunnar Myrdal's point about the mutually reinforcing nature of developmental activities is indispensable for understanding the processes of sequential change, whether they be degenerative, cash income growth, or the structural changes entailed in successful development (Myrdal 1957: Chaps. 1–3).

plexity of the transformation processes and the long periods of time over which they take place. The traditional technique of fieldwork, one investigator making a single visit of a year or two in the field, continues to yield fruitful results in studying some of the problems. But for other problems different approaches are being used. So too, the use of historical records to describe sequential events before, during, and after culture contact, continues to be important (Schapera 1928, 1934). Here we will mention some of the newer techniques being used.

(1) Raymond Firth (1959, 1966) and others have returned to communities in which they did fieldwork twenty years or more earlier to study the socioeconomic changes in the intervening period. These direct comparisons have been illuminating (for an appreciation, see Beattie 1961), and we are fortunate to have in print the restudies of Tikopia and Malay fishermen.

(2) T. Scarlett Epstein's work (1962) deserves wide reading both for its content and its methods. She used the traditional fieldwork approach in a strategic way. She chose two agricultural village communities in India within six miles of one another, only one of which got irrigation (some twenty years earlier), and analyzed the socioeconomic changes in both villages. Enough time has elapsed so that important changes were discernible, and her training in economics allowed her to measure productivity, income, and expenditure so as to buttress her qualitative analysis of socioeconomic organization with quantitative data on economic performance. Her work should be recognized as a model of how the traditional fieldwork approach of anthropologists can be used to study socioeconomic change in peasant communities.

(3) Clifford Geertz's work in Indonesia on entrepreneurs (1962), and on agricultural development (1963), is noteworthy for the sensitive combination of historical and anthropological analysis and for his study of the economic growth of towns. (His more recent fieldwork in Morocco is designed to study socioeconomic change in depth by frequent residence over a ten-year period.)

(4) Collaborative fieldwork is another method of coping with the complicated problems of social and economic change. Several kinds of teams of researchers have done useful work in the field.

A group of anthropologists from Cornell (Holmberg 1965), in residence over several years, studied minutely the socioeconomic transformation of Vicos, a peasant hacienda community in Peru. Their work is unusual not only because of its collaborative nature, but also because the group itself initiated the basic technological and economic innovations (applied anthropology), because of the theoretical sophistication brought to bear, and because the work is described and analyzed at sufficient length and depth to allow the reader to learn some important lessons from Vicos.

A different kind of team approach is a recent piece of work sponsored by the World Bank (de Wilde et al., 1967). A group of economists and anthropologists studied problems of transforming agriculture in tropical Africa. They did field investigations in thirteen areas of varying ecological, cultural, economic, and technological conditions.

Socioeconomic change and development at the local community level is best regarded as a social science subject. It is, of course, an old focus of interest in anthropology (Bohannan and Plog 1967). But the *circumstances* of present-day change and development are sufficiently different so that new methods, theories, and policies are required. The nation-states of Africa and Asia in which the local communities exist are politically independent and their central governments are now explicitly commited to nationwide economic development and modernization. Moreover, international agencies as well as governments of North America and Europe are committed for a long time to come to give technical and economic aid to accelerate the transformations. What is also new is the extent to which social scientists of Europe, America, and the underdeveloped countries are engaged in the theory and practical problems of socioeconomic change. What used to be the exclusive preserve of anthropologists a generation ago is now a field of wide professional concern to economists, sociologists, psychologists, and others, all over the world, in universities and governments. The complexity of the processes and the long periods of time over which change and development take place have already brought forth new approaches, interdisciplinary sophistication, and some fruitful results. It is not farfetched to suggest that an increasing number of the young anthropologists emerging from university training with a specialist's interest in the subject will be New Men, combining the several talents necessary. They will be fieldworkers and historians, anthropological economists and economic anthropologists, theoreticians and practitioners.

APPENDIX

Ethnography and Analysis: A Bibliographical Note

On the *organization* of primitive economies with and without centralized polities, the analytical scheme of Karl Polanyi and his associates is useful. See Polanyi (1944: Chap. 4, 1947, 1957, 1963, 1966, 1968); Polanyi, Arensberg, and Pearson (1957); Bohannan (1959, 1960); Dalton (1961, 1962, 1965, 1967); see also, Smelser (1959), Sahlins (1960, 1966).

Among the best descriptive ethnographies of primitive economies with and without centralized polities, are Malinowski (1922, 1926, 1935), Firth (1929, 1939), Nadel (1942), Maquet (1961), and Bohannan and Bohannan (1968).

On measuring economic *performance*—aggregate output and its composition, holdings of tools and buildings, and the productivity of land and labor—in small-scale economies in which the bulk of labor, land, and produce is not transacted by purchase and sale, see Deane (1953), Salisbury (1962), and Samuels (1963). For analytical insights on traditional peasant economies (as distinct from cultures), one must turn to historians, economists, and rural sociologists as well as anthropologists. Among the best works are Chayanov (1966); Sorokin, Zimmerman, and Galpin (1931: Vol. 2 Chap. 11); Firth (1946); Tax (1953); Smith (1962).

On socioeconomic change, growth, and development in primitive and peasant economies, important theoretical insights are contained in Myrdal (1957), Hagen (1962), and Smelser (1963). Excellent ethnographic works with important theoretical conclusions, are Firth (1959) and Epstein (1962). The latter, as well as Hill (1963, 1966), are unusually thorough in their measurement of economic performance. Some very good writings of

journal article length are Linton (1952), Jaspan (1953), Bohannan (1959), Yudelman (1964), Douglas (1965), and Holmberg (1965).

Any anthropologist with a serious interest in present-day problems of socioeconomic change and development should be aware of the important literature outside of anthropology. "Convergence" still may be too strong a word to characterize what is happening, but certainly it is true that the areas of overlapping interest in anthropology, economics, sociology, and psychology—as these relate to change and development in Africa, Asia, Latin America, etc.—are growing larger and growing quickly. Some examples will be cited.

A number of economists have written works bearing directly on socioeconomic development at the local community level. Myrdal (1957, Chaps. 1–3), is concerned with the interaction of social and economic forces and makes points which are widely applicable. Hagen (1962), in what must be one of the most imaginative departures from conventional economics, employs psychoanalytical theory to trace out the intergenerational changes in personality formation necessary to produce persons capable of entrepreneurial initiative. It is an impressive piece of work for its method as well as its substance, drawing on all the social sciences. An early article of the economic historian Sawyer (1951) should be better known. It emphasizes the important connections between social organization and economic development. Several economists have written on the problems of transforming subsistence agriculture and increasing agricultural productivity (Jones 1961; Yudelman 1964; Fogg 1965). Seers (1963) and Myint (1965) consider the important question of the relevance of conventional economics to problems of socioeconomic change and development. Boeke (1942), of course, in his analysis of "dualism," was one of the first to point out how traditional primitive and peasant societies existed side by side with colonial-implanted commercial production. Lewis (1954), in a classic article, showed how development proceeded in dualistic economies.

As with the anthropologists and economists, the sociologists, psychologists, and political scientists perceive the processes of transformation from their special viewpoints:

Smelser (1958) has written on the social changes that accompanied the British Industrial Revolution, and the similar changes in the present-day transformations of underdeveloped areas (Smelser 1963). The rural sociologists have extended their interests from Europe and America to the underdeveloped world (Rogers 1960, see especially his bibliography). The psychologist McClelland (1961) has started a special line of investigation with his work on achievement motivation. Apter (1960), one of the most perceptive political scientists, has written on the connections between traditional and modern political leadership in the new continent of politically independent African states.

BIBLIOGRAPHY

ADELMAN, IRMA, and CYNTHIA TAFT MORRIS
   1965 Factor analysis of the interrelationship between social and political variables and per capita gross national product. *Quarterly Journal of Economics* 79:555–578.
   1967 *Society, politics, and economic development*. Baltimore, Johns Hopkins University Press.

APTER, DAVID E.
   1960 The role of traditionalism in the political modernization of Ghana and Uganda. *World Politics,* 13:45–68.

ARENSBERG, CONRAD M., and ARTHUR H. NIEHOFF
   1964 *Introducing social change*. Chicago, Aldine.

ARMSTRONG, W. E.
   1924 Rossel Island money: a unique monetary system. *Economic Journal* 34:423–429.
   1928 *Rossel Island*. Cambridge, Cambridge University Press.

ARNOLD, ROSEMARY
   1957a A port of trade: Whydah on the Guinea coast. In K. Polanyi, C. M. Arensberg, and H. W. Pearson, eds., *Trade and market in the early empires*. Glencoe, Ill., Free Press.
   1957b Separation of trade and market: great market of Whydah. In K. Polanyi, C. M. Arensberg, and H. W. Pearsons, eds., *Trade and market in the early empires*. Glencoe, Ill., Free Press.

BEATTIE, J. H. M.
   1961 Culture contact and social change. *British Journal of Sociology,* June, 165–175.
   1964 Bunyoro: an African feudality? *Journal of African History* 5, 1:25–36.

BELSHAW, CYRIL S.
   1965 *Traditional exchange and modern markets*. Englewood Cliffs, N.J., Prentice-Hall.

BENNETT, H. S.
   1962 *Life on the English manor, 1150–1400*. Cambridge, Cambridge University Press.

BESTOR, A. E., JR.
   1950 *Backwoods utopias*. Philadelphia, University of Pennsylvania Press.

BIEBUYCK, DANIEL (ed.)
   1963 *African agrarian systems*. London, Oxford University Press.

BISHOP, CLAIRE
   1950 *All things common*. New York, Harper.

BLOCH, MARC
   1961 *Feudal society*. London, Routledge and Kegan Paul.
   1966 *French rural history*. London, Routledge and Kegan Paul.

BOEKE, J. H.
   1942 *The structure of Netherlands Indian economy*. New York, Institute of Pacific Relations.

BOHANNAN, PAUL
   1954 *Tiv farm and settlement*. London, His Majesty's Stationery Office.
   1957 *Justice and judgment among the Tiv.* New York, Oxford University Press.
   1959 The impact of money on an African subsistence economy. *Journal of Economic History* 19:491–503.
   1960 Africa's Land. *Centennial Review* 4:439–449.

BOHANNAN, PAUL, and LAURA BOHANNAN
   1968 *Tiv economy*. Evanston, Ill., Northwestern University Press.

BOHANNAN, PAUL, and GEORGE DALTON
   1965 Introduction. In *Markets in Africa*. New York, Natural History Press.

BOHANNAN, PAUL, AND FRED PLOG (eds.)
   1967 *Beyond the frontier: social process and cultural change*. New York, Natural History Press.

BOULDING, KENNETH
   1957 The Parsonian approach to economics. *Kyklos* 10:317–319.

BROKENSHA, DAVID W.
   1966 *Social change at Larteh, Ghana*. Oxford, Clarendon Press.

BURLING, ROBBINS
   1962 Maximization theories and the study of economic anthropology. *American Anthropologist* 64:802–821.

CARR, E. H.
   1951 *The new society*. London, Macmillan.

CHAMBERLIN, E. H.
1932 *The theory of monopolistic competition.* Cambridge, Harvard University Press.

CHAYANOV, A. V.
1966 *The theory of peasant economy.* Homewood, Ill., Irwin. (First published in Russian, in 1925.)

CHEVALIER, FRANÇOIS
1963 *Land and society in colonial Mexico.* Berkeley, University of California Press.

CLOWER, R., G. DALTON, M. HARWITZ, and A. A. WALTERS
1966 *Growth without development: an economic survey of Liberia.* Evanston, Ill., Northwestern University Press.

COHEN, RONALD
1966 *The dynamics of feudalism in Bornu.* Boston University Publications in African History, Vol. II.

COLSON, ELIZABETH
1949 Assimilation of an American Indian group. *Human problems in British Central Africa (Rhodes-Livingston Journal)* No. 5:1–12.

COOK, SCOTT
1966 The obsolete "anti-market" mentality: a critique of the substantive approach to economic anthropology. *American Anthropologist* 68:323–345.

DALTON, GEORGE
1960 A note of clarification on economic surplus. *American Anthropologist* 68:483–490.

1961 Economic theory and primitive society. *American Anthropologist* 63:1–25.

1962 Traditional production in primitive African economies. *Quarterly Journal of Economics* 76:360–378.

1963 Economic surplus, once again. *American Anthropologist* 65:389–394.

1964 The development of subsistence and peasant economies in Africa. *International Social Science Journal* 16:378–389.

1965 Primitive money. *American Anthropologist* 67:44–65.

1965a Primitive, archaic, and modern economies: Karl Polanyi's contribution to economic anthropology and comparative economy. In *Proceedings of the 1965 annual spring symposium of the American Ethnological Society.* Seattle, University of Washington Press.

1965b History, politics, and economic development in Liberia. *Journal of Economic History* 25, 4:569–591.

1966 Bridewealth versus brideprice. *American Anthropologist* 68:732–737.

1967 Bibliographical essay. In *Tribal and peasant economies: reading in economic anthropology.* New York, Natural History Press.

DEANE, PHYLLIS
1953 *Colonial social accounting.* Cambridge, Cambridge University Press.

DE WILDE, JOHN C., et al.
1967 *Agricultural development in tropical Africa.* Baltimore, Johns Hopkins University Press.

DOMAR, EVSEY D.
1957 *Essays in the theory of economic growth.* New York, Oxford University Press.

DOUGLAS, MARY
1958 Raffia cloth distribution in the Lele economy. *Africa* 28:109–122.

1965 The Lele—resistance to change. In P. J. Bohannan and G. Dalton, eds., *Markets in Africa.* New York, Natural History Press.

EINZIG, PAUL
1948 *Primitive money.* London, Eyre and Spottiswoode.

EPSTEIN, T. SCARLETT
1962 *Economic development and social change in South India.* Manchester, Manchester University Press.

ERASMUS, CHARLES J.
1961 *Man takes control.* Minneapolis, University of Minnesota Press.

FALLERS, LLOYD A.
1961 Are African cultivators to be called "peasants"? *Current Anthropology* 2:108–110.

FIRTH, RAYMOND
1929 *Primitive economics of the New Zealand Maori.* Wellington, R. E. Owen, Government Printer.

1939 *Primitive Polynesian economy.* London, Routledge and Kegan Paul.

1946 *Malay fishermen: their peasant economy.* London, Routledge and Kegan Paul.

1951 *The elements of social organization.* London, Watts.

1958 Work and wealth of primitive communities. In *Human types,* rev. ed. New York, Mentor Books.

1959 *Social change in Tikopia.* London, George Allen and Unwin.

1957 The place of Malinowski in the history of economic anthropology. In R. Firth, ed., *Man and culture: an evaluation of the work of Bronislaw Malinowski.* New York, Harper Torchbooks.

1964 Capital, saving, and credit in peasant societies: a viewpoint from economic anthropology. In R. Firth and B. Yamey, eds., *Capital, saving, and credit in peasant societies.* Chicago, Aldine.

1965 Review of L. Pospisil's *Kapauku Papuan*

economy. *American Anthropologist* 67: 122–125.

1966 *Primitive Polynesian economy*, rev. ed. London, Routledge and Kegan Paul.

FIRTH, RAYMOND, and BASIL YAMEY
1964 *Capital, saving, and credit in peasant societies.* Chicago, Aldine.

FOGG, C. DAVIS
1965 Economic and social factors affecting the development of smallholder agriculture in eastern Nigeria. *Economic Development and Cultural Change*, 13, 3: 278–292.

FORTES, M., and E. E. EVANS-PRITCHARD
1940 *African political systems.* London, Oxford University Press.

FRANKEL, S. H.
1955 *The economic impact on under-developed societies.* Cambridge, Harvard University Press.

FROMM, ERICH
1941 *Escape from freedom.* New York, Rinehart.

FUSFELD, DANIEL B.
1957 Economic theory misplaced: livelihood in primitive society. In K. Polanyi, C. M. Arensberg, and H. W. Pearson, eds., *Trade and market in the early empires.* Glencoe, Ill., Free Press.

GEERTZ, CLIFFORD
1962 Social change and economic modernization in two Indonesian towns: a case in point. In Everett E. Hagen, *On the theory of social change.* Homewood, Ill., Dorsey Press.

1963 *Peddlers and princes.* Chicago, University of Chicago Press.

GERSHENKRON, ALEXANDER
1954 Social attitudes, entrepreneurship, and economic development. *International Social Science Journal* 6:252–258.

1962 *Economic backwardness in historical perspective.* Cambridge, Belknap Press of Harvard University Press.

GLUCKMAN, MAX, and I. G. CUNNISON
1962 Foreword. In J. P. Singh Uberoi, *Politics of the kula ring.* Manchester, Manchester University Press.

GODELIER, MAURICE
1965 Objet et méthode de l'anthropologie économique. *L'Homme*, V, No. 2.

GOODENOUGH, WARD HUNT
1963 *Cooperation in change.* New York, Russell Sage Foundation.

GOODFELLOW, D. M.
1939 *Principles of economic sociology.* London, Routledge.

GOODY, JACK
1963 Feudalism in Africa? *Journal of African History* 4:1–18.

GRAY, ROBERT F.
1960 Sonjo bride-price and the question of African "wife purchase." *American Anthropologist* 62:34–57.

GROSSMAN, GREGORY
1967 *Economic systems.* Englewood Cliffs, N.J., Prentice-Hall.

GRUCHY, ALLAN G.
1966 *Comparative economic systems.* Boston, Houghton Mifflin.

GULLIVER, P. H.
1965 The Arusha—economic and social change. In P. J. Bohannan and G. Dalton, eds., *Markets in Africa.* New York, Natural History Press.

HAGEN, EVERETT E.
1962 *On the theory of social change: how economic growth begins.* Homewood Ill., Dorsey Press.

HARRIS, MARVIN
1959 The economy has no surplus? *American Anthropologist* 61:185–199.

HARROD, R. F.
1952 An essay in dynamic theory. In R. F. Harrod, *Economic essays.* New York, Harcourt, Brace.

HERSKOVITS, MELVILLE J.
1940 Anthropology and economics. In *The economic life of primitive peoples.* New York, Knopf.

1941 Economics and anthropology: a rejoinder. *Journal of Political Economy* 49: 269–278 (reprinted in Herskovits, 1952).

1952 *Economic anthropology*, rev. ed. New York, Knopf.

HILL, POLLY
1963 *Migrant cocoa-farmers of southern Ghana.* Cambridge, Cambridge University Press.

1966 A plea for indigenous economics: the West African example. *Economic Development and Cultural Change* 15:10–20.

HOLMBERG, ALLAN R.
1965 The changing values and institutions of Vicos in the context of national development. *American Behavioral Scientist* 8:3–8.

HOMANS, GEORGE C.
1958 Social behavior as exchange. *American Journal of Sociology* 62:597–606.

HUNTER, MONICA
1961 *Reaction to conquest*, 2nd ed. London, Oxford University Press.

JASPAN, M. A.
1953 A sociological case study: communal hostility to imposed social changes in South Africa. In Phillips Ruopp, ed., *Approaches to community development.* The Hague, W. Van Hoeve.

JONES, WILLIAM O.
1961   Food and agricultural economies of tropical Africa: A summary view. *Food Research Institute Studies* (Stanford University) 2, 1:3–20.

KEYFITZ, NATHAN
1959   The interlocking of social and economic factors in Asian development. *Canadian Journal of Economics and Political Science* 25:34–46.

KEYNES, JOHN MAYNARD
1936   *The general theory of employment, interest, and money.* New York, Harcourt, Brace.

KNIGHT, FRANK
1941   Anthropology and economics. *Journal of Political Economy* 49:247–268 (reprinted in Herskovits 1952).

LECLAIR, EDWARD E.
1962   Economic theory and economic anthropology. *American Anthropologist* 64: 1179–1203.

LEWIS, W. ARTHUR
1954   *Economic development with unlimited supplies of labor.* Manchester, Manchester School.
1955   *The theory of economic growth.* London, Allen and Unwin.
1962   Foreword. In T. Scarlett Epstein, *Economic development and social change in South India.* Manchester, Manchester University Press.

LIENHARDT, R. GODFREY
1956   Religion. In Harry L. Shapiro, ed., *Man, culture, and society.* New York, Oxford University Press.

LINTON, RALPH
1952   Cultural and personality factors affecting economic growth. In B. F. Hoselitz, ed., *The progress of underdeveloped areas.* Chicago, University of Chicago Press.

MACIVER, R. M.
1933   *Society, its structure and changes.* New York, R. Long and R. R. Smith.

MALINOWSKI, BRONISLAW
1921   The primitive economics of the Trobriand islanders. *Economic Journal* 31:1–15.
1922   *Argonauts of the western Pacific.* London, Routledge.
1926   *Crime and custom in savage society.* Paterson, N.J., Littlefield, Adams (1959 edition).
1935   *Coral gardens and their magic,* Vol. 1. New York, American Book Company.

MAQUET, JACQUES
1961   *The premise of inequality in Ruanda.* London, Oxford University Press.

MARSHALL, ALFRED
1920   *Principles of economies.* London, Macmillan.

MAUSS, MARCEL
1954   *The gift: forms and functions of exchange in archaic societies.* Glencoe, Ill., Free Press.

MCCLELLAND, DAVID C.
1961   *The achieving society.* Princeton, N.J., Van Nostrand.

MYINT, H.
1965   Economic theory and the underdeveloped countries. *Journal of Political Economy* 68, 5:477–491.

MYRDAL, GUNNAR
1957   *Rich lands and poor.* New York, Harper.
1960   *Beyond the welfare state.* New Haven, Yale University Press.

NADEL, S. F.
1942   *A black Byzantium, the kingdom of Nupe in Nigeria.* London, Oxford University Press.

NASH, MANNING
1966   *Primitive and peasant economic systems.* San Francisco, Chandler.

NEALE, WALTER C.
1957   Reciprocity and redistribution in the Indian village. In K. Polanyi, C. M. Arensberg, and H. W. Pearson, eds., *Trade and market in the early empires.* Glencoe, Ill., Free Press.
1957a The market in theory and history. In K. Polanyi, C. M. Arensberg, and H. W. Pearson, eds., *Trade and market in the early empires.* Glencoe, Ill., Free Press.

NORDHOFF, CHARLES
1961   *The communistic societies of the United States.* New York, Hillary House Publishers (first published in 1875).

NOVE, ALEC
1962   *The Soviet economy.* New York, Praeger.

NOYES, JOHN HUMPHREY
1870   *American socialisms.* Philadelphia, Lippincott.

NYERERE, JULIUS K.
1964   Ujamaa. In William H. Friedland and Carl G. Rosberg, Jr., eds., *African socialism.* Stanford, Stanford University Press.

OKIGBO, PIUS
1956   Social consequences of economic development in West Africa. *Annals of the American Academy of Political Science:* 125:133.

PEARSON, H. W.
1957   The economy has no surplus. In K. Polanyi, C. M. Arensburg, and H. W. Pearson, eds., *Trade and market in the early empires.* Glencoe Ill., Free Press.

PIRENNE, HENRI
1936 *Economic and social history of medieval Europe*. London, Routledge and Kegan Paul.

POLANYI, KARL
1944 *The great transformation*. New York, Rinehart.
1947 Our obsolete market mentality. *Commentary* 13:109–117.
1957 The economy as instituted process. In K. Polanyi, C. M. Arensberg, and H. W. Pearson, eds., *Trade and market in the early empires*. Glencoe, Ill., Free Press.
1963 Ports of trade in early societies. *Journal of Economic History* 23:30–45.
1966 *Dahomey and the slave trade*. Seattle, University of Washington Press.
1968 The semantics of money uses. In G. Dalton, ed., *Primitive, archaic, and modern economies: essays of Karl Polanyi*. New York, Natural History Press.

POLANYI, K., C. M. ARENSBERG, and H. W. PEARSON
1957 *Trade and market in the early empires*. Glencoe, Ill., Free Press.

POSPISIL, LEOPOLD
1963 *Kapauku Papuan economy*. Yale University Publications in Anthropology No. 67.

POSTAN, M. M.
1966 *The agrarian life of the Middle Ages*. Volume I of *The Cambridge economic history of Europe*, 2nd ed. Cambridge, Cambridge University Press.

QUIGGIN, A. H.
1949 *A survey of primitive money*. London, Methuen.

REDFIELD, ROBERT
1956 *Peasant society and culture*. Chicago, University of Chicago Press.

REYNDERS, H. J. J.
1963 The geographical income of the Bantu areas in South Africa. In L. H. Samuels, ed., *African studies in income and wealth*. Chicago, Quadrangle Books.

RICHARDS, AUDREY I.
1939 *Land, labor and diet in Northern Rhodesia*. London, Oxford University Press.

RIVERS, W. H. R.
1922 *Essays on the depopulation of Melanesia*. Cambridge.

ROBBINS, LIONEL
1935 *An essay on the nature and significance of economic science*. London, Macmillan.

ROBINSON, JOAN
1933 *The economics of imperfect competition*. London, Macmillan.

ROGERS, EVERETT
1960 *Diffusion of innovations*. Glencoe, Ill., Free Press.

ROTTENBERG, SIMON
1958 Review of trade and market in the early empires. *American Economic Review* 48:675–678.

SAHLINS, MARSHALL D.
1960 Political power and the economy in primitive society. In Dole and Carneiro, eds., *Essays in the science of culture in honor of Leslie White*. New York, Crowell.
1966 The sociology of economic exchange. In M. Banton, ed., *The relevance of models in social anthropology*. London, Tavistock.

SALISBURY, R. F.
1962 *From stone to steel*. London and New York, Cambridge University Press.

SAMUELS, C. H.
1963 *African studies in income and wealth*. Chicago, Quadrangle Books.

SCHAPERA, I.
1928 Economic changes in South African native life. *Africa* 1:170–188.
1934 *Western civilization and the natives of South Africa*. London, Routledge.

SCHAPERA, I., and A. J. H. GOODWIN
1937 Work and wealth. In I. Schapera, ed., *The Bantu-speaking tribes of South Africa*. London, Routledge and Kegan Paul.

SEERS, DUDLEY
1963 The limitations of the special case. *Institute of Economics and Statistics, Oxford, Bulletin* 25, 2:77–98.

SENGHOR, LEOPOLD S.
1964 *On African socialism*. New York, Praeger.

SMELSER, NEIL J.
1958 *Social change in the industrial revolution*. London, Routledge and Kegan Paul.
1959 A comparative view of exchange systems. *Economic Development and Cultural Change* 7:173–182.
1963 Mechanisms of change and adjustment to change. In B. F. Hoselitz and W. E. Moore, eds., *Industrialization and society*. UNESCO-Mouton.

SMITH, M. G.
1962 Exchange and marketing among the Hausa. In P. J. Bohannan and G. Dalton, eds., *Markets in Africa*. Evanston, Ill., Northwestern University Press.

SOROKIN, P. A., C. C. ZIMMERMAN, and C. J. GALPIN
1931 Rural economic organization. Chapter II of *A systematic source book in rural sociology*, Vol. 2. Minneapolis, University of Minnesota Press.

SOUTHALL, AIDAN
1961 *Social change in modern Africa*. London, Oxford University Press.

STEINER, FRANZ
1957 Toward a classification of labor. *Sociologus* 7:112–129.

TAX, SOL
1963 *Penny capitalism*. Chicago, University of Chicago Press (first published in 1953).

UBEROI, J. P. SINGH
1962 *The politics of the kula*. Manchester, Manchester University Press.

UNESCO
1963 *Social aspects of economic development in Latin America*. New York, UNESCO.

UNITED NATIONS
1954 *Enlargement of the exchange economy in tropical Africa*. New York, United Nations.

WEBER, MAX
1950 *General economic history*. Glencoe, Ill., Free Press.

WILSON, GODFREY
1941 *An essay on the economics of detribaliza-* tion in Northern Rhodesia. The Rhodes-Livingstone Papers No. 5. Manchester, Manchester University Press.

WOLF, ERIC R.
1966 *Peasants*. Englewood Cliffs, N.J., Prentice-Hall.

WORSLEY, PETER
1957 *The trumpet shall sound: a study of "cargo" cults in Melanesia*. London, MacGibbon and Kee.
1957a Millenarian movements in Melanesia. *Rhodes-Livingstone Institute Journal*:18–31.

YANG, MARTIN C.
1945 The family as a primary economic group. In Martin C. Yang, *A Chinese village*. New York, Columbia University Press.

YUDELMAN, MONTAGUE
1964 *Africans on the land*. Cambridge, Harvard University Press.

CHAPTER 25

The Political System

RONALD COHEN

THE BASIC PROBLEMS OF POLITICAL ANTHROPOLOGY

The problems of data collection and theory testing among those phenomena accompanied by the term "political" are fairly new in anthropology. Only in the last few years have authors devoted themselves to any systematic approach to the subject, and there are, as yet, no well-established conventions as to what such a sub-field includes and excludes or what should be the basic methodological attack on the subject matter. Furthermore, with the notable exceptions of M. G. Smith (1956, 1960, 1966), David Easton (1959, 1965), Swartz, Turner, and Tuden (1966), and to a lesser extent Marion J. Levy (1966, 2:436–502), there have been no serious attempts at developing a set of conceptual tools that can provide workers in the field with a useful guide to the recording, description, and analysis of political life as it is experienced by the anthropological investigator. This makes comparisons difficult since the data recorded tend to emerge from whatever the particular field situation most obviously throws into relief, tempered by the range of the reading background of the particular field worker concerning "political organizations" or the "political system." The most immediate need, then, is to consolidate what is known and attempt to provide field workers with a conceptual framework that does justice to the complexity of political phenomena. Such a schema or model should also provide enough flexibility for the basic

concepts to be applied comparatively while leaving room as well for the schema to grow and develop as research proceeds. This chapter is not designed, however, as a review article, and the job of consolidating present knowledge must be left to another publication. Some general understanding of this can be obtained by consulting Fortes and Evans-Pritchard (1940), Schapera (1956), Middleton and Tait (1958), Easton (1959), Mair (1962), Gluckman (1965), Swartz, Turner, and Tuden (1966), Cohen and Middleton (1967). All of these publications synthesize materials from varying ranges of complexity although a systematic propositional inventory is as yet to be attempted. The present essay is directed not to this task, but specifically at elucidating a set of categories that form a working model of the political system which can be applied cross-culturally as a guide to data collection.

Elsewhere (Cohen 1965) I have discussed the scope of political anthropology and indicated that as a sub-field it comprises a wide range of political systems running all the way from the family level of organization, where the family is the largest permanent social unit in the society, to highly centralized non-Western states and empires in which there are central government structures, a permanent bureaucracy, and a means of maintaining some organized political life over a wide territory containing many local communities. One major methodological problem, then, is to obtain a set of concepts which can adequately cope with a very large range of variance in the data so that each individual case study adds to a corpus of

The author wishes to thank Professor Paul F. Kress for many helpful suggestions in the preparation of this paper.

materials that are comparable with one another.

In this same article, I also pointed out that indigenous political systems are all undergoing some form of rapid change today as they become incorporated within the boundaries of the modern nation-state. In other words the contemporary field situation is one of increased rates of social, political, and economic change when these societies are compared with the kinds of influences and changes they have adapted to in the past. Thus, another methodological problem involves the attempt to include in our thinking some means for discussing change since the observer in the field situation has to cope with this quality as he becomes acquainted with the culture and social system in which he is conducting his study.

Finally, and perhaps most basic of all, is the problem of what is "political" and what is not. Closely related to this is the question of whether or not we can speak realistically of a "system" or the political system as a special feature of social life. This is most difficult when it is realized that there are many societies which have no separate political sector with specialized political roles; instead political actions seem to be enmeshed in the entire social life of the people. The fact that anthropologists have not paid much attention to this problem has meant that their data are less easily used for comparative purposes and they have not developed many distinguishing theoretical thrusts or problems, beyond the level of taxonomy, which have provided us with an ongoing research tradition in the political life of non-Western peoples.

POLITICS AS A SYSTEM

If we look at political activity as a system, this means we are making a number of assumptions which should be clearly pointed out.[1] Basically, a system (a) has units that are (b) interconnected in a demonstrable way such that (c) segments (i.e., groups of units) within the system affect one another in knowable ways, and (d) there are

[1] For a detailed discussion of the systems approach to political life, see Easton (1965) and Rapoport (1966); for some of the difficulties involved see Dahl (1963), especially Chapters 4 and 5.

known and knowable relations between the system and/or its parts with other systems and/or their parts. Another feature is important because it often leads to misunderstandings. As I have pointed out in Chapter 2 above, although all systems have boundaries, it is unnecessary to think of any particular system as a kind of "black box" which must be very sharply separated from its context. The permeability of a system boundary is a variable characteristic, and an important one, since it defines how often, and how effectively, the system responds as *whole* to influences coming into it from the outside. Thus "system" is an analytic device for separating off from its context a set of phenomena that we wish to study. It can, of course, refer to a set of phenomena that are already separated out empirically from their context—but it may not, nor is this a necessary quality in a systems approach to analysis. Thus the concept of a system is most usefully thought of as an analytical distinction that is being applied in this case to political life in order to abstract it from its context while submitting it to study.

Another feature of systems analysis—which the approach commits us to—is a functional one in the teleological sense. The system as a whole does something. It can be characterized as having an activity or activities, and its various parts contribute to the fulfillment of these ends. Indeed systems designers are quite clear on this point when they invent systems, since they start with the functions and then work back to create a set of interrelationships that will, in fact, describe the carrying out of these ends. (See Boguslaw 1965.) This can be said as well, of course, when we speak for the parts of the system since they, too, must operate to fulfill its over-all ends. Logically, then, to say we are dealing with political life as a system involves us in two kinds of functional analyses. First, since parts are interrelated and the system itself is part of a larger whole, i.e., the society, we are forced to think about the relation of parts to one another in an analytical or mathematical sense such that any part, or the system as a whole, becomes the function of a series of other determinants. Secondly, the system is, after all, political in nature and therefore must be thought of as exercising a political function as its over-all activity. A political function refers to the operation and consequences of power and authority relations in a society. In summary, then, a systems approach to political life does little more than the usual social scientific approach to sociocultural behavior. It separates off a particular set of these data for study, enjoins us to conceptualize them as doing something—i.e., fulfilling some stipulated set of purposes—and points our attention at the relationships within the system, and between the system and its context in the sociocultural milieu.

WHAT IS POLITICAL?

As late as 1959 a political theorist surveying political anthropology was left to conclude that for the most part anthropologists did not bother to define what they meant when they wrote about political organization (Easton 1959). He then analyzed some of the work that had been directed toward definition and showed it be to sadly lacking in generality and logical cohesiveness. He summarized his findings in the following words:

It is ironic that anthropology, which has been optimally situated because of the breadth of its interests, should be so tardy in transcending the ethnocentric limits of past conceptualization. . . . A more useful conceptualization of the character of political interaction seems long overdue in anthropology.

The difficulty with much of the work lies in its lack of comparability. This can be seen by looking first at the various descriptions of political organization by anthropologists in which some things are included in some studies and left out in others. Thus one of my students, in trying to obtain data on coalition formation in the non-Western polities, found it extremely difficult to find comparable data across a sample of ethnographies. Secondly, the problems involved become clearer when we look at the few attempts that have been made to set up conceptual tools for dealing with political analysis—in other words, when we ask how politics is conceptualized in anthropology. Radcliffe-Brown (1940) suggests that politics refers to (a) the territorial rights of groups, (b) the maintenance of order by means of either personal or group action, (c) supernatural sanctions and/or processes of adjudication, (d) the accepted and prompt use of

violence, and (e) a set of rules dealing with the functions of (a) through (d). Unfortunately this breaks down when political analysis is attempted on groups such as the Bergdama (Schapera 1956) or the Siane (Salisbury n.d.), in which the organized control of coercive force is not present, or among the Shoshone (Steward 1938), where there is no continuing sense of territoriality.

This same kind of criticism, although it is applicable to a much lesser extent, can be leveled at Fried (1964), who suggests that there are three qualities differentiating political phenomena. First, he claims quite rightly that politics can be embedded into actions whose means and ends are extremely various. Secondly, like Radcliffe-Brown, he sees political action or the political sphere as having an attribute of compulsion or coercion such that members of a society must, on pain of punishment, comply with rules and the wishes of superiors. This, to Fried, is *the* basic quality of political activity. Thirdly, he suggests that societies differ in the degree in which compulsion of others is allowed. This allows for a varying scale of action which is necessary for comparative analysis, but it also produces the logical result that, depending upon the degree of compulsion of others which is allowed in the society, a political activity can vary from close to zero, all the way to very high. In other words, some societies have a lot of politics and others very much less. Perhaps this is true, but (a) we have no large body of systematic data on "allowable degree of compulsion of others," and (b) we have no idea whether or not a taxonomy of political systems based upon these criteria would have any reasonable appearance empirically. On this last point we should ask whether Fried's definition would lump the agricultural Siane with the hunting and gathering Bergdama and, if so, whether this would serve any useful purpose.

One of the few anthropologists to have created a well-thought-out conceptual model of the political system is M. G. Smith (1956, 1960, 1966). He argues that politics refers to a set of actions by which public affairs are directed and managed. He then calls the functioning of the system the governmental activity and divides it into administrative and political spheres. The former deals with the authoritative structuring of governmental roles while the latter refers to the exercise of, and competition for, power in the system. Administrative roles are of necessity hierarchically arranged while political interactions can take place between or among people playing these roles. This results from the fact that Smith conceives of power as influence over decisions and policy formation and thus as something never stabilized in the role structures of society. Anyone placed anywhere in the political system can try as best he can to achieve power and the competition is a continuous and constant ingredient of political life. Smith's schema is certainly a large step in the right direction. He has tried to characterize all political activity, no matter what the societal type, and he directs our attention toward rivalry and competition as universal features of all systems no matter what their scale. However, as Easton points out (1959:225), it may not be so easy to apply Smith's schema to the simpler societies. I would add that the distinction between "administrative" and "political" acts could conceivably disappear in some of the very simple societies or in those New Guinea groups in which authoritative leadership is a constantly unstable result of personal achievement and influence (Langness, personal communication). Finally, when Smith (1960) did apply his political theory to a society, he neglected to carry the application beyond the formal authority structure in Zazzau so that we are left guessing about the power of nongovernmental interest groups in the society and their relation to the formally constituted and recognized political system of the emirate.

Easton has also attempted to conceptualize political action and the political system so that both anthropologists and political scientists can utilize his model as a methodological approach to their data. Basically he distinguishes political from nonpolitical by suggesting that political activity relates to the formulation and execution of binding or authoritative decisions for a social system (1959:226). He goes on to define "decision" as an act that allocates valued things among persons and groups, and authoritative decisions occur when persons affected by them feel bound to carry them out. He realizes that such behavior takes place at all levels of society among all kinds of groups but limits his analysis to the widest-scaled social system of the society to which decisions apply—which for him becomes *the* political system. He then describes a series of categories of inputs and outputs which start with demands operating on a political organization and end with political acts in the form of decisions and policies. The process is seen as adaptive and circular so that outputs (i.e., decisions or policies) can create new demands on the system. As a set of categories there is little to criticize in Easton's approach in detail, yet I believe anthropologists must in the end find it less useful than Smith's concept of political action. This results from the fact that in ordering the data of political anthropology for study and presentation anthropologists find it difficult to get away from the structural features of the systems they are dealing with (cf., Smith 1966). The reason for this is that structural characteristics (i.e., the authority system) of the various non-Western political systems present us with the most clear-cut taxonomic distinctions of the variety of phenomena that we are dealing with. At the very least they serve as the indicators of our variance. For this reason most anthropologists would favor a definition of the "political system" that focuses attention immediately upon the structural features of political systems (for example the distinction between chief and non-chief societies) rather than on the nature of the political act itself. As Dahl (1963:26) suggests, there is no "best" way to classify political systems. Differences among the various approaches have to do with the purposes of research. In my view the roster of societies dealt with by the anthropologist approximates to a set of varieties similar in many respects to those of traditional biology. Just as the phenotypic qualities and structure of organisms provide a basis for simplifying their differences, i.e., classifying them, so too the arrangement of authority roles in a society provides a theoretically useful way of classifying political systems. However, it should be made clear that classification not only simplifies and provides a basis for analysis, it also determines the kinds of questions we ask. Thus classifying political systems on the basis of their authority structure highlights questions concerning differences in these structures while possibly obscuring other questions about other variations such as types of political ideology or the personalities of leaders which thus must be brought into the analysis in other ways; or, if considered of vital interest, then these qualities must eventually become another way of classifying political systems. In other words, I have chosen to use authority structures as a basis for the analysis of political systems because questions about variation in these structures, and the theories that help to explain such differences, appear to be important and central to the study of politics. It is with this in mind that I have tried to systemize the rest of this chapter. Although I have had to start my analysis with political activity, it moves directly to the study of authority structures, using these as the major dependent variable in the study of political systems.

Summarizing work already done we can define political, as opposed to nonpolitical, activity, as an aspect of social relations (cf., Smith 1956, Easton 1959, Fried 1964). In this sense it is distinctive or separable as a category of social life in an analytic sense, but may not be represented by a separate and differentiated role network on its own within the society. Those aspects of social relations that can be identified as political are specifically concerned with power and authority when these occur in social relations. Power is an ability to influence the behavior of others and/or gain influence over the control of valued actions. Like Professor Smith I see power as available at all times, in some measure, to everyone in a society so that there is always some competition between members of the society for it.[2] Furthermore, it is not necessarily hierarchically arranged. Thus a subordinate might, for example, try to gain power over his superior. Authority is legitimate power, and it is an aspect of all hierarchically arranged social relations in which the superior has a recognized right to a stipulated amount of power over subordinates. Both superiors and subordinates may try to increase their power, and thus the relations between power and authority are not necessarily stable or constant through time. This distinction between power and authority means as well that it is quite apparent what is meant by the "authority structure" in society but much less easy to observe and record a "power structure." This is because authority structures refer to a formally recognized role network while the power structure refers to a set of interrelations among those wielding power. Since this "structure" may or may not be present or

[2] It should be noted that this involves the assumption that to a variable degree people, or at least some people, in all societies desire power as this is defined in their culture.

easily apparent, the term "power structure" should be used only after careful definition of the units and some known or hypothesized stipulation concerning their interrelations has been made by the researcher.

As others have pointed out, this type of delineation of "the political" can apply to all social groupings in all societies since all social interactions have a political aspect, i.e., power and authority feature. For example, this means that we can ask, "What are the political aspects of family life or of the religious and economic organizations in a society?"; indeed all formally organized groups may be thought of as forming a part of the political system since they all involve social relations containing some power and authority aspects. Most writers get around this difficulty explicitly or implicitly by having the political system refer to the most inclusive set of authority relations in the society. When such a definition is applied to the nation-state, there is very little difficulty since boundaries of central government control are so easily marked. However, in hunting and gathering bands, or in acephalous tribal societies, the boundaries of the widest-scaled social system may not be so clearly apparent. Thus, in order to clarify the differentiation in scale of social relations and the variance in specialization of political roles found among anthropological data, I suggest the concept of "polity." "Polity" refers to the size and nature of the jural community and varies from society to society and sometimes within the same society over time. As it has been defined elsewhere (Middleton and Tait 1958), a jural community is the widest-scaled network of authority relations affecting a set of interrelations among roles. These may be activated only on occasion as in the case of communal hunt leadership among the Shoshone or again in the case of a person who is entitled to settle a feud among a set of Lugbara lineage groups. Conversely, the jural community may operate continuously as in the hierarchical administrative system of the preindustrial state. Whatever the scale of the polity, at any particular time, its boundaries are clearly marked by the fact that beyond it there is little and often no institutionalized means of settling disputes, i.e., there is no authority that links a polity with others such that both are subordinate systems.

It is important to realize here that "polity,"

then, does not necessarily coincide with "society" or with "economic system," or any other analytically important social category. It may do so, and obviously that strengthens the boundaries of both, or it may not, which makes the boundaries between ethnic units or parts of the same ethnic unit less distinct. Thus using "polity" as the social entity in which the political system manifests itself means that it is quite possible to speak of a tribe as having a number of constituent polities, or conversely to speak of a tribe as part of a larger, multi-ethnic polity. Finally, then, we can define "political system" as an aspect of social relations. This aspect is concerned with the power and authority relations affecting the social life of a polity, as that group is defined in the traditions and practices of the society.

One of the research problems that such a conceptualization throws into relief is that of the distribution of power and authority within so-called nonpolitical organizations in the society and their character and connection to the political system as it becomes progressively differentiated into a separate role network of the society. In very simple societies a limited set of roles incorporate all activities including those having political significance. Thus the relation of behavior in the political system to that in other sectors such as the kinship, economic, or religious systems is easily accomplished because it all takes place within a few roles. Indeed this integration is sometimes observed in the same act as in cases where economic redistribution by a leader is also a demonstration of the political obligations of leaders to those over whom they have authority.[3] However, as societies become more complex, the relation of behavior excluded by definition from the political system to behavior in that system becomes an interesting problem to investigate in order to shed light on the political culture, i.e., the ideology and practice of power and authority relations in the culture as a whole.

AUTHORITY RELATIONS

Authority relations in a political system make up its constitutional features. When an anthropologist lays out the nature of the stipu-

lated and legitimate power distinctions among the roles of a polity, he is, in fact, drawing up a constitution for that particular society. In this sense Rattray (1929) is quite right to call his book *Ashanti Law and Constitution* when describing the authority relations of the Ashanti. Furthermore to the extent that authority relations form a network among roles, then to that extent we can speak of an authority structure. As already noted, the authority structure is at present the basic identifying feature for taxonomic categories by which anthropologists label and distinguish one kind of polity from another among the roster they generally study. With special reference to the African societies, I have divided these up into centralized and non-centralized systems (Cohen 1965). The non-centralized polities are then further divided into types of ecological adaptations as follows: (a) those based on domesticated plants and/or animals, and (b) those based on hunting and gathering. Further sub-division is then provided for on the basis of the structural units that make up the organizational basis within which the authority relations operate; specific examples are patrilocal bands, village councils, segmentary lineages, etc. The centralized polities differ (a) with respect to the degree of autonomy of local groups and (b) the mode of recruitment into politically relevant roles. These two factors interrelate to produce a continual variation from extremely centralized to highly decentralized types of authority relations among the states.

As already noted above, whether this classification system or some other (cf., Vansina 1962, Mair 1962, Gluckman 1965, etc.) is used, this variance among authority relations provides us with a central problem to be explained. It is not the only possible approach (cf., Swartz, Turner, and Tuden 1966), but it flows logically from the idea of classifying political systems by their differences and similarities in authority structures.

To delimit this variable it is necessary to ask who can do what to whom at any particular level of the polity. What we are looking for is a set of rules explicitly stated or implicit in practice which indicate how scarce values are allocated among superiors and subordinates. What are the recognized rights of superiors and subordinates? By a "recognized right" I mean a behavior associated with

[3] Correlating such categories in cross-cultural studies must be done with the conscious understanding that the same behavior may be counted as an indicator of two or more variables.

some role or group which no individual or group successfully opposes. Members of the polity may support the right strongly or be noncommital in their feelings about it or even dislike it. However, as long as they do not actively, and successfully, oppose the prerogative so that it cannot be practiced by its present holders, it is, operationally speaking, a recognized right. It should be noticed that this is something like the concept of legitimacy in political science, but it is also different because legitimacy may have wider connotations, at least as it is used by some theorists. For example, in defining this term, S. M. Lipset suggests that legitimacy refers to "the capacity of the system to engender and maintain the belief that the existing political institutions are the most appropriate ones for the society" (Lipset 1960:74). In this sense, legitimacy refers to recognized rights as here defined and the beliefs of a population in the rightness of these practices. Recognized right more circumspectly denotes the fact that the role or group enjoys certain prerogatives. The reasons why this is so may include people's beliefs, a leader's political skills, his coercive powers, fear of outside enemies, etc. By limiting the concept of recognized right in this way we can allow for a wider variation of the conditions that might create such rights and include a wider variety of authority structures. Thus a conquering tyrant may not be the "legitimate" ruler of a polity, but his superior force provides him with the recognized right to rule, creating thereby a type of authority structure that is important in the evolution of political systems.

A further set of indicators which help delimit the authority relations stems out of the range of sanctions that are set into motion when authority relations are abrogated by subordinates, but under conditions in which recognized rights are still in operation. These may range all the way from individual action by the superior against the person or persons neglecting to act in the role of subordinate to retaliatory measures through special institutions that perform the function of protecting and maintaining authority relations in the polity. Besides actually observing such cases, this particular category of data is very well suited to the technique of the "hypothetical case." Informants can generally agree on what should be done when such and such a rule is broken, and it is much easier to obtain a wide range of sanctions by asking about them than by waiting to observe real instances of rule abrogation.

Just as constitutional history is one of the basic research strategies for understanding the development and nature of the modern nation-state, so, too, it is important in political anthropology to trace out whenever possible the past history of the authority structure isolating the major changes that have occurred. Work in such a framework has been carried out by Barnes (1954), Fallers (1956), Smith (1960), Pedrasco (1961), Bailey (1963), Cohen (1966), and others. Such an approach is extremely important since it is very often difficult to interpret or theorize about contradictory reports when diachronic studies have not been carried out. Thus Maquet (1961) and Codere (1962) have quite different views of the authority structure in Rwanda, and only when we have the historical material (Des Forges 1966) do we understand that both authors are essentially correct, but each reports on a different time period in Rwanda history. In more specific terms it is important to know whether: (1) authority roles have increased or decreased their power through time; (2) the subordinates have maintained a constant or changing response to their superiors; (3) there has been any significant role differentiation such that new political roles have been created; and (4) there have been any changes in the relation of the polity under study and the parts of it to other polities or their parts in the interpolity environment. It is, of course, crucial as well to ask what historical events seem to have preceded and stimulated these changes, for only in such a way are we able to know whether there is any rational explanation for the developments that have occurred.

One of the shortcomings in the work already done by anthropologists on political systems has been a tendency on the part of some writers to limit the recording of information to a description of the authority structure, and this is then assumed to comprise the political analysis of the field ethnographer. But as already suggested above in terms of the political system, this set of data deals with the constitutional framework only. To understand the system fully we must know how it changes and why, how it works in practice, and what influences are playing upon it to facilitate and restrain the change in any direction. The remainder of this chapter will concern itself with the processual and dynamic features of the system—in other words, the major independent variables associated with the authority structure conceived of as the major dependent variable.

THE ATTRIBUTES OF POWER

As already defined above, power is conceived of here as the ability to influence the behavior of others or influence the control over valued actions. As Smith (1956) has ably pointed out, power is "segmentary." That is to say it can never be fully contained within the authority relations, or if you like, within the constitution of the polity. There are always ways and means, some idiosyncratic to individuals, others more patterned and widespread, for individuals and groups to compete for greater amounts of power than is legitimately their right under the authority relations operating in the system at any particular point in time.

Why this should be so is an interesting question and one anthropologists could take advantage of in making a contribution to general political theory. In many of the traditional political theories from Machiavelli to the present, an original motor force is assumed into existence in order to provide the energy that makes for political activity in social life. Thus W. T. Bluhm (1965:249), in comparing Machiavelli with Neustadt's work on the power of the presidency, claims that both these writers feel that concern or desire for power is the basic motive of political action. More cogently for our purposes L. H. Riker (1962:22) suggests that a politically rational man is one who would rather win than lose, regardless of the stakes. In other words, according to political theorists in Western culture, a political system requires a certain type of motivation at the psychological level among at least some of its members in order to function. Here is a classical anthropological problem. How universal is this assumption? Is it indeed a constant? There are already available techniques for measuring "need for power" motivation in projected materials such as stories, folklore, dreams, etc. (see Atkinson 1958, Cohen and VanStone 1963). It is therefore reasonable to ask whether or not variation in the intensity of power motivation is related to differences in the na-

ture of political systems in general and authority relations in particular when comparisons are made across the entire gamut of polities known to the anthropologist.

The question of measuring or recording information on power is a more complex and subtle problem than that of authority. This is best seen if we analyze the concept of influence which is the operative or action component of power in interpersonal relations. It has been defined as ". . . a *relation among actors* in which one actor induces others to act in some way they would not otherwise act" (Dahl 1963:47). As Dahl points out in the same passage, it is not so easy, however, to estimate precisely how people might have behaved if the condition you are measuring or observing is said to be absent. But it is not impossible. For example, one leader A organizes an activity and gets ten people to follow his lead; another leader B, playing the same role, organizes a similar activity and succeeds in obtaining twenty followers. Comparing A and B in a number of activities we find that this disparity generally seems to hold true and conclude that B is the more powerful leader. Unfortunately, this is the simplest case. It may be that A's smaller following lasts for a year while B's larger one for only a few months, or A may be more influential with respect to activities, a, b, and c, while B only so with respect to x, y, and z. Thus Dahl's methodological warning (1963:47) is worthwhile noting. When recording data on power we must look (a) for as many measures of relative influence as possible, and (b) state specifically what particular dimensions or activities the influence refers to, and what behaviors are being utilized to indicate or measure such influence.

Besides the basic questions of how much power is desired among members of a polity and how power is measured, it is important to understand and analyze the sources of power available to the members. These may be found in the bases of the status system and the political skills of the actors.[4] In order to discover the status system questions must

[4] By status system in a polity I mean the ranking of activities as more or less desirable by members of the population. In this sense these activities are values, and are by definition relatively scarce such that not everyone can achieve them, and those who do, therefore, have things that are universally recognized as worthwhile by those who do not. (Cf., Cohen 1970)

be asked about what qualities people recognize as instruments that give a man the ability to influence or attempt to influence others. These instruments may include personal success, powers of adjudication, supernatural power to predict the future or invoke the help of the supernatural, military prowess, success in the food quest, physical appearance, forming of successful coalitions, acting as a middleman between policies, etc. Whatever the list may be, and it may be the same throughout the polity or vary among different levels of the population, acquisition of such instruments provides the person with the ability to gain or maintain influence. Political skills can be derived from the examples given above concerning the measurement of power. Given identical or similar status bases in the same system, one person may exercise more power than another. If the instruments are in fact the same, we then conclude that the more powerful person is using his instruments to better advantage. Why this should be so becomes the basis for the description and analysis of political skills in the system under analysis.

In summary then, power stems out of the values of the culture in which the political system is enmeshed plus the skills that political actors bring to their activities in the political system. Because these vary through time in response to changing conditions and personnel in the political system they are never fully contained by the more stable and formal authority structure, i.e., the constitutional structure of the society; indeed the interaction between power relations and the authority structure forms a major basis of the political process, to which we now turn.

THE POLITICAL PROCESS

In the over-all political system the relation of power to authority can be seen in two ways; first, in the breakdown or decrease of authority, and secondly, in the legitimization of power such that new authority roles are created and/or older ones enhanced in the amount of power available to them. In the first case, in order to energize or propel the system into action, I would assume the presence of an entropy-like principle in authority relations; this means that there is at all times in political systems a tendency for subordinates to reject the authority of superiors. This could be due to psychological reactions to authority. It is not necessarily present, or present to the same extent, in all members, but there are always some entropy-like forces that tend to be operating in the polity. On the other hand, these are contained or held in check by forces of legitimacy, in other words, by the widespread operation of forces that engender a belief in the worthwhileness of the authority structure. The two forces, legitimacy and its entropic opposite, are in tension such that any increase in one equals a decrease in the other. Another way of saying this is to state that in all political systems there are persons, groups, or situations that tend to lessen the power of one or more of the authority roles in the political system. A full description and analysis of that system should uncover what are the varieties of entropy in the polity—how old are they? how successful? and under what conditions do they operate? Conversely, since the sources of power are never fully incorporated within authority relations, there is always the possibility that persons or groups in authority will attempt to increase and legitimize their powers or that persons and groups not recognized in the authority structure will attempt to create new authority roles that consolidate and make legitimate their hold on specific powers. This situation is most clearly seen during periods of rapid change when the sources of power may themselves undergo change. At such times people, or more correctly, roles not traditionally associated with the authority relations, may come to control recognized and therefore legitimated sources of power.

The political process is not simply an abstract relationship between power and authority. In action terms it manifests itself as a set of activities lumped under the general category of decision-making. A decision is defined as "some choice amongst alternatives," and an authoritative decision is a "choice amongst alternatives in which the choice has meaningful and binding effects on those members of the political system to whom it refers" (Easton 1959). Decisions are the result of demands being made on the system. Such demands vary in the manner in which they stimulate the system to act, and this variance produces different varieties of decisions. All political systems are adapted to coping with demands, but the way in which they handle them and therefore associate decision-making with various roles is a major determinant of the differences among authority structures.

Decision-making can be classified in a number of ways. Perhaps the most detailed model of the process has been put forward by Snyder (1958), in which almost every conceivable aspect of the activity and its relationships is delineated. However, anthropologists will probably find this approach too cumbersome since it essentially analyzes a total society and culture using decision-making as a focal point for study. From a more pedestrian and common-sense point of view, decisions observed by anthropologists can be separated into two major categories —those that are aspects of routine functioning of the political system, and those that are more often periodic and/or irregular but which come under the rubric of what I shall call crisis decisions. This dichotomy is not completely satisfactory because routine decisions may develop into crisis ones under certain conditions, yet it does point up something widely noticed by field workers. Events that derive from the operation of the political system tend to make it function with an increasing degree of scale and clarity. Thus the allocation of land-use rights by a chief may be a normal function of a West African village chief. It affects only a small number of people and unless the field worker is made aware of the decision beforehand or is on hand in the situation it is difficult to observe. On the other hand, a war, or the succession to office of a new chief, can activate the entire system, and is more clearly visible in its effects throughout the polity. I would argue that these different types of decisions vary in the scale and degree of salience they have in the polity, which means that the political participation associated with each decision-type varies as well. In other words, as we move from everyday or routine decisions to crisis ones, increasingly wide segments of the political system are involved.

Under routine decisions I would place administrative and adjudicative matters since these activities are part of the everyday operation of the political system. Under crisis decisions I place certain aspects of interpolity relations, abnormal ecological conditions, and succession to office. These are discussed briefly below.

Most administrative decisions refer to routine matters whose playing out involves the execution of the "public policy" of the polity. This includes things like deciding on the nature of the food quest under normal circumstances, distributing and overseeing the use of new land, collecting tributes for local leaders, deciding on the time and scale of ceremonials in the annual cycle (again, under normal circumstances). There are a number of things that must be done on a regular basis that affect or could affect the entire polity if not properly organized and carried out. The vast range of factors affecting these everyday affairs in any particular situation is the set of independent variables which determine the nature of administrative activity in the polity. For example, it is not only important to know the expectations of each role in the hierarchy of a particular authority structure, one should also understand how outside influences and pressures affect each role and how each role player utilizes his prerogatives in order to understand the outcome of these decisions by each decision-maker in the authority structure. Only then will tendencies to change, brought on by regular patterns of decision-making in the everyday affairs of the polity, become clear.

As a routine matter adjudicative decisions are necessary when infractions of rules have been made that require public action by the polity against miscreants. In a number of the very simple societies, many infractions are dealt with as interpersonal disputes to be settled by those in conflict themselves while the other members maintain a steadfast lack of interest, and certainly do not intervene in any meaningful way. On other occasions, however, the group as a whole, and the person or persons taking action against the miscreant, may have no personal dispute with him or her at all. They are, instead, executing the judicial decision arrived at by members concerned with the miscreant's behavior. In more complex societies rule infraction produces an activation of the judicial system which is for many societies identical with the authority structure, differentiating from it only at the most complex levels of the centralized state where writing and the accumulation of legal codification produce the possibility of a category of legal specialists.

The distinction between administrative and adjudicative decisions hinges on the quality of infraction and the nature of interpersonal conflict within the polity, that is to say, on the nature of the demand or stimulus to make decisions. In administrative matters a decision has to be made about whether, how, why, where, or when certain things should or should not be done. All of the alternatives are (usually) legitimate; the question is simply which alternative will have the most beneficial or rewarding results given the known conditions. However, the stimulus or demand in an adjudicative situation involves one or both of two conditions. First, something has gone wrong that is felt to be an infraction of law, and law must therefore be appealed to in order to set the matter right. What are the precedents in such cases? What rules have been broken? etc. These are the questions being raised, and they stand out clearly as the group and its leaders deliberate the case. Secondly, two or more persons may be involved in a dispute which they cannot settle themselves. Each feels he (or they) are right and seeks to legitimize their position through the appeal to an adjudicative decision.

In order to obtain a set of independent variables that explain these decisions it is important to ask the question: How are judicial decisions arrived at? As in the case of administrative decisions this means defining the role characteristics and the influences, both formal and informal, that affect such decisions.

A number of problems are so stressful that decisions concerning them are what I would call a matter of crisis. A crisis decision is one in which either the whole polity or a significant portion within it consider their interest in a decision to be vital. In other words, it involves the survival of their group with respect to its present prerogatives. Abnormal ecological problems such as droughts, famines, the dying off of a major food source, sudden floods are some of the major types of such crises. However, lesser and more common abnormalities such as an unequal distribution of productive resources in gardening, planting, or the hunt when such things are said to be caused by supernatural aids might produce a crisis in a polity whose ideology is based on a belief that malevolence is a cause of unequal productivity. In such cases the vital interests of the community are seen as having been invaded, and decisions must be made in order to arrange a greater equity

of nature's bounty to be forthcoming in the future. Such decisions often involve the setting up of judicial proceedings in order to diagnose the problem and then deciding what course of action to follow when the causes become known—the causes being sought for in the gamut of cultural explanations for such disturbances. A second set of crises revolves around interpolity relations. This topic is discussed more fully below, but for the present it should be noted that relations between one polity, or part of it, and other political entities outside the political system can result in crises for which decisions must be made. Examples of such crises are rivalry among polities over access to resources, or trade, or competition over the dominant position in an emerging alliance among local polities. Again crises can arise over the operation of, or the reaction to, interpolity raiding for booty or people (slaves). A final example that comes to mind is the situation in which one person or a faction within a polity seeks to increase local power and solicits aid from outside the polity in order to strengthen his (their) internal position. Much of the exact form such crises takes depends upon the structure of interpolity relations which have been established in the past between the political systems concerned.

A third set of crises revolves around the succession to office in the authority structure (cf., Goody 1966). In modern complex political systems such as those of Western democracy such crises are alleviated by the widespread use of either electoral procedures, appointment by merit, or a well-organized patronage system, all of which are interrelated in intricate ways by the constitutional necessity for elections and the operation of political parties.

In most of the polities dealt with by anthropologists, such complex means of succession are not practiced. However, in all systems, whether electorally based or not, succession to office brings into sharp focus the various political segments of the polity who view succession as a possible expansion or contraction of their power. Thus succession always affects vital interests and is in this sense a crisis. On the other hand, because it is a crisis and involves access to the authority structure, succession involves decisions that very clearly isolate the political process by bringing into clear focus the rivalry over recruitment and the means by which such competition is resolved.

A number of factors influence succession although they vary enormously depending upon the complexity of the polity and its authority structure.[5] First of all, there are the rules governing succession; these may be complex or very simple, and they include as well precedents for exceptional events such as a regent who can rule for a monarch while that monarch is too young because of a rule of primogeniture. Perhaps the most important feature of succession rules is the degree of rivalry among candidates that is allowed for in terms of who makes the final decisions and what type of status requirements are mandatory and/or desirable on the part of the candidates. Even offices that must remain within one descent group allow for competition as long as the rules allow for the availability of a group of eligibles rather than just one. An interesting theoretical problem emerges here in the relationship of different types of succession rules and different types of authority structures (see Cohen 1966). A second set of influences on succession crises and the subsequent decisions that must be made arises from the type of interests that are involved in the succession, and who and what they represent. Concerning the same set of influences, it is important for those in control of the situation to take into account the requirements of office and the qualities of candidates and to try within the pressures of all other influences to choose the best man. In very simple polities it may be two powerful and successful men who have the qualifications, but only one of whom can have the job. Each may try to obtain supporters; often (but not always) the interests of their supporters as opposed to nonsupporters are only minimally served by giving support to one or the other. Instead it is the welfare of the entire polity that is involved as well as the individual desires of the candidates. On the other hand, in those cases in fairly simple societies such as the Tiwi where successful men have highly desirable patronage to dispense, then the interests of the supporters must be regarded as a factor influencing succession decisions. Of course, if an entire lineage group within a clan is being

[5] See Goody (1966) for a more complete discussion of the nature and effects of succession problems on the structure and process of the political system.

cut off from access to office for either a short time or for good because their lineage candidate is not chosen, then the entire lineage plus those dependent upon it become vitally concerned in the decision. In the same vein it is important to know how much power the incumbent of the office has in choosing his own successor, through his formal authority or his informal control of the decision-making even though he may be dead or infirm when the decision is actually made.

A third set of influences in succession crises is critical yet difficult to get at. This is the degree of commitment given by the members to their own political system or part of it since that commitment may vary for various offices in the authority structure, and vary across segments of the polity. I assume that this set of influences is, in fact, an unknown or at least not widely agreed upon quality by the people themselves in all societies. Thus it is always open to question "whether or not we can get away with it," when a person or group is thinking about succession and/or usurping an office or set of them, or imposing a new set of offices or officeholders on the polity. People tend to support their own system when asked if they believe in it, but they may or may not actively oppose a change in the system when it occurs. If, of course, change is accompanied by sufficient power, either through conquest or some other means, there is no difficulty. However, when succession problems arise, even without conquest, there is a tendency for candidates, excluded formally by the rules, to desire that rules be changed or expanded to include some or all of those previously excluded. This follows simply from the assumption that power is an attractive and desirable end, and succession rules are constantly under attack when groups or individuals who wish positions of authority are left out of the succession.

POLITICAL SOCIALIZATION

Given the fact that there are large numbers of authoritative decisions made in a polity, it is important to know how and why the actors in a political system accept such direction and indeed believe that to do so is the right way to act. Although some of the explanation lies in the coercive powers available to most, not all, authority structures, this is obviously not the whole answer since many people in any polity need not be forced to accept the outcome of decisions even when their own lives are at stake, as in the case of warfare. In other words: How do people learn to be active and believing members of the polity and what is it they must learn if they are to take part in the political life of the system? The assumption here is that, although there may be something as universal as "political man" (i.e., a person activated to win, or a person oriented toward gaining power), it is likely that the form, content, and intensity of such psychological qualities vary among political systems. Furthermore, a systems approach leads us to consider this variance in its relation to our major focus for comparative analysis, namely, the authority structure. The first thing to discover here, then, is what kind of political culture exists for the political system we are interested in.

By political culture I mean a set of ideals and symbols that describe the aims and goals of political life in terms of the traditions of the members. In practice this also means the way in which power and authority are conceived and practiced in the culture as a whole. Such cultural data should answer the question: "What is good, bad, and acceptable political behavior in this particular system?" Only when this is done can we infer more clearly the nature of "political man" in the system. An interesting comparative question then becomes: "What political cultures are correlated with varying types of authority structures?" (See LeVine 1966.) I would suggest that hunting and gathering societies stress egalitarianism because each man eventually comes to be an important political actor in the system. Acephalous sedentary societies stress high achievement because most members of the political system can, through effort, obtain an important political office. On the other hand most primitive states have limited access to authority positions as a quality of their constitutional make-up. Thus striving is emphasized among the political elite while, in the culture as a whole, good followership or the norms and rewards of proper subordination are stressed as values in the political culture.

Political socialization is, however, strongly time based. People learn about proper political behavior during their youth and then attempt to apply this learning as fully practicing members when they become adults. It is important to note how congruent socialization experience is with the actual practices of the authority structure since the possibility of change is always present given the time lag between learning and the adaptability of members to many pressures beside ideological ones once they become actors and decision-makers in the system. The more congruent socialization is to the actual practice, then the more stable and persistent is the political system and vice versa. The more socialization does not predict to adult experience, the less stable is the system. Ameliorating this instability are new types of learning which provide those being socialized with novel and sometimes more adaptive goals. Such things as Western schooling and urban experience, etc., are doing just this in many parts of the world today, but gaps still remain. Thus many northern Nigerian parents know their children will learn things in Western schools which could enable the youngsters to become "big men." However, they also know that a minute percentage of students ever get enough education to qualify for the few positions of power and authority open in society. The result is ambivalence about school and less than universal acceptance of its adequacy as a new means of socializing the young and providing opportunity for access to important jobs.

Finally it is important to understand how and what people who are eligible for office learn when attempting to gain the position and what political skills they must learn on the job in order to carry out their office successfully. Anthropologists have often described the qualities of political leadership either in particular by referring to a specific person, or in general terms thus characterizing the role. What is needed is some understanding of the forces that create good leadership and the way in which the people themselves and the leaders come to know and accept these standards. This latter point is very important in situations of rapid change as exemplified in most of the new nations. We still do not know what produces stable leadership in such situations, even though there are a number of well-documented cases of both stable (Smith 1960) and relatively unstable (Epstein 1958) political situations in the modern world.

INTERPOLITY RELATIONS

Interpolity relations vary with respect to boundary maintenance of the political system. At one end the polity acts as a whole unit through its authority structure, while at the other end of the variance, only parts of the political system interact with parts of other authorities. It is true whether we are dealing with small hunting bands, autonomous village units, small chieftaincies, or centralized states. Furthermore the interpolity relations are complicated by the fact that some polities are interacting horizontally, that is to say, with other units that are independent and roughly equal in status. Thus bands are relating to other bands, or villages with other villages, although some units of one scale, like autonomous villages, may have relations with centralized states, or small chieftaincies with big chieftaincies, etc. On the other hand polities also deal with one another when one of them is a small yet bounded part of the other, such as family units with a larger band organization, or wards with villages, or villages with central governments, and so on. This latter type of interpolity relation is generally referred to as "vertical."

In horizontal interactions it is necessary to understand what is the object of interrelation. Whatever the reason for interaction— be it warfare, raiding, competition for scarce resources, or cooperation for achieving a common goal—the goal or goals themselves tend to determine the nature of the interaction which generally involves the polity as a whole. The same is true when a part of the polity interacts with a part of another. Whether it is raiding, trading, joking relationships or blood brotherhood between members of adjacent tribal groupings, what is important is an understanding of the reasons why the interaction is taking place. What are its results and what are the influences playing upon these results? For example, the members of segmentary societies interact with neighboring groups who are acephalous, the latter practicing village autonomy and a non-ramifying (spatially) kinship structure. The result is that segmentary societies having larger groups of allies to call upon through their descent rules and tend therefore to expand into the territory of non-segmentary neighbors (Sahlins 1961). Or again, the

level of hierarchy stressed among the acephalous Mbembe of southern Nigeria, whether it is ward-level politics or over-all village level, was dependent upon their patterns of conflict and evacuation away from hostile groups to the north of them (Harris 1962). In the Mbembe example, the authority structure of the polity is affected by horizontal relations between polities, while in the segmentary lineage examples cited by Sahlins (1961), the authority structure itself tends to determine the outcome of hostilities between polities.

From the horizontal point of view it is important to know what are the relations, their goals, and effects, when parts of a polity relate to the whole, given the fact that the parts have some degree of autonomy—that is to say they can be thought of as political systems in their own right. For some types of analyses this job would already be done if the entire polity were studied as a whole and each part related. However, in anthropology we most often deal with parts of societies incorporated into larger entities. Thus the relations of the political systems we observe to the larger ones such as the nation-state into which they have been absorbed become an important task and have been discussed in detail by a number of writers (e.g., Apter 1961, Geertz 1963). The interrelations of different types of traditional authority systems within incorporating new nation-states has hardly begun, and it is difficult as yet to see any general pattern emerging in these kinds of investigations. What is needed here are sets of case studies showing the relations of traditional, non-Western polities to their newer national and regional areas of governmental organizations so we may begin to see which variables are associated with what range of response and which major type of authority structure (c.f., Cohen and Middleton 1970).

CONCLUSION

As we have defined it here, the political system comprises the authority structure of a society in its relation to the distribution of power, and these interrelations are played out in decision-making concerning the day-to-day life of a polity. The over-all or macro-evolution of political systems is a matter of comparative analysis as this subject is treated in Part IV of this book, both through controlled comparisons and aggregate data analysis of large samples of societies. On a local or micro level the strategy of attack on the study of political systems is not simply the description of static entities. By looking at the authority structure as a dependent variable in the political process, and including as well political socialization and interpolity relations as a set of practices that both stem from *and* affect the authority structure, we have, in effect, set up a model for depicting the dynamics of the system.

This model of analysis does not commit us to exclude anything in particular, thus the systems approach is not necessarily in contradiction to the older holistic strategy of ethnographic field work. Instead it simply asks that we focus on one problem area for investigation and explanation, and then find the answers wherever they happen to be in the operation of social and cultural life within the polity. The fuller the explanation, the more widely the entire sociocultural milieu will be searched and examined for correlates to the structure and processes we are interested in. In other words, we have gone a long way toward holistic anthropology if we continue to insist that the political system is not simply the authority structure but its operation, development, and persistence in a polity.

BIBLIOGRAPHY

APTER, D. E.
  1961 *The political kingdom in Uganda.* Princeton, N.J., Princeton University Press.
ATKINSON, J. W. (ed.)
  1958 *Motives in fantasy, action, and society.* Princeton, N.J., Van Nostrand.
BAILEY, F. G.
  1963 *Politics and social change: Orissa in 1959.* Berkeley, University of California Press.
BARNES, J. A.
  1954 *Politics in a changing society.* London, Oxford University Press.
BLUHM, W. T.
  1965 *Theories of the political system.* Englewood Cliffs, N.J., Prentice-Hall.
BOGUSLAW, R.
  1965 *The new utopians: a study of system design and social change.* Englewood Cliffs, N.J., Prentice-Hall.
CODERE, H.
  1962 Power in Rwanda. *Anthropologica* 4:45–85.
COHEN, R.
  1965 Political anthropology: the future of a pioneer. *Anthropological Quarterly* 38:117–131.
  1966 *The dynamics of feudalism in Bornu.* Boston University Publication in African History, Vol. 2.
  1970 Social stratification in Bornu. In A. Tuden and L. Plotnicov, eds., *Social stratification in Africa south of the Sahara.* New York, Free press.
COHEN, R., and J. MIDDLETON (eds.)
  1967 *Comparative political systems: studies in the politics of pre-industrial societies.* New York, Natural History Press.
  1970 *From tribe to nation in Africa.* San Francisco, Chandler.
COHEN, R., and J. L. VANSTONE
  1963 Dependency and self-sufficiency in Chipewyan stories. *National Museum of Canada, Bulletin* 194:29–55.
DAHL, R. A.
  1963 *Modern political analysis.* Englewood Cliffs, N.J., Prentice-Hall.
DES FORGES, ALISON
  1966 *The impact of European colonization on the Rwandan social system.* Paper delivered at the African Studies Association Meetings, Bloomington, Ind. Mimeo.
EASTON, DAVID
  1959 Political anthropology. In B. J. Siegel, ed., *Biennial review of anthropology.* Stanford, Stanford University Press.
  1965 *A framework for political analysis.* Englewood Cliffs, N.J., Prentice-Hall.
EPSTEIN, A. L.
  1958 *Politics in an African urban setting.* Manchester, Manchester University Press.
FALLERS, L. A.
  1956 *Bantu bureaucracy.* Cambridge, England, Heffer.
FORTES, M., and E. E. EVANS-PRITCHARD
  1940 *African political systems.* London, Oxford University Press.
FRIED, M. F.
  1964 Political anthropology. In Sol Tax, ed., *Horizons in anthropology.* Chicago, Aldine.

GEERTZ, CLIFFORD (ed.)
1963 *Old societies and new states: the quest for modernity in Asia and Africa.* New York, Free Press.

GLUCKMAN, MAX
1965 *Politics, law, and ritual in tribal society.* Chicago, Aldine.

GOODY, J. R. (ed.)
1966 *Succession to high office.* Cambridge Papers in Anthropology No. 4. Cambridge, Cambridge University Press.

HARRIS, R.
1962 The influence of ecological factors and external relations on the Mbembe tribes of south-east Nigeria. *Africa* 32:38–52.

LEVINE, R. A.
1966 *Dreams and deeds: achievement motivation in Nigeria.* Chicago, University of Chicago Press.

LEVY, MARION J., JR.
1966 *Modernization and the structure of societies.* 2 vols. Princeton, N.J., Princeton University Press.

LIPSET, SEYMOUR M.
1960 *Political man: the social bases of politics.* Garden City, N.Y., Doubleday.

MAIR, L.
1962 *Primitive government.* Baltimore, Penguin.

MAQUET, J. J.
1961 *The premise of inequality in Rwanda.* London, Oxford University Press.

MIDDLETON, J., and D. TAIT
1958 *Tribes without rulers.* London, Routledge and Kegan Paul.

PEDRASCO, P.
1961 The civil-religious hierarchy in Mesoamerican communities: Pre-Spanish background and colonial development. *American Anthropologist* 63:483–497. Reprinted in R. Cohen and J. Middleton (1967).

RADCLIFFE-BROWN, A. R.
1940 Preface. In M. Fortes and E. E. Evans-Pritchard, eds., *African political systems,* London, Oxford University Press.

RAPOPORT, A.
1966 Some system approaches to political theory. In D. Easton, ed., *Varieties of political theory.* Englewood Cliffs, N.J., Prentice-Hall.

RATTRAY, R. S.
1929 *Ashanti law and constitution.* Oxford, Clarendon Press.

RIKER, L. H.
1962 *Theory of political coalitions.* New Haven, Yale University Press.

SAHLINS, M. D.
1961 The segmentary lineage: an organization of predatory expansion. *American Anthropologist* 63:332–345. Reprinted in R. Cohen and J. Middleton (1967).

SALISBURY, R.
n.d. *Political organization in Siane society.*

SCHAPERA, ISAAC
1956 *Government and politics in tribal society.* New York, Humanities Press.

SMITH, M. G.
1956 On segmentary lineage systems. *Journal of the Royal Anthropological Institute* 86: 39–80.

1960 *Government in Zazzau.* London, Oxford University Press.

1966 A structural approach to comparative politics. In D. Easton, ed., *Varieties of political theory.* Englewood Cliffs, N.J., Prentice-Hall.

SNYDER, RICHARD
1958 A decision-making approach to the study of political phenomena. In Roland Young, ed., *Approaches to the study of politics.* Evanston, Ill., Northwestern University Press.

STEWARD, J. H.
1938 *Basin-plateau aboriginal socio-political groups.* Bureau of American Ethnology, Bulletin 120.

SWARTZ, M., V. W. TURNER, and A. TUDEN (eds.)
1966 *Political anthropology.* Chicago, Aldine.

VANSINA, J.
1962 A comparison of African kingdoms. *Africa* 32:324–335.

CHAPTER 26

The Religious System

JOHN MIDDLETON

DEFINING THE "RELIGIOUS"

This paper deals with a single problem: what data are relevant to an anthropological study of "the religious system" of a given people. I shall not discuss problems of gaining rapport so as to be able to attend rituals, nor of how to collect myths, nor of how to learn sufficient of a language to be able to comprehend the concepts behind a series of cosmological notions. This is a chapter in a book on methods, not one on techniques. What I shall discuss, on the other hand—or at least refer to by implication—includes such questions as what aspects of a rite may be considered important for anthropological analysis of the total society, and what is the anthropological significance of a myth or of a series of cosmological notions.

This chapter starts with three assumptions. The first is that in order to study such an all-pervasive part of human culture and experience as religion one must have a reasonable idea as to what is comprised under that rubric. The second is that anthropologists accept the view that religion is a social fact and so needs analysis in sociological terms. That it can also be analyzed in other terms is, of course, true, and must be recognized by us; this is one aspect of defining the bounds of the religious as it is anthropologically relevant. And the third assumption is that there is a particular anthropological way of analyzing religious phenomena that is implicit in the phrase "the religious system": we assume that these phenomena do in some way form a system and thus have an underlying pattern or structure.

There are many ways of viewing the field of religion. To some, religion consists of a narrow range of cultural data, mainly exotic beliefs which the anthropologist himself cannot accept as being "scientifically" true and which are as a consequence grouped together as a kind of rag-bag category. For others, the religious includes virtually every aspect of human life that is not specifically technical. In neither case is there any agreement as to a definition of "religious." It is noticeable, and significant to this chapter, that early anthropological studies were largely devoted to building up evolutionary schemes of the religious life. But in recent years, when anthropology has become a fairly rigorous discipline based on field research rather than on armchair conjecture, and when evolutionary studies have as a result lost much of their former importance, since many of the "facts" on which they were based have been shown to be untrue, studies of the specifically religious have become fewer. Far more effort has been devoted to accounts of social structure and organization in the fields of politics, kinship, economics and the rest. This has been a consequence of two main factors. One is that rapidly changing societies, those that are by necessity the ones mainly studied by anthropologists, would seem to present better opportunities for research in these particular fields than in the religious sphere. The other is the difficulty of defining a "religious sphere" of social life at all.

There have been many attempts to define the "religious," and I can see no useful purpose served by adding to them here, nor in commenting upon them; the most useful summary is that by Goody (1961), and Horton (1960a), Geertz (1966) and Spiro (1966) have interesting discussions on the subject.

In "common-sense" terms we know that we can include certain social phenomena under that rubric—myths and cosmologies, rituals, beliefs in gods, spirits, ancestral deities and the like, beliefs in magic, oracles, witches, sorcerers. Obvious peripheral phenomena include folk tales and legends, ideas of morality and ethics, ceremonial activities that are not specifically "ritual" ones, notions of taxonomy and classification (although in some senses these are at the very heart of religious analysis), naming systems, many aspects of art, music and dancing. We can observe these activities and beliefs in action and from discussion with informants.

We can accept, for our purposes, the central attribute of the religious to be the concept of a "spiritual being" or power which is thought to stand outside human society, which can create and destroy it. A belief in a power of this kind appears to be universal, although it may not be clearly defined, may be attributed to many forms, may be thought to act in many ways and situations, and may be considered by the anthropologists to represent various kinds of social forces and experience. This power has been expressed and analyzed in various ways by various writers: Tylor (1873) referred to the "belief in Spiritual Beings" as being the core of the religious, Durkheim (1912) referred to the attribute of sacredness as a symbol for the power of society and human interdependence, Otto (1917) referred to the attribute of holiness, and so on. All are in one way or another unsatisfactory when we come to consider any particular religion. Yet we have to come back, when we try to define the bounds of the religious, to the notion of a spiritual, divine power at the center.

If we accept the nature of the center of the religious sphere, we must then try to define its limits. It is here that there has been most of the uncertainty, disagreement, and controversy in anthropological thinking on the subject. It is usually very difficult to have the boundaries of the religious defined by the people we are studying, if their culture is a non-literate one, even if we can translate the concept of "religion" at all—and obviously if the "religious" is a symbol for some kind of social reality then we should hardly expect it to be definable.

The situation is obviously somewhat different, in a formal sense, if a society possesses sacred writings and an institutionalized priest-hood. But here there is the problem of the difference between the formal bounds (in theological terms) of the religious and what might be called its sociological bounds, which may be quite distinct. Every culture, whether literate or pre-literate, may define the bounds differently, as far as its own religion is concerned. The empirical fact that this is so, and the forms in which these differences are expressed, are highly significant, although there has really been very little comparative work done on this particular problem. It is important to recognize that if we ourselves do the defining in respect of the culture which we are studying, we thereby risk omitting much at the periphery of the religious sphere. If we take as one of the more important tasks in anthropology the discovery of interrelationships between cultural phenomena, the identity and relationship between independent and dependent variables, and the ways in which institutions function in relationship to other institutions of the same society, then we may easily miss the relationship between the religious and other phenomena if we try to delimit any one sphere too strictly or too arbitrarily.

This is perhaps another way of saying that to try to define the "religious" is in any event a false problem and so an insoluble one. Also, logically, to find a core of the religious and to work out from it to other items of social behavior may be incorrect and based on a misunderstanding of the nature of religion, although it is, I think, what we all tend to do in practice. The point here is that we may argue that the religious is an aspect of virtually all social relations—although not of all purposive social activities (see Nadel 1951)—and so to look for relationships between it and other aspects of social life is to ask the wrong question. One of the more obvious weaknesses in the anthropological study of religion has been the tendency to see various phenomena, which have traditionally been gathered under the rubric "religious," as being virtually unconnected except by being put under that rubric. They have not been put together as a single system, nor related to other systems. Yet we must, as I have mentioned, assume that in any one society they do have a single structure.

A basic problem is that of the observer's own approach to and degree of acceptance of the religious beliefs and practices he observes. It may be that in many field situations he will accept, in the sense of believing as an article of faith, the religion in question. Such would be the case of a Christian working in a Christian community or a Muslim working in a Muslim one. Even if not an active believer, the concepts and assumptions of the faith he observes would be immediately comprehensible to him. But in these cases, of course, an anthropologist is looking for a pattern of social relations between the people who hold that particular faith. He may or may not accept the ethics, notions of causation, and the sanctions, which are part of it. His objectivity consists in understanding the functions of these phenomena irrespective of their theological truth, even if he himself accepts this truth.

In many ways the situation is a simpler one when the field worker does not accept the theological truth of the religion he is observing, as he can then merely disregard any possible involvement, in that sense, in the situation. By "involvement" here I refer particularly to the difficulty of recognizing that a belief which one holds to be true may have a sociological function quite apart from its religious one. In the case of a faith other than one's own, one may assent to it without believing it (see Lienhardt 1954). One can accept an "as-if" attitude, in both field observation and in analysis (see Firth 1959).

RITUAL, MYTH AND MAGIC

Traditionally, anthropologists have in practice divided the field of the religious into the three central elements of ritual, myth, and magic. Each is related to the others, and each has close ties with several of the more "peripheral" phenomena mentioned above: for example, ritual with ceremonial and art, myth with cosmologies and taxonomic classifications, and magic with sorcery and divination. I think it is useful to discuss these three aspects of religion as though they were distinct, for the simple reason that this is the way in which most anthropological studies have been made (and most anthropology taught). In this way, also, some of the main methodological problems associated with them may be mentioned.

Having said this, however, one general point should be mentioned immediately, since its implications are significant throughout the rest of this discussion. It is clear that an anthropological analysis of the religious system can approach religious activity, of whatever kind, as having two main functions. These may be called the instrumental and the expressive. Theoretically they are two poles of a single continuum rather than distinct items of behavior. We may call an activity instrumental if it is performed to achieve a particular and purposive end; we may call it expressive if it is performed to express certain relations, that is, if it is primarily symbolic. There is clearly a difficulty here, in that "expressive" acts, as so defined, may be performed by the actors as though instrumental ones. Indeed, if they are symbolic then it could be argued that they are bound to be regarded as instrumental by the actors. I return to this point later, but the distinction is an important one. It is, of course, a reflection of the old argument about the relationship between magic and religion (see especially Malinowski 1948), and the distinction is in some ways a false one (see Homans 1941). Both functions may be found together, and we are here dealing with aspects of the same activities rather than with any basic differences. Acts that can be called magical and those that can be called religious have both functions, although the weighting of the instrumental to the expressive may vary from one act to another. The best discussion of this whole matter is probably that by Beattie (1964).

The first of the three central elements of the religious is ritual. Ritual refers to formalized, institutionalized, and usually (although not necessarily) group activity; it is thus usually the activity of a cult. From Durkheim onwards the relationship between it and ceremonial has been a point of argument. Probably the most generally accepted viewpoint is that ritual is religious ceremonial; that is, it is ceremonial whose ostensible purpose, as distinct from its secondary or latent function, is activity directed toward a spiritual power outside men. Leach (1954), Wilson (1957), Goody (1961), and Gluckman (1962) come near to this view, although each would like to refine it in one way or another. The argument is based on the expressive nature of ritual and ceremonial: they are performed with the social function of stating, reaffirming, creating, or enhancing certain relations between social statuses. The distinction is that ritual involves spiritual power.

Accounts of ritual activities are legion in

the anthropological literature. Here it is perhaps useful to mention a few of them, since they give a picture of the kinds of problems in which anthropologists have been and are interested and the kinds of solutions to them that have been put forward.

We may recognize three main interests of recent anthropologists in this field, although to distinguish them rigidly would in most cases be misleading; there is far more common ground than disagreement among them.

The first may be called the ideational, concerned primarily to demonstrate that religious beliefs and actions form logically coherent systems; the writers with this interest are concerned also, of course, to show the relationship between religion and social organization. This approach goes back to Radcliffe-Brown, with his classic study of the rites and myths of the Andaman Islanders (1922). Perhaps the best-known example of this approach is Evans-Pritchard's account of the religion of the Nuer (1956). This is a detailed analysis of Nuer religious beliefs, of the way in which they conceive of their God and the aspects, manifestations, or refractions of its power, of their own place in the world, and so on. Evans-Pritchard is at home with, and not frightened of, theological concepts, and he shows how Nuer religious beliefs and acts form a single, logically coherent system. He shows that this is congruent with their particular form of social organization, that, for example, the refractions of divine power are linked to the segments of their society. He presents Nuer theology as a closed system of thought, and he does not make very explicit the link between it and the social structure. It is a superb account of a theological system, but it is not essentially a sociological analysis. Other examples, which deserve fuller treatment than can be given in this necessarily brief essay, include Lienhardt's work on the Dinka (1961) and Turner's on the Ndembu (1962, 1964, and others). These are basically works that show the structure of theological systems. The relationship between these systems and the social structures of the societies in question are assumed to exist, and stated in general terms; but details of it, as part of the social process, are not shown.

There is a larger corpus of recent analyses in which the relationship is considered to be the central problem. Here the theological structure, although assumed to exist in its turn, is not regarded as being of primary importance for the anthropologist. The most solidly grounded on this viewpoint is the work by Leach on the Kachin of Burma (1954); others in which the link between religious and social structures are shown in considerable detail are by Goody on the Lodagaa (1962), Middleton on the Lugbara (1960), and the contributors to the book edited by Gluckman (1962). Middleton and Goody, in particular, make extensive use of case histories as a basis for their analyses. These are all more sociological in intent than theological, and they attempt to demonstrate the assumption of Radcliffe-Brown that ritual and myth have as a main function the cohesion and solidarity of social groupings, a hypothesis that is as a general statement beyond proof or disproof. Other works that are basically similar but in which the structural approach is not so pervasive (and which all merit discussion that cannot be given to them here), include the works of Srinivas on the Coorgs (1952), Wilson on the Nyakyusa (1957, 1959), Horton on the Kalabari (1960b), Fortes on the Tallensi (1959), Worsley on cargo cults in Melanesia (1957), Geertz on Java (1960), and Richards on the Bemba (1956). There are many other anthropological analyses that could be added to this list; I have here selected only a few of the better-known and more easily available monographs.

Lastly there is the tradition of analysis in which the role of the individual as well as the social system is regarded as being of primary interest. The writing of Malinowski already mentioned is relevant here, and later works which have clearly been influenced by him include the books of Fortune (1935), Bateson (1936), and Firth (1940), Hsu (1948), and Nadel (1954). In all of these the important but difficult problem of the individual's purpose and aims in ritual activity is explicitly recognized; the books mentioned in earlier paragraphs are not concerned with this question except by occasional implication.

Besides ritual, however it may be defined by any individual observer with reference to any particular society, the anthropologist has always been interested in myth. Throughout the development of anthropological studies of religion, myth has been regarded as a counterpart of ritual. Early evolutionist studies were much concerned with the problem of whether ritual or myth were the historically prior phenomenon: Fustel de Coulanges (1864), Tylor (1873), Smith (1889), Durkheim (1912), Frazer (1922) and others all proposed solutions to the problem. We need not concern ourselves with their work here. Since the writings of Radcliffe-Brown (1922) and Malinowski (1926), based on field research, the study of myth has been grounded on a greater sense of social reality, and four points are now generally accepted.

The first is that the historical truth or otherwise of myth, as its defining characteristic, is irrelevant; some myths may be historically or scientifically correct, others may not (although to define historical "correctness" is hardly a simple problem). Myths may be used to tell of recent historical events, and the mythical idiom used precludes any attempt to tell of them in historiographical terms. Examples could be given from many writers; here we may mention Middleton (1960) and Firth (1961). The second point is that the question of the priority of myth and ritual is an unrewarding one, mainly because it is largely a false problem. This has been shown, again, by many writers, but we may here mention the work of Leach (1954) on the Kachin, who make "statements" in both myth and ritual about the same social events and statuses. A third point is that myths have a very widespread function of providing a "charter" for a social belief, activity, institution, or relationship. This goes back particularly to the work of Malinowski (1926). A fourth point is associated especially with the work of Lévi-Strauss (1958, 1962, 1965), who has shown that myths are not mere tales, nor always mere charters for social institutions. They may also be attempts to resolve the paradoxes of human experience. Lévi-Strauss has been particularly interested in schemes of cosmological classification, a basic phenomenon in any religious system. This was seen long ago by Durkheim and Mauss in their essay on primitive classification (1903). Lévi-Strauss shows that such systems of classification are basic to all systems of religious thought, and that it is by them the people bring a sense of order and of control over their own experience of society and of an extrasocial universe. Myths and cosmologies have certain structures, which have an internal consistency and which are also related

to the basic principles of social organization of the communities concerned. Lévi-Strauss' work has been carried further by recent work of Leach (e.g. 1961).

The third main part of the "religious" is that of magic. Magic played a large part in the writings of the early evolutionist anthropologists. But in recent years there has been less interest shown in it. This has been due to the realization that it cannot easily be distinguished as a field apart from ritual, and, perhaps more important, from the fact that most interest has been expressed in the structural aspects of the religious; magic is less rewarding as an object of study from this particular viewpoint, in that it is not so directly expressive in function as is ritual. A third reason is possibly that in actuality magic is of far less importance in most societies than it was once thought to be; there are simply not the data to be observed in this field (see, however, Malinowski 1935).

There is one obvious exception to this last remark. Recent field studies (starting with Fortune 1932) have made notable analyses of witchcraft and sorcery; we may include the latter as part of magic, and the former is certainly closely related in thought and action. Witchcraft and sorcery are found, as systems of belief, in almost all societies, although they are sometimes of minimal importance. We may accept Evans-Pritchard's distinction between a witch as a person believed to be able to harm others or to influence "natural" events by the action of a mystical power within himself, and a sorcerer as a person believed to harm others by the use of material objects (Evans-Pritchard 1937). We may also accept that these are systems of belief—we need not accept the actual existence of witches, and even if there are literally sorcerers in a few cases, it is still the belief in them rather than their actuality that is of sociological significance. We may understand witchcraft and sorcery as systems of belief, that have an internal logical consistency and that have certain functions to play in the total belief system and social organization of the people who hold them.

Basically these are beliefs for explaining the occurrence of evil. This is so especially when the total religious system does not include the concept of a single deity responsible for all everyday human and extra-human events. They are found, as might be expected, in societies where close interpersonal ties provide the fundamental social structure, and their efficacy as a social mechanism depends largely on the fact that they enable the victim of evil to personalize its cause and so to cope with it by direct action.

There are three main problems in the anthropological analysis of witchcraft and sorcery. The first is whether or not these beliefs form coherent systems. Since Tylor's pioneer work on magic we have known how magical beliefs may be accepted as being true by the people who hold them, despite their lack of "scientific" foundation. And since Evans-Pritchard's work on the Azande (1937), where he so beautifully showed the logical consistency of Zande beliefs on these matters, it has been generally accepted that they everywhere form logical systems. The second problem is to analyze the variations in these beliefs from one society to another, and to explain these variations in terms of the forms of social relationships between the persons who are considered to be the agents, victims, or accusers, in cases of witchcraft and sorcery. This has been the theme of much recent work: besides Evans-Pritchard, we may mention the work of Wilson (1951), Mayer (1954), Marwick (1965), and the writers in the volume edited by Middleton and Winter (1963). An example is that of the apparent relationship between the patterns of inheritance and marital residence, on the one hand, and the sex of supposed witches and sorcerers, on the other. The third problem is that of the degree to which these beliefs, and especially the suspicions and accusations that arise from them, are functional or dysfunctional. Following Evans-Pritchard, several writers, especially Kluckhohn (1944), Nadel (1952), and Gluckman (1955) have shown that although disruptive at one level they may usually be considered cohesive at higher levels of organization, and that in addition their functional or dysfunctional significance may vary within the same social grouping at different times.

RITUAL ACTIVITIES AND STATEMENTS OF BELIEF

I have discussed, very briefly (and with the invidious omission of mention of many anthropological writings of interest and importance), some of the more obvious problems in the anthropological study of religious systems. To do so I have described some of the questions that arise in studies of ritual, myth, and magic. But as I have mentioned, this is mainly a convenient distinction made for discussion, and for ease of observation. The social reality is different. These distinctions are made primarily by the observer, not by the people themselves. In actuality the observer is confronted with two orders of social phenomena: the performance of religious activity, and the holding and statement of religious belief. Both act and belief are complementary to each other, and indeed may usually be considered as aspects of the same item of social behavior —although there are, of course, many cases of ritual without an accompanying myth and of myth without accompanying ritual.

There are clearly several general problems as to the nature and social functions of a religious system—and I stress that here I am writing from the viewpoint of method rather than of hypothesis or analysis, as such.

The first problem is that of the instrumental-expressive content of rite and belief, of where on the instrumental-expressive continuum a particular item of religious behavior may be placed. In some elements of behavior, in particular those to do with "magic," the instrumental content is primary; in others, in particular those to do with "ritual" in Leach's sense, the expressive content is primary. A task of the anthropologist is to determine, by the comparison of religious systems, what are the relevant variables that determine in each case where on this continuum the behavior lies. Another way of saying this is to pose the question asked by Gluckman (1962): What are the factors, presumably standing outside the religious system proper, that make for a greater or less degree of "ritualization" of social relations? It is obvious, in general, that preindustrial societies have a greater tendency to ritualization than have those of industrial societies. Gluckman, following Van Gennep (1909), suggests that ritual is used to separate and so to define clearly between undifferentiated and overlapping (multiplex) roles, so that ritualization becomes less necessary with increasingly secular differentiation of roles.

It is necessary also for us to realize that the degree of ritualization, and the varying weight given in any one ritual situation to the instrumental or expressive content of a set of ritual activities, may vary at different levels of organization within a single social system. In this regard it is clear that a knowledge of the main principles and aims of a society, in terms of its social organization and cohesion, is essential. In one case individual segments of a society may be in mainly competitive relations with each other. We should expect that this would be reflected in ritual activities: the objects of sacrifice would be seen as mutually antagonistic, or the antagonism between persons and groups be expressed overtly in some parts of the rites. On the other hand, greater emphasis may be placed on the need for social cohesion and amity, and the nature of the deities and the ritual acts directed toward them would reflect this. We may assume, of course, that in general such principles and aims are not necessarily in contradiction: there may be, for example, competition at the lower levels of organization of a society but the recognized need for cohesion at its higher levels.

What, then, is the unit of study and analysis, other than a total religious system, which is too large for detailed study? Turner has suggested (1964) that the smallest unit of ritual is the symbol. This is, I think, patently true when we are concerned with the expressive content of a religious act or statement. And it would seem to be valid also when we are concerned with the instrumental aspect. This aspect of religious behavior is never technical only: it has always some symbolic content. The symbols we are referring to here are used to represent certain things and events, but particularly social statuses and relationships. Religious phenomena are, from the anthropological viewpoint, to be considered as symbolic representations of social relations. They are also, of course, many other things besides. But to anthropologists this is probably their most meaningful feature. This is to say, the "religious system" comprises not things, but relations. People do not "have" ritual or myth or magic in the same sense that they "have" spears or huts (and, of course, to a social anthropologist the social significance of spears and huts lies largely in their symbolic aspects). People have social relations, of which much of the content is symbolized in ritual terms.

There are two more points to be made about the study of religious symbols. As Turner has pointed out, they have two poles. The one is ideological and refers primarily to social relations; the other is sensory, and refers primarily to individual psychological and physiological experience. The analysis of the former is the work of the anthropologist, the latter is more likely to be that of the psychoanalyst—we return here to our previous point, that of the bounds of the religious system. The second point is that in analyzing these symbols there are three main levels of interpretation needed. The first is analysis in the categories recognized by the people themselves—here we return to the study of systems of taxonomy and classification, mentioned above. The second is by the observer, who tries to comprehend the elements of the network of social relations and concepts to do with social relations that are symbolized; he makes overt what the people themselves take for granted. And third, there is a further level of analysis by the observer, who builds up an interrelation between the symbols and the network of social relations: both have structures which must be interrelated. Each element of the symbolic structure has associations with other elements, so that the networks or patterns form sub-structures in the mind of the user of the symbols. Human social experience is ever changing, and the associations between one set of experiences and others, or between one set of social relations and others, are never fixed for long. The associations can, as it were, be switched from one experience or relation to another as situations warrant it. This discussion has been carried furthest by Turner (1962, 1964).

A last and related problem is that of the degree to which a belief is held by the members of a given society. When I write that "the Lugbara believe that the dead send sickness to the living," to what extent is this statement true? Do all the Lugbara believe this, or do only a few of them, or only the elders who actually perform sacrifices to the dead? Although in general terms such a loosely worded statement is often sufficient, it is not always so. It depends largely on the purpose for which we make the statement. If we are trying to analyze a set of beliefs as a logically coherent system, then the statement is adequate, especially when we are referring to a society in which people either hold the belief and can discuss its tenets or are unsure of the details but can conceive of no other belief as possible. One of the marks of a "primitive" religion is that its adherents and their society admit no heresy. But this statement is not sufficient if we wish to show, let us say, the relationship between beliefs and practices and various groupings of persons within the community. This is particularly likely to be the case when we are studying situations of rapid and radical change, in which beliefs may be introduced by religious leaders and may be at variance with the traditionally held beliefs of the society. As Firth has pointed out (1959), we must analyze these situations most carefully when we are considering phenomena such as spirit possession and mediumship, which are almost by definition individual phenomena.

In conclusion, I have one point to make. This chapter may be criticized for being too "structural" in its approach, as an essay in somewhat extreme "social anthropology"; it may be said that the study of religion should be more eclectic, and in particular a paper on methodology should give equal weight to all "schools" of anthropology and to all ways of studying religious systems. Such a criticism would be a correct one. But that does not mean it would be valid or justified. I have mentioned at the beginning of the essay, the subject is not "religion," but "the religious system," and the two are not the same. "Religion" may be studied from many viewpoints—theological, historical, "comparative," psychological; but "the religious system" is a sociological system, an aspect of social organization, and can be studied properly only if that characteristic be accepted as a starting point.

BIBLIOGRAPHY

BATESON, G.
1936 *Naven.* Cambridge, Cambridge University Press.

BEATTIE, J.
1964 *Other cultures: aims, methods and achievements in social anthropology.* New York, Free Press of Glencoe.

DURKHEIM, E.
1903 *De quelques formes primitives de la classification.* Paris. (English translation, *Primitive classification.* M. Mauss, 1963. Cohen and West, London.)
1912 *Les formes élémentaires de la vie religieuse.* Paris. (English translation, *The elementary forms of the religious life.* London, 1915.)

EVANS-PRITCHARD, E. E.
1937 *Witchcraft, oracles and magic among the Azande.* Oxford, Clarendon Press.
1956 *Nuer religion.* Oxford, Clarendon Press.

FIRTH, R. W.
1940 *The work of the gods in Tikopia.* London, Monographs on Social Anthropology, Nos. 1 and 2, London School of Economics and Political Science.
1959 Problem and assumption in an anthropological study of religion. *Journal of the Royal Anthropological Institute* 89, 2: 129–148.
1961 *History and traditions of Tikopia.* Wellington, New Zealand, Polynesian Society. Memoir, No. 33.

FORDE, D. (ed.)
1954 *African worlds: studies in the cosmological ideas and social values of African peoples.* London, Oxford University Press.

FORTES, M.
1959 *Oedipus and Job in West African religion.* Cambridge, Cambridge University Press.

FORTUNE, R.
1932 *The sorcerers of Dobu.* London, G. Routledge & Sons, Ltd.
1935 *Manus religion.* Philadelphia, The American Philosophical Society.

FRAZER, SIR J.
1922 *The golden bough* (abridged edition). London, MacMillan.

FUSTEL DE COULANGES, N. D.
1864 *La cité antique.* Paris. (English translation, *The ancient city.* London, 1873.)

GEERTZ, C.
1960 *The religion of Java.* Glencoe, Ill., Free Press.
1966 Religion as a cultural system. In M. Banton, ed., *Anthropological approaches to the study of religion.* London, Tavistock.

GLUCKMAN, M.
1955 *Custom and conflict in Africa.* Glencoe, Ill., Free Press.
1962 (ed.) *Essays on the ritual of social relations.* Manchester, Manchester University Press.

GOODY, J.
1961 Religion and ritual: the definitional

problem. *British Journal of Sociology* 12, 2:142–164.

1962 *Death, property and the ancestors.* Stanford, Cal., Stanford University Press.

HOMANS, C. G.

1941 Anxiety and ritual: the theories of Malinowski and Radcliffe-Brown. *American Anthropologist* 43:164–172.

HORTON, R.

1960a A definition of religion, and its uses. *Journal of the Royal Anthropological Institute* 90, 2:201–226.

1960b *The gods as guests.* Lagos, Nigeria, Marina Lagos.

HSU, F. L. K.

1948 *Under the ancestors' shadow.* New York, Columbia University Press.

KLUCKHOHN, C.

1944 *Navajo witchcraft.* Boston, Beacon Press.

LEACH, E. R.

1954 *Political systems of Highland Burma.*

1961 Lévi-Strauss in the Garden of Eden. *Transactions of the New York Academy of Sciences* 23:386–396.

LÉVI-STRAUSS, C.

1958 *L'anthropologie structurale.* Paris, Plon. (English translation, *Structural anthropology.* New York, Basic Books, 1963.)

1962 *Le totemisme aujourd'hui.* Paris, Presses universitaires de France. (English translation, *Totemism.* Boston, Beacon Press, 1963.)

1965 *La pensée sauvage.* Paris, Librairie Plon. (English translation, *The savage mind.* London, Weidenfeld and Nicolson, 1966.)

LIENHARDT, R. G.

1954 Modes of thought. In E. E. Evans-Pritchard, ed., *The institutions of primitive Dinka.* Oxford, Oxford University Press.

1961 *Divinity and experience: the religion of the Dinka.* Oxford, Oxford University Press.

MALINOWSKI, B.

1926 *Myth in primitive psychology.* London, W. W. Norton.

1935 *Coral gardens and their magic.* London, Allen and Unwin.

1948 *Magic, science, and religion and other essays.* Glencoe, Ill., Free Press.

MARWICK, M.

1965 *Sorcery in its social setting: a study of the Northern Rhodesia Cewa.* Manchester, University of Manchester Press.

MAYER, P.

1954 *Witches.* Inaugural lecture delivered at Rhodes University, Grahamstown.

MIDDLETON, J.

1960 *Lugbara religion: ritual and authority* among an East African people. London, Routledge and Kegan Paul.

MIDDLETON, J., and E. H. WINTER (eds.)

1963 *Witchcraft and sorcery in East Africa.* New York, Praeger.

NADEL, S. F.

1951 *The foundations of social anthropology.* Glencoe, Ill., Free Press.

1952 Witchcraft in four African societies: an essay in comparison. *American Anthropologist* 54, 1:18–29.

1954 *Nupe religion.* Glencoe, Ill., Free Press.

OTTO, R.

1917 *Das Heilige.* Breslau, Trewendt und Gramer. (English translation, *The idea of the holy.* London, Oxford University Press, 1923.)

RADCLIFFE-BROWN, A. R.

1922 *The Andaman Islanders.* Cambridge, Cambridge University Press.

RICHARDS, A. I.

1956 *Chisungu.* London, Faber and Faber.

SMITH, W. R.

1889 *Lectures on the religion of the Semites.* New York, D. Appleton.

SPIRO, M. E.

1966 Religion: problems of definition and explanation. In M. Banton, ed., *Anthropological approaches to the study of religion.* London, Tavistock.

SRINIVAS, M. N.

1952 *Religion and society among the Coorgs.* Oxford, Clarendon Press.

TURNER, V. W.

1962 Ndembu circumcision ritual. In M. Gluckman, ed., *Essays on the ritual of social relations.* Manchester, Manchester University Press.

1964 Symbols in Ndembu ritual. In M. Gluckman, ed., *Closed systems and open minds.* Chicago, Aldine.

TYLOR, SIR E.

1873 *Primitive culture.* London, J. Murray.

VAN GENNEP, A.

1909 *Les rites de passage.* Paris, É. Nourry. (English translation, *The rites of passage.* London, Routledge and Kegan Paul, 1960.)

WILSON, M.

1951 *Good company: a study of Nyakyusa age-villages.* London, Oxford University Press.

1957 *Rituals of kinship among the Nyakyusa.* London, Oxford University Press.

1959 *Communal rituals among the Nyakyusa.* London, Oxford University Press.

WORSLEY, P.

1957 *The trumpets shall sound.* London, MacGibbon & Kee.

CHAPTER 27

The Personality as a System

DANIEL R. MILLER

In asking a psychologist to write this chapter, the editors probably made a number of assumptions about the topic: that personality is basic to some of the subjects studied by other social scientists; that interdisciplinary research is a fruitful field of endeavor in which many anthropologists are interested; that anthropologists should become familiar with some of its constructs and methods of measurement in order to use them in empirical work or to understand the findings of collaborators; and that the topic should be described by a specialist in the study of individual psychology who has worked with social scientists. Other assumptions would make it difficult to see why it is necessary to include a chapter on personality.

As a matter of fact, some writers disagree with one or more of the assumptions. Devons and Gluckman (Gluckman 1964) disagree with most of them. In their opinion, disciplines are defined in terms of their means of conceptualizing their subjects. Anthropology has one viewpoint, personality another. It would not do to mix them; studying the theories and methods of another discipline impedes the understanding of one's own. Interdisciplinary research is described as a fruitless endeavor. Since the results of two disciplines cannot be summated, each specialist has to acquire expertise in another field. Even if he does he cannot be confident that the concepts and relations established by one discipline can be transposed into those of the other.

When personality must be considered by

I am very indebted to Robert Bocock and Owen Rossan for their many helpful suggestions, and to the National Institutes of Health for the support they provided in grant MH-13082-01.

anthropologists, Devons and Gluckman advocate that they apply the "rule of accepted naïvety." This justifies the use of assumptions which ignore the complexity that other disciplines have demonstrated to exist in other aspects of the facts being studied; the assumptions may even appear distorting or false to practitioners of other disciplines. The investigator, they warn, should recognize the limits of his naïvety and not draw conclusions about events involved in that naïvety. The limits, they concede, shift with the problem. Admitting that some of the most important innovations in social theory could not have occurred had the authors followed these principles, Devons and Gluckman (Gluckman 1964:261) conclude, nevertheless, that ". . . the different social and human sciences may be different realms in whose borderlands trespass is dangerous save for the genius."

Opinions like these, which are held by many social scientists, must be considered in order to justify the inclusion of information on personality in the last half of the chapter. The first half, then, will be devoted to an examination of the arguments against interdisciplinary research, or against the systematic study of personality as part of research on social phenomena.

One argument mentioned frequently is the difficulty of becoming proficient in more than one discipline. A more fundamental one postulates that it is not meaningful to phrase relationships between constructs that are parts of systems designed to investigate different kinds of issues and to classify different kinds of data. This assumption is often broken down into a group of subsidiary ones, each phrased as incompatible, dichotomous alternatives. According to one, for example, behavior is affected primarily by the setting and not by internal dispositions, or vice versa. Hence it is proper to concentrate either on the setting or on dispositions, depending on one's predilections, but it does not make sense to study both. Finally, there is the claim that it is not possible to translate the constructs that are part of different systems so that their relationships can be examined within the same realm of discourse.

Each of these assumptions will be considered in turn. The chapter begins with the difficulties of collecting data using the methods of different disciplines, reviews the dichotomous alternatives commonly applied to the contents of different disciplines, and examines, in some detail, the difficulties of converting the terminology of one discipline into the frame of reference of another. Data are divided into the types that can be related to one another directly, and those that need to be modified or amplified in order to be conceived within the same realm of discourse. Some procedures are then suggested for making conversions, and illustrated in a table. The chapter concludes with a discussion of three components of the table that deserve more consideration than they have been getting in interdisciplinary research: they are identity, social interaction, and social networks. Throughout, it is assumed that systems for analyzing social organization and personality are so interrelated that a partiality to a particular conception of either commits one to premises which set limits on the other. Hence the chapter is devoted to the phrasing of relationships between society and personality, not solely to the personality as a system.

DIFFICULTIES OF CONDUCTING INTERDISCIPLINARY RESEARCH

For more than thirty years investigators of topics like religion, economics, social change, bureaucracy, socialization, and delinquency have tried to account for their findings by introducing psychological variables. Many have labored valiantly in this vineyard, but the results have not been impressive: much imaginative speculation, a few promising results that raise many more questions than they answer, but nothing like the systematic exploration in depth that would have justified all the effort. It is becoming apparent that analysis based on artistic speculation is not sufficient, that some kind of systematic exploration of the data of different systems is required in order to facilitate the development of clear deductive relationships among hypotheses.

Just what are the problems that face the anthropologist who aspires to do interdisciplinary research? The most immediate one is created by the division of social behavior into empires. Members of different professions seem to have agreed that the specialist in personality concentrate on events within the "subject's" skin and that the social theorist concentrate on events outside the skin. It also seems to have been agreed that neither specialist will poach on the other's territory.

Some of the obvious connections between the two realms of discourse might lead one to expect considerable cooperation between anthropologists and psychologists in instances when the subject requires the exploration of topics in both territories. There has certainly been some cooperation, but interdisciplinary research has not flourished.

The most obvious reason is that few people have the interest, time, or talent to become proficient in more than one discipline. Working on interdisciplinary problems, one sometimes feels like the circus equestrian standing astride two trotting horses not yet sufficiently trained to run in tandem and wondering when they will separate. It is hard enough to retain control of the techniques in one's own discipline without having to worry about another. If only, the anthropologist thinks, someone would produce a neat system for classifying people. The psychologist, too, has daydreams about being handed an analytic system with a few variables that provide an acceptable basis for understanding society. Each is resigned, if not eager, to analyze his own subject in all its complexity.

While it is natural to wish for a handy do-it-yourself kit that permits the analysis of personality in terms of a few common denominators, there is little doubt that investigators of interdisciplinary phenomena will have to live with the discouraging complexity inherent in psychological events for some time to come. The primary questions facing those with the courage to study such topics pertain to procedures: What are the most fruitful means of defining problems and obtaining data?

Given the difficulties of clarifying the concepts within one's own discipline, it is not surprising that most investigators concentrate primarily on that task, and, giving little thought to the premises of the other discipline, employ those of its concepts that are most convenient to the task at hand. Even well-known theorists have been known to take this cavalier attitude to the alien discipline that results in the making of assumptions about it, usually on the basis of "common sense" rather than on a careful consideration of reported empirical data.

Convinced that their system is superior to all others, some theorists have chosen the alternative of translating other systems into their own terminology. Reductionists eschew the building of bridges between disciplines, justifying their position by the claim that it is more parsimonious, and ultimately more fruitful, to phrase all variables in the terminology of a particular system (Smelser and Smelser 1963). Within disciplines, too, some men, usually those partial to a particular philosophical position, have tried to eliminate the chaos of the Tower of Babel by translating the work of other investigators into the terminology of a favored system. Behaviorists are particularly prone to reducing the seminal constructs of other theorists to a language of observable action with minimal surplus meanings. Dollard and Miller (1950) have made one of the best-known attempts to "clarify" psychoanalytic hypotheses by phrasing them in the terminology of Hullian learning theory. Most readers are impressed more by the ingenuity of such reductionistic translations than by the fruitfulness of the products.

CONTRADICTORY PROFESSIONAL VIEWPOINTS

As will be shown, the problems entailed in studying the association between personality and society are ameliorated but not eliminated by additional training. The more serious complications can be traced to the decision by members of individual professions to restrict themselves to segments of the large jigsaw puzzle represented by social behavior. The resultant confusions bring to mind the old parable of the blind men and the elephant.

Consider two specialists, one devoted to an understanding of personality and the other to an understanding of society. Starting with his commitment, each naturally assumes that his topic provides the most fundamental explanations of behavior and looks for constancies in his material. But the decision to specialize in a system of a particular type and scope defines the limits of one's contents, labels, hypotheses, and methods. If, as in the case of personality, the system is contained within an individual man, its components must refer to internal events, and constancies must be sought in underlying mechanisms such as abilities, needs, and habits which show promise of providing keys to behavior. If the system is a social organization, its components can refer to interactions among members, and the constancies sought in the rules governing their relationships. Depending on his theoretical predilections, the psychologist explores the power of techniques to clarify internal experiences, elicit characteristic physiological reactions, or measure the strengths of dispositions. The social theorist explores the power of techniques to categorize the operations of organizations and the patterns of interaction in relationships, and to explain the rules governing these recurrent patterns of behavior.

When specialists in society and in personality both investigate problems of common interest, such as the family, crime, and psychopathology, the contrasting viewpoints create disagreements about theory and the interpretation of data. Because the disagreements pertain more to faith in particular concepts than to predictions, it is not possible to resolve them in the short run by appeal to data. Five of these moot issues are now reviewed in terms of their implications for psychosocial theory. Each is phrased in the dichotomous, and possibly exaggerated, version, employed by partisans within particular disciplines. In some instances the positions are held by only a small group within the discipline, yet it is important to examine them because they question either the fruitfulness or possibility of integrating data considered within the scope of different disciplines.

Disposition Versus Setting

According to the first dichotomous position, either internal dispositions or the social setting have the most effect on behavior. It is not uncommon for one to be favored as the sole object of study and for the other to be dismissed.

The specialist in personality must assume that at least a major part of the variance in social behavior is attributable to capacities or dispositions, or he would not be able to devote his career to the study of these subjects. Once committed, he can, with little effort, find many intrapersonal traits that vary little and are also related to ways in which man behaves. He then devotes his efforts to the study of individual differences in the traits shown under various conditions by carefully selected populations.

But constancy of traits means that they remain identifiable in different settings and in relationships with many people. A psychologist who observes that a boy is teasing his sister at the dinner table is disposed to identify a need that explains this act and related ones in different settings and with different objects. If he invokes the strength of the boy's need for aggression, he may also use it to explain roughness during a football game and crankiness with parents.

If the psychologist is sufficiently sophisticated to include differences in settings as part of his research, he is likely to report, with some surprise, that a motive such as degree of guilt about aggression varies with kinds of acts and of objects that have been hurt, and with the social class and moral standards of the subject (Allinsmith 1960). The omission of such information is probably handicapping in some studies, but not in others which are confined to questions about enduring, internal traits that are important in a number of settings: How popular is a man likely to be? How good a leader will he make? How does he react to threat? The quest for enduring characteristics ultimately seems to reinforce the tendencies to think of them as the primary causes of behavior, and to play down the influence of interpersonal events such as others' expectations and the structures of social relationships.

A very different picture of man emerges when the investigator restricts his research primarily to social organization. He seeks prime movers mostly in the social setting, and considers constancies in internal dispositions of little consequence. A social theorist who observes the teasing incident will probably explain it in light of social norms and sanctions appropriate to behavior with a younger sibling of a child of given age, sex, and social class, not in terms of the strength of an underlying disposition. This observer, unlike the specialist in personality, is not likely to look for common denominators in the teasing of younger sisters and the taunting of opponents in a baseball game, since he allocates these relationships to different role-sets and expects them to be governed by different norms. He may thereby handicap himself if the behavior he studies is significantly affected by internal dispositions, but he can often afford to sacrifice the information because he is most attracted to topics that can be investigated without reference to psychological data, topics such as bureaucratization and social change, or social position and voting record. A case could be made for the inclusion, even within such studies, of data on individual variation, just on the chance that they may be significantly related to the dependent variables, but, having committed themselves to the primacy of social causation, many theorists are convinced that it is not worth their effort to measure individual differences since they are insignificant compared to the social pressures defined by constructs like social roles (Goffman 1959, Brim 1960).

Probably the most extreme statement of this viewpoint is contained in a paper by Durkheim and Mauss (1963), who attribute so much of the nature of man to socialization that it became unnecessary for them to pay any attention to psychology. Anticipating the ideas of Whorf, they propose that systems for classifying parts of society are models for the ways in which man organizes his experience. In support of this claim, they cite abundant evidence that styles of thinking vary, in a predictable manner, with the types of classification used in the society. The fact that they confuse cognitive capacities with systems of classification is less relevant to this chapter than their final conclusion: sociological analysis is sufficient to explain the sources and structures of ideas of cause and substance, various modes of reasoning and affective states. As for internal structure, they think that, following sociological analysis, ". . . all these questions so long debated by metaphysicians and psychologists, will, at last, be liberated from the tautologies in which they have languished" (Durkheim and Mauss 1963:88).

Man as Agent Versus Man as Object

Once having taken a position, the investigator is attracted to compatible ones when he has to commit himself on other issues. In their conceptions of the nature of man, members of different disciplines again tend to take bipolar positions. Consistent with the psychologist's interests in dispositions and individual differences is the assumption that people are active agents. They differ in their reactions to the same kinds of information, and can exert considerable influence on those about them. Much of the terminology of personality theory is devoted to classifying man's formidable repertory of responses. He perceives, interprets, questions, misjudges, accepts and rejects communications; he yields to, retreats from, supports, resists, and opposes social pressures; he acknowledges, expresses, suppresses, and diverts his own impulses; he conceives, plans, and carries out his own actions.

Accustomed to think of men as being the products of their social environment, the social theorist is not very interested in their unique characteristics as agents of action. On the contrary, he is more prone to assume that they are innately similar and passive, and that, like malleable pieces of clay, they are molded into their ultimate social forms by the roles assigned in the drama of life.

An example of this position may be found in Linton's discussion of psychology (1936), in which he notes that man's outstanding quality as a species is his extreme teachability. Attributing this inherent potential to the establishment of conditioned reflexes, he divides their contents into habits, ideas, and conditioned emotional responses. He goes on to list a small number of universal tendencies, such as acquisition and need for company, and emphasizes that these are acquired by means of conditioning. The total repertory of human potential, innate and acquired, is thus reduced to the four fundamental categories of conditioning, habits, ideas, and emotions. The poverty of this picture, which is more suitable to the description of passive animals in the restricted

environments of mazes than to men in communities, stands in marked contrast to the rich chapters on society, which contain many implicit assumptions about personality.

Abstract Versus Concrete Descriptions of Man

Associated with the aforementioned dichotomous viewpoints are three that point to more difficult problems in the integration of psychological and social phenomena. The disagreements are predicated on presumed incompatibilities between abstract and concrete terms for describing people, temporal and atemporal analysis, and interpersonal and intrapersonal problems.

The specialist in personality finds it necessary to employ very abstract language to convey the generality of relatively constant, internal states that are manifested when feasible. He is partial, therefore, to global labels like nurturance, endomorphic, anality, valence, and extratension. The terms are shorn of the concrete descriptions that might imply certain settings, and in line with the academic affiliations of most personality theorists, tend to have polysyllabic forms with Greco-Latin roots. Some motives, particularly interests and values, do refer to objects and actions and are less abstract than most, but even they are defined in broad categories, like the goodness of all actions labeled as honest, or an interest in all topics classified as part of aesthetics.

An interest in describing behavior as a product of the setting prompts the social theorist to employ specific references to agents, acts, objects, and goals. Sometimes he inveighs against what he thinks of as the vague, general dispositions of personality theory, which he compares invidiously with the concrete acts that he can observe and measure objectively.

Temporal Versus Atemporal

It is hard enough for the student of psychosocial topics to phrase relationships between abstract and concrete terms without having to face the additional hurdle of deciding between temporal and atemporal definitions of problems. In line with his tradition, the psychologist concentrates on differences among his subjects, which he explains in epigenetic terms: he looks for an earlier condition that accounts for the present reaction. The condition may have been one he created an hour earlier or it may have occurred during the subjects' infancy. An analysis of teasing at the dinner table inevitably entails references to the earlier conditions, such as deprivation of love or serious failure. The large literatures on trauma, psychosexual theory, learning theory, indeed the entire field of developmental psychology, testify to the prominence of the temporal dimension in psychological theories of behavior.

Atemporal analysis of the structure and function of social systems is more common in the writing of the social theorist. When accounting for particular kinds of behavior, he usually takes a contemporaneous viewpoint. When he observes teasing at the dinner table he is most likely to inquire into current details of that setting.

Interpersonal Versus Intrapersonal

Probably the most serious barrier to interdisciplinary research is created by the divergent attitudes within professions toward reciprocality in social behavior. The social theorist conceives of organizations in terms of coordinated group effort and reciprocal activities. As is often emphasized in the literature on organization, each person's rights are the responsibilities of people in reciprocal positions. It is often impossible to describe a position or a group without implying something about the features of complementary positions or groups. To convey the meaning of a supervisor's duties, one must include descriptions of the work of the employees being supervised; to convey the picture of parents' roles, one must include descriptions of the sexes and ages of the offspring. The nature of the reciprocal rights and obligations tends to be specific to the setting. The amount of deference that a son is expected to show his father, for example, may vary depending on whether they are alone or in the presence of strangers. Reciprocality is not pertinent to psychological systems which are restricted to the individual person and are designed to analyze behavior primarily in terms of generalized internal tendencies. Consequently, little attention is devoted to the interplay of partners' acts, an omission that makes most theories of personality seem solipsistic in comparison

with theories of social organization. Knowing only the strength of a disposition, such as the need for affiliation, for example, provides no hints of the specific kinds of relationships in which the person is involved; nor is it much help in interpreting acts the meaning of which is contingent on the pattern of social interaction.

RECONCILING DICHOTOMOUS ALTERNATIVES

Five pairs of ostensibly incompatible approaches have been mentioned. They include the opposition of setting and disposition as primary determinants of behavior, of man as agent and object, of temporal and atemporal analysis, of abstract and concrete descriptions of individual behavior, and of intrapersonal and interpersonal constructs. The advocates of one set of approaches tend to be in the professions devoted to the study of society, and the advocates of the other set of positions tend to be in the professions devoted to the study of personality. Investigators who assume incompatible, dichotomous alternatives are the ones who work within the confines of their own discipline or resort to reductionism. If the analysis of the conditions for phrasing interdisciplinary connections is not to be stillborn, it must be preceded by an examination of the dichotomous approaches.

Even a cursory examination of the disagreements about setting and disposition and about man as agent and object reveals little basis for conceiving them as dichotomous alternatives. Resolving the disagreements about temporal analysis, level of abstraction, and interpersonal analysis, is, however, a more complicated task.

How accurate is it to assume, as some theorists do, that social behavior is affected primarily by the interactions prescribed by the setting, and that individual variations in disposition and reaction have little significance? Or to assume, as others do, that it is the individual differences in attributes of personality that are most significant, and that what is socially prescribed can be ignored for all practical purposes? On the one hand, while roles set considerable limits on certain kinds of behavior, they permit much latitude in the initiation of activities, timing and rate of reactions, choice of partners, and the expression of values and skills.

A physician can meet his medical obligations to his patients and still develop very different relationships with them. On the other hand, despite marked individual differences, the members of a group display uniform responses to some of the predictable social pressures.

Considering setting and disposition as incompatible alternatives rules out the study of obvious interactions between constructs like identity, roles, and needs. Conformity to the pressures of one's role provides direct satisfaction of needs such as affiliativeness and affection, and is instrumental to the gratification of other needs like those for increased status and power. Acceptance by the group also affirms one's roles and self-identity. It is by living with others in his family that a father can remain clear about others' expectations, the standards they use in judging his behavior, his adequacy in meeting them, and ways in which he is pictured. It thus seems most fruitful to assume that the pressures of the setting and the traits of personality contribute to variance in behavior, both independently and in interaction with one another.

The conceptions of man as either an active, resourceful agent or a passive object that bends like a bough with every breeze are also phrased in a manner that places undue emphasis on their incompatibility. This is just as much reason to assume compatibility. Man is a willingly passive object in that he is responsive to the social pressures that mold him. He also takes advantage of the latitude they afford him to express unique personal characteristics that can have a discernible impact on his social group.

Professional bias about temporal analysis seems to be a matter of tradition. Psychologists work in a neo-Darwinian tradition which places great store in the study of individual adjustment and stages of development. The other social sciences have tended until recently to reject the temporal approach and the analysis of developmental stages, possibly because they were employed in the early part of the century to demonstrate the superiority of certain races and societies over others. Neither temporal nor atemporal analysis seems inherently more suited to either personality or society. Although they are not common, outstanding historical research has been performed on societies (Eisenstadt 1963), and outstanding contemporaneous research has been performed on personality (Lewin 1935).

RESEARCH STRATEGY

In terms of the dichotomous choices described thus far, a generic problem of interdisciplinary research is posed by the partiality of scholars in different professions to non-overlapping sets of positions. One group of psychologists and psychiatrists, and they are not necessarily the majority in their professions, explains behavior primarily in terms of generalized internal dispositions, concentrates on individual differences, studies both active and reactive psychological characteristics, is partial to abstract terms and historical explanations, and is relatively indifferent to reciprocality in social behavior and to the features of settings. Another group, consisting of some anthropologists and sociologists, explains behavior primarily by the contemporaneous analysis of social pressure, favors a concrete and interpersonal description of behavior, views men as being essentially alike and malleable, and is relatively disinterested in individual differences. Partiality to either set of positions is typically associated with a rejection of the other.

How does one answer this formidable challenge to the building of relationships between society and personality? An investigator's answer determines his strategy for designing research. The easiest solution is to accept the dichotomous definition of alternatives and to delimit research within the confines of a single discipline. If anthropologists wish to define related psychological variables, the strategies of choice are naïvety and reductionism. It is hard to work up much enthusiasm for this solution. To begin with, the linking of variables from different disciplines defines some problems that seem crucial to the understanding of society, and the social theorist is often reluctant to forget about them solely because someone has arbitrarily defined them as meaningless. Moreover the strategies have their own special deficiencies. Inkeles (1963) has shown in detail how Durkheim's naïve use of psychological concepts created fundamental distortions in his sociological thinking. As for reductionism, the painstaking translation of constructs does not seem to yield a sufficient harvest of new insights to justify the effort.

Reconciling the seeming incompatibilities between disciplines requires other strategies. The two discussed here are the blind exploration of a large group of relationships and the attempt to construct a miniature system.

When an investigator has little information about a general topic, he strives for broad coverage by selecting a considerable number of variables and analyzing the associations among the lot. Since he is seldom confident enough to make specific predictions and there are so many possibilities, he does not worry much beforehand either about interpreting significant results or about the problems he faces in understanding relationships between variables derived from different systems or defined at different levels of abstraction.

Typical of such research is a study of socialization in which this writer participated (Miller and Swanson 1958). To explore the associations between the family's position in the society and its methods of rearing children, the researchers obtained information about the techniques employed with children at different stages of development by interviewing a stratified sample of adults in the general Detroit area. The techniques chosen are included in many such studies; examples are timing and harshness of weaning, favored methods of discipline, and ages at which certain duties are assigned. Except for the categories of entrepreneur and bureaucrat, the demographic variables were also standard ones, such as social class, religion, and mobility. In the analysis of data all interrelationships were computed including many interactions.

If an investigator wants to do more than fish at random in unknown waters, he maps the region by constructing a system of interrelated principles. He begins by establishing an empirical foundation. Once he has some significant associations, he can use them to derive additional hypotheses. Consider the finding that within the middle class, the wives of entrepreneurs use harsher methods of weaning than do the wives of bureaucrats (Miller and Swanson 1958). Many possible interpretations come to mind, each of which suggests new hypotheses to be tested. Harshness is consistent with the entrepreneur's style of life; he has a clear picture of the goals he must attain to improve his status, he believes in sacrificing in the present for future gains, he is certain about his moral standards. Consistent with these views is the setting of high standards of performance for one's offspring and their enforcement by clear-cut rewards and punishments.

Questions for the reason for the association suggest new directions of research. The most obvious question pertains to the means by which the style of life associated with the father's type of employment comes to be expressed in the mother's method of weaning. Although the data provide no direct clues, there are many testable possiblities: the mother favors her method of weaning because she was talked into using it by other women in her neighborhood, was directed by her husband, read about it in articles on pediatrics, heard about it from her own mother, or is expressing her high standards of accomplishment in a particular sphere.

Another obvious question pertains to the possible connections between weaning and personalities in adulthood of the entrepreneurs and bureaucrats. No one postulates that experiences with weaning "cause" the traits of the adult's personality, but again, there is no dearth of hypotheses pertaining to weaning as an experience that sets standards, defines the nature of relationships, and develops identities. The original association between weaning and social integration suggests so rich a cluster of potential hypotheses that some method of pruning and organizing them is necessary before a circumscribed group of empirical studies can be planned. Some suggestions bearing on this process are provided by an examination of the remaining dichotomies.

CONVERSION

Temporal and atemporal, intrapersonal and interpersonal, concrete and abstract—despite the fashion in some quarters to consider each pair incompatible and to take strong positions in favor of one alternative, empirical work with social phenomena is leading many investigators to seek relationships between members of the same pairs. Their problem is to find ways of defining the connections between change in process over time and events at a particular moment in time, between the internal properties of the person and social relationships, and between abstract and concrete concepts. Common sense suggests that these must be associated. Past events must have some effects on the dynamics of current ones; individual properties like loyalty seem to affect properties of social relationships, such as stability; abstract concepts, like the category of Negro, seem related to concrete actions, like joining the Black Muslims. These all make sense, but rephrasing and amplification are required to clarify the associations between variables from different realms of discourse.

An Example of Conversion

Conceptual systems can be pictured schematically as spheres with overlapping volumes. It is only in the overlapping regions that connections can be meaningfully phrased. The characteristics of these regions must be understood in order to develop criteria for phrasing relationships. Some suggestions of the characteristics are provided by the attempt to interpret the results of a specific study (Miller and Swanson 1960), which pertained to social position, child rearing, and resolution of inner conflict. Subjects were preadolescent, white, normal boys from the middle and working classes in Detroit. Compared with children from the middle class, those from the working class were significantly more inclined to employ the defense mechanism of denial. This association was anticipated on the basis of the assumptions that hardship in the early years reinforces the defense, and is most common in families with the lowest incomes.

The results support the assumptions, but consideration of next possible steps made it obvious that the abstractness of the variables permitted many possible interpretations that had not been visualized when the research was designed. An example is provided by the concept of social class. Once a standard definition is chosen, it is a simple matter to categorize subjects. The trouble is that there are so many definitions—status, social access, power, education, income, residential area, and deference—and that each has a number of connotations. Though the intercorrelations among the criteria are high, there is also considerable independence, and it is far from an automatic task to explain the reasons for an association between social class and some other variable.

To account for the difference between boys from different social classes, one must translate the variable to one that is less abstract. *Conversion* is the term employed here for the rephrasing. Early hardship was visualized as a condition that might differ by social class and be associated with the defense. But this term, while less abstract than social class, is still too vague to clarify the reasons for denial. Hardship must, then, be converted to its more concrete manifestations. Poor diet and inadequate space constitute one form of hardship that is the lot of the lower working class. So are the anxiety of the child who is left alone for certain hours by his working mother, and the anticipation of unpredictable and harsh physical punishment, which is often administered without explanation. All of these conditions differ from those faced by the middle class, but their association with a predilection for denial is yet to be tested. It is even possible that the defense is associated with conditions other than hardship that are characteristic of the families of blue-collar workers. One is indoctrination in the use of the defense. Many mothers in the working class agree that it is good to retreat into one's daydream because the world is so difficult a place in which to live; most women in the middle class disagree strongly with this sentiment.

Problems in interpretation are also created by the abstractness with which denial is defined. In the study, the primary criterion for the defense was a misinterpretation which gave a difficulty its opposite meaning. The difficulties were all serious failures, which sons of the blue-collar workers were more inclined to deny than did the sons of white-collar workers. The common assumption about the generality of the defense having been accepted without question, it was taken for granted that the results were applicable to all cases of denial. It seems more probable, in retrospect, that each child's experiences reinforce the denial of only the kind of insoluble problems that he faces in his daily life. Possibly boys in the working class are partial not to denial in general, but only to the denial of evidence that they have failed. Boys in the middle class may also deny problems that they find hard to resolve, possible fear of physical danger or hostility to authority. Had such themes been used in the study, the trends might have been reversed.

Defining denial with respect to general content like failure or anger, is still not specific enough to permit a visualization of behavior associated with the defense. A further conversion is required. Denial of failure may be converted to optimistic aspirations based on misinterpretations of poor performance, denial of danger to counterphobic bravery.

The association between social setting and disposition requires an analysis of face-to-face interaction. In addition to forming a theoretical bridge to family and community, interaction defines the conditions under which a disposition is elicited and can be expressed legitimately. A child finds it easy to deny scholastic failure and play up his athletic accomplishments if his mother agrees with his high estimate of himself, demeans the importance of education, or claims the teachers are discriminating against him. He cannot persist in the use of the defense if she insists that he is responsible for the failure, that his athletic successes do not compensate for the poor academic performance, and that his grades raise a serious problem about his future. His use of the defense is thus contingent on the compatibilities of his values, cognitive organization of events, and actions with those of his mother. Hers reflect her other dispositions, her reactions to the setting, and, ultimately, her social background. Information about face-to-face interaction thus provides a bridge between socioeconomic status and parental behavior, on one hand, and the frequency of children's experience with failure and the inclination to misinterpret it by denial, on the other.

In planning a study, the researcher typically selects a segment from the lengthy chain derived by means of the conversions. Depending on his interests, he explores subjects like the association between denial and its evaluation by parents, or between the defense and discrepancies in the standards of parents and teachers. If he wants to concentrate on networks, he can postulate that the more frequent the contact among the members, the greater is their conformity to the group's norms, and the stronger is the conflict created by belonging in groups with contradictory ideologies. Tight networks

of family and peers can then be linked to splits in identity, and, by means of additional conversions, to the favoring of denial. The process of conversion thus provides a group of testable associations that are implicit in an initial hypothesis relating two abstract variables.

When an abstract variable is converted to a more concrete one, both can be used in an analysis of interaction. When socioeconomic status is converted to degree of hardship, it is meaningful to study the amount of denial employed within both social classes by boys exposed to few and many hardships.

Conversion of the Dimensions of Time and Abstraction

Constructs designed to analyze changes from one time to another cannot be related directly to constructs designed for purposes of atemporal description. Yet it is sometimes necessary to study such relationships. In the contemporaneous investigation of a small work group, the observer may wish to take into account the anxiety that everyone is showing about an earlier event when the foreman was humiliated by one of the workers. To do this, he must convert all concepts to the same span of time. He can make them all contemporaneous by converting the dimensions of the earlier incident to such current manifestations as the workers' aversion to mentioning the touchy topic, the split in the group's structure, or the current public identity of the foreman. The observer can also rephrase all constructs in temporal terms. The kind of conversion he chooses is dictated by the type of problem he wants to study.

When constructs differ in abstractness, it is necessary to convert one to the same level as the other in order to clarify the predicted relationship between them. The lower the common level of abstraction, the easier it is to visualize the nature of the asssociation. When constructs are parts of different systems, they must be converted to observable behavior, the region of intersection between the systems.

THE PROCESS OF CONVERSION

To achieve maximal generality of their findings, scholars are often inclined to phrase hypotheses in terms of abstract variables, such as power, flexibility, and ego strength. In some instances, these can be related to one another without modification. In others, they need to be converted to chains of interrelated, testable associations. When engaged in this procedure, the social scientist employs principles of the type listed in the previous section. The steps required in the process of conversion are the subject of the following table, which summarizes some of the variables that should be considered when one is attempting to phrase relationships between systems at different levels of abstraction.

The table illustrates the interaction of type of system with level of abstraction.[1] System varies in size, from the individual column at the left to the societal column at the right. Level of abstraction varies from observable actions in the top row to general concepts in the bottom one. The combinations of system and level of abstraction are illustrated by terms derived from various theoretical systems. Each category seems to be sufficiently different in quality from all others to merit separate considerations in the process of conversion.

Neither the columns nor the rows are viewed here as constituting separate "levels," a term that connotes the logical impossibility of relating them. Categories are

[1] Detailed versions of the columns pertaining to the individual and to the face-to-face relationships may be found in Inkeles (1963) and in Miller (1963).

assigned to levels either because the theorist subscribes to the double aspect theory, which defines them as different versions of the same event, or to the theory of emergence, which defines them as belonging to qualitatively different systems that do not intersect.

An examination of the table conveys the opposite impression: that it is easy to visualize meaningful associations among virtually all categories. An analysis of social climates in small industrial groups, for example, could easily involve the study of such diverse topics as degree of bureaucratization, the members' recurrent actions, and the integration of the community. Moreover, considerable information would be sacrificed if the interaction of system and level of abstraction were ignored and they were analyzed separately. The individual categories created by the interaction vary increasingly in complexity starting in the upper left and either descending or crossing to the right. The most extreme shifts in complexity can be traced by the diagonal path starting with individual behavior in the upper left and ending with analysis of the society in the lower right.

Only variables that permit the phrasing of contemporaneous psychosocial analysis are included in the table. Omitted are variables pertaining to subjects like physiology and factor analysis, which are not directly relevant to interdisciplinary subjects, and variables from historically oriented and devel-

Table 1   Two Types of Data Involved in Psychosocial Relationships

TYPE OF SYSTEM

LEVEL OF ABSTRACTION	Individual	Face-to-Face Relationship	Large Organization	Community and Society
Action	Recurrent responses	Sequence of acts	Organizational activities	Social programs
Cognition	Self-identity, self-esteem	Social climates	Ideology, group identity	Nationalism, community identification
Description	Cathexes	Patterns of interaction	Bureaucratization	Networks, distribution of power
Analysis	Motives, defenses	Cohesiveness, group structure	Roles, legitimacy	Integration, heterogeneity

opmental systems. The latter must be converted to contemporaneous terms when it is necessary to relate them to categories in the table.

The table lists only formal characteristics of hypotheses, not their contents. It is difficult to visualize principles pertaining to content, since its conversion is so much a matter of the researcher's theoretical preferences. There is one general principle to which he should be sensitive: the inclusion of a particular set of constructs in any category diminishes the degrees of freedom in the remaining categories.

Conversion is necessary because the average hypothesis is phrased as an association between relatively abstract variables, like social category and personality trait, that are closer to the bottom than the top rows of the table. To be theoretically fruitful, the process must include a definition of each construct and a description of its contribution to an understanding of the relationship under investigation. If he thus attributes the different behaviors of people in two social classes to memberships in contrasting kinds of networks, he defines that construct, specifies his operations, and explains its connection with socioeconomic status. Each conversion thus implies an hypothesis which determines the direction of the next step. To be clear about his reasons for anticipating the association, the investigator must make a group of conversions that enable him to phrase each variable in the language of behavior. He begins by locating the original independent and dependent variables in the proper categories of their respective columns and then converts each to the category above it, continuing one step at a time until he reaches the top row of the table. By descending the ladder of abstraction and forging a chain of associate links, he finally derives the implications for social action of the initial, abstract variables. Once the behavior is defined, it can be connected with the action in other columns. Movement between the columns is legitimate only at the row of behavioral variables, which are common to all four types of system.

THREE CATEGORIES IN THE TABLE: THEORY AND METHOD

The remainder of the chapter is devoted to identity, face-to-face interaction, and so-cial networks, three topics which, despite their relevance to many psychosocial hypotheses, have suffered an undeserved neglect in the empirical literature. In part, this is because they are vaguely defined or oversimplified. Identity, for example, is often presented as a global concept akin to ego, self, or soul, and seldom is an attempt made to differentiate the structural components. In each of the following sections, a system of classification is proposed, associations with other categories in the table are discussed, and empirical methods described.

Identity

Identity is one aspect of the more generic category of cognition, which describes the manner in which events are subjectively organized: how they are experienced, interpreted, and judged. Cognition is very much the concern of certain personality theorists and of symbolic interactionists (Stryker 1959), who assume that awareness, interpretation, evaluation, and action are indissolubly linked.

When people work in groups each participant is aware of himself, of the others, and of the group as an entity. Depending on their commitment to the enterprise, members blend their efforts to fulfill the group's purposes and to enable the various individuals to regard themselves with adequate respect. In light of their conceptions of the group's goals and activities, the members judge how well it and the various individuals are meeting their responsibilities.

As used here (Miller 1961), identity refers to a system of concepts which represent a proliferation of what is traditionally labeled as "self." Identity is inseparable from social interaction. Consider an encounter between two men. From countless previous experiences, each has developed an internal picture of communities, organizations, families, informal groups, and personal relationships. This total cognitive organization, entitled here the *internal society*, provides a frame of reference in terms of which each participant in the encounter views the other and himself, conceives of their roles, judges the adequacy of their behavior, and makes inferences about underlying personalities. Experienced as the center of the internal society is the self-identity, around which everyone organizes his life and values.

An identity is a socially labeled object defined by the pattern of attributes in terms of which a person or group is pictured. An attribute can be physical, such as color or skin; social, such as the status of one's family in the community; psychological, such as warmth. If it affects people's relationships, it is labeled, and is evaluated in line with its social consequences.

The picture that a group has of a member is his *public identity*. The ways in which a storekeeper behaves with his customers defines his identity for that public. The identity is formulated, in part, with reference to their norms. Possibly they think of him as outgoing and attractive because he participates in long, pleasant conversations. This sociability may earn him a different identity in the eyes of another public, his family, who consider him inefficient because the time he spends talking to customers keeps him from doing his other work. The same behavior thus creates different identities for two different publics, depending on their categories of meaning and of values.

As an entity, identity exists in the eye of the beholder. Because the beholder can have many vantage points, it is possible to differentiate the *objective public identity*, which is a man's pattern of traits as they actually appear to a public; *communicated public identity*, the picture conveyed by the public's behavior when they are with him; *subjective public identity*, the person's conception of his identity for a particular public; and *self-identity*, his private conception of what he is actually like. Discrepancies between different pairs are indexes of various kinds of stress. A discrepancy between objective and subjective public identities often results from the person's inability to tolerate his low status in the eyes of his public.

To explain phenomena like conflict and fluctuations in esteem, it is necessary to analyze the structure of identity, structure being defined in terms of the relationships among the parts. An identity can be diagramed as a circle that is divided by two internal concentric circles into three major regions. The innermost area is the core, or organizing part, the traits of which interact with those of the other regions. The core is experienced as the "truest, strongest, deepest self" (James 1890), and includes traits that affect one's reactions in most settings.

Examples are sexual identity, body image, and feelings of control and responsibility.

Outside the core, the circle is divided into a number of segments, each representing a *subidentity*. The subidentity is a cluster of traits that a person manifests in particular types of relationships. With colleagues, he is an engineer; with his children he is a father; with his wife he is a husband. Roles and categories create the conditions under which subidentities are defined. A role defines the expectations others have about the ways a man in a particular social position or category, should behave; the subidentity defines the unique cluster of traits he alone manifests when he is in the role.

Each subidentity is divided into the persona (Jung 1953) or presented self (Goffman 1959), which is at the peripheral part of the segment of subidentity in the diagram, and the private self, which is in the next arc of the segment. The persona is the portion of identity that each person is most inclined to display in public. The remainder is kept private to avoid interference with ongoing activities or exposure of undesirable attributes. Both presented and private portions have conscious and unconscious components.

The measurement of different structures requires a common set of categories. A group conceives of its members' identities in terms of *dimensions*. These are sets of alternative traits having common cores of meaning and constituting linear scales. Each trait has a *location* on at least one dimension, usually more.

Associated with each dimension of traits is a parallel dimension of values. The more significant a dimension is to the group's goals, the more *salient* it is: the more effect fluctuations in the trait are likely to have on one's status. Dimensions are often divided into segments, each defining a group of traits with roughly similar values. Segments may be labeled as ideal or acceptable or undesirable, depending on their significance.

The value assigned to a trait weighted by the salience of the dimension determines the height of a person's standing on a scale of esteem. The addition of results for all dimensions of a public subidentity produces his level of public esteem. Parallel processes are used to compute the levels of *communicated public esteem, subjective public esteem,* and *self-esteem.*

The level of a man's *objective public esteem* can have considerable consequences for the rewards and punishments he obtains from others and for the influence he can exert over them (Goffman 1959). Because he ". . . experiences himself . . . not directly but . . . from the particular standpoint of other individual members of the same social group . . ." (Cooley 1922), his level of *self-esteem* is often influenced considerably by *communicated public esteem* and *subjective public esteem.* By providing a basis for regulating his behavior, the internalization of the group's norms as part of the awareness of self and society also enables each person to act autonomously in accordance with the necessities of the social system (Hallowell 1955, Wallace 1956).

The analysis of the subjective and objective public identities, and of the self-identity with respect to realization of potential, yields four additional versions of each. A person and his public conceive of an *actual* identity, which is what he is like at the present time; a *potential* identity, which is what he can realistically hope to attain if he works at this goal; an *inadequate* or bad identity, which is what he is like when he is at his worst; and an *ideal* identity, which consists of a "set of to-be-strived-for but forever not-quite attainable ideal goals for the self" (Erikson 1956).

Potential realization of a man's pattern of accomplishment is analyzed by computing discrepancies: between actual and potential subidentities, which indicates how realistic he is in setting his aspirations; between inadequate and actual identities, which indicate how much he is inclined to backslide.

Ideally, the associations between columns are analyzed in terms of commensurate dimensions. Because identities, roles, and personality have in common traits and values, all of which are conceived in terms of the same or similar dimensions, it is possible to devise scales that have the same meaning for all three. A man is expected to show a certain degree of warmth in his role as husband; for example, he tries to meet that standard in his presented self, his family locates him on the dimension in defining his public identity, and he has conscious and unconscious impressions of his warmth, and experiences conflict because of discrepancies in its various manifestations. All can be located on the same scale.

If one just wants to learn about the traits required for leadership in a corporation, why does one have to complicate a simple problem by research on identity? There is no way of knowing beforehand whether the relationship really is as simple as it seems. Identity is often so interrelated with role and personality that two groups of people with the same compatibility between role and personality may differ in their capacity to perform a job because members of one group use high standards to judge themselves and members of the other use low standards.

Empirical work on identity has revealed its relevance to a variety of psychosocial phenomena (Miller 1961). In the literatures on socialization, perception, motivation, and pathology, the self is mentioned with increasing frequency in connection with such topics as identification, morality, conformity, reference groups, guilt, mourning, cultural discontinuities in adolescence and old age, depersonalization and splitting in compulsion and hysteria.

Once the structure of identity is clarified, its components suggest many methods of measurement. Objective and subjective public identities and the presented self-identity can be appraised by means of rating scales, which require subjects to locate the actual, worst, and ideal selves of themselves and others on given dimensions, and to rate the salience. The dimensions can be defined on the basis of earlier interviews or by means of Kelly's REP Test (1955). Cross-cultural use of scales has shown that they can produce valid results with subjects from other societies, psychiatric patients, and preadolescents.

When scales cannot be used, information about identity can be collected by tabulation or rating of behavior, the open-ended interview, or subjective observation. Private and unconscious regions of subidentity are best studied by means of projective tests. Verbal techniques, such as the completion of stories (Miller and Swanson 1960) and interviews in depth about assigned topics (Berman and Miller 1967) elicit many facts that subjects are unable or unwilling to report on objective forms. Such methods achieve the intended purposes only if codes are carefully standardized.

Face-to-Face Interaction

Interrelationships among the identities of participants represent a common focus in the study of social interaction. Others picture it in terms of the exchange of resources, compatibilities of roles or needs, and systems of communication. Although there is little consensus about problems, investigators often select similar populations and study the same kinds of problems. Usually this is the contemporaneous analysis of voluntary relationships, such as marriage and friendship. Less attention is paid to development, to involuntary asssociations such as those between patients in hospitals, or to relationships between people differing in status.

Degree and sources of stability are frequent objects of study. There are many definitions of stability; its measurement usually entails some index of adequacy with which people in a relationship fulfill their responsibilities in the face of disruptive events. The more adequate the performance, the greater is the capacity to attain common goals. Some of the common criteria of stability are productivity, efficiency in meeting qualitative standards, performance during stress, and the participants' desire to continue their association. Among the sources of stability are compatibility, obligations of roles, and mutually accepted barriers to the performance of proscribed activities.

There are three seemingly contradictory conceptions of compatibility. Some writers (Izard 1960) attribute it to the similarity of partners' traits: friends enjoy going to concerts together when both are interested in music. Other writers (Winch 1958) think of compatibility in terms of oppositeness: a pair like to work together when one is high and the other low in dominance. Still other writers (Beisser 1953) stress complementarity on different dimensions: the traits fit well if one partner likes to show off and the other is inclined to be deferential. In descriptions of the second and third positions, it is often postulated that compatibility depends on the gratifications each person obtains from the other's actions.

All three conceptions seem applicable to some aspects of mutual endeavor. In the sexual relationship, husband and wife are compatible if they are similar in the strength of the sexual drive, opposite in degree of dominance, and complementary in terms of initiative and passivity. In a mutually contingent system (Jones and Thibaut 1958), the three kinds of compatibility can affect stability. In general, similarity is necessary for recruitment to voluntary relationships; oppositeness or complementarity are necessary to the performance of tasks requiring asymmetry in authority.

Compatibility indicates the goodness of fit between psychological characteristics, some of which are particularly pertinent to the structure of groups. A *valence* is an inclination to engage in a specific activity with a particular person: a man likes to go walking with his wife. An *aversion* is a disinclination to engage in the activity with the person: he does not like to play bridge with her. An *interference* is an inclination to engage in an act that prevents the other person from obtaining a particular goal. A *bond,* or mutual valence, is the motivational building block of the voluntary relationship. A *conflict,* or mutual interference, is the most potent source of instability. A *divergence* is a mutual aversion, and an *incongruence* is a discrepancy between one partner's valence and the other's aversion or interference.

All these terms are cognitive and are specific to the agents, behaviors, objects, affects, and goals of motivational states with given strengths. The terms are also interpersonal, so they are readily related to some of the structural characteristics of relationships. Stability is enhanced by valences, bonds, and mutual aversions, and diminished by aversions, incongruences, and conflicts. In other words, valences and bonds enhance the gratifications obtained from shared activities; aversions, incongruences, and conflicts diminish gratifications, and create a reluctance to engage in the shared activities. Such hypotheses are based on the premises that the attainment of each person's goals is contingent on the traits of his partners, and that the products of mutual action either bind the participants together or prompt them to separate.

Flexibility, another attribute of the social relationship, refers to its capacity to retain its primary attributes when external conditions require changes in its functions. Sometimes the changes are necessitated by entering another stage of development, such as childbirth or retirement in the family. An inflexible system that remains stable while the social environment is constant, may dissolve in the face of pressures created by a new stage of development.

Flexibility varies with the participants' control of their identities and the permeability of barriers to activities with people outside the system. The more conscious a man is of his private subidentities and bonds, the more control he has over them when they must be altered in adjustment to new social situations. The more permeable the barriers, the easier it is to initiate new activities in relationships when old activities are eliminated and old bonds are dissolved. Other conditions affecting flexibility are ranges of social skills and of alternative activities, legitimacy of bonds, number of bonds with people inside and outside the system.

The measurement of flexibility requires the identification of the kinds of change required of the system. These are most often defined by the shifts in stages of development. In the family, the couple have to alter their identities when completing courtship and beginning married life, or when child rearing is completed and the children have left home. Stages in the life cycle of working relationships are not labeled as consistently as stages of marriage, probably because there are more variations in the structure, but their development is usually as clear. Workers are recruited, serve apprenticeship, are assigned to teams, and progress through a sequence of stages that culminates in retirement.

Roles and cognitive reactions, such as valences, divergences, and interferences, can be studied by means of rating scales, open-ended interviews, and projective tests. Research on flexibility is more difficult. If an experimental technique is used, the members of a group are given tasks which are solved in one way and then conditions are changed so that the group's methods are no longer effective. If the group is flexible, they change their method. It is also possible to determine if they know that their performance has deteriorated and what has gone wrong. In a more naturalistic approach, a study is made of a group's reactions to various crises or reactions to changes in stages of development.

Networks

When it is necessary to concretize abstract concepts containing implications about social access and influence, the network often proves a fruitful avenue of conversion to behavior. In contrast with an organized group, whose members have common aims and independent roles, a network is typically a looser association of people only some of whom have contact with one another (Barnes 1954). A man may know many people, for example, who see each other only when they visit him. Although the apparent aims of a network are often as vague as social expression, they may be a potent force in socialization and social control when they are close-knit and cut across many formal organizations. A study of socialization in the university, in which the writer has been participating, reveals that the girls are recruited to various residences because of differences in social values and backgrounds, and that the residences are the sites of networks with subcultures that profoundly affect the members' future lives. Information that girls are in a particular residence permits the prediction, with considerable confidence, of such characteristics as the social class of the families, whether or not they are from a minority group, the kind of subjects in which they are likely to specialize, the kind of men to whom they are attracted, the places where they dine, their taste in music and films, and the voluntary groups they are likely to join.

The literature on networks, other than references in descriptive accounts, is very small, and there are no published systems of classifications to which one can refer. A promising typology, which divides networks into tight-knit and loose-knit, is proposed by Bott (1957). In a network that is maximally tight-knit, all members see one another regularly and no pair needs to be brought together by a third person. In a diagram of a tight-knit network with seven members, lines representing regular associations connect each member with the other six, so there can be as many as forty-two avenues of communication. In a loose-knit network, the average member meets most others when he visits the one or two whom he sees regularly. A diagram of a loose-knit network with seven members can contain as few as six lines.

In a study of social networks that link the family to various parts of the community the writer has been using a number of additional categories, such as recruitment, qualifications for membership, differences in the statuses of members, activities, ideology, weight as a reference group, splits in the network, attitudes to outgroups, sanctions, and overlaps in networks and in ideologies of different networks. This information can be obtained by a questionnaire. The data permit the analysis of such topics as overlaps in husband's and wife's networks, and in the ideologies of their networks. When tight-knit networks show a maximal overlap in membership, as sometimes happens in small, isolated communities, each person sees everyone else frequently. If members have the same social status, the mutual support can be very strong, but, as noted by Bott (1957), since even minor deviations in behavior become known to the total community, it is very difficult for anyone to change. Providing they are heavily weighted as reference groups and are not split, overlapping, tight-knit networks are tradition-oriented, while non-overlapping, loose-knit networks permit social change.

SUMMARY

Conceptions of society and personality are so interdependent that both must be considered in the planning of psychosocial research. Certain members of different professions divide the source of variance of social behavior into pairs of variables. One member of each pair is favored either because it is conceived as having exclusive relevance to the subject being studied or because the presumed incompatibility of alternatives necessitates a choice. There appears to be no incompatibility between the analysis of behavior in terms of general psychological dispositions and the social setting, or between conceptions of man as agent and as object. There is some difficulty in integrating the three other dichotomies—temporal and atemporal analysis, abstract and concrete definitions, and concepts derived from social and psychological systems—but again there is no reason to be restricted to any member of the pair. An integration of temporal and atemporal variables requires that they be converted to the same time span. An integration of abstractly defined social and psychological variables requires that they be converted to the terminology of observable action, which is common to the two systems. As an aid in the making of conversions a table was provided which lists some of the primary categories created by the interaction between level of abstraction and systems varying in size from the individual to the society. Methods were then suggested for classifying and measuring components of three categories in the table: identity, face-to-face interaction, and social networks.

BIBLIOGRAPHY

ALLINSMITH, W.
  1960 The learning of maoral standards. In D. R. Miller and G. E. Swanson, eds., *Inner conflict and defense*. New York, Holt, Rinehart and Winston.

BARNES, J. A.
  1954 Class and committees in a Norwegian island parish. *Human Relations* 7:39–58.

BEISSER, P. T., *et al.*
  1953 *Classification of disorganized families*. New York, Community Research Associates.

BERMAN, E., and D. R. MILLER
  1967 The matching of mates. In S. Feshback and R. Jessor, eds., Cognition, personality and clinical psychology, a symposium held at the University of Colorado. San Francisco, Jossey-Bass.

BOTT, E.
  1957 *Family and social network*. London, Tavistock.

BRIM, O. G.
  1960 Personality development as role learning. In I. Iscoe and H. Stevenson, eds., *Personality development in children*. Austin, University of Texas Press.

COOLEY, C. H.
  1922 *Human nature and social order*. New York, Scribner's.

DEVONS, E., and M. GLUCKMAN
  1964 Conclusion: modes and consequences of limiting a field of study. In M. Gluckman, ed., *Closed systems and open minds*. London, Oliver and Boyd.

DOLLARD, J., and N. E. MILLER
  1950 *Personality and psychotherapy*. New York, McGraw-Hill.

DURKHEIM, E., and E. MAUSS
1963 *Primitive classification*. London, Cohen and West.

EISENSTADT, S. N.
1963 *The political systems of empires*. New York, Free Press.

ERIKSON, E. H.
1956 The problem of ego identity. *Journal of the American Psychoanalytic Association* 4:56–121.

GOFFMAN, E.
1959 *The presentation of self in everyday life*. Garden City, N.Y., Doubleday.

HALLOWELL, A. I.
1955 *Culture and experience*. Philadelphia, University of Pennsylvania Press.

INKELES, A.
1963 Sociology and psychology. In S. Koch, ed., *Psychology: a study of science*. New York, McGraw-Hill.

IZARD, C. E.
1960 Personality similarity and friendship. *Journal of Abnormal Social Psychology* 61:47–51.

JAMES, W.
1890 *The principles of psychology*, Vol. 1. New York, Holt, Rinehart and Winston.

JONES, E. E., and J. W. THIBAUT
1958 Interaction goals as bases of inference in interpersonal perception. In R. Taguiri and L. Petrullo, eds., *Person, perception and interpersonal behavior*. Stanford, Stanford University Press.

JUNG, C. G.
1953 *The development of personality*. New York, Pantheon.

KELLY, G. A.
1955 *The psychology of personal constructs*. New York, Norton.

LEWIN, K.
1935 *A dynamic theory of personality*. New York, McGraw-Hill.

LINTON, R.
1936 *The study of man*. New York, Appleton-Century.

MILLER, D. R.
1961 Personality and social interaction. In *Studying personality cross-culturally*. Evanston, Ill., Row, Peterson.
1963 The study of social relationships. In S. Koch, ed., *Psychology: a study of science*. New York, McGraw-Hill.

MILLER, D. R., and G. E. SWANSON
1958 *The changing American parent*. New York, Wiley.
1960 *Inner conflict and defense*. New York, Holt, Rinehart and Winston.

SMELSER, N. J., and W. T. SMELSER
1963 *Personality and social systems*. New York, Wiley.

STRYKER, S.
1959 Symbolic interaction as an approach to family research. *Marriage and Family Living* 21:111–119.

WALLACE, A. F. C.
1956 Revitalization movements. *American Anthropologist* 58:264–281.

WINCH, R. F.
1958 *Mate selection: a study of complementary needs*. New York, Harper.

CHAPTER 28

Methodology in the Study of Literate Civilizations

FRANCIS L. K. HSU

The place of literate civilizations has for long been anomalous in the world of anthropology. On the one hand, there are anthropologists who think that students of literate civilizations have contributed practically nothing to theory and they are, therefore, prepared to ignore it (Beals and Hoijer 1965:731–732). On the other hand, a considerable number of anthropologists have devoted all or most of their research energies to literate civilizations. There are today quite a few anthropologists or prospective ones whose areas of specialization are Japan, India, or even France (see Hsu 1968a:19–21). World War II gave a special impetus to Western anthropologists in the study of literate civilizations, due to the need for understanding the principal enemies —hence Japan and Germany were objects of a flurry of anthropological literature.

However, so far the two lines of inquiry have not met. In fact there has been little attempt in that direction. Furthermore, the science of anthropology appears today to be at a major crossroad. After it had outgrown its earlier antiquarianism, the anthropology of yesterday continued to produce works which were very long on generalization and very short on methodology. In the process of the discipline's coming of age and under the critical pressure of sciences that consider themselves more advanced, many of us have tended to swing to the other extreme, hiding our ineptitude behind a smoke screen of scientific respectability and overemphasizing localized details at the expense of a wider perspective. Thus we have today many tribal, village, and community studies but little to show in the way of an overall synthesis—

by nation, by region, or in terms of mankind as a whole. The older concepts, like culture area and the sketchy manner in which they deal with human behavior, are now practically out of date except in small pockets of academic resistance. The study of national character, an approach central to the understanding of large literate societies, seems to be losing adherents every year. Since there has been nothing positive to fill the vacuum, some anthropologists have simply devoted themselves to the minutiae (Hoebel 1967), hence we have the new subdiscipline, ethnoscience.

Some studies of the latter type have yielded interesting data, as have certain British anthropologists before them who devoted their entire creative energies to describing and analyzing one or two small tribes. The British scholars have given us infinitely rich details and insights into the life of the small groups of humans about which they write. But no matter what theoretical points they make, their central (and sometimes only) illustrations seem to be drawn from the one tribe or two tribes they have intimately studied. Some of them seem not only to avoid comparison between societies but seem consciously to believe that there should be no such comparison. It is perhaps not unfair to suggest that theirs is another form of ethnocentrism—not that of their mother cultures but that of the societies they have studied. The newer practitioners of ethnoscience seem to be even more restricted. They do not generalize about whole societies at all.

As a result many an anthropologist who concentrates on the single village or confines himself to minutiae pleads that we must wait for more localized or village studies before making any overall generalizations about any society, region, or people. They dwell on the complexity of each society, on the variations in details, and in the case of India or China seem to think that all generalizations about Hindu India are a long, long way off.

These scholars have not reflected on two facts. First, there are about 500,000 villages in India. Even if we can expect fifty village studies a year, it would take ten centuries to complete ten per cent of Indian villages, by which time the earlier monographs would likely need some revision before they could be used for synthesis with the later products. The task is simply impossible.

The second fact that these scholars need to reflect upon is that, whether they like it or not, they and their colleagues, even if they have done only as much as one village study in India or China, will be called upon to teach courses on "Indian Culture," "Chinese Family," "Indian Political Institutions," "Chinese Village Life," etc., or from time to time, either for scientific or practical reasons, they will be forced to react to one or more cultures as wholes. Is it not a matter of scientific necessity for such scholars to become a little better prepared by looking into the connections between their own villages and the wider society?

What we must do with reference to large literate societies is twofold. On the one hand we need the localized work in the form of village studies or ethnoscience. On the other hand we need researches of a broader nature, aimed at understanding each literate society as a whole. The second line of inquiry does not negate or replace the first; the two will complement each other. Overall synthesis is impossible without localized details. But localized materials are made more meaningful when they are set in the wider perspective of overall synthesis. The hallmark of anthropology is the study of societies or cultures as wholes and that hallmark should not be forsaken when we extend our attention from the non-literate to the literate world.

For a more comprehensive statement of my approach and methodology the reader is referred to my book *The Study of Literate Civilizations* (Hsu 1968a). In the present paper I shall confine myself to a few basic considerations.[1]

In the first place, we should have some traditional anthropological data from participant-observation in villages, tribes, or small geographical areas, supplemented by other data gathered with an eye on sampling procedures and quantitative aspects. Both sources are important. The former may include case studies, biographies and autobiographies, life cycles, conflicts and their resolution, aside from the usual patterns of life and work in the local community in general. The latter may include questionnaires (especially administered among college students), newspaper and magazine materials, police files and reports, as well as certain projective instruments such as the TAT or a modified form of it.[2]

In the second place, the main effort should be concentrated neither on the overall idea, pure and simple, nor on the localized reality of any particular time and place, but on the interaction between the ideal and reality and on the significance of both in terms of the whole. For example, in the case of India, the sacred books and most of the literary creations such as myths, folk tales, dramas, novels, etc., probably express aspects of the ideal more than reality. The contemporary facts garnered in different parts of the country, either by the sociological technique of topical inquiry or by the anthropological technique of community study, naturally approximate reality more than the ideal. It is imperative that we attempt to ascertain the link between them in any literate society.

Some students of Hindu folklore or history may be interested, for example, in what gods or goddesses worshiped today are survivals of which gods or goddesses in the ancient lores, or in the marriage of Draupadi to the five Pahdava brothers reported in the epic Mahabharata, which is an instance of tribal polyandry prevailing at the time. Other students of caste in India are interested in tracing how the Gujara group, through a

[1] This is a revised version of "Data and Methodology," Chapter II of Hsu 1963:12–26.
[2] I find the TAT highly useful. But for studying the cultural orientation of a society rather than the psychological make-up of an individual I find it is better to use only a few cards administered in a group situation. (For a fuller explanation see Hsu 1963:Annex, 263–311).

continuous process of spread and absorption, came to include diverse castes of different statuses (from Kshatriyas to near Untouchables) and in diverse localities (from Maharashtra to Delhi to Punjab). None of these particularistic researchers may be aware of any or all of the others. But the student of the culture of a large literate society must be primarily oriented toward the comparison of data, wherever they are found, in terms of the similarity or differences in underlying patterns or ideas. Dumont and Pocock, in their summary of and comment on Bouglé's and Hocart's theories on caste, which I dealt with elsewhere (Hsu 1963: 123–137), define the position succinctly: "Here texts are used not as historical evidence with which it is presumed that the present must accord but rather as offering certain systems of ideas with which the present may be compared."

It is the relationship between the texts or historical data and the present events which is basic for the understanding of every society, unless we assume little or no integrative process in each social system. Before one succumbs to the feeling that the Hindu sacred books have little relationship to the life of the common people, he should reflect for a moment on the following well-known fact in Western society. The actual behavior of the nominally Christian peoples may not be very Christian; but there are few scholars or laymen who will insist that the Bible and other religious writings emanating from it have no relationship with the common people born in Christianity. Illiteracy on the part of the common people of India has been no bar to knowledge of the ancient heritage. The Vedas and other sacred literature are constantly recited and explained by traveling *kathaks* (storytellers) and holy men all over India, while the epics are dramatized and told in a thousand ways to all types of audiences.

Likewise, the Confucian precepts in China were certainly not all original creations of the sage himself. Some of the mores and customs he endorsed and propounded must have existed long before him in some parts of China, but after his teachings were widely known they, in turn, affected and reshaped the mores and customs of the Chinese as a whole. This process is essentially similar to what folklorists describe as "circular flow,"

which requires "time to simmer . . . to integrate . . . to rework" (Foster 1953: 159–173).

Third, it is important that sequences of facts and events, from historical to modern, are compared in an ahistorical and genetic frame of reference. The numerous characteristics which distinguish one biological organism from another are usually absent in early life. In fact the embryos of frogs and human beings in their earliest stages look remarkably similar. At birth the differences between a human being and a chimpanzee are also negligible. But the emergence of physical or behavioral characteristics which distinguish some biological organisms from others require, in some instances, a few months and in other instances scores of years. Hence a science of living things must be based on the characteristics of adults, although those of infants are also of interest.

The characteristics which distinguish one society from another develop as a result of interaction among forces within the same society or as a result of mutual pressures between different societies. Sometimes these characteristics emerge quickly, but more often they do not do so for a long time— not infrequently centuries. The French Revolution cannot be understood sociologically if we study only the facts pertaining to the reign of Louis XVI, for the simple reason that it was not only related to a wider European development which sprang from seeds sown in the region of Louis XVI and earlier, but also to the Magna Carta, the Enlightenment philosophies, the Industrial Revolution and the American Revolution. In turn the forces underlying the revolutions in the West had a great deal to do with the Chinese revolutions, the Meiji Restoration of Japan, and the independence movements in India and other colonies. It is, therefore, methodologically sound to relate the French Revolution to the Magna Carta, even though the two events occurred nearly six centuries apart, and to relate the American Revolution to the Chinese and Japanese developments even though they occurred at different times and on different continents. For this reason social scientists can speak of the repetitive social or cultural process; processes which are repetitive through time are not the specific events and personalities but the patterns and ideas behind the events, or the roles and thought patterns molding or motivating the individuals.

Fourth, regional variations within the same society must be examined for their unitary features in terms of the society as a whole. Too often scholars have merely seen the trees for the forest, or even individual trees but never the forest, and critcize others for wanting to know something about the forest at all.

We have to realize that scientific anthropology consists of more than the exact counting of heads. Internal variation is to be assumed in any human group, however small, for the capacity to vary is one of the basic characteristics of man. In fact, no two individuals are alike. But not all individual peculiarities are relevant to his life as an active member of his society. Since the science of man is not one of individual differences we must deal with individuals in terms of larger or smaller collectivities which must, by definition, ignore some of the factors making for variation within each collectivity.

Of even greater importance here is the fact that anthropology is not the study of mere social and cultural life. It must ultimately unravel the ideas about such life which make it meaningful. The reason that Ruth Benedict gave us a masterly piece of work on the Japan she had never seen (though had she seen it a few of her emphases might have been corrected) was that she never for a moment ceased dealing with the ideas in terms in which the Japanese see their lives and life.

Anthropology brings to social science *not* merely scientific rigor on a small scale, for that it shares with sociology or psychology. What it really brings is a scientific framework for studying the sweep of ideas that makes a people memorable, that enlightens our way of life (or any other), and that brings richness to human perception of the universe. To say that anthropology cannot study anything beyond the range permitted by a single field job is to confuse anthropology with one of its component fields— ethnography. Ethnography has its place.

Unless we want to reduce a civilization like that of Hindu India or China to no more than a collection of local details we must be interested in the broader ideas which are the backbone of each major way of life affecting hundreds of millions of people. We go wherever we are likely to find such ideas in theory and as they are expressed in concrete acts: from the mouths of illiterate peasants or tribesmen in villages and back hills; from the testimony of merchant princes or Brahman priests in commercial centers and sacred places; from the great writings of ancient sages and modern pandits; and from the music, drama, and scenes in temple grounds no less than from ceremonials, pilgrimages, or public adorations to holy men. If the illiterate peasant of India can tell us the benefit of *sila* (stone object of worship) and the spiritual relationship between *devadasis* (temple ladies) and the gods, such information is important. But if the sophisticated Hindu intellectual can tell us that all *sadhus* (holy men) are fakes, or Hinduism is basically the same as Christianity, he is equally worth listening to. Ideas of a people can and must be studied on every social level. While genealogical tables and a knowledge of mother-in-law avoidance may be of help in our attempt to understand people's ideas, we should certainly not be tied to them. On the contrary, unless anthropologists can raise their sights and go beyond regional variation or community studies, anthropology will never be fit for anything but the study of small and isolated societies. It is simply impossible to study a subject of broad scope without employing a method suited to it.

Indeed, the pitfall of trying to fathom a broad subject with myopic techniques can be illustrated by all too many examples. In Oscar Lewis's work on religion in a village of north India, the author begins by questioning Morris Opler's statement that:

The fact that the highest goal of the Hindu is to eliminate earthly concerns, desires, and personal existence itself introduces a large element of asceticism, intellectualism, detachment, and withdrawal into Hindu religious philosophy. In no other country have so many men renounced the world, and in no other place is there so much fasting and mortification of the flesh. The world is considered transitory and an appearance. . . . (1958)

Lewis presents "some quantitative data relating to the religious views of the people of Rampur," secured by a questionnaire filled in by twenty-five individuals, with no mention of the method of their selection. He modestly states that although his study "cannot be considered definitive, it does set forth a method of investigation which could be applied elsewhere for further research." But what are the results? On the basis of such returns Lewis concludes, after a discussion of the differences between Brahmans and Jats, etc., that "the evidence from Rampur does not seem to support Opler's generalizations."

That Lewis's conclusion may not even apply at the village level has been shown by Morris Opler in a subsequent article (Opler 1959). My relatively brief personal sojourns in villages in several scattered parts of the subcontinent and information from many villagers in cities also convince me that Lewis's conclusion on the subject is questionable. But there is no doubt that Lewis received answers to his questionnaires from twenty-five persons in Rampur; there is no doubt that his conclusion is based on the nature of the returns; and there is no doubt, too, that the facts gathered, such as they are, are exact. However, what would we think of a study of the place of Christianity in medieval Europe or modern America based on one set of questionnaire returns from twenty-five individuals living in Belle-Île-en-Terre, Brittany, or Orchardville, Illinois? If such a study should reveal that the inhabitants of one of these localities knew little about the recorded doings of Jesus and his disciples, would our theologians, priests, mission board members, and even ordinary citizens who only occasionally see the inside of a church concede the unimportance of Christianity in medieval Europe or contemporary America?

A somewhat different pitfall awaits relatively intensive community studies such as that by Bernard S. Cohn and others of the village of Senapur in Uttar Pradesh. Here we have rich details in a series of articles by Cohn, and by Opler and Singh, of the castes, the law ways, the pasts, and the impact of Western forces and colonialism. Yet when some generalizations are called for on the interrelationship between modernization and the attachments to pasts, Cohn explains his inability to reconcile them in the following terms:

In a changing social situation we expect to find a transitory attachment to the past, often in the *irrational* form of a nativistic movement. It is significant that the anthropological literature on this sort of attachment to a revitalization of the past has focused on the more spectacular messianic cults such as the Ghost Dance, cargo cults, and the Mau Mau. But we have not yet analysed the complex interaction of modernization and traditionalization, such as is found in the Arya Samaj, or the traditionalization of Chamar religious life as a result of literacy and urban experience. The apparent conflicting values, institutions, and behavior found in India seem to our minds *rationally incompatible. We cannot build their coexistence into our theories of change;* we can only describe them. Perhaps it is characteristic of members of modern societies to believe that consistency in social and intellectual life is a prerequisite to efficient functioning of either a social system or a theory. (Cohn 1961: 248–249; italics mine)

The words "irrational" and "rationally incompatible" are obvious expressions of Cohn's Western bias which, unless defined precisely, will befuddle any scientific analysis, for what looks rational to an American scholar may not look rational to his Hindu counterpart, though they may both possess college degrees in Western terms. But of more immediate concern here is Cohn's admitted inability or refusal to build any theory because of inconsistencies, or incompatibilities in his data. The function of a theory or hypothesis is precisely to connect data which may be widely scattered, divergent, and incompatible. There would be no need for theory if all the data were uniformly consistent. The incompatibilities in the data may be more apparent than real. Or they may be more real than apparent. If they are the former, they should be reconciled; if they are the latter, they may possibly be linked. A single phenomenon may be correlated with many different manifestations. The role of the scientist is to find the intermediary steps which link divergent phenomena, even complete opposites.

In the present instance the incompatibilities Cohn finds impossible to incorporate into one theory can easily be so encompassed if we examine them in a wider perspective and introduce the concepts of status-seeking and time lag. In a wider perspective the low-caste Chamars of Senapur move toward greater traditionalization as a result of modernizing forces such as literacy and urban experience because they, like their low-caste brethren elsewhere, wish to raise their status wherever and whenever they feel they can do something about it. The means they resort to in this status-raising effort is strongly determined by their model of high status.

They will move toward greater traditionalization as a means (whether it is forbidding widow remarriage or creation of a fictitious Brahmanic past) as long as the modernizing forces have stimulated their aspirations but have not made any inroads on their model of high status. The Thakurs also wish to raise their status, or at least to maintain it. But being way above the Chamars on the caste hierarchy, economically better off and more powerful, the Thakurs have had more opportunity for contact with modernizing forces, and their model of high status has already been affected by some of the modernizing forces including those originating from Western missionaries and churches.

Yet a group can no more completely abandon its past than can an individual. In seeking a modernized model of high status the Thakurs have to use the old as well as the new. As time rolls on and as modernizing forces expand their spheres of influence, the attainable model of high status for the low-caste Chamars may well merge into some of the modernized features currently associated with the Thakur model. When that happens, we can expect the Chamars, too, to move toward status symbols which are mixtures of modernization and traditionalization.

These processes have been and are being repeated, with more or less intensity, in various societies in transition, but will be difficult to see until we raise our sights from the localized particulars.

These points, though they make up a research procedure drastically different from the modern anthropological emphasis on localized details, are closely related to the notion (first expressly stated by Robert Redfield) of continuous interaction between a Great Tradition as abstracted and systematized by the specialist literati, mainly in urban centers, and the Little Traditions of little village communities. The essential emphasis is not on the detailed data in any one time or place but the interrelatedness of different varieties of data to each other in terms of some central orientation which seems to represent the whole. The scientific universe is the whole of Hindu society instead of a single village. Therefore, while the bulk of the data in support of my hypothesis on Hindu family, clan, and caste (Hsu 1963) chiefly applies to those caste Hindus who

are the relatively more active (in literary, religious, economic, political areas) elements of Indian society, and is not concerned with the Sudras and the Untouchables except where specifically noted, it must in the long run approximate the permanent aspects of the Hindu way of life through the processes of Sanskritization (Srinivas 1952:30), and Parochialization and Universalization (Marriott 1955:197–201). Sanskritization is the process whereby a low caste has adopted the customs, rites, and beliefs of the higher-caste Brahmans in order to rise to a higher position. Parochialization supplements the process of Sanskritization. It refers to the fact that in its downward spread, the Great Tradition is obstructed or transformed by the indigenous Little Tradition. Universalization is the process whereby the materials of a Little Tradition are carried forward to form a relatively more articulate and refined indigenous civilization.

Redfield's conception of a continuous interaction between a Great Tradition and a Little Tradition is well expressed by Singer in his preliminary report on his Madras study:

> But if such a unit (a village or a cluster of villages) is to disclose the cultural links with the past and with other regions, it cannot be regarded as an isolate but must be considered rather as one convenient point of entry to the total civilization. . . . Different field studies may of course choose different points of entry—in terms of size, character, location—but the interest in comparing their results will not be to count them as instances for statistical generalization but rather to trace the actual lines of communication with one another and with the past. The general description of this organization in its most embracing spatial and temporal reach will then be a description of the culture pattern of the total civilization. (Singer 1955: 34)

However, while this line of thought helps us to ascertain the specific ways in which the Great and the Little Traditions interact, or how each is modified by the other, it does not lead us to an understanding of the overall pattern of Hindu society or any other. We are closer to some of the mechanisms as to how the parts of a given literate culture integrate themselves, but we are not clear as to the whole. For the latter purpose we must pay heed to a final methodological necessity: systematic and explicit comparison. I wish to emphasize the words "systematic" and "explicit" here, for casual or implicit comparison seems to be done all the time by most anthropologists, even among those who assiduously avoid literate civilizations (Hsu 1968a:79–82). But systematic and explicit comparison has not been central in anthropological thinking at all. What I propose is that the ethnography of every society and culture must of necessity be set in the comparative framework of another society and culture. In this way the significance of every major ethnographic observation of a qualitative nature will be easier to see in terms of continua, instead of in terms of absolutes. This will provide cross-cultural generalizations with possibly firmer bases, since such generalizations will then enjoy a closer accord with reality.

I firmly believe in the importance of the comparative approach, whether in studying single institutions or whole societies and cultures. Lacking precise measurements in most areas, our qualitative descriptions of facts often suffer from extreme ambiguity, thus rendering generalizations based on them to be of doubtful value. How permissive must child-rearing practices of a people be to be designated as permissive? How oppressive must a political regime be to merit the adjective "oppressive"? The terms "individualistic," "freedom-loving," "superstitious," "authoritarian," "industrious," "status-conscious," and scores of others including such commonplaces as "intensive" or "centralized" have been applied to many peoples in many parts of the earth, but one will be extremely hard put to find any reliable criteria for any of them in anthropological writings. A sure remedy to this situation is to be found in the comparative approach, so that instead of saying "A is oppressive," we can say "A is more oppressive than B but less oppressive than C." In this way, while still wanting in exactitude in the strictly quantitative sense, our statements at least gain in relative perspective.

The other advantage of the comparative approach is that it will enable us to avoid generalizations based on data from a single example or society. The importance of this is so basic to science, and so well propounded by scholars from Durkheim to MacIver, that it is hard to see why so many scholars have continued to ignore it. The least it will do is to reduce the chances for the anthropologist to replace one sort of ethnocentrism by another, a point already mentioned before. But it will certainly make ethnographic data across societies more usable for building general theories, and help to stop the futile argument on the part of some that anthropology is not a science. Anthropology will not become a science if we consciously stay away from even the elements of scientific method.

In suggesting that ethnographic observations and generalizations be set in a comparative framework, I am aware of certain possible objections. One of these is: How can every beginning anthropologist put his observations in a comparative framework when he has just studied one society and culture?

My response to this objection is simple and direct. Every prospective anthropologist is a product and active member of a society and its culture. He knows its language and its ways well, and is its participant observer for many years. This rich source of ethnographic data has so far been ignored except in a few rare instances. And the anthropologist's first field work among any other people should stimulate him at every turn to structure what information he already possesses of his own society and its culture. Every anthropologist can do this, and will do some of it unconsciously anyway even if he is opposed to it. The difference between doing this consciously and systematically and doing it unconsciously and casually is that the latter runs a greater danger of misleading himself and his readers. Psychoanalysis has long been built on the assumption that to understand his clients' problems the analyst must understand his own first. Why not anthropology?

There are roughly three stages that a student may have to go through as an anthropologist. At first every prospective anthropologist must do some intensive work on some aspect of his own society and culture (or at least read about it with some intensity) as part of his training. Secondly, when he goes to work in a society and culture not his own he must systematically and consciously compare what he observes and records in the field with what he has learned of his own society and culture. At the third stage, when he has re-entered his own society and culture, he should examine them in the light of his intensive field experience elsewhere.

It is therefore obvious that every anthropologist has ready access to at least two societies and cultures, and every ethnographical effort can be made to do double duty. We will undoubtedly have a richer store of ethnography than what we have at present.[3]

The procedure outlined here is drastically different from a view expressed by Singer:

Some anthropologists advised me before I went to India not to spend much time preparing myself by studying the history of Indian civilization or reading the Indian epics and other texts. A field study, they said, has a strict obligation to record only those realities which the field worker himself can observe within a limited area and what is within the living memory of the people he interviews. Historical and literary research would only clutter the mind with preoccupations, and if done at all, should be done after the field work is finished. Although I did not take this advice the course of the study would seem to justify it: I was compelled to limit my attention to a particular group of people within a region restricted enough to be brought under a single conspectus of interrelations. I had to set aside generic conceptual categories about total civilizations in favor of concrete units of observation like cultural performances, and even the analysis of these cultural performances runs in terms of constituent factors like cultural media institutions, cultural specialists and cultural media which in part, at least, are amenable to the direct observation and interview of the field worker. (Singer 1955:34)

In my view, this notion contains several fallacies. As we have already seen, no field worker can go to the field with an entirely open mind. Indeed, his mind is cluttered with assumptions from his own cultural background and/or those from his scientific training. His scientific training is supposed to help reduce the biases of his particular cultural background which have "cluttered up" his mind and fill it with an outlook which is commensurate with the assumptions and methods of modern science. But however hard the field worker tries, the chances are that he is not likely to be entirely free from all the hidden assumptions of his own cultural background. How, then, can he be worse off as a field worker if he has some of his Western assumptions at least checked a little, before he goes to the field, by some thinking about the history and literature of the people he intends to study?

Furthermore, if the notion of "cluttering up" the mind were true, then scholars of India would no longer be able to study Hindu civilization, and their counterparts of

[3] For the use of the comparative approach focused on one aspect of a literate society see Hsu 1952; on entire societies see Hsu 1953, 1963, and 1968b.

the United States would similarly be disqualified from studying American life. This would just about write off the bulk of our published works on most literate societies. I doubt if the anthropologists who hold the "cluttering up" of the mind notion are prepared to grant this. Fortunately they do not have to. The primary objective of the anthropologist is to ascertain the psychocultural commitment of the people he hopes to understand and to communicate something of his understanding to others. My view is that his understanding of the society and culture, and his explanation of that understanding to others, will be greatly enriched and much more scientific if he also has an understanding of his own society and culture. This augmented anthropological training should enable him to perceive different ways of life, by acquiring as full a knowledge of each society and culture as possible but, in his academic exercises, reducing emotional commitment to any of them, as far as the results of his research are concerned.

Another problem is the possibility of cultural shock, which causes some newcomers to a strange society and its culture to develop a neurotic and devastating reaction to it. There is less possibility of this among trained anthropologists than among others, but this is probably because anthropologists are better prepared. Traditionally preparation means not only knowing something about the diet and etiquette of the people to be studied, but also gaining as much familiarity as possible with their historical and literacy background. Our proposal here that this traditional preparation of anthropology be augmented by the student's systematic and conscious understanding of his own society and culture will lessen even further the possibility of cultural shock.

The student will not only have been prepared for possible differences and emotional conflicts when he goes to the field, but also will have gained some idea concerning the roots of his reactions.

Two final objections must be dealt with. One is that a study of the pattern of life of a large literate society as a whole is bound to be more superficial than a study of a single village or community—that it fails, for one thing, to take into consideration all internal variations within the same culture. We already discussed the fallacy of equating sound anthropology with the counting of heads. But superficiality depends upon our level of abstraction. And intensity is a matter of degree, even in the case of localized community studies.

Understandably most anthropological field studies leave something to be desired in this regard. We do not have to speak of vast African societies like the Yoruba or Baganda, which number millions. Cora DuBois obtained life histories of eight somewhat misfit Alores and thirty-seven Rorschach protocols of others in a population of less than 600; John Honigmann registered among the Kaska Indians not more than six brief life histories and only twenty-eight Rorschach protocols among a population of 175; while Oscar Lewis's restudy of Tepoztlán, carried out with the aid of a number of students and over a protracted period involving many visits, refers to Rorschach protocols on one hundred individuals and intensive data on seven families out of a village population of 4,000. Many anthropological field reports are far less explicit in quantitative terms, even though the need for quantitative evaluation was stressed by individual anthropologists long ago.

These facts are pointed out not to justify the present state of affairs but to underscore the lack of any clear criterion upon which a judgment of the intensity of anthropological field studies can be made. Lacking such a criterion, the one that we presently employ to evaluate the worth of a given field study is primarily qualitative: the fullness of the descriptive material, the extent of internal consistency, the training of the field worker, the conditions under which his field work was carried out, and in general, how his results compare with other results from a similar area. Some reports may provide more details than others but there is no reason to suppose that details as such are equivalent to intensity.

The final objection is a trite but recurring one. This is that such and such a work is defective because its author is selective in presenting his data—that is, they are arranged to suit his purposes. Students of large literate societies, since they must cover ground much more vast than those of most non-literate societies, are bound to be even more selective in their inclusion of data. My response to this objection is, of course, that no scientific study can use all data without discrimination. Even a descriptive monograph of a single village must perforce be restricted in its coverage. A complete coverage of all facts about all Hindu India or any other large literate society is an impossibility. The only practical criteria for judging the soundness of the selection are these: (1) Do the selected data make sense in terms of the thesis they are supposed to support? (2) Are there significant or obvious facts of comparable order which contradict them but which have been left out? The significance of the first criterion is obvious. Upon the second criterion rests the distinction between demonstrating a thesis and illustrating a thesis. In demonstrating a thesis the adequacy of the work is measured not only by how well it is supported by the data assembled but also by how well it can stand up against other data which contradict it. The critics of any such work must do more than merely voicing dissatisfaction on the general ground that the facts are selected. It is up to them to advance other facts, show how their new facts are contradictory to the thesis demonstrated, or help lead to an alternative and better hypothesis.

BIBLIOGRAPHY

BEALS, RALPH L., and HARRY HOIJER
 1965 *An introduction to anthropology.* New York, Macmillan.
BOUGLÉ, C.
 1908 *Essais sur le régime des castes.* Paris, *Travaux de l'annee sociologique.* F. Alcan.
COHN, BERNARD S.
 1961 The past of an Indian village. In *Comparative Studies in Society and History,* II, No. 3:241–249.
DUMONT, LOUIS, and D. POCOCK
 1958 *Contributions of Indian sociology.* No. 2, an irregular publication. Paris and The Hague, Mouton.
FOSTER, GEORGE M.
 1953 What is fold culture? *American Anthropologist* 55:159–173.

HOCART, A. C.

1950 *Caste, a comparative study*. London, Methuen.

HOEBEL, E. ADAMSON

1967 Anthropological perspectives on national character. *Annals of the American Academy of Political and Social Science* 370 (March):1–7.

HSU, FRANCIS L. K.

1952 *Religion, science and human crises*. London, Routledge and Kegan Paul.

1953 *Americans and Chinese: Two Ways of Life*. New York, Schuman.

1963 *Clan, caste and club*. New York, Van Nostrand.

1968a *The study of literate civilizations*. New York, Holt, Rinehart and Winston.

1968b Japanese kinship and iemoto. New chapter for Japanese translation of *Clan, Caste and Club*. Tokyo, Baifukan.

LEWIS, OSCAR

1958 *Village life in northern India*. Urbana, University of Illinois Press.

MARRIOTT, MCKIM

1955 Little communities in an *indigenous* civilization. In McKim Marriott, ed., *Village India*. Memoir No. 83, pp. 197–201. Washington, D.C.: American Anthropological Association.

OPLER, MORRIS

1959 The place of religion in a north Indian village. *Southwestern Journal of Anthropology* 15:3:219–226.

OPLER, MORRIS, and RUDRA DATT SINGH

1948 The division of labor in an Indian village. In Carleton S. Coon, ed., *A Reader in General Anthropology*. New York, Holt.

SINGER, MILTON

1955 The cultural pattern of Indian civilization: a preliminary report of a methodological study. *Far Eastern Quarterly* 15:1:34

SRINIVAS, M. N.

1952 *Religion and society among the Coorgs of South India*. Oxford, Oxford University Press.

CHAPTER 29

Method and Theory in Ethnoscience or Ethnoepistemology

OSWALD WERNER and JOANN FENTON

INTRODUCTION AND AIMS

'Ethnoscience' has recently become a fashionable word among anthropologists and other social scientists. Some of us pursue ethnoscience with the fervor of a 'true believer'; for others it is anathema. The aim of this paper is, in part, to highlight the relationship ethnoscience establishes between linguistics and more traditional ethnography.

The term 'ethnoscience' is used in a multiplicity of senses. The word itself is derived from the Greek *ethnos* 'nation' and the Latin *scientia* 'knowledge' (and related senses). We therefore conceive of ethnoscience as the ethnography and/or ethnology of knowledge, or as descriptive epistemology.[1]

This work was in part supported by a grant from the NIMH:MH-10940–3 and is based on insights gained during previous support, especially Werner's NSF Post-Doctoral Fellowship and MH-11912–01. Our joint authorship worked out as follows: whereas Oswald Werner bears most of the responsibility for Sections 1 and 2, Joann Fenton researched and wrote most of part 3. We would like to acknowledge valuable criticisms and suggestions made by Ethel Albert, P. J. Bohannan, R. Cohen, R. Naroll and D. Sade from the Department of Anthropology at Northwestern University and D. Hymes from the University of Pennsylvania. They are, of course, not responsible for any of the views expressed in this paper.
[1] In discussing knowledge we should keep in mind that what I know is knowledge. I know the culture in which I am living. I use this knowledge as a means of getting by. A Navajo's knowledge may be knowledge because he knows his culture and I do not. But much of his knowledge is to me his belief, because I doubt the validity of his knowledge. If my doubts are great I call his beliefs qua knowledge superstitions, or silly beliefs. Some of us believe— because we doubt our knowledge—that the virgin birth is a superstition, but we know others who believe in it. This belief of the believer is more than knowledge

Because all cultural knowledge is a composite of many individual competences, the description of knowledge is that of a potentially omniscient native speaker-hearer, who knows all of his culture (see p. 540).

Ethnoscience at present is largely a method. It is applicable by any anthropologist who finds it to his advantage to discover the meanings of native terms.

The power of the method can be illustrated anecdotally: Kluckhohn (1944) has reported his difficulties in eliciting Navajo witchcraft information. His eliciting was largely in English. By asking only questions which have been constructed and judged appropriate by native speakers of Navajo, we have collected witchcraft information without too much difficulty. Although we do not know at present why the Navajo questions are appropriate, or why they are better than English queries, it appears that there are culturally appropriate ways of asking for information concerning witchcraft without at the same time implying that the informant is a witch. Although Navajos have on occasion refused to answer questions about witchcraft, we have *never* encountered the stereotyped response Kluckhohn reports: "Why do you ask *me!*"

Ethnoscience method is applicable to the ethnographer's own culture. This permits validation of field techniques and theoretical claims publicly in one's native language.

because it is given by supernatural sanction in *our* culture. Even those who believe it to be a superstition will grant that for many it is a belief, not a superstition. We are more cavalier with the Navajo or most non-Occidentals. In short, the scale of knowledge, belief, and superstition is full of ethnocentric booby traps. Knowledge as used here includes all three: knowledge, belief, and superstition (silly belief).

Schneider's (1964:302) endorsement of Goodenough (1964) stresses the value of an intelligent informant for eliciting kinship knowledge. We think Schneider misses the important point that Goodenough does his analysis of the Yankee kinship system in English, presents it in English to an audience of native speakers of English all familiar with the Yankee kinship system from childhood. Goodenough's statements are vulnerable to an extent unheard of in the analysis of the kinship system of the Usurufa. The principle may be generalized: All ethnoscience universal claims in method and theory must be demonstrably applicable to English or the language of the investigator. It is most instructive for ethnographers to find themselves at times in the informant's role.

The above considerations make Schneider's remarks even more pertinent to ethnoscience:

> It is of great methodological significance to consider the time and work which went into the many interviews with many different people, the collection of genealogies, accounts of weddings and funerals and family squabbles, visiting patterns, residence patterns and religious affiliation and so forth on which I think I am basing my ethnographic statement, and then to see how closely they agree with Goodenough, whose statements are based on work with a single intelligent informant. (Schneider 1964:302)

Critiques of ethnoscience fall generally into three classes:

(1) "Ethnoscience does not deal with what I am interested in." Since it would be absurd to require all anthropologists to 'do' ethnoscience exclusively, the only possible answer is to encourage all anthropologists to find their own theories, methodologies, and field techniques.

(2) "Ethnoscience does not explain everything (does not give us, or has yet to give us, a 'complete' [sic] ethnography)." There does not exist a scientific theory that explains everything. The better theories usually apply to an explicit relatively narrowly circumscribed range of phenomena: Air resistance is excluded from classical considerations of gravity and the theory of relativity does not account for telekinesis. On more ethnographic grounds, a 'complete' ethnography is quite unthinkable. Few ethnographies do justice to native terminology or to native terminological systems; in some, transcriptions of native terms are so inadequate that they cannot be re-elicited.

(3) "It is impossible to elicit knowledge," or "eliciting knowledge is unscientific." The charge is unanswerable. This point of view and the point of view pursued in this paper are not reconcilable.

Any framework that promises either speed, ease or accuracy, in however a narrow segment of culture, deserves to be taken seriously and is worthy of further development.

We present ethnoscience in three parts. The first section deals with basic assumptions and is an attempt to demonstrate that ethnoscience is the link between ethnography and linguistic theory. The second section deals with the formal nature of the better-known lexical and/or semantic fields. Preoccupation with 'fields' and their formal characterization are central to ethnoscience. Readers unfamiliar with elementary set theory may want to skip the second section. We repeat informally some of the formal aspects of taxonomies that are relevant to eliciting in the last section. The third and last deals with the field techniques of ethnoscience.

BASIC ASSUMPTIONS

ETHNOGRAPHIC ETHNOSCIENCE includes such sub-areas as ethnoanatomy, ethnobotany, . . . , ethnozoology, ETHNOLOGIC ETHNOSCIENCE is a theoretical science which is comparative in the sense that it seeks to formulate universal laws of knowledge. It is META-EPISTEMOLOGY because it deals with formal and substantive constraints of particular descriptions in ethnographic ethnoscience.

The best we can hope for at present is a SYSTEMATIZED ETHNOSCIENCE—a step in the direction of SYSTEMATIC ETHNOSCIENCE, a universal theory of knowledge.[2]

Systematization implies preoccupation with *ad hoc* methodology rather than theoretically motivated methodology. Without theory, methodology is blind, and no matter how rigorous, it will not lead to better theory. Development of theory is imperative.

Ethnoscience deals with the Ideational Or-

[2] The problem (and/or impossibility) of a universal theory of knowledge is indirectly, but most suggestively, discussed by Bronowski (1966). We are reasonably certain that his arguments based on the work of Church, Goedel, and Tarski apply to the problem. How it can be demonstrated specifically that this is indeed the case is beyond our competence and sophistication.

der (in the sense of Goodenough 1964), primarily with cultural knowledge rather than cultural behavior; observation is used predominantly to generate further questions about the informant's knowledge. Ethnoscience description attempts to specify explicitly what a native speaker knows about his culture. This is to be sharply distinguished from what he can casually report of such knowledge. At some point, description of knowledge and description of behavior must fit without contradiction. However, questions of this theoretical fit are beyond the scope of this paper.[3]

Ethnoscience need not necessarily be restricted to 'culture through language,' although this paper deals exclusively with linguistic ethnoscience. Since it is linguistic, it should be congruent with linguistic theory. Our goal is a loose integration with transformational generative grammar.

Explicit Culture Which Is Language

Linguistic ethnographic ethnoscience deals with that part of cultural knowledge which is accessible through the language of the informants. The nonverbal implicit parts of a culture (e.g., kinesics) are considered neither unimportant nor unnecessary; they are simply outside of the self-imposed limitations. Since very large parts of any culture are transmitted through language, this restriction is not too limiting.

Language Which Is a Set of Sentences

A language may be defined as a potentially infinite set of sentences. Sentences are either grammatical or ungrammatical. Ungrammatical sentences differ among themselves in the degree of their ungrammaticality or deviance from theoretical well-formedness.

Recent investigations into the nature of grammars demand that grammars should generate grammatical *and* ungrammatical

[3] The description of knowledge as discussed in this paper falls generally in the category of a 'competence theory.' Theories of behavior are seen as theories concerning the use of cultural knowledge. We demand that theories of cultural knowledge and theories of cultural behavior (including theories dealing with the acquisition of such knowledge) do not contradict each other but form a unified system. This does not mean that cultural knowledge and cultural behavior will necessarily fit consistently. The above-mentioned theories should account for such inconsistencies.

sentences (e.g., Lakoff 1966). The ungrammatical sentences are assigned an index of deviance. This provision is important for semantic investigations. Part of human linguistic competence is the ability to interpret sentences which are slightly ungrammatical, for example, much of ordinary conversation or the speech of foreigners speaking English.

Sentences Which Are Culturally Appropriate

Semantically interpretable sentences contain a subset which is culturally appropriate, and another which is not appropriate (in some contexts). It is only necessary that the two sets be separable in principle.[4] The sentence, "I walked Sigmund home" is grammatically interpretable, and culturally appropriate. "I walked Sigmund" is culturally appropriate only if Sigmund is a dog. "I ambulated Sigmund" is appropriate if I am a nurse and Sigmund is recovering from an operation. If Sigmund is a dog, the sentence is culturally bizarre (inappropriate). Similarly, "Bobby is a square" is appropriate only if square designates certain qualities of Bobby, a man or a boy, but is inappropriate if it applies to some square on the piece of paper in front of me which I decided to call Bobby. A 'play suit' is a suit to play in, but a snowsuit is to be used in snow and not to snow in. Neither is it made out of snow as 'asbestos suit' would imply. Culturally inappropriate sentences may be either shocking, e.g., "I admired Mary's clitorectomy" (which may, however, be appropriate in aboriginal northern Australia), or amusing, e.g., "Don't let your snowsuit melt." The large gray area of sentences with undecidable status is interesting to the extent that the nature of the gray area needs to be examined.

Restriction of the investigation to sentences does not preclude the investigation of 'folk taxonomies' or folk classifications. Taxonomies can be interpreted as chains of sentences: 'A cherry tree is a fruit tree,' 'A fruit tree is a tree,' 'A tree is a plant,' . . . Such linked

[4] Dell Hymes (personal communication) suggests that culturally appropriate sentences intersect rather than are a subset of semantically appropriate sentences, as we here suggest. The relationship of the two sets is certainly complex and it may be premature to assert the relationship one way or the other. The most important aspect at present is the fact that at least in principle the two sets are separable.

sentences define a special lexical field (see pp. 543–566). Perhaps the most important lexical fields are taxonomies, but by far not the only ones. Most other lexical fields remain to be discovered.

Since ethnoscience theory is concerned with the characterization of lexical and/or semantic fields, it is concerned with a systematization of lexicography, or the systematization of (ethnologic) dictionaries.

Sentences Which Are Produced by an Ideal Speaker-Hearer

Ethnoscience, in common with standard ethnography and linguistics, is potentially exhaustive (holistic). Exhaustiveness of description is a principle which, in practice, may be approximated to some degree.

The knowledge of informants varies with their intelligence, interest, opportunity, and with the facts of the social division of labor. No informant has a total knowledge of his culture. A full description approaching a 'complete' description must be a composite picture of the cultural competence of many informants. Such a complex picture is conceivable only as the supra-individual record of an ideal 'omniscient' native speaker-hearer.

Culture may be viewed as the common element which all members share, or the set

theoretical INTERSECTION of individual competences. In ethnographic ethnoscience, as in traditional lexicography, the complementary view is taken: the description is an attempt to characterize the set theoretical UNION of all individual competences. These two definitions of the range of culture can be pictured as follows: 1, 2, . . . i, . . . n are competences elicitable from individual members of a culture.

The first crude approximation of a description of Anglo-American culture in terms of linguistic ethnographic ethnoscience is *Webster's Unabridged Dictionary*. The dictionary is 'omniscient' in that it contains many entries which are outside the competence of most individual speakers. The approximation could be improved by merging the *Unabridged* with technical dictionaries; further, by merging the result with the *Encyclopedia Britannica*. In the end, the ideal 'omniscient' native hearer-speaker emerges as a supra-individual who has read, remembered and mastered at least the contents of the entire Library of Congress. Even then, much of simple everyday knowledge would have been left out.[5]

The enormity of such a description is over-

[5] This includes much of the synchronization and distribution of individual competences (Roberts *et al.* 1963), 'scheduling' (Hockett 1964), 'plans' (Werner 1966), and 'rules of use' (Hymes, personal communication).

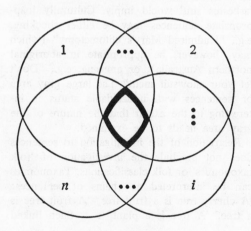

FIGURE 1 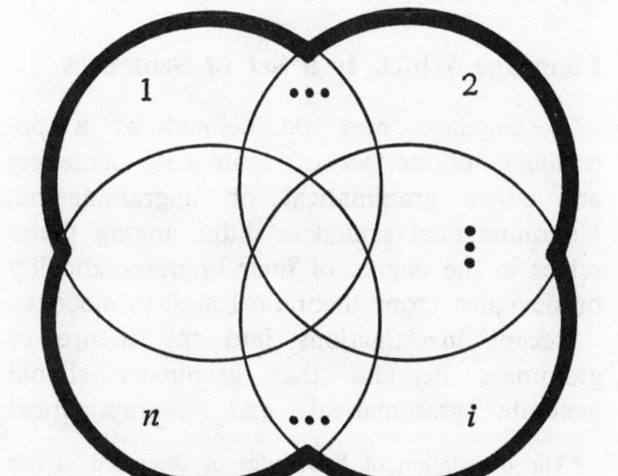   FIGURE 2

Figure 1. The range of culture as defined by the competences common to all members (intersection of individual competences).
Figure 2. The range of culture as defined by an ideal 'omniscient' native speaker-hearer (union of individual competences).

whelming. In simpler cultures, the task may be smaller by several orders of magnitude; nevertheless, the bulk and complexity of the knowledge of Homo sapiens anywhere is enormous.

One possible solution may be concentration on the properties of lexical-semantic fields rather than lexical domains; in other words, concern for the ORGANIZATION or the structure of knowledge rather than the SUBSTANTIVE EXTENT or more detailed (sub-) lists of knowledge.

Limiting the analysis to the highest, or near highest, level terms embedded in folk taxonomies may be another possible method for a systematic reduction of bulk and complexity.[6]

Sentences Which Are Judged Relevant by the Informant

Traditionally in ethnography, the judgment of what is relevant and what is not is a decision left, in the end, to the ethnographer. In ethnographic ethnoscience, however, the decision concerning importance, relevance, and appropriateness is left to the informant. This assertion needs to be put into proper perspective.

Ethnography: First-Level Anthropological Theory

Ethnography is considered by some anthropologists to be 'purely' descriptive; that is, some kind of *a priori* description is possible without theoretical orientation (e.g., Hoebel 1966:8, Keesing 1960:5, Honigmann 1959:5, Herskovits 1955:8). However, a theoretical statement is a proposition, or, better, a set of propositions, which makes certain claims about nature; in the case of anthropology, about the nature of culture. A proposition, or assertion, in an ethnography, is theoretical vis-à-vis a particular culture (e.g., Goodenough 1957; Frake 1962; Hymes 1962, 1964b:15; Bohannan 1963:11; Conklin 1964:25–26). It is an empirical hypothesis that the members who subscribe to this culture will act and react in asserted and, therefore, predicted manner (see Chapter 2 by Cohen in this volume).

The first problem of traditional ethnography is that FALSIFICATION OF ETHNOGRAPHIC HYPOTHESES IS EXTREMELY DIFFICULT: if

later restudies are made, the variable of time is not held constant. If synchronic restudies are carried out, the geographical (including social geography) variables are not constant. In order to evaluate two contradictory ethnographic assertions, we must undertake an analysis of the ethnographers' concepts and their internal consistency (e.g., the Goodenough-Fisher controversy). If one is inconsistent, the decision is in favor of the consistent. If both are consistent, or if consistency cannot be ascertained, we have to go to indirect criteria, such as the length of stay in the field, or the control of the native language, etc. (Naroll 1962).

Ethnology: Meta-Theory or the Theory of Culture

Regardless of their theoretical notions, anthropologists seem, by and large, to agree that, in a minimal sense, 'culture is like the table of contents of a book' (Kroeber 1948:5).[7] The most comprehensive and explicit 'table of contents' is Murdock's "Outline of Culture Materials." Most anthropologists are further interested in 'structure,' 'function,' 'integration,' 'system,' the 'configurations,' etc., or some theory of culture. In specific ethnographies, the ethnographer must make up much of his theory of his people as he goes, and in so doing, he makes more or less overt his theory of culture. Like all theory building, this is an intuitive and artistic intertwining of two sets of perception, the ethnographer's and the informant's, which makes every ethnography a unique document. A good ethnography is an aesthetic experience. This is also true of many good theories in other sciences, but our meta-theories, or theories of culture, are not sufficiently explicit or general to command professional consensus.

The second problem of traditional ethnography is that ETHNOGRAPHERS OPERATE WITH A WEAKLY DEVELOPED UNIVERSAL META-THEORY, OR THEORY OF CULTURE.

Michael Polanyi's (1956:4) analogy be-

[6] This may be somewhat analogous to Bohannan's "relatively few" 'key terms' (1963:11–12) of a culture.

[7] "Kluckhohn (1953) examined the content of ninety ethnographic reports published [in English, O.W.] during the last twenty years and found that they all followed a 'stereotype scheme' having 'numerous but comparatively minor variations'" (Keesing 1960:189). The implication is that regardless of some professed theoretical orientation, anthropologists writing in English bring a certain basic theoretical orientation about the nature of culture to the formulation of ethnographic theories of individual cultures.

tween a map and a theory may be extended as follows: an ethnography is a theory in the sense that a map is a theory of an area. The ethnography is like a guide map of a particular culture. Following this map will result in appropriate behavior. What we call 'universal meta-theory' are, then, the principles and constraints governing ethnographic description. The analogy may be pushed further: maps have scales. A very detailed description of ethnographic ethnoscience may include every splinter of firewood, as the 1:25,000 maps of parts of the Navajo Reservation show every hogan. Perhaps it is possible to construct ethnoscience descriptions using only 'keywords' (see footnote 6) and their structural relations analogous to a map indicating merely the major topological features of an area.

It is customary in this context to speak of the 'emic-etic' distinction (since Pike 1954). The 'etic' is a universal typology applicable to all cultures. The 'emic' structural units are significant only to the description of a particular culture, but representable in the 'etic' vocabulary.

There are many problems with this terminology: the 'etic' units are generally conceived as some kind of rock-bottom empirical units untouched by theoretical considerations. In fact, the 'etic' is ambiguous. The choice of a theory determines both 'etic' and 'emic' units. For example, the 'emic' units of transformational generative grammar may be the abstract underlying sentence-like structures of the deep structure. Are the 'etic' units the derived observable sentences of the surface structure ('allo-sentences'), or the formal and substantive universals of language? For the structuralist, the 'etic'' units were various substantive universals vis-à-vis several levels of 'emic' units (e.g., phonemes, morphemes, tagmemes, etc.). Ethnology is 'etic' vis-à-vis a particular ethnography, but 'emic' in relation to a theory of culture (the nature of culture). First, these multiple levels of theory make the application of the 'emic-etic' principle difficult; second, there is an inherent ambiguity of the 'etic' between the universal (highest) and the empirical (lowest) levels. Furthermore, both levels are theory-dependent. Relevant universals and relevant observations will shift as our theories of culture shift.

The 'emic-etic' distinction therefore appears to be in the vocabulary of the theory of theories. The abstraction of such meta-meta theoretical labels seems overwhelming.

Ethnoscience: Toward an Explicit Meta-Theory

For a description of the ethnoscience approach, the most primitive point of departure is the explicit meta-theory of the *Outline of Cultural Materials*. The list was provided by G. P. Murdock (1960) and his collaborators. If the ethnographer uses this list as an outline of a particular culture, he uses Murdock's meta-categories. The ethnoscience *analogue* is a similar list (because cultures are similar) consisting ENTIRELY OF NATIVE TERMS. The relative importance or generality of the natives' categories is based on judgments (for example, taxonomic judgments) of the informants. The relative importance or generality of Murdock's categories was judged to be so by Murdock and his collaborators, based on the cumulative experience of anthropologists over the years. That ethnographers using non-ethnoscience methodology achieve a close approximation of the judgments of their informants is explainable due to the fact that (1) anthropologists are trained to become sensitive to the native or a non-Western point of view and not to judge on ethnocentric grounds; (2) human beings immersed in another culture as ethnographers (or in other roles), if they are willing to learn (as anthropologists should be), will acculturate to the view of their host culture; and (3) the process (2) is accelerated by knowledge of the native language. That (2) is taking place is attested by the many private reports of anthropologists that they suffered shock upon *return* to the United States. Naroll's (1962) high positive correlations (although made only in relation to witchcraft reports), if generalized, support (2): quality (detail) of the report increases with length of stay in the field; and (3) quality (detail) of the report increases also with the knowledge of the native language; that is, in terms of ethnographic ethnoscience, an ethnographer who learns the native language with reasonable proficiency, and who stays in the field at least a year (following Naroll's measure) will, on the average, approximate the judgments of importance, relevance, and appropriateness of native speakers and may even surpass them.

The ethnographer, at some time, reaches the point where he feels he has grasped the integrating 'forces' of a culture, or the 'system'; and can now not only predict appropriate behavior in all situations he has experienced, but can extrapolate (generate) verbal and nonverbal situations not encountered before. But the ETHNOGRAPHER'S THEORETICAL INTEGRATION, OR SYSTEM FOR INTERRELATING CATEGORIES, IS HIS OWN, WITH HELP FROM INFORMANTS.

The ethnoscience achievements are at present much more pedestrian. They are small, but most promising. ALL PRINCIPLES OF INTEGRATION, SUCH AS THE UNIVERSAL PRINCIPLE OF FOLK TAXONOMIES, ARE TO BE PART OF A UNIVERSAL META-THEORY, OR THEORY OF CULTURE. THE CONTENT, THAT IS, UNDERLYING FEATURES, DIMENSIONS, OR WHICH TERMS ARE TO BE INTEGRATED SYSTEMATICALLY WITH WHICH OTHER TERMS, INTO SPECIFIC TAXONOMIES, FOR EXAMPLE, DEPENDS ENTIRELY ON THE JUDGMENT OF THE INFORMANTS.

To date, however, only the principles of taxonomic systems are well established. The work of Frake (1964), Williams (1966), Kay and Berlin (Kay 1965), Casagrande and Hale (1967), and Werner (1966, 1967a) and the following section, "Some Theoretical Insights," to mention a few, indicates that other general principles of integration of lexical domains are called for.

The falsification of hypotheses of ethnographic ethnoscience, of the form, for example, "X is a kind of Y," is simpler only because of the relative simplicity of the proposition. The geographic-synchronic and diachronic variations are as serious as they are in traditional ethnography. However, meta-theoretical hypotheses are now much easier to falsify, particularly since these are explicit and often formal. Such hypotheses make claims to be universal cultural propositions: "In ALL cultures, large parts of lexicon are taxonomically ordered." Only in this sense is ethnoscience more rigorous than traditional ethnography. Meanwhile, it should be remembered that most of what ethnoscience (ethnographic and ethnologic) claims remains to be done.

SOME THEORETICAL INSIGHTS

The tremendous complexity of cultural knowledge ranging from the esoteric to the seemingly mundane and trite especially (for members of the culture) places a tremendous burden on the investigator. Admitting that the complexity of simpler societies which anthropologists usually study is considerably less than the cultural information available to the investigator of high cultures does not get the ethnographer off the hook. He must make judgments concerning what is important and what is not, or what is to be abstracted and what ought to be reported in full. Some suggestions as to how the abstracting may become more rational at least as far as linguistic ethnographic ethnoscience is concerned is taken up later (see pp. 556–557).

Since the content of cultural knowledge is largely unmanageable the emphasis in this section will be on systems for the organization of cultural knowledge. We assume that knowledge is organized into semantic or lexical fields.

Intermediate between the individual lexical items and the totality of the vocabulary, Trier recognizes the existence of several 'concept fields' or 'lexical fields' ('Sinnbezirke,' 'Wortfelder'). It is this which constitutes the most original and fertile aspect of Trier's theory for semantics: "Felder sind die zwischen den Einzelworten und dem Wortganzen lebendigen sprachlichen Wirklichkeiten, die als Teilganze mit dem Wort das Merkmal gemeinsam haben, dass sie sich ergliedern, mit dem Wortschatz hingegen, dass sie sich ausgliedern" (as quoted by Lyons 1963:45).

Lyons continues in a footnote; "The sentence quoted (Trier 1963:430) is translated by Ullmann in his general account of Trier's theory, with the just comment that "in the German original, the difference [between the part-whole relation of single words to the fields and the fields to the vocabulary, on the one hand, and the whole-part relation of vocabulary to the fields and the fields to single words] is brought out more pregnantly by the opposition of 'sich ergliedern'–'sich ausgliedern,' which also imply an articulateness not conveyed by the English terms" (Ullmann 1957:157). (Ullmann's translation of Trier's quote: "Fields are linguistic realities existing between single words and the total vocabulary; they are parts of wholes and resemble words in that they combine into some higher unit, and the vocabulary in that they resolve themselves into smaller units.")

Research concerning field properties has just begun. To date in ethnoscience the cross-cultural universality of only two structures is fully recognized: taxonomies (in the strict sense) and paradigms (also in the strict sense).

The word 'taxonomy' is used here in a technical sense strictly as Aristotelian class inclusion. It does not include all possible ways of folk-classification. It is the relation aTb where a and b are representations of the content (meaning) of concrete nouns (most usually) and where T="——— is a (kind of) ———." The word 'paradigm' is also used in a technical sense, to denote a special non-hierarchic intersection of classes. It is not to be confused with 'grammatical paradigm' to which it bears some resemblance (see below), or paradigm in the general sense as used by T. Kuhn (1956) in "paradigm of science." The latter use seems to me to be synonymous with Bohannan's use of 'idiom' in "culture as the idiom of society" (1963:23). Both structures will be given rigorous definitions in the following sections (see also Werner 1967a). Although research in the extension of the notion of semantic fields is not lacking, none of this work has reached a stage at which the uncovered structures are formally characterizable (e.g., Frake 1963, Bendix 1966, Williams 1966, Casagrande and Hale 1967, Perchonock and Werner 1967). A discussion of these inchoate analyses of semantic fields beyond taxonomies and paradigms will conclude the present section (see pp. 561–566).

Paradigms are slightly more abstract than taxonomies. However, since the discussion of paradigms is basic and logically prior to that of taxonomies, we shall present it first.

Paradigm

A paradigm may be defined as follows:

(1) A paradigm is a relation of the form aPb (or (a,b) ϵP). We call P the relation of paradigm. It may be represented in natural language by the form "———and ———." (Conjunction of a and b—*note that this is not a sentence.*)

(2) If U (=Universe) is the set of all components of a paradigm and if P is the relation of paradigm then the paradigm is a subset of the Cartesian product U×U.

(3) The particular subset of U×U in order to qualify as a paradigm must have the following properties:

a) aPa is not a member of the paradigm. A paradigm is irreflexive, or an attribute conjoined with itself is meaningless.

b) If aPb is a member of a paradigm then bPa is also a member. A paradigm is symmetric, or two attributes are conjoined in either order aPb or bPa.

c) The relation P of a paradigm is not transitive.

d) Because of b) and c) a paradigm P is not an order and therefore it is also non-hierarchic.

(4) To define a paradigm by means of an operation we start with a set U (=Universe) of the components which make up this paradigm.

The set U is then partitioned into subsets, generally called dimensions in such a way that no two sets have any members in common and that the sum of all subsets is the set U. In other words, we partition U into subsets

D_i such that $\bigcap_{i=1}^{n} D_i = \emptyset$ (The intersection of all dimensions is the null or empty set) and $\bigcup_{i=1}^{n} D_i = U$ (the union of all dimensions is the set U itself).

Definition: A paradigm is the set of all subsets C_i of U containing exactly one element from each dimension.[8]

Represented in formulaic form, a paradigm of n dimensions is defined by the following 'star' operation:

$D_0 * D_1 * D_2 * \ldots * D_i * \ldots * D_n = \{\{d_0, d_1, d_2, \ldots, d_i, \ldots, d_n\}: d_i \epsilon D_i\}$

In a simple example:
$U = \{a_1, a_2, b_1, b_2\}$
with two dimensions $D_1 = \{a_1, a_2\}$ and $D_2 = \{b_1, b_2\}$ we get U×U.
As shall be seen (pp. 548–553) this accounts for the greater cohesion of the $C_i = a_i b_i$, which are linked by the abstract star operation.

Note also that this operation is related to Cooper's operation of interconcatenation (1964:29): $S \cdot T = \{x \frown y : x \epsilon S \text{ and } y \epsilon T\}$

[8] The formal arguments in this section are in part based on my paper "Taxonomy and Paradigm: Two Semantic Structures" (Werner 1967a) but contain several extensions and substantial corrections based on work done since that paper was written.

	a_1	a_2	b_1	b_2
a_1			a_1b_1	a_1b_2
a_2			a_2b_1	a_2b_2
b_1	b_1a_1	b_1a_2		
b_2	b_2a_1	b_2a_2		

Table 1. The star operation as a subset of $U \times U$.

Cooper's formula is the definition of a grammatical paradigm where for example 'book-s' is the plural of the word 'book' but '-s book' is not English. In semantic paradigms as defined by the star operation the order of elements is not relevant.

The Hanunóo pronominal set (Conklin 1962:135) will serve as an example of a paradigm:

$U = \{p, m_1, m_2, s_1, s_2, h_1, h_2\}$

$D_0 = \{p\}$ (expresses the fact that all combinations of components are pronouns)

$D_1 = \{m_1, m_2\}$ (minimal membership versus non-minimal membership)

$D_2 = \{s_1, s_2\}$ (inclusion of speaker versus exclusion of speaker)

$D_3 = \{h_1, h_2\}$ (inclusion of hearer versus exclusion of hearer)

Assuming further that there is some word in Hanunóo equivalent or similar to ($\{p\}$, ['PRONOUN']) and reserving the arrow '→' as a symbol for the relation of taxonomy (or "——— is a (kind of)———"), then the above paradigm represents one level of a taxonomic structure.

$\{p\} \rightarrow \{p\} * \{m_1, m_2\} * \{s_1, s_2\} * \{h_1, h_2\}$ and/ or pictured as a tree graph:

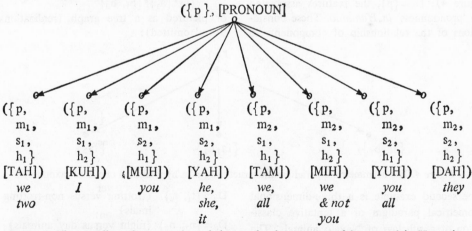

Figure 3. The paradigmatic structuring of the one-level taxonomy of 'pronouns' in Hanunóo. On the lower level the usual form of a lexical item (C, P) where C=semantic representation, and P=phonetic (graphemic) form is vertical (C, P) in order to conserve space.

We will call a paradigm with this characteristic symmetry of its dimensions a symmetrical or complete paradigm. Symmetrical paradigms seem to be exceedingly rare. Pronominal sets seem to be the favorite examples. In addition to Conklin's Hanunóo (1964), see Buchler (1966).

The fact that some of the kinship terminologies (or at least sub-parts of kinship terminological systems) have been analyzed in the literature of componential analysis as symmetrical paradigms is, as Werner tried to demonstrate (Werner 1967a), due to the fact that taxonomic considerations were often excluded. That is, the existence of additional relations between singular and collective kinship terms has been overlooked. Kay and others quoted by him have also concerned themselves with this problem (Kay 1966:21). As will be seen below, the clarification of the relationship of semantic paradigm to taxonomy is one of the major aims of this section.

Paradigmatic Definition. If a paradigm is the sematic representation of a single level taxonomy, then the unique combination C_i for each lexical item on one level of a taxonomy is a kind of definition which distinguishes a lexical item from all other lexical items on that particular level of the taxonomy. We will call such a definition:

P-DEF: A paradigmatic definition of a lexical item equals the corresponding set C_i. The set of all sets C_i is the result of the star operation on the dimensions of D_j of the paradigm.

The sets D_j include the dimension D_0 which was informally designated as the set which attaches the component or components $\{f\}$ of the immediately dominating node to all subordinate nodes. In the Hanunóo example (Figure 4), $D_0 = \{p\}$, the features associated with 'pronounness' *in Hanunóo*. These considerations of the relationship of components to hierarchy introduce problems of the relationship between paradigm and taxonomy which will be taken up in detail later (pp. 550–553).

Asymmetrical Paradigm. Considerably more important are asymmetrical or incomplete paradigms. The definition of an asymmetrical paradigm is identical with the definition of a symmetrical paradigm to which conditions of neutralization are added. An incomplete paradigm is the result of the fact that in certain sets C_i, or combinations of elements, one from each dimension, some of the dimensional contrasts become neutralized. This may be expressed in most general terms as:
$$D_0 \rightarrow D_0 * D_1 * D_2 * \ldots * D_i * \ldots * D_n$$
and the neutralization condition:
$D_k \overset{\rightarrow}{} \phi$ for $k \neq o$, and $D_i \overset{\rightarrow}{} D_i', \ldots, D_j \overset{\rightarrow}{} D_j'$ and all D' similar to D but have fewer members than D, and $i, \ldots, j \neq k$. The boldface arrow '$\overset{\rightarrow}{}$' represents the mapping of D_k onto ϕ, or D_i onto D_i', etc.

The first example of an asymmetrical paradigm is hypothetical:
$U = \{f, a_1, a_2, b_1, b_2\} D_0 = \{f\}$, $D_1 = \{a_1, a_2\}$ and $D_2 = \{b_1, b_2\}$
$$\{f\} \rightarrow D_0 * D_1 * D_2$$
Neutralization condition:
$D_2 \overset{\rightarrow}{} \phi$ and $D_1 \overset{\rightarrow}{} \{a_2\}$ which means that
$\{f\} \rightarrow \{f\} * \{a_2\} * \phi$
$\{f\} * \{a_1\} * \{b_1, b_2\}$
or pictured as a tree graph (realizations of 'form' omitted):

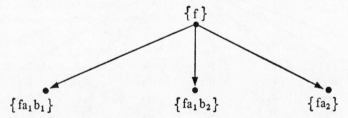

$$\{f\}$$

$$\{fa_1b_1\} \qquad \{fa_1b_2\} \qquad \{fa_2\}$$

Figure 4. The asymmetrical paradigmatic structuring of a hypothetical one-level taxonomy.

The second example is a three-dimensional asymmetrical paradigm of a tentative classification of a subclass of Navajo animals. The three-dimensionality of this example should permit a comparison with the three-dimensional symmetrical Hanunóo paradigm.
$U = \{f, d_1, d_2, t_1, t_2, n_1, n_2\}$
$D_0 = \{f\}$ (expresses *walker*ness)
$D_1 = \{d_1, d_2\}$ (dangerous versus nondangerous animals)

$D_2 = \{t_1, t_2\}$ (trotting versus non-trotting animals)
$D_3 = \{n_1, n_2\}$ (night versus day animals)
$\{f\} \rightarrow D_0 * D_1 * D_2 * D_3$
Neutralization condition:
$D_2, D_3 \overset{\rightarrow}{} \phi$ and $D_1 \overset{\rightarrow}{} \{d_1\}$; $D_3 \overset{\rightarrow}{} \phi$, $D_1 \overset{\rightarrow}{} \{d_2\}$ and $D_2 \overset{\rightarrow}{} \{t_1\}$; $D_2 \overset{\rightarrow}{} \{t_2\}$ and $D_1 \overset{\rightarrow}{} \{d_2\}$: +
Or $\{f\} \rightarrow \begin{Bmatrix} \{f\} * \{d_1\} \\ \{f\} * \{d_2\} * \{t_1\} \\ \{f\} * \{d_2\} * \{t_2\} * \{n_1, n_2\} \end{Bmatrix}$
Or pictured as a tree graph:

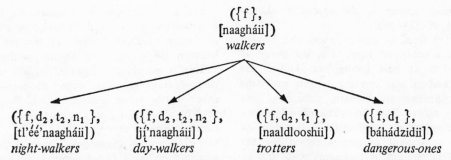

$$(\{f\},$$
$$[\text{naagháii}])$$
walkers

$(\{f, d_2, t_2, n_1\},$ $(\{f, d_2, t_2, n_2\},$ $(\{f, d_2, t_1\},$ $(\{f, d_1\},$
$[\text{tl'ée'naagháii}])$ $[\text{jí'naagháii}])$ $[\text{naaldlooshii}])$ $[\text{báhádzidii}])$
night-walkers   *day-walkers*   *trotters*   *dangerous-ones*

Figure 5. The asymmetrical three-dimensional paradigm structure of a Navajo one-level taxonomy.

In a more concrete manner, the two structures of the symmetrical paradigm of Hanunóo 'pronouns' and the asymmetrical paradigm of the Navajo 'walkers' may be represented following Conklin (1962:135):

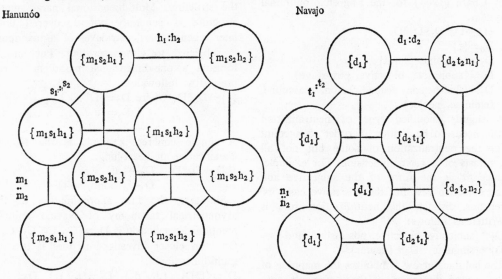

Figure 6. Picturing of a symmetrical and an asymmetrical paradigm following Conklin (1962: 135). (The D_0 dimensions which mark "pronounness" and "walkerness" are omitted)

Hanunóo

$(\{m_1 s_1 h_1\},$ $[\text{TAH}])$ *we two*
$(\{m_1 s_1 h_2\},$ $[\text{KUH}])$ *I*
$(\{m_1 s_2 h_1\},$ $[\text{MUH}])$ *you*
$(\{m_1 s_2 h_2\},$ $[\text{YAH}])$ *he, she, it*
$(\{m_2 s_1 h_1\},$ $[\text{TAM}])$ *we all*
$(\{m_2 s_1 h_2\},$ $[\text{MIH}])$ *we, not you*
$(\{m_2 s_2 h_1\},$ $[\text{YUH}])$ *you all*
$(\{m_2 s_2 h_2\},$ $[\text{DAH}])$ *they*

Navajo

$(\{d_1\},$ $[\text{báhádzidii}])$ *dangerous-ones*
$(\{d_2, t_1\},$ $[\text{naaldlooshii}])$ *trotters*
$(\{d_2 t_2 n_1\},$ $[\text{tl'ée'naagháii}])$ *night-walkers*
$(\{d_2 t_2 n_2\},$ $[\text{jí'naagháii}])$ *day-walkers*

Note that the English translation labels are not definitions. The dangerous-ones include bears, coyotes, wolves, etc., the trotters include sheep, cows, horses, deer, elk and moose, etc., the night-walkers include kanga-

roo rats, mice, etc., and the day-walkers include chipmunks, squirrels, etc. With these Navajo translation labels as well as with the translation labels provided by us for the Hanunóo pronouns all precautions should be taken in order to avoid the pitfalls of reckless generalization. Conklin's warnings and discussion are most relevant for all translation la-

† The last type of neutralization condition is discussed below.

bels which appear in the examples of this paper (1964:29–30).

Another word of caution about the Navajo taxonomy presented here: The taxonomy of walkers is at best incomplete. Under the same heading and creating serious problems of classification are humans, cats, dogs and possibly others. The three-dimensional assymmetrical paradigm used here is therefore at best a convenient oversimplification for the sake of illustration. A taxonomy with four or more paradigmatic dimensions may in the end approximate more closely the actual Navajo classification.

A second type of neutralization is reported by Chafe (1964) for the English pronominal system:

$$\{f\} \rightarrow D_0 * D_1 * D_2 * D_3$$
$$D_0 = \{f\}$$
$$D_1 = \{\text{singular, plural}\}$$
$$D_2 = \{\text{subjective, objective, possessive}\}$$
$$D_3 = \{\text{first-person, second-person, masculine, feminine, neuter}\}$$

A slightly modified type of neutralization rule needs to be written in order to account for the neutralization of some but not all contrasts of a given dimension. For example, since 'it' is the form of the subjective and the objective case but the possessive case 'its' remains distinct, the neutralization rule is written as follows:

$$D_2 \blacktriangleright \{\text{subjective-objective, possessive}\} \text{ and}$$
$$D_1 \blacktriangleright \{\text{singular}\}; D_3 \blacktriangleright \{\text{neuter}\}$$

The boldface arrow symbolizes the mapping of the second dimension of three elements onto two, by collapsing the first two elements and the reduction of the first and third dimension to one element. The neutralization of the third–person plurals (they, them, their) in regard to masculine, feminine and neuter, the third–person feminine singular (her) in regard to the objective and possessive, etc., can be handled in the same way. Chafe's English example is used here for illustration only. Alternate analyses are possible.

Summary of Neutralization conditions:

(1) TOTAL NEUTRALIZATION of a dimension.

The neutralization of a dimension D_i of a paradigm is total if $D_i \blacktriangleright \phi$

This is usually accompanied by a partial neutralization of some other dimension. In other words, an intradimensional contrast set (a dimension) may be completely eliminated in certain combinations of components.

(2) PARTIAL NEUTRALIZATION of a dimension.

The neutralization of a dimension D_i of a paradigm is partial if $D_i \rightarrow D_i'$, where D_i' is similar to D_i but some of the contrasts between the elements in D_i are neutralized.

This is usually accompanied by the partial neutralization of some other dimension. In other words, some intradimensional contrasts may be eliminated (but not others) in certain combinations of components.

One-Dimensional Paradigm. A special case of a paradigm is a one-dimensional paradigm. Generally when an investigator first proposes a taxonomy for some folk domain he will postulate, as a first approximation, a one-dimensional paradigm for the description of the structure. Multidimensional paradigmatic structure is generally not discovered until later when a particular level of a taxonomy is subjected to closer scrutiny. Put into a formula a one-dimensional paradigm is expressed as follows:

$$\{f\} \rightarrow D_0 * D_1 \text{ where } D_0 = \{f\}$$
$$D_1 = \{d_1, d_2, \ldots, d_i, \ldots, d_n\}$$

A simple concrete example is the Navajo classification of heart-lung:

$$\{hl\} \rightarrow D_0 * D_1 \quad D_0 \rightarrow \{hl\}$$
$$D_1 \rightarrow \{\text{round, soft}\}$$

Similarly, the first approximation of the asymmetrical taxonomy of Navajo animals mentioned previously is $D_1 = \{C_1, C_2, C_3, C_4\}$. Only on closer investigation does it become multidimensional:

$$D_0 = \{f\} D_1 = \{d_1, d_2\}, D_2 = \{t_1, t_1\}, D_3 = \{n_1, n_2\}$$ and $C_1 = \{f, d_1\}$, $C_2 = \{f, d_2, t_1\}$, $C_3 = \{f, d_2, t_2, n_1\}$ $C_4 = \{f, d_2, t_2, n_2\}$ and asymetrical (see Figure 6). The above structure in Figure 6 is a single-level taxonomy where the order of the nodes is irrelevant. That is, the above paradigmatic definitions C_1, C_2, C_3, may be presented in any order. This is, of course, also true of multidimensional paradigms. There are taxonomic levels where the ordering of the nodes is non-arbitrary. It is governed by an ordering relation. This is most simply 'C_1 precedes C_2' (e.g., from left to right).[9]

[9] The structural description of sentence in a transformational generative grammar is a combination of two relations: One, similar to the taxonomic relation, consisting of '————is a constituent of————,' establishes the hierarchy; the other, '————precedes ————', establishes the order of constituents. Thus the now famous formula S →NP⌢VP states that a sentence has the constituents of Nounphrase and Verbphrase and that the order is Nounphrase first followed by the Verbphrase.

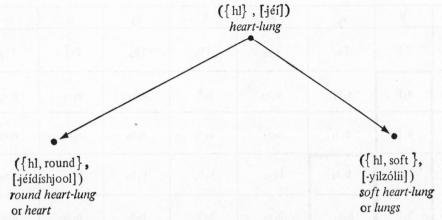

$(\{\,\text{hl}\,\}\,,\,[\text{-jéí}])$
heart-lung

$(\{\,\text{hl, round}\,\},$
$[\text{-jéídíshjool}])$
round heart-lung
or *heart*

$(\{\,\text{hl, soft}\,\},$
$[\text{-yilzólii}])$
soft heart-lung
or *lungs*

Figure 7. The simple one-dimensional paradigm structure of the one-level taxonomy of Navajo heart-lung.

Taxonomy

A taxonomy may be defined as follows:

(1) A taxonomy is a relation of the form aTB (or (a,b) ϵT). We call T the relation of taxonomy which is in natural language of the form "———is a (kind of)———', 'all——— are———', 'the class of———is a———' and possibly others.

(2) If U (=Universe) is the set of all nodes of the taxonomy and if T is the relation of taxonomy then the taxonomy is a subset of the Cartesian product U×U.

(3) The particular subset of U×U in order to qualify as a taxonomy must have the following properties:

a) aTa is not a member of the taxonomy, or a taxon cannot be a superordinate taxon of itself. A taxonomy is irreflexive.[10]

b) If aTb is part of the taxonomy then bTa cannot be. That is, a taxon cannot be simultaneously subordinate and superordinate. A taxonomy is asymmetric.

c) If aTb and bTc are in the taxonomy then aTc is also a member. This is the condition of transitivity, perhaps the most far-reaching formal characteristic of taxonomies.

d) An irreflexive asymmetric and transitive relation determines a partial order. The par-

tial order and transitivity define a hierarchy.

(4) A picture of a simple binary two-level taxonomy may look as follows:
U={F, a_1, a_2, b_1, b_2, c_1, c_2}
U×U and the members meeting the condition of taxonomy are marked in boldface squares in the following table.

The relation of taxonomy is essentially a relation between lexical items of the normal form (C, P) where C is a semantic representation of the 'content' and P is the representation of the physical (phonological or graphemic) 'form.' The matrix of the Cartesian product U×U in Figure 10 therefore represents the semantic relation of taxonomy which is inferred from actual sentences of the language under investigation. Thus if we designate semantic representations by lower-case letters and representations of 'form' (phonological or graphemic) symbolized by upper-case letters and in square brackets (suggestive of phonetic transcription) we may represent the taxonomy as pictured by the following graph of a two-level taxonomy (Figure 8). The interpretation of the graph is as follows: The nodes are all labeled by $(x_i, [X_i])$, a semantic representation x_i and a representation of 'form' $[X_i]$ of the identical index. The lines connecting the nodes are interpreted as the taxonomic relation T. The semantic relation of taxonomy with another node $(y_j, [Y_j])$ namely x_iTy_j is inferred from the existence of an actual sentence of the form $[X_iTY_j]$. More concretely the English sentence "A [CAT] is an [ANIMAL]" with the lexical entries (c, [CAT]) and (a, [ANIMAL]) is a representation in the English language of the

[10] Although this condition does seem to preclude the occurrence of grammatical sentences of the form 'a rose is a rose,' this is not the case. The latter sentence receives the interpretation similar to the interpretation of the sentence 'this rose is a rose,' that is, a specific rose belongs to the class of all roses; and 'a rose is a rose is a rose' as 'this rose like that rose belongs to the class of thing designated as 'rose.' The mechanics of such interpretations are far from clear.

	F	a_1	a_2	b_1	b_2	c_1	c_2
F	F,F	Fa_1	Fa_2	Fb_1	Fb_2	Fc_1	Fc_2
a_1	a_1F	a_1a_1	a_1a_2	a_1b_1	a_1b_2	a_1c_1	a_1c_2
a_2	a_2F	a_2a_1	a_2a_2	a_2b_1	a_2b_2	a_2c_1	a_2c_2
b_1	b_1F	b_1a_1	b_1a_2	b_1b_1	b_1b_2	b_1c_1	b_1c_2
b_2	b_2F	b_2a_1	b_2a_2	b_2b_1	b_2b_2	b_2c_1	b_2c_2
c_1	c_1F	c_1a_1	c_1a_2	c_1b_1	c_1b_2	c_1c_1	c_1c_2
c_2	c_2F	c_2a_1	c_2a_2	c_2b_1	c_2b_2	c_2c_1	c_2c_2

Table 2
THE CARTESIAN PRODUCT U × U

[Boldface line delimits the members of the taxonomy.]

universal semantic relation cTa. In Hungarian presumably the same semantic relation holds with lexical entries (c, [MACSKA] and a (a, [AALAT]) and the Hungarian sentence "Egy [MACSKA] egy [AALAT]", *a cat (is) an animal*.

The Relationship Between Taxonomies and Paradigms

Before continuing, the relationship between taxonomy and paradigm needs to be resolved.

A paradigm displays formally the structuring of a single level of a taxonomy. One type of lexical field can therefore be viewed as an alternation of taxonomic levels with paradigms. Each level of the taxonomy is semantically structured by a paradigm. The star operation of the paradigm constructs the paradigmatic definitions C_i out of the di-

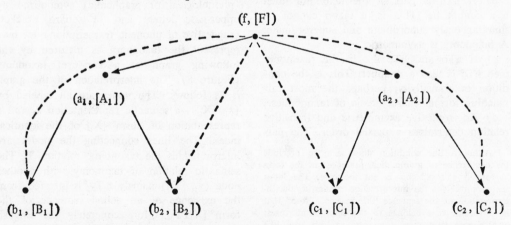

Figure 8. The representation of the taxonomy of Table 2 in the form of a graph. The solid lines are the usual tree representation. The condition of transitivity demands that the dotted lines also be part of the relation of taxonomy.

mensions D_1. Every node on one level of the taxonomy is assigned a paradigmatic definition C_1. If taxonomies and paradigms are firmly linked in this manner (alternation), then the componential part of Figure 8 may be represented in formulaic form as follows:

1.1. $f \rightarrow \{a_1, a_2\}$
1.2. $a_1 \rightarrow \{b_1, b_2\}$
1.3. $a_2 \rightarrow \{c_1, c_2\}$

The set notation is justified on the grounds that the items on a particular level of a taxonomy are usually not ordered. Note that this notation is consistent with the semantic notation that was used for paradigms. This notation is analogous to that used in linguistics (e.g., Chomsky 1965) which is of the form:

$$f \longrightarrow \begin{bmatrix} 1\alpha \\ 2\beta \\ 3\gamma \\ \ldots \end{bmatrix}$$

If the branching is binary, 1 and 2 are commonly replaced by + and − respectively. This corresponds in the notation used here to:

$$f \rightarrow \{1\alpha, 2\beta, 3\gamma, \ldots\}$$

The sets on the right side of the arrow imply that the internal structuring of each level of this taxonomy is by a one-dimensional paradigm. If c_1 and c_2 respectively are paradigmatic definitions as Figure 8 implies, then $\{c_1 T a_2\}$ and $\{c_2 T a_2\}$, semantic relations of taxonomy, are true. However, this interpretation of c_1 and c_2 is not consistent with formula 1.3. The interpretation of this formula must be that the only dimension of the paradigm which distinguishes C_1 from C_2 by means of the components c_1 and c_2 is D_1 (of a_2) $= \{c_1, c_2\}$. If this is the case then $c_1 T a_2$ and $c_2 T a_2$ are certainly false.

Therefore Figure 8 is only correct if c_1 and c_2 are interpreted as complex and contain more components that just the two which distinguish between C_1 and C_2.

If c_1 and c_2 are the paradigmatic components which contribute only to the distinction between the lexical items C_1 and C_2 on this particular level of this taxonomy, we must rewrite the labels on Figure 8 as follows:

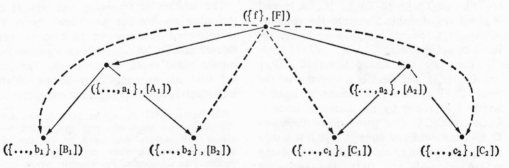

Figure 9. A Reinterpretation of Figure 8.

The '. . .' indicates in the case of $(\{. . . , c_2\}, [C_2])$ for example that as we descend the taxonomic tree structure additional components are 'picked up' at each level of the taxonomy. These could be simple components as in the above case or complex components if the particular level of a taxonomy displays a multidimensional paradigmatic structure.

The same condition can be expressed in formulaic form:

2.1. $\{f\} \rightarrow \{. . .\}^* \{a_1, a_2\}$
2.2. $\{. . . , a_1\} \rightarrow \{. . .\}^* \{b_1, b_2\}$
2.3. $\{. . . , a_2\} \rightarrow \{. . .\}^* \{c_1, c_2\}$

This convention seems awkward at best. Another convention may be to add the successive dimensions as they accrue, that is, each subordinate node is marked for the distinctive features of its superordinate node:

3.1. $\{f\} \rightarrow \{f\}^* \{a_1, a_2\}$
3.2. $\{f, a_1\} \rightarrow \{f, a_1\}^* \{b_1, b_2\}$
3.3. $\{f, a_2\} \rightarrow \{f, a_2\}^* \{c_1, c_2\}$

The first term in each line of (3) corresponds to the dimension D_o as it was introduced earlier (pp. 544–545). This 'zero dimension' is one of the paradigmatic definitions from the superordinate level of the taxonomy. Note that this set C_l must be treated as different from the dimensions D_l under the star operation: Whereas in D_l each element of the set contributes to a different C_l on that level, the paradigmatic definitions C_l are an indivisible unit. Although the C_l from the immediately superordinate level may itself consist of components, within the C_l of the subordinate level, it must be treated as an unanalyzable whole. The paradigmatic definitions C_i and the C_j on the next lower level are 'natural' bundles of components which are matched with lexical items (physical 'form') and are therefore not ordinary sets but special sets which are the result of the star operation (see pp. 544–545).

If we perform the star operation (pp. 544–545) above the following taxonomic tree results:

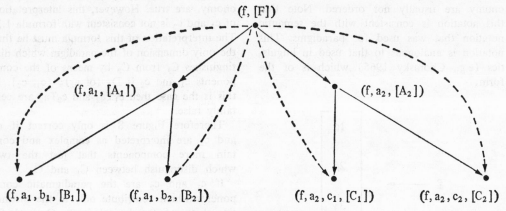

Figure 10. Correction of Figure 8.

Since we know that Figure 10 is a taxonomy, that is, sentences of the form $[A_1TF]$, $[A_2TF]$, $[B_1TA_1]$, $[B_2TA_1]$, $[C_1TA_2]$ and $[C_2TA_2]$ are elicitable, therefore the semantic relation of taxonomy is equivalent to the relation of set inclusion:

If there are two lexical items $(C_i, [P_i])$ and $(C_j, [P_j])$ and there is a sentence of the form $[P_iTP_j]$, then the semantic relation which is expressed by the above sentence is $C_j \subset C_i$ or $C_i \supset C_j$ (the paradigmatic definition C_j, of the subordinate node $(C_j, [P_j]$, is a subset of the paradigmatic definition C_i of the subordinate node $(C_i, [P_i])$. The notion of 'taxonomy' and set inclusion of semantic components are synonymous.

The above result seems to indicate that taxonomies and paradigms are relatively independent of each other. Paradigms seem to explain the location of lexical items in a complex multidimensional semantic field which is determined by the putatively universal semantic features or components and the star operation. The feeling of this apparent independence is enhanced by the rules for asymmetrical paradigms developed earlier (pp. 545–548). By far the large majority of

semantic fields consists of asymmetrical paradigms.[11]

The relation of taxonomy and with it all the other possible but less known or as yet undiscovered relations are now to be considered strictly lexical relations superimposed on the paradigmatic semantic grid. The lexical field of taxonomy may be particularly important because its semantic representation

[11] In Werner (1967) Werner has failed to see the distinction between taxonomies and asymmetrical paradigms. This mistake was aided by the fact that asymmetrical paradigms are often very easily convertible into taxonomies. For example, having established the fact that Navajo has animals called *'dangerous ones'* it would be easy to think up the *'harmless ones,'* namely the *trotters, night-walkers,* and *day-walkers* (say by inventing a folk tale "The harmless animals gathered in the forest to discuss what to do about the depradations suffered at the hand of the dangerous ones . . ."). It would be much more difficult to invent new superordinate nodes of a taxonomy if the paradigm is symmetrical. A second notion which supported my mistake was the notion of 'no lexeme.' The solution presented in these pages calls a taxonomy a taxonomy only if there *is* a 'lexeme.' The absence of a lexeme is extremely difficult to attest. Whenever possible, solutions without zero lexemes are preferable. The notion of an asymmetrical paradigm gives the analyst the formal tools to eliminate most if not all cases of 'no lexeme.'

is closely linked to the paradigm by the condition of set theoretical inclusion discussed above. The taxonomic field is therefore the automatic by-product of the correct componential paradigmatic solution. This is highly significant because one possible empirical attestation of the correct fit of a paradigm is given by the fact that it reflects correctly the taxonomic relations which are elicitable in the language under investigation.

The rules (3) (see Figure 10) of the two-level taxonomy can now be interpreted as follows:

$\{f\} \rightarrow \{f\} * \{a_1, a_2\} * \{b_1, b_2\} * \{c_1, c_2\}$

With $D_0 = \{f\}$, $D_1 = \{a_1, a_2\}$, $D_2 = \{b_1, b_2\}$, $D_3 = \{c_1, c_2\}$

and the neutralization conditions:

(1) $D_2 D_3 \twoheadrightarrow \phi$ which yields $\{f, a_1\}$ and $\{f, a_2\}$
(2) $D_3 \twoheadrightarrow \phi$, $D_1 \twoheadrightarrow \{a_1\}$ which yields $\{f, a_1, b_1\}$ and $\{f, a_1, b_2\}$
(3) $D_2 \twoheadrightarrow \phi$, $D_1 \twoheadrightarrow \{a_2\}$ which yields $\{f, a_2, c_1\}$ and $\{f, a_2, c_2\}$

In addition to $\{f\}$ this series of paradigmatic rules yields all the necessary paradigmatic definitions of Figure 10 and the paradigmatic definitions display automatically the proper taxonomic lexical relationship to each other.

Implicitly at this point there are three possible solutions to the problem of the interrelation between taxonomy and paradigm:

(1) to continue assuming that taxonomic levels and paradigms alternate throughout the entire system. The distinctions between lexical entries on one level of a taxonomy are resolved by the paradigm which structures that level.

(2) That solution (1) is essentially correct

except that the alternation does not necessarily have to be worked out for each level of a taxonomy. That is, some levels may present natural boundaries between paradigms underlying several levels of taxonomy. Although there is no evidence for this kind of a "boundary level" of a taxonomy and formally this is not necessary, this solution is perhaps the most conservative one.

(3) Finally the solution we favor most at present: various reasons presented in the above discussion and several additional arguments which will follow, assert the relative independence of paradigms and taxonomies. The paradigmatic dimensions and components provide paradigmatic definitions and represent one type of semantic field. The paradigmatic definitions are the semantic representation of lexical items which make up a lexical field; especially by the relation of set inclusion which may hold between the semantic representation of lexical items and which is, of course the relation of taxonomy. The manifestation of other lexical relations discussed in this paper and their manifestation in the semantic (paradigmatic) structure is not known and represents one of the most urgent research problems in semantics.

The entire following discussion will assume for the time being the correctness of solution (2).

The notation presented (pp. 548–549) will be adopted but only for paradigmatic definitions C_1 if an associated tree structure is drawn. This is simply a matter of conserving space.

Thus Figure 10 is redrawn as follows:

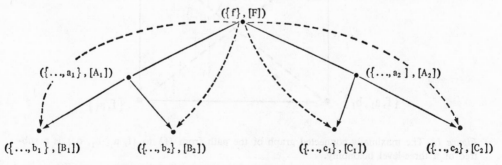

Figure 11. Demonstration of the abbreviated notation.

Consequences of Transitivity

The transitivity of the relation of taxonomy has important implications:

Theorem: The nodes on a path from the

origin $\{f\}$ of the taxonomy to any other node of the taxonomy are completely connected.

Instead of a proof we present the following informal demonstration: Assuming a three-level taxonomy where all paradigmatically derived nodes are represented by words,

$\{f\} \rightarrow \{f\}*\{a_1, \ldots\}*\{b_1, \ldots\}*\{c_1, c_2, \ldots\}$
$D_0 = \{f\}$, $D_1 = \{a_1, \ldots\}$, $D_2 = \{b_1, \ldots\}$ and
$D_3 = \{c_1, c_2, \ldots\}$

and the neutralization conditions:

(1) $D_2, D_3 \rightarrow \phi$ which yields $\{f, a_1\}$ and $\{\ldots\}$
(2) $D_1 \rightarrow \{a_1\}$, $D_3 \rightarrow \phi$ which yields $\{f, a_1, b_1\}$ and $\{\ldots\}$
(3) $D_1 \rightarrow \{a_1\}$, $D_2 \rightarrow \{b_1\}$ which yields $\{f, a_1, b_1, c_1\}$ and $\{f, a_1, b_1, c_2\}$

The second element c_2 is added in order to make the picture of the tree slightly more representational; the lower-case letters represent universal semantic features; the indication of phonological 'form' is omitted.

The semantic condition of a taxonomy was the set theoretical relation of inclusion:

(i) $\{f\} \subset \{f, a_1\} \subset \{f, a_1, b_1\} \subset \{f, a_1, b_1, c_1\}$.

but also because of the transitivity of T,

(ii) $\{f\} \subset \{f, a_1, b_1\}$, $\{f\} \subset \{f, a_1, b_1, c_1\}$ and $\{f, a_1\} \subset \{f, a_1, b_1, c_1\}$.

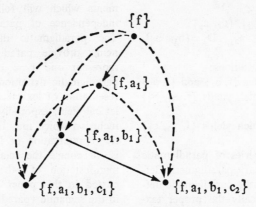

Figure 12. The graph representation of all possible relations of taxonomy in a subtree of a three-level taxonomy.

In Figure 13, the path from $\{f\}$ to $\{f, a_1, b_1, c_1\}$ is redrawn as the sides of a square:

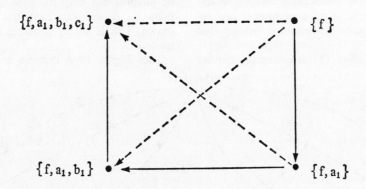

Figure 13. The maximally connected graph of the path from $\{f\}$ to $\{f, a_1, b_1, c_1\}$ is a subtree of a three-level taxonomy.

The combined graph of solid and dotted lines in Figure 13 represents a completely connected graph.

From this fact stem two important generalizations about taxonomies:

(1) The formal transitive nature of taxonomies affects the nature of definitions.

(2) This also accounts for the empirical fact that informants agree on some general and the most specific nodes. They may

greatly differ, however, in their knowledge of the intermediate classifications customary in their culture. This is especially true if they are compared with 'specialists' in the field under study (Landar *et al.*, 1960, Perchonock and Werner 1969). In other words, as long as members of a culture generally agree on some nodes of the taxonomy of an ideal speaker-hearer, minimally on one specific and the most general node, they will be able to communicate because there will always be a path from the specific node to the most general node regardless of their disagreement on the depth (number of levels) of intermediate or intervening classifications.

Putting it still another way, as long as there is some overlap in the taxonomic knowledge of two speakers of the same language, and if because of specialization (division of labor or curiosity) one has a deeper taxonomy with more levels than the other, this fact will not interfere with communication. On the contrary, since this situation is the rule, rather than the exception, it makes communication possible.

Definitions. Aristotle's profound interest in 'forms' which allows classification of things in terms of common attributes into genera and species is a kind of taxonomic definition. I will call it here Aristotelian definition or A-DEF. A species-genera type definition is a definition which is based on the dominance and subordination principle of taxonomies and parts of taxonomies. Adding to this the transitive character of the relation of taxonomy, it follows that:

Every lexical item in a folk taxonomy is multiply ambiguous because every possible path and sub-path from the term to be defined to any superordinate node (genus) is a separate Aristotelian definition. I will therefore define an Aristotelian definition in this extended sense which includes all possible paths to any superordinate node, or all possible genus-species relations (taxonomic relations). The Aristotelian definition of a linguistic term occurring at node $\{f, a_1, b_1, c_1\}$ in Figure 12 is therefore as follows: If C_1 is the composite semantic representation of the semantic content of the lexical item, whereas $[P_1]$ is the actual language form, and f' is the abbeviation for $\{f\}$, a'_1 for $\{f, a_1\}$; b'_1 for $\{f, a_1, b_1\}$ and c'_1 for $\{f, a_1, b_1, c_1\}$, then

$$\text{A-DEF }(C_1, [P_1]){:}C_1 = \left\{ \begin{array}{l} \{c'_1 Tf'\} \\ \{c'_1 Tb'_1, b'_1 Tf'\} \\ \{c'_1 Ta'_1, a'_1 Tf'\} \\ \{c'_1 Tb'_1, b'_1 Ta'_1, a'_1 Tf'\} \end{array} \right\}$$

This corresponds to the four different paths that can be taken from the node c'_1 to the origin f' of the tree.

$$\left\{ \begin{array}{l} \{c'_1 Tb'_1, b'_1 Ta'_1\} \\ \{c'_1 Tb'_1\} \\ \{c'_1 Ta'_1\} \end{array} \right\}$$

In addition there are the sub-path definitions The large braces { } are to be interpreted as disjunction: take one of these definitions (one line) at a time.

A concrete example may be a possible Aristotelian definition of the English word 'lion' (given in sentences of English, rather than an abstract semanic code):

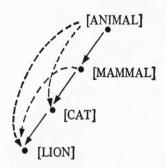

Figure 14. Some hypothetical taxonomic relations between [ANIMAL] and [LION].

A-DEF $(C_1, [\text{LION}]):C_1 =$

(1) "A lion is an animal"

(2) "A lion is a cat,"
"A cat is an animal"

(3) "A lion is a mammal,"
"A mammal is an animal"

(4) "A lion is a cat,"
"A cat is a mammal,"
"A mammal is an animal"

(5) "A lion is a cat,"
"A cat is a mammal"

(6) "A lion is a cat"

(7) "A lion is a mammal"

The subdefinition (4) is the definition one would minimally expect of an ideal native hearer-speaker (if the above definition were reasonably complete, which it is not since it is meant only as a hypothetical example). However, since the ideal native speaker-hearer must be able to communicate with all nonideal hearer-speakers, his competence must naturally include all other possible sub-definitions. The requirements of successful communication are therefore merely that two speakers agree at least on one of the definitions (1) to (7). This is aided by the fact that the less complete definitions are logically contained in the more complete definitions.

Since all relations of taxonomy that can be made are implicitly contained in the fourth subdefinition we could exclude sub-definitions (1), (2), (3), (5), (6), and (7) by an appropriate convention, i.e., that all other paths implied by the longest possible path are understood. The difficulty is of course that we never know if we have reached the most general node of any taxonomy.

One possible way of reducing the enormous complexity of cultural knowledge may be to concentrate on discovering the set of most general concepts which dominate all taxonomies. This has, to my knowledge, never been tried. Nor do we know if this is possible in principle (see pp. 541–542).

The justification of definitions of this type can best be comprehended if one tries to understand the interpretation of the following group of sentences:

(8) "A lion escaped from the city zoo. (9) The animal is large, carnivorous and potentially dangerous; we suggest you stay indoors. (10) So, if you see a large cat, call the police at HYper 2-5402."

The word 'animal' in sentence (6) must be interpretable as a 'lion' or by definitional sentence (1); more adequately perhaps by the inverse of (1): "A lion is an example of an animal." In abstract form 1_1 is the paradigmatic definition of 'lion' in abridged form and a_1 of 'animal': $a_1 \bar{T} 1_1$ ($\bar{T}$ is the inverse of T). Similarly in sentence (10) the definition of 'cat' follows (2) or (6): (k is the paradigmatic definition of 'cat') $k_1 \bar{T} 1_1$ and $k_1 \bar{T} a_1$, or simply $k_1 \bar{T} 1_1$. (See also T-SYN-ONOMY below.)

This raises questions about the identity or distinctness of C_1 (above in the A-DEF) and 1_1. Whereas 1_1 is the paradigmatic definition (see pp. 546–547) given in semantic components, the concept 'lion' may obviously contain further structure. It is in general a complex set derived by the star operation of the paradigm. Thus 1_1 could be called the paradigmatic definition which distinguishes 1_1 from $1_2 \ldots 1_n$ on the same level of the taxonomy. C_1 is even more complex and specifies the position of the word [LION] in the lexical taxonomic field. (Other field relations will be discussed later, pp. 565–566.)

An expanded Aristotelian definition defines a term and its embeddedness in a taxonomy only in part. Just as important for the proper understanding of a word as is the path from the highest dominating node to the term to be defined is the sub-tree which in turn is dominated by it. If we assume that $\bar{T}$ is the inverse of the taxonomic relation such that $a\bar{T}b$ represents approximately "a is included in b" or "a is an example of b" then I will call the following definition a taxonomic definition, or T-DEF of node $\{f, a_1, b_1\}$ in Figure 12 (abbreviations are the same as for A-DEF):

$$\text{T-DEF} (B_1, [P_2]):B_1 = \left\{ \begin{array}{l} [\, b'_1 \bar{T} f' \,] \\ [\, b'_1 \bar{T} a'_1, a'_1 \bar{T} f' \,] \\ [\, b'_1 \bar{T} a'_1 \,] \\ \text{and (any subset of)} \\ [b'_1 \overline{Tc}'_1, b'_1 \overline{Tc}'_2, \ldots] \end{array} \right\}$$

Whereas the first three lines of the definition represent the Aristotelian extended definition, the last line is a definition by enumeration of the members of the class b'_1 which is to be defined. Note that the two types of definitions complement each other.

A taxonomic definition is the disjunction of a set of Aristotelian definitions *and* a definition by enumeration. The enumerated level of the taxonomy may contain further structure. The internal semantic structuring of a taxonomy by a paradigm is an attempt to replace a definition by enumeration, or a list, by a definition by rule, that is, the dimensions, the star operation on the dimensions and the neutralization conditions.

This bundle of features states the necessary and sufficient conditions which an object must satisfy if it is to be a DENOTATUM of the term so defined. Terms having single denotata are the exception; multiple denotation is more generally the case. The class of all possible denotata constitutes its DESIGNATUM. The defining features of a class—the necessary and sufficient conditions for membership in it—are its SIGNIFICATUM. The componential definition of a term is the expression of its significatum.[12]

The relation of the definition by enumeration and the paradigmatic definition which specifies the significata of the class to be defined are apparently in complementary distribution. That is, the presence of the paradigmatic definition obviates the necessity of a definition by enumeration (and to a weaker degree vice versa). In reality the relationship may not be that simple. It appears that the paradigmatic definition compared with the definition by enumeration contains the complex problem of reference. Lounsbury's reduction rules (1964a, 1965) are such rules of reference. That is, the rules specify what the

[12]"(The use of these terms derives from C. W. Morris [1938] and [1946].)" (Lounsbury 1964:1074).

distinguishing characteristics of a set of relatives are in order to be included under one kinship term (within the kinship terminology of a society). The rule itself is therefore a semantic component. In other domains where paraphrases are not as easily elicitable as in the domain of kinship or where criteria of distinctness are nonverbal (Polanyi 1956:49–65; see the discussion on pp. 565–566 about the two possible paths by which any kinship node may be reached in any culture), the problem of reference is much more complex. Therefore for the time being I will include both, paradigmatic definition and definition by enumeration, under the general concept of definition.

The other part of every general definition is an Aristotelian expanded definition for the specification of the dominance relations upward. The taxonomic relation upward is also given by the paradigmatic definitions. Note, however, that it is given by the entire set of paradigmatic definitions and not by a single paradigmatic definition. *This is evidence concerning the logical primacy of semantic and lexical fields over definition.*

Among definitions the taxonomic definition consisting of the Aristotelian and the definition by enumeration are the first empirical steps toward a paradigmatic definition. But the paradigmatic definition (with the star rule) is the definition of an entire semantic-lexical field and not of a single lexical item.

However if we construe the P-DEF narrowly as the definition of one lexical item by a set C_i of semantic components, then the taxonomic definition is complementary and is the explication of a lexical field formed by but one out of the many possible other lexical field relations. The P-DEF as defined earlier (pp. 546–547) was used in this narrow sense.

In its most general form a paradigmatic-taxonomic definition PT-DEF may be specified as follows:

$$\text{PT-DEF } (C, [P_1]) = \text{P-DEF and T-DEF:}$$

$$\left.\begin{array}{c} C = C_i = \{\, d_1, d_2, \dots d_i, \dots d_n \,\} \\ \\ \text{the P-DEF,} \end{array}\right\} \text{ and}$$

$$\left.\begin{array}{c} \{\, C_i \text{Tf} \,\} \\ \dots \dots \text{ and all taxonomic relations} \\ \text{upward, or the A-DEF subpath} \\ \text{of T-DEF,} \end{array}\right\} \text{ and}$$

$$\left.\begin{array}{c} \{\, C_i \overline{\text{T}} p, C_i \overline{\text{T}} g, C_i \overline{\text{T}} r, \dots \,\} \\ \text{the enumeration of all or} \\ \text{part of the members of class } C_i. \end{array}\right\}$$

Any one of the three parts of this definition is retrievable from the field paradigm

$$\{f\} \rightarrow \{f\}*D_1*D_2* \ldots *D_i* \ldots *D_n$$

and the appropriate neutralization conditions. This corresponds to the aforementioned logical primacy of the field paradigm over definitions.

The problem of how the phonological or graphemic 'form' gets 'hooked up' with the C of the PT-DEF is problematic and beyond the scope of this paper.

The PT-DEF given above is complex. Dictionary definitions even in the best of dictionaries appear to be simple by comparison. The reason for this is that dictionaries seem to relate entries only to their nearest neighbors in the network of lexical fields.[13] The complex paradigmatic-taxonomic definition includes such definitions by immediate neighborhood (insofar as the lexical field is paradigmatic-taxonomic). It demonstrates,

[13] The PT field of paradigm and taxonomy is only one out of many possible fields. See pp. 560–561.

however, that such dictionary definitions are at best only partial definitions.

Supertaxonomies

Superficial investigation of natural languages seems to reveal that 'pure' paradigm-taxonomy fields are relatively rare. A much more common form assumed by lexical fields linked by the relation of taxonomy is more complex than ordinary taxonomies. I propose the term 'supertaxonomy' for their designation. Supertaxonomies may be defined in two ways; I will call the first type a *componential supertaxonomy*, the second a *phonological supertaxonomy*:

C-Supertaxonomy. If two subtaxonomies are dominated by a common superordinate node and if the two subtaxonomies have any nodes with identical paradigmatic definitions C_i, then the union of the two taxonomies forms a C-supertaxonomy.

It is illustrated with a simple binary two-level taxonomy below:

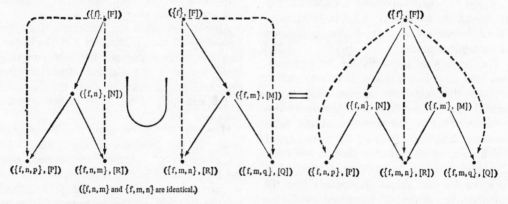

($\{f, n, m\}$ and $\{f, m, n\}$ are identical.)

Figure 15. The union of two taxonomies resulting in a C-supertaxonomy.

A concrete example of a C-supertaxonomy is found in a subsystem of the Yankee kinship terminology:

The paradigmatic representation of the C-supertaxonomy in Figure 16 is:

$\{f\} \rightarrow \{f\}*\{n, 1\}*\{m, w\}$

$D_0 = \{f\}$; $D_1 = \{n, 1\}$; $D_2 = \{m, w\}$

(1) $D_1 \rightarrow \phi$ will yield $\{f, m\}$ and $\{f, w\}$

(2) $D_2 \rightarrow \phi$ will yield $\{f, n\}$ and $\{f, 1\}$

(3) No terminal conditions (execute star operation without neutralizations) with yield:

$\{f, n, m\}$, $\{f, n, w\}$, $\{f, 1, m\}$ and $\{f, 1, w\}$

The paradigmatic definitions C_i exhibit all the proper taxonomic relations by set inclusion.

P-Supertaxonomy. Any taxonomy in which a particular node may be reached by more than one path from the root of the tree, some yielding at least partially different paradigmatic definitions C_i, is a phonological or P-supertaxonomy.

A concrete example of a supertaxonomy comes from Conklin (1962:89). (This is an adaptation of the taxonomy in his Figure 1 as a supertaxonomy; abbreviations as used previously, p. 545.)

This C-supertaxonomy takes into account the fact that both (1) "one dollar is a bill" and (2) "one dollar is a coin" are sentences of English. This situation needs to be distin-

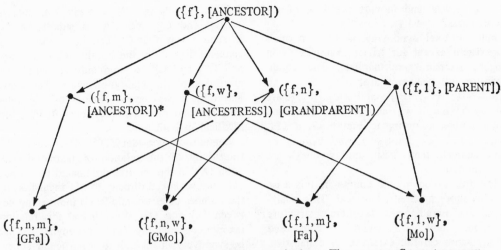

Figure 16. A fragment of the Yankee kinship terminology: The ancestor C-supertaxonomy.
* also [FOREFATHER]

guished from the synonymous paraphrases of (1a) "A buck is a bill" and (2a) "A buck is a coin" and (3) "A buck is a deer." Whereas (1a) and (2a) are part of a supertaxonomy similar to the one depicted in Figure 17, (3) belongs to another taxonomy. The association between (1a), (2a) and (3) is *strictly* phonological and entirely non-semantic. Poets' use of language may exploit phonological as well as semantic associations.

Supertaxonomies and their role in lexical fields need to be investigated in greater detail.

Synonymy

Taxonomies display by force of their structural characteristics two types of synonymy.

This is primarily due to the existence of several paths from a subordinate node to a superordinate node. This fact makes it easy for informants to 'mix levels' of a taxonomy; a particular annoyance in the elicitation of folk taxonomies. For example, to the question in English "What kind of money is there?" an informant may answer "Bills, quarters, dimes and nickels" (see Figure 17); a perfectly reasonable answer explainable entirely by the structural characteristics of taxonomies. The mixing of taxonomic levels is difficult to detect and/or eliminate. Closely linked is the problem of all informants' 'lack of exhaustiveness.' Both of these problems will be discussed later (pp. 570–571). The various types of synonyms explain the nature of

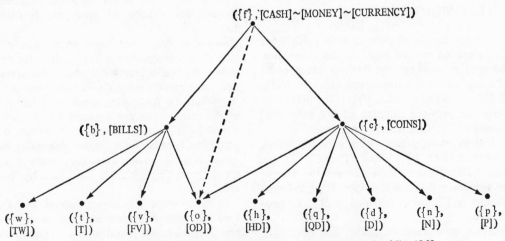

Figure 17. Illustration of a P-supertaxonomy adapted from Conklin 1962.

'mixing levels' and in part the 'lack of exhaustiveness.'

Full or total synonymy is rare, perhaps nonexistent except for trivial examples as in English [ikənámɨks=ekənámɨks]. The conditions for full synonymy are:

SYNONYMY: $(C_1, [P_1])$ and $(C_2, [P_2])$ are full synonyms if C_1 and C_2 are identical. For example, according to Figure 17, if $(F_1,$ [CASH]) and $(F_2,$ [MONEY]), and F_1 and F_2 are identical, then 'cash' and 'money' are full synonyms.

The full synonymy of course in this case may be more apparent than real. This analysis of the paradigmatic taxonomic structure of 'money' and 'cash' cannot be considered in any sense careful, extensive or exhaustive. Similarly:

PARTIAL SYNONYM: $(C_1, [P_1])$ and $(C_2, [P_2])$ are partially synonymous if C_1 is fully contained in C_2. For example, $(B_1,$ [BILL]): $B_1 = \{bTf\}$ as a partial definition; and $(T_1,$ [TEN DOLLARS]); $T_1 = \{tTb, bTf\}$ (again partial definition); and since B_1 is a subset of T_1, 'bill' and 'ten dollars' (perhaps more appropriately and excluded only for the sake of brevity; 'ten-dollar bill') are partial synonyms.

Partial synonymy therefore holds for any two lexical items in the same taxonomy if there is a path from one to the other. For example, 'animal' is a partial synonym of 'lion' (see Figure 14). The relation of synonymy strictly holds only for the partial definition. The situation appears to be more complex particularly for the kind of complex definitions discussed earlier (pp. 555–556):

$(B_1,$ [BILL]): $B_1 = \{bTf\}$ and
$$\{bTo, bTv, bTt, bTw\}$$
$(T_1,$ [TEN]): $T_1 = \{tTf\}$
$$\{tTb, bTf\}$$

We can for the moment exclude $\{tTf\}$ from consideration on the basis of the convention adopted earlier, namely that all other paths are implied by the transitivity of $\{tTb, bTf\}$.

For $B'_1 = \{bTf\}$ and $T'_1 = \{tTb, bTf\}$ we have the previous situation of B'_1 fully contained in T'_1, thus partial synonymy.

For $B'_1 = bTf$, and/or $\{bTo, bTv, bTt, bTw\}$ and $T'_1 = \{bTf, bTt\}$ since tTb and bTt are identical); if the relation includes the inverse of taxonomy then the condition of partial synonymy is T'_1 'fully contained in B'_1'; or generally:

PARTIAL SYNONYMY: $(C_1, [P_1])$ and $(C_2, [P_2])$ are partially synonymous if C'_1 is fully contained in C'_2 and C''_2 is fully contained

in C''_1. (If C'_1 and C''_1 are given as subsets of C_1, and C'_2 and C''_2 as subsets of C_2 in such a way that C'_1 and C'_2 contain only elements linked by the relation of taxonomy, and C''_1 and C''_2 contain only elements that are linked by the relation of inverse taxonomy, and only such elements linked by the relation of taxonomy (if they occur) that are identical in both.)

Let us now consider $\{tTf\}$. Because of the transitivity of the relation of taxonomy any node $\{X\}$ in the sub-tree dominated by a node $\{f\}$ may be linked directly to $\{f\}$ regardless of the number of taxonomic levels intervening between $\{x\}$ and $\{f\}$. We will call this relation taxonomic-synonymy (or T-synonymy). That is, synonymy in relation to a particular superordinate node $\{f\}$.

T-SYNONYMY: (C_1, P_1) and (C_2, P_2) are taxonomically synonymous, if there are two subsets $C'_1{''} = \{c_1Tf\}$ and $C'_2{''} = \{c_2Tf\}$ of C_1 and C_2 respectively. Example: $(B_1,$ [BILL]) and $(T_1,$ [TEN]) are taxonomically synonymous because there exists a subset $B_1{'''} = \{bTf\}$ and a subset $T_1{'''} = \{tTf\}$.

That semantic interpretation of sentences must often operate with the notion of T-synonymy may be seen in sample sentences as the following: "The Batman piggy bank contained bills, quarters, and pennies. The children inserted the money through a slot in Batman's head." That is, the interpretation rests on the T-synonymy of $\{bTf\}$ with $\{gTf\}$ and $\{pTf\}$. (Figure 17.)

The definitions of 'bill' and 'ten' are both partially synonymous and T-synonymous. If the definitions had been more complete the picture would no doubt be more complex. Further investigation of synonymy is called for.

Antonymy. Antonymy seems to be a special case of partial synonymy. That is, if in the definition there is a binary branching in a taxonomy or a paradigmatic dimension which is binary then the contrasting terms on either side of the dichotomies are considered to be antonyms. In this sense 'mother' and 'father' are antonyms because both display essentially the same features except for the binary taxonomic branching which is dominated by 'parents.'

In taxonomies T-synonymy seems to be a kind of multiple antonymy. All terms that are T-synonymous constitute a contrast set, or are mutually exclusive. The common superordinate concept, 'parent,' in the above example, and 'money' in the previous examples, neutralize the T-synonymy of their subordinate taxa. Respectively, 'father,' 'mother,' and 'bill,' 'ten,' are therefore partially synonymous with their subordinate taxa. The superordinate forms are pro-forms which may be used for the entire contrast set of the entire sub-tree dominated by them.

Another type of antonymy seems to be of the type where the antonym is the negation of the other term. This negation seems to be selective in regard to some of the semantic features and does not affect others. For example, 'good' is the negation of 'bad' (or vice versa). The fact that both are evaluative adjectives is not negated—the antonym is not non-evaluative—only the feature of negative or positive evaluation (depending on the direction) seems to be negated.

The rather complex nature of synonymous sets is not exhausted and further investigation is necessary. Additional characteristics of synonymy which in this paper would take us beyond our scope are treated by Weinreich (1963) and Ullmann (1957 and 1963).

Other Relations

The relation of taxonomy may be the most important semantic relation. The semantic theory proposed by Katz, Fodor, and Postal and the revisions by Weinreich rely heavily on taxonomic (dictionary) definitions. All other relations in the Katz and Fodor (1963), Katz and Postal (1964), Weinreich (1966) scheme are relegated to the so-called semantic distinguishers. This wastebasket category is necessary because virtually nothing is known about the structure of semantic fields outside of taxonomies. Katz, Fodor, Postal, and Weinreich emphasize the notion of dictionary definitions in their approaches to semantic theory. This seems misguided. It was seen earlier (pp. 554–555) that definitions based on the paradigmatic-taxonomic fields were *derived* or *retrieved* from the field structure and that definitions were quite complex and redundant in relation to the associated paradigmatic-taxonomic field structure. I therefore once more assert the logical primacy of the field relations over definitions.

It is a fact that all human beings are more or less capable of providing definitions if asked to do so.

This takes cognizance of the fact that a desired definition may not be more sophis-

ticated, than, if queried about a rose, we get the answer: "A rose is a rose (what else, you silly!)." Such lack of sophistication is by no means universal.

However, all definitions are secondary or surface semantic phenomena. They require the prerequisite existence of semantic fields or semantic associations. The evidence for this is based on the greater formal simplicity of field structures. Definitions may be derived from paradigm-taxonomies (including supertaxonomies) but it *is* possible to elicit other kinds of definitions. For example we may define taxonomically the ear as (a kind of body part, or as a (kind of) organ, and especially a (kind of) sense organ. On the other hand we may define it in a functional sense: "The ear is used for hearing," or even "My ears hear (the noise)." Although most educated people will not accept this second sentence on the grounds that it is persons or organisms who hear and not ears, there is no guarantee that this insight is universal either in Western culture or cross-culturally.

Other semantic relations and possible definitions derivable from them will be discussed below.

Part to Whole. The part to whole relation is manifested by the English sentences such as "B is a part of A," or in Navajo in verbal Venn diagrams "hálátł'ááh hála'ḅąąh łahgo bił haz'ą́," *a person's palm occupies somewhere part of the space (surface) occupied by the (surface) of a person's hand.* This is one of the most important relations in eliciting anatomical parts. It may be equally useful in eliciting technology.

The relation displays all the formal characteristics of the relation of taxonomy. Often it is more or less freely convertible into a relation of taxonomy. Sometimes such conversions sound awkward. For example, while "an ear is part of the head" is acceptable, "the ear is a (kind of) head part" is odd. Navajo names for body parts that denote three-dimensional entities, that is, entities that have volume, are freely convertible into taxonomies. Body parts which refer to surfaces of the body are so convertible. Whole to part definitions follow analogously out of the taxonomic definitions. It seems that most whole to part systems display the same type of complexity as was found with supertaxonomies. Figure 18 illustrates this point. The example is from *The Anatomical Atlas of the Navajo* (Werner and Begishe 1966).

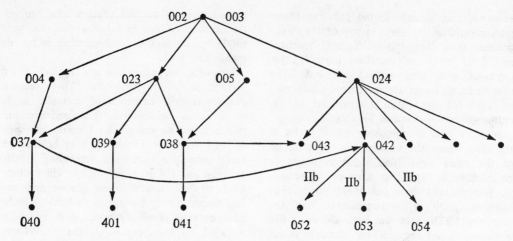

Figure 18. A Sub-tree of Navajo Anatomical Parts from Werner and Begishe (1966).

002 hats'íís bąąh
  (*on*) *body*
003 t'áájizííńt'éę́
  (*on*) *body*
004 hadááhdéę́'
  (*from*) *front of body*
023 hagaan bąąh
  (*on*) *arm*
005 hane'déę́'
  (*from*) *back of body*
024 hála' bąąh
  (*on*) *hand (incl. fingers)*
037 hagaandááhdéę́'
  (*from*) *front of arm*
039 haghosgi
  (*on*) *shoulder*
038 hagaan bine'déę́'
  (*from*) *back of arm*

043 hála'binedéę́'
  (*from*) *back of hand*
042 hálátl'ááh
  palm
040 hadohgi
  (*on*) *biceps*
401 haghostis
  (*on and over*) *shoulder*
041 hach'oozhla'gi
  (*on*) *elbow*
052 hálátl'ááh haldzisí
  hollow of palm
053 hálák'ool
  major lines of palm
054 hála'hada'neests'ee'ígóó
  (*on*) *whorl of finger*

II. *y x* łahgo bił haz'ą́ ⌘ (unlabeled lines)
IIb: *y x* -gi łahgo bił haz'ą́ ⌘ (labeled lines)

The relatedness of the taxonomic and the whole to part relation remains problematic. For example, among the Navajo anatomical parts the taxonomic 'is a kind of' and the relation 'is a part of' alternate seemingly unpredictably, but together form a unitary connected tree structure of the Navajo body parts. What semantic characteristics of the individual entries accounts for this alternation on different levels is not clear. In most cases the taxonomic relation occurs on the lowest levels of the 'part to whole' tree structure.

The interaction and connection of different principles of organization of semantic fields remains one of the foremost problems of semantics and ethnoscience.

Folk Definitions and Lexical Fields. Frake (1964), Williams (1966), and Casagrande and Hale (1967) have proposed other field relations. The work of the latter two authors is particularly interesting because they derive and classify their scheme of defining relations on the basis of empirically obtained folk definitions from Papago informants. The definitional principles obtained from Papago informants coincide with types of word pairs found in word association tests. This further strengthens the notion that definitions are partial retrievals from more complex, more fundamental field structures. The Casagrande and Hale categories of defining statements are listed below in the form of English sentences. These sentences were derived in part by applying the Casagrande and Hale categories to dictionary entries in monolingual English dictionaries. As the authors have predicted, the categories derived from Papago seem to be universal and apply equally well to Papago, Navajo, and English. The total number of relations of this kind seems to be very large. This gives rise to the speculation that if indeed semantic relations beyond taxonomy are a part of the semantic distinguishers, then the distinguishers are very large. *The semantic interpretation of every sentence involves therefore very large parts of the speaker-hearer's knowledge.* Monolingual dictionaries give only the barest minimum of this knowledge because they assume that the users control large parts of the prerequisite knowledge for full understanding. The Casagrande and Hale categories make it clear that the information contained in the semantic distinguishers is more of an encyclopedic character than definitions found in standard dictionary entries. Since encyclopedias are not particularly or notably systematic, the major theoretical goal of ethnoscience which emerges from these considerations remains research into the principles of the organization of knowledge.

Dictionary definitions are then simply partial retrievals from an even more complex network of knowledge than more taxonomies. In this paper terms like the 'network of knowledge,' 'lexical' and 'semantic fields' are used almost interchangeably. The justification of such looseness seems questionable. At least semantic fields seem to be more deeply embedded into mental processes. The precise nature of relationships and the characterization involved in their description need further illumination. Similarly the relationship of lexical and semantic fields, the organization of knowledge and its congruence with current theories of language and semantics, and the highly problematic and uncertain 'psychological reality' of lexicons or dictionaries in the base component of an integrated theory of language, remain unexplored.

The lexical relations proposed by Casagrande and Hale (1967) are shown in the following table.

Class inclusion is the relation of taxonomy discussed above. The spatial relations include the 'part to whole' relation and many others. "Attributives," especially inherent ones, may well be closely linked to the relation of taxonomy, or else it may be the relation which assigns attributive components in the dimensions of a paradigm.

The single-dimension paradigmatic structure of the Navajo taxonomy for heart-lung is based on 'attribution':

$$f \rightarrow \{f\} * D_1$$

where D_1 = dijool *it is ball-shaped (chunky)*, yilzooł (yilzhólí) *it is soft (spongy)* the attributive, hajéídijool *a person's heart-lung is ball-shaped,* hajéídishjool *a person's heart;* the attributive, hajéí yilzoolh *a person's heart-lung is soft,* and hajéíyilzólii *a person's lung.*

The two subordinate taxa *heart* and *lung* are derived by nominalization of the attributive relation. The relation of 'function' and 'operation' respectively specify the possible subjects and objects of verbs. From the specification are derived 'functional' and 'operational' definitions. For example "hammer: it hits" is a 'functional' definition and "whiskey: it is drunk," 'operational.'

'Comparison' is possibly the most important relation used in explanation. It permits the comparison of something unknown with something that is well known. It explains the unknown by the 'comparison.'

At least some form of 'exemplification' seems to be the inverse of the taxonomic relation. The example "sour: lemon" shows that attributives and possibly other relations may be explained by 'exemplification.'

'Provenience' is the most useful relation in recipes and technology. 'Grading' is important in linear orderings on one level of a taxonomy, for example the ordering of the colors of the spectrum from left to right; it is important in scales of evaluation and in the elicitation of verbal Plans. For example, hauling wood precedes chopping it into stove-size pieces. 'Precedes' and 'follows,' however, may have temporal implications not mentioned by Casagrande and Hale. 'Synonymy' and 'antonymy' were discussed previously.

Papago informants used 'contingency' primarily for defining verbs ("if you are hungry you eat"). However, the proper evaluation of this relation is at present problematic.

Frake (1964) introduces the interesting idea of finding inverses to some of the semantic relations. He uses specifically five interlinkages:

?k/?w species-genus or the inverse taxonomic relation and taxonomic.

Name	Relation	Example
Class inclusion (Taxonomy)	___ is ___ NP NP	lion: animal
	___ is a kind of ___ NP NP	
	All ___ are ___ NP NP	
Spatial	___ is part of ___ NP NP	street: city
	and a large number of relations such as	
	___ is above ___ NP NP	
	___ is below ___ NP NP	
	___ is next to ___ NP NP	
	___ connects ___ & ___ NP NP NP	
	___ is between ___ & ___ NP NP NP	
	___ passes through ___ NP NP	blood: heart
	___ is found throughout ___ NP NP	fat: body
Attributive	___ is ___ NP Adj	grass: green
	___ has ___ NP NP	spider: web
	___ make ___ NP NP	bees: honey
Evaluative attributive	___ is ___ NP Adj	honey: good
Function	___ is for the use of ___ NP· V-ing	hammer: hit (ting)
	___ is used for ___ NP V-ing	
Operation	___ is the object of ___ NP V-ing	whiskey: drink
Comparison	___ is like ___ NP NP	butterfly: moth
	___ is not like ___ (?)	woman: man
Exemplification	___ is exemplified by ___	sour: lemon
	___ is an example of ___	lemon: sour
Provenience	___ comes from ___ NP NP	mutton: sheep
	___ is made from ___ NP NP	cheese: milk
	___ comes out of ___ NP NP	gold: mountain
Contingency	if ___ then ___ S S	hungry: eat
	(the slots imply propositions rather than lexical items: e.g., if /lemon is sour/ then /lemon is an example of sour/.)	
Grading	___ precedes ___	Sunday: Monday
	___ follows ___	Monday: Sunday
	___ is almost ___	yellow: white
	(the first two may be spatial, temporal, conceptual)	
Synonymy	___ means ___	command: order
Antonymy	___ means the opposite of ___.	dark: light

ʔk/ʔu species-use	or the inverse taxonomic and function (?)
ʔi/ʔu species-use	or (?) and function (?) and operation (?)
ʔp/ʔs part-source	or part to whole and provenience
ʔu/ʔs use-source	function (?) and operation (?) and provenience.

Similarly the interlinkages (Query-Response networks) of Williams (1966) are also in large part adaptable to the Casagrande and Hale list of relations: 'kind' is the taxonomic relation, 'part' and 'include' (?) is the part to the whole relation, 'from' is provenience, 'for' perhaps function or operation, 'name' maybe synonymy or a new relation of naming. 'Fruit' may represent two relations, one of provenience ("mandarin orange comes from a mandarin orange tree") and taxonomy ("mandarin orange is a kind of fruit"). 'Bloom' and 'which' are perhaps new relations which could be called temporal contingency: "flowers are blooming in spring" or "if it is spring then flowers are blooming," "if it is spring and if it rains then the rain is (called) spring rain." The translations are not easy because both Frake and Williams are considering relations only in terms of the Investigative Unit which is a question-and-answer frame and the appropriate filler terms. They do not focus on the relation proper. Athough question-and-answer frames may be important for eliciting (see pp. 569–570) they are derived from underlying relations. The question "What kinds of x are there?" and the response "There are $y_1, y_2, \ldots y_n$" are derived from the existence of structures linked by $y_1 Tx, \ldots, y_n$. This is again indirect evidence for the logical primacy of lexical fields and semantic fields over the derived question-and-answer frames by which they are elicited.

One of the central problems of these lexical field relations beyond the paradigmatic-taxonomic field is their relative inapplicability to verbs and/or abstract concepts. Except for the small but important contribution of Bendix (1966) (see pp. 575–576) little has been accomplished.

Lounsbury's Expansion Rules. The set of all affinal and consanguineal relatives of an ego form a complex genealogical network or matrix (Hammel 1965). The nodes represent universal classes of relatives. For example, one node may represent all older brothers of ego because no human society distinguishes terminologically between older brothers. Should some anthropologist discover a society where the firstborn or oldest brother is distinguished from other brothers the universal schema will have to be revised.

This universal grid may be called etic network in analogy to the universal phonetic theory which is independent of individual languages. The emic grid by contrast is the respective culture- or language-specific kinship network. A problem of this nomenclature seems to be that, if it is extended to kinship terminologies, as Burling's experiment (1965) seems to indicate and on the basis of my own casual observation of Navajo kinship behavior, there are at least two ways to reach every node in a universal kinship network in every society. One is by the path of the 'regular' kinship terminology and another by 'descriptive' (relative product) combinations of terms close to ego. Thus in Navajo instead of the cousin term shizeedí *my 'cousin'* a Navajo may say shimá bitsílí bighc' *my mother's younger brother's son.* Burling remarks that this latter method of explaining kinship terms seems to have more reality for the Burmese because it may represent the actual way in which the kinship terminology was learned. Whether this is 'psychological reality,' or a culture-specific method of explanation remains to be seen. Certainly the aspect of how the 'regular' kinship terminology is explained in a given society may have important implications and may independently verify the reduction rules postulated by Lounsbury (e.g. 1964a, 1964b, 1965).

The nodes of a universal kinship network are linked by lines which symbolize four relations: (1) parenthood (ascending direction), (2) childhood (descending direction), (3) siblinghood (horizontal consanguineal link), and (4) marriage (horizontal affinal link). The nodes may further have attached attributes: (1) sex (male or female), and (2) relative age (elder or younger).

The expansion rules specify how the complex network of universal kin is to be collapsed so that only the 'regular' kinship terminology remains. This is accomplished by explicit rules which state how certain kinship terms close to the nuclear family are to be expanded in their content in order to include a potentially infinite segment of the kinship network. Lounsbury has demonstrated, especially in Lounsbury (1964a) and (1965), that this kind of analysis has important sociological implications and is a logical prerequisite to extended sociological analysis of kinship.

Whether the method is applicable in lexical domains outside kinship is questionable.

Similarly the position of expansion rules vis-à-vis general ethnoscience and linguistic theory and methodology remains problematic. They are rules by which potential candidates for class membership are evaluated. Although they are of the form of relations these seem to be relations between one set of lexical items of the 'regular' kinship terminology and a set of lexical items of the 'descriptive' kinship terminology. As such they are conversion rules from one system to the other. Implicitly these rules contain the semantic components of the 'descriptive' terminology. That the rules themselves qualify as semantic components of the 'regular' kinship system seems likely but remains at present problematic.

Since the method is highly specialized the reader is referred in particular to the work of Lounsbury (1964a, 1965). His analysis is lucid and contains extensive sociological justification, which is largely absent, for example, in Hammel (1965), whose goals are more formal.

ETHNOSCIENCE ELICITING TECHNIQUES

Although anthropologists have emphasized the role of methodology in the development of ethnoscience (e.g., Frake 1962, 1964), there are to the best of our knowledge no practical guides to ethnoscience field techniques (however, see Samarin 1967). Most publications are not overly clear in the discussion of their techniques. This gap in the literature became evident when we attempted to compile for this section specific illustrations of ethnoscience techniques.

In the 'discovery procedure' controversy we are firmly on the side of stressing the primacy of explanatory theories and the dependence of methodology and field techniques on the former. This does not mean that we consider field techniques unimportant. However, we consider them more as a 'bag of tricks,' of the order of such skills as to know how to read a galvanometer, to build a Wheatstone bridge, to construct a linear accelerator, or to find numerical solutions to a given equation. What galvanometers, Wheatstone bridges, linear accelerators, and equations should be used for is not entirely or even predominantly a question of method or methodology.

The need in ethnoscience is for better theory which will guide us in the selection of the most appropriate techniques. The selection of techniques does not, of course, depend solely on theoretical considerations. There are times in the field when one technique fails—often for reasons of the human field equation—and another needs to be substituted. Aside from theoretical considerations, the ultimate selection of a technique will depend on its fruitfulness.

Native Consultant

Because of the inclusion of lexical-semantic fields, ethnoscience goes beyond conventional lexicography. Subtle investigations of the lexicon of a language are impossible without knowledge of the language with native-like proficiency. Few anthropologists acquire this kind of proficiency during their brief stay in the field. Many semantic subtleties are learned after one has mastered most rules of grammar. After fifteen years in the United States I (Werner) still find myself using English words in a composite of their Hungarian, Slovak, German senses (languages given in order of acquisition). This is true in spite of the fact that today I consider English my language of greatest proficiency.

Claims that one can learn with any kind of subtlety a field work language in a few months smack of intellectual neo-colonialism. Even documented facile language learners who have learned a field language relatively early in life encounter the discouraging native speaker's response, "I know what you mean, but I wouldn't say it that way" (Ken Hale, personal communication, with respect to Papago).

There are two types of contribution to ethnoscience: (1) theoretical contributions independent of the language which is investigated or through which the investigation proceeds; and (2) substantive contributions dependent on the subtle knowledge of a native language. Although the two types may overlap in particular investigations to a considerable extent, type (1) is predominantly the job of trained professional anthropologists, whereas type (2) is best left to a native speaker.

In substantive contributions in the field language, the native consultant acquires a decisively important role. In terms of training, he assumes an intermediate role between the university-trained anthropologist and the native layman of his culture. His education is the responsibility of the anthropologist. As a person on an intermediate level, he becomes akin to what may be called an anthropological technician. In terms of his effort alongside the anthropologist, he becomes a bilingual colleague, a linguistic-cultural expert who can lead the anthropologist through the intricacies of his native culture. It may not be possible to acquire a person like this in all cultures of the world. Wherever this is the case, the anthropologist will be able to proceed far less surely in his research.

Some of the characteristics of such a person are as follows: (1) he must be highly articulate and preferably interested in his native language and culture. In American Indian communities, such persons are available, although their incidence may vary from culture to culture. Among the Navajo, for example, the incidence seems high; among the Hopi, much less frequent. (2) He should be very humble about his cultural-linguistic knowledge. He must display willingness to learn more about his own culture; that is, willingness to consult the experts in cases where interpretation of the data is in doubt.

No interpreter or native consultant is proficient in the vocabulary of every domain of his culture. Due to the division of labor and interest, specialists are to be found even in the simplest of cultures. Besides monitoring formal interviews, the native consultant should be allowed time to converse informally with experts in cultural domains of interest to the anthropologist. Interest in one's specialty is a universal form of flattery. The success of the consultant with the experts will increase as he increases his vocabulary of the field, barring of course exclusions of esoteric discourse from public domain.

The native consultant's willingness to learn from others must coordinate with all his other skills. Deficiencies in lexical specialization are extremely difficult to detect (see the discussion pp. 553–554). Persons who share just a few nodes of a taxonomy can converse successfully because of the transitivity of the taxonomic relation: all subordinate terms can be directly connected to any term which is more general. Often only the consultant's willingness to learn stands between the eliciting of a superficial taxonomy of the native lay person with few intermediate taxonomic levels and the rich stratification of the expert. As far as we know today, the lay taxonomy is (again because of the transitivity of the relation of taxonomy) but one of many possible subsystems of the expert.

(3) The native consultant—in the role of the technician—must be willing to learn the technical vocabulary of the anthropologist (see Hale 1966). This is best accomplished in staff seminars and informal sessions and in the context of actual data.

Native Informants

In addition to one or a few consultants, other native informants should be consulted. These consultations may utilize any of a number of techniques listed below. Informants should be experts in the domain of eliciting, and highly articulate. It is an old lexicographic tradition to consult the most articulate members of the speech community. Although in anthropology more controls are needed and careful records of the provenience, training, age, etc., of informants should be kept, inarticulate informants rarely do more than confirm the evidence. Often their response upon presentation of data from experts is akin to saying, "I wish I had said that."

With any sizable number of informants, the anthropologist faces the problem of agreement. Little work has been done in this area. Perchonock's work (in Perchonock and Werner 1969) shows that there is general agreement on the most general and some of the most specific terms. The expert differs most from the layman in his richness of intermediate-level classifications. Other problems of agreement reflect differential acceptance of classificatory schemes from other languages due to the acculturational situation. In our own work with monolingual Navajos, there are very few unambiguous disagreements between informants. The absence of controversy is the more disturbing since the responses were elicited almost exclusively by non-directed interviewing, or open-ended questions.

Interviews

All interviews by any member of the anthropologist's staff (minimally, the anthropologist and his consultant) should be tape-recorded: first, to allow the consultant to hear interviews where he was not present; second, a few interviews periodically should be recorded *in toto*. This is possible today with portable recorders at $1\frac{7}{8}$ or at $15\frac{5}{16}$ inches per second speeds on thin tape. Such records allow evaluation of interviews.

Transcription

Transcription for ethnoscience work should be as accurately phonemic as possible. If the language under investigation possesses a practical orthography, then it should be used, particularly if consultants and informants are literate. Unless the anthropologist is reasonably skilled in phonemic analysis, this job is better left to a linguist. Pike (1954) is a good guide to the reduction of a language to writing. The Voegelins' guide to transcription (1959) contains many useful hints, particularly short-cuts which today are possible because of typological knowledge about the languages of the world. On the strength of this information, it is possible to exclude phonetic distinctions not found in human languages. The anthropologist with a tape recorder can thus begin eliciting with a broad (few distinctions and few symbols) transcription. If the transcription needs narrowing (more distinctions), then previous transcriptions can be edited by going over the tape record.

Consultants should be or should become (under the direction of the anthropologist) literate in their language. One of the best ways to teach writing to consultants, particularly in contexts where formal study is unknown, is as follows: once the anthropologist has mastered the transcription, the consultant is given a sizable number of sentences to copy. If the consultant has problems wth fine hand motor coordination, substitution of the pencil by a typewriter may help. As the consultant copies a sentence, he should listen to the tape recording of the same sentence. The initial learning session may require great investments of the anthropologist's time. However, finding a consultant and teaching him to write has high priority in any ethnoscience research scheme.

Our experience with native Navajo secretaries has demonstrated that native speakers, once they have been taught to write their language, are more accurate and more proficient transcribers (e.g., of interview protocols) than an anthropologist or linguist coming from the outside.

The anthropologist can teach himself the transcription of a new language in a number of ways. We have found success in the construction of programmed guides to transcription (Werner, Frank, and Begishe 1967). The principle of these guides is simple, if a phonemization of the language is available: A list is made of all the phonemes and their allophones. The phonemes are then sorted into sets. Usually the largest set is a list of phonemes with an allophonic distribution closest to the language of the investigator (English) and is presented first. Either by eliciting, or by excerption from existing dictionaries, monosyllabic or very short words containing only phonemes of the first subset are selected. We have found it most useful to present the words first in the form of a list accompanied by a tape recording of the list. The student learning to transcribe listens to the tape and writes the words. Since the phonemes of the first subset or list are those most similar to the investigator's language (English), the early success in transcription is most rewarding. The second step is to elicit simple sentences containing the words of the first list. The students again listen to a tape of the sentences but fill in only the words from the first list. The third and subsequent steps depend more or less on intuitive judgments regarding the exoticity of the rest of the phonemes. Phonemes that are considered relatively easy from the learner's point of view are presented first; subsequent phonemes follow in increasing order of complexity. Distinctions which are usually not made in the learner's language require special attention. Every effort should be made to heighten the contrast. In our Programmed Guide to

Navajo Transcription we accomplish this by juxtaposition: minimal pairs are presented together whenever possible; Navajo tone is presented in bisyllabic words where one of the two syllables is high, the other always low.

The initial success of our transcription guide in teaching Navajo transcription seems to warrant extension of the method to other exotic languages.

Adaptation of Transcription. For a number of reasons it may be advantageous to adapt a transcription to the typewriter (see p. 568). There are a number of ways to do this. Most transcriptions in Pike (1954) are adapted to typewriters. However, for semantic and/or ethnoscience work, the investigator must work with large bodies of texts or other elicited materials, which are most easily managed by computerized indexing or concordance procedures. It is therefore useful to adopt a transcription on the typewriter in such a way as to facilitate keypunching. Two things need to be kept in mind: (1) ease of typing and (2) the transcription should follow standard transcription and/or orthography as closely as possible. Persons who know how to write the language should require a minimum of retraining time.

For Navajo, we have accomplished this by writing only lower-case symbols. We have replaced all diacritical marks by numbers: '8' preceding a vowel is nasalization, '7' following a vowel is high tone. Fortunately, in Navajo the Bureau of Indian Affairs transcription (Young and Morgan 1942) and the most popular God Bizaad (Navajo Bible) transcription use two- and three-letter clusters for some of the more exotic Navajo phonemes. Thus 'gh' for 'gamma' is well established and does not need further explanation. In other languages, departures from standard orthography may vary. The major advantage of the Navajo computerized transcription system is that the transcriber finds all his symbols on the lower case of the typewriter. All tiresome shifting is eliminated.

Eliciting Techniques

Below we will discuss some of the techniques discussed in the literature, most of which we have tried successfully.

Question and Answer. As members of a cultural system are able to acquire and to transmit knowledge from one generation or from one individual to another, it may be assumed that the ethnographer too can learn how to formulate questions which will elicit the kind of information he needs for an adequate ethnographic description. Every ethnographer encounters the problem of formulating questions in the field which will be meaningful to those being studied. In traditional ethnography, the anthropologist usually attempts to learn and communicate in the native language, asking questions relevant to his own research needs, his observations, and the native's interpretations of particular events. In this broad sense, the approach of traditional ethnography differs little from the 'new ethnography.' Ethnographic ethnoscience, however, further assumes that decisions concerning relevancy and appropriateness, aside from questions concerning meta-theory (see discussion pp. 541–542), must be left to the informant. That is, culturally appropriate answers are elicitable only by culturally relevant questions in the native language.

The initial task, therefore, in ethnographic ethnoscience, is one of ascertaining how a native speaker-hearer finds out what another native speaker-hearer knows. Parenthetically, the question-and-answer technique is often most successful if the anthropologist (or his consultant) and informant assume the fictitious roles of a child (anthropologist) learning from an adult (informant). In many cultures, large domains of questions seem inappropriate without such a fiction.

Frake (1962, 1964) and Metzger and Williams (1963, 1966) are most responsible for developing and illustrating one technique an ethnographer may use to find culturally appropriate questions and answers—the question-and-answer technique. The initial step is to collect questions which seem to be potentially productive in eliciting responses from informants about a particular domain. These may be obtained from casual conversations overheard or recorded, from informants or, most successfully, from a bilingual native consultant, who, if properly briefed on the goals and needs of the research program, can formulate in the native language questions relevant to both the ethnographer's research problems and the cultural system being investigated. These culturally appropriate questions in the question-and-answer procedure constitute *frames* which are utilized to elicit responses from any number of subjects.

Many question-frames evoke lists of items; for example, the taxonomic frame, 'What kinds of————are there,' or the frame of 'provenience,' 'What is————made of.' These lists may increase in number of items with each successive application of a question-frame. Lists in themselves are of relatively little interest for most purposes. More important is the organization of culturally derived categories and/or terms—that is, lexical-semantic fields. For this reason, isolated question-frames are of limited use until interlinked—in some culturally appropriate way. Commonly, an answer elicited by one question will prompt the asking of another question by a native speaker-hearer. An ethnographer may obtain, then, from his informants a set of sequentially ordered questions and answers which are related in some systematic way. This set of interlinked question-frames can be used not only to establish classificatory relations among categories (by way of one pass), but may also serve as a kind of program which can be employed repeatedly for the purpose of establishing consistency and variation.

Restricted to taxonomic eliciting, the question-and-answer method works as follows: (1) Anthropologist and consultant agree on a cultural domain labeled by the native term X. (2) A taxonomic question, analogous in meaning to 'What kinds of X are there?' is elicited in the native language. (3) The question is presented to informants. With proper precautions, the answers will constitute a list. Now the taxonomic relation holds between the term X and the first list of Y's: 'Y is a kind of X.' (4) The question frame from (2) is now applied to the items Y and the question 'What kinds of Y are there?' is presented to informants. Thus, the second, third, . . . , levels of a taxonomy are elicited. The method applies analogously to other kinds of question-frames, based, for example, on the Casagrande and Hale list (1967; see pp. 563–564 of this paper). Obviously, the direction of the eliciting could be reversed from specific to general instead of the usual general to specific. Frake (1964), in particular, has explored some of these inverse relationships.

Some anthropologists, especially Metzger (1964, casual papers), consider the question-frame and the answers as their investigative unit. Our emphasis in this paper is on lexical and/or semantic fields. Lexical items in the fields are all firmly linked by relations, for example, the taxonomic relation (see pp. 548–549). The questions are derived from the underlying lexical and/or semantic fields by a simple question transformation of representative sentences linking lexical items. In other words, *the principal concern of ethnoscience is the organization of knowledge, not the acquisition of knowledge* (questions). In this pursuit, the ethnographer constantly shifts from questions to statements to formal representation.

The application of the question-and-answer frame is well established for taxonomic eliciting. For the elicitation of paradigms or the discriminations of items on one level of a taxonomy, the method is problematic. Perhaps questions of the order of 'What are the attributes of X?' or, if X and Y are on the same level of a taxonomy, 'In what way does X differ from Y?' or 'How can you tell X and Y apart?' may work. However, lexical paraphrase seems to be a more direct way to proceed in the elicitation of the contrast on one taxonomic level (see below). The formal aspects of lexical and/or semantic relations beyond taxonomies and paradigms are not sufficiently known to serve as guides for eliciting.

Advantages. The great strength of the question-and-answer technique is that it is entirely conducted in native language with a minimum need for translation. This is particularly true of taxonomic eliciting. As the ethnographer proceeds with his elicitation, he constructs taxonomic tree structures. As we demonstrated earlier (p. 555), part of the definition of every term in a taxonomy is its position within the tree. This can be grasped almost nonverbally, or with a minimum of information about the distinguishing criteria on one taxonomic level. The necessary minimum may often be merely a translation label.

By interlinking reciprocal series of questions and answers which are derived from relational sentences linking lexical items and their *inverse* (for example, in taxonomies, the inverse of 'What kind of X are there?' may be 'What is Y an example of if Y is a kind of X?'), one may be led to other principles of classification since the inverses are rarely as symmetrical as is the case with taxonomies. Relations linking lexical items beyond taxonomies have important implications for the existence of semantic-lexical fields.

The advantage of the question-and-answer technique as a contextual control (by questions specific to a sociocultural context), as a means to replicability (many informants can be asked the same questions expeditiously), and for the establishment of intracultural similarities and differences (such as those resulting from the division of labor, personal interests, or the acculturational situation), have been mentioned above.

Problems. The question-and-answer technique was only marginally useful in the investigations of Navajo foods by Perchonock (Perchonock and Werner 1969). Naive informants (traditional Navajo housewives) found it difficult to formulate questions in a systematic way. Most of the elicited questions were unproductive for further work. The formulation of questions was more a test of the informant's memory and inventive capacity than her knowledge of the domain of foods. The Navajos' extreme reluctance to expose themselves to failure, real or imagined, further curtailed their readiness to respond.

This implies that skillful formulation of questions is crucial to the question-and-answer method. The formulation of questions worked out in advance in cooperation with the native consultant (see pp. 569–571 and the example concerning Navajo witchcraft eliciting p. 537).

It is difficult to list specific problems in the elicitation of relations beyond taxonomies (see pp. 561–563) because their formal structures are not yet understood. The remaining problems are predominantly relevant to taxonomic eliciting only.

The question-and-answer method is often used to control the informants' responses in such a way that at each application of the taxonomic query they respond with a list. The individual items of the list are then used for further questioning in the same question-frame. It is difficult to constrain articulate informants' responses to mere lists. The resulting texts contain the required lists but with a great deal of supplementary in-

formation. We have found such texts extremely useful as sources for further questioning along other than taxonomic lines. Often the most culturally revealing information came to our attention through such 'unsolicited' textlets. We will list methods for analyzing texts below.

The transitivity of the taxonomic relation (see pp. 553–554) presents three major problems to eliciting:

(1) *Non-exhaustiveness.* Regardless of how many informants the ethnographer consults, one additional informant may be *the* specialist who knows a given cultural domain in greatest detail. There is no formal indication when the analysis is complete. Exhaustiveness is approached only asymptotically. The best indicator of completeness seems to be diminishing returns. In the *Anatomical Atlas of the Navajo* (Werner and Begishe 1966) the field work of the second summer yielded less than ten new terms (out of five hundred already in the *Atlas*). Since then, during another year of analysis, less than five, predominantly synonyms, were added.

(2) *The ambiguity of levels.* This problem of transitivity was discussed with examples earlier (pp. 553–554). Briefly, since every subordinate term in a taxonomy is linked by the taxonomic relation to every superordinate node, any item of an elicited list given in response to a taxonomic query may be on any level of the sub-tree dominated by the superordinate term. It is this feature by which the detailed taxonomy of the expert includes as a special case the subtaxonomy of the layman. But even the best specialist may have lapses of memory or attention and overlook possible intermediate levels. As a result, any elicited list consists of items of very different degrees of generality. Only repeated questioning in both directions from general terms to specific and from specific to general, will gradually clarify the complexities. Unfortunately, this is by no means an automatic process. Every new informant may add to the complexity, which in turn will require extensive further questioning.

Although in work with the *Anatomical Atlas of the Navajo,* we assume, because of diminishing returns, that the lists are reasonably exhaustive, the last four revisions (not counting minor revisions) were essentially reorganizations of the structure of the taxonomic (or more precisely, the 'part to whole') tree structures. Only the fact that the entire system is getting relatively simpler (more clear) seems to indicate that we are approaching the optimal solution.

The ambiguity of levels concerns also supertaxonomies, or the intersection of two subtaxonomies. The problem is discussed in detail earlier (pp. 558–559). In eliciting, such intersections are troublesome because at first sight they often appear to be different systems of classification of two different informants.

(3) *The most general node.* Similar to the indeterminancy of exhaustiveness is the indeterminancy of the highest node elicited in any taxonomy. There is no assurance when the highest node is reached or how the highest nodes of several taxonomies in a culture interrelate. This is one of the acute research problems of ethnoscience (see also discussion, pp. 542–543). The nature of the terms used to label the most general nodes of a taxonomic tree structure is a closely related problem. Some terms are monomorphemic, others utilize multiple morpheme constructions. Still others may consist of entire phrases. The relation of the 'naming units' to each other may be significant, as Mathiot has demonstrated (Mathiot 1962). In Navajo, at least upon cursory examination, only specific terms are monomorphemic or nontransparent in their morphemic structure. All abstract terms or general terms are aggregate. This situation may be responsible for the opinion that languages associated with simple cultures lack abstract (read: abstract monomorphemic) terms.

Card-Sorting. Literate informants are given a set of filing cards on each of which is written a native term of a given domain. The terms may be compiled beforehand from native language dictionaries, ethnographies and so forth, or in the field from informants. An informant is then asked to sort into groups those cards he feels belong together, for whatever reason. The sorting generally proceeds from general categories to specific terms; that is, from large piles (or a few subdivisions of cards) to small piles (or a larger number of subdivisions). At each successive stage or level of subdivision, the informant is asked if there is a name which will cover all the cards in each pile. These

terms are recorded. The process is continued until the finest subdivision is reached.

Perchonock and Werner (1969) found that the sorting scheme could be represented in all cases by a tree structure. The nodes of the tree were labeled by lexical items and the branches of the tree by sentences expressing the relation which holds between two nodes. The sentences of classification were elicited after the sorting of the cards was complete and the nodes labeled. Different principles of classification (i.e., different relations between nodes) were pictured by branches of different colors.

Advantages. The card-sorting technique

(1) gives each informant complete freedom to classify the cards according to any principle he sees fit. This is extremely useful in testing for intracultural variation. For example, the card-sorting process was found to be useful in mapping the effects of acculturation. Navajos who spoke little or no English considered neest'ą̈ *domesticated edible ripeables* (a major category of Navajo foods) as a single category. Those Navajo who speak English frequently or predominantly, consistently divided neest'ą̈ into two groups which were equivalent to the English categories of fruits and vegetables. Some of these acculturated Navajo labeled these two categories by their English terms, while others expressed a vague feeling that somehow neest'ą̈ should be divided into two categories, but had no terms for them. These and other findings help further to substantiate the idea that the ways in which people structure their universe is influenced by the language, or languages, they know.

(2) provides a comparatively expeditious way of eliciting classificatory tree structure. Perchonock was able to obtain a classification of several hundreds of food terms in a single afternoon.

(3) has revealed some interesting features regarding the way in which taxonomies can overlap or intersect—a property of taxonomies less readily apparent in data elicited by the question-and-answer method (Perchonock and Werner 1969).

Problems. The major drawback of the method is that it depends on the literacy of the informants. For eliciting in certain domains pictures instead of words may be substituted (e.g., pictures of 'animals') and mounted on the cards. Picture representation, however, adds a new dimension to the problems: the intercultural translation of visual representations. Photographs or representational illustrations may be used safely in cultures where photographs are viewed regularly.

Tree-Drawing. Informants, especially consultants (see pp. 567–568), appear to grasp easily the principle of classificatory tree structures. This lends support to the impression that these semantic structures—possibly representing only one of several organizations of semantic fields—are language universals. The informant may do the drawing and labeling of the tree entirely on his own, or as he draws the tree structures the ethnographer may record the labels for the nodes. Classificatory sentences may be elicited at this time or left for another pass through the tree structure.

Advantages. Perhaps the main advantage in contrast to the question-and-answer technique and one that this method shares with card-sorting is that the entire classificatory structure is seen at once and inconsistencies are readily apparent. The tree diagrams furnish excellent stimuli for discussion between informant and interviewer or anthropologist and his consultant.

Problems. The problems of this method are also a mixed blessing—at least at the present time. Informants will often link nodes even if a sentence expressing a classificatory relation is unelicitable. The significance of non-verbalizable linkages is not yet clear. The absence of linking sentences, or at least of transitive relations (e.g., taxonomies: X is a Y) is striking in abstract vocabularies such as the terminology of values. Informants will often draw pictures representing hierarchic (i.e., transitive) trees even if the relation among two terms in question is non-hierarchic, but rather, for example, the relation of synonymy.

Paraphrase. Various forms of paraphrase relations are important in the elicitation of paradigmatic components (see p. 544). In Werner & Campbell (Chapter 22) (in this volume) we suggest the following method for eliciting components:

Queen$_1$: Paraphrase$_1$: a female king
Queen$_2$: Paraphrase$_2$: the wife of a king

The paraphrases indicate that while both senses contain the component (or aggregate of components) 'king,' the first contains only the component of femininity; the second, 'feminine,' 'wife' and the relation holding between 'king' and 'wife' which is possibly contained in the components of 'wife' or 'wife to a ———.'

Lounsbury (1956) uses the paraphrase relation to get from covert semantic relations to overt relations by the following formula:

King: Queen: : Lion: Lioness

From the formal marking of lioness for 'femininity,' Lounsbury deduces the marker 'femininity,' for Queen.'

LeVine and Campbell (1965) suggest translation as a special kind of interlanguage paraphrase to get at definitions quickly. By translating key terms of their interest into the informant language, they obtain a set of possible native terms. The native terms are back-translated into an English set of terms. The two sets may then be compared in their referent ranges. Several steps of translation in both directions are possible. Although the method is effective in de-emphasizing the ethnocentric dominance of the English (language of the investigator) vocabulary over the native terms by matching a set of terms in one language by a set in the other, its success depends heavily on the proficiency of the interpreter in English. Rather than being culturally relevant, the two sets may represent the interpreter's idiosyncratic interpretation of English terms. The Voegelins (1960) recognize this problem as one aspect of 'back-translation' (translation from imperfectly known language [vocabulary] of the investigator into the native language).

Folk Definitions. Articulate informants tend to answer questions with small texts. Without exception, these are highly informative. The textlets often contain extensive 'folk definitions.' Following the lead of Ken Hale (Casagrande and Hale 1967) we have found it most useful to ask directly for definitions. The results are most encouraging (e.g., see Werner 1965). The definitions may then be analyzed by the method suggested by Casagrande and Hale (see also pp. 562–563).

We were often able to obtain from Navajo informants up to twenty-minute dissertations on the definition of one lexical item. The informant was permitted to talk freely as long as he kept to or near the topic being investigated. These interviews, consisting of lists, explanations, discourse and definitions, were taped and subsequently transcribed. The average interview ran about twenty typewritten pages, but some spread over several hundred. *Systematization of Folk Definitions.* The principle is simple: Folk definitions and other textual material in the form of complex sentences appearing in regular discourse, are analyzed into simple constituent sentences.[14] Until good transformational grammars are available in the native languages, this is best done intuitively by a competent native speaker (preferably the native consultant see pp. 566–567). The resulting simple sentences are arranged into types of definitional statements given by Casagrande and Hale (see pp. 562–563). Ancillary taxonomic eliciting may be used to ascertain the position of lexical items in a hierarchic tree structure. The sorting out of the various types of definitional statements constitutes systematization of definitions. Since theoretical underpinnings are as yet lacking, we prefer to call them systematized and to contrast them with systematic definitions which would be fully theoretically justified. Thus, paradigmatic (pp. 545–546) and taxonomic definitions (pp. 555–558) may be considered systematic; definitional statements other than these, merely systematized.

In accomplishing the above task, the use of a concordance computer program is most helpful (for an extended explanation of this procedure see Werner 1967). Definitions and texts from transcribed interviews are keypunched onto IBM cards. The output is essentially a KeyWord in Context (KWIC) format.[15]

The concordance program lists all the occurrences of particular lexical items in a given text, in alphabetical order. Each oc-

currence is centered on an output page and flanked by a context of one line (a total of 120 characters including spaces).

From the concordance actual encyclopedic definitions may be excerpted and utilized in three ways:

(1) All textual material may be combined. Sampling problems or sampling bias is ignored since we operate on the assumption that cultural competence is the sum total of all relevant competences. This view of competences is important because of the fact that the division of labor and differences in interest exist even in the least complex of societies, and implies differential knowledge. In an encyclopedic dictionary definition the cultural competence described is that of an omniscient ideal native speaker-hearer (p. 540). This encyclopedic knowledge transcends that of any one individual. Contradictions, of course, must be further investigated.

(2) The definitions may be arranged according to different individuals. This allows one to investigate individual differences of knowledge and their characteristics. Significant points to look for would be: are the differences due to chance or lapses of memory; are they systematic or random; are the different versions relatable by some rules, and so forth.

(3) The sum total (set theoretical union) of encyclopedic definitions from different sources may be compiled, as in (1), and compared with individual versions, as described in (2). For an example of a sample encyclopedic definition see Werner (1967).

Advantages. As has been pointed out, the method is encyclopedic, that is, helps in the construction of extremely complex definitions. Thus, it yields extremely detailed knowledge of the cultural ramifications of given lexical items. The data base is available for ancillary projects (e.g., problems of individual variation).

Problems. This method is extremely time-consuming. However, it is extravagant by anthropological standards only. By the standards of the lexicographers, who are engaged in the making of dictionaries in the major languages of the world, and dependent on the efforts of a large staff, the investment of time and effort is still small.

The method works well only with items that can be defined ostensively, that is, concrete nouns and their general classes. Abstract

---

[14] Some older texts in American Indian languages give the impression that the Indians talk only in simple sentences (e.g., Sapir and Hoijer 1942). Actual live tape recordings of interviews indicate a complex and involved sentence structure. Our explanation is that anthropologists working in exotic languages before the general use of tape recorders had to constrain the informants to short sentences. When these 'abbreviated' texts are read to informants, the effect on them is similar to the 'Dick and Jane' primers on most of us.

[15] We actually prefer to use the NU-CRUDEN program, a recreated and improved version of Martin Kay's CRUDEN from the RAND Corporation. The major advantage of the CRUDEN and NU-CRUDEN programs over KWIC is the use of all eighty columns of the card for data input. This reduces the size of input data decks by 30 percent. Our NU-CRUDEN now also accepts punched paper tape, an input medium preferable in a field operation.

nouns and verbs present special difficulties. At present, not even the precise nature of the problem is clear. The concordance and the method of reducing complex sentences may help to gain insight into the problem, too. Another serious problem is that the set of the Casagrande-Hale principles do not fit into any of the currently proposed semantic theories (these are summed up in Weinreich 1966 together with extensive revision by the author).

Componential Analysis. This is a very specialized method of elicitation, analysis, and display. The steps outlined below are, with one major and some minor modification, the directions given by Wallace and Atkins (1960:60):

(1) The recording of a complete set (or a defined subset) of the terms. . . . In all application of componential analysis outside of the domain of kinship a few components are identified and the domain of these must be established by tedious testing (for example, Werner 1965 and Bendix 1966). Various boundary testing criteria are employed, such as, constant syntactic context, a type of pragmatic situation. A very important but often neglected aspect is the identification of collective terms and the establishment of the existing taxonomic relations. Wallace and Atkins suggest the inclusion under just one cover term 'kinsmen' in the analysis of kinship. We want to urge emphatically the establishment of all collective kinship terms, such as in the Yankee terminology, 'parents,' 'children,' 'grandparents,' 'grandchildren,' 'ancestors,' 'descendants,' and possibly others, as well as the taxonomic relations holding between these and the singular kinship terms. (For a partial taxonomy of Yankee terms see Figure 16, p. 559).

(2) The definition of these terms in the traditional kin-type notation (i.e., as Fa, FaBr, Da, Hu, Br) in the domain of kinship. Note the existence of two possible nomenclatures for kinsmen (see pp. 565–566). The 'real' kinship network may be explained by the 'descriptive' network; the more complex by the simpler closer at hand. The English kin-type notation is thus the second descriptive system of the Yankee terminology. Such descriptive systems may contain universal features which are in need of investigation. In eliciting in non-kinship domains this step may have to be replaced by paradigmatic questions mentioned earlier (p. 570) and/or eliciting by paraphrase. Bendix (1966) was interestingly led to the conclusion that his components in the definition of verbs are relational rather than features. Note that the taxonomic definitions (p. 555) seem to bear out this insight. Only paradigmatic features serving as discriminators on one level of taxonomy seem to be attributive features.

(3) The identification, in the principles of grouping of kin-types, of two or more conceptual dimensions each of whose values ('components') is signified by one or more of the terms. Whereas in the domain of kinship this search (grouping) is restricted to a closed set, outside of kinship the set may be open. If a taxonomy is elicitable the search may be restricted to a single level or a few levels of the taxonomy. The set containing a common component in abstract terminologies seems to be always open. Abstract terms rarely fit taxonomic structures in any revealing sense.

(4) The definition of each term, by means of a symbolic notation, as a specific combination, or a set of combinations of components. This is of course the description of a paradigmatic definition (p. 546). The introduction of taxonomic relations which are often overlooked in componential analyses of kinship produce asymmetrical paradigms (p. 546) and definitions which contain paradigmatic and taxonomic definitions (p. 546 and p. 555).

(5) A statement of the semantic relationship among the terms and the structural principles of this terminological system. In particular, this involves the representation of taxonomic relations as a tree graph. Paradigms are not representable graphically (see p. 544).

BIBLIOGRAPHY

BENDIX, E. H.
1966 *Componential analysis of general vocabulary: the semantic structure of a set of verbs in English, Hindi and Japanese.* Publication 41, Indiana University Research Center in Anthropology Folklore and Linguistics.

BOHANNAN, P. J.
1963 *Social anthropology.* New York, Holt, Rinehart and Winston.

BRONOWSKI, J.
1966 The logic of the mind. *American Scientist* 54:1–14.

BUCHLER, I., and R. FREEZE
1966 The distinctive features of pronominal systems. *Anthropological Linguistics* 88: 78–105.

BURLING R.
1965 Burmese kinship terminology. In E. A. Hammel, ed., Formal semantic analysis. *American Anthropologist* 67:5, Part 2.

CASAGRANDE, J. B., and K. L. HALE
1967 Semantic relations in Papago folk definitions. In D. Hymes, ed., *Language in culture and society.* New York, Harper and Row.

CHAFE, W. L.
1965 Meaning in language. In E. A. Hammel, ed., Formal semantic analysis. *American Anthropologist* 67:5, Part 2.

CHOMSKY, N.
1965 *Aspects of the theory of syntax.* Cambridge, Mass., M.I.T. Press.

COLBY, B. N.
1965 Ethnographic semantics (and CA treatment). *Current Anthropology* 7:3–3.

CONKLIN, H. C.
1962 Lexicographical treatment of folk taxonomies. In *Householder and Soporta,* 1962, pp. 119–141.
1964 Ethnogenealogical methods. In W. H. Goodenough ed., *Explorations in cultural anthropology.* New York, McGraw-Hill.

COOPER, W.
1964 *Set theory and syntactic description.* Cambridge, Mass., Mouton.

FRAKE, C. O.
1962 The ethnographic study of cognitive systems. In T. Gladwin and W. C. Sturtevant, eds., *Anthropology and human behavior.* Washington, D.C., Anthropological Society of Washington.
1964 Notes on queries in ethnography. In A. K. Romney and R. G. D'Andrade, eds., Transcultural studies in cognition. *American Anthropologist* 66, Part 2.

GARVIN, P. L. (ed.)
1957 *Report of the seventh annual round table meeting on linguistics and language study.* Washington, D.C., Georgetown University Press.

GLADWIN, T., and W. C. STURTEVANT (eds.)
1962 *Anthropology and human behavior.* Washington D.C., Anthropological Society of Washington.

GOODENOUGH, W. H.
1957 Cultural Anthropology and Linguistics. In P. L. Garvin, ed., *Report of the seventh annual round table meeting on linguistics and language.* Washington, D.C., Georgetown University Press. Reprinted in Hymes 1964.
1964 *Explorations in cultural anthropology.* New York, McGraw-Hill.
1965 Yankee kinship terminology: a problem in componential analysis. In E. A. Hammel, ed., *Formal semantic analysis. American Anthropologist* 67:5, Part 2.

GREENBERG, J. (ed.)
1963 *Universals of language.* Cambridge, Mass., M.I.T. Press.

GUMPERZ, J. J., and D. HYMES (eds.)
1964 The Ethnography of communication. *American Anthropologist* 66, Part 2.

HALE, K. L.

HAMMEL, E. A. (ed.)
1966 The use of informants in field work. *Canadian Journal of Linguistics* 10:108–119.
1965 Formal semantic analysis. *American Anthropologist* 67:5, Part 2.

HERSKOVITS, M. J.
1955 *Cultural Anthropology.* New York, Knopf.

HOCKETT, C. F.
1962 *Scheduling.* Paper prepared in advance for participants in Burg Wartenstein Symposium No. 21. "The determination of the philosophy of a culture." Wenner-Gren Foundation for Anthropological Research.

HOEBEL, E. A.
1966 *Anthropology: the study of man.* New York, McGraw-Hill.

HONIGMANN, J. J.
1959 *The world of man.* New York, Harper.

HYMES, D.
1962 The ethnography of speaking. In T. Gladwin and W. C. Sturtevant, eds., *Anthropology and human behavior.* Washington, D.C., Anthropological Society of Washington.

1964a Toward ethnographies of communication. In J. J. Gumperz and D. Hymes, eds., The ethnography of communication. *American Anthropologist* 66, Part 2.

1964b (ed.) *Language in culture and society.* New York, Harper and Row.

1967 (ed.) *Studies in Southwestern ethnolinguistics.* Cambridge, Mass., Mouton.

KATZ, J. J.
1963 The structure of a semantic theory. *Language* 39:170–210.

KATZ, J. J., and P. POSTAL
1964 *An integrated theory of linguistic descriptions.* Cambridge, Mass., M.I.T. Press.

KAY, P.
1965 Comment on Colby, Ethnographic semantics. *Current Anthropology* 7:21.

KEESING, F. M.
1960 *Cultural anthropology.* New York, Rinehart.

KLUCKHOHN, C.
1944 *Navaho Witchcraft.* Papers of the Peabody Museum, Harvard University, Vol. 22.

KROEBER, A. L.
1948 *Anthropology:* race, language, culture, psychology, prehistory. New York, Harcourt, Brace.

KROEBER, A. L., and C. KLUCKHOHN
1953 (1963 ed.) *Culture: a critical review of concepts and definitions.* New York, Vintage Books.

KUHN, T. S.
1956 *The structure of scientific revolution.* Chicago, University of Chicago Press.

LAKOFF, G.
1965 *On the nature of syntactic irregularity.* The Computation Laboratory of Harvard University. NSF 16.

LANDAR, H., SUSAN M. ERVIN, and A. E. HOROWITZ
1960 Navaho color categories. *Language* 36:368–382.

LEVINE, R. A., and D. T. CAMPBELL
1965 *Ethnocentrism field manual.* Evanston, Ill., Northwestern University.

LOUNSBURY, F. G.
1956 A semantic analysis of Pawnee kinship usage. *Language* 32:158–194.

1964a A formal account of the Crow and Omaha type kinship terminologies. In W. H. Goodenough, ed., *Explorations in cultural anthropology.* New York, McGraw-Hill.

1964b The structural analysis of kinship semantics. In H. G. Lunt, ed., *Proceedings of the Ninth International Congress of Linguists.* Cambridge, Mass., Mouton.

1965 Another view of Trobriand kinship categories. In E. A. Hammel, ed., Formal semantic analysis. *American Anthropologist* 67:5, Part 2.

LUNT, H. G. (ed.)
1964 *Proceedings of the Ninth International Congress of Linguists.* Cambridge, Mass., Mouton.

LYONS, J.
1963 *Structural semantics.* Oxford, Basil Blackwell.

MATHIOT, MADELEINE
1962 Noun classes and folk taxonomy in Papago. *American Anthropologist* 64:340–350.

METZGER, D. G.
1964 Several informal papers. Dittoed.

METZGER, D. G., and G. E. WILLIAMS
1963 A formal ethnographic analysis of Tenejapa Ladino weddings. *American Anthropologist* 65:1076–1101.

1966 Procedures and results in the study of native categories: Tseltal firewood. *American Anthropologist* 68:389–407.

MORRIS, C. W.
1946 *Sign, language and behavior.* New York, Prentice-Hall.

1938 Foundation of the theory of signs. *International Encyclopedia of Unified Science,* Vol. 1. No. 2. Chicago, Chicago University Press.

MURDOCK, G. P.
1960 *Outline of cultural materials.* New Haven, Human Relations Area Files.

NAROLL, R.
1962 *Data quality control.* Glencoe, Ill., Free Press.

NORTHROP, F. S. C., and H. H. LIVINGSTON (eds.)
1964 *Cross cultural understanding: epistemology in anthropology.* New York, Harper and Row.

PERCHONOCK, NORMA, and O. WERNER
1969 *Navaho systems of classification: some implications for ethnoscience.* 1969 Ethnology 8:229–242.

PIKE, K. L.
1947 *Phonemics.* Ann Arbor, University of Michigan Press.

1954– *Language is relation to a unified theory*
1955– *of the structure of human behavior,* Parts
1960 I, II, IV (Preliminary ed.). Glendale, Calif., Summer Institute of Linguistics.

POLANYI, M.
1956 (1964 ed.) *Personal knowledge.* New York, Harper Torchbooks.

ROBERTS, J. M., B. SUTTON-SMITH, and A. KINDON
1963 Strategy in games and folktales. *Journal of Social Psychology* 63:185–99.

ROMNEY, A. K., and R. G. D'ANDRADE
1964 Transcultural studies in cognition. *American Anthropologist* 66, Part 2.

SAMARIN, W.
1967 *Field linguistics.* New York, Holt, Rinehart and Winston.

SAPIR, E., and H. HOIJER
1942   *Navaho texts.* Linguistic Society of America.

SCHNEIDER, D. M.
1965   American kin terms and terms for kinsmen: a critique of Goodenough's Componential analysis of Yankee kinship terminology. In Hammel 1965:288–308.

SEBEOK, T. A.
1966   *Current trends in linguistics,* Vol. 3. Cambridge, Mass., Mouton.

TRIER, J.
1931   *Der Deutsche Wortschatz im Sinnbereich des Verstandes: die Geschichte eines Sprachlichen Feldes.* Heidelberg.

ULLMANN, S. DE
1957   *The principles of semantics. A linguistic approach to meaning.* Oxford, Basil Blackwell.
1963   Semantic universals. In J. Greenberg, ed., *Universals of language.* Cambridge, Mass., M.I.T. Press.

VOEGELIN, C. F., and FLORENCE M. VOEGELIN
1959   Guide for transcribing unwritten languages in field work. *Anthropological Linguistics* 1.1:1–28.
1960   Selection in Hopi ethics, linguistics and translation. *Anthropological Linguistics* 2.2:48–77.

WALLACE, A. F. C., and J. ATKINS
1960   The meaning of kinship terms. *American Anthropologist* 62:58–80.

WEINREICH, V.
1963   On the semantic structure of language. In J. Greenberg, ed., *Universals of language.* Cambridge, Mass., M.I.T. Press.
1966   Explorations in semantic theory. In T. A. Sebeok, ed., *Current trends in linguistics.* Cambridge, Mass., Mouton.

WERNER, O.
1965   Semantics of Navaho medical terms: I. *International Journal of American Linguistics* 31:1–17.
1966   Ethnoscience and pragmatics. *Anthropological Linguistics* 8.8:42–65.
1967a Taxonomy and paradigm: two semantic structures. MS.
1967b Systematized lexicography or ethnoscience: the use of computer-made concordances. *American Behavioral Scientist* 10:5–8.

WERNER, O., and K. BEGISHE
1966   *The anatomical atlas of the Navajo,* 3rd rev. preliminary version. MS.

WERNER, O., JEANETT FRANK, and K. Y. BEGISHE
1967   *A programmed guide to Navajo transcription,* 2nd ed. Evanston, Ill., Northwestern University.

WILLIAMS, G. E.
1966   Linguistic reflection of cultural systems. *Anthropological Linguistics* 8.8:13–21.

YOUNG, R. W., and W. MORGAN
1942   *The Navaho language.* United States Indian Service.

PART V

Comparative Approaches

CHAPTER 30

Comparativists and Non-Comparativists in Anthropology

ANDRÉ J. F. KÖBBEN

THE ESSENCE OF GENERALIZATION

As I pointed out in Chapter 4, many statements have been made in anthropology of the type "where A, there B," or again, "where A, there B, there C, . . ."—statements concerning the functional relationship between two, three, or a whole series of social phenomena. What do we do when formulating regularities of this kind? Do we *create* order in what is *factually* chaos, or do we *describe* order in what is *apparently* chaos? Obviously the answer is that we do both. Or, to put it differently, that we in fact create order, but that social phenomena are such that they allow us to do so. Take as an example Radcliffe-Brown's (1952) article about the mother's brother in Africa. He claims that in different patrilineal societies the relations of ego vis-à-vis his mother's brothers are of a similar kind. What justification has he for his conclusions? He derives his most outstanding example from Junod's (1927:267–271) description of the Ba-Thonga.

The uterine nephew all through his career is the object of special care on the part of his uncle. . . . The latter has a special right of intercession on behalf of his nephew and . . . is charged to sacrificing for him. Of the uterine nephew it is said, "he is a chief! He takes any liberty he likes with his maternal uncle" . . . In religious ceremonies he cuts the prayer and steals the meat or the beer of the sacrifice and runs away with them. As to inheritance, the sons of the deceased have the sole right of property, but the uterine nephews refuse to be left out. You will find them everywhere, trying to get something for themselves. They were already planning with the mother's brother's wives to take them as spouses after the death of their husband; they tease the whole family on the day of the distribution of the widows.

When we compare this situation with, say, that among the Bete (Köbben 1956:114–115; Paulme 1962:69–72), the Bwamba (Winter 1957:181–191), the Kgatla (Schapera 1940: 111–113), and the Nuer (Evans-Pritchard 1951:162–167), we see very different pictures! Ego's behavior toward his mother's brother among the Thonga would be thought shocking by the other tribes mentioned, at least in some of its details (different details in different societies): the effrontery of a Thonga's sister's son is absent among most of them, especially among the Nuer, who would have to fear the mother's brother's curse when so acting. The Kgatla do not abuse their mother's brothers, although ego may steal some of his mother's brother's possessions as does his Thonga counterpart. Among the Bete there is good-natured banter from both sides, but no stealing; here the relationship is much more reciprocal than among the Thonga.[1]

In every one of the cases mentioned there are still other distinctive features, so that with regard to this relationship an individual from one society would not be able to behave adequately in any of the other societies. In other words, in all these cases the relationship is truly "unique."

Still Radcliffe-Brown is justified in putting

This paper was originally prepared for Proceedings, Symposium on Cross-Cultural Research Tools in Comparative Social Anthropology (Paris, September 19–22, 1966).

[1] At least this is how I described the ego versus maternal uncle relationship among the Bete (district of Gagnoa). Paulme, however, who did her fieldwork in Daloa district, depicts a situation which is much more reminiscent of the Thonga one.

all these cases, as well as untold others,[2] into one category. But he can put these cases into one category only on condition that he chooses a high-enough level of abstraction (Evans-Pritchard 1963:4): "affection, cordiality, relative indulgence" on the one hand, versus "respect, formality, rigidity" on the other. In Radcliffe-Brown's (1952:21) own words: "the father's sister is (the relative) to be respected and obeyed. The mother's brother is the relative from whom he may expect indulgence, with whom he may be familiar and take liberties."

Operating thus on a higher level of abstraction is the essence of all generalizing and not "leaving out the details" as is sometimes alleged. Richards (1957:28), after having remarked that modern fieldwork "finds more and more details about more and more," alleges that such methods make ambitious comparisons impossible. If, however, the categories we construe are broad enough, innumerable details may well be subsumed. Of course, the comparativist may, and often does, decide "to leave out details," that is, put a case into a category notwithstanding minor contrary evidence—that is what footnotes are for—but apart from the fact that it is not essential to the operation, he should not carry this process too far.

To avoid misunderstanding let me make it clear that I do not suggest that *all aspects* of a society should be assessed when comparing, rather *all the details* of the particular aspects that are the subject of comparison. As Popper (1959:420–422) phrases it so aptly: "Two things (e.g., societies) which are similar are always similar in certain aspects. Similarity . . . always presupposes the adoption of a point of view." The five societies mentioned which we put into one category as to ego–mother's brother relationships would have to be put into quite different categories as to means of livelihood, political structure, social stratification and what not.

What is true for *inter*cultural comparisons is equally true for *intra*cultural comparisons: we impose order but the property of social phenomena is such that it allows us to do so. The relations between any pair of ego and maternal uncle in a particular society have their distinctive characteristics (are unique)

and it needs an operation of the mind to put them all into one category. Thus among the Bete ego may be richer than his maternal uncle, which may affect the reciprocal character of the relationship; or he may be educated and therefore feel too "civilized" to act according to all the niceties of custom; or he and his mother's brother may be partners in some sort of commercial venture which may become the overriding bond between them; or the mother's brother may simply live too far away from ego for any real relationship to develop (Köbben, field notes; Paulme 1962:72).

Generalization, then, entails the loss of uniqueness and variegation; a monotony is suggested which does not really exist in social behavior. If we nevertheless generalize and thereby accept the loss, it is in order to gain. What we do gain is not only order but also the *explanation* of order: we note not only the uniformity in the ego–mother's brother relation, but also that it occurs in patrilineal societies and we lay a causal or functional nexus between the two phenomena. Or take as another example Ruth Benedict's (1934: Chap. 4) classical description of Pueblo Indian culture. She depicts it as a unique configuration ("Apollonian": no excesses, aversion of individualism, no striving for power and leadership) and as such she cannot and does not try to explain it otherwise than as an internally consistent system. One may well argue that Benedict's picture of Pueblo society is one-sided and that some of her evidence may be differently interpreted (Li-An-che 1937), also that what she describes as internalized behavior is at least partly enforced by the rigorous Pueblo judicial system (Hoebel 1969), but that is beside the point here. Her purpose is merely to point out the existence of an internally consistent system, and she leaves her readers wondering why it should have come about. In a paper by Thoden van Velzen and Van Wetering (1960), however, Pueblo culture is treated as one of a class of societies: those which avoid uncontrolled force internally while allowing for aggression externally. The authors have found twenty of these societies which they compare with a control group of other societies, and thereby look for causal relations. The causal nexus in this case appears to lie in the fact that these societies are non-stratified and matrilocal. They cannot af-

[2] Not *all* patrilineal societies, however! Among the Mende a man should show marked respect toward his mother's brother (Little 1954:110).

ford to allow aggression to exist. Again, what we get is not only order but also its explanation.

THE REASONS FOR AND AGAINST COMPARISON

We may well ask whether the sacrifice of uniqueness is worth the price. In the anthropological fraternity there are two constantly warring factions which we may label the comparativists and the non-comparativists, and they would give a totally different answer to this question. The non-comparativists plead its inadvisability; some of them would even go further and question its admissibility.

This dichotomy—comparativists versus non-comparativists—is by no means to be found only in our discipline. In fact, it has a long standing in the history of science. In a chapter of his *Critique of Pure Reason* Kant deals with it, distinguishing between two groups of scholars, one following the principle of "specification," the other following the principle of "homogeneity."

This distinction shows itself in the different manner of thought among students of nature, some . . . being almost averse to heterogeneousness, and always intent on the unity of genera; while others . . . are constantly striving to divide nature into so much variety that one might lose almost all hope of being able to distribute its phenomena according to general principles. [in Cassirer 1955: 5–6]

Kant points out that both attitudes are not really in conflict with one another, as they do not express any fundamental ontological difference. They rather represent a twofold interest of human reason. Jones (1961:20–23), in about the same way, constructs an order-disorder continuum and formulates the difference between its two extremes:

Some individuals prefer system, clarity and structure, what we may call the neat package; others enjoy complexity, fluidity and disorder. Those who prize order usually put a high premium on conceptual analysis; those who prize disorder minimize or distrust analysis. Where the former aim at a systematic pigeonholing and classifying of experience, the latter exclaim "we murder to dissect." What the former reject as hopelessly chaotic, the latter will describe as a fruitful mess. On the other hand, explanations satisfying the former are

likely to be criticized by the latter as "oversimplified" or "false to the facts."

Jones compares William James and Munsterberg and quotes the former as saying: "I want a world of anarchy, Munsterberg one of bureaucracy, and each of us appeals to nature to back him up. *Nature partly helps and partly resists each of us*" (my italics).

Thus, this distinction is not the same as that between "ideographic" and "nomothetical" sciences (Windelband 1904), or that between "individualizing" and "generalizing" sciences (Rickert 1926) as in the latter cases the distinction is not between minds of scientists but an alleged ontological difference between the phenomena itself. This Windelband-Rickert distinction is not wholly without its base: when examining molecules, cells, beetles or quails, what strikes the eye is uniformity. It is only recently that zoologists with highly refined observation methods have succeeded in noticing *differences* in behavior between individual beetles. When studying human beings it is no longer so difficult to see idiosyncrasies; conceivably, a psychologist may study individuals as easily under the head of uniformity as under that of difference. But our subject matter, which is groups and institutions with different cultural background, asks for a mental effort to see the *uniformities*.

Anthropology is more plagued by this controversy than any of the other social sciences with the possible exception of history (Romein 1946:11–12). There are many confirmed non-comparativists among anthropologists and we may ask why this should be so. It has, first of all, something to do with our subject matter, which admittedly does not lend itself easily to generalization. Secondly, it has to do with the traumatic experience—fieldwork—anthropologists have gone through which makes them unwilling to see the society, whose uniqueness they have established with such infinite care, treated as just one more specimen of a genus. It is much the same as the individual in a hospital who does not like to hear himself being referred to as just "a case." Thirdly, it has to do with the kind of personalities who choose anthropology as a career (compare the personnel of any department of anthropology with, say, that of economics). Many—but not all—anthropologists are essentially romantic and appreciate social phenomena rather from the aesthetic than from the scientific point of view. As Bohannan (1957:vii) has put it: "Anthropology provides an artistic impression of the original, not a photographic; I am no camera." Our distinction is, of course, far too clear-cut and has, in fact, all the qualities which make the non-comparativist shudder. Take Malinowski, in whose breast two souls seemed to live; he says on the one hand that ". . . in the science of culture to tear out a custom which belongs to a certain context leads nowhere," whereas on the other hand he contends that "unless we use the comparative method from the functional point of view, and through this obtain the laws of correlation we shall inevitably be building our vast edifices of philosophical reflection on sand" (Malinowski 1932:xxv).

Others at least theoretically acknowledge the need for generalization but think that we are not yet ready for it (note that they never specify when that blessed moment will arrive). Holleman (1963:5–6), talking about acculturation, says: "We should fix our attention much more thoroughly upon diversity before we can hope to generalize with any amount of certainty; *until then we remain visitors of Babel*" (my italics).

The comparativists, on the contrary, argue that we cannot escape generalizing anyhow and that we might therefore better do it as explicitly and systematically as possible, so as to avoid Babel and the confusion it stands for. When so generalizing, however, they would do well to pay attention to the protestations of their opponents so that these may play the part of the devil's advocate and help to avoid the many possible pitfalls, thereby promoting the sake of comparison, however indirectly. We will discuss the non-comparativists' objections under the following headings (not all non-comparativists would agree to all of these): a) the allegation that cross-cultural generalizations based on comparison amount to trivialities or tautologies only; b) the allegation that generalizations should be arrived at by analyzing thoroughly one society rather than a great number of societies; c) the allegation that the comparing of elements from different societies leads to inadmissible distortions of reality.

THE ALLEGATION OF TRIVIALITY

Let us take as our starting point Evans-Pritchard's (1965: Chap. 1) recent essay on "the comparative method in social anthropology." In it he discusses at length Nieboer's early attempt to explain why in some types of society slavery exists whereas in others it does not. He duly praises Nieboer for the care and sublety with which this author assesses his data, but he judges his final outcome as being most disappointing: "his conclusions take us little beyond what one might have expected: that as a rule slaves are not kept when there is no use for them." This would indeed have been a poor result for a 474-page book based on years of patient research, but Evans-Pritchard does Nieboer an injustice in so summing up his position. Nieboer's (1910: Part 2) main thesis is: "where slavery, there open resources"; by "open resources" in an agricultural society he means a situation where there is land in plenty, or where, at least, not all land is being used, and where few capital goods are required to till the soil. He reasons that in such societies there are no economic reasons for a man to volunteer to work for another. Accordingly, when you want someone to work for you, you have to force him; hence slavery. As a cause of slavery this may seem self-evident, but it had never before been recognized as such, so that by pointing to it Nieboer really added to our insight into the functioning of human society. What is more, Nieboer's rule does not hold good for all cases (societies): presumably when a rule or law is trivial it is at the same time without exception. In a recent retesting of Nieboer's hypothesis, it appeared to be true for one type of society only (i.e., a stratified society) and even then only in the sense that there is a statistically significant correlation between the two phenomena (slavery and open resources) (Bax 1966:90–107; Köbben 1967:4–5, 12, 13, 15). So in order to explain the phenomenon of slavery, at least the additional factor of stratification has to be taken into account. Therefore: "where slavery, there stratification (apart from slavery itself) *and* open resources." I predict that this additional factor will again seem self-evident to many a reader. But the fact remains that neither Nieboer nor

Evans-Pritchard nor anyone else has clearly seen this causal nexus before.

Often, if a proposition seems trivial and self-evident it is simply a function of its having been suggestively presented and aptly illustrated by data from one or two societies, that fit well. Take the hypothesis that societies with a high degree of political complexity lack feuding. A number of writers have argued that where societies become politically more complex, courts intervene in the case of murder and prevent the relatives of the victim from taking direct revenge. This argument seems so reasonable, and indeed self-evident, that until recently nobody bothered to test it. When it was tested, however, no statistically significant relation was found between level of political integration and presence of feuding (Otterbein and Otterbein 1965:1475–1476). Or take Fallers' (1956:242) proposition "that societies with hierarchial, centralized political systems incorporate the Western type of civil service structure with less strain and instability than do societies having other political systems." This sounds quite convincing and even trivial . . . until one meets with exactly the opposite proposition (Apthorpe 1959:xiv), again backed up by empirical data from a handful of societies ("it is in societies which are not hierarchically centralized that Western ideas of bureaucracy can be more speedily adopted"); then one realizes that this sounds no less convincing than the earlier proposition.

All this is not to deny that sometimes trivial generalizations *are* formulated in comparative anthropology. The higher our level of abstraction, the greater the danger that our generalizations are commonplace (cf. Boas as cited in Lévi-Strauss 1963:13). In my very first lectures to first-year students, I use highest-level generalizations, such as: "where tribal societies, there less calculating and organizing than in Western society." Or even: "where human society, there. . . ." It is exceptional indeed when generalizations on this level manage to whet the curiosity of professional anthropologists. As an example we may take Foster's (1962: Chap. 3) rule to the effect that "where peasant community, there interpersonal relations strained: suspicion, enmity, envy, lack of cooperation." This embraces the greater part of the world population; and if it nevertheless arouses our interest it is only because of the far too rosy view of group life in small-scale societies that was until recently prevalent among anthropologists, as exemplified by the following quotation (Murdock 1949:83):

. . . the members of a community form an in-group, characterized by internal peace, law, order, and cooperative effort. Since they assist one another in the activities which gratify basic drives, and provide one another with certain derivative satisfactions obtainable only in social life, there develops among them a collective sentiment of group solidarity and loyalty.

If Foster's evaluation of community life in peasant societies is going to be shared by most anthropologists, his rule will soon be thrown on the scrap heap of trivialities. There is only one way to escape this fate, and that is by pointing to exceptions to his rule; only by questioning its general validity can its viability be assured. The prospects for Foster's rule seen in this light are not too gloomy. In his original presentation Foster (1959:175) himself mentions one exception and there are undoubtedly others.

GENERALIZATION WITHOUT COMPARISON?

A belligerent non-comparativist is Edmund Leach, whose *Rethinking Anthropology* (1961: 1–27) is pertinent to our subject. He distinguishes between two varieties of generalization: one, which he claims to dislike, allegedly deriving from the work of Radcliffe-Brown, the other, which he claims to admire, from that of Lévi-Strauss. Leach emphasizes that his concern is with *generalization,* not with *comparison:*

Comparison and generalization are both forms of scientific activity, but different. Comparison is a matter of butterfly collecting,—of classification, of the arrangement of things according to their types and subtypes. The followers of Radcliffe-Brown are anthropological butterfly collectors. . . . Arranging butterflies according to their types and subtypes is tautology, it merely reasserts something you know already in a slightly different form (Leach 1961:2–5).

This is somewhat of a caricature of comparativists. *First,* as I pointed out above (p. 582) the concern of most of them is not merely in classifying, but primarily in explaining things. They try not only to establish the relationship of two (or more) factors in a significant number of cases, but to postulate a causal and/or functional nexus between them. Although mere "butterfly collecting" occurs, it is so rare, that it is not simple to find pure examples (whereas there are hundreds of propositions of the type "where A, there B"). As a case in hand Hewes' (1955:231–234) article on postural habits may be mentioned. He simply lists standing, sitting, kneeling, crouching and squatting postures as they occur in about 480 cultures. Though it is curious to learn that people from different cultures sit differently and even urinate in different positions, I agree with Leach (1961:3) that classifications of this kind have limited uses only.

A not-so-pure further example is Goldman's (1955) paper, in which he classifies Polynesian societies into three types (Traditional, Open and Stratified). Compare this with Sahlins' (1958) book on *Social Stratification of Polynesia,* which offers a threefold typology of Polynesian societies closely resembling Goldman's. Sahlins, however, does not stop at classification but proceeds to explanation. He shows, in fact, that the degree of stratification varies with productivity and he considers surplus output as the cause—albeit an indirect one—of stratification. Regardless of whether the explanation offered is a correct one, we see here the difference at its clearest: classifying versus classifying-plus-explanation.

Secondly, when Lévi-Strauss (1963: Chap. 8) classifies a number of very different societies into the one category of dual societies, he acts as a comparativist and performs, moreover, essentially the same operation that Radcliffe-Brown does, i.e., concentrating upon the cultural elements appropriate to his subject and choosing a high enough level of abstraction. In Lévi-Strauss' (1963:21) own words: "We must analyze each dual society in order to discover, behind the chaos of rules and customs, a single structural scheme existing and operating in different spatial and temporal contexts." If Leach likes Lévi-Strauss' generalizations and dislikes Radcliffe-Brown's he should look for other grounds than the methodological one he mentioned.

Generalizations—at least well-founded ones —are impossible without comparison. Amusingly, in the final pages of his *Rethinking Anthropology* Leach implicitly corroborates this assertion by proffering a generalization *based on comparison.* That is, Leach would

not have been able to formulate his theory without making use of comparisons. However, his rule, being based on the data of five societies only, is highly dubious as a general proposition. Including more societies in the comparison would have sharpened his theory and indicated its limitations.

Leach's proposition runs as follows: "In any system of kinship and marriage there is a fundamental ideological opposition between the relations which endow the individual with membership of a 'we-group' . . . and those other relations which link 'our group' to other groups of like kind (relations of alliance), and in this dichotomy relations of incorporation are distinguished symbolically as relations of common substance, while relations of alliance are viewed as metaphysical influence" (1961:21).

As a hypothesis this is not easy to test as it contains an almost tautological element. Take the Nuer, who are partly a clear-cut confirmation of Leach's theory. Ego and his maternal uncle, who are in a relation of alliance according to Leach's definition, are metaphysically dangerous to one another. Were a man to bury his maternal uncle he would die; a man and his maternal uncle may not tether their cattle together, nor may they use the same sleeping-hide or sleep in the same hut; an uncle may not give his sister's son a spear shaft, for the gift might cause him serious injury, etc. (Evans-Pritchard 1951:164). Leach (1961: 25), in this connection, distinguishes between *uncontrolled mystical influence* denoting a relation of alliance and *controlled supernatural attack* denoting a relation of potential authority of attacker over attacked or vice versa. Now, in the Nuer case, apart from the instances of uncontrolled mystical influence referred to above, controlled supernatural attack exists; ego and his maternal uncle may curse each other and, as Evans-Pritchard says (1951:164–165),

the maternal uncle's curse is believed to be among the worst, if not the worst, a Nuer can receive, for unlike the father, a maternal uncle may curse a youth's cattle, as well as his crops and his fishing and hunting. . . . Nuer, therefore, however angry they may be, avoid swearing at their maternal uncles . . . you might think of swearing at your father, but never, never at your maternal uncle.

One may, of course, contend that this curse does not derive from the alliance relation but points to a position of authority of the maternal uncle. But this would be a case of *circulus in probando,* as there is nothing to prove that the maternal uncle has a position of authority over ego, let alone of more authority than ego's father, apart from the very fact of his having the power to curse him.

Anyway, apart from the Nuer case, Leach's generalization does not hold good for at least one of the societies I know by personal acquaintance (the Bush Negroes of Surinam). And what about Western societies?

Thirdly, Leach (1961:5) blames Meyer Fortes—who in this essay functions somewhat as his private bête noire—for using "contrived" rather than "natural" category distinctions, implying that his own method provides him with the latter variety. Categories may be practical or impractical—that is, well-chosen or ill-chosen for the problem in hand—but *they are of necessity all "contrived":* all categories, either inside or outside of anthropology, are creations of the human mind. What Leach calls "natural" categories are presumably the ones he is especially familiar with.[3]

GENERALIZATIONS BASED ON THE SINGLE CASE

Meanwhile I have not yet really refuted Leach's and Lévi-Strauss' contention that general laws may be and should be perceived in the circumstances of one special case. These men are by no means the first to recommend such a procedure. In 1912 Durkheim had already written:

On objectera qu'une seule religion constitue une base étroite pour une induction. Mais . . . quand une loi a été prouvée par une experience bien faite, cette preuve est valable universellement. Si, dans un cas même unique, un savant parvenait à surprendre le secret de la vie . . . les vérités ainsi obtenues seraient applicables à tous les vivants. (Durkheim 1960:593–594)

(It will be objected that a single religion constitutes a narrow base for an induction. But . . . when a law is demonstrated by one well-conducted observation, this demonstration is universally valid. If, in a single case, a scientist would succeed in capturing the secret of life . . . the truth thus obtained would be applicable to all living things.)

[3] Only after I wrote this chapter was my attention drawn to Barnes' (1962) witty review article in which he questions Leach's arguments along lines similar to the ones above.

Apropos of this contention: one wonders what would have happened to Durkheim's theory ("religion represents the collective life of the group") if his one case had derived not from the Australian aborigine but from the individualistically colored religion of the Crow Indians (Lowie 1956: Chap. 11).

Much in the same vein Lévi-Strauss (1963: 288) places before us the dilemma:

either to study many cases in a superficial and in the end ineffective way, or to limit oneself to a thorough study of a small number of cases, thus proving that in the last analysis one well done experiment is sufficient to make a demonstration. . . . We remain . . . confronted with only one alternative, namely, to make a thorough study of one case.

Now, we may concede these authors two things. The first is that in the past cross-cultural comparisons involving hundreds of cases have, in fact, sometimes been done in a superficial manner, the comparativists in question making use of third-rate source material and assuming all too lightheartedly that their errors in classifying would average out, given the great number of societies involved (Köbben 1952, 1967b:4). However, this is far from saying that the Murdockian approach is worthless per se. With the growing body of adequate ethnographic literature and with more refined classifying procedures (Köbben 1967b:4–12) one may even predict that more complicated and subtle questions may in the future be investigated in this way, such as, for example, Leach's hypothesis mentioned above, much to his dismay, perhaps.

Given, however, scarcity of time, money and adequate ethnographic sources, it is true that for many intercultural problems one can better restrict oneself to a limited number of strategically chosen cases, even if the results one thus arrives at will never constitute a proof in the mathematical sense of the word. It may even be predicted that this instrument will never be removed from the anthropological tool kit, because new questions will always be asked which cannot be answered from the columns of even a much perfected *Ethnographic Atlas* (Murdock 1967).

The second point is that the initial hunch about the interrelationship between social phenomena is mostly provided by the thorough analysis of one society—with the analyst's knowledge of other societies in the background. Mostly, the source of inspiration is the society the author himself did fieldwork in, but not invariably so: though Elisabeth Colson (1953) demonstrated how conflicting loyalties in Plateau Tonga society are their chief element of social control, it was Gluckman (1955: Chap. 1), inspired by her exposition, who proclaimed this a general rule for acephalous societies, which theory is by now a commonplace of anthropology.

With the introduction of the computer in anthropology (Coult and Habenstein 1965; Textor 1967) statistically significant correlations will conceivably be discovered in the future by the machine. Those correlations may be translated by man into meaningful functional relations. However, one may predict that even with perfect machines most relevant questions will remain to be asked by the human mind, analyzing the one case with which he is thoroughly familiar. There is, therefore, nothing against a general hypothesis based on a single society, *as long as it is clearly presented as such*. Holmberg (1950:92–99) did fieldwork among the Siriono in order to investigate intense hunger frustration and its relation to culture. He concludes his analysis by presenting seventeen broad generalizations, such as: "In hunger societies prestige will be gained and status maintained largely by food-getting activities"; he says that these generalizations can and should be tested in other societies where similar conditions exist. Testing Holmberg's hypotheses is a revealing experience. Some of them, which seem eminently logical and even self-evident in the framework of Siriono society, do not fit into other societal systems; others do, but with modifications (cf. also Needham 1954 and de Josselin de Jong 1957, whose judgments on Holmberg's hypotheses seem, however, too harsh). The lesson we can draw from this experience is that by testing such hypotheses we come to modify, specify and refine them. So comparative activities, when properly done, do not create trivialities, but help to avoid them.

In sum, my objection is not so much against generalizations based on a limited number of cases, but against those based on the single case (except as a provisional hypothesis). Note how Lévi-Strauss in the above quotation (1963:288) almost imperceptibly shifts from "a small number of cases" as

the basis for a generalization to "one case." His argument is at least partly valid for the former contention, not for the latter one.[4]

Let me demonstrate the imperfections of generalizing on the basis of one or too few cases by offering an example of theories on modernization. I define a society as modernized when its individual members feel that it is within their power to improve their own position and that of their children by working harder, investing and getting a better education (Köbben 1964:55–57). It is an often observed fact that some societies offer an almost insuperable resistance to modernization as here defined, whereas others readily accept it. Why should this be so? When searching the literature for general factors I found the following pairs of mutually contradictory statements:

1 a: population pressure has a positive effect on modernization (Ottenberg 1959:142).

  b: population pressure has a negative effect on modernization (Wertheim 1964:5).

2 a: political stratification has a positive effect on modernization, as modern ideas may be forcefully introduced to the masses from the top (modernizing autocracy) (Apter 1961:8–9, 86–87; see also, though reasoning along slightly different lines, Balandier 1956:502–504; cf. Köbben 1964:70–72).

  b: political stratification has a negative effect on modernization, as it is in the interest of the leading elite to maintain the status quo and as the lower classes are used to a situation in which any suggestion of change is made in the interest of the rulers (Sjoberg 1960:355).

3 a: an integrated society, such as the Zuni, offers high resistance to change (Adair and Vogt 1949:550–551, 558–559).

  b: an atomistic society, such as the Thai, offers high resistance to change and economic advance (Hauser 1959:82).

4 a: peasant societies lack the necessary minimum of cooperation: hence modernization is difficult (Foster 1962: Chap. 3).

[4] An intermediary position is taken by Devereux (1955:vii): ". . . the intensive analysis of the context and implications of a particular institution in a single tribe . . . can yield universally valid conclusions, (but) . . . the selfsame proposition could also be derived from a study in breadth of the variations of the same culture-trait or institution in a large number of societies."

b: peasant societies have a shared poverty system: hence modernization is difficult (Geertz 1963).

5 a: emigrant groups, being no longer subject to the social control of the home-group and being in a competitive situation vis-à-vis the autochtonous population, are bound to be progressive (Raulin 1957:99).

b: emigrant groups, being transplanted into a strange and inimical social milieu, are apt to stress their own identity and emphasize traditional social values: hence they are conservative (de Waal Malefijt 1963:190–191).

6 a: in the focal aspects of a culture, as people will think and talk them over continually and thereby see possibilities of realignment the resistance to change will be minimized (Herskovits 1955:484–497).

b: in the focal aspects of a culture, as these will be particularly dear to a given population, the resistance to change will be maximized (Albert 1960:69).

7 a: a social structure which permits the incorporation of new alternates, such as the Navaho's, offers stubborn resistance to change (Shepardson and Hammond 1964:1048–1049).

b: a social structure which permits the incorporation of new alternates, such as the Papuan, is especially open to change and modernization (Held 1951).

8 a: a society, such as the Ibo, where a father allows his son autonomy, is likely to produce men high in achievement motivation; hence is open to modernization (LeVine 1966:5).

b: a society, such as the Hindustani's, where the father is an authoritarian figure, produces aggression in the sons, who become, thereby, highly ambitious; hence is open to modernization (Speckmann 1963:466).

Which of these paired statements are true and which are not? Presumably they are all partly true *and* untrue (although some contain more truth than others). Each of them is inspired by the analysis of one special case for which the presence together of two stated elements is well established. Thereby a false sensation of "fit" and of inevitability is cre-ated, which remains undisturbed as long as one remains blissfully ignorant of societies offering contrary evidence (Merton 1949:90–91). The statements are exclusively based on ex post facto explanations; once one tries to predict on the basis of them, one realizes how defective their validity is. All the theories upon which these statements are based suffer from what Hempel (1964:318–319) calls *the inadequate specification of scope,* i.e., the failure to indicate clearly the range of situations (the limits of tolerance) to which the statements refer. They are only valid provided a number of subsidiary conditions are fulfilled.

But what these subsidiary conditions are is never indicated and without systematic comparisons it is indeed forever impossible to do so (Köbben 1964:76–82). Also, much depends on the *intensity* of the factors mentioned. For example, as to the first one on population pressure: conceivably population pressure in a moderate degree, such as among the Ibo of Nigeria, may be a stimulus to modernization as it obliges people to look for new opportunities (Ottenberg 1959:140). Heavy population pressure, on the other hand, may contribute to an "involution process" (Geertz 1963; Wertheim 1964:11) and may even lead to a fatalistic acceptance of the status quo. Unfortunately, to assess the nature of this factor (whether it is positive or negative) we are dependent on subjective impressions rather than quantifiable criteria (Köbben 1964:65–67).

As long as contradictions of this kind abound, one cannot but agree with the lament that the literature on social change, though extensive, is of a noncumulative nature (Beals 1953:638). Again, valid theories, on social change or on any other subject, can only be developed on a comparative basis.

THE ALLEGATION OF DISTORTION

The most formidable and at the same time the most reiterated objection against comparison is that it violates the articulated whole ("configuration," "pattern," "arrangement") of a culture. This objection was eloquently worded by Durkheim as early as 1912:

. . . les faits sociaux sont fonction du système social dont ils font partie; on ne peut donc les comprendre quand on les en détache. C'est pourquoi deux faits qui ressortissent à deux sociétés différentes ne peuvent pas être comparés avec fruit, par cela seul qu'ils paraissent se ressembler. . . . Que d'erreurs n'a-t-on pas commises pour avoir méconnu ce précepte. (1960:133)

(. . . social facts are functions of the social system of which they are a part; therefore they cannot be understood when they are detached. For this reason, two facts which come from two different societies cannot be fruitfully compared merely because they seem to resemble one another. . . . How many errors have been made from misunderstanding this rule.)

Mauss, in 1925, made a passionate plea for anthropologists to study "total phenomena" and not separate unduly the various elements of a society (Mauss 1954:76–81). Ruth Benedict's (1934) simile of anthropologists building up a Frankenstein monster by comparing disparate traits from different societies is well enough known that I need not repeat it here. But the most incisive criticism from the older generation of anthropologists is the one made by Lowie (1948:51–53), although he was too eclectic to be averse to comparison himself. He presents us with surveys of two primitive religions, Crow and Ekoi, and then proceeds to compare these. He points out how very different they are, the essence of Crow religion lying in the visionary experience of the individual, that of Ekoi being centered around witchcraft and sorcery beliefs.

When from such general impressions we turn to concrete elements, a fact of the utmost significance confronts us. Most of the phenomena that occur in either tribe are also found in the other, *but they are quite differently weighted.* For example, the individual psychic experience . . . is not lacking among the Ekoi, wraiths of dead friends appear in the dark to warn of danger or to demand offerings . . . but they are far from having the pivotal significance attaching to them in the Plains of North America. On the other hand . . . evil magic, though sporadic, was not wholly absent among the Crow, but it was not often leveled against a tribesman, let alone a relative. Furthermore, Crow sorcery is practically always linked with the favoritism displayed by the tutelary spirit acquired in a vision, so that its associations are quite different from those in West Africa. . . . So merely to catalog the occurrence of such and such beliefs and observances is a futile enterprise. When we know that a tribe practices witchcraft, believes in ghosts, or, it may be, the supremacy of some one supernatural being, we know precisely nothing concerning the religion of the people concerned. Everything depends on the interdependence of the several departments of supernaturalism, on the emotional weighting that attaches to each and every one of them.

Leach (1965:299) seems to be making the same point:

Murdock's World Ethnographic Sample and all the work that derives from it rest on the assumption that tribes or cultures . . . are "species objects" which can be described taxonomically by a list of characteristics. Just as species of beetle may be described. This is a proposition which I simply do not accept. If I write a monograph on the Kachin (as I have done) and Murdock chooses (as he has done) to have that book treated as it were a taxonomic description, he is acting within his rights, but from my point of view he is producing tabulated nonsense.

Let this stand for statements by others in this same vein (Nader 1965:11; cf. Gluckman 1965:251–267) albeit less outspoken. The only variant that needs to be mentioned separately is the concern of some authors not to do violence to the "folk system" (Bohannan), the "unconscious model" (Lévi-Strauss) of a culture. As Bohannan (1957:47–51, 212, 214), discussing Tiv law, says:

To think that there are similarities and differences between English and Tiv law, and that all one has to do is compare them is sociological oversimplification of the most blatant sort. Rather, there are two idioms and two sets of images in which peoples see their jural institutions and their institutions of social control.

For instance, the English word "lie" may be translated by Tiv "yie," but the two concepts, though overlapping, do not coincide. So with the words "tort," "contract," "law," and the like, which leads Bohannan to the conclusion that jamming Tiv notions into Western juridical categories would lead only to confusion and distortion.

THE ALLEGATION OF DISTORTION: ITS REFUTATION

What defenses can the comparativist muster against this massive attack upon his activities? Let the first be one of elastic retreat: as I conceded in my first paragraphs, comparisons and generalizations, in fact, do injustice to the uniqueness of the individual case. But then, as Kroeber (1954:258) once said, "Our concern is with differences *and* likenesses." It is not science's sole, nor even, I submit, its prior aim to copy pieces of reality as faithfully as possible, but rather to provide valid explanation; to investigate not only *how* people behave, but also *why* people behave as they do.[5]

As to taxonomy, the objections of Leach and company seem to be not so much against taxonomy per se, but against bad taxonomy (and I share their feelings). Conceivably, a student may put Crow and Ekoi religion into one category ("visionary experiences present; sorcery present"), but I would fail him for lack of discernment. So with polygyny; one might put Javanese society (less than 2 per cent of adult males polygynously married; large sections of the population very much against the practice) and Mende society (almost 50 per cent of adult males polygynously married; plural marriages the *sine qua non* for gaining prestige (Little 1954:5, 140–141) into one category: "polygyny present," but a sensible scientist would make more and finer distinctions. He would put Javanese society into the category "polygyny slight," or better: "less than 5 per cent of adult males polygynously married"; Mende society into "polygyny high," or better: "between 40 per cent and 50 per cent of adult males polygynously married." As to attitude, he would class the Javanese under "attitude divided," the Mende under "attitude positive." Admittedly, even these classifications would distort reality—all classification does and we all classify—but they cannot legitimately be dubbed "tabulated nonsense."

It is, of course, true that such strategy cannot always be followed, as anthropologists still have the unfortunate habit—though at present much less so than formerly—of classing their cases on an all-or-nothing basis (Köbben 1967b:7). Also, whereas such finer classifications can only be carried out successfully with the help of operational definitions, not all social phenomena lend themselves easily to operationalization. Take Foster's hypothesis: "In peasant society jealousy is intense." One might operationalize this as: "In peasant societies more than *n* percent of all illnesses and deaths are attributed to witchcraft and/or sorcery." Difficult to ascer-

tain but possible. (There are however, many pitfalls: Some peasant societies may not believe in witchcraft and sorcery at all.) Perhaps witchcraft accusations are essentially different: is death attributed vaguely to an unknown evildoer, or is a particular individual accused and persecuted (Redfield 1941:332). Such differences should be accounted for in our tabulations. Other propositions are still tougher. Take: "In such and such a society the incidence of gossip is high" (Köbben 1969). This makes sense only if it means: "The incidence of gossip is higher than in another type of society," but I do not see at all what yardstick to apply for this case.

All this is to say that a taxonomy of social phenomena meets with many more technical obstacles than one of beetles, *not* that the behavior of human beings is for ontological reasons barred from classification.

As to the charge that comparativists isolate traits from their context, this censure was more justified in a former generation than it is now. After all, Benedict (1934), when blaming comparativists for building a Frankenstein monster, was thinking of such studies as *The Golden Bough*. Nowadays, at least in serious comparativist work, isolated traits are no longer compared, but rather, clusters; not: "where A, there B," but rather: "where A, there B, there C . . . there N"; *lumps* of society are compared, so to say, or syndromes, to use a medical term. It is true that even so the integrity of culture is violated; what we do when comparing is still some form of "dissection." But then, even the confirmed configurationalist is a perpetrator of the same sin: every so-called description of a society involves organizing the data, carving up the culture, doing violence to "living reality." As soon as one translates a Tiv concept into, say, English, the Tiv folk system is deformed. But one has to do these things in order to escape solipsism, or to escape writing an ethnography comprehensible only to the fellow anthropologist who also did fieldwork among the Tiv. The question therefore is not *whether* we dissect, but *how much* and *how*, which cannot be answered in the abstract.

So let us turn to an example. When formulating a rule like: "where (a certain type of) matrilineal society, there (a certain type of) tensions" (Köbben 1964: Chap. 2), this is a shorthand way of expressing ourselves,

[5] Evans-Pritchard (1965:25) claims that he would like to place emphasis on the importance for social anthropology as a comparative discipline, of differences (*not* of similarities). Although one-sided, this is, of course, a legitimate preoccupation. Lévi-Strauss (1963: 14) refers to anthropology as a discipline "whose main if not sole [sic] aim is to analyze and interpret differences"; see also Needham (1961:94).

which gives the false impression of two isolated traits being compared. In fact, however, what we do compare when testing this rule, is not only part of the kinship structure—say, the relation between ego, his maternal uncle and his maternal uncle's son—and the tensions therein, but also the economic, juridical, political, supernatural (witchcraft and sorcery) and moral connotations of these tensions. It would be very difficult to ignore the similarities, not only of the matrilineal conflict itself, but also of its impact on the various domains of life. Also, there is no denying that this whole complex is very much part of the folk system. Fortes (1950:270–273) cites Ashanti proverbs that refer to the matrilineal conflict and he tells how it is continually discussed by them. The Agni (Köbben 1956: Chap. 1) and the Plateau Tonga (Colson 1958:230–236, 254–255) and many other matrilineal societies have similar discussions, often with very similar expressions and arguments—so much so that when one has read the reports on some of these societies, one has the sensation of *déjà vu* when reading the others.

Today *complexes* of traits, not isolated traits, are compared. From Sjoberg (1960) I could have listed here the variations concomitant with the preindustrial city (where preindustrial city, there A, there B, there C . . . there Z). Sjoberg himself remarks:

It is only by abstracting out the universal, or near-universal traits in preindustrial cities that one really discovers and explicates what is unique. The more materials on cities around the world that I examine, the more I am convinced that too many social scientists assume uniqueness where this does not exist. (1960:322)

After the defense the attack. It is my contention (negatively) that comparative studies need not be detrimental to the configurationalistic viewpoint, and (positively) that they may make a real contribution to configurationalistic studies. Conceivably, a prime aim of the configurationalist (I use this term for want of a better one) is to assess the total number of factors, the knot of functional relations, which together form a given social reality. By means of a comparative study a factor (or factors) may be added that has been overlooked by the configurationalist when concentrating upon his society.

Evans-Pritchard, whom we may well take as an example, as he is very suspicious of comparisons (1965:27–28), assumes in his book on the Nuer a direct relation between their egalitarian political institutions and certain personality traits.

The lack of governmental organizations among the Nuer and . . . of developed leadership . . . is remarkable. The ordered anarchy in which they live accords well with their character, for it is impossible to conceive of rulers ruling over them. . . . The Nuer is a product of hard and egalitarian upbringing, is deeply democratic and is easily roused to violence. His turbulent spirit finds any restraint irksome and no man recognizes a superior. They strut about like lords of the earth, which, indeed, they consider themselves to be. . . . Never are they truckling or sycophantic. (1940:181–183)

As Evans-Pritchard does not mention other factors contributing to their personality structure nor does he give any restrictive clauses, one is entitled to elevate this relationship to the status of a general rule: "where egalitarian political institutions, there fierce and independent personality." However, even by a superficial reconnaissance of the literature, one learns of societies having acephalous political institutions, but whose members have quite a different personality. This is not to deny that the two phenomena in question *have* some functional relation: one could not conceive of, say, the Javanese, who have lived for more than three centuries under a feudal system, with that kind of personality. Egalitarian political institutions thus seem to be a necessary but not sufficient condition for the said personality traits. To indicate the necessary *and* sufficient conditions, at least one more causative element needs to be traced.

LeVine (1960:51–55) provides us with this missing element: he compares the Nuer with the Gusii, who are similar in many aspects of indigenous sociopolitical organization. However, the Gusii appear to have strongly authoritarian values:

Command relationships are a part of every-day life and are morally valued by the Gusii . . . orders are given in imperative terms and often in harsh tones, yet this is considered normal and proper conduct.

As an explanation of this difference LeVine turns to parent-child relations and aggression training:

The Nuer, who as adults have egalitarian values, grow up with warm, demonstrative fathers, who do not beat them. The Gusii who exhibit authoritarian behavior as adults, have experienced, as children, fathers who are remote, frightening and severely punitive. Further . . . Nuer children are from their earliest years encouraged by their elders to settle all disputes by fighting. With the Gusii, on the other hand, parents do not encourage their children to fight but rather to report grievances to the parent.

So, by this comparative study, the picture of Nuer society has been made more complete. Far from having been impoverished by the comparison, the man-of-one-society has been enriched: his attention has been drawn to factors he had not been aware of before.[6]

CONCLUSION

Is the bitter feud between comparativists and non-comparativists in the interest of anthropology? Although the expressions of aggressiveness by the sharp-witted and sharp-tongued gentleman from Cambridge are among the joys of the discipline, the answer cannot be entirely in the affirmative. The two parties should realize that both approaches, the comparative and the structuralist, are legitimate, provided they do not neglect each other. When I am doing field-work, say, among the Bush Negroes, or writing up my materials about them I am primarily concerned with getting a hold on their folk system and their social structure in all its uniqueness, as well as presenting this faithfully. But meanwhile I should not forget the comparative viewpoint, on penalty of two

[6] For another example, coincidentally also referring to Evans-Pritchard's study on the Nuer, see Goldschmidt (1966:15).

things: of laying causal or functional links between phenomena which are only coincidentally together in that society; *and* of not seeing certain other relations which are, in fact, present. Without knowledge of other societies I do not even know where to look or what to look for. The Bush Negroes, though a matrilineal society, have not the matrilineal conflict: without knowing of other matrilineal societies I could not possibly have noticed this for the curious fact it is. So I disagree wholeheartedly with Lévi-Strauss where he says:

On the observational level, the main, one could almost say the only rule is that all the facts should be carefully observed and described without allowing any theoretical preconception to decide whether some are more important than others. (1963:280)

If one literally followed the advice of noting "all the facts," irrespective of relevancy, one would have to fill a library with what happens in one village in one day. The field worker needs a point of view (points of view), which only comparison can give him (Köbben 1967a:41). On the other hand, when doing a comparative study, one should not forget the structuralistic viewpoint, on penalty of violating too much the living reality, which must be the basis of all our generalizations.

Let us, therefore, try to mold ourselves and our pupils into that harmonious kind of individual who combines in his personality the positive sides of both parties: the comparativists and the non-comparativists (Köbben 1966a, 1966b; Pouwer 1966a, 1966b).

BIBLIOGRAPHY

ADAIR, F., and C. VOGT
    1949   Navaho and Zuni veterans. *American Anthropologist* 51:547–561.
ALBERT, E. M.
    1960   Socio-political organization and receptivity to change. *Southwestern Journal of Anthropology* 16:46–75.
APTER, D.
    1961   *The political kingdom in Uganda.* Princeton, N.J.: Princeton University Press.
APTHORPE, R. (ed.)
    1959   *From tribal to modern government.* Lusaka, Northern Rhodesia, Rhodes Livingstone Institute.

BARNES, J. A.
    1962   Rethinking and rejoining: Leach, Fortes and filiation. *Journal of the Polynesian Society* 71:403–410.
BALANDIER, G.
    1955   *Sociologie actuelle de l'afrique noire.* Paris, Presses Universitaires de France.
BAX, C., J. C. BREMAN, and A. T. J. NOOIJ
    1966   Slavery as a system of production in tribal society. *Bijdragen Taal-Land-en Volkenkunde* 122:90–109.
BEALS, R.
    1953   Acculturation. In A. L. Kroeber, ed.,

Anthropology today. Chicago, University of Chicago Press.

BENEDICT, R.
1934 *Patterns of culture.* New York, Mentor.

BOHANNAN, P.
1957 *Justice and judgment among the Tiv.* London, Oxford University Press.

CASSIRER, E.
1955 *The myth of the state.* Garden City, N.Y., Doubleday.

COLSON, E.
1953 Social control in Plateau Tonga society. *Africa* 23:199 ff.

1958 *Marriage and the family among the Plateau Tonga of Northern Rhodesia.* Manchester, University Press for Rhodes Livingstone Institute.

COULT, P. D., and R. W. HABENSTEIN
1965 *Cross tabulations of Murdock's World Ethnographic Sample.* Columbia, University of Missouri Press.

DEVEREUX, G.
1955 *A study of abortion in primitive society.* New York, Julian Press.

DURKHEIM, E.
1960 *Les formes élémentaires de la vie religeuse.* 4th ed. Paris, Presses Universitaires de France.

EGGAN, FRED
1950 *Social organization of the Western Pueblos.* Chicago, University of Chicago Press.

EVANS-PRITCHARD, E. E.
1940 *The Nuer: a description of the modes of livelihood and political institutions of a Nilotic people.* Oxford, Clarendon Press.

1951 *Kinship and marriage among the Nuer.* Oxford, Clarendon Press.

1965 The comparative method in social anthropology. In E. E. Evans-Pritchard, *The position of women in primitive society and other essays in social anthropology.* New York, Free Press.

FALLERS, L. A.
1956 *Bantu bureaucracy.* Cambridge, England, W. Heffer for East African Institute of Social Research.

FORTES, M.
1950 Kinship and marriage among the Ashanti. In A. R. Radcliffe-Brown and D. Forde, eds., *African systems of kinship and marriage.* London, Oxford University Press.

FOSTER, G. H.
1960 Interpersonal relations in peasant society. *Human Organization* 19:174–178.

1962 *Traditional cultures and the impact of technological change.* New York, Harper.

GEERTZ, C.
1963 *Agricultural involution; the process of ecological change in Indonesia.* Berkeley, University of California Press.

GLUCKMAN, M.
1955 *Custom and conflict in Africa.* Glencoe, Ill., Free Press.

1965 *The ideas in Barotse jurisprudence.* New Haven, Yale University Press.

GOLDMAN, I.
1955 Status rivalry and cultural evolution in Polynesia. *American Anthropologist* 57: 680–697.

GOLDSCHMIDT, W.
1966 *Comparative functionalism. An essay in anthropological theory.* Berkeley, University of California Press.

HAUSER, PHILLIP M.
1959 Cultural and personal obstacles to economic influence in the less developed areas. *Human Organization* 18:2, 78–84.

HELD, G. J.
1951 *De Papoea, cultuur-improvisator.* 's Gravenhage/Bandung.

HEMPEL, C. G.
1964 The logic of functional analysis. In C. G. Hempel, *Aspects of scientific explanation and other essays in the philosophy of science.* New York, Free Press.

HERSKOVITS, J.
1955 *Cultural anthropology.* New York, Knopf.

HEWES, G. W.
1955 World distribution of certain postural habits. *American Anthropologist* 57: 231–245.

HOEBEL, E. A.
1969 Keresan Pueblo law. In H. Nader, ed., *Law and culture in society.* Chicago, Aldine.

HOLLEMAN, J. F.
1963 *Verkenningen in het Babel der acculturatie.* Leiden.

HOLMBERG, A. R.
1950 *Nomads of the long bow; the Siriono of Eastern Bolivia.* Washington, D.C., Smithsonian Institution, Institute of Social Anthropology Pub. 10.

JONES, W. I.
1961 *The romantic syndrome: toward a new method in cultural anthropology and the history of ideas.* The Hague.

JOSSELIN DE JONG, P. E. DE
1957 *Enige richtingen in de hedendaagse culturele anthropologie.* 's Gravenhage.

JUNOD, H. A.
1927 *The life of a South African tribe,* 2nd rev. ed. 2 vols. London, Macmillan.

KÖBBEN, A. J. F.
1952 New ways of presenting an old idea: the statistical method in social anthropology. *Journal of the Royal Anthro-*

pological Society of Great Britain and Ireland 82:129–146.

1956 Le planteur noir. *Etudes Eburnéennes* 5:7–181.

1964 *Van primitieven tot medeburgers.* Assen, van Gorcum.

1966a Structuralism versus comparative functionalism; a comment. *Bijdragen Taal-Land-en Volkenkunde* 122:145–151.

1966b Structuralisme en functionalisme; dupliek. *Bijdragen Taal-Land-en Volkenkunde* 122:379–381.

1967a Participation and quantification. In P. C. W. Gutkind and D. G. Jongmans, eds., *Anthropologists in the field.* Assen.

1967b Why exceptions? The logic of cross-cultural analysis. *Current Anthropology* 8:3–19.

1969 Law on the village level; the Cottica Djuka of Surinam. In L. Nader, ed., *Law and culture in society.* Chicago, Aldine.

KROEBER, A. L.
1954 Critical summary and commentary. In R. F. Spencer, ed., *Method and perspective in anthropology.* Minneapolis, University of Minnesota Press.

LEACH, E. R.
1961 *Rethinking anthropology.* London, University of London, Athlone Press.

1965 Comment. *Current Anthropology* 5:299.

LEVINE, R. A.
1960 The internalization of political values in stateless societies. *Human Organization* 19:51–55.

1966 *Dreams and deeds; achievement motivation in Nigeria.* Chicago, University of Chicago Press.

LÉVI-STRAUSS, C.
1963 *Structural anthropology.* Trans. from French by Claire Jacobson and Brooke G. Schoepf. New York and London, Basic Books.

LI-AN-CHE
1937 Zuni: some observations and queries. *American Anthropologist* 39:62–77.

LITTLE, K. L.
1954 *The Mende of Sierra Leone. A West African people in transition.* London, Routledge and Kegan Paul.

LOWIE, R. H.
1948 *Primitive religion.* New York, Liveright.
1956 *The Crow Indians.* New York, Rinehart.

MALINOWSKI, B.
1932 *The sexual life of savages in Northwest Melanesia.* London, Routledge.

MAUSS, M.
1954 *The gift.* Glencoe, Ill., Free Press.

MERTON, R. K.
1949 *Social theory and social structure.* Glencoe, Ill., Free Press.

MURDOCK, G. P.
1949 *Social structure.* New York, Macmillan.
1967 *Ethnographic Atlas.* Pittsburgh, University of Pittsburgh Press.

NADER, L.
1965 The anthropological study of law. *American Anthropologist* 67:3–32.

NEEDHAM, R.
1954 Siriono and Penan: a test of some hypotheses. *Southwestern Journal of Anthropology* 10:228–236.

1961 Notes on the analysis of asymmetric alliance. *Bijdragen Taal-Land-en Volkenkunde* 117:93–117.

NIEBOER, H. J.
1910 *Slavery as an industrial system,* 2nd rev. ed. The Hague, M. Nijhoff.

OTTENBERG, S.
1959 Ibo receptivity to change. In W. R. Bascom and M. J. Herskovits, eds., *Continuity and change in African cultures.* Chicago, University of Chicago Press.

OTTERBEIN, K. F., and C. OTTERBEIN
1965 An eye for an eye, a tooth for a tooth; a cross-cultural study of feuding. *American Anthropologist* 67:1470–1482.

PAULME, D.
1962 *Une société de Côte d'Ivoire: les Bété.* The Hague.

POPPER, K.
1959 *The logic of scientific discovery.* New York, Basic Books.

POUWER, J.
1966a The structural and functional approach in cultural anthropology. *Bijdragen Taal-Land-en Volkenkunde* 122:129–145.

1966b Referential and inferential reality. *Bijdragen Taal-Land-en Volkenkunde* 122:151–157.

RADCLIFFE-BROWN, A. R.
1952 The mother's brother in Africa. In A. R. Radcliffe-Brown, *Structure and function in primitive society.* London, Cohen and West.

RAULIN, H.
1959 *Problèmes fonciers dans les régions de Gagnoa et Daloa.* Paris.

REDFIELD, R.
1941 *The folk-culture of Yucatan.* Chicago, University of Chicago Press.

RICHARDS, A. I.
1957 The concept of culture in Malinowski's work. In *Man and culture.* London.

RICKERT, H.
1926 *Kulturwissenschaft und Naturwissenschaft,* 6th ed. Tübingen.

ROMEIN, J.
1946 *Theoretische geschiedenis.* Groningen.

SAHLINS, M.
1958 *Social stratification in Polynesia.* Seattle, University of Washington Press.

SCHAPERA, I.
1940   *Married life in an African tribe.* London, Faber and Faber.
SHEPARDSON, M., and B. HAMMOND
1964   Change and persistence in an isolated Navaho community. *American Anthropologist* 66:1029–1049.
SJOBERG, G.
1960   *The preindustrial city.* Glencoe, Ill., Free Press.
SPECKMANN, J. D.
1963   De positie van de Hindostaanse bevolkingsgroep in de sociale en ekonomische struktuur van Suriname. *Tydschrift Aardrijkskundig Genootschap* 80:459–466.
TEXTOR, R.
1967   *Computer summarization of the coded cross-cultural literature.* New Haven, Human Relations Area Files Press.

THODEN VAN VELZEN, H. U. E., and W. VAN WETERING
1960   Residence, power groups and intra-societal aggression. *International Archives of Ethnography* 49:169–200.
WAAL MALEFIJT, A. DE
1963   *The Javanese of Surinam.* Assen.
WERTHEIM, W. F.
1964   *East-West parallels.* The Hague.
WINDELBAND, W.
1904   *Geschichte und Naturwissenschaft,* 2nd ed. Strassburg.
WINTER, E. H.
1956   *Bwamba: a structural-functional analysis of a patrilineal society.* Cambridge, England, W. Heffer for East African Institute of Social Research.

CHAPTER 31

A Critical Evaluation of Concomitant Variation Studies

REMI CLIGNET

INTRODUCTION

Scientific explanations involve the isolation of invariant relationships among the facts analyzed. The first step toward the achievement of this goal requires the use of experimental methods, including concomitant variations, which facilitate the elimination of irrelevant circumstances and thus of unwarranted hypotheses. Their use leads to a definition of the *necessary* conditions under which associations between *n* series of phenomena take place, but it is not conducive, however, to a determination of the relevant sufficient circumstances (Cohen and Nagel 1934:245–272).

The application of experimental methods in the field of social sciences raises several difficulties. The definition of "invariant relations" is necessarily looser than that used in other disciplines: correlations between social phenomena are never perfect. In addition, social sciences are hardly in a position to meet all the prerequisites of an experimental method. First, the very nature of anthropology or sociology forbids the *a priori* introduction of systematic variations in the phenomena treated as independent variables. Indeed, systematic variations are applied only on an *ex post facto* hypothesis, as far as sociology and anthropology are concerned; and the properties of the variables under investigation cannot be manipulated freely (Selvin 1957:519–529). It is obviously impossible to create a matrilocal patrilineal society, holding every other variable constant, if this category, for example, is needed in order to make a comparative analysis meaningful.

Second, circumstances surrounding social

phenomena are difficult to operationalize. Most of the time, they are defined in qualitative terms which are not entirely unequivocal. Further, in the context of experimental methods, qualitative terms should be translated into quantitative expressions, and such a translation raises obstacles which are difficult to overcome.

Third, anthropologists dispose of a limited number of solutions to eliminate circumstances which are irrelevant for the purposes of the comparative analysis. One solution is to neutralize the potential effects of these irrelevant circumstances by the use of cross-cultural research. The constitution of a large sample of units derived from a variety of geographic, historical and social environments maximizes the properties attached to a random distribution and minimizes accordingly the significance of irrelevant circumstances. Under such conditions, correlations cannot be the product of chance.

An alternative solution consists in the use of the method termed "controlled comparison" by Eggan (1954:747) or "concomitant variation studies" by Durkheim (1927:163) or Nadel (1951:223). This second solution, in its original definition, consists of examining regularities in the distribution of selected traits among a limited number of units which are usually located within a single geographical, historical or social whole. The examination by Bascom of the linkages between size, density, and heterogeneity among Yoruba cities is an illustration of this method (1962:699–709). In Bascom's study, observed variations cannot be explained in terms of contrasts in geographical factors (climate and soil hardly vary); nor in terms of cultural differences (all cities are located in Yoruba land); nor in terms of inequalities in the level of economic development (the general level of economic development in this particular subregion of Nigeria is somewhat homogeneous). Thus the potential significance of social variables deemed to be irrelevant are minimized by holding them constant. As we will see, however, an alternative strategy developed in the context of the concomitant variations method consists in showing that variations in the social variables deemed to be irrelevant do not modify the direction or the intensity of the association between the dependent and independent variable. Whatever the specific strategy they use, all the comparisons which involve the systematic manipulation of constants are "controlled."

The present chapter presents some problems raised by anthropologists' use of concomitant variations. First, a brief review of these anthropological concomitant variations studies.

SCOPE OF CONCOMITANT VARIATION STUDIES

Studies of concomitant variations can be classified into two types according to their scope. A first type is *narrow in scope* and is concerned with an examination of the relationships among limited segments of a social system. A second type is *broad in scope,* more ambitious and deals with an analysis of the interaction between social systems and other elements of the cultural and ecological contexts in which these systems are located.

Examples of Studies of the Narrow Type

Some explore the antecedents of religious activities. Wilson (1951:307–313) compares the Pondo and the Nyakyusa, to determine how differences in territorial organization are associated with contrasts in incentive to witchcraft activities. Nadel (1952:18–29) analyzes the impact of discrepancies in the social and physical definition of age categories, and of discrepancies in the normative and actual definitions of sex roles upon the type of witchcraft accusations observable in four African tribes.

Others examine the variations in the organization of familial structures. Radcliffe-Brown (1931) measures the degree to which

variations in kinship terminology among a number of Australian tribes are accompanied by corresponding variations in the institutional and non-institutional forms of sociability. Clignet (1968) analyzes how changes in the residential and occupational characteristics of two Ivory Coast peoples, one matrilineal and the other patrilineal, affect the child-rearing practices of the women of these two peoples. Mead (1935) challenges the universality of the principles underlying role differentiation along sex lines and examines the variations which characterize the definition of sex roles among three peoples of New Guinea: the Arapesh, the Tchambuli and the Mundugumor.

Some controlled comparison studies evaluate variations in educational development. Clignet and Foster (1964:349–362) analyze how differences in the length of the colonial period and in the cultural characteristics of the colonial power account for differences in the recruitment patterns, and in the functions of the secondary school systems of two adjacent African countries: Ghana and the Ivory Coast. Clignet (1967:360–378) attempts to go further in this type of analysis and to determine whether the propositions derived from an examination of these two countries are independent of the size of the units studied. Are the contrasts between nations analogous to the contrasts between the ethnic components of those nations?

Examples of Studies of the Broad Type

These investigate a larger number of phenomena. Goldschmidt and his associates (1965:400–447) examine linkages between ecological and cultural variations on the one hand, and variations in patterns of social interaction on the other. Similarly, Spicer (1956) attempts to show the pre-eminence of ceremonialism over the other components of a single cultural system: the Yaqui of Sonora. In a diachronic perspective, Eggan (1950) studies the impact of the differentiation in the territorial arrangements of the Western Pueblos upon other components of their social organization, more specifically on their mechanisms of social integration. Cohen (1966: 53–76) and Redfield (1941) are concerned with a more specific aspect of social change: urbanization. Cohen examines how urbanization has changed the familial organization of the Athapascan-speaking peoples of Northern Canada, whereas Redfield studies the integrative and disintegrative effects of the forces accompanying urbanization on four communities of Yucatan.

The variety of instances where controlled comparisons have been used makes it easy to review the types of problems and difficulties which accompany this particular method.

The purpose of controlled comparisons is to test the validity of the conditions deemed necessary to uphold a hypothesis, after irrelevant circumstances have been eliminated. In order to accomplish this, two basic requirements must be fulfilled. First, units compared must be typical examples of the range of possible variations in the series of phenomena investigated. Second, variables which are held constant and whose possible influence is thus seen to be irrelevant must also be clearly defined and assessed.

TYPICALITY OF THE COMPARISON UNDERTAKEN

Typicality pertains to the possibility of generalizing the results derived from the controlled comparison. For example, we may ask whether the significant differences between Merida and Tusik, the two extremes of the continuum analyzed by Redfield in Yucatan, characterize contrasts between folk and urban societies or between Spanish and Mayan cultures. We may ask whether the differences in social organization among the Zuni, Hopi, Acoma, and Laguna noted by Eggan suggest a definition of the stages by which social systems shift from one stable configuration to another. Or do they merely reflect the individual contact differences of these four Western Pueblos subgroups and their Spanish and American colonizers?

We may ask about the similarities and differences which characterize the patterns of behavior of the white and Negro segments of the population of a single North American community. Do Negroes present inherently distinctive psychological traits? An assumption that they do requires investigation of the relevant patterns of behavior among other Negro samples, derived from other geographic, historical, and cultural environments. Conversely, it may be argued that the observed differences between Negroes and whites are the product of a situation where relations

between subordinate and superordinate groups are of a certain nature. In this case the step following the initial comparison should consist of the examination of the patterns of behavior of social or ethnic groups other than white and Negro, but occupying similar positions within a social structure somewhat analogous to that of the United States. Generally speaking, the problem of typicality pertains to the significance of the differences and similarities observed. What seems to be alike may, on deeper analysis, prove to be different; and what seems to be different may, on deeper analysis, prove to be alike.

Definition of the Typicality of the Comparison Undertaken

An assessment of the typicality of the comparison undertaken requires a definition of the various aspects of this term. Typical by reference to what? An evaluation of the typicality of a study necessitates a definition of the variability of (1) each one of the phenomena investigated; (2) the empirical units in which these phenomena will be measured or tested; and (3) the form and the intensity of the relationship between the n series of phenomena analyzed.

In turn, the definition of this variability depends upon the system of categorization used by the investigator. The general issues associated with the use of systems of categorization are presented and discussed in broad terms by LeBar (Chapter 38) and by Tatje (Chapter 36). I will consider here the specific application of such systems to concomitant variation studies.

Primarily, a system of categorization is adequate insofar as it rests upon the application of a universal principle.

(1) As far as the phenomena under investigation are concerned, categories must rely upon the assumption that psychological and social needs are limited in number and are satisfied through the use of few alternative solutions. Indeed, the number of strategies that men have available to solve their problems is not infinite.

(2) The universality of the system of categorization of empirical units implies that their boundaries should be constant through time and space. This particular requirement limits the circumstances under which empirical

units other than territorial ones can be compared. For example, a controlled comparison of familial roles rests upon the hypothesis that nuclear families are universal in nature. First, we may argue that familial functions are stable throughout space and time. Yet, there is no agreement as to the nature and number of the basic functions performed by this particular group (Murdock 1949:1–16; Winch 1964:4–32; Bohannan 1963:98–99; Spiro 1954:838–846). To be sure, we may overcome this difficulty by defining the universality of the nuclear family in other terms, for example by stressing the universal character of the dyadic relations found in this particular group. We are still unable, however, to assess the comparability of such dyadic relations when the nuclear family is a minimal discrete unit and when it is embedded within a larger extended kin group. Do the functions and the organization of an atom differ when it is completely isolated and when it is not detachable from the molecule in which it is found (Levy and Fallers 1959:647–651; Murdock 1949:1–16; Zelditch 1964:462–500)? As long as there is no definite answer to this question, nuclear families cannot be properly used as valid empirical units for comparison. Territorial units are often chosen instead of organizational units like the nuclear family because their boundaries can be easily identified, both by their own members and by outside observers. Even when these territorial units are investigated, there still remains the problem of ascertaining the boundaries between the community in which it is found and the entire people of which this community is just a subpart. For example, the use of "case histories" by Nadel to describe the psychological components of witchcraft among the Nupe and the Gwari raises the problem not only of assessing the relative positions occupied by the two types of informants he used in their participant community, but also of evaluating the comparability of these communities themselves.

(3) The categorization of the form and intensity of the relationship between the n series of phenomena investigated, must be derived from a universal principle insofar as the differentiation which characterizes both categorizations and comparisons requires *a priori* generalizations. In statistics, we know that correlations, while chronologically anterior

to factor analysis, are nevertheless the product of one or several "factors," which we assume to be stable throughout space and time. Similarly, in comparative analysis, the isolation of regularities in the distribution of a series of social facts implies *a priori* assumptions about the "determinateness," that is, the direction and the insignificance of such regularities (McEwan 1963:155–169). For example, when we assume that a significant proportion of variations in the personality types and social systems examined result from variations in the concomitant cultural systems, we implicitly posit three universals: (1) systems of personality, society and culture are always organized into a single supersystem; (2) all three systems are interdependent; (3) among the three, culture is preeminently important.

The problem remains, however, to determine the level of abstraction at which integrative and generalizing principles should be defined. Lévi-Strauss (1958:326–351) suggests that a comparative analysis is meaningful only when it concerns structures—that is, the models derived from an examination of the concrete social relations evident in a particular setting rather than these concrete social relations themselves. Lévi-Strauss suggests that the concept of communication is a common denominator of all cultures. Comparisons may, then, concern the specific, concrete and easily observable forms of communication found in a variety of cultures: for example, language (communication of words), marriage (communication of women) and economic exchanges (communication of goods and services). Lévi-Strauss argues, however, that the results yielded by comparative analysis are more meaningful when instead of being concerned with the concrete forms of communication suggested above, this analysis deals with an exploration of the systemic properties of the rules applicable to them (i.e., grammar, kinship arrangement and economies). Thus, if communication presents universal prerequisites, these rules should present identical traits or trends (Lévi-Strauss 1958:326–342).

Difficulties Associated with the Definition of Typicality

The categorization of the relationships between the n series of phenomena investigated raises, however, a fundamental difficulty. As we have seen, Lévi-Strauss argues that comparisons should deal with structures, that is, with models underlying concrete and specific forms of communication or organization. What is then the nature of such models? It reflects, to be sure, an ultimate purpose. But should we take under consideration the explicit purposes of the actors involved, or the more abstract purposes that we observers find illustrated by the nexus of patterns of behavior investigated (Nadel 1951:265–276)? To be sure, an assessment of any type of social relations must begin by an evaluation of the conscious models elaborated by the actors of the groups which are compared. Yet, the function of these models is to perpetuate beliefs and techniques rather than to explain them. Further, although these models reflect the social organization in which they are produced, they might also be dissonant with or independent from some other aspects of this organization (Lévi-Strauss 1958:144, 308–310). In this context, the full acceptance by the researcher of the conscious models elaborated by the culture he analyzes forbids systematic comparisons between the data that he has gathered and data collected on other cultures. The very nature of conscious models makes them hardly comparable, and to paraphrase the words of Mannheim, "We must find a formula for translating the content of one model into that of the other and to discover a common denominator for these varying viewpoints" (1936:270). The task of finding this common denominator should not be equated, however, with the substitution of the folk views prevailing in the empirical units compared by those prevailing in the culture from which the observer himself is derived. "The most common anthropological errors," writes Bohannan, "are (1) explaining the descriptive data of the societies compared in terms of the folk systems prevailing in the observer's own group (2) explaining the folk systems of the groups under analysis in terms of the folkviews of the observer without first determining that the former can be derived from the descriptive data pertaining to the groups compared" (1963:13).

Scholars may be tempted to overcome the difficulty suggested above by formulating the terms of their comparison, regardless of the relevant norms and imagery current in the social groups analyzed. Thus, we might measure, among a variety of peoples, the influence of the economic independence of a married woman upon the power structure of the domestic group into which she has married. We could do so by comparing families in which wives exert an economic activity independent of their husbands, with families where wives do not exert such activities. Yet, potential contrasts between these two types of family are affected by the social values attached to the economic independence of married women. In a study comparing the functioning of polygynous families within two peoples of the Ivory Coast, the matrilineal Abure and the patrilineal Bete, Clignet (1968) suggests that the contrast between the relative power of married women earning independent incomes and that of housewives is greater among the Bete than among the Abure. This differential reaction of the two cultures to the gainful employment of married women may be interpreted in terms of the differing expectations attached to dissimilar degrees of absorption. Bete women, whose degree of absorption into their affinal group is high, are not expected to have an independent occupation, and deviate accordingly from prevailing norms when they enter into the labor market. This study would suggest, then, that it is not the participation of women in the labor market which is the most significant variable in this context but, rather, as Chombart de Lauwe indicates (1964:14–15), the degree to which this participation is consistent with the traditional organization of the peoples under investigation.

If, as Lévi-Stauss suggests (1963:91), comparisons require the researcher to isolate the relations of opposition, inclusion and coordination which exist among institutions, values and situations, what are the strategies that he can use to synthetize these various relations? Psychoanalysis may provide an adequate framework to shift from conscious to unconscious models, but the limits within which the use of this tool is valid have still to be ascertained. Nonetheless, Tillon (1966:15) suggests that we can use the equivalents of Freudian slips at the societal level to analyze the patterns of development and differentiation of human groups. This proposition rests upon the assumption that individual and social structure present parallel features, and remains therefore problematic for the time being.

Concrete Steps to Be Taken to Evaluate the Typicality of the Comparison

According to Lévi-Strauss (1963:16–17), the building of a meaningful comparative framework requires several steps. Although his argument primarily pertains to cross-cultural comparisons, his recommendations seem to be applicable as well to the method of concomitant variation. The steps are:

(1) Definition of the phenomenon studied as a relation between two terms, real or supposed. Thus, totemism is defined by Lévi-Strauss as a relationship between two series: one *natural* and the other *cultural*. Similarly Louis Wirth (1938:1–24) defines urbanism as an interrelationship between *size, density,* and *heterogeneity* of human groupings; this is the interrelationship that Bascom (1962) has tested in the article about Yoruba cities quoted above. This step also involves a categorization of the form and the intensity of the association investigated: the purpose of controlled comparison is to test the system of categorization suggested by a logical examination of the phenomenon, or alternatively to derive such a system from the empirical data available.

(2) Construction of a table of possible permutations between these terms. Thus, in his discussion of totemism, Lévi-Strauss argues that the *natural series* involves a distinction between categories and individual animals, whereas the *cultural series* comprises a distinction between groups and persons. There are then four possible types of interaction taking place between these two series in the context of totemism: a) interaction between a particular animal and a particular person; b) interaction between a category of animals and the same particular person; c) interaction between a particular animal and a whole group of persons (an entire social category such as the elders for example); d) interaction between a category of animals and a group of persons. Similarly, although they are not arranged in this particular way, Bascom's data about the size density and heterogeneity of the areas that he has investigated could be categorized in quantitative terms (high, medium, and low). Such as a quantitative categorization requires, however, that the qualitative definition of the categories utilized in this context be unequivocal. This is not always so, and many of the followers of Wirth, including Bascom, have undertaken controlled comparisons in order to identify the components of heterogeneity.

(3) Examination of the table of possible permutations as a general object of analysis which at this level can only yield necessary connections. The empirical phenomenon considered at the starting point of the analysis is only one possible combination among others, the complete system of which must be reconstructed *a priori*. For example, the variations in the size, density and heterogeneity of Yoruba towns represent only a limited range of variations along these three dimensions; the entire scale of the values that each one of these three dimensions can take must therefore be determined before the actual comparison takes place. Although Lévi-Strauss does not mention this particular prerequisite, I would add that the categorization of the empirical units used in the comparison must intervene at this point.

We have seen that the significance of a concomitant variation study increases when the conditions underlying a further testing of the association between dependent and independent variables are clearly spelled out. This testing depends on how well the problem of typicality is solved. It depends also on the definition of the irrelevant circumstances and thus of the *ceteris paribus*. (*Ceteris paribus* means "other things being equal.") In effect, the duplication of any comparison is likely to yield similar results only insofar as the nature and the number of variables held constant in both cases are identical. We must therefore turn our attention now to the problem of constants.

DEFINITION OF THE CONSTANTS

A problem accompanying possible duplication of the comparison undertaken concerns the definition of the units.

Constant Nature of the Units

I have stressed the importance of a clear-cut definition of the boundaries of the empirical units used in the context of controlled comparison, because we must answer the question of whether the associations demon-

Table 1

A TABLE OF POSSIBLE PERMUTATIONS—SYSTEMATIC PRESENTATION OF THE INTERACTION BETWEEN SIZE, DENSITY AND HETEROGENEITY IN BASCOM'S ANALYSIS OF YORUBA URBANISM

Heterogeneity (Occupational)*	*Heterogeneity* (Demographic)	Low									Medium									High								
		Low			Med.			High			Low			Med.			High			Low			Med.			High		
		Low	Med.	High	Low	Med.	High	Low	Med.	High	Low	Med.	High	Low	Med.	High	Low	Med.	High	Low	Med.	High	Low	Med.	High	Low	Med.	High
Low	Low																											
	Medium																											
	High																											
Medium	Low																											
	Medium																											
	High																											
High	Low																											
	Medium																											
	High																											

*Heterogeneity can be measured in two independent ways; the more farmers there are, the more there is occupational homogeneity (low occupational heterogeneity); the more even sex ratio, the more there is demographic homogeneity (low demographic heterogeneity).

strated or tested are independent of the size and the other characteristics of such empirical units. Thus, when we say with Redfield that secularization and social disorganization accompany urbanization, is this proposition true at the level of an entire country, of a single community, or of a particular individual? In a similar manner, when we note with Wirth that size, density, and heterogeneity co-vary as fundamental characteristics of urbanism, we must also recognize with Bascom that the association among these three dimensions is not alike (1) for cities located in Yoruba land and outside of it; (2) for cities with a majority of Yoruba and cities with a minority of them; and (3) for cities located inside and outside the cocoa belt of the Yoruba country. Another example concerns the examination of social selectivity and its incidence on patterns of recruitment into the secondary schools of two countries with differing enrollments and differing exposure to colonial influences. Whereas social selectivity seems in general to be greater in the Ivory Coast than in Ghana, it nevertheless seems to be less among the Agni and the Bete of the Ivory Coast than among the Ashanti and the Ewe of Ghana (Clignet and Foster 1964; Clignet 1967).

These examples of possible inconsistencies in the results produced by comparative methods illustrate clearly the need for a careful definition of the empirical units compared. These inconsistencies may imply that, in the duplication of the initial concomitant variation, *"ceteris"* have ceased to be *"paribus."* As Popper points out, "It is only experiments which lead us to discover changes in social conditions," and he argues that it is impossible to decide *a priori* whether any observed difference or similarity, is relevant for the purpose of reproducing an experiment (1964: 93–97). He implies then that our definition of constants is as important as our categorization of independent and dependent variables. We must further investigate their role in the context of concomitant variations and analyze how they are used in the design of the research itself.

Role of the Constants

The purpose of controlled comparisons is to establish not only that there is an association between the variables deemed to be in-

dependent and dependent, but also to establish that variations in the independent variable *alone* produce corresponding variations in the dependent variable. The fulfillment of this twofold purpose requires two distinctive strategies: a) the demonstration that while holding everything else constant, variations in the independent variable will produce related variations in the dependent variable; b) the demonstration that systematic variations in the variables deemed to be irrelevant do not modify the form nor the intensity of the association between the independent and the dependent variables. These two strategies have been suggested by Eggan (1954), Lewis (1953), and Nadel (1951).

The first strategy consists of the examination of a single community or a single culture or a single geographical zone at a particular time, and the comparison deals in this case with variations in particular modes of action or social organization. Thus, the absence of variations in the ecological and economic organization of the Australian tribes analyzed by Radcliffe-Brown facilitates the isolation of the relationship between the kinship terminology of these tribes and their social institutions. More specifically, it enables us to see how variations in kinship terminology lead to variations in the number of persons with whom a given individual enters into direct or indirect relations; further, how such variations, in turn, are associated with distinctive mechanisms of social integration. It also enables us to identify the variations in the social mechanisms derived from the equivalence of brothers. These variations are easy enough to identify because uniformities in ecological and economic conditions limit interindividual psychological differences and minimize accordingly the variability of the roles held by individuals. Similarly, the geographic isolation of Yucatan facilitates Redfield's examination of the processes by which the dominant traits of an urban system diffuse from a central place. Indeed, the political and cultural isolation of the area makes external influences very unlikely. Its homogeneity in this regard implies that, originally, all the units compared have an equal chance of acquiring a given pattern of organization. Under such conditions, differences in the social organization of the four communities compared should primarily reflect inequalities in their relative exposure to urbanization. The strategy used by Cohen is similar in his article analyzing modernization in the northern part of Canada. The population of this area is derived from a similar Athapascan background, had been originally engaged in similar hunting and gathering activities, and its isolation prevented its exposure to uncontrolled extraneous influences. In this uniform setting, Cohen is able to argue that the differences in the familial organization, the number of job opportunities and the income per capita of these three communities are attributable to differences in their size, the number of European Canadians who reside in them and other indicators of exposure to modernization.

The second strategy involves examination of social groups which differ in terms of a variety of dimensions but present at least two traits in common. This strategy is used by scholars who want to establish the concrete limits within which institutions, beliefs or techniques can vary or develop. This is the purpose of Rand and Riley (1958:274–297) in their article on the development of the blowgun in three different areas of the world. Showing the limits of diffusionist hypotheses, these authors demonstrate that the use of this blowgun has followed a similar pattern of development in three cultural zones which present distinctive organizations and have not entered into contact with one another. Independent invention in this context results from the simultaneous presence of the three following conditions: a) there is no other meat except small animals which live high in the trees; b) the people are already using bamboo for other things; and c) the people have nothing else with which to kill these animals high in the trees.

In this instance, then, the purpose of a controlled comparison is to demonstrate that differences among the units examined in terms of the variables deemed to be irrelevant do not affect the form nor the intensity of the association between independent and dependent variables. Regardless of other differences among the three cultural areas investigated, the presence in them of the three conditions described above shapes the patterns of possible uses of blowguns. In this particular case, the units investigated are not temporally nor spatially juxtaposed: they have been chosen because of the maximal differences which oppose them to one another.

Similar is the strategy used by Spicer in his examination of the social organization of the Yaqui. In order to demonstrate the preeminence of ceremonialism in this particular cultural system, the author shows that the relative position occupied by ceremonialism in the entire cultural organization of the villages investigated is independent of their degree of autonomy. Thus, we discover that there are two possible uses of constants in the context of controlled comparisons: the first strategy implies the manipulation of *similarities* between units whereas the second one requires the manipulation of *differences* between these units.

Other research designs rest upon a combination of the two strategies. Thus the purpose of Eggan in his study of the Western Pueblos is 1) to define the common features of the social structure and 2) indicate the nature of the variations which occur in this framework. The first task requires the demonstration that "despite opportunities for contacts and similarity in environment" there are significant differences between the Pueblos and other peoples housed in the same zone (1950:4). In other words, Eggan is concerned with an examination of the remarkable unity which characterizes the material culture, ideas, beliefs and sentiments of the variety of Pueblo subgroups. Yet, at the same time, the uniformity of the environment of these subgroups—communities are compact, built on the same style and include similar objects —and of their adjustment to material conditions facilitates an assessment of the divergent routes followed by them to achieve their identical goal of social integration.

In the first step of his demonstration, Eggan uses as constants historical *differences* between Pueblo subgroups to show that these historical differences do not prevent them from showing common traits which distinguish them as a group from their non-Pueblo neighbors. In his second step, however, he uses as constants *similarities* between these same subgroups to show that there are variations in their respective mechanisms of social integration. Köbben (1956) follows the same strategy in his analysis of the responses of the patrilineal Bete and matrilineal Agni of the Ivory Coast to the introduction of cash crops. His initial hypothesis is opposite of that of Redfield; whereas the latter assumed that before the introduction of his independent variable (urbanization), all his units had an identical organization, Köbben posits that before the introduction of industrial crops there are marked contrasts in the traditional organization of the two peoples compared. His examination of the *convergences* in the changes of the social organization of these two peoples leads him to use these original contrasts as constants: the purpose of the comparison is to demonstrate that, regardless of the initial contrasts between Agni and Bete, their exposure to a cash economy has similar effects upon them. Alternatively, however, Köbben's purpose is also to analyze the *divergences* in the changes of the social organization of these two peoples. This implies that he uses as constants the similarities of the two peoples in terms of their exposure to a cash economy to show that initial contrasts between the two cultures persist or increase throughout time. Clignet, in his examination of the child-rearing practices of urban and rural Abure and Bete women of the Ivory Coast, follows an identical strategy. In his examination of the urban-rural contrast among these women, again the variables used were the initial differences between the two peoples compared, and the constant used was their similar degree of exposure to environmental change.

Last, we should also note that constants do not involve only the manipulation of similarities and contrasts between the sole empirical units investigated. Contrasts and similarities may refer to the relation of these units with a third category. For example, the association between the choice of a particular animal as a totem and the particular form of ancestor cult found in a given cultural setting is often interpreted as a result of perceived psychological similarities between the animal chosen and the ancestors (Fortes 1945:141–145). Yet, Lévi-Strauss (1963:77) counterargues that these psychological similarities are not meaningful in absolute terms: "On the one hand totemic animals differ from others in that they belong to a particular species which has its own physical appearance and mode of life. On the other hand, ancestors differ from other categories of men in that they are distributed among different segments of the society." Thus, although A (totemic animal) is distinctive from B (ancestors), the relationship between A and C (other animals) is equivalent to the relationship between B and D (other human beings). It is this equivalence which is most significant. Although it pertains to the examination of independent and dependent variables, this notation of Lévi-Strauss is also appropriate for the investigation of constants.

Systematic Use of Constants

In the three research designs described above, the purpose of the analyses is to establish that, *ceteris paribus,* there is an association between independent and dependent variables. However, no concomitant variation study has yet used great care to check systematically these "other things." An example of a standard which might reasonably be expected from the researcher, is the work of Kroeber and his associates of the University of California—the *Culture Element Distribution* studies (done there in the thirties), and discussed further in Chapter 32.

These studies of cultural diffusion use check lists of several thousand traits which can be completed in a matter of one or two weeks per community studied. Similar check lists can be used readily for concomitant variation studies, even though their use raises the following important difficulties.

First, there is the question of deciding whether a cluster of patterns should be divided into more analytical categories. Second, the check list gives a static image of the patterns of action to be performed and fails to designate their sequential order. A third difficulty concerns the determination of the most adequate informants. What solution is appropriate when the item recorded is performed by specialists to whom the informant has only a restricted access either because of his sex or his social affiliation? For example, a description of the functions performed by African minstrels is likely to vary with the nature of the informant: social distance between minstrels and other social categories is large enough to distort the information desired in unexpected directions. There are no perfect solutions to alleviate this particular difficulty. On the one hand, an increase in the number of informants accentuates random errors in the recording of the distribution. On the other hand, the introduction of systematic errors due to the inadequacies of a limited number of informants diminishes the general reliability of the information collected.

Fourth, this check list indicates the central tendencies of a trait but gives hardly any clue as to the amount of dispersion observable around these central tendencies. Last, we must decide: Which trait, the archaic item of behavior or the modern one, should be recorded when the empirical unit investigated is undergoing transition? Nevertheless, these check lists are tools which should be used to a greater extent. In most concomitant variation studies undertaken so far, "*ceteris*" are not really "*ceteris*" but only "*aliis,*" i.e. "other things." That is, as long as there is no systematic investigation of constants, our propositions are shown to hold "*some other things being equal*" rather than "*all other things being equal.*"

MEASURING CONSTANTS AND VARIABLES

Present-Absent Dichotomies

In most studies, constants are defined by the presence or absence of traits. Thus, the "*ceteris paribus*" used by Wilson (1951) in her study of witchcraft among the Pondo and the Nyakyusa lie in the fact that "both peoples are cattle raising and engaged in subsistence agriculture, although an increasing number of individuals is now participating in a cash economy as labor migrants." Yet, it is not proven that the participation of these two peoples in cattle-raising activities and subsistence agriculture is alike. Neither is it demonstrated that their involvement in a modern economy is comparable. In effect, as long as we use dichotomies—whether as 1) constants, 2) as independent variables, or 3) as dependent variables—a concomitant variation tends to be a misnomer. Whereas the method of agreement and the method of difference demonstrates the occurrence or nonoccurrence of a particular phenomenon in conformity with the occurrence or nonoccurrence of others, the concomitant variations method requires a measurement of *quantitative* co-variations. A simple statement is therefore not enough to hold a variable constant; more refined statistical indicators are needed to determine the degree to which constants are really constants or the extent to which the independent variable influences the variable deemed to be dependent.

Statistical Measures

The use of such measures raises an initial problem. We must have some *a priori* idea about the characteristics of the distribution of traits used as constants or alternatively as independent and dependent variables. For example, an analysis of the consequences attached to a division of cities by size demands an *a priori* decision about whether these cities should be differentiated in terms of classes or along a continuum.

Means are the most frequent statistical measures used in the context of controlled comparisons. For example, the assumption that Ghana and the Ivory Coast present enough similarities for an examination of patterns of recruitment in their secondary school system rests, among other things, on the observation that their gross national products per capita are similar (Clignet and Foster 1964). The use of arithmetic means presupposes, however, that we have clear ideas about the limits beyond which differences become significant. Most of the time, the definition of these limits varies with the purpose of the analysis undertaken. Thus, slight differences, as they exist between the gross national products of Ghana and the Ivory Coast, are disregarded when the object of the comparison is between these two countries and the less developed nations of West Africa. The significance of such differences might be different when we want to focus our attention on the internal differences between these two nations, regardless of their position in the general scale of development of West Africa.

The standard deviation is another important measure used in the definition of constants, dependent and independent variables. Of course, this statistic measures the spread of variation, or variance. Thus, the comparison between two social classes of *n* cultures whose similarities and differences are controlled, remains limited, as long as we have not determined the degree to which these two social classes occupy a similar relative position in the social hierarchy of the cultures investigated. Although the mean incomes or mean occupational scores of the *n* distributions may be alike, their respective standard deviations may vary markedly. Another example of the importance of standard deviation in this regard concerns the examination of similarities and contrasts in the organization of polygynous families derived from a variety of ethnic groups. On the one hand, we may argue that the number of women present in a household is the only variable likely to influence the concrete exercise of domestic power. Or we may argue that the significance of this number varies with the distribution of polygynous families within each one of the peoples investigated. The position occupied by families including three wives is not similar when the incidence and the intensity of polygyny in the community at large is low or high.

Indicators of Change

The examination of patterns of change requires more subtle indicators or measurement. For example, Goode (1963:2) notes that even though family systems in distinctive areas of the world are moving toward similar patterns, they nevertheless begin from different points. If modernization is associated with a trend toward the emergence of a uniform level of divorce or illegitimacy across human societies, this may imply a decrease in such levels as far as some countries are concerned, but an increase in others. Thus, Goode indirectly suggests that we can compare levels of divorce by holding rates constant, or alternatively compare rates by disregarding the problem of differences in levels. In this general area of comparative analysis concerned with patterns of growth and differentiation, Moore and Feldman (1962:151–163) have suggested the following measures:

(1) Rates of change. For example, we can compare two countries which have a similar or a different level of urbanization and hold constant their rate of change of level of urbanization. Or we can examine variations in rate of change and disregard differences in levels.

(2) Timing. Given the fact that two societies present a common trait, the length of time necessary for them to acquire the trait may differ. Such differences or similarities between societies constitute a fruitful ground for comparisons.

(3) Sequential orders. For example, we may intend to compare two societies with similar levels of complexity, as defined by the indicators used by Freeman and Winch (1957:461–466). Thus, the two societies may

each have a cash economy and a secularized system of punishment. Yet, these two societies may differ in the order in which they have acquired these two "complex" features. We may then compare them, holding constant their differences as to sequential order, and examine the consequences attached to the similarity of their position in a scale of societal complexity. Alternatively, we may disregard such similarities and analyze how their differences in terms of sequential order induce other difficulties.

EVALUATING DATA QUALITY

So far we have shown how the significance of a concomitant variation study depends on the typicality of the various components entering into the analysis and also on the accuracy of the instruments used to measure constants, dependent, and independent variables. Of course, this significance is also a function of the validity of the data collected by the investigator. This problem of data quality control is treated by Naroll in Chapter 44. I consider here its specific relevance to concomitant variation studies. The first question concerns an evaluation of the various biases which affect these studies. More specifically, can we analyze the factors likely to produce such biases?

Biases Arising from the Investigator's Field Role

An initial type of bias can be the result of the position occupied by the investigator within the social structure examined. He may come as a missionary, he may come as an administrator, or he may come as a scholar. These three different roles produce very different sorts of relations with his social environment. Informants often give the type of answers that they think the investigator wants to hear; the nature, the direction and the degree of their distortions are likely to vary with the perceived attributes of the investigator and hence with his activities.

For a similar reason, while holding every other variable constant, it seems important to determine the degree to which the data gathered by male and female anthropologists in similar societies are comparable. Of course, a thorough examination of this problem requires a comparison of sex roles both within the cultures investigated and within the culture from which these anthropologists come. It also requires an analysis of the degree to which ethnic differences override sex differences in the perceptive processes of the actors involved. It is probably not an effect of sheer chance that so many female anthropologists have been concerned with an investigation of the "male viewpoint" of the cultures that they have studied. Was this viewpoint more accessible to them than the female viewpoint? Indeed, a particularly talented field worker shows quite explicitly that her acceptance by the women of the culture in which she was interested could only take place after she had been able to establish workable relations with the elder male members of the community (Bowen 1964).

Biases Arising from Scholar's Theoretical Orientation

A scholar's perceptions may be distorted by his theoretical orientation; he may be oversensitive to events and patterns which correspond to his theoretical orientations and underrate the facts which jeopardize his assumptions. Although his perceptions may be correct, he may also overemphasize events and patterns which support his theoretical propositions. Lastly, he may simply falsify his data.

Biases Arising from Informant's Errors or Prejudices

A third source of possible bias stems from the informant himself. He may be misled by the conscious models produced by his culture. He may also be unable to give a full account of the facts that the analyst is desirous to know. Among societies where sex roles are sharply differentiated, it seems obvious that male informants will give a male viewpoint about social relations developed along sex lines. For example, we often view polygyny in male terms and consider this institution as leading to a merciless domination of women by men. Yet, an examination of the female perception of this problem may lead the investigator to realize that there is large variance in the organization of such families and that the corresponding contrast between monogamy and polygyny is not as systematic as it appears to be at first glance. In general,

the information of the informant may be inaccurate, due to the marginal nature of the position he occupies in his culture (Zelditch 1962:566–576). Lastly, an informant may give erroneous information simply because he cannot remember the event. Many authors have suggested that information about child-rearing practices is unreliable, since memories in this area are often distorted by normative considerations. Accordingly, the only valid method of data gathering in this particular field is longitudinal analysis.

Data Quality Control Techniques

There are various techniques to measure the amount of errors produced by the introduction of these three types of bias (Naroll 1962:77–105). Thus it is possible to compare the similarity of information gathered through reports and through participant observation. It is also possible to measure how the length of stay and the perceived role of the investigator affect the quantity and the richness of the information that he gathers. And it is possible to measure the influence of investigators' linguistic skill on the validity of the data that they collect. Of course, the use of the test-retest method is also relevant in this context. This use can be refined. If it is true that the order in which compared empirical units are investigated affects the investigator's perceptions, it should be fruitful to introduce systematic variations in this order to measure the amount of distortions so produced. Lastly, while there are techniques available to measure the distortions in the information collected by field workers, there are also definite means to limit them. The "personal equation" of the field worker can be neutralized by psychoanalytical training or by the use of group field parties. The control over the situation can be increased by a systematic use of standardized materials (Lewis 1953:452–475). The data to be compared can be presented in the form of ratings made by judges independent both of the field workers and of one another (Whiting and Child 1953). In the specific field of the analysis of local politics, Hanna (1966:1–16) has indicated, for each step of the study, what kind of biases were likely to be introduced, and what precautionary measures should be taken to diminish their effects.

ANALYSIS OF ASSOCIATIONS

So far our concern has been to review the various steps of concomitant variation studies. Although all of them examine association among variables, the nature of these associations differs and we must therefore turn our attention to a definition of their typology. Some associations are studied synchronically —at a single point in time; others, diachronically—at two or more points in time. This distinctive use of time leads to the isolation of various sorts of associations.

Synchronic Studies

When conducted at a single point in time, most concomitant studies tend to identify the "laws of social statics," to use the terminology proposed by Radcliffe-Brown (1951:15–22). The purposes of these studies is to show how social functions are interdependent. Taking the Yaqui culture as an illustration, Spicer has attempted to identify the various forms of this interdependence. Thus, the Yaqui kinship terminology is not only used to refer to associations within and among households; it also defined relationships which take place in ceremonial activities. The use of a single set of symbols in a variety of situations helps to ensure the continuity of a culture, in spite of the dispersion of its members both throughout time and space. This use is called *formal linkage* by Spicer. It can be contrasted with *functional linkages,* which lead various members or subsegments of a single culture to gather at a particular point in space to coordinate their activities; in this case, cultural integration results from an increase in the physical and social density of interactions between individuals and groups. These linkages are, however, closely related to the conscious models of the culture investigated.

At a more abstract level, it is possible to analyze the hierarchy underlying the mechanisms by which a given culture achieves its integration. Through a diachronic analysis, the effects of the erosion of cultural institutions by time can be assessed and the cultural elements which have remained the most intact can be defined as the core of the cultural system. An examination of settlements differentially located, engaged in a variety of economic activities, may enable the researcher to achieve the same goals. Thus Spicer compares Pascua and Potam and shows that variations in economic exploitation and in degree of autonomy are not associated with basic changes in the ceremonial institutions of the Yaqui. He concludes that ceremonialism occupies a superordinate position among other components of this particular culture and he defines this pre-eminence as *compendance.*

The various components of a cultural system are not, however, systematically interrelated and Spicer suggests that it is possible to analyze their interrelations by building a scale measuring their consistency. Going from most to least, this scale comprises four points: (a) *Reinforcement,* which occurs when participation in a number of social activities reinforce one another. Thus among the Yaqui participation in labor ceremonial, *Fiestas* and *Pascuolas* tend to be mutually inclusive. (b) *Consistency,* which characterizes all situations where beliefs and patterns of actions do not interfere with one another. (c) *Inconsistencies,* which take place when these beliefs and patterns of action interfere with one another. Thus, there are inconsistencies in the demands of ceremonialism and of land tenure or between ceremonial labor and the activities necessary to make a living. (d) *Incompatibilities,* which occur when two beliefs or practices are in open conflict with one another. The presence of Mexican officers in Potam is incompatible with the belief that only Yaqui can live in Yaqui territory. Since incompatibilities threaten the functioning of the whole system, perceptions have to be rapidly modified.

In another context, Goldschmidt and his associates intend to underscore how determinants of social interaction are articulated. Social interaction is influenced by institutionalization of social requirements. That institutionalization depends in turn on other cultural and structural factors. Considering two pairs of African tribes—the Sebei and the Pokot which belong to the Kalenjin cluster, and the Kamba and the Hehe of the Bantu cluster—the authors intend to measure the relative impact of farming and pastoralism on the one hand, and of cultural and language factors on the other, upon social organization and hence upon patterns of social interaction. Further, the authors are not concerned with an examination of pure pastoralism versus pure farming, but rather with varying degrees of each. Data will be analyzed therefore in terms of "range and degree," making the study the best example, to my knowledge, of an adequate application of the concomitant variation method, as originally labeled by Stuart Mill.

Another function of synchronic studies is to test the universality of a proposed distinction. Thus, although the biological determinants of temperament probably make this variable evenly distributed across human societies, cultures do not stress equally a similar temperamental form. Neither do they attach similar significance to the two ends of the continuum of temperamental variations. Nor do they use analogous rewards and punishments to skew in a particular direction the distribution of temperaments among their members. Under such conditions, differentiation of roles along sex lines has more social than physical determinants and presents variable features. To show the variability of this distinction is Margaret Mead's main purpose in her study of three New Guinea tribes. Her results are summarized in Table 2.

In this context the method of concomi-

Table 2

DISTRIBUTION OF "MASCULINE" AND "FEMININE" ORIENTATIONS
AMONG FOUR DISTINCT CULTURES

| | | MEN | |
		"Masculine" Orientations	"Feminine" Orientations
WOMEN	"Masculine" Orientations	MUNDUGUMOR	TCHAMBULI
	"Feminine" Orientations	U.S.A.	ARAPESH

tant variations leads to the elimination of the possible influences exerted by geographical and historical factors. Tribes are from the same area and are considered at one single point in time, demonstrating that contrasts in some of the social organization traits of these three peoples are associated with variations in the allocation of "masculine" and "feminine" roles along sex lines. This study enables us to evaluate the variability of the socially acceptable types of personality across cultures, even though it does not necessarily enhance our understanding of the determinants of this variance.

In all these cases there is a complete "fit" between the purposes of the analysis and the strategy which supports it. Authors eliminate the time dimension because they are concerned with the isolation of timeless associations between various social phenomena.

Studies conducted at a single point in time, however, may also be substitutes for longitudinal studies which are too costly to undertake or too difficult to build because of a lack of basic information concerning independent and dependent variables. Thus Redfield uses a spatial axis of differentiation in lieu of the inaccessible but essential axis of growth and differentiation which is really the main object of his investigation. His technique is summarized in Table 3.

Clignet proposes the same type of equation in his analysis of the impact of urbanization on the child-rearing practices of the Abure and the Bete. Yet the validity of this equation is not demonstrated. In effect, differences in the recruitment of the various types of migrants investigated may account for a larger part of the variance in the distribution of the traits analyzed than differences in the organizational requirements of urban and rural communities or of occupations.

Diachronic Studies

The use of the time dimension can serve either one of the two following functions: (a) The second time period is *not* taken as

Table 3
GRAPHIC REPRESENTATION OF THE IMPLICIT EQUATION PROPOSED BY REDFIELD

Spatial Typologies at Time T4

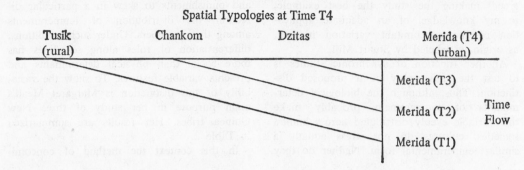

Tusik (rural)	Chankom	Dzitas	Merida (T4) (urban)

Merida (T3)

Merida (T2)   Time Flow

Merida (T1)

a result of the first time period. If functional linkages can be isolated through the comparison of two units located in the same general geographical and cultural whole at a single point of time, then the same can theoretically be achieved by comparing the same social units at different times. In this context, the time dimension is not treated as irreversible and historical, but rather as empty and mechanical, to use here the expression of Lévi-Strauss (1963:313–314). Insofar as they are concerned with an examination of the distinctive requirements of an industrial and nonindustrial social system rather than with an analysis of the processes by which these requirements change, comparisons of traditional and modern societies can be entered in this category. (b) The second time period is taken as a result of the first time period. Usually, the main function of diachronic studies is to determine patterns of growth and social differentiation, laws of "social dynamics" as Radcliffe-Brown calls them. This use of diachronic studies raises several difficulties.

First, the models likely to be used in this context are variable. Moore (1964:38–40) has identified at least three possible models likely to be used in the context of these analyses: linear, stairlike, and threshold. However, Clignet has suggested that the validity of these models vary both with the patterns of behavior investigated and the nature of the social organization studied, as it actually precedes change. Thus he observes that, as their level of exposure to environment change increases, Abure co-wives are less likely to cooperate, whereas their Bete counterparts are less likely to compete with one another. On the other hand, among the two peoples

investigated, there is a curvilinear relation between level of exposure to environmental change and incidence of polygyny; the minimal level of plural marriage is found for an intermediate level of exposure to environmental change.

A second difficulty concerns the definition of the two ends of the continuum of the social phenomena analyzed. Thus, Moore (1964:331–338) suggests that the rate of economic development of a given country changes as the process begins later in history, making it difficult to compare rates of development over time. Further, Moore tries to identify the various discontinuities which underlie social processes. Such discontinuities may account for inconsistencies in observations made on the patterns of behavior of social groups which hold relatively similar positions in cultures with differing levels of economic and social development. Thus, the observations of Clignet (1967b) and LeVine (1967) on the child-rearing practices of Ivory Coast "modern" parents in one case and of Nigerian "modern" parents on the other are contradictory: the limits of maximal exposure to environmental change do not coincide in the two studies.

In addition, the isolation of patterns of growth presupposes a valid definition of what is "primitive" and what is "modern." It is not clear whether the traits characteristic of the folk end of the continuum are uniformly antecedent to those attached to the urban end. Lévi-Strauss has demonstrated that it is often impossible to assert whether a division into two social categories is more primitive than a division into a multiple of two. This is the type of difficulty that Redfield has met in his analysis of the Yucatan communities described above. According to his model, "local variants of a given pattern of behavior should be less between any two of the four communities under study which are locally adjacent than between the two which are separate" (1941:78). Yet there are many errors in his model and the problem remains to interpret them correctly. Do they reflect discontinuities in the processes of growth or inadequacies in the models at hand?

The variety of associations derived from diachronic studies has been summarized by Eggan (1954:757). His summary is presented in Table 4.

Table 4
ASSOCIATIONS ISOLATED BY DIACHRONIC STUDIES

Type	Units	Time 1	Time 2	Example
Fusion	A	plus[a]	plus	
	B	minus[a]	plus	Eggan (1937)
Differentiation	A	plus	plus	
	B	plus	minus	Bellah (1952)
Persistence of Differences	A	plus	plus	
	B	minus	minus	Kluckhohn (1954)
Accentuation of Differences	A	plus	plus	
	B	minus	minus	?

[a] plus and minus refer to the absence or presence of the traits investigated.

SIGNIFICANCE OF THE ASSOCIATION

Having reviewed the variety of associations isolated by concomitant studies, I now turn to the problem of evaluating their significance. What are the causal implications of associations in concomitant variation studies? Of course, correlations among variables are not necessarily indicators of causal relationships among them. Correlations may be spurious, either because empirical units are not really independent or because there are intervening variables whose influence has not been properly detected.

Galton's Problem

The problem of common borrowing or common cultural heritage as a possible source of spurious correlation is often called Galton's problem. It is discussed at length in Chapter 47. Galton's problem is as important to concomitant variations studies as it is to cross-cultural surveys. Thus, even in such surveys it is difficult to ascertain the degree to which an association is the product of a functional linkage or of a process of diffusion. For example, do the contrasts among the traits found in Tusik, Chan Kom, Dzitas, and Merida reflect the processes by which urban cultures diffuse from their centers toward their periphery or do these contrasts reflect cleavages in the structural requirements of cities of varying size and varying complexity? The solution to this problem is made more difficult by the fact that various patterns of behavior or of organization do not diffuse at the same rate. In this context, the negative association between amount of brideprice and incidence of divorce, as it is suggested by a comparison between Abure and Bete, does not necessarily result from contrasts in the demands of matrilineal and patrilineal descent groups but rather from how far apart these two particular peoples are from a single center of diffusion.

Limits of the Concomitant Variations Studies

There is a more serious limitation in the results produced so far by concomitant variations studies in the field of anthropological investigations. According to the requirements of experimental method, we must demonstrate both that our hypothesis holds true each time that Variable 1 occurs and never holds true each time that Variable 1 does not occur. When we translate these requirements into a chart, we observe that most studies provide us with information about cells *a* and *d* but do not tell us anything about cells *b* and *c:*

VARIABLE 1

VARIABLE 2

	Plus	Minus
Plus	a	b
Minus	c	d

From Nadel's article on witchcraft (1952:18–29), a classic illustration of the concomitant variations method, we can derive the general proposition that *ceteris paribus,* divergences between two cultures in terms of the relative position occupied by their female members, are accompanied by further contrasts concerning the perceived role of women in witchcraft activities. Nupe women who are able to perform activities and exert demands which are inconsistent with the relevant expectations of their male counterparts, are viewed, for this very reason, as sources of frustrations and are accordingly accused of witchcraft activities. Occupying a different position in the social structure, Gwari women are not treated as potential witches. In this particular instance, we have collected information about the cells *a* and *d* of a table analyzing interrelation between the domestic status of women and the perceptions of witchcraft activities. Thus cell *a* tells us that the existence of inconsistencies between female activities and corresponding male expectations is associated with accusations of witchcraft against women. Correspondingy cell *d* tells us that the absence of such inconsistencies is associated with the absence of corresponding accusations. Yet we do not have any information about instances where such inconsistencies exist without being accompanied by the development of the relevant accusations (cell *b*)—or about instances where women are accused of witchcraft in spite of the fact that their actual status is not inconsistent with male expectations (cell *c*). Are there cases in *b* and *c?* What is their number? Are these numbers proportionately smaller than these observed in *a* or *d?* Are the characteristics of the cultures to be found in these cells such that we can establish meaningful contrasts between them and the Gwari or the Nupe?

The same observation holds true for Wilson's article concerning the Pondo and the Nyakyusa. In this instance we establish that a particular type of territorial organization is associated with the emergence of strains concerning the distribution of food or alternatively with the development of anxieties concerning sexual relations. We should, however, demonstrate that all peoples who do not follow either one of the rules of residence of the Pondo and the Nyakyusa do not present either one of the psychological symptoms of these two particular peoples. We should also demonstrate that there are no empirical instances where the first type of territorial organization is accompanied by sexual anxieties. In addition, we should demonstrate symmetrically that there are no instances where the second type of territorial arrangement is accompanied by strains concerning the distribution of food.

When we examine the contrasts between Gwari and Nupe, we note that these contrasts are manifold. Thus, the political, religious, familial and economic organization of these two peoples is similar, but the scale of the economy is greater among the Nupe than among the Gwari. This is accompanied by a high participation of Nupe women in activities deemed to be traditionally masculine. In addition, the sleeping arrangements of these two groups differ. Nupe women visit the bedroom of their husbands, whereas the pattern is reversed among the Gwari. Although this point is disputed by Nadel, it can be argued that Gwari children are directing their aggressiveness against their fathers whom they perceive as an intruder, whereas Nupe children hate their mothers who have abandoned them (LeVine 1961:49–88). Last of all, Nupe are characterized by a high discrepancy between the distribution of power and authority along sex lines. All these contrasts are summarized in Table 5. Table 5 suggests that the

Table 5

A SYSTEMATIZED APPROACH TO THE COMPARISON BETWEEN THE GWARI AND THE NUPE*

	FAMILIAL ORGANIZATION^a (+)							
	Scale of the Economy^b (+)				Scale of the Economy^b (−)			
	Differentiation of role along sex lines^c (+)		Differentiation of role along sex lines^c (−)		Differentiation of role along sex lines^c (+)		Differentiation of role along sex lines^c (−)	
Distinction between power and authority^d	Sleeping Arrangements^e (+)	Sleeping Arrangements^e (−)						
(+)								
Sleeping Arrangements^e (+)		Nupe: (identification of witches by sex)	Gwari: (no identification of witches by sex)					
(−) Sleeping Arrangements^e (−)								

Legend:

a. *Familial organization:* + refers to peoples having a patrilineal, patrilocal organization with localized extended families.

b. *Scale of the economy:* + refers to the importance of a cash economy, (involving long-distance exchanges) in the general outlook of the economic organization of the society analyzed.

c. *Differentiation of roles along sex lines:* − refers to the participation of women in activities that their own society deems to be male attributes (e.g. trading).

d. *Distinction between power and authority:* + refers to the fact that the distributions of authority (legitimized power) and power in domestic groups coincide.

e. *Sleeping arrangements:* + refers to the fact that wives visit their husbands.

*Note that the chart does not take into account variations in political and religious organizations.

comparison between the Nupe and the Gwari is but one subpart of a thirty-two-cell table of which only two cells are filled. It implies that we should consider these two people as only two discrete instances derived from a much larger distribution concerned with the variety of possible interactions between selected patterns of social organization. In other words, these instances do not constitute the two sole components of an entire universe. Thus, the comparison between Gwari and Nupe does not represent an end in itself, but rather constitutes an illustration of how, under a set of highly specific conditions, the emergence of certain strains in social structure lead the members of this structure to identify in a particular manner the sources of their frustration.

To give another example of the limitations of the results brought about in concomitant variation studies, we can examine the difficulties underlying the interpretation of the comparison undertaken by Köbben on the two peoples of the Ivory Coast already mentioned above. Köbben compares the impact of one single independent variable—the introduction of cash crops—on the social organization of the matrilineal Agni and the patrilineal Bete. In this case the dependent variables are familial relations on the one hand and land tenure on the other. However, these two peoples have the following dissimilarities: (a) Political organization. The first group represents a complex political organization whereas the second is politically segmented. (b) Type of descent. Agni are matrilineal, Bete patrilineal. (c) Territorial exogamy. The dense type of settlement prevailing among these Agni enables them to marry within the village, whereas both a low density and the complexity of kinship arrangements oblige Bete individuals to marry outside of their village of origin. (d) Degree of social absorption of married women into their affinal group. In more specific terms Bete women constitute the backbone of the labor force which their husbands control. Agni women are entitled to a certain amount of economic independence. (e) Exposure to the colonial system. The Agni were colonized at least fifty years before the Bete.

The problem is to ascertain which one of these five contrasts accounts for the difference in impact exerted by the introduction of industrial crops on the dependent variables

selected by Köbben. To be sure, some of the variables listed above vary both within and among the two peoples compared (for example, some Bete villages are large enough to allow marriages among their inhabitants). It is therefore possible to control more tightly their impact and to measure their relative weight in the variance of the distribution of the dependent variables. The fact remains, however, that these two ethnic groups do not constitute a single universe. Consequently we are wrong when we put *their* names at the top of the columns which list their traits. The object of the comparison is not to assess the similarities and contrasts between Agni and Bete alone. The object is to ascertain how economic changes affect various patterns of familial relations and of land tenure in general. Those of the Bete and the Agni merely constitute two examples. These traits themselves should therefore constitute the headings of the rows and columns used for comparative purposes. In this way and this way only, we may acquire an understanding of the dimensions of the comparison undertaken and achieve a better assessment of the limits of the concrete study examined. In short, we must cease to regard the empirical units as the objects of our examination; they are instruments of measurement and not what we want to measure.

CONCLUSIONS

Improvement in research which uses the concomitant variation method depends upon 1) a more systematic definition of the requirements attached to the operationalization of independent and dependent variables and of constants; 2) the introduction of more quantitative measurements in the treatment of these three parameters. True enough, the fulfillment of these conditions raises many difficulties and varies with the investigation. Thus the use of longitudinal or diachronic studies is more urgent in some areas of research than in others. Similarly, as contacts between cultures increase in frequency and intensity, the participation of the various groups found in these cultures becomes more uneven. It is therefore crucial to introduce measures of dispersion in the comparative analyses dealing with processes of change. It is equally important to introduce a larger number of more differentiated indicators of trends rather than to stick to static measures of central tendencies or to sheer dichotomies.

Concomitant variations studies represent the third stage in the series of operations which can lead us to scientific explanations. The first stage is the intense observation of several instances of the phenomenon in which we are interested. The second stage involves the establishment of a systematic typology derived from our observations. The validity of the third stage depends upon the validity of the typology developed in the second stage of scientific explanations. Indeed the validity of our typologies determines our assessment of the typicality of the comparison undertaken and our choice of constants. The purpose of concomitant variation method, however, is to offer provisional hypotheses, and its application cannot close all the loopholes present in our reasoning.

Thus the comparison of Clignet and Foster between Ghana and the Ivory Coast is incomplete in the sense that we still do not know whether the differences observed between the two countries reflect differences in the length of the colonial period or in the cultural characteristics of the models of colonization developed by French and British administrations. Similarly, as already mentioned, Redfield's analysis does not enable us to decide whether the differences observed among the four communities compared are the result of disparities in structural requirements, of differential frictions between Spanish and Maya cultures, or simply reflect different stages of diffusion. His work has gained from the analyses conducted later by Miner in Timbuctoo (1953), by Bascom in Yoruba land, and by Eggan in the Philippines (1961:11–18).

The necessity of duplicating such experiments must be particularly stressed at a time when replication is not fashionable and is instead perceived as unimaginative. A succession of valid concomitant variation studies will eliminate many preliminary and useless steps for succeeding generations of scholars. They will be able to move on to larger-scale comparisons like that between Australian and Californian tribes suggested by Eggan (1956) or like the studies done by Whiting and Child. Later scholars will also be able to consider wider or narrower conceptualizations of the variables treated in the original concomitant variations studies. Such larger-scale comparisons are the fourth stage in the series of operations leading to scientific explanations. The task which lies ahead is to introduce a systematic methodology with which we can move from the third to this fourth stage in the series of operations.

BIBLIOGRAPHY

BASCOM, WILLIAM
1962 Some aspects of Yoruba urbanism. *American Anthropologist* 64:699–708.

BELLAH, ROBERT
1952 *Apache kinship system*. Cambridge, Harvard University Press.

BOHANNAN, PAUL
1963 *Social anthropology*. New York, Holt, Rinehart and Winston.

BOWEN, ELENORE SMITH (pseudonym)
1954 *Return to laughter*. New York, Harper.

CHOMBART DE LAUWE, PAUL
1963 *Images de la femme dans la société*. Paris, Editions Ouvriers.

CLIGNET, REMI
1967 Ethnicity, social differentiation and secondary schooling in West Africa. *Cahiers d'Etudes Africaines* 7:360–378.
1968 Environmental change, types of descent and child-rearing practices. In H. Miner, ed., *The city in modern Africa*. New York, Praeger.

CLIGNET, REMI, and PHILIP FOSTER
1964 Potential elites in Ghana and the Ivory Coast: a preliminary comparison. *American Journal of Sociology* 70:349–362.

COHEN, MORRIS, and ERNEST NAGEL
1939 *An introduction to logic and scientific method*. New York, Harcourt, Brace.

COHEN, RONALD
1966 Modernism and the hinterland; the Canadian example. *International Journal of Comparative Sociology* 7:52–75.

DURKHEIM, EMILE
1958 *The rules of the sociological method*. Glencoe, Ill., Free Press.

EGGAN, FRED
1937 Historical change in the Chocktaw kinship system. *American Anthropologist* 39:34–52.

1941 Some aspects of culture change in the northern Philippines. *American Anthropologist* 43:11–18.

1950 *The social organization of the Western Pueblos*. Chicago, University of Chicago Press.

1954 Social anthropology and the method of controlled comparisons. *American Anthropologist* 56:743–761.

FORTES, MEYER

1945 *The dynamics of clanship among the Tallensi*. Oxford, Oxford University Press.

GOLDSCHMIDT, WALTER, et al.

1965 Variability and adaptability of cultures. *American Anthropologist* 7:400–447.

GOODE, WILLIAM

1963 *World revolution and family patterns*. New York, Free Press.

HANNA, WILLIAM

1966 The cross cultural study of local politics. *Civilizations* 16:1–16.

KLUCKHOHN, CLYDE

1954 Southwestern studies of culture and personality. *American Anthropologist* 56:688–697.

KÖBBEN, ANDRÉ

1956 Le planteur noir. *Etudes Eburnéennes* V (Abidjan Centre IFAN).

LEVINE, ROBERT

1961 Africa. In F. Hsu, ed., *Psychological anthropology*. Homewood, Ill., Dorsey Press.

1968 Urban father-child relationships; an exploration of Yoruba culture changes. In H. Miner, ed., *The city in modern Africa*. New York, Praeger.

LÉVI-STRAUSS, CLAUDE

1958 *Anthropologie structurale*. Paris, Plon.

1963 *Totemism*. Boston, Beacon Press.

LEVY, MARION, and LLOYD FALLERS

1959 The family; some comparative considerations. *American Anthropologist* 61:647–651.

LEWIS, OSCAR

1953 Control and experiments in fieldwork. In A. Kroeber, ed., *Anthropology today*. Chicago, University of Chicago Press.

MANNHEIM, KARL

1935 *Ideology and utopia*. London, Routledge and Kegan Paul.

MCEWEN, WILLIAM

1963 Forms and problems of validation in social anthropology. *Current Anthropology* 64:165–183.

MEAD, MARGARET

1935 *Sex and temperament in three primitive societies*. New York, Morrow.

MINER, HORACE

1953 *The primitive city of Timbuctoo*. Princeton, N.J., Princeton University Press.

MOORE, WILBERT, and ARNOLD FELDMAN

1962 Industrialism and industrialization; convergences and differentiation. *Transactions of the Fifth World Congress of Sociology* II:151–169.

1964 The McIver lecture. Predicting discontinuities in social change. *American Sociological Review* 29:331–338.

MURDOCK, GEORGE PETER

1949 *Social structure*. New York, Macmillan.

NADEL, S. F.

1949 *The foundations of social anthropology*. London, Cohen and West.

1952 Witchcraft in four African societies: an essay in comparison. *American Anthropologist* 54:18–22.

NAROLL, RAOUL

1962 *Data quality control*. New York, Free Press.

POPPER, KARL

1957 *The poverty of historicism*. Boston, Beacon Press.

RADCLIFFE-BROWN, A. R.

1931 The social organization of Australian tribes. *Oceanic Monographs* 1:3–123.

1951 The comparative method in social anthropology. *Journal of the Royal Anthropological Institute* 81:15–22.

RANDS, ROBERT, and CAROLL RILEY

1958 Diffusion and discontinuous distributions. *American Anthropologist* 60:274–287.

REDFIELD, ROBERT

1941 *The folk culture of Yucatan*. Chicago, University of Chicago Press.

SELVIN, HANAN

1957 A critique of tests of significance in survey research. *American Sociological Review* 22:519–528.

SPICER, EDWARD

1954 *Potam, a Yaqui village in Sonora*. Memoir No. 77 American Anthropological Association. *American Anthropologist* 56, No. 4, Part 2.

SPIRO, MELVIN

1956 Is the nuclear family universal? *American Anthropologist* 54:839–846.

TILLON, GERMAINE

1966 *Le harem et les cousins*. Paris, Le Seuil.

WHITING, JOHN, and IRVING CHILD

1953 *Child development and personality*. New Haven, Yale University Press.

WILSON, MONICA

1951 Witchbelief and social structure. *American Journal of Sociology* 56:307–313.

WINCH, ROBERT

1962 *The modern family*. New York, Holt, Rinehart and Winston.

WINCH, ROBERT, and LINTON FREEMAN

1957 Societal complexity; an empirical test. *American Journal of Sociology* 52:461–465.

WIRTH, L.
1938 Urbanism as a way of life. *American Journal of Sociology* 44:1–24.

ZELDITCH, MORRIS
1962 Some methodological problems of field studies. *American Journal of Sociology* 67:566–576.

1964 Cross cultural analyses of family structure. In Harold Christensen, ed., *The handbook of marriage and the family. handbook of marriage and the family.* Chicago, Rand McNally.

CHAPTER 32

Statistical Studies of
Continuous Geographical Distributions

HAROLD E. DRIVER

This essay is arbitrarily limited to comparative studies of continuous distributions of cultural objects or behaviors in regions ranging from a single culture area to a continent. Such studies include all or nearly all the ethnic units in the region and the generalizations arrived at are usually regarded as limited to the region. When the region is an entire continent, however, some of the generalizations may also apply to the entire world. Although such studies do not always exhaust all the available evidence in the region, they may operate with such large samples of ethnic units that sampling variability is not a crucial issue. When the time level is limited to some period in the past, say the nineteenth century, it is possible to assemble a large enough corpus of data to make it difficult for a critic to find enough additional information to seriously alter the principle generalizations.

The earliest study of this type is that of Boas (1894). Boas assembled a total of 214 elements (motifs, incidents, and tale types) of Indian myths and tales among twelve ethnic units on the Northwest Coast and adjacent Plateau area and three widely scattered peoples (an interior Athapaskan group, the Ponca, and Micmac) to serve as a geographical control. He first presented the raw frequencies of elements shared by each combination of two tribes in a rectangular matrix. But since the number of pages of folklore material varied considerably among the fifteen ethnic units, he corrected for this uneven quantity in the following manner. On the assumption that the available data on all ethnic units totaled 100 pages and that the relation of the number of elements to the

number of pages was positive and linear (a perfect correlation), he corrected upward each raw frequency of shared folklore elements with the following formula:

$$\frac{100}{40} \times \frac{100}{17} \times 4 = 60$$

where 100 is the hypothetical number of pages, 40 the actual number of pages for the Kwakiutl, 17 the actual number of pages for the Tlingit, 4 the actual number of elements shared by the two groups, and 60 the corrected number of elements shared by the two groups. He then arranged the corrected values in a rectangular matrix in such a manner that areal clusterings emerged. Thus he treated the tribes as variables and the folklore elements as cases (observations).

These are his principal conclusions. 1. Neighboring peoples share more folklore inventory than distant peoples. The ethnic units in the continuous area on the Northwest Coast and Plateau share more with each other than with the Ponca, Micmac, and interior Athapaskan group. Therefore very strong diffusions among neighboring peoples have taken place. 2. Tribes speaking languages of the same family show significantly greater internal similarity with each other. Thus Boas distinguishes the culture heritage–migration explanation of resemblances from the diffusion one which must be postulated for elements spilling over language family fences. 3. Most resemblances do not arise independently from "elementary ideas" shared by all peoples on earth, but are determined by contacts of peoples.

In his later and much larger study centered on the Tsimshian, Boas (1916) collected the largest corpus of folklore material of its time, but did not apply any statistical concepts to it. This material supported the conclusions derived from the early (1894) work and added a few more. 4. The elements (motifs) of a particular tale type or tale cycle tend to diffuse independently of each other as well as independently of the larger tale unit, which never diffuses as a whole. 5. The elements assembled in a tale type of a single society, however, are reinterpreted and integrated into each local literary style. 6. There is no way to tell which version of a tale type is prior historically and by this means to arrange them in a historical or evolutionary sequence. These and the earlier conclusions of 1894 gave rise to the theory of culture which Lowie (1920:441) phrased as "that planless hodgepodge, that thing of shreds and patches called civilization. . . ."

The next application of statistics to a comparative problem in a restricted region is that of Czekanowski (1911). His data were those assembled by Ankermann (1905) in his "Kulturkreise und Kulturschichten in Africa." Czekanowski intercorrelated seventeen variables of material culture among forty-seven African ethnic units (cases) using Yule's Q coefficient, and clustered the coefficients in a rectangular matrix. A second matrix was constructed in which the coefficients were grouped into class intervals and each class was represented by a shade of gray, thus producing a graphic device for quick comprehension of the relationships. The entire matrix divided neatly into two principal clusters which, when mapped, formed two areal units, a tropical forest culture and a Sudan–East African culture. Czekanowski assumed, as did Ankermann, that all resemblances were due to historical factors, but no clear distinction was made between diffusion and culture heritage –migration. Although Czekanowski presented a fairly simple technique for demonstrating the authenticity of *Kreise* or *Schichte,* no member of this school ever applied it. Czekanowski did not cite Boas' (1894) work on folklore but did cite Tylor's (1889) world-wide study on social organization.

Kroeber and Holt (1920) tested the correlation in North America of two variables, masks and moieties, which Foy of the *Kulturkreis* school had postulated as positive. Although they did not use a phi coefficient

or chi-square, they computed the expected frequencies for each cell in the 2×2 table from a sample of seventy-two ethnic units and showed that they matched the observed frequencies exactly, thus yielding a zero correlation. They interpreted this to mean that there was no historical connection between masks and moieties; that they had not spread together by migration or diffusion. Schmidt (1920) wrote a reply but, as he changed the description of the moiety variable, made a number of errors in his coding, and did not use any probability theory, he accomplished nothing of interest here.

As the *Kreise* and *Schichte* were extended to larger and larger regions and finally to the whole world, they became progressively more speculative and few of them have been confirmed by more recent correlation methods.

The next statistical regional study is that of Clements, Schenck, and Brown (1926), which was begun in a seminar conducted by Kroeber at the University of California at Berkeley. Using the comparative data on Polynesian material culture in the table at the end of Linton's (1923) monograph, they distributed 282 presence-absence traits among six island groups in Polynesia. They compared each combination of two island groups in terms of the amount of this cultural inventory shared, thus treating ethnic units as variables and the culture traits as cases. Instead of describing the frequencies in their 2×2 tables with a phi coefficient, they computed only chi-squares. Because some of the chi-squares were quite high, they were forced to carry out the probabilities of the chi-squares arising from sampling variability to six decimal places in order to distinguish the higher relationships from one another.

Because chi-square had no sign, they used the "excess of agreements over disagreements" as a sign marker. If we adopt Karl Pearson's symbols, Table 1, then the excess of agreements over disagreements becomes $(a+d)-(b+c)$. This is a poor measure of relationship and even a poor sign marker because it does not adjust for sample size or for asymmetry in either or both variables of the 2×2 tables. The hypothetical frequencies in Table 2 make the latter point. Here the excess of agreements over disagreements is $(1+81)-(9+9)=64$, or 64 per cent of the maximum, yet the relationship is one of chance and both phi and chi-

Table 1
PEARSON'S SYMBOLS FOR 2 × 2 TABLE

	Presence +	Absence −	
Presence +	a	b	a + b
Absence −	c	d	c + d
	a + c	b + d	n

square equal zero. The amount of asymmetry in the Polynesian data was not as extreme as that in the above example, but it was sufficient to show that chi-square and the above algebraic summation were not functions of one another and were not measuring the same thing. Clements *et al.* classified the six island groups into three areal classes of two members each and explained the relationships in terms of both culture heritage–migration and subsequent diffusion. Three time levels were distinguished in a "layer cake" diagram in which the most widespread traits were regarded as the older, thus using the age-area hypothesis.

Wallis (1928) wrote a detailed criticism of Clements *et al.* (1926). First he criticized all attempts to infer history from synchronic geographical distributions, and argued that generalizations about change should be made only from diachronic dated information. He forgot to say that the amount of documentary material on pre-European Polynesian and other non-literate cultures is too little to produce significant generalizations about culture change, and that rules worked out for change in the advanced cultures of Europe would not necessarily apply to those of Poly-

nesia. Wallis next argued that generic traits were stronger evidence of culture contacts than specific traits, which is just the opposite of the view shared by most ethnologists then and now. He made the further point that common absences should not be given the same weight as common presences in historical inference. This issue will recur in several places in this paper.

Clements' (1928) reply to Wallis was the best methodological statement up to that date on areal classification and historical inference. He mentioned sampling procedures for the first time, saying that the trait sample should be as large as possible, that traits should be chosen from as many different aspects of culture as possible, that all traits should be split into the smallest units possible, and that specific traits are more valuable than generic traits for inferring common origin. Without hazarding a precise threshold for the quantity of traits necessary to prove historical connection, he suggests that, if 300 out of 500 traits are shared by two ethnic units, common history is the only explanation. He admits that some of the resemblances may be of independent origin, but says that they will be few in number. He agreed with

Table 2
HYPOTHETICAL FREQUENCIES

	Presence +	Absence −	
Presence +	1	9	10
Absence −	9	81	90
	10	90	100

Wallis that all available documents on culture change should be used, but disagreed on the importance of common absences, which he argued were significant within a limited geographical and historical frame such as that of Polynesia in the last thousand years. He further acknowledged that while statistics can indicate the amount of historical relationship it cannot give the direction of diffusion or migration.

The impact of the sober method of Clements' 1928 paper was diminished somewhat after his (1931) study of the Sun Dance of the Plains Indians appeared. Using the trait distribution table of Spier (1921) and a little additional data, he compared the Sun Dance inventories of the eighteen tribes by means of Yule's Q coefficient. He again treated the tribes as variables and the traits as cases. Because of unevenness of reporting as well as large real differences in the number of traits possessed by the various tribes (the range was 57 to 10), many of the 2×2 tables were highly asymmetrical. It so happened that most of the ten traits reported for the Plains Ojibwa were shared with most of the other tribes, thus raising these Q coefficients to high positive values. One such value achieved unity (Table 3). The result was that the algebraic sums of all

Table 3

ONE SUN DANCE RELATIONSHIP

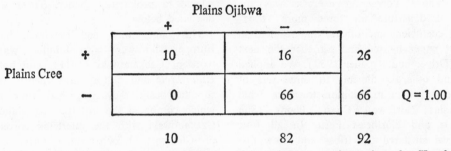

Plains Ojibwa

	+	−	
Plains Cree +	10	16	26
Plains Cree −	0	66	66 Q = 1.00
	10	82	92

the Q values of each tribe showed a higher positive value for the Plains Ojibwa than for any other tribe. Along with the Assiniboin and Plains Cree, the Plains Ojibwa was assigned a major role in the development of the Sun Dance. This is very unlikely in view of the marginal position and late arrival of the Ojibwa and Cree to the Plains area. More about the Q coefficient later.

In 1931 Kroeber finished his volume on *Cultural and Natural Areas of Native North America* and sent it to the Bureau of American Ethnology for publication. Although it was nonstatistical, except for summations of population estimates, it is mentioned here to make the point that areal classification and historical inference were his principal interest from about 1925 to 1931.

At some time between 1926 and 1931, Kroeber arranged the fifteen Polynesian interisland relationships, derived from chi-square and its probabilities, in a new rank order from high to low. He was not satisfied with the statistical scheme, and worked out another rank order impressionistically, but did not publish it. In the spring of 1931, I participated in a seminar given by Kroeber on the culture area and related problems. In this seminar, I came up with a new coefficient of interrelationship, and Kroeber suggested I apply it to the Polynesian data of Clements, Schenck, and Brown. This I did, and when Kroeber arranged my results in rank order, they matched exactly his own impressionistic rank order. Thus, by using statistical methods, a first-year graduate student, who knew nothing about Polynesia, was apparently able to equal a seasoned ethnologist in the task of grouping territorial units into meaningful relationships.

In the symbolism of Karl Pearson's 2×2 table, the new coefficient, called G, devised to eliminate common absences, is the following:

$$G = \frac{a}{\sqrt{(a+b)(a+c)}}$$

This is identical to the theoretical formula for Karl Pearson's linear r from the factor theory of Charles Spearman and others, where a equals the number of factors common to both variables, b the number belonging exclusively to the first variable, and c the number belonging exclusively to the second variable. It goes back at least to Thomson (1916:275) and I found it for the first time in 1931 in a book by Kelley (1924).

I learned later of the relation of G to phi. If G is rotated around the 2×2 table it takes on four forms which, collectively give phi (Table 4). (G has recently been rediscovered by Ellegard (1959) and labeled R_n.)

Table 4
RELATION OF G TO PHI

$$G_a = \frac{a}{\sqrt{(a+b)(a+c)}} \qquad G_b = \frac{b}{\sqrt{(a+b)(b+d)}}$$

$$G_c = \frac{c}{\sqrt{(a+c)(c+d)}} \qquad G_d = \frac{d}{\sqrt{(b+d)(c+d)}}$$

$$G_a G_d - G_b G_c = \frac{ad - bc}{\sqrt{(a+b)(a+c)(b+d)(c+d)}} = \phi$$

The above Polynesian exercise was the point of departure for three more "tests" of my coefficient and others, and resulted in a joint paper by me and Kroeber the next year (Driver and Kroeber 1932). We applied this and other coefficients to three sets of ethnological data in addition to those from Polynesia: Northwest Coast; Plains (Sun Dance); and Northeast Peru. In all four cases we clustered the tribes and drew historical inferences from the clusterings.

This was Kroeber's major statement on the subject of statistical ethnology. I did the library work, prepared the tables of data, and computed the coefficients, but he wrote the first draft, which was little changed in the published form. Our general conclusion was that statistics were ancillary to the other ethnological methods and should not be divorced from a thorough knowledge of the cultures of the region, a careful coding of the data, and an awareness of geographical relations of the ethnic units. In our concluding paragraph we emphasized that nearly all ethnological data are faulty for comparative purposes because they mention positive occurrences almost exclusively and leave it up to the comparativist to decide whether an unmentioned trait is actually absent or merely unobserved by the field worker. This uncertainty looms just as large in non-statistical as in statistical comparisons, however. Kroeber devised three other formulas for the 2×2 table, but these involve certain crude summations of the frequencies, which do not adjust to asymmetry and cannot be

related to probability theory. These will be discussed below.

This paper was read by three men in Europe who were also familiar with the work of Czekanowski (1911), and both the *Kulturkreis* and culture area theory. Almost simultaneously they published four papers which combined the intertrait correlations of Czekanowski with the intertribe correlations of Clements, Kroeber, and Driver. These papers are those of Fürer-Haimendorf (1934), Klimek (1935), Milke (1935), and Klimek and Milke (1935). The coefficient they used was a trigonometric function of phi called Q_6 by Karl Pearson:

$$Q_6 = \text{Sin} \ [(90°)(\phi)]$$

This coefficient gives values identical with those of tetrachoric r when there is perfect symmetry in both variables of the 2×2 table. It was devised by Pearson as a substitute for tetrachoric r because the latter was much more time-consuming to compute. Where one or both variables are strongly skewed, however, its results are closer to those of phi than to tetrachoric r (Driver 1939: 300–302).

The three Europeans computed three sets of coefficients: intertribe, intertrait, and tribal cluster with trait cluster. All three assembled their coefficients in rectangular matrices, and constructed a second matrix where the values were grouped in class intervals represented by varying shades of gray for quick comprehension, as Czekanowski had done in 1911. Then they returned to their rectangular distribution tables showing presences and absences of all the traits among all the tribes and 1) rearranged the order of the traits to match that of the clustered variables in the table of intertrait correlations and 2) rearranged the order of the tribes to match that of the clustered tribes in the table of intertribal correlations. Finally they mapped their major clusters. A simplified explanation of this technique still in print is that of Driver (1961).

Knowledge of statistical mechanics was so rare among ethnologists at that time that few understood that these studies integrated the approachs of the American culture area and the German *Kulturkreis* schools. They offered an objective method for determining both intertribal (culture area) and intertrait (*Kulturschichte-Kulturkreis*) clusterings. If every writer in these schools had empirically demonstrated his intertribe and intertrait groupings in this manner, the differences between the schools would have been less marked and a lot less paper and ink would have been wasted on polemics. Differences in interpretation of the data clustered in these ways could still have existed, but the authenticity of the clusters themselves could have been agreed upon.

The paper of Klimek (1935), the largest and most impressive of the four, will be described in more detail because it relates to the University of California culture element survey. Klimek obtained a Rockefeller fellowship for research at the University of California at Berkeley and, soon after his arrival in September 1933, Kroeber generously gave him a list of about 800 culture traits compiled by Kroeber for a comparative synthesis of California Indian cultures that had not yet got off the ground. Klimek, with the aid of Philip Drucker, then a graduate student at Berkeley, worked out the geographical distributions of about 400 of these traits among sixty ethnic units. As it was next to impossible to intercorrelate each combination of two culture traits among a sample of 400 at that time, Klimek topically divided the total into five sections, averaging 80 traits each, and computed the intercorrelations of the traits within each of these sections. He then equated the trait clusters in the five sections impressionistically. All resemblances were regarded as caused by migration or diffusion; parallelism and convergence were not mentioned. Klimek's text included a recitation of the groupings of data apparent

from an inspection of the tables and figures, plus a historical reconstruction. He called his historical inferences historical facts. However, he was the first to offer numerical correlations between culture clusters and language family groupings, which he regarded as resulting from common history. His areal classification matched that of Kroeber (1920) amazingly closely, and demonstrated again that a novice with a quantitative method can obtain taxonomic results comparable to those of a seasoned master.

Klimek's historical reconstruction, based on the intertrait clusters as well, which he called strata, differed so much from Kroeber's view that the latter wrote four pages in a preface to Klimek's (1935) work in order to keep the two sets of interpretations separated. This example emphasizes an important point. Two or more researchers, working with correlation methods from the same corpus of data, are likely to show a high degree of agreement in the clusters of tribes or traits they discover, yet may differ considerably in the historical inferences drawn from the clusters. The objective part of the procedure is the taxonomy, not the historical inferences derived from it. Therefore, a culture area scheme which claims to be only a taxonomy is likely to be more objective and demonstrable than one which is thought to be historical or genetic. Kroeber's insistence (1939a) that culture area classification must reflect historical factors introduces a subjective element which leaves room for disagreement.

Routil (1936) wrote a critical review of applications of statistics to ethnological problems and rejected forms of r and Q after showing instances where they worked badly. He introduced two new measures, Z and A; the latter is identical to Kroeber's W; both are given in Table 5. He favored A

TABLE 5 Other formulas for 2×2 table.

$$\text{Yule's } Q = \frac{ad-bc}{ad+bc}$$

$$\text{Kroeber's } A = \tfrac{1}{2}\left(\frac{a}{a+b} + \frac{a}{a+c}\right)$$

$$\text{Kroeber's } T = \frac{a}{a+b+c}$$

$$\text{Kroeber's } W = \text{Routil's } A = \frac{a+d}{n}$$

$$\text{Routil's } Z = \frac{(a+d)-(b+c)}{(a+d)+(b+c)}$$

Formula for Pearson's tetrachoric r*:

$$\frac{d}{n} - \frac{c+d}{n}\frac{b+d}{n} = r + xy\frac{r^2}{2!}$$

$$z_x z_y$$

$$+ (x^2-1)(y^2-1)\frac{r^3}{3!} + (x^3-3x)(y^3-3y)\frac{r^4}{4!}$$

$$+ (x^4-6x^2+3)(y^4-6y^2+3)\frac{r^5}{5!} \cdots$$

(W), but Milke (1937) in a reply to Routil showed that A (W) also behaved badly under certain conditions.

THE CULTURE ELEMENT SURVEY

The fact that Klimek, with the aid of Philip Drucker, was able to work out fairly complete geographical distributions for only about half of Kroeber's original list of culture traits called attention to the gaps in knowledge. To remedy this defect in data, Kroeber organized questionnaire field work in California and later expanded it under the name of the Culture Element Survey to an area west of the Rocky Mountain divide, stretching from the Mexican border to Alaska. This program, described by Kroeber (1939b), was aimed at the collection of data of sufficient comparability to revolutionize comparative ethnology in western North America.

The field work was done from 1934 to 1938 among 254 territorial units by thirteen field workers. Of these thirteen field workers, only five were seasoned ethnologists with the Ph.D. or the equivalent; the rest were graduate students. Most of the thirteen did not approve of quantification in ethnology and knew little about it. They accepted the grants because they had no better opportunity to upgrade themselves in the profession. If given the same sum of money and the choice of the kind of field inquiry to pursue, I doubt if more than two or three would have chosen the questionnaire plan of the Culture Element Survey. There was a lack of morale and of standard procedure in carrying out the plan.

Although the Culture Element Survey was

* x is the deviation of one variable from its mean in terms of standard deviation, y the same for the other variable, $z_x = \frac{1}{\sqrt{2\pi}} e^{\frac{-x^2}{2}}$ which is the ordinate of the normal probability distribution at x, z_y the same for the other variable at y.

principally a salvage program to obtain as much nineteenth-century information as possible from old informants in the 1930s, before they died, some work of theoretical interest emerged. The first was that of Kroeber (1937) on the Pomo. A short quotation in a section on reliability will show that Kroeber was still employing only indirect and subjective means of determining the reliability of the data.

Reliability of the 20 lists is presumably not equal: informants will vary in degree of knowledge, precision, cooperation, suggestibility. Their respective reliability may be objectively tested in two ways: by the nature and appearance of each list as such; and, after a classification has been made, by the degree of fit of each list to what is expectable on the basis of geographical proximity, linguistic relation, and, above all, concordance with the totality of the results obtained. (1937: 223)

Kroeber had only a single informant from each of the twenty localities and was unable to separate the reliability of response from various interpretations of the data.

In analyzing the data, Kroeber exhibited several matrices of numerical relationships from tribe with tribe comparisons, using Yule's Q and his W measure. These matrices revealed only a slight tendency to cluster and were more remarkable for their even variation from one locality to another.

. . . there normally appears to be a nearly equal step-by-step progression from community to community, so that the fifth from a given starting point can be predicted with certainty, and the fourth with high probability, to be more different than the third. Where this is not so, the "irregularity" almost invariably coincides with either an environmental or an ethnic break. (1937:244)

On my northwest California field trip I occasionally interviewed two informants from the same language group and had, in addition, a fair amount of previously published data to compare with my questionnaire responses. The result was "The Reliability of Culture Element Data" (Driver, 1938). In this study I measured reliability by correlating the responses of two informants from the same locality, using tetrachoric r, thus divorcing reliability from ethnographic interpretation. My principal conclusions were these:

Compared with data of other social sciences, the reliability of culture-element material is fairly high. Reliability coefficients . . . of the entire body of data examined range from .87 to .97. . . . The low values are likely to be nearer the true reliability because higher ones are from data collected by a single ethnographer [Driver] who may have possessed a bias of some kind.

Within the limits of personal variation among the present ethnographers and informants, the personal equation of the ethnographer seems to be as important as that of the informant. . . . No one major division of culture, material, social, or religious, shows any higher reliability than any other. . . . Illustrations [photographs and drawings shown informants] apparently do not increase reliability. Generic or specific elements show no significant differences in reliability from each other or from the data as a whole. Widely distributed elements are apparently more reliable than the unselected elements in the list; narrowly distributed elements less reliable. (Driver 1938: 213)

I also pointed out that if errors tended to be randomly distributed in the data, as I suspected they were, they would "attenuate" (lower) correlation coefficients. The true values would, therefore, be higher, and obtained values could be corrected upward with the formulas given by Spearman (1907).

In the introduction to my northwest California field report (Driver 1939a:297–306) I made a number of methodological and theoretical points. I showed with a series of diagrams that tetrachoric r, phi, Q, Q_6, G, and three other coefficients (A, T, W) of Kroeber give parallel results when there is perfect symmetry in both variables in the 2×2 tables, and that differences sufficient to seriously alter groupings in correlation matrices are caused by asymmetry in one or both variables of the 2×2 table. The additional formulas (not given above), in Karl Pearson's symbolism for the 2×2 table, are given in Table 5 above).

A (Kroeber's), T, W, and G all vary from zero to +1.00; they have no negative values. Q, Q_6, tetrachoric r, and phi vary from −1.00 to +1.00.

W (Routil's A) is especially deceiving because it can show a high relationship between two traits when there is not a single instance of their co-occurrence. The following data in Table 6 (Driver 1941: Table 13) will illustrate this point.

Table 6
GIRLS' PUBERTY DATA

Sun symbol on girl's head or face

		Present	Absent		
Tortoise Shell Rattle	Present	0	5	5	
	Absent	4	140	144	W = .94
		4	145	149	

Q and r are also misleading in this example because they give perfect negative values (−1.00). A, T, and G give zero values; phi is −.03 and Q_6 is −.05.

The correlations between membership of ethnic units in a language family and two culture areas will illustrate further unacceptable behavior of Q and tetrachoric r. These data in Table 7 are taken from my North American avoidance study (Driver 1966: Table 6; the phi coefficients are given in Driver and Sanday 1966: Table 3).

If the concept of correlation or association is to have a useful meaning in comparative ethnology, two variables which correlate or associate perfectly and positively with a third

variable must correlate or associate perfectly and positively with each other. This does not hold true for Q and r. The Yukon Subarctic culture area and the Mackenzie Subarctic culture area both correlate or associate perfectly and positively with the Athapaskan language family, yet their relationship is perfect and negative with each other, according to Q and r. Such incongruities in a correlation matrix make it impossible to run matrix reduction analyses, such as factor analysis. Driver and Sanday (1966:174) found it impossible to get an accurate inversion of their phi correlation matrix because of a modest amount of irregular behavior comparable to that for phi in the above three

Table 7
CULTURE AREA AND LANGUAGE FAMILY RELATIONSHIPS

Yukon Subarctic culture area

		Present	Absent	
Athapaskan Language Family	Present	7	25	32
	Absent	0	245	245
		7	270	277

Mackenzie Subarctic culture area

		Present	Absent	
Athapaskan language family	Present	10	22	32
	Absent	0	245	245
		10	267	277

Yukon Subarctic culture area

		Present	Absent	
Mackenzie Subarctic culture area	Present	0	10	10
	Absent	7	260	267
		7	270	277

	ϕ	Q_6	Q	r	A	G	T
First relationship	.45	.65	1.00	1.00	.61	.47	.22
Second relationship	.54	.75	1.00	1.00	.66	.56	.31
Third relationship	−.03	−.05	−1.00	−1.00	.00	.00	.00

relationships. Tetrachoric r would be impossible to deal with in a factor analysis of such a matrix and Q could not be clustered in any meaningful manner.

That asymmetry is common enough in actual data to seriously alter classifications into tribal clusters or trait clusters was shown by Clements' (1931) Sun Dance article and by my monograph on girls' puberty rites (1941). In the table of intertrait correlations (Table 11) in the latter study, 80 per cent of the 1891 intercorrelations among the 62 variables were skewed more than 80:20 or 20:80 per cent in one or both variables. All of the correlations involving language family and culture area membership in Driver and Sanday (1966: Table 3) would also be skewed more than this amount. The skewness difficulty is, therefore, a real one and not just an imaginary monster.

In this same introduction (Driver 1939a: 304–305) I wrote a sharp criticism of the Driver and Kroeber (1932) paper. This was, of course, directed at Kroeber, with whom I had disagreed on a number of points when the joint paper was written in 1931.

In a section on historical inference I challenged the view that "all correlations in any body of data are caused by purely historical factors. Although this statement does seem to be true of the majority, nevertheless such 'functional' factors as the compatibility of the trait with the rest of the culture may determine its acceptance in a number of cultures and its rejection in many others exposed to it. . . . One of the most interesting but heretofore almost untouched fields of correlation is the determination of these mutual-compatibility patterns by a combination of functional and historical theory" (Driver 1939a:305–306).

Kluckhohn (1939) wrote a review article on the application of statistics to ethnological data, with the emphasis on the period from 1932 to 1937. As he was not aware of the effect of skewness on the various coefficients applied to the 2×2 table, his comments on the formulas are immature. He tended to favor W and Z over forms of r and Q, and concluded that "the use of formulae based upon probability theory must be regarded with scepticism" (p. 366). Nevertheless he made some good points: that correlation may be due to functional cohesion of traits as well as to purely historical factors; that

convergences may arise independently in multiple localities; that analysis of variance might separate historical factors from those of social interaction (function) and ecology. In general, he was more sympathetic to applications of statistics to ethnological problems than nine out of ten ethnologists at the time.

The Culture Element Survey produced a few statistical areal classifications in small areas in the field reports, but only two more quantitative papers of theoretical interest, those of Driver (1941) and Chretien (1943). Kroeber (1940, 1941) wrote two short descriptive papers based on the survey, but used no statistics.

My monograph (1941) on girls' puberty rites is still the largest statistical study emanating from the Culture Element Survey. Using the phi coefficient, I intercorrelated 118 traits and 159 tribes by pooling highly correlated traits and tribes and representing each pool by a single variable. Thus I dealt with 18,762 bits of information, while Klimek had operated with about 24,000 (60×400). I used a technique similar to that of Klimek, Milke, and Fürer-Haimendorf; after computing the two sets of correlations (phis), I rearranged the presence-absence entries in a large table so that the order of both tribes and traits matched that in their respective clustered correlation matrices.

My interpretation, however was much more eclectic: I distinguished between universals, cultural heritages spread by migration, relayed diffusions, and convergences. I pointed out 1) that elements of universal or near universal occurrence should not be used to establish historical connection between ethnic units in limited areas, 2) that elements closely associated with a language family might be regarded as a cultural heritage from the proto-culture associated with the proto-language of the group, 3) that continuously distributed resemblances which crossed over language family fences were best regarded as borrowings, 4) that the ceremony for multiple pubescent girls among the Apacheans represented an independent origin and a convergence with that in southern California for multiple girls. I also wrote a chapter on the psychological aspects of menstrual taboos, described the functional position and significance of the girls' puberty rite in each of the sub-areas in which the entire area of occurrence had been divided, assessed the influence of geographical environment on the data, and computed phi coefficients between language family groupings and the puberty material. The following theoretical statement assesses the relation of the shreds and patches theory of culture to functionalism.

How much of the form and content of girls' puberty rites is consistent with the concept of functional wholes, and how much with the idea that culture is a randomly associated conglomerate? From the viewpoint of a single tribe at a single point in its history, no doubt every element of its puberty rite is believed or felt to be an integral part of a unified whole. Any good informant, if pressed hard, would probably construct enough rationalizations to make any ceremony appear to have functional unity. . . . The broader the comparative universe in either space or time, the looser the integration of single parts of single cultures at a single point in history will appear to be. The reason is that the elements which constitute a small spatial and temporal unit of culture are almost invariably found to have wider distributions and different associations in a broader spatial and temporal frame. Natives have less comparative knowledge than ethnologists and consequently they would be expected to believe or feel the presence of a relatively small number of integrating impulses in their cultures which to them produce or maintain the harmonious whole. An ethnologist cannot really believe or feel such unity unless he suddenly develops a state of mind in which he eliminates his comparative knowledge. The description of relationships within single folk cultures as seen by native participants is an important task for ethnology, but it will never be complete description or a substitute for the broader relationships that are revealed by comparative studies. (Driver 1941:51)

Chretien (1945) challenged Kluckhohn's (1939) skepticism about the conventional formulas (Q, Q_6, r, phi, chi-square) based on probability theory. Applying chi-square first to some of the data of Driver (1938) he corrected two errors in that paper. Then he launched on a general discussion of the 2×2 table and showed for the first time in anthropology the close relation of phi to chi-square.

$$X^2 = \phi^2 N$$

This was followed by a description of Yates' correction for chi-square which, when applied to Driver's (1939) northwest California data, only slightly altered the uncorrected chi-square values. Chretien next computed all Q_6 values for the same sample and for a second sample, that of Barnett (1939) on the Gulf of Georgia Salish, and also gave their relevant levels of significance according to

chi-square. Although Driver (1938) had used the standard error of tetrachoric r to determine the significance of differences between pairs of values of that coefficient, Chretien (1945) emphasized in greater detail that some test of significance is necessary in all statistical inference in order to distinguish between differences due to sampling variability and those that are probably true differences in the parameters sampled. He concluded that coefficients of intertribal relationship are meaningful if based on five hundred or more culture traits.

OTHER STATISTICAL STUDIES

Although Clark Wissler never employed any statistics to describe his geographical distributions of cultural material, he, nevertheless, conceptualized the ideal distribution form as that of a right circular cone. This cone was sliced horizontally into a number of time levels, with the oldest and most widespread culture traits at the bottom and the youngest and least widespread at the top. The dynamics of the model required a perpetual generation of new cultural behaviors in the center of the area and their subsequent diffusion outward in all directions at approximately the same rate, such that the age of a given trait or assemblage would be positively correlated with the size of the area in which it occurred. This view was most elaborated by Wissler in his 1926 book, which was heavily criticized by Dixon in 1928. Wissler asserted that the trait frequencies given in Spier (1921) for the Sun Dance of the Plains Indians, when plotted on a map, approximated the shape of a right circular cone and Dixon argued that the reverse was true, that the higher frequencies lay at some distance from the center, thus forming a concave geometric model.

I (Driver 1939b) assumed that the centers of the tribal territories were points on a plane and that each point was weighted according to the number of Sun Dance traits present. The weights varied from 54 for the Arapaho to 5 for the Whapeton (Plains Dakota). I then found the center of gravity of these weighted points and measured the distance of each tribe from the center of gravity. If the distribution were an exact fit to a right circular cone, there would be a perfect negative correlation (linear r) between distance from the center of gravity and the number of traits present. The actual correlation was only $-.3$, thus lending only a little support to Wissler.

Because the geographical distribution of the Sun Dance was obviously greater in a north-south than in an east-west direction, I decided to test it for fit to a right elliptical cone. This required the determination of the line about which the sum of the squares of the deviations perpendicular to it was least. This line differs from the conventional regression lines on a scatter diagram, where only vertical and horizontal deviations are considered, neither of which are perpendicular to their respective regression lines. Having found this special least squares line, I used the standard deviation from it to give the short axis of the ellipse and the standard deviation from a line perpendicular to it to give the long axis. The ratio of the long to the short axis of the ellipse was 1.9 to 1. I then measured the relative distance of each tribe from the center of gravity in terms of its position in a series of concentric ellipses. The correlation between this elliptical distance and frequency of Sun Dance traits was $-.7$, a substantial increase from the $-.3$ of actual distance. Therefore the Sun Dance distribution was a fairly close fit to a right elliptical cone.

Milke (1949) measured the relation between amount of cultural similarity and geographical distance. After citing an earlier and briefer study of Keiter (1938:207 f.), he chose Driver's G, Pearson's Q_6, and phi as measures of similarity between tribal trait inventories and compared their values with the geographical distances of the ethnic units from each other. The data used were those of Klimek (1935) in California, Burrows (1938) in Polynesia, Klimek and Milke (1935) in South America, and Milke (1935) in Melanesia. Most of the curves showed a sharp drop in similarity with increasing distance in the beginning, but as distance became greater they dropped at a less rapid rate and eventually tended to almost level off. This is the familiar die-away curve, generically similar to those of glottochronology and carbon-14 radiation. Milke found that G and phi approximated hyperbolas, while Q_6 matched a deformed sine curve more closely. In California and Melanesia he then chose a single ethnic unit near the center

of the culture area as a point of reference and drew a series of isopleths, which showed that the drop-off in similarity of the other tribes to this tribe conformed closely to the shape of the culture area in which the original tribe was located. Finally he demonstrated differences in Q_6 values between adjacent California ethnic units by using five weights of lines; the heavier the line the lower the amount of similarity and the greater the cultural barrier. Although no one has ever challenged the general idea that similarity tends to decrease with distance, Milke refined it by giving the equations of the curves and showing the shapes of culture areas in a new way.

In 1950 I and Riesenberg challenged Nordenskiöld's theory that many of the cultural parallels in the southern marginal area of South America and in the California, Great Basin, and Plains areas of the United States were best explained by a single origin, that they were marginal survivals of a formerly continuous distribution of early culture. We assembled data on 485 ethnic units and found that the phi coefficient between hoof rattles and a girl's first menstruation rite was .13. We concluded that these two traits did not belong to an old stratum of culture which was once widespread or which diffused as a unit from North to South America. The great amount of variation in forms and functions of this rattle on both continents seemed to us to refute that view. I was too cavalier at the time to compute the chi-square, and no one since has bothered to do so. At a later date I found that the chi-square is 8.24, significant at less than .01. However, there are so many factors other than historical connection that can produce a significant relationship that I still doubt the common origin of the two traits or assemblages. For instance, the ready availability of hoofs in hunting societies and the tendency for greater attention to menstruation at the same ecological level might account for the correlation in the two continents without historical connection between the two.

Clements (1954) applied the numerical cluster analysis techniques of Holzinger (1937), Holzinger and Harmon (1941), and Tryon (1939) to the culture element data of northwest California collected by Driver (1939) and correlated and clustered by inspection by Kroeber (1939c). The groupings of ethnic units of Clements matched exactly those of Kroeber (1939c) and the completely intuitive classification of Kroeber (1920). This was the first application of an automatic clustering technique to anthropological data.

Schuessler and Driver (1956) and Driver and Schuessler (1957) factor-analyzed the same data (Driver 1939) that Clements had clustered. This was the first factor analysis of ethnological data. It employed the phi coefficient, the Q-technique (which means that the ethnic units were treated as variables and the culture traits as cases), and the centroid method of Thurstone with orthogonal factors. Its aim was areal classification, as was the work of Clements. The areal classification matched that of Clements (1954) and Kroeber (1920, 1939c) so closely that for all interpretive purposes the three may be considered identical. The groupings of ethnic units were so unquestionably historical as well as geographical that this interpretation was taken for granted and scarcely mentioned in these statistical papers.

I (Driver 1956) made the first statistical attempt to integrate the culture area–diffusion approach of Wissler and Kroeber with the cross-cultural–evolutionary method of Murdock and Whiting. The subject coverage of this paper included division of labor in subsistence pursuits, residence, land tenure, descent, and kinship terminology, and the sample was 280 North American ethnic units. Intertrait correlations (phis) were computed for twenty-five variables, clustered by inspection, and exhibited in a single matrix. The phis were next grouped in class intervals, according to magnitude, and each class interval was represented by a shade of gray in a rectangular intercorrelation diagram like that of Czekanowski (1911). Because this sample included a whole continent, all of the significant correlations were interpreted as cross-cultural regularities of multiple independent origin. This interpretation was originally derived in part from writings of Lowie and also from Murdock's (1949) *Social Structure;* it has more recently been supported by Coult and Habenstein's (1965) computer print-out of correlations derived from Murdock's (1957) world-wide sample of 565 ethnic units. My study largely confirmed the developmental cycle postulated by Murdock (1949: Chap. 8): from division of labor to residence to descent to kinship terminology.

My interpretation departed from Murdock's in its greater emphasis on historical factors, of which diffusion off the top of a developmental cycle without the recipient society going through the several antecedent stages, in the proper sequence, was the dominant innovation. An example of this diffusion off the top (or near the top) of such a cycle is the postulated diffusion of the weak matrilineal descent system of the Athapaskans in the Yukon Subarctic from the Tlingit Haida, and Tsimshian on the coast without most of these Athapaskans first going through stages of matridominant division of labor and matrilocal residence. Murdock (1955), in contrast, postulated matrilineal descent as part of the proto-culture of all Athapaskans, and explained its absence among at least half of the Athapaskan ethnic units in terms of loss. My (1956) paper offered no explicit technique for measuring historical influence and, therefore, fell short of its goal. It did succeed, however, in showing how continuous distributions of data make possible interpretations that cannot be made from discontinuous samples, such as those of Murdock and Whiting.

Driver and Massey (1957) presented a descriptive comparative summary of North American Indian cultures with the aid of 163 maps. Although the maps are too small (one to a page would have been far better) they succeed in giving the geographical distributions of about five hundred culture variables in the nineteenth century or earlier. It was originally intended to collect about twice this quantity of data and to run off a massive correlational analysis of all of it, but other things interfered and the project was never completed. The data do show conclusively, however, the non-random character of all of the distributions and suggest that quantitative analysis would reveal many distinct clusters of ethnic units and of culture traits as well. Now that Murdock, the world's greatest and most energetic coder of ethnographic data, has coded an additional corpus of data of comparable magnitude for North America, a combination of these two samples should produce a grand slam of intercorrelations that would go beyond anything achieved to date.

Driver's (1961) *Indians of North America* gives the broad outlines of the geographical distributions of traits on additional subjects and these might be used as a point of departure for the coding of more variables among the specific ethnic units of the continent, and the testing statistically of the impressionistic generalizations he made.

Although Ellegard (1959) limited himself to linguistic classification, he rediscovered both the G and T formulas of Driver and Kroeber (1932). He used the symbol r_n for G, and p for T. He also worked out a sampling error for r_n (G) for the first time. His argument for the superiority of r_n (G) over phi as a measure of similarity of languages could be transferred with little change to comparisons of the cultural inventories of ethnic units. It seems to this reviewer, however, that the problem of the significance of common absences and the best formula to use for a particular corpus of data is still unsettled. It is saying too much of any formula to claim that it is best for all ethnological purposes. Perhaps it can be said that r_n (G) is the best of the unconventional formulas discovered and used by ethnologists and linguists.

Blalock (1960), with the help of David Aberle, developed a new causal model for a part of the data in one of Driver's (1956) correlation matrices. He showed that a rectangular model with matridominant division of labor having a direct effect on matricentered land tenure, rather than through the intervening variable of matrilocal residence, gave a better fit to the correlations than the causal chain proposed by me (Driver 1956). In playing around with my 1956 correlations since Blalock's demonstration, I have found that, when the variables chosen are division of labor, residence, descent, and kinship terminology for only one generation (bifurcate merging for the matricentered matrix, Omaha for the patricentered, and Hawaiian for the bicentered), the causal chain model fits better than for the four variables he chose. Then when I averaged the phi values in the three matrices, on the assumption that observational, coding, and sampling errors were having considerable adverse effect on the correlations and that an average would tend to iron these out, I found quite a close fit to a causal chain model (Table 8).

Table 8

AVERAGE PHIS FROM 3 MATRICES: MATRICENTERED, PATRICENTERED, AND BICENTERED (DRIVER 1956).

	D.L.	Res.	Desc.
Division of labor			
Residence	.24		
Descent	.11	.36	
Kin terms	.00	.13	.43

Actual	Expected
.11	.09 = (.24)(.36)
.13	.15 = (.36)(.43)
.00	.04 = (.24)(.36)(.43)

Because it is better to average phi-square than phis, I averaged the phi-squares in the same matrices and then took the square root of the averages to get a value comparable to the original phis. This resulted in a poorer fit to the causal chain model (Table 9).

The Simon-Blalock technique is of limited utility because it is practical for only a few variables, and makes the assumption that no other variables have any influence at all on

the ones being compared. It seems to me that the exhibition of the relationship of one variable to many others in a large matrix, the larger the better, will throw more light on its causal connections than the arbitrary selection of three or four variables with which to compare it.

The Aschers (1963) offered a computer program for chronological ordering and applied it to two archaeological interrelationship matrices and to two of Driver's (1956)

Table 9

SQUARE ROOTS OF AVERAGE PHI-SQUARES FROM 3 MATRICES: MATRICENTERED, PATRICENTERED, AND BICENTERED.

	D.L.	Res.	Desc.
Division of labor			
Residence	.30		
Descent	.22	.37	
Kin	.00	.14	.44

Actual	Expected
.22	.11 = (.30)(.37)
.14	.16 = (.37)(.44)
.00	.05 = (.30)(.37)(.44)

matrices. In every case it confirmed the sequence previously established by less refined methods. This has nothing directly to do with causal models but shows that Driver's "serial" order was correct.

Naroll (1961, 1964) and Naroll and D'Andrade (1963) were the first since Tylor's time to make probabilistic statements about the Tylor-Galton problem, the problem of the relation of historical-diffusion to psychofunctional-evolutionary factors in culture change. In general they found that both kinds of factors are involved in most correlations. A weakness of Naroll's techniques is that he measured only linear order along artificial arcs or strips of latitude and longitude. Some of his methods could certainly be extended to two-dimensional areas on continents without getting involved in the spherical geometry of the entire world. D'Andrade's method attempts to assess more directly the problem of whether historical-diffusion or functional-evolutionary factors are more important in the explanation of a correlation, and can handle ethnic units in a continuous two-dimensional area or spaced apart in any shape of space. He also found that each kind of interpretation is of about equal weight. Both of these authors, however, used samples in which the ethnic units were spaced well apart. Had they worked with continuously distributed ethnic units, the historical-diffusion factor would have loomed larger.

Chaney and Driver (MS.) tested the correlation of .40 in North America between mother-in-law son-in-law avoidance and bifurcation in kinship terminology in either ego's generation or in the first ascending

generation by D'Andrade's matched pair technique. They applied it to two sets of pairs of ethnic units: adjacent pairs and randomly matched nonadjacent pairs. In most cases the ethnic units in the adjacent pairs also belonged to the same culture area and the same language family. Those in the nonadjacent pairs had to be from different culture areas and language families and were paired from a table of random numbers. Historical factors won by a wide margin over functional-evolutionary ones for adjacent pairs as was anticipated. The surprise came when historical factors won by a definite but narrower margin for nonadjacent, extra-culture area, and extra-language family random pairs. We have as yet no explanation of the dominance of historical factors in the random pairs but are mentioning this apparent defect of the method here to call attention to it. For further discussion of the Tylor-Galton problem see Naroll, pp. 974–989, this volume.

Driver (1966), with the help of Jorgensen (1966), Sanday (Driver and Sanday 1966), D'Andrade, and other commentors threw additional light on the Tylor-Galton problem. For the first time culture areas and language families were treated as variables and correlated with variants of residence, descent, kinship terminology, and avoidance. When the correlations between avoidances and the other variables were first given one at a time, correlations with culture areas (borrowing) were highest, language families next highest (culture heritage), kinship terminology third, and residence and descent still lower. It was further shown (Driver 1966: Table 6, Fig. 1) that avoidances were most heavily concentrated in the California and the Plains-Prairies areas, and it was also noted that they occurred among five language families in California and six (counting Kiowa and Tonkawa) in the Plains-Prairies. Borrowing, therefore, becomes a necessary part of the explanation. If one does not assume borrowing across language family fences in these culture areas, the next best alternative is as many independent origins as there are language families in the areas, with avoidance being a part of the proto-culture associated with each proto-language of each family and being passed on as a culture heritage within each family and spreading by migration. In light of the geographical pattern of avoidances and language families in other areas, this becomes a totally untenable theory. A much more extreme alternate theory would call for as many independent origins as positive instances reported, in this case eighty-four, a ridiculous interpretation.

By adding geographic position to culture area and language family membership, many instances of borrowing were postulated without their being challenged by any of the commentors. The case for borrowing was finally settled by some partial correlations (Driver 1966:157) between mother-in-law son-in-law avoidance, the three culture areas above, the four language families with the heaviest loadings of avoidances, and bifurcation in kinship terminology (the absence of bifurcation gave a negative value whose sign can be changed by changing the label to bifurcation). Culture areas correlated highest with avoidances, when the other two variables were held constant, bifurcation second highest but much lower, and language families lowest. This suggests that borrowing is the most powerful determiner. Driver tended to think that bifurcation represented lag from unilineal descent, but D'Andrade (Driver 1966:149) thought the correlation was much stronger and more pervasive than a lag theory would predict.

Driver (1966:145) postulated five independent origins of avoidances in native North America (including Mexico and Central America), with subsequent dispersal by migration within each of the "donor" language families, and by borrowing or acculturation from the "donor" group of twenty-seven ethnic units to the "recipient" group of fifty-seven ethnic

units. Avoidances may have diffused simultaneously with unicentered forms of residence, descent, and kinship terminology, or may have diffused more easily to those ethnic units which possessed in advance some of these cultural behaviors.

CONCLUSIONS

As Oscar Lewis (1956) pointed out, comparisons may range from two ethnic units to hundreds, and they may be concentrated within a single culture area, spread over two or more cultural areas, or cover an entire continent or most of the world. The peoples may be adjacent to each other and form a continuous area, or they may be spaced some distance apart. Perhaps a fourfold division into studies of 1) continuous distributions in one to several culture areas, 2) discontinuous distributions over the entire world, 3) continuous distributions over an entire continent, and 4) continuous distributions over the entire world will facilitate this discussion.

1. Statistical studies of continuous distributions in small areas offer fewer problems than those in larger areas. Although the aim of nearly all these studies has been limited to historical inference, the reconstructions offered are in the main plausible and acceptable today. The greatest emphasis was on material culture, with religion and ceremony second, and social organization third. Barnett (1964), in his historical review of the diffusibility of different aspects of culture, rates material culture as most diffusible, religion and ceremony intermediate, and social organization as least diffusible. Because the traits selected in small area studies matched the planless hodgepodge theory of culture better than the functional integration theory, the emphasis on the former was not entirely a misplaced one, although it is not considered sufficient at this date. These small statistical studies also dealt with continuously distributed ethnic units and generally interpreted continuous distributions of cultural variables as evidence of a single origin and subsequent diffusion. The statistics employed were largely descriptive; only a few authors made tests of significance. Attempts to sample a wide range of culture, such as that of Klimek (1935), seem overschematic and lacking in many subjects of interest today, yet the taxonomies they achieved would probably not be seriously

altered if redone today from fuller material.

Trait lists may be compared to the parts of an automobile completely dissembled and spread out on a garage floor. A trained automotive engineer can look at the parts in an arbitrary linear order, measure and otherwise observe their specifications and, in the end, predict a great deal about the performance of the assembled car. A seasoned ethnologist, in an analogous way, can comprehend and infer a great deal from trait lists that a novice would fail to learn because the latter lacks the knowledge to integrate the data in a meaningful manner.

The principal weakness of such small area studies is that it is difficult, if not impossible, to determine what Steward called cross-cultural regularities from them. Multiple correlation clusters of functionally related variables that appear to have arisen independently more than once, as a result of like causes or causal chains producing parallel evolutionary sequences, seldom show up in small areas. Even when the number of ethnic units is considerable, as is the case with Klimek's (1935) sixty ethnic units, the entire area may reveal only a single areal cluster of a phenomenon, for instance, kin avoidances (Driver 1966: Fig. 1). The associated cultural behaviors cannot be unequivocally assumed to represent a causal complex unless the cluster is replicated in another region far enough away to rule out culture contact.

2. World-wide studies of discontinuous distributions, such as those of Murdock, Whiting, and Naroll, can establish cross-cultural regularities with some assurance if the samples are large enough. Murdock's samples of 250 ethnic units (1949), 565 (1957), and nearly 1000 (1962–1967) have done this. The small samples of fewer than 100 ethnic units of Whiting and his followers are on shakier ground but have, nevertheless, produced some plausible interpretations. Unless these samples are very large, it is difficult to determine how many distinct areal clusters of a phenomenon and its correlatives occur and how many independent origins seem likely. The lack of continuity makes it difficult to establish diffusion or ecological determinism within a single cluster, not to mention possible diffusion between apparent clusters. A 10 per cent or even a 25 per cent random sample of the world is about as useful for tracing geographical and historical continuities

as a 10 per cent or 25 per cent random sample of human beings in a single community is for tracing genealogical connections. Everyone agrees that it would be impossible to make a meaningful genealogical study from a simple random sample of a community because most of the connecting links between the members would be lost. That is exactly what happens in hop-skip-and-jump cross-cultural samples, even though the ethnic units run into the hundreds and cover much of the world.

The screening of ethnic units so as to eliminate most of the duplication in the same culture area and language family, as Murdock (1966) has done, can lessen the effect of historical factors but can scarcely eliminate them. Many documented diffusions, such as that of the alphabet, spread over many culture areas and language families. The same is true for the less completely documented dispersals of domesticated plants and animals. Granting that social structure is less diffusible than the above assemblages, it can still spill over culture area boundaries and language family fences, and continuity of the details is the best evidence of such diffusion or acculturation.

3. Studies of continuous distributions over entire continents, such as those in North America (Driver 1956, 1966; Driver and Massey 1957; Driver and Sanday 1966), have both some of the advantages and disadvantages of types one and two above. Where the continent extends from the arctic to the equator and contains sharp differences in geography (such as arctic, desert, and tropic environments), as does North America, the total range of culture variation may approach that of the entire non-literate world. Under such conditions, cross-cultural regularities may appear in a number of clusters well separated from each other. An example would be the patrilineal descent systems of California, Plains-Prairies, and the Mayans. Continuous distributions of continental scope can distinguish culture heritages within language families from diffusions across language family fences as I (Driver 1966) have done, and can employ partial correlations, multiple correlations, factor analyses, and other multivariate techniques that require sizable samples.

4. Studies of continuous distributions over the entire world or non-literate world have

not yet been achieved, but would have all the advantages of the three kinds of studies mentioned above without any of the limitations. The increasing availability of high-speed computers and the amazingly large sample that Murdock (1962–1967) has coded will make such research practical in the near future.

BIBLIOGRAPHY

ANKERMANN, B.
1905 Kulturkreise und Kulturschichten in Africa. *Zeitschrift für Ethnologie* 37:54–84.

ASCHER, MARCIA, and ROBERT ASCHER
1963 Chronological ordering by computer. *American Anthropologist* 65:1045–1052.

BARNETT, HOMER G.
1939 Culture element distributions: IX Gulf of Georgia Salish. *University of California Anthropological Records* 1:221–296.

BLALOCK, HUBERT M., JR.
1960 Correlational analysis and causal inferences. *American Anthropologist* 62:624–631.
1961 *Causal inferences in non-experimental research.* Chapel Hill, University of North Carolina Press.

BOAS, FRANZ
1894 *Indianische Sagen von der Nord-Pacifischen Küste Amerikas.* Berlin, Asher.
1916 *Tsimshian mythology.* Bureau of American Ethnology Annual Report 31:27–1037. Washington, D.C., Government Printing Office.

BURROWS, E. C.
1938 Western Polynesia, a study in cutural differentiation. *Ethnologiska Studier* 7:1–192.

CHANEY, RICHARD P., and HAROLD E. DRIVER (MS.)
The Tylor-Galton problem for avoidance data.

CHRETIEN, C. DOUGLAS
1945 Culture element distributions: XXV Reliability of statistical procedures and results. *University of California Anthropological Records* 8:469–490.

CLEMENTS, FORREST E.
1928 Quantitative method in ethnography. *American Anthropologist* 30:295–310.
1931 Plains Indian Tribal Correlations with Sun Dance Data. *American Anthropologist* 33:216–227.

CLEMENTS, FORREST E., EGBERT SCHENCK, and THEODORA BROWN
1926 A new objective method for showing special relationships. *American Anthropologist* 28:585–604.

COULT, ALLAN D., and ROBERT W. HABENSTEIN
1965 *Cross tabulations of Murdock's world ethnographic sample.* Columbia, University of Missouri Press.

CZEKANOWSKI, JAN
1911 *Objektive Kriterien in der Ethnologi.* Korrespondenz-Blatt der Deutschen Gesellschaft für Anthropologie, Ethnologie und Urgeschichte 42, August to December, 1–5.

DIXON, ROLAND B.
1928 *The building of cultures.* New York.

DRIVER, HAROLD E.
1938 Culture element distributions: VIII The reliability of culture element data. *University of California Anthropological Records* 1:205–220.
1939a Culture element distributions: X Northwest California. *University of California Anthropological Records* 1:297–433.
1939b The measurement of geographical distribution form. *American Anthropologist* 41:583–588.
1941 Girls' puberty rites in western North America. *University of California Anthropological Records* 6:21–90.
1956 *An integration of functional, evolutionary, and historical theory by means of correlations.* Indiana University Publications in Anthropology and Linguistics, Memoir 12. Partly reprinted in Harold E. Driver and Wm. C. Massey, Comparative studies of North American Indians. *Transactions of the American Philosophical Society* 47:421–439.
1961 Introduction to statistics for comparative research. In Frank W. Moore, ed., *Readings in cross-cultural methodology.* New Haven: Human Relations Area Files. Also reprinted by Bobbs-Merrill as No. A-53 of their Reprint Series in the Social Sciences.
1966 Geographical-historical versus psychofunctional explanations of kin avoidances. *Current Anthropology* 7:131–160.

DRIVER, HAROLD E., and A. L. KROEBER
1932 Quantitative expression of cultural relationships. *University of California Publications in American Archaeology and Ethnology* 31:211–256.

DRIVER, HAROLD E., and WM. C. MASSEY
1957 Comparative studies of North American Indians. *Transactions of the American Philosophical Society* 47:165–456.

DRIVER, HAROLD E., and S. H. RIESENBERG
1950 *Hoof rattles and girls' puberty rites in*

North and South America. Indiana University Publications in Anthropology and Linguistics, Memoir 4.

DRIVER, HAROLD E., and PEGGY R. SANDAY
1966 Factors and clusters of kin avoidances and related variables. *Current Athropology* 7:169–176.

DRIVER, HAROLD E., and KARL F. SCHUESSLER
1957 Factor analysis of ethnographic data. *American Anthropologist* 59:655–663.

ELLEGARD, ALVAR
1959 Statistical measurement of linguistic relationship. *Language* 35:131–156.

FÜRER-HAIMENDORF, CHR. VON
1934 Völker- und Kulturgruppen im westlich Hinterindien, dargestellt mit Hilfe des statistischen Verfahrens. *Anthropos* 29: 421–440.

HOLZINGER, K. J.
1937 *Student manual of factor analysis,* Chapter III. Chicago, Department of Education, University of Chicago.

HOLZINGER, K. J., and H. H. HARMON
1941 *Factor analysis.* Chicago, University of Chicago Press.

JORGENSEN, JOSEPH G.
1966 Geographical clusterings and functional explanations of in-law avoidances: an analysis of comparative method. *Current Anthropology* 7:161–169.

KEITER, FRIEDERICH
1938 *Rasse und Kultur.* Stuttgart.

KELLEY, TRUMAN L.
1924 *Statistical method.* New York, Macmillan.

KLIMEK, STANISLAW
1935 The structure of California Indian culture. *University of California Publications in American Archaeology and Ethnology* 37:1–70.

KLIMEK, STANISLAW, and WILHELM MILKE
1935 An analysis of the material culture of the Tupi peoples. *American Anthropologist* 37:71–91.

KLUCKHOHN, CLYDE
1939 On certain recent applications of association coefficients to ethnological data. *American Anthropologist* 41:345–378.

KROEBER, A. L.
1920 California culture provinces. *University of California Publications in American Archaeology and Ethnology* 17:151–169.
1937 Part II: Analysis. In E. W. Gifford and A. L. Kroeber, Culture element distributions: IV Pomo. *University of California Publications in American Archaeology and Ethnology* 37:117–253.
1939a Cultural and natural areas of native North America. *University of California Publications in American Archaeology and Ethnology* 38:1–242, 28 maps.

1939b Tribes Surveyed. *University of California Anthropological Records* 1:435–440.
1939c Local ethnographic and methodological inferences. In Harold E. Driver, Culture element distributions: X northwest California. *University of California Anthropological Records* 1:297–433.
1940 Stepdaughter marriage. *American Anthropologist* 42:562–570.
1941 Salts, Dogs, Tobacco. *University of California Anthropological Records* 6:1–20.

LINTON, RALPH
1923 *The material culture of the Marquesas Islands.* Hawaii, Memoirs of the B. P. Bishop Museum, Vol. 8, No. 5.

LOWIE, ROBERT H.
1920 *Primitive society.* New York, Liveright.

MILKE, WILHELM
1935 *Südostmelanesien, eine ethnostatistische Analyse.* Würzeburg Dissertations-druckerei und Verlag Konrad Triltsch.
1937 Statistische Forschungs-methoden. *Mitteilungen der Anthropologischen Gesellschaft in Wien* 67:119–121.
1949 The quantitative distribution of cultural similarities and their cartographic representation. *American Anthropologist* 51: 237–252.

MURDOCK, GEORGE P.
1949 *Social structure.* New York, Macmillan.
1955 North American social organization. *Davidson Journal of Anthropology* (Seattle) 1:85–95.
1957 World ethnographic sample. *American Anthropologist* 59:664–687.
1962– Ethnographic Atlas. *Ethnology* 1–6:
1967 end.
1966 Cross-cultural sampling. *Ethnology* 5:97–114.

NAROLL, RAOUL
1961 Two solutions to Galton's problem. *Philosophy of Science* 28:15–39. Also in Frank W. Moore, ed., *Readings in cross-cultural methodology.* New Haven, Human Relations Area Files, 1961.
1964 A fifth solution to Galton's problem. *American Anthropologist* 66:863–867.

NAROLL, RAOUL, and ROY D'ANDRADE
1963 Two further solutions to Galton's problem. *American Anthropologist* 65:1053–1067.

ROUTIL, R.
1936 Statistische Forschungsmethoden in Natur- und Geisteswissenschaftderen Anwendung in der Anthropologie und Ethnologie. *Mitteilungen der Anthropologischen Gesellschaft in Wien* 66:231–261.

SCHMIDT, WILHELM
1920 Die kulturhistorische Methode und die nordamerikanisch Ethnologie. *Anthropos* 14–15:546–563.

SCHUESSLER, KARL F., and HAROLD E. DRIVER
1956 A factor analysis of 16 primitive societies. *American Sociological Review* 21: 493–499.

SPEARMAN, CHARLES
1907 Demonstration of formulae for true measure of correlation. *American Journal of Psychology* 18:161–169.

SPIER, LESLIE
1921 The Sun Dance of the Plains Indians. *American Museum of Natural History Anthropological Papers* 16:451–527.

THOMSON, GODFREY H.
1916 A hierarchy without a general factor. *British Journal of Psychology* 8:271–281.

TRYON, ROBERT C.
1939 *Cluster analysis*. Ann Arbor, Mich., Edwards Brothers.

TYLOR, EDWARD B.
1889 On a method of investigating the development of institutions; applied to laws of marriage and descent. *Journal of the Royal Anthropological Institute of Great Britain and Ireland* 18:245–272.

WALLIS, WILSON D.
1928 Probability and the diffusion of culture traits. *American Anthropologist* 30:94–106.

WISSLER, CLARK
1926 *The relation of nature to man in aboriginal America*. New York.

CHAPTER 33

The Human Relations Area Files

FRANK W. MOORE

The Human Relations Area Files (HRAF) is a nonprofit cooperative organization of twenty-three universities and research institutions with central headquarters in New Haven, Connecticut. HRAF's principal activity is supplying organized bodies of primary ethnographic and other data to its member and associate member HRAF-Microfiles institutions. Members have complete sets of full-size files and representatives on HRAF's governing board. Associate members have HRAF-Microfiles sets—microcard copies of the full-size files.

Stated in the broadest terms, the function of HRAF is to contribute to an understanding of human behavior and to stimulate research in this area through its organized materials.

In addition to the file materials supplied to the member institutions (listed below) HRAF prepares and publishes bibliographies, ethnographic surveys, monographs, gazetteers, and other research materials.

REGULAR MEMBERS

University of Chicago
Chicago, Illinois
University of Colorado
Boulder, Colorado
Cornell University
Ithaca, New York
Harvard University
Cambridge, Massachusetts
University of Hawaii
Honolulu, Hawaii
University of Illinois
Urbana, Illinois

Indiana University
Bloomington, Indiana
University of Iowa
Iowa City, Iowa
Kyoto University
Kyoto, Japan
Maison des Sciences de l'Homme
Paris, France
University of Michigan
Ann Arbor, Michigan
State University of New York at Buffalo
Buffalo, New York
University of North Carolina
Chapel Hill, North Carolina
University of Oklahoma
Norman, Oklahoma
University of Pennsylvania
Philadelphia, Pennsylvania
University of Pittsburgh
Pittsburgh, Pennsylvania
Princeton University
Princeton, New Jersey
U. S. National Museum
Washington, D.C.
University of Southern California
Los Angeles, California
Southern Illinois University
Carbondale, Illinois
University of Utah
Salt Lake City, Utah
University of Washington
Seattle, Washington
Yale University
New Haven, Connecticut

ASSOCIATED UNIVERSITY

Northwestern University
Evanston, Illinois

ASSOCIATE (HRAF-MICROFILES) MEMBERS

University of Alaska
  College, Alaska
University of Alberta, Calgary
  Calgary, Alberta, Canada
Antioch College
  Yellow Springs, Ohio
Brandeis University
  Waltham, Massachusetts
Brigham Young University
  Provo, Utah
The University of British Columbia
  Vancouver, British Columbia, Canada
University of California
  Davis, California
University of California, Los Angeles
  Los Angeles, California
University of California
  Santa Barbara, California
Carleton College
  Northfield, Minnesota
Catholic University of Nymegen
  Nijmegen, Holland
Columbia University
  New York, New York
The University of Connecticut
  Storrs, Connecticut
University of Copenhagen
  Copenhagen, Denmark
Dalhousie University
  Halifax, Nova Scotia
Dartmouth College
  Hanover, New Hampshire
Dickinson College
  Carlisle, Pennsylvania
The University of Florida
  Gainesville, Florida
Florida Atlantic University
  Boca Raton, Florida
The Florida State University
  Tallahassee, Florida
Franklin and Marshall College
  Lancaster, Pennsylvania
University of Göteborg
  Göteborg, Sweden
University of Guelph
  Guelph, Ontario, Canada
Universität Heidelberg
  Heidelberg, Germany
Hunter College
  New York, New York
Indian School of International Studies
  New Delhi, India

The Institute of Asian Economic Affairs
  Tokyo, Japan
The University of Kansas
  Lawrence, Kansas
University of Kentucky
  Lexington, Kentucky
Korea University
  Seoul, Korea
Louisiana State University
  Baton Rouge, Louisiana
University of Louisville
  Louisville, Kentucky
University of Manitoba
  Winnipeg, Manitoba, Canada
McMaster University
  Hamilton, Ontario, Canada
University of Maryland
  College Park, Maryland
University of Massachusetts
  Amherst, Massachusetts
Memorial University of Newfoundland
  St. John's, Newfoundland, Canada
Michigan State University
  East Lansing, Michigan
University of Minnesota
  Minneapolis, Minnesota
University of Missouri
  Columbia, Missouri
Missouri State Library
  Jefferson City, Missouri
University of Montreal
  Montreal, Canada
National Library of Nigeria
  Lagos, Nigeria
National Museum of Canada
  Ottawa, Ontario, Canada
University of New Hampshire
  Durham, New Hampshire
University of New Mexico
  Albuquerque, New Mexico
The New York Public Library
  New York, New York
New York University
  New York, New York
State University of New York at Albany
  Albany, New York
State University of New York at Stony Brook
  Stony Brook, New York
The Ohio State University
  Columbus, Ohio
University of Oregon
  Eugene, Oregon
The Pennsylvania State University
  University Park, Pennsylvania

Portland State College
Portland, Oregon
Purdue University
Lafayette, Indiana
University of Queensland
Brisbane, Queensland, Australia
Rice University
Houston, Texas
Universität des Saarlandes
Saarbrücken, Germany
Saint Louis University
Saint Louis, Missouri
San Diego State College
San Diego, California
Stanford University
Palo Alto, California
Syracuse University
Syracuse, New York
Temple University
Philadelphia, Pennsylvania
University of Tennessee
Knoxville, Tennessee
Tohoku University
Sendai City, Japan
The University of Tokyo
Tokyo, Japan
University of Toronto
Toronto, Canada
U. S. Army Human Engineering Laboratories
Aberdeen Proving Ground, Maryland
University of Waikato
Hamilton, New Zealand
University of Waseda
Tokyo, Japan
Washington State University
Pullman, Washington
Washington University
Saint Louis, Missouri
The University of Western Ontario
London, Ontario, Canada
The University of Wisconsin—Milwaukee
Milwaukee, Wisconsin
University of Freiburg
Freiburg in Breisgau, Germany

The HRAF grew out of the Cross-Cultural Survey founded in 1937 at Yale. HRAF was incorporated in 1949 with 5 members and has since enjoyed a steady growth in membership (approximately 100 in 1966), amount of available file material (267 files with over one-half million text pages), and rate of utilization.

The entire HRAF file system is based on two universal codes—the *Outline of Cultural Materials* (*OCM*) (Murdock *et al.* 1965) and the *Outline of World Cultures* (*OWC*) (Murdock 1963). The classification and codes for ethnic and political units are contained in the *OWC*, which is the universe from which societies are selected for processing. The *OCM* is the subject code and classification device. All aspects of human behavior, institutions, artifacts, and ecology are described under 710 category headings. The code numbers for these categories are applied by analysts to each paragraph of the source materials processed and the pages are then printed in 5×8 format in sufficient quantity to permit actual filing of each page behind the appropriate subject divider card (representing an *OCM* category) in each file. (For a description of research techniques see *Guide to the Use of the Files,* which may be obtained, without charge, from HRAF or any member institution.)

The *OCM* as it stands today is the result of thirty years of constant experimentation, revision, and testing. The original version of the *OCM,* first devised in 1936 for use with the Cross-Cultural Survey, was based on experience with the literature. The ultimate test of the *OCM* in all its forms has been its utility as a classification device for ethnographic material. Since the *OCM* is intended to be and is used as a universal system, i.e. not specific to any one source or type of source, revisions cannot be made in light of the difficulty encountered with a single specific source. With thousands of sources already classified and processed for the files, revisions in general must be in terms of classification and greater degree of specificity rather than major shifts, which would invalidate the work previously accomplished. New concepts and approaches to describing and interpreting field observations in some cases pose problems for analysis into *OCM* categories. In these cases, somewhat more significant changes and extensions of meaning and content of certain categories have had to be made. To date it has not been necessary (since 1949) to revise to the point that earlier analysis has become outdated. Revisions are always cross-referenced to related categories to prevent confusion on the part of researchers. In the future, major shifts in concepts and reporting may force dating of revisions in the *OCM* to indicate new analysis decisions.

The *OCM* has been fairly described as

"an empirical construct, not entirely without logic." As such, it is essential for research users to consult all details of the *OCM*— table of contents, index, category descriptions, and cross references. It should be pointed out that very rarely will a researcher's information needs coincide with the *OCM* categories to the extent that he will be able to find all the desired material in a single category. In this connection it should also be pointed out that practically all *OCM* categories have at least one or two cross references to related categories, and that the approximate number of cross references to the average category is seven. The number of cross references and index entries for specific activities, institutions, and objects is continually growing as more experience in analysis accumulates.

How good is the *OCM?* For many research purposes it is very good indeed. The fact that it has become (with individual modifications in many cases) a standard device for use in field ethnography testifies to its utility. Certain areas in the *OCM,* particularly those outside the central interests of anthropologists (political science, law, etc.) have become somewhat dated in light of theoretical and conceptual advances. In a few cases, major revisions and reorganizations are needed for maximum utility to all social scientists. In general, however, it is safe to say that the *OCM* has stood the test of time and use well. In fact, on several occasions in recent years, organizations other than HRAF have adopted the *OCM* as their standard classification device simply on the grounds that "it works."

The selection of societies for inclusion in the HRAF sample (HRAF has never intended to analyze and process all material on all societies) has always been a problem. Since the HRAF sample tends to be the universe from which most cross-cultural studies are drawn, the responsibility for maintaining a dispersed representative sample has always weighed heavily in decisions to start new files. Certain programs in the past which were supported by government agencies with specific missions in view, have tended to skew the sample, especially toward advanced cultures of Asia and the Middle East. Since 1954, however, most HRAF efforts have not been specifically oriented, and a continual improvement in sample distribution both in terms of area and culture type has been accomplished. Other factors, such as language problems and uncertain ethnic unit identification, have tended to reduce relative coverage of areas such as Central and North Asia and South America. The South American problem is now being reduced by an intensive program, and it is expected that the remaining poorly-covered areas will be improved in the near future.

In selection of specific societies for processing, a variety of factors are considered. First, culture areas are considered, especially in the light of the classification of culture areas in Murdock's *World Ethnographic Sample* (1961). For example, if file work on the Central Bantu of Africa were being considered, Murdock's listing of ten groups in that area would be considered first. Four files out of the ten listed by Murdock would be considered an adequate sample for most purposes. In this case, all groups in the area speak closely related dialects, so language would not be a factor. Environments are also similar throughout the region. The political level ranges from autonomous local communities (A) to states of at least 100,-000 population (S). Accordingly, all A, M (minimal states), L (little states), and S groups would be surveyed for other factors of dispersal. Seven of the ten are matrilineal, and two groups would be selected with matrilineal descent, each with a different political and economic base if possible. In this case the Bemba and Yao (both matrilineal) were selected. The Bemba are S on political level and the Yao are M. Both have a seed-agriculture-based economy with subsidiary fishing and, in the case of the Yao, some hunting. The Liumbe are also matrilineal with an A political rating and a fishing economy, the only one of the seven matrilineal groups to have other than an agricultural economy. The scanty literature on the Liumbe, however, rules it out as a possible file. Of the remaining three groups, not matrilineal, the Ila were selected for the example of double descent and A political status. The Ngoni were selected for their pastoral economy, bilateral descent, and L political features. If a fifth group were to be selected in the future on a new round of file building, probably another matrilineal group with L political and a different economy would be selected—in this case most likely the Chokwe.

An attempt is always made to balance out all factors, including the amount of literature available. No one of the five major factors —language, environment, economy, descent, or politics—is considered more significant than the others, though language is usually the first factor considered when it differs significantly from group to group in an area.

A negative factor in file selection is the existence of large, diverse, and fragmented groups. Generally speaking, with everything else being equal, HRAF tends to select smaller, more homogeneous, culture groups whenever possible in terms of the sample. Highly fragmented and differentiated groups tend, of course, to have a larger gross population, but population in terms of number of individuals is not in itself a factor.

It should also be emphasized that file building and selection is not now and never has been limited to Murdock's or anyone else's listings. A special effort has been made in recent years to discover and process the literature on well-described societies which are, however, not commonly utilized by comparativists, in an attempt to broaden our ethnographic horizons. Examples of these are: Malta (an excellent but little-known or used literature); Sarakatsani (a nomadic herding people of Greece); and Yanoama (South America).

An inevitable consequence of these selection techniques is that a fair number of "ethnographic standards," i.e. cultures which are very much a part of every anthropologist's vocabulary, are not included in the files. For example: Haida, Hopi, and Kiowa in North America; Zulu, Ibo, and Herero in Africa; and Tahitians and Palauans in Oceania are not included in the files for various reasons.

The maximum dispersal factor may in some cases produce a slight imbalance, in regional terms, of exotic or atypical societies. For example, the Goajiro, Dorobo, and Bush Negroes are represented in the files, though each is far from typical of the general culture areas in which they are located.

The HRAF's aim is in effect to provide not a sample, but a limited sampling universe from which a researcher may draw. To this end, maximum dispersal is essential if the limited HRAF universe is to be representative of the total cultural universe, in terms of diversity if not in a statistical

sense. That is to say, no effort has been made to evaluate the world's supply of cultures and to reproduce a miniature model in the HRAF files of this world of cultures. No attempt has been made, for example, to count the number of societies in the entire world with autonomous local communities as the highest form of political organization, extract a percentage, and make the HRAF files conform to this percentage. What has been done, is to survey the world, area by area, and produce files representative of the range of variation within each area.

The HRAF would certainly not claim that its sampling universe is statistically representative in any respect or that it constitutes a random sample. The HRAF sampling universe is, however, representative of the range of variation of human culture in most respects, and a representative sample can be drawn from it for most cross-cultural research purposes.

One of HRAF's problems has been the lack of resources to provide for adequate and systematic updating of files. In some cases, the most recent source is a decade or more old. Over the years, with constant pressure to produce a large dispersed sample, all available resources have been devoted to producing new files to complete the sampling universe. However, HRAF is now in a position to begin to bring all files up to date in a systematic fashion. In the near future, English-language materials may be expected to lag from four to eight months from the time of first appearance until they become available in the files. Foreign-language materials will probably take a year or more for processing.

Along with continual updating of files, HRAF expects to add more nonconventional and difficult-of-access materials. Color slides, for example, can now be incorporated into the files. More and more original, unpublished materials will also be added, along with rare and little-known materials.

The utility of HRAF as a research tool for cross-cultural statistical studies has been established for many years. The usefulness of HRAF as a teaching and training device is also clear. The value of HRAF as a sort of gigantic ethnographic encyclopedia is not as well known or appreciated. Several factors have contributed to this. The specialist, seeking information on "his" people, has often been disappointed since, as discussed above, HRAF makes no effort to be all-inclusive in terms of coverage of ethnic and political units. Even if a file is available, however, it may be substantially less complete *in terms of sources* than the specialist's own library or even his knowledge. As mentioned above, steps are being taken to correct this latter problem, although the files will probably never attain the level, individually, of the dedicated specialist's complete needs. The nonspecialist will, however, find the files a basic point of reference which, while not always able to supply all his information needs, will provide a starting point for conventional research.

In using and evaluating the files, the researcher must be aware of several basic facts. First, the files are nothing more nor less than a retrieval device, i.e. by utilizing the files rapid access to specific items of data can be obtained. Second, the organizational system of the files is determined by a convergence of research and retrieval factors. The files do not do research—they merely expedite it. Third, HRAF does not manufacture data—the files cannot contain more than

is known to the literature. Fourth, use of the files cannot substitute for reading and comprehending over-all descriptions and theoretical concepts. The HRAF is a "fact-finder," not a royal road to understanding. Fifth and last, use of HRAF in no way excuses the researcher from responsibility for his work. Bad research is bad research, whether it is based on books, HRAF, or hearsay.

Intelligent use of HRAF can provide far greater coverage of the literature than is possible and practical by any other means. Furthermore, use of HRAF can add a dimension to research in terms of subject relationships that would not ordinarily have been observed. Through HRAF, conflicts in observation and reporting are apparent that might not be discovered with conventional research techniques. (In at least one case, a prominent anthropologist is known to have spent a very considerable time checking the contents of an African file to discover discrepancies in his voluminous ethnographic publications.)

Following is a listing of HRAF files now available. It is not anticipated that this list will be added to in terms of new files to any considerable extent in the foreseeable future.

ASIA

OWC Code	Name of Society	No. of Sources	No. of Pages	OWC Code	Name of Society	No. of Sources	No. of Pages	OWC Code	Name of Society	No. of Sources	No. of Pages
AA1	Korea	55	5,362	AH6	Inner Mongolia	12	1,279	AR7	Khasi	14	557
• AB6	Ainu	10	1,407	AH7	Outer Mongolia	3	1,428	AU1	Afghanistan	74	6,234
• AC7	Okinawa	2	567	AI1	Sinkiang	3	860	AV1	Kashmir	6	2,006
AD1	Formosa	40	1,836	•• AJ1	Tibet	24	6,814	AV3	Dard	4	711
AD4	Formosan Aborigines	Subfile		•• AJ4	West Tibetans	20	1,590	AV4	Kashmiri	4	887
AE3	Sino-Tibetan Border	7	529	AK5	Lepcha	11	1,038	•• AV7	Burusho	8	2,157
AE4	Lolo	5	564	AL1	Southeast Asia	22	3,851	AW1	India	41	14,980
AE5	Miao	12	1,182	AM1	Indochina	152	19,633	AW2	Bihar	1	619
AE9	Monguor	5	1,221	AM4	Cambodians	Subfile		•• AW5	Coorg	4	802
AF1	China	80	19,442	AM8	Laotians	Subfile		AW6	East Punjab	3	1,106
AF12	North China	8	2,595	AM11	Vietnamese	Subfile		AW7	Gujarati	4	627
AF14	Central China	2	1,130	•• AN1	Malaya	193	10,142	•• AW11	Korala	13	989
AF15	East China	3	1,384	AN5	Malays	Subfile		AW17	Telugu	1	265
AF16	Southwest China	7	2,800	AN7	Semang	3	786	AW19	Uttar Pradesh	4	255
AF17	South China	8	1,846	AO1	Thailand	40	6,114	•• AW25	Bhil	7	1,069
AG1	Manchuria	6	1,250	AP1	Burma	31	4,680	AW32	Gond	4	1,552
AH1	Mongolia	9	1,358	AP4	Burmese	Subfile		AW37	Kol	1	347
				AP6	Kachin	Subfile		AW60	Toda	13	1,553
								AX5	Vedda	5	776
								AZ2	Andamans	10	1,057

AFRICA

OWC Code	Name of Society	No. of Sources	No. of Pages	OWC Code	Name of Society	No. of Sources	No. of Pages	OWC Code	Name of Society	No. of Sources	No. of Pages
F1	Africa	1	2,339	FJ22	Nuer	16	1,541	FO32	Mongo	9	773
FA8	Bambara	4	1,127	FJ23	Shilluk	29	1,073	FO42	Rundi	10	1,314
•• FA28	Mossi	11	885	FK7	Ganda	10	1,595	FP13	Mbundu	6	847
FC7	Mende	8	605	FL6	Dorobo	14	354	FQ5	Bemba	10	830
FE11	Tallensi	10	954	FL10	Kikuyu	8	1,438	FQ6	Ila	6	998
FE12	Twi	26	3,045	•• FL11	Luo	21	463	FR5	Ngoni	13	1,112
FF38	Katab	4	252	• FL12	Masai	16	938	FT6	Thonga	2	1,210
FF52	Nupe	9	858	FN4	Chagga	5	1,962	FT7	Yao	11	555
FF57	Tiv	29	3,063	FN17	Ngonde (Nyakyusa)	14	1,474	FX10	Bushmen	13	958
FF62	Yoruba	42	1,568	•• FO7	Azande	67	2,842	FX13	Hottentot	14	1,359
FH9	Fang	8	1,117					FX14	Lovedu	4	414
								FX8	Tanala	1	334

EUROPE

OWC Code	Name of Society	No. of Sources	No. of Pages	OWC Code	Name of Society	No. of Sources	No. of Pages	OWC Code	Name of Society	No. of Sources	No. of Pages
E1	Europe	9	1,599	EE1	Bulgaria	7	998	• EI9	Imperial Romans	2	711
E16	Slavic Peoples	7	903	EF1	Yugoslavia	13	2,765	EK1	Austria	6	1,334
EA1	Poland	31	3,940	•• EF6	Serbs	11	1,993	EO1	Finland	1	402
EB1	Czechoslovakia	75	6,491	•• EG1	Albania	9	1,975	EP4	Lapps	13	2,813
EC1	Hungary	16	1,401	• EH1	Greece	10	1,034	ER6	Rural Irish	15	1,494
ED1	Rumania	9	1,245	• EH14	Sarakatsani	2	441	• EZ6	Malta	9	1,069

MIDDLE EAST

OWC Code	Name of Society	No. of Sources	No. of Pages	OWC Code	Name of Society	No. of Sources	No. of Pages	OWC Code	Name of Society	No. of Sources	No. of Pages
M1	Middle East	70	13,891	MI1	Kuwait	7	877	MO4	Somali	17	1,138
MA1	Iran	72	7,000	MJ1	Saudi Arabia	30	3,371	MP5	Amhara	10	1,056
MA11	Kurd	6	703	MJ4	Bedouins	Subfile		MR13	Fellahin	9	1,262
•• MB1	Turkey	14	1,493	MK2	Maritime			MR14	Siwans	7	518
MD1	Syria	11	1,395		Arabs	4	103	MS12	Hausa	14	1,066
MD4	Rwala	2	1,042	MK4	Trucial Oman	3	256	•• MS25	Tuareg	8	1,225
ME1	Lebanon	11	657	ML1	Yemen	14	446	MS30	Wolof	42	1,382
MG1	Jordan	22	3,358	MM1	Aden	7	418	MS37	Senegal	23	849
MH1	Iraq	8	1,825	MM2	Hadhramaut	23	765	MX3	Rif	4	379
								MZ2	Bahrain	8	428

NORTH AMERICA

OWC Code	Name of Society	No. of Sources	No. of Pages	OWC Code	Name of Society	No. of Sources	No. of Pages	OWC Code	Name of Society	No. of Sources	No. of Pages
•• NA6	Aleut	69	2,003	• NP12	Winnebago	10	915	NT13	Navaho	146	11,626
NA12	Tlingit	17	1,489	NQ10	Crow	23	1,468	NT14	Plateau		
ND8	Copper			NQ12	Dhegiha	33	1,968		Yumans	13	807
	Eskimo	27	1,860	NQ13	Gros Ventre	8	1,085	NT15	River Yumans	6	561
ND12	Nahane	7	758	NQ17	Mandan	10	1,297	NT18	Tewa	15	1,274
NE6	Bellacoola	8	1,561	NQ18	Pawnee	13	1,178	•• NT20	Washo	8	316
NE11	Nootka	19	1,547	NR4	Plateau			NT23	Zuni	16	2,842
•• NG6	Ojibwa	26	4,354		Indians	4	303	•• NU7	Aztec	18	1,942
NH6	Montagnais	18	1,013	•• NR13	N. Paiute	15	910	NU28	Papago	17	1,899
NJ5	Micmac	8	1,016	NR19.	Southeast			NU31	Serl	9	514
NL7	Historical				Salish	7	945	•• NU33	Tarahumara	12	1,472
	Massachusetts	1	533	NS18	Pomo	22	1,220	NU34	Tarasco	10	612
NM7	Delaware	15	1,733	NS22	Tubatulabal	4	180	NU37	Tepoztlan	5	859
NM9	Iroquois	40	2,704	NS29	Yokuts	16	975	• NV10	Yucatec Maya	11	1,870
NN11	Creek	3	757	NS31	Yurok	13	1,101				
NO6	Comanche	10	745	• NT8	Eastern Apache	4	589				

OCEANIA

OWC Code	Name of Society	No. of Sources	No. of Pages	OWC Code	Name of Society	No. of Sources	No. of Pages	OWC Code	Name of Society	No. of Sources	No. of Pages
OA1	Philippines	58	7,451	OI19	Tasmanians	1	293	OQ6	Lau	10	997
OA5	Apayao	Subfile		OI20	Tiwi	13	563	OR11	Marshalls	21	2,199
OA14	Central Bisayan	Subfile		• OJ13	Kwoma	1	250	•• OR19	Truk	23	1,927
OA19	Ifugao	Subfile	.	OJ23	Orokaiva	4	652	OR21	Woleai	41	2,665
OB1	Indonesia	18	4,367	OJ27	Wogee	14	460	• OR22	Yap	11	1,535
OC6	Iban	17	1,162	•• OJ29	Kapauku	5	869	•• OT11	Tikopia	25	2,303
OF5	Alor	3	726	•• OL6	Trobriands	24	2,991	OU8	Samoa	19	3,008
OF7	Bali	9	1,297	OM6	Manus	7	1,639	OX6	Marquesas	13	1,163
OG6	Makassar	1	379	OM10	New Ireland	5	457	OY2	Easter		
OH4	Ambon	Subfile		ON6	Buka	5	721		Islanders	15	960
OI8	Aranda	40	3,259	• ON13	Santa Cruz	6	420.	OZ4	Maori	10	3,257
OI17	Murngin	15	1,731	OO12	Malekula	3	883	OZ11	Pukapukans	11	860

•New files in process

••New additions to old files in process

——————— Underlining of a file indicates that it is made up wholly or substantially of the old form of file slips

RUSSIA

OWC Code	Name of Society	No. of Sources	No. of Pages	OWC Code	Name of Society	No. of Sources	No. of Pages	OWC Code	Name of Society	No. of Sources	No. of Pages
R1	Soviet Union	81	11,987	RG4	Estonians	5	615	RR1	Siberia	4	609
RB1	Baltic			RH1	Caucasia	4	1,500	•• RU4	Samoyed	31	1,862
	Countries	3	211	RI1	Georgia	5	759	RV2	Yakut	31	733
RB5	Lithuanians	11	990	• R13	Abkhaz	4	207	•• RX2	Gilyak	3	1,929
RC1	Belorussia	5	191	RL1	Turkestan	4	707	RY2	Chukchee	21	2,191
RD1	Ukraine	20	2,219	RL4	Turkic Peoples	1	235	RY3	Kamchadal	11	840
RF1	Great Russia	4	386	•• RQ2	Kazak	7	969	•• RY4	Koryak	5	810

SOUTH AMERICA

OWC Code	Name of Society	No. of Sources	No. of Pages	OWC Code	Name of Society	No. of Sources	No. of Pages	OWC Code	Name of Society	No. of Sources	No. of Pages
SA15	Mosquito	3	263	SG4	Araucanians	11	1,167	SP17	Nambicuara	8	436
SA19	Talamanca	6	479	SH5	Tehuelche	6	611	SP22	Tapirapé	12	350
•• SB5	Cuna	34	3,932	SH6	Yahgan	3	1,700	• SP23	Trumai	1	120
SC7	Cagaba	7	1,134	SI4	Abipon	2	452	SQ13	Mundurucu	14	649
•• SC13	Goajiro	10	724	•• SI7	Mataco	8	595	• SQ18	Yanoama	9	542
• SC15	Paez	8	700	SK6	Choroti	2	523	SQ20	Tucuna	5	259
•• SD6	Cayapa	4	747	• SK7	Guana	6	327	• SR8	Bush Negroes	6	1,152
•• SD9	Jívaro	33	2,315	SM3	Caingang	4	308	SR9	Carib	1	317
•• SE13	Inca	13	2,646	SO8	Timbira	2	367	• SS16	Pemon	4	145
•• SF5	Aymara	11	894	SO9	Tupinamba	26	1,637	• SS18	Warao	6	680
• SF10	Chiriguano	7	1,197	• SP7	Bacairi	6	820	•• SS19	Yaruro	7	252
SF21	Siriono	5	692	• SP8	Bororo	6	303	ST13	Callinago	13	524
• SF24	Uru	8	385	• SP9	Caraja	9	677				

INCOMPLETE AND EXPERIMENTAL FILES

OWC Code	Name of Society	No. of Sources	No. of Pages	OWC Code	Name of Society	No. of Sources	No. of Pages	OWC Code	Name of Society	No. of Sources	No. of Pages
A1	Asia	1	6	EL11	East Germany	1	336	RK5	Tat	1	22
AE1	Greater			MK1	Oman	4	158	RN1	Uzbekistan	1	26
	China	3	47	MZ1	Middle East			RO1	Tadzhikstan	1	18
AE2	Hainan	2	143		Islands	1	13	RP1	Kirgizstan	1	23
AE6	Yao	1	37	RB4	Letts	4	269	RP2	Kirgiz	1	4
AE7	Pai-i	3	58	RD2	Cossacks	1	13	RQ1	Kazakhstan	1	24
AF13	Northwest			RE1	Moldavia	1	21	RU2	Ket	1	5
	China	2	579	RG2	Cheremis	1	145	RU3	Ostyak	2	231
AH4	Khalkha	1	47	RG5	Karelia	2	236	RU5	Tungus	3	74
AH5	Kalmyk	1	46	RG6	Mordva	1	134	RW1	Buryak		
AT1	Pakistan	1	227	RG7	Votyak	1	160		Mongolia	3	138
AW10	Kanada	2	230	RG8	Zyryan	1	172	RX1	Southeast		
AW12	Marathi	2	267	RH2	Historical				Siberia	1	12
E13	Balkan				Caucasia	1	544	RX3	Goldi	1	78
	Peoples	3	311	RH8	Dagestan	1	32		Primate	18	344
EE2	Historical			RJ1	Armenia	2	258		Theoretical	136	2,213
	Bulgaria	1	489	RK1	Azerbaijan	1	24				

SUMMARY

Total number of Major Files available (including in process)	267	Total number of incomplete and experimental files	42
Total number of text pages	436,608	Total number of text pages	8,214
Total number of sources in Files	3,906	Total number of sources	216
Total number of file slips in each set (estimate)	2,620,000	Total number of file slips (E)	45,300

BIBLIOGRAPHY

MURDOCK, GEORGE PETER
  1963 *Outline of world cultures*, 3rd ed., revised. New Haven, Human Relations Area Files.

MURDOCK, GEORGE PETER, *et al.*
  1965 *Outline of cultural materials*, 4th revised ed. New Haven, Human Relations Area Files.

CHAPTER 34

The Methodological Findings of the Cross-Cultural Summary

TERRENCE A. TATJE, RAOUL NAROLL and ROBERT B. TEXTOR

INTRODUCTION

Analysis of the intercorrelations of methodological variables included in *A Cross-Cultural Summary* (Textor 1967) supports four general findings relevant to the use of the cross-cultural survey method. Briefly stated, these are: 1) A general lack of evidence of "error biases" when cultures are classified on the basis of the nationality of the principal ethnographers; 2) a general lack of evidence of "error biases" when cultures are classified on the basis of the period of publication of the principal ethnographic materials; 3) strong indication of "biases" in the selection of survey samples; and 4) clear evidence of "significant" correlations between given cultural traits, even after the factor of random occurrence has been controlled. Each of these findings is discussed separately below.

A Cross-Cultural Summary presents a very large number of intercorrelations of substantive variables (culture traits), in addition to a number of methodological variables, which are the subject of this chapter. The array of statistical data is made possible by the use of the electronic computer, specifically by the use of the Pattern Search and Table Translation Technique which was previously employed in *A Cross-Polity Survey* (Banks and Textor 1963).

The *Summary* utilizes a world-wide culture sample consisting of four hundred cultures recommended by Murdock's "Ethnographic Atlas" as a "representative sample of the world's known cultures." These are the first four hundred cultures listed in the "Ethnographic Atlas," as published in *Ethnology* (1:113–134, 265–286, 387–403, 533–545;

2:109–133). For this sample the *Summary* presents intercorrelations on 480 culture traits or "finished characteristics" (Paragraphs 1 through 480), and 56 methodological variables (Paragraphs 481 through 536). The 480 substantive variables are based on the defined culture traits coded in thirty-six different cross-cultural studies, plus those traits tabulated by Murdock (1957) in his "World Ethnographic Sample" (WES), and those tabulated in the "Ethnographic Atlas" (EA). Of these 480 traits categories, 259 were run as "both subject and predicate" in the *Summary* print-out (i.e., as both "column headings" and "row headings," respectively); 150 were run as "subject only"; 19 as "predicate only"; and 52 as "neither subject nor predicate" (i.e., 52 of the traits included are in the *Summary* with coding assignments but were not included in the correlation matrices). Thus for the substantive variables alone the computer calculated a total of 113,443 intercorrelations ($[409 \times 278]-259$). For a description of these variables, and of the Pattern Search and Table Translation Technique, see Textor 1967.

The methodological control variables employed in the *Summary* are of four kinds: variables concerning the nationality of the principal ethnographers who have published descriptions of the 400 societies in the sample; variables concerning the samples used by the thirty-six "contributors" to the *Summary;* and ten random nonsense variables, the so-called "whiskers" variables. For the latter a table of random numbers was used to arbitrarily assign each of the 400 societies either to the group which sports whiskers of a certain color, or to the group which does not, e.g., 120 societies (30 per cent) were randomly chosen as those which have green whiskers (Textor 1967:55).

THE SAMPLE

The reader is cautioned to bear in mind throughout the following discussion that the sample upon which *A Cross-Cultural Summary* is based is *not* a random one. The first four hundred societies included in the "Ethnographic Atlas" were selected by the editors of *Ethnology* as a proportional, representative sample of well-described cultures from the total ethnographic universe (Murdock *et al.* 1963:109 f.). As such, this sample reflects Murdock's judgment—acquired over more than thirty years of cross-cultural experience —as to what ought to comprise a balanced sample of the known cultural types.

The nonrandomness of the sample means that the use of probability values in the *Summary* print-out and in the tables of this analysis is technically unwarranted. The reader must therefore decide for himself how he will regard these probability values: as measures or indicators of significance, of unusualness, of remarkability, of strength of association, and so forth. Naroll (1962:25–26) has suggested that such probability values can be taken as measures of the likelihood of a similar outcome occurring by chance if a random sample had been drawn from a universe in which no correlations exist. But this position assumes that the observed probability value is that found *in a single trial*. This is not the case with the "significant" correlations found in the print-out of *A Cross-Cultural Summary*. The Pattern Search and Table Translation Technique is specifically designed to "comb" through a large number of correlations; in all, more than 130,000 possible intercorrelations were "combed" for the *Summary*. The computer was programmed to retain all those with p values of a certain order, and to translate these into sentence statements.

In this situation we must face squarely the question of how many "significant correlations" one would expect merely by chance—in a maximum total of 130,000 correlations—if a random sample had been drawn from a universe in which no real relationship exists between the correlates. Obviously the number is large; the "combing

hypothesis" predicts that by random chance alone one would theoretically expect, on the average, 1300 "significant" correlations from a total of 130,000 at the 0.01 probability level. How then are we to decide whether the correlations printed out in the *Summary* actually reflect some real relationship between the variables, and not random chance? We suggest that an examination of the random "whiskers" variables offers a procedure for controlling the "combing" factor.

RANDOM "WHISKERS" VARIABLES

The ten "whiskers" variables included in *A Cross-Cultural Summary* enable us to test the "combing" hypothesis. Since the whiskers traits are purely random, any "significant" correlations between them and the finished characteristics used in *A Summary* can only be due to chance. Table 1 tabulates the number of "significant" intercorrelations for each of the methodological variables of the *Summary*, and a list of the column headings ("subjects") for each of the fifty-six methodological variables is given in Appendix I. The rows in Table 1 corresponding to Paragraphs 527 through 536 show the number of such "significant" correlations for the ten whiskers traits.

The first column in Table 1 identifies the paragraph, i.e., the "subject" variable being correlated with the other finished characteristics used in the *Summary*. The second column gives the toal number of possible intercorrelations computed for that "subject." The last four columns of the table tabulate the number of correlations of this total which had extremely small expected probability values. These are divided into four interval categories: The figures under the column heading "0.01" indicate the number of correlations with an expected probability value of "less than 0.01, but not less than 0.001"; the figures under the heading "0.001" give the number of correlations with an expected probability value of "less than 0.001, but not less than 0.0001"; and so forth. Thus, for example, from the row corresponding to Paragraph 532 we read that there were 4 correlations out of a possible 278 with expected probability values between 0.01 and 0.001, and none with an expected probability value of less than 0.001.

The "combing hypothesis" predicts that in

Table 1

SUMMARY OF INTERCORRELATION DATA FOR METHODOLOGICAL VARIABLES, FROM A CROSS-CULTURAL SUMMARY

PARAGRAPH NO.	TOTAL NO. OF INTER-CORRELATION	NO. OF INTERCORRELATIONS WITH P LESS THAN:			
		0.01	0.001	0.0001	0.00001
Nationality					
481	281	4	7	6	9
482	281	2	6	0	2
483	281	2	3	2	8
484	278	2	1	0	1
485	278	1	1	1	0
Date					
486	281	3	0	0	0
487	281	1	0	0	0
488	281	9	0	0	0
Contributors					
489	319	2(9)	0(4)	0(5)	0(6)
490	319	11(3)	2(4)	0(1)	2(26)
491	319	3(7)	1(2)	0(4)	0(14)
492	319	3	1(3)	0(4)	0(24)
493	319	4(3)	1(1)	2(2)	0(29)
494	319	2(4)	1(3)	0(1)	0(20)
495	319	1(1)	0(5)	0(4)	0(22)
496	319	2(2)	0(3)	0(2)	0(25)
497	319	1(3)	1(3)	0(6)	0(19)
498	319	6(2)	2(3)	0(2)	0(26)
499	319	16(1)	1	0(1)	0(30)
500	319	0(3)	0(3)	0	0(26)
501	319	8(1)	1(2)	0(2)	0(28)
502	319	2(3)	0(2)	0	0(25)
503	319	1(2)	0(5)	0(6)	0(20)
504	319	1(3)	1(1)	0(6)	0(20)
505	319	0(4)	0(6)	0(2)	0(3)
506	319	1(3)	0(5)	0(1)	0(22)
507	319	1(2)	1(5)	0(3)	0(23)
508	319	4(1)	1(3)	0(2)	0(22)
509	319	1(6)	2(4)	0(2)	0(1)
510	319	0(4)	0(7)	0(5)	0(5)
511	319	9(4)	1(4)	2(4)	0(21)
512	319	2(3)	2(2)	1(4)	0(22)
513	319	4(5)	0(8)	0(4)	0(11)
514	319	3(1)	0(2)	0	0(32)
515	319	3(4)	3(2)	0(3)	0(26)
516	319	0(10)	1(3)	1	1(2)
517	319	2(6)	0(9)	0(7)	1(4)
518	319	3(3)	0(4)	0(4)	0(23)
519	319	2	0(7)	0(1)	0(19)
520	319	3(3)	1(2)	0(4)	0(22)
521	319	2(2)	0(3)	0(1)	0(27)
522	319	3(2)	0(4)	0	0(28)
523	319	6(2)	1(3)	0(2)	0(25)
524	319	1(4)	0(3)	1(4)	0(22)
525	278	1	0	1	0
526	320	4	0	0	0
Whiskers					
527	278	0	0	0	0
528	278	0	0	0	0
529	278	0	0	0	0
530	278	0	1	0	0
531	278	0	0	0	0
532	278	4	0	0	0
533	278	3	0	0	0
534	278	0	0	0	0
535	278	0	0	0	0
536	278	0	0	0	0

NOTE: For Paragraphs 489 through 524, the numbers in parentheses indicate the number of intercorrelations between "contributor's" samples for each of the four probability value intervals. Thus, for example, in the row corresponding to Paragraph 489 (cultures in Ackerman's sample) two correlations between this variable and substantive characteristics *plus* nine correlations between Ackerman's sample and another "contributor's" sample had expected probability values "less than 0.01 but not less than 0.001"; there were no correlations with substantive traits that had p values less than 0.001, but four of the intercorrelations with other samples had p values falling between 0.001 and 0.00001; and so forth.

one thousand random correlations we should expect on the average nine with expected probability values falling between 0.01 and 0.001; i.e., in the "0.01" column of Table 1. *But this expectation can only be realized if the probability values for the correlations are free to take infinitely small values.* Taking the ten "whiskers" runs together, we should expect about twenty-five random correlations to fall into the "0.01" probability interval under these conditions $(2780 \times 9/1000 = 25.02)$. Reading down column 3 of Table 1 we see that only seven observed correlations fall into the "0.01" interval for the ten "whiskers" variables (Paragraphs 527–536).

This unexpectedly low random frequency is caused by two factors. Most important is the fact that the observed p values are not free to take infinitely small values. The expected probability value of a 2×2 correlation matrix is a function of N, or the total number of cases in the four cells. Where N is small, the expected p value— even in the case of a "perfect correlation"— cannot achieve an exceedingly small value. This can be illustrated by the following matrix from the *Summary* print-out: In Statement 444 of Paragraph 530 there is a perfect negative correlation between "having purple whiskers" and the "use of dreams to seek and control supernatural powers."

	cultures that have purple whiskers	cultures that do not have purple whiskers	totals
use of dreams is high	0	3	3
use of dreams is low	4	0	4
totals	4	3	7

While the matrix shows a perfect correlation, only seven cases were coded for the "use of dreams" variable; thus the expected probability (by Fisher's exact test) is relatively large: 0.0247. For many of the characteristics used in the *Summary,* codings were available for only a small proportion of the four hundred societies. Therefore the total N for many of the correlation matrices is too small to permit p values to reach levels of 0.01 or less, as in the above example.

There is a second factor working to reduce the number of random correlations with small expected probability values. It sometimes happens, especially where the N is small, that all of the societies for which there are codings on a particular culture trait happen by chance to fall into one or the other of the "whiskers" categories. In this event there is no variance, and thus, the correlation matrix does not constitute a trial at all. This factor perhaps considerably reduces the actual number of correlations for each of the "whiskers" runs from the maximum possible number of 278.

Both these factors work in the same direction, i.e., they both tend to reduce the number of random correlations with p values of the order shown in Table 1. Consequently, estimates of the number of "significant" correlations due merely to chance are biased in a *conservative* direction. For any of the "subject" variables used in the *Summary* the number of such correlations predicted by the "combing hypothesis" is greater than the actual possible number.

Another important fact from the analysis of the whiskers correlations allows us to define what we mean by a "significant correlation." In only one case—from a maximum possible total of 2780—does a random correlation have an expected probability value of less than 0.001. Likewise, in only this one case is there an observed chi-square value of greater than 9.00 (with one degree of freedom). We therefore feel safe in asserting that any correlation from the *Summary* with a chi-square value greater than 9.00 and/or an expected probability value less than 0.001 is almost certainly due to some other factor than chance. This is not to say that the correlations with p values falling between 0.01 and 0.001 do not reflect some real relationship between the correlates; however the possibility of chance association cannot be discounted at this level. For the remainder of this analysis we shall use a conservative interpretation, and only consider correlations with p values less than 0.001 and/or chi-square values greater than 9.00 as "significant."

NATIONALITY VARIABLES

Paragraphs 481 through 485 of the *Summary* contrast the four hundred societies of the sample with respect to the nationality of the principal ethnographers. A society is considered as falling into one of the "nationality" categories only if all the principal ethnographic materials about it—as listed in the "Ethnographic Atlas"—were written by persons who were enculturated in the nation concerned and, if trained, were also trained in that nation. (For a full explanation of these definitions, see Textor 1967:177 f.) As we might expect, the classification of cultures in this way reveals some significant differences between the groups of cultures studied by ethnographers of the same nationality or school of training. *But analysis of these significant correlations lends no support to the hypothesis that such differences are due to systematic "error biases" on the part of ethnographers of the same cultural background and/or training.*

In Table 1 the rows corresponding to Paragraphs 481 through 485 show the number of cases in which it was found that cultures described primarily by ethnographers of a particular nationality differ significantly —with respect to some other trait—from cultures not studied primarily by ethnographers of that nationality. In general there are two alternative explanations for these cases. First, they may be due to a "sampling bias," e.g., American ethnographers tend to study indigenous North American Indian cultures significantly more frequently than do non-Americans. Secondly, such correlations may be due to a particular "error bias." By "error bias" we mean a tendency for ethnographers of a given nationality to consistently overlook certain kinds of information, to consistently concentrate and search for information on other topics, or to erroneously report information about still others. Presumably such "error biases" reflect the ethnographers' cultural background and/or professional training. As a hypothetical example, suppose that American ethnographers, as a group, tend to ignore evidence of witchcraft in the cultures they study, and consequently tend to report witchcraft as absent or unimportant; assume further that British ethnographers, on the other hand, pay special attention to evidence of witchcraft, and in fact tend to infer a high incidence of witch-

craft even when the evidence is scanty. Such a situation constitutes a clear case of "error bias." In comparative cross-cultural studies the researcher need not be overly concerned about "sampling bias" of the sort described, but he must guard against possible error biases. The "sampling bias" factor would be of real concern only if the researcher restricted his own sampling to societies described in a certain language—and presumably most often described by ethnographers of the nationalities corresponding to that language—e.g., if the researcher decided to use only monographs written in French, most of the ethnographic materials would be those written by French and Belgian ethnographers. From our hypothetical example, for instance, the results of a cross-cultural study of witchcraft practices would be significantly altered by the over-inclusion of societies described by either British or American ethnographers.

One of the major conclusions of this analysis of the methodological variables of *A Cross-Cultural Summary* is that there are very few such "error biases" due to cultural background of the ethnographer. Almost all of the significant correlations between nationality characteristics and substantive culture traits can easily be explained as artifacts of various "sampling biases." To illustrate this fact, Table 2 presents all the significant correlations from Paragraph 481 of the *Summary*. This paragraph contrasts those cultures which have been principally described by Americans with those described chiefly by ethnographers who are other than American. Other paragraphs of the *Summary* present similar correlations for British, German, and French ethnographers (Textor 1967:177 f.).

Statements /3 and /8 of Table 2 are clearly the most important. These tell us that American ethnographers tend significantly more than others to study cultures outside of Africa, and that they tend (in 57 of 113 cases) to study American Indian cultures. Obviously statements /13, /14, /15, /16, and /42 reflect this "sampling bias." That is, the facts that the cultures studied by Americans are significantly more often nontropical, and tend to be located in the more extreme latitudes, merely reflect the fact that Americans tend to study American Indian societies rather than African ones. Similarly, the correlations with basic subsistence techniques (statements /51, /54, and

Table 2
SIGNIFICANT CORRELATIONS FROM PARAGRAPH 481 OF A CROSS-CULTURAL SUMMARY*

PARA 481	LEFT COLUMN AMERICAN ETHNOGRAPHERS (113)	RIGHT COLUMN OTHER THAN AMERICAN (275)	MATRIX	XSQ	PHI	XP/EP
/3	More outside Africa (320) 0.98 of 113	Less outside Africa (320) 0.73 of 275	2 74 / 111 201	30.56	−0.281	0.0000001
/8	Located in N. Amer. (70) 0.50 of 113	Located outside N. A. (330) 0.95 of 275	57 13 / 56 262	110.13	0.533	0.0000000
/13	Less where latitude is less than 40 degrees (329) 0.65 of 113	More where latitude is less than 40 degrees (329) 0.89 of 275	40 29 / 73 246	32.16	0.288	0.0000000
/14	Latitude is 30 degrees or greater (119) 0.59 of 113	Latitude is less than 30 degrees (281) 0.82 of 275	67 49 / 46 226	63.77	0.405	0.0000000
/15	Latitude is 20 degrees or greater (183) 0.69 of 113	Latitude is less than 20 degrees (217) 0.64 of 275	78 100 / 35 175	33.11	0.292	0.0000000
/16	More where latitude is 10 or greater (277) 0.82 of 113	Less where latitude is 10 or greater (277) 0.63 of 275	93 174 / 20 101	12.64	0.180	0.0004
/42	More where environment is non-tropical (244) 0.73 of 113	Less where environment is non-tropical (244) 0.55 of 275	31 123 / 82 152	9.30	−0.155	0.0023
/51	Subsistence is primarily by food gathering (147) 0.56 out of 113	Subsistence is primarily by food production (253) 0.70 of 275	50 193 / 63 82	21.92	−0.238	0.000003
/54	Less where food production is by intensive or simple agriculture rather than by incipient food production (192) 0.65 of 62	More where food production is by intensive or simple agriculture, rather than by incipient food production (192) 0.87 of 171	40 128 / 22 23	12.80	−0.234	0.0003
/56	Food production is by incipient food production, rather than by simple agriculture (46) 0.59 of 37	Food production is by simple agriculture, rather than by incipient food production (101) 0.79 of 108	15 85 / 22 23	17.01	−0.343	0.00004
/71	More where metalworking is absent (153) 0.80 of 75	Less where metalworking is absent (153) 0.54 of 173	15 80 / 60 93	14.16	−0.239	0.0002

*Only correlations with chi-square values of 9.00 or greater are included in this table.

Table 2 (continued)

	AMERICAN ETHNOGRAPHERS (113)	OTHER THAN AMERICAN (275)	MATRIX		XSQ	PHI	XP/EP
481 /109	More where castes are absent (317) 0.95 of 106	Less where castes are absent (317) 0.50 of 260	5 44	101 209	9.13	−0.160	0.0025
/110	Slavery is absent (218) 0.73 of 110	Slavery is present (163) 0.50 of 260	30 130	80 130	15.35	−0.204	0.00009
/186	More where kin group other than exclusively patrilineal (250) 0.78 of 113	Less where kin group other than exclusively patrilineal (250) 0.57 of 275	25 118	88 157	13.99	−0.190	0.0002
/188	Kin group is exclusively cognatic (148) 0.51 of 113	Kin group is other than exclusively cognatic (252) 0.68 of 275	58 88	55 187	11.94	0.175	0.0006
/190	Kin group is matrilineal, rather than patrilineal or double-descent (61) 0.50 of 54	Kin group is patrilineal or double-descent, rather than matrilineal (186) 0.83 of 183	27 151	27 32	21.87	−0.304	0.000004
/192	Less other than where only kin group is kindred or else bilateral descent inferred (289) 0.58 of 113	More other than where only kin group is kindred or else bilateral descent inferred (289) 0.77 of 275	47 62	66 213	13.46	0.186	0.0002
/209	Less where marital residence is patri-, viri-, or avunculocal rather than matri- or uxorilocal (270) 0.68 of 88	More where marital residence patri-, viri-, or avuncu-local rather than matri- or uxorilocal (270) 0.85 of 235	60 200	28 35	10.63	−0.181	0.0011
/210	Less where marital residence is patrilocal rather than matrilocal (169) 0.62 of 42	More where marital residence is patrilocal rather than matrilocal (169) 0.91 of 149	26 135	16 14	18.27	−0.309	0.00001
/213	Where first cousin marriage is not permitted (198) 0.66 of 107	Where first cousin marriage is permitted (172) 0.52 of 252	36 131	71 121	9.43	−0.162	0.0021
/262	Less where wives obtained by means involving presence of some consideration (305) 0.62 of 112	More where wives obtained by means involving presence of some consideration (305) 0.84 of 271	69 227	43 44	20.92	−0.234	0.000005
/263	Wives obtained by relatively easy means (162) 0.57 of 112	Wives obtained by relatively difficult means (223) 0.65 of 271	48 177	64 94	15.58	−0.202	0.00008

Table 2 (continued)

	AMERICAN ETHNOGRAPHERS (113)	OTHER THAN AMERICAN (275)	MATRIX	XSQ	PHI	XP/EP
481 /370	More where segregation of adolescent boys is absent (148) 0.83 of 69	Less where segregation of adolescent boys is absent (148) 0.51 of 170	12 80 57 90	17.01	−0.267	0.00004
/377	More where male genital mutilation is absent (242) 0.92 of 95	Less where male genital mutilation is absent (242) 0.68 of 222	8 71 87 151	18.50	−0.242	0.00002
/459	Games, if present, include games of chance (82) 0.77 of 62	Games, if present, do not include games of chance (89) 0.69 of 107	48 33 14 74	32.28	0.437	0.0000000
/460	Games, if present, are not limited to games of skill only (104) 0.81 of 62	Games, if present, are limited to games of skill only (67) 0.50 of 107	12 54 50 53	14.68	−0.295	0.00013

/56) are artifacts of the "sampling bias"; hunting and gathering, and incipient food production are prevalent among indigenous North American cultures, but less common among cultures outside this region. Reference to Paragraph 8 in the *Summary*, which contrasts cultures located in North America versus all others, in every instance supports similar conclusions about the other significant correlations listed in Table 2; i.e., absence of metalworking (statement /71), social stratification variables (/109 and /110), kin group organization (/186, /188, /190, and /192), residence rules (/209 and /210), cousin marriage (/213), marriage payments (/262 and /263), and male puberty rites (/370 and /377). The one possible exception is in the study of games (statements /459 and /460). The difference here may be due to the fact that Americans seem to pay more attention to this topic than do other ethnographers. In all these cases the difference between the group of cultures studied by Americans, and the other cultures of the sample, reflect the differences in indigenous North American cultures from the world-wide pattern.

The apparent lack of "error bias" by nationality in ethnographic materials is heartening. It should reassure the comparativist that he is not contaminating his findings by using a wide variety of sources for his world-wide samples.

DATE OF PUBLICATION VARIABLES

Paragraphs 486 through 488 of the *Summary* contrast the sample societies on the basis of the period in which the principal ethnographies describing them were written. In such a classification we might well expect significant correlations that reflect changing interests, as well as "sampling" and "error biases" of different generations of ethnographers. Thus such correlations are interesting from the standpoint of the sociology of knowledge as well as for detecting possible "error bias." From Table 1, it is noteworthy that none of the correlations for Paragraphs 486, 487, and 488 have expected probability values of less than 0.001 (only two correlations have chi-square values that are greater than 9.00). In fact, the total number of correlations in the "0.01" category is only slightly greater than we would expect by chance from a total of 843 possible correlations. Table 3 presents all the correlation matrices with p values of less than 0.01 for the three "publication" variables. As with the nationality variables, analysis of these correlations suggests a general lack of "error biases"; most of the correlations in Table 3 reflect the changing interests of anthropologists since they began doing systematic field work.

For example, statement /483 of Paragraph 486 (which contrasts cultures described before 1930 with those for which the principal monographs have been published since 1950) reflects the facts that the British were among the first to carry on systematic field work, and that an increasing proportion of field workers are now Americans. Similarly, from Paragraph 488, statements /51, /79, /84, /94, /95, and /109 all seem to reflect a growing trend among anthropologists toward the study of more complex, less isolated and "primitive" societies.

Although the evidence is hardly conclusive, statement /428 of Paragraph 486 may reflect an "error bias." This statement says that in considerably more cases in which high gods are present in cultures described before 1930, these gods are reported to be non-supportive of human morality; whereas in cultures with high gods described since 1950 such gods are reported to be supportive of human morality. One possible explanation is that a greater percentage of early monographs were written by missionaries, who may have been biased in their understanding and reporting of native cosmologies; this tendency may have been true of other early ethnographers as well. Alternatively this association may reflect an actual change in native religious conceptions; contact with Christianity during the last forty years may have stimulated increasing reference to morality in the natives' explanations of their religious beliefs. A more plausible explanation, however, is simply that these more recent studies have tended to concern more complex cultures with more advanced subsistence technology, and that these cultures tend to be the ones that, if they have high gods at all, have high gods supportive of morality. (Readers may check this in the Summary by referring to Statements 486/84, 85, 105, 53, 72; and 428/85, 86, 96, 105, 51, 53, 54, 55, 63, 64, 66, 72.)

The general lack of significant correlations for the "publication" variables, and especially the apparent lack of "error biases," is important. In almost every case, cross-cultural

comparativists have utilized ethnographic materials from a wide range of time periods. To date, no one to our knowledge has questioned whether this practice has introduced possible error biases. The relevant data from A Cross-Cultural Summary indicate that it does not.

CONTRIBUTORS' SAMPLES

Paragraphs 489 through 524 of the Summary contrast the cultures (of the four hundred) included in each of the thirty-six contributors' samples with those (of the four hundred) not so included. For each of these paragraphs Table 1 shows both the number of significant correlations with substantive characteristics, and the number of significant intercorrelations between the samples themselves. It is clear from Table 1 that many of these thirty-six cross-cultural samples differ significantly from the four-hundred-society sample of the "Ethnographic Atlas" with regard to one or more cultural traits. It is even more clear, from the figures in parentheses, that these samples are not mutually independent. It is useful to keep the intercorrelations between samples distinct from the significant correlations with the substantive culture traits coded in the Summary. Table 4 presents all of the significant correlations ($X^2 > 9.00$) between each of the contributors' samples and the culture traits; significant intercorrelations between samples are not included in Table 4.

There are several reasons for the high intercorrelations between the contributors' samples. In the first place, many of these studies used the same, or partially the same, samples to begin with. Thus we can identify "families" of related samples. For instance, all thirty-six of the sample societies in Veroff's study (Paragraph 519) are among the forty societies of McClelland's sample (Paragraph 508). All of McClelland's forty societies in turn are included in the Bacon, Barry and Child sample (508/493). This latter sample overlaps substantially with the Whiting and Child sample (493/523). The largest family of samples is that which has historically stemmed from the work of Whiting and Child, and from the Bacon, Barry and Child studies (Paragraphs 490, 491, 492, 493, 494, 495, 496, 501, 502, 506, 508, 512, 515, 519, 522, 523, and 524).

The practice of using the same sample for

Table 3

SIGNIFICANT CORRELATIONS FROM PARAGRAPHS 486, 487 AND 488 OF A CROSS-CULTURAL SUMMARY*

PARA	LEFT COLUMN	RIGHT COLUMN	MATRIX	XSQ	PHI	XP/EP
486	PUBLISHED BEFORE 1930, RATHER THAN IN 1950 OR AFTER (32)	PUBLISHED IN 1950 OR AFTER, RATHER THAN BEFORE 1930 (72)				
/110	Slavery is present (163) 0.65 of 31	Slavery is absent (218) 0.66 of 67	20 23 / 11 44	6.67	0.261	0.0098
/428	A high god, if present & active, does not support human morality rather than support it (26) 0.60 of 5	A high god, if present & active supports human morality, rather than not (61) 1.00 of 17	2 17 / 3 0	7.27	−0.575	0.0065
/483	Principal ethnographers have been British, rather than American (52) 0.58 of 12	Principal ethnographers have been American, rather than British (113) 0.88 of 34	5 30 / 7 4	8.17	−0.421	0.0053
487	PUBLISHED BEFORE 1930 (32)	PUBLISHED IN 1930 OR AFTER (227)				
/5	Less located outside of East Eurasia (330) 0.59 of 23	More located outside of East Eurasia (330) 0.82 of 227	13 40 / 19 187	7.76	0.173	0.0053
488	PUBLISHED BEFORE 1950 (185)	PUBLISHED IN 1950 OR AFTER (72)				
/51	Less where subsistence is primarily by food production (253) 0.54 of 185	More where subsistence is primarily by food production (253) 0.74 of 72	99 53 / 86 19	7.85	−0.175	0.0051
/79	More where no city is present (201) 0.94 of 95	Less where no city is present (201) 0.73 of 44	6 12 / 89 32	9.93	−0.267	0.0016
/84	More where level of political integration is other than states of 100,000 or more (262) 0.92 of 158	Less where level of political integration is other than states of 100,000 or more (262) 0.74 of 39	12 10 / 146 29	8.53	−0.208	0.0035
/94	More where hierarchy of national jurisdiction has 2, 1, or no levels (296) 0.94 of 149	Less where hierarchy of national jurisdiction has 2, 1, or no levels (296) 0.79 of 57	9 12 / 140 45	8.58	−0.204	0.0034

*All correlations with an expected probability value of less than 0.01 are included in this table.

Table 3 (continued)

	MATRIX		XSQ	PHI	XP/EP

488

PUBLISHED BEFORE 1950 (185)

/95 More where hierarchy of national jurisdiction has one or no levels (254)
0.85 of 149

/107 More where class stratification, if present, is based on something other than occupational status (160)
0.86 of 86

/109 More where castes are absent (317)
0.92 of 172

/220 More where first cousin marriage in some form or other is not prescribed or preferred (273)
0.81 of 167

/241 More where family, if extended, is large or small, rather than stem (187)
0.92 of 92

PUBLISHED IN 1950 OR AFTER (72)

Item	MATRIX		XSQ	PHI	XP/EP
/95 Less where hierarchy of national jurisdiction has one or no levels (254) 0.67 of 57	23	19	7.07	−0.185	0.0078
	126	38			
/107 Less where class stratification, if present, is based on something other than occupational status (160) 0.62 of 39	12	15	8.12	−0.255	0.0044
	74	24			
/109 Less where castes are absent (317) 0.75 of 64	14	16	10.48	−0.211	0.0012
	158	48			
/220 Less where first cousin marriage in some form or other is not prescribed or preferred (273) 0.62 of 65	32	25	8.39	−0.190	0.0038
	135	40			
/241 Less where family, if extended, is large or small, rather than stem (187) 0.73 of 37	85	27	7.08	0.234	0.0078

several comparative studies has both advantages and disadvantages. The chief advantage is that it allows the researcher to utilize previously coded data. The principal danger is that any "biases" in the original sample will be carried over from one study to the next. One case of this seems to be present in the large family of samples just mentioned. In ten out of the seventeen samples in this family the incidence of relatively strong food taboos (Statement 449 or 450) is significantly greater than among the cultures not included in these samples. (See Table 2, and Paragraphs 490, 491, 493, 501, 502, 512, 515, 523, 524.)

A second reason for the high intercorrelations among the contributors' samples is the fact that many of them were drawn from the same sampling "universe." For example, in his study of divorce Ackerman (Paragraph 489) restricted his sample to societies included in WES, in order to make use of Murdock's codings on social organization variables. Similarly, many of the samples were drawn solely from the Human Relations Area Files (HRAF), e.g., the studies of sex by Ford, and Ford and Beach (Paragraphs 498 and 499, respectively). The practice of relying on an established "universe" for sample selection has the same advantages and disadvantages as using a previously reported sample. Usually, as with WES and HRAF, the ethnographic materials have already been compiled and codings are readily available for many traits. But here again there is the danger that these "universes" are biased. This seems particularly true of the Human Relations Area Files.

Finally, the use of judgmental sampling accounts for the frequent occurrence of the same societies in many cross-cultural samples. In part, this reflects the uneven coverage of the ethnographic literature—for the most part, only the best known and most adequately described societies are chosen for inclusion in such samples. This can be demonstrated for the thirty-six studies considered in the *Summary* by reference to a list of the best-described cultures recently issued by the directors of the Human Relations Area Files (1967). The HRAF list included 208 societies which meet stringent bibliographic requirements: at least 1200 pages of cultural data; substantial contributions from at least two different authors; a basic ethnographic account considered reliable by the profession;

well-rounded coverage of all major aspects of social organization; a major portion of the ethnographic evidence must have been gathered while the group was a viable functioning culture; and at least one hundred years of historical depth.

Of the 208 societies which meet these data requirements, 143 are included in the four-hundred-society sample used in *A Cross-Cultural Summary*. Table 5 contrasts these 143 cultures with the remaining 257 with respect to the number of contributors' samples in which they occur. The best-described societies (those included in the HRAF list) are significantly more often included in the samples of the thirty-six contributors.

We turn our attention now to Table 4, to the significant correlations between a particular contributor's sample and some substantive cultural trait. Table 4 shows all those cases in which a given contributor's sample has a frequency distribution of a given substantive cultural trait which differs significantly from the frequency distribution of that same cultural trait among the remaining societies of the four hundred—those not in his sample. For example, take item 490/73. This item refers to Anthony's sample on male initiation rites. One hundred thirteen of the four hundred societies were in Anthony's sample; so that leaves 287 others out of four hundred which were not in Anthony's sample. Eighty-eight of the 113 tribes in Anthony's sample had information about whether the people wove cloth or not; and 160 of the 287 others also had this information. (In all four hundred tribes, weaving was coded present among 118; it was coded absent among 130; and it was not coded at all among the remaining 152.) Now the point of item 490/73 is this: of the 88 tribes *in* Anthony's sample, two-thirds *did not* weave cloth; but of the 160 *not in* Anthony's sample, more than half (55 per cent *did* weave cloth. This difference between only 34 per cent of cloth weavers among the tribes *in* Anthony's sample compared to 55 per cent of cloth weavers among the tribes not in Anthony's sample is too great to be explained by chance. We would expect so great a difference would occur in either direction through chance in only five samples out of a thousand. Therefore, the only sensible conclusion is that sampling bias of some kind must have affected either Anthony's sample, or Murdock's sample (the four hundred), or both.

Table 4

SIGNIFICANT CORRELATIONS FROM PARAGRAPHS ON CONTRIBUTOR'S SAMPLES, PARAGRAPHS 489 THROUGH 524 OF A CROSS-CULTURAL SUMMARY*

PARA	LEFT COLUMN	RIGHT COLUMN	MATRIX	XSQ	PHI	XP/EP
489	IN ACKERMAN'S STUDY OF DIVORCE (57)	NOT IN ACKERMAN'S STUDY OF DIVORCE (343)				
	NOTE: There are no correlations with chi-square values of 9.00 or greater					
490	IN ANTHONY'S SAMPLE ON MALE INITIATION RITES (113)	NOT IN ANTHONY'S SAMPLE ON MALE INITIATION RITES (287)				
/4	More located outside Circum-Mediterranean (355) 0.97 of 113	Less located outside Circum-Mediterranean (355) 0.85 of 287	3 42 / 110 245	10.48	−0.162	0.0012
/73	Weaving is absent (130) 0.66 of 88	Weaving is present (118) 0.55 of 160	30 88 / 58 72	9.13	−0.192	0.0025
/234	Cousin terminology is of Crow, Omaha, or Iroquois type, rather than Eskimo or Hawaiian (152)	Cousin terminology is of Eskimo or Hawaiian type, rather than Crow, Omaha, or Iroquois (170)	65 87 / 38 132	14.44	0.212	0.00015
/370	Segregation of adolescent boys is complete or partial (95) 0.52 of 90	Segregation of adolescent boys is absent (148) 0.69 of 153	47 48 / 43 105	9.49	0.198	0.0021
/391	Premarital sex relations are punished only if pregnancy results, or freely permitted (90) 0.66 of 65	Premarital sex relations are strongly punished and in fact rare, or weakly punished and in fact not rare (89) 0.59 of 114	22 67	9.32	−0.228	0.0023
/426	A high god is absent (104) 0.54 of 90	A high god is present (156) 0.68 of 170	41 115 / 49 55	11.06	−0.206	0.0009
/450	More where observation of food taboos is high or medium, rather than low (60) 0.86 of 43	Less where observation of food taboos is high or medium, rather than low (60)	37 23 / 6 20	9.32	0.329	0.0023
/473	Sensitivity to insult is moderate or negligible (56) 0.76 of 58	Sensitivity to insult is extreme (32) 0.60 of 30	14 18 / 44 12	9.49	−0.328	0.00

*Only correlations with chi-square values of 9.00 or greater are included in this table.

Table 4 (continued)

			MATRIX	XSQ	PHI	XP/EP
490	IN ANTHONY'S SAMPLE ON MALE INITIATION RITES (113)	NOT IN ANTHONY'S SAMPLE ON MALE INITIATION RITES (287)				
/482	Less where principal ethnographers are other than British (336) 0.72 of 112	More where principal ethnographers are other than British (336) 0.92 of 276	31 21 / 81 255	25.95	0.259	0.0000005
/483	Less where principal ethnographers are American rather than British (113) 0.54 of 68	More where principal ethnographers are American rather than British (113) 0.78 of 97	37 76 / 31 21	9.53	−0.240	0.0020
/488	More those about which principal ethnographies were published before 1950 (185) 0.91 of 79	Less those about which principal ethnographies were published before 1950 (185)	72 113 / 7 65	19.40	0.275	0.00001
491	IN APPLE'S STUDY OF GRANDPARENTHOOD (49)	NOT IN APPLE'S STUDY OF GRANDPARENTHOOD (352)				
/449	Observation of food taboos is high, rather than medium or low (25) 0.69 of 16	Observation of food taboos is medium or low, rather than high (61) 0.80 of 70	11 14 / 5 56	12.74	0.385	0.0004
/481	Less where princ. ethnographers are other than American (275) 0.51 of 47	More where princ. ethnographers are other than American (275) 0.74 of 341	23 90 / 24 251	9.11	0.153	0.0025
492	IN AYRES' STUDY OF FEMALE INITIATION RITES (39)	NOT IN AYRES' STUDY OF FEMALE INITIATION RITES (361)				
/108	Class stratification, if present, is based on a hereditary aristocracy (74) 0.79 of 19	Class stratification, if present, is based on something other than a hereditary aristocracy (129) 0.68 of 184	15 59 / 4 125	14.38	0.366	0.00015
493	IN BACON, BARRY & CHILD'S STUDY OF CHILD REARING (78)	NOT IN BACON, BARRY & CHILD'S STUDY OF CHILD REARING (322)				
/4	In all cases located outside of Circum-Mediterranean (355) 1.00 of 78	Less located outside of Circum-Mediterranean (355) 0.86 of 322	0 45 / 78 277	10.92	−0.165	0.0010

Table 4 (continued)

	Left condition	Right condition	MATRIX	XSQ	PHI	XP/EP
492	IN BACON, BARRY & CHILD'S STUDY OF CHILD REARING (78)	NOT IN BACON, BARRY & CHILD'S STUDY OF CHILD REARING (322)				
/449	Observation of food taboos is high, rather than med. or low (25) 0.53 of 38	Observation of food taboos is med. or low, rather than high (61) 0.90 of 48	20 5 / 18 43	16.34	0.436	0.00006
/450	Observation of food taboos is high or med., rather than low (60) 0.95 of 38	Observation of food taboos is low, rather than high or med. (26) 0.50 of 48	36 24 / 2 24	18.06	0.458	0.00002
494	IN BARRY'S STUDY OF ART (29)	NOT IN BARRY'S STUDY OF ART (371)				
/325	Degree of diffusion among infant's nurturant agents is high (42) 0.81 of 27	Degree of diffusion among infant's nurturant agents is low (32) 0.57 of 47	22 20 / 5 27	9.06	0.350	0.0025
/449	Observation of food taboos is high, rather than medium or low (25) 0.80 of 10	Observation of food taboos is medium or low, rather than high (61) 0.78 of 76	8 17 / 2 59	11.58	0.367	0.0007
495	IN BROWN'S STUDY OF FEMALE INITIATION RITES (65)	NOT IN BROWN'S STUDY OF FEMALE INITIATION RITES (335)				
		NOTE: There are no correlations with chi-square values of 9.00 or greater.				
496	IN D'ANDRADE'S STUDY OF DREAMS (55)	NOT IN D'ANDRADE'S STUDY OF DREAMS (345)				
		NOTE: There are no correlations with chi-square values of 9.00 or greater.				
497	IN EVAN'S STUDY OF LAW (61)	NOT IN EVAN'S STUDY OF LAW (339)				
/180	Community is commonly exogamous, rather than non-exogamous (124) 0.52 of 61	Community is commonly non-exogamous, rather than exogamous (258) 0.71 of 321	32 92 / 29 229	12.18	0.179	0.0005
498	IN FORD'S STUDY OF SEX (51)	NOT IN FORD'S STUDY OF SEX (349)				
/391	Premarital sex relations are punished only if pregnancy results, or freely permitted (90) 0.76 of 37	Premarital sex relations are strongly punished and in fact rare, or weakly punished and in fact not rare (89) 0.56 of 142	9 80 / 28 62	10.79	−0.245	0.0010

Table 4 (continued)

			MATRIX	XSQ	PHI	XP/EP
498	IN FORD'S STUDY OF SEX (51)	NOT IN FORD'S STUDY OF SEX (349)				
/488	More those about which principal ethnographies were published before 1950 (185) 0.97 of 39	Less those about which principal ethnographies were published before 1950 (185) 0.67 of 218	38 147 1 71	13.32	0.228	0.0003
499	IN FORD & BEACH'S SAMPLE ON SEXUAL EXPRESSION BY THE YOUNG (86)	NOT IN FORD & BEACH'S SAMPLE ON SEXUAL EXPRESSION BY THE YOUNG (314)				
/6	Less located outside insular Pacific (330) 0.71 of 86	More located outside insular Pacific (330) 0.86 of 314	25 45 61 269	9.16	0.151	0.0025
/107	More where class stratification, if present, is based on something other than occupational status (160) 0.98 of 44	Less where class stratification, if present, is based on something other than occupational status (160) 0.74 of 159	1 42 43 117	10.63	−0.229	0.0011
/186	More where kin group is other than exclusively patrilineal (186) 0.78 of 86	Less where kin group is other than exclusively patrilineal (186) 0.58 of 314	19 131 67 183	10.27	−0.160	0.0013
/342	Child's inferred anxiety over performance of nurturant behavior is high (18) 0.59 of 29	Child's inferred anxiety over performance of nurturant behavior is low (28) 0.94 of 17	17 1 12 16	10.40	0.475	0.0013
/390	More where premarital sex relations are weakly punished and in fact not rare or punished only if pregnancy results, or freely permitted (132) 0.90 of 59	Less where premarital sex relations are weakly punished and in fact not rare or punished only if pregnancy results, or freely permitted (132) 0.66 of 120	6 41 53 79	10.56	−0.243	0.0012
/391	Premarital sex relations are punished only if pregnancy results, or freely permitted (90) 0.71 of 59	Premarital sex relations are strongly punished and in fact rare, or weakly punished and in fact not rare (89) 0.60 of 120	17 72 42 48	14.17	−0.281	0.0002
500	IN FREEMAN & WINCH'S STUDY OF SOCIETAL COMPLEXITY (40)	NOT IN FREEMAN & WINCH'S STUDY OF SOCIETAL COMPLEXITY (360)				

NOTE: There are no correlations with chi-square values of 9.00 or greater.

Table 4 (continued)

			MATRIX	XSQ	PHI	XP/EP
501	IN GOODMAN'S STUDY OF ASCETIC MOURNING BEHAVIOR (67)	NOT IN GOODMAN'S STUDY OF ASCETIC MOURNING BEHAVIOR (333)				
/107	In all cases class stratification, if present, is based on something other than occupational status (160) 1.00 of 33	Less where class stratification, if present, is based on something other than occupational status (160) 0.75 of 170	0 43 33 127	9.13	−0.212	−.0025
/450	More where observation of food taboos is high or medium, rather than low (60) 0.91 of 32	Less where observation of food taboos is high or medium, rather than low (60) 0.57 of 54	29 31 3 23	9.00	0.323	0.0027
/488	More those about which principal ethnographies were published before 1950 (185) 0.94 of 47	Less those about which principal ethnographies were published before 1950 (185) 0.67 of 210	44 141 3 69	12.07	0.217	0.0005
502	IN HARLEY'S STUDY OF ADOLESCENT PEER GROUPS (57)	NOT IN HARLEY'S STUDY OF ADOLESCENT PEER GROUPS (343)				
/449	Observation of food taboos is high, rather than medium or low (25) 0.54 of 28	Observation of food taboos is medium or low, rather than high (61) 0.83 of 58	15 10 13 48	10.39	0.348	0.0013
503	IN HICKMAN'S STUDY OF FOLK-URBAN CONTINUUM (54)	NOT IN HICKMAN'S STUDY OF FOLK-URBAN CONTINUUM (346)				

NOTE: There are no correlations with chi-square values of 9.00 or greater.

			MATRIX	XSQ	PHI	XP/EP
504	IN HORTON'S STUDY OF ALCOHOLISM (49)	NOT IN HORTON'S STUDY OF ALCOHOLISM (351)				
/36	Less where natural environment is other than "very harsh" or subtropical bush, or temperate grassland (292) 0.51 of 49	More where natural environment is other than "very harsh" or subtropical bush, or temperate grassland (292) 0.76 of 351	24 84 25 267	12.45	0.176	0.0004
505	IN JACKSON'S STUDY OF CRIMINAL LAW AND MEDICINE (20)	NOT IN JACKSON'S STUDY OF CRIMINAL LAW AND MEDICINE (380)				

NOTE: There are no correlations with chi-square values of 9.00 or greater.

Table 4 (continued)

			MATRIX	XSQ	PHI	XP/EP
506	IN LAMBERT, TRIANDIS & WOLFE'S STUDY OF SUPERNATURAL BEINGS (36)	NOT IN LAMBERT, TRIANDIS & WOLFE'S STUDY OF SUPERNATURAL BEINGS (364)				
	NOTE: There are no correlations with chi-square values of 9.00 or greater.					
507	IN LEARY'S STUDY OF FOOD TABOOS (86)	NOT IN LEARY'S STUDY OF FOOD TABOOS (314)				
/62	More where husbandry of some kind is present (228) 0.73 of 86	Less where husbandry of some kind is present (228) 0.53 of 314	63 165 / 23 149	10.98	0.166	0.0009
508	IN McCLELLAND'S STUDY OF ACHIEVEMENT MOTIVATION (40)	NOT IN McCLELLAND'S STUDY OF ACHIEVEMENT MOTIVATION (360)				
/8	Less located outside North America (330) 0.63 of 40	More located outside North America (330) 0.85 of 360	15 55 / 25 305	10.82	0.164	0.0010
509	IN MONI NAG'S STUDY OF FERTILITY (25)	NOT IN MONI NAG'S STUDY OF FERTILITY (375)				
/3	Less located outside Africa (320) 0.52 of 25	More located outside Africa (320) 0.82 of 375	12 68 / 13 307	11.27	0.168	0.0008
/366	Dissociation of the sexes at adolescence is high (16) 0.88 of 8	Dissociation of the sexes at adolescence is medium or low (41) 0.82 of 49	7 9 / 1 40	13.03	0.478	0.0003
510	IN NAROLL'S STUDY OF SOCIETAL COMPLEXITY (20)	NOT IN NAROLL'S STUDY OF SOCIETAL COMPLEXITY (380)				
	NOTE: There are no correlations with chi-square values of 9.00 or greater.					
511	IN ROBERTS, ARTH & BUSH'S SAMPLE ON GAMES, AS MODIFIED BY EA (189)	NOT IN ROBERTS, ARTH & BUSH'S SAMPLE ON GAMES, AS MODIFIED BY EA (211)				
/8	Less located outside North America (330) 0.76 of 189	More located outside North America (330) 0.88 of 211	45 25 / 144 186	9.07	0.151	0.0026
/51	Less where subsistence is primarily by food production, rather than gathering (253) 0.52 of 189	More where subsistence is primarily by food production, rather than gathering (253) 0.73 of 211	99 154 / 90 57	17.33	−0.208	0.000035

Table 4 (continued)

No.	(left description)	(right description)	MATRIX	XSQ	PHI	XP/EP
511	IN ROBERTS, ARTH & BUSH'S SAMPLE ON GAMES, AS MODIFIED BY *EA* (189)	NOT IN ROBERTS, ARTH & BUSH'S SAMPLE ON GAMES, AS MODIFIED BY *EA* (211)				
/183	Less where largest non-cognatic kin group is smaller than a moiety (218) 0.78 of 110	More where largest non-cognatic kin group is smaller than a moiety (218) 0.93 of 142	24 10 / 86 132	10.36	0.203	0.0013
/196	Less where individual rights in real property, and rules for inheritance are present (194) 0.57 of 138	More where individual rights in real property, and rules for inheritance are present (194) 0.81 of 143	78 116 / 60 27	18.74	−0.258	0.000018
/263	Less where wives are obtained by relatively difficult means (233) 0.50 of 189	More where wives are obtained by relatively difficult means (233)	95 138 / 94 68	10.72	−0.165	0.0011
/377	More where male genital mutilation is absent (242) 0.82 of 186	Less where male genital mutilation is absent (242) −.65 of 139	34 49 / 152 90	11.17	−0.185	0.0008
/426	Less where a high god is present (156) 0.52 of 169	More where a high god is present (156) 0.74 of 91	89 67 / 80 24	9.98	−0.196	0.0016
512	IN SHIRLEY & ROMNEY'S STUDY OF LOVE MAGIC (33)	NOT IN SHIRLEY & ROMNEY'S STUDY OF LOVE MAGIC (367)				
/6	Less located outside insular Pacific (330) 0.58 of 33	More located outside insular Pacific (330) 0.85 of 367	14 56 / 19 311	13.65	0.185	0.0002
/108	Class stratification, if present, is based on hereditary aristocracy (74) 0.76 of 17	Class stratification, if present, is based on something other than hereditary aristocracy (129) 0.67 of 186	13 61 / 4 125	11.01	0.233	0.0009
/449	Observation of food taboos is high rather than med. or low (25) 0.71 of 17	Observation of food taboos is med. or low, rather than high (61) 0.81 of 69	12 13 / 5 56	15.29	0.422	0.00010
513	IN SIMMON'S STUDY OF TREATMENT OF THE AGED (43)	NOT IN SIMMON'S STUDY OF TREATMENT OF THE AGED (357)				
/33	Less where natural environment is other than "very harsh" (341) 0.67 of 43	More where natural environment is other than "very harsh" (341) 0.87 of 357	14 45 / 29 312	10.62	0.163	0.0011

Table 4 (continued)

			MATRIX	XSQ	PHI	XP/EP
513	**IN SIMMON'S STUDY OF TREATMENT OF THE AGED (43)**	NOT IN SIMMON'S STUDY OF TREATMENT OF THE AGED (357)				
/487	Less those about which principal ethnographies were published in 1930 or after (227) 0.63 of 19	More those about which principal ethnographies were published in 1930 or after (227) 0.90 of 240	7 25 / 12 215	9.04	0.187	0.0026
514	**IN SLATER'S STUDY OF NARCISSISM (90)**	NOT IN SLATER'S STUDY OF NARCISSISM (310)				

NOTE: There are no correlations with chi-square values of 9.00 or greater.

			MATRIX	XSQ	PHI	XP/EP
515	**IN STEPHENS' SAMPLE ON AVOIDANCE RELATIONSHIPS (52)**	NOT IN STEPHENS' SAMPLE ON AVOIDANCE RELATIONSHIPS (348)				
/6	Less located outside insular Pacific (330) 0.65 of 52	More located outside insular Pacific (330) 0.85 of 348	18 52 / 34 296	10.80	0.164	0.0010
/63	Husbandry, if present, is principally in the form of pigs, sheep, or goats, rather than bovine, equine, camel-like, or deer-like animals (74) 0.55 of 40	Husbandry, if present, is principally in the form of bovine, equine, camel-like or deer-like animals, rather than pigs, sheep or goats (152) 0.72 of 186	18 134 / 22 52	9.74	−0.208	0.0018
/449	Observation of food taboos is high, rather than medium or low (25) 0.57 of 28	Observation of food taboos is medium or low, rather than high (61) 0.84 of 58	16 9 / 12 49	13.91	0.402	0.0002
/450	More where observation of food taboos is high or medium, rather than low (60) 0.96 of 28	Less where observation of food taboos is high or medium, rather than low (60) 0.57 of 58	27 33 / 1 25	12.18	0.376	0.0005
516	**IN SWANSON'S SAMPLE ON LOCAL JURISDICTION, AS MODIFIED BY ETHNOGRAPHIC ATLAS (331)**	NOT IN SWANSON'S SAMPLE ON LOCAL JURISDICTION, AS MODIFIED BY ETHNOGRAPHIC ATLAS (69)				
/54	Food production is by intensive or simple agriculture, rather than by incipient food production (192) 0.83 of 229	Food production is by incipient food production, rather than by intensive or simple agriculture (46) 0.78 of 9	190 2 / 39 7	16.78	0.266	0.00005

Table 4 (continued)

		MATRIX	XSQ	PHI	XP/EP
516 IN SWANSON'S SAMPLE ON LOCAL JURISDICTION, AS MODIFIED BY *ETHNOGRAPHIC ATLAS* (331)	NOT IN SWANSON'S SAMPLE ON LOCAL JURISDICTION, AS MODIFIED BY *ETHNOGRAPHIC ATLAS* (69)				
/56 Food production is by simple agriculture, rather than by incipient food production (101) 0.72 of 140	In all cases food production is by incipient food production, rather than by simple agriculture (46) 1.00 of 7	101 0 / 39 7	12.96	0.297	0.0003
/62 Animal husbandry of some kind is present (228) 0.68 of 331	Animal husbandry of any kind is absent (172) 0.94 of 69	224 7 / 107 65	86.69	0.466	0.0000000
517 IN SWANSON'S SAMPLE ON HIGH GODS, AS MODIFIED BY *EA* (260)	NOT IN SWANSON'S SAMPLE ON HIGH GODS, AS MODIFIED BY *EA* (140)				
/62 Husbandry of some kind is present (228) 0.67 of 260	Husbandry of any kind is absent (172) 0.61 of 140	174 54 / 86 86	28.70	0.268	0.0000001
518 IN UDY'S STUDY OF WORK ORGANIZATION (105).	NOT IN UDY'S STUDY OF WORK ORGANIZATION (295)				
/488 More those about which principal ethnographies were published before 1950 (185) 0.87 of 70	Less those about which principal ethnographies were published before 1950 (185) 0.66 of 187	61 124 / 9 63	9.95	0.197	0.0016
519 IN VEROFF'S STUDY OF ACHIEVEMENT MOTIVATION IN FOLK TALES (36)	NOT IN VEROFF'S STUDY OF ACHIEVEMENT MOTIVATION IN FOLK TALES (364)				

NOTE: There are no correlations with chi-square values of 9.00 or greater.

		MATRIX	XSQ	PHI	XP/EP
520 IN B.B. WHITING'S STUDY OF SORCERY (40)	NOT IN B.B. WHITING'S STUDY OF SORCERY (360)				
/333 In all cases age at beginning of training in heterosexual play inhibition is 8 yrs. or higher (8) 1.00 of 7	Age at beginning of training in heterosexual play inhibition is lower than 8 years (8) 0.89 of 9	7 1 / 0 8	9.14	0.756	0.0014

Table 4 (continued)

	IN-group	NOT-IN group	MATRIX	XSQ	PHI	XP/EP
520	IN B.B. WHITING'S STUDY OF SORCERY (40)	NOT IN B.B. WHITING'S STUDY OF SORCERY (360)				
/428	A high god, if present and active, does not support human morality, rather than supporting it (26) 0.80 of 10	A high god, if present and active, supports human morality, rather than not supporting it (61)	2 59 / 8 18	10.98	−0.355	0.0009
/488	In all cases those about which principal ethnographies were published before 1950 (185) 1.00 of 25	Less those about which principal ethnographies were published before 1950 (185) 0.69 of 232	25 160 / 0 72	9.29	0.190	0.0023
522	IN M.G. WHITING'S STUDY OF DIET (82)	NOT IN M.G. WHITING'S STUDY OF DIET (318)				
/306	Early dependence satisfaction potential is high (28) 0.69 of 36	Early dependence satisfaction potential is low (24) 0.81 of 16	25 3 / 11 13	9.51	0.428	0.0020
523	IN WHITING & CHILD'S STUDY OF CHILD TRAINING & PERSONALITY (61)	NOT IN WHITING & CHILD'S STUDY OF CHILD TRAINING & PERSONALITY (339)				
/6	Less located outside insular Pacific (330) 0.67 of 61	More located outside insular Pacific (330) 0.85 of 339	20 50 / 41 289	10.43	0.162	0.0012
/450	More where observation of food taboos is high or medium, rather than low (60) 0.96 of 24	Less where observation of food taboos is high or medium, rather than low (60) 0.60 of 62	23 37 / 1 25	9.05	0.325	0.0021
/488	More those about which principal ethnographies were published before 1950 (185) 0.96 of 45	Less those about which principal ethnographies were published before 1950 (185) 0.67 of 212	43 142 / 2 70	13.65	0.230	0.0002
524	IN WHITING, KLUCKHOHN AND ANTHONY'S STUDY OF MALE INITIATION CEREMONIES (44)	NOT IN WHITING, KLUCKHOHN AND ANTHONY'S STUDY OF MALE INITIATION CEREMONIES (356)				
/449	Observation of food taboos is high, rather than medium or low (25) 0.71 of 17	Observation of food taboos is medium or low, rather than high (61) 0.81 of 69	12 13 / 5 56	15.29	0.422	0.00010

Therefore cases of significant differences do not necessarily indicate that the contributor's sample is biased with respect to the culture trait in question; but to the extent that the four-hundred-society sample is taken as representative, this conclusion is at least suggested. Our main concern here is with sampling biases which may affect the conclusions derived from a cross-cultural study of some topic. Thus we are particularly interested in cases where the contributor's sample and the four-hundred-society "Ethnographic Atlas" sample differ significantly with respect to a variable theoretically connected with the topic of the study. A number of such cases occur in the data, and will be mentioned below. We leave it to the reader to assess the importance of the other correlations shown in Table 4. Obviously, some are of little interest, and perhaps should not have been included at all; the tendency for several of the studies to include societies described before 1950, rather than after, is generally explained by the year in which the study was published —Simmons (Paragraph 513) could not have used monographs published after 1950 since his study of the aged was published in 1945.

In singling out the following correlations our aim is to demonstrate the existence of possible biases in cross-cultural studies. We have not attempted an exhaustive analysis of all the correlations shown in Table 4. No doubt the reader will find others which seem to him theoretically important.

Our first example comes from Anthony's study of male initiation rites (Paragraph 490). Statement /370 indicates that the segregation of adolescent boys is significantly more frequent among the societies of Anthony's sample than among those not considered by Anthony. Theoretically, this difference may have had an important bearing on Anthony's conclusions about male initiation practices.

Certain correlations from the studies of sex by Ford (498) and Ford and Beach (499) also deserve attention. In both, the samples used include a significantly higher percentage of cultures with permissive attitudes toward premarital sexual relations than is found among cultures not considered in these studies (see Statements 498/391, 499/390, and 499/391). The samples for both these studies were drawn from the Human Relations Area Files, which cannot be taken as a representative sampling universe. One indication of a sampling bias comes from Statement /6 of Paragraph 499; i.e., the sample for the Ford and Beach study includes considerably more societies from the insular Pacific—societies with generally permissive attitudes toward sex —than does the four-hundred-society sample from the "Ethnographic Atlas."

Our final example comes from Simmons' study of the treatment of the aged (Paragraph 513). In a considerably greater proportion of cases Simmons' sample includes societies with "very harsh" natural environments. (See Statement /33.) We cannot say for certain what effect this has on his results, but it does seem worthy of consideration.

Table 5
FREQUENCY OF INCLUSION OF SOCIETIES IN CONTRIBUTOR'S SAMPLES

	In from 6 to 27 Contributor's Samples[1]	In from 1 to 5 Contributor's Samples[2]	Not in any Contributor's Samples[3]	Totals
In HRAF List	71	50	22	143
Not in HRAF List	37	87	133	257
Totals	108	137	155	400

c .392 χ^2 73.69   p 0.0000001

[1] These cultures are listed in the left column of Paragraph 526, Textor 1967.
[2] These cultures are listed in the right column of Paragraph 526, Textor 1967.
[3] These cultures are listed in the right column of Paragraph 525, Textor 1967.

Appendix I   Subject (Column) Headings for the Methodological Variables used in *The Cross-Cultural Summary*

PARA. NO.	RIGHT COLUMN	LEFT COLUMN
481	Cultures where the principal ethnographers have been American	Cultures where the principal ethnographers have been other than American
482	Cultures where the principal ethnographers have been British	Cultures where the principal ethnographers have been other than British
483	Cultures where the principal ethnographers have been American, rather than British	Cultures where the principal ethnographers have been British, rather than American
484	Cultures where the principal ethnographers have been German	Cultures where the principal ethnographers have been other than German
485	Cultures where the principal ethnographers have been French	Cultures where the principal ethnographers have been other than French
486	Cultures about which the principal ethnographies were published before 1930, rather than in 1950 or after	Cultures about which the principal ethnographies were published in 1950 or after, rather than before 1930
487	Cultures about which the principal ethnographies were published before 1930	Cultures about which the principal ethnographies were published in 1930 or after
488	Cultures about which the principal ethnographies were published before 1950	Cultures about which the principal ethnographies were published in 1950 or after
489	Cultures included in Ackerman's study of divorce	Cultures not included in Ackerman's study of divorce
490	Cultures included in Anthony's sample on male initiation rites	Cultures not included in Anthony's sample on male initiation rites
491	Cultures included in Apple's study of grandparenthood	Cultures not included in Apple's study of grandparenthood
492	Cultures included in Ayres' study of female initiation rites	Cultures not included in Ayres' study of female initiation rites
493	Cultures included in Bacon, Barry and Child's study of child rearing	Cultures not included in Bacon, Barry and Child's study of child rearing
494	Cultures included in Barry's study of art	Cultures not included in Barry's study of art
495	Cultures included in Brown's study of female initiation rites	Cultures not included in Brown's study of female initiation rites
496	Cultures included in D'Andrade's study of dreams	Cultures not included in D'Andrade's study of dreams
497	Cultures included in Evan's study of law	Cultures not included in Evan's study of law
498	Cultures included in Ford's study of sex	Cultures not included in Ford's study of sex
499	Cultures included in Ford and Beach's sample of sexual expression by the young	Cultures not included in Ford and Beach's sample on sexual expression by the young
500	Cultures included in Freeman and Winch's study of societal complexity	Cultures not included in Freeman and Winch's study of societal complexity

PARA. NO.	RIGHT COLUMN	LEFT COLUMN
501	Cultures included in Goodman's study of ascetic mourning behavior	Cultures not included in Goodman's study of ascetic mourning behavior
502	Cultures included in Harley's study of adolescent peer groups	Cultures not included in Harley's study of adolescent peer groups
503	Cultures included in Hickman's study of the folk-urban continuum	Cultures not included in Hickman's study of the folk-urban continuum
504	Cultures included in Horton's study of alcoholism	Cultures not included in Horton's study of alcoholism
505	Cultures included in Jackson's study of criminal law and medicine	Cultures not included in Jackson's study of criminal law and medicine
506	Cultures included in Lambert, Triandis, and Wolf's study of supernatural beings	Cultures not included in Lambert, Triandis, and Wolf's study of supernatural beings
507	Cultures included in Leary's study of food taboos	Cultures not included in Leary's study of food taboos
508	Cultures included in McClelland's study of achievement motivation	Cultures not included in McClelland's study of achievement motivation
509	Cultures included in Moni Nag's study of fertility	Cultures not included in Moni Nag's study of fertility
510	Cultures included in Naroll's study of societal complexity	Cultures not included in Naroll's study of societal complexity
511	Cultures included in Roberts, Arth, and Bush's sample on games, as modified by the Ethnographic Atlas	Cultures not included in Roberts, Arth, and Bush's sample on games, as modified by the Ethnographic Atlas
512	Cultures included in Shirley and Romney's study of love magic	Cultures not included in Shirley and Romney's study of love magic
513	Cultures included in Simmons' study of the treatment of the aged	Cultures not included in Simmons' study of the treatment of the aged
514	Cultures included in Slater's study of narcissism	Cultures not included in Slater's study of narcissism
515	Cultures included in Stephen's sample on avoidance relationships	Cultures not included in Stephen's sample on avoidance relationships
516	Cultures included in Swanson's sample on local jurisdiction, as modified by the Ethnographic Atlas	Cultures not included in Swanson's sample on local jurisdiction, as modified by the Ethnographic Atlas
517	Cultures included in Swanson's sample on the high gods, as modified by the Ethnographic Atlas	Cultures not included in Swanson's sample on the high gods, as modified by the Ethnographic Atlas
518	Cultures included in Udy's study of work organization	Cultures not included in Udy's study of work organization
519	Cultures included in Veroff's study of achievement motivation as revealed in folk tales	Cultures not included in Veroff's study of achievement motivation as revealed in folk tales
520	Cultures included in B: B. Whiting's study of sorcery	Cultures not included in B. B. Whiting's study of sorcery

PARA. NO.	RIGHT COLUMN	LEFT COLUMN
522	Cultures included in M. G. Whiting's study of diet	Cultures not included in M. G. Whiting's study of diet
523	Cultures included in Whiting and Child's study of child training and personality	Cultures not included in Whiting and Child's study of child training and personality
524	Cultures included in Whiting, Kluckhohn, and Anthony's study of male initiation ceremonies	Cultures not included in Whiting, Kluckhohn, and Anthony's study of male initiation ceremonies
525	Cultures included in at least one contributor's sample (disregarding samples expanded by the Ethnographic Atlas)	Cultures not included in any contributor's sample (disregarding samples expanded by the Ethnographic Atlas)
526	Cultures included in between six and twenty-seven contributor's samples (disregarding samples expanded by the Ethnographic Atlas)	Cultures included in between one and five contributor's samples (disregarding samples expanded by the Ethnographic Atlas)
527	Cultures that belong to the fifty percent that have purple whiskers (200)	Cultures that belong to the fifty percent that do not have purple whiskers (200)
528	Cultures that belong to the fifty percent that have purple whiskers (where N equals 200 and there is a residue of 200) (100)	Cultures that belong to the fifty percent that do not have purple whiskers (where N equals 200 and there is a residue of 200) (100)
529	Cultures that belong to the fifty percent that have purple whiskers (where N equals 100 and there is a residue of 300) (50)	Cultures that belong to the fifty percent that do not have purple whiskers (where N equals 100 and there is a residue of 300) (50)
530	Cultures that belong to the fifty percent that have purple whiskers (where N equals 50 and there is a residue of 350) (25)	Cultures that belong to the fifty percent that do not have purple whiskers (where N equals 50 and there is a residue of 350 (25)
531	Cultures that belong to the fifty percent that have purple whiskers (where N equals 25 and there is a residue of 375) (13)	Cultures that belong to the fifty percent that do not have purple whiskers (where N equals 25 and there is a residue of 375) (12)
532	Cultures that belong to the forty percent that have blue whiskers (160)	Cultures that belong to the sixty percent that do not have blue whiskers (240)
533	Cultures that belong to the thirty percent that have green whiskers (120)	Cultures that belong to the seventy percent that do not have green whiskers (280)
534	Cultures that belong to the twenty percent that have pink whiskers (80)	Cultures that belong to the eighty percent that do not have pink whiskers (320)
535	Cultures that belong to the ten percent that have yellow whiskers (40)	Cultures that belong to the ninety percent that do not have yellow whiskers (360)
536	Cultures that belong to the five percent that have white whiskers (20)	Cultures that belong to the ninety-five percent that do not have white whiskers (380)

BIBLIOGRAPHY

ANONYMOUS
1967 The HRAF quality control sample universe. *Behavioral Science Notes* 2:81–103.

BANKS, ARTHUR S., and ROBERT B. TEXTOR
1963 *A cross-polity survey.* Cambridge, Mass., M.I.T. Press.

MURDOCK, GEORGE PETER
1957 World ethnographic sample. *American Anthropologist* 59:664–687.

1962– Ethnographic Atlas. *Ethnology* 1:113–
1963 134, 265–286, 387–403, 533–545; 2:109–133.

NAROLL, RAOUL
1962 *Data quality control.* New York, Free Press.

TEXTOR, ROBERT B.
1967 *A cross-cultural summary.* New Haven, HRAF Press.

CHAPTER 35

Societal Research Archives System: Retrieval, Quality Control and Analysis of Comparative Data

DOUGLAS R. WHITE

INTRODUCTION

The Societal Research Archives System was created by the author in 1966 as a computer-based retrieval and research facility for comparative data in social science.[1] The basic idea was to integrate all of the available cross-societal coded data from published and unpublished sources into a single data base, and secondly to develop computer programs which would facilitate all of the steps in comparative research, from sample selection and data retrieval to correlation, data quality control, and testing for genetic, diffusional, or functional sources of correlation. This paper will serve to explain the present operation of the system. Additional work began in 1968 at the University of Pittsburgh's Cross-Cultural Cumulative Coding Center on the refinement and expansion of the system, which will be the subject of a future report.

SCOPE OF MATERIALS INCLUDED IN S.R.A.S.

As of fall, 1967, the comparative ratings from fifty-six of the major books and articles in the cross-cultural field have been incorporated into the S.R.A.S. computerized archive (see Appendix; and White 1967a). This represents 40 per cent of the approximate

total number of such publications, but over 90 per cent of the actual ratings, since the remaining publications contain fairly scanty data.

Three major cross-polity surveys (Banks and Textor, Rummel, and Russett *et al.*) have also been incorporated on an experimental basis. Ultimately, it is expected that S.R.A.S. will be entirely cross-disciplinary, including data on all types of social units from nations, states and cities to villages, tribes and bands.

Comparative psychology, sociology, political science, and anthropology are already well represented by the research topics presently included and rated in the archive. Also planned by the author is the addition of data which would be of use in the study of social change and in comparative history. The first involves delimiting a sample of the societies presently in the archive which can be re-rated for a second time-period, or of drawing up a new sample of societies in which change has been well documented. The second involves adapting the data of comparative history so that it may be coded for successive periods in the great historical traditions. Kroeber's data from *Configurations of Culture Growth* have already been key-punched to form one nucleus of coded material for a comparative historical data pool which will be expanded over the next two-year period.

S.R.A.S. AS A REACTIVE RETRIEVAL-RESEARCH SYSTEM

A common dilemma in the use of computers for social research has been that designs were applied to retrieval of informa-

[1] A portion of the funds were available through an NIMH Predoctoral Fellowship Grant #5-F1-MH-25, 516-03; another portion through the University of Minnesota Graduate School. The author would like to thank Dr. E. Adamson Hoebel, whose sponsorship was instrumental in establishing the project, in addition to others who worked on the project. The Societal Research Archive System, begun at Minnesota, has been transferred to the University of Pittsburgh Department of Anthropology.

tion, instead of to the research process itself. The real potential for the computer in social science, largely untapped as yet, lies in the areas of communication: 1) communication between a researcher and a "reactive" system which can provide an information pool, research procedures and results in a form selected by the user; 2) communications *between* researchers, and storing of information and research programs via telecommunications and time-sharing computer systems; and 3) educational communications, or the use of a select body of data and retrieval or research procedures for individual or classroom "reactive" learning, or question-and-answer exchange between learner and the learning system, or computerized consoles.

The technological component—or console —must be backed up by a well-designed "Reactive Retrieval-Research System" (with the appropriate acronym of the "3 R's") which is a complex of data-storage equipment, retrieval and analytic programs, and a mediator language very close to plain English which enables the user to ask questions or to request that operations be done with the data and available programs, and to specify how the results be returned to him. Behind the ultimate simplicity of a user at a keyboard, communicating in his native language, there is of course a technological mazeway of which he need not be aware in all its detail. The ultimate technological simplicity, however, is that once a single such system is established (and hopefully this will be the case at the University of Pittsburgh), it is accessible to anyone, no matter how far away, through telecommunications (telephone or telegraph dial-ups), just as though he were in an office adjoining the computer center on one side, and the S.R.A.S. staff on the other.

It must be stressed that while all of the operational programming for such a "3 R's" console system has been completed (i.e., programs which do the required operations for each step in comparative research), the development of this system by the author is still in its experimental stages, supported by the Cross-Cultural Cumulative Coding Center at Pittsburgh. Since the "mediator language" for the reactive console system has not yet been translated into "plain English" with built-in programmed-learning devices to aid the uninitiated user, those desiring to use the system in its present state should have a fair

amount of technical sophistication in computer languages. Anyone seriously interested in establishing telecommunication linkage with the console system, or in using these facilities at the University of Pittsburgh, now or in the future, should contact the author. With the coming diffusion of console units across the country, it will not be long before the console system is available for research and experimental teaching use on a national basis. This will be one of the objectives of the Center at Pittsburgh.

THEORETICAL CROSS-CULTURE RESEARCH STRATEGIES

There are two kinds of strategies for research underpinning the existence of S.R.A.S. The first involves the possibility of culling out the statistically significant correlations from the consolidated data pool containing all available cross-cultural studies. After this step, a variety of control variables can be applied to determine whether a particular correlation is probably due to historical factors (common origin or common diffusion for those societies in which the correlations hold good), or may be due to kinds of systematic error endemic to comparative data (errors in data collection, bias or inadequacy in ethnographies, or misinterpretation by coders). Naroll's work on "Galton's Problem" (1965) and *Data Quality Control* (1962) has shed sufficient light on these problems that they need not be discussed here in detail. Suffice it to say that *only after the influence of spurious or historical factors has been screened out can the remaining correlations legitimately be considered the subject for functional explanation.* It is, of course, also possible that a correlation is due to chance, a possibility which can be evaluated statistically by the null hypothesis, but is ultimately subject to retest using a new sample. Such a rigorous culling out of "genuine" correlations is the first research strategy which is facilitated by S.R.A.S. The extreme laboriousness of compiling "control variables" and of amassing statistical computations prevents a culling out in most contemporary cross-cultural studies. By use of the computer, S.R.A.S. goes one better: given a correlation between two variables, A and B, the entire data matrix can be searched for any other variables which correlate highly with both, and which thus may play the role of "intervening variables," or account for the correlation between A and B. The pooling of all comparative coded data, with a present inventory of over two thousand variables, gives great depth to this possibility. Thus, three dimensions of refinement in research have been added which were not formerly feasible in cross-cultural methodology: intensive historical and data quality controls, and identification of other intervening variables. Each of these points are discussed in the paragraphs below, under the heading Steps in Research Using S.R.A.S., steps 2, 3 and 4, 6 and 7.

A second research strategy made possible through S.R.A.S. (in White n.d.) operates on the Bayesian principle of seeking correlations which do not confirm theoretical expectations. This becomes a take-off point for testing the extensibility of present theoretical models versus the need for developing alternative models which would differ in their deductive implications and so might better incorporate a range of facts and correlations which the older model could not explain adequately. Strodtbeck (1964) has noted the suitability of the cross-cultural method to this kind of "discovery procedure," but in labeling the technique "retroduction" or "abduction," in the tradition of C. S. Pierce, he loads the dice in favor of always extending our existing models instead of working out better alternatives which may start from different assumptions. (For a discussion of a Bayesian view contrary to Strodtbeck and Pierce see White n.d.)

CROSS-CULTURAL RESEARCH STRATEGIES APPLIED

The S.R.A.S. materials are not by any means limited in their use to world-wide or "hologeistic" comparisons or the standard "cross-cultural methods." The author, for example, has applied such coded material toward an interregional analysis of differences in the organization of kinship systems in North American and African cultures (White 1967a), establishing correlations which hold for one continent but not for another. A regional comparison on the order of Driver's (1957) work on North America, or Murdock's (1959) on Africa, could be attempted from the cumulative results of cross-cultural investigations, selecting out the societies for that

area. Such regional studies could also serve as a checkpoint for the reliability and validity of the existing cross-cultural codes and categories, and would undoubtedly raise significant new ones.

It is equally feasible to do studies of particular types of societies drawn from the world's population, such as the Aberle (1961) study of matrilineal societies. Variables in the S.R.A.S. data pool could be used, if applicable, as the basis for drawing such specialized samples.

Time-depth studies, using data coded from periods of history as known for a sample of societies, will also be feasible through S.R.A.S., although such data in coded form is only beginning to be available (see p. 676 on plans for developing such a data pool).

Since S.R.A.S. is intended for use by social scientists without any specialized computer training (to the specialists, a USER-ORIENTED RETRIEVAL-RESEARCH SYSTEM), the remainder of the paper presents, step by step, a cross-cultural research procedure using the S.R.A.S. retrieval and research analysis programs.

STEPS IN RESEARCH USING S.R.A.S.

The steps in cross-cultural research using S.R.A.S. are outlined below. The operating programs essential to steps 1, 4 and 5 are presently installed and workable, while the "control variable" programs of steps 2 and 3 are projected on the basis of data pertaining to these control factors, which will be added within the two-year period 1970–1972. Step 6 is simply the result of having screened out spurious or historically-produced correlations in steps 2, 4 and 5, and is in this sense operational. Step 7 still awaits programming, but presents no theoretical problems. Step 8 does not rely on programming, and is in this sense workable, but will be fully significant only when all the other steps are operational.

All of the programming necessary for these steps—both retrieval and analytic procedures —will ultimately be written up in the form of a manual.

1. Sampling and Integrating Data from Different Sources

For most cross-cultural research designs using precoded data, the problem is to draw a *representative* sample from the available two thousand societies and yet, through a strategic choice of societies, to maximize the amount of coded data relevant to the research topic. The use of three retrieval programs, DRT I, II, and III, is sufficient for all possible permutations of this sampling dilemma: DRT I establishes the *minimal criteria* for inclusion of a society (e.g., that it has been rated in certain of the studies) and culls out all societies which fit the criteria; DRT II then retrieves selected ratings for only these societies; and DRT III accepts criteria for a stratified sample (e.g., one society per culture area) and chooses the specified number of societies per strata by taking those societies which are most complete for the specified variables. DRT I and II are both operational; DRT III is being programmed at Pittsburgh. As discussed previously, regional samples and special-purpose samples (e.g., matrilineal societies) can easily be drawn using these retrieval programs.

2. Data Quality Control

Differences in the ethnographic material on societies can originate from five major classes of systematic error in comparative codes: a) differences in the *quantity* of material may reflect a selection preference for certain types of societies which are then overrepresented in a sample; b) differences in the *quality* of the material may lead to error such as the case where a cultural feature is rated as present because it is described in more complete ethnographies, and rated as absent where there has simply been a failure to report on this subject at all; c) differences in *coding techniques* may compound error, such as the case where a coder's "hunches" are followed in those descriptions which are more scanty and subject to interpretation; d) differences in ethnographers' techniques may lead to *source* errors, such as the case where ethnographers who speak the language tend to obtain better data on witchcraft, so that witchcraft ratings can be biased by this factor; and e) differences in the type of primary field data which the ethnographer has used may reflect actual vs. verbal behavior in the society, and can produce *origin error,* as in the case where ethnographers using informants' reports tend to describe a lower incidence of drunkenness than those ethnographers using an actual case-incidence method.

For shorthand purposes, these can be referred to as selection bias (quantity errors), quality errors, coding errors, source errors, and origin errors. "Data quality control" for these factors can be rated as they apply to the ethnographic material of a society *in toto,* or as they apply to material on a particular cultural domain.

Naroll (1962) has developed the technique of data quality analysis, through intercorrelation of coded ratings (on cultures) with quality control ratings (on sources and techniques in each of the five classes of systematic error). As he has recently pointed out (1967:77–78), the influence of systematic error on coded ratings need not be a simple monotonic correlation, and the possibility of curvilinearity should be investigated as well.

The S.R.A.S. is designed to accumulate and facilitate the use of quality control ratings, such as planned for the new HRAF Quality Control Sample of sixty societies (*Behavioral Science Notes* 2:63–69 and 81–88). Pittsburgh's Cross-Cultural Cumulative Coding Center will also begin to provide such ratings (Murdock and White 1969). A matrix of all codes correlated with all quality ratings can be computer-generated and updated as part of the S.R.A.S. data pool. Any coded cultural variable which has been found to correlate with a source of systematic error will be *tagged* so that the user is aware of this limitation. The user must then be particularly circumspect in drawing interpretations from data which have been so tagged. In the extreme case, where the independent *and* dependent variables or a correlation have been tagged by the same systematic error source(s), the correlation may be completely spurious, or be a by-product of such systematic error.

In an optimally designed reactive console system, the quality control tag-search would be performed as a matter of course, and the user would be automatically notified of possible sources of error in his variables.

3. Structural Controls for Comparability of Societal Units

A "world sample" of societies, primitive and peasant, ancient and modern, has been the tool of most cross-cultural studies in attempting to generalize about cultural processes. A true world sample presupposes a diversity of conditions: some societies are indigenous and autonomous, others acculturated and dependent; some societies are actual communities, others are networks of shifting political alliances, still others highly complex centralized administrative structures.

There are many reasons why a researcher may want to select or control certain "strata" of the world's societies for comparative purposes (e.g., to study peasants, or politically autonomous peoples): a) the importance of such structural variables for cultural processes might suggest that these strata be examined separately (e.g., the hypothesis that societies may behave differently at different "levels of integration"); b) as a preliminary to construction of a societal typology and test of the coherence of such types; and c) the possibility that the definition of boundaries of the societies in the sample may have produced a bias in the cultural characteristics which are being analyzed. Leach (1960:137–138), for example, has said that the meaning of a "custom" when comparing the Tikopia (pop. 1,800) and the mainland Chinese (pop. 650 million odd) is so radically different—one being normative in the community sense, the other in a statistical sense—that quite different explanations are required.

To aid in dealing with the problem of definition of the social units in comparative studies, two classificatory devices have been included in the design of S.R.A.S.: 1) a typology of levels of integration (band/tribe/chiefdom/state, etc.); and 2) a trichotomy of the six "boundary" criteria by which social units are often defined (e.g., territorial, political, linguistic boundaries, etc.) as to whether the society is a *subset,* a *singular unit* or a *heterogeneous unit* with respect to each. This information is included along with other background data, in the codebook of societal characteristics.

4. Distributional Analysis: Diffusion and Historical Clusters

The problem of diffusion, or historical relations between cultures producing common constellations of social forms, has been one of the most besetting problems of comparative research ever since Galton raised the issue in 1889 when E. B. Tylor presented the first paper using statistics in cross-cul-

tural tabulations. The problem in the use of statistics to draw generalizations about "functional" relationships between traits, to quote Mr. Galton, is ". . . the degree to which the customs of the tribes and races which are compared together are independent. It might be that some of the tribes had derived them from a common source, so that they were duplicate copies of the same original" (in Moore 1961:26).

Stratified sampling from different culture areas has been used to circumvent the problem, but more recently Naroll (1961, 1964; Naroll and D'Andrade 1963) has proposed five solutions designed to sift out diffusion effects entirely; in three cases his method provides a relative evaluation of diffusion vs. functional hypothesis (i.e., the Cluster, Matched Pair, and Linked Pair methods).

A computer program by Naroll and Morrison has been incorporated into S.R.A.S. to calculate the "Linked Pair" (Naroll 1964) solution to Galton's problem by evaluation of the type of diffusion which has occurred with each pair of traits being investigated. The "Linked Pair" solution is the most elegant, but since it requires that societies must be aligned on a diffusion arc, it will be more convenient for some samples to have programs which utilize other solutions (this programming will be done at Pittsburgh, 1969–1971).

Naroll's solutions, however, are based upon the assumption that diffusion or common origin of traits will be reflected in geographical clustering of traits. Under conditions of migration or separation of historically related peoples, the most likely clustering of traits is not by geographic but *linguistic* propinquity, as an indication of past historical relationship. The case of sibling terminology (Murdock, 1968) is an excellent example of high genetic clustering, with a low incidence of borrowing.

The author has developed a method for calculating the degree of clustering of traits in branches of the world linguistic tree, as classified by continental affiliations, phyla, families and subfamilies (White 1966b). A computer program called "treesort" is being developed which summarizes the levels and particular branches at which such clustering is greatest. This will provide a more refined measure of true genetic common origin of trait clusters, as opposed to Naroll's measures of geographic clustering.

5. Mapping Data and Results

For distributional and historical analysis, there is perhaps no technique more useful than simply the mapping of trait distributions or of trait co-occurrences and clusters. This time-consuming process has also been transformed through the application of computer programming. The S.R.A.S. mapping program will plot society locations, trait and cluster distributions, continent by continent, at the rate of hundreds of maps per minute. Plots for sequential time-periods can also be prepared for diachronic analysis. Rough outlines of each continent and a wide choice of representational symbols are a feature of these maps.

6. Culling Out Likely "Functional Associations"

The quality control and distributional programs can be used to screen out those correlations which have possible functional significance barring those which are the result of selection bias, quality errors, coding errors, source errors, origin errors, and distributional clustering. Analogous to the results of *A Cross-Cultural Summary* (Textor 1967), but considerably refined, this can help to establish empirical materials for building of more sophisticated theories in comparative research.

7. Third Factor Controls

Having found a correlation between A and B which has potential functional significance, the researcher is in a position to ask whether there is any third variable, X, which might possibly "intervene" or be correlated with both A and B, and possibly be a "hidden factor" accounting for the association.

A computer program is currently being prepared which will intercorrelate *all* of the variables in the archive, similar to the results of Textor's (1967) undertaking. In this case, however, the results (some 36 *million* corre-

lations) would be packed in binary code on a magnetic tape with entry procedures for searching any given row or column of the matrix.

When this gigantic matrix is produced, the researcher will be able to utilize a second program which will "search" for all the X's which satisfy the condition of being correlated with both traits A and B. He will receive a print-out with an exhaustive list of all such possible "intervening variables" among the already coded cross-cultural variables. He can then apply the data quality control and distributional tests to determine whether any of these is a likely functional determinant of A and B.

This addition of an exhaustive "third factor" search is another example of the increase in sophistication of research design made possible through S.R.A.S.

8. Reformulation of Study Design

The most critical part of comparative research is the establishment of theoretical models and postulates. Once certain hypotheses have become provisionally accepted on the basis of S.R.A.S. correlational procedures and control tests, then the researcher may wish to construct a hypothetico-deductive model in which additional hypotheses, derived deductively, are to be tested. The S.R.A.S. is an ideal environment for this kind of "feedback" from the guidance of theoretical models, since it is easy to reformulate and test the new hypotheses through the same steps which have just been surveyed.

As S.R.A.S. expands or articulates with optimally researchable bodies of coded and descriptive materials, a computerized system for assaying previous results in theoretical domains (e.g., an inventory of hypotheses) could also be developed, to accelerate the feedback and reformulation process. Effective organization of our theoretical knowledge (discussed in White n.d.) would also aid greatly in the evaluation and construction of theoretical models. Such theoretical development will also suggest improved ways to generate new variables, by applying new coding procedures to the descriptive materials, as is planned in the Cross-Cultural Cumulative Coding Center at Pittsburgh.

MAKING S.R.A.S. AVAILABLE

The results of this experiment in comparative research are presently available to the academic community in three forms: 1) requests for information on specific variables can be automatically processed, given a sampling plan, or whole data decks for particular studies can be obtained; 2) S.R.A.S. user manuals are available, including prospecti, reference manuals for codes, variable names, society lists, cultural and linguistic classification, and papers on theoretical and applied problems associated with research methodology and developing the retrieval-research system (see White 1965, 1966a, 1966b, 1966c, 1967a, Gold and White 1966); 3) the entire archive and associated computer programs can be distributed, via magnetic tape, for those who want to experiment with their own procedures at another computer center. Dartmouth's Department of Anthropology and Project IMPRESS, for example, have installed a reactive research system using some of the S.R.A.S. cross-cultural materials.

Requests for information retrieval, punched-card decks, S.R.A.S. manuals, copies of the archive on magnetic tape, and information concerning the present and future development of the system and reactive console facilities should be directed to the author.

The development of the console system for reactive retrieval-research, including long-distance dial-ups from remote consoles at other institutions, will be part of the program of the Cross-Cultural Cumulative Coding Center (C⁵) at the University of Pittsburgh.

The C⁵ Center will also disseminate results of the project in another way, through publication in the journal *Ethnology* of significant correlations between variables in the data pool, and tests of whether these are likely due to systematic error, historical factors, or possible functional relationships. The C⁵ Center will provide the next needed step in the expansion of new codes, coding of new ethnographies, and extension of the existing codes in the literature to larger samples of societies. Expansion of the data base itself will provide the needed multiplicative effect of increasing the sample size for any given correlation, and increasing the capabilities and the pay-off of research through a reactive system such as the one described.

Appendix I

Bibliography of cross-cultural studies incorporated in S.R.A.S. as of mid-1967. Figures in parentheses indicate size of samples (s) and number of variables (v) per study.

ADDISS, PENNY, and CAROL FRIEDMAN
1963 *Cross-cultural data on marriage and divorce.* Unpublished study. Pittsburgh, University of Pittsburgh. (s–53; v–11)

APPLE, DORIAN
1956 The social structure of grandparenthood. *American Anthropologist* 58:656–663. (s–75; v–4)

AYRES, BARBARA C.
1954 *A cross-cultural study of factors relating to pregnancy taboos.* Unpublished doctoral dissertation. Cambridge, Mass., Radcliffe College. (s–35, 467; v–10)

BACON, M. K., I. L. CHILD, and H. BARRY III
1963 A cross-cultural study of the correlates of crime. *Journal of Abnormal Social Psychology* 66:291–300. (s–48; v–10)

BACON, MARGARET K., HERBERT BARRY III, IRVIN L. CHILD, and CHARLES SNYDER
1965 A cross-cultural study of drinking. *Quarterly Journal of Alcohol Studies* (Special Issue) Supplement No. 3. (s–111; v–99)

CARNEIRO, ROBERT L., and STEPHEN F. TOBIAS
1963a Application of scale analysis to the study of cultural evolution. *Transactions of the New York Academy of Sciences* 26:190–207. (s–100; v subset of item below)
1963b *Trait list to be used for the study of cultural evolution. Accompanying data.* Unpublished Mimeograph. New York, American Museum of Natural History. (s–100; v–354)

COHEN, YEHUDI A.
1964a The establishment of identity in a social nexus: the special case of initiation ceremonies and their relation to value and legal systems. *American Anthropologist* 66:529–552. (s–66; same data as below)
1964b *The transition from childhood to adolescence: cross-cultural studies of initiation ceremonies, legal systems and incest taboos.* Chicago, Aldine. (s–65; v–11)

DRIVER, HAROLD E.
1966 Geographical-historical versus psychofunctional explanations of kin avoidances. *Current Anthropology* 7:131–160. (s–277; v–6)

FISCHER, JOHN L.
1961 Art styles as cultural cognitive maps.

American Anthropologist 63:79–93. (s–29; v–4)

FORD, CLELLAN
1964   *A comparative study of human reproduction.* New Haven, Human Relations Area Files Press. (s–48; v–60)

FREEMAN, LINTON C.
1957   *An empirical test of folk-urbanism.* Ann Arbor, Mich., University Microfilms No. 23502. (s–52; v–48)

FREEMAN, LINTON C., and ROBERT F. WINCH
1957   Societal complexity: an empirical test of a typology of societies. *American Journal of Sociology* 62:461–466. (s–48; v–7)

HICKMAN, JOHN M.
1962   Dimensions of a complex concept: a method exemplified. (folk-urban continuum) *Human Organization* 21:214–218. (s–70; v–12)

HOBHOUSE, L. T., G. C. WHEELER, and M. GINSBURG
1915   *The material culture and social institu-*
(1965) *tions of the simpler peoples: an essay in correlation.* London, Routledge and Kegan Paul. (s–687; v–64)

HOMANS, GEORGE C., and DAVID M. SCHNEIDER
1955   *Marriage, authority and final causes.* Glencoe, Ill., Free Press. (s–31; v–3)

HORTON, DONALD
1943   The functions of alcohol in primitive societies. *Quarterly Journal of Alcohol Studies* 4:199–320. (s–77; v–10)

LAMBERT, WILLIAM W., LEIGH M. TRIANDIS, and MARGERY WOLF
1959   Some correlates of beliefs in the malevolence and benevolence of supernatural beings: a cross-cultural study. *Journal of Abnormal and Social Psychology* 58: 162–168. (s–62, 43; v–35)

MCCLELLAND, DAVID C.
1961   *The achieving society.* Princeton, N.J., Van Nostrand. (Nations s–50; v–8. Tribes s–52; v–11)

MURDOCK, GEORGE PETER
1949   *Social structure.* New York, Macmillan. (s–250; v–11)
1957   World ethnographic sample. *American Anthropologist* 59:664–687. (s–565; v–20)
1962– Ethnographic Atlas. In sequential issues
1967   of *Ethnology.* (s–1182; v–94)

MURPHY, H. B. M., E. D. WITTKOWER, and N. A. CHANCE
1964   Cross-cultural inquiry into the symptomatology of depression. *Transcultural Psychiatric Research* 1:5–18. (s–96; v–36)

NAROLL, RAOUL
1956   A preliminary index of social development. *American Anthropologist* 59:687–715. (s–30; v–4)
1960– *Northridge deterrence project: Reports*

1964   *1–34.* Mimeograph. Evanston, Ill., Northwestern University. (s–16; v–29) Uncoded. A revised version: *Military deterrence in history.* Albany, State University of N. Y. Press, 1971. With Vern Bullough and Frada Naroll.
1966   *Warfare, peaceful intercourse and territorial change: a cross-cultural survey.* Mimeograph. Evanston, Ill., Northwestern University. Summary published as: Does military deterrence deter? *Transactions* 3:14–20. (s–48; v–27)
1966   *Imperial cycles and world power.* American Anthropological Association Meetings, Pittsburgh. (s–28; v–18) An expanded version: Imperial Cycles and World Order. *Papers,* Peace Research Society (International), Vol. VII (1967); 83–101.
1969   *Thwarting disorientation and suicide: a cross-cultural survey.* Mimeograph. Evanston, Ill., Northwestern University. (s–58; v–9) A shortened version: Cultural determinants and the concept of the sick society. In Robert F. Edgerton and Stanley C. Plog, eds., *Changing perspectives in mental illness.* 1969. New York, Holt, Rinehart and Winston.

ROBERTS, JOHN M., MALCOLM ARCH, and ROBERT BUSH
1959   Games in culture. *American Anthropologist* 61:597–605. (s–51; v–2)

ROBERTS, JOHN M., and BRIAN J. SUTTON-SMITH
1962   Child training and game involvement. *Ethnology* 1:166–185. (s–56, 111; v–28)
1966   Cross-cultural correlates of games of chance. *Behavior Science Notes* 1:134–144. (Uses data from earlier studies via Textor's Cross-Cultural Summary tables; total of two hundred societies in all Robert's studies.)

ROBERTS, JOHN M., BRIAN SUTTON-SMITH, and ADAM KENDON
1963   Strategy in games and folktales. *Journal of Social Psychology* 61:185–199. (s–141, 25; data combined with the above)

SCHWARTZ, RICHARD D., and JAMES C. MILLER
1964   Legal evolution and societal complexity. *American Journal of Sociology* 70:159–169. (s–51; v–3)

SIMMONS, LEO W.
1945   *The role of the aged in primitive society.* New Haven, Yale University Press. (s–71; v–113)

STEPHENS, WILLIAM N.
1961   A cross-cultural study of menstrual taboos. *Genetic Psychology Monographs* 64:385–416. (s–71; v–20)
1962   *The Oedipus complex.* Glencoe, Ill., Free Press. (Includes D'Andrade's Kin Avoidances) (s–139; v–48)

1963 *The family in cross-cultural perspective.* New York, Holt, Rinehart and Winston. (s–29; v–50)

SWANSON, GUY L.
1960 *Birth of the gods.* Ann Arbor, University of Michigan Press. (s–50; v–41)

SWEETSER, DORRIAN APPLE
1963 Asymmetry in intergenerational family relationships. *Social Forces* 41:346–362. (s–18; v–6)

1966a On the incompatibility of duty and affection; a note on the role of the mother's brother. *American Anthropologist* 68: 1009–1013. (s–102; v–see above)

1966b Avoidance, social affiliation, and the incest taboo. *Ethnology* 5:304–316. (s–110; v–see above)

TATJE, TERRENCE A., and RAOUL NAROLL
1970 See Chapter 40 of this handbook. Two measures of societal complexity: an empirical cross-cultural comparison. (s–58; v–14) See Chapter 40.

UDY, STANLEY H.
1959 *The organization of work; production in non-industrialized societies.* New Haven, Human Relations Area Files Press. (s–150; v–26)

1962 Administrative rationality, social setting and organizational development. *American Journal of Sociology* 68:299–308. (s–34; v–12)

WHITING, BEATRICE B.
1950 *A cross-cultural study of sorcery and social control. Paiute Sorcery.* Viking Fund Publications in Anthropology 15: 82–91. (s–50; v–4)

WHITING, JOHN W. M.
1959 Sorcery, sin, and the superego: a cross-cultural study of some mechanisms of social control. In Marshall R. Jones, ed.,

Nebraska symposium on motivation. Lincoln, Neb., University of Nebraska Press. (s–36; v–17)

1964 The effects of climate on certain cultural practices. In Ward H. Goodenough, ed., *Explorations in cultural anthropology.* New York, McGraw-Hill. (s–177; v–11)

WHITING, JOHN W. M., and IRWIN L. CHILD
1953 *Child training and personality.* New Haven, Yale University Press. Paperbound. (s–75; v–35)

WHITING, JOHN W. M., RICHARD KLUCKHOHN, and ALBERT S. ANTHONY
1958 The function of male initiation ceremonies at puberty. In E. E. Maccoby, T. M. Newcomb, and E. L. Hartley, eds., *Readings in social psychology.* New York, Holt, Rinehart and Winston. (s–55; v–7)

WHITING, MARJORIE
1956 *A cross-cultural study of nutrition.* Cambridge, Harvard University (doctoral dissertation). (s–118; v–23)

WITTKOWER, M. D., H. B. MURPHY, and J. FREID (eds.)
1960 *Special issue on schizophrenia.* Review and Newsletter: Transcultural Research on Mental Health Problems 9. (s–90; v–39)

YOUNG, FRANK
1962 The function of male initiation ceremonies: A cross-cultural test of an alternative hypothesis. *American Journal of Sociology* 67:379–396. (s–62; data incorporated with item below)

1965 *Initiation ceremonies: A cross-cultural study of status dramatization.* New York, Bobbs-Merrill. (s–77; v–67)

YOUNG, FRANK, and ALBERT S. BACDAYAN
1962 Menstrual taboos and social rigidity. *Ethnology* 4:225–240. (s–65; v–5)

BIBLIOGRAPHY

ABERLE, DAVID F.
1961 Matrilineal descent in cross-cultural perspective. In David M. Schneider and Kathleen Gough, eds., *Matrilineal kinship.* Berkeley and Los Angeles, University of California Press.

ANONYMOUS
1967 Summary of a conference discussion on cross-cultural research. *Behavior Science Notes* 2:63–69.

BANKS, ARTHUR S., and ROBERT B. TEXTOR
1963 *A cross-cultural survey.* Cambridge, Mass., M.I.T. Press.

DRIVER, HAROLD, and WILLIAM MASSEY
1957 Comparative studies of North American Indians. *Transactions of the American Philosophical Society* 47:165–456.

GOLD, GERALD L., and DOUGLAS R. WHITE
1966 *Dictionary of societal variables used in cross-cultural studies.* Mimeograph. Minneapolis, University of Minnesota.

HUMAN RELATIONS AREA FILES
1967 The HRAF quality control sample universe. *Behavior Science Notes* 2:81–88.

KROEBER, ALFRED
1944 *Configurations of culture growth.* Berkeley, University of California Press.

LEACH, EDMUND
1960   Review of Stanley Udy, *Organization of work. American Sociological Review* 25: 136–138.

MOORE, FRANK
1961   *Readings in cross-cultural methodology.* New Haven, HRAF Press.

MURDOCK, GEORGE R.
1959   *Africa: its peoples and their culture history.* New York, McGraw-Hill.
1968   Patterns of sibling terminology. *Ethnology* 7:1–32.

MURDOCK, GEORGE R., and DOUGLAS WHITE
1969   Standard cross-cultural sample. *Ethnology* 8:329–369.

NAROLL, RAOUL
1961   Two solutions to Galton's problem. *Philosophy of Science* 28:15–39.
1962   *Data quality control.* New York, Free Press.
1964   A fifth solution to Galton's problem. *American Anthropologist* 66:863–867.
1965   Galton's problem: the logic of cross-cultural analysis. *Social Research* 32: 428–458.
1967   The proposed HRAF probability sample. *Behavior Science Notes* 2:70–80.

NAROLL, RAOUL, and ROY D'ANDRADE
1963   Two further solutions to Galton's problem. *American Anthropologist* 65:1053–1067.

RUSSETT, BRUCE M., et al.
1964   *World handbook of political and social indicators.* New Haven and London, Yale University Press.

RUMMEL, RUDOLPH
1965   The Dimensionality of Nations Project. In Richard Merritt and Stein Rokkan, eds., *Comparing nations.* New Haven, Yale University Press.

STRODTBECK, FRED L.
1964   Consideration of meta-method in cross-cultural studies. *American Anthropologist* 66:223–234.

TEXTOR, ROBERT B.
1967   *A cross-cultural summary.* New Haven, HRAF Press.

WHITE, DOUGLAS R.
1965   *Prospectus: Societal Research Archives System.* Ditto. Minneapolis, University of Minnesota.
1966a   *Index of societal samples used in cross-cultural studies.* Mimeograph. Minneapolis, University of Minnesota. (2nd edition, 1967.)
1966b   *Linguistic and areal classifications of world cultures and a new refinement of Galton's problem.* Mimeograph. Minneapolis, University of Minnesota.
1966c   *Problems of cross-cultural research.* Ditto. Minneapolis, University of Minnesota.
1967a   *Compendium of coded materials from cross-cultural literature: the Societal Research Archives System.* Mimeograph. Minneapolis, University of Minnesota.
1967b   *Concomitant variation in kinship structures.* Master's thesis. Minneapolis, University of Minnesota Microfilms.
n.d.   *Cybernetics and social research.* Unpublished MS.

PART VI

Problems of Categorization

CHAPTER 36

Problems of Concept Definition
for Comparative Studies

Terrence A. Tatje

OPERATIONAL DEFINITIONS

Concept definition is a general problem of social science. In anthropological theory many of the basic concepts have been arrived at inductively through empirical observation; however, the starting point for theory building remains a logically deductive system of concepts, definitions and principles. It is from these theoretical building-blocks that "hypotheses" are generated. Such theoretical propositions are usually not in themselves testable however. Usually they must first be operationalized.

There is no clear procedure for linking theoretical and operational definitions. Blalock (1960:9–11) points out that operational definitions can be thought of in several ways: as alternative definitions for theoretical concepts; as wholly different kinds of concepts; or as "indices" that imperfectly measure some underlying variable. However one chooses to view operational definitions, they share three attributes. First, they are stated in terms of the actual measurement procedure. Thus, for example, an operational definition of "intelligence" might be "that which is measured by an IQ test." Secondly, as a minimum, operational definitions involve classification. Ideally the measurement procedures are defined with enough precision so that any competent researcher can make unambiguous classifications of every case. Thirdly, the notions of validity and reliability are inherent in all operational definitions. These concepts refer to two related questions: Does what is being measured reflect the underlying variable? And how accurately or consistently does it do so? (Bag-

galey 1964:60–90; Campbell 1957). The questions of validation of concepts will be taken up below.

It is important to emphasize that actual hypothesis testing is always conducted in terms of operationally defined variables. Propositions stated in theoretical terms are usually not directly testable (Blalock 1960: 10–11).

In comparative research different operational measures of the "same" theoretical concept are often employed. Where this is the case each such measure should be regarded as a separate variable. For example, in Chapters 41 and 40 of this handbook three different operational definitions of "social complexity" are described and compared (by Carneiro, and Tatje and Naroll). Naroll's Social Complexity Index yields information not on "social complexity" per se, but on social complexity defined as the weighted average score on the variables settlement size, number of team types, and number of craft specialties (which in turn are operationally defined). Likewise, Carneiro's scale of "social complexity," and Freeman's folk-urban scale, involve other operational variables. Each is a distinct concept. Whether or not these three operationally defined concepts can all be linked to the same underlying theoretical abstraction—social complexity—is another question, one of validity. In this case the high correlations among the results of these different procedures for measuring "social complexity" provide evidence of the validity of each—they do indeed seem to be measuring much the same thing.

It is not uncommon to find different operational measures of the "same" theoretical concept yielding conflicting results. There are several possible explanations for such an outcome: 1) different theoretical variables, or unclearly defined ones, are involved; 2) the operational measures have low reliability; or 3) the results are based on unrepresentative samples.

CONCEPTUALIZATION AND OPERATIONALIZATION IN CROSS-CULTURAL STUDIES

The following discussion deals with some particular problems of conceptualization and operationalization in cross-cultural comparative research. I shall begin with a few basic assumptions about the comparative method and the kinds of problems for which it is useful, and then consider some specific tactics for minimizing the difficulties in defining operational concepts.

Cross-cultural comparative studies are usually undertaken for the following purposes: to test general hypotheses about social or cultural phenomena, to establish the range of variation of such phenomena, or to demonstrate relationships among different aspects of culture or social organization. Such studies involve *within culture* correlations, and correlations among arrays of cultures. The cross-cultural survey method is a technique for testing essentially functional hypotheses (functional in the sense that relationships among elements of the same culture are sought).

There are certain implicit assumptions of the comparative approach which should be made clear. First, the theories being tested are not theories about any particular culture, as are ethnographies; instead, they are *generalizations about phenomena believed to hold true, or vary in predictable (or at least discernible) ways for a range of human societies*. The cross-cultural survey is thus a method for testing more broadly the scope, validity and generality of theories developed within the context of a single culture.

Implicit also is the assumption that certain phenomena are common to all organized ways of human social life; i.e., all societies must face certain "problems"—such as procurement and distribution of subsistence needs, socialization of new members, maintenance of social norms, satisfaction of human social needs, etc. Each separate cul-

ture can be thought of as an "independent solution" to these and other problems of human organization. From this assumption it follows that the universe of known cultures—past and present—is also the known universe of solutions to organized human life. (It should be realized that while the cultural configurations of each society are taken as independent, most specific elements within each configuration tend to be functionally related.)

In a lucid critique of the cross-cultural comparative method Köbben (1952) presents two sets of arguments against its use. The first, which Köbben calls "culture-historical," relates mainly to the assumptions just stated. Among these are the problems of statistically valid sampling, and comparability of cultural units. Another is the problem of independence raised by Sir Francis Galton in response to Tylor's (1889) paper introducing the method. Simply stated, Galton questioned whether every culture represents an *independent* way of life. Naroll addresses himself to these topics in other chapters of this volume.

Köbben's second set of arguments against the statistical comparative method is referred to as "functionalist." Basically, the functionalist argument is that the tabulation and comparison of "trait" configurations taken out of their cultural context violates their meaning, and cannot hope to produce meaningful results. In support of this position Köbben cites a statement by Lowie concerning the religion of the Crow and Ekoi which bears repeating:

Most of the phenomena that occur in either tribe are also found in the other, *but they are quite differently weighted* . . . merely to catalogue the occurrence of such and such beliefs and observations is a futile enterprise. When we know that a tribe practices witchcraft, believes in ghosts, recognizes the mysterious potency resident in inanimate nature . . . we know precisely nothing concerning the religions of the people concerned. (Lowie 1948:53; in Köbben 1952:179; the italics are Lowie's)

In part, the objection of the functionalists is a valid one. Too often the operational categories employed in cross-cultural surveys have been so gross as to lose all meaning. But this shortcoming can be remedied by the use of more adequate procedures for defining operational variables. To a large extent, however, the functionalist argument fails to take into account the purpose of comparative studies, and the kinds of problems for which they are undertaken. Whereas Lowie is concerned to point out very real differences between the religions of the Crow and the Ekoi, despite the occurrence of some of the same beliefs and practices (one level of generalization), a comparativist would be concerned with contrasting societies such as the Crow and Ekoi, which have certain common religious traits, with societies that do not have these traits (another level of generalization). For the comparativist the fact that there is within-group variation is not critical. The test of the usefulness of his operational definitions (sets of categories) is whether they show significant correlations for which he can provide plausible explanations within the context of his theoretical framework. The analysis of variance model of inductive statistics provides a good general frame of reference for approaching cross-cultural comparative studies.

The concepts most useful for a full ethnographic description of a single society are not necessarily most useful for comparative studies. As Ward Goodenough states:

. . . What we do as ethnographers is, and must be kept independent of what we do as comparative ethnologists. An ethnographer is constructing a theory that will make intelligible what goes on in a particular social universe. A comparativist is trying to find principles common to many different universes. His data are not the direct observations of an ethnographer, but the laws governing the particular universe as an ethnographer formulates them. It is by noting how these laws vary from one universe to another and under what conditions, that the comparativist arrives at a statement of laws governing the separate sets of laws which in turn govern the events in their respective social universes. (Goodenough 1956:37)

Ethnographers are interested in the fullest possible description and explanation of the social organization of a particular society; comparativists are interested in generalizations and comparisons among social systems. This must involve some simplifications of the data —the problem for the comparativist is to strike a balance between the conflicting goals of goodness-of-fit to the data, and parsimony. An ethnographer's description represents a generalization at one level of abstraction; the comparativist makes higher-level generalizations. The value of such generalizations depends largely on the categories and concepts which are used.

PROBLEM: COMPARABILITY OF CONCEPTS

A major problem in the theoretical development of anthropology is the lack of comparability of concepts. Many terms are used in different ways by different theorists, and often without any clear definition to indicate which usage is intended. This is particularly a problem for comparativists. Consider the term "clan." This widely used term has had several different meanings in the literature. In his *Social Structure,* Murdock (1949:47; 65 ff.) found it necessary to make a clear distinction between extended consanguineal kinship groups, which he calls "sibs," and *compromise kin groups* based upon both a rule of descent and a rule of residence, for which he used the word "clan." In compiling his data, however, Murdock had no assurance that the ethnographers' uses of these terms agreed with his own definitions. Thus it was necessary to examine the description of the social organization of each individual society reported to have "clans" or "sibs" to determine the actual nature of these groups.

Often the meaning of terms used by ethnographers are altered by the cultural context in which they are used. Most often this reflects cultural variation among similar institutions. For example, the terms "headman" and "chief" are widely used in the description of the political organization of tribal societies, but the meanings of these terms vary greatly from society to society. Chiefs and headmen had wide authority in many African societies, e.g., Bunyoro, Chagga, and Azande, with powers to exact taxes or tribute, enforce decisions, and mete out punishment for offenses. In contrast, "chiefs" among the Orokaiva of New Guinea, the Malekulans of Eastern Melanesia, and the Western Apache of the Southwest, had few if any of these powers. In each of the six societies mentioned there existed a recognized role of "chief," but the content of this role varied greatly. Clearly, noting the presence or absence of "chiefs" in a society tells us little about that society's political authority structure; but this does not necessarily lead us to Lowie's conclusion that comparative studies can be of little value. The solution is to seek more meaningful operational concepts for comparison rather than simply abandon the whole effort. In the case of political authority figures a useful variable might be a typology of authority roles based on both theoretical and empirically observed variation; presumably the roles called "chiefship" in the ethnographic literature would include several of the types.

The comparability of concepts, then, is one major problem of conceptualization in comparative studies. Difficulties arise either because concepts have been used to mean different things, or where they are universally applicable—have meaning in many cultures—exhibit functional variation which should be taken into consideration if meaningful comparisons are to be made.

MISUSE OF CULTURALLY BIASED CONCEPTS

Even more distressing has been the use (or misuse) of culturally biased concepts. That is, concepts which are not universally applicable because their meaning is specific to one culture or related group of cultures. For example, the use of the term *mana* to describe magical beliefs in cultures outside of Polynesia involves a distortion and conveys a misleading impression. Many concepts must be considered culturally biased because they are value-loaded or have specific connotations in Western culture. Bohannan and Dalton (1965:1–32) point out that many of the terms used in economic anthropology, such as "money," "barter," and "market," are misleading when applied to the economics of primitive societies because of their specific meanings in our own society. "Economic surplus" is another such term (Dalton 1960, 1963).

Perhaps the classic example of a culturally-biased concept is the term "cannibalism." The Second Edition of Webster's New International (1957) gives the following definition of cannibalism:

Act or practice of eating human flesh by mankind, or of any animal by its own kind. The use of human flesh as an ordinary article of food is very rare. Among most cannibals the practice is a religious or sacramental rite, the belief being, usually, that the eater acquires the soul, or some of the powers of the victim. Usually, persons eaten are enemies captured in war. Often only warriors or chiefs share the feast.

Despite this enlightened definition, I submit that in common Western usage, particularly of a few generations ago, cannibalism meant the active pursuit of human flesh as an article of diet. While dietary cannibalism has been practiced in some societies, e.g., the Orokaiva, the number is small. Nevertheless, M. R. Davie (1929) found enough references to the practice to persuade him that not only was dietary cannibalism widespread among primitive peoples, it was the original cause of war! One can well imagine the vivid images in the minds of nineteenth-century missionaries and travelers—upon whose reports Davie's conclusions are largely based—when told that the local natives occasionally dined on human flesh!

Comparative studies must begin with theoretical propositions stated in terms of culture-free concepts—that is, in terms of concepts that have meaning in any social system. A good example is the term "patrilineal descent."

OPERATIONAL PROBLEMS ARISING FROM THE NATURE OF THE DATA

It is at the operational level that the most formidable problems of conceptualization in comparative research become apparent. Four considerations guide the formulation of operational variables for cross-cultural research. These are: 1) the nature of the data itself, 2) concern for bias, 3) concern for validity and reliability, and 4) concern for functional variation in the phenomena under investigation.

The basic datum of comparative studies is the ethnographic report. Generally, the comparativist does not deal with actual social and cultural phenomena, but only with the statements about such phenomena formulated by ethnographers. These reports vary in their inherent trustworthiness and accuracy. (For a discussion of this topic see Chapters 8 and 44, and Naroll 1962.) Ethnographic reports also vary greatly in terms of the interests and theoretical point of view of the ethnographer. As we have already seen, the comparativist must interpret not only the ethnographer's data, but the concepts as well.

Unfortunately, ethnographic reports often fail to provide the kind of data most useful for operationalized comparative concepts. For many research problems the comparativist desires interval scale data, i.e., rates of occurrence of cultural or social phenomena. As a hypothetical example, suppose we wish to use the cross-cultural survey method to test the hypothesis that frequent warfare leads to increased political authority and organization. Ideally we would like information on the rates of occurrence of wars among the societies samples, i.e., data such as the average number of months per year or decade that the society is "at war," and information on the number of war casualties per 100,000 population per year. Obviously such precise data are not often found in ethnographic monographs. What we do find are statements such as "warfare is uncommon," or "warfare is frequent," or "the people are continually at war." Thus in studying warfare as a cultural variable, the operational measures of warfare frequency must be stated in terms of such categories as "rare," "infrequent," "common," and "continuous," and not as precise rates.

From this example it should be evident that *the available kinds of data are the limiting factor on operational concepts for comparative research—operational variables must be defined in terms of the available information.*

To a considerable degree the limitations of the data used in cross-cultural surveys—ethnographic reports—make the formulation of operational variables a trial-and-error process. One begins with tentative operational measures of the variables which are considered theoretically important. Almost invariably these operational concepts must be altered to meet the limitations of the data; sometimes a potentially important variable must be dropped entirely. Both situations are well illustrated in Naroll's (1962) monograph on culture stress research. He began with a number of theoretical variables which appeared to be possible indicators (symptoms) of culture stress; among these were alcoholism and stuttering. In the course of the data collection process, however, both alcoholism and stuttering were found to be useless as operational concepts. Naroll notes that "data on pathological alcoholic addiction as distinguished from mere use of alcohol is very rare in existing ethnological literature" (Naroll 1962:53). Consequently he was forced to modify the theoretical variable alcoholism, settling finally on the operational concept of "drunken brawling"—reports of overt physical aggression following the use of alcohol—as a symptom of culture stress. The stuttering variable had to be abandoned altogether because of a lack of data (Naroll 1962:48–49).

One useful and statistically valid procedure

for minimizing the difficulties of poor or insufficient data is to include in the sampling universe only societies for which some information on the desired topics is available. This form of stratified sampling represents a departure from "true randomness," since it is highly likely that those societies for which certain specific aspects of culture have been well described vary systematically from societies not so described. However, since this departure from randomness is known, it can be controlled (see Chapter 43).

For some research problems large-scale field studies represent an ideal (though costly) solution to the problems imposed by the nature of the existing ethnographic literature. Where teams of investigators enter the field with the same set of concepts, problems, and data-gathering procedures, we can expect much greater comparability of data than is presently possible. The world-wide study of ethnocentrism proposed by Campbell and LeVine (1961) is such an undertaking. Coordinated, problem-oriented field research is not a complete answer however. For many cultures the record is already "closed." Field restudies cannot tell us much more about the social systems of the Incas, the Tasmanians, or most of the indigenous societies of North America. For these and many other cultures we cannot expect much more data than already exists. For this reason, the comparativist who wishes to utilize truly world-wide random samples of societies, at all levels of complexity and from many time periods, must continue to rely chiefly upon the existing literature, and focus his attention on improving available techniques for manipulating the data at hand.

OPERATIONAL PROBLEMS ARISING FROM BIAS

Bias is a second major concern of the comparativist as he sets about operationalizing his theories. There are several sorts of "biases"; each must be dealt with separately. First, the comparativist must guard against statistical bias—i.e., non-representativeness and non-randomness in sampling procedures. This is essential if the usual statistical measures of association are to have any meaning. Secondly, there are possible biases in the data, conscious or unconscious errors in ethnographer's reports. These are best dealt with by the technique of data quality control (see Naroll 1962 and Chapter 44). A third source of bias is the comparativist himself. Ambiguities in written ethnographic reports make independent judgments by the comparativist almost inevitable; but careful development of operational concepts can do much to limit this source of bias. For obvious reasons, the less the researcher is called upon to exercise his own judgments in the data-collecting process, the better. To achieve this, three basic rules should be followed:

1) *Culturally-biased concepts should be avoided.* Such concepts not only have the disadvantages already noted; they also increase the likelihood of arbitrary judgments by the comparativist. The term "money" is an example. Money has particular uses and meanings for Westerners—including field anthropologists—which are not usually found in "primitive" societies (Dalton 1965:44). In using "money" as an operational concept the comparativist would be called upon in many cases to interpret whether a particular commodity, e.g., Rossel Island shells, *kula* valuables, or *potlatch* coppers, are "really" money.

2) *Concept definitions should be made in advance of the actual data collection.* As far as possible the trial-and-error process of developing operational categories should be worked out in preliminary investigations of the kinds of data which are available. To return to our earlier example of warfare, the comparativist should state in advance whether a statement such as "The Navaho sometimes carried out punitive expeditions against their neighbors" is to be classified as a case of "frequent" or "infrequent" warfare.

3) *Definitions of operational concepts should be complete and precise.* What is meant by warfare? How frequent is "frequent"? The meaning of every term used in a concept definition should be made explicit. This alone will go a long way to clear up ambiguities both in the mind of the researcher and in the minds of his readers.

OPERATIONAL PROBLEMS ARISING FROM FUNCTIONAL VARIATION

Related to these considerations is another major concern of the comparativist: concern for the functional variation in the phenomena under investigation. Simple dichotomies, such as presence or absence of chiefs, frequent or infrequent warfare, and so on, often mask as much as they reveal. Wherever possible, the comparativist should try to expand his categories; a valid ordinal scale is more powerful (statistically) and more valuable (theoretically) than a nominal scale or dichotomy (Blalock 1960:12 f.). Interval scales, of course, are even more desirable.

As an example of ethnographic report scaling, I offer a four-category typology developed in connection with a cross-cultural study of warfare and culture stress conducted by Naroll (n.d.). This typology began with a dichotomy of societies classified as having "frequent" or "infrequent" warfare. It is designed to be a measure of the extent to which warfare is a potential event in daily life. The four types are:

Type I. Societies which consider themselves to be in a constant state of war with some or all of their enemies, and in which punitive expeditions or enemy attacks might occur at any time—those societies which are never "at peace" with their neighbors; e.g., Cheyenne, Western Apache.

Type II. Societies which fight frequent wars, but usually only at certain known intervals or upon formal declaration, with intervening periods of "peace"; e.g., Callinago, United States.

Type III. Societies which fight only "sporadic" or "occasional" wars, but where warfare is still frequent enough to be a recognized group activity; e.g., Central Wintun, Gilyak.

Type IV. Societies in which warfare is "extremely rare" or unknown; e.g., Yagua, Semang, Tikopia.

The operational definitions of these four scale types are stated in terms of the kinds of ethnographic statements that are to be accepted as evidence for each category. For example, statements such as "incessant strife," "continuously at war," "no interludes of peace," "made frequent raids throughout the year," typify the societies of Type I. It is not necessarily true that all societies classified as Type I have more warfare (actual fighting) than all of the societies of Type II; this is impossible to determine in the absence of data on rates of occurrence. Nevertheless, it seems likely that *on the average,* societies of Type I have more frequent warfare than those of Type II.

The techniques of componential analysis are useful for developing ethnographic report scales, particularly when complex variables are involved. It often proves easier to define mutually-exclusive categories if each "component" or "element" of a complex concept is singled out and treated separately. Ancestor worship is such a concept. The technique is illustrated by the following six-type classification of ancestor spirit beliefs, developed for a study of ancestor worship and kinship (Tatje and Hsu 1969). The six categories used in this study are:

1) *Absence of Spirits*—people generally do not believe in the existence of human "spirits," "souls," "ghosts," etc.

2) *Neutral Spirits*—there is a general acceptance of the existence of spirits of dead human beings, but such spirits are believed not to have any active influence on the affairs of the living.

3) *Undifferentiated Spirits*—belief that the spirits of dead human beings exist, and are a potential source of help or harm to the living, but no specific importance is attached to the spirits of ancestors or close kinsmen;

if worshiped at all, spirits are worshiped generally without specific reference to ancestors or departed kinsmen.

4) *Negative Ancestor Spirits*—belief in the existence and special importance of ancestral spirits on the affairs of their descendants, accompanied by the fear of harm or retribution from the spirits of dead ancestors or kinsmen.

5) *Concerned Ancestor Spirits*—belief in the existence of ancestral spirits, who are generally helpful to their descendants but may punish neglect or serious moral or ritual transgressions.

6) *Positive Ancestor Spirits*—belief in the existence and special importance of ancestral spirits on the affairs of their descendants, with no fear of retribution or harm; i.e., belief in the absolute benevolence of departed ancestors toward their descendants.

The definitions of these six categories incorporate six separate elements of belief about spirits of the dead, three general and three specific elements. It is helpful to show these belief elements diagrammatically. A plus (+) indicates the presence of a given element; a minus (−) indicates its absence:

Type of Spirit Beliefs	Elements of Beliefs About Spirits of the Dead					
	existence of spirits of the dead	influence of spirits on affairs of living	special importance of *ancestral* spirits	ancestral spirits usually a source of harm to descendents	ancestral spirits usually helpful but may punish descendents	ancestral spirits always helpful to their descendents
1) Absence of Spirits	−	−	−	−	−	−
2) Neutral Spirits	+	−	−	−	−	−
3) Undifferentiated Spirits	+	+	−	−	−	−
4) Negative Ancestor Spirits	+	+	+	+	−	−
5) Concerned Ancestor Spirits	+	+	+	−	+	−
6) Positive Ancestor Spirits	+	+	+	−	−	+

RELIABILITY AND VALIDITY

This brings us to a final concern of the comparativist regarding the formulation of operational concepts: their reliability and validity. The concepts of reliability and validity are too complex to be discussed fully here. I shall merely point out that significant correlations are in themselves some evidence of validity. As Blalock put it, "If the classification is a useful one, the categories will also be found to be homogeneous with respect to other variables" (1960:12). While the comparativist should concern himself with the statistical and theoretical questions of validity and reliability, the burden of proof should be shifted from the researcher to the critic. It is up to the latter to furnish plausible alternative explantions for the correlations reported in cross-cultural surveys.

BIBLIOGRAPHY

BAGGALEY, ANDREW R.
1954 *Intermediate correlational methods.* New York, Wiley.

BLALOCK, HUBERT M., JR.
1960 *Social statistics.* New York, McGraw-Hill.

BOHANNAN, PAUL, and GEORGE DALTON (eds.)
1965 *Markets in Africa; eight subsistence economies in transition.* Garden City, N.Y., Doubleday.

CAMPBELL, DONALD T.
1957 Factors relevant to the validity of experiments in social settings. *Psychological Bulletin* 54:297–312.

CAMPBELL, DONALD T., and ROBERT A. LEVINE
1961 A proposal for cooperative cross-cultural research on ethnocentrism. *Journal of Conflict Resolution* 5:82–108.

DALTON, GEORGE
1960 A note of clarification on economic surplus. *American Anthropologist* 62:483–490.
1963 Economic surplus, once again. *American Anthropologist* 65:389–394.
1965 Primitive money. *American Anthropologist* 67:44–65.

DAVIE, M. R.
1929 *The evolution of war.* New Haven, Yale University Press.

GOODENOUGH, WARD
1956 Residence rules. *Southwestern Journal of Anthropology* 12:22–37.

KÖBBEN, ANDRÉ J.
1952 New ways of presenting an old idea; the statistical method in social anthropology. *Journal of the Royal Anthropological Institute of Great Britain and Ireland* 82:129–146. (Reprinted in F. W. Moore, ed., *Readings in cross-cultural methodology.* New Haven, HRAF Press.)

MURDOCK, GEORGE PETER
1949 *Social structure.* New York, Macmillan.

NAROLL, RAOUL
1962 *Data quality control.* New York, Free Press.
n.d. *Warefare, peaceful intercourse and territorial change: a cross-cultural survey.* Mimeograph.

TATJE, TERRENCE A., and FRANCIS L. K. HSU
1969 *Variations in ancestor worship practices and their relation to kinship beliefs. Southwestern Journal of Anthropology* 25:153–172.

TYLOR, EDWARD B.
1889 On a method of investigating the development of institutions applied to laws of marriage and descent. *Journal of the Royal Anthropological Institute of Great Britain and Ireland* 18:245–272.

CHAPTER 37

Taxonomy in Comparative Studies

MELVIN EMBER

Ever since the first anthropologist published his account of some hitherto undescribed people, the data on cultural variation has been steadily accumulating. Yet even today few anthropologists do much more than add to the mountain of descriptive material. Although there has been a slight increase in comparative studies recently, the amount of such work has scarcely tapped the descriptive resources available. This paper suggests that a number of confusions and misunderstandings concerning classification may lie behind our reluctance to do cross-cultural research.

The word "taxonomy" in the title of this paper is used in the same sense that some philosophers of science use it, namely, to refer to the theory of classification (cf. Hempel 1965). What follows then is a review of some aspects of that theory which have implications for the taxonomic problems of comparative studies.

THE NATURE AND PURPOSE OF CLASSIFICATION

To classify in empirical science is to partition a set or class of objects into two or more subclasses. Each subclass is defined by specifying the attribute(s) a given object must possess in order to be said to belong to that subclass, just as the entire class is defined by specifying the attribute(s) all of the subclasses possess (Hempel 1965). So, for example, we might want to speak of a class of "unilineal" societies, those which have groups of kin whose members trace descent from a common ancestor through links of one sex; and we might partition this class into two subclasses, "patrilineal" and

"matrilineal," the former tracing descent through males only and the latter tracing descent through females only.

Philosophers of science have written extensively about the principles of classification (see Hempel 1965 and the sources referred to therein). This section emphasizes two of these principles, which are particularly relevant to the current state of comparative studies: 1) that all classifications are equally "natural"; and 2) that to classify things is to hypothesize about the relations between things.

At least as far back as the time of Aristotle, thoughtful men have realized that there is no knowledge or meaningful assertion about any particular except in terms of abstractions, i.e., words or other symbols (Cohen 1931). We may in a dumb way point to a particular object or phenomenon, but we cannot even say "this" about it without using a word which is applicable to other particulars. Even if we use a proper name, it has meaning only by convention—and all convention ultimately involves abstractions such as words. If I want to talk about "Miles Standish," I may say that he was a man from the Massachusetts Bay Colony with a yen for a girl named Priscilla—all of which words can also be applied (individually) to other men (or women). Only because they are so applicable can my statement about "Miles Standish" have any meaning to somebody else. But, paradoxically, my meaning can never be completely unambiguous. This is because the definition of a word is not that definite. That is, the definition or meaning of a word is actually an approximate rule of use, whose limits are not absolutely defined. It is this paradoxical quality of words, their somewhat ambiguous generality, that enables men to analyze and categorize the aspects of reality which to them seem repeated. Were it not for the generality of symbols, all things, events, and feelings would remain unique and hence incommunicable.

What has been said so far about symbols in general also applies to scientific concepts, e.g., classificatory terms, in particular. All experience is private to begin with, but symbols in general and scientific concepts in particular permit the communication of at least some aspects of experience. This fact disposes of one of the hoariest and silliest objections to cross-cultural research—namely that cultures are incomparable because the unique content of each cannot be completely described and hence is knowable only by the person who directly experiences it. The fallacy in this objection is the assumption that cultures are incomparable because they are not completely describable. Snowflakes too are individually unique, and hence not completely describable, but we can still say that they are all hexagonal, more or less white, and likely to be transformed into water at temperatures above 32 degrees Fahrenheit. The point is: If we can talk about something, i.e., if we can specify some of its attributes, we can compare it with other things we think it is like. As Pratt (1939: 106–107) put it: "If an operation for penetrating privacy were self-contradictory, no intelligible communication of any kind could ever take place between two individuals. All symbols, all gestures, all languages of every kind would be meaningless. There could be no such thing as science. Each individual would organize his own experience according to his own private fashion, and it would remain forever impossible for him or anyone else to discover whether two people could know the same thing. Since such impenetrable privacy is manifestly and fortunately not the rule of human life, it must mean that operations *do* exist which make it possible to bring private experience out into the open." Classification is possible, and therefore comparison is possible, because speech is possible. Things may not be completely comparable, because they are individually unique, but they are not thereby completely incomparable.

We sometimes hear the statement that a particular classification is "artificial," that it does not capture the "essence" of that which is classified. Such a statement implies that the essence of something is objectively ascertainable, in the same way that an attribute such as temperature is ascertainable. But this is not true. We could agree that the temperature of a given fluid is 75 degrees Fahrenheit, but we would probably not agree that the essence of water is its potability (or anything else). Nevertheless, though the essence of something is nonobjective, its meaning is like the meaning of "temperature" in one important sense, namely that it is arbitrary. Just as there is no compelling or "natural" reason that the word "dog" should refer to a smallish four-legged carnivore who is the bane of postmen, so there is no "natural" justification for any symbol or set of symbols. Classifications and words in general should be recognized for what they are —man-made devices that more or less facilitate communication. Sapir (1937:157) said: "[the forms of language] predetermine for us certain modes of observation and interpretation." This statement describes the language-culture relationship ontogenetically, from the viewpoint of the individual and how he acquires language. But the relationship can also be described phylogenetically, from the viewpoint of the culture and how language evolves, which is more to the point here. That is, it is appropriate to say that conventional modes of observation and interpretation determine whether we retain a term or classification in current usage, or change its meaning to conform to new modes of observation and interpretation, or stop using it altogether because its frame of reference is no longer important to us. Hardly anyone speaks of "running boards" any more.

All classifications are equally "natural," then. But they are not on that account equally useful, which brings us to the purpose of classification in empirical science. To put the matter simply, the purpose of a classification is to aid us in our pursuit of understanding. Let us take a moment to recall what the term "understanding" means in empirical science. To begin with, we have to remember that a classification by itself does not help us to understand anything. It merely partitions a set of phenomena. If it partitions ambiguously, i.e., if we cannot decide whether case X belongs to subset A or to subset B, the classification cannot be very useful in any sense. Even if it partitions unambiguously, it may still not be particularly useful, except perhaps as a purely mnemonic device. Now, to understand something scientifically is to explain it, ". . . to show that it occurs in accordance with general laws or theoretical principles" (Hempel 1965:139). Hence a scientifically useful classification (or concept) is one that lends itself ". . . to the formulation of general laws or theoretical principles which reflect uniformities in the subject matter under study, and which thus provide a basis for explanation, prediction, and generally scientific understanding" (Hempel 1965:146).

In other words, to classify things is to hypothesize about the relations between things; and to classify usefully is to hypothesize verifiably. The familiar distinction between "natural" and "artificial" classifications may accordingly be interpreted as

. . . referring to the difference between classifications that are scientifically fruitful and those that are not: in a classification of the former kind, those characteristics of the elements which serve as criteria of membership in a given class are associated, universally or with high probability, with more or less extensive clusters of other characteristics. For example, the two sets of primary sex characteristics which determine the division of humans into male and female are associated, by general laws or by statistical connections, with a large variety of concomitant physical, physiological, and psychological traits. It is understandable that a classification of this sort should be viewed as somehow having objective existence in nature, as "carving nature at the joints," in contradistinction to "artificial" classifications, in which the defining characteristics have few explanatory or predictive connections with other traits; as is the case, for example, in the division of humans into those weighing less than one hundred pounds, and all others. (Hempel 1965:146–147)

If a classification does not prove to be useful, it is abandoned—at least ultimately. The Greek division of the elements into earth, air, fire, and water was replaced by the periodic table—not because the latter is any more "natural," but because Mendeleev derived a set of highly specific predictions from it that were confirmed by subsequent research.

Even though scientific classifications are heuristic devices that can be abandoned if useless, and even though we now have an enormous body of ethnographic information that is largely unexplained, some anthropologists are still inclined to think that it is premature to classify cultural things. Their stated reason for thinking so is the assumption that the quality of our descriptive data is not yet adequate to the task of classifying. As Sturtevant (1964:101) says: "What is needed is the improvement of ethnographic method, to make cultural descriptions replicable and accurate, so that we know what we are comparing." In other words, it is assumed that our ethnographic literature is so full of error and incommensurability that any efforts to classify cultural things at this time in order to test hypotheses are doomed to failure, that any findings we may happen to come up with will be suspect because "their descriptive foundations are insecure" (Sturtevant 1964:100).

This assumption—that it is premature to classify cultural things—is questionable on two grounds. First, it implies that if we are skeptical about some proposed explanation of some particular finding, this means that the finding itself is suspect—which is not true so long as the variables involved are measured validly and reliably and so long as the rest of the research procedure (e.g., sampling method, statistical analysis) cannot be faulted. (For an introduction to the general principles of research design in behavioral science, and for the meaning of such terms as "validity" and "reliability," see Selltiz et al. 1961; see also the relevant papers in this volume.) We may reject the theory that gremlins were responsible for the collapse of a given bridge, but we are not thereby entitled to deny that the bridge did collapse. A second reason for questioning the assumption that it is premature to classify cultural things is suggested by Merton's (1957) discussion of "self-fulfilling prophecy." If we believe that our available data are inadequate to the task of classifying and hypothesis-testing, we shall not attempt the task; and if we do not make the attempt, we give ourselves no chance to be disabused of our pessimism.

In point of fact, whether or not it is premature to classify cultural things usefully is a pragmatic matter. It may or may not be true that some particular set of cultural phenomena, as classified in some particular way, is related to some other particular set(s) of phenomena. Moreover, it cannot ever be proved that it is impossible to classify some set of phenomena usefully. Even if that set, as classified in some particular way, is not found to be related to other things, we cannot be sure that different classifications of the same phenomena would also not be related to those other things. The only way to find out if they are is to act on the intuition that they are and conduct the inquiries called for. After all, the only thing we can lose is our ignorance.

But do we want to? I would guess that our reluctance to classify and hypothesize is not merely a function of the supposed inadequacy of our data. The assumption of inadequacy may reflect two more deep-seated attitudes that are widely held in cultural anthropology and that may explain the present underdeveloped state of comparative research. One of these attitudes may be called the "strictly empiricist" view of scientific method. The other attitude is an incomplete commitment to, or complete rejection of, the idea of a deterministic universe. Let me now try to show how these two attitudes may be inhibiting our efforts to understand cultural variation.

According to the strictly empiricist view of scientific method, the essence of that method is to mistrust all *a priori* reasoning and to rely on the facts only (cf. Sturtevant 1964:101). The motto "Don't think, find out!" illustrates this attitude. Scientific method is assumed to begin by banishing all preconceptions of nature. In the first stage it simply collects the facts. In the second stage it classifies them in natural ways. And in the third stage it lets the facts themselves suggest the laws that explain them. But this scheme does not agree with actual practice in empirical science. As Morris Cohen (1931:76–77) so eloquently noted:

Begin with collecting the facts? Ay, but what facts? Obviously only with those that have some bearing on our inquiry. Attention to irrelevant circumstances will obviously not help us at all, but will rather detract us from our problem. Now, the relevant facts of nature do not of their own accord separate themselves from all the others, nor do they come with all their significant characteristics duly labelled for us. Which of the infinite variety of nature's circumstances we should turn to as relevant to or bearing upon any specific problem depends upon our general ideas as to how that which is sought for can possibly be related to what we already know. Without such guiding ideas or hypotheses as to possible connection we have nothing to look for.

Even if we do not think we are collecting data to test hypotheses, we are still likely to be collecting selectively. One always observes on the basis of hypotheses, albeit unconscious ones that are produced by perceptual habits and cultural expectations. How could it be otherwise? Human beings are not cameras or tape recorders, and even they do not record everything that is to be seen or heard.

One could say there are two kinds of useful research, which are sometimes combined in one study. On the one hand there is research that tests hypotheses. Needless to say, this kind of research is appropriate whenever we have hypotheses to test. On the other hand, there is exploratory research, the goal of which is the formulation of hypotheses. Such research is appropriate whenever we become interested in phenomena we know little about. So, for example, the recent "ethnoscientific" studies of cognition (Romney and D'Andrade 1964) have directed our attention to behavior that had not been well described previously. The advantage of exploratory research is its openness, its potential for reaching out in new directions. The disadvantage is that we do not readily see what we are not looking for (cf. Krech *et al.* 1962 for a review of studies of selective perception). For example, Driver (1966) computed the intercorrelations among a large set of variables in an effort to discover whether "geographical-historical" factors predicted kin avoidances better than certain "psycho-functional" factors. (The "geographical-historical" factors turned out to be the better predictors.) But let us imagine that kin avoidances are really caused by elements X and Y. No matrix of intercorrelations will suggest such a relationship to us if we have not included measures of X and Y in the set of variables to be intercorrelated. Thus, exploratory research is not guaranteed to further our understanding of cultural variation, and it will be even less likely to do so if it is strictly empiricist in orientation. No matter how much we describe or intercorrelate, the laws of nature will not reveal themselves.

Now, if we are to maximize our chances of doing useful exploratory research, comparative or otherwise, we have to assume the operation of causality in our data, as a special case of the belief in a deterministic universe. But this is something that many in cultural anthropology are still not prepared to accept (which may account for the continuing popularity of the strictly empiricist orientation). Even if an investigator poses a question for himself, it is not very likely that he will be able to formulate an answer to that question without believing in causality (Where would the answer come from?). And if he could not come up with an answer, it is hardly likely that he would be able to design a study that could confirm that answer. In Steward's (1949:1) unfortunately still timely words: "Reaction to evolutionism and scientific functionalism has very nearly amounted to a denial that regularities exist; that is, to a claim that history never repeats itself. While it is theoretically admitted that cause and effect operate in cultural phenomena, it is considered somewhat rash to mention causality, let alone 'law,' in specific cases. Attention is centered on cultural differences, particulars and peculiarities, and culture is often treated as if it developed quixotically, without determinable causes, or else appeared full-blown." (For a refutation of some popular arguments against causality in human behavior, see Grünbaum 1953.) It might be comforting to remember that the predisposition to think causally is probably just as likely to produce self-fulfilling prophecy as the reluctance to think causally.

In summary, then, classification is an arbitrary way of talking about the observable world. As such, it is merely a more systematic form of ordinary speech. We construct classifications because we think they will help us discover which things are related to which other things. The way of science, including the way we classify, is a game we play against our own ignorance. Judging by the success of the more developed sciences, it would seem that the more we deliberately play at that game, e.g., the more we deliberately try to classify cultural phenomena according to hypotheses as to the relations between cultural things, the more we shall find out about the causes of cultural variation.

THE TWO KINDS OF CLASSIFICATION

It is a sad commentary on the underdeveloped state of comparative studies that some of the classifications most frequently referred to are not or have not been shown to be scientifically useful. That is to say,

their usefulness for the prediction or explanation of other phenomena has not been demonstrated. Consider, for example, the ambiguous classification offered by Middleton and Tait (1958:12–16) of "segmentary lineage systems." Three types of such system are supposedly distinguished, but the defining features of each are not clearly or operationally given. Indeed, no one of the types is even given a name. Rather, the labels "Group I," "Group II," and "Group III" are used. If the authors are not clear about what they mean to distinguish, it is no wonder that they offer no suggestion as to what their types may be related to. Examples of less ambiguous, more operational, but still not demonstrably useful classifications are Murdock's (1949) typology of "social organization" and Freeman's (1957) Guttman scale of "societal complexity." Although both of these classifications are easily applied to individual societies, and although both in the future might be found to be scientifically useful, neither has as yet been shown to be related to phenomena other than those which are employed in the classifications. Hence to consider them now as scientifically useful would not be justified. If we were to consider them so, we would have to say also that the Greek four-part classification of the elements is scientifically useful—which of course it has not been shown to be. As was emphasized in the previous section, a scientifically useful classification does more than just allow us to assign objects to groups.

If we want to maximize our chances of classifying usefully, it seems advisable for us to be acquainted with the fact that there are two kinds of classification. This section discusses the differences between them. Two points are emphasized: 1) that the two kinds of classification are more or less primitive ways of measurement; and 2) that the two kinds of classification differ therefore in regard to their power to predict other things.

In the literature of social science, the term "measurement" is often used to refer to certain procedures that are less precise than those which are typically employed in the physical sciences. In this more general sense of the term, to measure some object is to say how it compares with others. So, for example, when we say that a given object is 21 inches long, we are saying that it is different (by 2 inches in length) from another object 19 inches long, according to that standard of comparison we call a "ruler." Similarly, when we say that a given object falls into some particular subset of a set of nonnumerically defined categories, we are saying that is is different (in the way the subset is defined) from another object that belongs to another subset of the classification. In short, to measure is to compare objects by locating them in the same or different subsets (e.g., intervals on a ruler) of some set of such categories.

There are four ways to compare or measure. These are conventionally distinguished according to the ways the subsets or categories involved are ordered or scaled. (See Blalock 1960:11–16 for a simple discussion of the four different kinds of scale.) Listing them in order of increasing complexity, we can measure nominally, ordinally, according to an interval scale, and according to a ratio scale. All classifications are either nominal or ordinal scales and hence more or less primitive ways of measurement. (When we say that one scale is more primitive or less complex than another, we mean that more powerful statistical tests can be used with the more complex scale. And by power we mean the probability of avoiding what is called a "Type II" error, i.e., failing to reject a null hypothesis which is in fact false. In other words, the more powerful test gives us a better chance to find support for some hypothesis that we are interested in finding support for. See Blalock 1960 for discussions of the Type II error and the power of a statistical test.)

The most primitive level of measurement is the nominal scale. Such a scale, e.g., Murdock's (1949) typology of "social organization," consists of a set of categories that are not ordered in any way. Thus, it makes no difference whether we list the "Crow Type of Social Organization" first or second or last. This is because no assumptions are made about relationships between the categories. No one category, e.g., "Crow," is said to be "greater than" or have more of something than any other category. The only conditions that must be satisfied, if a set of categories is to constitute a nominal scale, are: 1) that the categories are exhaustive, i.e., include all cases; and 2) that the categories are nonoverlapping or mutually exclusive, i.e., that no case belongs in more

than one category. The statistical tests which are most commonly applied to nominally scaled data are those which enable us to evaluate whether the proportions of cases with a certain characteristic (in the different subsets) differ significantly from the proportions that might be produced by chance fluctuations (see Blalock 1960:212 ff. for a description of such tests). So, for example, we might want to know if patrilocal societies have the custom of bride price significantly more often than matrilocal societies.

The next most primitive level of measurement is the ordinal scale. In such a scale, e.g., Freeman's (1957) Guttman scale of societal complexity, the sample cases are ranked in an ordered series with respect to the degree to which they possess a certain characteristic. The scale is ordinal rather than interval (see below) because we cannot be sure exactly how much of the given characteristic the sample cases possess. Even though we may have a score for each case, the numbers are not considered accurate enough for us to treat the scores as forming an interval scale; they are only accurate enough, we assume, to permit us to rank the cases. On Freeman's scale of societal complexity, for example, the Zulu are ranked higher (with a score of 8) than the Samoans (with a score of 5), but we cannot say that the difference between scores of 8 and 5 is the same as the difference between scores of 5 and 2 (e.g., the Nuer). (It should be noted, incidentally, that we may have an ordinal scale even with only two categories, e.g., "high" and "low.") Because an ordinal scale allows us to say that one case has more of something than another case, we can correlate one set of such ranked data with another such set for the same cases (Blalock 1960:317 ff.), as do Tatje and Naroll (in this volume) when they compute the Spearman rank-order correlation coefficient for the relationship between Freeman's scale of societal complexity and Naroll's (1956) scale of "social development."

The two most complex levels of measurement, which take us beyond the subject of classification per se, are the interval and ratio scales. When we can rank cases with respect to the degree to which they possess a certain characteristic, and when we can also indicate the exact distance between the cases, we have an interval scale. Needless to say, the interval-scale level of measurement ". . . requires the establishment of some sort of a physical unit of measurement [e.g., weight as measured in pounds] which can be agreed upon as a common standard and which is replicable, i.e., can be applied over and over again with the same results" (Blalock 1960:14). The advantage of an interval scale, over an ordinal one, is that we can say something like, "The difference between Zulu and Samoan complexity is the same as the difference between Samoan and Nuer complexity." Finally, if we can also locate an absolute or nonarbitrary zero point on an interval scale, we have a ratio scale, which is the highest level of measurement. It is highest because we can compare scores by taking their ratios. For example, we could say that the Zulu have twice the complexity of the Hopi (who have a score of 4 on Freeman's scale). It should be noted, however, that the distinction between interval and ratio scales is practically always an academic one, so that it is usually considered legitimate to use all of the ordinary operations of arithmetic, including the taking of ratios, whenever we have an interval scale.

Let us turn now to an empirical example that illustrates how ordinal classification allows us to say more about some body of data than nominal classification.

In his "World Ethnographic Sample," Murdock (1957) employs a classification of mode of marriage that consists of the following more or less conventional categories: 1) bride price; 2) bride service; 3) token bride price; 4) gift exchange; 5) exchange of women; 6) dowry; and 7) no transfer of women, labor or property. This classification satisfies the necessary conditions for a useful classification: it unambiguously partitions a set of phenomena into a number of subsets that presumably exhaust all the possibilities. Accordingly, it allows us to describe differences between cultures economically. But it is a nominal classification, its categories unordered. It is not obvious, therefore, that the phenomena classified can be interpreted in terms of some underlying variable, and hence it is difficult to hypothesize how mode of marriage might be related to other things.

Let us say now that we have an intuition that mode of marriage is somehow related to patterns of postmarital residence. We might check this intuition out preliminarily by turning to page 378 of Coult and Habenstein's (1965) "Cross Tabulations of Murdock's World Ethnographic Sample," where we find a large contingency table showing the association between the nominal classification of mode of marriage and the conventional and nominal classification of ultimate marital residence (patrilocal, bilocal, neolocal, matrilocal, avunculocal, duolocal). Judging from that table, there appears to be some support for the intuition that mode of marriage is somehow related to marital residence. The proportion of patrilocal cases with bride price is larger than would be produced by chance, the proportion of matrilocal cases with bride price is smaller than would be produced by chance, the proportion of patrilocal cases with no transfer of women, labor, or property is smaller than would be produced by chance, the proportion of matrilocal cases with no transfer of women, labor, or property is larger than would be produced by chance, etc. However, these departures from chance expectancies do not allow us to say anything more specific than that the conventional nominal classification of mode of marriage is in fact associated with the conventional nominal classification of marital residence.

If we are interested in discovering something more specific, i.e., more ordered, about the relation between residence and mode of marriage, we have to formulate some bivariate hypothesis (e.g., the more of A, the more of B) and test it against the sample cases which are reclassified accordingly. One such hypothesis is found in the literature (Murdock 1949:206–207), namely that when the couple settles down near or with the husband's kin, the wife's kin are compensated for the loss of her labor. This interpretation generates the following *ordinal* reclassifications of mode of marriage and marital residence. With regard to mode of marriage, the categories of bride price, bride service, and exchange of women all involve some kind of considerable compensation to the wife's kin, in contrast to token bride price, dowry, gift exchange (which, since it is reciprocal, does not compensate the wife's kin for the loss of her labor), and no transfer of women, labor, or property. Thus, we have a two-category ordinal classification of mode of marriage, defined in terms of the underlying variable of low versus high compensation to wife's kin. With regard to marital residence, we also have a two-category ordinal classification, defined in terms of the underlying variable of low versus high likelihood that couples will settle near or with the husband's kin. On the one hand, patrilocal and avunculocal residence can be grouped as generally locating the couple with or near the husband's kin. And, on the other hand, bilocal, neolocal, matrilocal, and duolocal residence can be grouped as not generally locating the couple with or near the husband's kin. Table 1 shows that low versus

Table 1

RELATIONSHIP BETWEEN MARITAL RESIDENCE AND MODE OF MARRIAGE[1]
(DATA FROM COULT AND HABENSTEIN 1965:378)

Compensation to Wife's Kin*

Likelihood of Residence With or Near Husband's Kin*		high	low	
	high	291 (245.89)**	104 (149.11)**	395
	low	52 (97.11)**	104 (58.89)**	156
		343	208	551

*For operational definitions of "high" and "low" see text.
**Chance expectancies in parentheses.
[1] The author is indebted to James M. Schaefer for checking the calculations here.

high compensation to wife's kin is indeed associated, as Murdock suggested, with low versus high likelihood of residence with or near the husband's kin (chi-square equals 75, p less than .001). Of the cases in which couples are likely to settle with or near the husband's kin almost two-thirds provide considerable compensation to the wife's kin at or around the time of marriage; in contrast, of the cases in which couples are not likely to settle with or near the husband's kin, almost two-thirds do not provide such compensation to the wife's kin.

Why this relationship exists is a problem beyond the scope of this paper. But the way it was revealed illustrates the advantage of classifying things ordinally rather than nominally—assuming, of course, the existence of *a priori* reasoning (in this case Murdock's) to direct our search for lawfulness. Although the table in Coult and Habenstein (1965) suggested some sort of relationship between

mode of marriage and marital residence, we would not have been able to discover anything more specific about the relationship if we had not hypothesized exactly how mode of marriage might be related to residence and accordingly reclassified the data ordinally. The moral is clear: If we want to discover the specific relations between things, we should try to classify or otherwise measure those things according to how we expect them to be related. More particularly, if we can think of an ordinal classification, we should use it.

THE ROLE OF CLASSIFICATION IN A DEVELOPING SCIENCE

In the preceding section, we have examined a number of principles of classification and discussed their implications for comparative studies, and we have compared the two kinds of classification we might employ in such studies. This section discusses one final principle of classification, namely that a scientifically useful one contains the germs of its own extinction.

It has been suggested (Northrop 1947, Hempel 1965) that the development of a science usually begins with a "natural history" stage, during which investigators try to describe the phenomena under study and to establish simple generalizations concerning them, and then proceeds to more and more "theoretical" stages, during which there is an increasing emphasis on the achievement of comprehensive theoretical accounts of the phenomena under study. Cultural anthropology, it seems to me, is nearing the end of its "natural history" stage, not only because there are fewer and fewer cultures that have not been described, but because we are beginning to gag on all of our undigested data. Our journals are still dominated by essentially descriptive articles, but more and more of them are being written with some comparative issue in mind. For example, an article on ambilineal descent groups in the Gilberts now asks how those groups differ from or resemble such groups elsewhere (Lambert 1966). We are no longer completely satisfied with purely descriptive writing, unless perhaps it is modishly garbed in the new "ethnoscientific" style. But even such new vessels for old data will begin to pall, I suggest, as we increasingly realize that the real frontier in our discipline, the exciting and wide-open challenge, is the colossal scale of our ignorance about why cultures are different and why they came to be that way.

In a discipline like cultural anthropology, which is just emerging from its "natural history" stage, most of the questions posed in research will refer to readily observable phenomena. As Hempel (1965:140) says: "The vocabulary required in the early stages . . . will be chosen so as to permit the description of those aspects of the subject matter which are ascertainable fairly directly by observation." This tendency to deal with observables rather than theoretical terms is exhibited in cross-cultural as well as in intra-cultural studies. Until we have achieved considerably greater understanding of cultural variation, the classifications we construct to generate or test hypotheses cross-culturally are likely to derive most of their categories from conventional modes of analysis and to employ concepts that are closely tied to the standard ethnographic observables, as in the example described in the previous section.

The time will come, however, when we will have accumulated a good deal of knowledge about the correlations among those standard observables. The correlations themselves will then become the "facts" we spend most of our time trying to explain. As we find ways to explain them, we shall find that the concepts we use will be changing. Our old (and successful) classifications will be replaced by more complex ways of measurement, just as our essentially descriptive terms will be replaced by more theoretical terms. It is ironic that, as our classifications prove more and more scientifically useful, they will become more and more obsolete. Quoting again from Hempel (1965:148–149):

. . . the concepts used in a given field of scientific inquiry will change with the systematic advances made in that field: the formation of concepts will go hand in hand with the formulation of laws and, eventually, of theories. . . . [The] laws may at first express simple uniform or statistical connections among observables; they will then be formulated in terms of the observational vocabulary of the discipline. . . . Further systematic progress, however, will call for the formulation of principles expressed in theoretical terms which refer to various kinds of unobservable entities and their characteristics. In the course of such development, classifications defined by reference to manifest, observable characteristics will tend to give way to systems based on theoretical concepts. This process is illustrated, for example, by the shift from an observational-phenomenal characterization and classification of chemical elements and compounds to theoretical modes of defining and differentiating them by reference to their atomic and molecular structures.

Let us be clear about the reason that a scientifically useful classification contains the germs of its own extinction. Classification is a "yes or no" affair. A given object either falls into a given subset or it does not, depending upon whether or not it possesses the defining attribute(s).

In scientific research, however, the objects under study are often found to resist a tidy pigeonholing of this kind. More precisely: those characteristics of the subject matter which, in the given context of investigation, suggest themselves as a fruitful basis of classification often cannot well be treated as properties which a given object *either* has *or* lacks; rather, they have the character of traits which are capable of gradations, and which a given object may therefore exhibit *more or less* markedly. As a result, some of the objects under study will present the investigator with borderline cases, which do not fit unequivocally into one or another of several neatly bounded compartments, but which exhibit to some degree the characteristics of *different* classes. (Hempel 1965:151–152)

Quantitative concepts have a further advantage over classificatory ones, even of the ordinal variety, namely that they allow us to use the powerful tools of quantitative mathematics. Laws and theories can then be expressed ". . . in terms of functions connecting several variables, and consequences can be derived from them, for purposes of prediction or of test, by means of mathematical techniques" (Hempel 1965:153).

In short, if the more mature sciences are any guide, the future development of comparative studies will probably show two trends: 1) a gradual shift from studies which deal with observable characteristics to studies which deal with theoretical concepts that have operational criteria of application; and 2) a gradual shift from nominal classificatory concepts and methods to ordering concepts and methods, both of the ordinal and interval scale varieties.

BIBLIOGRAPHY

BLALOCK, HUBERT M., JR.
1960 *Social statistics.* New York, McGraw-Hill.
COHEN, MORRIS R.
1931 *Reason and nature.* New York, Harcourt.
COULT, ALLAN D., and ROBERT W. HABENSTEIN
1965 *Cross tabulations of Murdock's World Ethnographic Sample.* Columbia, University of Missouri Press.
DRIVER, HAROLD E.
1966 Geographical-historical *versus* psychofunctional explanations of kin avoidances. *Current Anthropology* 7:131–148.
FREEMAN, LINTON D.
1957 *An empirical test of folk-urbanism.* Ann Arbor, Mich., University Microfilms, No. 23,502.
GRÜNBAUM, ADOLF
1953 Causality and the science of human behavior. In Herbert Feigl and May Brodbeck, eds., *Readings in the philosophy of science.* New York, Appleton-Century-Crofts.
HEMPEL, CARL G.
1965 Fundamentals of taxonomy. In Carl G. Hempel, *Aspects of scientific explanation.* New York, Free Press.
KRECH, DAVID, RICHARD S. CRUTCHFIELD, and EGGERTON L. BALLACHEY
1962 *Individual in society.* New York, McGraw-Hill.
LAMBERT, BERND
1966 Ambilineal descent groups in the Northern Gilbert Islands. *American Anthropologist* 68:641–664.
MERTON, ROBERT K.
1957 *Social theory and social structure,* revised and enlarged edition. Glencoe, Ill., Free Press.

MIDDLETON, JOHN, and DAVID TAIT (eds.)
1958 *Tribes without rulers.* London, Routledge and Kegan Paul.
MURDOCK, GEORGE PETER
1949 *Social structure.* New York, Macmillan.
1957 World ethnographic sample. *American Anthropologist* 59:664–687.
NAROLL, RAOUL
1956 A preliminary index of social development. *American Anthropologist* 58:687–715.
NORTHROP, F. S. C.
1947 *The logic of the sciences and the humanities.* New York, Macmillan.
PRATT, CARROLL C.
1939 *The logic of modern psychology.* New York, Macmillan.
ROMNEY, A. KIMBALL, and ROY GOODWIN D'ANDRADE
1964 Transcultural studies in cognition. *American Anthropologist* 66, No. 3, Part 2.
SAPIR, EDWARD
1937 Language. In Edwin R. A. Seligman, ed., *Encyclopedia of the social sciences* 9: 155–168. New York, Macmillan.
SELLTIZ, CLAIRE, MARIE JAHODA, MORTON DEUTSCH, and STUART W. COOK
1961 *Research methods in social relations,* revised one-volume edition. New York, Holt, Rinehart and Winston.
STEWARD, JULIAN H.
1949 Cultural causality and law: a trial formulation of the development of the early civilizations. *American Anthropologist* 51:1–27.
STURTEVANT, WILLIAM C.
1964 Studies in ethnoscience. In A. Kimball Romney and Roy Goodwin D'Andrade, eds., Transcultural studies in cognition. *American Anthropologist* 66, No. 3, Part 2:99–131.

CHAPTER 38

Coding Ethnographic Materials

FRANK M. LEBAR

Coding is commonly associated with global cross-cultural surveys of the statistical type—which Köbben (1966:169) has called hologeistic, and which Lewis (1966:63) calls atomistic. For the five-year period 1950–1954, Lewis was able to list ten dissertations and published studies of this type. In the ten-year period since 1954, a check of the literature reveals at least fifty studies of the global type using statistics. In the year 1965, the *American Anthropologist* alone published three such studies. In addition, there appeared in 1965 Coult and Habenstein's *Cross Tabulations of Murdock's World Ethnographic Sample* and in 1963 Banks and Textor's *A Cross-Polity Survey,* the latter a computer print-out, including cross-tabulations of some fifty-seven variables. Textor has ready for the press another massive computer print-out containing coded variables with cross-tabulations from some thirty-eight prior studies, published and unpublished (Textor 1967). And since 1962, G. P. Murdock has been publishing in *Ethnology* his "Ethnographic Atlas," a series of variables for (so far) over seven hundred societies in what is to be a "complete analysis of the ethnographic universe" (Murdock 1963:249). There seems little doubt, then, that studies employing new codes and/or using precoded data have increased markedly within the past decade—and that even more such studies will appear in the future.

In light of this obvious proliferation of coded data, and the wide use that is undoubtedly going to be made of it, there would

I am indebted to Frank W. Moore, John M. Roberts, Clellan S. Ford, Timothy J. O'Leary, and Robert O. Lagacé for their criticisms of earlier drafts of this paper.

seem to be a justification for an examination of the entire subject—the conceptual and methodological premises involved, the techniques employed, and the results achieved thus far. A few preliminary definitions are, however, in order.

PRELIMINARY DEFINITIONS

A *code* is a system of symbols that achieves some desirable advantage over common language in the communication process. (The definition of "code" and likewise of succeeding italicized concepts are borrowed from Kent 1962:163.) The particular set of symbols used to represent a code may be designated by the term *notation.* Codes are commonly used to reduce the space required to record information. Before any set of data can be coded it must be *analyzed,* i.e., broken up or sorted according to a conceptual scheme of some kind—commonly by indexing or classifying. *Classification* is the putting or arranging of data into classes, on the basis of resemblance or likeness.

The coding of ethnographic materials can be regarded as essentially a step in the information retrieval process, designed to short-cut the cumbersomeness of normal expression and to reduce the amount of space required to record a large corpus of information. Prior analysis and classification of data are often accomplished by the researcher himself. Within the field of cultural anthropology, however, the Human Relations Area Files has undertaken this phase of the process on a broad scale; the Area Files, a collection of preanalyzed data to which has been applied a simple substitution code, are available for research use at a number of universities and scholarly institutions (see Chapter 33).

This paper will approach the subject of coding from the point of view of (1) the nature of the ethnographic statement, the prime datum of comparative ethnology; (2) the task of getting ethnographic descriptions into a system such as the HRAF—essentially a problem of data analysis and classification, of pigeonholing data according to the conceptual categories of a "universal culture pattern"; (3) cross-cultural coding—essentially a problem of societal classification, of pigeonholing a society or ethnic unit according to a predetermined set of indicators or variables (which may be in the form of a typological classification, a scale or continuum, or a present-absent dichotomy); and (4) subsequent use of precoded data.

This developmental approach seems justified in view of the fact that the greater proportion of existing codes have been based, directly or indirectly, on data in the HRAF or its precursor, the Yale Cross-Cultural Survey. Additionally, it seems worthwhile to look at the nature and use of precoded data in view of the rapid proliferation of codes within the past decade and the cumulative effect of studies using precoded material of the kind to be found in Murdock's World Ethnographic Sample and his Ethnographic Atlas.

PROBLEMS OF CONCEPTUALIZATION

The application of a code, or notational system, to data presupposes some kind of prior analysis or sorting out of the data within classes or categories. These in turn must rest on a system or set of concepts. The ethnographer in the field organizes his data according to a set of concepts in his own mind—or he may attempt to organize the information according to native categories. Likewise, the formation of a data retrieval system such as HRAF requires a set of concepts (the classes of like data, or categories, of the *Outline of Cultural Materials*). And the researcher making a cross-cultural survey works with concepts (indicators, attributes, variables). We need, therefore, to examine the conceptualization of data at these various levels, in order to clarify our thinking about exactly what we are doing when we classify or code ethnographic data.

Goodenough (1956) has pointed out that much of ethnographic description to date has been couched within a conceptual framework derived from long-existing preoccupations within comparative ethnology; the field ethnographer reports that his group is "predominantly patrilocal" (perhaps supporting this statement with the results of a census) and feels that his tasks as a reporter are fulfilled. The comparativist, in turn, has made use of ethnographic statements of this order, since they predominate in the literature. Goodenough objects that what ethnographer Jones calls patrilocal in society A may not be the same as what Smith reports as patrilocal in society B (or at least that the criteria in terms of which the people within the two societies make residence choices may not be the same). But the fact remains that a comparativist such as Murdock, using ethnographic statements of the traditional sort to which Goodenough objects, was able to demonstrate significant associations among kinship systems, rules or residence, and forms of the family —and to go on to formulate important conclusions about the relationship of these social structural factors with economic and geographic factors. More important for the conduct of comparative research has been Goodenough's demonstration that two ethnographers, reporting on the same society within the space of three years, could come up with quite different statements as to prevailing residence rules within that society (1956).

Goodenough and his colleagues within the new "ethnographic semantics" emphasize the necessity for a clearer distinction between ethnography and (comparative) ethnology. They are attempting a new rigor in ethnographic reporting, wherein they go beyond the traditional ethnographic statement to an analysis (analogous to that employed in linguistics) and construction of a theoretical model that will most adequately and elegantly account for observed phenomena within a single society. As phrased by Goodenough (1964:9), they conceive their task as one of discovering "the most economical statements of laws governing behavioral events within one society." Their intent, insofar as it concerns cross-cultural research, is that (1) the comparativist may have at his disposal adequate information on which to classify societies within existing conceptual pigeonholes, and (2) from this new ethnography may emerge new concepts or new ways of looking at data that may have greater cross-cultural validity. Lowie's objection (Köbben 1966:172) that "when we know that a tribe practices witchcraft (and), believes in ghosts . . . we know precisely nothing concerning the religion of the *people concerned*" [my emphasis] is certainly true. But global statistical studies do not concern themselves with understanding the culture of any one group in a sample; they are concerned, rather, with problems of intercultural similarities and differences and with uncovering associations among cultural or other variables that might account for these. Goodenough's rule (1956:37) is applicable here, i.e., that the concepts that are suitable for describing particular cultures are not necessarily the same as those suitable for comparing these cultures with others. The problem is that the comparativist is working with traditional common-sense categories (e.g., witchcraft) derived from Western culture. Hence their usefulness as cross-cultural concepts—as truly comparable from one society to another—is questionable. And it is precisely here that Goodenough insists that truly comparable concepts will have to emerge from prior studies of cultures in their own terms—in terms of ethno-categories that will adequately and completely account for the observed behavior within each particular culture.

But until ethnographic semantics produces a corpus of ethnographic descriptions of whole societies (and not just minute analyses of drinking behavior, plant classification, kinship systems, and the like), the comparativist, if he is to operate at all, must perforce rely on the existing literature. The question then becomes: What are the pitfalls in classifying and coding this literature for cross-cultural survey purposes, and what means have been (or can be) taken to avoid or reduce the methodological hazards involved?

CLASSIFYING DATA: THE HRAF

The data in the HRAF are classified according to the *Outline of Cultural Materials*, published originally in 1938 and now in its fourth revised edition (Murdock *et al.* 1965). The 710 categories described in the *Outline* are intended as a guide to both input and retrieval of data. Major categories are numbered from 10 to 88, with up to nine three-digit subdivisions within each major division. For example, 86 is *Socialization,* 861 is *Techniques of Inculcation,* and 869 is *Transmission of Beliefs.* The system is multidimensional, allowing the same datum to be placed in more than one category; cross references direct the researcher to related categories. Finally, the categories are of the generic type, e.g., shamans and psychoanalysts are both filed under 756, *Psychotherapists.*

As stated in the preface to the *OCM,* the categories or classes of data found therein reflect the way in which ethnographic description is most frequently organized in the literature. The authors state that in this sense the classification is wholly pragmatic (Murdock *et al.* 1965:xxi). Kluckhohn, commenting on the categories of the "standard monograph," refers to them as "in the first instance common-sense concepts corresponding to nineteenth-century Western notions of the all-pervasive framework of human life . . . slightly modified in accord with changing theoretical fashions" (Kluckhohn 1966:90). The *OCM* category headings such as *Polygamy, Games, Slavery, Clans, Magic, Funeral,* etc., can be found in most nineteenth-century *Völkerkunde* and in the classic compilations by Spencer, Sumner and Keller, and others. They are well within the definition of Wissler's "universal culture pattern." Kluckhohn rightly criticizes these concepts from the point of view of their comparability for cross-cultural research purposes. Further examples of the prescientific nature of commonly used categories can be found in the psychoanalytically-oriented studies of Whiting, Child, and others, which use as measures of adult pathology factors such as high incidence of drunkenness or crime—presumed by Western standards to be deviant behavior indicative of psychopathology.

The immediate inspiration for the *OCM* and the Cross-Cultural Survey was undoubtedly Yale's Albert G. Keller, and through him William Graham Sumner. The six co-authors of the first edition of the *OCM* (Murdock, Ford, Hudson, Kennedy, Simmons, and Whiting) all received their Ph.D. degrees at Yale in either sociology or anthropology—Murdock in 1925 and the others in the 1930s. All six studied with Keller, who continued his influential teaching careeer at Yale until

1940. G. P. Murdock, the founder of the CCS and the principal author of the *OCM,* has acknowledged his intellectual debt to these men (Murdock 1965:358). If one compares the table of contents of Sumner and Keller's *Science of Society* (1927) with the categories in the *OCM* (discounting categories 01–18 and those not normally pertaining to preliterate societies, e.g., *Finance, Taxation, Delinquency,* and the like), one finds that only about twenty-four *OCM* (two- and three-digit) categories are not represented in the *SOS* table of contents. Nine of these twenty-four are, however, listed by name in the *SOS* index, often with numerous text references. The result is that only the following categories appear to be represented weakly or not at all in the *SOS: Material Culture, Diet, Settlement Pattern, Marketing, Travel, Daily Routine, Social Mobility, Ethnic Stratification, Kin Groups* (other than *Clan*), *Territorial Organization, Political Behavior, Numbers and Measures, Ethnobotany, Sexuality and Sexual Behavior, Socialization* (other than *Initiation*).

Sumner, stimulated by Spencer's *Principles of Sociology,* set out to outline a "science of society," to consist of generalizations about behavior arrived at inductively through the examination of case material. He died in 1910, leaving his junior colleague, Keller, a mass of notes and manuscripts. The latter finished the four-volume *Science of Society,* using essentially the system of presentation devised by Sumner (Keller's preface to *SOS,* Vol. 1, xxiii–xxxii). It is instructive to note that when Keller came to compile the fourth-volume casebook, he had on hand a great quantity of notes (collected for the most part by Sumner) composed of quotations and extracts from writings on societies, mostly preliterate, from around the world. In order to organize these voluminous notes, Keller one summer arranged for the use of Yale's Woolsey Hall. He then proceeded to distribute the notes on seats, letting aisle seats represent societies and row seats the topics under which he intended to organize the casebook. He had, thus, what Sumner once termed a "Laboratory without Walls"—a kind of primitive version of what Murdock later developed as the Cross-Cultural Survey, and which in turn was reorganized in 1949 as the Human Relations Area Files. (I am indebted to C. S. Ford for

this information.) And Murdock's goal, in setting up the CCS and in his subsequent work, has been essentially that of Sumner—to arrive at the "laws" of a "science of society" inductively through comparative analysis of case materials (Murdock 1965:297 ff.; and 1966:40 ff.). Murdock has added an element of statistical verification lacking in Sumner's work.

The *OCM* categories, then, are common-sense categories of the kind traditional to ethnography. As such, the system lends itself best to the analysis of traditional ethnography. This fact is reflected in the experience of analysts at HRAF over the years; the least "trouble" is experienced with the traditional comprehensive ethnography (e.g., Gusinde 1937). Analysts have the greatest difficulty in applying the *OCM* system to works produced by certain adherents of British social anthropology (e.g., Read 1956) and to results of some of the newer problem-centered research (e.g., Faron 1961). More general concepts, which crosscut the older established categories, e.g., authority, social control, integration, and social mobility, occasion much concern among HRAF analysts.

The ethnographic statement of the traditional sort is most often at the level of what Linton has called the "cultural construct" (Linton 1945:45). On the basis of what he has seen and heard, the ethnographer makes a generalizing statement. The full range of variation of behavior and the conditions governing choices, within a particular culture, may or may not be given.

Whether the ethnographic statement consists of an ethnographer's "construct," or of what he reports as ideational behavior (rules or standards in the minds of the people), or of what purports to be "actual behavior" makes no difference insofar as the HRAF classification system is concerned. The *OCM* categories provide for no systematic distinction among these levels of reporting, and it is up to the user to determine, by the nature of the statement or by internal analysis of the source, the level of reporting. The categories do vary as to the specificity or degree to which they break down a concept. Category 591, *Residence,* provides for any data on where a couple choose to live after marriage—regardless of how it is labeled. Category 61, *Kin Groups,* on the other hand, is broken down into 612 *Kin-*

dreds, 613 *Lineages,* 614 *Sibs,* and so on through 618 *Clans.* This means that in cases where the ethnographer has not already attached a conceptual label, the HRAF analyst must decide, for example, whether a given description should be coded for 614 *Sibs* or 618 *Clans.* It is true that cross-reference slips can be added in such cases and that the user would ordinarily be expected to look under both categories. Similarly, 596 *Extended Families* provides for data on any of various possible combinations of living arrangements, whereas types of religious experience are specified under such headings as 782 *Propitiation,* 783 *Purification and Expiation,* etc.

FORMAL ANALYSIS OF DATA

The researcher attempting to code ethnographic data (including those classified in the HRAF) is faced then, at the outset, with certain fundamental problems—in themselves a function of the complex nature of ethnographic statements per se, and the non-comparability of concepts in terms of which data are traditionally organized in the field and classified in a system such as HRAF. These problems have been attacked notably by C. S. Ford and J. W. M. Whiting in various papers on methods of formal analysis and on specificity of referents.

Both Ford and Whiting, in their comparative studies, have made wide use of biogenic and psychogenic variables. As noted by Kluckhohn (1966:92), the difficulties inherent in the comparability of data are predictably less in such instances. Nevertheless, it is instructive to examine the methods devised by these and other workers in comparative ethnology to attempt to control these inherent problems. Ford (1966a) starts off by defining *culture* as consisting of beliefs and rules (implicit or explicit standards of conduct) in contrast to *custom,* which he defines as the actual behavior of the members of a society. Working with what he has defined as rules, Ford then proceeds to a formal analysis in terms of their properties, i.e., *person, condition, emphasis, behavior, sanction,* and *meaning.* This analysis, published in 1939, closely approximates a listing under the heading of "general directions" in the 1938 (first) edition of the *OCM.* Later editions of the *OCM* have carried in their introductory pages a list of "seven major

facets" said to be characteristic of "any element of culture." These are presented as analytic concepts employed in defining or arriving at the categories within the *OCM* system. These are (1) *patterned activity,* a customary norm of motor, verbal or implicit behavior; (2) *circumstances;* (3) *subject,* a culturally defined class of persons; (4) *object* toward which an activity is directed; (5) *means;* (6) *purpose;* and (7) *result.*

Ford (1966a:153 ff.) demonstrates the use of such analytical concepts in a cross-cultural study of the rules governing behavior with respect to the biological activities that they forbid or prescribe. Combining meaning and sanction, for example, he comes up with categories such as "insulting another," which he feels are of a more general nature (and thus of greater cross-cultural utility) than statements of actual behavior. Ford also uses the concepts of "problem" and "problem solving," whereby customs are regarded as traditional problem solutions, e.g., those customs surrounding problems posed during conception, pregnancy, and childbirth (Ford 1945). In all such attempts he, like others, is attempting to get behind actual behavior (which varies in detail from society to society) to something that can be generalized cross-culturally and that is truly comparable as one moves from one society to another. As Ford has recently pointed out, the development of culture-free common referents for purposes of comparative research is one of the most difficult problems facing anthropology. There is no "royal road" to the collection and analysis of data by which we can hope to attain these ends. Descriptions in detail of actual patterns of behavior are needed, as well as construction of ideational concepts by means of which a people conceive of their universe and order their way of life (Ford 1966b).

Whiting (1966) takes as his basic unit what he likewise calls *custom,* defining it as referring to the behavior of a typical individual in a given society, with the qualification that its attributes—the agent, the act, and the circumstances—be recognized as categories by the members of the society. Whiting makes the further conceptual innovation of equating custom with habit: assuming that psychological principles (including learning theory) that apply to habit should also apply to custom, he and his colleagues have proceeded to test a variety of Hullian and Freudian hypotheses on a sample of the ethnographic literature.

Whiting further assumes that any custom is actually embedded in a complex of related customs—a *custom complex*. He then proceeds to a formal analysis of this concept, in a manner similar to Ford's analysis of rules. The attributes or properties of a custom complex may consist of *practices, beliefs, values, sanctions, rules, motives,* and *satisfactions* (Whiting and Child 1953:27 ff.). These attributes are all conceived of as customs. Thus, "Value is a custom whose response attributes goodness or badness to some event," or again, "Rules, beliefs and values are symbolic customs and form part of the stimulus pattern and of the motivation of a practice." These can all be "behavior of a typical individual in a given society." Culture in these terms is behavior, symbolic or otherwise. This kind of analysis affords a certain framework for cross-cultural comparison utilizing relatively culture-free referents. Typologies of sanctions or motives can be worked out and actual practices in individual societies then classed and compared under such headings.

If we take a closer look at what Whiting is actually dealing with when he analyzes and compares customs, we find that this is most often in the form of ethnographic generalizations or constructs—made either by an ethnographer on the basis of what he observes and what his informants tell him or by the comparative ethnologist (Whiting himself or his colleagues) on the basis of various kinds of information in the literature. Thus Whiting writes: "Our data are accounts given by anthropologists of customary behavior, based partly on observations of behavior of individuals and partly on statements by informants about how people typically behave or ought to behave" (Whiting and Child 1953:16–17). Or again, "A reasonably reliable estimate of the typical behavior of people in small homogeneous societies can be made on the basis of ethnographic data" (Whiting 1966:293).

This leads us back again to the observation that most ethnographic statements are in the nature of generalizations about cultural behavior, whether one chooses to call them "cultural norms," "customs," "rules," "patterns," or by any other term. This is the level of the data with which the comparativist ordinarily works. These are the kinds of statements which the cross-cultural survey method attempts to measure, scale, and code —either directly (based on an ethnographer's explicitly stated construct) or by making a kind of generalization-once-removed, on the basis of what scattered information can be found in the literature. The point is that the ordinary ethnographic report seldom distinguishes observed behavior from statements of ideal patterns in the minds of informants— or either of these from constructs made by the observer in terms of his own preconceptions and stereotypes. Elements of all three may be present in a typical statement. Although Murdock and Whiting are not unaware of these problems, they have gone ahead in their attempts to make do with what literature is available, and have proceeded on the assumption of a modal or average custom as the unit of comparison.

"In justification of our method, we can only say that in general what the sources report is what the informants said was supposed to be the case, so that the comparisons are generally between two supposed or ideal patterns. We have to assume, to make these results valid, that the difference between the ideal pattern and the manifest behavior is approximately the same from society to society, which is a very questionable assumption, I grant" (Murdock, reply to Erikson, pp. 40–41 in Senn 1951). The results of their work to date, although criticized (at times severely) from some quarters, are nevertheless impressive with respect to the sheer number of demonstrated correlations and the hypotheses as to the nature of culture which they have raised.

The assumption of a modal or average custom as the unit of comparison is perhaps the only practical procedure in light of the nature of the existing ethnographic data. But to assume that there are no significant differences between normative statements about behavior (standards of behavior) and the actual behavior itself runs counter to much of the experience of field ethnography. If one accepts the fact that differences do exist, then the implications of this for the theoretical results of correlational studies would seem to be considerable; for example, in correlating two variables within the same society, one's results might vary depending on whether the data were altogether at the normative level or partly at the level of observed behavior. The difficulty lies in actually testing the effects of differences in the level of reporting, using the (so often) undifferentiated statements in the existing literature.

At this stage it is perhaps premature to state categorically that any one approach to cross-cultural survey research is necessarily invalid. To quote Ford: "There seems to be no sure way of knowing in advance which approach or combination of approaches to identifying and classifying aspects of culture is going to be the most useful" (1966b:81). But, adds Ford, the underlying assumptions of the researcher regarding the nature of culture tend to favor some approaches over others. What is important is that the would-be researcher be aware of his underlying assumptions and that he make them explicit—both as an aid in his own research and to the reader who is attempting to evaluate the results. Ford, Whiting, and some others have attempted to do this and have evolved methods of formal analysis, deriving from such underlying assumptions, which they feel enable them to move with some assurance of comparability from one society to another.

A major move in this direction has been the attempt by the Whitings to apply uniform concepts and data-gathering techniques to six cultures in the field of child rearing and socialization (Beatrice Whiting 1963). Many workers in this field, on the other hand, appear to pay relatively little attention to such explication—and the reader is left to assume that they are simply taking the literature at some kind of face value. Their awareness, if any, of underlying assumptions within the ethnography itself or in their own analysis and coding of the data is left unstated.

CROSS-CULTURAL CODING

Thus far we have been discussing the more theoretical problems of conceptual levels and comparability of concepts as these apply to both raw and coded data. We now turn to an examination of some of the characteristics and special problems of codes as actually used in cross-cultural survey research.

Coding is normally employed in global- or random-type studies which quantify, measure, or scale data. Such studies normally utilize a sample of twenty-five or more societies, and

if a number of variables are investigated and if ratings are manipulated statistically there is the problem of presenting data in tabular form within a minimum of space. Studies of this type in general fall within one of three classes: (1) range of variability studies, (2) random correlation studies, and (3) postulational studies. Ford's research on human reproduction (1945) explores the range of beliefs and practices in regard to various phases of the reproductive cycle in man. Simple quantification is employed in order to demonstrate the relative strength of cross-cultural uniformities that point to generalizations about basic human behavior.

Random correlation studies, such as those by Simmons (1945) and Banks and Textor (1963), go a step beyond the simple normative type in that they attempt to get at the determinants of intercultural variation by looking for "adhesions" or correlations between variables. They are essentially exploratory in nature, without prior hypotheses. The unsympathetic critic might well term them "fishing expeditions."

Postulational studies set out to test specific hypotheses on a cross-cultural sample. As exemplified by the work of Murdock (1949), Horton (1943), Swanson (1960), and others this involves the prediction, on the basis of prior hypotheses, of positive correlations between variables. The data are analyzed and coded and the resulting scores or ratings then commonly subjected to one or another of various statistical tests to determine degree of association and level of significance. Depending on the outcome, the original hypothesis is considered to be supported or disproved. Studies of the postulational type are the most numerous in the literature; they hold the most promise of advancing a science of society, but at the same time they are plagued by the greatest number of methodological problems. (See Chapters 2 and 5.)

The notation systems employed in coding data for cross-cultural survey research can be either of two basic types: (1) ordinal or scalar, and (2) typological. The former ordinarily sets up a scale, continuum, or rank order and assigns units (societies, cultures, ethnic units) to points along this continuum. A notation of this type is commonly in terms of "pronounced-moderate-negligible," "dominant-strong-weak," or the like. The latter sets up types or categories within a given universe, e.g., "patrilocal-matrilocal-neolocal," and assigns a unit to one or another of these pigeonholes. The commonly used present-absent dichotomy, although seemingly simple to apply, presents special problems with respect to the determination of negative evidence, to be discussed below.

Any of the above notational types may be further classified as direct or indirect. That is to say, the coding of something like altitude or presence of plow agriculture rests on relatively direct evidence that can be and usually is unequivocably stated in the literature; a variable such as degree of anxiety, on the other hand, must be arrived at indirectly as a composite of several other scores (cf., Horton 1943) or by judgmental ratings of some sort (cf., Whiting and Child 1953). A common control in judgmental rating or scoring is the use of multiple judges, ideally with no prior knowledge of the hypotheses being tested. Tests of inter-rater reliability are normally reported in studies of this type. As a further control or check, the scores of raters can be compared as between those with prior knowledge of hypotheses and those without (cf., Swanson 1960).

A notational system commonly purports (whether so stated or not) to exhaust a particular universe. A given trait is either present or absent; a given society is either patrilocal, matrilocal, or neolocal. Whatever the attributes chosen for a particular notation, it is assumed that a given case will fall somewhere within the scale or typology chosen. There are (implicitly at least) no other logical choices. As pointed out by Banks and Textor (1963:8–9), typological coding tends to be relativistic, i.e., the assignment of a society or polity to a particular attribute is based on a consideration of that polity in relation to other polities within the sample universe, and does not necessarily represent a characterization of that polity in any absolute sense. The categories within a typology are usually considered to be distinctive and mutually exclusive. For a recent attempt to construct a typology of distinctive but overlapping types, see Spiro (1965).

These characteristics are most explicit in codes set up independent of the data—on the basis of a formal model or set of hypotheses. Such coding, of course, runs the risk of overlooking (or miscoding) cases which do not fit and which might suggest a logical extension of the notational system. A more serious problem is the possibility that the researcher may unconsciously tend to rate or score the data in a direction predicted by his prior hypotheses. One possible control here is to run a check on a sample of the sample, using raters with no knowledge of the hypotheses and thus no understanding of the significance of the notational system and no bias in the rating of variables (cf., Swanson 1960: 40–41). A further, somewhat related, method of checking the validity of ratings and of generalizations resulting from cross-cultural research is what Roberts and Sutton-Smith (1962) have called the technique of subsystem validation, utilizing as supplementary data those from well-documented societies.

Thus Roberts reports a positive association, based on a global-type, cross-cultural comparison, between certain child-training variables and types of game involvement. Societies that rated high in obedience and responsibility training rated high on games of strategy and chance, while those rating high on achievement training rated high on games of physical skill. Since these training variables have been shown to differ according to sex, Roberts reasoned that if a universal association does indeed exist between child training and game involvement, then the preferences by sex for different types of games should reflect this fact. He should, for example, be able to predict the game preferences of American boys and girls. Using results of existing grade school tests and questionnaires, he found that 37 out of 56 games were so predictive at the 5 per cent level, or better. As Roberts puts it: "Cultural variation occurs within, as well as between, social groups. Under favorable circumstances, therefore, it is possible to study the relationships among variables at two levels of generality, e.g., in a world sample of societies and in subcultures within a single national culture. If generalizations established on the basis of cross-cultural study are found to have predictive power within particular cultures, confidence in the cross-cultural generalizations is increased" (Roberts and Sutton-Smith 1962:170).

The mental processes associated with classification and coding, are above all, those of decision making.

In the classification of data in a system such as HRAF, the analyst must decide that a given block of data is or is not this or that; in judgmental coding there are often additional decisions as to ranking, ordering, measuring, or comparing. With respect to the analysis and classification of data for HRAF, at least, the intriguing possibility arises as to whether an analysis of the coding decisions of analysts might provide some insight into behavior in such situations and thus a potentially fruitful vantage point from which to evaluate the coded material already in the Files. The analyst is basically beset by two conditions—on the one hand, the requirements of the classification system (OCM), which demand decisions, and on the other his natural disinclination to make decisions. Do analysts in this situation tend to behave in a manner calculated to attain the greatest gain with the least risk? Alternate strategies available to analysts are either overmarking (coding) or undermarking. Do analysts tend to employ overmarking, for example, in order to maximize gain (avoid decision making) and minimize risk (getting out of line with the "system" or rendering the files useless for researchers)? Where there is an element of choice as between two or more categories (as in coding data for the HRAF files) or as between two or more attributes in a scale or typology (as in cross-cultural coding), the element of subjective judgment enters the picture. The effectiveness of the HRAF as a retrieval system assumes a level of consistency among those who do the analysis and coding of the data; the scientific results of a cross-cultural study rest on the assumption that the classification and coding is sufficiently objective so that a second rater or scorer, going through the same data, would agree in a significantly large number of cases with the original rating. Although some attention is paid this problem in the literature, it is not uncommon in cross-cultural research to find the author presenting his ratings without the original data which would allow an independent check of the ratings. In fact, in a study involving many societies, the presentation of the original data becomes almost a physical impossibility. In those cases where the study has utilized the HRAF, it is common practice to cite the HRAF source and page numbers; this at least allows the interested individual to read through the same material with a minimum of labor if he is so inclined.

The reliability of HRAF coding (i.e., con-sistency in coding expressed as measure of agreement among analysts) was examined in a test situation by Kay (1957). The results indicated a mean agreement among some twenty-seven analysts of between 80 and 83 per cent with respect to a predetermined list of preferred categories. This does not mean that material not assigned to preferred or prime categories is necessarily lost to the researcher, since the basic OCM classification is supplemented by an extensive system of cross references. The study did reveal that overcoding, rather than undercoding, may present a greater problem to the person using the Files. That is, the researcher is likely to find that in any particular category approximately 4 per cent of the slips will yield data unrelated to the stated contents.

Some redundancy is a common feature of retrieval systems employing other than machine coding, and in this respect the HRAF system appears no better and no worse than other systems. As Kent says: "It is not possible for a single analyst, much less a team of analysts, to exercise absolute consistency in the way in which they conduct analyses of graphic records. Some means must be considered for overcoming the effects of inconsistency, either through the use of some redundancy in analysis [or] through the use of a coding or cross-reference system which is superimposed after analysis." Concerning machine coding, Kent adds: "This absolute consistency [of machine coding] brings with it no guarantees whatever that the resulting analysis meets any of the purposes that are to be served by an information-retrieval system" (1962:84).

In cross-cultural studies employing judgmental-type variables (and usually multiple raters or judges), researchers attempt to make their coding criteria as explicit or "foolproof" as possible, and coding rules are normally included in the presentation of the results of cross-cultural research. The ideal here is that given the coding rules or "instructions to coders," an independent rater going over the same data would be bound to come up with identical results. Of course, the inability to completely objectify some types of variables and the unevenness of the ethnographic literature make the attainment of the ideal a virtual impossibility.

As a further control on consistency (replicability) of coding it is not uncommon to report results of tests on inter-rater reliability. Whiting (1964:511), for example, reports 83 per cent agreement on fifty-three overlapping cases as to presence or absence of circumcision rites between Murdock's determination and judgments made at the Laboratory of Human Development. In this same study, Whiting (1964:525) reports between 75 and 95 per cent agreement among judges at the Laboratory on variables involving various types of sleeping arrangements. Swanson (1960:222) reports a significant level of agreement between his ratings on 28 of 39 variables and the independent ratings of two students on the same variables. On the remaining eleven there was less agreement. Stephens (1962:51) reports disagreement among multiple coders "about 20 per cent of the time."

In general, inter-rater reliability is greatest on objective-type variables, but this is not necessarily the case; Swanson, for example, reports only 30 per cent agreement on amount of bride-price ("none-moderate-considerable") between himself and any one of two student judges. Moreover, his and his students' judgments on this variable disagreed with those of Murdock. It is my impression that an over-all figure for inter-rater reliability for all published studies might fall somewhere in the neighborhood of 80 per cent (i.e., agreement in scores or ratings in 80 per cent of all cases, as between any two raters).

SOME CODING PROBLEMS

Among the many special problems in coding, two will be singled out here for discussion: (1) the problem of negative data, and (2) the problem of temporal discrepancy. The former often arises in connection with notational systems requiring the rater to choose within a "present-absent" dichotomy, the basic problem being caused by the fact that ethnographies often do not report specific presence or absence of a trait. If ethnographies were conventionally written in the form of check lists of traits, in the manner of the California culture element distribution studies (see Chapter 32), this problem would not occur as frequently as it does.

The purists among cross-cultural researchers tend to throw out any case in which the trait in question is not specifically reported as either present or absent. Others have devised ways (often quite ingenious) to get around this problem. A frequent solution has been to examine each case within a larger whole—either the context of the entire ethnography or the totality of what the researcher already knows of the society or of the culture area of which it is a part. If in the light of this contextual examination the researcher concludes that a given trait is either present or absent, regardless of whether the ethnographer specifically says so, he will code it as such—normally using a special device to indicate a lesser degree of reliability. In addition, a content analysis of the ethnographic text may reveal that the ethnographer carefully and fully covered the context, e.g., puberty and religion, in which the trait, e.g., circumcision rites, would be expected to occur; in the absence of any mention of circumcision rites, the rater may feel justified in rating the trait as absent for that particular society.

Another way of getting around this problem is to construct a scalar notation, using attributes of degree such as "important-unimportant" or "very prevalent–less prevalent"—in preference to an absolute dichotomy of "present-absent." This "solution" of course involves a certain conceptual loss and the elimination of cases that might otherwise be included on the basis of inferential coding. The researcher in effect sacrifices the possibility of broader theoretical implications in favor of greater methodological rigor.

The problems of temporal discrepancy in the ethnographic data and the implications of this discrepancy for cross-cultural research have occasionally been voiced by critics but largely ignored by proponents of the method. It is commonly assumed by the latter, apparently, that one is coding data referring to the "ethnographic present"—a rather vaguely defined concept implying the description of a culture as an ongoing system, irrespective of time. Furthermore, it is usually assumed, and occasionally so stated, that the customs being measured are static—and pertaining to aboriginal or near aboriginal conditions. As often as not, the published results of cross-cultural research fail to specify a temporal referent or set a cutoff date or dates for the data included in the study. In actuality, the ethnographic literature may cover a considerable time period and may incorporate fundamental or extensive changes in customs, due to Western acculturation or other sources.

The categories in the HRAF reflect this situation; the categories in the Island Carib file, for example, contain firsthand descriptions by Breton dating from the 1630s, together with pages from Taylor's field work in the 1930s. Although it is true that each file slip heading includes the date of field work as well as date of publication, it is possible for the uncritical researcher to treat the material as a whole for purposes of coding or rating. This can have serious implications for the results of correlational studies, which assume the concurrence of traits in space and time.

A few simple examples will perhaps demonstrate the effect on research results of this temporal factor. Two cross-cultural studies of food habits, including food taboos, were done independently at HRAF some years ago. In comparing the results on an overlapping portion of the samples used, it was found that in a number of cases there was a considerable discrepancy in the reported number of food taboos per society. This at first seemed inexplicable in light of the fact that both studies utilized identical data in the HRAF files. It was finally realized that one study had utilized all the material in the relevant categories, irrespective of time period, whereas the other had adopted a cutoff date of approximately 1900, utilizing only data referring to twentieth-century conditions. As another example, one might cite the case of the New Georgian (Solomon) Islanders, who in the early 1900s were converted by Seventh Day Adventists and henceforth adopted a diet specifically precluding the use of pork. In coding any variables relating to diet or food habits, it obviously makes a difference in the case of the New Georgians whether one attempts to utilize all the data in the HRAF categories, or whether one sets his cutoff date pre- or post-1900 (see further Chapter 39).

USE OF PRECODED DATA

G. P. Murdock has thus far been the chief proponent and source of coded data on preliterate cultures. His Ethnographic Atlas has to date published coded ratings for some sixty-three characteristics (under each of which is subsumed two or more attributes) on more than seven hundred societies. Textor's forthcoming cross-tabulation of ethnographic codes will include precoded data on some 480 variables from well over thirty prior studies by other workers (Textor 1967). The prospect of the cumulative build-up of such material is an exciting one, but at the same time it is cause for a certain amount of apprehension. It is exciting to think of a continuous expansion of overlapping samples, such that one can quickly run through a correlation of, for example, house type with polygyny for a sizable sample of the world's cultures.

Whiting (1966:299) provides a nice demonstration of the potential research use of overlapping samples, in this case the relationship between sex anxiety and duration of postpartum sex taboo for twenty-nine societies. But one's enthusiasm is dampened somewhat by the realization that so many of the existing ratings have been made on the basis of the author-reseacher's own judgments. Probably one-half of all published codes are of this single-rater type. With due respect to the ethnographic know-how and honest intentions of the authors, the resulting ratings, per se, can hardly lay claim to any great degree of scientific respectability.

Murdock's ratings in his Ethnographic Atlas, although for the most part resting on the personal judgment of the author, were made with no particular theoretical scheme in mind; in this respect they are probably on the whole more objective than ratings made in conjunction with specific postulational studies.

Of those studies that have relied on multiple raters, it is furthermore the fact that a good proportion of such ratings have been done by graduate students under the direction of a senior author (cf., Swanson). This does not, of course, automatically invalidate the results, even though students cannot be expected to have the wide background in ethnography and the handling of ethnographic data of a Murdock or a Whiting. Apprehensions as to increasing use of these data are not lessened when one realizes that they will undoubtedly be put on punched cards and made available for machine handling. Faulty or incorrect ratings, once they are perpetuated in IBM decks or in compendia such as the Textor volumes, are extremely difficult to trace down and correct in any consistent fashion.

A badly-needed correction here is replication of existing coding. This would at least help to allay apprehensions as to the possibly subjective element in their derivation. There have been recent encouraging signs in this direction. Horton's ratings of drinking behavior and degree of insobriety (Horton 1943) have been compared with more recently derived ratings on a larger sample (Barry *et al.* 1965). Whiting and Child's (1953) socialization ratings may now be compared with independently derived ratings of the same type (Barry *et al.* 1957). Murdock (1962:533) reports the beginning of a project to check previous codings independently, using a research assistant. Murdock has also invited criticism and correction of his published ratings. These he conscientiously reviews and, where he considers it warranted, publishes the corrected rating. Under the existing arrangement of the Atlas, however, one in effect needs to have the data on cards for machine handling in order to keep up with additions and corrections.

Whiting's (1964) study of climate and some cultural practices associated with male circumcision affords an example of the use of precoded data and of the possibilities (in this case seemingly somewhat extreme) of exploratory research utilizing one's own codes in conjunction with precoded data on an overlapping sample. Whiting presents ratings and correlations on some thirteen variables, seven of which are taken essentially from Murdock's published ratings and two from abstracts published by G. Devereaux. The remaining four were done by personnel at Whiting's Laboratory for Human Development.

Starting off with a demonstratedly biased geographical distribution of male circumcision rites (i.e., confined largely to tropical areas, with the exception of tropical South America), Whiting examines three cultural variables that were shown in earlier cross-cultural studies to correlate with male circumcision: mother-infant sleeping arrangements, patrilocal residence, and a long postpartum sex taboo. In an attempt to see whether any of these associated factors might be related to climate and thus regarded as indirectly associated with the geographic distribution of circumcision, he correlates

mother-infant sleeping with temperature; long postpartum sex taboo with protein deficiency, and this, in turn, with tropical climates; and patrilocal residence with polygyny, and this, in turn, with long postpartum sex taboo.

Regardless of what one thinks of the involved reasoning in Whiting's demonstration of what he feels are possible ecological factors behind the distribution of circumcision rites, one can note the objective fact that his reasoning here is cumulative, and that at each successive step he is relying on ratings and measures of (often) elusive factors, such as those on nutrition and health for an entire society. Whiting rightly regards the paper under discussion as a demonstration of the usefulness of the correlational method of cross-cultural research in working out the knotty problem of causality—in this instance the indirect effect of climate on certain cultural practices and the relation of these in turn to circumcision rites. Whiting's demonstration of causality implies a developmental sequence and thus a time dimension. For a method of deriving explicit developmental sequence directly from correlational data, see Driver and Massey (1957:432 ff.).

In conclusion, there is ample evidence of increasing interest in cross-cultural survey research, and particularly in the prospect of the cumulative effect on research of an increasing corpus of precoded data on a truly broad perspective of variables. Some of the existing research has been done hastily, on poor data, and with inadequate controls. It is undoubtedly the case that some of the existing ratings will not stand the test of time. Replication of cross-cultural studies is badly needed so that, among other things, the doubtful ratings can be either corrected or eliminated (at least until more adequate data or more precise methodology comes along). What remains, however, is still impressive, perhaps as much as anything as a body of what Banks and Textor (1963:7) have aptly called *approximate knowledge*— a highly suggestive and potentially fruitful source for further hypothesis formation and testing under more controlled conditions. In this sense, if in no other, it can fairly be said that cross-cultural research in the past few decades has made a positive contribution to the goal toward which Sumner, and others before him, were striving—a science of society based on inductive examination of a broad sample of pan-human behavior.

BIBLIOGRAPHY

BANKS, ARTHUR S., and ROBERT B. TEXTOR
1963   A cross-polity survey. Cambridge, M.I.T. Press.

BARRY, H., III, MARGARET K. BACON, and I. L. CHILD
1957   A cross-cultural survey of some sex differences in socialization. Journal of Abnormal Social Psychology 55:327-332.

BARRY, H., III, C. BUCHWALD, I. L. CHILD, and MARGARET K. BACON
1965   A cross-cultural study of drinking: IV. Comparison with Horton ratings. Quarterly Journal of Studies on Alcohol, Supplement No. 3, 62-77.

COULT, ALLAN D., and ROBERT W. HABENSTEIN
1965   Cross tabulations of Murdock's World Ethnographic Sample. Columbia, University of Missouri Press.

DRIVER, HAROLD E., and WILLIAM C. MASSEY
1957   Comparative studies of North American Indians. Transactions of the American Philosophical Society 47:165-456.

FARON, LOUIS C.
1961   Mapuche social structure: institutional reintegration in a patrilineal society of Central Chile. Urbana, University of Illinois Press.

FORD, CLELLAN S.
1945   A comparative study of human reproduction. Yale University Publications in Anthropology No. 32. New Haven, Yale University Press.
1966a Society, culture, and the human organism. In Frank W. Moore, ed., Readings in cross-cultural methodology, 2nd printing, reset. New Haven, HRAF Press. (Originally published in the Journal of General Psychology 20 [1939]:135-179.)
1966b On the analysis of behavior for cross-cultural comparisons. Behavior Science Notes: HRAF Quarterly Bulletin 1:79-100.

GOODENOUGH, WARD H.
1956   Residence rules. Southwestern Journal of Anthropology 12:22-37.
1964   Explorations in cultural anthropology. Introduction, pp. 1-24. New York, McGraw-Hill.

GUSINDE, MARTIN
1937   Die Feuerland Indianer, 3 vols. Vol. 2, Die Yamana, vom Leben und Denken der Wassernomaden am Kap Hoorn. Anthropos-Bibliothek, Expeditions—Serie II. Mödling near Vienna, Anthropos Institut. (HRAF translation, 5 vols., 1961.)

HORTON, DONALD
1943   The functions of alcohol in primitive societies: a cross-cultural study. Quarterly Journal of Studies on Alcohol 4:199-320.

KAY, BRIAN
1957   The reliability of HRAF coding procedures. American Anthropologist 59:524-527.

KENT, ALLEN
1962   Textbook of mechanized information retrieval. New York, Wiley.

KLUCKHOHN, CLYDE
1966   Universal categories of culture. In Frank W. Moore, ed., Readings in cross-cultural methodology, 2nd printing, reset. New Haven: HRAF Press. (Originally published in A. L. Kroeber, ed., Anthropology today. Chicago, University of Chicago Press, 1953.)

KÖBBEN, ANDRÉ J.
1966   New ways of presenting an old idea: the statistical method in social anthropology. In Frank W. Moore, ed., Readings in cross-cultural methodology, 2nd printing, reset. New Haven: HRAF Press. (Originally published in Journal of the Royal Anthropological Institute of Great Britain and Ireland, 82 [1952]:129-146.)

LEWIS, OSCAR
1966   Comparisons in cultural anthropology. In Frank W. Moore, ed., Readings in cross-cultural methodology, 2nd printing, reset. New Haven: HRAF Press. (Originally published in William L. Thomas, Jr., ed., Current anthropology: a supplement to anthropology today. Chicago, University of Chicago Press, 1956.)

LINTON, RALPH
1945   The cultural background of personality. New York, Appleton-Century-Crofts.

MURDOCK, GEORGE P.
1949   Social structure. New York, Macmillan.
1962   Ethnographic atlas. Ethnology 1:533.
1963   Ethnographic atlas. Ethnology 2:249-268.
1965   Culture and society. Pittsburgh, University of Pittsburgh Press.
1966   The cross-cultural survey. In Frank W. Moore, ed., Readings in cross-cultural methodology, 2nd printing, reset. New Haven, HRAF Press. (Originally published in American Sociological Review 5 [1940]:361-370.)

MURDOCK, GEORGE P., et al.
1965   Outline of cultural materials, 4th revised

edition, second printing. New Haven, HRAF Press.

READ, MARGARET
1956 *The Ngoni of Nyasaland.* London, Oxford University Press for the International African Institute.

ROBERTS, JOHN M., and BRIAN SUTTON-SMITH
1962 Child training and game involvement. *Ethnology* 1:166–186.

SENN, MILTON J. E. (ed.)
1951 Problems of infancy and childhood. *Transactions of 4th Conference on Problems of Infancy and Childhood, March 6–7, 1950.* New York, Josiah Macy Jr. Foundation.

SIMMONS, LEO W.
1945 *The role of the aged in primitive society.* New Haven, Yale University Press.

SPIRO, MELFORD E.
1965 A typology of social structure and patterning of social institutions: a cross-cultural study. *American Anthropologist* 67:1097–1120.

STEPHENS, WILLIAM N.
1962 *The Oedipus complex: cross-cultural evidence.* New York, Free Press of Glencoe.

SUMNER, WILLIAM GRAHAM, and ALBERT G. KELLER
1927 *The science of society.* 4 vols. New Haven, Yale University Press.

SWANSON, GUY E.
1960 *The birth of the gods: the origin of primitive beliefs.* Ann Arbor, University of Michigan Press.

TEXTOR, ROBERT B.
1967 *A cross-cultural summary.* New Haven, HRAF Press.

WHITING, BEATRICE B. (ed.)
1963 *Six cultures: studies of child rearing.* New York, Wiley.

WHITING, JOHN W. M.
1964 Effects of climate on certain cultural practices. In Ward H. Goodenough, ed., *Explorations in cultural anthropology.* New York, McGraw-Hill.
1966 The cross-cultural method. In Frank W. Moore, ed., *Readings in cross-cultural methodology,* 2nd printing, reset. New Haven, HRAF Press. (Originally published in Gardner Lindzey, ed., *Handbook of social psychology,* Vol. 1. 1954.)

WHITING, JOHN W. M., and IRVIN L. CHILD
1953 *Child training and personality.* New Haven, Yale University Press.

CHAPTER 39

The Culture-Bearing Unit
in Cross-Cultural Surveys

RAOUL NAROLL

INTRODUCTION

This chapter is a discussion of the problem of defining the "tribe" or "society," conceived of as the basic culture-bearing unit—that group of people whose shared, learned way of life constitutes a whole "culture" rather than a mere "subculture" on one hand or a culture area or culture cluster on the other. I propose a general concept of such a unit, whose application to varying situations results in four types of culture-bearing units.

My interest in this problem first arose in connection with sampling design for cross-cultural surveys. In such research, three important problems present themselves. First, probability sampling theory requires that each sampling unit in the universe sampled have a mathematically definable chance of being selected. Obviously, the first step in meeting this requirement must be to define the units being considered. For cross-cultural surveys this task heretofore had never been rigorously accomplished. Secondly, the chief aim of cross-cultural surveys is to build theory by counting instances of culture trait types. But what constitutes one instance? Thirdly, the validity of results of cross-cultural surveys has been questioned in discussions with anthropologists on the ground that the units were not comparable. One man asked me at dinner table, with a note of disdain in his voice, "How *can* you compare a little tribe like the Yahgan with a complex people like the English?" (See further discussion in Whiting 1954:527–528 f.)

The Skin of Culture

Obviously, however, interest in this problem is not confined to those concerned with comparative method but is shared by all students of culture, since the nature of the culture-bearing unit is itself a scientific question of prime importance. As Ralph Gerard, a biologist who has worked seriously with cultural problems, asked in a seminar I attended: "Exactly where is the *skin* of culture?"

The truth of the matter is that cultures, unlike animals, do not necessarily have any skin. One distinct culture sometimes grades into another by slight, almost imperceptible degrees. Thus in Gabon, Fang culture grades into Ntumu culture and the people on the boundary are not sure whether they are one or the other (Fernandez 1963:8).

Furthermore, unlike biologists, in considering the ethnic unit definition problem, we must vary our unit definition concept according to the problem at hand. We must consider not only the nature of the particular data we are studying. We must also consider the level of generalization we seek. In thinking about ethnic unit definition, the general rule of Goodenough (1956:37) about concept development is especially applicable. The cultural or ethnic unit definition concepts useful for describing particular cultures may or may not be useful for comparing several cultures. *And vice versa!* Furthermore, the cultural or ethnic unit definition concept useful for comparing a few neighboring cultures may or may not be useful for global comparisons—

for cross-cultural surveys. And vice versa.

This chapter focuses its view upon the ethnic unit definition problem for cross-cultural surveys. We are here concerned with the unit definition problem in global comparisons only. But while global comparisons may or may not find the ethnic units of particular cultural descriptions useful, the global comparativist needs to consider them in his thinking, before finally deciding upon his unit of global comparison. We need not *adopt* the concepts used for particular descriptions. But we should not *ignore* them.

We seek, then, an ethnic unit definition concept especially for use in cross-cultural surveys, in global comparisons. Such surveys usually are studies of world-wide samples (see Chapter 43). The samples chosen are supposed to be representative of the larger universe from which they were taken. As shown in Chapter 43, most sampling experts now agree that probability sampling is the best way to get a representative sample. In order to take probability samples, sampling lists are needed. One must be able to define precisely what constitutes the unit sampled and one must be able to count the number of such units. Ways have been worked out to avoid the need for naming and counting *all* the units in the universe; but these ways call for counting all the units in randomly sampled blocks or clusters. So while we do not actually have to list and count all the ethnic units in the world, we do need to *know how to do so*. We therefore need a unit definition concept which can be applied to any of the diverse forms and types of culture all over the world.

Cross-cultural surveys have a second need for rigorous unit definition. Such surveys always have as a main part some sort of statistical comparison—that is to say, some sort of count of units. This counting may only amount to a simple statement of proportion: 23 per cent of the tribes studied had purple whiskers while 77 per cent had green whiskers. But usually coefficients of correlations are worked out to show the relationship between variables. All this counting work supposes that the counter knows what he is counting. As Fried (1966:527) has put it:

As we all know, statistical manipulations can be meaningless or worse if the units to which they pertain are ill-defined or quixotically variable.

Naroll and some others have set themselves to . . . state the boundaries of the culture-bearing units being compared and from this step to compute the number of cultural units in any sample, the indispensable denominator of all equations in this type of work.

The Nature of the Culture-Bearing Unit

The problems of ethnic unit definition faced at all levels arise from the peculiar nature of culture. These peculiarities are best observed by careful analysis of the mapped and tabulated results of culture element distribution studies (see Chapter 32, above). Native North America has been the region most thoroughly studied in this manner. See especially Kroeber (1936), Driver and Massey (1957) and Driver (1961). These studies show that the culture-bearing unit is a complex phenomenon rather than a simple one, that units are *not* congruent with regard to quality, quantity, or spatial extension. They show that language groupings are often not congruent with distributions of other important traits; neither are political organizations, endogamy groups, or largest meaningful social unit. Going beyond these North American trait distribution studies, looking at what is known of the histories of such tribal groups as the Iroquois, the West Greenland Eskimos, the Nguni-speaking peoples, and the Nahua-speaking peoples, I think it safe to say that culture-bearing units are also not congruent with respect to chronological position and duration or pattern of genesis and development. Culture-bearing units are not species-objects, in Leach's phrase; a cultunit specifies a particular culture-bearing group and not a category of such groups as a zoological species designates a category of animals. If neat congruencies between groups of traits were invariable, the problem of unit definition would be easy to solve, and there would be no need for such a discussion as this. Any particular world-wide definition of the culture-bearing unit is sure to be arbitrary, to follow some boundaries and hence to ignore others. Consequently, there cannot be any particular trait or trait group which will be universally suitable. But again remember Goodenough's rule: what we do as ethnographers is, and must be kept, independent of what we do as comparative ethnologists.

To vary the unit definition to suit the problem being studied is a sensible practice wherever it is feasible. But the feasibility is not merely a matter of devising theoretically suitable categories; it depends upon the ability of the investigator, with the resources at his disposal, to apply those categories in practice.

Thus the horizontal distribution of culture traits about the landscape is most untidy and gives us no end of trouble. But its "vertical" distribution is equally messy. There is no such thing as a culturally homogeneous community, or even a culturally homogeneous family. In all societies, division of labor and age-grading produce variations of culture from individual to individual within every human family. Some important things are known to men but not to women. Other important things are known to women but not to men. Always, there are important things known to older people but not yet taught to younger ones. In rapidly changing societies like our own, there may well be other important things better known to younger people than to older ones. Consider computer programming today, for example.

Among very simple societies, this local heterogeneity is small. But the higher we go in the scale of social development, the greater the heterogeneity. Civilized societies characteristically have cultures which are collectively immensely richer in information content than primitive societies. Occupational specialization makes the difference. But this richness is purchased at the price of wholeness. For collectively, the riches are parceled out among experts, none of whom has more than a small share. So no one person has more than a small piece of his culture among civilized societies. In contrast, an Eskimo man who prides himself on doing well any kind of man's work holds in his mind nearly all his culture.

Toward a Taxonomy

It seems clear that the final solution of the cultural unit definition problem requires not merely a single concept, but a hierarchy of concepts. We seek not merely a list of ethnic units, but a taxonomy. We already have in common use by anthropologists such a concept hierarchy. We think of subcultures born by social groups, cultures born by whole societies, culture clusters born by a small group of neighboring societies, culture areas encompassing a larger group of neighboring societies, and continental areas. Murdock (1963) has recently proposed a new taxonomic concept, the culture type. He defines "culture type" as "either a single unquestionably distinctive culture or a group of cultures which differ from one another to a degree not significantly greater than the local variations to be expected in the culture of any homogeneous society of substantial geographic extent." This definition has vague and undefined criteria: "unquestionably distinctive culture," "not significantly greater," "homogeneous society," and "substantial geographical extent." The use of this concept is illustrated by the presentation of forty examples from six widely scattered regions of the world. However, these examples are not yet supported by data: we are not yet told what traits characterize each type: what traits or trait combinations are found everywhere within each type and nowhere outside it. When Murdock publishes this supporting data, as he plans to, his work might well prove to be the most fruitful contribution of his amazingly fruitful career. The rigorous establishment of such a taxonomy through clearly defined traits would be of the greatest theoretical and practical value. That value would be still greater if the traits used to define types could in turn be related theoretically. Thus the Linnean classification was later seen to reflect evolutionary descent although Linnaeus had no such thought in mind. The periodic table of the physical elements was later seen to reflect the arrangement of subatomic particles, though these were undreamed of when the classification was first made.

The Comparability of Units

As we have remarked, there is a wide variety of scale among cultures. Some cultures are small in informational content, with hardly any occupational specialization. These cultures tend to be homogeneous with few subcultures, simple in team structure and small in population. Other cultures are large in informational content, with much occupational specialization. These cultures tend to be heterogeneous, with many subcultures, complex in team structure and large in population. So-called "primitive" societies are not alike in this respect, but form a scale or continuum of increasing complexity and heterogeneity, grading off into civilized cultures. (See Chapter 40 below.)

When we compare cultures differing little with respect to this scale of social and cultural development, the differences are easy to overlook. But when we compare cultures at extreme ends of the scale, differences are immense and obvious. Thus—as I said before—we may be asked: "Is a society like that of the English really comparable to another like that of the Yahgans?"

What is meant by comparability? Is an orange comparable to an apple? Is an orange comparable to the planet Mars, or the sun? To the extent that all these objects are spheres, or nearly so, they may be usefully compared with respect to the problem of computing their volume, given knowledge of their diameters. Oranges and apples may be usefully compared with respect to digestibility, taste, and food value.

If we compare English and Yahgan kinship, we find their differences in scale unimportant. The relationship between descent and residence and kin terms seems little related to these differences and we are comfortable about ignoring them. Clearly, the English, with all their complexities, are fairly uniform with respect to their ideas on these matters. If they differ slightly among themselves with respect to certain details, these differences are few and minor and like differences are found among the Yahgans.

If we compare English and Yahgan infant training, we find English practices varying somewhat according to social class, a difference unknown among the Yahgans.

If we compare English and Yahgan formal education systems, we have problems. The Yahgans have only one formal education system—and that a very simple one. It consists of a single course of study lasting only a week or two and held whenever a whale-stranding provides enough food to feed pupils and instructors. The English formal education system is so complicated and subtle no one person understands its whole social structure—and it would require at least a thousand carefully chosen people collectively to understand its curriculum.

Differences in scale, then, sometimes matter very little, other times very much. And so with other kinds of differences.

But these differences are not problems of comparative method at all. They are problems of theory. The question always is: What sort of differences matter for the problem at hand? Those which matter must form part of the theory being studied. If they do not, the man who plans the study does not know his theory well. If differences in scale—or in anything else—matter for his theory, then they matter for his method. Then they are relevant variables. Then he must consider them in his research design. He must collect data on them. He must measure their influence upon or at least relationship with the other variables he studies. For differences in scale, the problem of measurement is surveyed in Chapter 40 below.

But if for the problem at hand differences in scale—or any other particular differences which seem disquieting—do not matter for his theory, they do not matter for his method. Then they can be ignored in the research design.

In any cross-cultural survey which seeks to test ideas about functional links between traits, the man doing the study has the problem of discerning all the relevant variables.

This is equally true in any other kind of study which seeks to test ideas about functional links between traits. The man doing the study has exactly the same problem. If we say we want to understand some sort of behavior, we mean by that, we want to know what factors produce it, and how.

Therefore, I submit that the comparability issue is a false issue. There is no special problem of comparability of units among cross-cultural surveys. There is only the general problem in all scientific research of discerning which factors are relevant, which not. This is no more and no less true of cross-cultural surveys than of any other kind of comparative study or any other kind of theoretical analysis.

UNIT DEFINITION IN THE LITERATURE

Considerable attention to the problem of unit definition has been given by anthropologists. Brief surveys of opinions among them have been published by Schapera (1953), Berndt (1959), and LeVine (1961). See also Naroll (1964). In reviewing this body of thought, it is important to distinguish opinions about the nature of the basic culture-bearing unit from opinions about the proper unit to be used in comparative studies. The term "tribe" has often been used to mean a non-literate culture-bearing unit (Berndt 1959:81); but this usage is by no means universal. For example, Evans-Pritchard (1940:278–279 f.) uses "tribe" to designate a political unit within the Nuer people; but it is the Nuer as a whole of whom he regularly speaks in his descriptions of Nuer culture. Fried (1966) points up the confusion arising from the use of the term "tribe" to designate a culture-bearing unit and its use to designate a stage in social evolution.

Reichard (1938:413 f.) obviously has the basic culture-bearing unit in mind in her discussion of the primitive tribe as a unit. "By a tribe," she says, "we usually mean an economically independent group of people speaking the same language and uniting to defend themselves against outsiders." But she notes that some "tribes," like the Toda, are not economically independent, while other "tribes," like the Dobuans, act only rarely as a unit. Further, she adds, a tribe is a closed society, with laws and morals applying only to its members. Radcliffe-Brown (1940a:xii–xiii) speaks of Australian aborigines as "divided into some hundreds of separate tribes, each with its own language, organization, customs, and beliefs." To Fortes (1940:239) the term "tribe" likewise denotes a basic culture-bearing unit, a "well-defined political or cultural entity differentiated from like units." Fortes calls attention to the difficulty of using such a concept in discussing the Tallensi or their neighbors (1940:239):

. . . no "tribe" of this region can be circumscribed by a precise boundary—territorial, linguistic, cultural or political. Each merges with its neighbors in all these respects. In the transition zones between two "tribes" dwell communities equally linked by residential contiguity and by structural ties to both.

The concept of society as that of a basic culture-bearing unit is clearly expressed by Fortes and Evans-Pritchard (1940:23):

The social structure of a people stretches beyond their political systems, so defined, for there are always social relations of one kind or another between peoples of different autonomous political groups. Clans, age-sets, ritual associations, relations of affinity and of trade, and social relations of other kinds unite people of different political units. Common language or closely related languages, similar customs and beliefs, and so on, also unite them. Hence a strong feeling of community may exist between groups which do not

acknowledge a single ruler or unite for specific political purposes. Community of language and culture, as we have indicated, does not necessarily give rise to political unity, any more than linguistic and cultural dissimilarity prevents political unity.

These views may be compared with some others. Murdock (1953:478–479) proposes

to define a culture as including all local cultural variants exhibited by communities within a particular geographical area which speak mutually intelligible languages and have essentially similar forms of economic adjustment.

Ember (1963) difines his sampling unit as "a continuously distributed population whose members speak a common language or *lingua franca* which is different from the dominant languages of any neighboring societies."

One common thread runs through the foregoing comments. Reichard, Radcliffe-Brown, Fortes, Evans-Pritchard, Murdock, and Ember all conceive of the basic culture-bearing unit as a unit in which a common language is spoken. Had the Tallensi differed sharply from their neighbors in speech, instead of blending gradually along a linguistic continuum, Fortes would not have complained of the difficulty of defining "tribal" boundaries in the Tallensi country. On the other hand, none of these writers thinks that speech community alone can be relied on to define the basic culture-bearing unit, and they do not agree on what else needs to be considered. Recent studies by Leach (1954) and Moerman (1965) have pointed up the practical difficulties of ethnic unit definition in Southeast Asia. These writers ably study complex native concepts of the culture-bearing unit.

Another point of disagreement among anthropologists lies in the nature of the unit to be examined in comparative studies. Murdock and Ember wish to compare whole cultures. Radcliffe-Brown (1940:4–5) proposes we take "any convenient locality of a suitable size" and study "the structural system as it appears in and from that region, i.e., the network of relations connecting the inhabitants amongst themselves and with the peoples of other regions." Whiting (1954:526) likewise recommends the local community as the basic unit of comparative study. Nadel (1951:187) on the other hand recommends the "political group," that is the aggregate of human beings who coordinate their effort for the employment of force against others and for the elimination of force between them, and who usually count as their principal estate the possession and utilization of territory.

Schapera (1956:8–10) likewise favors the political unit, however small, as the basic unit of comparison. For the universe of study, within which comparisons are to be made, he, like Radcliffe-Brown and Leach (1954), favors the region. As Schapera (1953: 359–360 f.) explicitly pointed out, the results of these regional comparisons ultimately were themselves to be compared; but this presumably would be the work of future generations.

Driver's regional study (1956:15), comprising the entire North American continent,

divided extensive territorial groups into the minimum number of units necessary to display all the variation present in the data on the six topics under consideration. . . . Uniformity in trait inventory of two neighboring groups who spoke different languages was not regarded as sufficient reason to lump them.

Berndt (in Naroll 1964:292) proposes that we take the widest social unit relevant to the people concerned. In the eastern Highlands of New Guinea, language names distinguishing unintertelligible (mutually *un*intelligible) dialects serve as native names for native districts. The natives call such district names "big names"; local community names they call "small names." But above and beyond these "big name" districts is a wider unity. Throughout the whole area, Berndt says, "there is a more or less common culture. Members of contiguous districts combine or oppose one another across linguistic boundaries for fighting, intermarriage, and ritual purposes, and these shifting spheres of interaction are the widest social units relevant to these people."

Bessac (in Naroll 1964:293) and Moerman (1965) propose that we take the native name into consideration. However, they differ widely on how to go about doing so. Bessac suggests that we modify my cultunit concept (see below) by adding native name as an additional criterion; to do so gives us six cultunit types instead of four. Moerman suggests that we ignore all other criteria and use *only* native name in defining ethnic units.

Jaspan (in Naroll 1964:298) suggests that

among other things we consider "important elements of common folklore or history."

Hobhouse, Wheeler and Ginsberg (1930) simply followed the units used by the ethnographers they studied.

The unit definition problem is discussed further in essays by Fried, Hymes, Hoffman, Bessac, Naroll, Moerman and Nag in Helm (1968).

CRITIQUE OF CRITERIA

Thus we have at least ten criteria proposed for defining whole societies, or other units of comparison:

(1) Distribution of particular traits being studied.
(2) Territorial contiguity.
(3) Political organization.
(4) Language.
(5) Ecological adjustment.
(6) Local community structure.
(7) Widest relevant social unit.
(8) Native name.
(9) Common folklore or history.
(10) Ethnographers' units.

Before discussing the theory of ethnic unit definition or proposing my taxonomic scheme, let me review the theoretical and practical difficulties connected with these ten criteria from various points of view.

Distribution of particular traits being studied. Where the societies being studied include all those found within a single geographical area, this is operationally feasible and methodologically clean. For Driver's North American study, it seems to have been successful. But for comparative studies in which scattered samples are to be studied, the method is prohibitively expensive because it requires the study of all the neighbors of each society in the sample, and *their* neighbors, and *their* neighbors, until boundaries have been reached for all the traits being studied—or, if a linguistic criterion is also used, as by Driver, until a sharp language boundary is reached.

Territorial contiguity. This criterion seems important where neighboring societies have generally similar cultures and speak intertelligible (mutually intelligible) dialects but are separated by uninhabited geographical gaps, whether water gaps or wasteland gaps. Such gaps seem to be the crucial boundaries between many Polynesian and Eskimo groups. On the other hand, water gaps seem less important to peoples who share membership in a single political unit. Also, short gaps of water or wasteland obviously are unimportant; the gaps between the home islands of Japan or between the Samoan islands of Savaii, Upolu, and Tutuila obviously are inconsequential. Operationally, large gaps are usually easy to find out about.

Political organization. States—territorial units embracing a considerable number of local communities into a political unit wielding exclusive war-making authority—are generally treated by both the people involved and the ethnologists as distinct cultures. Murdock himself so treats neighboring states not differing importantly in ecological adjustment and speaking intertelligible dialects, e.g., Zulu and Swazi. On the other hand, where no such territorial units exist, and where each local community is politically independent, retaining full control over war-making, not only the people involved but also ethnologists commonly ignore the criterion of political organization in defining tribes. Thus to give only a few examples, the following societies aboriginally contained many independent political organizations (made up, in some, of the single nuclear family): Copper Eskimo, Hopi, Southern Paiute, Samoans, Ainu, Chuckchee, Nama Hottentots, Naron Bushmen, Yahgans, Onas. Data on political organization membership is usually easy to find and interpret.

Language. Where people are separated *either* by substantial water or wasteland gaps, *or* by state boundaries as above described, it is common for people speaking intertelligible dialects to deny membership in a common "tribe" and for ethnologists to treat them as belonging to distinct cultural units. Furthermore, it not seldom happens that people speaking intertelligible dialects are commonly classified as members of distinct cultural units if they differ markedly and obviously in their ecological patterns and occupy distinct and fairly large contiguous territories. On the other hand, it is rather uncommon to class a group of people as a single "tribe" who speak neither a generally intelligible dialect nor a lingua franca (understood as a second language by leading men in every local community). This uncommon classification is probably applied most frequently to simple foraging peoples like the Andamanese and the Yahgans.

However, the operational difficulties of applying the linguistic criterion are formidable, and neither Murdock nor Ember claims to have systematically examined the linguistic data of the societies in his sample to see whether in fact he meets the linguistic criteria proposed. If they had done so, they could hardly have avoided discussing the operational problems involved in working with linguistic continuums or in defining intertelligibility. I have systematically surveyed the linguistic evidence for the thirty tribes of my first pilot study (Naroll 1956). I found serious linguistic classification problems in eleven of the thirty: Yahgan, Yagua, Ona, Fiji, Lesu, Ramkokamekra Timbira, Hupa, Flathead, Ulithi, Nama, and Lepcha.

Although Yahgan dialects are said to be intertelligible, they are also said contradictorily to differ as much as Scottish and Cockney (Lothrop 1928:120). Nothing but formal linguistic experiments of the Voegelin-Biggs type would persuade me that Ayreshire rural Scottish and Cockney are intertelligible. Eastern Ona (Haush) and Western Ona differ similarly (Bridges 1948:92). It is easy to see that some nineteenth-century Fijian dialects were unintertelligible but it is not so easy to divide them up into intertelligible groupings (Williams 1858:216; Capell 1941:464; Fison 1886). The relationship of Yagua to other Peban dialects (Peba, Yameo, Tucuman) is not at all clear (Steward and Métraux 1948:713, 728–729 f.; Rivet 1911:176–177 f., 182). Eastern and Western Timbira probably are unintertelligible (what is our definition of intelligibility?) but clearly are on a linguistic continuum (Snethlage 1930:187–199; Nimuendaju 1915, 1946:6). According to Powdermaker (1933:15, 31), the Lesu dialect was understood only in four other nearby villages; but there seems reason to suspect that Lesu is on a linguistic continuum running not only the length of New Ireland but also New Britain (Capell 1962:89–94). Hupa seems to be intertelligible with neighboring Athapaskan dialects to the south (Leldin, Hleltin) and west (Whilkut) (Goddard 1903:7; 1911:92–93 f.). The Flathead dialect seems to be on a Salish linguistic continuum (Swadesh 1950:159) and evidently is readily intertelligible with Kalispel and Pend d'Oreille (Teit 1930:303). Ulithians speak a Central Caroline dialect; but these dialects are unintertelligible and it is an open question how intertelligible

Ulithi (Mogmog) is with the dialect of nearby Sorol or Fais (Damm 1938:230–231 f., 297 ff., 372 ff.; Kramer 1937:390 ff.; Cheyne 1852:195; Fritz 1911:6–7 f.).

Nama may or may not be intertelligible with Korana, Cape Hottentot or Gricqua but does seem to be readily intertelligible with Bergdama, although there are some differences (Schapera 1930:45, 224; Hoernlé 1925:3–4 f.; Stow 1910:265; Godée-Molsbergen 1916:215–233; Barrow 1801:382–383 f., 389; Beach 1938:8, 181; Wandres 1927). Lepcha seems to be unintertelligible with its nearest relatives among the non-pronominalized Himalayan dialects of the Tibeto-Himalayan group of the Tibeto-Burmese family but the evidence on this score is not from informants' statements nor from linguistic experiments but only from examining the available word lists (Hodgson 1857; Kunow 1906; Campbell 1868).

However, even where the linguistic data is clear, the classification problem often remains formidable. What do we do about one-way intelligibility, where speakers of Dialect A understand speakers of Dialect B but not vice versa? Operationally, linguistic classification is extremely technical and difficult at best; with the materials available in existing ethnographic literature it is often sheer guesswork. If, as seems to be the case, Eastern and Western Timbira are unintertelligible dialects but are connected by over a dozen geographically intermediate dialects, each of which is readily intelligible to its neighbor, where does Eastern Timbira stop and Western Timbira start? Where is the skin of the culture here? Paul Bohannan in conversation has spoken of linguistic continuums in Africa whose poles are radically different languages and yet which nowhere present a sharp linguistic break. Romance language peasant dialects seem to present a linguistic continuum including dozens of unintertelligible variants and including literary Portuguese, Spanish, French and Italian within their range. The German linguistic continuum is the classic example; how do we treat a village, all of whose members claim to speak intertelligible variants of German but who in fact do not? What is our operational definition of intelligibility and how do we apply it to the available word lists? Do we take an informant's word for it? Most Viennese claim to understand Tyrolean readily; but this is a myth; they usually cannot. What

do we do about bilinguality? trilinguality? Many Luiseño today seem equally at home in Luiseño, Spanish and English; many Hopi Tewa speak fluent Hopi and English as well as Tewa. A Western Papago man may speak fluent English, but his wife not a word of it. Is he a member of American society because he speaks the lingua franca and his wife not because she doesn't? And what about the children? In some Tyrolean villages, children of six or seven neither understand nor speak literary German, but only their local dialect. Their parents are bilingual and the children are expected to become bilingual.

Ecological adjustment. I know of no case involving societies who possess aboriginal states where this criterion has been considered important by the people themselves or by ethnologists. But it is a criterion applied to a number of fairly well known "tribes" which lack aboriginal states, a criterion distinguishing "tribes" who occupy contiguous adjacent territories and who speak intertelligible dialects. There are the desert-foraging Papago and the riverine-farming Pima; and similarly the desert-foraging Yavapai and the riverine-farming Havasupai; the cattle-herding Nama and the foraging Bergdama; the reindeer Chukchi and the maritime Chukchi; the reindeer Koryak and the maritime Koryak—to give the best-known examples.

Theoretically, this criterion is bothersome because it is ignored by everyone in considering the inhabitants of large, complex societies where division of labor is commonplace and no one follows a "typical" ecological adjustment. Operationally, it is formidable to apply; where societies get part of their subsistence from farming and part from foraging, it often becomes a problem to determine the predominant ecological pattern. Both Murdock (1957)—in his World Ethnographic Sample—and Hobhouse, Wheeler and Ginsberg (1930) have classified peoples widely by ecological criteria, but they have not presented evidence that their classifications are either reliable or trustworthy (which is by no means the same thing; see Chapter 44 below on data quality control). However, if this criterion were applied only to stateless societies, and even then only when its crucial importance is explicitly claimed by the ethnographer, this procedure would meet the need presented by the examples given and solve the operational problem.

Local community structure. Restricting the unit of study to certain local communities is clearly a good idea in certain kinds of comparative study but clearly impossible in certain other kinds. In a cross-cultural survey which seeks a random or stratified random sample (Ember 1963; Naroll 1961b), such a unit definition is operationally worthless. It is hard enough to get something resembling a complete list of societies, but impossible to get anything even vaguely like a complete inventory of local communities. Furthermore, to this operational difficulty must be added a theoretical one. Where the variable being studied is a political variable, often no single local community presents the trait as such. No one can understand race relations in Oxford, Mississippi, unless he is aware of the behavior of the Supreme Court in Washington, D.C., and vice versa. Both Ember (1963) and I (1956) are interested in the size of the largest settlement in a society as a variable for study; such a variable by its very definition requires a society comprising several local communities. Folk-urban interrelationships cannot be understood without considering both the city and its hinterland; a Tyrolean village like Feichten in Kaunertal cannot be understood without looking carefully at the small town of Prutz, the larger town of Landeck, and the cities of Innsbruck and Vienna. Finally, no one claims that the local community usually embodies the full society; proponents of that concept are talking about the design of comparative studies, not about the nature of the culture-bearing unit. However, most ethnographies in fact are chiefly descriptions of one or two particular communities. This fact usually holds even though title and preface alike speak of a whole political or linguistic group. Hence in fact cross-cultural surveys are largely comparing a cross-cultural sample of communities rather than whole tribes or nations.

Widest relevant social unit. For many people at higher levels of social development than the natives of Australia and New Guinea, the widest relevant social unit in Berndt's terms has long comprised whole subcontinents. Today, for most human beings, the widest relevant social unit in Berndt's terms comprises about 98 per cent of mankind. The participating citizens of states now in the United Nations or now eligible for possible admission to it collectively constitute a single such unit. These people today combine or oppose one another across linguistic boundaries for fighting, intermarriage, ceremony, trade, postal and telecommunications—and diplomacy. Six hundred years ago, all "Christendom" comprised one such unit; all India, another such unit.

Native name. Native name is, however, a common and widespread, if by no means universal ethnic unit definition criterion. Bessac's proposal (in Naroll 1964:293) thus has strong attraction, especially since the reference group of a native name is so often very easily identified. Bessac's proposal is to subclassify my Hopi type (as defined below) into those who have a name for themselves (Bessac's Hopi type) and those who do not (Bessac's Yuki type); and to subclassify my Flathead type (as defined below) into groups of linguistically homogeneous states who have a common name for themselves, presumably the same as their own name for their language (Bessac's Mongol type), and those in which language and state boundaries are coterminous (Bessac's Mohave type). Finally, as to linguistically heterogeneous states, Bessac retains my Aztec type (as defined below), but he substitutes for my Aymaran type (as defined below) his Kazak type in which peoples speaking a distinct language and having a name for themselves are lumped together regardless of state boundaries. Bessac's approach is promising, but it needs some more work. At present, it is not an exhaustive classification. What about two linguistically heterogeneous states having intertelligible lingua francas? The English-speaking peoples know themselves collectively as Anglo-Saxons, but they operate a number of linguistically heterogeneous states.

Moerman's proposal is however another matter. I do not think that native names alone would produce a useful ethnic unit concept for global comparisons. Moerman has been much influenced by recent linguistic theory (Moerman 1964:1–8). By and large, recent linguists are wise in urging ethnographers to seek out native concepts to use when describing native cultures. But even here, at the level of particular description, native concepts do not always serve. The natives sometimes are not aware of important elements in their own culture. Often they do not see the importance of relationships between two elements of that culture. For example, every human culture had phonemes as key elements in its speech; but no folk culture has a word for "phoneme." Two thousand years of grammatical analysis went on in India and the West before the phoneme was discovered. But even though the natives have no native name for "phoneme," linguists wisely seek out and report "phonemes" when they describe a language.

Even though native names for native concepts are usually valuable in describing particular cultures, they may not be so valuable when these same cultures are compared with others in a cross-cultural survey. Goodenough's rule again! The concepts which are useful for describing particular cultures may or may not be useful in comparing these cultures with others. For global comparisons, use of native name to define the ethnic unit compared brings on four main difficulties:

1. Some people have no name for themselves at all as an ethnic group. They simply call themselves "people"—"human beings." Thus behave the Eskimo, the Navaho, the Basin Shoshoneans, and the Yanomamö (Chagnon 1967:22 f.), for example, among many others.

2. Some people are not sure what ethnic labels apply to themselves. Consider once more the people of the Gyem area of the Gabor district of Gabon. This area is in effect the boundary between the Fang people and the Ntumu people. Both Fang and Ntumu are names of languages. Fang and Ntumu are along a single language chain (linguistic continuum). The Ntumu of Bitam call the Gyem people Fang. The Fang of Mitzik call them Ntumu. The Gyem people themselves say they do not know whether they are Fang or Ntumu (Fernandez 1963:8).

3. Most people have not only one ethnic label and concept for themselves, but two or more differing ones. These names designate native taxonomies. I have already spoken of the "big name" and "small name" ethnic labels among the people of the eastern Highlands of New Guinea. The people Moerman studied call themselves Ping, Phong, Lue, North Country People, Northern Tai and Tai. These six names designate increasingly general classes in an ethnic unit taxonomy. The peasants of the mountain hamlet in Tyrol my wife and I studied similarly call themselves by

many names. At the least general level, the people of a single farmstead have for that farmstead a special name pertaining to the real estate, not to the family. Thus the family of Joseph Praxmarer might live in the farmstead called Stotzner. Its head then would be known as "Stotzners Seppl." But if they moved away from that farmstead they would no longer be called "Stotzner." Then each hamlet of two to a dozen farmsteads has a name by which its inhabitants are collectively called; we stayed in Unterhäuser. But the people of all the hamlets of the Catholic parish of Feichten are known collectively by its name—*Feichtener*. Feichten in turn is part of the commune of Kaunertal, whose people call themselves *Kaunertaler*. Kaunertal is in Tyrol and Kaunertalers are more than anything else Tyroleans (*Tiroler*). I say nothing about the named judicial district of Ried and the named political district of Landeck, to both of which Kaunertal belongs because neither district yields a named group of people. Of course, people in Kaunertal know about the court in the village of Ried and the district headquarters building (*Bezirkshauptmannschaft*) in the town of Landeck; but most would think of these as places to go to for judicial and political services rather than as centers of a district of people. Furthermore, Kaunertalers are politically, and call themselves, Austrians (*Oesterreicher*) and they are linguistically and culturally, and call themselves, Germans (*Deutschen*). Beyond that, the Kaunertalers are emphatically Roman Catholics (*Katholiken*) and Christians (*Christen*), and call themselves by those names.

I submit that in cultures like these the notion of "native name" begs the question of ethnic unit classification. We must still decide on some consistent basis which of these named groups to choose. Moerman (1965: 1224 f.) urges us to make some choice but admits that he does not yet know how to do so.

4. Finally, native names may be used inconsistently by different people in the same region (Moerman 1965:1223).

Common folklore or history. It is their common history that makes Moerman's Lue a self-conscious unit. The Lue are the reputed biological and cultural descendants of the members of the nineteenth-century Lue State —now disappeared—or their spouses. That and that alone is who the Lue are. There are many such named and self-conscious units whose bonds of unity are the conditions of their forebears rather than their own conditions. Thus many people who call themselves Basques today do so because they claim descent from speakers of Basque. Millions of people in the United States today call themselves Jews but neither believe in the truth of the Jewish holy books nor attend Jewish religious services. They all however claim descent from people who did believe and did attend. These in turn claimed descent from members of the ancient Jewish states of Israel or Judah.

Jaspan's suggestion that we consider important elements of common folklore and history did not specify how we might tell important elements from *un*important ones. The "ex-tribe" concept would do so. For comparative purposes, however, it is often convenient simply to ignore "ex-tribes," as such. At other times, for comparative purposes, it may often be useful to think of ex-Lue, ex-Basques or ex-Jews. It depends upon the problem being studied.

Ethnographers' units. Ethnographers follow no consistent pattern of unit definition. The perils of following them blindly are best illustrated by the difficulties of Hobhouse, Wheeler, and Ginsberg (1930): for example, these men counted the Indians of Lower California collectively as one unit, and the Waicuri and Pericui of Lower California as two other units; the Hopi as one unit and the Moqui (another name for Hopi) as another unit; the Azande as one unit and Niamniam (another name for Azande) as another unit. In short, in ethnic unit classification as in other concept definition problems, again the rule by Goodenough (1956:37) applies: the concepts which are suitable for describing behavior patterns of particular cultures are not necessarily the same as those suitable for comparing these cultures with others.

THE CULTUNIT

I have proposed a concept of the culture-bearing unit—the *cultunit*—which yields four taxonomic classes.

Definition of the Cultunit

Cultunit. People who are domestic speakers of common distinct language and who belong either to the same state or the same contact group.

Distinct Language. In homogeneous languages, the language itself. In language chains, the chain link.

Homogeneous Language. A set of dialects such that: a) the speakers of any of the dialects can understand all the others in the set; and b) the speakers of any dialect not in the set cannot as such understand any dialect in the set.

Language Chain. A set of dialects which are arrangeable in sequences such that, while each dialect in the sequence is intertelligible with the preceding and the following dialect, and all such intertelligible neighbors are included, some dialects in the set are not intertelligible with others in the set.

(N. B. What I have here called a "language chain," following Voegelin, is nothing else but what I earlier called a "linguistic continuum," following Bloomfield. Notice that "Homogeneous Language" and "Language Chain" are mutually exclusive and collectively exhaustive categories. Every dialect must belong to one or the other of these; none can belong to both.)

Chain Link. One of a set of divisions of a language chain made in such a way as to produce the smallest possible number of divisions each containing only intertelligible dialects and, wherever consistent with the foregoing requirement, dividing neighboring dialects with maximum differences. (In other words, one seeks boundaries which separate comparatively dissimilar dialects wherever alternate division plans present themselves. This proposal assumes that language chains or dialect continuums do not proceed by exactly equal alternations in dialect from community to community, but rather that the amount of the difference varies considerably. I understand that the dialect maps of Germanic and Romance peasant dialects do reveal such variations.)

Domestic Speakers. People who predominately use a given dialect for speech within the nuclear family, that is, among husband and wife and their minor children.

State. A territorially ramified territorial team occupying at least ten thousand square kilometers of land whose leaders assert and wield the exclusive right to declare and conduct warfare.

Territorially Ramified. Made up of a num-

ber of component territorial teams. For example, the United States is made up of fifty territorially defined states.

Territorial Team. A group of people whose membership is defined in terms of occupancy of a common territory and who have an official with the special function of announcing group decisions—a function exercised at least once a year.

Common Territory. A geographically contiguous territory within which are found not only the dwellings of the people of the team but also the lands of their usual subsistence activities ashore.

Contiguous. Accessible without crossing the land territory of others. (N. B. Thus water gaps are ignored, however great.)

Warfare. Public lethal group combat between territorial teams. (N. B. Thus blood feuds between non-territorially defined kin groups are not considered warfare.)

Contact Group. People who belong to no state but who speak a common distinct language and who are all interconnected by successive contact links.

Contact Link. Two nuclear families constitute a contact link if every year one of the members of each speaks directly to one of the members of the other. As an operating presumption, in the absence of evidence to the contrary I take two nuclear families to be contact links if their dwellings are not more than two hundred airline kilometers apart at some time in their annual cycle. All the examples of the use of this presumption I know about involve water gaps or large uninhabited stretches of desert or tundra. Notice that the question of contact links and contact groups only arises in the absence of states. None of the people I know about where this question arises have any means of travel other than on foot or in pre-European boats.

Discussion of the Cultunit Concept

This concept of a cultunit as a basic culture-bearing group makes use of three of the ten criteria discussed earlier. The criteria of language and territorial contiguity are invariably used. The criterion of political organization is also used wherever there is a sufficiently authoritative political structure transcending the local community.

Deciding dialect affiliation according to the dialect predominately used domestically re-solves readily most questions of bilinguality or trilinguality. Occasionally, informants claim to belong to bilingual nuclear families which use two unintelligible languages with "equal" frequency. Mathematically, this claim seems implausible; such statements might mean only that the informant does not know which language is more frequently used in his household, or they might mean that a lower prestige language is used more frequently.

No precise definition of intertelligibility is stated above. The problem of dialect intelligibility has been studied in the field by several linguists whose interest in this problem was stimulated by Carl Voegelin (Voegelin and Harris 1951; Hickerson et al. 1952; Pierce 1954; Biggs 1957; Yamagirva 1967; see also Wolff 1959). These studies seem to suggest that where two dialects have approximately 90 per cent of their vocabulary cognate, little trouble is ordinarily experienced when speakers of one try to communicate with speakers of the other; apparently the substantial element of redundancy in language is able to accommodate itself to this much informational "noise." On the other hand these studies suggest that where two dialects have as little as 70 per cent of their vocabulary cognate, speakers of one commonly have great difficulty communicating effectively with speakers of the other. Strikingly similar results were obtained by random garbling of graphemes in printed English (Chapanis 1954). Two dialects with more than 70 per cent but less than 90 per cent of cognates may be termed "partially intelligible."

While the definitive solution of this problem must be left to linguists, as a practical working method for comparative ethnologists today, I propose the following: (1) Where comparative word lists including at least twenty words are available in a consistent phonetic notation, consider as "recognizable cognates" only those words which are reported to share at least one meaning in common and which also have 80 per cent of their phonemes in common and in the same order. (Where word lists exceed two hundred entries, use only those on the Swadesh glottochronology list [Hymes 1960].) If 80 per cent or more of the words examined constitute "recognizable cognates" consider the two dialects intelligible; otherwise, not. (2) Where no such comparative word lists are available, follow statements by informants or ethnographers about intelligibility. (Such statements can probably be trusted to agree with the "recognizable cognate" word-list method except when the dialects concerned are in the "partially intelligible" class.) Use availability or unavailability of such word lists as a data quality control factor (Naroll 1962:14–18).

Important: In cross-cultural surveys, it is necessary in practice to concern oneself with chain link classification only where it appears that neighboring links are each represented by bodies of ethnographic literature meeting the bibliographic criteria of the sample in question and not separated by state boundaries. For such chain links, the comparativist can usually expect to find or to be able to construct enough parallel word lists to permit him to make a chain link classification.

Classification of the Cultunit

It seems useful to distinguish four types of cultunit:

Hopi type. *People who belong to no state but who speak a common distinct language and who are all interconnected by successive contact links.* Examples: Hopi, Bella Coola, Naron, Hupa, Nuer.

Flathead type. *People who belong to a state all of whose members speak a common distinct language.* Examples: Flathead, Swazi, Tikopia.

Aztec type. *People who belong to a state in which unintertelligible dialects occur and who are domestic speakers of a dialect intelligible to speakers of the lingua franca of the state, that is, the dialect in which the state officials usually transact their business.* Examples: Aztecs, Incas, Zulus.

Aymaran type. *People who belong to a state in which unintertelligible dialects occur and who are domestic speakers of a dialect not intelligible to speakers of the lingua franca of the state.* Examples: Aymara, Zulu-ruled Thonga.

These four cultunit types emerge when we consider two different kinds of boundaries; a linguistic boundary and a communication-link (state or contact group) boundary. A cultunit boundary is formed by *either* of these boundaries. If a state has more than one distinct language spoken within it, then the political unit, as established by the political boundaries, is subdivided into cultunits by the linguistic boundaries within the state. That cultunit formed by the domestic speakers of the lingua franca of the state is classified as an Aztec-type cultunit; the other cultunits within that state are classified as Aymaran-type cultunits. Thus by definition we cannot have an Aztec-type cultunit except in association with Aymaran-type cultunits. (Theoretically, we could have a state made up entirely of Aymaran-type cultunits, provided the lingua franca of the state is not spoken domestically by anyone. This may indeed prove to be the case in Switzerland, where the predominant lingua franca may well be literary German; literary German seems to be spoken little if at all in the home by the Allemanic Swiss, who prefer one or another of the several unintertelligible varieties of Schweizerdeutsch. The question of identifying the actual lingua franca of supposedly multilingual states like Canada, Belgium, South Africa, and Switzerland who theoretically have more than one is a matter for research; presumably one language in each such state is most commonly used to transact business among officials.)

Where a state is linguistically homogeneous, the state boundary is followed and we get a Flathead-type unit. Where there is no state, linguistic boundaries only are followed unless contact gaps occur which break up speech communities into cultunits within which speech communication presumably flows freely but between which speech communication presumably is rare and unimportant; and the speech communication groups thus defined form Hopi-type cultunits—see examples below.

It is important to remember that some cultunits differ very little in culture from one another while others differ very much. Frequently, neighboring cultunits may differ not at all with respect to certain traits being studied. But methods of avoiding the fallacy of counting neighboring and closely related cultunits repeatedly as independent trials of a functional hypothesis being tested are presented in Chapter 47.

In evaluating the cultunit concept, anthropologists should bear in mind that it is offered primarily to solve sampling and counting problems in cross-cultural surveys. Field description units often will not correspond to the cultunit. The cultunit sometimes may be a genuine social system but often will be only theoretical—an analytical abstraction.

Considered as an analytical abstraction, the cultunit concept is valuable even though, as Leach (1954) points out, a given human being may function simultaneously as a member of two distinct societies, based on two distinct cultunits. Indeed, the distinction between *society* and *culture* becomes critical when we consider Leach's informant who functioned both as a Shan and a Kachin. A culture is a pattern, a set of plans, a blueprint for living. Every culture includes as an element a social system, that is, a plan for social interaction. A society is an actual system of social interaction. Among human beings, such a system usually resembles rather strikingly the plans in the minds of its members; but this resemblance seldom if ever attains complete identity. Social practice in most if not all societies departs somewhat from social theory. The distinction between culture and society becomes evident the moment we look at social insects. These have societies but lack cultures. The social organization plan, which in a human society is taught anew to each generation of children, is among social insects communicated genetically. The cultunit is offered as a unit of comparative statistical analysis of sets of *plans* —of social and cultural patterns as they exist in the minds of culture bearers. Study of actual social systems is of course relevant to the study of the plans which are supposed to govern them, but the unit of comparison is the plan, not the society.

That is why it is usually irrelevant how many people follow the plan—whether a few hundred only or many million. The idea of a comparative statistical study, a cross-cultural survey, is not to assess the general trends among the human race as a whole by counting heads, as Leach suggests (Leach 1960: 137). Instead, it is to compare culture patterns in order to see if there are general tendencies governing their construction. In *Social Structure,* Murdock had no interest in learning if bilateral descent was more characteristic of humanity as a whole than patrilineal descent, matrilineal descent, or double descent. Murdock was as much interested in double descent, a rare phenomenon found only among a few exotic peoples, as he was in bilateral and patrilineal descent, one or the other of which is found among the vast majority of mankind. Consequently, the number of people who model their behavior

upon a given culture pattern is irrelevant per se; if, as occasionally happens, a particular culture pattern varies in its social implications with the number of people involved, then but only then is the population of the culture-bearing group—the cultunit— relevant. In such a case, social population is *ex hypothesi* a factor influencing the situation being studied and needs to be considered in some sort of multiple variable analysis along with other factors being considered. If an investigator suspects that social population may be relevant to the problem he is studying, he should collect population data and test its relevance directly.

In one statement about comparative statistical studies, Leach (1963:174) points out correctly that social *facts* may be statistical phenomena like demographic or economic information, or they may be nonstatistical jural rules; for the statement of jural rules, Leach correctly reminds us, statistics are wholly irrelevant. From this he infers that statistical procedures are likewise irrelevant in testing theories about jural rules. Not so. Within each cultunit we search for the predominant jural rule. But in a statistical study of a number of cultunits, we may count the frequencies with which certain sorts of jural rules occur and may compare these frequencies with the implication of a theory about jural rules. Such a comparison is the usual purpose of a cross-cultural survey. A cross-cultural survey uses facts about particular cultunits to test theories about culture in general.

Since the cultunit concept is offered as a tool for comparative statistical studies, it is desirable to have that concept as nearly uniform as possible. I have thus reduced the number of proposed cultunit types to four, which seems to me the feasible minimum.

It is worth remarking that while the cultunit concept often diverges from the concepts used by natives to identify their own groups or by ethnologists to describe native cultures, yet these divergences are rarely extreme or arbitrary. Usually the divergences are moderate and within the range of variation of divergences among varying native and varying ethnographic concepts. The cultunit, I submit, generally resembles fairly closely at least *some* operating social unit within the society wherever these units have sharp boundaries. Its most arbitrary element is its delineation of boundaries along linguistic continuums from a bibliographic vantage point (see below).

The only ethnic unit definition criterion not considered in the foregoing discussion is that of religion. In most civilized parts of Eurasia, religion has long been an important ethnic unit identification criterion. Wherever Christianity, Islam, or Buddhism has spread, religious cult membership has involved major cultural differences. And we are all familiar with the cultural significance of such religious groups as Jews, Parsees, Sikhs, and Mormons. In the twentieth century, secular ideologies which embody many traditional Judeo-Christian moral attitudes often play a quasi-religious role: cultural differences between Communist and anti-Communist Koreans, Chinese, or Vietnamese seem parallel to seventeenth-century differences between Catholic and Protestant Germans, French, or Romansch. However, among the vast majority of native cultures, unconverted to religious or secular universal ideologies stemming from India, the Middle East, or Europe, ideological organization membership is almost never an ethnic definition criterion.

Finally, the cultunit concept is not entirely without theoretical interest. A culture is a plan of behavior. Although, as Schapera (1956:9) has pointed out, there are many Naron bands, there seems to be only one standard Naron plan for band organization which all the Naron band members seem to have in mind and which all Naron bands more or less model themselves upon. Culture patterns however are not fixed and immutable; on the contrary they are constantly changing, sometimes very slowly, sometimes very quickly. These changes presumably occur when opinion leaders deliberately or unconsciously change the rules or the texts in repeating them and when furthermore these changes are accepted by their associates, whether deliberately or tacitly. The communication nets through which these changes are passed from "mouth to mouth"—i.e., from mind to mind—are obviously key elements in defining the culture-bearing group. A speech community tends to form such a communication net, even though its boundaries may be blurry; translation problems constantly remind us that even closely related languages often lack equivalent terms for key cultural concepts. Thus literary German has no equivalent

for the English word "fair" as in "fair play"; nor has English any equivalent for the German *Heimat*, which is neither "home" nor "homeland," but a little of both. A political state, with its specialist leaders, forms a communication net of another sort, one in which key concepts can be coined and argued or ordered into use by the expert leaders of the state. In the absence of state organization, a gap of two hundred kilometers between the nearest settlements of technologically primitive people must ordinarily represent a clear break in the speech community's communication net. Samoans and Tongans spoke varieties of Polynesian sufficiently similar so that the crucial communication question was less often "Can you understand what they are saying?" than "Do you ever talk to them?"

The Cultunit in Time

The problem also arises of defining cultunits in time rather than space. This problem has often been neglected by comparativists in cross-cultural surveys, with results which are sometimes disastrous (Pilling 1962). The practical problems of time period definition differ greatly in civilized societies and uncivilized ones.

Uncivilized Societies. For uncivilized societies—those without native written literatures—the problem is relatively simple. For them I propose this rule:

Ethnographic Time Period. That period of time in which the cultunit type remains constant. The proposed periodization rule calls for us to distinguish, for example, pre-colonial, colonial and post-colonial periods, if the people belong to a Hopi-, Flathead-, or Aztec-type cultunit before and after colonial conquest. It also calls for us to distinguish changes in cultunit type in the formation of a native state; for example, when the Zulu state organized a Flathead-type unit from the undifferentiated eighteenth-century Nguni, who were then all members of a Hopi-type cultunit.

Civilized Societies. Societies which keep written records (including of course societies taught to do so by Europeans) present an entirely different problem of periodization. The only general attempts at periodization of history have been made in connection with theories of rise and fall of civilization, like those by Spengler (1926), Toynbee (1947), and Quigley (1961); of these, Quigley's is by far the most nearly acceptable scheme for me. Of course, conventional historians construct and reach fairly broad agreement on particular periodization schemes for particular historical traditions, although they commonly haggle over precise boundary lines; very often histories of monarchies are divided dynastically; and art styles are also commonly used as period markers.

The development of a satisfactory general theory of historical periodization is an urgent task, but one which I cannot attempt here. For sampling purposes, at least, it seems satisfactory simply to use arbitrary time units, like centuries. (Incidentally, for scientific purposes, it would be a vast improvement on time notation if the Christian era were dropped. Why not do so by commencing time reckoning from the year 10,000 B.C.? Thus the year 1 B.C. becomes the year 10,000 absolute; the year 1 A.D. becomes the year 10,001 absolute; the year 376 A.D. becomes the year 10,376 absolute; the year 1962 A.D. becomes the year 11,962 absolute; while the year 776 B.C. becomes the year 09,225 absolute. Such a system would encompass dates of all written records. Archaeologists might prefer to begin an archaeological reckoning 110,000 B.C. or 1,110,000 B.C., leaving all absolute historical dates unchanged in their last five digits while keeping all dates positive.)

The Cultunit in Cross-Cultural Surveys

Now some comments about the use of the cultunit concept in cross-cultural surveys. Ideally, random sampling should be made from a list of cultunits whose linguistic boundaries or characteristics are described and to which a bibliography of basic ethnographies is attached. Such a list should ideally include all cultunits about which a minimally acceptable ethnographic literature exists. The comparativist will find that many of the units randomly chosen must be rejected because they fail to meet bibliographic requirements. So sampling must continue in a predetermined manner until an acceptable number have been identified. (See Chapter 43 below.)

The bibliographic unit of examination must be the unit named in the sampling universe list. Only those ethnographies can be examined which purport to deal with the unit, or some portion of it; regional ethnographies which deal collectively with groups of sampling units (hence presumably with groups of cultunits) are not to be considered.

Some of these units will prove to embrace more than one cultunit as I have defined it above. Some of them will prove to constitute a cultunit as so defined. Some of them will prove to comprise only a part of a cultunit. Some of them will prove to be on linguistic continuums such that cultunit definition on the terms proposed here is not possible until a particular "stated dialect" is first specified. And some of them will prove impossible to classify because the necessary linguistic data is unavailable (in some case, *forever* unavailable because no informants survive). Cultunit classification should work with the dialect spoken by the people described in the monograph which qualified the sampling unit bibliographically. Rarely will more than one such monograph involving unintertelligible dialects turn up for a single sampling unit.

Since cross-cultural surveys usually seek correlations, the ethnic unit definition problems involved in them boil down to two. First, does the actual sampling unit definition used bias the sample and thus affect the correlations found in the study? Second, does variation in the type of unit studied affect the correlations found in the study? This second question is the classic problem of comparability of units—if the variation in type of unit does not affect the correlations, then the units are obviously comparable.

To answer the first question above, control the sample by classifying it into two groups: Group 1—those sampling units which clearly include all of one but no more than one bibliographically acceptable cultunit; Group 2 —the remainder of the sample, i.e., the sampling units which depart from the model or whose boundaries are not clear. Then correlate this dichotomy with the traits being studied to see if the two groups differ importantly and significantly. For example, in a study investigating the relationship between residence rules and descent rules, the sampling unit control consists in seeing whether Sampling Group 1 and Sampling Group 2 differ in their proportions of matrilineal, patrilineal, bilateral or double descent and in their proportions of matrilocal, patrilocal, neolocal or bilocal residence. If they do not so differ, no harm has been done by the departures from the model in Group 2. If they do so differ, then Group 2 should be examined to see whether it contains a higher proportion of "hits" (cases confirming the hypothesis being tested) than does Group 1. If not, then there is still no harm done; but if so, then sampling errors have biased the results of the study and the investigator must allow for these errors by differential weighting or by eliminating the excessive proportion of "hits" from Group 2. To answer the second question above, proceed similarly, seeing whether Hopi-type units, Flathead-type units, Aymaran-type units, Aztec-type units differ from one another with respect to the traits being studied, and if so, whether they differ likewise in proportion of "hits."

PROPOSED USE OF THE CULTUNIT CONCEPT BY COMPARATIVISTS AND FIELD WORKERS

I suggest that in any cross-cultural survey the comparativist note the cultunit boundaries associated with each unit in his sample. If he can use a sampling list made up of cultunits, so much the better. Thus by a distinct calculation the comparativist can see whether, in the unit of references of the ethnographers he studies, variations from the cultunit standard affect his correlations or not. In other words, I propose that we strive to order all data by cultunits for purposes of cross-cultural survey comparisons. (This is not to deny the value of other sorts or comparisons, which may well make use of other sorts of units.) To comparativists, then, I suggest that you arrange your data by cultunits as nearly as you can and take note of discrepancies which you cannot avoid.

My proposal to field workers is different. Following Goodenough's rule, I suggest that you determine your unit of study, of data collection, with primary regard to local cultural conditions. Field workers in parts of Australia or New Guinea, for example, might well need to pay greatest heed to marriage exchange grouping. However, I urge you also to ascertain and report the cultunit boundaries involved in your study (i.e., the linguistic boundaries and the state or contact group boundaries), so that your reports may be accurately classified by comparativists.

HOW TO FIND CULTUNITS

There are two contrasting situations in which a person might wish to identify cult-units. Each of these situations calls for a somewhat different work plan for greatest efficiency. The first is that met by a compiler of a reference work who wishes to map all the cultunits of a given region. The second such situation is that now met in an ordinary cross-cultural survey.

To Map All Cultunits in a Given Region

Step 1: Language Boundaries. Prepare a language map of the region. Linguistic surveys like that of the Voegelins (1966) and Meillet and Cohen (1952) and ethnographic maps will be indispensable. In the present state of the art, for most continental regions, the preparation from scratch of an accurate language map calls for one or two man-years of work. However, much work has already been done (*North America:* Driver *et al.* 1953. *South America:* Mason 1948, McQuown 1955, Murdock 1951. *Africa:* Murdock 1959, Baumann, Thurnwald and Westermann, 1939. *Oceania:* Brigham 1900, Greenway 1963, Capell 1962, Kennedy 1962, Conklin 1952. *Eurasia:* Buschan 1922–1925, Gerland 1892, Luzbetak 1951, Tolstov, Levin and Cheboksarov 1960, Levin and Potapov 1956, Lebar, Hickey and Musgrave 1964, Hodson 1937).

Where language chains (linguistic continuums) occur, it is necessary to divide them along isogloss lines in such a way as to produce the smallest number of chain links. Theoretically, this should be done in such a way as to make each chain link as homogeneous as possible. In practice, given the present state of dialect geography, this work will often be little more than educated guesswork.

It will be convenient to show language boundaries on the map in a distinctive manner—for example by *red lines.*

Step 2: State Boundaries. Map the boundaries of all the states in the area. This commonly is a lighter task than the language mapping. Two kinds of state boundaries need to be kept distinct. One kind is a boundary separating two states. Such a boundary could be shown for example by a *thick solid blue line.* The other kind of boundary is the boundary between a state on one hand and unorganized tribal territory on the other. By unorganized tribal territory is of course meant territory occupied by Hopi-type cultunits, by people not members of any state. Such a boundary could be shown for example by two parallel lines: *thin solid blue line alongside a thin dashed blue line*. The thin dashed blue line could run on the *tribal side*.

Step 3: Contact Gaps. Contact gaps need to be mapped only for tribal territory, for peoples not organized into states. Thus in the example given, if a map shows blue state boundaries, contact gaps need to be mapped only for areas bounded by dashed blue lines. As a practical matter, contact gaps should be mapped in two kinds of situations: 1) When within areas in which a single language is spoken, uninhabited areas (bodies of water, wastelands) wider than two hundred kilometers occur. Here the boundary—for example, a *green line*—is drawn across the language family in the middle of the unhabited territory. 2) When a single language is not found in a single contiguous area but is scattered into two or more areas, separated by people speaking other languages and more than two hundred kilometers apart. Draw a green line around the intervening strangers.

Step 4: Date Determination. After the first three steps have been attempted, the provenience date may be fixed. If reports lack indication of change in boundaries over time, or change in character of state organization, this date may well be put at the most recent period of independence prior to colonial conquest. Where reports call attention to changes of boundaries over time, the classifier must fix the point in time as of when all boundaries may confidently be mapped. If more than one such mapping is possible, then the point in time is to be preferred as of when most ethnographic information is available. Large areas like the continent of North America cannot be efficiently classified for cross-cultural survey purposes at any single point in time. But there is no reason why the mapper cannot map different peoples at different points in time, as long as these differences are reported. It may be convenient to show the date of provenience inside each language or state boundary, for example in like-colored ink.

Step 5: Mapping Cultunit Boundaries. When the first four steps have been performed, the fifth follows easily. Consider all three kinds of boundary lines, red linguistic ones, blue political ones, and green contact ones. Any one of these constitutes a cultunit boundary.

Hopi-type cultunits will be those with red, green or dashed blue boundaries, or combinations thereof. Flathead-type cultunits will be those with solid blue boundaries, which may or may not coincide with red ones. Aztec- and Aymaran-type cultunits will be partly bounded in solid blue, partly in red.

Given a Settlement, to Find Its Cultunit

Supposing that no cultunit map of the area exists, and a comparativist has an ethnographic report he wishes to classify by cultunit.

Step 1: Identify a settlement as a datum point. Most ethnographies reflect data chiefly gathered in a single community. That then constitutes the datum community. Otherwise, if the people studied fall on a linguistic continuum, it is essential that one particular community be so designated, in the center of the area in which data was collected, as a datum point. Where an ethnography is confined to the speakers of a single homogeneous language, no datum community is needed for cultunit definition; but one is always useful for data quality control.

Step 2: Identify linguistic boundary. If we have to deal with a single homogeneous language, the boundaries of that language of course form the linguistic boundaries of the cultunit. If instead we have to deal with a language chain (linguistic continuum), locate the points along the chain at which the dialect of the datum community becomes unintelligible. If copious word lists are available, this location can be done precisely by following the 80 per cent rule given above. If word lists are not available, this boundary will often need to be estimated from statements about dialect intelligibility of places on either side of the boundary.

Step 3: Identify political boundary. If datum settlement or datum homogeneous language lies within any organized state or states (as defined above), map the state boundaries. Sometimes all the speakers of the datum language are within a single state. If so, the language boundaries form the cultunit boundaries as well. At other times, the speakers of the datum language are found in more than one state. If so, there are as many distinct cultunits as there are states; within each state, the language boundary forms the cultunit boundary.

Step 4: Identify contact boundaries. For people within any state, skip this step. For people in unorganized tribal territory—that is, not within any state—look within the language boundaries for uninhabited water or wasteland tracts at least two hundred kilometers across. Such tracts constitute contact gaps where they completely separate or sever two groups of people speaking intertelligible dialects. Example: the Point Barrow Eskimo are separated from the Mackenzie Eskimo by many hundreds of kilometers of coastland uninhabited by Eskimos. Contact gaps may also occur if two groups of people speaking intertelligible dialects are separated by other people speaking other languages and occupying tracts of territory at least two hundred kilometers across. Example: the Navaho and the Apache seem to have been so separated at one time.

ILLUSTRATIVE EXAMPLES OF USE OF CULTUNIT CONCEPT

Civilized Societies

As an ethnographic classification, intended to serve for data on all the people, not merely on elites, the cultunit is defined in terms of spoken language, not written language. Consequently, the Chinese written language, which used to be as widely understood in Korea and Vietnam as in China (and quite widely understood in Japan as well), plays no part in the classification of the Chinese people. The Chinese Peoples Republic of 1950–1966 was a single state, as far as I know. Within its mainland boundaries, control of conduct of warfare was claimed and effectively exercised by the authorities in Peking. I would classify its inhabitants by their domestic speech into one Aztec-type cultunit (Mandarin speakers) and a considerable number of Aymaran-type cultunits, among which would be found speakers of such Chinese dialects as Cantonese, Hakka, Fukienese, etc. I would pay no attention at all to the fact that those inhabitants who are literate employ a single common ideographic script which they pronounce differently when reading aloud.

Similarly, I would divide the peoples of the United Kingdom into one Aztec type and a number of Aymaran types. The Aztec type would consist of those inhabitants of the U.K. who are domestic speakers of some English dialect intertelligible with that used to conduct business by Her Majesty's government. I would distinguish as Aymaran types, domestic speakers of those surviving dialects of English which are not intertelligible with the Queen's English (including one or more types of Cockney and one or more types of Lowland Scottish, and perhaps many others). I would also distinguish as additional Aymaran types the speakers of one or more varieties of Welsh and one or more varieties of Gaelic. Similarly in France, I would distinguish the domestic speaker of literary Parisian on the one hand and of unintertelligible provincial dialects (*patois*) on the other; and further distinguish as necessary among Breton and Basque speakers. In what is left of the overseas British and French empires (not counting militarily and diplomatically independent associates), I would consider as part of the metropolitan Aztec-type cultunit domestic speakers of standard English or literary Parisian, respectively, and sort out domestic speakers of other dialects (whether English or French pidgins or not) as so many Aymaran-type cultunits.

Kachin and Shan

The problem of classifying Kachin and Shan peoples of the Burma hills was the focus of the justly celebrated study by Edmund R. Leach (1954, 1964). The term *Shan* is the Burmese and English name for the inhabitants of Burma who call themselves Tai and speak Northern Tai dialects. The term *Kachin* is the English version of a Burmese name for a certain group of hill people. Because the group concerned includes speakers of unintertelligible dialects, Leach (1964:41) describes the group as polyglot and says that *therefore* the term Kachin was originally *not* a linguistic category. Nevertheless, Leach's own linguistic survey of the Kachin (1964:44 f.) as well as the survey of the Voegelins (1965:5:10–16), shows that whatever Leach may say in fact the term Kachin was and is a linguistic category. The peoples included in it originally (Leach 1964:41) and finally (Leach 1964:44 f.; Voegelins 1965:5:10–16) all speak closely related languages of a linguistic subfamily which both Leach and the Voegelins call by the name Kachin subfamily. The German language today includes many unintertelligible dialects, all whether spoken in Germany, Austria or Switzerland, called *deutsch* by laymen and scholars alike. "Kachin" is no less linguistic a category than "German," i.e., *deutsch*.

With these two terms Shan and Kachin are, however, associated a number of other traits, as well. The following statements are true of most if not all people called Shan, but of only a very few people called Kachin: the people live in the valleys, practice wet-rice agriculture, are Buddhists, belong to feudal "states" administered by Shan-speaking officials but including both Shan and Kachin subjects. Contrariwise, the following statements are true of most but not all people called Kachin but true of only a very few people, if any, called Shan: the people live in the hills, are pagans, and practice dry-rice agriculture. These trait contrasts are seen as important by the people involved; therefore a bilingual Kachin who takes up wet-rice agriculture, becomes a Buddhist and becomes an official of a Shan state would often be called a Shan by himself and others, even if he continued to speak Kachin in the home.

Neither the Kachins nor the Shans themselves operated true states as that term has been defined in this chapter. Shan princes were feudal underlings of Burmese, Chinese or British authorities; these princes never claimed, or effectively wielded, exclusive control of warfare in their territory. Kachin chiefs were ceremonial leaders with jurisdiction partly territorial, partly familial. Military operations under their aegis were between lineages rather than between territorial groups (Leach 1964:34, 185–187).

In order to classify these Shan and Kachin for a cross-cultural survey, we must look not only at them but also at the political authorities in Rangoon and Bangkok. At times, many of the Shan and Kachin peoples have been controlled from Rangoon in fact: they have acknowledged the authority of the Rangoon government and have submitted to its control over warfare, feuding and other kinds of homicide. But at other times, as apparently at present (1966), the Rangoon government has not effectively controlled them. Similarly, neighboring Tai-speaking peoples of Thailand have at times been effectively controlled by the Bangkok government; at other times, not.

Case 1: Communities not effectively controlled in fact by the Rangoon government.

These are classified according to language as Hopi-type cultunits. The linguistic data are sparse and poor. Therefore, the exact number and boundaries of these units are not yet known, nor is it known if the languages are discrete or if instead they are language chains—but the latter possibility seems a lively one. However, a reasonable estimate today might look toward approximately eight to ten Kachin cultunits: 1. Jinghpaw; 2. Marun proper (Laung); 3. Atsang (Maingtha, A'chang); 4. Lashi (Litsi); 5. Atzi (Tsaiwa); 6. Nung; 7. Rawang proper, said to include seventy-five to one hundred dialects, many of which may be unintertelligible; 8. Daru (may belong with Rawang group). For cross-cultural survey purposes, only those cultunits are of interest whose culture has been described in detail. For many such surveys, only Jinghpaw would qualify as sufficiently well described.

The Shan may constitute only a single cultunit; when Bangkok authority is not being widely exercised, most Shan form part of the Northern Tai cultunit extending into Thailand and beyond. One Shan dialect, Khün, is tentatively classified as a distinct language by the Voegelins (1965:3:8) but they warn the reader that this classification may be in error.

Case 2: Communities effectively controlled by the Rangoon government. Such communities are classified by language into Aymarantype cultunits. This may well mean, for example, that at certain times there are two Jinghpaw cultunits: a Hopi-type cultunit consisting of those Jinghpaw villages that manage their own military affairs, and an Aymarantype cultunit consisting of those other Jinghpaw villages which submit in fact to control from Rangoon.

Leach introduces the Kachin-Shan problem by discussing the case of a man named Hpaka Lung Hseng (1964:2). This man for the past seventy years has considered himself both a Kachin and a Shan. He claims to be a Kachin because his ancestors were typical Kachins and he traces membership in a Kachin lineage through actual biological descent. He claims to be a Shan because he was accepted as such by a Shan ruler, was adopted into a Shan clan, and embraced Buddhism. We are not told if this man practiced wet-rice agriculture but it seems likely that the village of which he served as headman is a wet-rice village. We are also not told what language(s) this man speaks;

perhaps he is bilingual, speaking both Shan and Kachin. Conceivably, he and his family might in fact prefer to speak lower-status Kachin but tell outsiders that they usually speak higher-status Shan. Or conceivably the man's wife may be a monolingual Shan—then they may speak only Shan in the home. I would for my purposes classify this man as a Kachin if the former situation were shown to be the case; as a Shan if the latter situation were shown. For cross-cultural survey purposes, a decision of this kind about a particular individual rarely needs to be made, but it is well to be able to make it when called upon. Ethnographers commonly avoid using men and women like Hpaka Lung Hseng as informants. Because they are to some extent members of two cultures, their concepts of either way of life are clouded by those of the other. It is better for comparative purposes to study reports compiled from particular cultures by using monolingual informants or at least those whose identity is clearly one or the other.

But the study of ambicultural people like Hpaka Lung Hseng might well form a special kind of study useful in many special ways. Such studies presumably would be best carried out after the cultures concerned have been reasonably well described from the viewpoint of monolingual informants.

The Lue

The Lue of Northern Thailand were the data base for an extended critique of the cultunit concept by Moerman (1965). To classify the Lue, it is necessary also to consult Moerman's doctoral thesis (1964). The Lue are best defined as the reputed biological or cultural descendants of the nineteenth-century Lue state (Moerman 1965:1219, 1226) or their in-marrying spouses. They are thus an ex-political category.

Lue Cultunit: Northern Tai, *ca.* 1960. This is an Aymaran-type cultunit. It consists of all those people who (a) speak Tai dialects intertelligible with Ban Ping Lue; and also (b) do not actually wage warfare independently of the Thailand authorities in Bangkok.

These authorities claim exclusive control of warfare throughout Thailand. Their state is considered to extend to those portions of Thailand where people do not openly defy this claim. (People openly defy this claim

who not only wage war independently of Bangkok but also publicly announce that they have done so.)

Since the Ban Ping Lue belong to the state of Thailand, the question of defining their contact group does not arise. That question arises only for people who belong to no state at all. But for purposes of illustration we could imagine a situation in which none of the Northern Tai people belonged to any state: neither to Thailand, Laos, Vietnam nor China. If this were so, I would presume that all these Northern Tai people belong to a single contact group; I would *presume* so since *presumably* at least one family from each such village speaks to at least one other family from each neighboring Northern Tai village at least once a year. Obviously, I do not have direct evidence to demonstrate the truth of this presumption, but make it because no two neighboring Northern Tai villages are separated by as great a distance as two hundred kilometers and I have no information inconsistent with this presumption. That is to say, in the absence of direct evidence otherwise, I presume villages in contact with their neighbors if these are within two hundred kilometers; if not, not.

The Northern Tai people seem to belong to a language chain which grades into Southern Tai (Standard Thai) of Bangkok. All Northern Tai dialects of Thailand appear to be intertelligible, not only those of Thailand, but also most of those of Vietnam, Laos, Burma and China. On the other hand, Bangkok Thai seems to be on the borderline of unintertelligibility; the Voegelins (1965:7 f.) tentatively classify it as a separate language.

The problem of determining the boundary between Southern Tai and Northern Tai for cultunit classification purposes arises only if there is another suitable monograph on another Tai community for the cross-cultural survey in question. In the present example, it would arise only if there were a monograph on a more southerly Tai community with useful information on land tenure and subsistence technology. If so, I must decide whether to treat that community as part of the same cultunit as the Ban Ping Lue, or as part of another cultunit.

If faced with this problem, I would deal with it in one of four ways, in order of preference.

Test 1. I would prefer to compare the

TABLE 1
CULTUNIT CLASSIFICATION, WAR, STRESS AND CULTURE SAMPLE
For approximate location of these cultunits see sketch map below

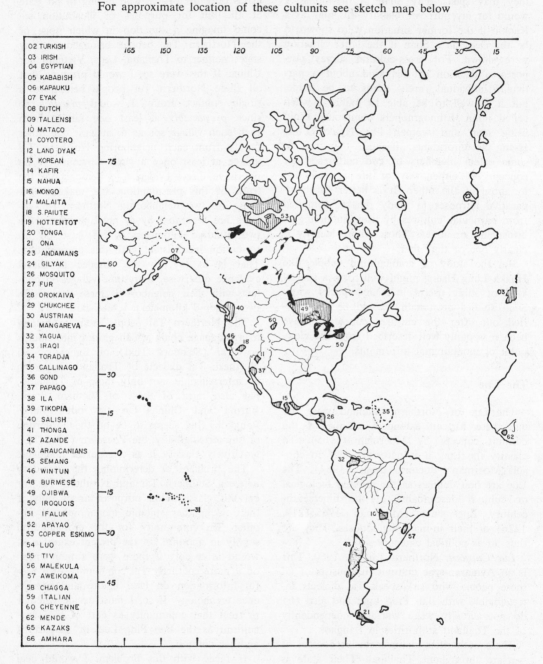

02 TURKISH
03 IRISH
04 EGYPTIAN
05 KABABISH
06 KAPAUKU
07 EYAK
08 DUTCH
09 TALLENSI
10 MATACO
11 COYOTERO
12 LAND DYAK
13 KOREAN
14 KAFIR
15 NAHUA
16 MONGO
17 MALAITA
18 S. PAIUTE
19 HOTTENTOT
20 TONGA
21 ONA
23 ANDAMANS
24 GILYAK
26 MOSQUITO
27 FUR
28 OROKAIVA
29 CHUKCHEE
30 AUSTRIAN
31 MANGAREVA
32 YAGUA
33 IRAQI
34 TORADJA
35 CALLINAGO
36 GOND
37 PAPAGO
38 ILA
39 TIKOPIA
40 SALISH
41 THONGA
42 AZANDE
43 ARAUCANIANS
45 SEMANG
46 WINTUN
48 BURMESE
49 OJIBWA
50 IROQUOIS
51 IFALUK
52 APAYAO
53 COPPER ESKIMO
54 LUO
55 TIV
56 MALEKULA
57 AWEIKOMA
58 CHAGGA
59 ITALIAN
60 CHEYENNE
62 MENDE
65 KAZAKS
66 AMHARA

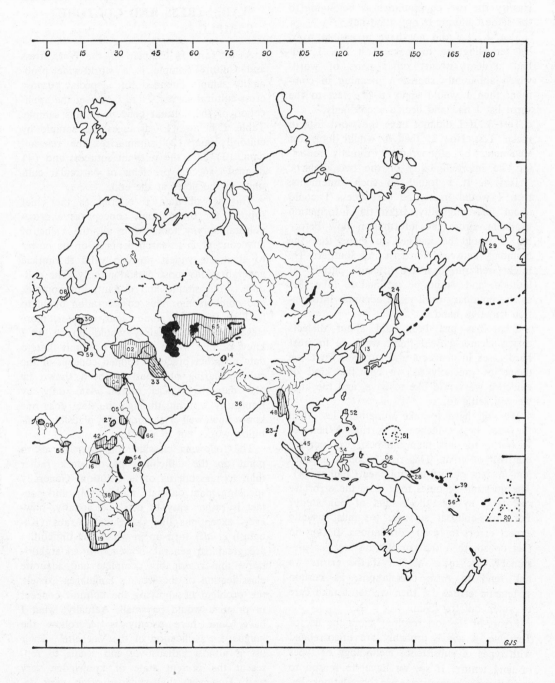

dialects of the two villages by comparing their words for the standard Swadesh two-hundred-word list (Hymes 1960:6). If at least 80 per cent of the corresponding words shared at least 80 per cent of their phonemes in the same order, I would classify them as dialects of a single language. Then I would classify the two communities as belonging to the same cultunit. If not, then not.

Test 2. If I did not have accessible word lists enabling me to make Test No. 1, but had at least twenty other pairs of words which apparently shared a meaning in common, then I would apply a like test to the word list I had and decide accordingly.

Test 3. If I did not have the word lists to make Test No. 2, then I would look for statements by ethnographers directly reporting the intertelligibility of the two dialects.

Test 4. If I found no such statements, then I would make the best guess I could about intertelligibility, from the information available. From the information now before me, I would be inclined to guess that the boundary between Northern and Southern Tai might well run near the fifteenth parallel of latitude, and would be inclined to take that as the boundary until more accurate information came to hand.

What has just been said about dialects makes clearer how I think we have to treat hard cases in cross-cultural surveys. First, we define as precisely as we can the kind of evidence we would like to have, and the kind we will settle for.

We will have to take something less than the very best evidence as a rule. Whenever we settle for less than the best, we increase our risk of error. This risk becomes a problem in data quality control (see Chapter 44). The question becomes this: does the error we risk tend to bias the results of our study? For cross-cultural surveys, we must usually expect errors to lower correlations. If they in fact do so, then the correlations we get presumably are too low. But if the errors we risk tend to *raise* correlations, as certain systematic errors do, then we must take care to watch out for them.

Errors of the sort resulting from the use of Test No. 4 above probably are uncorrelated with types of subsistence technology or types of land tenure. If so, we have no reason to expect such errors to *raise* correlations between these traits. Only if errors in intelli-

gibility inferences were correlated not only with land tenure codings but also with subsistence technology codings would we expect them to make for spurious correlations between the two traits (see Chapter 44).

CULTUNIT CLASSIFICATION OF THE WAR, STRESS AND CULTURE SAMPLE

As set forth in Chapter 43, the War, Stress and Culture Sample is a world-wide probability sample intended for a special purpose cross-cultural survey. Here I present the application of the cultunit concept to this sample. Table 1 below (1) arranges the sample by cultunit type; (2) summarizes the relevant data; (3) cites the relevant sources; and (4) discusses specific problems of particular cultunits in the notes at the end.

This set of data is offered as the chief support for the cultunit concept as a cross-cultural survey tool. After all, the value of any concept in research depends on its power to elicit the widest possible valid theoretical generalizations most parsimoniously. The cultunit is not simple and elegant, but complex and cumbersome. This consideration ought to lead us to prefer some other, simpler, more elegant one. I certainly would do so, if I knew of one which worked. I submit that to date no other precisely defined concept of the culture-bearing unit has yet been shown by like data to be as useful. And only by rigorously working through the data does one know how well a theoretically plausible definition works out in practice.

The following classification often serves to point up the difficulties of the task rather than to reassure us of its solution. Generally speaking, data on state membership and contact is rather easy to get; occasionally, however, exceptions like the Sudan Arabs (Kababish *et al.*) turn up in which the difficulties are great. In general, however, if an authoritative and reasonably complete and accurate classification of the world's languages existed, the problem of applying the cultunit concept in practice would be small. Actually, what I have done here usually is to follow the language classification of the Voegelins. Their list is almost exhaustive, and seems to represent the present state of knowledge very well. However, that state is often very defective. For example, the classification of colloquial Arabic into mutually unintertelligible dialects is hardly even begun. And it may be that such a classification, like that of dialects closely related to Burmese proper, may soon become utterly impossible by dialect comprehension tests in the future. Most people of Burma are learning Burmese proper as a second language, where it is not their first one. Most speakers of colloquial Arabic are learning literary Arabic as a second language. These learning processes interfere with dialect comprehension tests obviously. Thus, in the future, linguists may be forced to adopt some such percentage-of-cognate method as was first proposed by Hickerson *et al.* (1952:8).

For further information about languages named, see "Languages of the World," in C. F. and F. M. Voegelin, eds., *Anthropological Linguistics*, Vols. 6, 7, and 8; 1964–1966. For example, under HOTTENTOT, I cite AL VI, 5:271. This citation refers to *Anthropological Linguistics*, Volume 6, Number 5, page 271.

The classification of each tribe by Murdock, *Outline of World Cultures,* is given in parentheses after each cultunit name. For example, the HOTTENTOT are identified as FX–13. All but twenty-eight cultunits seem to agree with Murdock's classification, although linguistic data are often vague and uncertain. Twenty-one cultunits of mine form parts of a larger grouping by Murdock: 02 Turks; 03 Irish; 04 Egyptian; 12 Sadong Dyak; 14 Bashgali Kafir; 15 Aztec; 17 Lau Malaita; 19 Hottentot; 21 Ona; 23 Aka-Kora Andaman; 30 Austria; 33 Iraqi; 36 Hill Maria Gond; 38 Ila; 41 Western Thonga; 46 Wintun; 54 Jo-Lwoo; 56 Seniang of Malekula; 57 Aweikoma; 58 Chagga; 59 Italian. Seven cultunits of mine include more than one of Murdock's groupings: 09 Tallensi; 20 Tonga; 24 Gilyak; 37 Pima-Papago; 39 Tikopia; 40 Straits Salish; 53 Central Eskimo.

Information on cultunit areas, unless otherwise stated, comes from the ethnographic maps cited above, pp. 742–743.

HOPI-TYPE CULTUNITS

19 Hottentot	36 Hill Maria Gond	07 Eyak
41 Western Thonga	23 Aka-Kora Andaman	40 Straits Salish
38 Ila	45 Semang	46 Wintun
58 Chagga	52 Apayao	18 Southern Basin Shoshoneans
16 Mongo	12 Sadong Dyak	60 Cheyenne
62 Mende	34 Bare'e Toradja	49 Ojibwa
09 Tallensi	06 Kapauku	50 Western Iroquois
55 Tiv	28 Orokaiva	11 Western Apache
42 Azande	51 Wolea	37 Pima-Papago
54 Jo-Lwoo	17 Lau Malaita	35 Callinago
05 Sudan Pastoral Arabs	56 Seniang of Malekula	32 Yagua
14 Kati Kafir	39 Tikopia	43 Araucanians
65 Kazaks	20 Tonga	21 Ona
29 Chukchee	31 Mangareva	10 Mataco
24 Gilyak	53 Central Eskimo	57 Aweikoma

FLATHEAD-TYPE CULTUNITS

13 Koreans	26 Miskito

AZTEC-TYPE CULTUNITS

66 Amhara
27 Fur
04 Egyptians
59 Italians
03 Irish

08 Dutch
30 Austrians
02 Osmanli Turks
33 Iraqi
48 Burmese
15 Aztec (Tenochca)

HOPI-TYPE CULTUNITS

The HOPI TYPE of cultunit is defined as a group of people who:
(1) share mutually intelligible dialects of a single language
(2) are not members of any state (N.S.M.; see below)
(3) are interconnected by successive contact links.

Two neighboring nuclear families constitute contact links if every year one of the members of each speaks directly with one of the members of the other. In practice, we presume two neighboring families to be contact links if they are no more than two hundred kilometers apart.

Space does not permit detailed discussion of the often uncertain data. The citations given are to the most important passages found. Often the importance of the passage will not, however, be clear to one who has not familiarized himself with the culture concerned. For example, the citation on *N.S.M.* (No State Membership) of Wolea takes for granted that the reader is already aware that Wolea consists of several nearby small and politically autonomous atolls loosely linked by the so-called Gagil Empire of Yap. The key problem for Wolea is the nature of that Empire; if politically authoritative, controlling warfare, then it constitutes a state. If not, not.

Contact is assumed unless otherwise stated; N.S.M. means No State Membership

19 HOTTENTOT
(FX–13)

Ca. 1880

Language—The Hottentot consist of the speakers of the Nama, Korana, Gricqua and Cape dialects of Hottentot (Beach: 181; Stow: 11 f.; AL VI, 5:271). These dialects seem to be barely intertelligible. *N.S.M.*—"Nama chiefs or councils could not prevent . . . clans from conducting feuds" (Murdock:491). I presume other Hottentot chiefs could not do so either.

41 WESTERN
THONGA
(FT–6)

Ca. 1890

Language—The Western Thonga consist of those Tonga speakers not enslaved by the Zulu (omitted in AL; Johnston:281). *N.S.M.*—The Thonga outside the Zulu state occupy an area too small to be a state (*Encyclopaedia Britannica*, 11th ed., 11:544).

38 ILA
(FQ–6)

Ca. 1900

Language—The Ila consist of the speakers of the Ila language (Smith and Dale: xxv–xxvii; AL VI, 5:138). (Elizabeth Colson once told me in conversation that she suspected the Ila dialect to be on a dialect chain with the Plateau Tonga to the East.) *N.S.M.*—"There is not more than a congeries of communities loosely bound together by individual ties, not a nation welded together under a single head" (Smith and Dale 1:238).

58 CHAGGA
(FN–4)

Ca. 1900

Language—The Chagga consist of the Chagga (Caga) speakers of Kilimanjaro (AL VI, 5:116). *N.S.M.*—Total territory of 2,000 sq. km. is divided into twenty-eight principalities (Dundas:50).

16 MONGO
(FQ–32)

Ca. 1890

Language—The Mongo consist of the speakers of the various dialects of the Mongo language, among which "only insignificant differences . . . of language can be observed" (Hulstaert:2; AL VI, 5:107). *N.S.M.*— ". . . chiefs were totally unknown" (Boelaert:7).

62 MENDE
(FC–7)

Ca. 1920

Language—The Mende consist of the speakers of the various dialects of the Mende language (AL VI, 5:62, 63). *N.S.M.*—"Mende country is divided into sixty independent chiefdoms . . ." (McCulloch:16), none of which is large enough to be a state, as the total territory is about 25,000 sq. km.

09 TALLENSI
(FE–10)

Ca. 1900

Language—The Tallensi consist of those people speaking dialects of Mole-Dagbane which are intertelligible with the dialect of Tongo. (Such dialects include some but not all dialects of Kusai, Mamprusi, Tallensi and Gurunsi.) (Fortes: xii, 14, 16; AL VI, 5:672–675.) *N.S.M.*—"They share no apparent political unity" (Fortes:16).

55 TIV
(FF–57)

Ca. 1900

Language—The Tiv consist of the speakers of the Tiv language (Bohannan and Bohannan:11; AL VI, 5:45). *N.S.M.*—The Tiv are "without any internal cohesion" and have "no leaders" (East:406).

42 AZANDE
(FO–7)

Ca. 1900

Language—The Azande consist of the speakers of the several dialects of the Zande language, which are "mutually intelligible" (Baxter and Butt:14; AL VI, 5:50). *N.S.M.*—Toward the end of the nineteenth century there were six or seven chiefdoms occupying approximately 50,000 sq. km. in all (Evans-Pritchard:476). However, much of these 50,000 sq. km. were occupied by uninhabited bush separating these chiefdoms (Evans-Pritchard:15). From these two facts I infer that no Zande chiefdom occupied a territory of more than 10,000 sq. km.

54 JO-LWOO
(FL–11)

Ca. 1900

Language—The Jo-Lwoo consist of the speakers of the Jo-Lwoo dialect of Kaverondo (AL VI, 5:233). *N.S.M.*—"There is nothing that can be described as a political office in a Luo tribe" (Evans-Pritchard:28). *Contact*—The dialects of the Jo-Lwoo of Kaverondo and the Adhola of Uganda are probably intertelligible, but the two groups are not in contact.

05 SUDAN PAS-
TORAL ARABS
(MQ–5,
MQ–9,
MQ–10)

Ca. 1850

Exact limits of this cultunit are not known. *Language*—The Sudan Pastoral Arabs consist of the speakers of colloquial Arabic dialects intertelligible with Kababish (AL VI, 5:332, 334). *N.S.M.*—Namely, the Sudan Pastoral Arabs consist of such colloquial Arabic speakers who in 1850 conducted intratribal and intertribal raiding independently of the Turkish authorities (Parkyns:259, 275).

14 KATI KAFIR
(AU–6)

Ca. 1890

Language—The Kati Kafir consist of the speakers of Kati (Morgensterne:40, AL VII, 8:286), *N.S.M.*—There is no political organization beyond kinship grouping (Robertson:83–87; 434–442).

65 KAZAKS
(RQ–2)

Ca. 1800

Language—The Kazaks consist of the speakers of Kazak Turkish, North and West of the Caspian Sea (AL VII, 1:97–99). *N.S.M.*—Among the Kazaks there is infrequent effective rule of khans and the presence of internal war (Hudson:63, 66). *Contact*—The Azerbaijani probably speak intertelligible dialects but are not included in the cultunit because they have, for the past several centuries, belonged to a separate state. Furthermore, they are separated from the Kazaks by several hundred miles of Caspian Sea and Persian speakers.

29 CHUKCHEE (RY–2)

Ca. 1900

Language—The Chukchee consist of the speakers of the five dialects of the Chukchee language (AL VII, 1:131–136). *N.S.M.*—". . . there are to be found among the Chukchee living at the coast neither any recognized chiefs nor any trace of social organization" (Nordenskiold:492).

24 GILYAK (RX–2)

Ca. 1870

Language—The Gilyak consist of the Mainland (Amur-Gilyak) and Sakhalin Island Gilyak whose languages are mutually "understood after a fashion" (Seeland:60; AL VII, 1:139). *N.S.M.*—"Among these tribes there appeared to be no traditions of a great chief or king" (Hawes:209).

36 HILL MARIA GOND (AW–32)

Ca. 1880

Language—The Hill Maria Gond consist of the speakers of Hill Maria Gond. (Voegelin in AL VII, 4:44–46, lumps all Gond dialects as a single language, but Grigson:xx, 319, makes it completely clear that Hill Maria and Bison Horn Maria are completely unintertelligible.) *N.S.M.*—They are "aboriginals . . . who have maintained their primitive clan organization on to this day" (Buradkhar:127).

23 AKA-KORA ANDAMAN (AZ–2)

Ca. 1910

Language—The Aka-Kora Andaman consist of the speakers of North Andaman dialects intertelligible with the Aka-Kora (Radcliffe-Brown: vii–viii; AL VIII, 4:10–11). *N.S.M.*—"The head chief of the tribe . . . possesses no power to punish or enforce obedience to his wishes . . ." (Radcliffe-Brown:46).

45 SEMANG (AN–7)

Ca. 1920

Language—The Semang consist of the speakers of the Semang-Pangun language, which is unintertelligible with Sakai and Jukun (Skeats and Blagden 2:385–386; Al VIII, 4:8–9). *N.S.M.*—". . . no organized body of chiefs" (Skeats and Blagden, 1:494).

52 APAYAO (OA–5)

Ca. 1920

The Apayao consist of the speakers of the Apayao language which is unintertelligible with the neighboring Ibang and Kalinga (Wilson:136; AL VI, 4:90). *N.S.M.*—There is no more than a grroup of families joined together for mutual protection under one headman (Wilson:12).

12 SADONG DYAK (OC–8)

Ca. 1950

Language—The Sadong Dyaks consist of the Land Dyaks speaking dialects intertelligible with that of the Sadong of Mentu Tapuh (Geddes:6; AL VI, 4:71; AL VII, 2:14). *N.S.M.*—". . . Dyaks, in their different tribes, do not acknowledge the authority of one chief who has rule or influence over several of them . . ." (Low:290).

34 BARE'E TORADJA (OG–11)

Ca. 1890

Language—The Bare'e Toradja consist of the speakers of Toradja dialects which are intertelligible with the dialect of the Bare'e of Poro (Adriani and Kruyt 2:3; AL VII, 2:25). *N.S.M.*—The main function of the village chief is simply to follow the will of the people (Adriani and Kruyt 1:108).

06 KAPAUKU (OJ–29)

Ca. 1940

Language—The Kapauku consist of the speakers of Kapauku (Ekagi) dialects intertelligible with that of the Kamu valley (AL VII, 9:14). *N.S.M.*—There is no central political authority (Pospisil:15).

28 OROKAIVA (OJ–23)

Language—The Orokaiva consist of the speakers of Orokaiva dialects intertelligible with the Aiga (Binandere) (Williams:v; AL VII, 9:20).

Ca. 1910	*N.S.M.*—"There is no well-defined chieftainship among the Orokaiva" (Williams:104).
51 WOLEA (OR–21) *Ca.* 1900	*Language*—The Wolea consist of the speakers of Wolean dialects intertelligible with that of Ifaluk (Burrows:1; AL VI, 4:90). *N.S.M.*—The so-called "Yap Empire" seems to be simply an arrangement for giving and exchanging gifts (Bates and Abbot:169).
17 LAU MALAITA (ON–9) *Ca.* 1925	*Language*—The Lau Malaita consist of the Lau speakers of the Island of Malaita and nearby islands, but not the "hill people" of Malaita who speak a different and unintertelligible language (Ivens:23–28; AL VI, 9:45). *N.S.M.*—The power of the chiefs "was limited to their own particular adherents . . ." (Ivens:28).
56 SENIANG OF MALEKULA (OO–12) *Ca.* 1880	*Language*—The Seniang of Malekula consist of the speakers of the Seniang language and those dialects of Wilemp and Nahate which are intertelligible with Seniang (Deacon:5, 52; AL VI, 9:26, 27). *N.S.M.*—"There is no chieftainship" (Deacon:48).
39 TIKOPIA (OT–11) *Ca.* 1930	*Language*—The Tikopia consist of the speakers of Tikopia-Anuta, intertelligible dialects being spoken on both islands (AL VI, 4:28). *N.S.M.*—Tikopia and Anuta are politically independent and are too small to be a state.
20 TONGA (OU–9) *Ca.* 1800	*Language*—The Tonga consist of the speakers of Tongese (AL VI, 7:111). *N.S.M.*—The total area of Tonga (i.e., the island of Tongatapu, Hopai Island and Vavoo) is 385 sq. mi., which is less than 1,000 sq. km. (*Encyclopaedia Britannica*, 11th ed.: *s. v.* "Tonga").
31 MANGAREVA (OX–5) *Ca.* 1885	*Language*—The Mangareva consist of the speakers of Mangareva which is closely related to, but unintertelligible with that of the Tuamatu Archipelago (Paumotu) (AL VI, 4:44). *N.S.M.*—Mangareva has an area less than 5,000 sq. km.
53 CENTRAL ESKIMO (ND–5, ND–6, ND–8, ND–11, ND–13) *Ca.* 1910	*Language*—The Central Eskimo consist of certain speakers of Eskimo dialects intertelligible with the Copper Eskimo, possibly including the Baffin Land Eskimo, Caribou Eskimo, Mackenzie Eskimo and Netsilik Eskimo (AL VI, 6:81). *N.S.M.*—I find no evidence of formal political organization. *Contact:* The Central Eskimo consist of those speakers of the aforementioned Eskimo dialects in contact with the Copper Eskimo. There are contact gaps between the Mackenzie Eskimo and the Point Barrow Eskimo to the east; and other contact gaps between the Netsilik Eskimo and other Eskimo to the east.
07 EYAK (NA–7) *Ca.* 1880	*Language*—The Eyak consist of the speakers of Eyak, an Athapascan language, unintertelligible with the neighboring Atna (Birket-Smith and De Laguna:341; AL VI, 6:87). *N.S.M.*—The Eyaks constitute a single territorial team, not territorially ramified. They have moieties, each with its chief, but these moieties are not territorially organized (Birket-Smith and De Laguna:123).
40 STRAITS SALISH (NR–15) *Ca.* 1885	*Language*—The Straits Salish consist of all those speakers of Coastal Salish dialects which are intertelligible with that of the Klallam of Port Townsend (Gunther:181–182; AL VI, 6:95). *N.S.M.*—". . . chief gives advice but has no power beyond the backing of public opinion to enforce it" (Gunther:261).

46 WINTUN
(NS–26)

Ca. 1845

Language—The Wintun consist of the speakers of Wintun and Wintu who "more or less understand each other" but not the Patwin, whose language is unintertelligible (Kroeber:253; AL VI, 6:119). *N.S.M.*—"Their warfare was usually nothing more pretentious than a neighborhood feud. . . ." The decision to engage in such a "war" could be made by anyone who could gather enough followers (DuBois:30–31; 36–37).

18 SOUTHERN
BASIN
SHOSHONEANS
(NT–16,
NT–19,
NS–13)

Ca. 1845

Language—Southern Basin Shoshoneans consist of speakers of Shoshonean dialects intertelligible with Shivwits. According to the Voegelins, these include the Southern Paiute, the Ute, the Chemehuevi and the Kawaiisu (AL VI, 6:130). *N.S.M.*—"Political control was minimal" (Stewart:261). *N. B.* The Ute seem to have had some sort of band organization, at least for a time; it is conceivable, but doubtful, that they formed a distinct Flat-head-type cultunit in the 1840's.

60 CHEYENNE
(NQ–8)

Ca. 1840

Language—The Cheyenne consist of the speakers of the Cheyenne language, which was unintertelligible with the Arapaho, their nearest neighbors (Mooney:372; AL VI, 6:98). *N.S.M.*—There are no leaders who wield exclusive right to conduct warfare. Indeed "any properly qualified Cheyenne can assemble a war party; he need only engage the interest of a few friends . . ." (Hoebel:70).

49 OJIBWA
(NG–6)

Ca. 1800

Language—The Ojibwa consist of the speakers of the Algonquian dialects intertelligible with Chippewa, including Ottawa, Algonquin, and Salteaux (AL VI, 6:96, 97). *N.S.M.*—The Ojibwa bands had an independent status, and their chiefs had "feeble authority" (Jenness:102). (Data for the War, Stress and Culture survey was collected only from the Ojibwa proper of Wisconsin and Minnesota.)

50 WESTERN
IROQUOIS
(NM–9)

Ca. 1700

Language—The Western Iroquois consist of the speakers of Seneca-Cayuga-Onondaga (AL VI, 6:112). *N.S.M.*—The Seneca, Cayuga and Onondaga together with the Oneida and Mohawk formed the original Iroquois Confederacy, later joined by the Tuscarora. At one time this confederation controlled a large part of the Great Lakes region. However, any of the five (later six) could declare war separately; in fact, any warrior could organize a war party whenever he pleased (Morgan:26).

11 WESTERN
APACHE
(NT–21)

Ca. 1880

Language—The Western Apache consist of speakers of Apachean dialects intertelligible with San Carlos Apache. While differences from other Apachean dialects and Navaho are not great, the Voegelins follow Hoijer in considering Western Apache unintertelligible with them (AL VI, 6:88, 90). *N.S.M.*—Political organization was confined to the local group or band; even here the band chiefs "did not have supreme power, but instead led their people mainly by prestige and good example . . ." (Goodwin:57).

37 PIMA-PAPAGO
(NU–28)
Ca. 1880

Language—The Pima-Papago consist of speakers of Pima dialects that are intertelligible with the Papago of Topawa (AL VI, 6:131, 132). *N.S.M.*—"The Papago had no central government" (Underhill:70).

35 CALLINAGO
(ST–13)

Ca. 1490

Language—The Callinago consist of the speakers of so-called Island Carib (AL VII, 7:93). *N.S.M.*—"Except in war time, each Carib village seems to have been . . . independent. . . . Each island had one or two war chiefs" (Rouse:555).

32 YAGUA
(SE–20)

Ca. 1935

Language—The Yagua consist of the speakers of Yagua, Peba and Yameo, which are grouped in "an independent Peban linguistic family," not including Tucuna (Steward and Métraux:728; AL VII, 7, Part 1:72). *N.S.M.*—The Yagua live in a "series of essentially independent communities" (Fejos:15).

43 ARAUCANIANS
(SG–4)

Ca. 1800

Language—The Araucanians consist of the speakers of the dialect of Araucanian (Faron:268; AL VII, 7, Part 1:76). *N.S.M.*—". . . no aboriginal political divisions greater than autonomous local groups or lineage" (Faron:273).

21 ONA
(SH–4)

Ca. 1880

Language—The Ona consist of the speakers of the Shelknam, or Ona language, which seems to be unintertelligible with the Aush (Haush) or Eastern Ona, but may be "mutually intelligible with great difficulty" (Lothrop:48–49; AL VII, 7, Part 1:76). *N.S.M.*—". . . no chiefs, no ruling group or caste of any kind" (Cooper:116).

22 MATACO
(SI–7)

Ca. 1870

Language—The Mataco consist of the speakers of the Mataco language (Pelleschi:43; AL VII, 7, Part 1:61). *N.S.M.*—Aboriginally the Mataco seemed to have had war chiefs both for independent bands and groups of bands, but according to Pelleschi these chiefs had no real authority and functioned only as influential leaders (Pelleschi:47; Karsten:43).

57 AWEIKOMA
(SM–2)

Ca. 1930

Language—The Aweikoma consist of the speakers of the Chocren language, one of thirteen in the Kaingang family (AL VII, 7, Part 1:47). *N.S.M.*—". . . They have been in a state of perpetual feud with one another . . ." (Henry:49).

FLATHEAD-TYPE CULTUNITS

The FLATHEAD TYPE of cultunit is defined as a group of people who:
(1) are members of a single state
(2) speak mutual intelligible dialects of the single language
common to all members of that state.

13 KOREANS
(AA–1)

Ca. 1960

State—The Koreans consist of the members of the state of Korea (Kang:166; Kennan:310). *Language*—They speak dialects of the Korean language, some of which are "mutually intelligible only after considerable time" (AL VII, 1:112–114).

26 MISKITO
(SA–15)

Ca. 1850

State—The Miskito proper were united into a political confederacy under British patronage, but not formal control; British claim to suzerainty seems not to have been effectively exercised, since at the height of British power and prestige their claim was effectively disputed by United States diplomats (Kirchhoff:224; Thompson:593A). *Language*—Miskito is classed as a single language, distinct however from Sumo (AL VII, 7:30).

AZTEC-TYPE CULTUNITS

The AZTEC TYPE of cultunit is defined as a group of people who:
(1) are members of a single state

(2) speak dialects intertelligible with the lingua franca
of that state
(3) live in a state in which dialects unintertelligible
with the lingua franca occur.

By *lingua franca* I mean the dialect in which the state officials usually conduct
their business.

S stands for State Membership; LF stands for Lingua Franca; UD stands for
Unintertelligible Dialects

66 AMHARA
(MP–5)

Ca. 1880

S and LF—The Amhara consist of those members of the state of Ethiopia
who are Amharic speakers (State—Messing:6; *LF*—Plowden:45; AL VI,
5:338). *UD*—"There are three major linguistic families in Ethiopia:
Cushitic, Semitic and Nilotic" (Messing:4).

27 FUR
(MQ–8)

Ca. 1880

S and LF—The Fur consist of those members of the state of DarFur who
are speakers of the Fur language. I presume that Fur is the lingua franca
since the state is named for its speakers (State—Felkin:245; *LF*—AL VI,
5:207). *UD*—The Masalit, who also live in DarFur, speak an unintertelligible language (AL VI, 5:206).

04 EGYPTIANS
(MR–1)

Ca. 1950

S and LF—The Egyptians consist of those members of the state of Egypt
who speak dialects of Arabic intertelligible with the dialect of Cairo (State—
Statesman's Year-Book:1580; *LF*—*Encyclopedia of Islam* 1:575; AL VI,
5:333). *UD*—Also living in Egypt are the speakers of Siwa Berber
(*Encyclopedia of Islam* 1:575).

59 ITALIANS
(EI–1)

Ca. 1960

S and LF—The Italians consist of those members of the state of Italy
who are speakers of literary Italian (Tuscan). (State—*Statesman's Year-
Book*:1175; *LF*—Naroll: field notes; AL VII, 8:33). *UD*—There are many
well-known unintertelligible dialects. Sicilian is an example (Naroll: field
notes).

03 IRISH
(ER–1)

Ca. 1955

S and LF—The Irish consist of those members of the State of Ireland
who are speakers of English (Brian O'Kelly of the Consulate General of
Chicago told me that most government officials conduct their verbal
business in English. He states that some, however, do so in Gaelic, such
as the Education Department (State—Arensberg:xiii; *LF*—AL VII, 8:95).
UD—Gaelic (AL VII, 8:95).

08 DUTCH
(ET–4)

Ca. 1955

S and LF—The Dutch consist of those members of the state of Netherlands
who are speakers of Dutch-Flemish (State—*Statesman's Year-Book*:1244;
LF—AL VII, 8:45; Naroll: field notes). *UD*—From statements of an
urban Dutch and a Frisian informant, it is clear that there are at least
two unintertelligible dialect groups in Netherlands: the Dutch-Flemish
speakers and the Frisian speakers.

30 AUSTRIANS
(EK–1)

Ca. 1960

S and LF—The Austrians consist of those members of the state of Austria
who are speakers of literary German (State—*Statesman's Year-Book*:806;
LF—Naroll: field notes; AL VII, 8:45). *UD*—West Tyrolean and other
peasant dialects (Naroll: field notes).

02 OSMANLI
TURKS
(MB–1)

S and LF—The Osmanli Turks consist of those members of the state of
Turkey who are speakers of Osmanli Turkish, but not Yürük (State—
Royal Institute of International Affairs:511; *LF*—AL VII, 1:97). *UD*—A

Ca. 1955 native Turkish informant who lived for a time in Diyarbakir in Eastern Turkey told me that she could not understand the dialect of the nearby Yürüks. She said that she could understand all other varieties of Turkish spoken in Turkey. Kurdish is also widely spoken in parts of Eastern Turkey and a small Greek-speaking group still lives in Istanbul (Naroll: field notes).

33 IRAQI
(MH–1)

Ca. 1960

S and LF—The Iraqi consist of those members of the state of Iraq who are speakers of Arabic dialects intertelligible with the dialect of Bagdad (State—*Statesman's Year-Book:*1046; *LF*—Royal Institute of International Affairs:256; AL VI, 5:332). *UD*—Kurds speak an Iranian language in various forms. Armenian and Persian are also spoken (Royal Institute of International Affairs:256).

48 BURMESE
(AP–4)

Ca. 1850

S and LF—The Burmese consist of those members of the state of Burma who are speakers of Tibeto-Burmese dialects intertelligible with Standard Burmese (Hall:132–134; AL VII, 6:37 f.). *UD*—In 1931 about 60 per cent of the population of Burma were Burmese proper, as here defined, while about three-quarters of the remainder spoke Burmese as a second language (AL VII, 6:38).

15 AZTEC
(TENOCHCA)
(NU–7)

Ca. 1525

S and LF—The Aztecs consist of those members of the Tenochcan state of the Aztec Confederacy who were speakers of Nahua (State—Vaillant:109; *LF*—*Encyclopaedia Britannica,* 11th ed., 19:153; AL VI, 6:132). *UD*—Mazahua (Bassauri, 3:353–354).

An alphabetical cross reference of the ethnic unit and tribal names in the War, Stress and Culture sample, together with the identifying serial numbers. In the bibliography which follows, the tribes are in serial order. *N. B.* For maps of tribal locations, see pp. 742–743.

Name	Serial Number	Name	Serial Number
Aka-Kora Andamans (Andamans)	23	Egyptians (Egypt)	04
Amhara	66	Eyak	07
Andamans (Aka-Kora Andamans)	23	Fur	27
Apayao	52	Gilyak	24
Araucanians	43	Gond (Hill Maria Gond)	36
Austrians	30	Hill Maria Gond (Gond)	36
Aweikoma	57	Hottentot	19
Azande	42	Ifaluk (Wolea)	51
Aztec (Nahua) (Tenochca)	15	Ila	38
Bare'e Toradja (Toradja)	34	Iraqi	33
Burmese	48	Irish	03
Callinago	35	Iroquois (Western Iroquois)	50
Central Eskimo (Copper Eskimo)	53	Italian (Italians)	59
Chagga	58	Italians (Italian)	59
Cheyenne	60	Jo-Lwoo (Luo)	54
Chukchee (Chukchi)	29	Kababish (Sudan Pastoral Arabs)	05
Chukchi (Chukchee)	29	Kafir (Kati Kafir)	14
Copper Eskimo (Central Eskimo)	53	Kapauku	06
Coyotero (Western Apache)	11	Kati Kafir (Kafir)	14
Dutch	08	Kazaks	65
Egypt (Egyptians)	04	Klallam (Straits Salish)	40

Korea (Koreans)	13	Seniang of Malekula (Malekula)	56
Koreans (Korea)	13	Southern Basin Shoshoneans	
Land Dyak (Sadong Dyak)	12	(Southern Paiute)	18
Lau (Malaita)	17	Southern Paiute (Southern	
Luo (Jo-Lwoo)	54	Basin Shoshoneans)	18
Malaita (Lau)	17	Straits Salish (Klallam)	40
Malekula (Seniang of Malekula)	56	Sudan Pastoral Arabs (Kababish)	05
Mangareva	31	Tallensi	09
Mataco	10	Tenochca (Aztec) (Nahua)	15
Mende	62	Thonga (Western Thonga)	41
Miskito (Mosquito)	26	Tikopia	39
Mongo	16	Tiv	55
Mosquito (Miskito)	26	Tonga	20
Nahua (Aztec) (Tenochca)	15	Toradja (Bare'e Toradja)	34
Ojibwa	49	Turks (Osmanli Turks)	02
Ona	21	Western Apache (Coyotero)	11
Orokaiva	28	Western Iroquois (Iroquois)	50
Osmanli Turks (Turks)	02	Western Thonga (Thonga)	41
Papago (Pima-Papago)	37	Wintun	46
Piam-Papago (Papago)	37	Wolea (Ifaluk)	51
Sadong Dyak (Land Dyak)	12	Yagua	32
Semang	45		

BIBLIOGRAPHY FOR TABLE 1

Key to Abbreviation
V and V refers to the series: Voegelin, Carl F. and Florence M., *Languages of the world*. Anthropological Linguistics, Indiana, Publications of the Archives of the Languages of the World. For example: AL VII, 8, refers to Volume 7, No. 8.

02 Osmanli Turks
GOKCU, OYA
1961 Verbal communication.
NAROLL, RAOUL
1965 Field notes.
ROYAL INSTITUTE OF INTERNATIONAL AFFAIRS
1954 *The Middle East: a political and economic survey.*
London and New York.
1954 *The Middle East: a political and economic survey.* London and New York.
v and v
1965 *Boreo-Oriental.* AL VII, 1.
03 Irish
ARENSBERG, CONRAD
1940 *Family and community in Ireland.* Cambridge, Mass., Harvard University Press.
O'KELLY, BRIAN
1967 Verbal communication.
v and v
1965 *Indo.* AL VII, 8.
04 Egyptians

ANONYMOUS
1960 *Encyclopedia of Islam,* Vol. 1, new edition.

ANONYMOUS
1963 *The statesman's year book,* Vol. 100. London, Macmillan.

v and v
1964 *African.* AL VI, 5.

05 *Sudan Pastoral Arabs*

PARKYNS, MANSFIELD
1850 The Kabbabish Arabs between Angola and Kardofan. *Journal of the Royal Geographic Society of London* 20:254–275.

v and v
1964 *African.* AL VI, 5.

06 *Kapauku*

POSPISIL, LEOPOLD
1958 *Kapauku Papuans and their law.* Yale Publications in Anthropology No. 54. New Haven, Yale University Press.

v and v
1965 *Indo.* AL VII, 9.

07 *Eyak*

BIRKET-SMITH, KAJ, and F. DE LAGUNA
1938 *The Eyak Indians of the Copper river delta.* Kobenhavn: Levin and Munksgaard.

v and v
1964 *Native American.* AL VI, 6.

08 *Dutch*

ANONYMOUS
1959 *Statesman's year book,* Vol. 96. London, Macmillan.

KROONTJE, WIEBE
1956 Verbal communication.

MUNCK, MICHELINA DE
1960 Verbal communication.

NAROLL, RAOUL
1966 Field notes.

v and v
1965 *Indo-European.* AL VII, 8.

09 *Tallensi*

FORTES, MEYER
1945 *The dynamics of clanship among the Tallensi.* London, New York, Toronto, Publications for the international African Institute by the Oxford University Press.

v and v
1964 *African.* AL VI, 5.

10 *Mataco*

KARSTEN, RAFAEL
1932 *Indian tribes of the Argentine and Bolivian Chaco: ethnological studies.* Societas Scientarum Fennico, Commentationes Humanarum Litterarum, Vol. 4, No. 1. Helsingsfors, Akademische Buchandlung.

PELLESCHI, JUAN
1896 *Boletín del Instituto Geográfico Argentino,* Vol. 17. Buenos Aires.

v and v
1965 *Native American.* AL VII, 7, Part 1.

11 *Western Apache*

GOODWIN, GRENVILLE
1935 The social divisions and economic life of the Western Apache. *American Anthropologist* 37:55–64.

v and v
1964 *Native American*. AL VI, 6.

12 *Sadong Dyak*

GEDDES, W. R.
1954 Land tenure of land Dyaks. *Sarawak Museum Journal,* Vol. 6, No. 4.

LOW, HUGH
1848 *Sarawak: its inhabitants and productions.* London, Richard Bentley.

v and v
1964 *Indo-Pacific*. AL VI, 4.

v and v
1965 *Indo-Pacific,* AL VII, 2.

13 *Koreans*

KANG, YOUNGHILL
1931 *The grass roof.* New York, Charles Scribner's.

KENNAN, GEORGE
1905 Korea: a degenerate state. *The Outlook* 81:307–315. New York, Outlook Company.

v and v
1965 *Boreo-Oriental*. AL VII, 1.

14 *Kati Kafir*

MORGENSTIERNE, GEORG
1926 *A report on a linguistic mission to Afganistan.* Institutet for Sammenlignende Kulturforskning, Series C, Vol. I, Part 2. Oslo, Aschehoug.

ROBERTSON, SIR GEORGE SCOTT
1896–1900 *Kafirs of the Hindu Kush.* London, Lawrence and Bullen.

v and v
1965 *Indo-European*. AL VII, 8.

15 *Aztec (Tenochca)*

ANONYMOUS
1910 *Encyclopaedia Britannica,* 11th ed., Vol. 19. New York.

BASAURI, CARLO
1940 *La población de Mexico,* Vol. III. Mexico, Secretaria de education publica.

VAILLANT, GEORGE CLAPP
1944 *The Aztecs of Mexico.* Hammondsworth, Middlesex, Penguin Books.

v and v
1964 *Native American*. AL VI, 6.

16 *Mongo*

BOELAERT, E.
1940 De Nkundo-Mattschappij. (Nkundo Society.) *Kongo-Overzee,* Vol. VI. Antwerp, De Sikkel.

HULSTAERT, GUSTAVE E.
1930 *Le Mariage des Nkundo.* Institut Royal Colonial Belge. Section des Sciences Morales et Politiques, Memoires in 8°, Vol. VIII. Bruxelles, Libraire Falk Fils, George Van Campenhout, Successeur.

v and v
1964 *African*. AL VI, 5.

17 *Lau Malaita*

IVENS, WALTER G.
1930 *The island builders of the Pacific.* London, Seeley Service.

v and v
1964 *Indo-Pacific*. AL VI, 9.

18 *Southern Basin Shoshoneans*

STEWART, JULIAN H.
1939 Some observations on Shoshonean distributions. *American Anthropologist* 41:261–265.

v and v
1964 *Native American.* AL VI, 6.
19 *Hottentot*
BEACH, D. M.
1938 *The phonetics of the Hottentot language.* Cambridge, England, W. Heffer.
STOW, GEORGE W.
1905 *The native races of South Africa; a history of the intrusion.* . . . London, S. Sonnenschein.
MURDOCK, GEORGE PETER
1934 *Our primitive contemporaries.* New York, Macmillan.
v and v
1964 *African.* AL VI, 5.
20 *Tonga*
ANONYMOUS
1910 Tonga. *Encyclopaedia Britannica,* 11th ed., Vol. 27. New York.
v and v
1964 *Indo-Pacific.* AL VI, 7.
21 *Ona*
COOPER, JOHN M.
1946 The Ona. Handbook of South American Indians. *Bureau of American Ethnology, Bulletin* No. 143, 1:107–127. Washington, D.C., Smithsonian Institution.
LOTHROP, SAMUEL K.
1928 *The Indians of Tierra del Fuego.* New York, Museum of the American Indian. Heye Foundation:48–98.
v and v
1965 *Native American.* AL VII, 7, Part 1.
23 *Aka-Kora Andaman*
RADCLIFFE-BROWN, A. R.
1922 *The Andaman islanders: a study in social anthropology.* Cambridge, University Press.
v and v
1966 *Indo-Pacific.* AL VIII, 4.
24 *Gilyak*
HAWES, CHARLES H.
1903 *In the uttermost East.* London and New York, Harper.
SEELAND, NICOLAS
1882 Die Ghiliaken; eine ethnographische skizze. *Russische Revue,* Vol. 21. St. Petersburg, Carl Rottger.
v and v
1965 *Boreo-Oriental.* AL VII, 1.
26 *Miskito*
KIRCHOFF, PAUL
1948 The Caribbean Lowland Tribes; the Mosquito, Sumo, Paya and Jacaque. Handbook of South American Indians. *Bureau of American Ethnology, Bulletin* No. 143, 4:219–229. Washington, D.C., Smithsonian Institution.
THOMPSON, WALLACE
1946 Miskito coast. *Encyclopaedia Britannica,* 15:593a. Chicago, University of Chicago.
v and v
1965 *Native American.* AL VII, 7.
27 *Fur*
FELKIN, R. W.
1885 Notes on the Fur tribe of Central Africa. *Proceedings of the Royal Society of Edinburgh,* Vol. 13, No. 120:205–266. Edinburgh, Neill.

v and v
1964 *African*. AL VI, 5.
28 Orokaiva
v and v
1965 *Indo-Pacific*. AL VII, 9.
WILLIAMS, F. E.
1930 *Orokaiva society*. London, Oxford University Press.
29 Chukchee
NORDENSKIOLD, A. E.
1882 *The voyage of the Vega round Asia and Europe*. New York, Macmillan.
v and v
1965 *Boreo-Oriental*. AL VII, 1.
30 Austrians
ANONYMOUS
1957 *Statesman's year book*, Vol. 94. London, Macmillan.
NAROLL, RAOUL
1956 Field notes.
v and v
1965 AL VII, 8.
31 Mangareva
v and v
1964 *Indo-Pacific*. AL VI, 4.
32 Yagua
FEJOS, PAUL
1943 *Ethnography of the Yagua*. New York, Viking Fund Publications in Anthropology.
STEWARD, JULIAN H., and A. MÉTRAUX
1948 The Peban tribes. Handbook of South American Indians. *Bureau of Amercan Ethnology, Bulletin* No. 143, 3:128–136. Washington, D.C., Smithsonian Institution.
v and v
1965 *Native American*. AL VII, 7, Part 1.
33 Iraqi
ANONYMOUS
1936 *The statesman's year book*, Vol. 73. London, Macmillan.
THE ROYAL INSTITUTE OF INTERNATIONAL AFFAIRS
1954 *The Middle East: a political and economic survey*. London and New York.
v and v
1964 *African*. AL VI, 5.
34 Bare'e Toradja
ADRIANI, N., and ALB. C. KRUYT
1950 *De Bare'e sprekende Toradjas van midden-celebes (de Oost-Toradjas)*. Verhandelingen der Koninklijke Nederlandse Akademie van Wetenschappen, Afdeling Letterkunde, Niewe Reeks, Deel 54, 55, 56, (nos. 1–3). Amsterdam, Noord-Hollandsche Uuitgevers Maatschappij.
v and v
1965 *Indo-Pacific*. AL VII, 2.
35 Callinago
ROUSE, IRVING
1948 The Carib. Handbook of South American Indians. *Bureau of Ethnology, Bulletin* No. 143; 4:547–565. Washington, D.C., Smithsonian Institution.
v and v
1965 *Native American*. AL VII, 7.
36 Hill Maria Gond

BURADKHAR, M. F.

1947 The clan organization of the Gonds. *Man in India* 27:127–136. London, H. Milford, Oxford University Press.

v and v

1966 *Sino-Tibetan.* AL VII, 4.

37 Pima-Papago

UNDERHILL, RUTH MURRAY

1939 *Social organization of the Papago Indians.* Columbia University Contributions to Anthropology, Vol. 33. New York, Columbia University Press.

v and v

1964 *Native American.* AL VI, 6.

38 Ila

COLSON, ELIZABETH

Verbal communication.

SMITH, REV. EDWIN W., and CAPTAIN ANDREW MURRAY DALE

1920 *The Ila-speaking peoples of Northern Rhodesia.* 2 vols. London, Macmillan.

v and v

1964 *African.* AL VI, 5.

39 Tikopia

v and v

1964 *Indo-Pacific.* AL VI, 4.

40 Straits Salish

GUNTHER, ERNA

1927 Klallam ethnography. *University of Washington Publications in Anthropology,* Vol. 1, No. 5:171–314. Seattle, Washington, University of Washington Press.

v and v

1964 *Native American.* AL VI, 6.

41 Western Thonga

ANONYMOUS

1910 *Encyclopaedia Britannica,* 11th ed., Vol. 11. New York.

JOHNSTON, SIR HARRY H.

1919 *A comparative study of Bantu and Semi-Bantu languages,* Vol. 1. Oxford, Clarendon Press.

42 Azande

BAXTER, P. T. W., and AUDREY BUTT

1953 *The Azande and related peoples of the Anglo-Egyptian Sudan and Belgian Congo.* International African Institute Ethnographic Survey. London, Oxford University Press.

EVANS-PRITCHARD, EDWARD EVAN

1956 *A history of the kingdom of Gbudwe (Azande of the Sudan).* Zaire, Vol. 10, Nos. 5, 7, 8. Brussels, Editions Universitaires.

v and v

1964 *African.* AL VI, 5.

43 Araucanians

FARON, LOUIS C.

1956 Araucanian patri-organization and the Omaha system. *American Anthropologist* 68:267–283.

v and v

1965 *Native American.* AL VII, 7, Part 1.

45 Semang

SKEATS, WALTER W., and C. O. BLAGDEN

1906 *Pagan races of the Malay peninsula.* 2 vols. London, Macmillan.

v and v

1966 *Indo-Pacific.* AL VIII, 4.

46 Wintun

DUBOIS, CORA
    1935 Wintu ethnography. *University of California Publications in Archaeology and Ethnology,* Vol. 36. Berkeley, University of California Press.

KROEBER, A. L.
    1932 The Patwin and their neighbors. *University of California Publications in Archaeology and Ethnology,* Vol. 29, No. 4. Berkeley, University of California Press.

v and v
    1964 *Native American.* AL VI, 6.

48 Burmese

HALL, DANIEL G. E.
    1950 *Burma.* London, Hutchinson's University Library.

v and v
    1965 *Prosodic analysis and Burmese syllable-initial feature.* AL VII, 6.

49 Ojibwa

JENNESS, DIAMOND
    1935 *The Ojibwa of Parry Island, their social and religious life.* Bulletin of the Canada Department of Mines, No. 78. Ottawa, National Museum of Canada.

v and v
    1964 *Native American.* AL VI, 6.

50 Western Iroquois

MORGAN, LEWIS HENRY
    1901 *League of the Ho-De-No-Sau-Nee or Iroquois,* Vols. 1 and 2. New York, Dodd, Mead.

v and v
    1964 *Native American.* AL VI, 6.

51 Wolea

BATES, MARSTON, and DONALD P. ABBOTT
    1958 *Coral Island: portrait of an atoll.* New York, Charles Scribner's.

BURROWS, EDWIN GRANT
    1949 *The people of Ifaluk: a little disturbed atoll culture.* Unpublished manuscript submitted as a final report, Coordinated Investigation of Micronesian Anthropology. Washington, Pacific Science Board, National Research Council.

v and v
    1964 *Indo-Pacific.* AL VI, 4.

52 Apayao

v and v
    1964 *Indo-Pacific.* AL VI, 4.

WILSON, LAURENCE L.
    1947 *Apayao life and legends.* New York, South East Asia Institute.

53 Central Eskimo

v and v
    AL VI, 6.

54 Jo-Lwoo

EVANS-PRITCHARD, EDWARD EVAN
    1949 Luo tribes and clans. *The Rhodes-Livingstone Journal,* No. 7:24–40. Lusaka, Rhodes-Livingstone Institute.

v and v
    1964 *African.* AL VI, 5.

55 Tiv

BOHANNAN, PAUL and LAURA
    1953 *The Tiv of central Nigeria.* Ethnographic Survey of Africa, Western Africa, Part 8. London, International African Institute.

EAST, RUPERT
    1939 *Akiga's story: the Tiv tribe as seen by one of its members.* London, International Institute of African Languages and Cultures, Oxford University Press.

v and v
    1964 *African.* AL VI, 5.
56 Seniang of Malekula
DEACON, BERNARD
    1934 *Malekula, a vanishing people in the New Hebrides.* London, Routledge.
v and v
    1964 *Indo-Pacific.* AL VI, 9.
57 Aweikoma
HENRY, JULES
    1941 *Jungle people, a Kaingang tribe in the highlands of Brazil.* New York, J. J. Augustin.
v and v
    1965 *Native American.* AL VII, 7, Part 1.
58 Chagga
DUNDAS, HON. CHARLES
    1924 *Kilimanjaro and its people.* London, H. F. and G. Witherby.
v and v
    1964 *African.* AL VI, 5.
59 Italians
ANONYMOUS
    1963 *The statesman's year book,* Vol. 100. London, Macmillan.
NAROLL, RAOUL
    1966 Field notes.
v and v
    1965 *Indo-European.* AL VII, 8.
60 Cheyenne
HOEBEL, ADAMSON E.
    1936 Associations and the State in the plains. *American Anthropologist* 38:433–448.
MOONEY, JAMES
    1905–1907 The Cheyenne Indians. American Anthropological Association. *Memoirs,* 6:357–443.
v and v
    1964 *Native American.* AL VI, 6.
62 Mende
MCCULLOUGH, M.
    1950 *Peoples of Sierra Leone protectorate.* Ethnographic Survey of Africa, Western Africa, Part 2. London, International African Institute.
v and v
    1964 *African.* AL VI, 5.
65 Kazaks
HUDSON, ALFRED E.
    1938 *Kazak social structure.* Yale University Publications in Anthropology, No. 20: 1–109. New Haven, Yale University Press.
v and v
    1965 *Boreo-Oriental.* AL VII, 1.
66 Amhara
MESSING, SIMON DAVID
    1957 *The highland-plateau Amhara of Ethiopia.* Philadelphia, University of Pennsylvania Press.
PLOWDEN, WALTER CHICELE
    1868 *Travels in Abyssinia and the Galla Country with an account.* . . . London, Longmans, Green.
v and v
    1964 *African.* AL VI, 5.

BIBLIOGRAPHY

BARROW, JOHN
1801   *An account of travels into the interior of South Africa.* 2 vol. London, T. Cadell and W. Davies.

BAUMANN, HERMAN, RICHARD THURNWALD, and DIEDRICH WESTERMANN
1939   *Völkerkunde von Afrika.* Essen, Essener Verlagsanstalt.

BEACH, DOUGLAS M.
1938   *The phonetics of the Hottentot language.* Cambridge, England, Hefner.

BERNDT, RONALD M.
1959   The concept of "the tribe" in the western desert of Australia. *Oceania* 30:81–107.

BESSAC, FRANK
1968   Cultunit and ethnic unit—Processes and symbolism. In Helm 1968: 58–71.

BIGGS, BRUCE
1957   Testing intelligibility among Yuman languages. *International Journal of American Linguistics* 23, No. 2:57–62.

BRIDGES, THOMAS
1948   The Canoe Indians of Tierra del Fuego. In Carleton S. Coon, ed., *A reader in general anthropology.* New York, Holt.

BRIGHAM, WILLIAM T.
1900   *An index to the islands of the Pacific Ocean.* Bishop Museum (Honolulu), Memoirs. Volume 1, No. 2.

BUSCHAN, GEORGE (ed.)
1922–   *Illustrierte Völkerkunde.* 3 Vols. Stutt-
1925   gart, Strecker and Schroeder.

CAMPBELL, A.
1868   On the tribes around Darjeeling. *Transactions of the Ethnological Society of London* 7:144–159.

CAPELL, ARTHUR
1941   *A new Fijian dictionary.* Sydney, Australasian Medical Publishing Co.
1962   *A linguistic survey of the South-Western Pacific Noumea.* South Pacific Commission. Technical Paper No. 136.

CHAGNON, NAPOLEON A.
1967   Yanomamö—the fierce people. *Natural History* 76:22–31.

CHAPANIS, A.
1954   The reconstruction of abbreviated printed messages. *Journal of Experimental Psychology* 48:496–510.

CHEYNE, ANDREW
1852   *A description of islands. . . .* London, Potter.

CONKLIN, HAROLD C.
1952   *Outline gazetteer of native Philippine ethnic and linguistic groups.* Mimeograph. New Haven.

DAMM, HANS, *et al.*
1938   Zentralkarolinen. II: Part I. Halbband: Ifaluk – Aurepik – Faraulip – Sorol – Mogemog. In G. Thilenius, ed., *Ergebnisse der Südsee-expedition, 1908–1910,* Section B, Vol. 10, Part 2. Hamburg, Friederichsen, DeGruyt.

DRIVER, HAROLD
1956   *An integration of functional, evolutionary and historical theory by means of correlations.* Indiana University Publications in Anthropology and Linguistics, Memoir 12.
1961   *Indians of North America.* Chicago, University of Chicago Press.

DRIVER, HAROLD, JOHN M. COOPER, PAUL KIRCHHOFF, DOROTHY O. LIBBY, WILLIAM C. MASSEY, and LESLIE SPIER
1953   Indian tribes of North America. Memoir 9. *International Journal of American Linguistics,* Vol. 191, No. 3, Supplement.

DRIVER, HAROLD, and WILLIAM C. MASSEY
1957   Comparative studies of North American Indians. *Transactions of the American Philosophical Society,* Vol. 47. Philadelphia.

EMBER, MELVIN
1963   The relationship between economic and political development in non-industrialized societies. *Ethnology* 2:228–248.

EVANS-PRITCHARD, E. E.
1940   The Nuer of the Southern Sudan. In Meyer Fortes and E. E. Evans-Pritchard, eds., *African political systems.* London, Oxford.

FERNANDEZ, JAMES W.
1963   *Redistribution and ritual reintegration in Fang culture.* Ph.D. thesis. Department of Anthropology, Northwestern University.

FISON, LORIMER
1886   Specimens of Fiji dialects. Edited by A. S. Gatschet. *Internationale Zeitschrift für Allgemeine Sprachwissenschaft* 2:193–208.

FORTES, MEYER
1940   The political system of the Tallensi of the northern territories of the Gold Coast. In Meyer Fortes and E. E. Evans-Pritchard, eds., *African political systems.* London, Oxford.

FRIED, MORTON H.
1966   On the concepts of "tribe" and "tribal society." *Transactions of the New York Academy of Sciences,* Series II, 28:527–540. Reprinted in Helm 1968: 3–22.

FRITZ, GEORG
1911 *Die Zentralkarolinische Sprache.* Berlin, Reimer.

GERLAND, GEORG
1892 Atlas der Völkerkunde. In Berghaus, *Physikalischer atlas.* Abt. 7. Gotha.

GODDARD, PLINY E.
1903– Life and culture of the Hupa. Hupa
1904 texts. *University of California Publications in American Archaeology and Ethnology* 1:1–88, 89–368.

GODEE-MOLSBERGEN, EVERHARDUS C. (ed.)
1916 *Reizen in Zuid-Afrika in de Hollandse Tijd.* Vol. 11. 's-Gravenhage, Publication of the Linschoten Society.

GOODENOUGH, WARD H.
1956 Residence rules. *Southwestern Journal of Anthropology* 12:22–37.

GREENWAY, JOHN
1963 *Bibliography of the Australian Aborigines.* Sydney, Angus and Robertson.

HELM, JUNE, (ed.)
1968 *Essays on the Problem of Tribe.* Proceedings of the 1967 Annual Spring Meeting of the American Ethnological Society.

HICKERSON, HAROLD, *et al.*
1952 Testing procedures for estimating transfer of information among Iroquois dialects and languages. *International Journal of American Linguistics* 18:1–8.

HOBHOUSE, L. T., G. C. WHEELER, and M. GINSBERG
1915 *The material culture and social institutions of the simpler peoples.* London, Chapman and Hall.

HODGSON, BRIAN H.
1857 Comparative vocabulary of the language of the broken tribes of Nepal. *Journal of the Royal Asiatic Society of Bengal* 26: 317–349.

HODSON, T. C.
1937 *India. Census Ethnography 1901–1931.* Delhi, Manager of Publications.

HOERNLE, AGNES W.
1925 The social organization of the Nama Hottentots of southwest Africa. *American Anthropologist* 27:1–24.

HOFFMANN, HANS
1968 Mathematical structures in ethnological systems. In Helm 1968: 49–57.

HYMES, DELL
1960 Lexicostatistics so far. *Current Anthropology* 1:3–44.
1968 Linguistic problems in defining the concept of "tribe." In Helm 1968: 23–48.

KENNEDY, RAYMOND, *et al.*
1962 *Bibliography of Indonesian peoples and cultures,* 2nd ed. New Haven, Yale University, Southeast Asia Studies.

KRAMER, AUGUSTIN
1937 Zentralkarolinen. II, Part 1, Halbband:

Lamotrek-Oleai—Feis. In G. Thilenius, ed., *Ergebnisse der Südsee-expedition 1908–1910,* Section B, Vol. 10, II. Hamburg, Friedrichsen, DeGruyt.

KROEBER, A. L.
1936 Culture area distributions III: Area and climax. *University of California Publications in American Archaeology and Ethnology* 37:111–112.

KUNOW, STEN
1906 General introduction, Specimens of the . . . Himalayan dialects. . . . Part 1, Tibeto-Burman family. In George A. Grierson, ed., *Linguistic survey of India,* Vol. 3. Calcutta.

LEACH, EDMUND
1960 Review of *Organization of work: a comparative analysis of production among non-industrial peoples,* by Stanley H. Udy, Jr. *American Sociological Review* 25:136–138.
1963 Comment on *Forms and problems of validation in social anthropology,* by William J. McEwen. *Current Anthropology* 4:174.
1964 *Political systems of Highland Burma,* 2nd ed. Boston, Beacon Press.

LEBAR, FRANK M., GERALD C. HICKEY, and JOHN F. MUSGRAVE
1964 *Ethnic groups of mainland Southeast Asia.* New Haven, HRAF.

LEVIN, M. G., and L. P. POTAPOV (eds.)
1956 *Narodii Sibiri.* Moscow and Leningrad, Akademii Nauk SSR.

LEVINE, ROBERT A.
1961 Anthropology and the study of conflict: an introduction. *Journal of Conflict Resolution* 5:3–15.

LOTHROP, SAMUEL K.
1928 *The Indians of Tierra del Fuego.* New York, Museum of the American Indian, Heye Foundation:48–98.

LUZBETAK, LOUIS J.
1951 *Marriage and the family in Caucasia.* Studia Instituti Anthropos, Vol. 3. Vienna-Mödling, St. Gabriel's Mission Press.

MASON, J. ALDEN
1948 The languages of South American Indians. Handbook of South American Indians. *Bureau of American Ethnology, Bulletin* No. 143, Vol. 6:157–317. Washington, D.C., Smithsonian Institution.

MCQUOWN, NORMAN A.
1955 The indigenous languages of Latin America. *American Anthropologist* 57:501–570.

MEILLET, ANTOINE, and MARCEL COHEN (eds.)
1952 *Les langues du monde,* 2nd ed. Paris.

MOERMAN, MICHAEL
1964 *Farming in Ban Phaed.* Yale University

Ph.D. dissertation. University Microfilms, Ann Arbor.

1965 Who are the Lue? *American Anthropologist* 67:1215–1230.

1968 Being Lue: uses and abuses of ethnic identification. In Helm 1968: 153–169.

MURDOCK, GEORGE P.

1951 *Outline of South American cultures.* New Haven, HRAF.

1953 The processing of anthropological materials. In A. L. Kroeber, ed., *Anthropology today.* Chicago, University of Chicago Press.

1957 World ethnographic sample. *American Anthropologist* 59:664–687.

1959 *Africa: its peoples and their culture history.* New York, McGraw-Hill.

1963 Ethnographic atlas. *Ethnology* 2:249–253.

NADEL, SIEGFRIED F.

1951 *The foundations of social anthropology.* London, Cohen and West.

NAG, MONI

1968 The concept of tribe in the contemporary socio-political context of India. In Helm 1968: 186–200.

NAROLL, RAOUL

1956 A preliminary index of social development. *American Anthropologist* 58:687–715.

1961 *Two stratified random samples for a cross-cultural survey.* Mimeograph.

1962 *Data quality control.* New York, Free Press.

1964 On ethnic unit classification. *Current Anthropology* 5:283–291, 306–312.

1968 Who the Lue are. In Helm 1968: 72–82.

NIMUENDAJU, KURT

1915 Vokabular der Timbiras von Muranhao und Para. *Zeitschrift für Ethnologie* 47: 302–305.

PIERCE, JOE E.

1954 Crow vs. Hidatsa in dialect distance and glotto-chronology. *International Journal of American Linguistics* 20:134–136.

PILLING, ARNOLD R.

1962 Statistics, sorcery and justice. *American Anthropologist* 64:1057–59.

POWDERMAKER, HORTENSE

1933 *Life in Lesu.* New York, Norton.

QUIGLEY, CARROLL

1961 *The evolution of civilizations.* New York, Macmillan.

RADCLIFFE-BROWN, A. R.

1940a Preface. In Meyer Fortes and E. E. Evans-Pritchard, eds., *African political systems.* London, Oxford.

1940b On social structure. *Journal of the Royal Anthropological Institute* 70:1–12.

REICHARD, GLADYS A.

1938 Social life. In Franz Boas, ed., *General anthropology.* Boston, Heath.

RIVET, PAUL

1911 La famille linguistique Peba. *Journal de la Société des Americanistes de Paris,* N.S., 8:173–206.

SCHAPERA, I.

1930 *The Khoisan peoples of South Africa.* London, Routledge.

1953 Some comments on comparative method in social anthropology. *American Anthropologist* 55:353–362.

1956 *Government and politics in tribal societies.* London, C. Watts.

SNETHLAGE, HEINRICH

1930 Unter nordostbrasilianischen Indianern. *Zeitschrift für Ethnologie* 62:111–205.

SPENGLER, OSWALD

1926 *The decline of the West.* New York, Knopf. 2 vols. Trans. from German by Charles Francis Atkinson.

STEWARD, JULIAN H., and ALFRED MÉTRAUX

1948 The Peban tribes. *Handbook of South American Indians.* Smithsonian Institution. Bureau of American Ethnology Bulletin No. 143, Vol. 3:728–736. New York, Cooper Square.

STOW, GEORGE W.

1910 *The native races of South Africa.* London, Swan Sonnenschein.

SWADESH, MORRIS R.

1950 Salish internal relationships. *International Journal of American Linguistics* 16:157–167.

TEIT, JAMES A.

1930 The Salishan tribes of the western plateaus. *Annual Reports of the Bureau of American Ethnology* 45:37–197. Washington, D.C., U. S. Government Printing Office.

TOLSTOV, S. P., M. G. LEVIN, and N. N. CHEBOKSAROV (eds.)

1960 *Ocherki Obschii Etnografii.* Akademiya Nauk SSR. Institut Etnographii imeni N. N. Miklukho-Maklaya. Moscow.

TOYNBEE, ARNOLD J.

1947 *A study of history,* abridged ed. New York, Oxford.

VOEGELIN, C. F., and ZELLIG S. HARRIS

1951 Methods for determining intelligibility among dialects of natural languages. *Proceedings, American Philosophical Society* 95:322–329.

VOEGELIN, C. F., and F. M. VOEGELIN

1965 Sino-Tibetan Fascicle Five. *Anthropological Linguistics,* Vol. 7, No. 6.

1966 Index to languages of the world. *Anthropological Linguistics,* Vol. 8, Nos. 6–7. (These numbers index the nineteen earlier fascicles which together comprise the latest authoritative listing and classification of the languages of the world.)

WANDRES, C.
1927 Tiernamen in der Nama und Bergdama Sprache etymologisch erläutert. Festschrift Karl Meinhof. *Sprachwissenschaftliche und andere Studien*:125–233. Hamburg, Friederichsen, DeGruyt.

WHITING, JOHN W. M.
1954 The cross-cultural method. In Gardner Lindzey, ed., *Handbook of social psychology*, 1:523–531. Cambridge, Mass., Addison-Wesley.

WILLIAMS, ROGER J.
1958 Chemical anthropology—an open door. *American Scientist* 46:1–24.

WOLFF, HANS
1959 Intelligibility and inter-ethnic attitudes. *Anthropological Linguistics* 1:34–41.

YAMAGIRWA, JOSEPH K.
1967 On dialect intelligibility in Japan. *Anthropological Linguistics* 9:1–18.

CHAPTER 40

Two Measures of Societal Complexity:
An Empirical Cross-Cultural Comparison

TERRENCE A. TATJE and RAOUL NAROLL

INTRODUCTION

A leading problem of cross-cultural method is the measurement of variables. Most cross-cultural surveys use simple attributes: a trait is scored present or absent, high or low. Whiting and Child (1953) used artificial scales in which a rater arbitrarily assigned a tribe a score which reflected only the rater's subjective impressions. But this chapter, like the following one by Carneiro, demonstrates the application of more sophisticated techniques. Such techniques have long been used in other social sciences but are comparatively unfamiliar in cross-cultural survey work. The problem faced by both this chapter and the next is the classic anthropological one of measuring level of civilization, or degree of cultural evolution. In this chapter, a three-indicator index is compared with an eleven-step Guttman scale. In the following chapter, a far more elaborate Guttman scale is presented. All three measures produce highly correlated results. Thus the validity of all three is strongly supported.

The present paper serves incidentally to apply many of the points made in other chapters. Its data are derived from the probability sample described in Chapter 43; it deals with the units defined in Chapter 39; its major variables were subjected to quality control tests presented in Chapter 44; and

This work was supported by Grant G-21584, National Science Foundation. Ronald Cohen and Robert F. Winch made valuable comments and suggestions; however, we alone are jointly responsible for errors and shortcomings. Space limits prevent listing here the dozens of people who have contributed to the War, Stress and Culture project of which this study forms a part.

tests for interdependence in Chapter 47. Thus we can claim for these results greater rigor of demonstration than those of earlier studies.

The work presented in this chapter is a small part of a much larger whole—Naroll's War, Stress and Culture (WSC) study. The larger aim of that study is the general investigation of the role of warfare and culture stress in the processes of cultural evolution. But the methodological analyses of this chapter as well as of Chapters 39, 43, 44 and 47 all figure prominently in that study.

This chapter presents an empirical comparison of Freeman's (1957) scale typology and Naroll's (1956a) Social Development Index. It presents new social development data from Naroll's WSC study and fits the new data into the Social Development Index. Both schemes are devised to measure the relative complexity of societies in terms of increasing specialization of function, or the degree of elaboration and cumulation of cultural elements. Freeman's scale is based on twelve folk-urban variables; Naroll's index utilizes three general indicators of social development.

Social scientists have long recognized that much of culture is cumulative; as a society adds new traits to its cultural inventory many older traits tend to remain. Likewise, attempts to determine an ordered sequence of social development are not new. Indeed, social or cultural evolution was a major focus of early theorists such as Morgan (1877), Maine (1861) and Bachofen (1861). Each of these writers proposed a unilineal theory of cultural development; that is, a definite sequence of "stages" through which every culture was thought to progress. These theorists made selective use of ethnographic data to fit their schemes, and the rigidity of their concept of unilinear evolution made contradictions inevitable. For several decades anthropologists, disenchanted with these early formulations, abandoned cultural evolution and turned their attention to other problems in anthropological theory. Campbell (1961) discusses several reasons for this disenchantment. However, the basic question—the pattern of the development of cultural institutions—remained unanswered.

The last ten or twenty years have seen much renewed interest in cultural evolution (White 1943, 1960; Chapple and Coon 1942: 260 f., 452 f.; Coon 1948:612 f.; Steward 1955; Sahlins and Service 1960). In a survey of recent evolutionary literature Cohen (1961) states:

> . . . there is a need for some unifying theoretical approach that might bridge the gap between the constantly specializing and differentiating sub-branches of the discipline. Evolutionary theory not only unifies, it is a success, and it is therefore even more attractive as a generalizing and scientific approach which has already produced legitimate results in biology. . . . Ideally then, evolution is a method of coping intellectually with a changing world, and a theoretical framework for synthesizing and unifying disparate and differentiating aspects of knowledge. (Cohen 1961:323)

Cohen analyzes several approaches which have been taken in recent evolutionary studies, in terms of their underlying logical starting points and their scope. One leading approach employed by modern evolutionists is the cross-cultural survey. It is this method which is the principle concern here.

RECENT EVOLUTIONARY SCALES FOR CROSS-CULTURAL SURVEYS

By cross-cultural survey is of course meant a statistical study of culture traits from a world-wide sample of cultures. The cultural unit—"tribe," "society" or "culture" —is taken as the sampling unit, and inferences are made on the basis of a sample of such units from the universe of human cultures. Strict probability sampling of this universe is precluded by two difficulties: (1) the total universe of such cultural units has not been listed rigorously, although approximate listings of cultures known in modern times are available; and (2) most such cultures are insufficiently described to permit

adequate library study. However, techniques have been devised for stratified sampling of a bibliographically defined universe, in which all departures from randomness are indentified and hence susceptible of control for sampling bias (see Chapter 43). The statistical nature of such studies result in the illumination of cultural tendencies, i.e., correlations, and not absolute "laws."

The studies by Murdock (1949) and Whiting and Child (1953) are still probably the best known of this type. Murdock's (1949) study of social structure was one of the first to make use of a large sample of societies, albeit a judgmental one, to test hypotheses about the development of cultural institutions. Since that time there has been much more use of the cross-cultural survey to test evolutionary theories. Considerable interest has been shown lately in improving the cross-cultural method. (See Part VII, this volume.)

Many recent evolutionary studies have been concerned with the development of specific aspects of culture. Following the work by Naroll (1956a), Ember's (1963) study of the relation between economic and political development is a case in point. Ember's results, like Naroll's, show a general tendency toward simultaneous increase in the complexity of economic and political institutions among non-literate societies; and both factors are related to a general increase in cultural complexity. Similarly, Schwartz and Miller (1964) relate the development of legal institutions to increased complexity in other aspects of culture. Three legal characteristics —mediation, council, and police—are found to form a nearly perfect Guttman scale of development for a forty-eight society sample. The development of these traits is then related to the appearance of the traits employed by Freeman and Winch (1957) to construct their typology of societal complexity; Freeman and Winch found in another forty-eight society sample that six culture traits formed a Guttman scale of development. These traits, in the order of their occurrence, are: symbolic medium of exchange, punishment of crimes, full-time specialized real priests, full-time specialized teachers, full-time bureaucrats, and written language.

With the increase of such studies as these the need for some general measure of overall cultural complexity has become apparent.

In a pilot study of leadership in non-literate societies Moskos (n.d.) examines four general measures of societal complexity to "ascertain the degree to which leadership variables may be predicted from measures of societal complexity" (Moskos n.d.:1). The complexity measures used by Moskos include the typology of Hobhouse, Wheeler and Ginsberg (1915), Naroll's (1956a) Social Development Index, the empirical typology set forth by Freeman and Winch (1957), and a complexity index using three variables—political integration, settlement pattern, and social stratification—from Murdock's (1957) World Ethnographic Sample. Moskos finds considerable variation among these measures when applying them to his sample of six societies; he comments that "while it is true, that six societies are a very small sample, it would seem that constructing a valid scale of societal complexity is a problem which has not yet been satisfactorily resolved" (Moskos n.d.:5).

The most elaborate evolutionary scale has been that of Carneiro—see Chapter 41.

COMPARISON OF TWO COMPLEXITY MEASURES

This chapter is a comparison of two of these general measures of cultural complexity: Naroll's Social Development Index, and a Guttman scale of societal complexity presented in *An Empirical Test of Folk-Urbanism,* an unpublished Ph.D. dissertation by Linton C. Freeman (1957). There are good reasons for undertaking this comparison. Fundamental truths in the social sciences, as in the natural sciences, will be proven by different lines of research all pointing to the same generalizations. It is therefore valuable to know whether or not Naroll's Social Development Index and the Guttman scale of Redfield's folk-urban variables developed by Freeman will give substantially the same results when applied to an independent cross-cultural sample of societies. Substantial agreement between the two measures will provide much support for the validity of both schemes as measures of the concept of cultural complexity and development. At the same time any systematic differences between the two sets of results will call for an explanation and may well point to refinements in our conceptual model of

cultural development. Furthermore, the application of these two measures of social complexity to a new, comparatively unbiased sample will further support their validity, since both were originally tested on nonrandom, selective samples.

FREEMAN'S FOLK-URBAN STUDY

In its general approach the Freeman dissertation is the same as the earlier Freeman and Winch study cited above (Freeman 1957: 2). However, whereas the Freeman and Winch paper has no particular theory of cultural complexity as a referent, the Freeman study is an empirical test of Redfield's folk-urban typology.

Although Redfield himself did not explicitly acknowledge the evolutionary nature of his concept until *The Primitive World and Its Transformations* (Redfield 1953), the evolutionary implications of the folk-urban continuum have long been apparent. The evolution of societies toward greater functional complexity along the folk-urban continuum can be viewed in the same way that Morgan saw societies changing from savagery and barbarism to civilization. In his original statement, Redfield (1947) said:

Such a society is small, isolated, nonliterate, and homogeneous, with a strong sense of group solidarity. The ways of living are conventionalized into that coherent system which we call "a culture." Behavior is traditional, spontaneous, uncritical, and personal; there is no legislation or habit of experiment and reflection for intellectual ends. Kinship, its relationships and institutions, are the type categories of experience and the familial group is the unit of action. The sacred prevails over the secular; the economy is one of status rather than of the market (Redfield 1947:293).

After a careful analysis of Redfield's discussions of folk-urbanism, Freeman redefines the traits used by Redfield to differentiate his types and establishes categories useful for cross-cultural purposes. Since the technique he uses in analyzing his findings is scaling analysis, each variable is reduced to a dichotomy. The presence of a trait is taken to indicate greater complexity, or the urban pole; its absence indicates less complexity, i.e., folkism.

Freeman applies these categories to a sample of fifty-two societies, scoring the presence or absence of each trait for each society. The sample includes one selected society from each of the fifty culture areas described in Murdock's (n.d.) paper, "The Comparative Study of Cultures," plus two additional societies from the European culture area. For this sample eleven traits are found to fall into a nearly perfect Guttman scale of development (coefficient of reproducibility=0.96 [Freeman 1957:82]). In order of development these categories are:

1. Presence or absence of trade with other societies.
2. Presence or absence of a subsistence economy based primarily on agriculture or pastoralism.
3. Presence or absence of social stratification or slavery.
4. Presence or absence of full-time governmental specialists.
5. Presence or absence of full-time religious or magical specialists.
6. Presence or absence of secondary tools (tools fashioned exclusively for the manufacture of other tools).
7. Presence or absence of full-time craft specialists.
8. Presence or absence of a standard medium of exchange with a value fixed at some worth other than its commodity value.
9. Presence or absence of a state of at least 10,000 population.
10. Presence or absence of towns exceeding 1,000 in population.
11. Presence or absence of a complex, unambiguous written language.

Freeman dropped a twelfth variable, social integration, when it was found not to scale; i.e., social integration, as measured, varied independently of the other traits.

Freeman's study gives empirical evidence that eleven of the traits used to characterize the folk-urban continuum, at least as he redefined them, constitute a unidimensional concept. Twelve distinct scale types emerge, ranging from the least complex (no "urban" traits present) to the most complex (all eleven "urban" traits present). Thus, Freeman's study not only presents evidence supporting the unidimensionality of folk-urbanism, but also provides a typology for measuring societal complexity.

Freeman has not ignored the evolutionary implications of his results: "Such results are consistent with Redfield's typology, but they also lend credence to the schemes of the social evolutionists" (Freeman 1957:88). Guttman's scalogram technique arranges the variables as well as the societies in an ordered sequence of complexity of develop-

ment. (For a discussion of the use of scale analysis in evolutionary studies see Carneiro 1962, and Chapter 41.) Freeman notes that "from this arrangement a hypothetical sequence of development in the process of social change may be deduced" (Freeman 1957:87). This statement suggests a unilineal concept of the evolutionary process of cultural development from lower to greater complexity. Indeed, Freeman concludes:

This study, then, suggests the possible utility of reexamining some of the proposals made by Tylor, and perhaps also those made by Morgan, Spencer and other evolutionists (Freeman 1957:90).

NAROLL'S SOCIAL DEVELOPMENT INDEX

Naroll's Index of Social Development proceeds from the classic concept of social evolution of Spencer (1900:314) and Durkheim (1933:41): that is, progressive differentiation of function. "That society is the most evolved which has the highest degree of functional differentiation, whether in the form of occupational specialization or organizational complexity" (Naroll 1956a:687). Both the degree of occupational specialization and of organizational ramification are related to population size, or the degree of urbanization. The relationship between occupational specialization and urbanization has long been recognized: in Adam Smith's classic statement—the division of labor is limited by the extent of the market; and the extent of the market in turn is defined by problems of communication (Smith 1776: Book I, Chap. 3). Similarly, with regard to organizational complexity, Spencer (1898: 525–528) and Simmel (1902–1903) agree that an increase in size necessitates more complex forms of communication. The empirical study of Terrien and Mills (1955) suggests that this need is progressive: the larger the organization, the greater the proportion of control officials needed.

Naroll indicates an allometric relationship between social evolution and urbanization, that is, between occupational specialization or organizational ramification on one hand and size of settlement on the other (Naroll 1956a:689). Allometric growth is a familiar concept in biological evolution; it is defined as growth of one part relative to another part, or relative to the whole, at such a rate that there is a linear regression of the logarithms of the dimensions (Naroll and Bertalanffy 1956). Naroll's Social Development Index is based upon these relationships. The over-all index number for a society is a composite of scores on three indicators of social development. Two represent social evolution: a craft specialization indicator and an organizational ramification indicator. The third represents urbanization. These indicators are defined with five characteristics in mind: culture freedom, logical independence, adequate documentation, reliability, and convenience.

The craft specialization variable is taken as a measure of occupational specialization. To make the indicator useful to archaeologists, and to prevent overlapping with the organizational ramification variable through the counting of political or administrative specialists, only craft specialists, i.e., manufacturers or repairers of durable artifacts, are included. All craft specialties practiced in the culture unit are weighted equally, regardless of their extent; this rule simplifies the research process considerably, though it may produce some distortions.

The organizational ramification indicator is designed "to measure complexity in social organization from the viewpoint of structural ramification in group decision communication channels" (Naroll 1956a:695). This indicator employs the concept of a "team," that is, a functioning social group with a defined membership of three or more persons and some recognized leadership through which decisions are communicated. Three types of teams are distinguished: *kinship teams,* those whose membership is defined entirely in terms of common descent or marriage or some combination of the two; *territorial teams,* those whose membership criterion is expressible entirely in terms of standing occupancy of a common territory; and *associational teams,* those which are neither kinship nor territorial teams.

In computing the total team score *only the most highly ramified team of each type is counted.* The counting procedure takes account only of the extent of vertical organization, i.e., only the number of levels of subdivision are counted, not the total number of subdivisions. However, a given level is counted twice if either a council or a staff is present at that level, three times if both are present. The final indicator score is the combined total of the number of teams for the most highly ramified *kinship team, territorial team,* and *associational team.*

The urbanization indicator is simply the population of the largest (most populous) settlement in the culture unit. A settlement is defined in 1956 as a group of contiguous dwelling places none of which are more than two hundred meters from another. The over precision of this definition prevents ambiguity, but has the drawback that it cannot be applied to people such as the Todas, who have no settlements larger than the extended family, people who live in what Murdock calls dispersed neighborhoods. Where people have shifting or nomadic settlement patterns of varying size, the largest camp of the annual cycle is counted.

The three indicators are arbitrarily given equal weight, since there seems to be no obvious reason for doing otherwise. However, the *scores* on each indicator are weighted to make them comparable; the weighted scores are derived from the regression formula which describes the allometric relationship between the variables (described above). For every culture unit a raw score and a weighted score is obtained for each indicator. The mean of the weighted scores is defined as the Social Development Index score.

In its original presentation the Social Development Index is applied to a non-random, selected sample of thirty non-Western societies. The calculated indices of social development for these thirty societies range from 12 (for the Yahgan) to 58 (for the Aztec); the index scores thus form a continuum and provide a convenient measure of the relative complexity of each society.

Because the classification concepts were defined only after the data were collected, Naroll pointed out the need for a restudy (Naroll 1956a:710) in his original paper. The present chapter now reports the results of a restudy of Naroll's Social Development Index, on a new sample, his fifty-eight society WSC study. It embodies two modifications of the 1956 concepts, both adopted in advance of the restudy and indeed incorporated in Naroll's research proposals to the National Science Foundation. The first of these modifies the concept of a craft specialist from

Table 1
NAROLL'S SOCIAL DEVELOPMENT INDEX OF THE WSC STUDY

Society	Raw Scores			Weighted Scores			Index Score
	P	T	C	P	T	C	
Semang	54	2	3	17	0	19	12
Andamans	70	3	2	18	11	12	14
Aweikoma	300	3	2	25	11	12	16
Callinago	—	5	2	—	24	12	18
Coyotero	—	5	2	—	24	12	18
Copper Eskimo	—	2	8	—	0	36	18
Malekula	—	5	2	—	24	12	18
Yagua	50	3	5	17	11	28	19
Eyak	120	5	2	21	24	12	19
Apayao	—	4	3	—	18	19	19
Southern Paiute	—	6	2	—	29	12	21
Ona	500	3	4	27	11	24	21
Mataco	—	4	5	—	18	28	23
Klallam	200	7	2	23	33	12	23
Mosquito	600	6	2	28	29	12	23
Chukchee	142	4	5	22	18	28	23
Gilyak	200	5	4	23	24	24	24
Ifaluk	252	6	3	24	29	19	24
Kababish	—	9	2	—	39	12	25
Orokaiva	—	5	5	—	24	28	26
Land Dyaks	—	6	4	—	29	24	27
Luo	—	6	4	—	29	24	27
Chagga	—	6	4	—	29	24	27
Tiv	—	5	6	—	24	31	28
Ojibwa	—	6	5	—	29	28	29
Cheyenne	2,000	10	2	33	42	12	29
Mangareva	—	7	4	—	33	24	29
Kapauku	181	8	5	23	36	28	29
Wintun	1,000	7	5	30	33	28	30
Araucanians	360	6	7	26	29	34	30
Mongo	—	6	6	—	29	31	30
Azande	200	9	5	23	39	28	30
Ila	3,000	7	4	35	33	24	31
Kazaks	3,000	7	4	35	33	24	31
Fur	—	10	3	—	42	19	31
Toradja	600	6	8	28	29	36	31
Hottentots	2,500	9	4	34	39	24	32
Papago	800	9	5	29	39	28	32
Malaita	5,000	5	9	37	24	38	33
Kafirs	—	6	12	—	29	43	36
Tallensi	2,400	7	10	34	33	40	36
Iroquois	3,000	13	5	35	49	28	37
Tikopia	1,400	9	12	31	39	43	38
Gonds	—	11	7	—	44	34	39
Mende	2,545	9	13	34	39	45	39
Thonga	—	11	8	—	44	36	40
Tongans	5,000	10	16	37	42	48	42
Amhara	7,000	10	16	38	42	48	43
Burmese	293,316	16	28	55	54	58	56
Nahua (Aztec)	400,000	17	34	56	56	61	58
Iraqi	1,306,604	21	—	61	61	—	61
Egyptians	2,800,000	19	—	64	59	—	62
Irish	506,051	22	102	57	62	80	66
Koreans	1,710,242	30	—	62	71	—	67
Turks	1,000,000	33	284	60	73	98	77
Dutch	871,577	27	444	59	68	106	78
Italians	2,100,000	27	626	63	68	112	81
Austrians	1,667,000	25	1289	62	66	124	84

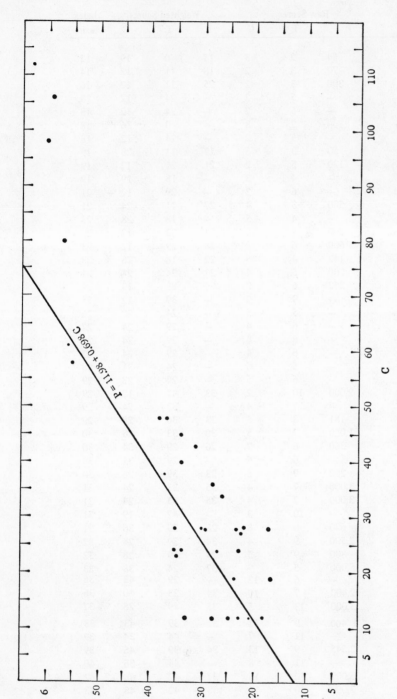

ORDINATE SHOWS SETTLEMENT POPULATION WEIGHTED SCORE GROUPS. WEIGHTED SCORE (P) IS DERIVED FROM RAW SCORE (X) BY THE FORMULA: P=10 LOG X.

ABSCISSA SHOWS CRAFT SPECIALTY WEIGHTED SCORE GROUPS. WEIGHTED SCORE (C) IS DERIVED FROM RAW SCORE (Y) BY THE FORMULA: C=40 LOG Y.

COEFFICIENT OF CORRELATION 0.8867.

FIGURE 1. RELATIONSHIP BETWEEN SETTLEMENT POPULATION AND CRAFT SPECIALTIES IN THE NAROLL WSC STUDY

that of a *role* to that of a *status*. A craft specialty has been redefined as the existence of a recognized status of manufacturer or repairer of a durable artifact for the use of some hale adult member of the unit studied other than the maker or repairer. The existence of a recognized status involves (a) a recognized title, usually in the form of a native name for the craft specialty; and (b) a recognized claim on society for some special treatment, e.g., payment of money, or gift in exchange by the holder

of the status. The second of these modifications has redefined the concept of settlement size as the most populous cluster of dwellings enclosable by a circle of six kilometer radius at any time in the regular annual cycle.

The new sample of fifty-eight societies in the Naroll WSC restudy uses the cultunit concept as the unit of study. The cultunit is defined as a group of people who are domestic speakers of a common distinct language and who belong to the same state

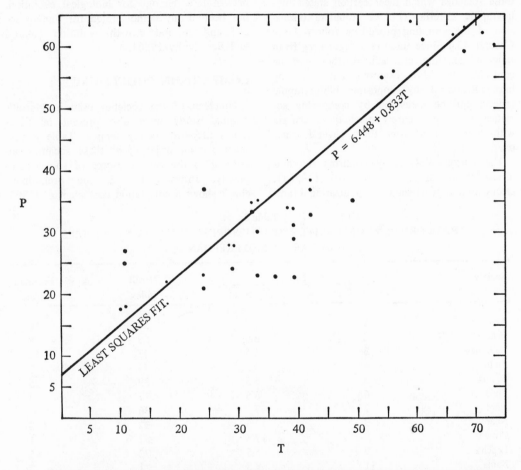

ORDINATE SHOWS SETTLEMENT POPULATION WEIGHTED SCORE GROUPS. WEIGHTED SCORE (P) IS DERIVED FROM THE RAW SCORE (X) BY THE FORMULA: P=10 LOG X.

ABSCISSA SHOWS TEAM TYPE WEIGHTED SCORE GROUPS. WEIGHTED SCORE (T) IS DERIVED FROM RAW SCORE (Z) BY THE FORMULA: T=6 LOG (Z/2).

COEFFICIENT OF CORRELATION: 0.9057.

FIGURE 2. RELATIONSHIP BETWEEN SETTLEMENT POPULATION AND TEAM TYPE COUNT IN THE NAROLL WSC STUDY

or the same contact group. (For a fuller explanation and detailed discussion of this concept see Chapter 39.)

The WSC sample of the Naroll restudy is a composite of two stratified probability samples: (1) a diffusion arc sample, and (2) a World Ethnographic Sample sub-sample. The sampling method used is a special type of stratified sampling, in which only one case is sampled from each stratum. In both samples the strata are geographically defined, and the sampling universe includes only those societies which meet certain stated bibliographic criteria. (For a complete discussion of the sampling procedure followed see Chapter 43.) Since these two departures from random sampling are defined, they can be controlled for. For example, any sampling bias introduced by imposing bibliographic criteria can be measured by comparing societies which just barely meet these criteria with those which meet them several times over.

The Naroll WSC study confirms the empirical results of his earlier work (1956a). Occupational specialization, organizational ram-ification and size of largest settlement are related allometrically: there is a linear regression of their logarithms and very high coefficients of correlation among them. (See Figures 1 and 2.) Furthermore, as previously reported (Naroll 1962b), there is a similar relationship between settlement population and dwelling floor area. Thus based on the archaeological and historical finding that maximum settlement size has been generally and markedly increasing over the past ten thousand years, a general pattern of allometric growth, a pattern like the one for biological evolution, has been firmly demonstrated for human social and cultural growth evolution (Naroll and Bertalanffy 1956).

COMPARISON PROCEDURE

Nineteen of the societies used in Naroll's original study were also present in Freeman's fifty-two society sample. Table 2 presents a rank ordering of these societies according to the two measures of social complexity. From Table 2, the preliminary check shows a correlation coefficient of 0.893.

Table 2
RANK ORDERING OF NINETEEN SOCIETIES PRESENT IN ORIGINAL STUDIES
BY NAROLL AND FREEMAN

Society	Rank Order		Naroll Index	Freeman Scale
	Naroll	Freeman		
Aztec	1	1.5	58	10
Inca	2	3.5	55	8
Dahomey	3	1.5	47	10
Zulu	4	3.5	44	8
Samoa	5	5.5	39	5
Cuna	6	8.5	37	3
Hopi	7	7	36	4
Nuer	9	12.5	32	2
Crow	9	17.5	32	1
Lepcha	9	5.5	32	5
Nama	11	8.5	31	3
Toda	12	12.5	29	2
Flathead	13.5	12.5	27	2
Bellacoola	13.5	12.5	27	2
Timbira	15	17.5	26	1
Kiwai	16	12.5	25	2
Vanua Levu	17	12.5	22	2
Ainu	18	17.5	21	1
Yahgan	19	17.5	12	1

Coefficient of rank-order correlation (rho) = 0.893

This value indicates reasonably high agreement between the two measures of complexity.

The two measures of societal complexity are further applied to Naroll's WSC study. Two of Freeman's trait categories—the presence or absence of secondary tools, and the presence or absence of towns exceeding 1,000 in population—are excluded from the analysis. The secondary tool variable was dropped because data were unavailable for some of the societies in the sample and could only be indirectly inferred for many others. The population variable was excluded because it is logically related to the settlement size indicator used in Naroll's Social Development Index; the 1,000 population cutoff point merely divides the population continuum into two parts.

However, the "full-time craft specialist" category was retained. This category is felt to measure a different aspect of craft specialization than the indicator used by Naroll; it measures *extent* of specialization rather than the total number of specialties ("full-time craft specialist" is interpreted to mean those who receive the major part of their subsistence in exchange for their craft production). Of the two, Freeman's dichotomous variable seems a less sensitive measure of craft specialization: in the Naroll WSC study literally hundreds of full-time craft specialties have been recorded for the Austrians, as well as many hundreds of part-time specialties, whereas only three craft specialties have been recorded in Fur society. Nevertheless, since blacksmithing represents a full-time occupation among the Fur, both the Austrians and the Fur are scored as having full-time specialists on Freeman's Guttman scale (see Table 3).

Ratings on the folk-urban variables were done by Tatje, who also made the comparisons between the Naroll index and the Freeman scale. Several sources were used for each society. In a few cases where there were data conflicts, or where information was ambiguous, an arbitrary decision was made. Such cases are indicated by a question mark (?) following the coding symbol (Appendix IV). As stated above, one variable—presence or absence of secondary tools—was dropped entirely because trustworthy data were not available for many of the sample societies.

Since twelve of the societies in the Naroll WSC study are also found in Freeman's sample, comparison of the separate ratings on these cases offers a partial check on the extent of agreement between Naroll's and Freeman's scores. Only six definite conflicts (out of 108 codings) were found. In six of the twelve societies—Semang, Copper Eskimo, Ojibwa, Hottentots (Nama), Tallensi, and Nahua (Aztec)—the codings agreed. Three other cases (Mende, Azande and Kababish) are unclear: In one place Freeman codes these societies as having political states of 10,000 or more (1957:78); in his final scale, however, political states are coded "absent" for the Mende and Azande, and the Kababish are omitted altogether (Freeman 1957:83). In the Naroll WSC study, states of 10,000 or more are coded as present among the Mende and Azande, but absent for the Kababish (see Table 3). Definite conflicts between Naroll's and Freeman's codings were found in four cases: Money and full-time craft specialists among the Tiv, and full-time religious specialists among the Chagga are scored "present" in Freeman and "absent" in Naroll; on the other hand, social stratification in Ifaluk, full-time craftsmen among the Mende, and political states of 10,000 among the Chagga, are scored "absent" in Freeman but "present" in Naroll.

These empirical errors may be due to the use of a different base year for rating these societies. However, a greater source of possible bias is ambiguous definition by Freeman of some of the dichotomous folk-urban variables. The use of the term "full-time" in defining several of the categories permits varied subjective interpretation. For this study, craftsmen are considered full-time specialists only if they receive the major part of their subsistence in exchange for their craft production; religious and governmental officials are considered full-time specialists only if (a) they receive their subsistence needs in exchange for their services, or (b) they do not devote any time to other subsistence-producing activities. For example, chiefs and *tendaanas* (cult priests) among the Tallensi are considered to be full-time specialists; though their main subsistence source is not direct payments for their services, they devote their time primarily to their official duties and do no farming themselves (Fortes 1940:250, 255–267).

The presence or absence of money also

Table 3
FREEMAN SCALE OF FOLK-URBAN VARIABLES
IN THE NAROLL WSC STUDY

| Society | Trait Present | | | | | | | | | Trait Absent | | | | | | | | |
	I	E	S	G	R	C	P	M	W	I	E	S	G	R	C	P	M	W
Andamans										X	X	X	X	X	X	X	X	X
Southern Paiute										X	X	X	X	X	X	X	X	X
Aweikoma	X										X	X	X	X	X	X	X	X
Coyotero	X										X	X	X	X	X	X	X	X
Copper Eskimo	X										X	X	X	X	X	X	X	X
Semang	X										X	X	X	X	X	X	X	X
Yagua	X										X	X	X	X	X	X	X	X
Ona	X										X	X	X	X	X	X	X	X
Mataco	X										X	X	X	X	X	X	X	X
Gilyak	X										X	X	X	X	X	X	X	X
Ojibwa	X										X	X	X	X	X	X	X	X
Cheyenne	X										X	X	X	X	X	X	X	X
Callinago	X		X								X		X	X	X	X	X	X
Eyak	X		X								X		X	X	X	X	X	X
Apayao	X	X										X	X	X	X	X	X	X
Orokaiva	X	X										X	X	X	X	X	X	X
Land Dyaks	X	X										X	X	X	X	X	X	X
Wintun	X		X								X		X	X	X	X	X	X
Klallam	X		X					X			X		X	X	X	X		X
Chukchee	X	X	X										X	X	X	X	X	X
Ifaluk	X	X	X										X	X	X	X	X	X
Kababish	X	X	X										X	X	X	X	X	X
Luo	X	X		X								X		X	X	X	X	X
Tiv	X	X	X										X	X	X	X	X	X
Mongo	X	X	X										X	X	X	X	X	X
Toradja	X	X	X										X	X	X	X	X	X
Hottentots (Nama)	X	X	X										X	X	X	X	X	X
Malaita	X	X	X										X	X	X	X	X	X
Papago	X	X			X							X	X		X	X	X	X
Malekula	X	X	X		X								X		X	X	X	X
Mosquito	X	X	X	X										X	X	X	X	X
Mangareva	X	X	X			X								X	X		X	X
Kapauku	X	X				X		X				X	X	X		X		X
Araucanians	X	X	X			X								X	X		X	X
Tikopia	X	X	X	X										X	X	X	X	X
Tallensi	X	X	X	X	X										X	X	X	X
Gonds	X	X	X		X	X							X			X	X	X
Thonga	X	X	X	X	X										X	X	X	X
Chagga	X	X	X	X		X	X								X			X	X
Azande	X	X	X	X	X		X									X		X	X
Ila	X	X	X	X	X	X											X	X	X
Kafirs	X	X	X	X	X	X											X	X	X
Kazaks	X	X	X	X		X	X	X							X				X
Iroquois	X	X	X	X	X	X	X											X	X
Mende	X	X	X	X	X	X	X											X	X
Tongans	X	X	X	X	X	X	X											X	X
Fur	X	X	X	X	X	X	X	X											X
Nahua (Aztec)	X	X	X	X	X	X	X	X											X
Amhara	X	X	X	X	X	X	X	X	X									
Burmese	X	X	X	X	X	X	X	X	X									
Iraqi	X	X	X	X	X	X	X	X	X									
Egyptians	X	X	X	X	X	X	X	X	X									
Irish	X	X	X	X	X	X	X	X	X									
Koreans	X	X	X	X	X	X	X	X	X									
Turks	X	X	X	X	X	X	X	X	X									
Dutch	X	X	X	X	X	X	X	X	X									
Italians	X	X	X	X	X	X	X	X	X									
Austrians	X	X	X	X	X	X	X	X	X									

presents some difficulties. Freeman defines this variable as "a standard medium of exchange with a value fixed at some worth other than its commodity value." But as Dalton (1965) and Bohannan (1959) have shown, many nonindustrial societies employ various commodities as a medium of exchange *only for a restricted sphere of transactions*. They term such items "special-purpose" monies. In coding this variable, money is considered present only if it is used as a medium of exchange for the full range of economic transactions. Thus such items as brass rods among the Tiv and ceremonial shell "money" in Malaita—which serve as a medium of exchange, standard of value, and means of payment only in the sphere of "prestige transactions"—are not considered "money" for the purposes of this study.

Lack of complete ethnographic data on the three indicators has made it difficult to apply the Social Development Index results. Although social organization is usually given a prominent place in ethnographic monographs, for many of the societies in the WSC study there was no information at all on settlement population size (Appendix III). But the greatest difficulty is with the craft specialty indicator. Undoubtedly some craft specialties for many of the societies in the WSC study sample have been overlooked—the craft specialty counts for the Malakulans, Klallam, Mosquito, Kababish, Cheyenne, Fur and Iroquois are especially suspect (Table 1 and Appendix II). Often ethnographers give only cursory attention to craft specialties, and describe the techniques of material culture with little or no indication of whether it involves specialized activities; furthermore, references to craft specialties are often scattered throughout the monograph.

A special procedure was used for compiling craft specialty data for several of the modern industrial societies, i.e., the Austrians, Dutch, Irish, Italians and Turks. For these societies, the occupational classified listings of the telephone directories for the largest cities were used. Beginning from a random start, all the craft specialties, as defined above and listed on every tenth page (every fifth page in the Turkish case) were counted. The total number of specialties counted by this procedure was then taken to be a 10 per cent sample of the total for the so-

ciety. Craft specialty counts have been omitted for modern Egypt, Korea and Iraq. These countries have very large urban population centers, and would be expected therefore to have a relatively large number of craft specialties. However, craft specialty data are available only for *rural* settlements in these societies; telephone directories from Cairo, Seoul and Baghdad were not available. Even if they had been, the telephone book sampling procedure might well have greatly underestimated the craft specialty count. For in these cities of comparatively underdeveloped countries, occupations seem especially likely to lack telephone installations.

The data on highly industrialized population centers of the order of a million or more (like the industrial cities of modern Italy and Austria) appear to indicate that the allometric relationship (linear log-log regression) between settlement size and number of craft specialists may not hold for populations of this magnitude. With the onset of industrialization there seems to be a proliferation in the number of craft specialists, and probably service occupations as well. What is involved may be a curved line of regression or it may be a step function, a jump from one allometric line to another, reflecting a sudden fundamental change in developmental dynamics. Such shifts in allometric growth rates occur in biological evolution, like that which occurs at the onset of puberty in the growth of the testes of mice (Bertalanffy 1942:280).

A change in the regression relationship between craft specialization and urbanization evidently comes with industrial technology and the rise of cities of more than a million population. The Naroll Social Development Index probably makes a biased estimate of the relative complexity of such modern industrial societies, since their weighted index scores are based upon the allometric regression formula described above. Nevertheless, the allometric relationship seems to be the best description of the relation between settlement size and the craft specialization indicator for most of its range.

Table 1 presents the raw scores, weighted scores (from Tables 1 and 2 of Naroll 1956a), and index scores for the WSC study (using the Social Development Index procedure of Naroll 1956a). Similarly, Table 3 presents a

Table 4
RANK ORDERING OF MEASURES OF SOCIAL COMPLEXITY IN THE NAROLL WSC STUDY

| Society | Rank Order | | Naroll Index | Freeman Scale |
	Naroll Index	Freeman Scale		
Semang	1	7.5	12	1
Andamans	2	1.5	14	0
Aweikoma	3	7.5	16	1
Callinago	5.5	15.5	18	2
Coyotero	5.5	7.5	18	1
Copper Eskimo	5.5	7.5	18	1
Malekula	5.5	32.5	18	4
Yagua	9	7.5	19	1
Eyak	9	15.5	19	2
Apayao	9	15.5	19	2
Southern Paiute	11.5	1.5	21	0
Ona	11.5	7.5	21	1
Mataco	14.5	7.5	23	1
Klallam	14.5	24	23	3
Mosquito	14.5	32.5	23	4
Chukchee	14.5	24	23	3
Gilyak	17.5	7.5	24	1
Ifaluk	17.5	24	24	3
Kababish	19	24	25	3
Orokaiva	20	15.5	26	2
Lank Dyaks	22	15.5	27	2
Luo	22	24	27	3
Chagga	22	40.5	27	6
Tiv	24	24	28	3
Ojibwa	26.5	7.5	29	1
Cheyenne	26.5	7.5	29	1
Mangareva	26.5	32.5	29	4
Kapauku	26.5	32.5	29	4
Wintun	30.5	15.5	30	2
Araucanians	30.5	32.5	30	4
Mongo	30.5	24	30	3
Azande	30.5	40.5	30	6
Ila	34.5	40.5	31	6
Kazaks	34.5	44.5	31	7
Fur	34.5	47.5	31	8
Toradja	34.5	24	31	3
Hottentots (Nama)	37.5	24	32	3
Papago	37.5	24	32	3
Malaita	39	24	33	3
Kafirs	40.5	40.5	36	6
Tallensi	40.5	37	36	5
Iroquois	42	44.5	37	7
Tikopia	43	32.5	38	4
Gond	44.5	37	39	5
Mende	44.5	44.5	39	7
Thonga	46	37	40	5
Tongans	47	44.5	42	7
Amhara	48	53.5	43	9
Burmese	49	53.5	56	9
Nahua (Aztec)	50	47.5	58	8
Iraqi	51	53.5	61	9
Egyptians	52	53.5	62	9
Irish	53	53.5	66	9
Koreans	54	53.5	67	9
Turks	55	53.5	77	9
Dutch	56	53.5	78	9
Italians	57	53.5	81	9
Austrians	58	53.5	84	9

Guttman scale for the same sample using nine of the variables originally developed by Freeman in his 1957 study. Table 4 shows a rank ordering of the fifty-eight societies in the WSC study according to the two measures of social complexity. For this set of paired ranks the Spearman coefficient of rank correlation, corrected for tied ranks, is: $r_s = +.865$. For a sample of this size, the obtained value of r is significant at $p < .0005$.

DISCUSSION

The high coefficient of correlation associated with the very high significance level allows the conclusion that the two measures of social complexity presented here yield much the same results. This fact strengthens confidence in the validity of both methods; i.e., both seem to be measuring the same concept.

However, the Freeman scale measures variations only within the range covered approximately by Naroll index scores 12–43. In all but one of the societies with a Naroll index score of 43 or higher all nine urban traits are clearly present. It is not clear whether the one exception, the Aztecs (Naroll index score 58) had a writing form adequate to express the full range of information conveyed by their speech (Soustelle 1955:265 f.).

The index numbers for the eleven societies in this category range from 43 to 84, indicating the need for more culture traits of the folk-urban type to allow differentiation among more complex societies. Such a trait list was first provided in the paper by Carneiro and Tobias (1963). They presented a scalogram of one hundred societies and 50 culture traits with a coefficient of reproducibility of 0.950. These 50 traits were those that manifested the best scaling from among a total trait list of 354 culture traits thought to be cumulative; i.e., traits which tend to be retained when further culture traits are added to a society's cultural inventory (Carneiro and Tobias 1963:200). It should be pointed out, however, that these results were tentative, since Carneiro and Tobias selected the traits used in this scale *a posteriori*, based on the data from their sample (see further Chapter 41).

Carneiro and Tobias used their 354-trait list as a measure of over-all cultural complexity; the greater number of listed traits found present in a society, the greater its relative complexity is taken to be. Fifteen societies in their sample were also present in Naroll's 1956 sample. Comparing the rank order of complexity for these societies using their trait inventory method with the rank order from Naroll's Social Development Index, Carneiro and Tobias reported a rank order coefficient of 0.891 (Carneiro and Tobias 1963: 203). An additional ten societies from their sample are found in the sample used in the Naroll WSC study; comparing these ten societies in the same way, the obtained rank correlation coefficient is 0.976 (Carneiro, personal communication). See the next chapter for a full discussion. This work by Carneiro and Tobias gives further, independent support of the validity of the Social Development Index as a measure of cultural complexity. Equally it supports the validity of the Carneiro and Tobias scale (see further Chapter 41).

However, it is important to differentiate between over-all complexity of social development, and the development of individual cultural elements. The former concept is essentially a unidirectional process of increasing specialization of function, and it is this concept which the Social Development Index is devised to measure. No assumptions are made as to the nature of the process of evolution of specific cultural features.

Trait-based typologies, on the other hand, generally assume a unilinear sequence of trait development. This assumption of unidimensionality is true of typologies of the Guttman scale type, where the defining traits are cumulative; and it is true of "stage" concepts where they are replacive, as in the dichotomy between agricultural societies and hunting and gathering societies. There is growing evidence, however, against this strict unilinear view of the evolvement of culture elements in human societies: for example, Hickman's (1962) factor analysis of twelve variables of the folk-urban concept reveals three main factors—kinship organization, size-complexity, and isolation.

Carneiro and Tobias provide further evidence that within the framework of generally increasing over-all complexity, cultural evolution is a multidirectional process. While conceiving of the fifty traits used in the Guttman scale described above "as constituting a *main sequence* of cultural evolution," they state:

Although only a fraction of the 354 traits on our list scaled very well when tested together with traits from all aspects of culture, we had reason to believe that many more traits would scale well if compared only with traits from the same aspect of culture as themselves. Since one of the bases of scaling is that some cultural elements are functional prerequisites of others (Carneiro, 1962, pp. 160–161), a group of traits among which functional relationship is especially strong is more likely to scale well than one in which traits are less closely related. (Carneiro and Tobias 1963: 203–204)

Carneiro and Tobias divide their total list of 354 culture traits into fourteen major categories of culture. The two categories—political organization and economics—which they have examined bear out their belief: thirty-one of the economic variables form a Guttman scale whose coefficient of reproducibility is 0.943; thirty-three of the political organization traits yield a coefficient of 0.960 (Carneiro and Tobias 1963:204). Continuing, they state:

Now if scaling is greater among closely related traits, then we may suppose that evolution within each category may, to a certain extent, proceed independently of evolution in other categories. This phenomenon, which we have observed in our data, may be termed *differential evolution*. (Carneiro and Tobias 1963:204)

This multidirectional or differential pattern of cultural evolution is illustrated by several examples. For example, the Maori, with a total of 92 of 354 traits present, have 17 from the Religion category and 3 from the Law and Judicial Process category. By contrast, the Bemba, with a total of 100 traits, have only 7 Religion traits but 14 Judicial traits (Carneiro and Tobias 1963:205).

Rose and Willoughby reach similar conclusions about the pattern of cultural evolution in their study, "Cultural Profiles and Emphases" (1958). Proceeding with a sample of twenty societies divided into those with an emphasis on modern traits and those with an emphasis on primitive traits, they find that "modern cultures seem to exhibit a correlation between extent and type of emphasis on modern categories of culture. No corresponding correlation between extent and type of primitive emphasis seems to hold for primitive cultures" (Rose and Willoughby 1958: 476).

All this is not to say that the evolution of various aspects of culture is not grossly interdependent, at least to some degree. Certainly it is. For example, an agricultural subsistence base is probably a functional prerequisite to the development of a complex hierarchy of religious specialists. Thus a scale typology relying on a limited number of culture traits, such as Freeman's typology, *can* differentiate the relative complexity of societies without agriculture, those with an agricultural subsistence base, and those with both agriculture and religious specialists. However, might not an agricultural economy also be the necessary prerequisite to an elaborate political hierarchy? Or to a complex system of craft guilds?

Considering the multidirectional nature of cultural elaboration we would expect to find the greatest amount of variation between the two measures of complexity in the middle range of Social Development Index scores. Very simple cultures, those with almost no specialization of function, are not likely to have much elaboration of cumulative culture traits in any aspect of culture. Very complex societies are likely to have relatively high elaboration in all aspects of culture, and the findings of Rose and Willoughby cited above indicate that the range of differential elaboration becomes narrower with greater complexity. Thus it is only in the middle range of complexity that we may expect to find considerable evolution in one aspect of culture and relatively little in another.

This expected difference in variation between middle ranges and extreme ranges clearly appears in Naroll's WSC study (Table 4). Considering the ties in ranks, this sample breaks down fairly obviously into approximate quartiles, with the lowest quartile containing the first sixteen societies and the highest quartile containing the last thirteen. The average rank difference between the Naroll index score ranks and the Freeman scale ranks among these twenty-nine societies in the extreme ranges is 5.72. The average difference between the twenty-nine remaining middle-range societies is considerably greater —8.28. The difference between these two means is shown by the *t* test to be significant at the 0.01 level.

One further problem in using Freeman's typology to measure social complexity emerges from this comparison study. Although the Guttman scale presented in Table 3 has a relatively high coefficient of reproducibility, 0.943, the sequence of development for two of the variables is reversed from that found by Freeman. In Freeman's sample fourteen societies have money and eleven have political states of 10,000 or more; in the Naroll WSC study fifteen societies have money (a general-purpose symbolic medium of exchange) and eighteen have political states of 10,000. In addition, whereas Freeman found religious specialists present in twenty-four of the societies in his sample and full-time craftsmen present in only sixteen, each of these traits is present in twenty-three of the societies in the WSC study. These differences can be accounted for in several ways: First, they may be due to random sampling variation; or to the use of different base years for scoring the societies; or to more complete data on craft specialization in the WSC study.

However, the most likely explanation is a difference between the interpretation of the meaning of the terms "money" and "full-time" (see above). These discrepancies point up the need for very explicit definitions of trait categories. A slight alteration of the definition (or interpretation) of a trait can change its position in the development scale. Schwartz and Miller (1964) make the same point when relating the trait sequence of the Freeman and Winch typology to the evolution of legal institutions.

OPERATIONAL CHARACTERISTICS OF THE NAROLL INDEX AND THE FREEMAN SCALE

There seem to be three difficulties to the use of Freeman's typology (or a similar trait-based typology): First, his trait categories have not yet been unambiguously defined. Secondly, enough traits are needed to allow differentiation at all levels of complexity; Freeman's typology fails to differentiate among societies beyond a certain level of complexity. Finally, the reliance on the presence or absence of a few "key" traits to measure cultural complexity may produce distortions due to the differential pattern of cultural evolution. This seems particularly true for societies in the middle range of complexity. Where the functional elaboration of a particular society occurs in aspects of culture other than those including these "key" traits, there may be a tendency to underestimate that society's relative degree of actual social complexity.

On the other hand, Freeman's typology, and others like it, have the not inconsiderable advantage of employing only a few dichotomous variables for which it is generally easy to find data in the ethnographic sources.

In the study cited above, Moskos considers lack of operational ease one of the chief weaknesses of Naroll's index:

. . . the methodological problems present in ascertaining the empirical variables used by Naroll as indicators of complexity are of some magnitude. There is also some question as to the reliability of Naroll's index in that subjective interpretations can easily enter in the selection of figures on the degree of craft specialization and organizational ramification. (Moskos n.d.:4)

While it is true that the craft specialization and the organizational ramification indicators are conceptually more complex than dichotomous variables, and probably require more ethnographic source data, careful adherence to the counting rules set forth in Naroll 1956a largely precludes the need for subjective judgments. Likewise, the Social Development Index is free from the other drawbacks of Freeman's scale. Futhermore, considering the present data, the urbanization indicator can be used alone as an adequate first approximation of relative cultural development. Variations in the craft specialty and team type counts from the allometric regression line relating these variables to the settlement size indicator may well reflect distortions introduced by the counting rules. Also, there may be a change in the relationship between occupational specialization and urbanization with the onset of industrialization as described above.

Finally, settlement size indicator as a rough measure of social complexity makes the Social Development Index especially useful to archaeologists. Naroll (1962b), as mentioned above, has shown that an allometric relationship exists between the population of a settlement and the total floor area under roof of the settlement. Thus settlement size can be estimated from floor area alone, and from this estimate a rough measure of minimum social complexity can be gauged for the largest known site of a given archaeological horizon.

CONCLUSIONS

The results of this study show a high degree of correlation between two measures of social complexity: Naroll's Social Development Index and Freeman's Guttman scale of folk-urbanism. A similar high correlation is also noted between Naroll's Social Development Index and another Guttman scale of cultural complexity developed by Carneiro and Tobias. The fact that all three of these measures, using three quite distinct trait inventories, reach much the same results, supplies strong support for the validity of all three. Like the three legs of a tripod, they are joined in their function though separate in their base; like the three legs of a tripod, they all stand firmly when linked together though none could stand alone.

Thus it appears that social and cultural evolution partakes of the various processes analyzed by all three measures. It consists of urbanization, measured directly in terms of settlement size by one of Naroll's indicators and indirectly in terms of the folk-urban continuum trait inventory by the Freeman scale. It consists of organizational ramification, measured by another of Naroll's indicators. It consists of occupational specialization, measured by a third of Naroll's indicators. Particular occupational specialties are directly or indirectly represented in many of the traits in the Freeman and Carneiro-Tobias scales. Finally, it consists of cumulative informational content of culture, measured most directly by the Carneiro-Tobias scale, but indirectly through occupational specialization by the Freeman scale and the Naroll index.

APPENDIX I
Team Type Counts in the Naroll WSC Study

AMHARA *ca.* 1880 Total: 10
admin. prov.; st.; dist.; st.; vil. (ham. grp.); ham.; ext.f.; pol.f.; n.f.; parish.
Sources: Messing 1957:4, 6, 76–80, 83, 281, 284, 396, 475; Alvarez 1881:45.

ANDAMANS *ca.* 1910 Total: 3
tribe; local grp.; n.f.
Source: Radcliffe-Brown 1922:22, 45–7, 83.

APAYAO *ca.* 1920 Total: 4
vil.; st.; hshd.; n.f.
Sources: Wilson 1947:12, 48; Vanoverbergh 1941:170, 213.

ARAUCANIANS *ca.* 1800 Total: 6
loc. setl.; co.; st.; ext.f.; pol.f.; n.f.
Source: Titiev 1951:38, 46–8, 52–7.

AUSTRIA *ca.* 1960 Total: 25
nat.; co.; st.; prov.; co.; commune; co.; st.; vil.; co.; n.f.; army; st.; div.; st.; brig.; st.; reg.; st.; bat.; st.; com.; st.; plat.; sqd.
Sources: SYB 1957:806; *World almanac* 1961:397; Rüstung 1934:22–7.

AWEIKOMA *ca.* 1930 Total: 3
ext.f. (joint marriage hshd.); pol.f.; n.f.
Source: Henry 1941:22–5, 29–37, 60–3, 97, 101–2, 161.

AZANDE *ca.* 1900 Total: 9
tribe; st.; co.; dist.; patri-clan; pol.f.; n.f.; army; com.
Sources: Evans-Pritchard 1937:15; Graffen

1906;784–6; Larken 1926–27:16, 101, 127; Seligman 1932:498–503, 506.

BURMESE *ca.* 1850 Total: 16
nat.; co.; st.; prov.; co.; st.; circle or twns.; vil.; co.; Buddhist Church; co.; church dist.; vil. monastery; matr. ext.f.; pol.f.; n.f.
Sources: Hall 1950:87–8, 131–5, 137; Brown 1925:51–7, 62–5.

CALLINAGO *ca.* 1700 Total: 5
island; st.; vil.-ext.f.; pol.f.; n.f.
Sources: Rouse 1948:555; Breton and La Paix 1929:15, 22.

CHAGGA *ca.* 1900 Total: 6
chft.; clan sib; ext.f.; pol.f.; n.f.; labor corvée
Source: Gutmann 1926:1, 11, 20, 81, 272.

CHEYENNE *ca.* 1840 Total: 10
tribe; co.; st.; band; co.; warrior soc.; co.; kin.; pol.f.; n.f.
Sources: Hoebel 1960:3, 6, 12, 21–31, 33–7, 45–7, 52; Grinnell 1923, I:337–40, 343–4; II:48–51; Mooney 1907:403.

CHUKCHEE *ca.* 1900 Total: 4
camp; ext.f.; n.f.; boat crew.
Source: Bogoras 1904–1909:5, 12–13, 542–4, 612, 628 f.

COPPER ESKIMO *ca.* 1910 Total: 2
pol.f.; n.f.

Sources: Stefansson 1913:286; Rasmussen 1932:19.

COYOTERO *ca.* 1900 Total: 5
vil. (local group); st.; ext.f.; st.; n.f.
Sources: Goodwin 1935:55–7; 1942:123–8, 146–7, 152, 165–8.

DUTCH *ca.* 1955 Total: 27
nat.; co.; st.; prov.; co.; st.; muni.; co.; st.; vil.; st.; ext.f.; n.f.; army; st.; army corps; st.; div.; st.; reg.; st.; bat.; st.; com.; st.; plat.; sqd.
Sources: SYB 1959:1244–6; Keur 1955:19, 37, 74–6, 106f; Rüstung 1934:116f; Dupuy 1939:42

EGYPT *ca.* 1955 Total: 19
nat.; co.; prov.; co.; st.; dist.; co.; hshd.; n.f.; army; st.; bat.; st.; brig.; st.; com.; st.; plat.; sqd.
Sources: SYB 1955:938–9; Ammar 1942: pref., 32, 49.

EYAK *ca.* 1880 Total: 5
vil.; ext.f.; pol.f.; n.f.; potlatch moiety.
Source: Birket-Smith and de Laguna 1938: 32–6, 126–31, 169–73.

FUR *ca.* 1880 Total: 10
tribe; st.; prov.; dist.; vil.grp.; vil.; pol.f.; n.f.; army (*dalimars*); st. (sub-chiefs).
Source: Felkin 1885:207–8, 211, 233–5, 240–2, 254.

GILYAK *ca.* 1870 Total: 5
vil.; co.; clan; pol.f.; n.f.
Source: Hawes 1903:200, 209, 263; Seeland 1882:40.

GOND *ca.* 1880 Total: 11
tribe; admin.div.; st.; vil.; st.; co.; clan; co.; ext.f.; pol.f.; n.f.
Sources: Russell 1916:45–6, 72, 82, 131–4, 795; Grigson 1949:28, 32, 37, 120, 131, 141–2, 238–40, 248–50, 256–60, 286–93; Cain 1881:411–2; Elwin 1943:12, 105–7, 119, 196, 361–4.

HOTTENTOT *ca.* 1880 Total: 9
tribe; co.; st.; kraal; co.; st.; clan; pol.f.; n.f.
Source: Schapera 1930:227, 251, 328–36.

IFALUK *ca.* 1900 Total: 6
atoll; co. of chiefs; dist.; st.; ext.f.; n.f.
Sources: Burrows 1949:85, 116–7, 130, 139–40; Damm *et al.* 1938:60–71, 76, 79; Spiro 1949:5, 131.

ILA *ca.* 1900 Total: 7
community; co.; commun.div.; clan; st.; pol.f.; n.f.
Source: Smith and Dale 1920, I:283–4, 293, 296–9, 308; II: 64.

IRAQI *ca.* 1935 Total: 21
nat.; co.; st.; prov.; dist.; sub-dist.; vil.; tribe; n.f.; army; st.; div.; st.; brig.; st.; bat.; st.; com.; st.; plat.; sqd.
Sources: SYB 1936:1046; Campbell 1949: 26–7; Dowson 1932:20; Ireland 1938:94; Longrigg 1953:22; Rüstung 1934:51; Dupuy 1939:22, 58

IRISH *ca.* 1955 Total: 22
nat.; co.; st.; cnty. borough; co.; admin. cnty.; co.; urban cnty. dist.; co.; town; st.; n.f.; army; st.; bat.; st.; brig.; st.; com.; st.; plat.; sqd.
Sources: SYB 1959:1137 f; Arensberg 1940: 210f; Rüstung 1934:51–2.

IROQUOIS *ca.* 1700 Total: 13
conf.; co.; st.; nat. or tr.; co.; st.; clan; co.; ext.f.; st.; n.f.; keepers of the faith; st.
Source: Morgan 1901, I:5–7, 58, 62–72, 75–7, 84–5, 94–5, 103–7, 177–204, 313–5; II: 215, 218–223.

ITALY *ca.* 1960 Total: 27
nat.; co.; st.; prov.; co.; st.; dept.; st.; vil.; ext.f.; n.f.; army; st.; field army; st.; army corps; st.; div.; st.; reg.; st.; bat.; st.; com.; st.; plat.; sqd.
Sources: SYB 1962:1150–1; Moss and Thomson 1959:37; Pitkin 1960:34; Dupuy 1939:37.

KABABISH *ca.* 1900 Total: 9
tribe; st.; tr. sect.; tr. subsect.; st.; hshd.; pol.f.; n.f.; encampment.
Source: Seligman 1918:105–12, 115, 117–8.

KAFIR *ca.* 1890 Total: 6
tribe; co.; st.; clan; pol.f.; n.f.
Source: Robertson 1900:18, 83–7, 305, 370, 434–9, 472–6, 534.

KAPAUKU *ca.* 1940 Total: 8
conf.; st.; vil.; lin.; sub-lin.; ext.f.; pol.f.; n.f.
Sources: Pospisil 1958a:81–4, 101, 273, 277; van Logchem 1958:44

KAZAKS *ca.* 1800 Total: 7
khanate; st.; loc.grp.; st.; ext.f.; pol.f.; n.f.
Sources: Hudson 1938:24–31, 35–6, 39–43, 61–3; Sabitov 1953:196–200; Krader 1953:411.

KLALLAM *ca.* 1885 Total: 7
tribe; vil.; st.; ext.f.; pol.f.; n.f.; secret society.
Sources: Gunther 1927:183–9, 245–6, 261f, 309; Stern 1934:7, 31–2, 72, 75, 86.

KOREA *ca.* 1955 Total: 30
nat.; co.; st.; prov.; st.; dist.; st.; twns.; st.; vil.; co.; st.; hshd.; n.f.; army; st.;

field army; st.; army corps; st.; div.; st.; battle grp.; st.; bat.; st.; com.; st.; plat.; sqd.
Sources: *SYB* 1958:1189; 1959:1190–1; Brunner 1928:11, 37, 40; Osgood 1951:20; Griffis 1882:231, 246; Heydrich 1931:18; Ha 1958:57.

LAND DYAK *ca.* 1950 Total: 6
dist.; st.; vil.; st.; hshd.; n.f.
Source: Geddes 1954:9–12, 34–5, 39–40, 45, 48–51

LUO *ca.* 1900 Total: 6
tribe; clan-dist.; lin.-vil.; ext.f.; pol.f.; n.f.
Sources: Butt 1952:109–10, 113; Wilson 1960:179–80; Roscoe 1915:277; Southall 1952:24; Bohannan 1960:191; Shaw 1932: 41.

MALAITA *ca.* 1925 Total: 5
island; st.; area (under single chief); pol.f.; n.f.
Sources: Hogbin 1937:364–6; Ivens 1930: 28, 65, 80, 88, 92.

MALEKULA *ca.* 1880 Total: 5
clan; vil.; pol.f.; n.f.; *nimangki* society.
Source: Deacon 1934:45–6, 52–4, 71, 81, 164–8, 219, 243, 272–3.

MANGAREVA *ca.* 1885 Total: 7
tribe; co.; dist.; sub-dist.; island; pol.f.; n.f.
Source: Buck 1938:135, 151, 157.

MATACO *ca.* 1870 Total: 4
sub-tribe (clan); vil.; matr. ext.f.; n.f.
Source: Karsten 1932:43, 49–50.

MENDE *ca.* 1890 Total: 9
chft.; co.; town; vil.; vil.sect.; ext.f.; pol.f.; n.f.; *poro* soc.
Source: Little 1951:98–101, 140f, 175–6, 182–3.

MONGO *ca.* 1890 Total: 6
vil.; co.; st.; hamlet; pol.f.; n.f.
Source: Muller 1956:15, 23–7.

MOSQUITO *ca.* 1725 Total: 6
tribe; st.; co.; dist.; vil.; n.f.
Sources: Conzemius 1932:101–2, 147; Kirchoff 1948:224; Pijoan 1946:16.

NAHUA (Aztec) *ca.* 1525 Total: 17
Aztec emp.; Mexican conf.; tribe; co.; st.; clan; co.; st.; ext.f.; pol.f.; n.f.; clergy; eccles. co.; temple; st.; temple school; st.
Sources: Prescott n.d.:314; Sahagun 1938, I:237–53; II:385ff; Vaillant 1950:115–24, 207.

OJIBWA *ca.* 1800 Total: 6
gens or vil.-band; co.; pol.f.; n.f.; *metawin* soc.; *metawin* sub-div.
Sources: Hilger 1939:114; Landes 1937a:

101; 13, 36; 1938:72; Jenness 1935:2, **3,** 101; Skinner 1912:155; 1913:482; Kinietz 1947:83; Barrett 1911:352.

ONA *ca.* 1880 Total: 3
tr. sect. (ext.f.); pol.f.; n.f.
Sources: Lothrop 1928:84; Cooper 1946: 116–7.

OROKAIVA *ca.* 1910 Total: 5
vil.; men's hse.; clan; pol.f.; n.f.
Source: Williams 1930:91–107, 131, 136, 151, 156–7.

PAPAGO *ca.* 1880 Total: 9
cntr. vil.; st.; co.; satellite vil.; st.; pol.f.; ext.f.; n.f.; hunting party.
Sources: Underhill 1946:6, 58–60; 1939:2, 70–7, 84–8, 118, 179, 203; Williams 1956: 58–9, 75–6, 90–2.

SEMANG *ca.* 1920 Total: 2
camp; n.f.
Source: Schebesta 1927:279.

SO. PAIUTE *ca.* 1850 Total: 6
nat.; tribe; st.; band; pol.f.; n.f.
Sources: Palmer 1928–9:35–6; Lowie 1924: 277–8, 283–5; Kelly 1934–554, 633–4.

TALLENSI *ca.* 1900 Total: 7
clan; st.; max. lin.; sub-lin.; ext.f.; pol.f.; n.f.
Sources: Fortes 1945:32, 37, 41–5, 182–3, 251; 1949:66, 74, 81, 269.

THONGA *ca.* 1890 Total: 11
clan; co.; st.; clan div.; vil.; co.; pol.f.; n.f.; army; bat.; com.
Source: Junod 1927, I:14, 126, 219, 310, 328–33, 356, 367–76, 406–10, 421–3, 434, 456–9, 470.

TIKOPIA *ca.* 1930 Total: 9
island; isl.dist.; clan; st.; co.; lin.; sub-lin. (ext.f.); pol.f.; n.f.
Sources: Rivers 1914:298–304, 309, 334, 399–44, 354; Firth 1930a:68, 73–7; 1930b: 105–15; 1936:565; 1959:180, 188, 205.

TIV *ca.* 1900 Total: 5
family grp.; co.; ext.f.; pol.f.; n.f.
Sources: Downs 1933:28–9; Abraham 1933: 147, 156, 200; Bohannan 1959:52f; East 1939:313.

TONGA *ca.* 1800 Total: 10
kng.; st.; area (under gt. chief); co.; dist. (under infr. chief); st.; vil.; st.; pol.f.; n.f.
Sources: Beaglehole 1941:7–8, 12, 25; Mariner 1820:110, 180–1, 318–22, 353–4, 428; West 1865:262–3; Gifford 1929:15, 16, 20.

TORADJA *ca.* 1890 Total: 6
princ.; vil.; co.; ext.f.; pol.f.; n.f.

Sources: Adriani and Kruyt 1950, I:103, 108–14, 119, 122–6, 148–9; Kaudern 1925a:37, 376.

TURKS *ca.* 1955 Total: 33

nat.; st.; co.; prov.; st.; co.; dist.; st.; cnty.; st.; city-admin. unit; st.; co.; vil.; co.; patr. ext. f.; n.f.; army; st.; field army; st.; army corps; st.; div.; st.; reg.; st.; bat.; st.; com.; st.; plat.; sqd.

Sources: Simmons 1944:229; *RIIA* 1954: 515f; Makal 1954:1–6; Rüstung 1934:184–5.

WINTUN *ca.* 1845 Total: 7

vil.; co.; f.soc.grp.; ext.f.; pol.f.; n.f.; *hesi* society.

Sources: DuBois 1935:28–32, 35, 54–5; McKern 1923:165, 238–44, 256.

YAGUA *ca.* 1935 Total: 3

clan; co.; n.f.

Source: Fejos 1943:76, 81–4, 104–5, 727.

Abbreviation Code for Team Type Count in the Naroll WSC Study

bat., battalion
brig., brigade
chft., chieftancy
cntr., central
cnty., county
co.*, council
com., company
commun., community
conf., confederacy
dist., district
div., division(s)
dept., department
eccles., ecclesiastical
emp., empire

ext.f., extended family
f., family
grp., group
gt., great
hse., house
hshd., household
ham., hamlet
infr., inferior
isl., island
kin., kindred
kng., kingdom
lin., lineage
loc., local
matr., matrilineal
max., maximum
muni., municipal
nat., nation
n.f., nuclear family
patr., patrilineal
plat., platoon
pol.f., polygynous family
princ., principality
prov., province
reg., regiment
sect., section
setl., settlement
soc., society, social
sqd., squad
st.*, staff
tr., tribe
twns., township
vil., village

*refer to staffs and councils of preceding team.

APPENDIX II
Craft Specialties in the Naroll WSC Study

AMHARA *ca.* 1880 Total: 16

m.c.; w.c.; ironsm.; tan.; tail.; *mano* mkrs.; pot.; sun umbrella mkrs.; saddle mkrs.; sil.sm.; gd.sm.; painter; weavers; bskt.; carpet mkrs.; *burnos*-mkrs.

Sources: Messing 1957:146f, 150, 153, 158–9, 167, 169–72, 174f, 183–215, 220–1, 231; Messing 1962:387, 391–4, 401.

ANDAMANS *ca.* 1910 Total: 2

m.c.; w.c.

Source: Man 1932:154, 180.

APAYAO *ca.* 1920 Total: 3

m.c.; w.c.; sm.

Sources: Wilson 1947:5, 9–10, 11; Vanoverbergh 1936:127, 129–30.

ARAUCANIANS *ca.* 1800 Total: 7

m.c.; w.c.; stone obj. mkrs.; wood obj. mkrs.; bskt.; pot.; sil.sm.

Sources: Titiev 1951:32–3; Hilger 1957: 231; Cooper 1946:708.

AUSTRIA *ca.* 1960 Total: 1289*

adding mach. reprs.; asbestos and cement mfrs.; asphalt kettles; asphalt uten.; ortho. appl.; bldrs.; skip loaders; concrete mixers; concrete slab mfrs.; concrete vibrators; sculp.; billiard cue mfrs.; billiard table reprs.; coop.; coop. tool mfrs.; mfg. twine;

mfg. bags; mfg. boring mach.; well-drillers; mach. shops; mfg. riveting equip.; mfg. office lamps; mfg. camping gear; mfg. camping stoves; mfg. camping furn.; mfg. camping umbrellas; mfg. Xmas tree orn.; mfg. contact lenses; dressmkrs.; mfg. clothing; mfg. graph paper; diamond cutting; mfg. diamond tools; mfg. filmstrips; refrig. reprs.; elec. supp.; elec. floor brushes; elec. drills; elec. iron reprs.; elec. appl.; elec. tool reprs.; mfg. elec. hand tools; mfg. elec. heaters; mfg. elec. motors; mfg. ribbon; mfg. fishing equip.; mfg. barbershop equip.; mfg. gas ranges; mfg. gas ovens; graphic arts designers; graphic arts mach. reprs.; mfg. elec. heating pads; mfg. children's beds; mfg. bicycles; mfg. chil. furn.; mfg. chil. hats; piano reprs.; mfg. carbon brushes; mfg. candy mach.; mfg. cranes; mfg. wheelchairs; mfg. hosp. equip.; mfg. balls; mfg. ballpoint pens; refrig. sys. designers; die moldings; mfg. cop. art.; mfg. Chinese lanterns; mapmkrs.; mfg. farm equip.; mfg. lea. gloves; mfg. *lederhosen;* scaf. bldrs.; mfg. mtl. wire; mfg. air heating equip.; mfg. blowers; mfg. paint sprayers; mfg. paint rollers; mfg. art supp.; mfg. manometers; mfg. cutlers; meas. tape reprs.; meas. tool reprs.; mfg. hats; motorscooter reprs.; power saw reprs.; mfg. garment bags; grain mill const.; oven fac.; mfg. opt. goods; excelsior; mfg. cardboard; mfg. pumps; spot welding equip.; mfg. doll clothes; mfg. dolls; mfg. razor blades; mfg. smoking art.; mfg. pipes; saw reprs.; mfg. sawdust; mfg. sawdust incinerators; millwork; mfg. record racks; mfg. carts; mfg. veils; mfg. lace art.; type foundries; mfg. welding equip.; mfg. stamps; mfg. sil. ware; silo const.; siren const.; mfg. furn.; mfg. sportswear; mfg. seals; tool mkrs.; mfg. drugs; tachographs; carpet reprs.; cab. mkrs.; vibrator mfrs.; mfg. lingerie; mfg. toys; mfg. tents; mfg. igniters; mfg. tongue depressors; tail.; m.c.; w.c.
Source: *Wien Telephonbuch (1960). 10% sample. (129×9.98=1287+m.c.+w.c.)

AWEIKOMA *ca.* 1930 Total: 2
m.c.; w.c.
Source: Henry 1941:15, 16, 164–72.

AZANDE *ca.* 1900 Total: 6
m.c.; w.c.; wdcrvs.; sm.; pot.; bskt.
Source: Evans-Pritchard 1937:17.

BURMESE *ca.* 1850 Total: 28
m.c.; w.c.; gilded box mkrs.; lacquerware

mkrs.; silk-wvrs.; pot.; b.sm.; gd.sm.; wdcrvs.; paper mkrs.; mat mkrs.; sculp.; coffin mkrs.; brick mkrs.; rope mkrs.; net mkrs.; umbrella mkrs.; sandal mkrs.; brnz. casters; sword sm.; tin sm.; sil.sm; carp.; iv. crvs.; painters; copyists; boat mkrs.; cartbldrs.
Sources: Scott 1882:431–2; Ferrars and Ferrars 1901:96–101, 103–8, 119–24, 133–6, 138–9; Dautremer 1913:356, 364–9; Orr 1951:27.

CALLINAGO *ca.* 1700 Total: 2
m.c.; w.c.
Sources: Rouse 1948:555; Ober 1895:300.

CHAGGA *ca.* 1900 Total: 4
m.c.; w.c.; c.c.; sm.
Source: Gutmann 1926:272.

CHEYENNE *ca.* 1840 Total: 2
m.c.; w.c.
Source: Grinnell 1923:171–2.

CHUKCHEE *ca.* 1900 Total: 5
m.c.; w.c.; iv. crvs.; fishnet mkrs.; skin dressers.
Sources: Bogoras 1904–09:215; Nordenskiold 1882:490f.

COPPER ESKIMO *ca.* 1910 Total: 8
m.c.; w.c.; lame m.c.; bow mkrs.; sled mkrs.; wd. art. mkrs.; pot.; lamp mkrs.
Sources: Stefansson 1914:102, 103; Jenness 1922:53.

COYOTERO *ca.* 1900 Total: 2
m.c.; w.c.
Source: Goodwin 1942:332–3.

DUTCH *ca.* 1955 Total: 444*
asphalt roads; mfg. storage batteries; poster printers; mfg. alum. art.; mfg. welding mach.; automat fac.; motorcycle reprs.; mfg. chem. art.; mfg. readymade clothes; mfg. shirts; mfg. dictating mach.; mfg. elec. solder pins; mfg. elec. motors; mfg. plaster bandages; mfg. gls.; mfg. ink; mfg. ink ribbon; mfg. wedges; mfg. badges; mfg. fiber rugs; mfg. wheelbarrows; mfg. artif. flowers; art printing; mfg. leather goods; mfg. books; mfg. air mattresses; furn. reprs.; auto reprs.; toy fac.; mfg. numbering mach.; license plate fac.; mfg. orthopedic art.; mfg. paper goods; mfg. doll clothes; doll reprs.; rainwear fac.; mfg. paint mach.; mfg. paint roller; mfg. paint sprayer; amplifier mfg. and repr.; mfg. lace curtain; mfg. flags; mfg. flag poles; washing mach. fac.; m.c.; w.c.
Source: *10% sample from Dutch tele-

phone book (1960). (44×10.05=442+m.c. +w.c.)

EYAK *ca.* 1880 Total: 2
m.c.; w.c.
Source: Birket-Smith and de Laguna 1938:74, 77, 80–1.

FUR *ca.* 1880 Total: 3
m.c.; w.c.; b.sm.
Source: Felkin 1885:248.

GILYAK *ca.* 1870 Total: 3
m.c.; w.c.; mtl. wrkrs.
Sources: Kreinovich 1934:22–3; Seeland 1882:27.

GOND *ca.* 1880 Total: 7
m.c.; w.c.; b.sm.; brass wrkrs.; iron wrkrs.; carp.; pot.
Sources: Grigson 1949:174–5, 179, 480; Russell 1916:62.

HOTTENTOT *ca.* 1880 Total: 4
m.c.; w.c.; wdcrvs.; Herrero sm.
Source: Schapera 1951:316–17.

IFALUK *ca.* 1900 Total: 3
m.c.; w.c.; carp.
Source: Burrows 1949:98, 116.

ILA *ca.* 1900 Total: 4
m.c.; w.c.; iv. turning; sm.
Source: Smith and Dale 1920:180, 187.

IRISH *ca.* 1955 Total: 102*
printers; weighing mach. mfrs.; clothing mfrs.; radio and TV mfrs.; mantle mfrs.; stationers; skirt mfrs.; contractors; carpet reprs.; cab. mkrs.; children's clothing mfrs.; boat mfrs.; meter mfrs.; corset mfrs.; sloth mfrs.; umbrella mfrs.; woolen mfrs.; appl. mfrs.; opticians; auto reprs.; m.c.; w.c.
Source: *20% sample from Irish telephone directory (1960). (20×5=100+m.c.+w.c.)

IROQUOIS *ca.* 1700 Total: 5
m.c.; w.c.; wampum mkrs.; sil.sm.; mask mkrs.
Source: Morgan 1901: v.II, 50, 52, 280; Fenton 1940:424.

ITALY *ca.* 1960 Total: 626*
mfg. bridal clo.; mfg. men's clo.; mfg. calendars; mfg. bowling balls; mfg. confect. box.; mfg. mail box.; mfg. packing box.; mtl. molds; safes; mfg. elec. cable; cab. mkrs.; mfg. furnaces; mfg. ovens; mfg. naval furn.; mfg. office furn.; mfg. hotel furn.; mfg. bars; mfg. indus. furn.; stoneware mfrs.; mfg. cranes; mfg. generators; mfg. gloves; mfg. work gloves; mfg. indus. gloves; mfg. wardrobe closets; sign mkrs.; intercom. bldrs.; mfg. inst. for irri.; mfg. files and rasps; mfg. mattresses; mfg. bed

springs; mfg. mica; mfg. microfilm; gd.sm.; mfg. steel furn.; foundry molds; tail.; grinding wheel oper.; mfg. mill acces.; monument bldrs.; tombstone mkrs.; mfg. mosaics; mfg. folding beds; mfg. packing nets; mfg. sandblasting mach.; sack fac.; mfg. paper sacks; mfg. plastic bags; mfg. soldering irons; mfg. welding mach.; welders; mfg. saws; mfg. signaling devices; saddle mkrs.; mfg. cement and abestos; mfg. iron tanks; mfg. drafting equip.; mfg. drafting tables; mfg. telephones; mfg. gls. lab. equip.; mfg. showcases; mfg. concrete vibrators; m.c.; w.c.
Source: *Roma Categorico, 1960–61. 10% sample. (62×10.06=624+m.c.+w.c.)

KABABISH *ca.* 1900 Total: 2
m.c.; w.c.
Source: Seligman 1918:173–9.

KAFIR *ca.* 1890 Total: 12
m.c.; w.c.; pot.; brass wrkrs.; lea. wrkrs.; mech.; wdcrvs.; sil. wrkrs.; b.sm.; dagger mkrs.; iron wrkrs.; carp.
Source: Robertson 1900:99, 443–5, 477, 511.

KAPAUKU *ca.* 1940 Total: 5
m.c.; w.c.; bowmkrs.; netmkrs.; counterfeit cowry shell mkrs.
Sources: Smedts 1955:96; Pospisil 1958a: 14, 118, 121, 127.

KAZAK *ca.* 1800 Total: 4
m.c.; w.c.; b.sm.; carp.
Source: Hudson 1938:29f.

KLALLAM *ca.* 1885 Total: 2
m.c.; w.c.
Source: Stern 1934:88.

LAND DYAK *ca.* 1950 Total: 4
m.c.; w.c.; e.c.; c.c.
Source: Geddes 1954:81.

LUO *ca.* 1900 Total: 4
m.c.; w.c.; apron mkrs.; iron forging.
Sources: Hobley 1902:27, 29; Shaw 1932: 43.

MALAITA *ca.* 1925 Total: 9
m.c.; w.c.; 'alavolo (war club) mkrs. fishnet mkrs.; canoe mkrs.; crvs.; hse. bldrs.; shell money and orn. mkrs.; artif. island bldrs.
Source: Ivens 1930:7, 34, 179, 306.

MALEKULA *ca.* 1880 Total: 2
m.c.; w.c.
Source: Deacon 1934:36.

MANGAREVA *ca.* 1885 Total: 4
m.c.; w.c.; c.c.; carp.
Sources: Buck 1938:148; Laval 1938:240.

MATACO *ca.* 1870 Total: 5
m.c.; w.c.; weapon mkrs.; canoe bldrs.; net mkrs.
Source: Pelleschi 1896:116–118.

MENDE *ca.* 1920 Total: 13
m.c.; w.c.; b.sm.; weavers; dyers; gd.sm.; mat mkrs.; bskt.; raffia cloth mkrs.; net mkrs.; tail.; canoe mkrs.; pot.
Sources: Staub 1936:37; Little 1951:69, 79, 121, 134, 142, 284, 288, 290.

MONGO *ca.* 1890 Total: 6
m.c.; w.c.; basketry; sm.; wood sculp.; *lokole* mkrs.
Sources: Gutersohn 1920:2, 9, 13; Hulstaert 1938:11.

MOSQUITO *ca.* 1725 Total: 2
m.c.; w.c.
Sources: Pijoan 1946:19; Conzemius 1932: 49–53.

NAHUA (Aztec) *ca.* 1525 Total: 34
m.c.; w.c.; mtl. wrkrs.; go. leaf mkrs.; lapidary wrkrs.; feather wrkrs.; carp.; mas.; tail.; pot.; sculp.; *chicuite* bskt.; other bskt.; *cotaras* mkrs.; *serape* mkrs.; paper mkrs.; stone knife mkrs.; mat mkrs.; mirror mkrs.; needle mkrs.; rubber mkrs.; broom mkrs.; pipe mkrs.; candle mkrs.; bag mkrs.; ribbon mkrs.; fur.; glove mkrs.; vase mkrs.; manuscript writing; mosaic mkrs.; sandal mkrs.; jew.; woodwrkrs.
Sources: Prescott n.d.:314; Sahagun 1938, I:237–53: II:385ff; III:29–75; Torquemada 1943, I:291, 527; II:174, 176, 183–191, 544f; III:208–10: Vaillant 1951:115–23, 127, 144, 147, 156–61, 207.

OJIBWA *ca.* 1800 Total: 5
m.c.; w.c.; pipestem mkrs.; net mkrs.; arrow mkrs.
Sources: Hilger 1951:119, 129, 134; Densmore 1929:238; Landes 1938:125–6, 132.

ONA *ca.* 1880 Total: 4
m.c.; w.c.; bow mkrs.; fishnet mkrs.
Sources: Gusinde 1931:355; Lothrop 1928: 71.

OROKAIVA *ca.* 1910 Total: 4
m.c.; w.c.; stone club mkrs.; wooden bowl mkrs.
Source: Williams 1930:76.

PAPAGO *ca.* 1880 Total: 5
m.c.; w.c.; weavers; lea. tan.; rope braiders.
Sources: Underhill 1939:49; Naroll (unpublished field notes).

SEMANG *ca.* 1920 Total: 3
m.c.; w.c.; bow mkrs.

Sources: Williams-Hunt 1952:60; Schebesta 1927:56.

SO. PAIUTE *ca.* 1850 Total: 2
m.c.; w.c.
Source: Lowie 1924:225.

TALLENSI *ca.* 1900 Total: 10
m.c.; w.c.; b.sm.; lea. wrkrs.; pot.; sewer of caps; hencoop mkrs.; bskt.; bow mkrs.; adze-shaft mkrs.
Source: Fortes 1945:9–10; 1949:47f.

THONGA *ca.* 1890 Total: 8
m.c.; w.c.; y.c.; crvs.; pot.; b.sm.; bskt.; boat mkrs.
Source: Junod 1927, I:91, 338; II:112, 125–7, 135, 138.

TIKOPIA *ca.* 1930 Total: 12
m.c.; w.c.; canoe bldrs.; wdcrvs.; stone crvs.; net mkrs.; cooking pot mkrs.; mtl. mortar mkrs.; bow mkrs.; bowl mkrs.; sinnet mkrs.; bonito hook lashing.
Sources: Firth 1930b:109f; Firth 1936:51–71, 131, 364, 439, 461; Firth 1939: 40, 43, 113, 120, 135–6, 142, 166, 187f, 295–8, 342.

TIV *ca.* 1900 Total: 6
m.c.; w.c.; bskt.; pot.; brass sm.; b.sm.
Sources: Bohannan 1958:295, 305, 306; East 1939:55, 60.

TONGA *ca.* 1800 Total: 16
m.c.; w.c.; crvs.; stone mas.; net mkrs.; fortif. bldrs.; rope mkrs.; bow and arrow mkrs.; club and spear mkrs.; *gnatoo* mkrs.; mat mkrs.; bskt.; thread comb mkrs.; dugout canoe mkrs.; hse. bldrs.: whale teeth cutters.
Sources: Beaglehole 1941:20, 41–2; Mariner 1820:318–22, 416.

TORADJA *ca.* 1890 Total: 8
m.c.; w.c.; e.c.; wd. ves. mkrs.; b.sm; cop. orn. mkrs.; skin dres.; tipi mkrs.
Source: Adriani and Kruyt 1950, III:301, 309–11, 316–7, 330, 334–5.

TURKS *ca.* 1955 Total: 284*
wood lathwkrs.; mfg. belts and suspenders; sharpeners; mfg. bicycles; mfg. gls. obj.; mfg. gls. bottles; mfg. steel; mfg. bags; marine const. docks; mfg. marine suppl.; mfg. elec. mchry. and devices; mfg. T-shirts; mfg. brushes; oven bldr.; engravers; mfg. carpets and rugs; mfg. perfumery supp.; mfg. rope; wood laminators; mfg. beds; mfg. safes and steel cab.; mfg. paper bags; mfg. locks; mfg. compressors; mfg. ribbon and cord; mfg. plastic; mfg. pails and buckets; mfg. bird feathers; mfg.

jewelers obj.; mfg. met. obj.; mfg. musical inst.; mfg. faucets; mfg. jew.; mfg. hdwr.; mfg. nylon; car assemblers; crvs.; mfg. toys; mfg. measuring inst.; mfg. cloth; mfg. plastic obj.; mfg. porc. obj.; watchmkrs.; mfg. chairs; mfg. saddler's equip.; saddlers; mfg. hse. heating staves; photo shops; tech. job shops; mfg. wire; mfg. med. tools; mfg. pins; lathe shops; mfg. razor blades; mfg. cotton; mfg. wool; m.c.; w.c.

Source: *Istanbul Telefon Rehberi, 1960–61, yellow pages. 20% sample. (56×5.04= 282+m.c.+w.c.)

WINTUN *ca.* 1845 Total: 5

m.c.; w.c.; rope mkrs.; bskt.; bow and arrow mkrs.

Source: DuBois 1935:21–4, 134.

YAGUA *ca.* 1935 Total: 5

m.c.; w.c.; clay ware mkrs.; blowgun dart mkrs.; wdcrvs.

Source: Fejos 1943:113.

Abbreviation Code for Craft Specialties in the Naroll WSC Study

acces., accessories
alum., aluminum
appl., appliances
art., articles
artif., artificial
bldrs., builders
box., boxes
brnz., bronze
bskt., basketry, basket makers
b.sm., blacksmith
cab., cabinet
carp., carpenter
c.c., children's crafts
chem., chemical
chil., children
clo., clothes, cloth
cob., cobbler, shoemaker
confect., confectionary
const., construction
coop., cooper
cop., copper
crvs., carvers
dres., dressing, dresser
e.c., elders' crafts
elec., electrical
equip., equipment
fac., factory
fortif., fortifications
fur., furrier
furn., furniture

gd., gold
gls., glass
hat., hatter
hdwr., hardware
hosp., hospital
hse., house
indus., industry
inst., instruments
irri., irrigation
iv., ivory
jew., jewelry, jeweler
lab., laboratory
lea., leather
mach., machines, mechanics
mas., mason
m.c., men's crafts
mchry., machinery
meas., measure, measuring
med., medical
mfg., manufacture
mfrs., manufacturers
mkrs., makers
mtl., metal
obj., objects
oper., operator
opt., optical
orn., ornaments
ortho., orthopedic
porc., porcelain
pot., pottery, potter
prod., products
refrig., refrigerator, refrigeration
reprs., repairers
scaf., scaffolding
sculp., sculptor, sculpture
sil., silver
skl., skilled
sm., smith
supp., supplies
sys., system
tail., tailor
tan., tanner
tech., technical
uten., utensils
ves., vessels
w.c., women's crafts
wd., wood
wdcrvs., woodcarvers
wrkrs., workers
wvrs., weavers
y.c., youth's crafts

*based on percentage samples from telephone directories.

APPENDIX III
Largest Settlement Population Data in the Naroll WSC Study

SOCIETY	NAME OF LGST. SETTLEMENT	POP. OF LGST. SETTLEMENT	TYPE OF ESTIMATE	SOURCES
Amhara ca. 1905	Gondar	7,000	—	Enc. Brit. (11th ed.), vol. 12:232.
Andamans ca. 1925	—	70	lgst. mentioned	Man 1932:62
Araucanians ca. 1920	—	360	estimate	Faron 1959:268f.
Austrians ca. 1960	Vienna	1,667,000	census estimate	World Alm. 1961:397
Aweikoma ca. 1930	—	300	lgst. mentioned	Henry 1941:50
Azande ca. 1910	—	200	—	Czekanowski 1924:40
Burmese ca. 1911	Rangoon	293,316	census estimate	Dautremer 1913:145
Cheyenne ca. 1800	—	2,000 (220 lodges)	census estimate (9/lodge)	Grinnell 1923:20.f.; Grinnell 1918:365–366
Chukchee ca. 1900	Ircowin	142	—	Bogoras 1904–1909: 30, 172
Dutch ca. 1960	Amsterdam	871,577	govt. census	World Alm. 1961:398
Egypt ca. 1960	Cairo	2,800,000	—	World Alm. 1961:397
Eyak ca. 1885	Algonik	120	lgst. mentioned	Birket-Smith and de Laguna 1938:20, 32
Gilyak ca. 1880	Vaida	200	—	Seeland 1882:36
Hottentot ca. 1880	—	2,500	—	Schapera 1930
Ifaluk ca. 1950	Ifaluk	252	ethno. census	Bates and Abbott 1958:32f., 25, 28, 252; Spiro 1949: 5–6
Ila ca. 1910	Kasenga	3,000	—	Smith and Dale 1920: 313
Iraqi ca. 1960	Baghdad	1,306,604	census	World Alm. 1961:398
Irish ca. 1950	Dublin	506,051	census	World Alm. 1952:353
Iroquois ca. 1850	—	3,000	—	Morgan 1901, II:229
Italy ca. 1960	Rome	2,100,000	govt. census	World Alm. 1961:398
Kapauku ca. 1955	Botukebo	181	ethno. census	Pospisil 1958a:102
Kazak ca. 1860	—	3,000	estimate	Hudson 1938:24; Kostenko 1880:99, G-4, G-5

SOCIETY	NAME OF LGST. SETTLEMENT	POP. OF LGST. SETTLEMENT	TYPE OF ESTIMATE	SOURCES
Klallam ca. 1885	Port Angeles	200	—	Gunther 1927:184–186
Korea ca. 1960	Seoul	1,710,242	—	World Alm. 1961:1, 397
Malaita ca. 1930	Little Mala	5,000	—	Ivens 1930:17
Mende ca. 1945	Kailahun	2,545	—	Little 1951:65
Mosquito ca. 1945	—	600	lgst. mentioned	Pijoan 1946:18
Nahua (Aztec) ca. 1565	Tenochtitlan	400,000	estimate	Cook and Simpson 1948:34f.
Ona ca. 1880	—	500	—	Gusinde 1931:824n (cf. 203)
Papago ca. 1940	Sells	800	ethno. estimate	Joseph, Spicer and Chesky 1949:4f.
Semang ca. 1920	Teladn	54	lgst. mentioned	Schebesta 1927:109
Tallensi ca. 1925	Tongo	2,400	lgst. mentioned	Fortes 1945:159
Tikopia ca. 1930	Whole Island	1,400	ethno. estimate	Firth 1959:182
Tonga ca. 1850	Nukualofa	5,000	lgst. mentioned	West 1865:44
Toradja ca. 1920	Bolapapol	600 (30 houses)	est. lgst. mentioned	Kaudern 1925:37
Turks ca. 1950	Istanbul	1,000,000	—	Simmons et al. 1944: 206
Wintun ca. 1845	—	1,000	lgst. mentioned	McKern 1923:256
Yagua ca. 1930	—	50	estimate	Fejos 1943:15f.

APPENDIX IV
Trait Codings of the Freeman Scale in the Naroll WSC Study

IV–A: Intersocietal Trade (I)

X=present
O=absent

CODE	SOCIETY	STATEMENT	REFERENCE
X	Amhara	"Certain basic trade routes have not changed between Ethiopia and surrounding areas in thousands of years. . . ."	Messing 1957:27
		"In the past, most imports were for the top feudal chiefs and the clergy. . . ."	Messing 1957:227

CODE	SOCIETY	STATEMENT	REFERENCE
O	Andamans	Gift exchange between local groups is the only form of economic exchange (i.e., no intersocietal trade).	Radcliffe-Brown 1922: 83–84
X	Apayao	"They obtain their clothing, pots, salt and other materials from Ilocano traders in exchange for their honey. . . ."	Wilson 1947:5
X	Araucanians	"They carried on considerable 'foreign' trade. . . . There were no established markets or market days."	Cooper 1946:728
		"The oldest informants recalled the days when the trade of the Araucanians extended from the Atlantic to the Pacific."	Hilger 1957:356
X	Austrians	International trade present.	Naroll 1956b:34–35
X	Aweikoma	". . . steal from the Brazilian settlers" . . . also trade with them.	Henry 1941:101, 105
X	Azande	". . . many of them have visited foreign lands where they . . . purchase, or receive as gifts, commodities difficult to acquire in their own country."	Evans-Pritchard 1937: 277–279; also Graffen 1906:777
		Chiefs maintained a monopoly on trade of slaves and ivory to the Arabs.	Baxter and Butt 1955: 60; also, Reining 1962: 544
X	Burmese	Regular trade was carried on between the British and the Kingdom of Upper Burma.	Scott 1882:527
		"The import of iron and steel began centuries ago. . . ."	Ferrars and Ferrars 1901:105
X	Callinago	"They trade with everyone with whom they are at peace."	Breton and De La Paix 1929:21
X	Chagga	Traded slaves and ivory to the Swahilis.	Stahl 1964:247f.
X	Cheyenne	Traded with French and Mexican traders.	Grinnell 1923, I:35–36
X	Chukchee	Traded with Eskimos, neighboring tribes, and with the Russians.	Borgoras 1904–1909: 12, 46–58, 65–66; Sverdrup 1938:96–97
X	Copper Eskimo	"There is always much trade . . . between neighboring groups. . . ."	Jenness 1922:53
		Sleds are traded to the Victoria Indians.	Stefansson 1914:82
X	Coyotero	Traded with Navaho, Zuni, etc.	Goodwin 1942:72–73, 76
X	Dutch	International trade present.	*SYB* 1964:1256f.
X	Egyptians	Cotton is the chief export.	*SYB* 1955:941
		". . . cotton . . . (provides) 60 per cent of the proceeds of visible exports."	*MENA* 1967:742; 746
X	Eyak	"The Eyak also traded with the Atna. . . ."	Birket-Smith and de Laguna 1938:150
X	Fur	"Exchange of goods is carried on with several of the surrounding tribes, and with the Arabs."	Felkin 1885:249

CODE	SOCIETY	STATEMENT	REFERENCE
X	Gilyak	Furs were used as barter with other tribes. . . . They also traveled up the Amour to trade furs with Chinese merchants.	*Ak. Nauk SSR*, 92f.
X	Gond	Traded for weapons "in or near the bazaar villages of the plains. . . ." "At every market . . . in the valleys and plains below there are potters who do a considerable trade with the Hill Marias. . . ."	Grigson 1949:81 Grigson 1949:180
X	Hottentots	Traded cattle to Europeans for guns, alcohol, tobacco and other articles. "There was a certain amount of trading between the Naman and the Bantu tribes. . . ."	Schapera 1930:331 Schapera 1930:317
X	Ifaluk	The natives of Ifaluk made trading expeditions to Guam.	Bates and Abbott 1958: 170, 177f.
X	Ila	Traded with neighboring tribes for cattle; traded ivory to the Mambari for European glass beads.	Smith and Dale 1920, I:106
X	Iraqi	International trade is carried on.	MENA 1967:284
X	Irish	International trade present.	*SYB* 1959:1148; Arensberg 1940:297
X	Iroquois	". . . launched a series of wars . . . to control the fur trade. . . ." Traded furs to the French.	Noon 1949:109
X	Italians	"Italy's imports normally exceed her exports. . . ."	*SYB* 1964:1172
X	Kababish	cloth, weapons, grain, etc. ". . . obtained by exchange from the neighboring tribes. . . ."	Seligman 1918:172
X	Kafirs	"The greater part of the external trade of Kafiristan is carried on through the Musalmah villages on its frontiers." Trade is carried on with other tribes.	Robertson 1900:540 Robertson 1900:543f.
X	Kapauku	Traded with coastal peoples and Europeans for metal axes, etc.	Pospisil 1958a:68; 121; 126–128
X	Kazaks	"The time and place for trade is not limited by any rules." Traded with neighboring peoples, Mongolia and China.	Grodekov 1889:112–113 Hudson 1938:77
X	Klallam	"Barter relations were maintained with neighboring tribes. . . ."	Stern 1934:7; also, Gunther 1927:212, 218
X	Koreans	"Korea . . . was in 1876 forced by Japan to open its ports to Japanese shipping and trade." "In 1962 the total exports were equal to US $57m."	*SYB* 1964:1190 *SYB* 1964:1193
X	Land Dyaks	Traded with Malays.	Low 1848:243
X	Luo	". . . canoes bought from Baganda or Basoga."	Hobley 1902:26

CODE	SOCIETY	STATEMENT	REFERENCE
X	Malaita	". . . markets are held in which vegetables from the bush are exchanged for fish from the salt-water people."	Hogbin 1937:296; also, Ivens 1930:262
		Traded with whaling ships and foreign traders during the nineteenth century.	Hogbin 1937:283–284
X	Malekula	". . . the Malekulans used undoubtedly . . . to trade even with other islands."	Deacon 1934:203
X	Mangareva	Traded with Europeans after 1824.	Buck 1938:98
X	Mataco	Intertribal trade existed with the tribes to the north.	Karsten 1932:183
X	Mende	"Slaves . . . were bartered and exchanged for goods, notably for salt from the coast."	Little 1951:37; 202–203
X	Mongo	"Copper is brought in from other peoples. . . ."	Hulstaert 1938:11
X	Mosquito	"the Miskito . . . sold them [war captives] to Jamaican traders for arms and ammunition."	Conzemius 1932:85
		Traded with neighboring tribes.	Conzemius 1932:40
X	Nahua (Aztec)	Traded with foreign tribes.	Bandelier 1880:128
		Regular long-distance trade was carried on between the Aztecs and Mayans.	Chapman 1957:114f.
X	Ojibwa	"Their first contact with the white man was usually through the medium of trading goods. . . ."	Barnouw 1950:10
X	Ona	Traded and intermarried with the Yaghan.	Cooper 1946:107
X	Orokaiva	Informal exchanges with neighboring groups were by barter or gift-exchange.	Williams 1930:317f.
X	Papago	"They sold them [Apache war captives] in Sonora. . . ."	Underhill 1939:135
X	Semang	Traded with Malays.	Schebesta 1927:32
O?	So. Paiute	There is no evidence of intertribal trading.	
X	Tallensi	Trade present—often buy grain in foreign markets.	Fortes and Fortes 1936:246
X	Thonga	Have traded with Europeans since the sixteenth century.	Junod 1927, I:542; II:141–142
X	Tikopia	"Such exchange with other native communities as can take place is sporadic. . . . It consists in the rare barter. . . ."	Firth 1939:47
X	Tiv	"Salt was formerly acquired by trade from the Jukun and the salt-producing peoples of the upper Benue. . . ."	Bohannan and Bohannan 1953:52
X	Tongans	Traded for sandalwood in the Fiji Islands.	Mariner 1820:69

CODE	SOCIETY	STATEMENT	REFERENCE
X	Toradja	Traded goods with other tribes.	Adriani and Kruyt 1950, 3:339–346
X	Turks	"In recent years new products are accounting for more and more exports."	*MENA* 1967:695; also, Dunn 1952:23
X	Wintun	Traded with neighboring subgroups and tribes.	Washington 1909:93
X	Yagua	Obtained canoes by barter with neighboring tribes.	Fejos 1943:46

IV–B: Producing Economy (E)

CODE	SOCIETY	STATEMENT	REFERENCE
X	Amhara	Agriculture and animal husbandry are the main subsistence activities.	Messing 1957:168; 1962:407
O	Andamans	Hunting is the chief subsistence activity.	Radcliffe-Brown 1922: 41
X	Apayao	Agriculture is the dominant subsistence mode. "Rice . . . is the basic food of the people."	Vanoverbergh 1941: 324f. Wilson 1947:8
X	Araucanians	Agriculture is the dominant activity.	Titiev 1951:36; Latcham 1909:343
X	Austrians	Agriculture and animal husbandry dominant food-producing activities.	*SYB* 1964:807–808; Naroll and Naroll 1962:6
O	Aweikoma	Hunting is the main source of subsistence.	Henry 1941:26, 49
X	Azande	". . . Azande are good agriculturalists, and to possess good gardens . . . is the principal objective of every male Zande."	Baxter and Butt 1953: 42
X	Burmese	Agriculture is the major subsistence activity.	Orr 1951:24; Scott 1882:243f.
O	Callinago	"The staple food of the *Carib* was the crab, which was hunted at night. . . ." Hunting and fishing were more significant than agriculture.	Rouse 1948:550 Rouse 1948:550–551
X	Chagga	Banana cultivation is the primary source of subsistence. Animal husbandry also important: "The introduction of cattle farming brought about . . . the distinction between rich and poor. . . ."	Gutmann 1926:371; Raum 1940:204f. Gutmann 1926:35
O	Cheyenne	Fishing and hunting are the major sources of subsistence.	Grinnell 1923:49f.; Hoebel 1960:2, 58f.
X	Chukchee	Herding. ". . . the reindeer who to him means food, clothing, shelter and transportation."	Srevdrup 1938:62
O	Copper Eskimo	The Copper Eskimo depend entirely on hunting and fishing for their subsistence.	Jenness 1922:93, 158

CODE	SOCIETY	STATEMENT	REFERENCE
O	Coyotero	Hunting and food gathering are the chief subsistence activities.	Goodwin 1935:55, 57
X	Dutch	Farming and animal husbandry are the main subsistence activities.	Keur and Keur 1955: 77f., 148f.
X	Egyptians	Agriculture is the main subsistence source.	Blackman 1927:169; *MENA* 1967:742
O	Eyak	Hunting and fishing economy.	Birket-Smith and de Laguna 1938:10f.
X	Fur	The economy is based on farming.	Felkin 1885:211, 240, 254
O	Gilyak	Subsistence is based on hunting and fishing.	Hawes 1903:258–259; Kreinovich 1934:3–5, 20–22
X	Gond	Practice slash-and-burn agriculture. Depend on crop raising for subsistence.	Grant 1870:xiv Grigson 1949:141–142
X	Hottentots	Cattle nomads who live mainly off their herds.	Schapera 1951:235f.
X	Ifaluk	"Breadfruit in its season . . . is the staple food . . . the main food varieties are seedless, completely dependent on man for reproduction. . . . Almost as important as breadfruit were the two taros." Fishing is also an important source of food.	Bates and Abbott 1958: 72, 74 Bates and Abbott 1958: 77
X	Ila	Agriculture is the dominant activity; cattle herding is also important.	Smith and Dale 1920: 320f.
X	Iraqi	Agriculture provides the bulk of subsistence; the Kurdish and Arab nomads are pastoralists. ". . . the majority of workers are engaged in subsistence agriculture."	Clark 1951:33; *IBRD* 1952:141; Longrigg 1953:22 *MENA* 1967:279
X	Irish	Farming and animal husbandry are the main economic activities.	Arensberg 1940:5
X	Iroquois	Although hunting and fishing were important, agriculture provided the basic food supply.	Morgan 1901:229
X	Italians	". . . the vast majority of those engaged in agriculture rent their land for money or kind."	Lopreato 1961:586; also, *SYB* 1964:1169–1170
X	Kababish	Animal husbandry provided the main source of subsistence.	Seligman 1918:105–107
X	Kafirs	"Farm and dairy work is done by the people, who are all equally expert."	Robertson 1900:546
X	Kapauku	Pig raising and gardening are the main subsistence activities.	Smedts 1955:50; Pospisil 1958a:14, 104–106

CODE	SOCIETY	STATEMENT	REFERENCE
X	Kazaks	Semi-nomadic herders; they depend almost entirely on their herds of goats, sheep and horses for subsistence.	Hudson 1938:24
O	Klallam	Hunting, fishing and gathering subsistence.	Gunther 1927:214; Stern 1934:7
X	Koreans	". . . this land has produced plentiful rice which has served as the main food."	Ha 1958:65
X	Land Dyaks	Horticulture is the chief subsistence activity.	Geddes 1954:94
X	Luo	Agriculture is the dominant activity; cattle keeping is also important.	Owen 1933:243f.
X	Malaita	". . . most of the natives were subsistence horticulturalists and pig-keepers."	Hogbin 1958:153
X	Malekula	Horticulture is dominant; pig raising is also important.	Deacon 1934:199
X	Mangareva	Horticulture is the basic subsistence-activity, though fishing is quite important.	Laval 1938:240f.
O	Mataco	". . . looking for roots . . . is women's work. Hunting, fishing . . . are men's business. . . ."	Pelleschi 1896:77
X	Mende	"Essentially the Mende are an agricultural people whose staple crop and food is rice."	Little 1951:77f.
X	Mongo	"The Tumba are agriculturalists, hunters, and fishing people. . . . Every family has its plantation of manioc, the staple diet. . . ."	Brown 1944:431
X	Mosquito	"Agriculture is not highly developed . . . it furnishes, nevertheless, the principal means of subsistence." Hunting and fishing are also important.	Conzemius 1932:60 Conzemius 1932:65f.
X	Nahua (Aztec)	"Theirs was a highly stratified and complex society, based on agriculture."	Chapman 1957:119
O	Ojibwa	Hunting, gathering and fishing economy.	Jenness 1935:3f.; Landes 1937b:87
O	Ona	Nomadic hunters and gatherers.	Gusinde 1931:193–194
X	Orokaiva	Horticulture is the dominant subsistence activity.	Williams 1930:317
X	Papago	"Flood water" agricultural activity was the basis of the subsistence economy.	Williams 1956:66, 72
O	Semang	They lead a nomadic existence, gathering wild foods and hunting game in the forest.	Evans 1937:33

CODE	SOCIETY	STATEMENT	REFERENCE
O	So. Paiute	Economy based on hunting and gathering.	Lowie 1924:284
X	Tallensi	Agriculture is the basic subsistence activity. "The Tallensi are peasants farming mainly cereal crops."	Fortes and Fortes 1936:246f. Fortes 1940:248
X	Thonga	"The basis of economic life in Bathonga is in agriculture and husbandry of livestock. . . ."	Goldman 1961:355
X(?)	Tikopia	Plant cultivation seems to be the dominant subsistence source, although fishing and gathering make important contributions.	Firth 1936:23–24, 373f., 416
X	Tiv	"They are prosperous subsistence farmers. . . ."	Bohannan 1958:492
X	Tongans	Agriculture provides the major part of their subsistence needs.	Mariner 1820:322
X	Toradja	Agriculture is the dominant activity, although hunting is important.	Adriani and Kruyt 1950, I:108–114, 164–166
X	Turks	"Turkey is predominantly an agricultural country. . . ."	*MENA* 1967:691
O	Wintun	Hunting and gathering economy.	Washington 1909:94
O	Yagua	"As hunting is the most important institution in the life of the Yagua. . . ."	Fejos 1943:104

IV–C: Social Stratification or Slavery (S)

CODE	SOCIETY	STATEMENT	REFERENCE
X	Amhara	". . . the complex social system, with its ethnic division of labor and the noble-commoner class distinctions." "Though actual slavery has now been abolished its recent existence still affects the pattern of . . . labor."	Messing 1962:403 Perham 1948:217
O	Andamans	No social stratification or slavery.	Man 1932:41
O	Apayao	Wealth brings status, but there are no distinct social classes.	Wilson 1947:15
X	Araucanians	"Sometimes captives . . . kept as drudge slaves. . . ." Some captive slaves, but no real slave class. "Within the Araucanian settlements there was some social stratification based on both kinship status and wealth. . . ."	Padden 1957:112 Cooper 1946:729 Faron 1959:279
X	Austrians	"Austrians mark status differences sharply in titles and forms of address and in manner of personal transportation. . . ."	Naroll 1956b:79
O	Aweikoma	". . . no social stratification."	Henry 1941:29, 30–33
X	Azande	People conquered by Azande often ". . . remained on as slaves and serfs of the new rulers."	Czekanowski 1924:22

CODE	SOCIETY	STATEMENT	REFERENCE
		Three main classes: rulers, ordinary freemen, and slaves and serfs.	Czekanowski 1924:40f.
		Male child born of adultery is considered a slave.	Lagae 1926:176
X	Burmese	Both debt slavery, and hereditary outcaste groups of "pagoda slaves" existed: "Pagoda slaves are still universal at all the greater shrines."	Scott 1882:429, 427–434
		". . . private property of the king . . . cultivated . . . by the outcaste *lamaing,* crown praedial slaves."	Scott 1882:535
X	Callinago	"There was a slave class composed of captive women, but their children were free."	Rouse 1946:556
X	Chagga	"At the court of a chieftain there were many . . . slaves."	Gutmann 1926:51
		"Related to these captured children are the serfs of the Chagga aristocrats. . . ."	Gutmann 1926:203
O	Cheyenne	". . . no class distinctions."	Hoebel 1960:94
X	Chukchee	"The term for a male slave was pu'rel . . . a captive of another tribe. . . ."	Bogoras 1904–1909: 659
		". . . only certain individuals were recognized as of a higher condition. . . ."	Hooper 1853:59–61
O	Copper Eskimo	There is no rank or class stratification among the Copper Eskimos.	Jenness 1922:42
O	Coyotero	No social stratification or slavery.	Goodwin 1942:541
X	Dutch	"There is recognition throughout Drente of a different and 'higher' status for the group of professionals who bear titles—. . . class distinctions within the farm villages were formerly much more rigid and stringent."	Keur and Keur 1955: 148; also, pp. 102, 112, 149–150
X	Egyptians	"The poorer classes lived in tumble-down dwellings. . . ."	Blackman 1927:281
		"The *fellahin* (peasant class) form the bulk of the population. . . ."	Blackman 1927:25
		". . . many Egyptian ladies of the upper classes."	Blackman 1927:36
X	Eyak	"All the slaves . . . are said to have been Eskimo."	Birket-Smith and de Laguna 1938:139
		There were class distinctions between commoners and wealthy.	Birket-Smith and de Laguna 1938:127f.
X	Fur	". . . not large slaveholders . . . do not . . . make slave raids; but they are permitted to capture slaves in war."	Felkin 1885:234
		The regular soldiers ". . . are divided into two classes; the one . . . of well-to-do men, the other of common soldiers."	Felkin 1885:240

CODE	SOCIETY	REFERENCE	STATEMENT
		"The chiefs and rich men . . . usually have one or two eunuchs, who are slaves, to look after their women."	Felkin 1885:233
O	Gilyak (Sakhalin)	"There have never been any (slaves) among these people."	Kreinovich 1934:20
		"There are no privileged classes or families. . . . There are no slaves. . . ."	Seeland 1882:42
X	Gonds	". . . a number of separate castes have naturally developed. . . ."	Russell 1916:62
		"Among the Gonds proper there are two aristocratic subdivisions. . . ."	Russell 1916:63
X	Hottentot	"The Bushman occupies the lowest place . . . slaves. . . ."	Schultze 1907:121
X(?)	Ifaluk	"As individual rank is so largely settled by birth, a man cannot do much to improve his position."	Burrows 1949:201–202
		Part-time craft specialists share "a common status, next to that of the chiefs. . . ."	Burrows 1949:98
		"All of this indicates . . . the absences of social classes based on wealth."	Spiro 1949:44
X	Ila	". . . two classes—free-men and slaves."	Smith and Dale 1920, I:299; also, 283–284
		"Slavery . . . has always been an institution among the Ba-ila. . . ."	Smith and Dale 1920, I:398
X	Iraqi	"The near famine conditions among the poorer classes. . . ."	Longrigg 1953:348
		"Among the upper class women. . . ."	Longrigg 1953:204, 170f.; also, Warriner 1948:106
X	Irish	Social stratification is based mainly on wealth and occupation.	Arensberg 1940:65f., 293
X	Iroquois	War captives are kept as laboring slaves.	Quain 1937:253; Morgan 1901, I:277
X	Italians	". . . the social system . . . was stratified along the three estate lines of professionals and 'nobles,' artisans and merchants, and peasants."	Lopreato 1961:586
X	Kababish	"All camel-owning nomads possess slaves. . . ."	Seligman 1918:107
		"Only Negroes are slaves . . . slaves cannot be made at the present day and any slave who demands it shall be given his freedom."	Seligman 1918:116
X	Kafirs	". . . the lowest class are . . . the slaves."	Robertson 1900:83
O	Kapauku	"There are no castes, slaves, or social classes."	Pospisil 1958a:16
X	Kazaks	A slave was ". . . usually a war captive. Also . . . born into slavery	Kostenko 1880:36

CODE	SOCIETY	STATEMENT	REFERENCE
		of slave parents, or . . . sold into slavery by his own parents. . . ."	
		"Class stratification . . . first by blood related groupings in the sense of an hereditary caste, and second by economic position in the community."	Hudson 1938:55
X	Klallam	"The Klallam are divided into two groups, an upper and a lower class."	Gunther 1927:260
		". . . women and children of the vanquished were brought back . . . as captive slaves."	Stern 1934:7
		"All *siem* (rich men) have slaves."	Stern 1934:74
X	Koreans	"If our boy belongs to the higher class, he will not be expected to work. . . . If he belongs to the middle or lower class, he will be compelled at an early age to take part in the struggle for rice."	Moose 1911:91–93
O(?)	Land Dyaks	". . . egalitarian society . . . no true indications of rank. . . ."	Geddes 1954:86
		"Though slavery is not practiced . . . system of slave-debtors is carried on . . . to a very small extent."	Low 1848:302
O(?)	Luo	Wealth is necessary for high status, but there are no distinct social classes.	Evans-Pritchard 1949: 28; Southall 1952:24
X(?)	Malaita	"The Lau chiefs are chiefs by virtue of their birth. . . ."	Ivens 1930:84
		". . . the name given to a fighting man—a champion, is namo. These men might be either chiefs or commoners. . . ."	Ivens 1930:199
X	Malekula	". . . in the north and northwest . . . something in the nature of class distinctions exist . . . in the south and southwest the social status of a man is entirely dependent upon his ability to purchase membership of a high rank in the two graded societies. . . ."	Deacon 1934:47–48
X	Mangareva	"Nobles and commoners were the two primary divisions of society by birth. . . ."	Buck 1938:142, 144f.
O	Mataco	"The lower Chaco tribes . . . do not know of any distinctions between rich and poor. . . ."	Karsten 1932:94
		". . . slavery, an unknown phenomenon amongst them."	Pelleschi 1896:122
X	Mende	"One of the aims of war . . . has always been to acquire slaves. . . ."	Crosby 1937:252
		". . . slaves were allocated land to cultivate as their own. . . ."	Little 1951:83

CODE	SOCIETY	STATEMENT	REFERENCE
		Social status depended on wealth, hereditary position, and membership in the many secret societies.	Little 1951:80, 140f., 182f., 240f.
X	Mongo	"The female slaves who were taken in war were given by the polygynist to his male slaves as wives."	Kapstein 1922:3; cf. also Hulstaert 1938: 145, 226, 369
		Pygmies form a subservient class in part of Mongo territory.	Hulstaert 1938:3
X	Mosquito	". . . captive women and children were either kept as slaves or they were sold."	Conzemius 1932:83–84
X	Nahua (Aztec)	". . . there developed a social class of people who had . . . become slaves."	Vaillant 1941:118
		". . . property in the form of rights to use land . . . created a social stratification. . . ."	Vaillant 1941:113
O	Ojibwa	"There was . . . no rankings within the tribes."	Kinietz 1947:69
O	Ona	". . . there were no social classes. . . ."	Cooper 1946:116
		". . . no slavery or slave labor."	Cooper 1946:119
O	Orokaiva	Social classes and slaves are absent.	Williams 1930:311–317
O(?)	Papago	There is no evidence of social stratification or slavery.	
O	Semang	There is no social stratification or slavery among the Semang.	Schebesta 1927:279
O	So. Paiute	No social stratification or slavery.	Murdock 1964:200
X	Tallensi	"Slaves were never natives of Taleland but hapless strangers. . . ."	Fortes 1945:25
		"There are no economic classes cutting across and detracting from the solidarity of lineage, clan, and local community. . . ."	Fortes 1940:250–251; also, Fortes 1945:240
X	Thonga	". . . marriages between relatives are sanctioned in the royal families. The chiefs of Mpfumo generally marry into the reigning families of Mabota and Matjolo, and these latter seek their wives at the court of Maputju."	Junod 1927, I:377
X	Tikopia	"Wealth, rank and clan membership are all primarily determined by the *paito* into which he may be born."	Firth 1936:346
		"Formerly there was a barrier on marriage between chiefs and commoners. . . ."	Firth 1936:373
X	Tiv	"A man became a slave either by being captured by Tiv . . . or through sale by his agnates. . . ."	Bohannan and Bohannan 1953:45

CODE	SOCIETY	STATEMENT	REFERENCE
X	Tongans	Highly stratified society. ". . . the Tongans recognize three general classes. . . ."	Mariner 1820:180f. Gifford 1929:128
X	Toradja	Young women and children war captives were used as slaves.	Adriani and Kruyt 1950, I:236f.
X	Turks	"The obvious careers for the upper class are the civil service."	*RIIA* 1954:520
X(?)	Wintun	"Wealth and chieftainship were correlated. . . ." Chiefship was hereditary.	DuBois 1934:31–32
O	Yagua	"There are no social strata. . . ."	Steward 1963:727; also, Fejos 1943:84

IV–D: Full-time Government Specialists (G)

CODE	SOCIETY	STATEMENT	REFERENCE
X	Amhara	". . . the Emperor . . . was always recognized in theory as absolute . . . and the disposer of all lands and offices." ". . . the former feudal structure . . . is retained in the old Amhara provinces, despite the official break-up of the system at the top levels."	Perham 1948:267 Messing 1957:83; also, 75f., 281f.
O	Andamans	No full-time government specialists present.	Radcliffe-Brown 1922: 45–46
O	Apayao	Village headmen were not full-time government officials.	Wilson 1947:12
O	Araucanians	No full-time leaders except in wartime. The titular head of the tribe is "the descendant of the founder. . . . No tribute is paid him. . . ."	Cooper 1946:724, 726; also Latcham 1909:355
X	Austrians	Full-time government officials present.	*SYB* 1957:806
O	Aweikoma	No political leaders of any sort.	Henry 1941:xii, 36
X	Azande	The paramount chief and other important chiefs and officials were full-time government specialists.	Seligman and Seligman 1932:506; Graffen 1906:784f.; Lagae 1926:18–19, 25; Czekanowski 1924:38, 50
X	Burmese	"King Mindon abolished the tithe system as far as the payment of local officials was concerned, and arranged to give them fixed salaries. . . ." "The central government consists of the king . . . and the council of ministers. . . ."	Scott 1882:523; 431–432, 490f., 509f. Fielding-Hall 1917:81; 82f.; also, Hall 1950: 131f.
O	Callinago	"Outside of war, the chiefs have no authority over the others."	Breton and La Paix 1929:21
X	Chagga	Chagga chiefs were full-time specialists—they exacted compulsory labor,	Gutmann 1926:337, 342, 486

CODE	SOCIETY	STATEMENT	REFERENCE
		tax tribute and one-half of all war booty from their subjects.	
O	Cheyenne	"It brings respect and honor, but nothing else. There are no economic advantages; quite to the contrary, being a chief means having a drain on one's resources."	Hoebel 1960:46
O	Chukchee	There were no full-time political authorities in the indigenous Chukchee social organization.	Bogoras 1904–1909: 542–543, 612; Nordenskiold 1882:492
O	Copper Eskimo	"Established authority among the Copper Eskimos is unknown."	Jenness 1917:86; also, Jenness 1922:94–96
O	Coyotero	Coyotero "chiefs" and "subchiefs" were informal leaders, not full-time specialists.	Goodwin 1942:132f., 164–168
X	Dutch	Full-time government officials present.	*SYB* 1959:1244–46
X	Egyptians	Full-time government officials present.	*SYB* 1955:938–940; *MENA* 1967:755f.
O	Eyak	The hereditary moiety heads were "chiefs." They do not seem to have been full-time specialists.	Birket-Smith and de Laguna 1938:127– 130
		". . . the chief . . . hunted. . . ."	Birket-Smith and de Laguna 1938:128
X	Fur	"The Furs have had a long hereditary line of despotic sultans. . . . The Arab tribes . . . [are] compelled to pay them taxes. . . ."	Felkin 1885:244–245
O	Gilyak	". . . there appeared to be no traditions of a great chief or king. Each village has its council of elders to whom the injured apply."	Hawes 1903:209
		The informal council of local family heads (elders) was the widest authority recognized by the Gilyak; there were no full-time political officials.	Seeland 1882:37–38; Hawes 1903:209f.
O	Gond	"The tribes have *panchayats* or committees for the settlement of tribal disputes or offences . . . generally there does not seem to be a recognized head of the *panchayat.*"	Russell 1916:132–134; also, Grigson 1949: 284f.
O	Hottentots	No full-time specialists—the political leaders were the elders of the various clans.	Schapera 1930:225– 228
		"The chief of the tribe was little more than *primus inter pares.* . . . The whole conduct of affairs in the tribe was—and still is—the concern of the older men."	Schapera 1930:227
O	Ifaluk	"The bonds that unite it [the group of chiefs] are common rank, a common	Burrows 1949:85, 130f.; also, Spiro 1949:

CODE	SOCIETY	STATEMENT	REFERENCE
		part-time occupation . . . that of governing. . . ."	15–18
X	Ila	Community chiefs seem to be full-time officials.	Smith and Dale 1920, I:305–308, 350f., 385
X	Iraqi	Full-time government officials present.	*SYB* 1936:1046; *MENA* 1967:286
X	Irish	Full-time government officials present.	*SYB* 1959:1137–39
X	Iroquois	Sachems were full-time specialists.	Morgan 1901, I:68–70
X	Italians	Full-time government officials are present.	*SYB* 1964:1161–63, 1167
O(?)	Kababish	The leaders of the tribal groupings and clans (sheykhs) were not full-time specialists.	Seligman and Seligman 1918:114f.
X	Kafirs	"The affairs of a tribe . . . are managed by the *Jast* nominally, but actually by a small group of grey-beards, who at ordinary times rule in a more or less absolute way."	Robertson 1900:434, also, 433–437
O	Kapauku	Political leadership is completely informal and is based on having previously acquired wealth.	Pospisil 1958a:15, 95; 77f. Van Logchem *ca.* 1958:35–38
X	Kazaks	The Khans were full-time government specialists; they were supported by tribute and taxes.	Hudson 1938:63–64
O	Klallam	No full-time government specialists.	Stern 1934:7; Gunther 1927:261–263
X	Koreans	Full-time government officials present.	*SYB* 1964:1191; Kennan 1905:310
O	Land Dyaks	The village headmen are not full-time government specialists.	Geddes 1954:48–51
X	Luo	Village chiefs are full-time governing specialists who are supported economically by their followers.	Roscoe 1915:277; Hobley 1898:34
O	Malaita	"The chiefs are the wealthy members of the community. . . . There is no paying of tribute to chiefs in Lao and Tolo. . . . The Lao chiefs work hard and are never idle. . . ."	Ivens 1930:86–87; also, Hogbin 1958:157–159
		"Every leader had his following of relatives and other individuals."	Hogbin 1937:364
O	Malekula	There are no political specialists; wealthy men have the leading role in community affairs.	
		". . . such high rank carries with it considerable influence, but probably nothing which could be truly regarded as authoritative powers."	Deacon 1934:47–48
O(?)	Mangareva	Buck mentions "chiefs" but there is	Buck 1938:142–157

CODE	SOCIETY	STATEMENT	REFERENCE
		no indication that they were full-time specialists, as defined.	
O	Mataco	"There is no use looking for chiefs or captains with any authority, for among them there are neither those who give orders or any who obey them. . . ."	Pelleschi 1876:47
X	Mende	"the [Paramount] Chief . . . acted as the principal adjudicator in the case of complaints and disputes. . . . the fees and fines gained in the hearing of court cases . . ." (were an important source of his income).	Little 1951:182
		"Districts added to the chiefdom by conquest . . . were expected to pay tribute to him" [the Paramount Chief].	McCulloch 1950:18
O	Mongo	". . . chiefs were totally unknown in native society."	Boelaert 1940:7; also, Hulstaert 1938:11f.; Brown 1944:432
X	Mosquito	"Hereditary chiefs did not rule the Mosquito Coast until after the establishment of British influence."	Conzemius 1932:101; also, Kirchoff 1948: 224
		"On June 25, 1720, a convention was signed between . . . Governor of Jamaica, and . . . 'King' of the Mosquito. . . ."	Conzemius 1932:87
		NOTE: Full-time governmental specialists were present as of *ca.* 1725.	
X	Nahua (Aztec)	(A portion of the harvest) . . . was paid as tribute-tax to the central tribal council for the maintenance of . . . the 'king' and his various non-taxpaying staff. . . ."	Von Hagen 1961:87
O	Ojibwa	Band chiefs were not full-time specialists.	Jenness 1935:102f.; Hilger 1939:12; Kinietz 1947:69
		"There were no real chiefs among the Chippewa, and political authority . . . was almost nonexistent. . . ."	Barnouw 1950:34
O	Ona	No political leaders with authority beyond their own family group.	Cooper 1946:116–117
O	Orokaiva	". . . there is no such thing as a central authority to enforce the law. . . ."	Williams 1930:325
O	Papago	Hereditary officials were part-time specialists.	Underhill 1946:5; Underhill 1939:76
O	Semang	". . . the individual camps have no recognized rulers."	Schebesta 1927:279; also, Skeats and Blagden 1906, I:494
O	So. Paiute	". . . neither sub-chief nor great chief has any salary."	Lowie 1924:283; 284–285

CODE	SOCIETY	STATEMENT	REFERENCE
X	Tallensi	"Chiefs . . . have no over-riding rights of ownership entitling them to rent, tax or tribute for land. They have, indeed, no more land than they have acquired in the same way as any other elder." However, Tallensi chiefs do not engage in any subsistence activities.	Fortes 1940:250; also, 255–261
X	Thonga	Thonga chiefs were full-time specialists supported by levies on their subjects.	Junod 1927, I:280f., 380, 405f.
X	Tikopia	Chiefs were full-time specialists.	Rivers 1914:145
O	Tiv	"In the indigenous Tiv system nothing resembling an [political] office existed. . . ." "There is no tribute labor among Tiv."	Bohannan and Bohannan 1953:33 Bohannan 1957:56A
X	Tongans	The hereditary Tongan chiefs were full-time rulers supported economically by their subjects.	Mariner 1820:158–159
O	Toradja	Village "chiefs" were family headmen; certain "princes" among the eastern Toradja tribes received tribute but did not govern.	Adriani and Kruyt 1950, I:110–122
X	Turks	Full-time government officials present.	*RIIA* 1954:511–520; *MENA* 1967:701–703
O	Wintun	"The chief possessed little but nominal authority. . . ." The "chief" was not a full-time specialist.	Washington 1909:94–95 DuBois 1934:31–32
O	Yagua	Clan chiefs are not full-time specialists; there are no other political authorities.	Fejos 1943:83

IV–E: Full-time Religious Specialists

CODE	SOCIETY	STATEMENT	REFERENCE
X	Amhara	Full-time Coptic priests are present; they are supported by revenue from Church lands.	Messing 1962:389–390; Messing 1957:249–250, 291; Rey 1924:176–177
O	Andamans	Medicine men are not full-time religious specialists.	Radcliffe-Brown 1922: 222, 623
O(?)	Apayao	Shamen are women—that is no indication that they are full-time specialists, or that they support themselves through their religious activities.	Vanoverbergh 1936: 131–133; Wilson 1947: 24, 27
O	Araucanians	Shamen were not full-time specialists.	Faron 1959:270
X	Austrians	"Normally the priest [of a Tyrolean parish] has two full-time subordinates. . . ."	Naroll and Naroll 1962:20
O	Aweikoma	No religious specialists.	Henry 1941:xii

CODE	SOCIETY	REFERENCE STATEMENT	
X	Azande	"(Doubtful cases) . . . are decided by oracle tests, carried out under the orders of the chief by his special diviners."	Seligman and Seligman 1932:504; also, Lagae 1926:23–24; Evans-Pritchard 1937:75; 1965:347–348
		"The witch doctor is a professional specialist. . . ."	Baxter and Butt 1953: 84
X	Burmese	"Every village had its pagoda and at least one resident monk . . ." (supported by the villagers).	Hall 1950:137; cf. also, Scott 1882:124, 127f.; Fielding-Hall 1917:87
O	Callinago	Shamen were not full-time specialists.	Rouse 1948:562–563
		"There were . . . no household idols or priests. . . ."	Rouse 1948:563
O(?)	Chagga	Chagga diviners and sorcerers do not appear to be full-time specialists.	Raum 1940:114–121, 368; Gutmann 1926: 611
O	Cheyenne	The religious leaders of the tribe are chosen from among the forty-four peace chiefs—"There are no economic advantages . . . [in] being a chief."	Hoebel 1960:44–45, 46
O(?)	Chukchee	Shamen do not seem to be full-time specialists.	Bogoras 1904–1909: 484–507
O	Copper Eskimo	The shaman is a part-time specialist, who also hunts for a living.	Rasmussen 1932:51
O	Coyotero	There were no full-time religious specialists.	Gifford 1941:71–75
X	Dutch	Full-time religious leaders present.	Keur and Keur 1955: 150
X	Egyptians	Full-time Muslim religious leaders are present.	Blackman 1927:25, 95, 109–110; *MENA* 1967: 763
		Full-time magicians also present.	Blackman 1927:184, 201
O	Eyak	Shamen were not full-time specialists—they trapped and hunted like other Eyaks.	Birket-Smith and de Laguna 1938:208–229
X	Fur	The puggees—religious leaders and judges—are full-time specialists.	Felkin 1885:223, 245
O(?)	Gilyak	There is no evidence that shamen are full-time practitioners, or that they receive remuneration for their activities from the community.	Cf. Bush 1871:101f.; Seeland 1882:42f.
X	Gond	"Pardhans or priests and minstrels. . . ." form a separate caste.	Russell 1916:62; also, Grigson 1949:196–197, 199–200
O(?)	Hottentots	Diviners and curers do not seem to have been full-time specialists.	Schapera 130:389–395
O(?)	Ifaluk	No full-time religious specialists.	Burrows 1949:197

CODE	SOCIETY	STATEMENT	REFERENCE
O(?)	Ila	"The profession (of diviner) is handed down from older men to younger on payment of fees."	Smith and Dale 1920, I:266
		". . . the services of the diviner are called in. The first thing invariably to be done is to pay a fee—large or small according to the ability of the applicant. . . ."	Smith and Dale 1920, I:266
		"Doctors (magical practitioners) do not practice for nothing. The fee is termed. . . ."	Smith and Dale 1920, I:275; also II:187–189
X	Iraqi	Full-time religious specialists are present.	*MENA* 1967:289–290
X	Irish	Full-time Catholic priests are present.	Arensberg 1940:136–137
X(?)	Iroquois	". . . there was a select class appointed by the several tribes to take charge of their religious festivals and the general supervision of their worship."	Morgan 1901, I:177
X	Italians	Full-time Catholic bishops and priests present.	*SYB* 1964:1166
O	Kababish	No full-time religious specialists.	Seligman 1918:112, 118f.
X(?)	Kafirs	Full-time hereditary priests are present: ". . . the priest takes two shares of every animal sacrificed, and has other perquisites."	Robertson 1900:138, 334–335, 415f.
O	Kapauku	Part-time specialists only. Shamen and sorcerers are paid for their services, but do not depend upon this income: "All the shamans the writer saw were . . . usually rich and successful in their economic and political pursuits."	Pospisil 1958a:24; 25–30
O	Kazaks	They are nominally Muslims despite ". . . complete absence of a Muslim ecclesiastical hierarchy. . . ."	Kostenko 1880:36
O(?)	Klallam	No full-time religious specialists.	Stern 1934:8
X	Koreans	Full-time religious monks are present. "Skill in the cult (Confucianism) practically guaranteed a good livelihood. . . ."	Clark n.d.:49 Clark n.d.:107
O	Land Dyaks	Indigenous "spirit-mediums" are not full-time religious specialists.	Geddes 1954:32
O	Luo	Religious and magic practitioners are not full-time specialists.	Hobley 1898:32; Northcote 1907:63
O	Malaita	"The only experts were the priests, magicians, and certain craftsmen . . . and even these practiced their specialty solely as a spare-time occupa-	Hogbin 1958:154–155

CODE	SOCIETY	STATEMENT	REFERENCE
		tion. Thus the community priest and woodcarvers spent most of their days gardening, fishing, or hunting like everyone else."	
X(?)	Malekula	Private magicians seem to be full-time specialists: ". . . wealth also enables them to purchase the services of highly skilled magicians. . . ."	Deacon 1934:49
		". . . a sorcerer must not cohabit with any woman; he must not even approach a woman. . . . The sorcerer marks himself off from the rest of the community—removes himself from the 'secular' or 'profane' world. . . ."	Deacon 1934:685–686
O	Mangareva	Religious experts were not full-time specialists.	Buck 1938:148f.
O	Mataco	Shamen and "witch doctors" are not full-time specialists.	Pelleschi 1896:10, 110
X	Mende	"Broadly speaking, a medicine man is simply a professional worker of (supernatural) medicine. . . ."	Little 1951:229f.
		". . . among the specialists in supernatural power come the officials and senior graduates of the secret societies, like . . . Sande. . . . Senior Sande women rely for a substantial part of their personal income on the perquisites gained from initiates and from fees and fines rendered by other individuals requiring the offices of the society."	Little 1951:128, 228
O(?)	Mongo	No evidence of full-time religious specialists.	
O(?)	Mosquito	Hereditary "priest-doctors" were not full-time specialists.	Conzemius 1932:140f.
X	Nahua (Aztec)	Full-time religious priests present.	Vaillant 1941:111; Sahagun 1938:52; von Hagen 1961:82
O	Ojibwa	Shamen and medicine men were not full-time specialists.	Landes 1937b:112; Barnouw 1950
O	Ona	Shamen are present, but they are not full-time religious specialists.	Cooper 1946:121
O	Orokaiva	The "taro men" (cult leaders) are not full-time specialists.	Williams 1928:56–66
		"The question of payment for the semi-professional services of the Taro doctor is not an easy one."	Williams 1928:61
X(?)	Papago	Papago ceremonial officials—"Keepers"—seem to be full-time specialists.	Underhill 1939:73–76; 1946:6, 167–168, 278
O	Semang	No religious specialists—shamen were part-time practitioners.	Evans 1923:158–160

CODE	SOCIETY	STATEMENT	REFERENCE
O(?)	So. Paiute	No evidence of religious specialists.	
X(?)	Tallensi	Diviners are only part-time specialists. The earth cult priests (*tendaanas*) do seem to be full-time specialists; they are not paid directly for their services, but they do not seem to engage in any other subsistence-producing activities.	Fortes 1945:10 Fortes 1940:250, 255–267
X	Thonga	"These diviners work for a fee. . . ." The chief is the priest of the national gods.	Goldman 1961:373 Goldman 1961:368; Junod 1927, II:403–404, 412
O	Tikopia	There are no full-time specialists among the "magicians."	Firth 1954:100
O	Tiv	". . . there is no priesthood. . . ." Religious activities are performed or led by lineage elders, not full-time specialists.	Bohannan and Bohannan 1953:93 Bohannan and Bohannan 1953:84–93
X	Tongans	Full-time religious leaders are present.	Mariner 1820:318–322
O	Toradja	Religious practitioners—magicians, diviners and "medicine men"—are only part-time specialists.	Adriani and Kruyt 1950, I:240, 246, 259, 284; III:113–115, 117, 119
X	Turks	Full-time religious specialists (Christian and Muslim) are present.	*RIIA* 1954:510–511; *MENA* 1967:706
O(?)	Wintun	Shamen do not seem to have been full-time specialists.	DuBois 934:112f.
O	Yagua	Shamen are not full-time specialists.	Fejos 1943:83
		IV–F: Full-time Craft Specialists (C)	
X	Amhara	Saddle makers are full-time specialists: ". . . some are so proficient that they do nothing else as long as the demand lasts." Weavers are also full-time specialists.	Messing 1962:392; also, Messing 1957: 168–171 Messing 1962:393
O	Andamans	There are no craft specialists.	Man 1932:154, 180
O	Apayao	"Perhaps the only kind of work that is performed among the Isneg by special craftsmen, and not by everyone indifferently, is that of the blacksmith. . . . And occupations are not monopolized by a few individuals . . . but are professed by the whole settlement or at least by several families. . . ."	Vanoverbergh 1936: 130
X(?)	Araucanians	". . . one gathers that Araucanian craftsmen formerly manufactured many objects. . . . At present a specialist here and there continues one or another of the traditional crafts. . . ."	Titiev 1951:32–33; also, Faron 1959:276–277

CODE	SOCIETY	STATEMENT	REFERENCE
X	Austrians	Full-time craft specialists present.	Naroll and Naroll 1962:11–12; Naroll 1956b:51–52
O	Aweikoma	No craft specialists.	Henry 1941:15–16
O(?)	Azande	Craftsmen do not seem to have been full-time specialists.	Evans-Pritchard 1937: 17, 48; Baxter and Butt 1953:19, 46
X	Burmese	"Professional artisans such as carpenters, blacksmiths, gold and silver smiths occupy a lower position."	Orr 1951:24; also, Scott 1882:427f.; Ferrars and Ferrars 1901:96f.
O	Callinago	There were no specialist craftsmen.	Rouse 1948:555; Taylor 1946:192
X(?)	Chagga	Chagga smiths seem to be full-time specialists: "The Malisa sib. . . . Although they are smiths, and therefore held a position as serfs under the Masai. . . ."	Gutmann 1926:27; also, Raum 1940:188
O	Cheyenne	No full-time craft specialists.	Hoebel 1960:60f.
O	Chukchee	All specialists were part-time activities.	Bogoras 1904–1909: 215
O	Copper Eskimo	There are no full-time craft specialists; old and lame men work at various crafts but are dependent upon able-bodied hunters of the group.	Rasmussen 1932:51; Stefansson 1914:102f.
O	Coyotero	The only division of labor is by sex; there were no full-time specialists.	Goodwin 1942:332–333
X	Dutch	Full-time craft specialists present.	Keur and Keur 1955: 54f.
X	Egyptians	Shoemakers, blacksmiths, etc. are full-time craft specialists.	Ammar 1954:19–21; also, Blackman 1927: 167, 282
O	Eyak	No full-time craft specialists are found.	Birket-Smith and de Laguna 1938:74–87
X	Fur	"The blacksmiths are the only class of special workers who do nothing but follow their own trade."	Felkin 1885:249
O	Gilyak	"Those who are too aged to hunt are supported by the exertions of the younger generation. . . ." "... every Gilyak man and woman knows how to do all the work necessary for their existence. . . ."	Hawes 1903:258–259 Seeland 1882:27
X	Gond	Blacksmiths, potters and brass workers have become separate castes.	Grigson 1949:50, 175f.; also, Russell 1916:62
O	Hottentots	"... no fixed division of labour, save as between the two sexes." "... craftsmen devoting themselves exclusively to the continuous manufacture of special objects for barter do not exist among the Hottentots."	Schapera 1930:316 Schapera 1930:317

CODE	SOCIETY	STATEMENT	REFERENCE
O	Ifaluk	Craft specialties are part-time occupations.	Burrows 1949:85
X	Ila	Professionals in ivory-turning, iron-smelting and smithery.	Smith and Dale 1920, I:180
X	Iraqi	There are ". . . nearly 50,000 [manufacturing and handicraft workers] . . . in the four largest cities alone."	IBRD 1952:129; also, Harrison 1924:116
X	Irish	Full-time craft specialists present.	Arensberg 1940:239–245
X	Iroquois	Full-time craftsmen present.	Noon 1949:84; Morgan 1901, 2:50
X	Italians	Many full-time craft specialists are found.	STTR 1960–1961; also, Lopreato 1961:586f.
O	Kababish	Certain crafts are practiced, but there are no full-time specialists.	Seligman 1918:173–179
X	Kafirs	"All the craftsmen of the Kafirs, carpenters, dagger makers, iron workers, and weavers, are slaves. . . ."	Robertson 1900:99; also, 543–546
X	Kapauku	Full-time netmakers, bowmakers and counterfeit cowry-shell makers are present.	Pospisil 1958a:121, 127
X	Kazaks	Carpenters and blacksmiths are full-time specialists.	Hudson 1938:70, 77
O	Klallam	No full-time craftsmen.	Gunther 1927:214, 219–224
X	Koreans	Many kinds of full-time craftsmen.	Osgood 1951:57–58; Hulbert 1902:275
O	Land Dyaks	". . . practically no occupations are confined to one sex or to any single age group."	Geddes 1954:81
O(?)	Luo	Craftsmen were not full-time specialists.	Hobley 1902:27f.
O	Malaita	"The only experts . . . such as the wood-carvers and the supervisors in house building and canoe construction . . . practiced their specialty solely as a spare-time occupation."	Hogbin 1958:154–155
O	Malekula	". . . there is little or no specialization of occupation. . . ."	Deacon 1934:202
X	Mangareva	"Craftsmen and artists were paid for their services in food, cloth and other material property."	Buck 1938:166
		"If individual members (of the artisan class) acquired a comfortable revenue from the exercise of their trade or profession, they merged into the *pakaora* middle class. . . ."	Buck 1938:150
O	Mataco	". . . nor were there any craftsmen who made their whole living by specialized trades. . . ."	Cooper 1946:119

CODE	SOCIETY	STATEMENT	REFERENCE
X	Mende	"With the exception of . . . a few specialized occupations, such as blacksmithing, goldsmithing, etc., most Mende men, from the chief downwards, either have their own farm. . . ."	Little 1951:79; also, 121, 284, 290
O	Mongo	"There are no laborers and . . . no artisans."	Gutersohn 1920:2
		"The people make their own tools. . . ."	Brown 1944:431
		Craft specialties were only spare-time activities.	Gutersohn 1920:9; Maes 1924:81; Hulstaert 1938:11
O	Mosquito	There were no full-time craft specialists—specialties were part-time activities of either men or women, depending on the craft.	Conzemius 1932:39, 47, 50–55
X	Nahua (Aztec)	Full-time craftsmen present; paid out of the national treasury.	Vaillant 1941:117; von Hagen 1961:87, 152–158
O	Ojibwa	Ojibwa craftsmen were not full-time specialists.	Landes 1938:125–126
O	Ona	No full-time specialist craftsmen.	Cooper 1946:119
O	Orokaiva	No full-time craft specialties: "The only labour division of any great interest is the habitual one between the sexes."	Williams 1930:76
O	Papago	". . . there are no full-time specialists of any kind among unassimilated Papagoes. . . ."	Fontana 1962:21
O	Semang	There are no full-time craft specialists.	Evans 1937:60; Schebesta 1927:56
O	So. Paiute	There were no full-time craft specialists.	Lowie 1924:225–226, 237f.; also, Steward 1942:299
O	Tallensi	"Craft specialists work at their crafts only in their spare time . . . when there is no farm work."	Fortes 1945:9–10; also, Fortes 1940:248
O	Thonga	Craftsmen were not full-time specialists.	Junod 1927, II:125–137
O	Tikopia	"Differentiation of function is merely temporary. . . ."	Firth 1939:112
O	Tiv	Craftsmen are only part-time specialists.	Bohannan 1959:491f.
X	Tongans	Certain specialists worked full-time at their crafts.	Mariner 1820:318–322
O	Toradja	Craft specialties are part-time activities.	Adriani and Kruyt 1950, III:301, 309–311, 316–317, 330, 334–335
X	Turks	Full-time craft specialists present.	Fisher 1950:334
O	Wintun	Craft specialties were not full-time occupations.	DuBois 1934:22–24

CODE	SOCIETY	STATEMENT	REFERENCE
O	Yagua	No one works full-time at any special craft.	Fejos 1943:113–117; Stewart 1963:727
X	Amhara	*IV–G: Political State of 10,000 (P)* "For many centuries Abyssinia was a confederation of states governed by princes, who recognized the superiority of one of them—the 'king of kings.' . . ."	Messing 1957:238
		"The Amhara number about two million . . . and have in the past formed the ruling class."	*MENA* 1967:193
O	Andamans	The local group was the war-making unit, and the largest political entity.	Radcliffe-Brown 1922: 28, 85
O	Apayao	The village is the largest political unit.	Wilson 1947:12
O	Araucanians	"Each settlement [up to about 360 individuals] was politically autonomous."	Faron 1959:268f.; also, Titiev 1951:53
X	Austrians	Independent republic of several millions.	*SYB* 1957:806
O	Aweikoma	There was no social unit beyond the extended family.	Henry 1941:36
X	Azande	"The Azande are governed by chiefs or sultans . . . they can unite at one time no more than 20,000 warriors."	Graffen 1906:786
X	Burmese	Large independent kingdom before British occupation in nineteenth century; population in 1891 was over six million.	Fielding-Hall 1917: 81–84; Ferrars and Ferrars 1901:212
O	Callinago	"Except in war times, each Carib village seems to have been an independent organization."	Rouse 1948:555
X	Chagga	"The Chagga country is now divided up into twenty-eight small states, the population of which varies from one to 20,000 inhabitants; in three it exceeds 10,000. . . ."	Dundas 1924:50
O	Cheyenne	The total population of the Cheyenne in 1800 was about 2,000.	Grinnell 1923, I:20f.; Grinnell 1918:365–366
O	Chukchee	No organization beyond the local camp.	Bogoras 1904–1909: 542–543
O	Copper Eskimo	"Established authority among the Copper Eskimos is unknown. . . ."	Jenness 1917:46
		The population in 1914 was between 700 and 800.	Jenness 1922:174
O	Coyotero	The total population of the Western Apache in 1890 was about 1,400.	Goodwin 1942:582–585
X	Dutch	"The Netherlands is a constitutional and hereditary monarchy."	*SYB* 1964:1254
		Population (1962): 11,889,962	*SYB* 1964:1256

CODE	SOCIETY	STATEMENT	REFERENCE
X	Egyptians	Egypt is an independent state. ". . . the population—numbering around 30 million in mid-1965. . . ."	*MENA* 1967:754 *MENA* 1967:742
O	Eyak	One of the nineteenth-century estimates of the Eyak population is more than a few hundred.	Birket-Smith and de Laguna 1938:24
X	Fur	". . . one of the three great Negro Mohammedan kingdoms. . . . The whole population of Dafur may be roughly estimated at from 3 to 5 millions, about half that number being Fors. . . ."	Felkin 1885:206
O	Gilyak	"Among these tribes there appeared to be no traditions of a great chief or king." Each village and clan is politically autonomous. ". . . on the island [Sakhalin] . . . more than 2,000 Gilyaks. . . ."	Hawes 1903:209f. Hawes 1903:116
O	Gond	". . . the clans . . . are . . . practically political units. . . ." The Gonds were divided into a large number of independent clans; they had no centralized political state during the nineteenth century.	Grigson 1949:236 Grigson 1949:235–238, 240–243, 284–297
O	Hottentots	". . . the tribes have for a long time been independent of one another. . . . The tribes do not seem to have been at all large. The number of people in each ranged apparently from several hundreds to a couple of thousand."	Schapera 1930:225
O	Ifaluk	"The 252 natives on Ifaluk live on two islands. . . ."	Spiro 1949:5
O	Ila	Local "communities" were independent political units—"They vary in size and population, the largest being Kasenga with about 3000 people."	Smith and Dale 1920, I:299
X	Iraqi	"The Iraqi Republic is a democratic socialist state, fully sovereign." ". . . her present (population of) six and a half million."	*MENA* 1967:286 *MENA* 1967:276
X	Irish	"The Irish Republic is a sovereign independent, democratic state. . . . The population . . . 2,898,264 in 1956."	*SYB* 1964:1137, 1140
X	Iroquois	Political confederacy of more than 10,000 people.	Morgan 1901, I:58–59, 226–230
X	Italians	"On 10 June 1946 Italy became a republic. . . ." Population (1961): 50,463,762.	*SYB* 1964:1161 *SYB* 1964:1164

CODE	SOCIETY	STATEMENT	REFERENCE
O	Kababish	Kababish tribes numbered less than 10,000 individuals.	Seligman 1918:114f.; MacMichael 1912: 186f.
O(?)	Kafirs	The Kafir tribes are independent war-making units; none seem to include more than 10,000 people.	Robertson 1900:85–86, 561f.
O	Kapauku	"Several villages are united into a political confederacy which represents the largest unit in the political organization."	Pospisil 1958a:15
		"The five main villages of the confederacy boast a total population of four hundred and seventy-six individuals. . . ."	Pospisil 1958a:67
X(?)	Kazaks	"The Khanates . . . were not, except for brief periods under an exceptional ruler, strong centralized states . . . (the usual situation was) . . . tribal confederacy and feudal union. . . ."	Hudson 1938:63
X	Koreans	South Korea was declared a self-governing republic on July 20, 1948.	*SYB* 1964:1191
		"A census in Dec. 1960 showed a population of 24,994,117." (So. Korea)	*SYB* 1964:1191
O	Land Dyaks	". . . the Land Dyak villages are economically, politically, and in religious practices, separate from one another. There are no social groupings wider than the village complex."	Geddes 1954:12
O	Luo	States of 10,000 are absent.	Butt 1952:110; Evans-Pritchard 1949: 28
O	Malaita	"The widest community with a coherent system for the maintenance of internal order rarely exceeded three hundred members and was often much smaller."	Hogbin 1958:152
		"There were no paramount chiefs . . . no council of elders in the various places, who could be entrusted with the establishment of law and authority. . . ."	Ivens 1930:86
O	Malekula	Each clan was an independent war-making unit: "Between different clans within a single district hostilities not infrequently did arise. . . ."	Deacon 1934:212; 45–49
O	Mangareva	Estimates of the total population of Mangareva range from 1,275 to 8,000.	Buck 1938:11
		"Anua-Motua was the first chief to have extended power over the Mangareva Island. . . ."	Buck 1938:143: 157f.

CODE	SOCIETY	STATEMENT	REFERENCE
O	Mataco	There is no political integration beyond the local group.	Pelleschi 1896:47
X	Mende	"Luawa is the largest chiefdom in the Protectorate with a population estimated at over 26,000 (1941)."	Little 1951:63; 65–66
O	Mongo	There was no political authority above the head of the extended family.	Hulstaert 1938:11
O	Mosquito	"In 1725 the Moskito numbered about 2,000 men altogether and were ruled by three chiefs (Lade)."	Conzemius 1932:13
X	Nahua (Aztec)	Large theocratic empire. The population of the Valley of Mexico at the time of the Spanish conquest was about 2 million.	Vaillant 1941:240 Cook and Simpson 1948:27–28
O	Ojibwa	"The political unit among the Chippewa was the band. A band comprised from five to fifty or more families. . . ."	Hilger 1951:150
		"The tribe as a whole had no organization at all."	Kinietz 1947:69
		Each band was politically independent.	Jenness 1935:102f.
O	Ona	No political organization beyond the extended family.	Cooper 1946:116
O	Orokaiva	Political integration did not extend beyond the local clan group.	Williams 1930:101–104, 156
O	Papago	Village was the largest functioning political unit.	Underhill 1946:5
		". . . there was no tribal government as such."	Joseph et al. 1949:104
O	Semang	No organization beyond the local group.	Schebesta 1927:279
O	So. Paiute	The sovereign body is the localized band—(composed of less than 100 individuals).	Stewart 1942:299
O	Tallensi	"They had, in short, no 'tribal' government or 'tribal' citizenship, no centralized state. . . ."	Fortes 1940:241
		"Small fights were more frequent, both between Tale clans and between Tale and neighboring non-Tale clans."	Fortes 1940:241
		NOTE: The 10,000 "real Talis" were divided among twenty-five clans.	Fortes 1940:244
O	Thonga	". . . the true national unit is the clan."	Junod 1927, I:356
		". . . the typical Bantu clan, that small community of some hundreds or thousands of souls, with its hereditary chief. . . ."	Junod 1927, I:367
		". . . normal political state of the	Junod 1927, I:359

CODE	SOCIETY	STATEMENT	REFERENCE
		Bantus; small tribes of some thousand persons with a tendency to break up when they become too numerous. . . ."	
O	Tikopia	The total population of Tikopia is about 1,300.	Firth 1939:39
O	Tiv	Segmentary lineage system: there was not ". . . any position of leadership attached to any absolute lineage span. The only Tiv group of which one could say 'there must be someone responsible' was the compound. . . ."	Bohannan and Bohannan 1953:35, 19–26, 30–35
X	Tongans	The island of Tonga is a single political kingdom; the population was estimated to be 18,500.	Mariner 1820:318; *BRT* 1956:7
O	Toradja	Villages were independent political units.	Adriani and Kruyt 1950, I:110–122, 126
X	Turks	"The republic was founded in 1923. . . . The population in 1960 . . . 27,809,831."	*MENA* 1967:691
O	Wintun	"Each village was politically independent of every other village. . . ."	McKern 1922:242
O	Yagua	No political organization beyond the local clan (extended family group). ". . . the tribe as a whole numbers at present possibly one thousand individuals."	Fejos 1943:83; 733

Fejos 1943:15–16 |

IV–H: Monetary Exchange System (M)

CODE	SOCIETY	STATEMENT	REFERENCE
X	Amhara	"Money is used as both medium of exchange and standard of value."	Messing 1962:387; 406–407
O	Andamans	Money is absent.	Radcliffe-Brown 1922: 83–84
O(?)	Apayao	There does not seem to be any symbolic medium of exchange in the indigenous system.	Vanoverbergh 1936: 156f.
O	Araucanians	Certain commodities had traditionally set equivalences ". . . but a more specific currency was absent."	Cooper 1946:728
X	Austrians	"The Austrian unit of currency is the *schilling* of 100 *groschen*."	*SYB* 1964:809
O	Aweikoma	Money was unknown.	Henry 1941:101
O	Azande	"Money has been introduced relatively recently . . . only since the 1920's has coinage become widely used."	Reining 1962:550
X	Burmese	Taxes were paid in both money and kind. "In 1798 a call of thirty-three rupees was made from every house in the country."	Scott 1882:524–528

Scott 1882:526 |

CODE	SOCIETY	STATEMENT	REFERENCE
O(?)	Callinago	No evidence of the use of money.	Breton and La Paix 1929:21; Du Tertre 1667:20
O	Chagga	"Under the old Chagga economy one piece of value was exchanged for another . . . when suddenly confronted with money, the natives were unable to grasp its value. . . ."	Gutmann 1926:422
O	Cheyenne	All transactions were by barter or gift exchange.	Grinnell 1923, I:35f.
O	Chukchee	"Money is quite unknown."	Bogoras 1904–1909:67
O(?)	Copper Eskimo	All trade seems to be by direct barter; there is no mention of any general currency.	Jenness 1922:53f.; Stefansson 1914:82, 102–103
O(?)	Coyotero	Barter was the principle of exchange; there is no evidence of the use of a standard currency.	Goodwin 1942:72–76
X	Dutch	Money present.	Keur and Keur 1955: 72–73
X	Egyptians	Money is used.	Blackman 1927:92, 95; *MENA* 1967:744f.
O(?)	Eyak	No mention of currency—all trade was by direct barter.	Birket-Smith and de Laguna 1938:149–151
X	Fur	". . . the standard money being damoor cloth, but in the large towns imported cloth and Maria Theresa dollars are used."	Felkin 1885:250
O	Gilyak	". . . the bear festival is a sort of fair, where various things are bartered."	Seeland 1882:46
		Carried on barter trade with Chinese, and neighboring tribes.	*Ak. Nauk SSR* 1956: 92f.
		NOTE: No mention of use of money; all exchanges seem to be by direct barter.	
O	Gond	". . . a race that had no use for copper coin . . ." (no monetary system present).	Grigson 1949:13
O	Hottentots	Economic exchange was by direct barter.	Schapera 1930:317–319
O(?)	Ifaluk	No evidence of any symbolic medium of exchange.	Spiro 1949:9–10; Burrows 1949:105–106; Damm *et al.* 1938: 79
O(?)	Ila	There was no general-purpose money in the indigenous system—cattle and salt served as a medium of exchange for certain transactions.	Smith and Dale 1920, I:130, 148, 180
X	Iraqi	"The Indian rupee currency . . . was superseded early in 1932 by an Iraqi currency. . . ."	Longrigg 1953:202; also, *MENA* 1967:283

CODE	SOCIETY	STATEMENT	REFERENCE
X	Irish	Money is used.	*SYB* 1959:1149
O(?)	Iroquois	Wampum beads do not seem to have been a general-purpose currency.	
X	Italians	"The standard coin is the *lira* of 100 *centesimi*."	*SYB* 1964:1173
O(?)	Kababish	The Kababish do not seem to have had any general symbolic medium of exchange—trade was by bartering, and payments were generally made in livestock.	Parkyns 1850:254, 256–257; Seligman 1918:172
O(?)	Kafirs	"Among the Kafirs themselves all business is done by barter." NOTE: Cows and rupees serve as a standard of value, but are not used as a medium of exchange.	Robertson 1900:543
X	Kapauku	"The Kapauku economy is a money economy. Cowries provide the standard currency. . . ."	Pospisil 1958a:117
		". . . one can sell his labor to another individual."	Pospisil 1958a:119
		Land may be purchased for cowrie shell money.	Pospisil 1958a:124
		"As compared with sale, barter is a rather rare contract."	Pospisil 1958a:125
X(?)	Kazaks	". . . the buyer can refuse the animal or demand the return of the money payed. . . ."	Grodekov 1889:112–113
X(?)	Klallam	Dentalia shells seem to have been a general medium of exchange.	Gunther 1927:218; Eells 1889:647
X	Koreans	"On 10 June 1962 the *hwan* was revalued at the rate of 10 *hwan*=1 *won* (130 *won*=US \$1.)."	*SYB* 1964:1194
O(?)	Land Dyaks	The use of money appears to have been recently introduced; formerly no symbolic medium of exchange was employed.	Geddes 1954:90–96
O	Luo	Money was introduced by Europeans; formerly barter prevailed.	Northcote 1907:59; also, Owen 1933:243
O	Malaita	The shell disc money and porpoise teeth used on Malaita and Guadalcanal are a special-purpose currency within the sphere of "prestige goods" transactions:	
		"The chief functions of the discs and teeth are ceremonial. . . . It is also true that the valuables serve as a unit of account, though here the field is highly restricted. . . . Further, discs and teeth are not interchangeable. . . . Each traditional transaction requires its own kind of object. . . ."	Hogbin 1964:48

CODE	SOCIETY	STATEMENT	REFERENCE
		"The uses to which the traditional valuables could be put were so restricted that the owner had little temptation to keep them. Instead, he preferred to acquire prestige by giving them away. . . . Money is different. . . ."	Hogbin 1958:187
O	Malekula	All transactions are either gift exchanges or direct barter; pigs serve as a standard of value, but are in no sense a true currency.	Deacon 1934:199–200, 202–205
O	Mangareva	"In Mangareva . . . there was no money. . . ."	Buck 1938:165
O	Mataco	"They do not indulge in commercial enterprises. . . . However they do practice barter on a small scale. . . ."	Pelleschi 1896:119
O	Mende	General-purpose money was introduced by the British.	Little 1951:255
		Slaves, native cloth, and iron bars served as standards of value and mediums of exchange for a limited range of transactions.	Little 1951:37, 255, 289
O	Mongo	Money was first introduced by the Europeans.	Hulstaert 1938:114, 119
		". . . before the introduction of legal tender . . . salt played a much more important part in the economic life. . . . At the present time, it is used only in local transactions . . . frequently . . . saltmakers sell their surplus as a mere commodity to the highest bidder."	Maes 1924:81
O(?)	Mosquito	"The interchange of commodities was generally effected by barter."	Conzemius 1932:40
X	Nahua (Aztec)	"Cacao beans, along with other objects, were used both in exchange and for payment of fines, debts and tribute."	Chapman 1957:127, 119, 128, 134; also, Bandelier 1880:602
		"The long-distance traders used only the cacao bean as money."	Chapman 1957:134
O	Ojibwa	Formerly all trading was done by barter or gift-giving.	Densmore 1929:150; Landes 1937b:112
O	Ona	Economic exchange by barter; no currency.	Lothrop 1928:171
O	Orokaiva	All economic exchanges took the form of gifts and countergifts— money is absent.	Williams 1930:316–317
O	Papago	Money was introduced by Europeans; formerly barter and gift-exchange prevailed.	Underhill 1939:90, 102; Williams 1956:66, 71f.

CODE	SOCIETY	STATEMENT	REFERENCE
O	Semang	All exchanges are direct barter, or gifts.	Schebesta 1927:32; Evans 1937:33
O(?)	So. Paiute	No evidence of the use of any kind of currency.	
O(?)	Tallensi	"Peace and the introduction of British currency have brought about a tremendous expansion of local trade. . . ."	Fortes 1940:248; also, Fortes and Fortes 1936:246
O	Thonga	Currency was introduced by Europeans; indigenously, direct barter prevailed.	Junod 1927, II:140f., 626; I:376
		Hoes were a special-purpose currency used in bridewealth transactions during the nineteenth century.	Junod 1927, I:276–277
O	Tikopia	"This absence of money in Tikopia has a bearing on several situations."	Firth 1936:7
O	Tiv	". . . the economy of the Tiv . . . is what can be called a multi-centric economy."	Bohannan 1959:492
		". . . there was no money of any sort in this (subsistence goods) sphere—all goods changed hands by barter."	Bohannan 1959:493
		". . . brass rods were a general purpose currency *within the prestige sphere.*"	Bohannan 1959:498
O	Tongans	The Tongans did not use money.	Mariner 1820:158–159, 352; Simkin 1945–1946:112
O	Toradja	Money was not used before the coming of the Dutch.	Adriani and Kruyt 1950, I:126, 206
X	Turks	"The Turkish lira (pound), which is, in practice, employed as the monetary unit, is made up of 100 kurus."	*MENA* 1967:694
O	Wintun	Clam disk money did not have a set value.	DuBois 1935:24–25
O	Yagua	Money absent; trade by barter.	Fejos 1943:46

BIBLIOGRAPHY

ABRAHAM, ROY CLIVE
1933 *The Tiv people.* Lagos, The Government Printer.

ADRIANI, N., and ALB. C. KRUYT
1950 *De Bare'e Sprekende Toradjas Van Midden-Celebes (De Oost-Toradjas).* Verhandelingen der koninklijke Nederlandse akademie van wetenschappen, Afdeling Letterkunde, Niewe Reeks, Deel LIV, LV, LVI (No. 1–3). Amsterdam, Noord-Hollandsche Uitgevers Maatschappij.

ALVAREZ, FRANCISCO
1881 *Narrative of the Portuguese embassy to Abyssinia during the years 1520–1527.* London, Hakluyt Society.

AMMAR, ABBAS M.
1942 *A demographic study of an Egyptian province.* Monograph on Social Anthropology, No. 8. London, Percy Lund, Humphries.
1954 *Growing up in an Egyptian village, Wilsa, Province of Aswan.* London, Routledge and Kegan Paul.

ANONYMOUS
1956 Narodia Siberia. *Akademia Nauk SSR*, Vol. 56. Moscow and Leningrad.

1960 *Amtliches Telephonbuch, Wien, 1960 II.* Teil: Berufs-und Branchenverzeichnis. Wien, Post-und Telegraphendirektion für Wien, Niederösterreich und Burgenland.

1960 *Beroepenlijst voor de Plaatselijke Telefoondienst, Amsterdam No. 110—Sept. 1960.* Amsterdam, Staatsbedrijf der Posterijen, Telegrafie en Telefonie.

1956& *Biennial Report: Tonga, 1956 and 1957.*
1957 London, Her Majesty's Stationery Office.

1960– *Elenco Categorico Roma e Lazio,*
1961 *1960–61,* Vol. II. Società Telefonica Tirrena, Roma, Italy.

1910 *Encyclopaedia Britannica,* 11th ed. Vol. 12. New York, Encyclopaedia Britannica.

1952 *International Bank for Reconstruction and Development: The economic development of Iraq.* Baltimore, Johns Hopkins Press.

1960 *Istanbul Telefon Rehberi, Meslekler Kismi, 1960–61.* Istanbul, Dogan Kardes Yayinlari A. S.

1967 *Middle East and North Africa, 1966–1967,* 13th ed. London, European Publications.

1954 Royal Institute of International Affairs. *The Middle East: a political and economic survey.* London and New York.

1934 *Rustung und abrüstung,* Vol. 1. Berlin.

1936 *Statesman's year-book,* Vol. 73. London, Macmillan.

1955 *Statesman's year-book,* Vol. 92. London, Macmillan.

1957 *Statesman's year-book,* Vol. 94. London, Macmillan.

1958 *Statesman's year-book,* Vol. 95. London, Macmillan.

1959 *Statesman's year-book,* Vol. 96. London, Macmillan.

1962 *Statesman's year-book,* Vol. 99. London, Macmillan.

1964 *Statesman's year-book,* Vol. 101. London, Macmillan.

1960 *Telephone directory, Deireadh Fomhair, October, 1960.* Dublin, Cahill.

1957 *United Nations demographic yearbook.* New York, Statistical Office of the U.N., Department of Economic and Social Affairs.

1952 *World almanac.* New York, New York World-Telegram.

1961 *World almanac.* New York, New York World-Telegram.

ARENSBERG, CONRAD
1940 *Family and community in Ireland.* Cambridge, Harvard University Press.

BACHOFEN, J. J.
1861 *Das mutterrecht.* Stuttgart.

BANDELIER, ADOLPH
1880 On the art of war and mode of warfare of the ancient Mexicans. On the distribution of tenure of lands. On the social organization and mode of government of the ancient Mexicans. *Reports of the Peabody Museum of American Archaeology and Ethnology in connection with Harvard University,* 2:95–161; 385–448; 557–699. Cambridge, Harvard University Press.

BARNOUW, VICTOR
1950 *Acculturation and personality among the Wisconsin Chippewa.* American Anthropological Association, Memoir 72.

BARRETT, S. A.
1911 The dream dance of the Chippewa and Menominee Indians of northern Wisconsin. *Bulletin of the Public Museum of the City of Milwaukee,* Vol. 1, Part 2, 251–406. Milwaukee, Wisconsin.

BATES, MARSTON, and D. P. ABBOTT
1958 *Coral Island: portrait of an atoll.* New York, Charles Scribner's Sons.

BAXTER, P. T. W., and AUDREY BUTT
1953 *The Azande and related peoples of the Anglo-Egyptian Sudan.* International African Institute Ethnographic Survey. London, Oxford University Press.

BEAGLEHOLE, ERNEST and PEARL
1941 *Pangai: vllage in Tonga.* Memoirs of the Polynesian Society, Vol. 18. New Zealand, The Polynesian Society.

BERTALANFFY, LUDWIG VON
1942 *Theoretische biologie.* Berlin, Borntraeger.

BIRKET-SMITH, KAJ, and FREDERICA DE LAGUNA
1938 *The Eyak Indians of the Cooper River Delta, Alaska.* Copenhagen, Levin and Munksgaard.

BLACKMAN, WINIFRED S.
1927 *The fellahin of Upper Egypt.* London, George G. Harrap.

BOELAERT, E.
1940 De Nkundo-Maatschappij (Nkundo society). *Kongo-Overzee* 6:148–161. Antwerp, De Sikkel.

BOGORAS, WALDEMAR
1904– The Chuckchee. *American Museum of*
1909 *Natural History Memoirs,* Vol. 7, Part 1 (The Jesup North Pacific Expedition). New York.

BOHANNAN, PAUL
1957 *Tiv farm and settlement.* Colonial Research Studies, No. 15. London, Her Majesty's Stationery Office.

1958 *Tiv Bibliography.* Unpublished MS. New Haven, Human Relations Area Files.

1959 The impact of money on an African subsistence economy. *Journal of Economic History* 19:491–503.

1960 *African homicide and suicide.* Princeton, N.J., Princeton University Press.

BOHANNAN, PAUL, and LAURA BOHANNAN

1953 *The Tiv of Central Nigeria.* Ethnographic survey of Africa, Western Africa, Part VIII. London, International African Institute.

1958 *Three source notebooks in Tiv ethnography.* Unpublished MS.

BRETON, RAYMOND, and ARMAND DE LA PAIX

1929 Relation de l'île de la Guadaloupe (An account of the island of Guadaloupe). In Les Caribes, La Guadaloupe, 1635–1656, Joseph Rennard, ed., *Histoire Coloniale,* 1:45–74. Paris, Librairie Générale et Internationale.

BROWN, H. D.

1944 The Nkumu of the Tumba: ritual chieftanship on the Middle Congo. *Africa* 14: 431–446. London, Oxford University Press for the International Institute of African Languages and Cultures.

BROWN, R. GRANT

1925 *Burma as I saw it, 1889–1917.* New York, Frederick A. Stokes.

BRUNNER, EDMUND DE SCHWEINITZ

1928 Rural Korea; a preliminary survey of economic, social and religious conditions. *The Christian Mission in relation to rural problems,* Vol. VI, No. 2. N.Y., International Missionary Council.

BUCK, SIR PETER H.

1938 *Ethnology of Mangareva.* B. P. Bishop Museum Bulletin No. 157. Honolulu.

BURROWS, EDWIN GRANT

1949 *The people of Ifaluk: a little-disturbed atoll culture.* Unpublished manuscript submitted as a final report, Coordinated Investigation of Micronesian Anthropology. Washington, Pacific Science Board, National Research Council.

BUSH, RICHARD

1871 *Reindeer, dogs and snow-shoes: a journal of Siberian travel and explorations.* New York, Harper.

BUTT, AUDREY

1952 The Luo of Kenya. *Ethnographic Survey of Africa: East Central Africa, Part IV: The Nilotes of the Anglo-Egyptian Sudan and Uganda.* London, International African Institute.

CAIN, REV. JOHN

1881 The Koi, a southern tribe of the Gond. *Journal of the Royal Asiatic Society,* New Series 2, 13:410–425. London, Trubner.

CAMPBELL, C. G.

1949 *Tales from the Arab tribes.* London, Lindsay Drummond.

CAMPBELL, DONALD T.

1961 *Evolutionary theory in social science: a reappraisal.* Mimeograph.

CARNEIRO, ROBERT L.

1962 Scale analysis as an instrument for the study of cultural evolution. *Southwestern Journal of Anthropology* 18:149–169.

CARNEIRO, ROBERT L., and STEPHEN F. TOBIAS

1963 The application of scale analysis to the study of cultural evolution. *Transactions of the New York Academy of Sciences,* Ser. II, 26:196–207.

CHAPMAN, ANNE C.

1957 Port of trade enclaves in Aztec and Maya civilizations. In K. Polanyi, C. M. Arensberg, and H. W. Pearson, eds., *Trade and market in the early empires.* Glencoe, Ill., Free Press.

CHAPPLE, ELIOT D., and CARLETON S. COON

1942 *Principles of anthropology.* New York, Holt.

CLARK, CHARLES ALLEN

n.d. *Religions of old Korea.* New York, Fleming H. Revell.

CLARK, VICTOR

1951 *Compulsory education in Iraq.* Studies on Compulsory Education IV. Paris, United Nations Educational, Scientific and Cultural Organization.

COHEN, RONALD

1962 The strategy of social evolution. *Anthropologica* N.S., 4:321–348.

CONZEMIUS, EDUARD

1932 *Ethnographical survey of the Mosquito and Sumu Indians of Honduras and Nicaragua.* Bureau of American Ethnology, Bulletin No. 106. Washington, D.C., Smithsonian Institution.

COOK, SHERBURNE F., and LESLEY BYRD SIMPSON

1948 *The population of Central Mexico in the 16th century.* Berkeley, University of California Press.

COON, CARLETON S.

1948 *A reader in general anthropology.* New York, Holt.

COOPER, JOHN M.

1963 The Ona. *Handbook of South American Indians.* Smithsonian Institution Bureau of American Ethnology Bulletin 143, 1:107–127. New York, Cooper Square.

1963 The Araucanians. *Handbook of South American Indians.* Smithsonian Institution Bureau of American Ethnology Bulletin 143, 1:687–760. New York, Cooper Square.

CROSBY, K. H.

1937 Polygamy in Mende country. *Africa* 10: 249–264. London, International Institute of African Languages and Cultures.

CZEKANOWSKI, JAN
1924 *Forschungen im Nil-Kongo zwischenge-biet, Wissenschaftliche Ergebnisse der Deutschen Zentral Afrika Expedition, 1907–1908, unter Führung Adolf Fried-rich, Herzogs zu Mecklenburg,* Vol. 6. Part 2:21–110. Leipzig, Klinkhardt und Bierman.

DALTON, GEORGE
1965 Primitive money. *American Anthropolo-gist* 67:44–65.

DAMM, HANS, *et al.*
1938 *Zentralkarolinen, Part II: Ifaluk, Aurepik, Faraulip, Sorol, Mogemog* (The Central Carolines Part II). Ergebnisse der Sudsee-Expedition 1908–1910, Section B, Vol. 10, Part 2. Hamburg, Friederichsen, De Gruyter.

DAUTREMER, JOSEPH
1913 *Burma under British rule.* Trans. by G. Scott. London, T. Fisher Unwin.

DEACON, BERNARD
1934 *Malekula, a vanishing people in the New Hebrides.* London, Routledge.

DENSMORE, FRANCES
1929 *Chippewa customs.* Bureau of American Ethnology, Bulletin No. 86. Washington, D.C., Government Printing Office.

DOWNES, R. M.
1933 *The Tiv tribe.* Kaduna, The Government Printer.

DOWSON, ERNEST
1932 *An inquiry into land tenure and related questions.* Bagdad, Government of Iraq.

DUBOIS, CORA
1935 Wintu ethnography. *University of Cali-fornia Publications in American Archae-ology and Ethnology* 36:1–147. Berkeley.

DUNDAS, HON. CHARLES
1924 *Kilimanjaro and its peoples.* London, H. F. & G. Witherby.

DUNN, READ P., JR.
1952 *Cotton in the Middle East.* Memphis, National Cotton Council of America.

DUPUY, R. ERNEST
1939 *World in arms: a study of military geog-raphy,* Harrisburg, Pa., Military Service Publishing Co.

DURKHEIM, EMILE
1933 *The division of labor in society.* Trans. by George Simpson. Glencoe, Ill., Free Press.

DU TERTRE, JEAN-BAPTISTE
1667 *Histoire générale des Antilles Habitées par les français,* Vol. 2. Paris.

EAST, RUPERT (ed.)
1939 *Akiga's story: the Tiv tribe as seen by one of its members.* London, Interna-tional Institute of African Languages and Cultures, Oxford University Press.

EELLS, MYRON
1889 The Twana, Chemakum and Klallam In-dians of Washington territory. In *Smith-sonian Institution Annual Report for 1887.* Washington, D.C.

ELWIN, VERRIER
1943 *Maria murder and suicide.* Bombay, Ox-ford University Press.

EMBER, MELVIN
1963 The relationship between economic and political development in non-industrial-ized societies. *Ethnology* 2:228–248.

EVANS, IVOR H. N.
1923 *Religion, folklore and customs in North Borneo and the Malay Peninsula.* Lon-don, Cambridge University Press.
1937 *The Negritos of Malaya.* London, Cam-bridge University Press.

EVANS-PRITCHARD, EDWARD
1937 *Witchcraft, oracles and magic among the Azande.* Oxford, Clarendon Press.
1965 Consulting the poison oracle among the Azande. In W. Lessa and E. Vogt, eds., *Reader in comparative religion: an an-thropological approach,* 2nd ed. New York, Harper and Row.

FARON, LOUIS C.
1959 The Araucanians: Chilean farmers and pastoralists. In *Native peoples of South America.* New York, McGraw-Hill.

FEJOS, PAUL
1943 Ethnography of the Yagua. *Viking Fund Publications in Anthropology* 1:15–128. New York.

FELKIN, R. W.
1885 Notes on the Fur tribe of Central Af-rica. *Proceedings of the Royal Society of Edinburgh,* Vol. 13, No. 120:205–266. Edinburgh, Neill.

FENTON, WILLIAM N.
1940 *Masked medicine societies of the Iro-quois.* Annual Report of the Smithso-nian Institution, pp. 397–429. Washing-ton, D.C. Government Printing Office.

FERRARS, MAX, and BERTHA FERRARS
1901 *Burma.* London, Sampson Low, Marston.

FIELDING-HALL, HAROLD
1917 *The soul of a people.* London, Macmil-lan.

FIRTH, RAYMOND
1930a A dart match in Tikopia. *Oceania,* Vol. 1, No. 1:64–96. London, Australian Re-search Council.
1930b Report on research in Tikopia. *Oceania,* Vol. 1, No. 1:105–117. London, Austral-ian Research Council.
1936 *We, the Tikopia: a sociological study of kinship in primitive Polynesia.* London, Allen and Unwin.

1939 *Primitive Polynesian economy.* London, Routledge.

1954 Anuta and Tikopia: symbiotic elements in social organization. *Journal of the Polynesian Society,* Vol. 58, No. 2.

1959 *Social change in Tikopia: restudy of a Polynesian community after a generation.* London, Ruskin House, Allen and Unwin.

FISHER, W. B.

1950 *The Middle East, a physical, social and regional geography.* London, Methuen.

FONTANA, BERNARD L., et al.

1962 *Papago Indian pottery.* Seattle, Washington University Press.

FORTES, MEYER

1940 The political system of the Tallensi of the Northern territories of the Gold Coast. In M. Fortes and E. E. Evans-Pritchard, eds., *African political systems.* London, Oxford University Press for the International African Institute.

1945 *The dynamics of clanship among the Tallensi: being the first part of an analysis of the social structure of a Trans-Volta tribe.* London, Oxford University Press for the International African Institute.

1949 *The web of kinship among the Tallensi: the second part of an analysis of the social structure of a Trans-Volta tribe.* London, Oxford University Press for the International African Institute.

FORTES, MEYER, and SONIA FORTES

1936 Food in the domestic economy of the Tallensi. *Africa* 9:237–276. London, Oxford University Press.

FREEMAN, LINTON C.

1957 *An empirical test of folk-urbanism.* Ann Arbor University Microfilms, No. 23, 502.

FREEMAN, LINTON C., and ROBERT F. WINCH

1957 Societal Complexity: an empirical test of a typology of societies. *American Journal of Sociology* 62:461–466.

GEDDES, W. R.

1954 Land tenure of Land Dyaks. *Sarawak Museum Journal,* Vol. 6, No. 4. Singapore.

GIFFORD, EDWARD W.

1929 *Tongan society.* Bernice P. Bishop Museum, Bulletin 61, Bayard Dominick Expedition, Pub. No. 16. Honolulu.

1941 Culture Elements Distributions: XII Apache-Pueblo. *Anthropological Records* IV, No. 1:1–208.

GOLDMAN, IRVING

1937 The Bathonga of South Africa. In Margaret Mead, ed., *Cooperation and competition among primitive peoples.* New York and London, McGraw-Hill.

1961 The Bathonga of South Africa. In M. Mead, ed., *Cooperation and competition among primitive peoples,* rev. ed. Boston, Beacon Press.

GOODENOUGH, WARD

1944 A technique for scale analysis. *Educational and Psychological Measurement* 4:179–190.

GOODWIN, GRENVILLE

1935 The social divisions and economic life of the Western Apache. *American Anthropologist* 37:55–64.

1942 *Social organization of the Western Apache.* Chicago, University of Chicago Press.

GRAFFEN, ENRICO, and EDOARDO COLUMBO

1906 Les Niam-Niam. *Revue Internationale de Sociologie* 14:769–799. Paris, International Institute of Sociology and Society of Sociology of Paris.

GRANT, CHARLES

1870 *The gazetteer of the central provinces of India.* Nagpur, Bombay, Education Society's Press.

GRIFFIS, WILLIAM

1882 *Corea: the hermit nation.* New York, Charles Scribner's Sons.

GRIGSON, SIR WILFRID

1949 *The Maria Gonds of Bastar.* London, Oxford University Press.

GRINNELL, GEORGE B.

1918 Early Cheyenne villages. *American Anthropologist* 20:359–380.

1923 *The Cheyenne Indians, their history and ways of life.* New Haven, Yale University Press.

GRODEKOV, N. I.

1889 Kirgizy i Karakirgizy Syr-Dar'inskoi Oblasti (The Kazakhs and Kirgiz of the Syr-Darya region). *Juridical life,* Vol. 1. Tashkent, S. I. Lakhtin.

GUNTHER, ERNA

1927 Klallam ethnography. *University of Washington Publications in Anthropology,* Vol. 1, No. 5:171–314.

GUSINDE, MARTIN

1931 *Die Feuerland Indianer.* 1. Band. *Die Selk'nam.* Mödling-bei-Wein, Anthropos.

GUTERSOHN, TH.

1920 Het economisch leven van den Mongo-Neger (The economic life of the Mongo Negro). *Dongo* 1:92–105. Brussels, Goemaere. Imprimeur du Roi.

GUTMANN, BRUNO

1926 *Chagga law* (translated from German). Muenchen, C. H. Beck.

HALL, DANIEL G. E.

1950 *Burma.* London, Hutchinson's.

HARRISON, PAUL W.

1924 *The Arab at home.* New York, Crowell.

HA TAE HUNG
1958 *Folk customs and family life.* Korean Cultural Series, Vol. III. Seoul, The Korea Information Service.

HAWES, CHARLES H.
1903 *In the uttermost east.* London and New York, Harper.

HENRY, JULES
1941 *Jungle people, a Kaingang tribe in the highlands of Brazil.* New York, J. J. Augustin.

HEYDRICH, M.
1931 *Koreanische Landwirtschaft: Beiträge zur Völkerkunde von Korea I.* Leipzig, Druck und Kommissionsverlag von B. G. Tuebner.

HICKMAN, JOHN M.
1962 Dimensions of a complex concept: a method exemplified. *Human Organization* 21:214–218.

HILGER, M. INEZ
1939 *A social study of one hundred fifty Chippewa Indian families of the White Earth reservation of Minnesota.* Washington, the Catholic University of America Press.
1951 *Chippewa child life and its cultural background.* Bureau of American Ethnology Bulletin 146. Washington, Smithsonian Institution.
1957 *Araucanian child life and its cultural background.* Smithsonian Miscellaneous Collection, Vol. 133. Washington.

HOBHOUSE, L. T., G. C. WHEELER, and M. GINSBERG
1915 *The material culture and social institutions of the simpler peoples.* London, Chapman and Hall.

HOBLEY, C. W.
1898 Kavirondo. *Geographical Journal,* Vol. XIII, No. 4:361–372.
1902 *Eastern Uganda: an ethnological survey.* London, Anthropological Institute of Great Britain and Ireland.

HOEBEL, ADAMSON E.
1960 *The Cheyennes: Indians of the Great Plains.* New York, Henry Holt.

HOGBIN, IAN
1937 Guadalcanal and Malaita. *Geographical Magazine* 5:279–296, 351–368.
1958 *Social change.* London, Watts.
1964 *A Guadalcanal society: the Kaoka speakers.* New York, Holt, Rinehart and Winston.

HOOPER, WILLIAM HULME
1853 *Ten months among the tents of the Tuski, with incidents of an Arctic boat expedition in search of Sir John Franklin, as far as the Mackenzie River and Cape Bathurst.* London, John Murray.

HUDSON, ALFRED E.
1938 Kazak social structure. *Yale University Publications in Anthropology* 20:1–109.

HULBERT, HOMER B.
1902 The status of woman in Korea. *Korea Review* II:1–8; 53–59; 97–101; 155–159. Seoul, Methodist Publishing House.

HULSTAERT, GUSTAVE E.
1938 *Marriage among the Nkundu.* Institut Royal Colonial Belge, Vol. 8. Bruxelles, Librairie Falk fils, Georges Van Campenhout, Successeur.

IRELAND, PHILIP W.
1938 *Iraq: a study in political development.* New York, Macmillan.

IVENS, WALTER G.
1930 *The island builders of the Pacific.* London, Seeley, Service.

JENNESS, DIAMOND
1917 The Copper Eskimos. *Geographical Review* 4:81–91. New York, American Geographical Society.
1922 *The life of the Copper Eskimos, report of the Canadian Arctic Expedition, 1913–18.* Vol. 12, Part a. Ottawa, F. A. Acland.
1935 *The Ojibwa Indians of Parry Island, their social and religious life.* Bulletin of the Canada Department of Mines, No. 78. Ottawa, National Museum of Canada.

JOSEPH, A., R. B. SPICER, and J. CHESKY
1949 *The desert people: a study of the Papago Indians.* Chicago, University of Chicago Press.

JUNOD, HENRY A.
1927 *The life of a South African tribe.* 2 vols. London, Macmillan.

KAPSTEIN, GREGORIOUS
1922 Familieleven en seden bij de inboorlingen van den Evenaar. *Congo,* Vol. 3, Part I:531–549. Brussels, Goemaere, Imprimeur du Roi.

KARSTEN, RAFAEL
1932 *Indian tribes of the Argentine and Bolivian Chaco: ethnological studies.* Societas Scientarum Fennico, Commentationes Humanarum Litterarum, Vol. 4, No. 1. Helsingfors, Akademische Buchhandlung.

KAUDERN, WALTER
1925 *Structures and settlements in Central Celebes.* Ethnographical studies in Celebes. Göteborg, Elanders Boktryckeri Aktiebolag.

KELLY, I. T.
1934 Southern Paiute bands. *American Anthropologist* 36:548–560.

KENNAN, GEORGE
1905 Korea: a degenerate state. *The Outlook* 81:307–315. New York, Outlook Co.

KEUR, JOHN Y., and DOROTHY L. KEUR
1955 *The deeply rooted, a study of a Drents community in the Netherlands.* Monograph of the American Ethnological Society XXV.

KINIETZ, W. VERNON
1947   *Chippewa village: the story of Katiki-
       tegon.* Cranbrook Institute of Science,
       Bulletin No. 25. Bloomfield Hills, Cran-
       brook Press.

KIRCHOFF, PAUL
1948   The Caribbean lowland tribes: the Mos-
       quito, Sumo, Paya and Jicaque. *Bureau
       of American Ethnology Bulletin* No. 143,
       Vol. 4:219–229. Washington, D.C.,
       Smithsonian Institution.

KNOX, THOMAS W.
1870   *Overland through Asia.* Hartford, Amer-
       ican.

KOSTENKO, L. F.
1880   *Turkestanskiy kray. Opyt voennon-sta-
       tistischeskago obozreniia Turkestans-
       kago voennago okruga* (Turkestan Re-
       gion: Military statistical survey of the
       Turkestan Military District), Vol. I, Parts
       2 and 3. St. Petersburg, A. Transchel.

KRADER, LAWRENCE
1953   *Kinship systems of the Altaic-speaking
       peoples of the Asiatic steppe.* Unpub-
       lished Ph.D. dissertation, Harvard Uni-
       versity.

KREINOVICH, E. A.
1934   The fishing industry of the Gilyaks in the
       village Kul. *Sovetskaia Ethnografiia* 5:78–
       96. Leningrad, Akademiia Nauk SSR.

LAGAE, C. R.
1926   *Les Azande ou Niam-Niam; croyances
       religieuses et magiques, coutumes famili-
       ares.* Bibliothèque—Congo XVIII. Bru-
       xelles, Vromant.

LANDES, RUTH
1937a *Ojibwa sociology.* Series of the Columbia
       University Contributions to Anthropol-
       ogy, Vol. 19:1–144. New York.
1937b The Ojibwa of Canada. In Margaret
       Mead, ed., *Cooperation and competition
       among primitive peoples.* New York, Mc-
       Graw-Hill.
1938   *The Ojibwa woman.* New York, Colum-
       bia University Press.

LARKEN, P. M.
1926– An account of the Zande. *Sudan Notes
1927   and Records* 9:1–55; 10:85–134. Khar-
       toum, McCorquodale.

LATCHAM, RICHARD
1909   Ethnology of the Araucanos. *Journal of
       the Royal Anthropological Institute of
       Great Britain and Ireland* 39:334–370.

LAVAL, HONORÉ
1938   *Mangareva: L'histoire ancienne d'un peu-
       ple polynesien.* Braine-le-Compte, Bel-
       gium.

LEE, HOON K.
1936   *Land utilization and rural economy in
       Korea.* Chicago, University of Chicago
       Press.

LITTLE, KENNETH L.
1951   *The Mende of Sierra Leone.* London,
       Routledge and Kegan Paul.

LONGRIGG, STEPHEN H.
1953   *Iraq, 1900 to 1950.* London, Oxford Uni-
       versity Press.

LOPREATO, JOSEPH
1961   Social stratification in a South Italian
       town. *American Sociological Review* 26:
       585–596.

LOTHROP, SAMUEL K.
1928   *The Indians of Tierra Del Fuego.* New
       York, Museum of the American Indian,
       Heye Foundation:48–98.

LOW, HUGH
1848   *Sarawak: its inhabitants and productions.*
       London, Richard Bentley.

LOWIE, R. H.
1924   *Notes on Shoshonean ethnography.* An-
       thropological papers of the American Mu-
       seum of Natural History. New York.

MCCULLOCH, M.
1950   *Peoples of Sierra Leone Protectorate.*
       Ethnographic Survey of Africa: Western
       Africa. Part II. London, International Af-
       rican Institute.

MCKERN, W. C.
1922   Functional families of the Patwin. *Uni-
       versity of California Publications in
       American Archaeology and Ethnology*
       20:235–258. Berkeley.
1923   Patwin houses. *University of California
       Publications in American Archaeology
       and Ethnology* 20:159–171. Berkeley.

MACMICHAEL, H. A.
1912   *The tribes of northern and central
       Kordofan.* Chapter 10:172–198. Cam-
       bridge Archaeological and Ethnological
       Series. Cambridge, University Press.

MAES, J.
1924   *Notes sur les populations des Dassins du
       Kaisai, de la Lukenie et du Lac Leopold
       II.* Annales du Musée du Congo Belge,
       Nouvelle Série, Miscellanées, Vol. I,
       Fascicule 1. Brussels.

MAINE, HENRY SUMNER
1861   *Ancient law.* London, J. Murray.

MAKAL, MAHMUT
1954   *A village in Anatolia.* Trans. by Sir
       Wyndham Deedes. London, Vallentine,
       Mitchell.

MAN, EDWARD HORACE
1932   *On the aboriginal inhabitants of the An-
       daman Islands.* London, Royal Anthro-
       pological Institute of Great Britain and
       Ireland.

MARINER, WILLIAM
1820   *An account of the natives of the Tonga
       Islands in the South Pacific Ocean.* Bos-
       ton, Charles Ewer.

MESSING, SIMON DAVID
1957 *The Highland Plateau Amhara of Ethiopia*. Philadelphia, University of Pennsylvania.
1962 The Abyssinian market town. In Paul Bohannan and G. Dalton, eds., *Markets in Africa*. Evanston, Ill., Northwestern University Press.

MINER, HORACE
1952 The folk-urban continuum. *American Sociological Review* 17:529–537.

MOONEY, JAMES
1905– *The Cheyenne Indians*. American An-
1907 thropological Association Memoirs, Vol. 6.

MOOSE, J. ROBERT
1911 *Village life in Korea*. Nashville, M. E. Church.

MORGAN, LEWIS HENRY
1877 *Ancient society*. New York, Holt.
1901 *League of the Ho-De-No-Sau-Nee or Iroquois*, Vols. 1 and 2. New York, Dodd, Mead.

MORSE, EDWARD S.
1897 *Korean interviews*. New York, Appleton.

MOSKOS, CHARLES C., JR.
n.d. *A comparative study of leadership in non-literate societies*. Mimeograph.

MOSS, LEONARD, and W. THOMSON
1959 The South Italian family: literature and observation. *Human Organization* 18: 35–40.

MULLER, ERNST W.
1956 Soziologische Terminologie und soziale organisation der Ekonda (Sociological terminology and social organization of the Ekonda). *Zeitschrift für Ethnologie* 81:188–202. Braunschweig (Brunswick).

MURDOCK, GEORGE PETER
1949 *Social structure*. New York, Macmillan.
1957 World ethnographic sample. *American Anthropologist* 59:664–687.
1964 Ethnographic Atlas. *Ethnology* 3:199–217.
n.d. *The comparative study of cultures*. Mimeograph.

NAROLL, RAOUL
1956a A preliminary index of social development. *American Anthropologist* 58:687–715.
1956b *WHRAF Monograph: Area Handbook for Austria*. Washington, D.C., WHRAF.
1961a Two solutions to Galton's problem. *Philosophy of Science* 28:15–39.
1961b *Two stratified random samples for a cross-cultural survey*. Mimeograph.
1962a *Data quality control: a new research technique*. New York, Free Press.
1962b Floor area and settlement population. *American Antiquity* 27:587–589.

1964a On ethnic unit classification. *Current Anthropology* 4:283–312.
1964b A fifth solution to Galton's problem. *American Anthropologist* 66:863–867.
n.d. Unpublished field notes.

NAROLL, RAOUL, and ROY G. D'ANDRADE
1963 Two further solutions to Galton's problem. *American Anthropologist* 65:1063–67.

NAROLL, RAOUL, and FRADA NAROLL
1962 Social development of a Tyrolean village. *Anthropological Quarterly* 35:103–120.

NAROLL, RAOUL, and LUDWIG VON BERTALANFFY
1956 The principle of allometry in biology and the social sciences. *General Systems* 1:76–89.

NOON, JOHN A.
1949 *Law and government of the Grand River Iroquois*. Viking Fund Publications in Anthropology, No. 12. New York.

NORDENSKIOLD, A. E.
1882 *The voyage of the Vega round Asia and Europe*. New York, Macmillan.

NORTHCOTE, G. A. S.
1907 The Nilotic Kavirondo. *Journal of the Royal Anthropological Institute of Great Britain and Ireland* 37:58–66.

OBER, FREDERICK A.
1895 Aborigines of the West Indies. *Proceedings of the American Antiquarian Society* 9:270–313. Worcester, Mass.

ORR, KENNETH
1951 *Field notes on the Burmese standard of living as seen in the case of a fisherman refugee family*. Rangoon, Notes of the Burma Commission Research Project, Department of Anthropology, University of Rangoon.

OSGOOD, CORNELIUS
1951 *Koreans and their culture*. New York, Ronald Press.

OWEN, W. E.
1933 Food production and kindred matters along the Luo. *Journal of the East Africa and Uganda Natural History Society*, Nos. 49–50:235–249.

PADDEN, RICHARD CHARLES
1957 Cultural change and military resistance in Araucanian Chile, 1550–1730. *Southwestern Journal of Anthropology* 13:103–121.

PALMER, W. R.
1928– Paiute Indian government and laws.
1929 Utah Indians past and present. *Utah Historical Quarterly* 1:35–53; 2:35–42. Salt Lake City, Utah State Historical Society.

PARKYNS, MANSFIELD
1850 The Kabbabish Arabs between Dongola and Kordofan. *Journal of the Royal Geographical Society of London* 20:254–275.

PELLESCHI, JUAN
1896 Los Indios Matacos y su lengua (The Mataco Indians and their language). *Boletín del Instituto Geográfico Argentino* 17:559–622; 18:173–350. Buenos Aires.

PERHAM, MARGERY
1948 *The government of Ethiopia.* New York, Oxford University Press.

PIJOAN, MICHEL
1946 *The health and customs of the Miskito Indians of Northern Nicaragua: interrelationships in a medical program.* Mexico, Instituto Indigenisto Interamericano.

PITKIN, DONALD S.
1960 Marital property considerations among peasants: an Italian example. *Anthropological Quarterly* 33:33–39.

POSPISIL, LEOPOLD
1958a *Kapauku Papuans and their law.* Publication in Anthropology, 54. New Haven, Yale University.
1958b Kapauku Papuan political structure. In Verne F. Ray, ed., *Systems of political control and bureaucracy in human societies.* Proceedings of the 1958 Annual Spring Meeting of the American Ethnological Society: 9–22. Seattle.

PRESCOTT, WILLIAM H.
n.d. *History of the conquest of Mexico.* New York, Modern Library.

QUAIN, B. H.
1937 The Iroquois. In Margaret Mead, ed., *Cooperation and competition among primitive peoples.* New York, McGraw-Hill.

RADCLIFFE-BROWN, A. R.
1922 *The Andaman Islanders: a study in social anthropology.* Cambridge, Cambridge University Press.

RASMUSSEN, KNUD
1932 *Intellectual culture of the Copper Eskimos.* Report of the Fifth Thule Expedition, 1921–1924. Vol. IX. Copenhagen.

RAUM, O.
1940 *Chaga childhood: a description of indigenous education in an East African tribe.* London, Oxford University Press for the International Institute of African Languages and Culture.

REDFIELD, ROBERT
1947 The folk society. *American Journal of Sociology* 52:293–308.
1953 *The primitive world and its transformation.* Ithaca, N.Y., Cornell University Press.

REINING, CONRAD C.
1962 Zande markets and commerce. In P. Bohannan and G. Dalton, eds., *Markets in Africa.* Evanston, Ill., Northwestern University Press.

REY, CHARLES F.
1924 *Abyssinia as it is today.* Philadelphia, Lippincott.

RIVERS, W. H. R.
1914 *The history of Melanesian society.* 2 vols., 1:298–362. Cambridge, Cambridge University Press.

ROBERTSON, GEORGE SCOTT
1900 *The Kafirs of the Hindu Kush.* London, Lawrence and Bullen.

ROSCOE, JOHN
1915 *The Northern Bantu: an account of some Central African tribes of the Uganda Protectorate.* Cambridge, Cambridge University Press.

ROSE, EDWARD, and GARY WILLOUGHBY
1958 Culture profiles and emphases. *American Journal of Sociology* 62:476–490.

ROUSE, IRVING
1948 The Carib. *Handbook of South American Indians.* Smithsonian Institution Bureau of American Ethnology Bulletin No. 143, 4:547–565. New York, Cooper Square.

RUSSELL, R. V.
1916 *The tribes and castes of the central provinces of India.* 4 vols., 3:39–143. London, Macmillan.

SABITOV, N.
1953 Etnografisheskaia exspeditia v. Merkenskii Raion Oshambulskoi oblasti. *Sovietskaia Etnografiia* 3:196–200.

SAHAGUN, BERNARDINO
1938 *Historia general de las cosas de Nueva España,* 6 vols. Joaquin Ramirez Cabanez, ed. Mexico City, Robredo.

SAHLINS, M. D., and E. R. SERVICE
1960 *Evolution and culture.* Ann Arbor, University of Michigan Press.

SCHAPERA, ISAAC
1930 *The Khoisan peoples of South Africa: Bushmen and Hottentots.* London, Routledge. (Reprinted 1951.)

SCHEBESTA, PAUL
1927 *Among the forest dwarfs of Malaya.* London, Hutchinson.

SCHULTZE, LEONHARD
1907 *In Namaland and the Kalahari.* Jena, Gustave Fischer.

SCHWARTZ, RICHARD D., and JAMES C. MILLER
1964 Legal evolution and societal complexity. *American Journal of Sociology* 70:159–169.

SCOTT, SIR JAMES GEORGE
1882 *The Burman: his life and notions.* London, Macmillan.

SEELAND, NICOLAS
1882 Die Ghiliaken: eine ethnographische skize. *Russische Revue* 21:97–130, 222–254. St. Petersburg, Carl Rottger.

SELIGMAN, C. G.
1918 *The Kababish, a Sudan Arab tribe.* Har-

vard African Studies, Vol. II. African Department of the Peabody Museum of Harvard University. Cambridge, Mass.

SELIGMAN, CHARLES GABRIEL, and BRENDA Z. SELIGMAN
1932 Pagan tribes of the Nilotic Sudan. London, Routledge.

SHAW, K. C.
1932 Some preliminary notes on Luo marriage customs. Journal of the East Africa and Uganda Natural History Society 45–46: 39–50. Nairobi, Kenya.

SIMKIN, C. G.
1945– Modern Tonga. New Zealand Geographer
1946 I and II:99–118.

SIMMEL, GEORG
1902– The number of members as determining
1903 the sociological form of the group. Trans. by A. W. Small. American Journal of Sociology 8:1–46; 158–196.

SIMMONS, JAMES S., TOM F. WHAYNE, GAYLORD W. ANDERSON, HAROLD MACLACHIAN HORACK, RUTH ALIDA THOMAS, et al.
1944 Global epidemiology: a geography of disease and sanitation. The Near and Middle East, Vol. III. Philadelphia. Lippincott.

SKEATS, WALTER W., and C. O. BLAGDEN
1906 Pagan races of the Malay Peninsula. 2 vols. London, Macmillan.

SKINNER, ALANSON
1912 Notes on the Eastern Cree and Northern Salteaux. Anthropological Papers of the American Museum of Natural History 9:1–177. New York.
1913 Political and ceremonial organization of the Plains-Ojibwa. Anthropological Papers of the American Museum of Natural History 11:475–511. New York.

SMEDTS, MATTHEW
1955 No tabacco—no hallelujah: a tale of a visit to the Stone Age Capaukoos. London, William Kimber.

SMITH, ADAM
1776 Inquiry into the nature and causes of the wealth of nations. London.

SMITH, REV. EDWIN W., and CAPTAIN ANDREW MURRAY DALE
1920 The Ila-speaking peoples of Northern Rhodesia. 2 vols. London, Macmillan.

SOUSTELLE, JACQUES
1955 La vie quotidienne des Azteques à la veille de la conquête espagnole. Paris, Hachette.

SOUTHALL, A.
1952 Lineage formation among the Luo. International African Institute Memorandum 26. London, International African Institute.

SPENCER, HERBERT
1898 Principles of sociology, Vol. 1. New York, Appleton.
1900 First principles. 6th ed. Akron, Ohio, Werner.

SPIRO, MELFORD E.
1949 Ifaluk: a South Sea culture. Unpublished manuscript submitted as a final report, Coordinated Investigation of Micronesian Anthropology. Washington, Pacific Science Board, National Research Council.

STAHL, KATHLEEN M.
1964 History of the Chagga people of Kilimanjaro. The Hague, Mouton.

STAUB, J.
1936 Beiträge zur Kenntnis der materiellen kultur der Mendi in der Sierra Leone (Contributons to a knowledge of the material culture of the Mende in Sierra Leona). Solothurn, Buchdruckerei Vogt-Schild.

STEFANSSON, VILHJALMUR
1913 My life with the Eskimo. New York, Macmillan.
1914 The Stefansson-Anderson Arctic Expedition of the American Museum: Preliminary Ethnological Report. Anthropological Papers of the American Museum of Natural History XIV, Part 1. New York.

STERN, BERNHARD J.
1934 The Lummi Indians of Northwest Washington. New York, Columbia University Press.

STEWARD, JULIAN H.
1955 The theory of culture change. Urbana, University of Illinois Press.

STEWARD, JULIAN H., and ALFRED MÉTRAUX
1963 The Peban tribes. Handbook of South American Indians. Smithsonian Institution Bureau of American Ethnology Bulletin No. 143, 3:727–736. New York, Cooper Square.

STEWART, OMER C.
1942 The Ute-Southern Paiute. Anthropological Records 6:231–350. Berkeley, University of California Press.

SVERDRUP, HARALD ULRICH
1938 Hos Tundrafolket (With the people of the Tundra). Oslo, Gyldendal Norsk Forlag.

TAYLOR, DOUGLAS
1946 Kinship and the social structure of the Island Carib. Southwestern Journal of Anthropology 2:180–212. Albuquerque, University of New Mexico Press.

TERRIEN, FREDERICK W., and DONALD L. MILLS
1955 The effect of changing size upon the internal structure of organizations. American Sociological Review 20:11–13.

TITIEV, MISCHA
1951 *Araucanian culture in transition.* Occasional Contributions from the Museum of Anthropology of the University of Michigan 15. Ann Arbor, University of Michigan Press.

TORQUEMADA, JUAN DE
1943 *Monarquia Indiana.* 3 vols. 3rd ed. Mexico City, Calvador Chavez, Hayhoe.

UNDERHILL, RUTH MURRAY
1939 *Social organization of the Papago Indians.* Columbia University Contributions to Anthropology 30. New York.
1946 *Papago Indian religion.* Columbia University Contributions to Anthropology 33. New York.

VAILLANT, GEORGE CLAPP
1941 *Aztecs of Mexico: origin, rise and fall of the Aztec nation.* New York, Doubleday, Doran.

VANOVERBERGH, MORICE
1936 The Isneg life cycle. *Publications of the Catholic Anthropological Conference* 3: 81–86; 187–280. Washington, D.C.
1941 The Isneg farmer. *Publications of the Catholic Anthropological Conference* 3: 281–386. Washington, D.C.

VON HAGEN, VICTOR W.
1958 *The Aztec: man and tribe.* New York, Mentor.
1961 *The ancient sun kingdoms of the Americas.* Cleveland and New York, World.

VON LOGCHEM, J. T. H.
ca. *Gegevens ontrent de socio-politische or-*
1958 *ganisatie der Kapauko.* Mimeograph.

WARRINER, DORREEN
1948 *Land and poverty in the Middle East.* London, Royal Institute of International Affairs.

WASHINGTON, F. B.
1909 Notes on the northern Wintun Indians. *Journal of American Folklore* 22:92–95.

WEST, REV. THOMAS
1865 *Ten years in south-central Polynesia.* London, James Nisbet.

WHITE, LESLIE A.
1943 Energy and the evolution of culture. *American Anthropologist* 45:335–356.
1960 *The evolution of culture.* New York, McGraw-Hill.

WHITING, J. W. M., and IRVIN L. CHILD
1953 *Child training and personality.* New Haven, Yale University Press.

WILLIAMS, F. E.
1928 *Orokaiva magic.* London, Humphrey Milford; Oxford University Press.

WILLIAMS, THOMAS RHYS
1956 *Socialization in a Papago Indian village.* Ph.D. dissertation. Syracuse University.

WILLIAMS-HUNT, P. D. R.
1952 *An introduction to the Malayan aborigines.* Kuala Lampur, Government Press.

WILSON, G. M.
1960 Homicide and suicide among the Joluo of Kenya. In Paul Bohannan, ed., *African homicide and suicide* (179–213; 273–274; 287–288). Princeton, N.J., Princeton University Press.

WILSON, LAURENCE L.
1947 *Apayao life and legends.* New York, South East Asia Institute.

CHAPTER 41

Scale Analysis, Evolutionary Sequences, and the Rating of Cultures

ROBERT L. CARNEIRO

INTRODUCTION

One of the main concerns of cultural anthropology during the nineteenth century was the formulation of evolutionary sequences. These sequences were not limited to general stages, but often comprised series of particular traits as well. Thus the transitions from one stage to another in Lewis H. Morgan's famous sequence of Savagery, Barbarism, and Civilization were marked by the successive introduction of such traits as fire making, the bow and arrow, pottery, the domestication of animals, the smelting of iron ore, and the use of writing (Morgan 1909:9–12).

The sequence of traits proposed by Morgan was not, in his view, a chance historical succession of events which might just as readily have occurred otherwise, but rather, a closely determined evolution in which the order of appearance of traits was fixed by the nature of the traits themselves. Each succeeding trait in some way depended on those preceding it, but at the same time marked an advance over them. Such a sequence of traits was thought not only to epitomize the cultural development of mankind as a whole, but also to provide a scale against which the degree of evolution of particular societies could be measured. Thus when Morgan selected the Australian aborigines to represent the stage of Middle Savagery and the Homeric Greeks to represent the stage of Upper Barbarism, he was in effect assigning these societies a position on an evolutionary scale.

In the general reaction against evolutionism that began around the turn of the century the

evolutionary sequences of the earlier anthropologists were rejected, and no attempt was made to formulate new ones. Indeed, the feeling prevailed for a time that, as Edward Sapir (1920:378) expressed it, "evolutionism as an interpretative principle of culture is merely a passing phase in the history of thought. . . ."

The force of this reaction was so strong that it was not until the mid-1940's that the pendulum began to swing back. Since then, however, interest in cultural evolution has grown steadily, and the reality and validity of evolutionary sequences has now gained considerable acceptance.

Expressing the renewed confidence in the existence of such sequences, Leslie A. White (1947:175), the leader of contemporary evolutionism, wrote: ". . . few would admit that banking may precede barter, or that parliaments and proportional representation might precede tribal councils. Who is willing to concede that hereditary kings might have preceded elective chiefs in the course of human history?" Similarly, Melville Jacobs (1948: 567) affirmed that "the possibilities are good for finding regularities . . . in sequences such as those from shamanism to priesthood, mythology to theology, democratic to less democratic patterns, small-scale to large-scale fighting, gift-giving to trade, killing of captives to retention of captives as slaves, classes to castes, and many others."

The recognition of such sequences of traits leads us again to the same conclusion drawn by Morgan: if culture traits can be arranged on a scale from earlier and simpler to later and more advanced, then societies too can be arranged along an evolutionary scale according to how many, or which, of these traits they possess.

Before proceeding to discuss particular sequences I would like to make clear my own views on the relationship between evolutionary sequences and the data of ethnography, history, and prehistory. It seems advisable to do so since this issue is in dispute in modern evolutionism. I do not accept the view that a general evolutionary sequence is somehow entirely separate and distinct from the culture history of particular peoples. Such evolutionary sequences as exist do so only by virtue of the fact that many societies have evolved in similar ways during the course of their individual histories. An evolutionary sequence is thus a generalization of the order of development that societies by and large have tended to follow. Individually, societies *exemplify* this sequence; together they *constitute* it.

It is in the nature of things that simplicity precedes complexity. Were we to regress all cultures back to the start of the Paleolithic they would become exceedingly simple, and, in their simplicity, essentially alike. The process by which societies have become progressively more differentiated and more complex is, of course, *evolution*. All societies have evolved, but not all have done so to the same degree: some have evolved more than others. Fortunately for anthropology, those societies which survived into historic times reveal very wide differences in their degree of evolution. Not every phase of evolution can, of course, be illustrated by examples drawn from historically known cultures, since all existing societies—even the simplest—are more complex than their early Paleolithic forebears. Nevertheless, historically known societies do range from very simple to extremely complex, and by studying societies spanning this broad range of complexity anthropologists have been able to infer a great deal about the process which brought it about.

I have spoken of societal complexity and degree of cultural evolution more or less interchangeably. A society's "level of complexity" and its "degree of evolution" can be said to be the same thing looked at in different ways. The first of these expressions focuses on a society as a structural end-product; the second focuses on the process which gave rise to that end-product. This equation of increased complexity with higher evolution is, naturally, based on a certain view of the evolutionary process. The conception of evolution which I hold is essentially that first set forth by Herbert Spencer (1863:216; 1898:353; 1912:367): *Evolution is a change from a state of relatively indefinite, incoherent homogeneity to a state of relatively definite, coherent heterogeneity, through continuous differentiations and integrations.*

If we accept this view of evolution, then the task of working out evolutionary sequences can be seen to proceed hand in hand with the assessment of cultural complexity. In the parts of this paper to follow I present and discuss some recent work on the determination of evolutionary sequences and the rating of cultures.

SCALE ANALYSIS

The method by means of which the 1963 study of evolutionary sequences was carried out is Guttman scale analysis. How this form of scale analysis can be applied to cultural evolution was discussed in detail in an earlier paper (Carneiro 1962), and some preliminary results of this application were presented in a more recent one (Carneiro and Tobias 1963). Here I will explain scale analysis briefly, describe some of the results already obtained through its use, and present additional results not previously reported.

To carry out scale analysis one needs a sample of units from some population and a selection of attributes of these units. In the present case, the units are human societies and the attributes are culture traits. The first step is to list the societies chosen for the study along the bottom of a sheet of graph paper and to list the traits along the side. At this stage it makes no difference in what order the societies or the traits are listed. Next, the presence or absence of each trait among every society is ascertained from the ethnographic literature and indicated on the graph by a plus (+) or a minus (−).

Figure 1 shows a matrix made from a sample of twelve societies and a selection of eleven traits. Since both the traits and the societies were listed in random order, no

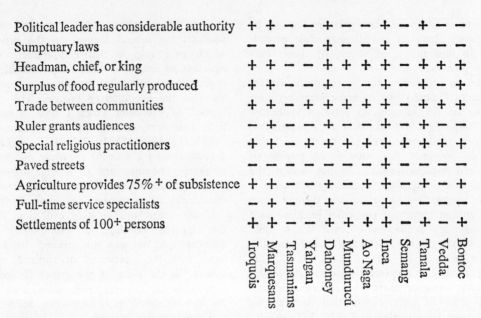

Figure 1. Matrix showing the presence (+) and absence (−) of 11 selected culture traits among a sample of 12 societies. The order of both the traits and the societies is random.

particular pattern appears in the matrix. The next step is to record the number of plusses for each trait and for each society. A new matrix is then constructed, the traits being rearranged so that the one occurring most frequently is listed at the bottom of the graph and the one occurring least frequently appears at the top. The societies are also rearranged so that the one with the smallest number of traits is at the left-hand end, and the one with the largest number is at the right. The matrix resulting from this rearrangement is called a *scalogram* (Figure 2). We see immediately that this scalogram has

	Tasmanians	Semang	Yahgan	Vedda	Mundurucú	Ao Naga	Bontoc	Iroquois	Tanala	Marquesans	Dahomey	Inca
Paved streets	−	−	−	−	−	−	−	−	−	−	−	+
Sumptuary laws	−	−	−	−	−	−	−	−	−	−	+	+
Full-time service specialists	−	−	−	−	−	−	−	−	−	+	+	+
Ruler grants audiences	−	−	−	−	−	−	−	−	+	+	+	+
Political leader has considerable authority	−	−	−	−	−	−	−	+	+	+	+	+
Surplus of food regularly produced	−	−	−	−	−	−	+	+	+	+	+	+
Agriculture provides 75%+ of subsistence	−	−	−	−	−	+	+	+	+	+	+	+
Settlements of 100+ persons	−	−	−	−	+	+	+	+	+	+	+	+
Headman, chief, or king	−	−	−	+	+	+	+	+	+	+	+	+
Trade between communities	−	−	+	+	+	+	+	+	+	+	+	+
Special religious practitioners	−	+	+	+	+	+	+	+	+	+	+	+

Figure 2. Scalogram showing a perfect scale produced by rearranging the traits and societies of the matrix in Figure 1.

an absolutely regular stairstep profile. A scalogram with such a profile is said to constitute a perfect scale.

It is important to understand that scaling does not result automatically from the mere manipulation of traits and societies in the manner described. Scaling must be inherent in the data if it is to be made to appear. If it does not inhere in the data, no amount of rearranging of the traits or societies will produce it. One can readily demonstrate this for himself by filling out a matrix in some random way, as by tossing a coin or a die, and then rearranging the traits and societies as described above. The result will be a slight tendency for plusses to cluster toward the lower right-hand corner of the scalogram, but nothing like a clear scale pattern will emerge.

The very orderly arrangement of plusses appearing in Figure 2 tells us nothing directly. It has to be interpreted. The question is, how? What explanation are we to give for the occurrence of such a regular pattern of stairsteps? I can think of only one that accounts for the pattern simply, plausibly, and fully. This is an interpretation in terms of evolution.

The evolutionary explanation of a scalogram is as follows: the order in which the traits are arranged, from bottom to top, is the order in which the societies have evolved them. Those traits toward the bottom of the scalogram are earlier and simpler, and consequently more societies have them. Those near the top are later and more complex, and therefore are possessed by fewer societies. By the same token, the order on the scalogram of the societies themselves represents their relative degrees of evolution. Those toward the left have fewer traits and are thus simpler and less evolved, while those on the right have more traits and are therefore more complex and more evolved.

From an examination of Figure 2 we would conclude, for example, that sumptuary laws develop after surplus food production, and that surplus food production develops after special religious practitioners. At the same time, we could say that the Iroquois are more evolved than the Semang, and the Inca more evolved than the Iroquois.

Although this scalogram employs actual data, the traits and societies appearing on it were, for purposes of demonstration, selected

to exhibit perfect scaling. Were we to begin adding more traits and societies to the scalogram we could expect that irregularities would start to appear in the profile: plusses would occur where we expected minuses, and minuses where we expected plusses. The question then becomes: For a large sample of societies is there a substantial number of traits which will show a reasonably close approximation to perfect scaling? It is this question that our research was designed to answer.

Our first step was to make a sampling of societies and a selection of traits. Choosing the societies to include was facilitated by the fact that Guttman scale analysis does not require a random sample. If scaling exists, any sample of societies should manifest it. In sampling societies, then, we concentrated on obtaining a broad geographic distribution and a wide range of culture levels. The sample of one hundred societies that was finally selected exhibited both these characteristics.

Formulating traits to test for scaling was decidedly more difficult. Theoretically, we could have begun with a list of all known culture traits, and, using the scalogram as a sorting device, successively separated out the traits that scaled poorly, eventually ending up with only those that scaled well. In practice, however, such a procedure was obviously out of the question. In order to avoid testing thousands upon thousands of traits, we began with a list of traits having what seemed to be a good antecedent probability of scaling. How were such traits identified?

The principal attribute to look for in traits when selecting good candidates for scaling is *retentiveness*. In order to scale well, a trait, once developed by a society, must tend to be retained indefinitely. If, on the contrary, a trait is liable to be discarded at any time following its adoption, then it will not scale well. Its "cultural spectrum line"—the row of plusses and minuses showing its presence or absence among the societies on the scalogram—would show an irregular pattern. Instead of a series of consecutive minuses followed by a series of consecutive plusses, indicating perfect scaling, we would have, with a poorly scaling trait, an irregular distribution of plusses and minuses.

Retentiveness is, admittedly, a relative matter. Traits which, late in their histories, are discarded or replaced may nevertheless have been retained for centuries or millennia before they were given up. Since our intention was to study cultural evolution only through preindustrial civilizations, and not beyond this point, we included in our list traits which we thought were generally retained through this level, whatever fate befell them thereafter.

At this point it might be asked: What is the relationship between retention and cumulation? *Retention* is an attribute of individual traits. When all of a number of successively developed traits are retained by a society, we speak of *cumulation*. Cumulation, then, is the retention of existing traits along with the development of new ones.

Although retention and cumulation are prerequisites for scaling, they are not in themselves sufficient conditions for it. Even if certain traits are retained indefinitely by all societies developing them they still will not scale well if they arose at different stages in the culture history of those societies. Only if traits emerge in approximately the same relative order in each society, and then are retained for long periods, will they exhibit good scaling.

Deciding whether a trait seemed likely to scale well was done on the basis of a general knowledge of ethnography, history, and prehistory. No strict rule was applied. Doubtful traits were sometimes included in the knowledge that, if their evolutionary histories proved irregular, scale analysis would reveal it.

The list of traits originally drawn up was revised three times before the version used in this study finally emerged. The fourth edition of the list contains 354 traits, arranged in fourteen categories (see Table 1).

TABLE 1
CATEGORIES OF TRAITS INCLUDED ON THE FOURTH EDITION OF THE SCALE ANALYSIS TRAIT LIST (THE NUMBER OF TRAITS IN EACH CATEGORY IS SHOWN IN PARENTHESES)

Subsistence (27 traits)
Settlements (29 traits)
Architecture (27 traits)
Economics (40 traits)
Social Organization and Stratification
  (19 traits)
Political Organization (51 traits)
Law and Judicial Process (20 traits)

Warfare (31 traits)
Religion (32 traits)
Ceramics and Art (16 traits)
Tools, Utensils, and Textiles (13 traits)
Metalworking (22 traits)
Watercraft and Navigation (9 traits)
Special Knowledge and Practices (18 traits)

Once the hundred societies had been selected and the 354 traits drawn up and scored for each society, the societies and traits were arranged to form a matrix. Following the rules already described, the traits and societies were then rearranged to form a scalogram. As expected, not all traits scaled well, but a considerable number did. Of these, we selected the ninety that scaled best and made a second scalogram with them. This scalogram had a coefficient of reproducibility of .938. This coefficient is a measure of the degree of scaling: 0 indicates no scaling at all, and 1.000 is perfect scaling. How this coefficient is calculated is explained in Carneiro (1962:155–157). Guttman (1950:

77) considers a coefficient of reproducibility of .90 or better to be "an acceptable approximation to a perfect scale."

The ninety-trait scalogram proved to be somewhat too large for convenient publication, and a selection was made from it of fifty of the best-scaling traits. The scalogram containing these fifty traits appears as Figure 3.

The coefficient of reproducibility of this scalogram is .950. This is even higher scaling than in the previous one, but it is still not perfect scaling. And without perfect scaling we cannot say that the order in which the traits appear on the scalogram represents an invariant sequence. What we can say is that it represents the most probable order in which the societies have evolved them. Thus there is a strong presumption that most societies have developed social segmentation before craft specialization, craft specialization before the corvée, the corvée before sumptuary laws, sumptuary laws before cities, and so on.

MAIN SEQUENCE OF CULTURAL EVOLUTION: UNILINEAR EVOLUTION

The order in which the traits appear on the scalogram may be thought of as a *main sequence* of cultural evolution, analogous to the main sequence of stellar evolution recognized in astronomy (Icko 1967:788–792). This main sequence is a developmental series which most societies appear to have followed most of the time. There are exceptions to it, but the existence of exceptions should not be allowed to obscure the fact that regularity predominates.

The idea of a main sequence of cultural evolution is closely related to the familiar notion of *unilinear* evolution. According to both there is a discernible regularity in the way in which societies develop, and this regularity is substantially duplicated by all societies if and as they evolve. But there is also a difference. Instead of saying that societies *tend to go through the same stages*, we say that societies *tend to evolve certain traits in the same order*.

It seems to me that cultural anthropologists rejected the idea of unilinearity in cultural development too quickly and without sufficient analysis of the facts. The premise on which they seem to have acted is that if evolutionary regularity could be disproved for *some* traits, it could not be established for *any*. In scale analysis we now have an instrument for testing unilinearity rigorously and objectively. If some degree of unilinearity exists, we can be sure that scale analysis will reveal it.

Indeed, the scalogram in Figure 3 is evidence that unilinearity of a sort does exist. There appears to be a line or sequence of development along which most societies have traveled most of the time.

As we noted earlier, at the same time that a scalogram arranges traits in their order of appearance, it also grades societies according to their respective degrees of evolution.

Looking at Figure 3 we can say, for example, that the Kwakiutl are more evolved than the Bushmen, the Batak more evolved than the Kwakiutl, the Bemba more evolved than the Batak, and the Aztecs more evolved than the Bemba.

SCALOGRAM AS A PREDICTOR IN THE CASE OF ANGLO-SAXON ENGLAND

The contention I am making in this paper is that by means of scale analysis synchronic cultural data can be made to yield a diachronic sequence of traits. This sequence, moreover, is one which I take to represent the way in which individual societies, by and large, have actually evolved these traits. In my opinion it is not only a logical sequence, but a temporal one. In a very real sense, then, we are wringing history out of ethnography. Of course this "history" is inferential, and like all inferences should be submitted to a test against the facts. The "facts" in this case would be the order of development of these same traits among one or more societies for which documentary history was available.

In a separate study designed to ascertain the rate of cultural development in Anglo-Saxon England (Carneiro 1969:1017–1018) data were obtained that enabled us to perform such a test. Our study of the Anglo-Saxons employed a revised version of the trait list containing 618 traits. Enough information could be found about 317 of these traits to permit us to say approximately when they first appeared in Anglo-Saxon England. Thus any selection of traits from these 317 could be arranged in the order of their actual historical appearance in England. Of these 317 traits 34 also appear on the 50-trait scalogram. Accordingly, the test consisted of comparing the actual order in which these 34 traits had developed in England with the order of development "predicted" for them by the scalogram.

The method chosen to make this comparison was a diagram resembling a mileage chart (Figure 4). The thirty-four traits used in this diagram are listed in the order in which they arose in Anglo-Saxon England, the earliest appearing at the bottom, and the latest at the top. Any pair of traits can be

Figure 3. Scalogram of 50 high-scaling traits taken from various aspects of culture. Only plusses are shown; minuses have been omitted. The wording of the traits is an abbreviation of their definition on the trait list. The figures preceding the traits indicate their frequency, and those preceding the societies indicate the number of traits they possess.

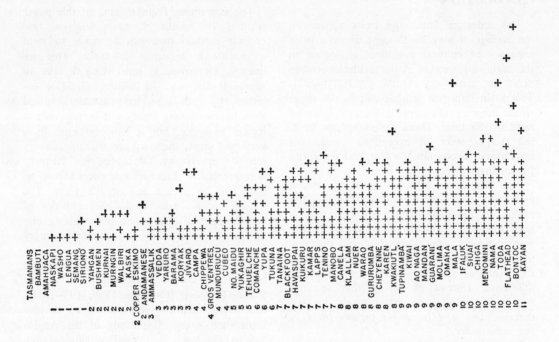

compared by finding where they intersect on the diagram. If the relative order of appearance of the two traits in Anglo-Saxon history was the *same* as that predicted by the scalogram, a check (√) was entered at their point of intersection. If the relative order of appearance of the two was the *reverse* of that predicted, a cross (X) was entered.

When the historical sources did not permit us to ascertain which of two traits appeared earlier in Anglo-Saxon England, an S was entered where they intersect. If two traits had the same frequency on the scalogram, thus preventing us from predicting which should have arisen first, a half-circled S was entered. And if the relative order of appearance of two traits could be determined in neither the Anglo-Saxon sequence nor the scalogram, then a fully-circled S was entered.

The large number of S's occurring in the lower left-hand corner of the diagram is due to the fact that the traits they represent were already present among the Anglo-Saxons when they arrived in England around 450 A.D., and thus their relative order of origin could not be ascertained.

Two examples will clarify how Figure 4 is to be read. We see on the scalogram in Figure 3 that "Code of Laws" is higher than "Military Conscription," and on the basis of this fact we predict that a code of laws should have developed later than military conscription in Anglo-Saxon England. Since, as we see from the order of the traits in Figure 4, this was indeed the case, a check occurs where these two traits intersect. On the other hand, the prediction that the corvée would appear later in Anglo-Saxon England

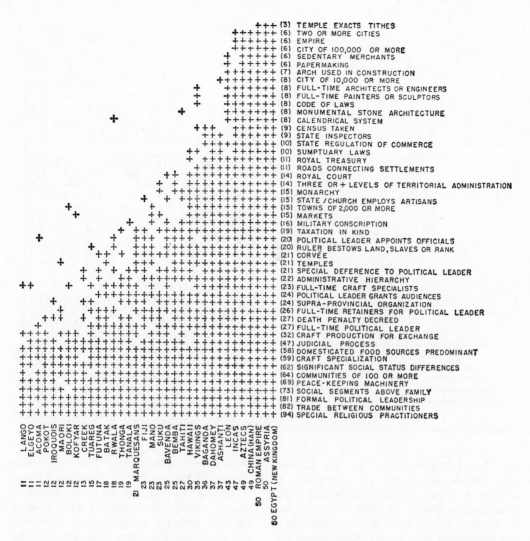

than craft production for exchange was not borne out. The order of appearance in England of these two traits was reversed. Consequently a cross has been placed at their intersection.

The results of tabulating the checks and crosses in Figure 4 are as follows: of the 418 pairs of traits for which the relative order of appearance could be determined in both Anglo-Saxon England and on the scalogram, 355 (84.9 percent) developed in the order predicted, while 64 (15.1 percent) did not. Insofar as one test case can provide it, this is verification of a fairly high order that the evolutionary sequence derived by comparing synchronic data from many societies represents historical reality for individual societies.

Although scale analysis is usually carried out with a considerable number of traits, it can be done with as few as two. To determine if two traits scale well in relation to each other we need not construct a scalogram, but can use a 2×2 table. Such a table, moreover, enables us to learn more about the relationship between two traits than merely which precedes the other.

The four cells of a 2×2 table yield the four logical possibilities of occurrence for any two traits, A and B: (1) A present–B present, (2) A present–B absent, (3) A absent–B present, and (4) A absent–B absent. Assuming that the trait we label A occurs more frequently than B, then the two traits scale perfectly if no cases appear in the third cell (A absent–B present). Such a distribution of cases would mean that some societies lacked

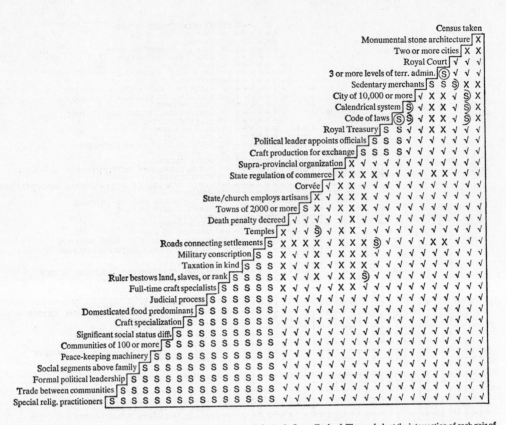

Figure 4. Diagram showing the order of development of 34 selected culture traits in Anglo-Saxon England. The symbols at the intersection of each pair of traits shows whether their relative order of appearance corresponds with that predicted by the scalogram in Figure 3. (See text).

both A and B, some had A but not B, some had both A and B, but no society had B without A. The inference we would draw from this distribution of cases would be that A always precedes B. As we have seen, it is this relationship between two traits that is the basis of perfect scaling.

Let us now examine two 2×2 tables constructed from data taken from the scalogram in Figure 3 to see what they reveal (see Figure 5). The first of these tables compares "Agriculture" with "Cities," while the second compares "Taxation" with "Sumptuary Laws."

Looking at the former we see that it shows perfect scaling: some societies lack both agriculture and cities, some have agriculture but not cities, some have both, but none has cities without agriculture. Let us study this table more closely. The fact that 67 societies (8+59) of the 100 in the sample have agriculture indicates that it is a fairly common trait and therefore relatively simple and early.

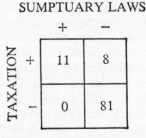

Figure 5. Two-by-two tables showing the relationship between the occurrence of Agriculture and Cities, and Taxation and Sumptuary Laws.

On the other hand, the fact that only 8 of the 100 societies have cities indicates that the presence of cities is uncommon and that it is therefore a relatively late and advanced trait. The number of cases in Cell 2 (societies with agriculture but without cities), 59, thus provides a measure of the *evolutionary distance* between the two traits. For agriculture and cities this distance is relatively great.

Next let us look at the table for "Sumptuary Laws" and "Taxation." The absence of cases in Cell 3 shows that we again have an instance of perfect scaling. The fact that only 19 societies have taxation and only 11 have sumptuary laws indicates that neither is a very common trait among the 100 societies in the sample and thus that both are high-level traits, sumptuary laws being the higher of the two. Furthermore, the fact that only 8 cases appear in Cell 2, representing "Taxation present–Sumptuary Laws absent," tells us that the two traits are not very far apart in the stage of cultural development at which they appear.

These results can be summarized and generalized as follows:

1. The smaller the number of cases in Cell 3, the higher the degree of scaling. If the frequency in this cell is zero, the scaling is perfect.
2. The larger the number of cases in Cells 1 and 2 (or 1 and 3), the earlier the development of the trait represented by them.
3. The smaller the number of cases in Cells 1 and 2 (or 1 and 3), the later the development of the trait represented by them.
4. The larger the number of cases in Cell 2, the greater the difference in cultural level between the two traits.
5. The smaller the number of cases in Cell 2, the less the difference in cultural level between the two.

DIFFERENTIAL EVOLUTION: PARALLEL EVOLUTION

In an earlier paper (Carneiro and Tobias 1963:204) we spoke of the phenomenon of "differential evolution." By this we meant that, up to a point, evolution within one aspect of culture may proceed independently of evolution in other aspects.

This unequal advance within their parts which societies sometimes display should, the-

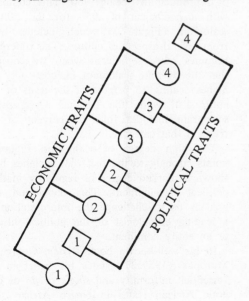

SOCIETY A

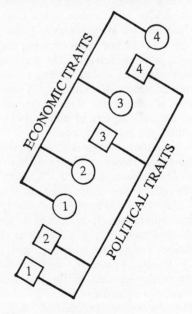

SOCIETY B

Figure 6. Diagram showing two possible relative orders of development for Economic and Political traits among two hypothetical societies.

Figure 7. Scalogram of 33 traits of Political Organization. Only plusses are shown; minuses have been omitted. The figures preceding the traits indicate their frequency, and those preceding the societies indicate the number of traits they possess.

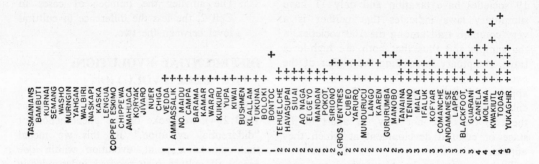

oretically, affect scaling. Since traits from the same aspect of culture are functionally more closely related than traits from different aspects, we should expect better scaling among the former than among the latter. Indeed, it is conceivable that we might find a high degree of scaling among traits from a particular aspect of culture even though the degree of scaling for these traits and others from different aspects of culture, when taken together, was relatively low.

A simplified hypothetical example of this possibility is shown in Figure 6. Here we see that Economic traits 1, 2, 3, and 4 have developed in the same order in Society A and Society B. We also see that Political Organization traits 1, 2, 3, and 4 have likewise developed in the same order in both societies. Taking the economic and political traits together, however, we see that their order of development in the two societies is substantially different.

The theoretical expectation that scaling should be higher among traits from a single aspect of culture than among traits of diverse aspects is borne out by additional scalograms we have made. For example, a scalogram including 33 of the 51 traits on the list in the category of Political Organization (Fig-

ure 7) shows very good scaling, its coefficient of reproducibility being .960. This compares with a coefficient of .950 for the 50-trait scalogram (Figure 3) which includes traits from several aspects of culture. This difference becomes more significant when we consider that the 50-trait scalogram includes only the highest-scaling 15 percent of the traits on the entire list, while the Political Organization scalogram includes fully 65 percent of the traits in that category.

The high degree of scaling in Figure 7 points strongly to the fact that societies have shown a marked degree of regularity in their political development. This conclusion emboldens us to challenge the interpretation of a leading ethnologist of the political history of an entire continent.

In his well-known book *Africa,* George P. Murdock (1959:37) states his belief in the "essential uniformity and *single origin* of despotic African states in Negro Africa . . ." (emphasis mine). This belief rests on the fact that native African kingdoms share many traits of political organization. These traits (of which eighteen are listed by Murdock [1959:37–39]) include Monarchical Absolutism, Divine Kingship, Insignia of Office, Royal Court, Territorial Bureaucracy, and

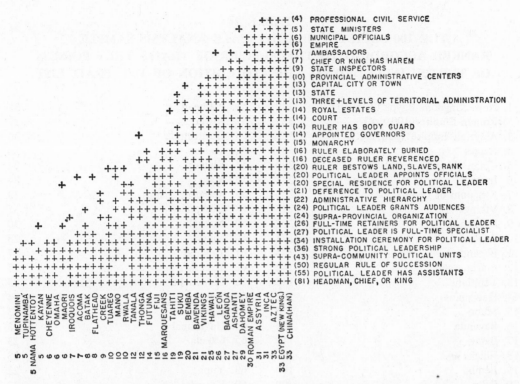

(4) PROFESSIONAL CIVIL SERVICE
(5) STATE MINISTERS
(6) MUNICIPAL OFFICIALS
(6) EMPIRE
(7) AMBASSADORS
(7) CHIEF OR KING HAS HAREM
(9) STATE INSPECTORS
(10) PROVINCIAL ADMINISTRATIVE CENTERS
(13) CAPITAL CITY OR TOWN
(13) STATE
(13) THREE + LEVELS OF TERRITORIAL ADMINISTRATION
(14) ROYAL ESTATES
(14) COURT
(14) RULER HAS BODY GUARD
(14) APPOINTED GOVERNORS
(15) MONARCHY
(16) RULER ELABORATELY BURIED
(16) DECEASED RULER REVERENCED
(20) RULER BESTOWS LAND, SLAVES, RANK
(20) POLITICAL LEADER APPOINTS OFFICIALS
(20) SPECIAL RESIDENCE FOR POLITICAL LEADER
(21) DEFERENCE TO POLITICAL LEADER
(22) ADMINISTRATIVE HIERARCHY
(24) POLITICAL LEADER GRANTS AUDIENCES
(24) SUPRA-PROVINCIAL ORGANIZATION
(26) FULL-TIME RETAINERS FOR POLITICAL LEADER
(27) POLITICAL LEADER IS FULL-TIME SPECIALIST
(34) INSTALLATION CEREMONY FOR POLITICAL LEADER
(36) STRONG POLITICAL LEADERSHIP
(43) SUPRA-COMMUNITY POLITICAL UNITS
(50) REGULAR RULE OF SUCCESSION
(55) POLITICAL LEADER HAS ASSISTANTS
(81) HEADMAN, CHIEF, OR KING

MENOMINI, TUPINAMBÁ, NAMA HOTTENTOT, KAYAN, CHEYENNE, OMAHA, MAORI, IROQUOIS, ACOMA, BATAK, FLATHEAD, CREEK, TUAREG, MANO, RWALA, TANALA, THONGA, FUTUNA, FIJI, MARQUESANS, TAHITI, SUKU, BEMBA, BAVENDA, VIKINGS, HAWAII, LEÓN, BAGANDA, ASHANTI, DAHOMEY, ROMAN EMPIRE, ASSYRIA, INCA, AZTEC, EGYPT (NEW KING), CHINA(HAN)

Ministers. Murdock holds that the co-occurrence of these elements among many African kingdoms points to diffusion from a single source, which he believes to have been the western Sudan, although he allows for the borrowing of additional monarchical traits from Egypt.

To me, however, an evolutionary explanation of these resemblances seems more reasonable than a diffusional one. My reasons for believing this are as follows. Of the eighteen traits listed by Murdock some thirteen are essentially the same as ones appearing on our scale analysis list. These thirteen traits common to both lists are by no means restricted to Africa, but, on the contrary, are normally found wherever kingdoms occur. In fact, they are the very traits which *constitute* kingdoms. Their common occurrence among African monarchies, then, seems to me to point, not to a single origin and subsequent diffusion, but rather, to parallel evolution. (For similar interpretations see Posnansky [1966] and Ogot [1964].)

CARNEIRO STUDY OF CULTURAL ACCUMULATION

We have noted that in addition to arranging traits in the order of their development a scalogram ranks societies according to their degree of evolution: the greater the number of cumulating traits a society has, the more evolved it is. Since we have equated degree of evolution with level of complexity we can take the number of a society's scale traits as a measure of its cultural complexity: the more such traits it has, the more complex it is. If this is sound, then the societies in the scalogram in Figure 3 are arranged in the order of increasing complexity since they are listed according to how many of the fifty traits they possess.

With only fifty traits available to order one hundred societies, instances are bound to occur in which two or more societies have the same rank. Greater discrimination between societies can be achieved by using more traits. In order to obtain finer gradations in ranking societies we decided to use the full list of 354 traits.

Now, it is true that not all of these 354 traits scaled well. But traits used to measure the degree of cultural complexity of societies, rather than to establish a general sequence of traits, need not show high scaling. It is sufficient that they exhibit a high degree of cumulation. This is because a society manifests increasing complexity merely by orig-

TABLE 2

**THE 100 SOCIETIES IN THE SCALE ANALYSIS SAMPLE
RANKED ACCORDING TO THE NUMBER OF TRAITS THEY POSSESS
OF THE 354 INCLUDED ON THE 4TH EDITION OF THE TRAIT LIST**

1. New Kingdom Egypt (1350 B.C.)	329	51. Flathead	38
2. Roman Empire (100 A.D.)	323	52. Kiwai	37
3. Assyrian Empire (650 B.C.)	311	53. Gururumba	36
4. Aztecs	303	53. Todas	36
5. China (Han Dynasty)	299	55. Klallam	34
6. Incas	288	55. Mala	34
7. Kingdom of León	271	57. Reindeer Lapps	33
8. Vikings	225	58. Guaraní	31
9. Dahomey	202	59. Yukaghir	30
10. Ashanti	198	60. Nuer	28
11. Baganda	181	61. Tanaina	27
12. Marquesans	142	62. Tukuna	25
13. Tahitians	140	62. Comanche	25
14. Hawaiians	127	64. Tenino	24
15. Mano	126	65. Blackfoot	23
16. Bavenda	124	65. Havasupai	23
17. Batak	119	65. Canela	23
18. Fijians	114	65. Warao	23
19. Bemba	100	69. Yupa	22
20. Suku	99	69. Koryak	22
21. Tanala	94	69. Jívaro	22
22. Maori	92	72. Kamar	21
23. Pokot	86	73. Kuikuru	19
24. Acoma	82	74. Tehuelche	18
25. Rwala	79	74. Mundurucú	18
26. Creek	77	74. Gros Ventres	18
27. Tuareg	76	74. Barama River Carib	18
28. Kayan	72	78. Campa	17
29. Futunans	71	79. Yaruro	16
30. Kofyar	70	80. Cubeo	14
31. Thonga	68	81. Northern Maidu	13
32. Iroquois	64	82. Amahuaca	11
33. Bontoc	60	83. Copper Eskimo	10
33. Boloki	60	83. Chippewa	10
35. Kwakiutl	57	83. Andamanese	10
36. Molima	56	83. Ammassalik	10
37. Elgeyo	55	87. Lengua	9
38. Chiga	52	88. Sirionó	7
39. Karen	51	88. Vedda	7
40. Lango	50	88. Kaska	7
41. Ao Naga	49	91. Naskapi	6
42. Mandan	47	92. Bushmen	5
43. Omaha	45	92. Yahgan	5
43. Ifaluk	45	92. Walbiri	5
45. Nama Hottentot	44	92. Murngin	5
46. Menomini	43	96. Washo	4
47. Manobo	41	97. Semang	3
48. Tupinambá	40	97. Kurnai	3
49. Siuai	39	97. Bambuti Pygmies	3
49. Cheyenne	39	100. Tasmanians	0

inating and retaining traits, regardless of whether or not it develops those traits in the same order as other societies. If all evolving societies do develop the traits in the same order, this indicates parallel evolution. But evolution need not be parallel to be evolution.

The question, then, is: How much cumulation do the 354 traits show? No final answer can be given to this question, but evidence bearing on it can be adduced from our study of Anglo-Saxon England. This study, it will be recalled, was carried out with an expanded version of the trait list containing 618 traits. Of the 317 traits on this list of known and datable presence in Anglo-Saxon England, 310 were retained from the time they first appeared to at least the end of the period, while only 7 dropped out. This represents a striking degree of cumulation.

Of the 317 traits just referred to, 178 were among the 354 traits on the earlier version

of the list. The remaining 176 traits (of the 354) that did not figure in the Anglo-Saxon study either did not occur in England during this period or else insufficient evidence was available to permit us to date their appearance. There is no reason to believe that these 176 traits would show any less cumulation than the other 178. Thus it seems to me that we are justified in using all 354 traits in attempting to measure societal complexity.

Table 2 shows how the hundred societies in our sample rank on the basis of how many of the 354 traits they possess. For convenience we will refer to the number of such traits a society has as its Index of Cultural Accumulation.

In computing this index all traits were weighted equally. This does not mean, of course, that we regard them all as of equal importance. Everyone would agree, I think, that Markets (No. 105) are more important

TABLE 3
COMPARATIVE RANKING OF 24 NORTH AMERICAN INDIAN SOCIETIES ACCORDING TO THE INDEX OF CULTURAL ACCUMULATION AND KROEBER'S LEVELS OF CULTURAL INTENSITY

INDEX OF CULTURAL ACCUMULATION		LEVEL OF CULTURAL INTENSITY	
1. Aztecs	303	1. Aztecs	7
2. Acoma	82	2. Acoma	5+
3. Creek	77	3. Creek	4+
4. Iroquois	64	3. Kwakiutl	4+
5. Kwakiutl	57	5. Iroquois	4
6. Mandan	47	5. Mandan	4
7. Omaha	45	5. Omaha	4
8. Menomini	43	8. Menomini	4–
9. Cheyenne	39	9. Cheyenne	3+
10. Flathead	38	9. Blackfoot	3+
11. Klallam	34	9. Gros Ventres	3+
12. Tanaina	27	12. Comanche	3
13. Comanche	25	13. Klallam	3–
14. Tenino	24	13. Northern Maidu	3–
15. Havasupai	23	15. Flathead	2
16. Blackfoot	23	15. Tenino	2
17. Gros Ventres	18	15. Chippewa	2
18. Northern Maidu	13	15. Copper Eskimo	2
19. Chippewa	10	19. Tanaina	1+
19. Copper Eskimo	10	19. Havasupai	1+
19. Ammassalik	10	19. Kaska	1+
22. Kaska	7	22. Ammassalik	1
23. Naskapi	6	22. Naskapi	1
24. Washo	4	22. Washo	1

to a society than Minstrels (No. 354), and Law Courts (No. 198) more important than Jewelry (No. 326). But how does one weigh a market against a minstrel? Indeed, by what set of rules can we assign differential numerical weights to any set of culture traits? Rather than attempting to devise some elaborate but still arbitrary and subjective system of weighting we decided to follow the simple expedient of weighing every trait the same.

Admittedly there is bias in this procedure too. But this bias is partially mitigated by the fact that complex cultural features are often represented on the list by more than one trait, while this is not true of simple features. Thus there are two traits dealing with markets and three dealing with law courts, but only one deals with minstrels or with jewelry.

Despite some imprecisions in the ratings I would venture to say that the order in which societies are arranged in Table 2 probably accords well with the subjective judgment of most anthropologists. This is not sheer conjecture on my part; there is evidence to support it. For example, A. L. Kroeber (1939: 225), acting on what he considered to be "feeling or intuition," once graded the ab-

original cultures of North America into several "levels of cultural intensity." Of the societies so graded by Kroeber, 24 also occur in our sample, and in Table 3, we compare Kroeber's rankings of these societies with our own. An inspection of the parallel lists shows that the two rankings are very close. Measuring their similarity statistically we find that the coefficient of rank correlation between them is +.878.

It is not enough, however, to show that our rankings of societies accord well with subjective anthropological opinion, even if it is the opinion of someone so exceptionally well informed as Kroeber. To establish the objectivity and reliability of our findings we need to compare them with other ratings which also have a claim to objectivity. The best known and most carefully devised of these is Raoul Naroll's Index of Social Development. Of the thirty societies rated by Naroll (1956:705), fifteen occur in our sample as well. How the two indexes rate these fifteen societies is shown in Table 4. The coefficient of rank correlation between the rankings is +.885, indicating a high degree of correspondence. Each index thus helps to

TABLE 4

COMPARATIVE RANKING OF 15 SOCIETIES ACCORDING TO THE INDEX OF CULTURAL ACCUMULATION AND NAROLL'S INDEX OF SOCIAL DEVELOPMENT

INDEX OF CULTURAL ACCUMULATION		INDEX OF SOCIAL DEVELOPMENT	
1. Aztecs	303	1. Aztecs	58
2. Incas	288	2. Incas	55
3. Dahomey	202	3. Dahomey	47
4. Acoma	82	4. Hopi	36
5. Nama	44	5. Crow	32
6. Ulithi	39	5. Nuer	32
7. Crow	38	7. Nama	31
7. Flathead	38	8. Toda	29
9. Kiwai	37	9. Ulithi	28
10. Toda	36	10. Flathead	27
11. Nuer	28	11. Ramkokamekra	25
12. Ramkokamekra (Canela)	23	11. Kiwai	25
13. Ammassalik	10	13. Egedesminde	23
14. Bushmen	5	14. Naron	14
14. Yahgan	5	15. Yahgan	12

NOTE. The Acoma and Hopi, Ammassalik and Egedesminde, and Bushmen and Naron are not identical but are here taken as equivalent. The Ulithi and the Crow are not among the 100 societies used in our scale analysis sample, but they were included in the preliminary sample and trait lists had been completed for them.

validate the other, and together they serve to strengthen the belief that societal complexity is something real, objective, and measurable.

NAROLL INDEX OF SOCIAL DEVELOPMENT COMPARED TO CARNEIRO SCALE

An index of cultural complexity should do more than simply rank societies in a serial order, however. It should also indicate the magnitude of the differences in culture level between them. We want to know not only that Society A is more complex than Society B, but also by what margin. Thus we can ask of any index how well it discriminates among societies. In this regard there is a perceptible difference between Naroll's index and ours. For example, Naroll's Index of Social Development assigns the Yahgan—the simplest society in our joint sample—a score of 12, and the Aztecs—the most complex— a score of 58. Our Index of Cultural Accumulation, on the other hand, rates the Yahgan at 5 and the Aztecs at 303.

There is of course no absolute measure of the complexity of societies against which to judge our respective ratings. Thus there is no way to determine objectively which index gives the truer picture of these cultural differences. Nevertheless, it seems to me that anyone familiar with the culture of both the Yahgan and the Aztecs would be likely to agree that the ratio of 303 to 5 more closely reflects the magnitude of their difference in complexity than that of 58 to 12.

Yet it seems to me that even the margin between 303 and 5 fails to do justice to the magnitude of the cultural difference involved. The failure of our index to fully express this difference is due in part to the limited number of traits employed. If more cumulating traits were added to the list there is every reason to believe that the gap between the Aztecs and the Yahgan would widen. But there is a more subtle, and at the same time more fundamental, reason than the limitation in the number of traits for our underestimating the magnitude of differences in complexity between societies. Let us examine what it is.

As we have seen, the Index of Cultural Accumulation takes account only of the presence or absence of qualitative features. A society receives a plus for having aqueducts, temples, markets, or governors, but is given no credit for *how many* of each of these it has. Yet who would deny that a society is more complex by virture of having many temples or markets than by having only one? Certainly the Roman Empire was more complex because it had some fifty provinces and two thousand judges than it would have been had it had only two or three.

Since our aim is to measure a society's level of cultural complexity precisely we should, ideally, take account of the quantitative incidence of qualitative features. In fact it can be argued that an index which fails to do so does not measure a society's cultural evolution fully. The process of evolution, as Herbert Spencer (1866:133n.) observed, comprises two sub-processes: *growth* and *development*. Growth is an increase in *substance*, and development is an increase in *structure*. In the present context growth would be the numerical increase in existing culture traits, while development would be the emergence of new traits. Clearly, then, as our index stands now, it measures only a society's cultural development and not its growth. Thus it fails to present a complete picture of its degree of evolution.

Yet being aware of our shortcomings does not necessarily permit us to overcome them. The extensive quantitative data required for an index that would measure growth along with development are seldom to be found in the available ethnographic and historical literature. Therefore we seem to be limited to the use of indexes which, for the most part, take account of only the presence or absence of qualitative features.

RANKING SOCIETIES IN CULTURAL CATEGORIES: CORRELATION WITH COMPLEXITY INDEX

In addition to ordering societies in terms of their overall complexity the Index of Cultural Accumulation enables us to rank these societies in each of various aspects of culture. What we dealt with earlier as differential evolution now manifests itself as differential ranking: the same society may rank rather differently in one aspect of culture than it does in another. In Table 5 we have listed the fifteen highest-ranking societies in our sample in each of the following four cate-

TABLE 5
RANK ORDERING OF THE HIGHEST-RANKING 15 SOCIETIES IN THE SCALE ANALYSIS SAMPLE IN EACH OF FOUR CULTURAL CATEGORIES

Architecture	Political Organization	Economics	Religion
1 Roman Empire (27)	1 New Kingdom Egypt (48)	1 Roman Empire (39)	1 Aztec (31)
2 Assyrian Empire (26)	1 Han China (48)	2 Han China (38)	2 New Kingdom Egypt (29)
2 New Kingdom Egypt (26)	3 Inca (47)	2 Assyrian Empire (38)	3 Inca (27)
4 León (25)	3 Aztec (47)	4 New Kingdom Egypt (37)	3 Roman Empire (27)
4 Aztec (25)	5 Assyrian Empire (43)	5 León (35)	5 Assyrian Empire (26)
6 Inca (22)	6 Roman Empire (40)	6 Aztec (32)	6 Baganda (23)
7 Han China (19)	6 Dahomey (40)	7 Ashanti (30)	6 León (23)
8 Vikings (10)	8 Baganda (39)	8 Dahomey (29)	8 Ashanti (20)
9 Acoma (9)	9 Ashanti (38)	9 Vikings (25)	8 Dahomey (20)
10 Marquesans (8)	10 León (34)	10 Inca (24)	10 Marquesans (19)
11 Tahiti (7)	10 Hawaii (34)	11 Baganda (23)	10 Tahiti (19)
12 Ashanti (6)	12 Vikings (32)	12 Mano (19)	12 Maori (17)
13 Kwakiutl (3)	13 Tahiti (29)	13 Suku (17)	13 Vikings (15)
13 Kofyar (3)	14 Bavenda (28)	14 Marquesans (15)	14 Hawaii (14)
15 Batak (2)	14 Bemba (28)	15 Tuareg (14)	15 Acoma (13)

gories: Architecture, Political Organization, Economics, and Religion.

Careful examination of this table reveals a number of variations in rankings. For example, the Inca, who are third in Political Organization, are tenth in Economics, while the Kingdom of León, fourth in Architecture, is only tenth in Political Organization. And Han China, second in both Economics and Political Organization, fails by one rank to appear among the fifteen highest societies in Religion.

How well the entire hundred societies intercorrelate in rank order for some of the major categories of culture is shown in Figure 8. Each cell of this table shows the coefficient of rank correlation between the rankings of the hundred societies for the two cultural categories that intersect in that cell.

It will be seen that the highest degree of

							Religion
Warfare							.713
Law and Judicial Process						.804	.735
Political Organization					.875	.834	.708
Social Organization and Stratification				.804	.803	.826	.648
Economics			.813	.791	.815	.751	.721
Subsistence		.773	.707	.737	.787	.764	.673

Figure 8. Chart showing the coefficient of rank correlation between the rank orders of 100 societies in each of seven categories of culture.

correlation is that between Political Organization and Law and Judicial Process, with a coefficient of +.875. The lowest coefficient is that of +.648 between Social Organization and Stratification and Religion. Religion, in fact, consistently correlates less well with the other cultural categories included in the table than the latter do among themselves.

Still another way of comparing societies is by means of a bar graph in which the height of each bar is proportional to the number of traits a society has in the cultural category represented by that bar. A diagram so constructed yields what might be called the "Cultural Profile" of a society. By matching the profiles of two or more societies we

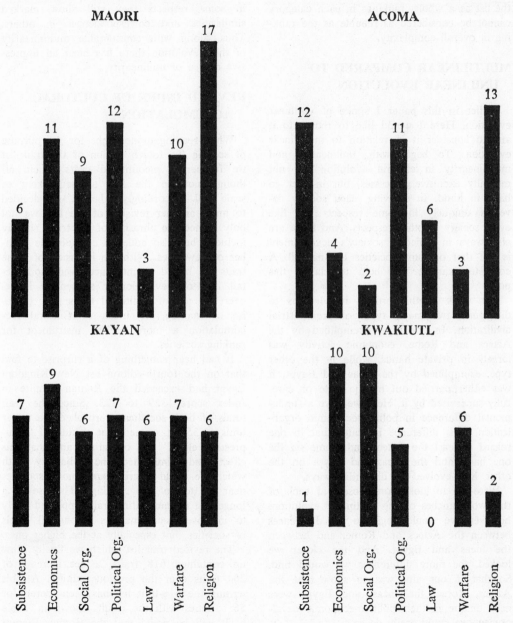

Figure 9. Bar graph showing the "cultural profile" of four societies based on the number of traits they possess from each of seven selected categories of culture.

can directly compare their relative degrees of complexity in each category. Figure 9 shows the cultural profiles of four societies: Maori, Acoma, Kayan, and Kwakiutl.

Of course, it should be borne in mind that since the number of traits used to rank a society in each cultural category is relatively small compared to the number of traits on the list as a whole, rankings in each category cannot be considered as reliable as the ranking in overall complexity.

MULTILINEAR COMPARED TO UNILINEAR EVOLUTION

Earlier in this paper I spoke of unilinear evolution. Here I would like to return to it and to consider it in relation to multilinear evolution. To begin with, unilinearity and multilinearity in cultural evolution are not mutually exclusive processes, but in fact go hand in hand. In evolving, each society develops uniquely in some respects but like every society in other respects. And there are also ways in which a society's development is like that of some societies but not all. A concrete example will help to clarify this point.

Our work in this project has led us to distinguish two major types of preindustrial civilization. In one type, exemplified by the Aztecs and Rome, economic activity was largely in private hands, while in the other type, exemplified by the Incas and Egypt, it was either carried out by the state or carefully supervised by it. Here we have a fundamental difference in politico-economic organization. This difference indicates that in one regard at least the Aztecs and Rome on the one hand and the Incas and Egypt on the other had evolved in dissimilar ways.

Were we to look more closely at each of the two branches of this "bilinear" evolution, however, we would begin to see differences between the Aztecs and Rome, and between the Incas and Egypt. And the closer we looked, the more differences we would find. So that if our aim was to show that the Aztecs, Rome, the Incas, and Egypt were each unique in their politico-economic development we could easily do so.

Yet all of these differences are accompanied by numerous and striking similarities— similarities which can be given numerical expression. Of the cumulating traits possessed by these societies—329 by Egypt, 323 by Rome, 303 by the Aztecs, and 288 by the Incas—no fewer than 241 were common to them all. Thus all four shared a very substantial core of evolutionarily significant traits. The conclusion seems inescapable that no matter how divergent or specialized these and other preindustrial civilizations may be in some respects they still show marked similarities and correspondences in others. Thus, along with considerable multilinearity in their evolution there has been an impressive degree of unilinearity.

REVISED INDEX OF CULTURAL ACCUMULATION

While reading monographs for the purpose of scoring the fourth edition of the trait list we frequently encountered traits which, although not on the list, seemed likely to scale well. Accordingly, when it was decided to make another revision of the list, we not only refined the phrasing of the traits already included but also added a considerable number of new ones. With the inclusion of these traits we hoped to introduce even more detail into our evolutionary sequences. Moreover, the use of additional traits gave promise of making the Index of Cultural Accumulation a more precise instrument for ranking societies.

It had been something of a surprise to find that on the fourth-edition list New Kingdom Egypt had exceeded the Roman Empire in Index score, 329 to 323. Since the trait totals of both societies approached the upper limit of 354 it seemed that a kind of "compression effect" was operating, and that this effect had diminished the reliability with which we could discriminate among societies near the top of the rankings. The use of a longer list of cumulating traits appeared likely to improve discriminations among all levels of societies, but especially at the higher ones.

The revised trait list which we finally drew up contained 618 traits, a net increase of 264 traits over the previous edition. At this writing the 618-trait list has been scored for 56 societies with the results shown in Table 6. It will be noted that the Roman Empire now surpasses New Kingdom Egypt in number of traits, 572 to 538, a margin wide enough to indicate a real difference between them.

TABLE 6
PROVISIONAL RANKING OF A SAMPLE OF 56 SOCIETIES BASED ON THE NUMBER OF TRAITS THEY POSSESS OF THE 618 INCLUDED IN THE 6TH EDITION OF THE TRAIT LIST

1. Roman Empire (125 A.D.)	572	31. Atayal	54
2. Ancient India (250 B.C.)	566	32. Omaha	51
3. New Kingdom Egypt (1350 B.C.)	538	33. Delaware	50
4. Athens (430 B.C.)	486	33. Tupinambá	50
5. Vikings	344	35. Cayapa	44
6. Tahiti	254	36. Guaraní	35
7. Baganda	253	37. Tukuna	32
8. Dogon	208	38. Blackfoot	31
9. Thonga	171	39. Kuikuru	28
10. Bavenda	170	39. Havasupai	28
11. Batak	160	39. Cubeo	28
12. Mangarevans	134	42. Yąnomamö	23
13. Creek	131	42. Zambales Negritos	23
14. Ao Naga	125	44. Chavante	22
15. Marshallese	122	45. Barama River Caribs	21
16. Masai	120	46. Murngin	17
17. Futuna	119	47. Ammassalik	16
18. Iroquois	96	48. Amahuaca	15
19. Kipsigis	90	48. Andamanese	15
20. Nootka	78	50. Vedda	14
21. Mandan	77	50. Pitjanjatjara	14
22. Callinago	75	52. Bushmen	13
23. Trobriand Islanders	74	53. Semang	12
24. Kiwai	71	54. Sirionó	10
25. Mala	66	55. Ona	7
26. Hottentot	62	56. Alacaluf	3
27. Manobo	59		
28. Toda	58		
29. Nuer	57		
30. Tolowa	55		

WHY MEASURE SOCIETAL COMPLEXITY

Devising an index of culture level and applying it to a sample of societies requires no practical justification. If differences in cultural complexity exist, they deserve to be revealed and measured for their own sake. But at the same time there is no reason to minimize the practical applications which such an index might have. In comparative studies of, say, cross-cousin marriage, ancestor worship, or any cultural phenomenon, one might wish to see how the occurrence of the phenomenon correlated with culture level. To do so an objective and precise index of cultural complexity would be required. For someone investigating such a problem it would be a convenience to have an index ready-made.

Moreover, for many types of problems it would be important to use an index of culture level that was independent of the phenomenon being studied. Suppose, for example, that one wanted to test White's law that culture evolves as the amount of energy harnessed per capita per year increases (White 1959:56). First of all, one would need to measure the total energy output of several societies and compute their energy expenditure per capita per year. But this would yield only one factor in the equation. There would still remain the problem of gauging each society's degree of evolution. Now, it is perfectly true that once White's law was verified the amount of energy harnessed per capita per year could be taken, not only as the *prime mover* of cultural advance, but also as a *measure* of it. However, so long as we were still testing the law it would be circular to measure cultural advance in terms of energy utilization. Clearly, we need a measure of culture level that is logically independent of energy use—a structural rather than a "metabolic" measure. The Index of Cultural Accumulation provides just such a measure.

CONCLUSIONS

Our findings in this paper point to the conclusion that human societies have evolved, and that to a considerable extent their evolution has proceeded in much the same direction. This direction is toward increased complexity, a phenomenon we found to be objective and measurable. But beyond this general trend we also discerned a specific sequence in the development of culture traits which societies, by and large, have consistently followed. This order of progression we have called the *main sequence* of cultural evolution.

The discovery and establishment of evolutionary sequences seems to me to rank high among the objectives of anthropology. Moreover, because this field was so long neglected, it can be expected to yield rich fruit in great abundance. Yet even today the number of scholars working along evolutionary lines remains surprisingly small. To many contemporary anthropologists it is incomprehensible that a previous generation could have virtually denied cultural evolution. The next generation may well ask why the present one has been so slow in seizing upon it and making it the guiding principle of its research.

APPENDIX I

The following list of 618 traits is currently being used in the study described above. It is the sixth edition of the list, and surpersedes the fourth edition (containing 354 traits) which was used in obtaining most of the data reported in this paper.

On the list below an attempt has been made to indicate those traits whose presence could be ascertained archaeologically. An "A" following a trait means that it should be possible to determine its presence in an archaeological site by direct examination of material remains. An "(A)" indicates that the presence of the trait, while not directly observable, may nevertheless be inferred from the presence of certain other traits which are themselves directly observable. Thus the presence of professional smiths (Trait 564) could be inferred from the amount and quality of metalwork found in an archaeological site. When no mark appears after a trait, its presence was judged not to be readily inferable from archaeological evidence, or, at best, to be inferable only with considerable uncertainty.

In distinguishing between traits which are archaeologically ascertainable and those which are not, I have had non-literate societies in mind. The reason for this is that for a society with written records the presence of any trait on the list could be ascertained if the trait was present, if it was recorded, and if the records were archaeologically recoverable. Thus, a trait has been marked "A" or "(A)" only if it could exist, and its presence could be detected, without the existence of any form of written records.

Subsistence

1. Agriculture (horticulture) present (i.e., domesticated food plants cultivated) A
2. Agriculture and/or domesticated animals provide the major part of subsistence (about 75% or more) (A)
3. Agricultural plots repeatedly cultivated except for periods of fallow (if they occur) A
4. Improved techniques of planting (e.g., mounds, planting in rows, breaking of clods, plowing, fertilization) A
5. Soil-working tools other than the digging stick (e.g., hoe, spade, rake, foot plow) A
6. Harvesting tools other than a simple beating stick used in reaping or threshing domesticated plants (e.g., flail, sickle, rice header, winnowing tray) A
7. Animal-drawn plow A
8. Fertilization of land with material other than wood ashes (e.g., animal manure, night soil, green manure, compost, fresh soil or mud) (A)
9. Fences built around fields or gardens to protect crops A

10. Men do as much or more of the agricultural work as women (beyond clearing) (A)
11. Drainage employed to increase the area of available agricultural land A
12. Irrigation of agricultural land A
13. Permanent dams or dikes to impound water for irrigation, drinking, etc. A
14. Terracing (including the erection of barriers to reduce soil slippage) A
15. Agricultural land reverts to kinship group (e.g., lineage, sib), chief or tribe, king or state, as personal property or for reassignment when owner or worker abandons the land or dies without heirs
16. Most of the agricultural land systematically reapportioned from time to time by the village, chief, tribe, or state to insure equitable distribution and/or a high degree of cultivation, rather than for services rendered
17. Chief, king, or other official(s) takes measures to promote or maintain agricultural production (e.g., requires land to be worked efficiently and punishes failure to do so)
18. Political or religious officials or other specialists determine the time of planting and harvesting
19. State or church provides farmers with seed or tools for agricultural purposes
20. State surveying of argicultural land
21. Surplus of food regularly accumulated over and above the annual subsistence needs of the food producers, and not consumed by them A
22. Agricultural estates which regularly produce a sizable surplus of food for sale to urban centers
23. Cash crops raised entirely or largely for sale rather than for domestic consumption
24. Granaries erected by the government and food distributed from them by a government official (A)
25. Domesticated animals serve as a source of food (exclude the eating during famines or other unusual occasions of domesticated animals not normally used as food) A
26. Domesticated animals used for packing (A)
27. Domesticated animals used for traction (A)

28. Domesticated animals used for riding (A)
29. Domesticated animals kept for wool or hair (A)
30. Selective breeding of domesticated animals (A)
31. Specialized herdsmen or dairymen
32. Fisheries or fish ponds stocked and maintained to provide a regular supply of fish for food (A)

Settlements

33. Settlements occupied for more than ten years, on the average (not necessarily all year around but at least 40 percent of the year) (A)
34. Settlements occupied for at least fifty years, (not necessarily all year around but at least 40 percent of the year) (A)
35. Settlement(s) arranged in regular pattern(s), (e.g., long house, houses in rows or streets, houses built around a square or plaza) A
36. Permanent communities (settled or nomadic) of about 100 or more members (A)
37. Permanent communities (settled or nomadic) of about 500 or more members (A)
38. Towns: nucleated settlements of 2,000 or more residents (A)
39. Two or more towns (A)
40. City: administrative and commercial population center of at least 10,000 residents (A)
41. Two or more cities (A)
42. City of 100,000 or more residents (A)
43. Planned cities A
44. Paved streets A
45. Paved sidewalks A
46. Paved plaza (exclude patios surrounded by house walls or exclusive to individual houses)
47. Civic or ceremonial structures (including men's house) not ordinarily used as dwellings by family units (excluding structures built for specific occasions and later abandoned, dismantled, or destroyed) A
48. Permanent cemeteries where the graves of the interred are marked A
49. Stone monuments or stelae (excluding cairns of unworked stones) to mark or

commemorate important persons or events (e.g., megaliths, obelisks, triumphal arches, pyramids) A

50. Grandstands, theaters, amphitheaters, or stadiums where spectators can witness contests or performances A
51. Formal or landscape gardens (A)
52. Ornamental fountains A
53. Aqueducts or conduits of stone or brick to supply water for domestic use A
54. Running water piped into dwellings or public buildings A
55. Cisterns: rain-catching or water-holding basins artificially lined with stone or other hard or impervious material (excluding clay) A
56. Baths of stone, brick, or tile A
57. Drains: lined channels, covered or uncovered, or pipes used to carry off rain or bath water A
58. Sewers: lined and covered channels or pipes, primarily for carrying away human waste A
59. Apartment houses: multistoried dwellings in which rooms are customarily rented to tenants (A)
60. Permanent fortifications (including palisades around settlements, blockhouses, citadels, and fortified boundaries, but excluding structures whose primary purpose is not defensive, e.g., compounds, fortifications around dwellings which are normally occupied by only one or a few families) A
61. Walls of stone, brick, adobe, or beaten earth (including earthworks) used in fortification A
62. Frontiers fortified with stone walls A
63. Moats (excluding dry ditches but including diverted rivers) used to protect settlements or fortifications A
64. Taverns, inns, or eating houses providing food, drink, and/or lodging (A)
65. Brothels (A)
66. Fire brigade
67. Broad and well-maintained roads connecting settlements A
68. Network of paved roads connecting settlements A
69. Bridges or causeways (excluding log spans, vine ropes, and simple pole frameworks) A
70. Way stations or resthouses, not necessarily staffed, which provide lodging for travelers A

Architecture

71. Rectangular ground plan for dwellings A
72. Substantial houses which are lived in for at least ten years without being permanently abandoned, dismantled, or rebuilt A
73. Interior space of houses permanently divided by means of walls or partitions (include lofts) A
74. Dwellings divided into three or more walled-off and separate rooms, with some degree of functional differentiation between them A
75. Dwellings which customarily house four or more family units A
76. Multistoried structures (not meant to include high storage platforms or lofts which do not form a complete story) A
77. Walls, ceilings, roof, or other part of dwellings or other structures extensively painted or carved A
78. Cut stone masonry A
79. Cut stone or brick substructures (e.g., platforms, truncated pyramids) used as bases for civic or ceremonial structures A
80. Dwellings (including walls) constructed of cut stone or fired brick A
81. Civic or ceremonial buildings constructed of cut stone or fired brick A
82. Monumental architecture of stone or brick (e.g., pyramids, palaces, temples, fortresses, amphitheaters, but excluding solid platforms) A
83. Quarrying of stone for construction (rather than merely dressing loose stones) A
84. Megalithic construction using blocks of stone too heavy to be moved without mechanical devices such as rollers, sledges, ramps, or pulleys A
85. Stone coursing (blocks of cut stone laid in successive horizontal layers) A
86. Rubble or some other fill used between walls in stone or brick construction A
87. Fired brick used in construction A
88. Walls of beaten earth or adobe A
89. True mortar (i.e., a plastic substance with a chemical bonding action) used in construction A
90. Facing of stone or brick walls or columns with plaster, alabaster, tile, etc. A
91. Roof of tile, brick, dressed stone,

planks, etc. (i.e., not bark, mud, thatching, or similar material) A

92. House floors made of stone, brick, tile, flagstone, or wood (including palm and bamboo) A
93. Stone lintels A
94. Arches of stone or brick (corbeled or keystone) A
95. True (keystone) arch A
96. Stone or brick pillars or columns used structurally A
97. Stone or brick stairways (of cut blocks, or carved into living rock) A
98. Buttresses used to strengthen stone or brick walls A
99. Ornamental carving of stone columns, walls, lintels, or other architectural features of stone A
100. Architectural features (e.g., tombs, stairways) cut into living rock A
101. Fortresses built of stone or brick (including walled cities and citadels, where people take refuge in time of war) A
102. Elaborations in fortified walls (including, e.g., towers, salients, merlons, but excluding loopholes) A
103. Professional (full-time) carpenters or woodworkers (excluding canoemakers and thatchers) (A)
104. Professional (full-time) stone masons or bricklayers (A)
105. Professional (full-time) architects or engineers (A)

Economics

106. Landed property: individual or familial ownership rights over improved land (e.g., cultivated plots, house sites) continue to be exercised, even if land ceases to be occupied or worked
107. Boundary markers (excluding growing crop plants but including hedges) set up in order to indicate the limits of a piece of private property or individually worked land (A)
108. Agricultural land commonly bought and sold
109. Economic speculation in land, foodstuffs, or other commodities a common practice
110. Inscription of land or other forms of property (registry of deeds)
111. Rental of land or dwellings by landlords to tenants as a system of tenure

112. Share-cropping: a system of land tenure in which the tenant (who is not a serf) pays the landlord a specific proportion or amount of the crop as rent
113. Leasing of land or dwellings: a formal agreement (not merely observance of custom) in which a tenant's right of occupancy is guaranteed for a specified period
114. Serfs: tenants and their descendants legally bound to land which they farm for the benefit of private persons or corporate groups (e.g., feudal lords, temples, monasteries)
115. Private ownership (not ownership by a sib or a local group) or government control exercised over scarce or limited natural resources (e.g., clay pits, clam beds, salt, water holes, mineral deposits, grove of wild fruit trees) rather than free access to them (A)
116. Seals, brands, or other distinctive marks used to indicate ownership of manufactured property A
117. Marked differences in wealth (e.g., real property, livestock, precious metals, slaves; but excluding wives, ceremonial bundles) among members of the society (other than the difference between the principal political leader or religious specialist and everyone else) A
118. Feasts or gift-giving ceremonies in which much wealth is displayed or consumed, including those for state purposes
119. Recorded inventories of property owned (e.g., with pebbles, knotted cords, notched sticks, clay tablets, ledgers) (A)
120. Most individual (not family) property owned and in the possession of a person at the time of his death (exclude property lent out and still outstanding) transmitted by inheritance rather than being buried, destroyed, or otherwise disposed of at the death of the owner (A)
121. Testamentary disposition of property, by a written will, through a formal executor, or orally in the presence of a witness (excluding incorporeal property)
122. Craft specialization: some craft(s) which only a limited number of persons in the society practice (excluding the making of religious or ceremonial objects by shamans or priests, or chiefs)
123. A significant amount of craft production primarily for economic exchange

rather than for personal consumption (A)

124. Full-time craft specialists (e.g., brewer, lapidary, tailor, baker, tanner) (A)
125. Service specialization: some services which only a limited number of persons in the society provide (excluding religious specialists and curers, but including clans or other groups that perform specialized services) (A)
126. Full-time service specialists other than religious practitioners (e.g., tattooer, barber, accountant, lawyer, physician) (A)
127. Professional barbers or hairdressers (A)
128. Professional porters or bearers (A)
129. Processing or preparation of food by full-time specialists (e.g., millers, butchers, cooks, bakers) other than household servants or slaves (A)
130. Professional brewers or wine makers (A)
131. Clothing or shoes manufactured by full-time specialists (A)
132. Medium of exchange, which is frequently used in trade for a variety of commodities A
133 Currency: a medium valued primarily for its use in economic exchanges rather than as an ornamental or consumable good, and which may be exchanged freely for any goods or commodities which are traded A
134. A significant amount of economic exchange carried out by means of currency or money (A)
135. Metallic currency valued according to weight (including coins) A
136. Two or more metals of different monetary value used as currency A
137. Coined money A
138. Coins of different denominations A
139. Animals, seed crops, or foodstuffs lent out at interest
140. Money or goods (not including animals or foodstuffs) lent out at interest
141. Professional moneylenders
142. Banks, which pay interest on deposits and make loans
143. Pledging of items of movable property as security on a debt
144. Pledging of oneself or members of one's family as security on a debt
145. Mortgage: a legal instrument offering land or houses as security to guarantee the repayment of a loan

146. Insurance: protection against calamities (e.g., fire, theft, loss of merchandise at sea) offered by an underwriter for a premium
147. Trade between communities (A)
148. Economically important trade carried out between communities or regions (including that conducted through itinerant merchants) (A)
149. Economically important trade in which finished goods (excluding food) are traded to other communities or societies (including exchanges conducted through itinerant merchants) (A)
150. Full-time specialist(s) in trade (A)
151. Trading outposts maintained outside the territory of the society
152. Markets, in which a variety of goods is traded (A)
153. Daily and permanent markets
154. Specialized market(s) within a town or city (e.g., fish market, cattle market, textile market, flower market) (A)
155. Itinerant merchants or specialized traders who are members of the society itself (rather than foreigners), and who remain such even if they trade outside the society (A)
156. Sedentary merchants who operate fixed commercial establishments outside the market area A
157. Wholesale merchants
158. Professional merchants undertake large-scale trading expeditions
159. Merchants form a significant segment of the society (A)
160. Merchants constitute a class, with prescribed advantages (e.g., exemption from military service or corvée labor) and/or disabilities (e.g., exclusion from holding office, subjection to discriminatory taxation)
161. Contracts: economic agreements legally enforceable by a higher authority (A)
162. Economic transactions formally witnessed or notarized
163. Commercial agreements negotiated between states
164. Seals, signatures, or individual marks used to authenticate commercial transactions
165. Commercial warehouses used to store privately-owned merchandise (A)
166. Bills of lading or other written docu-

ments used in large-scale shipments of goods

167. Long-term commercial records kept

168. Companies: private business enterprises including two or more persons who are organized to carry out commercial or industrial operations

169. Corporations: companies, chartered by the state, the members of which have limited liability

170. Labor mobilized by the offer of compensation (rather than by a kinship obligation), e.g., food and drink, payment in kind or money, salary (A)

171. Individuals commonly hired to perform unskilled manual labor

172. Wage labor, for which payment is made at definite rates and intervals

173. Enforced mobilization of labor for community, tribal, or state projects (excluding military conscription) (A)

174. Corvée (draft labor exacted by a supra-community authority or agency) (A)

175. Artisans and laborers attached to or employed on a regular basis (rather than under the corvée) by political or religious institutions (tribe or state, temple or church) (A)

176. Overseers, who superintend the labor of slaves or other workers (other than majordomos on private estates)

177. Factories: enterprises in which workers, under unified supervision, produce goods by performing differentiated tasks (including temple workshops) A

178. Trademarks placed on articles to identify the maker or manufacturer (e.g., potter's mark, swordsmith's signature, mint marks) A

179. Class of artisans who are freemen and who sell their products or services

180. Neighborhoods of specialized artisans within towns or cities A

181. Certain industries concentrated in particular villages, towns, or cities A

182. Guilds (i.e., cooperative associations) of craft or service specialists, including labor unions

183. Guilds of merchants or bankers

184. Taxation in kind (including produce from land farmed for the state, but excluding required contributions to community projects or ceremonies) (A)

185. Taxation in currency (A)

186. Official tax, tribute, or customs collectors (excluding local chiefs)

187. Collection of taxes in kind or currency on a regular schedule and at fixed rates

188. Special taxes, in addition to or instead of regular taxes, levied for special needs (e.g., war expenses, public works, royal marriages; but excluding primarily religious taxes)

189. Tax obligations commutable into service to the state or its representative

190. Assessors (as distinct from tax collectors) who appraise land or other property, and determine the amount of taxes to be paid

191. Taxes assessed on land

192. Taxes assessed on movable property (including crops and livestock)

193. Taxes on commerce (e.g., sales taxes, taxes on goods brought to market, ground rents on places in market)

194. Taxes on the manufacture, sale, or consumption of luxury goods

195. Inheritance taxes

196. Duties on goods imported, or transported across internal boundaries

197. Tolls collected for the use of roads, bridges, or ferries

198. Produce of certain privately worked lands set aside for the chief, king, tribe or state (excluding chief's land worked by the people at large for his support)

199. Superintendent who supervises the maintenance of royal or state herds, lands, or forests

200. The extent of landholdings limited by law or decree

201. State fixes rent or rent ceilings on privately owned lands or dwellings

202. Government operates industries or exploits resources directly (e.g., weaving, armoring, goldsmithing; mines, salt deposits)

203. Government derives revenue from industries and resources indirectly (e.g., licenses salt production, wine making, ironworking, mining)

204. Government registration or licensing of craft specialists, service specialists, or merchants for purposes of taxation or control

205. State lets out contracts to private enterprises for the performance of certain

functions (e.g., public works, tax collection) or the supply of certain goods
206. State sells or auctions public property (e.g., public lands, confiscated property, captured war booty) to raise revenue
207. Government buys or sells commodities on the open market
208. State obtains loans from private sources or from other states
209. Governmental supervision or regulation of commerce (e.g., inspecting weights and measures, maintaining order in markets, settling commercial disputes, enforcing payment of debts, fixing price levels)
210. Government inspection, licensing, or regulation of places of entertainment (e.g., taverns, gambling houses, brothels)
211. State-directed trade (i.e., trade carried on by agents of the state with other societies)
212. Wage levels of certain occupations fixed by law
213. Interest rates fixed by law and usury punishable
214. Distraint of property (by government officials, not private seizure) for default of debts or nonpayment of taxes
215. Government relieves conditions of food shortage or famine by distributing or selling foodstuffs
216. Public, government, or church support (as against support by kinsmen or tribesmen only) of the destitute (e.g., widows, orphans, aged, or infirm), excluding becoming wards or servants of the chief or king by indigent persons

Social Organization and Stratification

217. Social (rather than territorial) segments above the level of the extended family or household (e.g., lineages, sibs, moieties, marriage classes, social classes, castes, age grades, men's clubs, secret societies, warrior societies, ceremonial teams, craft guilds) (A)
218. Two or more different types of social segments (A)
219. Unilineal kin groups (segments) beyond extended families (including royal or chiefly lineages)
220. Genealogies traced back reliably for at least five generations

221. Voluntary associations, permanent and corporate, based on principles other than kinship or age
222. Blood brotherhood or other special friendships solemnized by ceremonies
223. Occupational classes, castes, or descent groups (excluding slaves, but including clans with specific duties)
224. Marriage formalized by bride price, bride service, or gift exchange between the bride and groom or their families
225. Dowry (as distinguished from the contribution of the bride or her family in gift exchange)
226. Marriage celebrated with a feast
227. Marriages performed or registered by priests or officials of the state (not including the mere blessing of the couple by a priest)
228. Well-defined and significant differences in social status (other than the difference between the principal political leader or shaman and everyone else, or differences based on age or sex) A
229. The accumulation of wealth in movable property or land, even without its redistribution, brings considerable prestige or influence (A)
230. Stratification of the society into distinct social classes (excluding status distinctions based only on age or sex, and the ranking of clans or subclans) (A)
231. Stratification of the society into at least three distinct social classes (A)
232. Differences of rank within the upper class(es) other than that based on political or religious office or sex
233. Class distinctions in legal liability for offenses (i.e., members of the various social classes have different rights under the law)
234. Special ornaments, differences in clothing, or other marks, which distinguish members of one class from the rest of the society (A)
235. Insignia of noble or high rank (e.g., earplugs, special hairdos, coats of arms) meant primarily to indicate status rather than being largely ornamental
236. Sumptuary laws concerning dress, adornment, or other manifestations of wealth and serving to maintain class distinctions
237. Some individual members of the society

(other than the political leader) have categorically superior residences A

238. Some individual members of the society (other than the political leader) own significantly more land than others (A)

239. Majordomos supervise staffs of private households or estates (other than that of the political leader)

240. Some members of the society (other than the political leader) have numerous wives or concubines (at least eight or ten) (A)

241. Some members of the society (other than the political leader) have permanent domestic servants or retainers (other than slaves) (A)

242. Persons of high rank (other than the political leader) have special privileges (e.g., exemption from taxation or corvée, right to hold political or religious office, right to remain seated in the king's presence) excluding privileges relating to dress and ornament

243. Competitive sports or spectacles staged by the political leader or members of the upper classes

244. Hunting primarily a pastime of the chief, king, or upper classes

245. Elaborate code of social conduct serves to distinguish between social classes or individuals of different social positions

246. Status (excluding age and sex) class, or caste differences in disposal of the dead (based on social rather than religious status; exclude shamans and priests) A

247. Some members of the society (other than the political leader) buried with large amounts of wealth, or have a considerable number of animals sacrificed at their death A

248. Some members of the society (other than the political leader) buried with or accompanied in death by wives, concubines, retainers, or slaves A

249. Some members of the society (other than the political leader) buried in elaborate tombs or graves (e.g., burial mounds, cist graves, thatched buildings) A

250. War captives or persons bought outside the society kept as slaves without subsequently being liberated, killed, or granted equal status with native-born members of the society (A)

251. Debtors or criminals made slaves, or other freeborn members of the society (including wives and children) sold into slavery

252. Slaves branded, tonsured, or otherwise identified

253. Some slaves kept as personal servants and not used in economically productive activities (including cooking)

254. Slaves as a class economically significant, i.e., they add to the economy more than they consume (produce food, make goods, or yield a product in significant amounts, rather than merely doing odd work)

255. Slaves bought and sold within the society (excluding the selling into slavery of freeborn members of the society)

256. Slave markets

257. Hereditary slavery

258. Manumission of slaves common

Political Organization

259. Communities (or camps) continuously grouped (year-round) into larger political units which recognize some central authority A

260. Districts or provinces, each comprising several villages or communities, are permanently grouped into a larger political unit (A)

261. Three or more levels of territorial administration above the community (e.g., 1. district, 2. province, 3. quarter, 4. kingdom)

262. State: permanent organization of a number of supra-community units (districts, tribes, or provinces) into a single political unit under centralized control, involving at least (a) some power to collect revenue, (b) the power to conscript men for work or war, (c) some centralized judicial authority, and (d) the power to formulate and execute policy (A)

263. Population of the state 100,000 or above (A)

264. Population of the state 1,000,000 or above (A)

265. Citizenship: citizens have certain rights under the law which noncitizens do not have

266. State or tribe has capital city, town, or village (A)

267. Towns or cities divided into quarters or wards for civil or judicial purposes

268. State endeavors to maintain administrative units of approximately equal size at each of several levels by redistricting or by the movement of populations

269. Government permission required to travel or move from one administrative unit to another

270. Colonists sent to settle in conquered or newly-opened territory

271. Young persons sent to capital for training or royal service or as hostages

272. A generally recognized agent or agency of the society (e.g., headman, chief, king, council of elders) makes decisions or policy affecting the society as a whole (A)

273. Political leader(s) has the power, by threat or exercise of active sanctions, to make individuals comply with his decisions (e.g., can assign tasks, draft labor, impose taxes, command military service) (A)

274. Political leader(s) exercises judicial power (decides guilt and decrees punishment, or settles cases appealed to him; does not merely mediate) (A)

275. Political leader(s) exercises supreme judicial authority, e.g., has the power to reverse decisions of inferior judges or courts in civil or criminal cases

276. Chiefly or kingly line through which political leadership is customarily transmitted

277. Heir apparent undergoes rigorous or intensive training or education as preparation for his future office, including, e.g., serving as governor of a province

278. Property qualifications required for appointment or formal election to public office

279. Secondary political leader(s) who have authority over segments of the society (e.g., sub-chiefs, house chiefs, clan chiefs, village chiefs, governors) (A)

280. Formally constituted council (permanent or *ad hoc*) or official who advises, deliberates with, or controls the political leader

281. Nonterritorial advisors or administrative civil officials: functionaries who advise or act at the direction of the political leader, but who are not personal servants or retainers (e.g., talking chiefs) (A)

282. Specialized official(s) in charge of one or more activities or enterprises controlled or supervised by the government

283. Hierarchy of nonterritorial administrative officials (excluding palace hierarchy) (A)

284. Secondary political officials may appoint their subordinates

285. Provincial or district administrative centers where officials appointed by the state (other than local chiefs) collect taxes or maintain order (A)

286. Towns or cities within a larger political unit have municipal governments

287. Secretariat, in charge of drafting, promulgating, and circulating laws or royal decrees

288. Accountant or treasurer who keeps track of the wealth accumulated by the chief, king, or state (A)

289. Inspectors, censors, or secret agents who examine records or investigate the functioning of officials, popular discontent, etc.

290. Census taken (including simple enumerations or head counts) (A)

291. Organized messenger or courier system which links together most of the society's territory (A)

292. Ministries: government departments headed by ministers and having full-time staffs of officials and clerks

293. Ministry of revenue or finance

294. Ministry of public works

295. Ministry of justice

296. Ministry of religious affairs, rites, or ceremonials

297. Ministry of foreign affairs

298. Ministry of war

299. Prime minister: principal administrative official below the ruler who initiates or executes policy

300. Council of ministers forming a regular advisory body to the ruler

301. Devices used to confirm or authenticate official orders, decrees, actions, and transactions (e.g., seals, signatures, rings, or other symbols)

302. Auditing procedures to check for errors or embezzlement in government financial accounts

303. Budget: a comprehensive and itemized estimate of anticipated revenues and expenditures, periodically prepared by government officials

304. Annals of state affairs regularly kept by official historian(s)

305. Archives in which official records and state papers are kept
306. State officials paid a fixed salary
307. Officials' salaries paid, at least in part, in currency rather than in kind
308. Codified regulations minutely govern the constitution and operation of the administrative structure
309. Political leader does not ordinarily engage in subsistence (A)
310. Political leader may not engage in certain common economic activities, which are considered to be beneath his status
311. Political leader entertains on a lavish scale
312. Political leader bestows land, slaves, wealth, women, or noble rank for services rendered
313. Political leader appoints and deposes subordinate political officials (A)
314. Political leader promulgates laws, issues decrees, or makes proclamations to the populace (not just orders that are obeyed) (A)
315. Political leader grants formal audiences to hear grievances or petitions (exclude appeal in legal cases)
316. Political leader makes regular visits to various parts of the kingdom to examine conditions, hear cases, collect taxes, awe his subjects, etc.
317. Political leader travels with a retinue
318. Political leader exercises considerable control over the activities of temples or the church (e.g., performs investiture of priests, endows temples)
319. Political leader performs rituals considered essential for the welfare of the society, and which only he can perform
320. Special ceremony for installation or investiture of new political leader (e.g., oath of office, coronation) (A)
321. Political leader has special symbols of office or authority (e.g., throne, crown, scepter, seal, robes) (A)
322. Displays of special deference to political leader (e.g., carrying in a litter, averting the eyes, bowing)
323. Officials, vassals, sub-chiefs, or courtiers swear allegiance to the chief, king, or state
324. Political leader addressed or referred to by various honorific titles
325. Lese majesty—an offense against the

dignity, person, or property of the ruler —severely punished
326. Political leader is considered divine, semi-divine, or sacred, or traces his descent from a god
327. Political leader buried with large amounts of wealth A
328. Wives, concubines, retainers, or slaves of political leader buried with him or otherwise killed at the time of his death A
329. Political leader buried in an elaborate tomb or grave (e.g., burial mound, cist grave, thatched building, pyramid) A
330. Special treatment (e.g., desiccation, embalming) to preserve the political leader's corpse or part thereof (not just the bones) A
331. Deceased former political leader especially reverenced (e.g., his spirit invoked or propitiated, monuments erected to his memory)
332. Chief or king receives large amounts of food and/or other goods as gifts, tribute, taxes, or fines (A)
333. Political leader lives in a special residence or compound categorically superior to any other residence A
334. Royal estates, residences, or preserves outside the capital which are the property of the ruler A
335. Political leader has full-time personal attendants or retainers (A)
336. Royal or chiefly household maintained by a steward and staff (A)
337. Court, a body of officials, members of upper classes, retainers, entertainers, etc., surrounding the chief or king (A)
338. Chief or king has significantly more wives or concubines than anyone else (A)
339. Chief or king has a harem (a special residence(s) supervised by a responsible official(s), e.g., a eunuch) (A)
340. Bodyguard to protect the ruler's person
341. Private tutors retained at court to instruct prince(s) and/or children of nobles
342. Political leader or state has storehouse or treasury (for hard goods or valuables, rather than for food) A
343. Formal treaties (recorded or witnessed and sworn) concluded between societies to establish alliances, to settle disputes, or to end wars
344. Ambassador(s): diplomatic representative

acting in regular relations with a foreign government

345. Diplomatic missions by government officials carried out for specific purposes

346. Passports, visas, or tallies to control the entry or exit of persons, native or foreign

347. Superordinate tribe or state which receives tribute, labor, soldiers, or other recognition of obligation from subordinate or vassal tribe(s) or state(s) (A)

348. Resident political officials who oversee native rulers of feudatory or tributary states

Law and Judicial Process

349. Composition: redress of death or bodily injury by payment of an indemnity to the victim or his relatives (with or without a formal judicial proceeding)

350. Ordeals or oaths to establish guilt or innocence or to settle disputes prescribed or enforced (exclude torture applied to extract a confession)

351. Mediation or formal legal procedure customarily used to settle at least one type of dispute within the political unit (A)

352. Disputes over land settled by political or judicial authority, rather than only by mediation or fighting (A)

353. Judicial process, in which an individual or limited group (e.g., council of elders, tribal chief, court of law) considers evidence and renders judgment in a dispute, or of an accused person, on behalf of the society (A)

354. Court trials, held under specialized judges or magistrates who hear testimony and weigh evidence, interpret the law or customary law, and render a decision in civil or criminal cases

355. Judicial system of higher and lower courts, cases being referred to one or the other according to their nature, with decisions of lower courts perhaps appealable to higher courts

356. Specialized courts (e.g., market courts, military courts, ecclesiastical courts, divorce courts)

357. Legal counsel: specialized advocates or lawyers who interpret the law or act for clients in legal cases

358. Oaths or affirmations of truthful testimony required of witnesses in legal trials

359. Oaths of compurgation accepted as evidence of innocence at legal trials

360. Perjury or false testimony in legal cases punishable by law

361. Judges: officials whose sole function it is to apply the law and render decisions in civil or criminal cases

362. Police: specialized individual or force charged with keeping the peace, enforcement of norms, or the apprehension and detention of offenders

363. Specialized public executioner

364. Law: a body of explicitly formulated secular norms, interpreted, applied, and enforced by a constituted authority (A)

365. Laws recurrently decreed by a ruler or enacted by a legislative body

366. Code of laws (explicit and recorded) which covers social, political, and/or economic relations

367. Offenses against persons (e.g., sorcery— if actually practiced, assault, maiming, rape, murder) punishable under law or custom by formal means (A)

368. Offenses against property (e.g., theft, arson, willful or inadvertent destruction) subject to indemnification or punishment under law or custom by formal means (A)

369. Obstruction of justice (e.g., harboring of criminals, refusing to give evidence) punishable under law

370. Laws governing marriage, divorce, abortion, infanticide, or adoption

371. Laws governing inheritance

372. Laziness, malingering, or vagrancy punishable by law

373. Libel, slander, or malicious lying punishable by law

374. Laws regulating borrowing and lending

375. Building codes: laws regulating house construction (e.g., prescribing building materials, limiting number of stories)

376. Sacrilege—irreverence or disrespect toward a sacred person, place, custom, or object—severely punished

377. Religious law enforced by political officials

378. Statute of limitations specifying the time within which offenders must be brought to trial to be punishable

379. Most offenses regularly punished by a specially designated or permanent agent

of the society rather than by the offended parties themselves (A)

380. Crimes legally punishable by public authorities only; private action illegal

381. Certain offenses punished by fines (in currency or in kind) paid to the lineage, sib or village, tribe or state, of which part may go to the offended party (including penalty feasts)

382. Certain offenses punished by confiscation of property, of which part may go to the offended party

383. Fines collected or property confiscated by political authority and not shared with the offended party (unless he is the political leader)

384. Corporal punishment (including mutilation, shaving off hair) meted out for certain offenses by an authorized agent of the society (other than the offended party or his kin unless he is the political leader) (A)

385. Incarceration of convicted offenders (in shackles, stocks, pens, cages, or prisons) (A)

386. Certain offenses punished by slavery or by terms at hard labor.

387. Death penalty decreed by custom or after judicial procedure for certain crimes, and exacted openly by someone acting with the explicit approval of the society (A)

388. Commutation of sentences for certain crimes may be granted upon payment of a fixed amount

389. Political leader sometimes pardons convicted offenders

390. General amnesties granted on special occasions

391. Violation of secular legal norms automatically incurs punishment by gods during the individual's lifetime, as well as secular punishment by a formally designated agent of the society

Warfare

392. Warfare initiated for considerations other than (or in addition to) the avenging of insults, personal injury, murder, witchcraft, the stealing of women, trespass, or forestalling an enemy attack (A)

393. Economic considerations (e.g., territorial acquisition, the capture of booty, the

taking of slaves) important in the initiation of warfare (A)

394. Warfare initiated in order to impose religious dogma or to make religious observances (e.g., human sacrifice)

395. Formal warning, challenges, or declaration of war, including the displaying of symbols, customarily given

396. Recognized war leader(s) (other than a political leader) who regularly leads the men of the society against the enemy (e.g., war chief, general)

397. Professional military commanders (e.g., generals) who regularly lead the army in time of war

398. Professional middle-level military officials (e.g., centurions, lieutenants, captains)

399. Body of specially trained or highly skilled warriors (as distinct from the rest of the fighting men)

400. Standing army, organized around a core of professional soldiers, and continuously maintained

401. Militia: a semimilitary organization with officers who keep its units in readiness to quell uprisings or repel invasions

402. Military conscription (those disinclined to fight either coerced into doing so, allowed to commute, or else subject to punishment) (A)

403. Substitutes may be hired or commutation paid to fulfill military or corvée obligations

404. Troops receive fixed pay (over and above, or instead of, a share of the booty)

405. Mercenaries (i.e., paid foreign troops) used in warfare

406. Soldiers or officers take oath of allegiance

407. Fighting force customarily divided into subunits

408. Army organized into groups of units which are successively more inclusive (e.g., platoons, companies, regiments, divisions)

409. Organized drills or exercises carried out to prepare for war

410. Differentiated military units (e.g., spearmen, bowmen, slingers, cavalry) A

411. Cavalry A

412. Military engineers (A)

413. Baggage trains used to transport the army's supplies

414. Pitched battles, involving considerable hand-to-hand fighting, initiated, in which the objective is to destroy or drive off the enemy fighting force, or capture (rather than merely raid) enemy settlements (A)

415. Fighters begin battle in formation (including arrangement in a straight line) (A)

416. Soldiers fight closely aligned or as compact units, rather than as separate individuals (A)

417. Formal rules governing conduct of soldiers and officers in war

418. Arsenals or armories where government stockpiles of weapons are maintained A

419. Cutting or thrusting weapons used in warfare A

420. Defensive body armor (exclude shields and helmets) A

421. Metal armor used in warfare A

422. Chariots used in warfare A

423. Emblems, banners, or special objects which serve to identify military units, or act as rallying points, are carried into battle (A)

424. Drums, horns, trumpets, etc., used to signal commands in battle or to encourage troops (excluding the use of these instruments merely to frighten the enemy)

425. Espionage, by special agents who gather strategic information in foreign territory by hiding their purpose and/or identity but not their persons

426. Sieges laid to enemy fortifications strong enough to resist immediate assault (A)

427. Permanently garrisoned forts (excluding observation posts, walled towns and cities) (A)

428. Battering rams A

429. Assault ladders or towers used in sieges A

430. Siege ramps

431. Catapult-type devices used as siege engines A

432. Body trophies (e.g., heads, scalps, hands) taken in war or from sacrificed prisoners A

433. Considerable booty taken during successful military campaigns (A)

434. Adult males frequently taken captive in warfare A

435. Cannibalism of war captives A

436. War captives regularly sacrificed to god(s) (A)

437. War captives kept for ransom or held as hostages

438. Special ornaments, insignia, or appellations awarded for prowess or wounds received in battle

439. Outstanding warriors rewarded with gifts of property, women, or slaves, or appointment to official positions

440. Nobility or distinctly high social status attainable through war exploits

441. Death, confiscation of property, or other severe punishment may be penalty for cowardice in battle, desertion, or insurrection

442. Formal ceremonies (including the making of treaties) to conclude hostilities with other societies

443. Military parades or reviews in which military skill and prowess are exhibited (excluding celebrations held for returning warriors)

444. Territory of vanquished enemy annexed (A)

445. Peoples of vanquished enemy subjugated and held under effective control (A)

446. Defeated political leader(s) or his relative(s) retained in authority over his territory on pledge of allegiance to conquerors

447. Indemnities or reparations (as distinct from tribute) exacted from defeated enemies

448. Permanent settlements built in conquered territory (A)

Religion

449. Supernatural being(s) who currently intervenes for the benefit of suppliants (A)

450. Ancestral spirits propitiated and invoked

451. God(s): specifically personified supernatural being(s) (not impersonal force) who is not particular to locations or to kinship segments (exclude, e.g., ancestral, guardian, and other personal spirits), to whom prayers are directed and who intervenes for the benefit of the society or its members (A)

452. Sun god worshiped (i.e., propitiated and invoked) (A)

453. God of war (not necessarily connected exclusively with war) worshiped (A)

454. Lawgiver god, who on more than one

occasion has enunciated extensive rules for governing human conduct, worshiped

455. Patron gods or saints (not including guardian spirits), who afford protection to groups of individuals engaged in particular occupations or activities (e.g., god of merchants, god of hunters, god of travelers, god of blacksmiths, god of war) (A)

456. Pantheon of gods worshiped (propitiated and invoked); (applies only to differentiated gods who actively control spheres of life or nature, e.g., rain god, war god, fire god, fertility goddess, love goddess) (A)

457. One god in the pantheon of differentiated gods worshiped as paramount (A)

458. Manner of living or dying affects the status or condition of the soul after death

459. Offerings (including libations and sacrifices) (A)

460. Libations: the ritual pouring, sprinkling, or drinking of a liquid

461. Animal sacrifices directed to supernatural beings to placate them or gain their favor (A)

462. Human sacrifice directed to supernatural beings to placate them or gain their favor (A)

463. Private worship of supernatural beings through personally owned (rather than societally maintained) idols, altars, or shrines (A)

464. Private ceremonies or sacrifices performed by priests (not shamans or medicine men) on behalf of individuals for payment

465. Priests conduct sacrifices on behalf of the society, or a significant segment thereof, to ward off calamities, solicit benefits, or offer thanks

466. Rites of passage performed by priests

467. Rites to promote fertility of the soil, to bring rain, or to celebrate the harvest performed seasonally (rather than merely when the crop is in danger)

468. Thank offerings to supernatural being(s)

469. Offerings, sacrifices, prayers, or other rituals carried out by religious specialists before battle

470. Victory offerings made to supernatural being(s) after successful military campaign (A)

471. Offerings or sacrifices made in connection with housebuilding or the erection of other structures

472. Religious pilgrimages to distant shrines or sacred places (A)

473. Votive offerings or ceremonies or votive pilgrimages made

474. Idols: durable representations made in the likeness of supernatural beings through or in which they are worshiped (A)

475. Oracles: shrines, places, or objects where, or by means of which, a medium transmits answers to questions posed to a god or spirit (exclude the use of animals for augury) (A)

476. Shrines, altars, ceremonial platforms, or other sacred places where religious practices (e.g., offerings, rituals, prayers) are regularly or repeatedly carried out A

477. Incense burned for ceremonial or ritual purposes A

478. Ritual or liturgical (written) texts

479. Special supernatural practitioners (e.g., shamans, diviners, priests, monks) (A)

480. Religious specialist(s) supported (fully or almost fully) by individuals, the community, tribe, or state (A)

481. Specialists (e.g., astrologers) concerned exclusively with divination and related activities (exclude shamans) are consulted before undertakings important to the society or the political leader

482. Priests: religious practitioners connected with specific gods or with society-wide ancestral cults (A)

483. Functionally specialized priests (e.g., interpreters of oracles or dreams, sacrificial priests, funerary priests, war priests) (A)

484. Priests formally invested in their office by chief, king, or higher priest

485. Head priest (including priest-chief or priest-king) has considerable political influence

486. Hierarchy of priests (A)

487. Different orders of priests

488. Women consecrated to a temple or to the service of a god (e.g., priestesses, virgins, nuns) (A)

489. Priests or monks always distinguished by specific visible marks of their status (e.g., tonsure, special garments)

490. Priests or monks ordinarily follow strict rules of discipline, including various

forms of abnegation (e.g., fasting, continence), purification, or mortification of the flesh

491. Training school for priests
492. Temple(s): structure(s), at least as large as dwellings, where priests worship gods or practice society-wide ancestral cults A
493. Temple has large staff of priests or attendants (more than ten) (A)
494. Temple owns considerable property (A)
495. Differentiated temples dedicated to specific gods or saints (A)
496. Monasteries, convents, or nunneries where priests, monks, priestesses, etc., live, and which, unlike temples, are ordinarily closed to laymen (A)
497. Ceremonial or religious center: a complex of temples and associated buildings having an important role in the religious life of the society A
498. Church: religious institution which encompasses a number of priests and temples (or monks and monasteries) and which is unified by a set of common beliefs and observances (A)
499. Temple or church receives donations (other than offerings left to supernatural beings)
500. Temple or church exacts tithes, receives the produce of a fixed portion of cultivated lands, or claims a set part of personal incomes
501. Church owns large amounts of land
502. Ecclesiastical courts

Ceramics and Art

503. Pottery (either made or commonly used) A
504. Painted pottery made A
505. Effigy vessels made A
506. Large ceramic vessels made expressly for storing or transporting grain or liquids A
507. Mold-made pottery A
508. Wheel-made pottery A
509. Pottery kilns A
510. Professional (full-time) potters (A)
511. Professional (full-time) painters or sculptors (A)
512. Terra-cotta (baked clay) figurines or statues as art or ceremonial objects (free-standing, not appliquéd on pots or walls) A

513. Statues or figurines carved in hard wood or ivory A
514. Stone statues (or figurines) as art or ceremonial objects A
515. Heroic or gigantic stone sculpture A
516. Reliefs, intaglios, or friezes carved into dressed stone surfaces A
517. Murals or frescoes painted on faced stone or fired brick walls A
518. Glass manufactured A
519. Mosaics of stone, brick, tile, or glass A

Tools, Utensils, and Textiles

520. Ground or polished stone or shell cutting tools A
521. Metal axes or adzes made A
522. Metal-pointed plowshares A
523. Animal-, wind-, or water-powered devices for grinding grain A
524. Mechanical devices for raising water (e.g., shadoof, water wheel, water screw) A
525. Wheeled vehicles A
526. Scales or balances A
527. Techniques of wood joining beyond lashing and gluing (e.g., use of pegs, nails, dovetailing, sewing) A
528. Furniture: e.g., stools, benches, platform beds, hammocks A
529. Lock and keys A
530. Mirrors A
531. Spindle A
532. Heddle loom A
533. Plant fibers woven into cloth A
534. Animal fibers (e.g., hair, wool, fur, silk) woven into cloth (exclude unraveling and reweaving of woolen cloth obtained by trade) A
535. Patterns (including warp and weft stripes) woven into cloth A
536. Garments (including capes and cloaks) made of woven cloth A
537. Garments made of bark cloth (including ceremonial garments)
538. Dyeing (not painting or smearing) of textiles, yarn, bark cloth, or pandanus leaves A
539. Fabrics for clothing ornamented with featherwork, elaborate painting, embroidery, jewelry A
540. Tapestries (woven or embroidered fabrics hung for decoration) A
541. Professional weavers (A)

Metalworking

542. Forging (hammering metal into shape while hot) A
543. Mining of ores (excluding placers) A
544. Mining of ores carried out as a continuing operation (i.e., not merely to meet the needs of the moment) (A)
545. Smelting of ores A
546. Furnaces for smelting ores A
547. Bellows used in working metal A
548. Indigenous copper worked (A)
549. Indigenous gold and/or silver worked (A)
550. Indigenous iron worked (A)
551. Alloying of metals A
552. Bronze or brass produced A
553. Casting in molds A
554. Lost-wax casting (cire perdue) A
555. Altering the hardness of metals by annealing (heating and slow cooling) or tempering (heating and rapid cooling by immersion in a liquid) A
556. Soldering, welding, or riveting used to join metals A
557. Decorative metalworking techniques (e.g., gilding, embossing, engraving, inlaying) A
558. Copper weapons, utensils, or instruments in common use A
559. Bronze or brass weapons, utensils, or instruments in common use A
560. Iron weapons, utensils, or instruments in common use A
561. Nonutilitarian metal objects (e.g., jewelry, figurines or statues, ceremonial chalices, solar disks) made or used A
562. Ornaments and jewelry of gold, silver, or other precious metals made or used A
563. Precious or semiprecious stones used for jewelry A
564. Professional smiths, who work metal primarily for exchange (A)
565. Professional goldsmiths, silversmiths, or jewelers (A)
566. Armorers: smiths specializing in making weapons (A)

Watercraft and Navigation

567. Watercraft (excluding floating logs and simple rafts) A
568. Vessel hulls built from several planks (excluding wash strakes) A
569. Vessels propelled by oars (not paddles) A
570. Vessels propelled by sails A
571. Steering oar or rudder A
572. Devices for stabilizing vessels (e.g., keels, centerboards, outriggers) A
573. Cabins on board vessels A
574. Decked vessels, with cabin or storage space below decks A
575. Merchant vessels, operated by professional merchants and specially designed to transport cargo (A)
576. Navy: fleet of specially designed warships maintained by the political unit (A)
577. Professional naval officers
578. Professional boatbuilders (including part-time specialists) (A)
579. Dry docks: permanent structures used during the construction and repair of vessels A
580. Professional sailors, pilots, or navigators (including part-time specialists) (A)
581. Professional boatmen, who earn a living ferrying passengers or goods over short distances
582. Voyages undertaken out of sight of land (A)
583. Canals built for navigation A

Special Knowledge and Practices

584. Traditions, events, etc., recorded by means of mnemonic devices (including writing, but excluding simple methods of recording elapsed time, events, or simple inventories) (A)
585. System of writing (including extensive systems of standardized pictographs)
586. Essentially phonetic system of writing
587. Scribes, secretaries, or clerks (other than priests)
588. Teachers: professional instructors, secular or religious, who are paid for their services and who instruct others than candidates for the priesthood
589. Schools for instruction in secular (i.e., nonreligious) subjects or for vocational training (including, e.g., school for brides)
590. Literacy general among the upper classes (not merely among scribes and priests)
591. Public primary schools
592. Secular professional schools (e.g., for the sudy of law, accounting, medicine, grammar)
593. Literature: speculative, aesthetic, or his-

torical writing as distinct from official records

594. Epic verse (excluding songs)

595. Philosophy: a system of beliefs about man's place in the world and about human conduct based on independent speculation and representing a departure from the prevailing or previously established system of beliefs

596. Technical treatises or manuals (e.g., on medicine, pharmacy, divination, agriculture, metalworking)

597. Standarized weights and measures (excluding measurement with parts of the body, and similarly variable measurements) A

598. System of numbers extending beyond 100 (A)

599. Mathematics (beyond simple arithmetic) (A)

600. Techniques of surveying and mensuration (including, e.g., plumb lines, knowledge of right angle, stretched cords, but excluding the swinging of circles by means of a cord) (A)

601. Astronomical observations regularly made by priests or other specialists (A)

602. Calendrical system, uniquely designating each day of the year (A)

603. Calendrically fixed days of celebration or religious observance recurring annually

604. Regular schedule of work and rest other than daily routine (e.g., one day off every five)

605. Musical instruments (excluding whistles) A

606. Games of calculation A

607. Team athletic contests in which there is coordination among the members of each side (A)

608. Professional athletes (e.g., gladiators, ballplayers, acrobats) (A)

609. Bards, minstrels, musicians, or storytellers, whose primary activity is to compose, play, or recite songs, poems, or stories

610. Professional dancers or musicians

611. Professional comic entertainers (e.g., clowns, buffoons, jesters, dwarfs)

612. Troupes of professional actors

613. Fermented beverages brewed from cultivated plants (A)

614. Midwives, wet nurses, or foster nurses who are regularly called upon and paid for their services

615. Physicians: specialists who treat patients primarily by rational (i.e., non-supernaturalistic) means (A)

616. Surgery practiced on human beings (excluding, e.g., the setting of broken bones, removal of arrows, bloodletting) A

617. Papermaking (including the making of papyrus, parchment, or vellum) A

618. Zoos or menageries in which a wide variety of wild animals are kept as curiosities

BIBLIOGRAPHY

CARNEIRO, ROBERT L.
1962 Scale analysis as an instrument for the study of cultural evolution. *Southwestern Journal of Anthropology* 18:149–169.
1969 The measurement of cultural development in the ancient Near East and in Anglo-Saxon England. *Transactions of the New York Academy of Sciences,* Ser. II, 31:1013–1023.

CARNEIRO, ROBERT L., and STEPHEN F. TOBIAS
1963 The application of scale analysis to the study of cultural evolution. *Transactions of the New York Academy of Sciences,* Ser. II, 26:196–207.

GUTTMAN, LOUIS
1950 The basis of scalogram analysis. In Samuel A. Stouffer *et al., Studies in social psychology in World War II: Measurement and prediction,* Vol. 4. Princeton, N.J., Princeton University Press.

ICKO, IBEN, JR.
1967 Stellar evolution: comparison of theory with observation. *Science* 155:785–796.

JACOBS, MELVILLE
1948 Further comments on evolutionism in cultural anthropology. *American Anthropologist* 50:564–568.

KROEBER, A. L.
1939 *Cultural and natural areas of native North America.* Berkeley, University of California Press.

MORGAN, LEWIS H.
1909 *Ancient society.* Chicago, Charles H. Kerr.

MURDOCK, GEORGE P.
1959 *Africa.* New York, McGraw-Hill.

NAROLL, RAOUL
    1956 A preliminary index of social development. *American Anthropologist* 58:687–715.

OGOT, B. A.
    1964 Kingship and statelessness among the Nilotes. In J. Vansina, R. Mauny, and L. V. Thomas, eds., *The historian in tropical Africa.* London, Oxford University Press.

POSNANSKY, MERRICK
    1966 Kingship, archaeology and historical myth. *Uganda Journal* 30:1–12.

SAPIR, EDWARD
    1920 Review of Robert H. Lowie's *Primitive society. The Freeman* 1:377–379.

SPENCER, HERBERT
    1863 *First principles,* 1st ed. London, Williams and Norgate.
    1866 *The principles of biology,* Vol. 1. New York, Appleton.
    1898 What is social evolution? *The Nineteenth Century* 44:348–358.
    1912 *First principles,* 6th ed. New York, Appleton.

WHITE, LESLIE A.
    1947 Evolutionary stages, progress and the evaluation of cultures. *Southwestern Journal of Anthropology* 3:165–192.
    1959 *The evolution of culture.* New York, McGraw-Hill.

CHAPTER 42

A Settlement Pattern Scale of Cultural Complexity

CHARLES W. MCNETT, JR.

INTRODUCTION

This study presents a five-rank ordinal scale of cultural complexity which was derived from a settlement pattern typology developed by Beardsley *et al.* (1956) for the 1955 Seminars in Archaeology (Wauchope 1956). The main purpose of the seminar's work was to define cultural types in such a way that the archaeologist—faced with the difficulty of inferring nonmaterial sociocultural traits— might be able to determine the existence of these customs. In order to do so, the seminar sought to show that cultural evolution and functionalism are opposite sides of the same coin in that evolutionary types are, in fact, functional systems in which specific ways of acting on the part of the culture are required by the integration of traits with settlement patterns. The latter arise out of the inter-action of technology with environment. Table 1 presents the seminar's system but lacks the first category, free wandering, since they feel it does not exist today and may never have (Beardsley *et al.* 1956:136).

Since the typology seemed to have a great deal of relevance both to anthropological theory and to practical application in archae-ology, the author attempted to empirically

This is a substantially revised portion of the author's dissertation which was submitted in partial fulfillment of the requirements for the degree of Doctor of Philosophy at Tulane University. Members of the committee were Arden R. King, chairman, Thomas Ktsanes, and Robert Wauchope. Most of the research was done while the author was a member of the faculty of Baylor University, and he would like to thank its administration for providing extensive computer pro-gramming and operating time. Finally, Michael Mick-lin, Albert Spaulding, and Raoul Naroll provided help-ful comments. Responsibility is retained by the author.

validate the typology and refine it, if possible. Statistical tests did give formal validation, and it was found that the original settlement patterns could be reduced to five ranks in an ordinal scale with pastoral and nonpastoral subtypes for each.

DEVELOPMENT OF THE SCALE

Full details of the development of the rank order scale will be found in McNett (1967). To summarize this process, a random sample of forty-eight cultures was drawn using an earlier version of the grid method presented in McNett and Kirk (1968). Data were gathered for all forty-eight cultures on twenty-seven traits taken from those suggested as significant by the seminar. In addition, three kinship traits (Numbers 28, 29, 30 be-low) were added in an effort to ascertain if these, too, were integrated into the same functional system as the others. The traits were cast into a dichotomous form to allow for ease of statistical manipulation. They are:

1. Is real estate owned by the community ("Defined as the largest grouping of persons in any particular culture whose normal ac-tivities bind them together into a self-con-scious, corporate unit, which is economically self-sufficient and politically independent" [Beardsley *et al.* 1956:133]) as a whole, or by an individual or group within the com-munity?

2. Are accumulated goods shared among members of the community, or are they hoarded by individuals or groups?

3. Is movable property destroyed at the death of its owner, or is it inherited?

4. Is each person a "jack-of-all-trades," or

Table 1
SOCIOCULTURAL CONCOMITANTS OF SETTLEMENT PATTERNS

Settlement Pattern	Economic	Political	Religious	Social
Restricted Wandering Wander within owned territory	Personal property primarily for food getting. Usually destroyed at death. Sharing practiced. Communal ownership of real estate.	Band of related or friendly families headed by advisory leader.	Vague beliefs with shamans who cure and bring luck.	No status differences.
Central-based Wandering Part of year sedentary at central base. Incipient Pastoral Nomadic Animals tolerate humans.	Community about the same size. Surpluses, if any, not used exclusively by any group.	Leader is community symbol.	Shamanism continues. More concern for the dead. Group ceremonies absent to frequent.	Status based on ability.
Semi-permanent Sedentary Move village whenever environment is exhausted. Equestrian Hunting Hunt herd animals on horseback.	Family land ownership. Surpluses acquired but redistributed. Some village specialization in manufacturing.	Clans or moieties generally basis of organization. Headman is agent for community.	More formal, with more life crises and common good ceremonies. Shamans have great power.	Status based upon surplus distribution.
Simple Nuclear Centered Self-sufficient village, or ceremonial and/or economic center and satellites. Diversified Pastoral Nomadic Herd a variety of domestic animals.	Private ownership of real estate. Full-time occupational specialization.	Chief with coercive power in a kinship-based system.	Formalized with priests, temples, common good ceremonies, and a pantheon of gods.	Stratification based on property.
Advanced Nuclear Centered Permanent administrative center.	Larger surplus controlled by the upper class.	Administrative centers with hierarchy controlled by a king. Law and politics supplant kinship organization.	Hierarchy of priests perform temple rites directed toward a pantheon of gods.	Hereditary classes.
Supra-nuclear Integrated Components integrated into state, typically by conquest.	Commercialism, large scale circulation of goods, much accumulated wealth, taxes.	Absolute power vested in ruler. Government manipulates population. Professional army.	Ruler identified with the gods.	Large lower class with many slaves.

are they specialized manufacturers of artifacts other than by sex?

5. Is trade with other communities sporadic and unimportant, or is it regular and important economically to the community?

6. Are there taxes, paid to the head of the community or his representative?

7. Is the political leader simply an adviser, or does he have the power to coerce obedience?

8. Is the largest level of organization of the community that of an organized and interacting family of whatever size, or do larger and non-kin organized entities exist?

9. Is social control performed only by kinship methods such as gossip and ridicule, or is there also a formal legal system, written or unwritten?

10. Is there a hierarchy of political leaders, with some having more coercive power than others within the same community?

11. Is there a year-round professional army supported by nonsoldiers?

12. Are the most important relations with the supernatural magical (coercive) or religious (supplicating) in nature?

13. Are the most important acts of the supernatural coercive toward man, or does the supernatural present ethical standards which may or may not be enforced?

14. Is the supernatural vaguely defined, or does it consist of clear and generally complex concepts?

15. Is the most important aspect of the supernatural in the form of spirits (relatively powerless beings who act much like humans) or gods (powerful cosmic figures), either of which may or may not be anthropomorphic?

16. Are the most important religious specialists shamans who deal with spirits, or priests who deal with gods?

17. Are some religious practitioners more powerful and of a higher rank than others? (Power gained by success in practice is not involved.)

18. Are individually-oriented or common weal rites more frequent?

19. Are group ceremonies infrequent or frequent?

20. Are death rites simple and relatively unimportant, or elaborate with long ritual, extensive burial furniture, mourning ceremonies, etc.?

21. Is ceremonial paraphernalia simple, consisting of a few objects, or is it elaborate,

consisting of many objects requiring significant time to manufacture?

22. Are there temples?

23. Is there a written calendar?

24. Is human sacrifice practiced?

25. Is status based upon personal ability, or upon wealth, heredity, or other similar factors?

26. Is there a simple, continuous and almost imperceptible status graduation, or are there formalized status divisions including hereditary classes, castes, or rich-poor divisions?

27. Is slavery usual and ordinary?

28. Is monogamy or polygamy (any form of multiple spouses) the common form of marriage?

29. Are families characteristically nuclear or extended?

30. Is descent primarily unilateral or bilateral in nature?

In many cases, the ethnographer does not report specific information, such as, "Group ceremonies take place thirty-five times a year." The trait questions were consequently phrased in such a way that the words "frequent," "slight," "unimportant," etc., would answer them. Little, if any, accuracy seems to have been lost by this procedure. The coded data are given in Table 2. The symbol "0" stands for the first or less complex half of the dichotomy where complexity is known; the symbol "1" for the second or more complex half. Dashes indicate no information. Two source abbreviations are used, with EA standing for Murdock et al. (1962–65) and WES for Murdock (1957). The settlement patterns are abbreviated to upper-case initials, such as restricted wandering—RW. Each pastoral subtype has been combined with its equivalent nonpastoral pattern, whose initials it bears.

In applying statistical techniques to this body of data, most tests involve the null hypothesis. Should it be possible to reject the null hypothesis because of significantly large differences, then one may accept the alternate hypothesis—that each settlement pattern is a distinct type differing from the others. A number of other factors can cause variation from chance, however, and it must be demonstrated that none have had an effect. These factors include systematically biased data, bias on the part of the investigator, and a biased sample.

Table 2
CROSS-CULTURAL DATA

Culture	Pattern	1	2	3	4	5	6	7	8	9	10	11	12	13	14	15	16	17	18	19	20	21	22	23	24	25	26	27	28	29	30	References
Abipon	S-PS	0	1	0	0	0	0	1	1	0	0	0	0	0	0	0	0	0	0	0	0	0	0	0	0	1	1	1	0	0	1	EA, WES, Métraux (1946)
Angmagsalik	C-BW	0	0	1	0	0	0	0	0	0	0	0	0	0	0	0	0	0	0	0	0	0	0	0	0	0	1	0	0	0	0	EA, Mirsky (1937)
Apinaye	SNC	1	1	1	1	0	0	0	0	0	0	0	0	0	0	0	0	0	1	1	1	1	1	0	0	0	1	1	0	1	1	EA, WES, Nimuendaju (1939)
Aymara	ANC	1	1	1	1	0	0	0	0	0	0	0	0	0	0	0	0	0	1	1	1	1	0	0	0	1	1	1	0	0	0	WES, Tschopik (1946)
Berabish	SNC	1	1	1	1	1	1	1	1	0	0	0	0	0	0	0	0	0	0	1	1	1	1	0	0	1	1	1	1	0	0	EA, WES, Miner (1953), Murdock (1959)
Bungi	S-PS	1	1	1	0	0	1	0	1	0	0	0	0	0	0	0	0	0	0	0	0	0	0	0	0	0	0	1	0	1	0	EA, Hesketh (1923), Howard (1961), Skinner (1914a,b)
Callinago	S-PS	0	0	0	0	0	0	0	0	0	0	0	0	0	0	0	0	0	0	0	1	0	1	0	0	0	0	1	0	1	0	EA, WES, Rouse (1948), Taylor (1946)
Chahar Mongols	SNC	0	1	1	1	1	1	1	1	1	0	0	0	0	0	0	0	0	0	1	1	1	1	0	0	1	1	1	0	0	0	EA, Vreeland (1957)
Cham	ANC	1	1	1	1	1	1	1	1	1	0	0	0	0	0	0	0	0	1	1	1	1	1	0	1	1	1	1	0	0	0	EA, LeBar, Mickey and Musgrave (1964)
Chichimec	RW	0	0	–	0	0	–	0	0	0	0	0	0	0	0	0	0	0	0	0	0	0	0	0	0	0	0	0	0	0	0	EA, Driver and Driver (1963), Kirchoff (1943)
Cuna	SNC	1	1	1	1	0	1	1	1	1	0	0	0	0	0	0	0	0	1	1	1	1	1	0	1	1	1	1	0	1	0	EA, WES, Nordenskiold (1938), Stout (1947)
Dogon	ANC	1	1	1	1	1	0	1	1	1	0	0	0	0	0	0	0	0	1	1	1	1	1	0	0	1	1	1	1	0	1	WES, Griaule and Dieterlen (1954), Murdock (1959)
Dusun	SNC	1	1	1	1	1	1	1	1	1	0	0	0	0	0	0	0	0	0	1	1	1	1	0	1	0	1	1	0	1	0	EA, WES, Williams (1965)
Ellice	ANC	1	1	1	1	–	1	0	1	1	0	0	0	0	0	0	0	0	1	0	1	1	1	0	1	1	1	1	0	1	0	EA, WES, Kennedy (1931)
Guahibo	RW	0	0	–	0	0	1	1	1	0	0	0	0	0	0	0	0	0	0	0	1	0	0	0	0	0	0	0	0	0	0	EA, WES, Kirchoff (1948), Wilbert (1957)
Javanese	ANC	1	1	1	–	1	1	1	1	1	1	0	0	0	0	0	0	0	1	1	1	1	1	0	1	1	1	1	0	1	0	EA, WES, Koentjaraningrat (1960)
Kababish	SNC	0	1	1	1	0	1	1	1	0	0	0	0	0	0	0	0	0	0	1	1	1	1	0	0	1	1	1	0	0	0	Seligman and Seligman (1918)
Kerala	S-NI	1	1	1	1	1	1	1	1	1	0	0	0	0	0	0	0	0	1	1	1	1	1	0	1	1	1	1	1	1	0	EA, WES, Gough (1961)
Koreans	S-NI	1	1	1	1	1	1	1	1	1	0	0	0	0	0	0	0	0	1	1	1	1	1	0	1	1	1	1	1	0	0	WES, Osgood (1951)
Kru	ANC	0	1	1	1	1	0	0	1	1	0	0	0	0	0	0	0	0	1	0	1	1	1	0	1	0	1	1	0	0	0	Schwab (1947)
Kwoma	SNC	0	1	1	1	0	0	1	1	0	0	0	0	0	0	0	0	0	0	1	1	1	1	0	0	1	1	1	0	0	0	EA, Whiting (1941)
Lesu	SNC	0	1	1	1	1	0	0	1	0	0	0	0	0	0	0	0	0	0	1	1	1	1	0	0	1	1	1	0	0	0	EA, WES, Powdermaker (1933)
Li	ANC	1	1	1	1	1	1	1	1	1	0	0	0	0	0	0	0	0	1	1	1	1	1	0	1	1	1	1	1	1	0	EA, LeBar, Mickey and Musgrave (1964)
Lifu	ANC	1	1	1	0	1	1	1	1	1	0	0	0	0	0	0	0	0	0	1	1	1	1	0	1	1	1	1	0	1	0	EA, WES, Ray (1917)
Lithuanians	S-NI	1	1	1	1	1	1	1	1	1	0	0	0	0	0	0	0	0	1	1	1	1	1	0	1	1	1	1	1	1	0	EA, Lambert (1964), Lambert (1966: pers. comm.)
Makin	ANC	1	1	1	0	0	0	0	1	1	0	0	0	0	0	0	0	0	1	1	1	1	1	0	1	1	1	1	0	1	0	EA, WES, Buck (1932)
Manihikians	SNC	1	1	1	0	0	1	0	0	1	0	0	0	0	0	0	0	0	1	1	1	1	1	0	1	0	1	1	0	1	0	Garvan (1941)
Manobo	S-PS	0	1	1	0	0	0	0	0	1	0	0	0	0	0	0	0	0	0	1	1	1	1	0	0	0	1	0	0	1	0	EA, WES, Mead (1937)
Manus	S-PS	1	1	1	1	1	0	0	0	0	0	0	0	0	0	0	0	0	0	0	1	1	1	0	0	1	1	0	0	1	0	EA, Hagen (1912)
Masa	SNC	1	1	1	1	1	1	1	1	1	0	0	0	0	0	0	0	0	0	1	1	1	1	0	0	1	1	1	0	0	0	EA, Krieger (1942), Kroeber (1919)
Moro	S-NI	1	1	1	1	1	0	1	1	0	0	0	0	0	0	0	0	0	1	1	1	1	1	0	1	1	1	1	1	0	0	Coon (1958)
Moroccans	S-NI	1	1	1	1	1	1	1	1	1	0	0	0	0	0	0	0	0	1	1	1	1	1	1	1	1	1	1	1	1	0	WES, Stephen (1936), Wedgewood (1936)
Nauruans	SNC	1	1	1	1	0	0	0	0	1	0	0	0	0	0	0	0	0	0	1	1	1	1	0	0	1	1	1	0	0	0	EA, Cameron (1890), Grant (1890)
Nipigon	C-BW	0	0	0	0	0	0	0	0	0	0	0	0	0	0	0	0	0	0	0	0	0	0	0	0	1	0	0	0	0	0	EA, WES, Hogbin (1961)
Ontong Java	ANC	1	1	1	0	1	1	1	1	1	0	0	0	0	0	0	0	0	1	1	1	1	1	0	1	1	1	1	0	1	0	EA, Atkinson (1953), Entwisle (1953)
Portuguese	S-NI	1	1	1	1	1	1	1	1	1	0	0	0	0	0	0	0	0	1	1	1	1	1	0	1	1	1	1	1	1	0	EA, WES, Deacon (1934)
Seniang	SNC	0	1	1	1	0	0	0	1	0	0	0	0	0	0	0	0	0	0	1	1	1	1	0	0	1	1	1	0	0	0	EA, WES, Lewis (1955)
Somali	SNC	1	1	1	0	0	1	1	1	1	0	0	0	0	0	0	0	0	0	1	1	1	1	0	0	1	1	1	0	0	0	EA, WES, Pitt-Rivers (1954)
Spanish	ANC	1	1	1	1	1	1	1	1	1	0	0	0	0	0	0	0	0	1	1	1	1	1	0	1	1	1	1	0	1	0	WES, Handy (1931)
Tahitians	ANC	1	1	1	–	1	1	1	1	1	0	0	0	0	0	0	0	0	1	1	1	1	1	0	1	1	1	1	0	1	0	
Culture	Pattern	1	2	3	4	5	6	7	8	9	10	11	12	13	14	15	16	17	18	19	20	21	22	23	24	25	26	27	28	29	30	References
Taino	ANC	1	1	1	1	1	1	1	1	0	0	0	0	0	0	0	0	0	0	1	0	1	1	0	0	1	1	1	0	0	0	WES, Rouse and Hostos (1948)
Tenino	C-BW	0	1	0	0	1	0	0	1	1	0	0	0	0	0	0	0	0	0	0	0	1	0	0	0	0	1	1	0	0	0	EA, WES, Murdock (1958, 1965), Ray (1942)
Tswana	ANC	1	1	1	1	1	1	1	1	0	0	0	0	0	0	0	0	0	0	1	1	1	1	0	0	1	1	1	0	0	0	EA, WES, Schapera (1953)
Tukudika	C-BW	0	0	0	0	0	0	0	0	0	0	0	0	0	0	0	0	0	0	0	0	0	0	0	0	1	0	0	0	0	0	EA, Steward (1938, 1943)
Ukrainians	S-NI	1	1	1	1	1	1	1	1	1	0	0	0	0	0	0	0	0	1	1	1	1	1	0	1	1	1	1	1	0	0	EA, Human Relations Area File (n.d.)
Uzbek	S-NI	1	1	1	1	1	1	1	1	1	0	0	0	0	0	0	0	0	1	1	1	1	1	0	0	1	1	1	1	0	0	WES, Coates and Coates (1951)
Yellowknife	RW	0	0	0	0	0	0	0	0	0	0	0	0	0	0	0	0	0	0	0	0	0	0	0	0	0	0	0	0	0	0	Mason (1946), Spencer (1965)
Yukaghir	C-BW	0	0	0	0	0	0	0	0	0	0	0	0	0	0	0	0	0	0	0	0	0	0	0	0	1	0	0	0	0	1	EA, WES, Jochelson (1926)

It is reasonable to assume that the multitude of sources used for the data in this study would not be systematically biased, although there might be random error. Naroll (1962:18) has pointed out that random error will usually make it less likely that the results will be significant. Fear of biased data in this sample is as unlikely, therefore, as it is in any cross-cultural study, while random error will only decrease the likelihood of significant results.

It is, however, a distinct possibility that I might have been biased in my recording of traits. Naroll's (1962) method of guarding against this was utilized by comparing my own evaluations with the independent ones of Murdock for Trait 1 and Traits 25–30. The 2×2 table yielded $\chi^2 = 101+$ with $p <$ .001, and an associated $\phi = +.8051$. A positive coefficient this large indicates essential agreement for these seven traits and, by extension, for the remainder.

The sampling procedure makes it unlikely that there is sample bias, but Naroll's (1964) fifth method of controlling for Galton's problem was utilized with only two sweeps instead of five. The trait, written calendar, which had significant ϕ's $= +.5763$ and $+.4286$, was dropped. It had apparently been defined in such a way that diffusion of the modern calendar was the only way it could occur.

One other trait had to be dropped when it was discovered that status and classes had identical χ^2 and ϕ values on each sweep. The two had been defined in such a way that the presence of one required the presence of the other. Status was, therefore, not used for further testing. No other anomalies were found.

The Kolmogorov-Smirnov test (Siegel 1956: 127 ff.) was chosen to test significance. It is extremely powerful and, in addition to rank order measurement, requires that the distribution be continuous. We assume that traits and settlement patterns do have a continuous distribution but are categorized because of our inability to measure them adequately. Should the assumption not be met, the test is conservative and more likely to cause acceptance of the null hypothesis (Blalock 1960: 205).

Table 3
ASSIGNMENT TO NEW RANK ORDER SCALE

Pattern	Culture	Score	Pattern	Culture	Score
Band Level	Nipigon	0	City Level	Taino	11
	Tukudika	0		Tswana	11
	Yellowknife	0		Li	11.2
	Angmagsalik	1		Lifu	11.8
	Guahibo	1.2		Makin	15.8
	Yukaghir	2		Kru	16
	Chichimec	3		Manihikians	16.6
				Somali	18
				Kababish	19
Village Level	Callinago	1.1		Dogon	19.6
	Manus	6		Ellice	19.8
	Tenino	6		Ontong Java	19.8
	Bungi	6.2			
	Manobo	7			
	Abipon	7.3	State Level	Cham	19.5
				Berabish	20
				Chahar Mongols	20
Town Level	Masa	7.2		Javanese	20
	Seniang	8.3		Aymara	21
	Cuna	9		Moro	21
	Lesu	9		Spanish	21
	Dusun	9.8		Kerala	22
	Nauruans	13.6		Koreans	22
	Apinaye	15		Lithuanians	22
	Kwoma	15		Moroccans	22
				Portuguese	22
				Tahitians	22
				Ukrainians	22
				Uzbek	22

Human sacrifice, slavery, and the three kinship traits were not significant and were dropped from further consideration. Of the remainder, 15 had $p < .001$; 7, $p < .01$; 1, $p < .02$; and 1, $p < .05$. Modal tests of economics, politics, and religion all had $p < .001$, while the social mode, with only two traits, was not significant. An overall $\chi^2 = 225.3136$ resulted. For two degrees of freedom, a $\chi^2 = 24$ has $p = .00001$ (Pearson and Hartley 1954:124). These results indicate that the types are valid.

Next, multiple discriminant analysis (Rao 1952:307 ff.) was used upon the randomly divided sample. In addition, linear regression (Blalock 1960:279 ff.) was applied to the entire sample. Both techniques were used to reassign the cultures to a set of ideal types based upon the number of complex traits each had. The new assignments were examined to see if refined definitions of the settlement patterns could be made which would fit the data better. Table 3 shows the results of this analysis, while Figure 1 is a linear regression of the cultures as finally assigned. The means of the scores of the newly defined patterns indicate an almost perfect relationship between each pattern and the average number of complex traits each culture possesses.

A further check of the validity of the new patterns was given by repeating the Kolmogorov-Smirnov test. Most traits had much higher χ^2's, especially in religion, while the overall χ^2 figure rose to 348.1805. All traits found to be nonsignificant earlier were unaffected.

SCALE DEFINITIONS

It is therefore possible to define the following rank order scale of cultural complexity, which does not include a tentative village subtype based upon commercial exploitation (see below, p. 878):

BAND LEVEL

Nonpastoral. The community as defined above changes its location more than once a year.
Pastoral. Communities get more than half of their food supply from domesticated or partially domesticated animals whose movements they are unable to control completely.

VILLAGE LEVEL

Nonpastoral. Communities do not move as often as once a year, but they do shift regularly at least once within a ten-year period due to depletion of natural resources. This reason may not be explicitly stated and can include moves due to deaths, etc.
Pastoral. Domesticated animals whose movements are controlled are ridden in search of wild animal food which makes up more than half of the subsistence of the community.

TOWN LEVEL

Nonpastoral. The community is not normally moved except in extreme circumstances. It is either self-sufficient, or it is made up of a center which performs religious and/or economic functions for satellite members of the community; the center has no primarily political function, however.
Pastoral. More than half of the food supply is gained from controlled movements of a variety of domesticated animals. There is a symbiotic relationship with nonpastoral towns.

CITY LEVEL

Nonpastoral. A center performs political, religious, and economic functions for surround-

Figure 1
DESCRIPTIVE REGRESSION

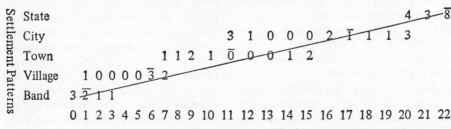

Number of Complex Traits (rounded to nearest whole number)

ing satellite members of the community. The primary function is usually political.

Pastoral. The same as towns, except that symbiosis is with cities.

STATE LEVEL

Nonpastoral. A number of cities, along with lower-level communities in many cases, are grouped together by a second level of political centralization. The state center performs the same functions for each component that the city center provides for its satellites.

Pastoral. The same as cities, except that symbiosis is with states.

DISCUSSION

Since the types have been validated, the seminar's system of dynamics which underlies them has at least partial validation as well. It might be instructive to review their dynamics and note alterations which result from the new scale. The seminar felt that their original categories had functional, evolutionary, and historical significance. In regard to the first consideration, they state that the major determinant is food production (Beardsley *et al.* 1956:150). The fact that there are so few types is taken to emphasize the existence of functional determinants which do not permit much variation in cultural features. They go on to point out that the similarities between the original sedentary and pastoral types result from, respectively, incipient domestication, exploitative plant or animal use, and intensive and conservational use of domestic resources. They conclude that the persistent recurrence of similar settlement patterns is a result not only of the functional relationships between traits but also between complexity and subsistence (Beardsley *et al.* 1956:152–153). Each category may be viewed as an evolutionary stage, but only a historical approach will also between complexity and subsistence area, where cultures may skip stages, progress, or regress according to their own unique histories. This history is explained by the form in which subsistence improvements are secured in a given community.

Thus, restricted wandering resulted from use of a relatively poor environment with a technology restricted to hunting, fishing, and gathering (Beardsley *et al.* 1956:136),

and central-based wandering from either a better environment, represented by a storable wild food harvest or a locally abundant food, or a better technology, represented by incipient plant domestication (Beardsley *et al.* 1956:138). Incipient pastoral nomadic is also the result of an improvement in technology in that domestication of animals has begun to take place (Beardsley *et al.* 1956: 147). The empirical evidence seems to indicate that all three may be combined into the band level since multiple discriminant analysis was unable to distinguish between them. It classified all representatives of these three types as C-BW, apparently on the basis of its slightly higher probability in the sample. It seems that this level of subsistence and the consequent wandering severely limit the number of complex traits that culture can possess, regardless of incipient domestication of either plants or animals.

Fewer changes were made in the seminar's semipermanent sedentary and equestrian hunting patterns. The former comes about when agriculture is improved but not to the point where soil fertility can be restored. A huge natural food supply which is eventually exhausted locally is an alternate cause, since either will allow permanence for a number of years. The pastoral pattern arises from the use of the horse as a technological device to improve hunting techniques. All three seem to result in the village level, in which subsistence is improved to the point where complexity begins to develop.

A problem was presented by Manus and Tenino. Both had sets of S-PS scores, yet they were classified SNC and C-BW respectively. Another look at the data revealed that Tenino served as middleman for the trade in their area (Murdock 1958:301), while Manus men were involved in commercial fishing and transportation (Mead 1937:211). This seems to indicate that commercial exploitation of the social environment has about the same result for complexity as exploitation of the natural environment. It allows a greater degree of permanence, however, since the social environment is not as easily exhausted. Only further study will reveal whether this subtype of the village level has validity.

Simple nuclear centered results from further improvements in agricultural technology which cause a dependence upon domesticated plants (Beardsley *et al.* 1956:141). The pastoral equivalent, diversified pastoral nomadic, is the result of the same dependence upon domesticated animals (Beardsley *et al.* 1956:148). Pastoral cultures, however, are unable to maintain themselves without symbiosis with agricultural peoples. Apparently the degree of nomadism necessary for pastoralism prevents the development of complexity unless there is an agricultural community to provide certain necessities. This is borne out by the fact that a diversified pastoral nomadic community will have the degree of complexity of the sedentary group with which it maintains symbiosis. Thus Kababish are symbiotic with both Negro and Arab advanced nuclear centers (Murdock 1959: 411); their scores are also advanced nuclear centered. On the other hand, the Berabish are symbiotic with a supra-nuclear integration (Miner 1953; Murdock 1959); their scores are S-NI.

Advanced nuclear centered is the result of further improvements in agriculture which lead to surpluses large enough to maintain specialized political groups who control them (Beardsley *et al.* 1956:142). Virtually no alteration of this type took place, although the pastoral subtype was added to create the city level.

Finally, supra-nuclear integrated apparently comes about from further improvements in agricultural technology that lead to essentially social causation, such as need for increased wealth, national morale, something for those freed from production to do, etc. (Beardsley *et al.* 1956:145). This type (state level) was broadened somewhat when it was discovered that the seminar's belief that members of an integration could be considered on the basis of their own settlement pattern (Beardsley *et al.* 1956:135) was incorrect. Membership at any time in an integration apparently leads to the possession of all of the traits that make up this type, except perhaps a professional army.

SOME THEORETICAL CONSIDERATIONS

The seminar's system is admittedly one of cultural evolution, a word which has had pejorative connotations in anthropology since the days of Boas. There are a number of specific objections which have been made against modern theories of cultural evolution which need to be answered.

White (1949, 1959) is one of the foremost exponents of general cultural evolution in the United States today. His main concern is with the evolution of culture as a whole, in which he sees a number of stages dependent upon the amount of energy available to man at any given time. This system owes a good deal to Morgan and Tylor, and White (1959:ix) acknowledges his debt. There is, however, a major difference in the levels of abstraction with which the old and new evolutionists deal. The latter feel that the former were on the right track but made the mistake of applying their findings to individual cultures with unique histories rather than to culture in the abstract. This fundamental difference has led Steward (1955: 16) to propose calling White and similar theorists "universal" evolutionists in order to distinguish them from the old, or "unilinear," evolutionists.

The chief criticism of universal cultural evolution has been that it is not applicable to individual cultures and, therefore, cannot tell us how they got that way (Steward 1955:18), nor is it easily tested by the use of empirical data (Naroll 1961:391). Neither of these criticisms can be applied to the typology presented here since it is applicable to individual cultures, can tell us how they got that way, and can be tested with specific cultural data.

Sahlins (1960) has pointed out that there is a difference between the biological evolution which leads to species and evolution as a whole. By analogy, White studies the latter in cultural evolution, while Steward (1955) prefers the former, which he calls "multilinear" evolution. This approach has been criticized because Steward is unwilling to do more than generalize in a very tentative fashion (Adams 1956; White 1957). This objection cannot be applied to the typology presented here either, because extensive generalizations about the causes of increasing cultural complexity have been made, and these generalizations have been tested.

Others object that the evolutionary approach, in whatever form it is applied, does not take into account other possible causes of cultural change. Opler (1964) may be taken as a typical example, and the answer to his objection will serve as a criticism of others who have offered similar arguments. He states that evolutionists do not consider the individual and his role in cultural growth. This is quite true, but it does not invalidate the typology.

Blalock (1964:20–21) has suggested that theories be considered as models of the "real" world. There are two ways to reject a model: show that it does not fit the facts, or show that another model fits the facts better or that it fits more facts just as well. The general way to test fit is to predict from the model and see if the predictions are borne out by the empirical data. This typology has been tested in just that way.

Goodman and Kruskal's (1954; 1963) measure of optimal prediction, L_a, was applied to the data. This coefficient measures the improvement, given the types presented here, of predicting the proper end of the trait dichotomy over prediction without knowledge of the type. In the latter case, we would be right about .5000 of the time by chance alone. If we know the type, the improvement is .4988±.0718 at the 95 per cent confidence interval. In other words, we would be right between .7135 and .7853 of the time in 95 per cent of our predictions. (This has important implications for the prediction of archaeological traits which are beyond the scope of this work and will be published elsewhere.)

If Opler were to present a model which explains as much about culture growth and which includes the effect of the individual, he would have grounds to demand the rejection of the evolutionary model—if he could show that his model fit the facts just as well. This is exactly what Dragoo (1961) had in mind when he demanded better theory rather than no theory from the critics of cultural evolution. Opler, however, has not done this; his criticism and others of the same kind may be rejected.

REPLICATION

Two means are available to replicate this study: the first is to compare it with similar studies to see if there is agreement among them; the second is to repeat the study, avoiding difficulties found in the original.

Tatje and Naroll, and Carneiro have presented three similar scales (Chapters 40 and 41) in this volume. We may compare cultures which occur both in the sample used in this study and in the other samples. Table 4 presents these common cultures, their scores in the various typologies, and their relative rankings. While the sample is somewhat small, we should be able to get an idea as to whether the scales agree with each other and are, therefore, measuring the same thing. Edwards (1954:194, 426 ff.) presents the rank order coefficient formulae, including corrections for tied ranks, which will give us this information. They are:

Table 4
COMPARISON OF FOUR ORDINAL SCALES

Culture	Ranks			Scores		
	McNett	Carneiro		McNett	Carneiro	
Angmagsalik (Ammasalik)	2	1		Band	3	
Nipigon (Chippewa)	2	2		Band	4	
Yukaghir	2	3		Band	5	
Tenino*	4.5	4		Village	7	
Manobo	4.5	5		Village	9	
Tahiti	6	6		State	27	
	McNett	Naroll	Freeman	McNett	Naroll	Freeman
Callinago	1.5	1.5	2	Village	18	2
Ojibwa (Bungi)	1.5	4	1	Village	29	1
Seniang (Malekula)	3	1.5	3.5	Town	18	3
Kababish	4	3	3.5	City	25	3
Korea	5	5	5	State	67	9

*Tenino are included as members of the commercial subtype of the village level. If classified according to the levels as defined, they would be town level and the coefficient would be somewhat lower. If omitted, the coefficient would be higher.

$$r' = \frac{\Sigma x^2 + \Sigma y^2 - \Sigma d^2}{2\sqrt{\Sigma x^2 \Sigma y^2}}$$

when

$$\Sigma x^2 = \frac{n^3 - n}{12} - \Sigma Cx$$

and

$$\Sigma y^2 = \frac{n^3 - n}{12} - \Sigma Cy$$

In each case, C indicates a correction factor for tied ranks (Edwards 1954: Table 19.6), while n represents the number of pairs of ranks and d the difference between each pair of ranks. Calculation of these coefficients gives the following assessments of agreement between the scales:

McNett-Carneiro $r' = +.9259$ $p < .0167$
McNett-Naroll $r' = +.5000$ $p < .1167$
McNett-Freeman $r' = +.9474$ $p < .0417$

These indicate that there is a high level of agreement between the four sets of scales; the least being with Naroll's index. Since Tatje and Naroll found $r' = +.865$ in their comparison of the Naroll and Freeman scales for the full sample (see p. 778), variability in the small sample used here could account for the smaller coefficient. Sample size also probably accounts for the nonsignificance of the McNett-Naroll coefficient.

In such a case, perhaps Kendall's Coefficient of Concordance (Edwards 1954:402 ff.) will give a better measure of agreement between McNett-Naroll-Freeman. This is a rank order technique in which the basic formula is:

$$W = \frac{Sum\ of\ squares\ between\ columns}{Total\ sum\ of\ squares}$$

Data are given in Table 5. Two correction factors must be used in the basic formula. The continuity correction involves subtracting $1/m$ from the *Between sum of squares* and

adding $2/m$ to the *Total sum of squares*. In addition, the *Total sum of squares* is corrected for ties by subtracting ΣC, which is derived in the same way as for r'.

$$Between = \frac{\overset{n\ m}{\Sigma}(\Sigma X)^2}{m} - \frac{mn(n+1)^2}{4}$$

$$Total = \frac{m(n^3 - n)}{12}$$

For our data:

$$W_c = +.6918$$
$$p < .05$$

This coefficient is of particular importance because, as Edwards (1954:403) notes, if we have no direct measure of complexity against which these scales can be compared, then comparison between the scales will show if there is a "community of agreement" which may be taken to demonstrate that the scales are, in fact, measuring complexity. A positive coefficient this high may be taken as such evidence.

Conversely, this study may be seen to replicate others. Thus, Tatje and Naroll suggest above (p. 779–780) that cultural evolution is a multidirectional process. This is borne out by the data presented here. During the development of the scale, it was discovered that linear regression of the total complexity score of a culture was more accurate than was multiple discriminant analysis. The latter assumes that a given culture type will have typical scores in religion, politics, and economics. Instead, some cultures in the sample had a high score in religion, others low, yet all were of the same type. If the course of cultural evolution were unidimensional, then any culture of a given type would have a high score in one mode, low in another. Upon entering the next stage, its score in the modes would rise, and so on. Apparently, cultures actually have a

Table 5
DATA FOR CALCULATING W_c AND $r_{\bar{x}\bar{x}}$

Judges (m)		Ranks (n)			
	Callinago	Ojibwa	Seniang	Kababish	Korea
McNett	1.5	1.5	3	4	5
Naroll	1.5	4	1.5	3	5
Freeman	2	1	3.5	3.5	5
$\Sigma n =$	5	6.5	8	10.5	15
$n =$	1.7	2.2	2.7	3.5	5

potential for complexity which each handles according to its own history, some concentrating in one mode, some in another, some in all three.

Moreover, Tatje and Naroll (p. 779) suggest that the middle range of the scale is likely to be the most variable. This, too, has been borne out by the present data. It was shown (McNett 1967) that archaeological traits can be predicted by the settlement pattern scale as defined above. In this process, the odds from the sampling distribution of the cultures themselves are used to indicate the reliability of such predictions. Cultures from types at the bottom and top of the scale have the best odds for correct prediction, while probabilities in the middle of the scale are often no better than pure chance. Figure 1 shows this variability as well. The total spread of scores at the band level is from 0 to 3; at the state level, 20 to 22. On the other hand, the spread at the town level is from 7 to 15, which is quite a wide range.

REPETITION

In replicating the study by repetition, there are a number of alterations in procedure which should be made. No one man can be an expert in every culture area, and I do not pretend to be one. There are undoubtedly classifications in this study which will horrify those with expertise in some areas. All assignments to type and classifications of traits should, therefore, be checked with experts in each area and, where possible, each culture. Moreover, a number of secondary sources were used due to the unavailability of some references through interlibrary loan. These references are more likely to be found at the institution or in the personal library of a real expert.

The sample should probably be larger, as well. Murdock (1966) suggests one hundred cultures as a minimum for cross-cultural studies. The problem is not that the sample is too small for the tests used; the Kolmogorov-Smirnov conversion of D to χ^2 is, in fact, conservative for small samples (Siegel 1956:134–135). Rather, a small sample is less likely to represent the universe of cultures adequately. More traits would also be useful, and it would be interesting to divide each into several subtypes rather than dichotomies. More subdivision of traits would also sacrifice less information, as Sawyer and Levine (1966) point out.

The method of drawing the sample for this study must also be examined. It varies from that presented in McNett and Kirk (1968) in that the five-degree latitude and longitude lines on a Mercator projection map were used to form the grid. Since degrees of longitude decrease as one proceeds away from the equator, the ten-degree blocks are quite small near the poles. It might be argued that this gives an unfair advantage to cultures in the sparsely settled north (the south is relatively uninhabited) at the expense of cultures in the more intensively settled areas nearer the equator. A check of the sample used in this study, however, shows that there were 12 points north of the forty-ninth parallel which touched upon some land mass and 51 south of that line. Six of the northern blocks went unfilled, while only 9 did in the south. It seems that the smaller blocks have less chance of containing a culture in sparsely settled areas, thus reducing the advantage gained from their size. If the equal-area projection map and non-degree grid suggested in the paper cited were used in replication, however, the sample would come closer to the ideal definition of randomness.

None of these suggestions can be taken as evidence that the types as presented do not have validity; they would, however, tighten the model further and make it more useful. Unless one wants to deny any validity to this sample and those used in the studies with which it was compared, it seems that the evidence in favor of the verification of this typology is quite strong. This is particularly true when it is remembered that violations of most assumptions underlying the tests would result in a lower, not higher, χ^2. Finally, it is unlikely, even if every procedure followed were biased, that a $\chi^2 = 348.1805$, whose probability approaches certainty, would be obtained.

ADVANTAGES

We are left with the decision as to which scale to use. The demands of a particular problem will undoubtedly determine this in large part, but there are objective criteria which may aid our decision if we have a choice. Edwards (1954:413) says, "Since each of the sets of ranks is an estimate of their order, we may inquire whether the various estimates may be combined to yield a single best estimate." The reason for this inquiry is that an average of several scales is a better estimate than any single scale. We can discover the reliability of the averaged ranks by computing (Edwards 1954:412 ff.):

$$r_{\bar{x}\bar{x}}=1-\frac{Sum\ of\ squares\ within\ columns}{(m-1)\ Sum\ of\ squares\ between\ columns}$$

where

$$Within=Total-Between$$

For our data, which are also given in Table 5:

$$r_{\bar{x}\bar{x}}=.78$$

We may conclude that the averaged ranks are quite reliable. We might now ask which of the three scales (McNett-Naroll-Freeman) is the best estimate of the average ranks. We calculate r' between each of the three scales and the set of averaged ranks (n in Table 5) to find out:

McNett	$r'=+.9744$	$p < .0417$
Naroll	$r'=+.6154$	$p > .1167$
Freeman	$r'=+.8718$	$p < .0667,\ p > .0417$

While small sample size has again had its effect, we may conclude that there is evidence that the settlement pattern scale conforms somewhat more closely to the reliable average ranks than do the other scales. We are unable to say what Carneiro's scale would do in a similar situation, since there are no common cultures between Mc-Nett-Naroll-Freeman-Carneiro. We note, however, that Carneiro's scale is even more highly correlated with the scale presented in this study than is Freeman's.

Another criterion may also be applied. Carneiro's scale requires gathering data on 50 traits for each culture; Freeman's uses 9. To apply Naroll's index, three separate sets of data must be gathered, including the counting of what may run into hundreds of groups. The settlement pattern scale requires only one set of data which is quite easy to get for most cultures.

In conclusion, the scale presented here has been empirically validated, has been shown to be measuring the same thing as other scales, may be the most reliable estimate of complexity of the four considered, and is certainly the easiest to apply to the data.

BIBLIOGRAPHY

ADAMS, ROBERT M.
1956 Review of Steward, *Theory of culture change. American Antiquity* 22:195–196.
ATKINSON, WILLIAM C.
1953 Institutions and law. In H. V. Livermore, ed., *Portugal and Brazil: an introduction.* Oxford, Oxford University Press.
BEARDSLEY, RICHARD K., PRESTON HOLDER, ALEX D. KRIEGER, BETTY J. MEGGERS, and JOHN B. RINALDO
1956 Functional and evolutionary implications of community patterning. In R. Wauchope, ed., Seminars in archaeology: 1955. *Memoirs of the Society for American Archaeology* 11:129–157.

BLALOCK, HUBERT M., JR.
1960 *Social statistics.* New York, McGraw-Hill.
1964 *Causal inferences in nonexperimental research.* Chapel Hill, University of North Carolina Press.
BUCK, P. H.
1932 Ethnology of Manihiki and Rakahanga. *Bishop Museum Bulletin* 99:1–238.
CAMERON, D.
1890 The Nipigon 1804. In L. F. Q. Masson, ed., *Les bourgeois de la compagnie du nord ouest,* 2:229–300. New York, reprinted by Antiquarian Press, 1960.
COATES, W. P., and ZELDA K. COATES
1951 *Soviets in Central Asia.* New York, Philosophical Library.

COON, CARLETON S.
1958   *Caravan.* New York, Holt.

DEACON, BERNARD A.
1934   *Malekula: a vanishing people in the New Hebrides.* London, Routledge.

DRAGOO, DON W.
1961   Comment on Sears, *The study of social and religious systems in North American archaeology. Current Anthropology* 2:232–236.

DRIVER, HAROLD E., and WILHELMINE DRIVER
1963   *Ethnography and acculturation of the Chichimeca-Jonaz of Northeast Mexico.* Indiana University Research Center in Anthropology, Folklore and Linguistics Publication 26.

EDWARDS, ALLEN L.
1954   *Statistical methods for the behavioral sciences.* New York, Rinehart.

ENTWISTLE, WILLIAM J.
1953   Religion. In H. V. Livermore, ed., *Portugal and Brazil: an introduction.* Oxford, Oxford University Press.

GARVAN, JOHN M.
1941   *The Manobos of Mindanao.* National Academy of Sciences Memoir 23.

GOODMAN, LEO A., and W. H. KRUSKAL
1954   Measures of association for cross-classifications. *Journal of the American Statistical Association* 49:732–764.

1963   Measures of association for cross-classifications. III: approximate sampling theory. *Journal for the American Statistical Association* 58:310–364.

GOUGH, KATHLEEN
1961   Nayar: Central Kerala. In D. M. Schneider and K. Gough, eds., *Matrilineal kinship.* Berkeley, University of California Press.

GRANT, P.
1890   The Sauteaux Indians about 1804. In L. F. Q. Masson, ed., *Les bourgeois de la compagnie du nord ouest* 2:303–366. New York, reprinted by Antiquarian Press, 1960.

GRIAULE, MARCEL, and GERMAINE DIETERLEN
1954   The Dogon. In C. Daryll Forde, ed., *African worlds: studies in the cosmological ideas and social values of African peoples.* London, Oxford University Press.

HAGEN, G. VON
1912   Die Bana. *Baessler-Archiv* 2:77–116.

HANDY, E. S. C.
1931   *History and culture in the Society Islands.* Bishop Museum Bulletin 79.

HESKETH, J.
1923   History of the Turtle Mountain Chippewa. *Collections of the North Dakota State Historical Society* 5:85–154.

HOGBIN, H. I.
1961   *Law and order in Polynesia.* Hamden, Conn, The Shoe String Press.

HOWARD, J. H.
1961   The identity and demography of the Plains Ojibwa. *Plains Anthropologist* 6:xiii.

HUMAN RELATIONS AREA FILES
1955   *Lithuania.* Subcontractor's Monograph 18.

n.d.   *Ukraine.* Subcontractor's Monograph 20.

JOCHELSON, W.
1926   *The Yukaghir and Yukaghirized Tungus.* American Museum of Natural History Memoir 13.

KENNEDY, D. G.
1931   *Field notes on the culture of Vaitupu.* Polynesian Society Memoir 9.

KIRCHOFF, PAUL
1943   Los recolectores-cazadores del norte de Mexico. In *Sociedad Mexicana de Antropología, El norte de Mexico y el sur de los Estados Unidos.* Mexico D.F., Tercera Reunion de Mesa Redonda sobre Problemas Antropológicos de Mexico y Centro América.

1948   Food-gathering tribes of the Venequelan llanos. In J. Steward, ed., Handbook of South American Indians. *Bureau of American Ethnology Bulletin* 143, 4:445–455.

KOENTJARAINGRAT, R. M.
1960   The Javanese of South Central Java. In G. P. Murdock, ed., *Social structure in Southeast Asia.* Viking Fund Publications in Anthropology 29:88–115.

KRIEGER, HERBERT W.
1942   Peoples of the Philippines. *Smithsonian Institution War Background Studies* 4:34–39.

KROEBER, ALFRED L.
1919   Kinship in the Philippines. *American Museum of Natural History Anthropological Papers* 19:69–84.

LAMBERT, BERND
1964   Fosterage in the Northern Gilbert Islands. *Ethnology* 3:232–258.

LEBAR, F. M., G. C. MICKEY, and J. K. MUSGRAVE
1964   *Ethnic groups of mainland Southeast Asia.* New Haven, HRAF Press.

LEWIS, I. M.
1955   *Peoples of the horn of Africa.* London, International African Institute.

MASON, J. A.
1946   Notes on the Indians of the Great Slave Lake area. *Yale University Publications in Anthropology* 34:1–46.

MCNETT, CHARLES W., JR.
1967   *The inference of socio-cultural traits in archaeology: a statistical approach.* Doctoral dissertation (Tulane University) to be published by University Microfilms.

MCNETT, CHARLES W., JR., and ROGER E. KIRK
1968   A suggested method of drawing random samples in cross-cultural surveys. *American Anthropologist* 70:50–55.

MEAD, MARGARET
1937.   Manus. In Margaret Mead, ed., *Cooperation and competition among primitive peoples.* New York, McGraw-Hill.

MÉTRAUX, A.
1946   Ethnography of the Chaco. In J. Steward, ed., Handbook of South American Indians. *Bureau of American Ethnology Bulletin* 143, 1:197–370.

MINER, HORACE M.
1953   *The primitive city of Timbuctoo.* Memoirs of the American Philosophical Society 32.

MIRSKY, J.
1937   Eskimo of Greenland. In Margaret Mead, ed., *Cooperation and competition among primitive peoples.* New York, McGraw-Hill.

MURDOCK, GEORGE P.
1957   World ethnographic sample. *American Anthropologist* 59:664–687.

1958   Social organization of the Tenino. In *Miscellanea Paul Rivet.* Mexico, D.F., XXXI International Congress of Americanists, 1:299–315.

1959   *Africa: its peoples and their culture history.* New York, McGraw-Hill.

1965   Tenino shamanism. *Ethnology* 4:165–171.

1966   Cross-cultural sampling. *Ethnology* 5:97–114.

MURDOCK, GEORGE P., et al.
1962–65 Ethnographic atlas. *Ethnology* 1–4: continuing series.

NAROLL, RAOUL
1961   Review of White's *Evolution and culture. American Anthropologist* 63:391.

1962   *Data quality control: a new research technique. Prolegomena to a cross-cultural study of culture stress.* Glencoe, Ill., Free Press.

1964   A fifth solution to Galton's problem. *American Anthropologist* 66:863–866.

NIMUENDAJU, C.
1939   *The Apinaye.* Catholic University Anthropology Series 8.

NORDENSKÏOLD, E.
1938   *An historical and ethnological survey of the Cuna Indians.* Comparative Ethnographic Studies 10.

OPLER, MORRIS E.
1964   The human being in culture theory. *American Anthropologist* 66:507–528.

OSGOOD, CORNELIUS
1951   *The Koreans and their culture.* New York, Ronald Press.

PEARSON, E. S., and H. O. HARTLEY
1954   *Biometrika tables for statisticians.* Cambridge, Cambridge University Press.

PITT-RIVERS, J. A.
1954   *The people of the Sierra.* Chicago, University of Chicago.

POWDERMAKER, H.
1933   *Life in Lesu.* New York, Norton Press.

RAO, C. RADHAKRISHNA
1952   *Advanced statistical methods in biometric research.* New York, Wiley.

RAY, S. H.
1917   The people and languages of Lifu, Loyalty Islands. *Journal of the Royal Anthropological Institute* N.S. 20:239–322.

RAY, V. F.
1942   Plateau. *Anthropological Records* 8:99–257.

ROUSE, IRVING
1948   The Carib. In J. Steward, ed., Handbook of South American Indians. *Bureau of American Ethnology Bulletin* 143, 4:547–565.

ROUSE, IRVING, and A. HOSTOS
1948   The Arawak. In J. Steward, ed., Handbook of South American Indians. *Bureau of American Ethnology Bulletin* 143, 4:507–546.

SAHLINS, MARSHALL D.
1960   Evolution: specific and general. In M. D. Sahlins and E. R. Service, eds., *Evolution and culture.* Ann Arbor, University of Michigan Press.

SAWYER, JACK, and ROBERT A. LEVINE
1966   Cultural dimensions: a factor analysis of the World Ethnographic Sample. *American Anthropologist* 68:708–731.

SCHAPERA, I.
1953   *The Tswana.* London, International African Institute.

SCHWAB, G.
1947   *Tribes of the Liberian hinterland.* Peabody Museum Papers 31.

SELIGMAN, C. G., and B. Z. SELIGMAN
1918   The Kubabish. *Harvard African Studies* 2:105–185.

SIEGEL, SIDNEY
1956   *Nonparametric statistics for the behavioral sciences.* New York, McGraw-Hill.

SKINNER, A.
1914a   The cultural position of the Plains

Ojibwa. *American Anthropologist* 16: 314–318.

1914b   Political and ceremonial organization of the Plains-Ojibwa. *American Museum of Natural History Anthropological Papers* 11:475–511.

SPENCER, ROBERT F.
1965   Athabascans of the Western Sub-Arctic. In R. F. Spencer and J. D. Jennings, eds., *The native Americans*. New York, Harper and Row.

STEPHEN, E.
1936   Notes on Nauru. *Oceania* 7:34–63.

STEWARD, JULIAN H.
1938   *Basin-Plateau aboriginal sociopolitical groups*. Bureau of American Ethnology Bulletin 120.

1943   Northern and Gosiute Shoshoni. *Anthropological Records* 7:263–392.

1955   *Theory of culture change*. Urbana, University of Illinois Press.

STOUT, D. B.
1947   *San Blas Cuna acculturation*. Viking Fund Publications in Anthropology 9.

TAYLOR, D.
1946   Kinship and social structure of the Island Carib. *Southwest Journal of Anthropology* 2:180–212.

TSCHOPIK, HARRY J.
1946   The Aymara. In J. Steward, ed., Handbook of South American Indians.

Bureau of American Ethnology Bulletin 143, 2:501–573.

VREELAND, H. H.
1957   *Mongol community and kinship structure*. New Haven, HRAF Press.

WAUCHOPE, ROBERT (ed.)
1956   *Seminars in archaeology: 1955*. Memoirs of the Society for American Archaeology 11.

WEDGEWOOD, C.
1936   Report on research work in Nauru Island, Central Pacific. *Oceania* 6:359–391; 7:1–33.

WHITE, LESLIE A.
1949   *The science of culture*. New York, Grove Press.

1957   Review of Steward, *Theory of culture change*. *American Anthropologist* 59: 540–544.

1959   *The evolution of culture*. New York, McGraw-Hill.

WHITING, JOHN W. M.
1941   *Becoming a Kwoma*. New Haven, Yale University Press.

WILBERT, J.
1957   Notes on Guahibo kinship and social organization. *Southwestern Journal of Anthropology* 13:88–98.

WILLIAMS, THOMAS RHYS
1965   *The Dusun: a North Borneo society*. New York, Rinehart and Winston.

PART VII

Special Problems of Comparative Method

CHAPTER 43

Cross-Cultural Sampling

RAOUL NAROLL

INTRODUCTION

This chapter reviews the sources of error in problems of cross-cultural sampling and proposes new methods of dealing with them. Sampling error can be divided into two kinds: random error, and systematic error, or bias. Size of sample affects random error; the larger the sample, the less net random error to be expected. Statisticians have developed many elaborate and sensitive methods of measuring random error risk; these methods are the familiar significance tests. But hitherto little has been done to measure systematic sampling error. Statisticians and sample survey experts have preferred to avoid such error entirely by using probability sampling methods. Few cross-cultural surveys have used probability sampling methods; most have used judgmental, expert, or quota samples. It is impossible to use conventional probability sampling methods in cross-cultural surveys because most societies in the universe are not sufficiently well known to study. On the other hand, judgmental, expert, or quota samples of the sort usually taken may have large and unmeasurable biases. The solution here proposed is twofold. First, to limit the sampling bias to a few well-defined restrictions and otherwise to use probability sampling. Second, to measure the biases involved in these restrictions and to control for their influence upon the variables being studied. This solution is tried out below on the author's fifty-eight-society War, Stress and Culture (WSC) sample. Sampling bias required for the method here proposed appears to be moderate and relatively unmalignant. Very large samples like the World Ethnographic Sample seem to be often equivalent to the entire universe for sampling purposes; this equivalence appears to hold whenever the investigator needs copious data on a culture in order to carry out his cross-cultural survey.

The role of sample size of stratification, and of diffusion (Galton's problem) in cross-cultural surveys is discussed. The reader is reminded that increasing the sample size does not decrease the risk of sampling bias, only that of random error. For problems involving correlations between two very widely diffused traits, the optimum sample size is held to be of the order of fifty or seventy-five. For narrowly diffused traits, the optimum number is between three and four hundred. Stratification is advocated not in order to reduce sampling costs or sampling variance but in order to reduce the effects of diffusion; therefore, stratification designs in cross-cultural surveys are advocated which differ from those in descriptive household or individual person sample surveys.

GENERAL THEORY OF SAMPLING

Sampling theory has been elaborately developed by sociologists, demographers and social psychologists in conventional sample surveys. (By conventional sample surveys, I mean those where the unit of study is an individual person. In cross-cultural surveys, on the other hand, as in cross-historical and cross-national surveys, the unit of study is an entire society or culture.) Three basic types of sampling methods have been extensively used in conventional sample surveys (Kish 1965:19 f.). (1) *Haphazard or fortuitous sampling*—sometimes called "bunch" or "grab" sampling. Such samples take information from whatever subjects come to hand, without any concern for their representativeness. (2) *Expert choice,* where a sample is assembled which some expert considers representative, without his stating precisely how he reached this conclusion. (3) *Quota sampling*—the universe to be sampled is classified according to several known characteristics believed to be important. (By *sampling universe* is meant of course the total collection of units which the sample is supposed to represent. Thus the Gallup poll interviews a thousand American voters—its sample—in order to make inferences about all American voters—its universe. The universe for a cross-cultural survey may perhaps be taken to be all known primitive societies, or perhaps all known human societies, past and present.) American voters thus can be classed by state of residence, sex, age, occupation, income, population of home town and so on. Primitive tribes can be classified by culture area or continental region, by level of social development, or by presence or absence of some other key trait of interest to the investigator. A quota sample fixes in advance the proportions of units having the stated characteristics. It then uses haphazard or fortuitous sampling to fill its quotas. Thus an interviewer may be instructed to find a housewife between the ages of thirty and thirty-five years living in Harlan County, Kentucky, in a town with a population of 2,000 to 5,000—a housewife who is at home when he calls. A cross-cultural survey designer may seek a Polynesian tribe with adequate literature on kinship. (4) *Probability sampling*—all units in the universe are considered in one way or another. Their names may be collected and listed; or their locations may be mapped. A selection procedure is followed which in some way or other enables the investigator to compute the probability (the gambling odds) that any particular unit will be chosen.

All samples purport to be representative of the universe sampled. That is the whole idea of sampling. In order to make her sample representative, the housewife stirs the stew before she tastes it and the painter stirs the paint bucket before he tries out its color.

After extensive experience with all these sampling methods, survey sample theorists seem to have become generally persuaded that only probability sampling is representative. Only probability sampling avoids sampling bias—that is, systematic sampling error. The key points to grasp firmly in mind about sampling theory are only two.

First key point: *random sampling error risk, and only random error risk, is measured by statistical significance tests.* (These tests measure the net risk of all kinds of random error—random sampling error, random reporting error and random classification error. See Chapter 44.) The larger the sample, the less the risk of net random error. But significance tests always take sample size into consideration; they measure the error risk for a sample of a stated size. By random errors are of course meant errors of a sort which when repeated tend to cancel each other out. In technical language, such errors have a mathematical expectation of zero. Such sampling errors always tend to lower correlations. They usually do not have any tendency to produce spurious correlations (see Chapter 44 below).

Second key point: *systematic sampling error—usually called sampling bias—is not controlled by ordinary significance tests and is not affected by sample size.* By systematic sampling errors are meant those whose effects tend to pile up or accumulate instead of canceling each other out. In technical language, such errors have a non-zero mathematical expectation. Such errors may well produce spurious correlations.

Probability sampling is thus preferred over the other kinds of sampling by sampling theorists for two reasons. It permits control of random error through use of statistical significance tests; such tests all assume probability sampling. Second, it gets rid of systematic sampling error. In a study of twelve leading textbooks on statistical theory, statistical practices, sample survey theory or sample survey practices, all the writers consulted without exception favored probability sampling and opposed the other kinds. The textbooks: Parten (1950:238), citing Neyman and Snedecor; Wallis and Roberts (1956: 117); Blalock (1960:410 f.); Kenney and Keeping (1951:151); Mood (1950:127); Duncan (1959:19); Walker and Lev (1953:172); Kish (1965:19–21); Cochrane (1963:10 f.);

Yates (1949:1 f., 9 f.); Hansen, Hurwitz and Madow (1953:9); Stephan and McCarthy (1958:47).

The opinions of these experts have been strongly supported by a number of studies of sampling bias in cross-cultural surveys. George P. Murdock (1957:644 f.), author of the best-known cross-cultural survey, *Social Structure*, himself reported a later study indicating spurious sampling bias in his work:

At one time the author believed that an adequate sample might be obtained merely by selecting a large number of cultures from a wide geographic range and avoiding excessive representation of any particular areas. A test conducted recently in a graduate class convinced him that this is not sufficient. In this test the major statistical correlations of *Social Structure* . . . were recalculated from two worldwide samples of 300 cultures each, one completely unselected and the other carefully chosen to give precisely equal representation to all the culture areas of the world. Though no startling reversals appeared, the results from the two samples differed so markedly in enough instances to demonstrate the imperative need for a much more systematic sampling procedure.

Another striking instance of acknowledged sampling error has arisen from the recent work of Melford E. Spiro. This distinguished anthropologist presented an important study in taxonomy, based upon a non-probability sample (Spiro:1965). However, Chaney (1966) showed that Spiro's sample was not representative of its universe. Spiro (1966: 1471 f.) conceded that his sample was not representative; further, he conceded that one of his propositions was clearly in error. Spiro's study had found that in societies with characteristically small, independent bilateral families, marriage tended to be monogamous. But this finding turned out merely to reflect sampling error (Chaney 1966:1461).

Köbben (1952:140) had previously pointed out wide discrepancies in earlier cross-cultural samples.

Yet are they in fact representative? The number of samples ranges from 56 with Horton to 250 with Murdock, whose choice may be examined from this aspect. There is little doubt that he has been guided more by the presence of good sources than by the proportional representation of each culture-area. Also he has not troubled himself with the question of whether too many peoples with the same mode of subsistence, e.g. hunting and collecting, occur in his list, which in fact contains no fewer than 70 North American Indian tribes. The value of the material may be tested by a comparison with that of others. Thus, Hob-house, Wheeler and Ginsberg find among their 643 tribes a proportion of ten with a matrilocal to thirteen with a patrilocal system (1930, p. 151). In Murdock's work this ratio is at best one to two (1949, p. 17). With Nieboer the proportions of slave-keeping to slaveless tribes are about equal and with Murdock, again, one to two (Nieboer, 1910, p. 166; Murdock, 1949, p. 87). Further suspicion of the unsatisfactory nature of Murdock's sampling is provided by a passage from his own book where he discusses two different explanations of the same phenomena by Lowie and Kroeber respectively. When he had treated 221 societies out of his 250, Murdock believed that in view of his figures something more was to be said for Kroeber's theory than Lowie's. Nevertheless, study of the remaining 29 societies was able to make him change his conclusion. What, then would remain of his theories if he undertook to deal with 643 tribes like Hobhouse, Wheeler and Ginsberg?

Murdock (1957:664 f.) himself later acknowledged these shortcomings.

However, the most massive demonstration of sampling inconsistencies is that in the magisterial study of Textor (see Chapter 34, above, Table 4, p. 661). Thus, for example, Anthony's cross-cultural sample on male initiation rites—as compared to Murdock's "Ethnographic Atlas"—overrepresented: (1) societies located outside the Circummediterranean area; (2) societies without weaving; (3) societies with cousin terminology of the Crow, Omaha or Iroquois type rather than of the Eskimo or Hawaiian type; (4) societies with segregation of adolescent boys; (5) societies where premarital sex relations were freely permitted or punished only if pregnancy resulted; (6) societies without high gods; (7) societies where food taboos were comparatively important, and (8) societies not keenly sensitive to personal insult. All these sampling preferences were so great as not plausibly to be explained as random sampling error, even after considering the very large number of correlations which Textor looked at. All these taken together make it clear that much sampling bias was present either in Anthony's sample; or else in the first four hundred societies of Murdock's "Ethnographic Atlas," with which it was compared; or in both. Chapter 34, Table IV, above, presents many dozen similar sampling biases, shown by comparing other studies with Murdock's "Ethnographic Atlas." Textor's work and Tatje's analysis of the random error problem combine to produce the most massive demonstration of sampling bias I know.

It is clear from this work of Textor and Tatje that much sampling bias exists in cross-cultural samples. However, it is never clear which samples, if any, are unbiased. From this evidence, we can never say for sure that any particular sample is biased. All we know is that two samples disagree and hence that at least one of them must be biased.

There are at this writing (1967) two and only two probability samples taken directly from bibliographically defined universes. These are (1) the Diffusion Arc Sub-Sample of Naroll's War, Stress and Culture Sample (see pages 908–909 below); and (2) the HRAF Quality Control Sample (see pages 910–912 below). At this writing, no studies have yet been made of the HRAF Quality Control sample, enabling comparisons of it with other samples. On the other hand, I have systematically compared sub-samples of the tribes in my War, Stress and Culture sample, seeking evidence of sampling bias. The size of sub-samples is too small to permit more than preliminary conclusions. These are offered for what they may be worth.

As explained below, pp. 908–909, my diffusion arc (DA) sub-sample was taken directly from a bibliographically defined universe. On the other hand my WES sub-sample was a stratified random sample from Murdock's quasi-universe, the World Ethnographic Sample (see pp. 905–906 below). My WES sub-sample and my DA sub-sample both were subjected to two similar biases. (1) They were subjected to identical bibliographic biases (see pp. 912–913 below). (2) They each in a different way tended to be biased in favor of societies occupying larger areas. In my DA sample, the sampling strata were of equal geographical area. Each society was represented by its northeasternmost point only. Consequently, all societies within any one stratum had an equal chance of selection regardless of area. But if one stratum tended to contain larger societies than another stratum, then the first would tend to have fewer societies than the second. Consequently societies in the first stratum would have a correspondingly better chance of being selected than those in the second. However, there were two countertendencies. First, sampling strata in the insular Pacific tended to favor a few *small-area* societies. Second, *very* large societies tended to be less likely to be chosen because they were more

likely to have their northeasternmost point outside the diffusion arc entirely. Murdock's WES quasi-universe sought to include the most populous society in each culture area, as one of his quota criteria. More populous societies of course tend to occupy larger territories than less populous societies; furthermore, if Murdock could not find population data, he simply chose the society with the largest area. Hence, about one-tenth of the societies in the WES quasi-universe were chosen with the criterion of size in mind; but this criterion was ignored in the other nine-tenths. Since my WES sub-sample randomly selected from strata of the WES quasi-universe, it presumably reflects this same bias.

Otherwise, the DA sub-sample is free of any of the biases of the WES quasi-universe. Otherwise, none of the quota criteria or other biases of the WES quasi-universe influenced the DA sub-sample. The DA sub-sample but not the WES quasi-universe was subjected to two other biases. I believe both of these to be trifling—of no importance. First, there were inconsistencies in the unit definitions of Murdock's *Outline of World Cultures* (Murdock 1963; see Chapter 39 above). Second, the DA sub-sample would be influenced by whatever bias, if any, results from culture trait distributions with a tendency to occur in geographical areas about eight hundred nautical miles in diameter. This bias would not affect distributions which tend to occur in geographical areas of varying size—as do all I know about. Nor in practice would it affect those which tend to occur in areas of some other regular size. (See for example the dozens of trait distributions mapped in Driver and Massey, 1957.)

These two samples were compared with respect to about one hundred culture traits reflecting aspects of culture stress (e.g. suicide, homicide, marriage and divorce rules), cultural evolution and warfare, as well as to characteristics of ethnic units (see Chapter 39 above) and data quality control factors (see Chapter 44 below). Because of variant codings, a total of about three hundred formal correlations were computed.

Only eight of these correlations attained nominal significance at the 5 per cent level. As discussed elsewhere in this *Handbook* (pp. 650–652 above and 941–942 below), it is not clear how many nominally significant correlations we really ought to expect by chance from these three hundred. The simple theoretical answer of fifteen (5 per cent of 300) is clearly too high. I think we may tentatively conclude that the eight nominally significant correlations out of a run of three hundred constitute no evidence of sampling bias at all. There is then some support for the following working hypothesis:

For sampling with bibliographic requirements as strict as those for the War, Stress and Culture (WSC) sample, probability samples from the WES quasi-universe are unlikely to differ from probability samples from the entire bibliographically defined universe. In other words, consider all the primitive tribes whose literature meets the bibliographic requirements of the WSC sample (see Appendix I, pp. 918–921 below). If we look at only those of them which appear in the WES quasi-universe, we will be looking at practically all of them. The few such tribes excluded will probably not differ enough from the large proportion included to matter.

Another sampling bias test was made of the societies in the War, Stress and Culture study. About half the societies in the WSC study turned out to be included in the Human Relations Area Files—HRAF (see above, Chapter 33 and see below, pp. 918–921). Again with respect to these same traits, the societies included in HRAF were compared to those not included.

Here I found nearly twice as many nominally significant correlations—fourteen. All but one of these came from the approximately 225 phi coefficients. It is clear that chance in fact would lead us to expect considerably fewer than eleven such (5 per cent of 226=11.25, but again, see pp. 650–652 above and 941–942 below).

Most of these fourteen correlations had to do with various measures of warfare scope and frequency. It seems likely that we can draw one of two conclusions about the original HRAF sample. Either (1) HRAF tended to select less warlike tribes and to pass over more warlike tribes; or else (2) information on warlikeness was more easily accessible and more likely to be found in works indexed by HRAF as a result of their index work but information on warlikeness was less easily accessible and more easily overlooked in works not so indexed. There seems good reason to suspect that both these effects may

be operating. If so, they indicate that the best strategy for studying warfare cross-culturally is to use the future HRAF quality control sample (see pp. 910–911 below) rather than the original HRAF sample.

It is important to bear in mind that all the sampling bias uncovered by the foregoing studies is bias in samples which it was hoped were representative—samples designed to be so. How much more sampling bias must we expect in studies which did not even try to be representative? As Clignet points out in Chapter 31 above, one major weakness of concomitant variation studies like Redfield's *Folk Cultures of Yucatan* is this very point of representativeness. In order to design such a study, very special requirements must be met. Meeting these requirements leaves the investigator very far from any claim that his few, specially chosen subjects of study are representative of human societies as a whole. Redfield himself (1941:343) was careful to make this very point by specifically disclaiming that his Yucatan findings could be generalized to culture as a whole without further research.

SPECIAL PROBLEMS OF SAMPLING IN CROSS-CULTURAL SURVEYS

The present chapter proceeds to a more detailed consideration of sampling problems in cross-cultural surveys and then proposes methods of avoiding sampling bias in the future. Cross-cultural survey work began in 1889, before the modern science of statistics was born. When Edward Tylor (1889) published the first cross-cultural survey, mathematicians had no measure of correlation and no tests of random error (i.e. tests of statistical significance). Pearson's product moment correlation coefficient, the phi coefficient, the biserial correlation coefficient, Yule's Q, Pearson's Q_6, Spearman's rank correlation coefficient—all these were undiscovered—the very word "regression" itself was not in use. "Student" had not yet discovered the t distribution, the cumulative binomial distribution—although known for centuries—had not been extensively tabulated and hence was in practice not available for regular use; in short, there was hardly any of the mathematical apparatus which today makes statistical inference so precise, so powerful and so convenient to use. Little wonder that neither Tylor nor his foremost critic Francis Galton worried about sampling theory. Until the 1930's, the aim of cross-cultural surveys was to study the entire universe of available data on primitive tribes. Such was Tylor's concept and such was the concept of Steinmetz (1896), of Nieboer (1910), of Hobhouse (1906), Hobhouse, Wheeler and Ginsberg (1915). Not until the 1930's, after probability sampling methods, sampling theory and statistical inferences had been refined and developed by biologists like Karl Pearson and R. A. Fisher, did the first cross-cultural sample appear. This sample was the work of Unwin (1934). Unfortunately, Unwin's study of the relationship between sexual restrictions and level of civilization was so deficient in other ways that the importance of his sampling method went unappreciated (Benedict 1935). It remained for George Peter Murdock and his associates at Yale to make popular sampling methods, correlational coefficients and statistical inference in cross-cultural survey work (Simmons 1937; Murdock 1937; Murdock 1949).

While Murdock may have been aware of the theoretical importance of probability sampling, several difficulties existed in the 1930's which made that kind of sample seem absolutely out of the question for cross-cultural surveys.

Units. To begin with, no satisfactory definition of the unit of study existed. Exactly what did one mean by a society, or a culture, or a tribe? (See Chapter 39 above.)

Universe Lists. Supposing that one did have such a definition, no lists of these units were available. Good ethnographic tribal location maps of entire continents were not available either. Thus probability sampling either by random selection of names from a list or random selection of points or areas on a map was not possible.

These matters are crucial. Only three basic approaches to probability sampling are known today. The first approach requires that the entire universe consists of small objects of like size and shape, all physically present. This approach obviously is of no use to us in cross-cultural work. The second approach requires a list of names of the units in the universe in some form or other. The third approach requires a map of the area in which the units are located. And unless the areas selected are to be personally visited by

the investigator or his staff, the location of the units within the selected areas must also be mapped. In the 1930's, neither such lists nor such maps were available to Murdock and his students.

Ethnographic Bibliography. But these difficulties, severe as they were, paled in the face of the truly central problem of cross-cultural sampling—bibliography. Cross-cultural survey work is usually library study work. Ordinarily, tribes can only be incorporated into cross-cultural statistical tabulations if adequate data on them are to be found in the libraries. But a random sample of primitive tribes will produce a high proportion—far more than half—of tribes about which not enough is known to permit study of any but the grossest and most obvious of characteristics. Information on such fine points as kinship terminology, descent rules, child training practices, occupational specialization, settlement population, law and religious beliefs is hardly to be had on the majority of primitive tribes.

One way of getting around the bibliography problem has long been used. Morgan (1871), Grant (1879), Magnus (1880, 1883) and Frazer in 1888 (Leach 1961:384 n.) sent questionnaires to missionaries and colonial administrators asking for information about natives in their locality. More recently, Paul J. Bohannan in an as yet unpublished study on divorce collected cross-cultural information by submitting questionnaires to a large number of anthropologists; he asked them to report on the natives they had studied. Currently, Donald T. Campbell and Robert A. LeVine are conducting a cross-cultural survey of ethnocentrism under a large grant from the Carnegie Corporation. They are contracting with ethnologists with ongoing field work to devote a month of their field stay to collecting data for the ethnocentrism study. This study was stimulated by the brilliant earlier work of Segall, Campbell and Herskovits (1966) on optical illusions; here anthropologists were commissioned to administer standard illusion tests to natives in widely scattered parts of the world. The result was massive documentation of the cultural relativity of many familiar optical illusions.

But we must not overestimate the importance for sampling theory of the success of the Segall, Campbell and Herskovits study of optical illusions. That study *did not need* representative sampling. It was neither a descriptive study nor a correlational study. It sought neither to infer the proportion of cultures deceived by the Müller-Lyer illusion nor to correlate this deception with other factors. *It only sought to show that variation existed.* It only sought to show that people of various cultures did not all react alike to these illusions. If we suppose, as well we may, that their sample was badly biased, this bias does not weaken the force of their findings. However, had they depended upon statistical manipulation of counts of societies it would have been another matter.

Wherever fresh data can be collected for a cross-cultural survey through fresh field work, such collection has obvious advantages. But the universe available for study through fresh field work is already a highly restricted and badly biased one. For example, most of the high-quality ethnology of native North America was recorded by professional American anthropologists between 1900 and 1940. These anthropologists worked with older informants who could still recall Indian life before the tribes concerned had their native culture largely destroyed by white conquest. No such informants are alive any longer. Primitive tribes in a state of cultural independence survive today in only a very few parts of the world; and elderly informants who still remember such conditions in only a few other parts. Already then cross-cultural survey work must restrict itself chiefly to library data if it considers problems related to warfare and political independence. Native oral tradition is hardly an improvement on written ethnographic literature.

Thus we cannot often avoid the bibliographic problem by collecting fresh data. The present chapter therefore concerns itself with the sampling problem of the investigator who wants to test a hypothesis in the library with library data.

We come back then to the basic bibliographic problem. The key sampling question for each investigator is: Which tribes have been described well enough for me and which tribes have not?

In the 1930's no answer to this question was at hand. To get such an answer above all an investigator would have needed ethnographic bibliographies—bibliographies ordered tribe by tribe. In the 1930's, those

available to Murdock and his associates were few and poor.

Sampling Materials Now Available

In the 1930's, then, Murdock and his associates lacked a clear concept of the tribe as a unit; they lacked tribal lists; they lacked tribal maps; and they lacked tribal bibliographies. Materials for all these existed, but they were scattered and hence inaccessible. Murdock himself is largely responsible for the fact that today we enjoy a radically different situation. His *Outline of World Cultures* (1963), with all its shortcomings, is nevertheless a workable tribal list for all the world except Australia and New Guinea. For these two areas, language lists in effect constitute tribal lists. We have Capell (1962) for New Guinea and Greenway (1963) for Australia. Murdock's *Outline of World Cultures* can serve the cross-cultural sampler as a city directory can serve a conventional sample survey man. The sample survey man would prefer a list of inhabitants of the city he studies. But he can make out very well with a list of its buildings. Some of the buildings on such a list have many residents; some have few; others have none at all. But if he takes a probability sample of the city's buildings, he can then count the number of residents in the buildings in his sample and weight his findings accordingly. Similarly, some of the categories in Murdock's *Outline of World Cultures* list or refer to many tribes, some list or refer to only one or two, a few refer to only a part of a tribe, and many refer to no contemporary society at all but to something else again entirely—to an entire region, or to historical or archaeological or even paleontological and ethological data. Such listings are analogous to uninhabited buildings in a conventional sample survey.

Adequate ethnographic bibliographies are now readily available for all the world except the Middle East, North Africa and Europe (see Chapter 7 above). This fact is in considerable extent again due to Murdock's own labors. He himself has compiled the standard ethnographic bibliography for North America; and directly stimulated those for South America, Africa, Southeast Asia, and Indonesia.

Tribal maps are now available for most of the world. However, few of these can be relied upon to follow adequate linguistic principles in mapping tribes whose boundaries are linguistic rather than political. See further discussion in Chapter 39, page 737, above.

Finally, Murdock has been responsible for the construction of two quasi-universes, the World Ethnographic Sample and the Ethnographic Atlas. As we shall see, these quasi-universes apparently can safely be used as equivalents for the entire universe of primitive tribes whenever the data requirements of the investigator are considerable. In other words, these quasi-universes turn out to include almost all the tribes there are with considerably large bodies of descriptive literature available on them. Consider an investigator who must in any case reject tribes from his sample whenever they lack copious descriptive literature listed in standard ethnographic bibliographies. If the literature is not so listed, he does not know it exists and has no time to hunt it out. If he cannot find enough data on a tribe, the tribe might as well not exist as far as he is concerned. As we shall see below, such an investigator is apparently wasting his time drawing a fresh sample from the entire universe of primitive tribes. As far as primitive tribes are concerned we shall see that he seems likely to do as well today if he sticks to those two quasi-universes of G. P. Murdock.

Thus, on one hand, for most investigators, a *bibliographic sampling bias* is unavoidable in cross-cultural surveys of primitive tribes. He cannot study tribes not already described. If the investigator seeks to collect fresh data in the field himself, or to question other anthropologists about their field notes, he only substitutes for the badly biased universe of the library an even more severely biased one of the tribes known to presently available anthropologists or those with living and presently available informants.

There is a second form of bibliographic sampling bias which also inevitably intrudes into cross-cultural survey work. This bias occurs in studying tribes like the Navaho, the Hopi, and the Iroquois with very large descriptive literatures. It reaches a crescendo in the study of civilized societies with native literatures. The comparativist cannot make himself responsible for examining all the available literature on such societies. Instead he must restrict himself to specified categories of reports among the mass available. This

simple fact should be obvious. Every investigator works with a budget. All or part of his budget may be in the form of his own working time; he must allocate whatever time he can to his task but some limit always must exist. For most working social scientists, one or two years of full-time work (spread perhaps over five or ten years of calendar time) is near to the feasible maximum the investigator can contribute of his own working time for any one study. To this, he can add the time of whatever other staff members he can raise funds to hire, or exercise enough charisma to lure for voluntary aid. Whatever an investigator's budget, he is not likely to be able to afford the luxury of carefully studying and comparing all the literature on a tribe like the Hopi. Such a task is a ten-year labor for a devoted scholar. He must rather search through a few leading general descriptions of them together with a few special treatises dealing with points of particular importance to him. The standards of ethnographic scholarship exemplified in works like Martin Gusinde's studies of Fuegian tribes are not for the likes of him. He may admire them but cannot hope to repeat them. Here is the key point. *The scholarly standards appropriate to a description of a single tribe are not those appropriate to a comparative study.* The comparativist must not only sample tribes from the universe of tribes, he must also sample reports on particular tribes from the universe of reports. And bibliographic characteristics of entire tribe and of particular report must consistently influence and bias these selections. There can be no question of a random choice between a copious description and a meager one, between a relevant report and an irrelevant one.

Galton's Problem

By Galton's problem is meant the problem of distinguishing between the influences of diffusion and functional association in cross-cultural surveys. The nature and importance of this problem, and ways to deal with it, are considered at length in Chapter 47, below. We are here concerned with only one aspect of Galton's problem, its effect on sampling. That effect is important.

The heart of the problem lies in the fact that most culture traits spread readily by borrowing or migration. Consequently, they tend to be found in clusters of neighboring societies. Intensive culture element distribution studies among the natives of particular regions like California have shown that very high correlations commonly occur among traits with little or no functional linkage. For example, among the tribes of southeastern California, there is a perfect correlation between tribes which play tunes on flageolets and tribes which use carrying frames made of sticks and cords, tribes which make oval plate pottery, tribes which use squared mullers, and tribes which favor twins. The tribes concerned are neighbors, speaking closely related languages. The fact that they are neighbors suggests diffusion by borrowing; the fact that they speak closely related languages suggests diffusion by migration. This sort of thing happens over and over again; see the further discussion in Chapter 47, below.

No student of culture trait distributions would think these perfect correlations anything out of the ordinary. Nor would he seek any further for their explanation than diffusion. The sole problem which might seem interesting is whether to explain the distribution of flageolets, carrying frames, squared mullers, and twin acceptance in California by borrowing, or by migration.

The rub comes when we examine similarly clustered culture trait distributions which seem to meet plausible functional needs. Consider now eight tribes of the Southeast United States: the Creek, the Cusabo, the Hichiti, the Timucua, the Alabama, the Chickasaw, the Choctaw and the Chakchiuma. These tribes too are all geographical neighbors, occupying a single continuous land area. They too all speak closely related languages. If we were to be told that all these eight southeastern tribes played tunes on flageolets, used squared mullers, made carrying frames of sticks and cords, baked oval plate pottery and favored twins, we should think no more of such a report than we do of the actual report that these traits are in fact found among the three neighboring, closely related tribes along the Colorado River in California. In fact, however, Driver (1956:36 ff.) reports that these eight southeastern tribes share five other traits. In all of them, women rather than men produce or collect most of the food. All of them have matri-

local residence. All of them have matrilineal descent. All of them have bifurcate-merging mother-aunt terms. All of them have Crow-type sister-cousin terms. This is precisely the sort of cluster of traits predicted by classical American kinship theory as argued by such people as Lowie, Eggan, Murdock and Driver. According to this theory, if women dominate in food production, residence tends to become matrilocal. If residence is matrilocal, descent tends to become matrilineal. If descent is matrilineal, then mother tends to be called by the same kinship term as mother's sister and mother's sister's daughter by the same term as sister, while father's sister tends to be called by the same term as father's sister's daughter. Widely scattered, unrelated tribes in other parts of the world also display association among some or all of these matricentered traits. Galton's problem is this: how many cases in support of classical kinship theory are offered by these eight southeastern tribes? Eight? If eight, why stop at eight? Why not make every Creek, Cusabo, Hichiti, Timucua, Alabama, Chickasaw, Choctaw and Chakchiuma household a case in support of the theory? Such a procedure makes no sense to anthropologists who contemplate the perfect correlation between flageolet playing, carrying frame design, pottery type, muller design and twin attitude among the Colorado River tribes. Not when they know they can find a thousand other like examples of co-distribution of traits with little or no functional relevance.

As explained in Chapter 47, below, the solution to Galton's problem lies in one way or another testing the hypothesis that functionally linked traits tend to diffuse together. In such a test, each single cluster of tribes with continuously distributed traits is a single case. Sampling design then depends upon which of the solutions to Galton's problem is chosen. In other words, before planning a sample for a cross-cultural survey, the investigator should think through his treatment of Galton's problem. The five solutions to Galton's problem discussed in Chapter 47 are adapted to four different sampling designs.

1. The cluster test and the bimodal sift test are adapted to very large samples, quasi-universes like the World Ethnographic Sample. Sample size should be at least four hundred. Coefficients of correlation within such samples will surely reflect diffusion to a high

degree. But the cluster test will provide a direct, clear and decisive test of the hypothesis that traits supposedly linked functionally tend to diffuse together. Although the study has not been made, I would predict no such tendency between flageolet playing, carrying frame design, pottery type, muller design and twin attitudes.

2. The matched pair test requires a specially designed sample. Pairs of neighbors (both meeting bibliographic requirements) are needed.

3. The interval sift method requires a widely scattered sample. Let us speak of sample neighbors. By sample neighbors I mean two tribes in the sample which have no third tribe in the sample situated between them. The interval sift method requires that sample neighbors *not* resemble each other with respect to the traits being studied more often than one would expect in a random distribution. Thus it would admit only one or at most two of the eight southeastern tribes to a study of kinship theory.

4. The linked pair method can be applied to any sample design. But the more that sample neighbors resemble each other, the greater the influence attributed to diffusion by partial correlations and the less the influence of functional relationship. Consequently, the linked pair method works best in a sample like that of the interval sift method, in which sample neighbors largely differ.

The advantage of the linked pair and interval sift methods over the other three lies in the fact that both produce conventional coefficients of correlation which are free from the influence of diffusion and which can be manipulated in conventional statistical ways: significance tests, factor analyses and the like. The key point in fitting sample design to Galton's problem is this. Unless the linked pair or the interval sift method is used, coefficients of correlation do not measure functional association alone; they measure both functional association and diffusion together. Thus significance tests of these correlations do not test the significance of functional hypotheses. The purpose of such a significance test is to see whether an observed correlation may be plausibly due to chance. If the correlation mixes functional and diffusional effects, a "significant" result may well merely reflect the existence of diffusion. Thus the significance of the functional association has not been tested. This important point is still widely ignored. For example, the significance tests in Coult and Habenstein (1965) are valueless if positive; they are only meaningful if negative. That is to say, it means nothing if these tests report a correlation as statistically significant. For that significance may merely reflect diffusion. It does mean something if the significance tests report a correlation statistically not significant. Such a report means that neither diffusion nor functional association tends to make the traits occur together.

It must be born in mind that in cross-cultural surveys, the larger the sample, the poorer must be the quality of scholarship. Time that is spent adding new tribes is time taken away from more thorough study of those already included. Other things being equal, an investigator can spend twice as much time per tribe collecting and coding data on fifty tribes as he can if he collects and codes data on a hundred.

Where increasing the size of a sample usually results in adding new tribes which resemble their sample neighbors in the traits being studied, this increase serves no purpose when the linked pair or the interval sift solution to Galton's problem is used. These solutions are clearly the most economical for a straight functional test of a hypothesis; and they are statistically the most flexible, permitting factor analysis, multiple and partial correlations, and the like. For very readily diffusing traits like those closely related to level of social development, the maximum useful sample size in such a cross-cultural survey is probably of the order of seventy-five or one hundred. My War, Stress and Culture sample, even though it had only fifty-eight societies, and even though it was specially planned to avoid sample neighbors at similar levels of social development—nevertheless despite all this it had many such neighbors. On the other hand, for a study of traits which do not diffuse so readily nor so easily, like suicide practices, a sample size of three or four hundred probably would be useful in a linked pair or interval sift design.

Where it is desired to measure the relative importance of diffusion and functional linkage in the universe, then the matched pair design is the preferred sampling design; see Chapter 47, below, for a demonstration.

Where it is desired to demonstrate directly that two traits tend to diffuse together, through the cluster test, the closer together the societies in the sample, the better. The most economical way of conducting such a test is to study societies along diffusion arcs such as those described in Naroll (1961a: 24 f.).

STRATIFIED SAMPLING

Stratification is a device often used in conventional sample surveys to reduce the sampling variance and hence the risk of random error. By *stratified sampling* is meant sampling randomly from groups of units of the universe. Stratified sampling is like quota sampling in that the units are classified according to criteria deemed relevant. But it is unlike quota sampling, in that from each group the sample is selected according to some probability sampling design, instead of opportunistically. For example, a universe of American college undergraduates could be stratified by sex and class. This would call for eight strata: freshman men, freshman women, sophomore men, sophomore women, and so on with juniors and seniors. A stratified random sample of this universe would sample randomly within each of the eight strata. The number chosen from each stratum might well be in proportion to number of students in that stratum. If 8 per cent of the student body being sampled were senior men, then 8 per cent of the sample would be chosen randomly from among the senior men.

Needless to say, by random choice is not meant haphazard choice. Random choice must be carefully done if hidden bias is to be avoided. The best method is to number the names of the units consecutively and then choose, using a table of random numbers. Most statistics textbooks have tables with several thousand random numbers; Rand Corporation (1955) has a million.

Need for Stratified Sampling

Stratified sampling then is needed for cross-culture surveys, not because it reduces sampling variance but because it tends to produce the maximum degree of independence from diffusion. Consider Ember's unstratified probability sample, from Murdock's World Ethnographic Sample. Ember sampled only twenty-four societies. Had he stratified by

culture area, he could have taken two culture areas per stratum. Thus he would have been sure not to have more than one tribe from the same culture area and perhaps half the time would not have had more than one tribe from any two neighboring culture areas. But by taking an unstratified random sample, he chose two nearby Bushman tribes (Xam and Naron); these two closely related tribes occupied adjacent positions in his two major rank order correlations (Ember 1963:238 f.).

Ember rightly urges that if geographical quota sampling is used, significance tests are not valid since these assume probability sampling. He fails to see that stratified probability sampling lets us have our cake and eat it too. Geographical stratification reduces the risk of including neighboring, closely related tribes in the sample. Random sampling within each stratum lets us use significance tests to measure random sampling error and eliminates unknown selection biases.

Geographical stratification is needed, either if the linked pair or the interval sift solution to Galton's problem is to be used. (As has just been pointed out, these two solutions are usually the most economical.) That is to say, the map needs to be divided into regions of such a size that the chance of similar sample neighbors is made as small as possible. What size this might be depends upon the traits being studied. Perhaps the trait is one of those whose distribution is mapped in Driver and Massey (1957). If so, a study of its distribution map there will suggest what size sampling stratum is most desirable.

Alternatives to Stratified Sampling

One seemingly plausible way to get around stratification is to reject sample neighbors with like codings. In practice this procedure turns out to be more difficult than it sounds. Each society has four sample neighbors and in even a random arrangement is likely to resemble at least one. It might not even be feasible to enforce a rule against any three societies in a row having like codings—a plan as yet untried.

Murdock (1966:113) recommends a two-hundred-mile rule of thumb as a diffusion screen. That is to say, he recommends rejecting any random choice whose geographical center is within two hundred miles of any previously chosen society. He recognizes that this rule of thumb will not always suffice and recommends that the comparativist "be on the alert to make other eliminations on the basis of general knowledge or common sense." In my view, both these proposals are unwise. Using the two-hundred-mile rule often will be helpful, but often quite inadequate, as in the thirteen North American culture types just discussed. "General knowledge and common sense" are needed to draw up the sampling plan. However, when they are used to justify departures from the plan once made, they convert a probability sample with clearly defined biases into an expert or judgmental sample, with undefined and unmeasurable biases.

Culture Areas as Sampling Strata

Ordinarily, the easiest way to set up sampling strata is to follow one or another of the culture area classifications of each major region of the world. (For surveys of these classifications, see Honigmann 1959:163 f.; and Hewes 1954.) Murdock's culture areas for his World Ethnographic Sample or his culture clusters for his Ethnographic Atlas also serve as useful sampling strata; but unfortunately neither set of classifications has been mapped. (Not all members of these classifications of Murdock's occupy a single mappable land area; but most of them do.) Thus it is easy and sensible to use these classifications of Murdock's when sampling from either of his quasi-universes; but difficult to use them otherwise.

It is true that all culture area classifications are more or less arbitrary and subjective. But they all tend to follow some important trait distribution boundaries and thus tend to make better sampling strata than like-size geographical units of a purely arbitrary sort, unrelated to culture distributions. The theoretical basis of all culture area classifications lies in the very facts of cultural diffusion which form the basis of Galton's problem. To some extent, at least, there is a tendency for traits with ecological relevance to spread over ecologically defined areas. Thus we get fairly sharp cultural boundaries for the Sudan, the North American Plains, the South American tropical forest cultures, the Asian Steppe cultures, and other associated clusters of traits which happen to fall into clearly mappable regions like Polynesia,

Micronesia, Melanesia, and the Far East (China proper, Japan, Korea and Vietnam). In any case, since the diffusion tests concerned measure the success of the stratification, no further validation of culture area classification is needed.

Coarse Classification vs. Fine Classification

If the comparativist has an idea about the ideal stratum size for his problem, he can use this idea to choose between fine classifications and coarse ones. For most parts of the world, there is a choice between finer and coarser culture area classifications. Thus Kroeber (1900) is a coarse classification of native North America while Murdock (1960) is a fine one. As already noted, Murdock's World Ethnographic Sample offers a coarse classification, suitable for studies of readily diffusing traits, while his Ethnographic Atlas (Murdock 1967) offers a fine classification, suitable for studies of traits diffusing less readily.

If one tribe only were chosen from each area of the World Ethnographic Sample, for example, only one of the eight southeastern tribes mentioned above could be chosen. Only one of the five northwestern California tribes discussed in pages 976–977, Chapter 47, below, could be chosen, and none at all of the three southeastern California tribes. If one tribe only were chosen from each of the 412 clusters of the Ethnographic Atlas (1967), again only one of the eight southeastern U.S. tribes could be chosen (Cluster 324). Only could be chosen (Cluster 332). But of the five northwestern California tribes, one is in Cluster 294 (the Tolowa) while the other four are in Cluster 293. Thus with bad luck, one could select say the Tolowa and the Hupa or the Tolowa and the Karok. If one tribe is chosen randomly from each of these two culture types and all meet the investigator's bibliographic requirements, we would expect such bad luck only eight times in one hundred tries.

The situation is different if one considers such widely diffused traits as descent type and sexual dominance in subsistence pursuits. All of the following culture types in the Ethnographic Atlas (1967) are found together in a single continuously distributed area of

North America and all have patridominated subsistence pursuits in association with bilateral descent: 278 Interior Eskimo; 279 Central and Eastern Eskimo; 280 Cree-Montagnais; 281 Maritime Algonkians; 283 Northeastern Athapaskans; 290 Kwakiutl-Bellacoola; 291 Nootka-Quileute; 292 Coast Salish; 310 Interior Salish; 311 Northern Plateau; 312 Kutenai; 313 Northwest Plains; 314 Northeast Plains. Obviously then for a study of the relationship between descent types and subsistence pursuits, it would not do to treat these as thirteen independent cases.

Treatment of Unequal Strata

One inconvenience arises from stratified probability sampling. Usually it is not convenient to have all the strata contain exactly the same number of societies. For example, suppose we are taking a stratified probability sample from Murdock's quasi-universe, the World Ethnographic Sample. His North Africa area, like most others, has ten societies; but his Overseas Europeans—as an exception—only five. If we take one society from each area, the Americans (New England) have one chance in five of being chosen while the Guanche of North Africa have only one chance in ten. Our final sample then will not meet the specifications for a random sample, since each member of the universe will not have an equal chance of selection. But it will still meet the specifications for a probability sample, since each member will have a *known* chance of selection (see Kish 1965:103; Cochrane 1963:10 f).

Weighting Unequal Strata. In a descriptive sample survey, where universe proportions are being inferred from sample proportions, one simply uses the formulas in Cochrane or Kish to weight the sampled units in order to compensate for the differences in probability. Thus if the Guanche were chosen, they would be weighted double the Americans because their chance of selection had been only half that of the Americans.

I have gone into such detail about stratification in conventional survey samples because that is the kind of sample for which statistical theory of stratification has been developed. To avoid confusion, it is important to bear in mind that in cross-cultural surveys, stratification serves a different purpose and hence may require different tactics and different statistical analysis.

As I said, the purpose of stratification in conventional survey samples is to reduce sampling variance and thereby to reduce risk of random error. In order to reap the fruits of such stratification, appropriate special statistical weighting methods must be used. So far, none have been so used in cross-cultural surveys. I suspect that it might sometimes be both feasible and profitable to do so in the future. However, for me now this is beside the point.

In a cross-cultural hypothesis test, however, I submit that weighting is not always necessary. The sampling bias of unequal strata may or may not affect the particular hypothesis test. If the societies favored by the bias systematically differ from those not favored by the bias in respect to the relationship tested, then the bias affects the test. If not, not. For example, suppose we are testing the correlation between residence rules and descent rules. Only 10 per cent of the North African tribes have neolocal residence. But 20 per cent of the Overseas Europeans have it—twice the proportion. Thus in measuring proportions, the selection bias in favor of Overseas Europeans is a selection bias in favor of neolocal residence. If the results of such a sample are unweighted, they would tend to overestimate the proportion of tribes with neolocal residence in the World Ethnographic Sample as a whole.

But the question we are asking in our hypothesis test is *not* what proportion of tribes have neolocal residence. The question we are asking is rather: What proportion of tribes with neolocal residence also have bilateral descent?

Stratification Bias Control. A simple way to control our sample for this bias is to classify the societies we choose according to the number of societies in the strata from which we chose them. Then make a test of the hypothesis that by and large societies from large strata differ with respect to the characteristics investigated from those from small strata. In the example, is it true that by and large the smaller strata tend to have more than their share of societies with neolocal residence? If not, we can henceforth ignore this sampling bias in our test of the residence/descent correlation. But if so, then we must also see whether there is a parallel bias in descent rules. If not, then the residence rule bias can still be ignored. But if so, then we must recompute the correlation, using weighted values (Kish 1965:103). For further discussion of sampling bias control see below, pp. 911–915.

The reader may ask: would it not be less trouble simply to weight the scores to begin with and then forget about the sampling bias test? Answer: No. Unweighted scores must be used for tests of Galton's problem. It seems likely that a far more serious source of sampling bias than unequal strata is the bibliographic sampling bias to be discussed presently. It therefore seems more convenient to include a control test for disproportionate strata allocation along with the many other tests proposed in this and other chapters and to take no further action unless bias is shown.

The War, Stress and Culture (WSC) sampling design is defective in that it does not readily permit a measure of stratification bias. It is possible to count the number of suitable rubrics from the *OWC*—the *Outline of World Cultures* (Murdock 1963)—in each sampling stratum of the diffusion arc sub-sample. But this count is not directly what is wanted; what is wanted rather is the number of adequately described cultunits per stratum. Inferences about such bias theoretically could be made indirectly, through a chain of correlations. We could compare strata having many *OWC* rubrics with those having few. We could compare strata in which the first or second trial revealed an adequately described tribe with those requiring more trials —thus indirectly comparing strata tending to have more adequately described tribes with those having less. Finally, we could and in fact have compared *OWC* rubrics which fitted the cultunit concept with those which did not (see Chapter 39 above).

It is far better to sample from an entire bibliographic universe like the PEPS universe or the HRAF Quality Control universe (see below). Such universes will inevitably have marked inequalities in the number of tribes per sampling stratum. For example, in the HRAF Quality Control universe (HRAF 1967:84–87), Stratum ⅟2 (Southern Bantu) has eight tribes to choose from while Stratum ⅟36 (Papuans) has only one.

To measure stratification bias, one has only to count the number of tribes per stratum, and (using a computer, presumably) correlate each substantive trait being studied with this variable—number of tribes per stratum. Unless both substantive traits in a hypothesis test are similarly related to stratification bias, it cannot be responsible for producing spurious correlations in substantive traits. If it is not so responsible, it does not matter to us. Testing to see whether spurious correlations may plausibly be ascribed to stratification bias constitutes *stratification bias control*.

SAMPLE SIZE

In all sampling work, sample size is influenced by two opposing and obvious considerations. First, the larger the sample, the smaller the risk of net random error and hence the more precise the sampling inferences. Second, the larger the sample, the more expensive. However, there is a third consideration which is as important but not as obvious. In no sampling work does increasing the sample size offer increased protection against systematic sampling bias. Thus the notorious *Literary Digest* sample of more than a million voters predicted that Alfred Landon would win the 1936 presidential election by a handsome majority; in fact Franklin Roosevelt beat him by a record landslide. The huge size of the *Digest* sample did not save it from absurd error because the sample had systematic biases which tended to favor supporters of Landon rather than supporters of Roosevelt.

Therefore, wise samplers prefer a smaller sample without systematic sampling bias to a larger one with it. Very significant results can often be obtained with quite small samples. For example, consider the relationship between settlement population and team type count (Naroll 1956:701). My original report on this relationship considered only twenty-six tribes. Yet Tukey's corner test shows a relationship significant at the .0001 level. By that is of course meant that not one random sample in 10,000 would be expected to produce so strong a relationship through random sampling error. The restudy of this relationship in the War, Stress and Culture sample included twice as large a sample (see Chapter 39, above). However, the restudy used a probability sample while the original study used an opportunistic one; and the restudy relationship, though still high, was not quite so high as that of the original study. The weak point in the original study was not its small sample size but its biases.

Let us recall to mind the influence of Galton's problem on sampling (pp. 896–898, above). Galton's problem tends to fix an optimum sample size for cross-cultural surveys. This optimum varies from trait to trait. It holds only for the linked pair or interval sift solutions. It depends upon the readiness with which the trait diffuses. In a test correlating two traits, the optimum size would be determined by that trait of the two which diffused less readily. For traits which diffuse very readily, like descent rules or subsistence technology, the optimum size may well be of the order of thirty to fifty. For traits which diffuse rather sluggishly, like suicide rates or kinship terms, the optimum may well be greater than three hundred tribes. It seems unlikely that any cross-cultural sample greater than four hundred can avoid including many more pairs of sample neighbors with like trait codings than would be expected from a random distribution.

The point to grasp firmly in mind when thinking about sample size is that significance test theory presumes that every one of the items in the sample is an *independent trial*. Because of Galton's problem this assumption is not plausible in cross-cultural surveys if sample neighbors tend frequently to have like codings.

To sum up considerations of sample size:

1. Other things being equal, the larger the sample, the less the net random error.

2. Sample size does not affect sampling bias. Therefore a small unbiased sample, or a small sample with known sampling biases, is better than a large sample with unknown sampling biases. Gallup does far better with probability samples of one or two thousand voters than the *Literary Digest* did with its opportunistic sample of over one million.

3. In the more economical solutions to Galton's problem, cross-cultural surveys cease to benefit from increased sample size when the new tribes chosen tend frequently to have trait codings like any of their sample neighbors. For in that case, the assumption of independent trials becomes untenable and hence tests of significance become useless.

4. In a cross-cultural survey, a sample size would appear to be too small if two things both were true: *one,* the hypothesis

tended to be supported but significance tests were unconvincing—in other words, random sampling error or other random error seemed a plausible rival explanation of the results —and *two,* the linked pair tests for one of the variables indicated no special tendency for tribes to resemble their sample neighbors.

TYPES OF CROSS-CULTURAL SAMPLES

This is a review of sampling procedures in formal cross-cultural surveys. I am here concerned then only with samples which purport to be representative of the entire universe of primitive tribes. (Some purport to represent only primitive tribes; others to represent all human societies, primitive and civilized.) Furthermore, I concern myself only with studies which make formal lists of their samples and use them to test functional hypotheses by statistical counts.

Expert Choice Samples

As already remarked, Unwin (1934) presented the first formal cross-cultural sample. Earlier cross-cultural surveys sought to include all known primitive tribes about which suitable information could be had (Tylor 1889; Steinmetz 1896; Neiboer 1900, 1910; Hobhouse 1906; Hobhouse, Wheeler and Ginsberg 1915). Unwin was followed by Murdock (1937); Simmons (1937); Horton (1943); Simmons (1945) and finally Murdock (1949). Although Unwin was reviewed at length in the *American Anthropologist* he was not cited either by Murdock, Simmons or Horton; like Steinmetz, his work dropped out of sight until recalled by the now classic review of cross-cultural surveys by Köbben (1952). Simmons and Horton were both students of Murdock at Yale. The influence of Murdock, exerted directly or through such able students as John W. M. Whiting, has been profound. The sampling plan taken for granted by the Yale school during the period 1935 to 1955 was much the one set forth in Simmons (1945: 6):

. . . a selection of tribes was made for intensive study. The plan was to limit these to the so-called primitive peoples, or those of antiquity, to try to make the selection world wide, and to cover as many significant variables as possible with respect to natural conditions, racial differences, cultural areas, manners of subsistence, social organization, and other general characteristics.

Notice that this is what Kish (1965:19) would call an "Expert Choice" sample. True, the ideal is a sort of quota sample considering "natural conditions, racial differences . . ." and the like. But there is no formal universe list. With one exception, "natural conditions, racial differences . . ." and the like are neither formally defined nor classified; we are not told what proportion of what types of each are included. The sample is not even classified by culture area. But it is mapped (pp. 8 f.) and classified by continent (p. 10) and climatic conditions (p. 11).

This "Expert Choice" sampling plan underlay the indexed data collection at Yale first called the Cross-Cultural Survey and later renamed the Human Relations Area Files. These data archives consist of drawers of $5'' \times 8''$ file slips. One or two drawers is given over to slips with data on each particular tribe or culture in the Files. To prepare a drawer, the most seemingly trustworthy and conveniently accessible primary sources on a tribe are collected. These writings are then indexed by writing topic numbers on the margin of each page. For example, if a page of an ethnography discusses suicide, homicide and witchcraft, the numbers 682, 754, and 762 would be written in the margin of the page. (See Chapter 33 above for further details, and Murdock et al. 1961 for the coding system.) If there are n index codes written on the margin, $n+1$ xerox photocopies are made of the page. One such copy goes into the drawer under the file section set aside for each index number and one copy into file section 116—the complete original text.

The convenience of this data archive has led to its widespread use in libraries around the world, either in its original form or in microcard copy. The Files indeed have become identified in many minds with the cross-cultural survey method itself. This confusion was inevitable, even though the leaders of the Yale school (Murdock 1949; Whiting and Child 1953) never confined themselves to the Files. Rather their strategy sent them first to the Files for what they could find of use there; and then beyond the Files to ordinary library research. This sampling strategy was set forth in Murdock (1949:viii–ix):

The author began the present study in 1941 by formulating a schedule of the data needed . . . and by abstracting such data from the files of the Cross-Cultural Survey on all societies for which sufficient information had been reported . . . he was able in this way to assemble the relevant materials for 85 societies. . . . This number, though large, still fell far short of the cases required for reliable statistical treatment, and the author set out to secure further information by the usual methods of library research. Eventually he secured data on 165 additional societies, making a total of 250 in all. . . . The present author has departed from the plan mainly in abandoning sampling technique in favor of using all available cases in areas such as South America and Eurasia for which there are too few sufficiently documented cases to obtain an adequate sample. In other areas, too, he has occasionally chosen a society because a good source was readily accessible rather than because a sample was demanded. He has, however, sought consciously to avoid any appreciable over-representation of particular culture areas. In short, departures from strict sampling, where they occur, reflect availability or non-availability of suitable sources and no other bases of selection.

The principles which underlay the dominant expert choice original sampling philosophy of the Yale school of Murdock and his followers then were three: (1) Cheating consists in accepting or rejecting a society because its data supports or fails to support a preconceived hypothesis. The sampler pledges his scientific word of honor that he has not cheated. (2) The sampler informally uses his best expert judgment to preserve what seems to him a reasonable distribution of the sample by continent and culture area, but no formal quotas are assigned. (3) Opportunistic convenience is a large factor in sampling decisions. For library research, this convenience usually means the presence of suitable books on library stack shelves. Books were treated as suitable if they were in a language the researcher could read and if by looking at their table of contents and index or by quickly flipping their pages the researcher found data on the topics he was studying. For the Human Relations Area Files as an institution, convenience often came to mean availability of funds to support the heavy cost of processing a file. Many Files were added because the United States Government was willing to pay for their cost. Thus it is that U.S.S.R. and its immediate neighbors are covered far better by the Files than is South America.

In such samples as these, four other principles were used rarely or never. (1) No formal universe lists were compiled. By that of course I mean lists of societies suitable for study from which a sample might be drawn. (2) Rarely was any formal classification (other than geographical) made of characteristics which were supposed to influence a sample. (3) No formal quotas were ever assigned in advance to such characteristics, and (4) no formal use was ever made of chance. There was no selection of names from a stirred urn of written slips; nor was there any use of random numbers tables; nor was there, needless to say, any systematic selection of every nth tribe from a universe list.

Two Opportunistic Samples

Such in general were the sampling procedures followed in American cross-cultural surveys from 1937 to 1957. Two minor variants may be mentioned. Whiting and Child (1953:48) describe their sampling procedure as "75 different primitive societies which were selected and used in our study as being the 75 for which the necessary material was available." They do not say exactly what they mean by *"available."* Are we to understand that these writers examined systematically all the ethnographic bibliographies then in existence, that they personally examined tens of thousands of ethnographic reports? Or do Whiting and Child simply mean that they opportunistically searched for suitable reports, and stopped looking when they had found 75? Quite evidently the latter. In a quick check of my own small (fifty-eight society) War, Stress and Culture sample I found at least eleven societies they omitted with data suitable for their purpose in print (in English except as otherwise noted) when they did their work. Ona (data in German), Eyak, Ila, Wintu, Ojibwa, Malaita, Tallensi, Chukchi, Toradja (data in Dutch), and Cheyenne. Now of these same fifty-eight societies of my War, Stress and Culture sample, twelve others *were* included by Whiting and Child. Mine was a probability sample with formal bibliographic screening for data on warfare, suicide and homicide (see below). Therefore, it seems reasonable to conclude that had Whiting and Child continued to search, they might have found at least seventy-five more societies with suitable data.

A similar sampling procedure was followed by Homans and Schneider (1955:31 f.). These authors render a more explicit account of what they did. They were concerned only with societies practicing some form of unilateral cross-cousin marriage. Thus of the 250 societies Murdock studied in *Social Structure,* only 15 were known to have this kind of marriage preference. Homans and Schneider set out to look for more cases. They reported: "We doubt that our search has been exhaustive. We got leads from Lévi-Strauss's book, from Murdock, and from others, and we followed them up to the point of diminishing returns, where the importance of this book did not, in our view, justify more work. But without question there are more societies practicing unilateral cross-cousin marriage than we have discovered." (*N. B.* The point of their study was to test correlations in which the dependent variable was the particular type of unilateral cross-cousin marriage: patrilateral vs. matrilateral.) Here we have an opportunistic sampling method frankly avowed. As in Whiting and Child there is no attempt at expert sampling; they take all suitable tribes they can find, and stop looking when their sampling budget runs out.

Quasi-Universes

Cross-cultural sampling methods were revolutionized in 1957 with the publication of Murdock's World Ethnographic Sample (latest version in Moore 1961:193–216). This selection of 565 tribes is important not only as a sample—as a sample it is too large for many purposes—but also and even more as a sampling universe. It is geographically classified by sixty culture areas, ten each for six major continental regions—the five familiar continents plus Circummediterranean (Europe, Caucasia, the Near East and North Africa). Each of the ten areas whenever possible includes: (1) The most populous society in the area (or if Murdock could not get census data, then the society occupying the largest territory); (2) the best-described culture in each of the cultural sub-areas. "Cultural sub-area" is not defined but apparently amounts to what Murdock would later call a "culture type." (3) One example of each basic type of subsistence technology present: a) farming, b) herding, c) fishing and d) foraging; (4) one example of each major rule of descent present: a) bilateral, b) patrilineal, c) matrilineal and d) double; (5) one example from each linguistic stock or major linguistic subfamily present. Furthermore, if Murdock happened to know of a particular culture which struck him as atypical or unusual, he tried to include that.

Thus, we have substituted for an expert sampling scheme, a quota sampling scheme. The quota selection criteria are clearly defined.

From the standpoint of survey sampling theory, this quota method does not seem exciting—far less revolutionary. Notice that no element of chance appears in the selection. Presumably, when all quota requirements have been satisfied, selection is by opportunistic accessibility. Thus we do not have a probability sample and nothing Murdock presents enables us to judge its sampling bias. We do not know from Murdock's work in what ways the tribes included in the World Ethnographic Sample differ from those omitted. Thus Murdock gives us no way of gauging its representativeness. This weakness would seem crucial to any sampling theorist; it was recognized immediately (Swanson 1960: 37; Naroll 1961a:6; Naroll 1961b:23; Ember 1963:237; Marsh 1967:291).

To a sampling theorist, Murdock's second quasi-universe, the "Ethnographic Atlas" (*Ethnology*, Vols. 1–5, throughout and especially Volume 6, Number 2, 1967) seems no improvement. His sampling principles continue to be opportunistic. He includes tribes because certain earlier writers have included them (1:265) or because authors of descriptions have sent him copies of their books (4:448). Nevertheless, he claims (1:533) to be paying "due regard to geographical distribution and cultural variation." No longer do we have an explicit set of quotas like those of the World Ethnographic Sample.

The final version of the "Ethnographic Atlas" (Vol. 6, No. 2) includes 862 societies, classified by culture type into 412 groups (some groups have only one member).

The value of these two quasi-universes nevertheless is great. But their value lies in their suitability as universes rather than in their precision as samples. This suitability cannot be deduced from a study of Murdock's work alone but requires comparison with other samples using stricter selection procedures. Such a comparison is made below.

Permanent Ethnographic Probability Sample (*PEPS*). In 1963, a committee of six behavioral scientists at Northwestern University planned a world-wide ethnographic probability sample (see p. 921). As a first step, it was decided to prepare a quasi-universe list of suitable tribes. The PEPS plan called for consideration of all the rubrics in Murdock's *Outline of World Cultures* (*OWC*) (1963), together with all the tribes listed in Greenway's Australian bibliography (1963) and all the language groups of New Guinea listed in A. Capell's *Linguistic Survey* (1962).

Five classes of listings in the *OWC* were to be ignored (skipped):

a. Listings which call for non-ethnographic data (either historical or archaeological).

b. Listings which call for *general* rather than *specific* data on a region or on the world as a whole.

c. Listings which obviously deal with a single community belonging to a larger cult-unit (doubtful cases will be included).

d. Listings on Indo-European–speaking peoples outside Eurasia.

e. Listings on societies commonly known to have professional recordkeeping specialists, including all modern nations rendering statistical reports to the United Nations or listed as an independent nation in the *Statesman's Year-Book*. The reason for making this exclusion is the belief that ethnographic research techniques are unsuitable for the general analysis of such societies.

From these lists, all tribes were to be taken which met three bibliographic requirements. The unit of evaluation of bibliographic requirements was the total calendared body of work of a particular ethnographer. By *calendared* is meant listed in one of the standard ethnographic bibliographies. So far these have been limited to O'Leary (1963), German Parra and Jimenez Moreno (1954), Murdock (1960), Wieschoff (1948) and Jones (1958, 1959, 1960, 1961); see Chapter 7 above. To be acceptable: (1) the ethnographer must have spent at least one year among the people of the *OWC* unit concerned; (2) the ethnographer must also make some pretension to a knowledge of their language, either by claiming to speak or understand it, or by publishing some sort of linguistic treatise, such as a dictionary or a phonetic or grammatical analysis (to qualify as a dictionary, a word list needs to have at least five thousand entries; there is no minimum length requirement, however, for the phonetic or grammatical analysis); and (3) it must be evident from an examination of the titles and tables of contents of the body of works that the ethnographer treats of at least ten different two-number categories (Murdock 1961).

The first two continents studied bibliographically to compile these lists were Africa and South America. For the remainder of the world our procedure was more complicated and is being reported elsewhere (see Naroll, Alnot, Caplan, Hansen, Maxant and Schmidt 1970). It was found that with but one or two exceptions, all tribes which qualified from these continents were listed in the 1967 revision of Murdock's World Ethnographic Sample. It should be noticed, however, that Murdock claims exhaustive coverage of Africa and the New World but *not* of Eurasia and Oceania (Murdock 1967:109). At present, the listings for North America and Central America have been completed as well. (For Central America, only tribes listed in the 1967 World Ethnographic Sample were considered.) While doubtless some obscure or recently published works have been overlooked, the listings may be taken as a nearly complete list of the qualified tribes described in readily identifiable and accessible ethnographies. While shortcomings and inadequacies remain, nevertheless about three thousand man-hours of library search time has been devoted to this task of combing the literature and examining all plausible candidates on the bookshelves of Chicago-area libraries. The listings of the tribes in this universe are given in Appendix II, below.

Bibliographic Probability Samples

Swanson's Birth of the Gods. The first cross-cultural probability sample was that of Swanson (1960). Swanson took as his universe a preliminary unpublished version of Murdock's World Ethnographic Sample. (I have not had access to a copy of this version.) Swanson is not himself an anthropologist; but he arranged to have WES edited for bibliographic coverage by anthropological consultants. There seems to have been one consultant for each of the six major continental regions (Swanson 1960:33 f., 233). The consultants were told the general problem Swanson wished to study and were asked to delete from the WES list two sorts of tribes. First, they deleted tribes which they felt were inadequately described. Second, they deleted those tribes which in their opinion had been so strongly influenced by a major world religion that they no longer had an independent religious life of their own.

From the remainder Swanson then chose at random one society "from those in each of the fifty 'world regions' into which Murdock divides his list." (In the published version, there are not fifty but sixty "world regions" or culture areas.) Of the fifty regions Swanson worked with, three had no available tribes. In these three regions, all tribes had been eliminated by the consultants. The total number of tribes in the version he worked with was 556; the final published version added 9 more. (Comparison of Swanson's list of selections [pp. 34 ff.] with the published version of WES makes it seem likely that the list Swanson worked from differed more widely in strata membership than did Murdock's final published list. For example, that final list includes twenty Polynesian tribes, grouped into two culture areas; but Swanson has only one Polynesian representative, from Eastern Polynesia. There is of course a rich literature on the native religions of such Western Polynesians as Samoa and Tikopia.)

Swanson's study included no control for unequal strata. Indeed, he did not publish the final, edited lists from which he sampled. Nor was there any attempt at measuring the bibliographic bias involved in the editing of Murdock's list by anthropological consultants. This editing process was judgmental. It could not even confidently be considered free of any inadvertent subconscious selection in favor of Swanson's hypothesis. After all, Swanson's consultants were furnished in advance with a statement of his problem (p. 33).

Futhermore, Swanson had no way of knowing what societies suitable for his study were *not* included in Murdock's list. Hence he had no way of measuring the non-bibliographic bias between Murdock's World Ethnographic Sample and the entire universe of primitive tribes.

Ember's Sample. Ember's 1963 study was a simple, unstratified random sample from Murdock's WES quasi-universe. He sought a sample of twenty-four societies. To get it, he considered in turn forty-one randomly selected societies. Ten of the forty-one were rejected because they were politically incorporated into some other society and hence lacked data on the political variable which interested Ember. One society (Japan) was industrialized and hence lacked data on the economic variable. Note that both these patterns of rejection are bibliographic ones. The politically incorporated societies had not always been subject to alien rulers. At some time in their past history they had been free. But the available literature on them covered them only as they were after alien conquest had obliterated their native political institutions. Similarly, Japan has not always been industrialized; her industrialization began only with the Meiji restoration in 1868. But the information conveniently available to Ember —an anthropologist, not a historian—covered Japan only after its industrialization. Finally, six other societies, though politically independent and unindustrialized, lacked enough data for Ember to classify them.

Like Swanson, Ember made no attempt to determine what proportion of societies *not* on Murdock's WES list had adequate coverage for his purpose. Because he did not stratify his sample, Ember was not concerned with the problem of unequal strata. But as remarked above, in a very small sample, two of his choices were neighboring Bushman tribes. On the other hand, it must be conceded that for a sample so small, stratification to avoid the effects of diffusion is far less important than it would be on larger samples.

Naroll's War, Stress and Culture Sample. This sample was completed in 1961. A mimeographed report (Naroll 1961b) was then distributed to a number of interested cross-culturalists, including Murdock and Ember. It consists of two parts, the diffusion arc sub-sample and the WES sub-sample.

Diffusion Arc Sub-Sample. This sample was originally designed as a forty-five strata probability sample. Each of the original strata consisted of a strip of the earth's surface along one of the author's Overland Diffusion Arcs (Naroll 1961b:24–29) three hundred nautical miles on either side of the arc and eight hundred nautical miles long. The arc boundaries perpendicular to each arc were laid out from a starting point chosen from a table of random numbers. The unit for sampling purposes was taken as the group or groups named in a given rubric of Murdock's *Outline of World Cultures* (*OWC*) concerning specific ethnographic data. Rubrics not calling for specific ethnographic data were ignored as were those calling for historical data or archaeological data. Ethnographic maps of the areas concerned were consulted; see Chapter 39, p. 737, above. The northernmost point of land occupied by the units named in the *OWC* rubric was treated as the location of the unit for sampling purposes. That point was called a *sampling point*. This rule reduced the sampling bias resulting from differences in land territory occupied. The rule also occasionally meant that a people might have most of their territory within the sampling arc, yet not be considered; this would happen if the northernmost point of their territory was outside the arc.

Each diffusion arc was divided into sampling blocks. Each sampling block was a rectangle six hundred nautical miles wide and eight hundred nautical miles long. Sampling search began at the near end of the block, i.e. the end nearest Cape Horn on the Cape Arc, nearest Ireland on the Island Arc. Each block was laid out in pencil on an ethnographic map. The block was then searched by moving a ruler across the map perpendicular to the long side of the block. The ruler was moved from the near end (see above) toward the far end. The first sampling point met by the ruler was the first candidate for selection. Then the research staff looked for the *OWC* rubric in the ethnographic bibliography serving its area. (See Appendix I, below, for the bibliographies used. For many parts of the world, of course, better bibliographies are now available than those I used in 1960.)

A strict protocol was followed in seeking ethnographic literature. This protocol is set forth in detail in Appendix I below. The bibliographic work was done not by me personally, but by several research assistants, most notably Barbara Steinberg, Stephanie Singer and Burton Siskin. These assistants had only a vague idea of the purpose of the sample or the hypotheses being studied. Thus that purpose and those hypotheses did not influence their work. Their task was clearly and objectively defined; were suitable works available for study at the library of the Los Angeles campus of the University of California? If so, the tribe concerned was accepted as the representative of the 600×800 mile sampling arc segment. If not, the tribe was rejected and the sweep continued. The next sampling point encountered was checked bibliographically in the same way and the process continued until a bibliographically acceptable society was found or the end of the sampling arc segment was reached. In nine of the forty-five segments, the first society checked was chosen. In twenty-four others, a choice was made in the arc segment before its end was reached; but in twelve arc segments, no society at all met the bibliographic requirements. In these twelve, the width of the arc segment was doubled, from six hundred miles to twelve hundred miles, and the arc segment reswept. Two of these resweepings produced selections; the other ten did not and so were abandoned. Thus the final result was to take a probability sample of a bibliographically defined universe. This subsample had as its random element the starting point of the arc segment.

WES Sub-Sample. The diffusion arc subsample was originally planned as the complete sample for the War, Stress and Culture study. Work on the selection of this sub-sample went on for many months. While it was going on, the idea struck me for using world-wide diffusion alignments to control Galton's problem (see Chapter 47, below, pp 982–983). Therefore, a world-wide sample now seemed feasible.

Futhermore, when the diffusion arc subsample was finished, a striking fact emerged. Although no use was made of the World Ethnographic Sample in the selection of the sub-sample, nevertheless, of the twenty-nine uncivilized societies chosen for the diffusion arc sub-sample, twenty-six of them, or 89.6 per cent were included in the World Ethnographic Sample.

In other words, whatever might be the biases of the World Ethnographic Sample, it seemed to include a large proportion of the bibliographic universe of the War, Stress and Culture study. Nearly all the tribes which met the bibliographic requirements of that universe apparently were to be found among the 565 tribes of the World Ethnographic Sample.

Clearly, then, using the World Ethnographic Sample as a quasi-universe would result in an enormous saving of sampling time for the War, Stress and Culture sample, at little cost in bias. This fact does not mean that the entire World Ethnographic Sample is equivalent to a probability sample. Nothing of the sort is here asserted. All it means is that among the 565 tribes of the World Ethnographic Sample are found practically all the primitive tribes in existence which meet the bibliographic requirements of the War, Stress and Culture sample. A large proportion—perhaps two-thirds—of the tribes in the WES do *not* meet these requirements and hence drop out of consideration. The WES is to be used not as a sample, but as a universe.

The key point to bear in mind is worth repeating. The less stringent the bibliographic requirements, and the higher the proportion of WES tribes which satisfy them, the higher the proportion of tribes not in WES which also satisfy them. Hence WES is suitable as a quasi-universe only for studies whose bibliographic requirements are so strict that a large proportion—perhaps two-thirds—of the tribes in WES fail to meet them.

In compiling the World Ethnographic Sample, Murdock clearly was influenced by a number of factors. He would include one tribe for this reason, another tribe for that. One factor which obviously seems to have influenced him strongly, whether he fully realized it or not, was the wealth of bibliographic coverage. Clearly, he was reluctant to pass over a tribe with an especially rich literature. So, while many tribes in WES do not have a rich coverage, very few primitive tribes with an especially rich ethnographic coverage are not in WES.

If a sampler needs to draw on primitive tribes with especially rich coverage, then, he can save much time and expense by checking those in WES and ignoring the others. This conclusion is one highly important finding of the diffusion arc sub-sample.

For the WES sub-sample, the sixty culture areas into which Murdock classified the world were taken as sampling strata. The fact that Murdock later became dissatisfied with this culture area classification need not trouble us. It is obvious that the sixty-area classification tends to group together tribes from the same corner of the world and with similar historical backgrounds. We need not worry further about the validity of this classification. As explained above, the main purpose in using it is to reduce the cultural similarity of sample neighbors. Certainly no one would deny similarity of sample neighbors. Certainly no one would deny that tribes in

WES tend to have closer historical connections with the other tribes in their culture area than with tribes in other culture areas. That this tendency does not hold good invariably and that some exceptions occur may be true. But as pointed out earlier, by stratifying in this way, we lose nothing over simple random sampling and gain whatever we gain. In other words, whenever the classification is successful in grouping together similar tribes, it helps us. Whenever it fails, it leaves us no worse off than before.

If the diffusion arc sample already had a tribe from a WES culture area, then that culture area was skipped. Only those areas were considered which were not represented in the diffusion arc sample. For each such area, one tribe was randomly chosen. If it met the bibliographic qualifications, it was selected for the WES sub-sample. If not, the next tribe after it in its culture area on the WES list was chosen in its place, and checked. Tribe after tribe in turn was checked until the last tribe of the culture area list was reached; then the search continued with the first tribe on that list, and then the second, and so on until a qualified tribe was found or until all were examined and rejected.

However, because sampling funds ran short, for four culture areas this random procedure was not used. On these four, tribes in the Human Relations Area Files had been studied in an earlier study (Naroll 1962) and were known to be bibliographically qualified. They were accepted accordingly. This departure was bad sampling practice and I now regret it.

In all, then, an attempt was made to choose a tribe from each of thirty-two of the sixty culture areas in WES. In four of these thirty-two, the choice was made opportunistically, non-randomly, because of budgetary pressures. In nine others, no choice at all could be made, since none of the tribes in the culture area qualified. In the remaining nineteen, a choice was successfully made following the procedure described above.

Table 2 below sets forth the tribes chosen in the two samples.

The HRAF Quality Control Sample. This sample was drawn not from a quasi-universe but from a complete, bibliographically defined one. The staff of the Human Relations Area Files,

including such experts as Clellan Ford, Frank Moore, Frank LeBar and Timothy J. O'Leary, combed the ethnographic literature for a complete list of societies with ethnological field studies meeting certain specifications. There were two sets of specifications. The ordinary quality, "Level B" specifications call for at least 1200 pages of cultural data, including one thousand pages of ethnological data; overlapping coverage by more than one reporter; at least one formal monograph; no serious challenge to the accuracy of the basic ethnographic account; well-rounded coverage of economics, sociopolitical organization and life cycle; reports chiefly based on field work done while culture was still functioning economically and politically; and some record of culture available for one hundred years before basic field work was done. The top quality, "Level A" specifications called for an additional one thousand pages of focused ethnological data; involvement of at least two professional anthropologists; one of these must have spent at least twelve months in the area and have had a working knowledge of the native language—or instead three professional anthropologists must have worked in the area (Human Relations Area Files 1967:81–83).

This procedure resulted in a total of 58 A level societies and 146 B level societies (HRAF 1967:84–88). These 204 societies were classified into sixty culture areas, or sampling strata, following Murdock's "Ethnographic Atlas." Within each stratum, which contained at least one A level society, a random choice was made among the A level societies; here B level societies were ignored. Where there were no A level societies, a random choice was made among the B level ones. In each of the twenty-five strata, there was one but only one A level society; such societies were of course automatically chosen. In each of six strata, there were no A level societies and only one B level society; again these six societies were of course automatically chosen. Hence random choice operated in twenty-nine of the sixty selections along with bibliographic bias; but in thirty-one selections, there was no scope at all for random choice. Users of this Quality Control sample would do well to compare the two groups with respect to the variables being studied, to see if the absence of the random principle is related to them.

SAMPLING BIAS CONTROL

Biases of Diffusion Arc Sub-Sample

The diffusion arc sub-sample of Naroll's War, Stress and Culture sample included four possible sources of bias, three unimportant but the fourth markedly important.

1. Because the samples began every eight hundred miles from a randomly chosen starting point, if there were any tendency for traits to be regularly distributed in eight-hundred-mile cycles, or some multiple of eight hundred miles, a selection bias would be introduced. But inspection of trait distribution maps like those in Driver and Massey (1957: throughout) gives us every reason to doubt that any such regularities occur. Trait distributions evidently are characteristically irregular rather than regular; hence a regular sampling interval cuts them randomly. Therefore, it seems most doubtful that the use of a regular eight-hundred-mile starting-point interval produced any systematic bias in the sample.

2. The sampling units varied greatly in geographical area. True, the use of single sampling points as selection triggers greatly reduced the effect of this bias. Nevertheless, some remained. This bias showed itself in the fact that some sampling arc segments included many sampling points (in these, there were many small tribes and few large ones); other sampling arc segments included fewer sampling points (in these, the tribes tended to be larger rather than smaller). The fewer the tribes in an arc segment, the greater the chance any one tribe had of its sampling point coming up first.

This sampling bias might have been controlled by correlating the number of tribes per arc segment with the traits being studied. For example, we would expect to find societies with higher levels of development and associated traits more frequently in arc segments with fewer tribes. However, as will be seen, a second sample of the remaining parts of the world was taken on different principles. This second sample had very little territorial bias. Nor were there any significant differences between the two samples with respect to any of the substantive traits studied. From this we can see that the bias arising from unequal territories did not affect the study for which the sample was drawn.

Curiously, an apparently significant relationship did emerge between the two sub-samples and another methodological control factor. Societies chosen by the diffusion arc method just described tended more toward having their ethnographic sources concentrated at a particular point in time. In contrast, those chosen from the World Ethnographic Sample quasi-universe tended more toward having their ethnographic sources spread over a greater period of time. But otherwise, no differences appeared between the two samples not plausibly attributable to chance. Forty-two other point biserial correlations were computed with as many quantified traits; of these only two were nominally significant at the 5 per cent level, and only one of these nominally significant at the 2 per cent level —just what we would expect from chance. One hundred and thirty-three phi correlations were computed; of these, not even one was nominally significant at the 5 per cent level. (This strikingly *low* result reflects the tendency of fourfold contingency tables between random numbers to produce markedly less than theoretically predictable levels of significance; this phenomenon is discussed further in Chapters 34 above and 44 below.)

3. A third source of possible bias arose from the inconsistencies in Murdock's *OWC* rubrics. These categories were impressionistic and subjective. However, every rubric selected was classified according to the cultunit concept of ethnic unit definition (see Chapter 39 above). In general, it may be said that Murdock rarely included more than one *bibliographically qualified* cultunit in the same *OWC* rubric. (This conclusion refers of course to the particular bibliographical qualifications set forth in Appendix I below. The less stringent the bibliographic qualifications, the more exceptions to this rule must be expected.) Each tribe in the War, Stress and Culture sample was classified according to the cultunit concept fit with Murdock's classification, regardless of bibliographic coverage. Thus the fit was said to be "too large" if the *OWC* rubric included more than one cultunit; "too small" if the *OWC* rubric included only a part of a cultunit; "OK" if it constituted a cultunit exactly. Correlations were then calculated by computer on all traits involved in the War, Stress and Culture study. Again, no significant relationships were found.

4. A fourth possible source of bias arose

in connection with the bibliographic bias involved in the bibliographic requirements. In effect, I sampled from a bibliographically defined sampling universe. This sampling universe (SU) consists of all those tribes which in 1960 met the bibliographical requirements set forth in Appendix I below.

How can these biases be measured? How can they be controlled? By *control* of a bias, of course. I mean a measurement of its tendency to make for spurious correlations among the traits being studied.

The chief bias is the bibliographic one. We proceed now to consider it.

Theory of Bibliographic Quality Control. We cannot of course assume that the well-described tribes constituting our sampling universe (SU) are typical of the larger universe (LU) we would like to know about. That larger universe (LU) consists of the perhaps six thousand to eight thousand human cultures of which some record survives. We study the War, Stress and Culture (WSC) sample in the hope of being able to make generalizations about the LU. The theory of mathematical statistics lets us make inferences from the WSC to the SU but says nothing about the resemblance or lack of resemblance between SU and LU.

However, since the SU was chosen from the LU by the use of explicit criteria all relating to the presence or absence of published ethnographic literature, we can by bibliographic quality control (BQC) tests investigate the similarities and differences between SU and LU. There are two types of such bibliographic quality control (BQC) tests possible. The first uses only data found in the WSC sample itself. The second goes beyond the WSC to the total corpus of ethnographic literature.

Both are concerned with what we may call *bibliographic selection bias.* Both ask what characteristics of human cultures encourage or discourage ethnographers from studying them and reporting upon them. For example, I suggest that ethnographers are more likely to study larger tribes than smaller, more likely to study tribes nearer the major routes of transcontinental communication than distant from them, more likely to study tribes resistant to colonial administration than those submissive to it, more likely to study warlike tribes than peaceful tribes, and more likely to study tribes with comparatively color-ful and vivid cultures like the Hopi than tribes with comparatively drab cultures like the Yavapai.

These suggestions present examples of the sort of thing I mean by bibliographic selection bias. If in fact these suggestions have merit, then the factors set forth constitute bibliographic quality control factors.

Of course, these suggestions need to be checked out by formal studies. Such studies would constitute bibliographic quality control research. That research can be carried out in the WSC sample itself. We can inquire whether in fact in that sample, the tribes with the greatest amount of ethnographic literature are larger than those with lesser, are nearer the major routes of transcontinental communication, and so on. If so, we can see whether among all known tribes this tendency also holds. For some parts of North America, for many traits, there is almost complete coverage of all tribes. A bibliographic bias found to exist not only in the WSC sample but also among all tribes in America north of Mexico would have strong evidence in favor of its universality.

But how do studies of this sort help? First, they tend to reveal the general character of bibliographic bias: whether strong or weak, whether common or unusual. Analogous data quality control tests, seeking for evidence of reporting bias of ethnographers, reveal that in general such bias is weak, not strong. (See Chapter 44, below.)

Second, where any of the variables in future research designs have been checked out here, they would tell the user whether or not he needs to worry about bibliographic bias.

Third, they would tell us not only whether bibliographic bias tends to be strong or weak but also whether it tends to be monotonic or nonmonotonic. This point is extremely important. For if bibliographic bias is monotonic, it can be controlled simply by the BQC of the WSC sample alone. But if it is nonmonotonic, then it can only be controlled by going beyond the WSC sample.

What is meant by the term *monotonic?* It has to do with the way in which two traits are correlated. A correlation between trait A and trait B is monotonic when it is true that the more we have of A the more we are likely to have of B. A correlation is also monotonic when it is true that the more we have of A the less we are likely to have of B. But a correlation is nonmonotonic if neither of these statements is generally true. For example, there is a nonmonotonic correlation in the human individuals between age and physical strength. During the earlier years of the life span, the older the person is, the stronger he is likely to be. But during the later years of the life span, the older a person is, the weaker he is likely to be.

For example, suppose it is true that more warlike tribes are more likely to be written up by ethnographers than less warlike tribes. Is this a monotonic relationship? Is it always true that the more warlike the tribe, the more likely it is to attract an ethnographer's attention? Or is there instead a certain point of warlikeness beyond which the attention attracted by the warfare is more than counterbalanced by the fear of danger frightening potential ethnographers away?

Now, if this certain point is reached outside the range of variation encompassed by the WSC universe, then BQC studies of that universe cannot reveal it. Only studies of all the tribes in a given region could do so. (For example, all the tribes in America north of Mexico could be rated on a scale of warlikeness and this scale correlated with the number of entries for that tribe in Murdock (1960).)

Thus we need to know if the variables we are studying (1) have a strong bibliographic bias or a weak one; (2) have a monotonic bias or a nonmonotonic one. If it is clear that the *dependent* variable in any study has only a weak bibliographic bias, no further BQC work is needed. For it would be an implausible rival hypothesis to explain away the correlations of the study as artifacts of bibliographic selection bias. If on the contrary there appears to be a strong bibliographic selection bias, then the user needs to know if it is a monotonic bias or a nonmonotonic one. If a monotonic bias, he is free to control it by studying only the tribes in the WSC sample or the WSC sampling universe. But if nonmonotonic, and if the point of change in character (point of inflection of regression curve) is outside the range of the SU, then he must look to the entire larger universe for his controls. It is to be expected that this latter situation will not often arise.

However, to make generalizations with confidence not only about the WSC sampling universe but also about the larger universe, bibliographic quality control needs to be part of a research design.

As studies of this sort accumulate, the task of later investigators will become progressively easier. Once the bibliographic bias of a trait has been established in one study, it is "cleared" for use again and again in others.

Application of BQC to the WSC Sample

For the WSC sample, wealth of bibliographic detail was measured by taking three steps. *First,* the number of items listed under the tribe in its ethnographic bibliography was counted. *Second,* that number was divided by the total number of entries from the bibliography concerned on all the tribes in the sample. In this way a measure of the relative wealth of description of each tribe as compared to the other tribes covered by the same bibliography was obtained. Thus the thirteen African tribes covered by Wieschoff's bibliography were compared with each other but not with other tribes covered by other bibliographies. In this way, differing bibliographic practices of different bibliographers and differing bibliographic coverages of different large regions were not permitted to affect the scoring. *Third,* all the scores were converted by a normalizing transformation into a normally distributed standard score.

This measure was then correlated by a product moment correlation with forty-four other similarly normalized scores of other quantified traits. Further it was correlated by a point biserial correlation with 135 dichotomized qualitative traits. Theoretically, we would expect from random chance only 2.2 product moment correlations nominally significant at the 5 per cent level; in fact there were 8. Molina's Poisson distribution tables tell us that we should expect through chance a group of forty-five correlations at least as unusual as this slightly less often than twice in a thousand such groups. We must conclude then that the hypothesis of systematic bias is strongly supported. The eight traits thus evidently biased include:

1 and 2. Two measures of time spread. Tribes whose sources are spread over longer periods of time tend to have larger bibliographies. This tendency is just what we would expect, of course. The longer that observers have been writing about a tribe, the more

they have had time to write. A trivial conclusion.

3. The earlier in time a tribe was described, the larger its bibliography tends to be. Like the preceding two, a trivial conclusion.

4. Aggression index. The larger the bibliography of a tribe, the more evidence of aggression was noted by the coders. Such evidence included attention to suicide, attention to homicide, allusion to witchcraft, mention of presence of drunken brawling, mention of presence of wife-beating, mention of presence of dog-beating, and words suggesting that warfare was frequently rather than infrequently practiced. The finding is certainly not unexpected; but it is important because it constitutes evidence of just the sort of systematic bias in the literature we would fear.

5. Population of largest settlement. (See Chapter 40 above.) The larger the settlement, the greater the bibliography. Since settlement size is a prime indicator of general social development, this finding probably indicates that more highly developed societies tend to be described more frequently than less highly developed societies of the same large region. A like tendency, but far weaker, was found with other measures of social development.

6 and 7. Territorial expansion in particular and territorial change in general tend to be reported more frequently among the more copiously described tribes than among the less copiously described ones.

8. The lower a tribe was placed on Tatje's Guttman scale of war frequency, the larger its bibliography. This relationship is related to Item No. 5. The smaller the largest settlement, the higher the score on Tatje's scale.

These eight associations lend themselves to three sorts of explanations. The first three associations seem most plausibly explained by a trivial relationship. By a trivial relationship is meant of course one that common sense would lead one to expect, without the need for tedious, expensive and complicated control tests. However, sometimes relationships of this sort turn out *not* to exist. For example, common sense would lead us to expect that the greater the bibliography, the more circumstances (folk explanations) of homicide would have been reported. But the coders found that, if anything, the tendency was

the reverse, although the results were not significant. Therefore, it is useful to have common-sense judgments confirmed. Thus, then we can confirm that the earlier a society was described and the longer a period of time its descriptions cover, the greater its total bibliography.

Two other correlations certainly appear to reflect sampling bias. Societies at higher levels of development—especially as reflected in larger settlement patterns—and societies with *less frequent* warfare tend to have more copious bibliographies. (The second conclusion is contrary to my original prediction about bibliographic sampling bias; the first was consistent with the original prediction.)

Finally, three correlations have two rival plausible explanations. We clearly have a bias, but it is not clear whether the bias is a sampling bias or a reporting bias.

Do more aggressive tribes attract more attention from ethnographers? If so, then we have a sampling bias. Or must we instead explain the relationship by supposing that the greater the bibliography, the greater the likelihood that aggressive behavior is noted? In my opinion, the phenomenon seems to be a sampling bias rather than a reporting bias. For the traits that contributed most to those correlations were the ones in which a specific report one way or the other was required for coding; and reports were dichotomized according to the content of the report.

Similarly, do territorially expanding tribes attract more attention than others? If so, we have a sampling bias. Or is territorial growth simply more likely to be reported if there is much literature than if there is little? My staff coded territorial change data two ways. In one, where growth was reported, I used a positive ratio; where contraction was reported, I used a negative ratio. Growth was reported far more often that contraction. In the other coding, I ignored these plus and minus signs; this coding then contrasted those tribes where any kind of change was reported with those where no change was reported. The fact that territorial growth was reported much more frequently than territorial diminution might be explained as a sampling bias—growing tribes attracted more attention. Or it might be explained as a reporting bias—informants might be more likely to boast of victorious expansion than to confess humiliating contraction. Now, unsigned territorial change had a slightly greater association with length of bibliography than signed territorial growth. This fact seems to argue in favor of another sort of reporting bias hypothesis—that by ethnographers. The more ethnographic reports there were, the more likely someone often was to mention territorial change.

To conclude, then, the War, Stress and Culture sample revealed eight presumably significant associations between extent of bibliography and other traits. Of these eight, five seem with varying degrees of plausibility to reflect sampling bias rather than reporting bias: (1) population of largest settlement; (2) frequency of warfare; (3) territorial growth; (4) territorial change; and (5) aggressive behavior, taken collectively. Thus we may tentatively conclude that the tribes in the sampling universe seem to be more aggressive, more highly evolved culturally, less frequently at war, more likely to expand territorially, or be otherwise territorially unstable than the remaining tribes in the larger universe we wish to describe.

Of 135 point biserial correlations, only 8 attained a nominal significance level of .05. This does not constitute persuasive evidence that any of these are significant, since we would expect 6.6 such correlations from chance alone.

We may now turn to consider those traits which seem clearly free from bibliographic bias. Which ones are they? To identify them would be helpful. Consider correlations of these traits either with each other or with other traits not free of bibliographic bias. Neither sort of correlation can be a spurious artifact of bibliographic sampling bias. How can we identify these unbiased traits? This is a problem in that branch of mathematical statistics called confidence interval estimation (Wallis and Roberts 1956:443 ff.; Kendall and Stuart 1961:98 ff.). Graphs have been prepared which let us make confidence inferences quickly and easily, by eye, without any arithmetic work. For our present task, the graph in Beyer (1966:301) is convenient. Mathematical statistics never let us be certain about anything; but we can reduce uncertainty to any desired tangible level. Now it is convenient for us to seek those traits which have no more than a 5 per cent chance of having a considerable true correla-

tion with bibliographic coverage. It is convenient to take a correlation with an absolute value of .4 or more as a considerable correlation. Hence we seek correlations in our sample so small that allowing for net random error (including random sampling error and random reporting and coding error) the odds are nineteen to one that the true correlation falls between $+0.4$ and -0.4.

Because our sample size is rather small, we are only able to make a few such inferences; see Table 1. Coding the World Ethnographic Sample or the Ethnographic Atlas for bibliographical coverage would permit many more, and would let us narrow our confidence interval from ±0.4 to ±0.2.

Of the 168 correlations attempted (other than with random-number Monte Carlo or "Whiskers" variables), 27 involved twenty-three or fewer cases. But we must have more than twenty-three cases; or else even a zero correlation would not permit an inference that the universe correlation had an absolute value of less than 0.4. Of the remaining 141 correlations attempted, 26 had correlations low enough to qualify for listing on Table 1. If in fact bibliographic bias affected *all* the traits in our sample, we would not expect so large a number to appear this little biased. We would expect only 7.05 (5 per cent × 141). In such a case, Molina's tables show us that we would expect as many as 26 in less than one group of 141 correlations out of a million (Molina 1942). So we may take this as firm evidence that some traits have no monotonic bibliographic bias. Any of the eighteen traits of Table 1 having a correlation coefficient with an absolute value less than 0.07 are particularly unlikely to have a bibliographic bias.

FURTHER WORK NEEDED

A most urgent task is the compilation of regional universe studies in Africa—almost the only part of the world where such studies still can be done in the field. For the western United States, and some adjacent parts of Canada and Mexico, the Culture Element Distribution studies of the University of California provide copious data on all the tribes of a large region (see Chapter 32 above). Like data on a much smaller area of South America was compiled by Tessman (1930); see also Driver and Kroeber (1932). If we

TABLE 1

TRAITS WITH LITTLE SAMPLING BIAS

**Traits with a probability of at least 0.95 that universe correlation
with bibliographic coverage has an absolute value of less than 0.4.**

TRAIT	NUMBER OF CASES	CORRELATION COEFFICIENT
Number of folk explanations of suicide	32	.0201
Craft specialty count (see Chapter 40, above)	45	.1031
Number of potential military rivals in political arena	39	.0715
Children not weaned from breast until at least twelve months of age, or until they can walk	27	.0000
Number of words devoted to discussion of suicide, dichotomized	40	.0948
Number of folk explanations of suicide, dichotomized	36	.0305
Either suicide wordage or homicide wordage high	40	.0600
Public expressions of grief at funerals is customary	41	.0845
Infanticide reported—infanticide either absent or unreported	44	−.0105
Number of cases of defiant homicide reported	24	−.0156
Only contact weapons used in warfare	38	.0622
Surprise always required to initiate warfare	28	.0098
Warfare usually fought by prearrangement (tournaments)	27	−.0037
Military expectations scale dichotomized	44	.0953
Political control an expectation of successful warriors	38	−.0518
Trophies (scalps, heads, etc.) an expectation of successful warriors	44	−.0377
Either trophies, coups, or trophy cannibalism an expectation of successful warriors	44	−.0562
Slaves kept	33	−.0050
Ascariasis endemic	44	.0326
Number of potential enemies, dichotomized	38	−.0480
Military preparations customary	43	.0956
Military obstacles customary	43	−.0745
Intertribal trade reported	43	−.0694
Western tools used	43	.0126
Unintermittent warfare reported	43	−.0336
Frequent warfare reported (civilized societies omitted)	43	.0942

had analogous ethnographic culture element distribution studies of entire large regions like Kenya and Tanganyika, it would give us an independent control for comparison. The use of these studies is to measure the bibliographic bias of readily observable traits, looking for indications of nonmonotonic bias. As explained in pp. 912–913 above, where the bias is monotonic, it can be measured within the sample studied itself. But where nonmonotonic, only observations of the entire universe are safe controls.

This major task, this work in Africa, falls under the category of urgent anthropology. Kroeber's California studies were done with elderly informants. As shown by Driver (1936, 1939)—see pp. 930–931 below—these studies were not notably reliable; errors up to 16 per cent may be presumed. The longer we wait, the older grow the informants who remember aboriginal culture; and in one or two decades more, it will be entirely too late.

TABLE 2
SAMPLING SELECTIONS

	OWC NO.	DIFFUSION ARC SAMPLE	WES SAMPLE	IN HRAF
Hottentot	FX–13	X		X
Thonga	FT–6		X	X
Ila	FQ–8	X		
Chagga	FN–4		X	X
Mongo	FO–32	X		X
Mende	FC–7		X	X
Tallensi	FE–11		X	X
Tiv	FF–57		X	X
Azande	FO–7		X	X
Luo	FL–11		X	X
Amhara	MP–5		X	X
Fur	MQ–8	X		
Kababish	MQ–9	X		
Egypt	MR–13		X	
Italy	EI–1		X	
Irish	ER–1	X		
Dutch	ET–4	X		
Austrians	EK–1	X		X
Turks	MB–1	X		X
Iraqi	MH–1	X		X
Kafir	AU–6	X		
Kazaks	RQ–2		X	X
Chukchi	RY–2	X		X
Gilyak	RX–3	X		X
Korea	AA–1	X		X
Gond	AU–32	X		X
Andamans	AZ–2	X		X
Burmese	AP–4		X	X
Semang	AN–7	X		X
Apayao	OA–5		X	X
Land Dyak	OC–8	X		
Toradja	OG–11	X		
Kapauku	OJ–29	X		X
Orokaiva	OJ–23	X		
Ifaluk	OR–21		X	X
Malaita	ON–9	X		
Malekula	OO–12		X	
Tikopia	OT–11	X		X
Tonga	OU–9	X		
Mangareva	OX–5	X		
Copper Eskimo	ND–8		X	X
Eyak	NA–7	X		
Klallam	NR–15	X		
Wintun	NS–26		X	
Southern Paiute	NT–16	X		
Cheyenne	NQ–8		X	
Ojibwa	NG–6		X	X
Iroquois	NM–9		X	X
Coyotero	NT–21		X	

	OWC NO.	DIFFUSION ARC SAMPLE	WES SAMPLE	IN HRAF
Papago	NU–28	X		X
Nahua	NU–7	X		X
Mosquito	SA–15	X		X
Callinago	ST–13		X	X
Yagua	SE–29	X		
Araucanians	SG–4	X		X
Ona	SH–4	X		
Mataco	SI–7	X		X
Aweikoma	SM–2		X	

APPENDIX I
Bibliographic Protocol for the War, Stress and Culture Sample

The following in effect constituted the plan followed by staff members in considering a society for selection in this sample. Societies were considered in a certain order derived from one of two stratified probability sampling plans, as described in the text above. If they qualified according to the following protocols, they were accepted as the representative of the stratum concerned. If not, the next society in order was considered. As explained above, the effect of this procedure was to impose an explicit, clearly defined bias on the selection procedure. This bias obviously was a function of the degree to which a society tended to attract the attention of anthropologists, missionaries or other ethnographers.

With the benefit of hindsight, it is clear that these protocols are too cumbersome and intricate. It would be better in every respect to use a simpler plan. The simpler the selection criteria, the easier it is to measure the sampling bias involved. The simpler the selection criteria, the less expensive the work of sampling.

BIBLIOGRAPHIC REQUIREMENTS

The study for which this sample was taken is a study of the interrelations between culture stress, warfare and social evolution. It was desired to include only societies with general ethnographic data and also with certain specific data on suicide or homicide and on warfare, accessible in a specified Los Angeles library. Ordinarily, in order for the data to be accessible, it had to be in a book or monograph calendared in one of the standard ethnographic bibliographies. The title had to give reasonable hope that the work might have general ethnograhic data or the specific data sought. The work had to be either in the Human Relations Area Files at the University of Southern California; or in the University of California, Los Angeles library, properly catalogued, and either in the stacks in its proper place or discoverable by the usual library stack search or recorded in the library's record of book loans. Such a work then had to be a topically organized ethnographic treatise with data of the sort required in passages indicated by the work's title, the table of contents, chapter subtitles, HRAF file key number or topic index. The sampling protocol defining these requirements precisely is set forth below.

Societies in the Human Relations Area Files, University of Southern California

When the sampling work was conducted, during the summer and fall of 1960 and the winter and spring of 1961, there were a total of 231 files and sub-files. Except for the 1957 sample, mentioned above, these were checked for bibliographic adequacy in their regular turn, as the societies in question came up along the diffusion arc segments or the World Ethnographic Sample lists. However, the nature of the files made determination of bibliographic adequacy simple.

1.1. A file had to include at least fifty pages of source material. All sampled met this requirement; the files themselves of course constitute a topical organization; therefore the organization of the original work (whether topical, geographical or chronological) was ignored.

1.2. All files consulted had at least fifty pages of material in the English language (original or translation); therefore, language of source was not a consideration.

1.3. A society in the files was rejected, however, unless it had *case reports* or *rate reports* on suicide or homicide in rubrics 682 or 762.

1.4. A society in the files was rejected unless it also had some data on warfare in rubrics 721, 725, or 726. A statement implying that the society in question, though free to make war, in fact did not practice warfare, constituted adequate data on warfare for the purpose of this rule, as did any data indicating that it did practice warfare.

Societies in the United Nations Demographic Yearbook

Those societies which maintain statistical bureaus and which turned in statistical reports on suicide or homicide among their people which were published in the 1958 *United Nations Demographic Yearbook* were considered *ipso facto* acceptable and were accordingly accepted if their turn came up, without further bibliographic requirements. (Ordinarily copious data is available on such societies, in library catalogues, under their name.)

Overseas Europeans

Nations outside of Europe which were settled by Europeans moving across the seas since 1492 were *ignored* in this study. This rule means for example that in considering the New World, only peoples speaking American Indian languages were sampled; domestic speakers of dialects of English, French, German, Dutch, Italian, Flemish, Spanish or Portugese in the New World, Africa, Asia and Oceania were ignored. This rule was adopted because of the disturbance to interdependence control (Galton's problem) which would have been produced by including them (see Naroll 1961a:23 f.).

Europe, Eastern Siberia and the Near East

In these areas, only societies in the Human Relations Area Files and *United Nations Demographic Yearbook* were considered; but *their* coverage here is almost complete.

2.1. *Europe.* Since the sample restricts itself to societies free to make war as such, the minority ethnic groups of Europe like the Basques, Bretons, Welsh, and Scottish Highlanders would be excluded in any case. The *United Nations Demographic Yearbook* covers acceptable European societies almost completely (omitting only societies *technically* free to make war but practically completely dependent upon large neighbors, like Monaco, Andorra, San Marino and Liechtenstein).

2.2. *Eastern Siberia.* Jakobson, Hütt-Worth and Beebe (1957) constitutes an excellent ethnographic bibliography for all the societies in Siberia on the diffusion arc except the Eastern Tungus (including Goldi). However, it was not necessary to use this bibliography for sampling purposes since the Human Relations Area Files has complete coverage of *all* Siberian peoples on this diffusion arc. (*N. B.* The Yukaghir group have their sampling point outside the arc.)

2.3. *Near East.* By the Near East is meant Persia, Iraq, Turkey, Syria, Lebanon, Israel, Jordan and all Arabia. No suitable ethnographic bibliography for this area was available; but the Human Relations Area Files and the *United Nations Demographic Yearbook* between them cover all the independent nations with regular diplomatic status, plus the Rwala Bedouin. There are no sub-files set up on other warring Arab nomadic tribes; or on the warring tribes of Iran—but whether any of these tribes could qualify if complete ethnographic bibliographies on them were available is a question.

Societies not in the Human Relations Area Files (HRAF) or the United Nations Demographic Yearbook (UNDY) Outside of Europe, Eastern Siberia and the Near East: For the New World, Africa, Oceania, and the rest of Eurasia—that is, for most of the world—societies not in HRAF or *UNDY* were sampled by a necessarily cumbersome bibliographic study. Rules were proliferated in an attempt to define as precisely as possible a procedure which would consider as large a number of promising leads as possible with as little waste motion as possible. For one of these societies to be accepted, one or more satisfactory ethnographic reports had to be listed in an ethnographic bibliography and located in the University of California, Los Angeles, library.

3.1. *Calendaring.* Works were required to be listed in one of the following ethnographic bibliographies or specialized surveys:

South America—Murdock, 1951

Mexico and Central America—German Parra and Jimenez Moreno, 1954

North America—Murdock, 1953; Voegelin, 1937

Greater China (including Manchuria, Mongolia, Tibet and Chinese Turkestan)—Cordier 1904–1924; Yuan, 1958.

Central Asia—Krader, 1956

Caucasus—Luzbetak, 1951

North Africa—Coon, 1958

Sahara—Briggs, 1960

Remainder of Africa—Wieschoff, 1948; Bohannan, 1960

Afghanistan—Wilbur, 1956

India, Pakistan and Indian Ocean—Fürer-Haimendorf, 1958

Mainland Southeast Asia—Embree and Dotson, 1950

Indonesia—Kennedy, 1955

Australia—Tindale, 1940

Remainder of Oceania—Taylor, 1950

At large—Wisse, 1933 (works considered if Wisse gave a case report on suicide)

3.2. Works were required to be in English, French, German, Spanish or Dutch.

3.3. *One* of the following requirements had to be met:

3.31. Suicide or homicide case report in Wisse (1933), Voegelin (1937) or Bohannan (1960); *or*

3.32. Title containing one of the following words: "suicide, homicide, death, murder, crime, blood revenge, law, justice, killings"; *or*

3.33. All of the following requirements:

3.331. Length as specified in bibliography not under fifty pages (if no length specified, this requirement ignored).

3.332. Title named the society, or some component thereof, as listed in Murdock 1958; *or* title had one of the following key words: "ethnology, ethnological, ethnography, ethno-

graphical, society, social, culture, cultural, tribe, tribes, people, village, men, head-hunters, fishermen, civilization, notes, peasant"; in either case in a context which did not indicate that the work dealt chiefly with material culture, aesthetics, religion, linguistics, folklore, folk tales, ethnobiology, biography or physical anthropology.

3.4. The work was required to be catalogued in the University of California, Los Angeles library, conformably to its listing in the ethnographic bibliography (i.e., under the title of the periodical as listed there, if part of a series; otherwise, under the name of the author as listed there).

3.5. The work was required to be present or accounted for in the University of California, Los Angeles collection (in the library stacks in its proper place or in the call slip file or located within two successive formal searches by library personnel).

3.6. The work was required to be topically arranged (not chronologically or geographically).

3.7. The work was required to contain at least fifty pages which dealt in name or in fact especially with the particular people being sampled (as listed in Murdock, 1958) or some portion of them—so that statements therein not applicable to these particular people were evidently so qualified and statements not specially qualified were intended to apply to these particular people.

3.8. The work was required to be a firsthand account (primary source) or a secondary source which cited primary sources by page reference for particular statements. (In fact, almost no secondary sources were used.)

3.9. The work was required to contain an indexed case report or rate report of suicide or homicide.

3.91. By a case report is meant a report of a particular instance of suicide or homicide.

3.92. By a rate report is meant a statement of the total number of suicides or homicides within a given community or group or per stated number of people (e.g., "no suicides in living memory," "three homicides in the last five years in A——," "five suicides per hundred thousand population per year").

3.93. By an *indexed* report is meant a report found in an article, chapter, work or passage whose presence is clued in the title of the work, or chapter, or table of contents entry covering the passage in question, by one of the key words listed in section 3.32 above, or some synonym of one of them.

4.0. The work, or some other work qualified under rules 3.1 through 3.8, had to have data on warfare sufficient to show that there was coverage of the society during a period when it was free to make war. Ordinarily, any sort of discussion of warfare met this qualification. Societies were rejected for lack of it in practice when it became clear that the period covered by otherwise qualified monographs was a period in which the society was under the *de facto* military control of some other society.

APPENDIX II
Permanent Ethnographic Probability Sample Universe
being the Standard Ethnographic Sample

The following list presents those tribes which meet the bibliographic criteria set forth in the text above, for Africa, North America, South America and Central America. Each listing gives the identification as contained in Murdock's *Outline of World Cultures*, together with the name of the author whose works were found to meet the standards of quality set forth. The reader is reminded that this list is necessarily incomplete for two reasons: (1) authors do not always conspicuously report their native language familiarity and length of stay in the field. Obviously, we could not read every page of every work cited in standard ethnographic bibliographies in search of this data but could seek it out only in the preface or introduction or other place clearly indicated by a table of contents; (2) ethnographic bibliographies are not complete. See further Naroll *et. al.* 1970

AFRICA

FA 8 Bambara — Monteil, Charles
FA 11 Bobo — Cremer, Jean
FA 16 Dogon — Griaule, Marcel
FA 17 Ewe — Spieth, Jacob
FA 18 Fon — Quenum, Maximilien
FA 21 Guro — Tauxier, Louis
FA 27 Malinke — Carreira, Antonio
FA 28 Mossi — Tauxier, Louis
FB 6 Pepel Tribes — Carreira, Antonio
FC 7 Mende — Little, Kenneth L.
FD 9 Vai — Ellis, George W.
FE 4 Birifor — Labouret, H.
FE 6 Ga — Field, J.
FE 11 Tallensi — Fortes, Meyer
FE 12 Twi — Rattray, Robert S.

FF 12 Bura — Helser, Albert D.
FF 21 Edo — Northcote, Thomas W.
FF 22 Ekoi — Talbert, Percy A.
FF 26 Ibo — Green, Margaret M.
FF 32 Nupe — Nadel, Siegfried F.
FF 51 Nsaw — Wuhrmann-Rein, Anna
FF 57 Tiv — Bohannan, Paul and Laura
FF 62 Yoruba — Ward, Edward
FH 9 Fang — Trilles, P. H.
FH 19 Ngangte — Lecoq, Raymond
FH 22 Tikar — Schmidt, Agathe
FH 24 Wute — Sieber, J.
FI 9 Baya — Tessman, Gunter
FJ 10 Didinga — Driberg, Jack H.
FJ 22 Nuer — Howell, P. P.
FJ 23 Shilluk — Hofmayer, Wilhelm
FK 5 Alur — Southhall, Aidan W.
FK 6 Chiga — May-Mandelbaum, Edel
FK 7 Ganda — Roscoe, John
FK 9 Lango — Driberg, J. H.
FK 11 Nyoro — Beattie, John
FK 12 Teso — Lawrence, J. C. D.
FL 4 Bantu Kavirondo — Wagner, Hunter
FL 6 Dorobo — Huntingford, G. W. B.
FL 7 Galla — Martial de Salviac, P.
FL 8 Gusii — Mayer, Philip
FL 9 Kamba — Lindblom, K. G.
FL 10 Kikuyu — Kenyatta, Jomo
FL 12 Masai — Hollis, A. C.
FL 13 Nandi — Huntingford, G. W. B.
FL 14 Nika — Ngala, Ronald
FL 17 Turkana — Gulliver, Philip H.
FN 4 Chagga — Gutmann, Bruno
FN 6 Fipa — Maurice, M.
FN 8 Haya — Cesard, Edmond
FN 9 Hehe — Culwick, A. T. and G. M.
FN 13 Makonde — Mackenzie, D. R.
FN 17 Ngonde — Wilson, Monica

FN 18 Nyamwezi — Blohm, Wilhelm
FN 21 Safwa — Kretschmer-Kootz, Elise
FO   7 Azande — Evans-Pritchard, E. E.
FO 10 Bashi — Colle, P.
FO 12 Boloki — Weeks, John H.
FO 17 Dinga — Mertens, Joseph
FO 18 Holoholo — Schmitz, Robert
FO 21 Kongo — Philippart, L.
FO 27 Luba — Colle, R. P.
FO 36 Ngbandi — Tanghe, Pere Basile
FO 42 Rundi — Van der Burgt, Jean M. M.
FO 49 Yaka — Plancquaert, M.
FO 50 Yombe — Bittremieux, Leo
FQ   5 Bemba — Richards, Audrey
FQ   6 Ila — Smith, Edwin W.
FQ   8 Lamba — Doke, Clement M.
FQ   9 Lozi — Gluckman, Max
FQ 12 Tonga — Colson, Elisabeth
FR   6 Tumbuka — Young, Callen T.
FS   4 Ndebele — Neville, Jones
FS   5 Shona — Holleman, J. F.
FT   4 Chopi — Earthy, Dora E.
FT   6 Thonga — Junod, Henri A.
FT   7 Yao — Mitchell, Clyde J.
FU   2 Swazi — Marwick, Brian A.
FV   6 Tswana — Schapera, Isaac
FW   2 Sotho — Casalis, Eugene Arnaud
FX   8 Ambo — Tonjes, Hermann
FX   9 Bergdama — Vedder, H.
FX 12 Herero — Brinckner, P. H.
FX 13 Hottentot — Hahn, Theophilius
FX 14 Lovedu — Krige, E. Jensen and J. D.
FX 16 Pedi — Harries, C. L.
FX 17 South Nguni — Soga, Henderson John
FX 19 Venda — Stayt, Hugh A.
FX 20 Zulu — Bryant, Alfred T.
FY   5 Imerina — Sibree, J.
MO   4 Somali — Lewis, Ioan M.
MP 19 Mao — Grotanelli, Vinigi
MP 23 Sidamo — Simoni, Antonio
MS 11 Fulani — Moreira, Mendes Jose
MS 12 Hausa — Mischlich, Adam
MS 20 Songhai — Rouch, Jean

NORTH AMERICA

NA   6 Aleut — Veniaminov, I.
NA   9 North Alaska Eskimo — Murdoch, J.
NA 12 Tlingit — Krause, A.
NA 13 West Alaska Eskimo — Nelson, E. W.
NB   5 Polar Eskimo — Rasmussen, K.
ND   6 Caribou Eskimo — Birket-Smith, K.
ND   8 Copper Eskimo — Stefansson, V.
NE   6 Bellacoola — McIlwraith, T. F.

NE   7 Carrier — Morice, A. G.
NE 10 Kwakiutl — Boas, F.
NE 12 Thompson — Teit, J. A.
NF   4 Assiniboin — Denig, E. T.
NG   5 Huron — Sagard-Théodat, C.
NH   6 Montagnais — Speck, F.
NJ   5 Micmac — LeClercq, C.
NL   4 Abnaki — Speck, F. G.
NM   7 Delaware — Heckeweder, J. G. E.
NM   9 Iroquois — Morgan, L. H.
NP   5 Fox — Jones, W.
NP   8 Menomini — Skinner, A.
NP 12 Winnebago — Radin, P.
NQ 10 Crow — Lowie, R. H.
NQ 11 Santee — Riggs, S.
NQ 12 Omaha — Fletcher, A. C., and
            F. La Flesche
NQ 14 Hidatsa — Matthews, W.
NR 15 Twana — Eells, M.
NS 11 Hupa — Goddard, P. E.
NS 14 Luiseño — Sparkman, P. S.
NS 18 Pomo — Barrett, S. A.
NS 31 Yurok — Kroeber, A. L.
NT   9 Hopi — Titiev, M.
NT 13 Navaho — Reichard, G. A.
NT 18 Tewa — Dozier, E.
NT 21 Coyotero — Goodwin, G.
NT 23 Zuni — Stevenson, M. C.
NU 28 Papago — Underhill, R. M.

SOUTH AMERICA

SC 11 Chibcha — Rochereau, H. J.
SD   9 Jivaro — Karsten, R.
SE 13b Inca — de la Vega, Garcilaso, and
            B. Valera
SE 13d Contemporary Quechua —
            Mangin, W.
SE 18 Piro — Matteson, E.
SF   5 Aymara — Tschopik, H., Jr.
SF 21 Siriono — Holmberg, A. R.
SG   4 Araucanians — Falkner, T.
SH   2 Alacaluf — Emperaire, J.
SH   4 S'elknam (Ona) — Bridges, E. L.
SH   6 Yamana (Yahgan) — Bridges, T., and
            M. Gusinde
SI   4 Abipon — Dobrizhoffer, M.
SI   8 Moscovi — Paucke, F.
SK 10 Moascoi — Grubb, W. B.
SK 11 Mbaya — Sanchez Labrador, J.
SM   2 Aweikoma — Henry, J.
SO   8 Timbira — Nimuendaju, C.
SO   9 Tupinamba — Sousa, G. S. de
SP   8 Bororo — Colbacchini, A., and
            C. Albisetti

SP 13 Northern Cayapo — Banner, H.
SP 17 Nambicuara — Lévi-Strauss, C.
SP 22 Tapirape — Wagley, Charles
SQ 18 Yanoama — Barket, J.
SQ 19 Tucano — Bruzzi, Alves da Silva
SS 18 Warao — Turrado Moreno, A.

CENTRAL AMERICA

NW 6 Chorti — Wisdom, Charles
SA 12 Black Carib — Taylor, D.

EURASIA

AB 6 Ainu — Batchelor, J.
AE 3 Minchia — Fitzgerald, C. P.
AE 9 Monguor — Schram, L. M. J.
AM 9 Mong Gar — Condominas, G.
AN 7 Semang — Schebesta, P.
AP 5 Chin — Lehman, F. K.
AP 6 Kachin — Leach, E. R.
AP 7 Karen — Marshall, H. I.
AR 5 Garo — Playfair, A.
AR 7 Khasis — Gurdon, P. R. T.
AR 8 Thado Kuki — Shaw, W.
AR 8 Lakher — Parry, N. E.
AR 13 Sema Naga — Hutton, J. H.
AV 3 Dard — Biddulph, J.
AV 7 Barusho — Lorimer, E. O.
AW 5 Coorg — Richter, G.
AW 24 Baiga — Elwin, V.
AW 25 Bhil — Naik, T. B.
AW 33 Ho — Majumdar, D. N.
AW 39 Oraon — Roy, S. C.
AW 42 Santal — Culshaw, W. J.
AW 60 Toda — Emeneau, M. B.
AZ 2 Andamanese—Radcliffe-
       Brown, A. R.
AZ 7 Nicobarese — Whitehead, G.
RV 2 Yakut — Jochelson, W.
RV 3 Yakaghir — Jochelson, W.
RX 2 Gilyak — Seeland, N.
RY 2 Chukchee — Bogoras, W.
EG 1 Gheg — Hasluck, M.
EP 4 Lapps — Whitaker, Ian

OCEANIA

OA 19 Ifugao — Barton, R. F.
OA 14 Sugbuhanon — Hart, D. V.

OA 28 Manobo — Garvan, J. M.
OA 38 Tinguian — Cole, Fay-Cooper
OC 6 Iban — Freeman, J. D.
OE 5 Javanese — Geertz, H.
OF 5 Alorese — DuBois, C.
OG 11 Toradja (Bare'e) — Adriani and
       Kruyt
OI 8 Aranda — Spencer, W. and Gillen, F.
OI 17 Murngin — Berndt, R. M. and C. M.
OI 10 Dieri — Gason, S.
OJ 29 Kapauku — Pospisil, L.
OJ 26 Waropen — Held, G. J.
OJ 21 Purari — Holmes, J. H.
OJ 13 Kwoma — Whiting, J. W. M.
OJ 12 Kiwai — Landtman, G.
OJ 30 Abelam — Kaberry, P. M.
OJ 18 Manam — Wedgwood, C.
— – Siane — Salisbury, R. F.
OL 6 Trobrianders — Malinowski, B.
OM 6 Manus — Mead, M.
ON 6 Kurtachi (Buka) — Blackwood, B.
ON 4 Siuai — Oliver, D. L.
ON 15 Ulawans — Ivens, W. G.
OO 2 Seniang — Deacon, A. B.
OP 5 Lifu — Hadfield, E.
OP 1 Aije (New Caledonia) —
       Leenhardt, M.
OQ 6 Lau Fijians — Hocart, A. M.
OX 5 Manga Reva — Laval, Honoré
OZ 4 Maori — Buck, P.
OZ 11 Pukapukans — Beaglehole, E. and P.

SPECIAL ACKNOWLEDGMENTS

PEPS has been an institutional project of Northwestern University. It was planned by a six-man committee: Paul J. Bohannan, Francis L. K. Hsu, Donald T. Campbell, Raoul Naroll, Richard D. Schwartz and Richard C. Snyder. It was supported by grants from two Northwestern University agencies: the Program of African Studies and the Council for Intersocietal Studies. The actual bibliographic search work was performed by Nancy Schmidt (Africa), Winston Alnot (South America) and Janice Caplan (North America; Central America)—all under the direction of Raoul Naroll.

BIBLIOGRAPHY

BENEDICT, RUTH
   1935 Review of Unwin's *Sex and culture.* *American Anthropologist* 37:691–692.

BEYER, WILLIAM H.
   1966 *Handbook of tables for probability and statistics.* Cleveland, Chemical Rubber Co.

BLALOCK, HUBERT M.
1960 *Social statistics.* New York, McGraw-Hill.

BOHANNAN, PAUL (ed.)
1960 *African homicide and suicide.* Princeton, N.J., Princeton University Press.

BRIGGS, LLOYD C.
1960 *Tribes of the Sahara.* Cambridge, Harvard University Press.

CAPELL, ARTHUR
1962 *A linguistic survey of the southwestern Pacific,* rev. ed. Noumea, South Pacific Commission.

CHANEY, RICHARD P.
1966 Typology and patterning: Spiro's sample reexamined. *American Anthropologist* 68: 1456–70.

COCHRANE, WILLIAM G.
1963 *Sampling techniques,* 2nd ed. New York, Wiley.

COON, CARLETON S.
1958 *Caravan,* rev. ed. New York, Holt. (Bibliography)

CORDIER, HENRI
1904– *Bibliotheca Sinica.* 5 vols. Paris, Geuth-
1924 ner.

COULT, ALLAN D., and ROBERT W. HABENSTEIN
1965 *Cross tabulations of Murdock's World ethnographic sample.* Columbia, University of Missouri Press.

DRIVER, HAROLD E.
1936 *The reliability of culture element data.* Ph.D. thesis. University of California at Berkeley, Department of Anthropology.
1939 Culture element distributions: VIII. The reliability of culture element data. *Anthropological Records* 1:205–219.
1956 *An integration of functional, evolutionary and historical theory by means of correlations.* Indiana University, Publications in Anthropology and Linguistics, Memoir 12.

DRIVER, HAROLD E., and ALFRED L. KROEBER
1932 Quantitative expressions of cultural relationships. *University of California, Publications in American Archaeology and Ethnology* 31:215–256.

DRIVER, HAROLD E., and WILLIAM C. MASSEY
1957 Comparative studies of North American Indians. Philadelphia, *Transactions of the American Philosophical Society* 47, Part II:165–456.

DUNCAN, ACHESON J.
1959 *Quality control and industrial statistics,* rev. ed. Homewood, Ill., Irwin.

EMBER, MELVIN
1963 The relationship between economic and political development in non-industralized societies. *Ethnology* 2:228–248.

EMBREE, JOHN F., and L. O. DOTSON
1950 *Bibliography of the peoples and cultures of the mainland of Southeast Asia.* New Haven, Yale University Press.

FÜRER-HAIMENDORF, ELIZABETH VON
1958 *An anthropological bibliography of South Asia.* Paris and The Hague, Mouton.

GERMAN PARRA, MANUEL, and WIGBERTO JIMENEZ MORENO
1954 *Bibliografia Indigenista de Mexico y Centroamerica, 1850–1950.* Mexico, Memorias del Instituto Nacional Indigenista, Vol. IV.

GRANT, ALLEN
1879 *The colour-sense: its origin and development.* London, Trübner.

GREENWAY, JOHN
1963 *Bibliography of the Australian Aborigines and the native people of Torres Strait to 1959.* Sydney, Angus and Robertson.

HANSEN, MORRIS H., WILLIAM N. HURWITZ, and WILLIAM G. MADOW
1953 Sample survey method and theory. In Vol. I, *Methods and applications.* New York, Wiley.

HEWES, GORDON W.
1954 A conspectus of the world's cultures in 1500 A.D. *The University of Colorado Studies, series in Anthropology* 4:1–22.

HOBHOUSE, LEONARD T.
1906 *Morals in evolution.* New York, Holt.

HOBHOUSE, LEONARD T., G. C. WHEELER, and M. GINSBERG
1915 *The material culture and social institutions of the simpler peoples.* London, Chapman and Hall.

HOMANS, GEORGE C., and DAVID M. SCHNEIDER
1955 *Marriage, authority and final causes.* New York, Free Press of Glencoe.

HONIGMANN, JOHN J.
1959 *The world of man.* New York, Harper.

HORTON, DONALD
1943 The functions of alcohol in primitive societies: a cross-cultural survey. *Quarterly Journal of Studies on Alcohol* 4: 199–320.

HUMAN RELATIONS AREA FILES
1967 The HRAF quality control sample universe. *Behavior Science Notes* 2:81–88.

JAKOBSON, ROMAN, GERTA HUTTL-WORTH, and JOHN F. BEEBE
1957 *Paleosiberian peoples and languages: a bibliographical guide.* New Haven, HRAF Press.

JONES, RUTH L.
1958 *Africa bibliography series. West Africa.* London, International African Institute.
1959 *Africa bibliography series. Northeast Af-*

rica. London, International African Institute.

1960 *Africa bibliography series. East Africa.* London, International African Institute.

1961 *Africa bibliography series. Southeast Central Africa and Madagascar.* London, International African Institute.

KENDALL, MAURICE G., and ALAN STUART
1961 The advanced theory of statistics. In Vol. II, *Inference and relationship.* New York, Hafner.

KENNEDY, RAYMOND A.
1955 *Bibliography of Indonesian peoples and cultures,* 2nd ed. New Haven, HRAF Press.

KENNEY, J. F., and E. S. KEEPING
1951 *Mathematics of statistics,* Part II, 2nd ed. New York, Van Nostrand.

KISH, LESLIE
1965 *Survey sampling.* New York, Wiley.

KÖBBEN, ANDRÉ J.
1952 New ways of presenting an old idea: the statistical method in social anthropology. *Journal of the Royal Anthropological Institute* 82:129–146.

KRADER, LAWRENCE
1956 *Annotated bibliography to handbook of Soviet Central Asia.* Soviet Central Asia, subcontractor's Monograph. New Haven, HRAF-49, 3:1041–1137.

KROEBER, A. L.
1947 *Cultural and natural areas of native North America.* Berkeley and Los Angeles, University of California Press.

LEACH, EDMUND
1961 Golden bough or gilded twig? Daedalus. *Proceedings of the American Academy of Arts and Sciences* 90:371–387.

LUZBETAK, LOUIS J.
1951 Marriage and the family in Caucasia. *Studia Instituti Anthropos,* Vol. 3. Vienna, Mödling, St. Gabriel's Mission Press.

MAGNUS, HUGO F.
1880 *Untersuchungen über den Farbensinn der naturvölker.* Jena.

1883 *Ueber ethnologische untersuchungen des Farbensinnes.* Breslaux.

MARSH, ROBERT M.
1967 *Comparative sociology.* New York, Harcourt and Brace.

MOLINA, E. C.
1942 *Poisson's exponential binomial limit.* Princeton, N.J., Van Nostrand.

MOOD, ALEXANDER
1950 *Introduction to the theory of statistics.* New York, McGraw-Hill.

MOORE, FRANK W. (ed.)
1961 *Readings in cross-cultural methodology.* New Haven, HRAF Press.

MORGAN, LEWIS H.
1871 *Systems of consanguinity and affinity of the human family.* Smithsonian Contribution to Knowledge, Vol. 17.

MURDOCK, GEORGE P.
1937 Correlations of matrilineal and patrilineal institutions. In G. P. Murdock, ed., *Studies in the science of society.* New Haven, Yale University Press.

1949 *Social structure.* New York, Macmillan.

1951 *Outline of South American cultures.* New Haven, HRAF Press.

1953 *Ethnographic bibliography of North America,* 2nd ed. New Haven, HRAF.

1957 World ethnographic sample. *American Anthropologist* 59:664–687.

1958 *Outline of world cultures,* 2nd ed. New Haven, HRAF.

1960 *Ethnographic bibliography of North America,* 3rd ed. New Haven, HRAF Press.

1961 *Outline of cultural materials,* 3rd ed. New Haven, HRAF Press.

1963 Ethnographic atlas. *Ethnology* 2:249–253.

1963 *Outline of world cultures,* 3rd ed. New Haven, HRAF.

1966 Cross cultural sampling. *Ethnology* 5:97–114.

1967 Ethnographic atlas: a summary *Ethnology* 6:109–236.

NAROLL, RAOUL
1956 A preliminary index of social development. *American Anthropologist* 58:687–715.

1961a Two solutions to Galton's problem. *Philosophy of Science* 28:15–39.

1961b *Two stratified random samples for a cross-cultural survey.* San Fernando Valley State College. Mimeograph.

1962 *Data quality control.* New York, Free Press.

NAROLL, RAOUL, WINSTON ALNOT, JANICE CAPLAN, JUDITH FRIEDMAN HANSEN, JEANNE MAXANT. and NANCY SCHMIDT
1970 A standard ethnographic sample. *Current Anthropology.*

NIEBOER, H. J.
1910 *Slavery as an industrial system,* 2nd ed. (1st ed., 1900). The Hague, Nyhoff.

O'LEARY, TIMOTHY J.
1963 *Ethnographic bibliography of South America.* New Haven, HRAF.

PARTEN, MILDRED
1950 *Surveys, polls and samples: practical procedures.* New York, Harper.

THE RAND CORPORATION
1955 *A million random digits with 100,000 normal deviates.* Glencoe, Ill., Free Press.

REDFIELD, ROBERT
1941 *Folk culture of Yucatan.* Chicago, University of Chicago Press.

SEGALL, MARSHALL H., DONALD T. CAMPBELL, and MELVILLE J. HERSKOVITS
1966 *The influence of culture on visual perception.* Indianapolis, Bobbs-Merrill.

SIMMONS, LEO W.
1937 Statistical correlations in the science of society. In George P. Murdock, ed., *Studies in the science of society.* New Haven, Yale University Press.

1945 *Treatment of the aged in primitive societies.* New Haven, Yale University Press.

SPIRO, MELFORD E.
1965 *A typology of social structure. . . . American Anthropologist* 67:1097–1119.

1966 A reply to Chaney. *American Anthropologist* 68:1471–74.

STEINMETZ, RUDOLF S.
1896 Endokannibalismus. *Mitteilungen der Anthropologischen Gesellschaft in Wien* 26: 1–60. Reprinted in *Gesammelte Kleinere Schriften zur Ethnologie und Sociologie.* Gronigen, Noordhhoff I:132–271, 1928–1935.

STEPHAN, FREDERICK F., and PHILIP J. MCCARTHY
1958 *Sampling opinions: an analysis of survey procedures.* New York, Wiley.

SWANSON, GUY
1960 *The birth of the gods.* Ann Arbor, University of Michigan Press.

TAYLOR, CLYDE ROMER HUGHES
1950 *A Pacific bibliography.* Wellington.

TESSMANN, GÜNTER
1930 *Die Indianer nordost Perus.* Hamburg, Friederichsen de Gruyter.

TINDALE, NORMAN B.
1940 Distribution of Australian aboriginal tribes. *Transactions of the Royal Society of South Australia,* Vol. 64, Part I, 40–231.

TYLOR, EDWARD B.
1889 On a method of investigating the institution applied to the laws of marriage and descent. *Journal of the Royal Anthropological Institute* 18:272.

UNITED NATIONS
1958 *Demographic yearbook.* New York, United Nations Department of Public Information.

UNWIN, JOSEPH D.
1934 *Sex and culture.* London, Oxford University Press.

VOEGELIN, ERMINIE W.
1937 Suicide in Northeastern California. *American Anthropologist* 39:445–456.

WALKER, HELEN M., and JOSEPH LEV
1953 *Statistical inference.* New York, Holt.

WALLIS, W. ALLEN, and HARRY V. ROBERTS
1956 *Statistics, a new approach.* Glencoe, Ill., Free Press.

WHITING, JOHN W. M., and IRWIN L. CHILD
1953 *Child training and personality.* New Haven, Yale University Press.

WIESCHOFF, HEINRICH ALBERT
1948 *Anthropological bibliography of Negro America.* American Oriental Series 23. New Haven, American Oriental Society.

WILBUR, DONALD M.
1956 *Annotated bibliography of Afghanistan.* New Haven, HRAF.

WISSE, JAKOB
1933 *Selbstmord und Todesfurcht bei den Naturvölkern.* Zutphen, Thieme.

YATES, FRANK
1949 *Sampling methods for censuses and surveys.* New York, Harper.

YUAN, TUNG-LI
1958 *China in Western literature: A continuation of Cordier's Bibliotheca sinica.* Yale University, Far Eastern Publications.

CHAPTER 44

Data Quality Control in Cross-Cultural Surveys

RAOUL NAROLL

INTRODUCTION

In this chapter, I argue: (1) We cannot assume the accuracy of field reports or cross-cultural codings by professional anthropologists or anyone else. (2) However, although errors are probably rather common, probably less than 16 per cent of cross-cultural codings involve random error. (3) Paradoxically, for cross-cultural surveys, the more random error, the *more* confidence can be placed in the correlations found. (4) Hence the problem is to detect non-random errors (also called systematic errors, or biases). (5) The control factor method of data quality control is a useful method of detecting such biases. (6) Control factors need to be used to detect informant error, ethnographer error and comparativist error. (7) Validating control factors is itself a major research problem, and for that purpose bias-sensitive traits should be studied. (8) A quality control study of bias-sensitive traits in the War, Stress and Culture sample (see pp. 907–910 above) supports the validity of at least six control factors: (a) scholarship of ethnographer; (b) native language familiarity; (c) use of non-native local resident helpers by ethnographer; (d) tendency of ethnographer to make clear commitments; (e) taking of ethnographic census by ethnographer and (f) ongoing ethnography as contrasted with its opposite, memory ethnography—by memory ethnography is meant the practice of describing a vanished culture by querying elderly informants about

The quality control study reported in this paper was supported by the National Science Foundation grant no. GS-773.

the days of their youth. (9) Control factors should be regularly used not only in the hope of finding systematic error in the few places where it is but also in the hope of creating a presumption of its absence in the many places where it is not. (10) Results so far suggest that bias is usually low and unimportant. These results, if confirmed, would be most reassuring.

The problem of trustworthiness of data is worrying social scientists more and more these days. Morgenstern (1950) presented a classic survey of the persistent difficulty of finding accurate economic data. For the laboratory experimenter and the sample survey worker, the difficulties and biases are well presented by Rosenthal (1966). Especially impressive is Rosenthal's own experimental data showing that even in the most strictly controlled laboratory situations, rats tend to be influenced in their behavior by the expectations of the experimenter (Rosenthal 1966:143–179). The pervasive influence of the research methods and theoretical orientations of political scientists and sociologists upon their findings has been strikingly demonstrated in two independent and parallel studies of the same problem by Gilbert (1968) and Walton (1966). Both Gilbert and Walton compared studies of community power structure made by sociologists and by political scientists according to (1) method of research and (2) findings. Sociologists tend to look for community influentials by asking knowledgeable people to tell them which of their fellow citizens had the *reputation* of being influential. Political scientists more often either surveyed documents to identify leading decision-makers or studied particular cases of community decisions to identify the community leaders. Using their methods, political scientists studying American cities usually found community power in the hands of at least two rival permanent factions or at least two temporary coalitions; seldom did they discern power concentrated in a single person, group or clique. Sociologists, using their methods, found single concentrations of power in nearly half the communities studied. Findings were a product of the research method rather than the discipline; sociologists who used non-reputational methods tended to find factions or coalitions. Two of the four political scientists in Walton's study who used reputational methods found single concentrations of power. Thus, the conclusions of such community studies seem to depend more upon the research method used than the community being studied.

The problem of data error in cross-national surveys is treated by Rummel in Chapter 45 and by Janda in Chapter 46.

A cross-historical survey by Naroll, Bullough and Naroll (1971) examined five characteristics of historical sources. While they did not find clear evidence of bias, there did seem to be a systematic tendency for historians to be influenced in certain ways by their sympathies—as would be expected.

I was once told in private by a well-known American anthropologist that credence belonged by right to any professional field worker who suffered hardships and took risks to get his field data. But consider another anthropologist, Allan Holmberg. In his vivid study of the Siriono Holmberg tells us of the severe difficulties of that field study. It was a constant problem for him to get enough to eat. And for several weeks, he went temporarily blind from a jungle infection. So severe was Siriono field work that Holmberg finally could stand it no longer and cut his visit short. Certainly we must all be grateful to Holmberg as a man and a colleague for struggling so manfully against such hardships to bring us back a fine report on an extremely interesting tribe. But when we put on our caps as cold-blooded scientists, should we credit Holmberg more because he spent half his time in an exhausting search for food? Did it make him a better observer to go temporarily blind?

THE PROBLEM OF ETHNOGRAPHIC ERROR

Occurrence of Field Work Error

Anthropologists have spent little time checking one another's field work for accuracy (see below). Even so, evidence is clear that even the best of field workers make mistakes. In particular, two major sources of bias appear even in the work of perceptive, well-trained and conscientious anthropologists. One is a tendency to select field data to fit some ideal conception or preconception of the culture studied. The other is a tendency to select field data which is conspicuous because exotic, but to overlook other field data which is inconspicuous because familiar to the ethnographer.

Preconception Bias. The best-documented instance of this sort is the study of Tepoztlán by Robert Redfield (1930). In an elaborate restudy, Oscar Lewis (1951:428 f.) found much evidence of a systematic bias in Redfield's work. Redfield presented the people of Tepoztlán in a much more favorable light than Lewis did. Redfield painted them as happy and friendly people. Lewis found much unhappiness and unfriendliness. Redfield stressed the cooperative and unifying elements in the life of Tepoztlán. Lewis called attention to its underlying individualism. Redfield reported a relatively homogeneous and smoothly functioning society. Lewis reported pervading tensions, conflicts, fears and unhappiness. Redfield reported a community of contented tillers of communally and privately owned lands. Lewis pointed out that over half the people had no privately owned lands and that violent quarrels took place over communally owned land. Redfield spoke much of the pleasant aspects of interpersonal relations. He said little about stealings and assaults. Lewis reports that 175 formal complaints of crimes and misdemeanors were filed in the village court during the year of Redfield's stay. To Redfield, local politics was an intriguing game. To Lewis, it was serious and often came to blows. Indeed, Lewis says (p. 430) that politics got so dangerous during Redfield's stay that the threat of harm from it drove Redfield away!

Another instance of preconception bias is found in the classic and magisterial Arapesh study by Margaret Mead (1935, 1938–1949).

Mead is concerned with the cultural roots of the differences in temperament between men and women. In our own traditional culture, until a generation or two ago, men were seen as constitutionally, innately violent and aggressive while women were seen as constitutionally peaceable and mild. Mead reported three New Guinea cultures in which the cultural origins of such tempermental differences were assertedly revealed. The Arapesh of both sexes, men and women, were said by Mead to conform to our own folk stereotype of womanly behavior: peaceable and mild. The Mundugumor of both sexes were said to conform to our own folk stereotype of manly behavior: violent and aggressive. The Tchambuli presented our own folk stereotypes in reverse: their women were violent and aggressive, their men peaceable and mild.

Mead's portrayal of Arapesh males was challenged by her coworker, Reo Fortune (1939). He reported that until it was suppressed by the Germans about 1910, intratribal warfare among the Arapesh was common. Fortune says (1939:27) he took a census of gray-headed men, those presumably old enough to have fought in wars before 1910. About half claimed to have killed at least one in battle. After presenting much case data about particular fights, Fortune (1939:36) rejected Mead's theory of Arapesh male temperament.

Exotic Data Bias. In a brief inspection trip, my wife and I found evidence of this bias in field reports on the Papago and the Nahua (Naroll and Naroll 1963). Some Papago villages are made up of houses scattered among the brush, each thus hidden from the other. But other villages lack brush between the houses; these rather are all in sight of one another. The former pattern is less like our own than the latter. The Papago study of Joseph, Spicer, and Chevsky (1949:60 f.) made much of the former type, describing it as the very archetype of Papago social attitudes. Yet it seems to long-time reservation residents no more common among the Papago than the less exotic types. We were told that the newer settlements are more likely to have brush between the houses; as time goes on, the Papago gradually clear it away. Secondly, Joseph, Spicer and Chevsky (51, 98 f., 122, 124 f., 132 and especially 166) say that the Papago seldom strike their children as punishment for offenses. Our Papago informants insisted that on the contrary the children were spanked whenever necessary "to show them that the old people mean business." Finally, Chevsky says (p. 123) that children are weaned "from eighteen to thirty months." We were told that while this statement was not strictly speaking inaccurate, it was misleading. Our informants insisted that Papago children usually were weaned when the mother was about five months pregnant with her next child; informants said this usually worked out to about eighteen months. However, a woman who did not become pregnant again might not wean her child until he was thirty months old. The impression Chevsky gives is misleading in the direction of greater contrast with the usual American or European practice.

Among the Nahua of Tuxpan, Jalisco, we found similar evidence of exotic bias in the report of Silva (1956). Our informant was not himself a Nahua but was their parish priest, who spoke fluent Nahua and had lived among them for more than thirty years. Silva reports the continued occurrence of three-generation extended family households (p. 47); the priest says this custom has died out, except in cases of advanced age or special difficulty. Silva says that sometimes the parents of a young man still select his bride for him; the priest denies that this happens at all any more. Silva says (p. 66) that the natives use native herbal remedies almost exclusively and very rarely use commercial pharmaceuticals from the drugstore; the priest says that both types are widely used. Thus in effect on all three points, the priest says that Silva presented native behavior as more exotic than it actually is.

After making these findings, my wife and I re-examined our own field reports on Kaunertal in the Austrian Tyrol (R. Naroll 1958, F. Naroll 1959, Naroll and Naroll 1962). In them, we found still more evidence of exotic bias. In them, we paid much attention to land titles for Alpine pastures, communal landrights different from anything we know about in the United States. But we did not look into land titles for croplands, because these seemed to be handled much as they were at home. We paid much attention to wayside shrines, not often found in the United States, but little attention to advertising signs offering Coca-Cola. We said something about the colorful and distinctive band and rifle company uniforms of our village. But we did not mention our visit to the Innsbruck tailoring firm which had designed them for our villagers a few years before. This firm (Lodenbauer) has a library of publications on Tyrolean folklore. If a village without a "traditional" uniform wants one, Lodenbauer designs it for them.

Edmund Carpenter tells me that like biases are common in field reports on the Central Eskimo. Carpenter says Central Eskimo make a great deal of use of manufactured goods bought in trading posts but that their use tends to be played down in field reports.

But these suggestive bits of data on exotic bias among the Papago, the Tuxpan Nahua, the Kaunertalers and the Central Eskimo are handsomely confirmed by an extensive and detailed study of Manu'a by Lowell D. Holmes (1957). Holmes spent five months of the year 1954 in the Manu'a group of Eastern Samoa, and another four months in Pago Pago. His interest focused on a restudy of the work done by Mead in 1925–1926. Holmes (pp. 194 f.) reports four major aspects of acculturation which Mead underemphasized: (1) The importance of Christianity in marriage and funeral ceremonies; (2) the effect of Christianity on the social and political life of Manu'a; (3) the disintegration of the *taupou* system, including the disappearance of a permanent society of unmarried women (*aualuma*); and (4) the importance of government schooling in altering the patterns of enculturation within the home.

Frequency of Field Work Error

Two systematic studies permit some preliminary estimate of the frequency of field work error. By far the more valuable of these is Driver (1936, 1939). Driver's study involved field data on four tribes of the central Pacific Coast of the United States: the Tolowa of Oregon, and the Yurok, Hupa and Karok of northern California. Using two separate informants from each tribe a single ethnographer obtained data on hundreds of traits from the Culture Element Distribution (CED) trait list (see Chapter 32 above). The statistical comparison of their answers constituted the core of Driver's study. Furthermore many of these answers could also

be compared with the reports by one other earlier ethnographer (presumably using other informants, although this is not stated) on each of the four tribes (Driver 1939: 205). Driver found a similar degree of variance between ethnographers as that between informants. Driver found percentages of agreement to range from .84 to .91. He believed the lower range to be the better measure. Driver also found that agreement between informants questioned by a single ethnographer was higher than between those questioned by two different ethnographers. He found further that no one major division of culture (material culture, social culture or religious culture) showed any higher reliability than any other. Large numbers of traits were involved in this study; they ranged from 1366 for the Galice to 2337 for the Yurok. The work of six ethnographers was compared: Driver, Kroeber, Goddard, Barnett, Drucker, and Curtis. The reputation of particular individuals was not called into question; the study thus was free of the emotional and personal undertones inevitably involved in restudies like those of Lewis, Fortune, Holmes, and the Narolls, discussed above.

However, the studies in question always involved at least one large set of data collected from informants not very well known and not very long worked with. This set was of course that for the Culture Element Distribution studies (see above) and involved data collected in brief field visits, of the order of a week or two. Furthermore, this set of the data was memory ethnography: aged informants were recalling the now shattered cultures of their youth. For these reasons, Driver's minimum percentage of agreement—84 per cent—seems like a safe minimum for field work by trained anthropologists.

There is no reason but professional pride and prejudice for anthropologists to assume that missionaries or government officials who lived for years among the people they describe have a greater proportion of errors in their reports than do trained anthropologists. In my earlier study (Naroll 1962:92 f.) I found that missionaries tended to report witchcraft more frequently than professional anthropologists. However—and this is the key point—if these data were controlled for length of stay in the field, the difference disappeared. A. L. Kroeber once said to me in a conversation concerning field data that he believed missionaries as a class were better informed on native cultures than anthropologists.

My wife and I (Naroll and Naroll 1963) found higher percentages of agreement than did Driver in our restudies of Papago and Nahua field reports. We found three discrepancies between our Papago informants' statements and those of Joseph, Spicer and Chevsky (1949) in sixty-six items; the other sixty-three items were confirmed by the informants. Our two informants agreed on all but one of these items. Thus we found 95 per cent agreement between informants and ethnographers; 98 per cent agreement between informants. The differences between our results and Driver's might be explained by: (1) sampling error, since our sample was so small; (2) ongoing ethnography, since our work concerned existing practices, not earlier ones; (3) field time, since Joseph, Spicer and Chevsky had spent an aggregate of more than a year in their Papago work, although ours involved only five days among the Papago; (4) lack of independence, since both our Papago informants had previously read the book by Joseph, Spicer and Chevsky. However, our Nahua work, which yielded quite similar results to our Papago work, was with a single informant who had been entirely unacquainted with Silva's (1956) ethnography.

Thus it appears that by and large ethnographic field reports are upwards of 84 per cent reliable, with 16 per cent or less of random error.

The crucial question for cross-cultural surveys becomes this: What percentage of error is *random* error? What percentage is *systematic bias?* For restudies may be taken as reasonable measures of random error. But they can be taken as measures of bias only where the two observers can be assumed to have differing biases. Restudies then are studies of reliability, not of validity. In other words, they are studies of consistency, not of accuracy.

Random Error and Bias

By a random error, I mean an error no more likely to be made in one direction than in another, nor to be any greater in one direction than another. Putting this idea into mathematical terms, a repetitive random error in a series of observations is defined as an error with net expectation of zero. A bias is defined as an error with a nonzero expectation. Thus a random error is one of a set of errors such that they tend to cancel each other out. A bias, on the other hand, is one of a set which tend to cumulate—a systematic error.

These two kinds of errors have radically different effects upon correlations. Random errors usually tend to lower correlations. If in fact two variables are correlated, random error in observations made on them will usually tend to lower the absolute value of the correlation coefficient; given enough random errors, the coefficient will usually tend to approach zero. A bias or systematic error in one but only one of two variables being correlated has a similar effect and, likewise, tends to make the absolute value of the correlation coefficient approach zero.

Hence, evidence of random error in a body of data of a cross-cultural survey or any other kind of study is usually evidence which paradoxically strengthens rather than weakens the case for any statistically significant correlations which that study might observe. For the clear implication is usually that if such errors had not been made, in all likelihood the correlation coefficients would have been even higher! This conclusion always holds good unless the random error made in one variable observation is somehow correlated with the other variable. Technically, it is possible to define a situation such that an error so correlated could be random, could have an expectation of zero—see below.

Our quality control problem then reduces itself to two cases.

First, the biased report. Consider witchcraft attribution, for example. In many societies where witchcraft is important, there is a tendency for informants to deny any knowledge of it. A man may be afraid of retaliation by witches if the witches think he talks too much. A man may be afraid of seeming knowledgeable about witchcraft because others may say he himself is a witch. Or he may simply view the whole topic with anxiety and discomfort and seek to avoid that embarrassing topic by denying he knows anything about it. These tendencies taken together mean that unwary field workers are likely to make the mistake of thinking witchcraft is not important when in fact it is. But there do not seem to be any contrary tendencies in other societies which would lead other anthropologists to think that witchcraft is important when in fact it is not.

Now consider weaning age. In many societies like the Papago, the people do not have any strong feelings about how old a child should be before his mother weans him from her breast; yet they *do* consider it unwise for a woman to be suckling more than one child at a time. Consequently their women usually wean one child when they are about five months pregnant with the next. Among the Papago and many other people, this system means that most children are weaned before they are two. The *last* child of any woman may not be weaned until he is even five or six years old.

An observer from the Western world in the last hundred years is used to children being weaned by the time they are two—often much earlier. Now take for example a man interested in formal kinship structure —clan organization, kinship terminology, and the like. He may give comparatively little time to studying the life cycle in general, or child-rearing in particular. Such an observer, among a people like the Papago, will tend to give more attention to four- and five-year-old children he sees suckling at the mother's breast than to eighteen-month-old children he sees chewing solid food. The suckling five-year-olds strike him as strange and exotic but the chewing toddlers strike him as natural and nothing out of the ordinary.

Less thorough and less accurate observers, then, are likely to underestimate the importance of witchcraft and overestimate weaning age. Might not such systematic tendencies, taken together, make for a spurious correlation? Might not a stream of such errors, coded and tabulated as hard facts, make it seem that in many tribes late weaning goes along with the absence of witchcraft? Certainly, in their study of *Child Training and Personality,* Whiting and Child (1953:283) reported such a correlation. They took this correlation to be evidence supporting an important theory in social psychology. There may in fact be such a correlation. But there is every reason for us to question

these findings until we are reassured that they are not simply a reflection of systematic factual errors—biases—in the field reports of anthropologists and other writers. In other words, a parallel bias in the data reports on both variables of a correlation can, if large enough theoretically, produce a spurious correlation. Such parallel biases then make up the first of our two chief data quality control problems in cross-cultural surveys.

The second of these data quality control problems seems far less menacing to me. This problem is that of *the correlated random error.* I know of no plausible example in the field data I have studied; I can only invent an imaginary one. Let us assume that ethnographers are as likely to overestimate population counts as to underestimate them. Let us also assume that ethnographers are as likely to list too many craft specialties as they are to list too few.

Finally, let us assume that city-bred anthropologists tend to *under*estimate both population counts and craft specialty counts while country-bred anthropologists tend similarly to *over*estimate both. In such a state of things, reports by city-bred anthropologists would tend to be higher on both variables, reports by country-bred anthropologists would tend to be lower. And so these tendencies taken together would make for a spurious correlation between craft specialty count and population count. Yet if there were equal numbers of both kinds of anthropologists, these errors would have a zero expectation.

There is, of course, one special case of the correlated random error which every well-trained behavioral scientist is on the watch for. That is the coding error where coders are aware of the theory or hypothesis being tested and interpret the doubtful cases consistently with that theory. This is, of course, usually guarded against by keeping coders ignorant of the purpose of the study.

THE CONTROL FACTOR METHOD

Control Factor Defined

I turn now to the control factor method of guarding against spurious correlations resulting from parallel bias or correlated random error. By a *control factor* is meant a characteristic of the data collection process which is related—or thought to be related— to the accuracy of the final data coding.

For example, most of us think that the longer an anthropologist stays in the field, the more complete and accurate his report is likely to be. Many anthropologists think that the better a field worker knows a native language, the more complete and accurate his report is likely to be. Many think that the more fully a field worker takes part in the daily life of the natives, the more complete and accurate his report is likely to be. Length of stay, native language familiarity, degree of participation are three examples of what I mean by control factors.

In this paper, when I speak of a *control factor,* then, I mean some characteristic of the data reporting process used as a variable in the hope that it will measure reporting bias. When I speak of a *trait,* on the other hand, I mean some variable intended to measure the behavior of the natives being studied. Thus ethnographer's length of stay in the field, his knowledge of the native language, his use of native assistants and the length of his report are examples of control factors. Suicide rate, settlement size, divorce rules and warfare characteristics are examples of traits.

Sources of Error

There are three distinct sources of error in cross-cultural surveys. These three error sources correspond to the three stages of the data collection process. The first source is in the mind of the informant. The second source is in the mind of the ethnographer. The third source is in the mind of the comparativist. For each of the three stages in the data collection process of a cross-cultural survey, there may well be specially related control factors. *Degree of participation* might well be related to frequency of informant error. In other words, the more fully an ethnographer takes part in the daily life of the natives, the more likely he presumably is to detect errors or misunderstanding which mislead his informants and give them an inaccurate mental picture of their own culture. The more complex and diverse a culture, the greater the likelihood of informant error. Use of probability sampling methods, stratified by area, greatly reduces the likelihood of such error; in very small societies, ethnographers may take a complete census, interviewing every member of the society. Use of such *census or sampling*

methods would presumably then also be related to informant error. In other words, we suppose as a working hypothesis that informant errors are less common and less serious in ethnographic reports based on extensive participation than those based on little or no participation; and less common and less serious in ethnographic reports based on probability samples or complete censuses than on those based on unsystematic selection of informants.

I turn now to the second stage of the data collection process—the ethnographer's mind. Ethnographers' errors might result from careless observation, incomplete or vaguely worded notes or careless and hasty writing of field reports. The evidence so far before us points also to field workers' gullibility as one of the chief sources of ethnographers' error. Informants may deliberately mislead ethnographers maliciously. They may do so to avoid an embarrassing topic or to keep themselves out of trouble. Or very often they may do so simply from politeness or from a desire to be pleasant: they tell the questioner what they think he wants to hear.

Two major precautions are usually taken by good field workers to guard against this kind of ethnographer's error. First, they question a number of informants about the same topics and compare their answers. This technique is most highly developed by military intelligence interrogators. A prisoner of war has an unusually strong motive to deceive his questioner. So a good intelligence officer begins by asking his prisoner about obscure facts the questioner already knows. The second precaution is equally important. The ethnographer selects a few people he believes especially knowledgeable and sympathetic and makes them his close personal friends. He "gains rapport," gains their confidence and trust, he leads them to value his friendship. Thus they are put in the position of having something to lose by misleading him and nothing to lose by confiding in him.

Length of stay seems one good measure of the rapport developed by a field worker with his informants, since such intimate relationships often take time to build up. *Native language familiarity* seems another good measure, since without it the informant must talk in a contact language foreign to him, or even worse, through an interpreter. Working through an interpreter is difficult and requires that the interpreter be carefully trained to give accurate interpretation—but worse than that, the interpreter is automatically a third person and thus makes the intimate two-person group impossible. "Under four eyes" say the Germans for a thing told in confidence. Confidence often disappears when they are not merely four eyes, but six.

Finally, there is the problem of comparativist's error. We ought first to consider the possibility of deliberate fraud. The Piltdown hoax reminds us of the pains some men will take to steal a scientific reputation. Among professional social scientists today, salary raises, promotion, tenure, job offers from more desirable employers—all these are often tied directly or indirectly to scientific publication.

It is, of course, easy to imagine a conspiracy among an investigator and his coders. The coders are told of the hypothesis being tested but are persuaded to keep this fact secret. They systematically bias the codings in favor of the investigator's hypothesis and compare their work in order to achieve high "reliability" ratings. All this is concealed and the investigator tells his public that on the contrary they worked independently and in ignorance of his theory. To an experienced policeman or police reporter, such a conspiracy would seem nothing out of the ordinary in the annals of crime. The main difficulty for the investigator scheming such a plot is to make the plan interesting enough to his coders. *His* rewards are uncertain and delayed. What is in it for the coders? And how can he stop their mouths later on from the belittling gossip which is the delight of academicians no less than other human beings? While I do *not* suspect that any such fraud has actually been committed, it is well for us to be on our guard.

There is a simple and age-old voucher to protect us from such frauds. Far more importantly, this voucher protects us against work which, although entirely honest and ethical, is careless and superficial in its data coding work. Careless and superficial data coding may unwittingly help the comparativist's subconscious mind to deceive his conscious mind as well as the mind of the reader. The voucher I have in mind is the classic voucher of humanistic scholarship, the precise source citation. For each coding, data source should be cited by page (see Chapter 40, for example). By spot-checking, it is then easy for a reader to catch sloppy work or

far-fetched interpretations—not to speak of actual cheating! Good vouchers make for more than good accounting; they make for honest and careful agents.

Unfortunately, the custom has grown of tabulating traits by tribe without giving any particular source citation. Sources are usually cited as in Murdock (1949:353) or Whiting and Child (1953:330) only for each tribe as a whole. If, for example, the reader wishes to check Murdock's classification of Zulu kinship terminology, the reader must search through all the works on the Zulu listed in Murdock's bibliography. In practice, then, only those who are already expert on the Zulu are likely to evaluate the trustworthiness of such coding. In contrast, the citations by Udy (1959:143) or Naroll (1962:142) tell the reader the particular pages on which the codings are based.

Well-trained, naïve, conscientious and independent coders may well be security against systematic bias stimulated by the investigator's theory. But they by no means guard against other sorts of systematic bias. Independent codings which strongly tend to agree with each other are said to be highly "reliable" but we know that in this sense *reliable* does not mean *trustworthy*, it only means *consistent*. The coders, commonly graduate students of a single academic discipline of a single university of a single city of a single society, share many common preconceptions and biased attitudes; they may well in all good faith and despite all training and skill consistently bias their codings. The tremendous power of a culture to consistently impose illusion has just lately been strikingly demonstrated in a cross-cultural study of optical illusions (Segal, Campbell and Herskovits 1966). These illusions, classic elements in the repertoire of experimental psychologists, affect people of different cultures to different extents. Certain illusions consistently fool urban Americans more than they fool primitive Bushmen; certain other illusions consistently fool Bushmen more than urban Americans. And these are simple illusions, simple line drawings! What about the illusions cast by verbal descriptions of vague social structures and vague moral attitudes?

To detect all sorts of bias by comparativists —at least all save mere fraud and forgery— a simple control factor seems clearly useful. That is the degree of precision and *clarity* —or in reverse, the degree of ambiguity and vagueness—*in the ethnographers' report*. I first used this test on my own codings of a pilot study. Of four traits thus tested, one showed a coding bias of mine at a 1 per cent significance level (Naroll 1962:97). Whatever else the comparativist and his staff are, if they are not consciously dishonest liars, their coding biases will affect the vague and ambiguous statements in their sources more than they will the clear and precise ones.

Sheer *length of ethnographer's report* is another factor whch seems likely to prove useful in detecting coding biases. This factor would seem appropriate where the variable being coded is almost never directly described by ethnographic reports but only inferred from their general drift or tenor by coders. One supposes on the average that the longer the report, the richer the data and less likely the bias.

Possible Control Factors

In the discussion of sources of error, I spoke in passing of six possible control factors. Actually, there are many more which might well prove useful. In the War, Stress and Culture sample quality control study, information was sought on a total of twenty-five such factors, as follows:

1. *Author's Role*

In what capacity did the author acquire his information? native of the culture? anthropologist? missionary? government official? trader? other?

2. *Field Time*

How many months did the author spend among the people? If there was a research team involved, how many people took part, and how many months did each stay in the field? Were the months consecutive or not? (For example, did the author spend six consecutive months or three months each for two summers?)

3. *Period of Work*

3.1. When was the author born? How old was he when he began field work?

3.2. When was the work written? When first published? Where some years have elasped between the completion of field work and the write-up, did the author state this lapse explicitly? Did he give a reason for this lapse?

4. *Field Experience*

Had the author previous field experience? How long? Where? When? Did he utilize

comparison with this previously studied group (groups) in describing his current field study?

5. *Field Team Composition*

How many persons composed the field team (*excluding* native assistants or non-team persons such as helpful missionaries, government officials, or resident Europeans)? What was the sex of each? What was the sex of the author? Was he accompanied by his spouse? By his child or children? If the latter, how many of what age?

6. *Nationality*

Where was the author born? Where did he grow up? What citizenship did he hold? Where was he educated? Likewise all other members of the field team.

7. *University*

What university did the author attend? What degrees did he hold? In what subject? Did he hold this degree before he began field work?

8. *Professor*

Who was/were the author's graduate professors? Whom did he cite as most influential in his education or intellectual development?

N.B. Where available, all above traits should be sought for each field team member.

9. *Financial Support*

From whom did the author secure financial support for his study? from a government? from a university? from a foundation? from a religious organization? from private resources? other?

10. *Purpose of Field Study*

Did the author indicate any purpose or goal of this field study? Any specific issue(s) which he proposed to investigate? for example the economic or kinship system. Was the study part of a program of study toward a graduate degree?

11. *Choice of Tribe*

Why was this particular culture or tribe chosen? Was it the author's personal choice? Choice of the author's academic superiors? Choice of other person or agency? What grounds for the choice were given? Was it first choice?

12. *Choice of Community*

Why was this particular community chosen for study? Was it the author's own choice or that of an outside source? Was it the first choice? What grounds were given?

13. *Number of Communities*

How many communities did the author visit? Did he name each of them? How much time did he spend in each?

14. *Personal Feelings*

Did the author indicate any personal feelings about the culture or the natives? Positive, negative, or neutral? Did he indicate personal feelings about some practice or culture trait? personality characteristics? other?

15. *Theoretical Orientation*

Did the author reveal any theoretical interests which might affect his study?
15.1. Did he see the people he studied as especially noble? especially depraved?
15.2. Did he see them as an instance of a social evolutionary stage?
15.3. Did he reveal any interest in economic theory, such as Marxism, or Social Darwinism?
15.4. Did he reveal any interest in psychological theory, such as Freudian theory?
15.5. Did he reveal any other particular interest or orientation such as medicine, law, or other?
15.6. Was the author's selection of topics influenced more by the orientation of the culture studied or by his own theoretical orientation?

16. *Native Language Familiarity*

What evidence did the author present of his familiarity with the native language?
16.1. What did he claim? Did he claim knowledge of the language? How did he qualify this claim?
16.2. Did he claim knowledge of a contact language? What was the extent of his claim?
16.3. Were there any indications that he carried on conversations in the native language? Was an interpreter used? always? Was the interpreter a native speaker? Did the author indicate the ability to check on the accuracy of the interpreter, though not himself fluent? Did he ever dispense with the interpreter? Did he ever take notes in the native language?
16.4. Did the author use native terms in the text? In the table of contents? In the index? How many words are in the table of contents? How many of these are native terms? How many words are in the index? How many of these are native terms?
16.5. Did the author include a glossary of word lists? How many words are given in such lists? Did the author include native language texts? With translation? How many words? Did the author claim to have recorded language texts or word lists although he did not include them in the text? Did he refer to other linguistic publications of his own?
16.6. Was there evidence that he translated any text into the native language? e.g. the Bible.

17. *Native Assistants*

Did the author use native assistants other than informants in his field work? In what capacity? How many? How were they paid? If he traveled to more than one community, did they accompany him? How did the author speak of native assistants? Did he discuss them as individuals? Did he skeptically assess their abilities to execute their duties? Did he indicate how much they contributed to the study?

18. *Non-Native Assistants*

Was the author assisted by persons outside the field team who were not natives? Who? e.g. trader? missionary? government official? resident European? (If the last, what was his role: plantation owner? retired colonial official? other?) Did the author skeptically assess the assistance or qualifications of such outside assistants?

19. *Informants*

Did the author name informants? How many informants did he name? Did he indicate there were others which he has left unnamed? Were statements identified as given by particular informants? All or most statements? or just those on which informants differ? Were informants paid? In what? e.g. trade goods? money? food? other? Did the author skeptically assess the qualifications of his informants?

20. *Field Station*

Where did the author/team live while conducting investigation? Within or without the community? In what sort of residence? e.g., government resthouse? mission? resident European's household? native household? native-style house? other? If within the community, where in relation to natives? on the edge of the village? in the center? or where? Note any observations made by the author on the advantages or disadvantages of the field station location.

21. *Genealogical Method*

Did the author use the genealogical method of inquiry? Did he reproduce genealogies in the text, or did he just state the use of this method? How many genealogies were reproduced? How many were taken?

22. *Participation*

22.1. Did the author visit the people about whom he writes? Did he consult secondary works exclusively or primarily? If the data are based primarily on field work, did the author refer to other works on these people? Did he consult informants who were native of the culture but not visit the place from which they came?

22.2. Did the author witness ceremonies? Did he participate in any ceremonies?

22.3. Did the author share meals with natives? occasionally or frequently? Did he live in the community he studied? in an occupied native household or in a separate residence?

22.4. Did the author assume some native economic, political, marital, military, or kinship role?

22.5. Was the author associated intimately with natives from early childhood, thus providing him with an ambicultural background?

22.6. Was the author born a native of that culture? If so, when (if ever) did he leave the culture, before returning for ethnographic field data?

23. *Enumeration*

Did the author use systematic investigation of quantitative data? For example, did he conduct a systematic census? Did he collect household budgets? Did he use systematic enumeration in any other way?

24. *Earlier Ethnographers*

Did the author refer to the works of earlier ethnographers? Was he critical of their work? Did he dispute specific statements? Did he corroborate specific statements?

25. *Wordage*

How many pages is the book? How many pages of actual text, excluding appendices, indexes, etc.? What is estimated total wordage?

A somewhat similar list was compiled by Hesung Koh (1966:157–159). Her system was aimed at being generally useful for any kind of social science source material rather than specifically aimed at ethnologists. Her list follows:

1. AUTHOR
   (a) sex
   (b) age
   (c) status (nationality, etc.)
   (d) professional training
   (e) role of the author (e.g. missionary, colonial officer, etc.)
   (f) knowledge of research language
   (g) world view, value orientation, interest, attitude, emotional state, assumption
   (h) previous works and experiences (publications, field work experiences, travel, etc.)
   (i) information concerning other research personnel, such as co-authors, interpreters, assistants, interviewers, etc.
   (j) research organization

2. SUBJECT OF INVESTIGATION
   (a) Subject coverage (following some social science classification system)
      (i) scope
      (ii) intensity of coverage
   (b) Unit identification
      (i) name and alternative names of the unit
      (ii) geographical location—general and specific
      (iii) population size, geographical area, boundary and other demographic data
      (iv) political unit identification
      (v) nature and characteristics of the unit (e.g. state, community, association, etc.)
      (vi) relationship with larger or related unit (e.g. suzerainty relationship)
      (vii) function of unit (e.g. clan studied is the primary unit of social control)
   (c) Time
      (i) time period covered
      (ii) field date
      (iii) number of years in the field (and also number of times in the field)
   (d) Language of the cultural group
      (i) major linguistic stock
      (ii) other languages

3. OBJECTIVES (implicit or explicit)
   (a) types of goals (propaganda, journalistic reports, policy-oriented or pure research, etc.)
   (b) hypothesis (if any)

4. RESEARCH METHOD
   (a) type of method used (field method, documentary method, combination, no method)
   (b) source (informants, oral tradition, folklore, types of documents used)
   (c) techniques used (e.g. interviewing, questionnaire, participant observation, sampling, etc.)
   (d) method of organization (any frame of

reference used, such as psychoanalytic
study)

(e) degree of documentation

(f) others (such as definition of concepts
used, etc.)

5. CONDITION OF RESEARCH

(a) author's definition of the situation (e.g.
friendly, unfriendly; war, fear of attack,
etc.)

(b) source of financial support

(c) time lapse between the field work and
the publication

6. RESEARCH RESULTS

(a) levels of organization (e.g. descriptive,
interpretative, theoretical, etc.)

Validating Control Factors

Intuitive Value of Some Control Factors. I
have just reviewed three stages in the data
collection process for cross-cultural surveys.
In these studies, data generally flow first
through the informant's mind, second through
the ethnographer's mind, and third through
the comparativist's mind. (Of course, *some*
data are directly observed by the ethnographer, and the comparativist himself may
well have firsthand knowledge of one or two
of the societies in his sample.)

For each of these stages, I have discussed
two control factors which have wide informal
acceptance in the profession. We take it for
granted that the greater the degree of participation by an ethnographer in native life,
the more he is likely to know about some
aspects of it. We take it for granted that a
systematic census or—in larger societies—
representative sample gives a more accurate
image of a society than dealings only with
people who are convenient to reach. We take
it for granted that the longer an ethnographer
stays in a community, the better he knows it
and the more expert on it he becomes. We
take it for granted that an ethnographer who
deals with the natives in their own language
is likely to know more about them than one
who does not. We take it for granted that a
comparativist is less likely to misclassify a
clear and precise statement than a vague and
ambiguous one. We take it for granted that
as a rule the longer a report is, the more
information it has.

We can all quickly think of exceptions to
these foregoing tendencies. Although Ruth
Benedict (1946) had never been to Japan, in

The Chrysanthemum and the Sword she told
us more about basic Japanese value orientations—especially those concerning personal
feelings of obligation—than many other writers who spent years in Japan. F. E. Williams
(1930:v) knew little of the Orokaiva language but his field report on Orokaiva society
is widely respected. By mere innuendo and
literary craftsmanship, Edmund Carpenter's
account (1960) of a Central Eskimo gives us
a more vivid and in many ways clearer report on a human being embedded in his
cultural setting than do many other less personal and more matter of fact accounts of
other men in other cultural settings. Perhaps
the most voluminous report on any primitive
tribe is the "five-foot shelf" of monographs on
the Kwakiutl by Franz Boas; for some purposes no doubt its wealth of loosely organized trivia is invaluable; but most comparativists have found this body of work extremely difficult to use because in it the trees
so effectively hide the forest. Another example: I looked in vain through Raymond
Firth's three celebrated reports (1936, 1939,
1940) on the Tikopia for a complete outline
of Tikopian formal social organization but
later on found it all neatly set forth in the
brief preliminary report he published (1930)
just after he got back from his first visit.

Nevertheless, despite these exceptions, the
six control factors just reviewed have, I think,
strong intuitive support. Until someone demonstrates the contrary, most of us, guided by
"common sense" and everyday experience with
our own observations of human affairs, will
still continue to take it for granted that together they form the *skeleton*—although
perhaps not the *heart* and *mind*—of good
field work.

Formal Validation of Control Factors. "Common sense" and everyday experience often are
wrong, however. Common sense led everyone
to believe that a ten-pound iron ball would fall
faster than a one-pound iron ball—until Galileo showed the contrary. "Common sense"
and everyday observation tell us that the earth
is flat, that the sun moves across the sky every
day, and the stars every night. Scientific progress has a way of making huge leaps forward
when basic "common-sense" propositions
seemingly supported by everyday experience
are shown up as false.

So we must seek for methods of testing
these and other propositions about field work,

in order to confirm or correct these "common-sense" beliefs and in order to find other sources of systematic error—of bias or correlated random error.

The control factor method of data quality control treats any supposed control factor like length of stay or native language familiarity as itself a hypothesis to be tested. The test consists in correlating the supposed control factor with some trait which the investigator believes is likely to be the subject of systematic error—like witchcraft attribution reports or weaning length reports. Under "Possible Control Factors," above, are listed a large number of observation conditions. Any of these may or may not prove to be a valid control factor. Research on data quality control itself is needed to test these hypotheses. Such research then consists in looking for bias-sensitive control factors and bias-sensitive traits. The studies by Walton (1966) and Gilbert (1968) discussed above (p. 927) are good examples of successful control factor validation. Ideally, the investigator predicts in advance a correlation between, for example, length of stay of ethnographer and importance of witchcraft in his field report. He then makes a cross-cultural survey to test this hypothesis.

In this way, correlations between conditions of observations (control factors) and types of trait reports can presumably be established. However, these correlations still need to be explained. A correlation between length of stay and witchcraft attribution reports might well reflect the "common-sense" interpretation that longer-stayers tend to report witchcraft attribution accurately while shorter stayers tend to overlook it. But in itself, this correlation equally well supports the contrary, "common-nonsensical" theory that shorter-stayers tend to report witchcraft attribution accurately while longer-stayers tend to exaggerate it. And there is a third, equally important possibility. It may be that this correlation reflects *no errors at all*; it may mean only this: societies with much witchcraft attribution are themselves more interesting, or tend to occur in more comfortable, pleasant and attractive surroundings, and so encourage ethnographers to stay longer among them; societies with little witchcraft are less interesting, or tend to be found in difficult and unpleasant places, and so dis-

courage ethnographers from staying long among them.

The way to solid scientific data quality control is thus a hard and long way—not a straight highway easily driven but a faint footpath through thicket and marsh. The thickets will be cleared; the swamps filled; the highway paved only when: (1) a number of bias-sensitive traits are found clearly correlated with a number of bias-sensitive control factors; and (2) the correlation matrix among all these variables is carefully analyzed for causal interrelations. Only thus can our tentative hypotheses about the nature and conditions of systematic error be confirmed.

The massive *Cross-Cultural Summary* (Textor 1968) includes two data quality control factor validation tests. (These are discussed at length in Chapter 34 above.) The two factors tested were (a) ethnographer's nationality and (b) ethnographer's time provenience. Thus the first factor tested for bias differing between ethnographers of one nationality and those of another—for example, between English field workers and American ones, or between French ethnographers and non-French ones. No evidence of such bias was found. Many differences in reporting patterns were observed, but these seemed readily explainable either by random variation among the very large number of correlations examined or by sampling biases among the nationalities. Thus American ethnographers, for example, tend to study North American tribes and thus their field reports as a group tend to reflect the cultural characteristics of these tribes. For example, collectively the tribes studied by North American ethnographers are more likely to live by hunting and gathering than those studied by ethnographers of other nationalities. The second factor which Textor tested for bias, ethnographer's time provenience, found no clear evidence of associated reporting bias. However, there was one tentative suggestion. There seems to be a clear tendency for ethnographies published before 1930 to differ from those published after 1930 on the role of high gods in public morality. Of the five ethnographies published before 1930 which reported a belief in high gods, three reported that such gods were *not* believed to support human morality; in contrast, all seventeen ethnographies published after 1930 reported that such gods were indeed believed to support human morality. (One would expect so great a difference to arise by chance less than seven times in a thousand random samples from a universe in which no real difference exists.) Two explanations for this difference seem plausible. (1) It may be that ethnographers publishing before 1930 tended to overlook the role of high gods in supporting public morality. If so, date of publication would have empirical support as a data quality control factor. Or (2) it may be that under the widespread influence of Christianity, in the early twentieth century the role of high gods in native religions tended to be expanded to include support for public morality. If so, the correlation would be telling us nothing about reporting bias, and thus nothing about the value of ethnographer's time provenience as a quality control factor. (But it *would* of course be telling us something important about diffusion of religious beliefs.)

Using Control Factors to "Clear" Trait Data

The ultimate use for control factors lies in their "clearing" particular traits or particular trait correlations from the suspicion of bias. If a control factor is presumed by "common sense" or better still shown by formal test to be in fact bias-sensitive, it is correlated with the traits of interest to the investigator. If there fails to be a substantial correlation between the control factor and the trait thus being controlled, a presumption is created that the trait being controlled is not substantially bias-sensitive and that hence correlations of that trait with other traits being investigated are not artifacts of reporting bias.

The same procedure may be used to control for correlated random errors. Let us return to our imaginary example of correlated random error between population reports and craft specialty counts. We imagined a tendency for city-bred anthropologists to underestimate both and a compensating tendency for country-bred anthropologists to overestimate both. Using "population of ethnographer's childhood home" as a control factor would reveal the error.

What if in fact both traits whose correlation interests an investigator are also correlated with a data quality control factor? Or likewise if a control factor test for correlated

random error shows the hit/miss dichotomy correlated with a control factor?

These results tend to *discredit* the correlation as a test of the theoretical hypothesis of intrinsic interest to the investigator. (They do, however, tend to *support* the hypothesis that the control factor is a useful tool in data quality control.) The investigator's attitude toward such a correlation may well be much like the industrial quality control engineer's attitude toward *his* statistical quality control tests (Duncan 1955). Both types of quality control, whatever their other differences, perform rigorous statistical tests looking for trouble. In both types of quality control, those who perform the tests hope these tests will turn out *un*interestingly. In quality control, those people look for trouble but hope they won't find any. Perhaps in this way a statistical quality control test is a bit like an alpinist's test of a glacier as he walks across it. He keeps probing the snow in front of him with his stick, probing for soft spots, for thinly covered crevasses. He hopes he will not find any. If he does, he has a problem. But not so much of a problem as if he had not probed first and only discovered the crevasse when he fell into it!

What can an investigator do if he has quality control trouble? That depends. The alpinist who finds a crevasse may be able to bridge it. Or he may be able to go around it. Or he may simply have to turn around and go back, if the crevasse is too wide, too deep and too long.

The investigator who has quality control trouble has, it seems to me, one of three possible ways out of his difficulty.

(1) He may feel justified in treating the control factor correlation as a measure of bias. This attitude would follow from a conviction that *some* of the reporters he is following are completely trustworthy and perfectly accurate. Given a feeling of entire confidence in the best group of reporters in his sample, the investigator can compute partial correlations, and thus determine the extent of relationship remaining between the traits of intrinsic interest, after allowing for the reporting bias. *N.B.* Unless the investigator is satisfied his correlations are linear, he should use non-parametric, partial correlations. See Kendall 1962:117–123; Quade 1967; and Naroll n.d.$_b$.

(2) Causal analysis of the relationship be-

tween the intrinsic traits and the control factor may support the hypothesis that at least one of these correlations reflects an actual association and not a reporting error at all. This would occur, for example, if an investigator explained a correlation between witchcraft attribution and length of stay by showing that in fact tribes which had more witchcraft attribution tended to attract ethnographers to stay longer among them.

(3) The investigator may be able to reconceptualize and recode at least one of his intrinsic traits in such a way as to eliminate the bias and thus eliminate the correlation with the control factor. (Obviously, the recoding should be done for him by naïve coders who do not know about the control factor problem he faces.)

If none of these three methods of dealing with the bias problem can be used, the investigator is baffled. He is in the position of the alpinist who can neither bridge nor go around a crevasse. Like the alpinist, he is frustrated but still better off than if he had fallen into the chasm.

The reader may wonder whether he might not always treat the control factor as a measure of bias. It cannot be so used if in fact all the reporters are subject to the bias in question, since there is no way to know how much of the bias is undetected.

Our quality control is strongest when the quality of our sources varies most. We should have a goodly proportion of sources—of the order of 10 per cent, perhaps—which have described the traits in question as trustworthily as possible; our top 10 per cent of sources should reflect the most rigorous and careful observation conditions. But our other sources should decrease in quality until the bottom 10 per cent reflects the poorest observation conditions represented in the literature. In this way we are most likely to discover systematic bias.

THE WAR, STRESS AND CULTURE STUDY

The cross-cultural sample described in Chapter 43, above, was studied with respect to about one hundred traits as well as the twenty-five control factors listed above. Variant codings on many traits raised the total number of traits correlated with the control factors to about two hundred and twenty-five. The number of nominally significant correlations did not exceed those theoretically expectable by chance. That is to say, not more than about 5 per cent of the correlations thus run were nominally significant at the 5 per cent level.

It is not yet at all clear what this result means. As pointed out in Chapter 34, in fact we really have to expect substantially fewer correlations from fourfold contingency tables (phi coefficients) than those predicted by theory. From the purely random-numbers "Whiskers" variables of Textor's, far less than 1 per cent of the correlations proved nominally significant at the 1 per cent level. This discrepancy in the case of the phi coefficients arises from the fact that the distribution of probabilities of the various possible arrangements in a contingency table is discrete rather than continuous.

Consider, for example, Table 1.

With the marginal totals given in that table, there are five possible outcomes of any trial of a hypothesis involving a correlation between two traits. Suppose that we predict a negative correlation between them. The most supportive outcome would be to find no cases at all in which both traits are present, a result significant at the .001032 level. Thus it is not possible for any outcome at all to be significant at the .001 level; it is not possible with these marginals to attain that level of significance no matter how high the true correlation is in the universe sampled. The next most favorable outcome would be to find only one case in which both traits were present, a result significant at the .031992 level. After that comes the outcome in which there were two cases where the traits were both present, a result significant at the .248710 level. The key point to grasp firmly in mind is here. This test cannot produce a result which just barely attains significance at the .05 level, or just barely misses significance at the .05 level. We cannot expect this particular set of marginals to yield results nominally significant at the 5 per cent level in more than 3.1992 per cent of trials. Either it does somewhat better than 5 per cent, or much, much worse. This state of affairs presumably goes far to explain the discrepancies between the theoretically expectable results of Textor's "Whiskers" values and the much lower frequencies of nominally significant values which Textor actually obtained.

So it is hard to say whether the number of nominally significant correlations on our data

TABLE 1

Trait "A"

		Present	Absent	Total
	Present	A	B	15
Trait "B"	Absent	C	D	5
	Total	4	16	20

Cell "A"	Cell "B"	Cell "C"	Cell "D"	Fisher's Exact Probability
0	15	0	1	.001032
1	14	3	2	.031992
2	13	2	3	.248710
3	12	1	4	.718226
4	11	0	5	1.000000

Source of Probabilities: Lieberman and Owen 1962:58, for values of N=20, n=16, k=5.

quality control tests can be explained away as the result of mere chance or if in fact it reflects some real relationship between some of the traits and some of the control factors.

All I can do now is to report the traits and the control factors which tended to produce the highest number of nominally significant correlations. These traits and factors, then, are the ones which are likely to be bias-sensitive, if any are.

At this writing (October, 1969), I am still working on the analysis of the bias-sensitivity of these traits and control factors. This *Handbook* has to go to press now. I am not yet ready to present firm results, correlation matrices and data tables.

To presume the traits and control factors I am about to discuss to be bias-sensitive is a cautious and conservative procedure. For a cross-culturalist to make this presumption where he tests other hypotheses is to presume the presence of bias where these traits and factors are concerned. This means the cross-culturalist should distrust generalizations made from correlations involving two presumably bias-sensitive traits listed below, or involving other traits found correlated with the presumably bias-sensitive control factors listed below.

Bias-Sensitive Traits

Seven traits seem to be especially bias-sensitive:

Craft Specialization. The number of formal statuses of manufacture or repair of durable artifacts.

Europeanization. Number of years elapsed between date of first European contact and midyear of dates of field work by author of major sources used.

Military Expectations. A five-item Guttman scale of expectations of successful warriors. First level—none at all. Second level—territorial defense. Third level—also subsistence wealth. Fourth level—also prestige. Fifth level —also political control (Naroll n.d.$_a$).

Suicide Wordage. Total number of words about suicide written by author of principle source of information on suicide.

Aggression Index. A Likert scale of the dichotomized scores of the following traits: (1) suicide wordage, as just defined; (2) homicide wordage, defined in the same way; (3) witchcraft—scored present if either of two conditions were met: (a) persons were reported executed as a punishment for witchcraft, or (b) deaths more frequently reported due to witchcraft than due to the activities of spirits; (4) wife-beating—scored present if explicitly reported, scored absent only if explicitly denied; (5) drunken brawling—scored present if people were reported to engage in brawls after drinking intoxicating liquors, but scored absent if use of intoxicating liquors were reported but brawls were unreported; and (6) dog-beating—scored like wife-beating.

Exchange Scale. A complex index of tendency for societies to accumulate wealth. Societies were classed I. as simple, dual or complex social class systems; II. as depending

(a) little or none, (b) moderately, or (c) chiefly upon agriculture or animal husbandry for subsistence; and III. as distributing goods and services (a) chiefly through the principle of reciprocity or (b) chiefly through either market exchange or redistribution or both. (The concepts for item III come from Polanyi 1944.) Scores on this scale were highly correlated with the craft specialty count.

Territorial Change. Where territorial change was reported, the area of original occupancy and the reported gain or loss was mapped as well as might be and the ratio of gain or loss computed. The aim was to compute the gain ratio or loss ratio over a one-hundred-year period. Sources were often vague and many standard presumptions needed to be made. Particularly, where no change was reported in certain common circumstances, it was presumed that no change took place. Evidently these coding procedures involved an important systematic bias of some kind.

Bias-Sensitive Control Factors

1. *Scholarship.* Presence in ethnography of citation to works of earlier ethnographers. Seems to be highly correlated with measures of warfare frequency, military expectations and territorial growth, as well as with sampling types.

2. *Native Language Familiarity.* There seems to be a threshold here, beyond which increasing claims of native language familiarity (NLF) do not constitute an effective control factor. A seven-level scale of NLF was tried. But the most sensitive measure of native language familiarity, in terms of correlations with substantive traits, turned out to be a simple dichotomy: on one hand, those ethnographers who had no claims at all to NLF except use of native terms in their reports; on the other hand, those ethnographers who had any one of the following greater claims to NLF: A. They compiled a formal glossary or word list. B. They recorded a native text. C. They claimed to be able to work without an interpreter, even if only at times, in relatively simple situations. D. They reported that their field notes were taken at least partially in the native language.

3. *Use of Non-Native Local Residents Helpers* as field assistants apparently tends to be associated with some measures of suicide frequency and social development.

4. *Tendency of Ethnographer to Make Clear Commitments* rather than to make only vague references to traits studied apparently tends to be associated with a wide variety of measures. In other words, where ethnographers tend to commit themselves, often this commitment tends to be in one particular direction of a scale rather than in either direction. For example, clear and precise descriptions of territorial change are more likely to report expansion than contraction; vague and imprecise descriptions are the other way about.

5. *Taking of Ethnographic Census by Ethnographer* seems for some reason to be highly related to frequency of witchcraft reports, although the sample involved is very small.

6. *Memory Ethnographies*—reconstructions of the days of their youth by elderly informants—tend to report fewer fine details such as craft specialties than do ethnographies describing ongoing cultures.

These results may be compared with those of an earlier study (Naroll 1962). There, three control factors were found to be useful: (1) length of stay in the field by ethnographer; (2) native language familiarity; and (3) tendency of ethnographers to make clear commitments. The first of these three early factors did better than chance in the present study, but not enough better to warrant inclusion on the later list of six just given. (When more is understood about the evaluation of probabilities of large runs of correlations, perhaps this judgment may be corrected.) The other two early factors appear again on a later list and thus are strongly supported.

For each stage of the data collection process, then, at least one control factor has been preliminarily validated: for control over informant's error, degree of participation of ethnographer; for control over the ethnographer's error, native language familiarity; and for control over comparativist's error, precision of ethnographer's report.

OTHER TOPICS

There is not space in this book to talk much about several other aspects of data quality control. I have discussed these topics in detail elsewhere.

One of these topics is the application of cross-cultural survey methods in general and the data quality control method in particular to comparative historical studies of the major higher civilizations. A classic problem of such historical studies is the problem of selection of data. This problem has been most exhaustively considered by Benedetto Croce (1921). I have elsewhere (Naroll, 1962:29 f.; Naroll, 1967; Naroll, Bullough and Naroll, 1971) argued that data quality control methods would enable us to escape the dilemma proposed by this problem in cross-historical surveys.

Another of these topics is the analogy between data quality control as described here and statistical quality control methods as widely used in industry. While there are important differences in the two methods, there are other important similarities. Hence the comparison is a useful one (Naroll 1962: 10–15).

A third such topic is the problem of making generalized inferences about rates from very small samples. For example, suppose that on an island there live 1000 people. An ethnologist is told that last year one and only one person on that island had committed suicide. Supposing that his informants are completely trustworthy, what can be said about the suicide rate on that island? Clearly it is unwarranted to extrapolate so high a rate as 100 suicides per 100,000 population— so high a rate is utterly unheard of among large populations. What can be said? I submit that for such rare events the use of sampling theory and the Poisson distribution lets us make inferences of some kind about such data. In the stated example, such reasoning would lead to the conclusion that the suicide rate on the island was probably greater than 20 per 100,000 per year (Naroll 1962: 107–114).

Finally, the application of data quality control methods to census data on primitive tribes presents special problems of considerable difficulty. Table talk among anthropologists suggests that government censuses tend consistently to underestimate the populations of primitive communities. However, a comparative study of government and ethnographic censuses on the same communities does not support this opinion (Naroll 1962:115–123).

CONCLUSION

The success of cross-cultural surveys requires that attention be paid to accuracy of data in the sources. There is much reason to believe that perhaps as much as one-sixth of the statements in the poorest-quality ethnographies may be inaccurate. On the other hand, only systematic biases need to worry us; random errors tend to lower correlations. Control factors offer a method of detecting possible biases in ethnographic reports. Seven bias-sensitive traits and six bias-sensitive control factors have been tentatively identified. Three control factors are more strongly supported, because confirming results of an earlier study on another sample: (1) degree of participation by ethnographer in native life; (2) native language familiarity; and (3) degree of precision of ethnographer's report on specific trait being coded.

BIBLIOGRAPHY

BENEDICT, RUTH
  1946 *The chrysanthemum and the sword*. Boston, Houghton Mifflin.
CARPENTER, EDMUND
  1960 Ohnainewk, Eskimo hunter. In Joseph Casagrande, ed., *In the company of man*. New York, Harper.
CROCE, BENEDETTO
  1921 *History: its theory and practice*. Trans. by Douglas Ainslee. New York, Harcourt and Brace.
DRIVER, HAROLD E.
  1936 *The reliability of culture element data*. Ph.D. thesis. Berkeley, University of California.

  1939 Culture element distributions: VIII. The reliability of culture element data. *Anthropological Records* 1:205–219.
DUNCAN, ACHESON J.
  1955 *Quality control and industrial statistics*. Homewood, Ill., Irwin.
FIRTH, RAYMOND
  1930 Report on research in Tikopia. *Oceania* 1:105–117.

  1936 *We, the Tikopia: a sociological study of kinship in primitive Polynesia*. London, Allen and Unwin.

  1939 *Primitive Polynesian economy*. London, Routledge.

  1940 *The work of the gods in Tikopia*. Monographs on social anthropology, Nos. 1 and 2. London, London School of Economics and Political Science.

FORTUNE, REO F.
1939 Arapesh warfare. *American Anthropologist* 41:22–41.

GILBERT, CLAIRE
1968 Community power structures. In Terry W. Clark, ed., *Community structure and decision making*. San Francisco, Chandler.

HOLMES, LOWELL D.
1957 *The restudy of Manu'an culture: a problem in methodology*. Northwestern University Ph.D. Thesis. Ann Arbor, University Microfilms, No. 23,514.

JOSEPH, ALICE, R. B. SPICER, and JANE CHEVSKY
1949 *The desert people: a study of the Papago Indians*. Chicago, University of Chicago Press.

KENDALL, MAURICE G.
1962 *Rank correlation methods*. Third Edition. London: Griffin.

KOH, HESUNG CHUN
1966 A social science bibliographic system: orientation and framework. *Behavior Science Notes* 1:145–163.

LEWIS, OSCAR
1951 *Life in a Mexican village*. Urbana, University of Illinois Press.

LIEBERMAN, GERALD J., and DONALD B. OWEN
1961 *Tables of the hypergeometric probability distribution*. Stanford University Press.

MEAD, MARGARET
1935 *Sex and temperament in three primitive societies*. New York, Mentor Books, New American Library.
1938– *The mountain Arapesh*. 5 vol. Anthropo-
1949 logical Papers of the American Museum of Natural History.

MORGANSTERN, OSCAR
1950 *On the accuracy of economic observation*. Princeton, N.J., Princeton University Press.

MURDOCK, GEORGE P.
1949 *Social structure*. New York, Macmillan.

NAROLL, FRADA
1959 Child training in a Tyrolean village. *Anthropological Quarterly* 32:206–214.

NAROLL, RAOUL
1958 German kinship terms. *American Anthropologist* 60:750–755.
1962 *Data quality control*. New York, Free Press.
1967 *Imperial cycles and world order*. Papers, Peace Research Society International, Vol. V.

n.d.$_a$ *Warfare, peaceful intercourse and territorial change*. MS.
n.d.$_b$ *An exact test of significance for ordinal measures*. MS.

NAROLL, RAOUL, VERN R. BULLOUGH, and FRADA NAROLL
1971 *Military deterrence in history*. Albany, State University of New York Press.

NAROLL, RAOUL, and FRADA NAROLL
1962 Social development of a Tyrolean village. *Anthropological Quarterly* 35:103–120.
1963 On bias of exotic data. *Man*, February, 1963, No. 25.

POLANYI, KARL
1944 *The great tranformation*. New York, Rinehart.

QUADE, DANA
1967 *Nonparametric partial correlation*. University of North Carolina. Institute of Statistics Mimeo, Series No. 526 (2nd ed.). Department of Biostatistics, University of North Carolina.

REDFIELD, ROBERT
1930 *Tepoztlán*. Chicago, University of Chicago Press.

ROSENTHAL, ROBERT
1966 *Experimenter effects in behavioral research*. New York, Appleton-Century-Crofts.

SEGAL, MARSHAL H., DONALD T. CAMPBELL, and MELVILLE J. HERSKOVITS
1966 *The influence of culture on visual perception*. Indianapolis, Bobbs-Merrill.

SILVA, ROBERTO DE LA CERDA
1956 *Los indigenas mexicanos de Tuxpan, Jal., Mexico, D.F.* Universidad Nacional de Mexico, Instituto de Investigaciones Sociales.

TEXTOR, ROBERT B.
1968 *A cross-cultural summary*. New Haven, HRAF Press.

UDY, STANLEY H., JR.
1959 *Organization of work*. New Haven, HRAF Press.

WALTON, JOHN
1966 Discipline, method and community power, a note on the sociology of knowledge. *American Sociological Review* 31: 648–649.

WHITING, JOHN M., and IRWIN L. CHILD
1953 *Child training and personality*. New Haven, Yale University Press.

WILLIAMS, F. E.
1930 *Orokaiva society*. London, Oxford University Press.

CHAPTER 45

Dimensions of Error in Cross-National Data

RUDOLPH J. RUMMEL

The influence of error is a major concern of those trying to analyze cross-national data statistically. Errors in the data, if serious enough, can completely distort the results of an analysis, leading to conclusions opposite to those the true values would give. Although the nature of data error thus plays a crucial role in the outcome of empirical research using cross-national data, little methodological or empirical research on such error has been done with a view to its control. The work of Raoul Naroll (1962) is a pioneering exception relevant to cross-national data.

This problem of error was of particular concern to the author and his colleagues, Harold Guetzkow and Jack Sawyer, when faced with assessing the effect of such error on a factor analysis of a large number of cross-national variables, such as population, GNP, infant mortality rate, telephones per capita, treaties, trade, area, etc. A description of the Dimensionality of Nations Project, of which this research is a part, is given in Rummel (1965). A consequent methodological analysis and a survey of the literature on error suggested several factor analyses of a large set of error scores. Two of the re-

This study was prepared in connection with research supported by the National Science Foundation, Contracts NSF-G24827, NSF-224, and NSF-GS-536. The author wishes to express his gratitude to Harold Guetzkow and Jack Sawyer, in collaboration with whom much of the methodological analysis was completed, the research design decisions made, and the results interpreted. Moreover, the author is indebted for many helpful suggestions on an earlier draft of this paper from Richard Chadwick, Raymond Tanter, and Dina Zinnes. The author alone, however, stands accountable for the results.

sulting dimensions or error were then included, along with several error measures, in the substantive factor analysis of the cross-national variables as a means of control for error.

The purpose of this paper is to report on the factor analysis of the error scores and the results of their inclusion in the substantive factor analysis. To give a context for these findings, however, a rough sketch of the methodology underlying the error analyses should be given. First, random and systematic error will be discussed in relation to single variable analysis. Such error will then be considered in the multivariate case as pertinent to several research models, with a focus on the correlation model which usually underlies the application of factor analysis.

UNIVARIATE RANDOM AND SYSTEMATIC ERROR

If the concern of the investigator is with analyzing a single variable, such as population, then error in the data collected on this variable may be *univariate random* or *univariate systematic*. Univariate random error is defined as

$$x = X + e \qquad E(e) = 0 \qquad (1)$$

where e denotes random error *in the case of a single variable analysis*, X is the true value, x is the empirical value, and E the expected value. In words, the definition asserts that an observation, x, is a sum of a true value and an error, and that the errors for *all* the true values vary in such a way that their average is zero. In practice, random error in international data on a variable would mean that one could get a world total for that variable which would be very near the true value, because of the cancellation of random error when the nation-by-nation statistics were aggregated. For a discussion as to how such errors combine see Bowley (1937) and Connor (1932).

Univariate systematic error is defined as

$$x = X + e, \qquad E(e) \neq 0, \qquad (2)$$

that is, the error on a variable tends to overestimate or underestimate the true value. Population data has this kind of systematic error, where the true values tend to underestimate the population estimates published (*Demographic Yearbook* 1960:1 ff.). If the amount of such systematic error is known, corrections easily can be made. When the systematic error can only be estimated, in terms of reliabilities, or error ranges, corrections cannot be made. Descriptive statistics based on data for which such error ranges are known, however, can and should include the range of error in a statistic, such as a world total or average.

The problem of univariate random and systematic error is straightforward enough and the analysis of such error in data is facilitated by the availability of several studies on the subject, and by the abundance of reliability codes, qualifications, and supplementary information that the United Nations attached to much of its published statistical data. (In general, see *Problems in the Collection and Comparability of International Statistics* 1948. For GNP and population see Studentski 1958 and *Demographic Yearbook* 1960, respectively. The introductory chapters of the *United Nations Demographic Yearbook* are especially rewarding with respect to possible error in demographic data. Morgenstern [1963] is an excellent source to consult for a general description of error in statistical data.)

regression model: $y = +bX - f^*$ (5)
structural model: $y = +bx + (be^* - f^*)$, $E(b) < E(B)$ (6)

For clarity, the residuals are assumed zero in (5) and (6). It is also assumed that errors e^* and f^* exist. Thus, in the case of the structural model when errors are in *both* variables, the empirical regression coefficient is an underestimate of the true regression.

If the structural model is the appropriate one for cross-national data when the concern is with unbiased regression coefficients, there are a number of techniques one may apply to correct the coefficient. Corrections are

MULTIVARIATE RANDOM AND SYSTEMATIC ERROR

The problem of error in the multivariate case is more severe. Dealing with the bivariate case for simplicity, bivariate random error is defined as

$$x = X + e^* \qquad\qquad y = Y + f^* \qquad (3)$$
$$\text{Cov}(e^*, Y) = \text{Cov}(f^*, X) = \text{Cov}(e^*, f^*) = 0 \ (4)$$

where the asterisk is used to distinguish univariate random error, e, from bivariate random, e^*, in the data on a variable whose relationship with another variable is being assessed. As a further simplification which leaves the conclusions unaltered, the values for the variables and errors are taken as deviations from their means. Covariance is defined in (7) below.

Just how the researcher will approach multivariate random error depends on the purpose of his investigation. If he is working with the *regression model*, then he must assume that his random error is contained in the dependent variable and that the independent variable is error-free. With error in only his dependent variable, he can derive an unbiased estimate of the regression coefficient.

When the error is contained in both independent *and* dependent variables, the investigator is working with the *structural model*. For a discussion of the structural model case, see Kendall and Stuart 1961, chap. 29. This chapter is excellent for discussing the statistical nature, effect, and controls of multivariate *random* error, and for the bibliography which allows one to trace the consideration of such error through the mathematical literature. The difference between the two models can be seen in (5) and (6) below for the true relationship $Y = +BX$ without error.

available (Kendall and Stuart 1961) if the variance of e^*, of f^*, or the ratio of these variances, can be estimated. If such estimates cannot be made, instrumental variables (Durbin 1954), or a grouping or ranking procedure (Mandansky 1959), might be applied. One might also "control" the independent variable (Geary 1953; Scheffé 1958) by selecting its values.

Often, however, the investigator using cross-national data is not concerned with the regression, but with the *correlation model*. He is interested in assessing the degree and direction of relationship, r, between two variables x and y, according to the formula,

$$r_{xy} = \frac{Cov(X,Y)}{\sigma_x \sigma_y}, \quad Cov(X,Y) = \frac{\Sigma XY}{N} \quad (7)$$

The denominators, σ_x and σ_y, are the standard deviations of X and Y, respectively. In the correlation model, the effect of

$$r_{xy} = r_{X+e^*}, \quad Y+f^* = \frac{Cov(X,Y) + Cov(e^*,Y) + Cov(f^*,X) + Cov(e^*,f^*)}{(\sigma_x + \sigma_e^*) \ (\sigma_y + \sigma_f^*)} \quad (8)$$

As can be seen from (10), when the covariances involving errors e* and f* are zero, the numerator is the same as in (7), the case of correlating true values, while the variances in the denominator have been increased by the addition of the error variances. Thus, if (4) is the case, and

$$(e^*)^2 \text{ and/or } (f^*)^2 \neq 0 \quad (9)$$

then

$$r_{xy} < r_{XY} \quad (10)$$

Where (10) holds for the samples one is analyzing, the significance level should be raised, say from .05 to .10, or even .20, depending upon the amount of error, to avoid rejecting a true hypothesis.

Mathematical studies of error begin with assumption (4) in addition to defining $E(e^*)$ and $E(f^*) = 0$. When assumption (4) is violated, that is

$$Cov(e^*,Y), \text{ and/or } Cov(f^*,X), \text{ and/or}$$
$$Cov(e^*,f^*) \neq 0, \quad (11)$$

the effect of error is more complicated. The situation indicated by (11) may be defined as bivariate *systematic error*, and results when one or more of the error covariances in (4) does not equal zero.

As can be seen from (8), whether or not bivariate systematic error will raise or lower the empirical correlation, r_{xy}, above its true value, r_{XY}, depends on the size and sign of the ratios of the error covariances to the standard deviations of x and y, which are $(\sigma_x + \sigma_e^*)$ and $(\sigma_y + \sigma_f^*)$, respectively. If, for example, Cov $(e^*,Y) \neq 0$, while Cov (f^*, Y) and Cov $(e^*,f^*) = 0$, then

$$r_{xy} < r_{XY}, \quad (12)$$

if

$$\frac{\sigma_e^*}{\sigma_x} > \frac{Cov \ (e^*,Y)}{Cov \ (X,Y)} \quad (13)$$

In words, the effect of bivariate systematic error in data for a variable on the assessment random errors, e* and f* in X and Y is to reduce the correlation. That is, r_{XY} is a *conservative* estimate of r_{XY}. Thus, for example, a correlation of .50 between telephones and vehicles would underestimate the true correlation if the error in both variables were random. This can be seen by replacing X and Y in the correlation formula (7) by the observations x and y with errors X+e* and Y+f* which, after algebraic manipulation, results in

of that variable's relationship with another is to lower the empirical correlation from the true correlation as long as the ratio of the standard deviation of the error to that of the true value is greater than the ratio of the covariance of its error with the other variable to the covariance of the true values of both variables. *The likelihood that systematic error will increase the empirical correlation over the true value is greater as the covariance between error and the other variable increases, relative to the true covariance.*

At this point it should be noted that *random error, in the univariate case, does not imply that this error will be random in a multivariate analysis, nor does systematic error in the univariate data mean that the error will be systematic in the multivariate case.* These distinctions get at the heart of much confusion over the role of error in assessing correlations among cross-national data. It has often been assumed that if error is random on a *variable*, the correlation of that variable with others will be a conservative estimate of the true value. This is not necessarily the case, since univariate random error may be correlated with the error or with the true values of another variable. Then, the correlations between the variables will be conservative *only* if (13) holds.

To summarize:

1. Bivariate random error in the data on one or two variables lowers the correlation between them.

2. Bivariate systematic error in the data on one or two variables will either lower or raise the correlation depending on the ratio of the covariances of error to the covariances of the true values.

3. Random error in the univariate case

may or may not act as random error in the bivariate or multivariate case.

4. Systematic error in the univariate case may or may not act as systematic error in the bivariate or multivariate.

DIMENSIONS OF ERROR

The researcher analyzing relationships among two or more variables for which cross-national statistical data are employed must determine whether the error that exists in his data is univariate or multivariate, random or systematic. Knowledge on this score should enable him to weigh the reliability of his results.

Concern with this question became uppermost in 1962 when Harold Guetzkow, Jack Sawyer, and Rudolph Rummel began the collection of 1955 data for an intercorrelation and factor analysis of 230 cross-national variables for eighty-two nations. For the variables, data sources and definitions, descriptive statistics on each variable, and full correlation matrix, see Rummel n.d.

Using the logic of the previous sections, it was thought that some way could be found for gauging the effect of systematic error in the data on these variables. One approach to assessing the reliability of such dimensions is to include in the factor analysis actual measures of the error contained in the variables. If the error measure is related (correlated in the orthogonal case) to a factor, then that factor should be interpreted with caution. If, however, the error measure is unrelated to the factor, one can have confidence that the factor is not an artifact of correlations between the error measure and the highly loaded variable.

This was the logic which informed a pilot factor analysis of twenty-two cross-national conflict variables in which two measures of systematic error—censorship and world interest—were included (Rummel 1963). See a similar analysis of error in such data by Tanter (1964b). Later studies by Rummel (1964) and Tanter (1964a) have followed similar procedures. An error factor independent of the substantive dimensions was extracted which showed that systematic error tapped by these measures was unrelated to the conflict dimensions. Consequently, the conclusions were stated with more assurance than

would otherwise be the case when working with such data.

For the 230 cross-national variable, eighty-two nation factor analysis, five kinds of error measures were developed; and these measures are set off by heavy horizontal lines in Tables 1A, B, C, and D. The first kind of error measure was an ordinal three point rating of nations on a variable according to the reliability and comparability of a nation's datum for that variable. Using the United Nations coding of reliability and their footnotes that give qualifications by which one can gauge the comparability and reliability of much of the data, it was possible to develop forty error ratings for forty variables. These error ratings were then named after the variables to which they relate. Hence, in the following Tables 1A, B, C, and D, where variables 18–45 are the error ratings, variable 42, called "infant mortality," is the error rating for the variable, "infant mortality."

For reasons of space the error measures given in Table 1A were limited to the same ones included in the subsequent analysis shown in Table 1B. Those included in the factor analysis of sixty-six measures, but not given in the table, are for off-1955 error measures: persons per dwelling room, divorce rate, per cent annual increase in national income and immigrants. For error ratings they are GNP per capita, per cent unemployed, national income per capita, library circulation, number of visitors, persons per dwelling room, per cent dwellings with running water, female workers, divorce rate, tuberculosis deaths, per cent food expenditure, and foreign mail.

Another possible source of error may be the result of data on a particular variable belonging to a year other than the base year of 1955 for the data collection. Since accumulated departures from the base year of data may increasingly distort the analysis, twenty-one "off-1955" error measures were calculated for twenty-one of the variables which had the largest variance in their off-1955 data. Each off-1955 error measure was determined by giving the absolute value of the difference between the base year and the year of datum for a country. These off-1955 error measures were given the name of the variable to which they relate and are numbered 1–17 in Tables 1A–D.

A missing data error measure was the

Table 1A   ERROR MEASURE   Including All 66 Error Measures

Error Measure #	1	2	3	4	5	6	7	8	9	10
1. illiteracy										
2. newsp. circ.		58					35			
3. radio rec.		44								
4. pupils per teacher					38					
5. life expect.							89			
6. inhab. per hosp.	−74									
7. inhab. per physician										
8. calories per cap.	67									
9. cinema att. per cap.		64								
10. female workers										
11. prim. & sec. stud.				−32						
12. % pop. Catholic				48						
13. # for.-born	−30			54						
14. defense exp.										
15. net value prod.							56			
16. % pop. econ. active										
17. % pop. < 15 yrs.		32		41						
18. birth rate		83	41							
19. econ. active		96								
20. agr. workers		76								35
21. % pop. econ. active										
22. mfg. employ.										
23. cost of living							50			
24. GNP/mfg.	44		31						60	
25. GNP	91									
26. book titles										
27. illiteracy		40							46	
28. letters				−93						
29. newsp. circ.										
30. radios								44		−33
31. pupils per teacher								84		
32. enroll. ratio								31		−45
33. exports	36									
34. college stud.										
35. % sci. & eng. stud.						30				
36. exchange rate	55									
37. sec. enroll. ratio										
38. marriage rate		78								
39. % law students	51									
40. prim. & sec. stud.										−81
41. life expect.			48							
42. infant mort.		82	37							
43. air pass. K.M.									41	
44. r.r. freight										
45. vehicles										
46. missing data	48	50								
47. % pop. error		48							40	
48. random normal					83					
49. random rect.										
50. random x⁻ᵃ							49			
Eigenvalue**	7.2	6.5	4.9	4.0	3.7	3.5	3.0	2.8	2.7	2.5
% Total Variance**	11.0	9.9	8.4	6.0	5.9	5.3	4.6	4.2	4.1	3.8

11	12	13	14	15	16	17	18	19	20	21	22	h²
				85								88
32									−34			76
												73
			−42							38		91
												100
						−37						88
											−86	91
										46		87
												81
					−98							105
										63		76
		42			−35							80
					−34							104
		−88										83
												90
					−91							93
		−40			−30	36						88
												104
												99
												97
									77			85
							46					97
42												77
												89
												98
							−74					84
				37	36							93
												95
										−63		82
												76
												80
					31							90
−33							−32	35	45			90
				45								83
					−37		66					103
							31	30				78
						104						128
												94
						−35	30	53				111
												88
						44			34			103
												98
			−32									81
									80			86
	90											91
		−40			34							107
					31	36	34					103
												84
			−81									76
						79	35					47
2.2	2.1	2.0	1.8	1.8	1.7	1.5	1.4	1.4	1.3	1.2	1.1	
3.4	3.2	3.0	2.8	2.8	2.5	2.2	2.1	2.1	2.0	1.8	1.7	98.8

Table 1B ERROR MEASURE   Excluding Error Measures with N<50

Error Measure #	1	2	3	4	5	6	7	8
1. illiteracy		37						
2. newsp. circ.	67		−28				−33	
3. radio rec.	37				−30			
4. pupils per teacher								72
5. life expect.							−68	
·6. inhab. per hosp.		−73						
7. inhab. per physician								
8. calories per cap.		81						
9. cinema att. per cap.	74							
10. female workers				86				
11. prim. & sec. stud.					−36			
12. % pop. Catholic					51			
13. # for.-born				35	65			
14. defense exp.								
15. net value prod.								
16. % pop. econ. active				90				
17. % pop. <15 yrs.	30				54			
18. birth rate	79		36					
19. econ. active	35		75					
20. agr. workers			88					
21. % pop. econ. active								
22. mfg. employ.			38				31	
23. cost of living							−70	
24. GNP/mfg.		42	50			−33		
25. GNP		84						
26. book titles								
27. illiteracy			44	−36				
28. letters					−81			
29. newsp. circ.				31				
30. radios								
31. pupils per teacher						60		
32. enroll. ratio				−47	36		36	
33. exports		49						
34. college stud.								
35. % sci. & eng. stud.		42						53
36. exchange rate		52						
37. sec. enroll. ratio						75		
38. marriage rate	75							
39. % law students		62						
40. prim. & sec. stud.								
41. life expect.	43							
42. infant mort.	79							
43. air pass. K.M.								
44. r.r. freight								
45. vehicles								68
46. missing data	42	32		−35				
47. % pop. error	50							
48. random normal							−34	
49. random rect.								
50. random x−a						67		
Eigenvalue**	5.7	4.9	3.1	3.1	2.8	2.6	2.0	2.0
% Total Variance**	11.5	9.7	6.1	6.3	5.7	5.1	4.1	4.1

9	10	11	12	13	14	15	16	17	h²
	37					35	−40		81
									70
	−36					43			84
									76
							31		91
									71
						78			74
									80
									77
									86
								58	72
			38				31		74
									81
			−85						75
56				41					83
									91
			−40						81
									86
									89
									93
		−83							81
					−43				85
									67
									74
									90
									75
					77				77
						31		32	79
									77
46	35								84
84									80
35									85
									76
									73
	79								86
							33		77
									71
					−44				80
									84
	31	32							77
					−34				94
				−77					82
				−64				−31	75
		−51							82
						43			73
							85		97
	−40								75
			−43						73
				32	−36				67
31				30			−31	−76	78
2.0	1.7	1.7	1.6	1.4	1.4	1.4	1.2	1.2	
3.9	3.5	3.5	3.1	2.8	2.8	2.7	2.4	2.4	79.7

Table 1C

ERROR MEASURE

Excluding Error Measures with N < 60

Error Measure #[a]	1	2	3	4	5	6	7	8	9	10	11	12	13	h^2
1. illiteracy	−36												73	80
2. newsp. circ.		51	−44											65
3. radio rec.		43		−41								34		74
4. pupils per teacher						52								67
5. life expect.														
6. inhab. per hosp.	69													63
7. inhab. per physician												84		79
8. calories per cap.	−82													80
9. cinema att. per cap.		64												71
10. female workers			40	42					34		48			82
11. prim. & sec. stud.									52		32			61
12. % pop. Catholic				73										72
13. # for.-born				83										76
14. defense exp.								79						72
15. net value prod.														
16. % pop. econ. active			39	59							40			91
17. % pop. < 15 yrs.				50				55						83
18. birth rate		89												84
19. econ. active														
20. agr. workers														
21. % pop. econ. active														
22. mfg. employ.														
23. cost of living			−40			33	34	39						59
24. GNP/mfg.														
25. GNP	−85													86
26. book titles										71				66
27. illiteracy							46	−32						69
28. letters														
29. newsp. circ.			76											71
30. radios			40		−35	45								70
31. pupils per teacher					−71									69
32. enroll. ratio					−82									84
33. exports	−50						−43			33				69
34. college stud.											−88			82
35. % sci. & eng. stud.	−49					54								79
36. exchange rate	−56									−48				73
37. sec. enroll. ratio														
38. marriage rate		85												83
39. % law students	−63					32					−36			76
40. prim. & sec. stud.														
41. life expect.														
42. infant mort.		82												78
43. air pass. K.M.														
44. r.r. freight						38						43	−48	77
45. vehicles						75								65
46. missing data		46		−53				41		−31				92
47. % pop. error		51												72
48. random normal										65				76
49. random rect.							−76							66
50. random x⁻a									89					85
Eigenvalue**	5.2	4.4	2.6	2.2	2.2	1.9	1.7	1.6	1.4	1.6	1.3	1.1	1.1	
% Total Variance**	13.7	11.5	6.8	5.9	6.9	5.0	4.6	4.3	3.6	4.3	3.4	2.8	3.0	74.8

*Decimals omitted from all loadings; only loadings ≥ |.30| are shown. N = 79.
**Eigenvalues and % of Total Variance are for *unrotated* factors.
[a]N = 38 error measures.

Table 1D

ERROR MEASURE

Excluding Error Measures with N < 70

Error Measure #b	1	2	3	4	5	6	7	8	h²
1. illiteracy		−33	58						60
2. newsp. circ.	73								66
3. radio rec.	54		49						71
4. pupils per teacher						−31		−57	50
5. life expect.									
6. inhab. per hosp.						67			64
7. inhab. per physician				−70					63
8. calories per cap.			37		−35	−53			70
9. cinema att. per cap.	79								74
10. female workers									
11. prim. & sec. stud.					−77				69
12. % pop. Catholic		−64							49
13. # for.-born									
14. defense exp.		65							56
15. net value prod.									
16. % pop. econ. active									
17. % pop. < 15 yrs.									
18. birth rate	67								63
19. econ. active									
20. agr. workers									
21. % pop. econ. active									
22. mfg. employ.									
23. cost of living									
24. GNP/mfg.									
25. GNP									
26. book titles									
27. illiteracy			80						69
28. letters									
29. newsp. circ.	−36			55				31	64
30. radios			43				55		69
31. pupils per teacher							80		69
32. enroll. ratio									
33. exports						−82			72
34. college stud.								71	58
35. % sci. & eng. stud.									
36. exchange rate									
37. sec. enroll. ratio									
38. marriage rate									
39. % law students									
40. prim. & sec. stud.									
41. life expect.									
42. infant mort.									
43. air pass. K.M.									
44. r.r. freight									
45. vehicles									
46. missing data	59	67							87
47. % pop. error	67								60
48. random normal				44				−45	55
49. random rect.					60	−38			63
50. random x⁻ᵃ					−55		53		67
Eigenvalue**	3.2	2.6	1.9	1.8	1.6	1.5	1.2	1.1	
% Total Variance**	14.1	11.2	8.1	7.6	7.1	6.3	5.3	4.9	64.6

*Decimals omitted from all loadings; only loadings ≥ |.30| are shown.
**Eigenvalues and % of Total Variance are for *unrotated* factors.
bN = 23 error measures.

third type of measure employed. Since the per cent of missing data for the 230 variable factor analysis was approximately 17 per cent, there was the possibility that missing data may have an adverse effect on the analysis. To assess this effect, a measure of missing data was calculated by summing the number of missing data cells for each country across the 230 variables. The resulting error measure is numbered 46 in the tables.

The fourth kind of error measure analyzed was the error ranges for each nation on its population data. This measure is numbered 47 in the tables. Derived from the United Nations coding of their population data and a formula they give for using the code to estimate the actual error, this measure gave an estimate of the per cent of error in the population data for each country (*Demographic Yearbook* 1960:8, and especially n. 11, 12). It was considered more important than any one of the other measures, since population entered into many of the variables as a denominator (e.g., GNP per capita), and the error in population data was similar to that in other census-derived demographic data.

It is important to recognize that these four types of error measures do not measure the e* and f* in (3) and (4) above. Rather, they measure the *variance* of e* and f* for each nation's values on x and y, or what might be termed the reliability of x and y. Consequently, the error equations we are dealing with are

$$x = X + |e^*|, \quad \sigma_e^* \geqq \sigma|e^*|, \quad (14)$$
$$\text{Cov}(e^*, Y) \geqq \text{Cov}(|e^*|, Y)$$
$$\text{Cov}(e^*, f^*) \geqq \text{Cov}(|e^*|, |f^*|)$$

These four types of measures then index the reliability of one's findings. A correlation between an error measure and the other variable or its error is a *sufficient* condition of systematic error affecting the assessment of their relationship. Similarly, a correlation between these error measures and a factor is a *sufficient* condition of systematic error influencing the cluster of relationships delineated by the factor.

A fifth type of measure, random number variables, was included to index the chance occurrence of a factor. They aid in interpreting lower bounds for the substantive meaning of the correlations and the factors. These measures were constructed by using random number tables and, except for chance

concomitance, should not be correlated with each other, or with the other measures. Their loadings in Tables 1A–D and Table 2 thus give one an idea of the level at which one can expect that the empirical correlations and loadings found among the other measures might well be the result of chance.

The five types of measures above totaled sixty-six—far too large a number to include in the factor analysis of 230 variables. Consequently, a prior factor analysis on only the error measures was computed to determine what *dimensions* of error existed. Then, error measures indexing the most important of these dimensions were included in the 230 variable factor analysis.

Values were not available for all countries on most of the error measures. In some extreme cases, fewer than 50 per cent of the countries had error scores on a measure. To guard against unreliable dimensions of error resulting from differential missing values for the error measures, it was decided to do four factor analyses and orthogonal rotations at different levels of missing data: one on all the error measures (Table 1A), one on error measures that have an N equal to or larger than 50 (Table 1B), a third on error measures that have an N equal to or larger than 60 (Table 1C), and a final analysis on those measures with an N equal to or larger than 70 (Table 1D). By comparing the orthogonally rotated (varimax) factor loadings between Tables 1A and 1D as is done in Table 2, it was possible to determine which of the factors remained stable at different levels of missing data.

Comparison of loadings $\geqq |.30|$ brings out four factors as appearing in each of the analyses. The factor which accounted for most of the variation among the error measures was Factor 2 of Table 1A. It includes among the high loadings both off-1955 and error score measures. In the subsequent analyses, it became Factor 1, 2, and 1, respectively. Error ratings numbered 18, 42, 38, and 47, which were for birth rate (.83, .79, .89, .67), infant mortality (.82, .79, .82, omitted), marriage rate (.78, .75, .85 omitted), and the population error measure (.48, .50, .51, .67), respectively, remained loaded across the analyses. The nature of these measures identified this factor as a *demographic error dimension* and indicated that the existence of this error *variance* and its effect on

Table 2
FACTOR SIMILARITY*

Analysis	Factor Numbers
All 66 Error Measures	1 2 3 4 5 6 7 8 9 10 11 12 13 14 15 16 17 18 19 20 21 22
Measures with N 50	2 1 3 5 7 12 4 6 14 8 10 11 13 15 16 17
Measures with N 60	1 2 ᵃ 4 3ᵇ 5 8 4 ᵃ 10 ᵃ ᵃ 6 11 ᵃ ᵃ 12 13 6 7 9 11 12 13
Measures with N 70	6 1ᵃ 2. ᵃ ᵃ 2 ᵃ ᵃ ᵃ ᵃ ᵃ 8 ᵃ ᵃ ᵃ 5 ᵃ

*Factor numbers appearing in the same column appear most similar to each other.
ᵃFactor lost definition through exclusion of measures loading highly on it in previous analyses.
ᵇThe similarity of this factor to the one above is questionable.

Table 3
CORRELATIONS AMONG ERROR MEASURES*

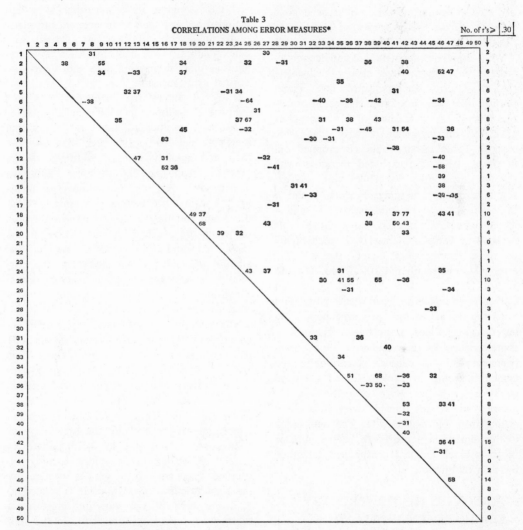

*Decimals omitted; only correlations ≥ |.30| are shown

substantive analyses would best be indexed by either error ratings on infant mortality or birth rate data, or a combined index of the standard scores of both. The latter alternative best approximates factor scores on this dimension.

The second factor to appear stable across the analyses was Factor 1 in Table 1A, which became Factors 2, 1, and 6 in the subsequent runs. This factor also accounted for much of the variation among the error measures and was general to both the error score and off-1955 ones. The measures which best identified the factor are numbered 25, 33, 6, and 8, which were the error ratings for GNP (.91, .84, −.85, omitted) and exports (.36, .49, −.50, −.82), and the off-1955 error measures for inhabitants per hospital bed

(−.74, −.73, .69, .67) and calories per capita (.67, .81, −.82, −.53), respectively. These off-1955 measures were of a welfare character, while the rating variables were economic. This factor thus was called an *economic-welfare error dimension*. The GNP error rating was the best single index to the dimension and a combined index of the GNP error rating and the inhabitants per hospital bed off-1955 error measure would be a good estimate of the factor scores of nations on the dimension.

While the above *demographic* and economic-welfare dimensions were clearly delineated, the other error factors were not. Either through the exclusion of measures in subsequent analyses, or because of the decreasing effect of missing data, factors that were clear in Table 1A or Table 1B dropped out in the analyses that excluded measures with the N's lower than 60. There was one example of factors merging. Factors 4 and 5 in Tables 1A and 1B, and Factors 16 and 4 in the same tables merged to become Factors 4 and 2 in Tables 1C and 1D. Loaded highly on these factors were mainly the off-1955 error measures numbered 10, 12, 13, 16, and 17 for female workers, per cent population Catholic, foreign-born, per cent population economically active and per cent population less than age fifteen, respectively. These were characteristics of a population most often enumerated in a census. Accordingly, the combined factors in Tables 1C and 1D were called a *census-lag error dimension*—a dimension which taps possible error in a study arising from old census data. The best index to this dimension appeared to be the number of years since the last census was taken of the data of interest.

CORRELATES OF THE PRIMARY ERROR DIMENSIONS AND MEASURES

As was mentioned above, intercorrelation and factor analysis of the error measures was carried out as a means of determining a small set of error measures which would generally index the variation in reliability of the 230 cross-national variables. This set could then be included in a factor analysis to determine the reliability of the factors extracted.

On the basis of the above analysis, it was decided to include in the set the *demographic error dimension*, which was indexed by summing the standard scores for the birth rate and infant mortality error ratings, and the *economic-welfare error dimension*, indexed by summing the standard scores for the GNP error rating and the off-1955 infant mortality error measures. The error rating on GNP and the population error measures were also included because their error entered into many ratios in which GNP or population were denominators. Two final measures were included—that for missing data and a random-normal error measure.

Table 4 shows the orthogonally rotated (varimax) factors on which the five error measures, excluding the random-normal measure, had loadings greater than .40 and their communality across the fifteen factors extracted from the 236 variables (230 plus 5 error measures, plus 1 random error measure). The first two factors, economic development and totalitarianism, were the only ones on which the five had loadings. These factors rank first and third, respectively, in the amount of variance extracted from the correlation matrix by the fifteen factors. From a consideration of Table 4, the interpretation of the error measures is clear.

The *economic development dimension* accounts for 38.5 per cent (loading squared) of the variation in scores on demographic error, 18.5 per cent of the variation in population error, and 39.9 per cent variation in the missing data. These percentages indicate that economic development has an important relationship to the reliability of demographic data and to missing data in general. Variance in reliability is also accounted for, and to a greater degree, by the *totalitarianism dimension*. It is related to 72.2 per cent of the variation in national scores on economic-welfare error, 74 per cent of the variation in GNP error ratings, and 27 per cent of the variation in missing data. Here, the assumed effect on cross-national data of political motives gains some statistical verification.

Missing data has a communality of .91, which means that 91 per cent of the variation in missing data is accounted for by the fifteen factors, 66.9 per cent of the variation being due to the *economic development* and *totalitarianism* dimensions. The

Table 4
LOADINGS OF ERROR MEASURES ON PRIMARY
ORTHOGONALLY ROTATED FACTORS OF 236 VARIABLE ANALYSIS*

Most Highly Loaded Variable**	F_1 Economic Development	F_2 Total- itarianism	
Many telephones per capita	.95		
Low ratio of agricultural population to population	−.92		
Many radio receivers per capita	.91		
Large GNP per capita	.91		
High energy consumption per capita	.90		
High ratio of English book titles translated to all translations		1.10	
High ratio of English book titles translated to English and Russian translations		1.07	
Western Bloc allegiance		.86	
Low ratio of Russian titles translated to all translations		−.83	
Much U.S. economic aid		.74	
High ratio of U.S. aid to U.S. and U.S.S.R. aid		.74	
Much freedom of opposition		.71	
Error Measures			h^2
Low on demographic error dimension	−.62		.75
Low on economic-welfare error dimension		−.85	.81
Low GNP error rating		−.86	.87
Low population error	−.43		.54
Little missing data	−.63	−.52	.91
% Total Variance for factor on 236 variables	26.0	9.0	

N = 82 nations for 1955

*Product moment correlations were factored with unities in the principal diagonal. Principal components factoring technique was employed; the factors (15) of all positive eigenvalues were orthogonally rotated using varimax. The raw data matrix had about 17% missing data.
**Adjectives are given to indicate the scaling of the variable.

amount of missing data for a nation is thus a function of both its degree of underdevelopment *and* its degree of totalitarianism. The more underdeveloped and totalitarian a nation, the less there are cross-national data for that nation. Because of the large percentage of variation that missing data have in common with economic development and totalitarianism, there is a danger that correlation or factor analysis studies centered on cross-national development and/or totalitarianism (and its correlates, such as ideology, or bloc allegiance), which have missing data, *may* end up with distorted results.

As shown in Table 4, the demographic error dimension has 38.5 per cent of its variation accounted for by economic development. With a communality of .75, 26.5 per cent of its variance is spread across the other fourteen factors. Economic development is

thus the most important correlate. Keeping in mind that the demographic error dimension reflects a large cluster of error ratings and off-1955 error measures, it follows that assessments of the substantive relationships among demographic data, or between these data and others, *may* well be distorted by systematic error. Because of the high relationship between the GNP error rating and the economic-welfare error dimension, on the one hand, and totalitarianism, on the other, the same distortion due to systematic error may result when economic or welfare data are related to each other or to other variables.

DISCUSSION

What this study has tried to show is that one should not carry out an analysis of cross-national statistical data without first trying to differentiate the kind of error involved. This can be done either by investigating the reliability and comparability of each datum if one is concerned with a univariate distribution, or by developing in the multivariate case measures of error which can then be correlated with each other and the measures to be used. When this was done with 230 cross-national variables, it was shown that such error was resolved into demographic, economic-welfare population, GNP, and missing-data error. It was further shown that such error was mainly related to the economic development of a nation and its degree of totalitarianism.

The question that naturally follows is what to do in an analysis once such errors and their correlates are determined. It is not within the scope of this paper to treat the subject at length, although several courses of action may be suggested (see Fiering 1962, Campbell and Fiske 1959, Kendall and Stuart 1961). If one is concerned with regression coefficients and can assume that the variance of error on a variable is less than the variance of the true value, one might trichotomize the data, throw out the middle group and use the high- and low-end groups (where 0=one end group, 1=the other). Then one can analyze the dichotomy through standard regression techniques with a high level of confidence in the results. This approach can be used on almost all cross-national economic and demographic data, where the ratio of true variance to possible error variance is quite high.

If the direction as well as size of error is known, another approach is to regress each of the variables on the set of error ratings or measures. The resulting "error free" residuals may be used in subsequent multivariate analysis. The results can thus be interpreted as being free of the error indexed by the error ratings and measures.

A similar approach would be to factor-analyze the variables along with their error ratings and measures. Then one might rotate the first factors through (colinear with) the error terms. The remaining substantive factors can then be interpreted as delimiting clusters of relationships among the variables with the error, indexed by the error measures and ratings, partialed out. Only these substantive factors now minus systematic error need then be rotated to some orthogonal or oblique solution.

This approach is also applicable if one is dealing with the variance in error—the reliability of the data. When one determines the factors to which the measures of reliability are most related, nations may be grouped as they are high or low on these factors, and a factor analysis carried on within each group. If factors similar to the global analysis are delineated, confidence in the global results is enhanced.

In summary, then, the researcher using cross-national data need not throw up his hands in dismay over the problems ensuing from error in his data. Nor need he be on the defensive in regard to the stated or implied critique, "Your data are too poor." There are methods he can use to determine the probable nature of such error; once determined, it may be controlled.

PROPOSITIONS

Several empirical propositions about error in cross-national data emerge from this study.

1. Two independent continua along which nations vary in the degree of systematic error in this data are *demographic error* and *economic-welfare* dimensions.
2. About a third of the variation of nations in the amount of their demographic error in international data is related to their level of economic development.
3. About three-fourths of the variation of nations in the amount of their error in economic-welfare data is related to their degree of totalitarianism.
4. About two-thirds of the variation of nations in the amount of their missing data is related to their level of economic development and totalitarianism.
5. About one-fifth of the variation of nations in their population data error is related to economic development; about half of the variation in such error appears to be random.

BIBLIOGRAPHY

BOWLEY, ARTHUR LYON
1937   *Elements of statistics*, 6th ed. London, P. S. King.

CAMPBELL, DONALD T., and DONALD W. FISKE
1959   Convergent and discriminant validation by the multitrait-multimethod matrix. *Psychological Bulletin* 56:81–105.

CONNOR, L. R.
1932   *Statistics in theory and practice*. London, I. Pitman.

DEMOGRAPHIC YEARBOOK
1960   New York, United Nations, Department of Economic and Social Affairs.

DURBIN, J.
1954   Errors in variables. *Revue of the International Statistical Institute* 22:23–32.

FIERING, MYRON B.
1962   On the use of correlation to augment data. *Journal of the American Statistical Association* 57:20–32.

GEARY, R. C.
1953   Non-linear functional relationship between two variables when one variable is controlled. *Journal of the American Statistical Association* 48:94–103.

KENDALL, MAURICE G., and ALAN STUART
1961   *The advanced theory of statistics*, II. New York, Hafner.

MANDANSKY, ALBERT
1959   The fitting of straight lines when both variables are subject to error. *Journal of the American Statistical Association* 54: 173–205.

MORGENSTERN, OSKAR
1963   *On the accuracy of economic observations*, 2nd ed. Princeton, N.J., Princeton University Press.

NAROLL, RAOUL
1962   *Data quality control*. New York, Free Press.

PROBLEMS IN THE COLLECTION AND COMPARABILITY OF INTERNATIONAL STATISTICS
1949   Papers presented at the Round Table on International Statistics, 1948. Conference of the Milbank Memorial Fund, November 17–18, 1948. New York.

RUMMEL, RUDOLPH J.
1963   Dimensions of conflict behavior within and between nations. *General Systems: Yearbook of the Society for General Systems Research* 8:1–50.

1964   *Dimensions of conflict behavior within nations*. Dimensionality of Nations Project. Mimeograph. New Haven, Yale University.

1965   The dimensionality of nations project. In Richard Merritt and Stein Rokkan, *Comparing nations*. New Haven, Yale University Press.

n.d.   *Dimensions of nations*. Forthcoming.

SCHEFFÉ, HENRY
1958   Fitting straight lines when one variable is controlled. *Journal of the American Statistical Association* 53:106–117.

STUDENTSKI, PAUL
1958   *Income of nations*. New York, New York University Press.

TANTER, RAYMOND
1964a *Dimensions of conflict behavior within and between nations*. Ph.D. dissertation. Bloomington, Indiana University.

1964b *Dimensions of conflict behavior within nations, 1955–60: turmoil and internal war*. Delivered before the Peace Research Conference, University of Chicago, November 16–17, 1964.

CHAPTER 46

Data Quality Control and Library Research on Political Parties

KENNETH JANDA

As introduced by Naroll in his book (1962) by that title, "data quality control" refers to the systematic evaluation of reliability among written reports of human behavior and social phemonena. In Naroll's words:

Data quality control deals not with individual reports but instead with groups of reports compiled by various authors under various conditions. It depends upon the assumption that some records are made under conditions of higher apparent trustworthiness than others. (p. 2)

For more than a century the only systematic method of evaluating the reliability of reports has been the method of internal and external criticism developed by classical historians. (pp. 1–2)

To evaluate report reliability, I propose instead to apply the general spirit and philosophy of statistical production quality control, as widely used in industry. The general spirit of such quality control is to test regularly, by sampling methods, the hypothesis that something is seriously wrong with production methods. (p. 10)

In data quality control the behavioral scientist working with written records tests indications of unreliability to see if something is seriously wrong with the statements in the records. To be sure, there is an essential difference in the position of the comparativist and the industrial quality control engineer. (p. 11) . . . Therefore I propose to use the term "control" somewhat more broadly than it is used in industry. By "control of errors" I shall mean not only their detection but also the methods taken to counteract their effect on the results of the study. (p. 12)

Naroll proceeded to demonstrate the utility of data control in a cross-cultural survey of

The International Comparative Political Parties project is supported by the National Science Foundation, Grant GS-1418. Northwestern University's Research Committee generously supported one year's work pre-testing the methodology before application was made to the National Science Foundation. Northwestern's Council for Intersocietal Studies graciously provided some data processing equipment to facilitate our research.

cultural stress in thirty-seven societies as reported in existing ethnographies. His study used six main control factors:

(1) collection of specific case reports by the ethnographer, (2) use by the ethnographer of direct observation and personal participation in an ongoing culture as a major source of field data, (3) length of stay in the field among the people studied by the ethnographer, (4) familiarity of the ethnographer with the language of the people studied, (5) role of the ethnographer among the people studied (such as social scientist, missionary, government official), and (6) explicitness and generality of the ethnographer's report on the trait in question, with the concomitant presence or absence of a need for inference by the comparativist in order to classify the report. (pp. 14–15)

Analyzing ethnographic data on cultural stress according to these control factors, Naroll found that some factors were "provisionally validated" as sources of reporting bias while others showed no significant relationship to reports of cultural stress. For example, the length of stay (control factor 3) was positively related to witchcraft attribution, but there was no evidence that professional social scientists were more trustworthy ethnographic reporters than missionaries (control factor 5).

As Naroll himself pointed out, most of his control factors were "characteristically applicable to the ethnographic data collection process and may be of little use in controlling other kinds of data reports" (p. 26). Nevertheless he proposed that the methodology of data quality control had general applicability to social science research based on library materials, and he suggested a number of control factors which might be applicable to historiography. More important than the specific control factors presented in the book was the attention called to the problem of data reliability and to methods of dealing with the problem.

The idea of data quality control has since been applied by Koh (1966) to social science bibliographic references on Korea and by Textor (1968) in his computerized *Cross-Cultural Survey*. This paper outlines another, and more extensive, application of data quality control methodology to literature on political parties under study in the International Comparative Political Parties Project. While the Project departs considerably from the methodology originally set forth by Naroll, it is inspired by the same philosophy in its treatment of data reliability problems.

THE INTERNATIONAL COMPARATIVE POLITICAL PARTIES PROJECT

The ICPP Project was established at Northwestern University in 1967 for the purpose of conducting the first comprehensive, empirically-based, comparative analysis of political parties throughout the world. Data for this analysis are being collected and managed through a variety of information retrieval techniques applied to published and unpublished writings on party politics in ninety foreign countries. The objectives and over-all design of the project are detailed in another place (Janda 1968). This paper will describe only those features of the project which are essential for understanding its data quality control methodology.

Contrary to most cross-national political research, our unit of analysis is the political party rather than the nation-state. Instead of drawing a sample of parties for analysis, we intend to gather data on the *universe* of political parties, defined as those whose candidates won at least 5 per cent of the seats of the lower house of a national legislature in two successive elections in the time period 1950–1962. (A complete list of the parties presently identified for inclusion in the study is given in Janda 1968.) We plan to code each of some 250 political parties on a series of variables (e.g., ideological orientation, centralization of power, method of leadership selection) for subsequent keypunching and statistical analysis. Our primary source of data for coding parties on these variables consists of such library materials as books, articles, theses, government documents, party documents and newspapers.

This material is stored in the information files of the ICPP Project as copies of the original pages tagged with three-digit code numbers in a fashion quite similar to the practice of the Human Relations Area Files (Murdock 1961). The methodology for handling our files, however, is quite different. We record the pages *and their corresponding code numbers* on 16-mm microfilm for instantaneous retrieval with Eastman Kodak's MIRACODE information retrieval system (Janda 1967a). The basic components of the MIRACODE system are a special microfilm camera and microfilm reader. A film magazine containing information on party politics in a given country can be searched by the MIRACODE reader for logical combinations of codes assigned to individual pages, which are then selectively displayed for the researcher. Approximately one thousand pages of material can be stored on one 100-foot magazine and searched for specified combinations of code numbers in ten seconds.

COVERAGE OF THE LITERATURE AND QUALITY OF THE DATA

Because our data are drawn from library materials, we are dependent upon both the *coverage* and *quality* of the literature on political parties. Coverage of the literature in our files can be assessed rather precisely by reference to the frequency distributions of coding categories across all the pages in a given country's information file. Table 1 shows that distribution for the file on party politics in Guinea, which contains 699 pages from thirty-four documents (Skogan 1967). The table shows, for example, that we have 134 pages in the Guinean files that deal with the party's "issue orientation" (code 530) but only 2 pages that discuss the way the party "raises funds" (code 260). A similar evaluation has been made for all nine countries processed for inclusion into the files to date (Janda 1967b). Our experience so far suggests that our missing data problems will be most severe for variables dealing with party organization and structure.

More relevant to the purpose of this paper is the separate question of the quality of the information that we do have in our files. We

Table 1
FREQUENCY DISTRIBUTIONS OF SUBSTANTIVE CODES USED IN INDEXING
ALL 699 PAGES OF LITERATURE FOR GUINEA

FREQUENCY OF USAGE BY ASCENDING CODE NUMBERS

Code	Description	FREQ.	PCT.
000	Definition of a political party	1	0.1
010	Typology of political parties	3	0.2
020	Purpose of studying parties	2	0.1
100	When it was formed	11	0.8
110	Who formed it, base of support	7	0.5
120	Why was it formed	1	0.1
130	How was it formed	5	0.3
140	Political history of party	8	0.6
150	Organizational history of party	12	0.8
200	Selects candidates, party officials	5	0.3
210	Conducts election campaigns	7	0.5
220	Builds party policy and organization	33	2.3
230	Influences government policy	17	1.2
240	Propagandizes its goals and activity	25	1.7
250	Discipline, maintains group unity	34	2.4
260	Raises funds	2.	0.1
270	Causes demonstrations, riots	2	0.1
280	Stands between gov't and citizen	14	1.0
290	Social activities of party	36	2.5
300	Party supporters	27	1.9
320	Party members	24	1.7
330	Party workers and activists	6	0.4
340	Party candidates	1	0.1
350	Party members in government posts	3	0.2
360	Party leaders and officials	120	8.3
370	Party factions	6	0.4
380	Organizational support	12	0.8
390	Group support	1	0.1
400	Local party organization	22	1.5
420	Regional party organization	17	1.2
430	National party convention, Congress	17	1.2
440	National party committee	34	2.4
460	Ancillary organizations	60	4.2
470	Party structure, functional or not	15	1.0
480	Articulation of party structure	22	1.5
490	Centralization of power	66	4.6
500	Gain control of government	6	0.4
520	Place members in government position	1	0.1
530	Issue orientation	134	9.3
540	Ideological orientation	37	2.6
550	Subvert the government	1	0.1
560	Efficiency and effectiveness	5	0.3
600	National crises	5	0.3
610	Issues of consensus or cleavage	14	1.0
620	Electoral system	6	0.4
630	Popular participation	7	0.5
640	Political norms and attitudes	24	1.7
650	Administrative bureaucracy	9	0.6
660	The executive	23	1.6
670	The legislature	11	0.8
680	Gov't. structure, political history	88	6.1
690	Geographical allocation of authority	13	0.9
700	Economic environment	76	5.3
710	Geographical environment	10	0.7

FREQUENCY BY RANK-ORDER OF USAGE

RANK	CODE	FREQ.	PCT.
1	530	134	9.3
2	360	120	8.3
3	680	88	6.1
4	700	76	5.3
5	720	68	4.7
6	490	66	4.6
7	460	60	4.2
8	890	41	2.8
9	880	38	2.6
10	540	37	2.6
11	290	36	2.5
12	250	34	2.4
13	440	34	2.4
14	220	33	2.3
15	300	27	1.9
16	240	25	1.7
17	320	24	1.7
18	640	24	1.7
19	660	23	1.6
20	400	22	1.5
21	480	22	1.5
22	770	21	1.5
23	760	20	1.4
24	230	17	1.2
25	420	17	1.2
26	430	17	1.2
27	850	17	1.2
28	750	16	1.1
29	470	15	1.0
30	280	14	1.0
31	610	14	1.0
32	690	13	0.9
33	150	12	0.8
34	380	12	0.8
35	740	12	0.8
36	100	11	0.8
37	670	11	0.8
38	820	11	0.8
39	860	11	0.8
40	710	10	0.7
41	730	10	0.7
42	840	10	0.7
43	650	9	0.6
44	140	8	0.6
45	110	7	0.5
46	210	7	0.5
47	630	7	0.5
48	810	7	0.5
49	330	6	0.4
50	370	6	0.4
51	500	6	0.4
52	620	6	0.4
53	130	5	0.3
54	200	5	0.3

Table 1 (continued)

		FREQ.	PCT.	RANK	CODE	FREQ.	PCT.
720	Social environment	68	4.7	55	560	5	0.3
730	Religious conditions	10	0.7	56	600	5	0.3
740	Social norms and attitudes	12	0.8	57	870	5	0.3
750	Activities of the military	16	1.1	58	10	3	0.2
760	Activities of the students	20	1.4	59	350	3	0.2
770	Activities of the trade unions	21	1.5	60	780	3	0.2
780	Volunteer activity, interest groups	3	0.2	61	830	3	0.2
800	Number of parties	1	0.1	62	20	2	0.1
810	Election results	7	0.5	63	260	2	0.1
820	Stability of parties in system	11	0.8	64	270	2	0.1
830	Interparty competition	3	0.2	65	0	1	0.1
840	Interparty cooperation	10	0.7	66	120	1	0.1
850	Origin, support, history of system	17	1.2	67	340	1	0.1
860	Status of the party in party system	11	0.8	68	390	1	0.1
870	Typology of party systems	5	0.3	69	520	1	0.1
880	International party system	38	2.6	70	550	1	0.1
890	Other parties	41	2.8	71	800	1	0.1

FREQUENCY DISTRIBUTIONS COMBINED INTO MAJOR CODING CATEGORIES

		FREQ.	PCT.	RANK	CODE	FREQ.	PCT.
000	Definitions, functions, theory	6	0.4	1	400	253	17.5
100	How does a political party begin	44	3.1	2	700	236	16.4
200	What does a political party do	175	12.1	3	300	200	13.9
300	Who belongs to the party	200	13.9	4	600	200	13.9
400	How is the party organized	253	17.5	5	500	184	12.8
500	What does party seek to accomplish	184	12.8	6	200	175	12.1
600	Conditions–political environment	200	13.9	7	800	144	10.0
700	Conditions–social, econ, geographic	236	16.4	8	100	44	3.1
800	Conditions–party system	144	10.0	9	0	6	0.4

approach the problem of data reliability (and validity) first by scoring each source document on a series of twenty-two "data quality" variables. Sample variables, which are analogous to Naroll's "control factors," are "place of publication," "original language of source," "position of author," "source of data," "scope of study," "field research," and subjective judgments of the document's over-all "quality," "ideological orientation," and "objectivity." A complete listing of the data quality codes is contained in the Appendix. For the most part, these coding categories constitute no more than nominal scales, although some of the scaling is ordinal, with higher numbers implying higher ratings on those variables.

Each document is scored on the data quality variables by the same analyst who indexes it for our MIRACODE system. As a matter of routine, approximately 10 per cent of the pages in our files are reprocessed by a second analyst who reindexes the pages done by the first analyst and recodes his data quality variables for the same document.

Two special computer programs are then used to calculate both inter*indexer* and inter*coder* reliabilities for the reprocessed material. In contrast to the rather low interindexer reliabilities around .50 that have characterized our indexing of test for MIRACODE retrieval, we have encountered more generally acceptable intercoder reliabilities above .80 for data quality variables. (The distinction between "interindexer" and "intercoder" reliabilities is discussed in depth in Janda 1967b. There a lower level of reliability is defended as being "acceptable" for indexing than for coding.)

CONTROLLING DATA QUALITY: THE PROBLEM OF BIAS

Once the data quality variables are assigned to the documents and keypunched for computer processing, they are used in two ways to "control" or monitor the quality of information in the files. First, usage of the codes is tabulated for all the documents on party politics in a given country. This pro-

Table 2

DATA QUALITY CODES APPLIED TO 34 DOCUMENTS INDEXED FOR GUINEA

DATA QUALITY CODES	MOST FREQUENT:	(N)	2nd MOST FREQUENT:	(N)	3rd MOST FREQUENT:	(N)	4th MOST FREQUENT:	(N)
Document Type	Section in book	12	Journal article	11	News feature	5	News item	2
Place of Publication	United States	25	Guinea	3	Other	3	France	2
Original Language of Source	English	29	French	5				
Position of Author	Academic	23	Party official	3	Journalist	3	Not applicable/no information	5
National Background	United States	24	Guinea	5	France	1	Geographical area	1
Language Resources	Cites native sources	17	Native sources	5	Not applicable/no information	12		
Date of Data	1960-1964	18	1955-1959	9	Post-World War II	6	Not applicable/no information	1
Data Source Types	Government or party document	19	Secondary sources	19	Electoral or ecological data	4	Personal experience	4
Quantitative Analysis	No quantification	23	Raw data in context	7	One table	3	Two or more tables	1
Theoretical Treatment	No propositions	33	1 + propositions	1				
Traditional Scholarship	No footnotes	17	Between one and two per page	6	Less than one per page	6	Between two and three per page	4
Nature of Sources Cited	No footnotes	17	Primary source—party document	15	Primary source—private record	1	Secondary source—news	1
Scope of Study	Single country	19	Single party	5	Area survey	1	Comparison of parties	1
Field Research	More than one year in country	10	None	8	Geographical area	5	Less than one year in country	4
Overall Judgment of Quality	Medium	16	High	11	Low	7		
Author's Ideology	Centrist	19	Leftist	5	Rightist	1	Not applicable/no information	9
Author's Objectivity	Objectivity not questioned	26	Value-oriented	6	Not applicable/no information	2		

vides a statistical profile of the file as given in Table 2, which shows the data quality summary of thirty-four documents indexed for Guinea. While this overview is useful for assessing the state of the literature on party politics in a given country, it can be misinterpreted because of its gross nature. Consider Skogan's comments on Table 2:

There appears to be a lack of extensive field research within Guinea itself. Although Table 2 lists "more than one year in country" as its most frequent document code, this is a reflection of work of one man, Victor DuBois, and the extensive contribution that his works have made to our files. Using authors rather than documents as our unit of analysis, we find that most do not appear to have spent much time in Guinea. (Skogan 1967)

Despite such possibilities for misinterpretation, this data quality summary has value for macro-level evaluations of the data in the files, although it does not readily allow for "control of errors" in Naroll's sense of "counteracting their effect on the results of the study."

The second usage of the data quality codes in controlling the quality of information obtained from the files—and certainly in keeping with Naroll's meaning of "control"—lies in the coding of individual parties on variables for comparative analysis. Here the data quality variables will facilitate decisions about the proper way to code or score a party on a given variable in the face of conflicting statements retrieved from our files by the MIRACODE system.

The MIRACODE equipment will retrieve varying numbers of pages containing information relevant to the coding of a given party on a given variable—e.g., "centralization of power" as measured on a three-point scale: "low," "medium," or "high." Insofar as the retrieved information is relevant to the decision, the researcher is expected, at the preliminary stage of coding, to score the party for each "hit" on the MIRACODE reader. As a result, he may record different scores on the party's coding sheet for "centralization of power" after searching all the material in the files.

When diverse sources disagree in statements about a party, we will seek to determine the basis of disagreement through a special analysis of variance computer program, which treats the data quality codes as independent variables predicting to varying party codes as the dependent variable. The program will try to identify the existence of systematic differences among data quality variables which account for variance in the dependent variable as coded from information in the files.

An example may clarify the procedure: the MIRACODE system may retrieve a total of thirty pages indexed for "party members" (code 320) pertaining to party X. Perhaps twenty-five of these pages would be relevant to coding the party on "severity of membership requirements." Assume that ten of these twenty-five report that membership in the party does *not* require the payment of dues, while fifteen other documents state that dues *is* a membership requirement. By analyzing the source of variance in our coding of this variable, we may discover that the discrepancy is explained by a data quality variable, e.g., "position of author"—with academics reporting no dues requirement and former party officials revealing that members are indeed required to pay dues to stay in good standing.

This example is offered only to illustrate the general procedure for using our data quality variables in "quality control" of the data we generate through library research. Even if we identify systematic sources of variance underlying disparate coding decisions, we have no method for "automatically" determining which coding decision is the *valid* one. With respect to judgments of validity, we are left in the age-old position of library researchers confronted with disagreeing sources; we use a variety of criteria, usually depending on the variable in question, to assess source validity. In the above example, we would probably decide to code "severity of membership requirements" according to the statements furnished by former party officials, who presumably constitute a "better" source for this variable than academics. Often, the disclosure of systematic differences among sources initiates focused analysis to resolve the discrepancy.

CONTROLLING DATA QUALITY: THE PROBLEM OF MEASUREMENT ERROR

In addition to guarding against the intrusion of bias or systematic error in the data generated through library research, there is the additional problem of guarding against more or less random measurement error, which is especially vexing in the age of team research, computer analysis, and data banks. Holes in punch cards and magnetic spots on computer tape convey an awful definitiveness and finality—regardless of the uncertainty that may have attended the actual coding process. Once a coding decision is reached, the variable score is enshrined in paper or plastic for subsequent analysis and, usually, unquestioned acceptance. In the ICPP Project, however, we recognize and allow for the fallibility of our data by means of an "adequacy-confidence" scale, which expresses our evaluation of the quality of the data in our files that underlie each variable code.

Our primary information resource for coding any party on any given variable will be the hundreds of pages we have indexed and microfilmed on party politics in the country under concern. Obviously, the literature will vary in its adequacy for providing information with which to make coding judgments, and our analysts will have more confidence in coding some variables than in coding others. We intend to reflect the adequacy of the documentation underlying any given variable and party and our analysts' confidence in their coding judgments by accompanying each variable with an "adequacy-confidence" rating, as scored by those who coded the variable.

Every variable for every party will be coded independently by each member of the two-man research team that has read and indexed the literature in the file for that country. The *variable* code that is eventually keypunched for statistical analysis derives from their independent coding operations. When the coders agree on a variable code, that code will obviously be entered for the variable. When they disagree over coding the variable, an attempt will be made to resolve their disagreement through discussion, involving outside coders if necessary. The *adequacy-confidence* code that is assigned to the final variable code also derives from both analysts' adequacy-confidence codes, which are independently assigned when the variable is coded. Intercoder conferences and involvement of outside coders are also used to resolve disagreements in rating variables on the adequacy-confidence scale.

The adequacy-confidence scale was de-signed to reflect four factors that seem especially important in determining the researcher's belief in the accuracy or truth value of the coded variable—as well as can be determined through library research. These factors are (1) the number of sources that provide relevant information for the coding decision, (2) the proportion of agreement to disagreement in the information reported by different sources, (3) the degree of discrepancy among the sources when disagreement exists, and (4) the credibility attached to the various sources of information.

The first three factors deal more with the "adequacy" of the literature that can be cited to document the variable code, and the fourth deals more with the analyst's confidence in coding the variable. In an effort to "objectify" our measure of the researcher's belief in the accuracy or truth value of the coded variable, we have operationalized the adequacy-confidence scale primarily in terms of the first three factors: (1) number of sources, (2) proportion of agreement, and (3) degree of discrepancy. However, this operationalization is intended only to guide the researcher in arriving at his adequacy-confidence rating when the fourth factor (source credibility) is held constant across documents. If the credibility factor, ignored in our operationalization, interacts sufficiently with the information sources to cause the researcher to be more or less confident in his coding than the operationalization formula would suggest, then he is free to revise the adequacy-confidence rating accordingly.

The credibility factor is kept out of the operationalization due to the great difficulty in fashioning an acceptable scale for a position in n-dimensional attribute space, created from the several subfactors contributing to source credibility, of which three seem especially important: (1) amount of attention given to the variable in the source, (2) adequacy of the research underlying the author's observation, and (3) the integrity and objectivity attributed to the author. These three factors, and certainly others, can interact in a variety of ways to affect the researcher's evaluation of source credibility, and we have not attempted to spell out rules for handling the combinations and subleties involved in any such evaluation. Instead, we are constrained to leave source credibility operate as a subjective variable in tempering the researcher's belief in the truth value or accuracy of the variable code after reference to the more objective operationalization.

In general, if the "credibility gap" between sources is not great, it is expected that the researcher will score the coding judgment according to the objective operationalization of the adequacy-confidence scale. But when he feels that the credibility of the sources is such that straightforward application of the operational definition results in a confidence code value that does not reflect his own belief in the truth value or accuracy of the variable code, then he should revise his adequacy-confidence code accordingly.

To guide the researcher in interpreting the graduations in the adequacy-confidence scale, a conceptual definition of each scale category is presented in Table 3 with the operationalizations of the coding categories.

The analysis of variance approach discussed earlier is in order only for variables that rated from "2" to "5" (and possibly "7") on the adequacy-confidence scale. Other scale values suggest a lack of disagreement within the literature, leaving no "variance" to be explained by the data quality codes through the analysis of variance model. Even for relevant adequacy-confidence codes, the analysis of variance approach is useless in detecting error if the observations in the literature are too few to support a statistical analysis. In these cases—which may turn out to be most cases—the adequacy-confidence scale is used in two less elegant methods for "control of errors" in Naroll's sense of "counteracting their effect on the results of the study."

The first and simpler method is to study scatter diagrams or contingency tables for the presence of deviant cases as disclosed by distance from the regression line or entries in cells off the diagonal. Assuming that the diagrams or tables are constructed to show

Table 3
ADEQUACY-CONFIDENCE SCALE

Code	Category label	Conceptual definition	Operational definition
BLANK	Inapplicable	Variable does not apply to the party coded	
1	Inadequate: no data	No information is contained in the file on the variable being considered	
2	Inadequate: disagreement	Disagreements are found in the file which are not resolvable by reference to source credibility. The disagreement might be resolved by more data, but the information in the file is inadequate	
3	Barely adequate: lowest confidence	It is possible to cite this code as the most probable among alternatives, but further research could easily produce a finding at great variance from this one	Two situations can produce this code: (1) There is a 1:1 division between sources with a "great" discrepancy* in the suggested codes, but one code can be favored on the basis of source credibility. (2) Data are incomplete in some way, but a code can be inferred from available information
4	Adequate: low confidence	There is a disagreement in the literature which suggests that the code might not be supported by further research, although the alternative is not greatly discrepant	There is a 1:1 division between sources with a "medium" discrepancy* in suggested codes, but one code can be favored on the basis of source credibility
5	Adequate: low to medium	There is no strong agreement in the literature on this particular code, but further research is likely to support the code or one close to it	Three situations can produce this code: (1) No source has complete information, but a summary code can be made from data from two or more incomplete sources. (2) There is a 2:1 division between sources without regard to degree of discrepancy. (3) There is a 1:1 division between sources with a "small" discrepancy* in suggested codes, but one code can be favored on the basis of source credibility
6	Adequate: medium confidence	The code is not extensively documented in the literature, but there is no disagreement in evidence. Further research would likely support the code, but there are no strong grounds to rule out possible disagreement	One source cites the summary code with no disagreement in evidence
7	Adequate: medium to high	Although the code is quite well documented, the judgment is placed in some doubt because it is not unanimous. Disagreements might occur in further research, but the code would likely be supported	There is at least a 3:1 division between sources, without regard to the degree of discrepancy, and the overwhelming evidence favors the code
Code	Category label	Conceptual definition	Operational definition
8	Adequate: high confidence	Since documentation of the code is good and no disagreements are apparent, it is probably accurate, although additional documentation is desirable	Two sources agree on the code and no source disagrees
9	Adequate: highest confidence	The variable code is extremely well documented and no disagreements are apparent; belief in the accuracy of this code is about as high as one could expect in the absence of original field research	Three or more sources agree on the code and no source disagrees

*The degree of discrepancy is applicable only to variables of an ordinal or interval nature. Whether a discrepancy is to be classified as "small," "medium," or "great" depends on the particular variable and is established in the operational definitions for each variable, which must be referred to in order to determine or interpret the degree of discrepancy.

the relationship between two variables linked by theory, the presence of deviant cases suggest either measurement error or exceptions to the theory. By examining the cases for their adequacy-confidence scale scores, which can be displayed by appropriate computer routines, the researcher might be able to determine if apparent exceptions to his theory rate low on the scale and represent probable measurement error or if the data seem solid and the theory dubious.

The second method of controlling error involves a "stepwise" approach to the calculation of correlation coefficients. By means of flexible computer programs for including and excluding cases from analysis on the basis of their adequacy-confidence scores, correlations can be calculated first for the "best" data, then again for progressively larger sets of data as the quality restriction

is relaxed. Assuming that measurement error (as expressed by the adequacy-confidence scale) is random and the hypothesized relationship is true, smaller correlation coefficients should be generated from each progressive relaxation of data quality. If the correlations should happen to increase, serious attention should be given to bias among data at the lower end of the adequacy-confidence scale.

Although problems inherent to library research are not unique to the ICPP Project, the scope of our activities is such that we must develop systematic procedures for evaluating the information that resides in and emerges from our files. We have adopted the methodology of data quality control to help us cope with the problem of data reliability.

APPENDIX

Data Quality Control Codes

Columns Variable

1–18 SENIOR AUTHOR'S LAST NAME AND INITIALS
19–20 YEAR OF ORIGINAL PUBLICATION
21–23 COUNTRY CODE
24–26 DOCUMENT CODE
27–29 INDEXER CODE
30 TYPE OF DOCUMENT
  0 not otherwise classified
  1 reference source—*Facts On File*, Keesings Archives, etc.
  2 newspaper or magazine item—popular periodical
  3 newspaper or magazine feature story—popular periodical
  4 party document—constitution, platform
  5 government documents—reports, statistical abstracts
  6 journal article
  7 article or chapter in book (used for reprints of journal article)
  8 thesis or monograph
  9 book
31–32 PERIODICAL CODE—specific for each country
33 PLACE OF PUBLICATION

  blank don't know (missing data)
  0 not otherwise classified (use also when not applicable)
  1 United States (except if 2 is applicable)
  2 in colonizing country (U.S., Britain, France, Germany, Spain, Portugal, Netherlands)
  3 in area of world where country exists—i.e., Latin America, Africa, Europe, Asia
  4 in country studied
34 ORIGINAL LANGUAGE OF SOURCE
  0 not otherwise classified
  1 English
  2 French
  3 Spanish
  4 German
  5 language of country studied (if two apply, favor using this code)
35 AUTHORSHIP
  0 no author named
  1 one author
  2 two authors
  3 three or more authors
  4 corporate author (e.g., Bulgarian National Committee)
36 POSITION OF FIRST-NAMED AUTHOR

(favor higher code if two apply)

blank no information (missing data)

0 not otherwise classified

1 journalist

2 government official in country studied

3 ex-government official

4 party official in country studied

5 ex-party official

6 academic

37 PRESUMED NATIONAL BACKGROUND—judged from last name and source of publication

blank not applicable—no author given

0 no judgment made/not otherwise classified

1 United States (except if 2 is applicable)

2 from colonizing country—U.S., Britain, France, Germany, Spain, Portugal, Netherlands

3 from area of world where country exists—e.g., Latin America, Africa, Europe (use if in doubt of 4)

4 from country studied

38 EVIDENCE OF USE OF LANGUAGE RESOURCES

blank not applicable (use for general theory, not country studied)

0 no information

1 coder infers author has no ability in native language

2 cites translated materials, worked with interpreter

3 cites native language sources, uses native language phrases in text (excluding the native names of political parties)

4 uses native interviewers to collect survey information

5 document itself translated from native language or written by native in English

39 DATE OF MAJOR PORTION OF DATA (code later period if other choice cannot be made)

blank not applicable (use for general theory)

0 not otherwise classified

1 prior to World War II (1939 or earlier)

2 1940–1944

3 1945–1949

4 1950–1954

5 1955–1959

6 1960–1964

7 1965–present

8 post–World War II (give preference to above categories)

40 NOT USED

41–49 CODE FOR DATA SOURCES (entered in columns 41–49, ranked by importance) blank not applicable (use for speeches, election reports, etc.)

0 no data sources revealed

1 not otherwise classified

2 secondary sources—newspapers, books, journals, broadcasts

3 government publications or party documents

4 election returns or ecological data

5 roll call votes

6 sample survey of individuals

7 interviews with party officials or leaders

8 personal experience as participant observer

50 NUMBER OF DATA SOURCES USED

51 NOT USED

52 QUANTITATIVE ANALYSIS SCORE

0 no quantification involved

1 raw data or per cents reported in text but not in tables

2 one raw data or percentage table reported

3 two or more raw data or percentage tables reported

4 bivariate measures of association reported

5 multivariate statistics reported

53 THEORETICAL TREATMENT SCORE

0 no explicit propositions advanced or tested

1 general theory that discusses "relevant" variables, but does not state relationships among them

2 one or more explicit propositions advanced but not statistically tested

3 one or more explicit propositions advanced and statistically tested

4 enumeration of three or more propositions with common concepts into a body of theory

5 incorporation of three or more propositions with common concepts into a body of theory

54 TRADITIONAL SCHOLARSHIP SCORE

blank not applicable (speeches, election returns)

    0 no footnotes cited or attribution of sources

    1 less than 1 footnote per page

    2 between 1 and 2 footnotes per page

    3 between 2 and 3 footnotes per page

    4 more than 3 footnotes per page

55 NATURE OF SOURCES CITED IN FOOTNOTES (enter the highest when appropriate)

blank not applicable—no footnotes

    0 not classified

    1 tertiary sources—encyclopedias, references only

    2 secondary sources—newspapers and magazines

    3 secondary sources—books, journal articles

    4 primary sources—party and government documents

    5 primary sources—personal records, memoirs, interviews, data from unpublished sources

56 CITATION OF DUVERGER (enter highest applicable)

blank not applicable—no footnotes in text

    0 footnotes, but none to Duverger

    1 one footnote to Duverger

    2 two or more footnotes to Duverger

    3 mentions Duverger in the text

    4 tests out Duverger's propositions or theory, modeled after Duverger's analysis, uses Duverger's concepts or "branch" and "caucus" parties, "majority bent" parties, etc.

57 SCOPE OF STUDY (use for whole document whether all is coded or not)

    0 not otherwise classified

    1 conceptual or theoretical, without emphasis on data and evidence

    2 survey of parties or politics in given area, e.g., Latin America

    3 comparative analysis of governmental systems

    4 comparative analysis of political parties

    5 study of a single country

    6 study of a single party

    7 news event

58–60 FOCUS OF STUDY—MOST FREQUENT SUBSTANTIVE CODING CATEGORY USED

61–63 NUMBER OF TIMES MOST FREQUENT SUBSTANTIVE CODING CATEGORY USED

64–66 FOCUS OF STUDY—SECOND MOST FREQUENT SUBSTANTIVE CODING CATEGORY USED

67–69 NUMBER OF TIMES SECOND MOST FREQUENT SUBSTANTIVE CODING CATEGORY USED

70 FIELD RESEARCH

blank not applicable or no information

    0 evidence of no work in country studied

    1 evidence of work in geographical area

    2 spent less than one year in country

    3 spent more than one year in country, or two trips of any length, or author writing in country

    4 author a nonresident native of a country

    5 author a resident of country

71 CODER'S SUBJECTIVE JUDGMENT OF QUALITY OF SOURCE

    1 low

    2 medium—code unless evidence points to high or low

    3 high

72 CODER'S SUBJECTIVE JUDGMENT OF IDEOLOGICAL ORIENTATION OF AUTHOR —

    0 not classified on left-right dimension

    1 leftist

    2 centrist—code unless evidence points to low or high

    3 rightist

73 CODER'S SUBJECTIVE JUDGMENT OF AUTHOR'S OBJECTIVITY

    1 antiseptically objective—e.g., "scientific" analysis, mainly tabular presentation of data

    2 no reason to doubt objectivity

    3 values detectable

    4 emotional language

74–76 NUMBER OF PAGES CODED

78–80 CODING TIME IN MINUTES

BIBLIOGRAPHY

JANDA, KENNETH

1967a Political research with MIRACODE: a 16-mm. microfilm information retrieval system. *Social Science Information* 6: 169–181.

1967b *A microfilm and computer system for analyzing comparative politics literature.* Paper delivered at the National Conference on Content Analysis, The Annenberg School of Communications, University of Pennsylvania, Philadelphia, November 16–18.

1968 Retrieving information for a comparative study of political parties. In William J. Crotty, ed., *Approaches to the study of party organization.* Boston, Allyn and Bacon. Reprinted in *Information retrieval: applications to political science.* Indianapolis, Bobbs-Merrill.

KOH, HESUNG CHUN

1966 A social science bibliographic system: orientation and framework. *Behavior Science Notes* 1:145–163.

MURDOCK, GEORGE P., *et al.*

1961 *Outline of cultural materials.* New Haven, Human Relations Area Files.

NAROLL, RAOUL

1962 *Data quality control: a new research technique.* Glencoe, Ill., Free Press.

SKOGAN, WESLEY

1967 *Bibliography on party politics in Guinea, 1950–1952.* In Kenneth Janda, ed., *ICPP Bibliography Series.* Evanston, International Comparative Political Parties Project, Northwestern University.

TEXTOR, ROBERT B.

1968 *A cross-cultural summary.* New Haven, Human Relations Area Files.

CHAPTER 47

Galton's Problem

RAOUL NAROLL

Galton's problem is widely considered to be a crucial weakness in the cross-cultural survey method. Galton raised his problem at the meeting of the Royal Anthropological Institute in 1889 when Tylor read his pioneer paper introducing the cross-cultural survey method (Tylor 1889:272). Tylor showed correlations ("adhesions," he called them) between certain traits; in the discussion which followed, Galton pointed out that traits often spread by diffusion—by borrowing or migration. Since this is often so, how many independent trials of his correlations did Tylor have? Boas, for decades the immensely influential dean of American anthropologists, once told his student Lowie (1946:227–230) that when he first read Tylor's paper, he became greatly enthusiastic. This seemed to him an ideal research technique. On reflecting further, however, Galton's objection seemed to him a devastating one; unless there was a solution to Galton's problem, Boas considered the cross-cultural survey method valueless.

Galton's problem is of great importance elsewhere as well. Whenever sociologists or political scientists test general theories about society or culture by correlations, they ought to be aware of Galton's problem. In such correlational studies cultural diffusion is often present as a possible third factor, a "lurking variable" which may explain away the correlation as a test of fundamental social theory.

For example, let me cite a research design once prepared by two colleagues of mine. A central hypothesis of the study was that there was a relationship between voting of Negroes in the United States and local prevalence of a one-party system rather than a two-party system. Of course there was a high negative correlation to be expected between proportion of Negroes voting and prevalence of the one-party system in the separate states. But this correlation merely reflected two of many characteristics of our Old South. As a theoretical investigation rather than a mere description of American behavior, such a correlation would establish nothing.

Social scientists often correlate particular traits in their own culture, or their own culture area (e.g., Western civilization), in order to test general theories about human behavior. Whenever they do so they should deal with the rival hypothesis that the correlations observed merely reflect characteristics of subcultures within the area studied. For subcultures (social classes, regional cultural variations, etc.) doubtless behave like primitive tribes with respect to the influence of diffusion-producing associations within themselves.

I believe that Boas' concept of independence of cases is an unfruitful approach to the solution of Galton's problem. The problem is to distinguish the effect of functional associations, of "adhesions" in Tylor's graphic term, from the effect of more common historical association through diffusion, whether through genetic relationship of common cultural ancestry or through borrowing from a common cultural center. The problem here is to control a cross-cultural (or cross-subcultural) correlation between factors considered related functionally to see whether this relationship is an artifact of common historical circumstances. Thus we have, conceptually speaking, a simple problem of partial association of the sort analogous to those discussed in detail in Zeisel (1947). For instance, Zeisel in one example shows that single people eat more candy than married people, but that if one controls for age, this relationship disappears; the apparent correlation between marital status and candy consumption merely reflects the fact that older people eat less candy than younger people and older people are more likely to be married than younger people. Now Galton's problem, as I see it, is to test apparently functional correlations between traits to see if they are mere artifacts of historical relationship—to control for diffusion. If the correlation merely reflects coincidences of borrowing or migration, I call the relationship a *hyper-diffusional* association, but if, after controlling for the effects of diffusion, the association remains significant, I call the relationship a *semi-diffusional* association. (If no diffusion were involved at all, I would call this an *un-diffusional* association; but I know of no such case.)

It is well to bear in mind that there are two distinct types of cross-cultural studies which use statistics, taking the "tribe" or society as a unit, and thus comparing the characteristics of a number of societies. First, there is the well-known cross-cultural survey, which seeks to test hypotheses about functional relationships in society and culture. (See Chapter 1, above.) Second, there are regional studies of trait distributions, like the magnificent, but little-appreciated, Culture Element Distribution studies conducted by Kroeber and his associates at the University of California a couple of decades ago. (See Chapter 32, above.) The object of the first is to discern "functional" relationships, associations of traits arising out of the nature of human personality, human society or human culture. The object of the second is to discern "historical" relationships, associations of traits spread through an area by borrowing or migration. Critics of each type of study have pointed out that an examination of either phenomenon ("functional" relationship or diffusion) needs to allow for the effect of the other. As already remarked, when Tylor introduced the cross-cultural survey method, Boas at first reacted with keen enthusiasm, seeing it as the answer to all problems; but

after he thought more about it, he came to feel that Galton's objection was deadly—if traits spread by diffusion, how many independent trials of the phenomenon did Tylor have? No one knew, and thus his statistics seemed meaningless (Boas 1927:120 ff.). Wallis (1928) likewise pointed out very early that the existence of a functional relationship between traits involved in a Culture Element Distribution study challenged the validity of its correlations taken as evidence of diffusion, an objection repeated by Kluckhohn (1939:359) and whose cogency with regard to the relationship between the distribution of girls' puberty rites and the distribution of religious cults in California was conceded by Kroeber (1936:111 ff.) himself.

THE SIGNIFICANCE OF GALTON'S PROBLEM

Some anthropologists still argue that wherever traits are found in association in a number of tribes, this association is evidence of some kind of functional linkage between the traits. In other words, they argue that if two traits are repeatedly found together, this alone shows that one trait has something to do with the other trait, that somehow the practice of one trait helps the people practice the other trait. Sociologists, who make extensive use of correlations among geographically distributed populations, have persistently ignored Galton's problem and in conversation many sociologists strongly resist any suggestion of its validity. They seem to feel that if two traits are correlated, such a correlation must constitute evidence that the traits are somehow functionally linked. That they may merely reflect joint diffusion without any functional linkage at all seems to many sociologists a most implausible argument.

Clear evidence that mere diffusional coincidence can produce not merely high but perfect correlations between traits was published by Klimek (1935). Klimek and his associates did not, however, call attention to this aspect of their findings, or consider it of much importance, because among these anthropologists at this time the overwhelming importance of diffusion was taken for granted. With them, as Kluckhohn (1939: 359 ff.) had to point out, the difficulty was the reverse: *they* had to be reminded that *some* traits might to *some* extent have some functional linkage.

In order to make clear the cogency of Galton's argument, we need only to look at Klimek's California Culture Element Distribution data. For example, Klimek shows that in aboriginal California, patrilinear totemic clans are to be found invariably and exclusively in tribes (namely the Mohave, the Yuma and the Kamia of the southeast corner of the state) which also play tunes of flageolets, use carrying frames made of sticks and cords, make oval plate pottery, use a squared muller, and favor twins.

Again, Klimek shows that in aboriginal California debt slavery was practiced only in the northwest corner of the present-day state, namely among the Tolowa, the Hupa, the Karok, the Yurok and the Wiyot. Thus in aboriginal California debt slavery is found invariably and exclusively among tribes whose women wear flat caps made of overlay twined basketry, whose men wear painted deerskin capes, who cook in low cooking baskets, who use pipes inlaid with haliotis and who levy a fine for adultery.

But patrilinear totemic clans are not peculiar to southeastern California. They are found scattered around the world in many other places. Would we expect that in Africa, in Eurasia or in Oceania, wherever we encountered patrilinear totemic clans, there and there only we would also find people playing tunes on flageolets? using carrying frames made of sticks and cords? making oval plate pottery? using a large fish scoop? using a squared muller? or favoring twins?

Again, debt slavery is not peculiar to northwestern California; it is found among peoples in several other parts of the world, notably in West Africa. Would we expect that wherever in West Africa we found debt slavery, invariably there but only there would we find women wearing flat caps made of overlay twined basketry? Women cooking in waterproof baskets using heated stones, rather than cooking in a metal pot? Men wearing capes of painted skin and using inlaid pipes? And the levying of fines for adultery?

Clearly we would not. The perfect correlations found between traits comprising selected elements of the southeastern California complex or the northwestern California complex are explained by joint diffusion and only by joint diffusion. How do we know then that correlations between matrilocal residence and matrilineal descent—traits which *seem* to have a clear functional linkage—might not likewise reflect the influence of joint diffusion, especially since they too are so often found in geographical clusters? (Driver and Massey 1957:421–439.) That is Galton's problem. It must be solved; it cannot merely be talked away.

The foregoing examples are merely illustrative suggestions; Klimek's tables show many other traits which are usually (although not invariably) associated with the southeast complex or with the northwest complex, as the case may be. Further, Klimek's tables show four or five *other* regional complexes within California, each of which has its clusters of highly correlated traits, like those of the northeast and the southwest. One can find for each a half-dozen or more traits which are invariably and exclusively found within each; and many other traits which are usually, though not invariably, associated with the complex.

Nor is this tendency for culture to occur in regional complexes a peculiarity of California Indians. So familiar was this phenomenon to anthropologists of a generation ago that they took it for granted. There have been many statistical studies directed toward classifying tribes regionally by counting Culture Element Distributions statistically. Boas (1895) studied thus the myths of the Northwest coast; Clements, Schenck and Brown (1926) analyzed thus Linton's data on Polynesia. Clements (1931) thus analyzed Spier's data on the sun dance of the Plains Indians. Tessmann (1930) collected data on 212 traits from thirty-four tribes of northeast Peru; Tessman's data were analyzed statistically by Driver and Kroeber (1932). Klimek and Milke (1935) studied sixteen Tupi tribes of eastern Brazil regarding the distribution of 125 traits of material culture, using Metraux's data. In many ways the most impressive studies are those by Driver (1956, 1961) of trait distributions among North American Indian tribes as a whole. The correlations I have selected from Klimek are merely the most striking ones I could find from the two extremities of California; one could find dozens of more perfect correlations in Klimek's data, and hundreds in the data of the other writers cited. For example, one could point out that there is a high correlation in Northeast Peru between tribes with exogamous clans (*Sippe mit exogamer Grundlage*) and tribes whose men wear narrow G-strings (*schmales Schamtuch*), who beat on wooden drums, and who use thin spears with pointed, poisoned tips (Driver and Kroeber, 1932:Table 7 and see Chapter 32 for still other compilations of such evidence).

Nor can these correlations be explained away merely as the few combings of nominally "significant" correlations taken from a large number of cases. I have listed seven traits from southeast California, all of which were present in all three southeastern tribes and absent from the remaining fifty-seven tribes, so far as is known. Fisher's exact test, as tabulated by Lieberman and Owen (1961), shows a probability of getting a result this unusual on a single try as less than three in a million (.0000029). Six other traits, making thirteen in all, had an identical distribution; I omitted them as having some conceivable plausible functional linkage with one of the seven listed. To find thirteen traits so distributed merely by combing a collection of random correlations, one would have to look at several millions. I looked at exactly 70; of the 411 traits considered by Klimek, only 70 occurred in any of the three tribes involved. Out of 70 traits, then, thirteen had a distribution so unusual as to be expected in random arrangements less than three times in a million; and of the remaining fifty-seven, most had obviously nonrandom distributions also. It seems evident from inspection that the vast majority of the thousands of correlations between the 411 traits which Klimek considered would have significant correlations either positive (occurring in the same region of California) or negative (occurring in different regions). Hundreds of these correlations were computed and shown in graphic form by Klimek (1935). It can hardly be supposed that these distributions are random; nor can it be doubted that the examples selected for presentation here are reflections—albeit extremely striking ones—of the general tendency for culture traits to occur in geographical clusters rather than to assume random geographical scattering.

It is also clear that many such traits owe their geographical clustering to the influence of diffusion rather than to their relationship to some geographically distributed feature of the natural environment. The natural environment of the Chemehuevi, who lack patrilinear clans, does not differ from that of their neighbors the Mohave and the Yuma, who do have them; but linguistically the Mohave and the Yuma are extremely close relatives, while the Chemehuevi are speakers of unrelated Shoshonean of the Southern Paiute group. Deer are found and hunted throughout California, but only the five northwestern California tribes make painted capes of their skins. No linkage between environment and twin frequency is known; but even if one were to be found, that would not explain twin *preference*, which is found only among the southeastern California tribes. Sticks and cord material are found throughout California, indeed in greater abundance in other parts than in the dry desert country of the southeastern Yumans, but carrying frames made of sticks and cords are found only among these southeasterners. And so on.

ATTEMPTS AT SOLUTION

As far as I know, nothing has been attempted by authors of trait distribution studies to allow for, or to measure the extent to which, "functional" relationships weaken the significance of correlations as evidence of diffusion. But there have been several attempts to deal with the converse problem of estimating the effect of diffusion on "functional" correlations. To supplement her study of Paiute sorcery, Beatrice Whiting (1950: 88 ff.) in a cross-cultural survey showed a negative correlation between presence of authoritative political officials and witchcraft attribution; in order to reduce the effect of diffusion, she recomputed her correlation using only one tribe from each culture area, and found the result statistically significant. A similar method was used by Whiting and Child (1953:184–187) in their study of child training and personality. They recomputed their correlations separately for each continent; however, these results did not prove statistically significant. Both these approaches use what I propose we call the *sifting* method, which has as its object the sifting out of duplications reflecting diffusion. These two attempts are vulnerable to the objection that diffusion cannot be assumed to stop at culture area or continental boundaries, but on the contrary is known to be often hemispheric or even world-wide in its scope. The distribution of the alphabet as a writing system, of the magic flight motif in folklore, of the bear cult in Siberia and northern North America, of tailored clothing throughout northern Eurasia and North America, of the wheat-cattle farming complex in most of the Eastern Hemisphere and the maize-beans-squash complex in most of the Western, are often-cited evidence of this tendency.

Another tack was taken in critiques of Murdock's *Social Structure* by Wilson (1952) and by Driver (1956). Wilson shows through statistical analysis of continental distributions and Driver through an illuminating set of trait distribution maps that kinship terminology and associated traits are affected by diffusion; both Wilson and Driver share Murdock's view that they are nevertheless "functionally" linked traits, but they offer no method of testing this hypothesis. However, their work, particularly Driver's maps, helps the student to grasp intuitively the nature of the diffusional process.

Driver (1966) recently attacked Galton's problem by attempting to reconstruct the actual diffusion patterns of the traits concerned. Interestingly, Driver worked on the specific question Tylor (1889) had studied and which had given rise to Galton's objection. This question is the relationship between descent rules and kin avoidance patterns. Thus Tylor held that in patrilocal societies a woman tends to avoid her husband's relatives, in matrilocal societies a man tends to avoid his wife's relatives. These patterns are by no means present in all such societies. But they are present in a larger proportion than we would expect by chance. Is this excess to be explained by mere accidents of diffusion or is it instead to be explained functionally, as Tylor suggested for matrilocal societies at least? Driver's study considers the total distribution patterns of both avoidance practices and descent rules throughout native North America. There (p. 145) he traces five separate independent inventions of avoidance practices and explains all other instances as diffusion. He thinks that avoidance practices did indeed tend to diffuse in company with related descent rules and that hence diffusion

patterns as well as independent invention patterns tend to support the hypothesis of functional linkage of these traits. But although he does a brilliant job of reconstructing the diffusion patterns, he offers no convincing evidence of functional association and concedes (1966:158) that the use of the propinquity methods described here are required to establish the functional relationship.

Galton's problem is especially perilous in very large samples, like Murdock's World Ethnographic Sample (Murdock 1961) or his Ethnographic Atlas (Murdock 1962). As I have shown, (Naroll 1961:29 ff.), certain traits in the first of these samples display very clear evidence of similarity among nearby tribes. Mere inspection of both these samples convinces me that most traits in both these samples reflect diffusion and would show significant evidence of resemblance among neighbors if tested by either the cluster test or the linked pair test. Thus correlations drawn from such world-wide samples (for example, Coult and Habenstein 1965) cannot be confidently viewed as evidence of functional association. Yet anthropologists still do so. And few of them face the problem.

Two men who recently made confident inferences of functional relationships from World Ethnographic Sample data are Jack Sawyer and Robert LeVine (1966). Sawyer and LeVine, unlike so many of their colleagues, do not, however, ignore Galton's problem. Instead they devote nearly half their paper (pp. 719–727) to a regional analysis of their data—an analysis whose chief purpose is an attempt to solve Galton's problem. They claim that regional differences in correlation patterns are more consistent with a functional than a simple diffusional explanation. Particularly, they find less average difference in correlations between Africa and South America than between Africa and East Eurasia. But they fail to make two essential points: (1) they do not show what the functional components of their correlation coefficients are and hence are unable to establish that the factor loadings in their factor analysis reflected functional rather than merely diffusional associations; and (2) they do not show whether these regional differences in correlations may not simply be chance variations and hence not significant of anything at all.

Let us consider this second point further.

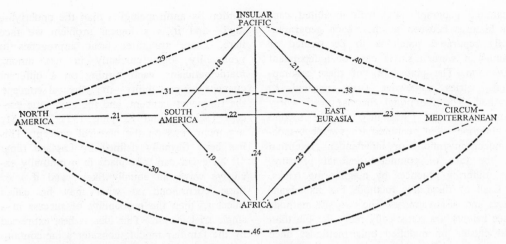

Figure 1. Average difference in correlations for each pair of regions, according to Sawyer and LeVine (1966:726).[1]

In all, Sawyer and LeVine (1966:726, Fig. 1) offer fifteen differences between six major world regions. Since each of these regions has more than one geographical neighbor, only five of the fifteen differences are differences between non-neighbors: (1) South America–East Eurasia; (2) Africa–East Eurasia; (3) North America–Africa; (4) South America–Circummediterranean; and (5) Insular Pacific–Circummediterranean. These five pairs have differences which rank respectively as numbers 5, 6½ (tie), 10, 12, and 13½ (tie). This ranking is on a scale from no. 1—least average difference hence greatest resemblance, to no. 15—vice versa. The sum of these ranks is 47; the Mann-Whitney test shows this result expectable by chance alone in twenty-two samples out of a hundred from a universe in which there is no difference at all. So Figure 1 may well mean nothing at all; but if it does mean anything at all, it means that regions are slightly more likely to resemble their geographical neighbors than their non-neighbors. In other words, if Sawyer and LeVine's figure means anything, it means just the reverse of what Sawyer and LeVine say it means.

For the average rank of these five pairs of non-neighbors is 9.2, while the average rank of all fifteen is of course 8. Thus we have a slight, perhaps merely chance, difference in the direction predicted by the diffusion hypothesis.

[1] Reproduced by permission of the American Anthropological Association from the *American Anthropologist,* Vol. 68 (1966), p. 726.

PROPINQUITY METHODS

Five* other solutions have recently been proposed to Galton's problem (Naroll 1961; Naroll and D'Andrade 1963; Naroll 1964). All five use geographical propinquity to measure diffusion. That is, they assume that similarities between neighbors are more likely to reflect diffusion than similarities among more widely separated peoples. One should note both limits to this assumption. They do *not* assume that all similarity between neighbors reflects diffusion. Nor do they assume that all similarity among widely scattered peoples reflects independent invention. These five methods are described below.

The diffusion model these five methods use envisions geographical patches of trait distributions. Many such patches are reported in great detail in the Culture Element Distribution studies of California and Peru already cited. One can, however, best understand the model by studying the maps of North American trait distributions by Driver (1961). The operating assumption of these methods is that whenever traits are found in continuous geographical distributions—solid patches on the map—such patches are to be treated as reflections of diffusion. Whenever traits are

* Since this manuscript was prepared for the press, a sixth and seventh propinquity solution have been devised. For the sixth, see the next chapter in this book, by Driver and Chaney. For the seventh, see Murdock and White (1969). The sixth is a modification of the matched pair method; the seventh though based on the linked pair method has some operational characteristics of the interval sift method. Both constitute distinct improvements.

scattered geographically, with inhabited gaps or hiatuses between patches, each geographically separated patch is to be treated as though it were a single case of independent invention. The plausibility of these assumptions varies somewhat from method to method. The functional theorist need worry only about the plausibility of the second assumption—that scattered traits reflect independent invention, or independent retention in the face of counter-diffusional pressure, i.e., differing practices by neighboring tribes.

Each of these five methods has its advantages and disadvantages. The two sift methods (see below) are statistically more flexible than the cluster or matched pair methods; once the validity of the sift has been verified, the sample can simply be treated statistically as though it were a sample from historically unrelated societies. The *bimodal sift* method is more sensitive than the *interval sift* method, but it is also considerably more expensive; for analyses which lean heavily on existing compilations of data, like those for Murdock, the bimodal sift method would be preferable, but for analyses which must make extensive new compilations of data, the interval sift method is recommended for its economy. The *cluster method* and the *matched pair* method are logically more rigorous but statistically less flexible than the sift methods; of the two, the cluster method might well prove to be the more sensitive statistically and, alone of the five, offers a direct test of the hypothesis that semi-diffusional associations actually diffuse together; but the matched pair method also measures the relative importance of diffusion and functional association in correlations. The *linked pair* method not only measures the relative importance of diffusion and functional association but also is statistically as flexible as the interval sift method. However, it is logically less rigorous than the cluster or matched pair methods. (This defect could be cured by following the example set by Driver (1966) of using language family affiliation as a control factor. Language family membership controls for diffusion among widely scattered peoples as a result of migrations like those of the overseas Europeans.)

The basic logic involved in all five of these methods needs explicit attention. As Kluckhohn (1939) pointed out, the mathematics of probability theory has been given more at-

tention by anthropologists than the underlying logic—and it is a logical problem we face here. There are three basic approaches to probability logic currently in use among mathematicians, each turning on a different concept of probability—the classical concept, the frequency concept, and the axiomatic concept (Kenney and Keeping 1951:2–5). My argument rests on the classical concept. This has been formally defined by Laplace thus: "If an event can take place in n mutually exclusive ways, all equally likely, and if r of these correspond to what may be called 'success,' then the probability of success in a single trial is r/n." This idea is best expressed by the familiar model: consider a jar containing a number (n) of spheres like ping-pong balls all absolutely identical in shape, size and other characteristics excepting only color—r of them are black, the others white. If the balls are thoroughly mixed and then a blindfolded person draws one ball out of the jar, the probability of the ball being black is r/n. That is the definition of the classical probability concept. When we say that the occurrence of an event has a probability of .05, we mean that event is as likely to occur as the blindfolded man is likely to get a black ball if there is one black ball to every nineteen white.

Where events being considered must occur in discrete units or bundles (or as the mathematician says, are discretely distributed), it is a relatively straightforward matter to work out correspondences between these discrete events and the model of a jar full of ping-pong balls. Where, instead, they can occur in magnitudes varying along a continual scale, such as height or weight or distance (that is, they are continuously distributed), the use of integral calculus and the probability density concept lets us work out correspondences between such situations and the model of a jar full of ping-pong balls.

The various statistical tests which are used to calculate probabilities can all be related to the ping-pong-ball jar model; the relationship is worked out mathematically and invariably involves certain stated mathematical assumptions. The logic of statistical inference involves inquiry as to the suitability of the mathematical model of the test being used. The test asks whether observed events can be explained by a given mathematical model. This question is the null hypothesis; if it is answered positively, the observations being tested are considered to lack statistic significance. For example, the chi-square test used by Murdock in *Social Structure* asks: would a random sample from a universe of two independent and continuously distributed phenomena be likely to produce an association of the kind observed?

Thus the key point is this: If an event being studied conforms in every way to the mathematical model of the statistical test being used, the result of a statistical test almost always must be to support the null hypothesis—to report the absence of a significant association, or a significant difference, or whatever. The point of the test is to establish the fact that the event being studied *cannot* plausibly be considered to conform to the mathematical model of the test.

It is then a logical and observational rather than a mathematical problem to explain the failure of the data to conform to the mathematical model. If ethnological observations are entirely independent of one another, then from the hypothesis itself neither historical nor sociological relationships exist among them, and the only plausible explanation for apparent relationships is sampling error. Where a statistically significant result is observed, then *random* sampling error is discredited as an explanation for the apparent relationship. In an ideally controlled experiment, only two possible explanations for any relationship are permitted—the hypothesis being tested and random sampling error. But in ethnological statistical studies, other hypotheses are also possible. We cannot plausibly explain the correlations in Murdock's *Social Structure* or Whiting and Child's *Child Training and Personality* or the University of California Culture Element Distribution studies as the result of random factors like sampling error. That is what the statistical tests tell us and that is all that they tell us.

How can we explain the correlations in *Social Structure?* Critics have pointed out that they might reflect sampling biases (since the sample was not random); or that they might reflect errors in the data (random errors tend to lower correlations but observational biases might produce spurious correlations, as has been elsewhere demonstrated —Naroll 1962); or that they might reflect inconsistencies in the unit of study.

This chapter concerns itself with the one remaining difficulty which would exist if these

others had been resolved—discriminating hyper-diffusional from semi-diffusional correlations. The tests here proposed can show that a statistically significant association cannot plausibly be explained as merely reflecting random sampling error or diffusion. What then is the best explanation remains a matter for further consideration. If these tests show that traits *A* and *B* are semi-diffusionally associated, then we must presume that they are somehow causally linked. *A* may be the cause of *B; B* may be the cause of *A;* or they both may be the effects of some third factor.

The methods summarized below are fairly simple and inexpensive (*very* simple and inexpensive when compared with such a technique as factor analysis). Most use non-parametric statistics, mathematical models which do *not* make any assumption that the variables studied are normally distributed, but only that they are continuous; most use a statistical method which has been mathematically demonstrated as closely approximating a normal distribution for samples above a minimum size and for which tables of exact probabilities have been computed for samples below the minimum.

It has been pointed out that the methods summarized below all rest upon the obvious fact that propinquity is usually a measure of diffusion. That is, the closer in space two societies are to each other, the more likely they are to resemble each other in any trait subject to diffusion. This is true whether the diffusion results from borrowing or migration and is the fact on which rest all studies of diffusion among peoples lacking written records. Obviously, people are more likely to borrow traits from their immediate neighbors than directly from more distant people; and obviously, societies which split up through migration or differentiation of dialects into several new societies are likely to be near each other and unlikely to be far distant. (This likelihood is far greater if we consider only trait distributions not borne by overseas Europeans after 1500 A.D., and accordingly, it is wise to omit overseas Europeans from consideration.) Of course, it is true that exceptions to this tendency are not uncommon; the use of coffee spread by direct borrowing all the way across the Indian Ocean from Arabia to Java; there is a gap of something like a thousand miles between the southern Athapaskans and the main body of this language family; and so on. But the methods here presented permit frequent exceptions; they simply rely on the fact that, by and large, diffusion is more likely to have taken place between nearby peoples than between distant ones.

True, the fact that two widely separated peoples have like traits does not necessarily rule out a connection through diffusion, even though many other societies with unlike traits lie between them. But such a separation does suggest that similar associations are not hyper-diffusional associations. The wide separation indicates that the traits, if not undiffusional associations, are semi-diffusional ones—if we cannot say with confidence that these traits have not diffused in the past, we can say that the societies which bear them have clung to them despite considerable time and the example of neighbors with other traits. Where we find many examples of widely separated peoples who cling to certain trait combinations, even though intervening groups have different trait combinations, we cannot accept hyper-diffusional association as the explanation for this phenomenon.

APPENDIX

Summary Description of Five Propinquity Methods

Space does not permit a full description here of all seven propinquity methods for the solution of Galton's problem. The interested reader should refer to the publications here cited for further details on the first four and demonstrations of each test by application to particular problems. See also Chapter 48 and Murdock and White 1969. Since the linked pair method can easily be used on any cross-cultural sample, large or small, it is described and demonstrated at greater length here than elsewhere.

The Bimodal Sift Method (Naroll 1961: 31–34). This method can be used for large samples where many of the tribes (subcultures) in the sample are geographical neighbors. It aligns the tribes geographically and counts the geographical rank order difference of recurrence between successive cases of the same type of association between the two traits being correlated. By rank order difference is meant the interval measured in number of other societies between each instance of a type and the next succeeding instance of the same type. If there are no societies of other types in the sample between the two societies of like type, I call this a rank order difference of 1. If there is one other society, I call this a rank order difference of 2, and so on. The counting scheme tells the number of societies there are on the way from the first society to the next one of like type. For a given geographical direction (e.g., along certain diffusion arcs: Naroll 1961:24–29; or simply along meridians of longitude from north to south; or along parallels of latitude from east to west), the rank order difference of recurrence is measured between each society and the next society of the same type. A frequency distribution of all these differences is compiled. If both diffusion and functional association are present, a bimodal distribution of these differences is to be expected. The second mode, reflecting the greater rank difference, is taken as reflecting the influence of independent invention. Cases of association involving lower rank differences than that in the trough between the two modes are taken as reflecting diffusion and are randomly dropped from the sample until the first mode disappears. The surviving sample is then treated as a collection of cases independent of diffusion.

The Interval Sift Method (Naroll and D'Andrade 1963:1058–1062). This method supposes that the investigator, in advance of his sampling selection, knows or can estimate fairly well the size of the diffusion patches of the traits he is studying. It is sufficient if he can do so with his dependent variables. For if he eliminates similarity of dependent variable type between neighbors in his sample, correlations between dependent and independent variables can hardly be explained away as mere reflections of diffusion. (Especially if his dependent variable is also unrelated *in his sample* to language type.) In accordance with this method, the sampling universe is divided into strata the approximate size of a diffusion patch of the dependent variable. If such diffusion patches are already mapped, they themselves should, of course, be used as sampling strata. If not, the sampling method should consider location of tribes within the strata, in order to draw a sample of tribes largely separated by the sift interval. The sift interval may be defined as the estimated diameter of the diffusion patch.

It is often convenient to take Murdock's World Ethnographic Sample or his Ethnographic Atlas (Murdock 1962) as a sampling universe. This procedure seems especially convenient in the case of a dependent variable which is treated in these works. Each of his culture areas can be taken as a tentative diffusion patch. By inspection of the similarities with respect to the dependent variable one can sometimes decide to accept each culture area as a sampling stratum. At other times, one might prefer to take only every other culture area, geographically checkerboarding them, in order to reduce similarity among neighbors.

However the sifting is done, its validity needs formal testing. *Some* neighbors could be expected to resemble each other through chance alone, even if no diffusion were involved. The run test for diffusion is a suitable test of the hypothesis that in the sifted sample, neighbors resemble each other with respect to a given variable type more often than would be expected by chance (Naroll 1961: 27–29).

The Cluster Method (Naroll 1961:34–38). This method, like the bimodal sift method, needs a large sample with many neighbors who resemble each other with respect to the traits being studied. To explain the method, it is essential to introduce two new terms. By a "hit" I mean a case in which the two variables are associated in the manner predicted by the functional hypothesis being tested, and which thus supports that hypothesis. By a "miss" I mean a case in which the two variables are not so associated, and which thus discredits the hypothesis. For example, in a test of the hypothesis that descent types are related to residence types, one sort of hit would be the case of a tribe in which matrilineal descent was associated with matrilocal residence; a second sort of hit would be the case of a tribe in which patrilineal

descent was associated with patrilocal residence; and a third sort of hit would be the case of a tribe in which bilateral descent was associated with neolocal residence. Similarly, one sort of miss would occur in a tribe where patrilineal descent was associated with matrilocal residence; a second sort of miss would occur in a tribe where matrilineal descent was associated with neolocal residence, and so on.

The cluster test concentrates on the peculiar character of semi-diffusional associations. In an undiffusional association, neither hits nor misses diffuse; the association of traits occurs geographically at random—by definition. In a hyper-diffusional association, hits and misses both diffuse with equal facility. Only in a semi-diffusional association is a difference to be expected between the diffusion rate of hits and misses. This difference is implied by the definition of a semi-diffusional association, one in which traits tend to diffuse together. If such a tendency exists, hits should form large diffusion patches, misses only small patches. If, on the other hand, the traits are simply accidental products of joint diffusion —hyper-diffusional associations—there is no reason why misses should not diffuse as readily as hits. The key variable becomes not the total number of hits and misses but their tendency to cluster. In a hyper-diffusional association both hits and misses should have a high tendency to cluster; in an undiffusional association, neither should have a tendency to cluster; in a semi-diffusional association, the hits should tend to cluster markedly more than the misses. In a Wald-Wolfowitz run test scheme, I predict relatively fewer runs of hits than of misses. A test of this hypothesis is a test of the semi-diffusional hypothesis; if there is no significant difference in the diffusion pattern, we are dealing with a hyper-diffusional distribution and the semi-diffusional hypothesis is refuted. It seems not at all unlikely that some phenomena should reveal a highly significant difference between the tendency of hits to cluster and the tendency of misses to cluster—and yet, because of other factors not involved in the study, display a low over-all association. Even so, a semi-diffusional relationship would have been established, while a high association without a significant difference in this clustering tendency would, in the presence of evidence that the individual traits diffuse, constitute evidence of a high hyper-diffusional association. This test, then, is a test of the diffusion process itself, and distinguishes hyper-diffusional associations from semi-diffusional associations. (It is not applicable to most undiffusional associations.)

The basic variable is the expected number of runs, as computed for the run test ($\bar{d}$ in the Mosteller-Bush notation). This is computed for each type of miss, and compared with the actual number of runs (in computing these runs, of course, we distinguish the type being studied, which we call X, and all other types, whether hits or misses, which we call Y).

If the hits tend to cluster more than the misses, then the ratio $d/\bar{d}$ (actual number of runs divided by expected number of runs) should be lower for the hits than for the misses. In order to apply the test successfully, one needs enough types of hits and misses so that the significance of the difference between these ratios can be computed. If in these circumstances it is clear that hits tend to cluster more than misses, it is logically very difficult indeed to avoid the conclusion that the hits tend to diffuse together and thus by definition reflect a semi-diffusional association.

The Matched Pair Method (Naroll and D'Andrade 1963:1062–1066). This method takes a cross-cultural sample of pairs of neighbors. Each pair is presumably separated from every other pair by a longer or shorter interval of space occupied by other tribes not in the sample. Let us suppose that the method is being applied to a test of the correlation between descent and residence. If the two tribes in a pair resemble each other with respect to descent rules, that is counted as one "win" for the historical-diffusion hypothesis. If they resemble each other with respect to residence rules, that, too, is counted as one win for the historical-diffusion hypothesis. If in the first tribe of the pair, descent and residence are hits, that is counted as one win for the functional hypothesis. If in the second tribe of the pair, descent and residence are hits, that, too, is counted as one win for the functional hypothesis. It is possible for both hypotheses to score two wins per pair; for both to score two losses per pair; for one to score two wins while the other scores two losses; or for each hypothesis to score one win and one

loss. Always the total number of wins and losses for each pair is four. This procedure is continued for successive pairs, with the wins and losses being tabulated in a fourfold table (resembling, but not to be confused with, a fourfold contingency table). When the wins and losses have been calculated, the proportions of each type give a measure of their relative importance and the sign test gives a test of statistical significance.

This method could be made much more sensitive by matching groups of three neighbors rather than groups of only two. Between two neighbors, only one comparison can be made, but among three, three. Thus instead of studying forty matched pairs we study forty groups of three neighbors, we collect data on sixty tribes rather than forty but have 120 tests of relative importance rather than 40.

The Linked Pair Method. Societies in a cross-cultural sample are aligned geographically, as for the interval sift diffusion test. With respect to each trait being studied, each tribe is correlated with its neighbor. For example, suppose we have ten tribes along a north-south line in Africa. We will call them tribes A, B, C, D, E, F, G, H, I, J. To begin with, we will call the northernmost tribe a case of Y1 and its neighbor to the south a case of Y2. Then for Case 1, the score of Tribe A is the Y1 score and the score of Tribe B is the Y2 score. Next, we move one tribe south. Now for Case 2, the score of Tribe B is the Y1 score while the score of Tribe C is the Y2 score. Thus we are getting a measure of similarity between neighbors. If the trait being measured is a dichotomy, we generate a fourfold contingency table in which cell *a* tabulates the number of cases where the trait was present in both tribes; cell *b* the number where it was present in the Y1 tribe but absent in the Y2 tribe; and so on. From this, phi coefficients and tests of significance can be computed in the usual way. If the trait measured is a ratio scale, or can be treated as one, product moment coefficients can be computed between the Y1's and the Y2's. If the trait is ranked, rank order correlations and rank order coefficients can be computed between the Y1's and the Y2's. In one of these ways, a coefficient of correlation is generated measuring the similarity between neighbors. This measure can be compared with similarly

Table 1
LINKED PAIR INDEPENDENCE TEST
NORTH-SOUTH-SOUTH-NORTH ALIGNMENT
TEAM RAMIFICATION COUNT

No.	Societal Name	Column 1 Latitude	Column 2 Longitude	Column 3 Team Ramification Score	Column 4 Neighbor's Team Ramification Score
08	Dutch	53°N	7°E	27	25
30	Austria	48°N	14°E	25	27
59	Italy	38°N	13°E	27	5
55	Tiv	7°N	9°E	5	9
19	Hottentot	26°S	18°E	9	7
38	Ila	16°S	27°E	7	6
16	Mongo	0°	20°E	6	9
42	Azande	5°N	27°E	9	10
27	Fur	12°N	24°E	10	9
05	Kababish	16°N	30°E	9	33
02	Turks	38°N	30°E	33	21
33	Iraqi	33°N	44°E	21	19
04	Egypt	30°N	31°E	19	10
66	Amhara	12°N	38°E	10	6
54	Luo	1°S	34°E	6	6
58	Chagga	3°S	37°E	6	11
41	Thonga	24°S	32°E	11	6
14	Kafir	36°N	71°E	6	7
65	Kazaks	48°N	70°E	7	11
36	Gond	21°N	80°E	11	2
45	Semang	5°N	102°E	2	3
23	Andamans	12°N	93°E	3	16
48	Burmese	20°N	95°E	16	6
12	Land Dyaks	0°	110°E	6	6
34	Toradja	2°S	121°E	6	4
52	Apayao	18°N	121°E	4	30
13	Korea	38°N	127°E	30	5
24	Gilyak	53°N	142°E	5	6
51	Ifaluk	7°N	147°E	6	8
06	Kapauku	4°S	136°E	8	5
28	Orokaiva	9°S	148°E	5	5
17	Malaita	9°S	161°E	5	4
29	Chukchi	66°N	177°E	4	9
39	Tikopia	12°S	168°E	9	5
56	Malekula	17°S	167°E	5	10
20	Tonga	20°S	174°W	10	5
07	Eyak	61°N	145°W	5	7
31	Mangareva	22°S	134°W	7	7
46	Wintun	39°N	122°W	7	7
40	Klallam	48°N	123°W	7	2
53	Copper Eskimo	70°N	115°W	2	6
18	Southern Paiute	36°N	115°W	6	5
11	Coyotero	34°N	110°W	5	9
37	Papago	31°N	112°W	9	17
15	Nahua	19°N	99°W	17	10
60	Cheyenne	39°N	104°W	10	6
49	Ojibwa	49°N	91°W	6	13
50	Iroquois	43°N	77°W	13	6
26	Mosquito	13°N	85°W	6	3
21	Ona	54°S	69°W	3	6
43	Araucanians	39°S	68°W	6	4
10	Mataco	24°S	63°W	4	3
32	Yagua	3°S	72°W	3	5
35	Callinago	15°N	61°W	5	3
57	Aweikoma	28°S	50°W	3	9
62	Mende	8°N	11°W	9	7
09	Tallensi	11°N	1°W	7	22
03	Irish	53°N	9°W	22	27

generated coefficients of correlation between substantive traits; and, where appropriate, first-order partial correlations can also be computed in which the influence of diffusion as measured by the linked pair method is the control factor.

The application of this linked pair method is illustrated in Table 1. This table tests my War, Stress and Culture sample (Chapter 43) to see whether I succeeded in my purpose of eliminating similarities in level of social development between neighbors, and if not, to measure the extent of the influence of diffusion between neighbors in the sample. By "neighbors" here is meant societies adjacent in the sample, ignoring other societies not in the sample and regardless of whether they have common boundaries or not. Thus the Klallam of the Olympic Peninsula of the state of Washington and the Wintu of central California are here considered neighbors because there are no other societies between them *in this sample*. This is true even though their tribal boundaries are hundreds of miles apart and many other societies not in this sample lie in between them.

The societies of my sample are arranged geographically in north-south lines. Beginning at the North Pole, and taking a strip 15° of longitude wide, societies are arranged in order of their latitude, moving from north to south, and continuing to the South Pole. Then we move east 15° of longitude and return to the North Pole, again arranging societies in order of their latitude, this time moving from south to north. Continuing in this way around the world, sweeping from north to south, then south to north, then north to south, moving 15° of longitude east each sweep, we group each society with its neighbors to the north and south, and the end societies in each sweep with its neighbor to the east or west.

Column 3 shows the team ramification score of each society as given in Table 1. Column 4 shows the team ramification score of the society's neighbor, usually its neighbor to the south. Notice that therefore each entry in column 4 is identical with the column 3 entry on the following line of the table.

Columns 3 and 4 have a rank order correlation of .23. Thus we see that the sifting attempt was not successful in removing similarity in social development level among neighbors but that on the contrary there is

a significant tendency for tribes in this sample to resemble their neighbors in team ramification.

However, as Figure 2 shows, this tendency is an allometric one. That is to say, there is a linear regression of the logarithms of the team ramification scores of the societies themselves (Table 1, column 3) as compared with their neighbors (Table 1, column 4). The product moment coefficient of correlation of these logarithms is .33. (Actually the logarithm used was that of team ramification score +1.001.) This coefficient is then a measure of linear regression. It thus meets the assumption of linearity required for partial correlations. There is a similarly linear correlation between the logarithms of the settlement sizes of these societies and those of their neighbors: .45.

Now the correlation between the logarithm of the settlement size and the logarithm of team ramification score is .87. What is the partial correlation between settlement size and team type count, after allowing for the resemblances in both traits among neighbors? Let t stand for team ramification score, p stand for population, and d stand for diffusional resemblance, as shown by similarities among neighbors. Then we have the following formula:

$$r_{cp.d} = \frac{r_{tp} - r_{td}\, r_{pd}}{\sqrt{1 - r^2_{td}}\ \sqrt{1 - r^2_{pd}}}$$

Substituting the values of the present problem, we have:

$$r_{cp.d} = \frac{.87 - (.33)\ (.45)}{\sqrt{1 - (.33)^2}\ \sqrt{1 - (.45)^2}}$$
$$= .86$$

0.86 fixes a reasonable minimum for the estimate of the *functional* team ramification score.

However the correlations between neighbors in my sample, r_{td} and r_{pd} is *not* a good estimate of the influence of diffusion on these traits, or of the tendency of one human society to resemble its actual, geographical neighbor with respect to them. I say this because my sampling method was designed to reduce this influence to a minimum. For a true measure of the relative importance of diffusion and functional association, the matched pair method is recommended. However, it cannot be applied to the War, Stress and Culture sample because that sample is not suitable for it. The matched pair test

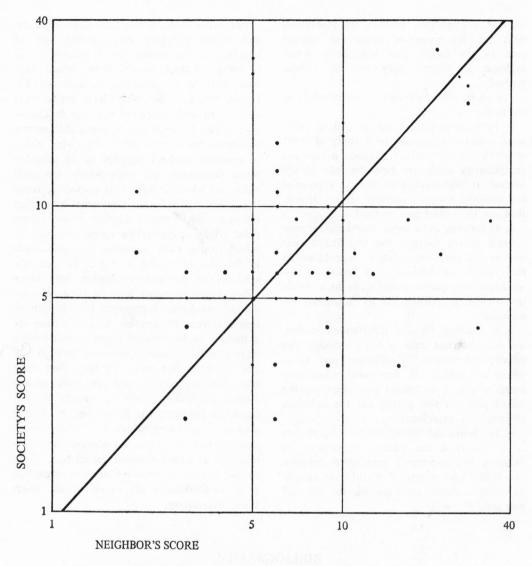

FIGURE 2 LINKED PAIR INDEPENDENCE TEST—NORTH-SOUTH-SOUTH-NORTH
ALIGNMENT—TEAM RAMIFICATION SCORE

needs a specially designed sample, one of pairs of actual, geographical neighbors.

The Five Propinquity Methods Compared

The writer considers the *linked pair* method the most frequently useful of the five for cross-cultural averages: (1) Unlike the matched pair, cluster or bimodal sift methods it does not require a special sample but can be used on any cross-cultural sample, large or small, world-wide or regional. (2) Unlike the *interval sift* method it is not dependent upon the assumption that a small, well-scattered, world-wide sample can sift out the effects of

diffusion and produce a geographically random distribution. True, for some traits at least—suicide for example—this assumption is justified. True also, the interval sift method does not require that this assumption be accepted arbitrarily but takes it as a working hypothesis which it subjects to formal test. But wherever the sample *fails its test,* the interval sift method is powerless.

However, the linked pair method is not an adequate test of the relative importance of diffusion and functional association; the matched pair method is superior for that purpose. Nor does the linked pair test offer direct evidence that two traits tend to diffuse together, a hypothesis which is the theoretical basis for inferences of functional linkage even in the linked pair test. Such direct evidence is offered only by the cluster method.

Therefore, the following recommendations are made:

1. In a cross-cultural survey with a fairly small world-wide sample, or a study of traits in which the influence of diffusion is believed exceptionally weak, try first the interval sift method. If that method confirms a successful sift, consider Galton's problem solved. If not, then use the linked pair method.

2. Otherwise, in a large world-wide cross-cultural survey sample, use the linked pair test to estimate the relative importance *in that sample* of diffusion and functional association. Use partial correlations to estimate the correlation attributable to functional association.

3. In Cultural Element Distribution studies, use the matched pair test to estimate the relative importance of diffusion and functional association. If functional association seems to play a significant part, then use the linked pair test and partial out the influence of functional association.

4. In theoretical studies whose central aim is to determine the relative importance of diffusion and functional association between two traits, take a special world-wide sample of widely scattered pairs and use the matched pair test.

Following these procedures leads to a result which probably errs on the side of caution. As the reader already knows, in all of these solutions, nearby tribes which have like traits are counted as instances of diffusion. Nearby tribes which have *unlike* traits are treated as instances of tests for functional association. It sometimes happens that widely separated tribes have like traits owing either to common cultural ancestry or to long-distance borrowing; but such widely separated tribes are likewise treated as displaying functional association. This treatment is justified because such similar although widely separated tribes obviously constitute instances in which traits have remained in association in the face of nearby examples of their absence. Thus the wide separation, with other tribes displaying other traits in between, constitutes evidence supporting the hypothesis that the traits in question tend to diffuse together, or to be retained together. But having once established such a tendency through any one of these five tests, we may then infer that this tendency is also at work among *similar neighbors,* which we usually do not count as evidence for it, as well as among *dissimilar neighbors,* which we usually do so count. Once we have established the existence of a semi-diffusional association, then, to use partial correlations as here suggested is to *underestimate* the extent of the functional association.

BIBLIOGRAPHY

BOAS, FRANZ
1895 Die Entwicklung der Mythologien der Indianer der nordpacifischen Küste Amerikas. *Zeitschrift für Ethnologie* 27:487–523.
1927 Anthropology and statistics. In W. F. Ogburn and A. Goldenweiser, eds., *The social sciences and their interrelations.* Boston, Houghton Mifflin.

CLEMENTS, FORREST E.
1931 Plains Indians tribal correlations with sun dance data. *American Anthropologist* 33: 216–227.

CLEMENTS, FORREST E., S. M. SCHENCK, and T. K. BROWN
1926 New objective method for showing spatial relationships. *American Anthropologist* 28: 585 ff.

COULT, ALLAN D., and ROBERT W. HABENSTEIN
1965 *Cross tabulations of Murdock's world ethnographic sample.* Columbia, University of Missouri.

DRIVER, HAROLD E.
1956 *An integration of functional, evolutionary and historical theory by means of correlations.* Indiana University Publications in Anthropology and Linguistics, Memoir 12. Bloomington, Indiana University Press.
1961 *Indians of North America.* Chicago, University of Chicago Press.
1966 Geographical-historical *versus* psycho-functional explanations of kin avoidances. *Current Anthropology* 7:131–148, 155–160.

DRIVER, HAROLD E., and ALFRED L. KROEBER
1932 Quantitative expressions of cultural rela-

tionships. *University of California Publications in American Archaeology and Ethnology* 31:211–256.

DRIVER, HAROLD E., and WILLIAM C. MASSEY
1957 Comparative studies of North American Indians. *Transactions of the American Philosophical Society* 47, Part 2:421–439.

DRIVER, HAROLD E., and KARL F. SCHUESSLER
1957 Factor analysis of ethnographic data. *American Anthropologist* 59:655–663.

KENNEY, JOHN F., and E. S. KEEPING
1951 *Mathematics of statistics,* Part Two, 2nd ed. New York, Van Nostrand.

KLIMEK, STANISLAUS
1935 The structure of California Indian culture. *University of California Publications in American Archaeology and Ethnology* 37: 1–70 (see especially Tables 2, 3, 5 and 6 facing pp. 36, 38, 42 and 44).

KLIMEK, STANISLAUS, and WILHELM MILKE
1935 An analysis of the material culture of the Tupi peoples. *American Anthropologist* 37:71–91.

KLUCKHOHN, CLYDE
1939 On certain recent applications of association coefficients to ethnological data. *American Anthropologist* 41:345–377.

KROEBER, A. L.
1936 Culture element distributions: II. Area and Climax. *University of California Publications in American Archaeology and Ethnology* 37:101–116.

LEVY, M. J., and L. A. FALLERS
1959 The family: some comparative considerations. *American Anthropologist* 61:648.

LIEBERMAN, GERALD J., and DONALD B. OWEN
1961 *Tables of the hypergeometric probability distribution.* Palo Alto, Calif., Stanford University Press.

LOWIE, ROBERT H.
1946 Evolution in cultural anthropology: a reply to Leslie White. *American Anthropologist* 48:227, 230.

MURDOCK, GEORGE P.
1949 *Social structure.* New York, Macmillan.
1957 World ethnographic sample. *American. Anthropologist* 59:664–687.

MURDOCK, GEORGE P. and DOUGLAS WHITE
1969 Standard cross-cultural sample. *Ethnology* 8:329–369.

MURDOCK, GEORGE P., et al.
1962 Ethnographic atlas. *Ethnology* 1:113–134.

NAROLL, RAOUL
1960 *Controlling data quality.* Series Research in Social Psychology, Symposia Studies Series, Vol. 4. National Institute of Social and Behavioral Sciences.
1961 Two solutions to Galton's problem. *Philosophy of Science* 28:16–39.
1962 *Data quality control.* New York, Free Press.
1964 A fifth solution to Galton's problem. *American Anthropologist* 66:863–867.
n.d. *Two stratified random samples for a cross-cultural survey.* Mimeograph.

NAROLL, RAOUL, and ROY G. D'ANDRADE
1963 Two further solutions to Galton's problem. *American Anthropologist* 63:1053–67.

SAWYER, JACK, and ROBERT A. LEVINE
1966 Cultural dimensions: a factor analysis of the world ethnographic sample. *American Anthropologist* 68:708–731.

STEPHENS, W. M.
1959 *Menstrual taboos and castration anxiety.* Ph.D. thesis, Graduate School of Education, Harvard University.

TYLOR, EDWARD B.
1889 On a method of investigating the development of institutions applied to the laws of marriage and descent. *Journal of the Royal Anthropological Institute* 18:272.

WALLIS, WILSON D.
1928 Probability and the diffusion of culture traits. *American Anthropologist* 30:94–106.

WHITING, BEATRICE
1950 *Paiute sorcery.* Viking Fund Publications in Anthropology, No. 15. New York, Wenner-Gren Foundation.

WHITING, JOHN W. M., and IRVING L. CHILD
1953 *Child training and personality.* New Haven, Yale University Press.

WHITING, J. W. M., RICHARD KLUCKHOHN, and ALBERT ANTHONY
1958 The function of male initiation ceremonies at puberty. In Eleanor Maccoby, T. M. Newcomb and E. L. Hartley, eds., *Readings in social psychology,* 3rd ed. New York, Holt, Rinehart and Winston.

WILSON, THURLOW R.
1952 Randomness of the distribution of social organization forms: a note on Murdock's social structure. *American Anthropologist* 54:134–138.

ZEISEL, HANS
1947 *Say it with figures.* New York, Harper.

CHAPTER 48

Cross-Cultural Sampling and Galton's Problem

HAROLD E. DRIVER and RICHARD P. CHANEY

INTRODUCTION

Historical factors (diffusion, acculturation, culture heritage–migration) must be considered in any comparative study, whether it includes only two or hundreds of variables, whether it is limited to two ethnic units or extended to hundreds, whether it covers a small area or the entire world, and whether it embraces a short or a long time span. The evolutionist or cross-cultural researcher who wishes to establish causal sequences among variables must commit himself with respect to the historical independence or dependence of his cases, as Tylor (1889) found out long ago when Galton challenged him. The diffusionist, aiming at establishing historical connection, must also control for independent origins, whether they be parallels or convergences.

Where ethnohistorical documents or carefully determined archaeological dates are available, the comparativist should make full use of such material and assign it priority over historical inferences derived from the analysis of essentially synchronic data. But because most of what we know about contemporary non-literate cultures has been collected within the last hundred years, time

This research was supported by a small grant from the Office of Research and Development at Indiana University, which the authors gratefully acknowledge. Chaney chose the two sets of matched pairs of tribes, tabulated the data, and computed the observed values for the D'Andrade technique. Driver devised the new technique for determining the expected values for all 16 outcomes and expressing the magnitude of the win in terms of the variance. He also wrote the first draft. The authors wish to thank Naroll, D'Andrade, and Joseph Jorgensen for reading the manuscript and offering suggestions.

depth is shallow and deeper levels must be inferred by indirect means.

Nearly everyone today agrees that the nineteenth-century evolutionists and the early-twentieth-century diffusionists of both the Kulturkreis and Culture Area schools failed to extricate themselves from the Tylor-Galton dilemma. Nor has the neo-evolutionary school of Leslie White really come to grips with this problem, although Sahlins' distinction between specific and general evolution has begun to divide up the continuum from the most specific to the most general evolutionary trends. Carneiro and Tobias' (1963) Guttman scales are further refining the views of this school, but are not able to be explicit about the number of independent origins among the cultural variables scaled. Steward's multilinear evolution likewise introduces more flexibility into the concept, but he and his followers also lack an explicit inductive technique for controlling historical factors in large samples.

The cross-cultural school of evolutionists led by Murdock and Whiting has consciously played down the effect of historical factors by choosing samples in which the ethnic units are spaced so that many fall into separate culture areas (or subareas) or separate language families (or subfamilies) or both. Murdock (1966) describes a world sample of about four hundred chosen by first grouping the world's ethnic units into culture types (subculture areas) and then choosing one ethnic unit in each type to represent it. The assumption is that diffusion and acculturation within each type are obvious and that by choosing only one ethnic unit for each type one can lessen the influence of historical factors. Diffusion between types is regarded as less frequent and less serious because the representatives of each type are spaced at a minimum distance of two hundred miles from each other. Although a separation of two hundred miles in native California would insure considerable historical independence because few persons before White contact had ever traveled that far, the same distance in the Plains area in the nineteenth century would not serve as a barrier to diffusion because few persons had *not* traveled much more than two hundred miles. A glance at Mooney's (1896) *Calendar History of the Kiowa* shows that members of this tribe in the nineteenth century traveled into Canada on the north and Mexico on the south. It would require nearer one thousand miles in a north-south direction on the Plains to eliminate a sizable portion of the more recent diffusions. Although Murdock's culture types are determined without any explicit inductive technique, his world ethnographic knowledge is conceded to surpass that of any other scholar by every comparativist known to the authors, and his world typology of cultures exceeds in importance at this time the more limited culture area schemes of the past, such as Kroeber's North American culture areas of 1939. Even though his types can eliminate only the more recent historical contacts of the last few centuries, they constitute an important taxonomical advance. But for those who think of historical independence in terms of several millennia (e.g., Driver, *et al.,* 1966:144–147), two hundred miles is not enough, and greater historical depths must be inferred by other means.

Whiting (MS.), on the other hand, has recently drawn a world-wide sample of 136 ethnic units, each a member of a separate language family or subfamily. Using the rough estimates of time from glotto-chronology, Whiting's units are separated by a minimum of one thousand years of linguistic distance. Whiting is assuming that language classification matches culture classification to a high degree and that linguistic distance and cultural distance are definitely related for all combinations of two ethnic units. A glance at the language family and culture area classifications and maps of almost any area in the world (e.g., North America, in Driver 1961) shows that this is far from true in every case. For instance, the Yurok, Karok, and Hupa not only belong to distinct language families but even to distinct phyla, yet their cultures are so close that repeated fieldwork has uncovered only trivial differences. In contrast, the Athapaskan languages form one of the most compact language families in North America with no more than two thousand to three thousand years of time depth, yet their cultures in the Subarctic, Pacific, and Southwest areas are so different that no one would have dreamed that they all stemmed from a single proto-culture in the north without the evidence from linguistics. The correlation between linguistic distances and cultural distances among the world's ethnic units is unknown because the latter have not yet been measured but, if it is positive, it is likely to be of low or at best medium magnitude. However, if Whiting's ethnic units tend to fall into many different culture areas and are spaced as far apart geographically as is feasible, his sample of only 136 will have more historical independence within it than Murdock's larger sample of about 400, and will be useful for his purposes.

NAROLL AND D'ANDRADE TECHNIQUE

Raoul Naroll (1961) was the first to offer explicit inductive techniques aimed at solving the Tylor-Galton problem. Roy D'Andrade (Naroll and D'Andrade 1963) joined him in a later paper on the same subject, and Naroll still later (1964) published another technique for this purpose, bringing the total to five. Naroll's techniques operate with strips of territory around the world and consider only the linear sequences of pairs of cultural variables along these continua. Naroll found non-random clustering of single traits and pairs of traits along his territorial strips. Clusterings between pairs of traits were labeled semi-diffusional, because they appeared to be caused both by functional adhesion and the tendency of such adhesions to diffuse together. He found that positive instances of both pairs of traits (presence-presence or absence-absence) clustered more markedly than negative pairs (presence-absence or absence-presence). His tests revealed no examples of hyper-diffusion (clusterings of non-functional or dysfunctional behaviors). He deserves the credit for the first major break-through in the solution of a problem which had confounded the best comparativists up to 1961.

D'Andrade's technique has the advantage that it is not limited to a linear arrangement of ethnic units along strips of territory. He compared the presence and absence of pairs of traits among pairs of ethic units belonging to the same culture area and the same language family. He found that the results confirmed both a diffusion hypothesis and a functional hypothesis and to about the same degree for Stephen's menstrual taboo data, but that a functional hypothesis won by a wide margin for social stratification and political complexity. Both Naroll and D'Andrade used samples of discontinuous ethnic units, those of Murdock (1957) and Stephens (1959).

DRIVER AND CHANEY TEST OF D'ANDRADE'S METHOD

We have recently tested D'Andrade's method on almost continuously distributed ethnic units in aboriginal North America. We selected two groups of paired ethnic units from a North American sample totaling 260: the first consisted of pairs of neighboring peoples located in the same culture area and speaking languages belonging to the same family; the second was made up of pairs of peoples not in the same culture area and same language family and paired randomly from a table of random numbers. Because such sampling techniques are seldom described in enough detail for the reader to replicate the experiment, we shall spell out our technique.

The 260 ethnic units in Driver's (1966)

avoidance study were chosen as the test sample. We began with the first ethnic unit listed in Driver's table (1966:Table 6). With the help of the maps in Driver's book (1961: maps 2, 37) and the large tribal map by Driver et al. (1953), we looked for an ethnic unit adjacent or as close as possible to the first and also in the same culture area and language family. If there was more than one such ethnic unit, we assigned a face of a die to each one and rolled the die; the one to come up first was chosen and paired with the first ethnic unit. If there was a conflict between language family and culture area, we gave priority to the former. Then we proceeded to the second ethnic unit and paired it with an adjacent society other than the first on the list. The same society often appeared in two adjacent pairs but in no case were both members of two pairs identical.

Distant pairs of ethnic units are defined as those not adjacent, not in the same language family, and not in the same culture area. They were chosen by first matching each of Driver's (1966:Table 6) ethnic units with a row in a table of random numbers. For each ethnic unit we proceeded from left to right across its row and stopped with the first three-digit number from 1 to 260. If this number matched that of a nonadjacent ethnic unit of different language family and different culture area, that unit was paired with the first. Thus the Aleut was paired with the Klallam. Then the second ethnic unit on the list was paired with a distant one by proceeding across its row of random numbers. Because the same three-digit number occasionally appeared more than once in the table,

TABLE 1

SAMPLE OF PAIRED SOCIETIES

SOCIETY	ADJACENT SOCIETY	DISTANT SOCIETY
1. Aleut	Eskimo: Chugach	Klallam
14. Ingalik	Tanaina	Shoshoni: Hukundika
25. Chipewyan	Beaver	Alabama
36. Montagnais-Naskapi	Algonkin	Cowichan
48. Bella Bella	Wikeno Kwakiutl	Mohave
59. Karok	Yurok	Kamia
69. Quinault	Twana	N. Yokuts
79. Wikeno Kwakiutl	Homalco	Otomi
89. Lillooet	Thompson	Picuris
99. Wishram	Chinook	Diegueno

TABLE 2
CORRELATION OF AVOIDANCE AND BIFURCATION
(EXPECTED PROBABILITIES IN PARENTHESES)

AVOIDANCE

		Present, A_1	Absent, A_0	Total
	Present, B_1	72 (.222)	120 (.517)	192 (.739)
BIFURCATION	Absent, B_0	6 (.078)	62 (.182)	68 (.260)
	Total	78 (.300)	182 (.699)	260 (.999)

$$\phi = .28 \qquad P < .001$$

or the researcher located the same number going through the table for another ethnic unit, the same ethnic unit might repeat several times as the random member of a pair; thus the Arikara appear three times as a random member of a pair and one time as an adjacent member of a pair, but none of the pairs are identical. Table 1 gives a small sample of ethnic units on the list with adjacent and distant pair-members.

Driver (1966:157, Table 15) gives a correlation (phi) of −.40 between mother-in-law son-in-law avoidance and generation and/or lineal and/or Eskimo and/or Hawaiian types of kin terms. Because all of these types of kin classification lack bifurcation and all other types recognize it, we can change the sign of the coefficient and say that there is a correlation of .40 between mother-in-law son-in-law avoidance and bifurcation, significant at less than the .001 level. The value of this same correlation (Table 2) is only .28. This difference is caused by a few languages

having multiple and overlapping terms for the same relative and being coded for more than one type of kinship terminology. (See Driver et al. 1966, Table 6.)

We shall first test the modest correlation (phi) of .28 between mother-in-law son-in-law avoidance and bifurcation. We give the raw frequencies of this relationship in Table 2 because the considerable asymmetry of both variables in opposite directions may influence the interpretation. Table 3 shows that the diffusion hypothesis wins for adjacent tribes by a ratio of 83:1 in the two quadrants where the contrasts occur (lower left and upper right). The bottom half of Table 3 gives an unexpected result: diffusion wins over function for distant tribes as well, where the ratio is 47:34. The implausibility of this second result suggests some flaw in the method. The clue to our more refined solution of the problem stemmed from D'Andrade's parenthetical statement:

(This form of summarizing the results is most applicable where about 50% of the sample has

TABLE 3
D'ANDRADE'S TEST FOR AVOIDANCE AND BIFURCATION

A. ADJACENT TRIBES

DIFFUSION HYPOTHESIS

		Wins	Losses	Total
FUNCTIONAL HYPOTHESIS	Wins	98	1	99
	Losses	83	6	89
	Total	181	7	188

B. DISTANT TRIBES

DIFFUSION HYPOTHESIS

		Wins	Losses	Total
FUNCTIONAL HYPOTHESIS	Wins	33	34	67
	Losses	47	4	51
	Total	80	38	118

each trait present. Where presence [or absence] is a rare occurrence, the table should be split by correct predictions for presence compared to correct predictions for absence.) [Naroll and D'Andrade 1963:1064]

The expected probabilities in our Table 2 were computed as follows: $A_1B_1 = (78/260)$ $(192/260) = .222$; $A_1B_0 = (78/260)$ $(68/260) = .078$; $A_0B_1 = (192/260)$ $(182/260) = .517$; $A_0B_0 = (68/260)$ $(182/260) = .182$. These are the expected probabilities for a single tribe.

Where pairs of tribes are involved, the probability of two of the above combinations occurring in both the first tribe and the second tribe is the product of the two probabilities for each of the single tribes. Table 4 gives the probabilities for all 16 outcomes for pairs of tribes. In row one the probability of A_1B_1 for the first tribe and A_0B_0 for the second tribe in the pair is $(.222)$ $(.182) = .040$. The first two values are given in Table 2. In this manner the probabilities

TABLE .4

CORRELATION OF AVOIDANCE AND BIFURCATION AMONG DISTANT PAIRS OF TRIBES (TABLE 2). A_1, TRAIT A PRESENT; A_0, TRAIT A ABSENT; B_1, TRAIT B PRESENT; B_0, TRAIT B ABSENT.

Position as in Table 3, and draws.	Pairs of tribes		Functional-causal hypothesis		Historical-diffusion hypothesis		Probability of occurrence	E. Expected frequency of pairs	O. Observed frequency of distant pairs	$\frac{(O-E)^2}{E}$	Proportion of total variance
	1st	2nd	Wins	Losses	Wins	Losses					
1. Upper right	A_1B_1	A_0B_0	2	0	0	2	.040	10.5	20.0	8.59	.147
2. Upper right	A_0B_0	A_1B_1	2	0	0	2	.040	10.5	14.0	1.16	.020
3. Upper left	A_1B_1	A_1B_1	2	0	2	0	.049	12.8	21.0	5.25	.090
4. Upper left	A_0B_0	A_0B_0	2	0	2	0	.033	8.6	11.0	.67	.011
5. Lower right	A_1B_0	A_0B_1	0	2	0	2	.041	10.5	3.0	5.36	.092
6. Lower right	A_0B_1	A_1B_0	0	2	0	2	.041	10.5	1.0	8.59	.147
7. Lower left	A_0B_1	A_0B_1	0	2	2	0	.267	69.5	46.0	7.94	.136
8. Lower left	A_1B_0	A_1B_0	0	2	2	0	.006	1.6	1.0	.22	.004
9. Positive	A_1B_1	A_0B_1	1	1	1	1	.115	29.9	32.0	.15	.003
10.	A_1B_1	A_1B_0	1	1	1	1	.017	4.5	0.0	4.50	.077
11. draws	A_0B_1	A_1B_1	1	1	1	1	.115	29.9	41.0	4.12	.070
12.	A_1B_0	A_1B_1	1	1	1	1	.017	4.5	2.0	1.39	.024
13. Negative	A_0B_0	A_1B_0	1	1	1	1	.014	3.7	2.0	.78	.013
14.	A_0B_0	A_0B_1	1	1	1	1	.094	24.5	34.0	3.68	.063
15. draws	A_0B_1	A_0B_0	1	1	1	1	.094	24.5	32.0	2.30	.039
16.	A_1B_0	A_0B_0	1	1	1	1	.014	3.7	0.0	3.70	.063
Totals							.997	259.7	260.0	$\chi^2 = 58.40$	.999

$P < .001$

TABLE 5
CORRELATION OF AVOIDANCES AND BIFURCATION
AMONG ADJACENT PAIRS OF TRIBES

	E. EXPECTED FREQUENCY OF PAIRS	O. OBSERVED FREQUENCY OF ADJACENT PAIRS	$\dfrac{(O-E)^2}{E}$	PROPORTION OF TOTAL VARIANCE
1.	10.5	0	10.50	.030
2.	10.5	1	8.60	.025
3.	12.8	50	108.11	.311
4.	8.6	48	180.51	.519
5.	10.5	2	6.88	.020
6.	10.5	4	4.02	.012
7.	69.5	82	2.25	.006
8.	1.6	1	.22	.001
9.	29.9	20	3.28	.009
10.	4.5	2	1.39	.004
11.	29.9	16	6.46	.019
12.	4.5	3	.50	.001
13.	3.7	0	3.70	.011
14.	24.5	12	6.38	.018
15.	24.5	19	1.24	.004
16.	3.7	0	3.70	.011
TOTALS	259.7	260	$\chi^2 = 347.74$	1.001

P<.001

for all 16 outcomes were computed and are given in Table 4, eighth column from the left. In the ninth and tenth columns from the left are given the expected frequency for pairs of tribes and the observed frequency of distant pairs of tribes. From these two sets of values the variance, $(O-E)^2/E$, is computed for each outcome, then its total which is chi-square and, in the last column, the proportion of total variance for each outcome.

The probability of obtaining a chi-square of 58.40 or higher from sampling variability is much less than .001, thus indicating a highly significant difference between the observed and expected values. If we single out the rows where diffusion and functional hypotheses show a contrast, rows one and two versus seven and eight, corresponding to the upper right and lower left quadrants of Table 3B, it is clear that the apparent victory of diffusion over function is reversed. The 47 wins for diffusion are definitely below the expected 71 while, in contrast, the 34 wins for function are above the expected 21. If we add the variance in rows 1, 2, 7, and 8, we may say that the functional hypothesis

wins over diffusion by a variance of 17.9, which is .307 of the total variance.

Table 5 gives parallel figures for adjacent pairs of tribes and the same correlation, that between kin avoidance and bifurcation. The apparent landslide victory of diffusion over function in Table 3A is reduced to a variance of 21.6 or .062 of the total variance. The enormous chi-square (347.7) is probably significant at less than one in a billion.

Table 6 introduces another correlation, that between kin avoidances and bifurcation only in sibling and cousin terms. Table 7 gives the results for pairs of adjacent tribes. Comparison of expected and observed frequencies in rows 1 and 2 shows that the observed values for the functional hypothesis are lower than the expected, while in rows 7 and 8 the observed values for the diffusion hypothesis are higher than the expected. A summation of the amount of variance in rows 1, 2, 7, and 8 shows that diffusion wins over function by 21.2 or .060 of the total variance.

Table 8 gives the results from the same correlation (Table 6) when distant pairs of tribes are tested. Function wins over diffusion by a variance of 31.6 or .551 of the total variance.

TABLE 6
CORRELATION OF AVOIDANCE AND BIFURCATION ONLY IN SIBLING AND COUSIN TERMS. (EXPECTED PROBABILITIES IN PARENTHESES)

		AVOIDANCE		
		Present, A_1	Absent, A_0	Total
BIFURCATION FOR SIBLINGS AND COUSINS	Present, B_1	53 (.130)	57 (.293)	110 (.423)
	Absent, B_0	27 (.178)	123 (.399)	150 (.577)
	Total	80 (.308)	180 (.692)	260 (1.000)

$$\phi = .32 \qquad P < .001$$

TABLE 7
CORRELATION OF AVOIDANCE AND BIFURCATION ONLY IN SIBLING AND COUSIN TERMS FOR ADJACENT PAIRS OF TRIBES

	PROBABILITY OF OCCURRENCE	E. EXPECTED FREQUENCY OF PAIRS	O. OBSERVED FREQUENCY OF ADJACENT PAIRS	$\dfrac{(O-E)^2}{E}$	PROPORTION OF TOTAL VARIANCE
1.	.052	13.5	3	8.17	.023
2.	.052	13.5	3	8.17	.023
3.	.017	4.4	34	199.18	.569
4.	.159	41.3	99	80.61	.230
5.	.052	13.5	1	11.57	.033
6.	.052	13.5	6	4.17	.012
7.	.086	23.4	34	4.80	.014
8.	.032	8.3	9	.06	.000
9.	.038	9.9	8	.36	.001
10.	.023	6.0	6	.00	.000
11.	.038	9.9	7	.85	.002
12.	.023	6.0	7	.17	.000
13.	.071	18.5	5	9.85	.028
14.	.117	30.4	17	5.91	.017
15.	.117	30.4	11	12.38	.035
16.	.071	18.5	10	3.90	.011
TOTALS	1.000	261.0	260	$\chi^2 = 350.10$	.998

$$P < .001$$

TABLE 8
CORRELATION OF AVOIDANCE AND BIFURCATION ONLY IN
SIBLING AND COUSIN TERMS FOR DISTANT PAIRS OF TRIBES

	E. EXPECTED FREQUENCY OF PAIRS	O. OBSERVED FREQUENCY OF DISTANT PAIRS	$\dfrac{(O-E)^2}{E}$	PROPORTION OF TOTAL VARIANCE
1.	13.5	25	9.80	.171
2.	13.5	26	11.57	.202
3.	4.4	9	4.81	.084
4.	41.3	54	3.90	.068
5.	13.5	6	4.17	.073
6.	13.5	7	3.13	.055
7.	23.4	14	3.78	.066
8.	8.3	1	6.42	.112
9.	9.9	11	.12	.002
10.	6.0	6	.00	.000
11.	9.9	14	1.70	.030
12.	6.0	8	.67	.012
13.	18.5	12	2.28	.040
14.	30.4	33	.22	.004
15.	30.4	22	2.32	.041
16.	18.5	12	2.28	.040
TOTALS	261.0	260	$\chi^2 = 57.17$	1.000
		P<.001		

Table 9 introduces still another correlation, that between bifurcation in terms for parents, uncles, aunts, with bifurcation in terms for siblings and cousins. Table 10 shows that for adjacent pairs of tribes diffusion wins over function by a variance of 7.0 or .016 of the total variance.

Table 11 reveals that for distant pairs of tribes function wins over diffusion by a variance of 64.5 or .474 of the total variance.

Table 12 summarizes the results for the matched pairs tests. Diffusion wins for all sets of adjacent pairs and function wins for all sets of distant pairs. It is impossible to generalize from such a small sample of tests, but there is a suggestion that diffusion is more likely to occur among adjacent pairs than distant pairs of tribes, a conclusion that Tylor would have endorsed nearly one hundred years ago. The contrast between diffusion and function can be sharpened by isolating the total variance (chi-square) of rows 1, 2, 7, 8, as given in Table 12, and testing it for significance with three degrees of freedom apart from the other 12 rows. All of the values in Table 12 are significant at less than .001 except that for the third

TABLE 9
CORRELATION OF BIFURCATION IN TERMS FOR PARENTS,
UNCLES, AUNTS WITH BIFURCATION IN TERMS FOR SIBLINGS
AND COUSINS. (EXPECTED PROBABILITIES IN PARENTHESES)

BIFURCATION FOR PARENTS, UNCLES, AUNTS

BIFURCATION FOR SIBLINGS AND COUSINS		Present, A_1	Absent, A_0	Total
	Present, B_1	103 (.299)	5 (.117)	108 (.416)
	Absent, B_0	84 (.420)	68 (.164)	152 (.584)
	Total	187 (.719)	73 (.281)	260 (1.000)
		$\phi = .44$	P<.001	

TABLE 10
CORRELATION OF BIFURCATION IN AVUNCULAR WITH BIFURCATION IN SIBLING AND COUSIN TERMS FOR ADJACENT PAIRS OF TRIBES

	PROBABILITY OF OCCURRENCE	E. EXPECTED FREQUENCY OF PAIRS	O. OBSERVED FREQUENCY OF ADJACENT PAIRS	$\dfrac{(O-E)^2}{E}$	PROPORTION OF TOTAL VARIANCE
1.	.049	12.7	11	.23	.001
2.	.049	12.7	8	1.74	.004
3.	.089	23.1	78	130.48	.287
4.	.027	7.0	49	252.00	.554
5.	.049	12.7	1	10.78	.024
6.	.049	12.7	0	12.70	.028
7.	.014	3.6	0	3.60	.008
8.	.176	45.8	54	1.47	.003
9.	.035	9.1	2	5.54	.012
10.	.126	32.8	12	13.19	.029
11.	.035	9.1	2	5.54	.012
12.	.126	32.8	20	5.00	.011
13.	.069	17.9	11	2.66	.006
14.	.019	4.9	0	4.90	.011
15.	.019	4.9	3	.74	.002
16.	.069	17.9	9	4.42	.010
Totals	1.000	259.7	260	$\chi^2 = 454.99$	1.002

$P < .001$

TABLE 11
CORRELATION OF BIFURCATION IN AVUNCULAR WITH BIFURCATION IN SIBLING AND COUSIN TERMS FOR DISTANT PAIRS OF TRIBES

	E. EXPECTED FREQUENCY OF PAIRS	O. OBSERVED FREQUENCY OF DISTANT PAIRS	$\dfrac{(O-E)^2}{E}$	PROPORTION OF TOTAL VARIANCE
1.	12.7	30	18.05	.133
2.	12.7	33	32.45	.239
3.	23.1	46	22.70	.167
4.	7.0	14	7.00	.051
5.	12.7	2	9.02	.066
6.	12.7	2	9.02	.066
7.	3.6	0	3.60	.026
8.	45.8	24	10.38	.076
9.	9.1	1	7.21	.053
10.	32.8	26	1.41	.010
11.	9.1	2	5.54	.041
12.	32.8	38	.82	.006
13.	17.9	20	.25	.002
14.	4.9	0	4.90	.036
15.	4.9	1	3.10	.023
16.	17.9	21	.54	.004
Totals	259.7	260	$\chi^2 = 135.99$	.999

$P < .001$

TABLE 12
SUMMARY OF RESULTS OF MATCHED PAIRS TESTS IN TOTAL AMOUNT OF VARIANCE IN ROWS 1, 2, 7, 8 (CHI-SQUARE), AND PROPORTION OF TOTAL VARIANCE (IN PARENTHESES)

	ADJACENT PAIRS OF TRIBES	DISTANT PAIRS OF TRIBES
First correlation	Diffusion wins by 21.6 (.062)	Function wins by 17.9 (.307)
Second correlation	Diffusion wins by 21.2 (.060)	Function wins by 31.6 (.551)
Third correlation	Diffusion wins by 7.0 (.016)	Function wins by 64.5 (.474)

correlation and adjacent pairs, which is significant at less than .10.

A comparison of Tables 4, 5, 7, 8, 10, 11 shows that chi-square values are much higher for adjacent pairs of tribes than for distant pairs. This is probably due to a combination of ecological and historical factors. Also, as correlations increase in positive magnitude, the frequencies of outcomes 3 and 4 will increase. The fact that these frequencies are higher for adjacent pairs suggests that functionally related traits tend to diffuse together, thus supporting the semi-diffusional nature of these data or of other variables which "cause" them.

In Tables 4 and 5, five of the expected values for the number of pairs of tribes fall below 5. If row 7 is combined with 8, 13 with 14, and 15 with 16 to eliminate the three lowest expected frequencies, the chi-square of Table 4 is reduced to 50.62, but with the degrees of freedom reduced from 15 to 12, it is still significant at much less than .001. Collapsing the same categories of Table 5 reduces its chi-square to 344.54, a difference of only about 1 per cent. Therefore the chi-squares in Tables 4 and 5 are essentially correct in spite of some low expected frequencies.

D'Andrade (personal communication) suggests that more light could be thrown on the relation of language and culture by comparing the following four sets of matched pairs:

1) geographically adjacent, same language family;

2) not geographically adjacent, same language family;

3) geographically adjacent, different language family;

4) not geographically adjacent, different language family.

The not geographically adjacent pairs could be chosen randomly. This is a good suggestion and will be followed at some time in the future.

An adequate solution to the Tylor-Galton problem by the matched pair method would also require a world-wide sample and a wide spectrum of culture inventory, such as that of Murdock (1967:109–236.). Murdock's sample is the largest and best so far, but its cultural inventory is largely lacking in so-called material culture, which is probably more diffusible than most of the categories he uses. Some of the categories in Driver and Massey's (1957) work would round out Murdock's trait coverage. If one chose to compare adjacent tribes, he would have to do a lot of additional coding, because Murdock's sample never includes two adjacent tribes. Nevertheless, it would be possible to match the nearest pairs obtainable from Murdock's (1967) sample and test them for a large number of correlations, perhaps a random sample of all possible dichotomous relationships. Needless to say, this would require a computer program.

DIFFUSION OF TRAITS

It further seems untenable to postulate that bifurcation can diffuse as a unit, or that any component of kinship semantics can diffuse as a unit. According to the lag theory, which is the one most generally accepted for kinship terminologies, economy or ecology would tend to change first, followed by residence, family organization, descent, and then kinship terminology. There is abundant evidence that tools, weapons, domesticated animals and plants, and knowledge of how to make use of geographical environment can and do diffuse. Residence and descent are certainly less diffusible, yet there is some evidence that they can diffuse without the ecological adjustment having been made (Driver 1956). But until someone can find a few morphemes shared by languages belonging to different families and a corresponding sharing of meanings not explainable in terms of residence, descent, or other aspects of social organization, the case for diffusion of semantic distinctions in kin terms apart from the features of social organization which seem to generate them is nonexistent. Our technique, therefore, hardly seems to be ferreting out diffusion. It seems to be measuring continuity of geographical distribution, which is often, but not always, caused by diffusion. (See Driver and Massey 1957, maps 160, 161, for continuity of distribution of types of kinship terminology, and Driver 1966:142 for continuity of kin avoidances.)

In Driver's paper on kin avoidances he has correlated all the material with culture areas and language families and his general conclusion (1966:157, Table 15) is that diffusion accounts for the greatest amount of mother-in-law son-in-law avoidance variance, bifurcation in kinship terminology the second greatest amount, and language family membership (as an indicator of culture heritage) the third greatest amount. With the change from .40 to .28 in the correlation mentioned above, bifurcation would take third place. Forms of residence and descent appear to have less causal potency, although as determiners of kinship terminology their roles may be greater than their correlations show. This last paper is too long and technical to review here in detail. Suffice it to say that we think he has given a general method applicable to all large-sample comparative studies where ethnic units are continuously distributed.

In simplified and brief form, this method begins with the correlation over the entire area of all the variables thought to be related to the variable the study seeks to explain. Those variables which show significant positive correlations with the phenomenon to be explained and lend themselves to functional interpretation are called the functional correlatives. The next step is to ferret out the negative instances where the phenomenon is present but where all or most of the functional correlatives are absent. If these negative instances occur among language families where the phenomenon is rare and not likely to represent a culture heritage from the protoculture associated with the proto-language, then the case for diffusion is strengthened. If at the same time these negative instances are geographically close to positive instances in other language families with well-developed functional syndromes, then the case for diffusion-acculturation becomes overwhelming. It is thus possible to establish diffusions of a phenomenon off the top so to speak, without the recipient society possessing any or many of the variables thought to generate or cause the phenomenon. There were many such negative instances for kin avoidances in North America. There were also many negative instances where the known functional correlatives were present and avoidances absent.

Diffusion may occur almost anywhere in some evolutionary sequences, as an inspection of the Guttman scale of Carneiro and Tobias (1963) suggests. For instance, diffusions for domesticated plants and animals have been worked out in greater detail than those of most cultural manifestations. Calendar systems, the arch, and papermaking, appearing higher up on the scale, exhibit much evidence of diffusion in areas of continental size, although the first and last seem to have been independently invented in the Old and New Worlds.

NUMBERS OF ORIGINS OF TRAITS

Those who argue that all we want to know is the general evolutionary sequence and that the number of origins of a phenomenon does not matter, because it will diffuse only to areas possessing functional correlatives capable of generating it independently anyway, are taking a much too cavalier attitude toward culture history. It surely makes a difference whether a widespread cultural behavior has a single, a dozen, or a hundred historically independent origins. Historical independence is also a matter of degree: every ethnic unit possesses some cultural behaviors which are unique to it and therefore historically independent of all other such unique behaviors among other ethnic units; every ethnic unit likewise shares some historically determined resemblances with its cultural or linguistic near neighbors, and still others with a larger number of ethnic units. An ethnic unit may be historically linked to others for some of its cultural inventory and be independent with respect to other aspects of culture. We can seldom determine the exact number of origins of the similarities we distribute in space and time in comparative studies, but we can choose between few and many, and between hundreds and thousands of years of independence.

IMPORTANCE OF CONTINUITY OF DISTRIBUTION

Continuity of geographical distribution is still one of the important clues to diffusion and numbers of origins. Comparative studies which deliberately separate the ethnic units in geographical, cultural, and linguistic space to lessen mutual historical influence are eliminating the connecting links needed to establish the amount of historicity involved and are thereby creating a biased sample. No one would think of taking a 10 per cent random sample of a single community to generalize about the kinship relations of that community, because the 90 per cent eliminated would remove the connecting links between the 10 per cent drawn in this manner for analysis. The same principle holds for comparative studies. Any sample which eliminates most of the geographical and historical connecting links is a biased sample and will be insufficient for assessing the importance of historical factors. The researcher needs the entire parameter or most of it to do this and no sample of any kind is as adequate for this purpose. Nevertheless, a sample can yield valid functional correlations, which are a necessary part of a program for ferreting out diffusions off the top, as Driver has applied it to kin avoidances.

Part of the difference between those who stress independent origin and innovation and those who emphasize diffusion is semantic. Even when a material object diffuses it must be preceded by a felt need and some lessons in its use and operation. If it is to be manufactured in the new area, the details of this process must be passed on also. If the materials available for manufacture in the new area are different from those in the donor area, this calls for innovation on the part of the maker. If the two cultures differ enough, the meaning, use, or function of the object may be changed by the recipient people. Diffusion is always accompanied by some innovation. A sufficient explanation of most cultural behaviors in most localities requires mention of the outside contact with the donor group which triggers the spread of the culture behavior, the inside innovations of the recipient groups which adapt it to their needs, and why it was needed at the particular time when it diffused instead of earlier or later.

RATES OF DIFFUSION

Different rates of diffusion are generally assumed to exist not only in different times and places, but also among differing aspects of culture in the same or adjacent sections of time and space. When documentary and accurately dated archaeological materials are lacking, rates are difficult to determine. Barnett (1964) suggests that material objects are generally most diffusible, social organization least diffusible, with organized religions taking an intermediate position. Although this generalization is arrived at by citing authoritative opinions rather than by assembling a large sample of datable diffusions, it may well be correct.

The maps on North American Indian culture assembled by Driver and Massey (1957) and Driver (1961) all show non-random areal clustering of all of the data. Although the multiple number of some of the clusters suggests multiple origins of these phenomena, the geographical continuity within clusters suggests diffusion within each cluster. Although significant positive correlations among functional correlatives have been established by many researchers in the field of social organization (e.g., Murdock 1949 and Driver 1956), some such correlations are based on as few as 60 per cent positive instances and as many as 40 per cent negative instances. The middle to low range of many of the correlations suggests that diffusion of one variable without the other is contributing to the number of negative instances.

SOCIAL ORGANIZATION AND KINSHIP TERMINOLOGY

The diffusion or acculturation of social organization would certainly require intimate and prolonged contact of the donor and recipient peoples. Intertribal marriages seem to have been not only common but universal in native North America (except for the Polar Eskimo who were isolated for centuries from all neighbors), and the assimilation of sizable parts of tribes decimated by war and disease by their conquerors or by friendly tribes was probably more common than the record shows. Ceremonies of adoption for foreign individuals were common, e.g., in the United States east of the Mississippi. We do not need to look far to find the ways and means for the diffusion of aspects of social organization.

Fifty years ago Lowie (1916) wrote a well-balanced paper on "historical and sociological interpretations of kinship terminologies." He pointed out certain features of kinship terminology which could be adequately explained by known variables of social organization and language family classification. At the same time he called attention to other components of kinship terminology which cross-cut language classification yet formed continuous areal clusters. Those which could not be explained by associated features of social organization or by correlations with language families were attributed to diffusion. Probably some of the features he attributed to diffusion could now be shown to correlate with some other social variable, but I suspect that no matter how exhaustive the analysis there are likely to be some details of kinship terminology that form areal clusters and cross-cut not only language family classification but also kinship typologies.

Although it has been said by a number of persons that social structure is comparable to language in its structural integration and resistance to change from without its system, linguists (e.g.. Emeneau 1956 and Taylor 1963) have given examples not only of words and phones but also of morphological features diffusing across genetic family boundaries. Kinship and social structure specialists might also find comparable diffusions in their fields if they searched for them.

The brief discussion by Köbben (1967) of the role of diffusion in creating exceptions to the general rules established by correlations and tests of significance is an excellent treatment of the subject and wholly in accord with the view expressed here. In addition he gives the most complete inventory so far of the many other ways in which negative instances may arise. Every cross-cultural researcher should examine his own data with these points in mind to see which ones may be applied to the interpretation of his exceptional cases.

Although the methods we have mentioned in this brief statement are complicated and subject to debate on many points, we believe that comparativists should debate them, refine them, and apply them, and not just relax and admit that they have made little progress in these matters since Tylor's and Galton's time.

BIBLIOGRAPHY

BARNETT, HOMER G.
  1964 Diffusion rates. In Robert A. Manners, ed., *Process and pattern in culture*. Chicago, Aldine.
CARNEIRO, ROBERT L., and STEPHEN G. TOBIAS
  1963 The application of scale analysis to the study of cultural evolution. *Transactions of the New York Academy of Sciences*, Ser. II, Vol. 26, No. 2:196–207.
DRIVER, HAROLD E.
  1956 *An integration of functional, evolutionary, and historical theory by means of correlations*. Indiana University Publications in Anthropology and Linguistics, Memoir 12.

DRIVER, HAROLD E., *et al*.
  1966 Geographical-historical versus psycho-functional explanations of kin avoidances. *Current Anthropology* 7:131–182.
DRIVER, HAROLD E., JOHN M. COOPER, PAUL KIRCHOFF, WM. C. MASSEY, DOROTHY RAINIER LIBBY, and LESLIE SPIER
  1953 *Indian tribes of North America*. Indiana University Publications in Anthropology and Linguistics, Memoir 9.
DRIVER, HAROLD E., and WM. C. MASSEY
  1957 Comparative studies of North American Indians. *Transactions of the American Philosophical Society* 47:165–456.

EMENEAU, MURRAY B.
1956 India as a linguistic area. *Language* 32: 3–16.

KÖBBEN, A. J. F.
1967 Why exceptions? The logic of cross-cultural analysis. *Current Anthropology* 8:3–34.

LOWIE, ROBERT H.
1916 Historical and sociological interpretations of kinship terminologies. In *Holmes anniversary volume: anthropological essays presented to William Henry Holmes . . . December 1, 1916 by his friends and Colaborers.* Washington, D.C.

MOONEY, JAMES
1896 Calendar history of the Kiowa Indians. *Bureau of American Ethnology, Annual Report,* No. 17, Pt. 1.

MURDOCK, GEORGE P.
1957 World ethnographic sample. *American Anthropologist* 59:664–687.
1966 Cross-cultural sampling. *Ethnology* 5:97–114.
1967 Ethnographic atlas: a summary. *Ethnology* 6:109–236.

NAROLL, RAOUL
1961 Two solutions to Galton's problem. *Philosophy of Science* 28:15–39. Also in Frank W. Moore, ed., *Readings in cross-cultural methodology.* New Haven, Human Relations Area Files.
1964 A fifth solution to Galton's problem. *American Anthropologist* 66:863–867.

NAROLL, RAOUL, and ROY G. D'ANDRADE
1963 Two further solutions to Galton's problem. *American Anthropologist* 65:1053–1067.

STEPHENS, WM. N.
1959 *Menstrual taboos and castration anxiety.* Ph.D. dissertation, Graduate School of Education. Cambridge, Harvard University.

TAYLOR, DOUGLAS
1963 The origin of West Indian Creole languages: evidence from grammatical categories. *American Anthropologist* 65:800–814.

TYLOR, EDWARD B.
1889 On a method of investigating the development of institutions; applied to laws of marriage and descent. *Journal of the Royal Anthropological Institute of Great Britain and Ireland* 18:245–272.

WHITING, JOHN W. M.
1968 Methods and problems in cross-cultural research. In Lindzey and Aronson, eds., *Handbook of social psychology,* 2nd ed. Reading, Mass., Addison-Wesley.

CHAPTER 49

On Museums and Anthropological Research

STUART D. SCOTT and PATRICIA K. SEGMEN

In a brief review of literature pertinent to the museum and anthropology, one finds both longer (Collier and Tschopik 1954, Fenton 1960, Frese 1960, Rainey 1955) and shorter (Colbert 1961, 1965, Collier 1962, Goldstein 1968, Guthe 1966, Kroeber 1954, Lindsay 1962, Mason 1960, Piddington 1950) discussions of American anthropology museums concerning: their relevance to the anthropological discipline both past and present; effective methods of exhibition and their educational aspects. Although there are a number of interesting elements to the problem of museum anthropology, the role played by the museum in anthropological research has received only a modicum of attention in recent years and would seem to be destined for a continuing position of low priority within the many generalized and programmatic interests of the anthropological discipline.

Museums, traditionally the places for storage of the material arts, prospered under the influence of strong interest in principles of evolutionism during the late nineteenth and early twentieth centuries. Much has been written about the historicalism of Boas, the collecting of objects for the study of technology, and the focus of anthropological interest on the so-called primitive peoples, all of which strongly influenced the development of anthropological museums and the world of culture as seen in natural history museums.

The influence of evolutionary anthropology on museums could be seen in displays which served to exhibit the linear development of culture as it was thought to have progressed through fixed stages. The principle of arranging artifacts in series with a view to showing their evolutionary development seemed to best fit the then present state of knowledge of anthropology and such display technique had its beginning through the pioneering work of General Lane-Fox Pitt-Rivers. His ethnological museum, which served as an example for the subsequent growth of natural history museums, is now preserved as the Pitt-Rivers Museum at the University of Oxford.

Another point of contact between museums and currents in the development of anthropology was the culture area concept. Here again the museum as utilized by Wissler (1912) served as an essential element in elaborating the similar and contrastive features of material culture and portraying large areas mapped in terms of distinctive culture complexes.

Reviewing the years of museum development, there are, among leading figures in anthropology, men and women whose careers in museums were made possible by those institutions in providing employment, time, and the general research base. Among many such names are those of Putnam, Tylor, Mason, Heye, Brinton, Powell, Hrdlicka, Holmes, Woolley, Mead, Vaillant, and numerous others.

Subsequent development of anthropology saw a decline of interest in classification and historical processes, followed by functionalist studies of social theory, and in general, an increased stress on investigating individual cultures as integrated wholes. Although anthropology continued to be museum-centered in some Western European countries, elsewhere university departments of anthropology and museums became separate institutions for research. In characterizing the present relation

SPECIAL PROBLEMS OF COMPARATIVE METHOD

between museum anthropology and anthropology at large, Frese (1960:69) notes that in the United States cleavage between university departments and museums reaches its greatest extent:

Indeed, over there [United States] anthropology has assumed unrivalled proportions. Studies of acculturation, of personality in culture, ethnopsychology, ethno-linguistics, race and culture and the most recent, joint field of anthropology and education, are among the many new subjects which have prospered in the U.S.A. more than anywhere else. However, it seems that sporadically a feed-back has taken place, fertilizing museum anthropology with the newer and wider insights. If it seems that in the U.S.A. the museums are lagging behind the development of cultural anthropology at large, it is not because the museums in that country are retarded in comparison with those in the other western countries. Instead, it indicates the exceedingly rapid development of anthropology in the United States.

It has been the natural tendency for museums to continue to collect examples of the material arts of the non-Western world regardless of the orientation of research. The result is that anthropology has marshaled its material resources consisting of thousands of institutionalized collections housed in several thousand museums in the United States (Anonymous 1965).

For anthropology to marshal its material resources is one thing; to determine how they can best be applied is another. What has happened in many museums is that although they have undergone a radical change in the educational and general public interest aspects, in the utilization of research collections for anthropology, many draw devastating criticism for their role in functioning only as repositories for memorabilia and white elephants. The big question therefore is whether the research collections which have served the course of development of anthropology, will also be capable of contributing to future anthropological research. We need to know if artifacts constitute a "useful, viable source for the understanding of the human past" (Hesseltine 1959:66), or must anthropologists accept the view which argues that the scientist or the historian cannot depend upon objects because the conclusions to be drawn from them are subjective.

The descriptive and interpretive analyses of archaeological and ethnographic collections suggest a continuing belief in the value of objects, as does the work of the art historian whose conclusions rest in recognition of the cultural data inherent in primitive art objects (Haselberger 1961). It is clear however that at the present time, object-oriented research is outside the mainstream of anthropological thought and research. The ascendency of "the New Anthropology" or perhaps better, Contemporary Anthropology, is reflected in such aspects as an increase in the use of statistics in the analysis of certain kinds of anthropological data; cross-cultural methodology; a sensitivity to observations that lie behind older ethnographic observations, the re-examination of generalizations about human behavior that once were regarded as unquestioned fact. Archaeological frontiers are advancing likewise through the articulation of excavation data with that of general ethnography and ethnology, and perhaps more important, through a strong new focus on the inferential aspects of archaeology.

The intermediary role of museums as the meeting place of anthropology and the public can be disregarded here in favor of a closer scrutiny of museums as scientific institutions with respect to anthropology. Collier and Tschopik (1954:773) observe that ". . . museums have not gone far in widening their programs in the direction of the current interests of anthropology." Frese notes further that developments in the study of man and culture appear to stay outside the orbit of most museums, in Europe as well as in the United States, and he asks (Frese 1960:107): "Are these traditional interests out of date now, representing a sluggish attitude on the part of the museums? . . . And does the advent of the divergent development of a later date imply that the process of increasing the significance of anthropology in the museums has been brought to a standstill?" Again, the question that is fairly before us, and posed by the refinement of research techniques resulting from the newer approaches in cultural anthropology, is the question as to whether artifacts are truly explanatory of the culture to which they are related and therefore of value as social documents, or should they perhaps be viewed in terms of future research as contributing little of scholarly importance. This issue is one that Hesseltine writes about, at first negatively (1959:68–69):

We have no techniques of internal criticism which will extract meaning and significance from these mute and inanimate objects. . . . By what means, by what processes of internal criticism, can these remains be made to divulge the parts they have shared in mankind's past? What questions can these walls answer? What, in fact are the questions which they should be asked?

Later, he adds (1959:70):

It is only that we cannot talk to them, cannot ask them questions, and cannot understand the answers. But until artifacts can be subjected to internal criticism and made to bear their witness, the task of historical methodology is unfinished.

For anthropology, Collier and Tschopik (1954:776) stated their view cogently and somewhat more optimistically when they observed:

We believe that material culture and technology have not yet lost their significance as subject matter for research. In fact, they offer a great potential for studies with a modern orientation. To point to a single example, anthropologists are showing an increasing interest in art—its history, as well as the problems of style, function, and values. At the same time, artists and art historians are becoming increasingly interested in anthropology.

Such a view reflects a tacit willingness among anthropologists to affirm and maintain museums for their traditional and still fruitful role in serving both anthropology and the public. But, if we expect to continue to support museums of anthropology and to encourage their use as a dynamic force in the anthropology of the future, we have to justify them primarily on the basis of collections. Anthropology having, at the same time, social, natural, and physical science attributes, exhibits an inherently variable susceptibility to understanding through material culture. For example, there is hardly any need to mention the material culture in the strategy of prehistory, e.g. its use in typology, dating and the myriad descriptive and interpretive devices of archaeology. For anthropological research outside of prehistory the utility of museums and their collections is less obvious; however, one recognizable trend within the last decade is toward the collection of descriptive materials, i.e., contemporary arts and crafts and contemporary technology in general. Following the example of other institutions, the State University of New York has begun modestly to make such collections in the belief that the "contemporaneity" of these non-Western cultures situated as they are just beneath the veneer of westernization

can profitably be studied from an essentially ethnographic point of view. Such an ethnographic point of view might differ in theoretical orientation from that of the 1920's in line with what Hesseltine (1959) considered the development of new techniques of studying artifacts. Collier and Tschopik (1954:775) write:

While foundations favor investigations of folk culture, community studies, applied problems, and the like, most social anthropologists concerned with the study of acculturated peoples are either disinterested in material culture or believe, erroneously, that "acculturated objects" hold no interest for museums.

Actually, with such collections museums could provide a hitherto unexploited potential in acculturation studies. Many aspects or processes of culture change can be studied concretely in terms of material culture, yet few modern studies of this nature have been made. Investigations of contemporary or recent acculturation would enrich our knowledge of change generally, and would add much to our understanding of changes in the past.

Beyond the use of artifacts for such acculturation studies and their use in anthropological art history, it is difficult and perhaps unwise to prognosticate for the future of museums and their collections as a force in anthropology. Arguments for a new "active anthropology" with more relevance of research to major problems of modern life (Goldstein 1968) calls for equivalent conceptual changes in museum display. Borhegyi (1964, 1968) among others urges the use of provocative or problem-oriented exhibits, among them "Prejudice," "The Urban Revolution," "Street-Corner Society," "The Wicked Age," "Narcotics and LSD," etc. Although Borhegyi is speaking here of the educational obligations of the museums of tomorrow, it seems to us that such "action-oriented" museum anthropology will serve the research interest of our field if only indirectly. By bringing to the attention of even greater numbers of anthropologists, both student and professional, the message of anthropology through the imaginative and yet substantive methods of communication that are uniquely those of the museum, it can only promote the feedback and interaction of ideas which is the inevitable and necessary consequence of all intellectual inquiry.

To conclude, we have organized several brief thoughts according to two matters: first, pro versus con on the value of artifacts in research; and second, the relative usefulness of object-oriented research within anthropology. What seems to us, however, another and more compelling argument for the museum and its role in anthropological research is the total resource aspect of anthropology. As anthropologists, we are taught and continue to teach that every cultural system is an interconnected series of ideas and patterns for behavior in which changes in one aspect generally lead to changes in other segments of the system. If we accept that, we cannot ignore material culture. We can see in man's

material heritage, spiritual, ethical, philosophical and social aspects. It is this concept of the totality of anthropology that carries its character.

Speaking eloquently of the whole world of man and his works which is our heritage, Frederica de Laguna in her presidential address of 1967 to the American Anthropological Association (1968:476) says:

It is not given to us, or at least to most of us, to be a Boas or a Kroeber who can work at first hand in all branches of our discipline. But we can share their vision and stand on the mountain top, surveying all the vast world laid out below.

BIBLIOGRAPHY

ANONYMOUS
1965 *Museums directory of the United States and Canada,* 2nd ed. Washington, D.C., American Association of Museums and the Smithsonian Institution.

BORHEGYI, STEPHAN F. DE
1964 Some thoughts on anthropological exhibits in natural history museums in the United States. *Curator* 7:121–127.
1968 Comment. In Marcus S. Goldstein, Anthropological research, action, and education in modern nations. *Current Anthropology* 9:255.

COLBERT, EDWIN H.
1961 What is a museum? *Curator* 4:138–146.
1965 The university in the museum. *Curator* 8:78–85.

COLLIER, DONALD
1962 Museums and ethnological research. *Curator* 5:322–328.

COLLIER, DONALD, and HARRY TSCHOPIK, JR.
1954 The role of museums in American anthropology. *American Anthropologist* 56:768–779.

FENTON, WILLIAM N.
1960 The museum and anthropological research. *Curator* 3:327–355.

FRESE, H. H.
1960 *Anthropology and the public: the role of museums.* Leyden, Rijksmuseum Voor Volkenkunde.

GOLDSTEIN, MARCUS S.
1968 Anthropological research, action, and education in modern nations: with special reference to the U.S.A. *Current Anthropology* 9:247–269.

GUTHE, ALFRED K.
1966 The role of a university museum. *Curator* 9:103–105.

HASELBERGER, HERTA
1961 Method of studying ethnological art. *Current Anthropology* 2:341–384.

HESSELTINE, WILLIAM B.
1959 The challenge of the artifact. In James H. Rodabaugh, ed., *The present world of history.* Proceedings, Conference on Certain Problems in Historical Society Work. Madison, Wisc. American Association for State and Local History.

KROEBER, ALFRED L.
1954 The place of anthropology in universities. *American Anthropologist* 56:764–767.

LAGUNA, FREDERICA DE
1968 Presidential address—1967. *American Anthropologist* 70:469–476.

LINDSAY, G. CARROLL
1962 Museums and research in history and technology. *Curator* 5:236–244.

MASON, J. A.
1960 Observations on the function of the museum in anthropology. In *Culture in history: essays in honor of Paul Radin.* New York, Columbia University Press.

PIDDINGTON, RALPH
1950 *An introduction to social anthropology,* Vol. 1. London, Oliver and Boyd.

RAINEY, FROELICH
1955 The new museum. *University Museum Bulletin* 19:1–53.

WISSLER, CLARK
1912 *North American Indians of the plains.* New York, American Museum of Natural History Handbook, Ser. 1:55.

INDEX OF PERSONS

Robinson, W. S., 99
Roe, A., 252
Rogers, C., and Frantz, C., 344
Rogers, E., 478
Romney, A. K., and D'Andrade, R. G., 333
Rose, E., 780
Rosenberg, J., 341
Rosenthal, R., 202, 285, 290, 381
Rossan, O., 509
Rummel, R., 119
Russell, B., 57, 76, 77
Russett, B., 122
Ryan, B., et al, 323

Sade, D. S., 537
Sahlins, M. D., 41, 477, 497, 586, 879, 990
Salisbury, R. F., 457, 463, 486
Samarin, W., 566
Sapir, E., 166
Sapir, E., and Hoijer, H., 574
Sawyer, J., 477, 978, 979
Schachter, S., 400, 414, 415
Schade, H., 321
Schapera, I., 92, 174, 321, 484, 486, 726
Schapera, I., and Goodwin, A. J. H., 462
Schenk, E., 621
Schleck, M., 90
Schmidt, W., 166
Schneider, D. M., 34, 48, 361, 537, 905
Schneider, D., and Homans, G., 449
Schnore, L., 121, 122
Schwab, W. B., 316, 326–27
Schwartz, R., 767
Schwitzgebel, R., 344
Scotch, N. A., 329
Scotch, N. A., and Geiger, H. J., 329
Segall, M. H., Campbell, D. T., and Herskovits, M. J., 25, 70, 199, 344, 367, 383, 384, 415
Selznick, P., 218
Senghor, L. S., 461
Seppilli, T., 329
Service, E. R., 18
Sherwood, E., 341
Simon, H. S., 99, 100, 102
Singer, M., 532, 534
Slobin, D. I., et al, 368
Smedslund, J., 73
Smelser, N. J., 460
Smelser, N. J., and Smelser, W. T., 465
Smith, M. G., 35–36, 173, 323, 328, 477, 484, 487, 488, 490, 491, 496
Smith, R. T., 276
Snyder, R., 493
Soares, G., 122
Sofer, C., and Sofer, R., 316, 326

Sorokin, P. A., Zimmerman, C. C., and Galpin, C. J., 477
Souriau, P., 59
Southall, A. W., 470
Southall, A. W., and Gutkind, P. C. W., 267
Spencer, H., 74
Spiegelman, S., 54
Spier, F. G., 42
Spier, L., 332
Spindler, G. D., 268, 339, 340
Spindler, G. D., and Spindler, L., 341
Spiro, M., 342, 500
Srinivas, M. N., 503, 532
Stavrianos, B. K., 33, 323
Steiner, F., 471
Stern, E., and D'Épinay, R. L., 414
Steward, J., 42, 330, 486, 701, 879
Stoetzel, J., 329–30
Stone, P., et al, 343
Streib, G. F., 320
Strodtbeck, F. L., 289, 342, 678
Stryker, S., 520
Sturtevant, E. H., 404
Sturtevant, W. C., 333
Stycos, J. M., 327, 341
Suggs, R. C., 167, 168
Sullivan, H. S., 285
Sumner, W. G., 91, 710
Sutton-Smith, B., 714
Sutton-Smith, B., and Roberts, J., 343
Swanson, G. E., 332, 907
Swartz, M., Turner, V. W., and Tuden, A., 484, 489

Tanter, R., 6, 20
Tax, S., 230, 259, 455, 456
Textor, R. B., 13, 707, 717, 897, 939
Thibaut, J. W., and Kelley, H. H., 288
Thompson, L., 216
Tobias, S., 779–80, 990, 1000
Tolman, E. C., and Brunswik, E., 74
Tremblay, M., 268
Trier, J., 543
Tschopik, H., 1005, 1006
Turnbull, C., 343
Turner, V. W., 503, 506
Tylor, E. B., 331, 501, 974, 978

Uberoi, J. P. S., 463
Uexküll, J. von, 73
Ullman, S. de, 543, 561
Underwood, B. J., 191

Vajda, L., 153, 154, 155
Van Bulck, G., 166
Van Gennep, A., 505
Vansina, J., 159, 161, 166, 168, 174, 175, 176, 489
Vidich, A. J., and Shapiro, G., 316, 321

Voegelin, C. F., and Voegelin, F. M., 407, 408, 568, 573
Vogt, E. Z., and Albert, E. M., 330, 353

Wallace, A. F. C., 268–69, 271, 339, 340, 522
Wallis, W. A., 622, 623
Wallis, W. A., and Roberts, H. V., 276
Walters, R. H., and Karal, P., 197
Walters, R. H., and Ray, E., 197
Watson, J. B., 367
Watson, J. B., et al, 382
Watson, O. M., and Graves, T., 342
Webb, E. J., et al, 202, 414, 417
Weber, M., 460
Weinreich, V., 561
Werner, O., 406, 407, 537, 540, 543, 544, 546, 552, 566, 573, 574, 575
Werner, O., and Begishe, K., 61
Werner, O., Frank, J., and Begishe, K. Y., 568
West, J., and Withers, C., 322
White, D., 14
White, L., 834, 879
Whiting, B., 286, 353, 355, 356, 359, 367, 713, 977
Whiting, B., and Whiting, J., 9
Whiting, J. W. M., 193, 292, 711, 712, 713, 718, 725, 991
Whiting, J. W. M., and Child, I. L., 332, 366
Whiting, J. W. M., et al, 188, 267, 270, 284, 285, 286, 288, 289, 290, 291, 293, 294, 353, 354, 356, 359, 367, 368, 381, 382, 383
Whorf, 512
Whyte, W. F., 24
Williams, G. E., 543, 544, 562, 565
Williams, H. H., and Williams, J. R., 340
Willoughby, G., 780
Wilson, E. G., 75, 80
Wilson, G., 323, 463
Wilson, M., 502, 503, 607
Wilson, T., 978
Winch, R. F., 523, 767
Wissler, C., 332, 630, 1104
Wittfogel, K. A., 91
Wolf, E., 455, 461
Worsley, P., 471, 472, 503
Wright, H. F., 284
Wright, S., 103–4

Yang, M. C., 473
Young, F., and Young, R., 324
Young, R. W., and Morgan, W., 569
Yudelman, M., 459, 469

Zelditch, M., 358
Zirkle, C., 63
Zubin, J., 340

INDEX OF SUBJECTS

Hyderbad, 328
Hyper-diffusion, Galton's problem, 975, 981, 982, 983–84
Hypotheses, multiplicity of, 193

Ibo, 229–30, 231, 343, 344
Identification problem, in dependence coefficients, 101–2
Identity, 520–23
    social, in unfamiliar culture, 424–27
Imbangala, 170
Immigrants, judgments of, 390–92
Inca, 466
Independence, sampling, 903
Index of Cultural Accumulation, 852
Indexes, multiplicity of, 192–93
India, 528
Influence analysis
    logical component, 109–10
    statistical component, 108–9
Innovation and diffusion, 1001
Interaction
    face-to-face, 523–24
    populations and experimental arrangements, between, 207
Interdisciplinary research, 510
International Comparative Political Parties Project (ICPP), 963
Interpersonal versus intrapersonal, 514
Inter-polity relations, 497
Interval scales, classification, 702, 703
Interval Sift Method
    Galton's problem, 982–83
    sampling, 898
Intervening variable, Societal Research Archives System, 681
Interview schedule, use of, with interpreter, 408–12
Iroquois, 238
Ivory Coast, 94, 601, 602, 605

Jamaica, 328
Japan, 36, 198, 318, 329, 330, 331, 341, 414, 416, 417, 475, 527, 529
Java, 323
Jinja, 326
Judgments, of visitors and immigrants, outsiders' judgments, 390–92
Juxtaposition, 94–95

Kachin, 503, 504
Kalabari, 503
Kalenjin, 396
Kamba, 344, 395
Kanuri, 36
Kaska, 266
Kaunertal, 929–30
Kigezi, 356
Kikuyu, 395
Kin avoidance, 993, 995, 1000
Kinship, 1000, 1002
Kipsigis, 396
Knowledge
    nature of, 28–29
    processes, 54–55
Kongo, 174
Kpelle, 197–98, 199, 206, 291, 503
Kuba, 168, 171, 175, 176
Kulturkreis, 990
Kwaio, 423–51
Kwakiutl, 174

Lango, 356
Language, 60–61
    activities (translation of) 406–7
    ambiguity, 403–4
    context, 407–8
    deep structure, 403
    transformational generative theory of, 400–2
Lapps, 174
Lele, 175, 176, 468
Linear regression, in cultural complexity scores, 881
Linearity, 17
Linked Pair method, 680
    Galton's problem, 980
    sampling, 898
    WC&C Sample, 984–87
Literate civilizations, methodology, 527–37
Locomotor devices, vicarious, 56–57
Lodagaa, 503
Luba, 176
Lue, 741, 743
Lugbara, 225–28, 488, 503, 506
Luo, 395

Machine coding, 715
Madras, 532
Magic, as psycho-physiological reaction, 95
Maharashtra, 530
Main sequence, cultural evolution, 854
Malay, 465, 476
Male circumcision, cross-cultural coding of, 718
Man
    abstract versus concrete descriptions of, 513
    as agent versus man as object, 513
Manu'a, 930
Mapping, trait clusters, Societal Research Archives System, 681
Marigoli, 290
Marquesan, 168
Marriage, mode of classification, 703, 704
Masai, 395, 396
Matched Pair method
    Galton's problem, 980, 984, 997
    sampling, 898
Mbembe, 497
Mbuti Pygmy, 343, 344
Melanesia, 93–94, 472
Menomini, 210, 219, 268
Meru, 395
Mestizo, social mobilization of, 113
Methodology
    field manual anthropology, in 378–84
    psychological anthropology, 337–52
    triangulational and validity, 67–71
Methods
    observing and recording behavior, 282–315
    survey research, review of literature, 320–31
Mexico, 171, 294, 306
Mnemonically supported thought, 58–59
Models
    descriptive, 33–37
    functional, 39–42
Mohave, 344
Mother's brother, in Africa, 581

Multi-ethnic field research, 330
Multi-universe validity, 21
Multivariate analysis, 20
Murngin, 344
Museums
    historical development in anthropological research, 1004
    Pitt-Rivers, 1004
    role of, in anthropological research, 1005–6

Nahua, 929
Nandi, 396
Naskapi, 369
National character, 329–30
Nationality (of ethnographer) variables, 653–56
Native informants, ethnoscience, 566, 567–68
"Natural" classifications, 698–99
Natural selection, orientation, 51–54
Navaho, 199, 230–37, 289, 320, 341, 405, 406, 407, 409, 410, 411, 412, 474, 537, 542, 546, 547, 548, 561, 563, 565, 567, 569, 571, 572, 573, 574
Ndembu, 503
Negative data, in coding, 716
New Guinea, Highland, entree, 220–25
Nilotic, 169
Nominal scales, classification, 702
Non-mnemonic problem solving, 55–56
Nonprobability sampling, 267–74
Notation systems, in coding, 713–14
Nuer, 463, 464, 468, 503, 586, 587, 592
Nupe, 465, 614, 616
Nyakyusa, 503
Nyamwezi, 395
Nyansongo, 286
Nyoro, 359

Observable concepts, classification by, 705–6
Observation
    behavior and situation, selecting, 270
    exploration, socially vicarious, 59–60
    length, 292
    people to study, selecting, 268–70
    problems in, 282–86
    recording, 291–92
    setting, choice of, 288–89
    types of systematic, 286–88
Ojibwa, 342
Okinawa, 291, 293
Operational definitions
    as classification, 689
    as measurement, 689
Optical illusions, sampling, 894–95
Oral traditions, 159–61
Ordinal scale, 702
Oshogbo, 327
Outline of Cultural Materials, 13, 642–43, 709, 711
Outsiders' judgments, 388–97

Pacific, bibliography, 144–45
Papago, 563, 929, 931, 932
Paradigm, ethnoscience, 544–53
Paraphrase, 404–6
Pare, 395, 396
Pathan, 276